Green Bay Packers

A Measure of Greatness

2nd Edition

Eric Goska

Published by

krause publications
An imprint of F+W Publications, Inc.

700 East State Street • Iola, WI 54990-0001
715-445-2214 • 888-457-2873
www.krause.com

Please call for our free catalog. Our toll-free number to place an order or obtain a free catalog is 800-258-0929 or please use our regular business telephone 715-445-2214 .

Library of Congress Catalog Number: 2004092773
ISBN: 0-87349-920-4

Printed in the United States of America

Edited by Dennis Thornton
Designed by Wendy Wendt

DEDICATION

To my wife, Ann, who graciously ran the household on her own these past few months so I could finish this book. I am deeply grateful. I couldn't have done it without you.

To my daughters, Nicole Marie and Rebecca Lynn, thanks for letting your Dad "do stats" every so often.

I love you all.

INTRODUCTION

It's great to be wanted.

A couple of years ago, it was me who had to convince Krause Publications that my statistical book on the Packers was worthy of publication. I made the phone calls, sent the letters and served up my best sales pitch.

My efforts paid off. In September 2003, *The Green Bay Packers: A Measure of Greatness* made its way to bookstores across the country. It also entered the realm of cyberspace.

About three months after the book debuted, I received a call from Paul Kennedy, acquisitions manager at Krause Publications. The book was selling well, he told me, so well in fact, that he was wondering if I could update it for the 2004 season.

Aha! The tables had turned. Now it was Krause's turn to take a stab at the art of persuasion. I was being pursued. They liked me. They really liked me.

The exchange went something like this.

"Eric, would you be able to update the book in the next couple of months so we could have a new book ready for training camp?"

Not wanting to tip me hand too early or appear too eager, I calmly replied: "Sure, when can we begin?"

So much for having to twist my chin strap.

The Power of Film

I recently watched the 1956 Packers highlight video. A No. 27 for the Packers played in both games on the West Coast. No big deal, except for the fact that a No. 27 does not show up on any roster that I am aware of.

What to do? I contacted my California connection, Coach T.J. Troup, who checked microfilm of the newspapers out there. Sure enough, Ken Gorgal, who was assigned No. 26 when he joined the team, switched to No. 27 for two games at least.

It was T.J. who discovered last year that Tom Finnin wore No. 71 for the Packers in 1957. Thanks for the help, T.J.

Games Played

When I first compiled the rosters that appear in this book, I relied on the NFL's Media Information Books to determine how many games each player played during the 1970s and early 1980s. The data came from the NFL so it had to be accurate, right? Not necessarily.

I had to change approximately 35 entries for the years 1970 through 1980 because of my reliance on those books. The most glaring mistake: Frank Patrick was credited with having played in 30 games between 1970 and 1972. He actually played in four. I regret the errors I perpetuated in previous editions.

Unfinished Business

Research, research, research. As you probably have surmised, writing about the Packers' past is an ongoing process. I will continue to dig deep into the team's rich history, not only to aid in the writing of my by-the-numbers columns during the season, but also to "add value" to this book.

Enjoy!

Eric Goska

Legendary Packers coach Curly Lambeau watches from the sideline at the old City Stadium during a game in 1940. From left are Lambeau, Gus Zarnas, Dick Weisgerber, Charley Brock, Champ Seibold, and Clarke Hinkle. Tom Pigeon Collection.

Packers end Milt Gantenbein breaks away for a big gain in a late 1930s game at the old City Stadium in Green Bay. Gantenbein, a Wisconsin graduate, played in 104 games from 1931-40. Stiller-Lefebvre Collection

Table of Contents

Acknowledgments

I have been fortunate to have received the assistance of many individuals in the years since I last published this work. My memory being what it is, I truly hope I do not leave anyone out.

Lee Remmel, former executive director of public relations for the Green Bay Packers and now historian, and his staff, especially Zak Gilbert, have been most helpful. I know Lee understands my obsession for all numbers football, and I thank him for letting me pursue my passion.

Art Daley, former sports editor of the Green Bay Press-Gazette, allowed me access to his play-by-plays and is always ready to answer any question I might have. Art is the one who first put me on to the idea of doing a book, and I am grateful for all the help he has given me.

The great photographs in this book were provided by the late Lee Lefebvre, Chip Manthey, and Tom Pigeon. Lee helped with many of the early team photos. Though I knew he had been battling cancer for some time, his death in June 2003 stunned and saddened me. Chip is a freelance photographer who came through with action and sideline shots from the '90s to the present. Chip, I've enjoyed working with you immensely. And Tom is a collector extraordinaire, who, fortunately, had the foresight to take pictures from his seat at Lambeau Field in the '60s and '70s. Tom, I always look forward to our football talks. Thank you, gentlemen.

Coach T.J. Troup, a fellow statistician and writer from California, cleared up a couple of issues with respect to Packers interceptions from the '40s and '50s. T.J., I wish you all the best wherever your research may take you.

I'd also like to thank John Carpentier, owner of Stadium Sports & Antiques, and Marv Niec, Vintage Specialist at Packer City Antiques. You have both provided invaluable insight and information over the years. You know I'm going to keep coming back to visit—and purchase.

Finally, I want to express my gratitude to Krause Publications, especially Paul Kennedy, acquisitions manager, and Dennis Thornton, book editor. The enthusiasm you have shown for this project has energized me, and I appreciate all the help you have given me. Thank you.

The following also provided assistance.

Mr. Don Langenkamp

Ms. Shirley Leonard

Mrs. Lois Lawniczak

Mrs. Dorothy Wittig

Mr. Steven P. Gietschier, *The Sporting News*

Mr. John Bostrom, Chicago Bears

Mr. Scott Berchtold, Green Bay Packers

Mr. Chuck Giordana, Green Bay Packers
Hall of Fame

Mr. Keith Newton, Indianapolis Colts

Mr. Mike Taylor, Los Angeles Raiders

Mr. Ed Croke, New York Giants

Mr. Jim Gallagher, Philadelphia Eagles

Mr. Bob Rose, Phoenix Cardinals

Mr. Dan Edwards, Pittsburgh Steelers

Mr. Jerry Walker, San Francisco 49ers

Mr. John C. Konoza, Washington Redskins

The Atlanta Falcons

The Cleveland Browns

The Detroit Lions

The Minnesota Vikings

The New England Patriots

The New York Jets

Mr. Solon S. Barnett, Jr.

Mr. John R. Biolo

Mr. Tony Canadeo

Mr. Lon Evans

Mr. Bob Kercher

Acknowledgments...continued

Mr. Darrell R. Lester

Mr. George McInerney

Mr. Bernard J. Scherer

Mr. Seymour Siwoff, Elias Sports Bureau

Mr. Steve Hirdt, Elias Sports Bureau

Mr. Chris Thorn, Elias Sports Bureau

Ms. Nancy J. Pierce, NFL Alumni

Mr. Joe Horrigan, NFL Hall of Fame

Ms. Leslie Hammond, NFL Promotions

Mr. Jim Heffernan, NFL Director of Public Relations

Mr. Paul Spinelli, NFL Properties

Ms. Carol O'Brien, University of Minnesota

Mr. Roger Wright

Mr. Jeff Ash, Green Bay Press-Gazette

The Sport Information Offices of:

Auburn University

Baylor University

Bucknell University

Catholic University

Duke University

Florida University

Fresno State University

Georgetown University

Indiana University

Kalamazoo University

Lincoln University

Memphis State University

Notre Dame University

Rice University

St. Mary's University (CA)

Southern Methodist University

Texas Christian University

Texas A&M University

University of Alabama

University of California-Los Angeles

University of Cincinnati

University of Iowa

University of Miami-Ohio

University of Michigan

University of Minnesota-Duluth

University of Missouri

University of Nebraska

University of New Mexico

University of San Francisco

University of Southern California

University of Utah

University of Washington

Washington & Jefferson

Forrest Gregg played offensive tackle for the Packers during the "Glory Years" of the 1960s, was elected to the Pro Football Hall of Fame, and later coached the team for four years. Stiller-Lefebvre Collection

Earl "Curly" Lambeau not only helped found the Green Bay Packers, he played from 1921-29 and coached the team until 1949. Yes, that's his name on Lambeau Field, which was named for him in 1965. Stiller-Lefebvre Collection

Explanation of Abbreviations

GB = Green Bay
OPP = opponents
Att. = attendance
Att = attempts
Yds = yards
Avg = average per attempt
LG = longest gain
TD = touchdown
No = number
Com = completions
In = number of passes had intercepted
YL = yards lost attempting to pass
Tk/Yds = number of times sacked and yards lost
Rate = player's passer rating
In20 = number of punts inside opponents' 20-yard line
TB = number of punts in end zone for a touchback
HB = number of punts had blocked
FC = number of fair catches
TDr = touchdowns rushing
TDp = touchdowns receiving
TDrt = touchdowns on returns and recoveries
PAT = points after touchdown
FG = field goals
S = safeties
TP = total points

Fum = number of fumbles committed
Ow = number of own fumbles recovered
Op = number of opponents' fumbles recovered
Tot = number of total fumbles recovered
W = wins
L = losses
T = ties
Pct = team's winning percentage
PF = points a team scored (points for)
PA = points a team gave up (points against)
Pos = position
Ht = height
Wt = weight
DOB = date of birth
G = number of games played
Rnd = round
Rush = number of yards rushing
Rec = number of yards receiving
P-rt = number of yards on punt returns
K-rt = number of yards on kickoff returns
Int = number of yards on interception returns
Fum = number of yards on recovered fumbles
Tot = total yards gained
100 = number of 100-yard games

THE TOWN TEAMS

Football and the city of Green Bay, Wis., have been intertwined for more than a century.

The first recorded semi-pro game in Green Bay took place on Oct. 1, 1896. Marinette, another Wisconsin city that boasted a team, defeated the locals 24-0. From that point forward, with the exception of 1916, Green Bay fielded a town team every year through the end of World War I.

In 1917, a group of "all-stars" from the city defeated the Badgers of Marinette 27-0. Nate Abrams played end. Playing right halfback for Green Bay was one Earl Louis (Curly) Lambeau.

On Sept. 15, 1918, a Green Bay team called the "Skidoos" beat De Pere 13-0. Nate Abrams again held down an end spot, while a Lambeau manned the right half back slot. (Whether that was Curly is unknown). The following week, many of the same players defeated Marinette 42-0 using the name "Whales." Lambeau was not among them.

Talent was scarce in 1918. A war raged overseas. A meeting was held on Oct. 9 in the editorial room of the Green Bay Press-Gazette. Football, it was decided, would continue. With Nate Abrams as captain, the city team played on through the end of November.

Two events occurred in 1919 that signaled the birth of the Packers. First, Curly Lambeau, and not Nate Abrams, was named captain of the squad on Aug. 14, 1919. And second, the city team was sponsored by the Indian Packing Company, leading to the nickname "Packers."

1919

Standing (L-R): Nichols, Powers, Coffeen, M. Zoll, Martin, Sauber, Martell, Leaper, Ladrow, Desjardins, C. Zoll, Muldoon, Rosenow, Petcka, George Whitney Calhoun. **Center:** Lambeau.
Sitting (L-R): Abrams, Gavin, McLean, Bero.

Results (10-1-0)

Date	GB		OPP
9/14	53	Menominee	0
9/21	61	Marinette	0
9/28	54	New London	0
10/5	87	Sheboygan	0
10/12	76	Racine	6
10/19	33	Ishpeming	0
10/26	85	Oshkosh	0
11/2	53	Milwaukee A.C.	0
11/9	46	Chicago A.C.	0
11/16	17	Stambaugh	0
11/23	0	Beloit	6
	565		12

The following played with the Packers in 1919.

Abrams, Nate
Bero, Henry (Tubby)
Bradlee
Coffeen, Jim
Desjardin, Jim
Dwyer, Dutch
Dwyer, Riggie
Gallagher, Jen
Gavin, Fritz
Ladrow, Wally
Lambeau, Curly
Leaper, Wes
Martell, Herm
Martin, Al
McLean, Ray
Muldoon, Andy
Nichols, Herbert L.
Petcka, Al
Powers, Sam
Rosenow, Gus
Sauber, Charlie
Wheeler, Lyle (Cowboy)
Wilson, Milt
Zoll, Martin
Zoll, Carl

1920

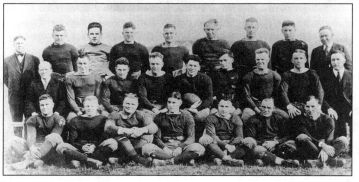

Front Row (L-R): M. Zoll, Leaper, C. Zoll, Martell, McLean, Abrams, Medley. **Second Row (L-R):** Tebo, Petcka, Gavin, Wheeler, Lambeau, Ladrow, Wagner, Dalton, Jonet.
Back Row (L-R): Delloye, Powers, Dwyer, Klaus, Nichols, Rosenow, Wilson, Sauber, Murphy.

Results (9-1-1)

Date	GB		OPP
9/26	3	Chicago	3
10/3	56	Kaukauna	0
10/10	3	Stambaugh	0
10/17	25	Marinette	0
10/24	62	De Pere	0
10/31	7	Beloit	0
11/7	9	Milwaukee	0
11/14	3	Beloit	14
11/21	19	Menominee	7
11/25	14	Stambaugh	0
11/28	26	Milwaukee A.C.	0
	227		24

The following played with the Packers in 1920.

Abrams, Nate
Bero, Henry (Tubby)
Buck, Howard (Cub)
Dalton, Jack
Dwyer, Dutch
Gallagher, Jen
Gavin, Fritz
Klaus, Fee
Ladrow, Wally
Lambeau, Curly
Leaper, Wes
Malis
Martell, Herm
McLean, Ray
Medley
Murphy
Nichols, Herbert L.
Petcka, Al
Powers, Sam
Rosenow, Gus
Sauber, Charlie
Smith
Wagner, Buff
Wheeler, Lyle (Cowboy)
Wilson, Milt
Zoll, Martin
Zoll, Carl

THE DOPE SHEET

OFFICIAL PROGRAM AND PUBLICATION, ACME-PACKERS FOOTBALL TEAM.

J. Emmett Clair, Mgr. Earl (Curley) Lambeau, Capt., Joe Hoeffel, Coach.
Harold T. I. Shannon and Associates, Advertising Agents.

SEASON 1921. GREEN BAY, NOV. 6, 1921. SEVENTH GAME.

HAMMOND TO BE HERE NEXT SUNDAY; ROCK ISLAND MAY RETURN

Charlie Mathys and his Hammond Professionals will be here next Sunday. They are one of the strongest elevens in the Western Professional Wheel and are meeting the Cardinals today. They will come into Wisconsin early in the week to train and are bent upon putting a crimp into the Packers championship hopes.

The Hammond game is as important ~~~~~~ land. Evansville lost its only game in 3 years to Hammond 3—0.

Charlie Mathys plays football to win and he will have no more scruples about dropping ~~~~~ over the Packers goal ~~~ ~~ over ~~~ other.

Charlie will get a ~~~~~~~~~~~ from home town fans ~~~~~~~ He is a great favorite and deserves it.

Hammond will be here n~~~ Sunday. They were scheduled for ~~~ day but owing to a downpour of rain in Chicago which cancelled their game with the Cardinals last Sunday they decided to ~~~~ the Cardinals today and secure ~~~~~~~~~~ their Green Bay ~~~~~~~~~~ than day.

Contracts have been mailed to Manager Flanigan of the Rock Island Independents for a return game either on Thanksgiving Day November 27th. The bigges~ item in the definite arrangements ~~ this game is the Packers insistence that Rock Island return here and the determination of the Islanders to bring the Green Bay team to their own grounds. The game will probably be played and the place announced next Sunday.

Cincinnati Celts, Columbus Pan-

(Turn to Page 5.)

SAMMY POWERS

If This Kid Had 40 Pounds More Beef—

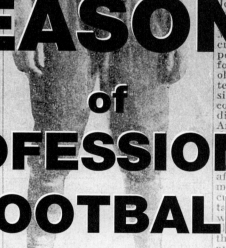

TEAM WANTS CHEER LEADER & NOISY FANS

—COACH HOEFFEL

The scrappy, peppy, scheming little "Cap'n" Joe Hoeffel of Varsity looked over one of the great team personnels of professional football in action Thursday afternoon and he was pleased. Never before had Wisconsin seen such a professional team in action and called it, her own.

It wasn't such a span since varsity days and the Badgers frenzied with joy over great conference victories paraded the striped surf of Camp Randall with their captain-idol on ~~~~~~ the stands or the campus was a mere echo compared to the "Wow, Dada!" posterity yowled forth at sundry midnight hours. The spirit of Little ~~~~~~~~~~~ again, schemy, peppy, ~~~~~~~~~~~~~~~ever.

~~~tta~~~~~~~~ a cheer leader. ~~~~~~~~ls. Bands, cheers, cr~~~~~~~~s yelling their support to the boys. That's all part of fotball and football isn't the same old game without it. We've got the team. There is no team in professional football anywhere in the country with a better galaxy of individual stars than the Packers. And never again will it be said that ~~~~lac~~~~nization. The boys ~~~~~~~~~~~~g the most intense ~~~~~~~~~~eek. They know that ~~~~~~~~~~~~ every week hereafter to stay with the team. That means stars and all. No man is excused from team practice. We'll ta~~ care of the team end of it but we~~ rather play football games with ~~~~ old yelling and fan support than exhibitions which are quiet and theatric. For the rest of the ~~~~~on ~~n't Green Bay or for that ~~~~~~ Fox River Valley take this ~~~~ up and cheer them ~~~ ~~~~ championship of our division of the league? The old college

(Turn to Page 5.)

</div>

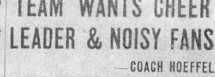

EIGHTY-THREE SEASONS of PROFESSIONAL FOOTBALL 1921 - 2003

(L-R): Herm Martell, Ray Lambeau, Jim Cook, Nate Abrams, Bill DuMoe, Lyle Wheeler, Buff Wagner, Frank Coughlin, Norm Barry, Joe Carey, Richard Murray, Curly Lambeau, Dave Hayes, Cub Buck, Art Schmaehl, Milt Wilson, Wally Ladrow, Grover Malone, Fee Klaus, Tubby Howard, Sammy Powers, Ray McLean, unknown, Emmett Clair.

3-2-1   1921   3-2-1

"In the greatest game of football ever seen on a Green Bay gridiron, the Packers celebrated their entrance into the Professional Football league by taking the far-famed Minneapolis Marines into camp to the tune of 7 to 6 before a crowd that jammed every corner of the field at Hagemeister Park."

That historic game, as described by Green Bay Press-Gazette sports editor George Whitney Calhoun, launched Green Bay and the Packers into the world of professional sport. The event lived up to its billing, particularly in the fourth quarter.

Cub Buck, Dave Hayes, Curly Lambeau, Buff Wagner, Fee Klaus and Art Schmaehl all played a role in the game-winning score. Midway through the final period, Hayes recovered Ben Dvorak's fumble. Lambeau and Wagner wasted no time as they collaborated on a pass play that reached the Marines' 14-yard line. Four plays netted 10 yards before Schmaehl, taking a direct center from Klaus, rumbled into the end zone. With Buck holding, Lambeau kicked the extra point.

The Packers then held the Marines scoreless for the final five minutes.

Green Bay had been home to a number of football teams as far back as the 1890s. In 1919, Lambeau convinced his employer, the Indian Packing Company, to sponsor a team. Lambeau was elected captain; Calhoun served as publicity director.

The team became known as the Packers. In its first year, the club blew out its first 10 opponents by a combined score of 565 to 6. A controversial, season-ending 6-0 loss to Beloit was the only setback suffered.

A year later, the Indian Packing Company sold out to the Acme Packing Corporation, which took up sponsorship of the team. Green Bay again fared well, going 9-1-1, with its only loss coming at the hands of Beloit.

The American Professional Football Association was born that year. In 1921, the entity reorganized itself, and John and Emmett Clair of the Acme Packing Corporation were given a franchise. The Packers were going professional.

Green Bay breezed through four games against non-league competition before hosting the Marines. The team beat Chicago 13-0, Rockford 49-0, Chicago-Hamburg 40-0, and Beloit 7-0.

In the weeks following the Minnesota game, the Packers lost to Rock Island 13-3, trounced Evansville 43-6, beat Hammond 14-7, and tied the Chicago Cardinals 3-3.

Green Bay endured a second loss on the final weekend of the season in what was the first exchange between two teams that would go on to become the oldest and fiercest rivals in professional football. On Nov. 27, Green Bay (3-1-1) traveled to Cubs Park to meet the Chicago Staleys (6-1). Chicago roared to a 14-0 halftime lead, then added a fourth-quarter score for good measure. On fourth down, Chick Harley tossed a short touchdown pass to George Halas to cap off that initial encounter. A year later, the Staleys became the Bears, and they and the Packers continue to do battle to this day.

1921

TEAM STATISTICS

Regular Season 3-2-1

Date	GB		OPP
10/23	7	Minneapolis Marines	6
10/30	3	Rock Island Independents	13
11/6	43	Evansville Crimson Giants	6
11/13	14	Hammond Pros	7
11/20	3	at Chicago Cardinals	3
11/27	0	at Chicago Staleys	20

Score By Periods

	1	2	3	4	Total
Packers	24	15	14	17	70
Opponents	13	14	7	21	55

INDIVIDUAL STATISTICS

Touchdown Passes

	No
Lambeau	1
Packers	**1**
Opponents	2

Scoring

	TDr	TDp	TDrt	PAT	FG	S	TP
Lambeau	2	0	0	7	3	0	28
DuMoe	0	1	1	0	0	0	12
Schmaehl	2	0	0	0	0	0	12
Abrams	0	0	1	0	0	0	6
N. Barry	1	0	0	0	0	0	6
L. Howard	1	0	0	0	0	0	6
Packers	**6**	**1**	**2**	**7**	**3**	**0**	**70**
Opponents	5	2	1	4	1	0	55

NFL STANDINGS

	W	L	T	Pct	PF	PA
Chicago Staleys	9	1	1	.900	128	53
Buffalo All-Americans	9	1	2	.900	211	29
Akron Pros	8	3	1	.727	148	31
Canton Bulldogs	5	2	3	.714	106	55
Rock Island Independents	4	2	1	.667	65	30
Evansville Crimson Giants	3	2	0	.600	87	46
Green Bay Packers	**3**	**2**	**1**	**.600**	**70**	**55**
Dayton Triangles	4	4	1	.500	96	67
Chicago Cardinals	3	3	2	.500	54	53
Rochester Jeffersons	2	3	0	.400	85	76
Cleveland Indians	3	5	0	.375	95	58
Washington Senators	1	2	0	.333	21	28
Cincinnati Celts	1	3	0	.250	14	117
Hammond Pros	1	3	1	.250	17	45
Minneapolis Marines	1	3	1	.250	37	41
Detroit Tigers	1	5	1	.167	19	109
Columbus Panhandles	1	8	0	.111	47	222
Tonawanda Kardex	0	1	0	.000	0	45
Muncie Flyers	0	2	0	.000	0	28
Louisville Brecks	0	2	0	.000	0	27
New York Giants	0	2	0	.000	0	72

ROSTER

Name	Pos	Ht	Wt	College	G
Abrams, Nate	E	5-7	160	No college	1
Barry, Norm	B	5-9	170	Notre Dame	5
Buck, Howard (Cub)	T	6-3	250	Wisconsin	6
Carey, Joseph	G	6-0	185	Illinois Tech	6
Cook, Jim	G	6-2	245	Notre Dame	2
Coughlin, Frank	T	6-2	215	Notre Dame	5
DuMoe, Bill (Gus)	E	5-11	165	No college	6
Hayes, Dave	E	5-11	165	Notre Dame	6
Howard, Lynn (Tubby)	B	5-11	210	Indiana	4
Keefe, Adolph	G	6-1	210	No college	1
Klaus, Feryl (Fee)	C	6-1	180	No college	4
Kliebhan, Roger	B	6-0	210	UW-Milwaukee	1
Ladrow, Wally	B	6-0	185	No college	1
Lambeau, Earl (Curly)	B	6-0	190	Notre Dame	6
Malone, John (Grover)	B	5-10	195	Notre Dame	6
Martell, Herman	E	6-0	160	No college	1
McLean, Ray (Toody)	B	5-9	165	No college	3
Murray, Richard (Jab)	C/T	6-3	250	Marquette	5
Powers, Sammy	G	6-0	150	Northern Michigan	4
Schmaehl, Art	B	5-10	165	No college	6
Smith, Warren	G	6-1	215	Western Michigan	2
Wagner, Almore (Buff)	B	5-9	165	Carroll	4
Wheeler, Lyle (Cowboy)	E	6-0	190	Ripon	3
Wilson, Richard (Milt)	G	6-1	200	UW-Oshkosh	6
Zoll, Martin	G	5-11	190	No college	1

The following also played with the Packers in non-league games.

Name	Pos	Ht	Wt	College
Douglas, George	C	6-2	200	Marquette
Elliott, Burton	B	6-0	185	Marquette
Gavin, Fritz	E	6-0	195	Marquette
Glick, Eddie	B	5-11	165	Marquette
Lande, Cliff	E	5-11	180	Carroll
Leaper, Wes	E	6-1	190	Wisconsin
Oakes, Bill	T	6-3	220	Haskell
Rosenow, Gus	B	6-0	185	Ripon
Sullivan, Walter	G	6-0	195	Beloit
Williams, Dick	B	6-1	180	Wisconsin
Zoll, Carl	G	5-11	240	No college

TOP ROW: (L-R) Tubby Howard, Jug Earp, Whitey Woodin, Dave Hayes
MIDDLE ROW: (L-R) Curly Lambeau, Cub Buck, Lyle Wheeler, Moose Gardner, Charlie Mathys
BOTTOM ROW: (L-R) Walter Niemann, Dewey Lyle, Stan Mills, Richard Murray

4-3-3 1922 4-3-3

In 1922, the Packers found out early and often that competition in the professional ranks was much tougher than that provided by the clubs they consistently overwhelmed in 1919 and 1920. Green Bay opened with three straight losses—nearly as many defeats as they had endured in three previous years combined—and didn't make it above the .500 mark until bouncing the Racine Legion 14-0 in the season finale.

Just that the Packers were playing football in 1922 was an accomplishment in and of itself. In January, the league expelled the team for using college players in its 20-0 loss to the Bears. John Clair surrendered the franchise at the winter AFPA meeting.

Curly Lambeau stepped in. He applied for the franchise and on June 24, the league granted Lambeau the right to field a team and compete in what had become the National Football League.

Green Bay's off-the-field woes, however, lingered throughout the season. Money was tight, and a rainy year kept attendance down. The team purchased rain insurance and was ready to cash in after a downpour drenched the Columbus game of Nov. 5, but the total that fell came up three one-hundredths of an inch short of the amount needed for a payout.

In November, a Thanksgiving Day game with the Bears failed to materialize because the Packers could not meet George Halas' request for a $4,000 guarantee. Green Bay hosted Duluth instead, but only after A.B. Turnbull, business manager of the Green Bay Press-Gazette, advanced the team enough money to meet its guarantee. Rain had caused Lambeau and George Calhoun to question whether or not to play the game.

Turnbull, who became the team's first president in 1923, also promised to rally support for the financially-strapped organization. Because of his intervention, the team finished out the year.

Three key players were added in 1922: Jug Earp, Whitey Woodin, and Charlie Mathys. Earp started the last seven games at right tackle after coming over from Rock Island. Woodin, who started the season with Racine, played six games at guard. Mathys, a hometown product who had starred at Green Bay West High School, started 10 straight for the Packers at quarterback.

The Packers dropped their first two games (to Rock Island 19-14 and Racine 10-6). In both, Green Bay failed to score a touchdown in the fourth quarter despite excellent field position. Eddie Novak batted down Lambeau's fourth-down throw in the last two minutes of the first game, and the Packers were left stranded at the Legion 20-yard line at the end of the second game.

Green Bay finally got into the win column on Nov. 5. Cub Buck kicked a field goal from the 25-yard line in the third quarter to defeat Columbus 3-0.

The Packers then won three of their last four games. In Week 9, Lambeau ran for a pair of touchdowns in a 13-0 romp over Milwaukee. Green Bay closed its season with a 14-0 victory over Racine, which left the team with a 4-3-3 record, good for a seventh-place tie with Dayton.

1922

TEAM STATISTICS

Regular Season 4-3-3

Date	GB		OPP
10/1	14	at Rock Island Independents	19
10/8	6	Racine Legion	10
10/15	3	at Chicago Cardinals	16
10/22	0	at Milwaukee Badgers	0
10/29	0	Rock Island Independents	0
11/5	3	Columbus Panhandles	0
11/12	14	Minneapolis Marines	6
11/19	3	at Racine Legion	3
11/26	13	Milwaukee Badgers	0
12/3	14	Racine Legion (at Milwaukee)	0

Score By Periods

	1	2	3	4	Total
Packers	6	24	3	37	70
Opponents	9	26	7	12	54

INDIVIDUAL STATISTICS

Touchdown Passes

	No
Lambeau	3
Packers	**3**
Opponents	1

Scoring

	TDr	TDp	TDrt	PAT	FG	S	TP
Lambeau	3	0	0	3	1	0	24
Mathys	0	2	0	0	1	0	15
Buck	0	0	0	3	1	0	6
Cronin	0	1	0	0	0	0	6
Taugher	1	0	0	0	0	0	6
Usher	1	0	0	0	0	0	6
Wheeler	0	0	1	0	0	0	6
Packers	**5**	**3**	**1**	**7**	**3**	**0**	**70**
Opponents	5	1	0	3	5	0	54

NFL STANDINGS

	W	L	T	Pct	PF	PA
Canton Bulldogs	10	0	2	1.000	184	15
Chicago Bears	9	3	0	.750	123	44
Chicago Cardinals	8	3	0	.727	96	50
Toldeo Maroons	5	2	2	.714	94	59
Rock Island Independents	4	2	1	.667	154	27
Racine Legion	6	4	1	.600	122	56
Dayton Triangles	4	3	1	.571	80	62
Green Bay Packers	**4**	**3**	**3**	**.571**	**70**	**54**
Buffalo All-Americans	5	4	1	.556	87	41
Akron Pros	3	5	2	.375	146	95
Milwaukee Badgers	2	4	3	.333	51	71
Oorang Indians	2	6	0	.250	69	190
Minneapolis Marines	1	3	0	.250	19	40
Louisville Brecks	1	3	0	.250	13	140
Evansville Crimson Giants	0	3	0	.000	6	88
Rochester Jeffersons	0	4	1	.000	13	76
Hammond Pros	0	5	1	.000	0	69
Columbus Panhandles	0	7	0	.000	24	174

ROSTER

Name	Pos	Ht	Wt	College	G
Buck, Howard (Cub)	T	6-3	250	Wisconsin	10
Cronin, Tommy	B	5-8	170	Marquette	
Davis, Pahl	G	6-1	185	Marquette	
Dunnigan, Merton (Pat)	E	5-11	210	Minnesota	2
Earp, Francis (Jug)	T	6-1	235	Monmouth	7
Faye, Allen	E	6-1	205	Marquette	1
Gardella, August (Gus)	B	5-10	185	No college	7
Gardner, Milton (Moose)	G	6-2	224	Wisconsin	9
Glick, Eddie	B	5-11	165	Marquette	
Hayes, Dave	E	5-11	165	Notre Dame	7
Howard, Lynn (Tubby)	E	5-11	210	Indiana	8
Lambeau, Earl (Curly)	B	6-0	190	Notre Dame	8
Lauer, Harold (Dutch)	B	5-11	184	Detroit	2
Lyle, Dewey	G	6-0	202	Minnesota	2
Mathys, Charlie	QB	5-8	165	Indiana	10
Mills, Stan	B	5-11	190	Penn State	8
Murray, Richard (Jab)	T	6-3	250	Marquette	3
Nadolney, Romanus (Peaches)	T/G	5-11	230	Notre Dame	8
Niemann, Walter	C	6-0	170	Michigan	8
Owens, Ralph (Rip)	G	6-0	210	Lawrence	3
Regnier, Pete (Doc)	B	5-11	170	Minnesota	5
Secord, Joe	C	6-1	190	No college	2
Smith, Rex	E	6-1	200	UW-LaCrosse	2
Taugher, Claude	B	5-10	185	Marquette	2
Usher, Eddie	B	6-0	195	Michigan	5
Wheeler, Lyle (Cowboy)	E	6-0	190	Ripon	8
Woodin, Howard (Whitey)	G	5-11	206	Marquette	6
Zoll, Carl	G	5-11	240	No college	1

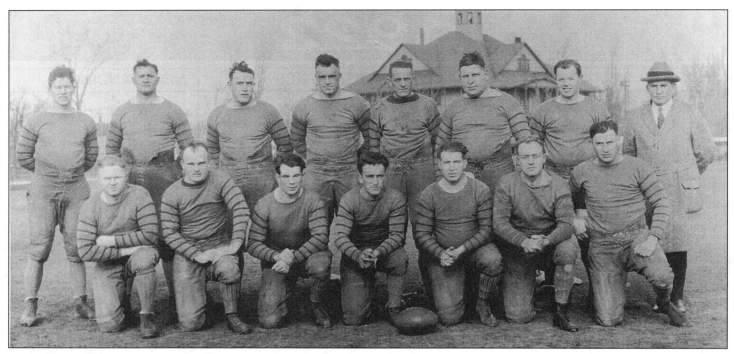

FRONT ROW: (L-R) Whitey Woodin, Norbert Hayes, Fritz Gavin, Charlie Mathys, Tommy Mills, Lyle Wheeler, Dewey Lyle.
BACK ROW: (L-R) Curly Lambeau, Richard Murray, Jug Earp, Moose Gardner, Walter Niemann, Cub Buck, Coach George Carey

7-2-1   1923   7-2-1

Professional football: a game or a business? The Packers aligned themselves more closely with the latter when on Aug. 18, 1923, the "Articles of Incorporation for the Green Bay Football Corporation" were filed with the State of Wisconsin. Andrew Turnbull was named president.

Turnbull, Leland H. Joannes, Dr. W. Webber Kelly, attorney Gerald F. Clifford, and Curly Lambeau were key players in the move to incorporate. Collectively, they became known as the "Hungry Five" because of their determination to keep the Packers solvent. The five spearheaded two sales of stock. The second—staged in late-summer—produced enough capital to ensure a third season of professional football in Green Bay.

With finances in hand, Lambeau promised to field a winner. Unlike the previous two years when more than two dozen players saw action in each season, only 17 suited up in 1923. With Jack Grey and Hal Hansen playing in only one game apiece and Wes Leaper making but two appearances, the bulk of playing time was logged by a mere 14 men. This reliance on a relative few peaked in Week 2 against the St. Louis All-Stars when all 11 starters played 60 minutes.

Green Bay played its home games at Bellevue Park in 1923. Hagemeister Park, which had been the team's field in 1921 and 1922, was gone, having been dug up to build a new Green Bay East High School. Bellevue Park served the Packers for two seasons, with the team compiling an 8-3-3 record there.

The Packers opened play against the Minneapolis Marines

as they had done in 1921. The result was equally satisfying. Two second-half touchdown runs by halfback Myrt Basing gave Green Bay a 12-0 win.

The team then entered a rough, four-game stretch in which it managed but one win. A scoreless tie with St. Louis was followed by a 3-0 loss to the Bears in which Ed Sternaman's field goal provided the difference. The Packers defeated the Milwaukee Badgers 12-0, but picked up a second loss when Racine's Milt Romney, Dick Halladay, and Al Elliott each threw a touchdown pass in a 24-3 rout.

The loss inspired Green Bay. The club won its last five games, including contests at St. Louis and Racine, where it made up for earlier failings. Cub Buck started the streak with a 28-yard field goal that sank the All-Stars 3-0 in a sea of mud at Sportsmen's Park on Nov. 4. A week later, Lambeau, Stan Mills, and Fritz Gavin each rushed more than 20 times in a 16-0 triumph in Racine.

Charlie Mathys and Lambeau worked some magic to garner a third consecutive win. Mathys tossed a third-quarter screen pass to Lambeau for the go-ahead score in a 10-7 decision in Milwaukee.

Green Bay wrapped up play with two late-November home contests. In the first, Lambeau's 40-yard scoring pass to Mills capped a 10-0 shutout of Duluth. In the second, Mathys, Mills, and Lambeau each scored touchdowns in a 19-0 victory over Hammond. With those wins, the Packers finished 7-2-1 to make good on Lambeau's preseason prediction.

1923

TEAM STATISTICS

Regular Season   7-2-1

Date	GB		OPP
9/30	12	Minneapolis Marines	0
10/7	0	St. Louis All-Stars	0
10/14	0	Chicago Bears	3
10/21	12	Milwaukee Badgers	0
10/28	3	Racine Legion	24
11/4	3	at St. Louis All-Stars	0
11/11	16	at Racine Legion	0
11/18	10	at Milwaukee Badgers	7
11/25	10	Duluth Eskimos	0
11/29	19	Hammond Pros	0

Score By Periods

	1	2	3	4	Total
Packers	18	10	36	21	85
Opponents	0	20	7	7	34

INDIVIDUAL STATISTICS

Touchdown Passes

	No
Lambeau	3
Mathys	2
Packers	**5**
Opponents	3

Scoring

	TDr	TDp	TDrt	PAT	FG	S	TP
Buck	0	0	0	5	6	0	23
Lambeau	1	2	0	0	0	0	18
Mills	1	2	0	0	0	0	18
Basing	2	0	0	0	0	0	12
Mathys	1	0	0	0	0	0	6
Wheeler	0	1	0	0	0	0	6
Niemann	0	0	0	0	0	1	2
Packers	**5**	**5**	**0**	**5**	**6**	**1**	**85**
Opponents	1	3	0	4	2	0	34

NFL STANDINGS

	W	L	T	Pct	PF	PA
Canton Bulldogs	11	0	1	1.000	246	19
Chicago Bears	9	2	1	.818	123	35
Green Bay Packers	**7**	**2**	**1**	**.778**	**85**	**34**
Milwaukee Badgers	7	2	3	.778	100	49
Cleveland Indians	3	1	3	.750	52	49
Chicago Cardinals	8	4	0	.667	161	56
Duluth Kelleys	4	3	0	.571	35	33
Columbus Tigers	5	4	1	.556	119	35
Buffalo All-Americans	4	4	3	.500	94	43
Racine Legion	4	4	2	.500	86	76
Toledo Maroons	2	3	2	.400	41	66
Rock Island Independents	2	3	3	.400	84	62
Minneapolis Marines	2	5	2	.286	48	81
St. Louis All-Stars	1	4	2	.200	14	39
Hammond Pros	1	5	1	.167	14	59
Akron Pros	1	6	0	.143	25	74
Dayton Triangles	1	6	1	.143	16	95
Oorang Indians	1	10	0	.091	43	257
Louisville Brecks	0	3	0	.000	0	90
Rochester Jeffersons	0	4	0	.000	6	141

ROSTER

Name	Pos	Ht	Wt	College	G
Basing, Myrt	B	6-0	200	Lawrence	9
Buck, Howard (Cub)	T	6-3	250	Wisconsin	10
Earp, Francis (Jug)	T/C	6-1	235	Monmouth	8
Gardner, Milton (Moose)	G	6-2	224	Wisconsin	9
Gavin, Patrick (Buck)	B	6-0	195	No college	9
Gray, Jack (Dolly)	E	5-11	180	No college	1
Hansen, Hal	B	6-3	220	Minnesota	1
Hayes, Norbert	E	5-10	200	Marquette	6
Lambeau, Earl (Curly)	B	6-0	190	Notre Dame	10
Leaper, Wes	E	6-1	210	Wisconsin	2
Lyle, Dewey	E/G/T	6-0	220	Minnesota	9
Mathys, Charlie	QB	5-8	165	Indiana	10
Mills, Stan	B	5-11	190	Penn State	9
Murray, Richard (Jab)	T/E	6-3	250	Marquette	9
Niemann, Walter	C	6-0	170	Michigan	10
Wheeler, Lyle (Cowboy)	E	6-0	190	Ripon	10
Woodin, Howard (Whitey)	G	5-11	206	Marquette	10

FRONT ROW: (L-R) Curly Lambeau, Dick O'Donnell, Verne Lewellen, Dutch Hendrian, Charlie Mathys, Walter Niemann, Lester Hearden, Myrt Basing.
BACK ROW: (L-R) Tillie Voss, Roman Rosatti, Moose Gardner, Jug Earp, Whitey Woodin, Cub Buck, Wilfred Duford, Richard Murray.

7-4-0 1924 7-4-0

In 1924, Green Bay opened with two consecutive road games for the first and only time in its history. The results were less than satisfactory.

On Sept. 28, the Packers traveled to Duluth where they lost five fumbles and threw two interceptions. Myrt Basing's early fourth-quarter fumble was turned into a touchdown by the Kelleys, who won 6-3.

In Chicago a week later, Green Bay missed five field goal attempts in a 3-0 loss to the Cardinals. Cub Buck misfired four times, and Curly Lambeau blew his lone attempt late in the fourth quarter. Chicago's success rate wasn't much better (1 of 5), but the Cardinals made Paddy Driscoll's 40-yarder in the first quarter hold up.

Saddled with two losses, the Packers were forced to chase the likes of Cleveland, Duluth, Rock Island, and the Bears in the race for the league crown. Six straight wins kept them within striking distance, but a 3-0 loss to the Bears on Nov. 23 all but ended their title dreams. A win over Kansas City and a season-ending loss to Racine gave Green Bay a 7-4 record, good for a sixth-place finish.

The loss to Chicago stood in stark contrast to what had transpired two months earlier. On Sept. 21, the Packers beat the Bears 5-0 for the first time ever, but the game didn't count in the standings. League play had not yet started. To this day, the NFL does not recognize the game; instead, the game with the Kelleys served as the Packers' official season opener.

Verne Lewellen was the most noteworthy addition to the team's roster. The running back from Nebraska played nine years in Green Bay and is considered one of the greatest punters of his era. He could score as well, and retired in 1932 with 51 touchdowns, then an NFL record.

The Packers opened their six-game winning streak with a 16-0 shutout of Kansas City. Tillie Voss initiated the scoring on a 45-yard touchdown pass from Curly Lambeau and Dutch Hendrian finished it off with his only field goal as a Packer. In between, Lewellen bagged his first touchdown on a short, third-quarter run.

Green Bay blanked its next two foes (Milwaukee and Minneapolis) as well. The first matchup featured a Buck pass to Lambeau for a touchdown on a fake field goal try, and the second saw Hendrian lead the way with two second-quarter touchdown runs.

Green Bay notched its fourth win against Racine. Lambeau and Voss opened the fourth quarter with a 40-yard scoring collaboration that beat the Legion 6-3.

Interceptions by Lambeau and Voss helped the Packers secure a fifth straight win. Lambeau converted both into points with passes to Voss and Mathys as Green Bay wrapped up its home schedule by beating Duluth 13-0.

Green Bay extended its run to six straight in Milwaukee. Buck kicked a field goal and both Hendrian and Lewellen found the end zone in a 17-10 conquest.

Chicago then reared its ugly head. Hendrian fumbled a punt and Jim McMillen recovered for the Bears at the Packers' 30-yard line. After three plays netted little, Joey Sternaman split the uprights with a field goal that effectively ended Green Bay's chances for a championship.

1924

TEAM STATISTICS

Regular Season 7-4-0

Date	GB		OPP
9/28	3	at Duluth Kelleys	6
10/5	0	at Chicago Cardinals	3
10/12	16	Kansas City Blues	0
10/19	17	Milwaukee Badgers	0
10/26	19	Minneapolis Marines	0
11/2	6	Racine Legion	3
11/9	13	Duluth Kelleys	0
11/16	17	at Milwaukee Badgers	10
11/23	0	at Chicago Bears	3
11/27	17	at Kansas City Blues	6
11/30	0	at Racine Legion	7

Score By Periods

	1	2	3	4	Total
Packers	20	19	26	43	108
Opponents	6	10	3	19	38

INDIVIDUAL STATISTICS

Touchdown Passes

	No
Lambeau	8
Buck	1
Packers	**9**
Opponents	2

Scoring

	TDr	TDp	TDrt	PAT	FG	S	TP
Voss	0	5	0	0	0	0	30
Hendrian	3	0	0	0	1	0	21
Buck	0	0	0	8	3	0	17
Lewellen	2	0	0	0	0	0	12
Mathys	0	2	0	0	0	0	12
Lambeau	0	1	0	1	1	0	10
L. Hearden	0	1	0	0	0	0	6
Packers	**5**	**9**	**0**	**9**	**5**	**0**	**108**
Opponents	2	2	0	2	4	0	38

NFL STANDINGS

	W	L	T	Pct	PF	PA
Cleveland Bulldogs	7	1	1	.875	229	60
Chicago Bears	6	1	4	.857	136	55
Frankford Yellow Jackets	11	2	1	.846	326	109
Duluth Kelleys	5	1	0	.833	56	16
Rock Island Independents	6	2	2	.750	88	38
Green Bay Packers	**7**	**4**	**0**	**.636**	**108**	**38**
Racine Legion	4	3	3	.571	69	47
Chicago Cardinals	5	4	1	.556	90	67
Buffalo Bisons	6	5	0	.545	120	140
Columbus Tigers	4	4	0	.500	91	68
Hammond Pros	2	2	1	.500	18	45
Milwaukee Badgers	5	8	0	.385	142	188
Akron Pros	2	6	0	.333	59	132
Dayton Triangles	2	6	0	.333	45	148
Kansas City Blues	2	7	0	.222	46	124
Kenosha Maroons	0	5	1	.000	12	117
Minneapolis Marines	0	6	0	.000	14	108
Rochester Jeffersons	0	7	0	.000	7	156

ROSTER

Name	Pos	Ht	Wt	College	G
Basing, Myrt	B	6-0	200	Lawrence	11
Beasey, Jack	B	6-2	195	South Dakota	1
Buck, Howard (Cub)	T	6-3	250	Wisconsin	11
Buland, Walter	T	5-11	240	No college	1
Duford, Wilfred	B	5-10	200	Marquette	3
Earp, Francis (Jug)	C	6-1	235	Monmouth	11
Gardner, Milton (Moose)	G	6-2	224	Wisconsin	11
Hearden, Lester	B	5-9	175	St. Ambrose	2
Hendrian, Oscar (Dutch)	B	5-10	200	Princeton	11
Lambeau, Earl (Curly)	B	6-0	190	Notre Dame	11
Lewellen, Verne	B	6-2	181	Nebraska	8
Mathys, Charlie	QB	5-8	165	Indiana	11
Murray, Richard (Jab)	T/E	6-3	250	Marquette	4
Niemann, Walter	C	6-0	170	Michigan	4
O'Donnell, Dick	E	5-10	196	Minnesota	9
Rosatti, Roman	T	6-2	210	Michigan	11
Usher, Eddie	B	6-0	210	Michigan	1
Voss, Walter (Tillie)	E	6-4	190	Detroit Mercy	11
Woodin, Howard (Whitey)	G	5-11	206	Marquette	11

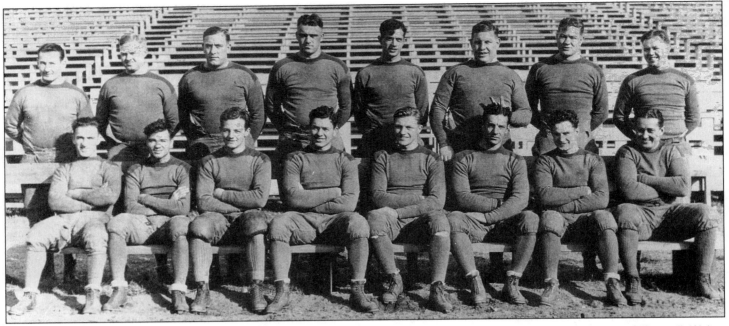

FRONT ROW: (L-R) Charlie Mathys, Marty Norton, Eddie Kotal, Curly Lambeau, Jack Harris, George Vergara, Dick O'Donnell, Walter LeJeune.
BACK ROW: (L-R) George Abramson, Whitey Woodin, Jug Earp, Moose Gardner, Verne Lewellen, Cub Buck, Fred Larson, Myrt Basing.

8-5-0   1925   8-5-0

City Stadium opened on Green Bay's east side behind the new East High School, and the facility brought a measure of stability to a team that had called two fields home in the previous four years. The executive committee of the Green Bay Packers Corporation, the city, and the local school board joined forces in building the structure, which opened with seating to accommodate more than 5,000 fans. The venue served as the Packers' home field for the next 32 years, attaining a seating capacity of 25,000 in the late 1930s.

Green Bay's first league game at City Stadium was a success. Approximately 3,000 fans saw the Packers dispatch the Hammond Pros 14-0 on the strength of a Charlie Mathys touchdown pass and a Myrt Basing run.

The team so treasured its new field, it went undefeated there in 1925. The Packers outscored the competition 119 to 23 and registered four shutouts in fashioning a 6-0 record at City Stadium.

The team's record on the road was another matter. Outside of Green Bay, the Packers notched just two wins in seven tries. Three tough losses at the end of November eliminated the team from the championship race, and ensured a less-than-stellar finish (ninth place) at 8-5-0.

In Week 2, Green Bay officially beat the Bears for the first time. Mathys and Verne Lewellen saved the day with a touchdown collaboration on the first play of the fourth quarter. Cub Buck added the extra point and, with the help of a Curly Lambeau interception in the waning moments, the Packers held on for a 14-10 win.

The Packers traveled to Rock Island on the first weekend in October. Rube Ursella's second-quarter, 20-yard field goal sent them home on the short end of a 3-0 count.

Green Bay returned for a three-game home stand. The Packers had little trouble handling Milwaukee (31-0), Rock Island (20-0), or Rochester (33-13). Marty Norton and Myrt Basing combined for 10 touchdowns in those contests as the Packers improved to 5-1.

Basing was the difference in Week 7 as the club grabbed its first win on the road, 6-0 in Milwaukee. The 200-pound fullback keyed a 13-play, 59-yard drive with 10 carries for 48 yards, including a 2-yard touchdown dive.

A week later, John (Paddy) Driscoll connected on a field goal late in the fourth quarter as the Cardinals edged Green Bay 9-6 in Chicago.

Green Bay entertained Dayton in its final home game on Nov. 15. Lewellen plowed into the end zone on the final play and added the point after for a 7-0 win.

The fourth-place Packers (7-2) closed out their schedule with four road games, three coming within a seven-day span. The Bears took revenge 21-0 in a game Lambeau missed due to injury. On Thanksgiving, Pottsville inflicted a 31-0 drubbing as George Vergara (arm/shoulder), Buck (knee), and Norton (ankle) did not play. Then, just two days later, a triple pass play—Henry Homan to Houston Stockton to George Sullivan—resulted in a fourth-quarter touchdown by Frankford that sank a battered Green Bay 13-7.

The Packers closed out with a 13-10 win over the Steam Roller in Providence.

1925

TEAM STATISTICS

Regular Season   8-5-0

Date	GB		OPP
9/20	14	Hammond Pros	0
9/27	14	Chicago Bears	10
10/4	0	at Rock Island Independents	3
10/11	31	Milwaukee Badgers	0
10/18	20	Rock Island Independents	0
10/25	33	Rochester Jeffersons	13
11/1	6	at Milwaukee Badgers	0
11/8	6	at Chicago Cardinals	9
11/15	7	Dayton Triangles	0
11/22	0	at Chicago Bears	21
11/26	0	at Pottsville Maroons	31
11/28	7	at Frankford Yellow Jackets	13
12/6	13	at Providence Steam Roller	10

Score By Periods

	1	2	3	4	Total
Packers	3	41	27	80	151
Opponents	24	24	13	49	110

INDIVIDUAL STATISTICS

Touchdown Passes

	No
Mathys	7
Lambeau	4
Packers	**11**
Opponents	7

Scoring

	TDr	TDp	TDrt	PAT	FG	S	TP
Basing	4	2	0	0	0	0	36
M. Norton	1	4	1	0	0	0	36
Lewellen	1	3	0	1	0	0	25
Abramson	0	0	0	2	2	0	8
Buck	0	0	0	8	0	0	8
Lambeau	0	0	0	5	1	0	8
Crowley	0	1	0	0	0	0	6
Gardner	0	0	1	0	0	0	6
Jack Harris	1	0	0	0	0	0	6
Kotal	0	0	1	0	0	0	6
O'Donnell	0	1	0	0	0	0	6
Packers	**7**	**11**	**3**	**16**	**3**	**0**	**151**
Opponents	6	7	1	11	5	0	110

NFL STANDINGS

	W	L	T	Pct	PF	PA
Chicago Cardinals	11	2	1	.846	230	65
Pottsville Maroons	10	2	0	.833	270	45
Detroit Panthers	8	2	2	.800	129	39
New York Giants	8	4	0	.667	122	67
Akron Pros	4	2	2	.667	65	51
Frankford Yellow Jackets	13	7	0	.667	190	169
Chicago Bears	9	5	3	.643	158	96
Rock Island Independents	5	3	3	.625	99	58
Green Bay Packers	**8**	**5**	**0**	**.615**	**151**	**110**
Providence Steam Roller	6	5	1	.545	111	101
Canton Bulldogs	4	4	0	.500	50	73
Cleveland Bulldogs	5	8	1	.385	75	135
Kansas City Cowboys	2	5	1	.286	65	97
Hammond Pros	1	4	0	.250	23	87
Buffalo Bisons	1	6	2	.143	33	113
Duluth Kelleys	0	3	0	.000	6	25
Rochester Jeffersons	0	6	1	.000	26	111
Milwaukee Badgers	0	6	0	.000	7	191
Dayton Triangles	0	7	1	.000	3	84
Columbus Tigers	0	9	0	.000	28	124

ROSTER

Name	Pos	Ht	Wt	College	G
Abramson, George	T/G	5-9	210	Minnesota	
Basing, Myrt	B	6-0	200	Lawrence	13
Buck, Howard (Cub)	T	6-3	250	Wisconsin	12
Crowley, Jim	B	5-9	165	Notre Dame	2
Earp, Francis (Jug)	T/C	6-1	235	Monmouth	13
Gardner, Milton (Moose)	G/T	6-2	224	Wisconsin	13
Harris, Welton John (Jack)	B	6-0	190	Wisconsin	11
Kotal, Eddie	B	5-10	165	Lawrence	5
Lambeau, Earl (Curly)	B	6-0	190	Notre Dame	11
Larson, Fred (O.J.)	C	6-0	215	Notre Dame	13
LeJeune, Walter	G/T	6-0	240	Heidelberg	9
Lewellen, Verne	B	6-2	181	Nebraska	10
Mathys, Charlie	QB	5-8	165	Indiana	12
Norton, Marty	B	5-8	165	Hamline	
O'Donnell, Dick	E	5-10	196	Minnesota	12
Vergara, George	E	6-1	190	Notre Dame	12
Wilkens, Elmer	E	5-10	195	Indiana	6
Woodin, Howard (Whitey)	G	5-11	206	Marquette	11

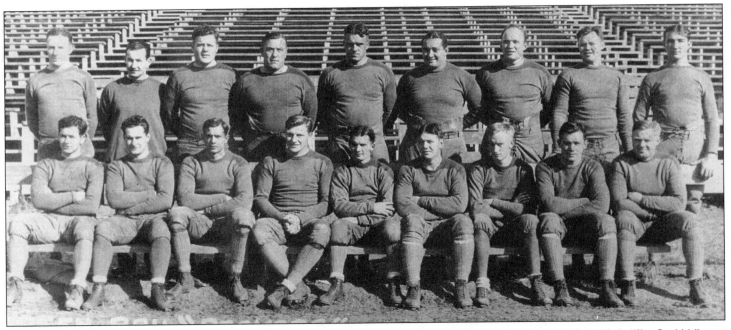

FRONT ROW: (L-R) Curly Lambeau, Dick O'Donnell, Verne Lewellen, Jack Harris, Pid Purdy, Rex Enright, Jack McAuliffe, Carl Lidberg, Whitey Woodin.
BACK ROW: (L-R) Dick Flaherty, George Abramson, Roman Rosatti, Jug Earp, Moose Gardner, Walter LeJeune, Ivan Cahoon, Myrt Basing, Hector Cyre.

7-3-3   1926   7-3-3

And then there was only Curly Lambeau. Howard (Cub) Buck's acceptance of a coaching position with the University of Miami prior to the start of the 1926 season left Lambeau as the only player remaining who had played every year with the Packers since the team turned pro in 1921. As important as Lambeau was, no player had participated in more games from 1921 through 1925 than had Buck.

For most of five seasons, the 6-foot-3, 250-pound lineman had owned the left tackle spot. He played in 49 of the team's first 50 games, making 47 straight starts (41 at left tackle) before a knee injury sidelined him for one game late in 1925. Besides playing in the trenches, Buck kicked and threw and caught an occasional pass. Hector Cyre (2 starts at left tackle), Ivan Cahoon (9) and Walter LeJeune (2) combined to fill Buck's shoes in 1926.

Two ties and a loss in the first four weeks of the season put Green Bay behind the eight ball early. The team then reeled off five straight wins to climb into fourth place by mid-November. But back-to-back losses to the front-running Bears and Yellow Jackets dashed the Packers' title hopes and the club's final 7-3-3 record was good only for fifth place.

Green Bay opened its season against the Detroit Panthers and won its seventh straight game at City Stadium. Two touchdown passes by Lambeau and one from Dunn highlighted the 21-0 rout.

A pair of no-decision games followed. In the first, the Bears escaped with a 6-6 tie after Lambeau's long, last-minute field goal attempt fell short. In the second, Green Bay's goal-line stand following an 80-yard interception return by Ernie Nevers was key in a 0-0 deadlock with Duluth.

Joseph (Red) Dunn, who would join the Packers in 1927, was nothing but trouble in Week 4. The back threw a touchdown pass, kicked two field goals, and added an extra point as the Cardinals prevailed 13-7.

Green Bay (1-1-2) ended its slide by going on a five-game tear. The Packers, who had never lost to Milwaukee, kept that record intact by edging the Badgers 7-0 on a 25-yard Lewellen touchdown run set up by Jug Earp's interception. A week later, the club blew away the Tornadoes 35-0. Pid Purdy's first-quarter field goal accounted for the third win (3-0 over the Cardinals) and Green Bay then blanked Milwaukee and Louisville in consecutive weeks.

After nine games, the Packers (6-1-2) were squarely in fourth place behind the Bears (9-0-1), Yellow Jackets (9-1-1), and Maroons (8-1). Two of Green Bay's final three games came against Chicago and Frankford.

No matter. Fourth-quarter mistakes doomed the Packers in consecutive weeks. First, John (Paddy) Driscoll returned Carl Lidberg's fumble for the decisive score in a 19-13 Bears' win. A week later, Houston Stockton fired a 39-yard touchdown pass to Henry Homan as Frankford prevailed 20-14.

Green Bay closed with a 7-0 win in Detroit, then agreed to appear in the Paddy Carr Christmas Basket benefit game at Soldier Field against the Bears on Dec. 19. There, Purdy and Driscoll traded field goals in a 3-3 tie.

1926

TEAM STATISTICS

Regular Season 7-3-3

Date	GB		OPP
9/19	21	Detroit Panthers	0
9/26	6	Chicago Bears	6
10/3	0	Duluth Eskimos	0
10/10	7	Chicago Cardinals	13
10/17	7	Milwaukee Badgers	0
10/24	35	Racine Tornadoes	0
10/31	3	at Chicago Cardinals	0
11/7	21	at Milwaukee Badgers	0
11/14	14	Louisville Colonels	0
11/21	13	at Chicago Bears	19
11/25	14	at Frankford Yellow Jackets	20
11/28	7	at Detroit Panthers	0
12/19	3	at Chicago Bears	3

Score By Periods

	1	2	3	4	Total
Packers	30	28	37	56	151
Opponents	19	10	6	26	61

INDIVIDUAL STATISTICS

Touchdown Passes

	No
Lambeau	3
Mathys	2
Kotal	1
McAuliffe	1
Purdy	1
Packers	**8**
Opponents	4

Scoring

	TDr	TDp	TDrt	PAT	FG	S	TP
Lewellen	3	3	1	0	0	0	42
Lidberg	4	0	0	0	0	0	24
Purdy	0	0	0	14	2	0	20
Flaherty	0	2	0	0	0	0	12
Jack Harris	2	0	0	0	0	0	12
Kotal	1	1	0	0	0	0	12
O'Donnell	0	2	0	0	0	0	12
Basing	1	0	0	0	0	0	6
Enright	1	0	0	0	0	0	6
Lambeau	0	0	0	4	0	0	4
Woodin	0	0	0	1	0	0	1
Packers	**12**	**8**	**1**	**19**	**2**	**0**	**151**
Opponents	2	4	1	4	5	0	61

NFL STANDINGS

	W	L	T	Pct	PF	PA
Frankford Yellow Jackets	14	1	1	.933	236	49
Chicago Bears	12	1	3	.923	216	63
Pottsville Maroons	10	2	1	.833	155	29
Kansas City Cowboys	8	3	0	.727	76	53
Green Bay Packers	**7**	**3**	**3**	**.700**	**151**	**61**
Los Angeles Buccaneers	6	3	1	.667	67	57
New York Giants	8	4	1	.667	147	51
Duluth Eskimos	6	5	3	.545	113	81
Buffalo Rangers	4	4	2	.500	53	62
Chicago Cardinals	5	6	1	.455	74	98
Providence Steam Roller	5	7	1	.417	99	103
Detroit Panthers	4	6	2	.400	107	60
Hartford Blues	3	7	0	.300	57	99
Brooklyn Lions	3	8	0	.273	60	150
Milwaukee Badgers	2	7	0	.222	41	66
Akron Pros	1	4	3	.200	23	89
Dayton Triangles	1	4	1	.200	15	82
Racine Tornadoes	1	4	0	.200	8	92
Columbus Tigers	1	6	0	.143	26	93
Canton Bulldogs	1	9	3	.100	46	161
Hammond Pros	0	4	0	.000	3	56
Louisville Colonels	0	4	0	.000	0	108

ROSTER

Name	Pos	Ht	Wt	College	G
Basing, Myrt	B/E	6-0	200	Lawrence	5
Bieberstein, Adolph	G	5-10	205	Wisconsin	1
Cahoon, Ivan (Tiny)	T	6-2	235	Gonzaga	11
Carlson, Wes	G/T	6-1	220	St. John's	
Cyre, Hector	T/E/G	6-2	216	Gonzaga	10
Earp, Francis (Jug)	C	6-1	235	Monmouth	12
Enright, Rex	B	5-11	195	Notre Dame	10
Flaherty, Dick	E	6-1	200	Marquette	12
Gardner, Milton (Moose)	G	6-2	224	Wisconsin	13
Harris, Welton John (Jack)	B/E	6-0	190	Wisconsin	10
Kotal, Eddie	B	5-10	165	Lawrence	10
Lambeau, Earl (Curly)	B	6-0	190	Notre Dame	12
LeJeune, Walter	G/T/C	6-0	242	Missouri	10
Lewellen, Verne	B	6-2	181	Nebraska	13
Lidberg, Carl (Cully)	B	6-0	200	Minnesota	11
McAuliffe, Jack	B	5-10	155	Beloit	8
Mathys, Charlie	B	5-8	165	Indiana	4
McGaw, Walter	G	5-10	195	Beloit	1
O'Donnell, Dick	E	5-10	196	Minnesota	11
Purdy, Everett (Pid)	B	5-10	175	Beloit	11
Rosatti, Roman	T	6-2	210	Michigan	10
Woodin, Howard (Whitey)	G	5-11	206	Marquette	

FRONT ROW: (L-R) Bruce Jones, Richard (Red) Smith, Whitey Woodin, Eddie Kotal, Pid Purdy, Thomas Hearden, Frank Mayer, Red Dunn, Claude Perry.
BACK ROW: (L-R) Roman Rosatti, Dick O'Donnell, Jug Earp, Verne Lewellen, Ivan Cahoon, Rex Enright, Lavvie Dilweg, Bernard Darling, Curly Lambeau.

7-2-1　　1927　　7-2-1

Though the Packers-Bears rivalry was in its infancy, Green Bay learned the price that could be paid for losing to the Monsters of the Midway. Green Bay stumbled only twice all year, both against Chicago, but those setbacks cost the Packers a championship, as Green Bay (7-2-1) had to settle for second place behind the Giants (11-1-1).

Green Bay almost pulled out a tie in its first meeting with Chicago. Down 7-0, the Packers mounted a 7-play, 57-yard drive that culminated in Verne Lewellen's touchdown plunge. But Pid Purdy didn't come close to making the extra point and the game ended shortly thereafter.

The rematch in Chicago on Nov. 20 was even more devastating. Green Bay (6-1-1) desperately needed a win in order to remain on the heels of New York (7-1-1) and break its second-place tie with the Bears (6-1-1). All went awry early in the fourth quarter when George Trafton blocked Red Dunn's field goal attempt from the 7-yard line. The Bears then proceeded to march 87 yards to pay dirt and secure a 14-6 decision.

Curly Lambeau inked a number of players in 1927 who would contribute in the championship years ahead. He secured Lavvie Dilweg and Red Dunn from the dissolved Milwaukee Badgers, and he gobbled up Claude Perry from the college ranks. Dilweg started 10 games at left end, Dunn opened at quarterback on six occasions, and Perry got five starts at tackle.

Green Bay opened with a pair of wins. Lambeau's two touchdown runs—the second coming on a short field after Jug Earp blocked Faye Abbot's punt and Ivan Cahoon recov-ered—beat Dayton 14-0. Cahoon recovered another blocked punt—this time for a touchdown—to spur the Packers past Cleveland 12-7 in Week 2.

After losing 7-6 to the Bears in Week 3, Green Bay rebounded to win four of its next five games. On Oct. 9, Dilweg returned an Ernie Nevers pass for a touchdown to cap the scoring in a 20-0 rout of Duluth. A week later, the Packers blanked the Cardinals 13-0 on the strength of touchdowns by Eddie Kotal and Verne Lewellen. Green Bay wrapped up its third win in a row with a 13-0 triumph over the Yankees.

Green Bay's run was then halted by a fired-up Cardinals team that tied the Packers in Chicago. Bill Springsteen blocked Dunn's extra point attempt after Lewellen's fourth-quarter touchdown plunge. The Cardinals then missed a late field goal themselves and the 6-6 score held up.

The Packers righted themselves with a 6-0 win over the Dayton Triangles in their home finale. Lewellen scored the only touchdown, and it was set up by a 53-yard pass from Dunn to Kotal.

That win was followed by a second loss to the Bears.

Green Bay closed out its season with a 17-9 victory at Frankford on Nov. 24. Dunn led the way with touchdown passes to Dilweg and Rex Enright.

While the Packers (7-2-1) were done, New York (8-1-1), the Bears (7-1-1), and others continued to play. When competition finally ceased on Dec. 11, Green Bay edged out the Bears (9-3-2) for second place, small consolation for the costly setbacks suffered earlier.

TEAM STATISTICS

Regular Season 7-2-1

Date	GB		OPP
9/18	14	Dayton Triangles	0
9/25	12	Cleveland Bulldogs	7
10/2	6	Chicago Bears	7
10/9	20	Duluth Eskimos	0
10/16	13	Chicago Cardinals	0
10/23	13	New York Yankees	0
11/6	6	at Chicago Cardinals	6
11/13	6	Dayton Triangles	0
11/20	6	at Chicago Bears	14
11/24	17	at Frankford Yellow Jackets	9

Score By Periods

	1	2	3	4	Total
Packers	7	32	28	46	113
Opponents	0	23	0	14	43

INDIVIDUAL STATISTICS

Touchdown Passes

	No
Dunn	3
Lambeau	1
Packers	**4**
Opponents	4

Scoring

	TDr	TDp	TDrt	PAT	FG	S	TP
Lewellen	5	0	0	0	0	0	30
Enright	2	2	0	0	0	0	24
Dunn	0	1	0	7	0	0	13
L. Dilweg	0	1	1	0	0	0	12
Lambeau	2	0	0	0	0	0	12
Purdy	1	0	0	1	1	0	10
Cahoon	0	0	1	0	0	0	6
Kotal	1	0	0	0	0	0	6
Packers	**11**	**4**	**2**	**8**	**1**	**0**	**113**
Opponents	2	4	0	4	1	0	43

NFL STANDINGS

	W	L	T	Pct	PF	PA
New York Giants	11	1	1	.917	197	20
Green Bay Packers	**7**	**2**	**1**	**.778**	**113**	**43**
Chicago Bears	9	3	2	.750	149	98
Cleveland Bulldogs	8	4	1	.667	209	107
Providence Steam Roller	8	5	1	.615	105	88
New York Yankees	7	8	1	.467	142	174
Frankford Yellow Jackets	6	9	3	.400	152	166
Pottsville Maroons	5	8	0	.385	80	163
Chicago Cardinals	3	7	1	.300	69	134
Dayton Triangles	1	6	1	.143	15	57
Duluth Eskimos	1	8	0	.111	68	134
Buffalo Bisons	0	5	0	.000	8	123

ROSTER

Name	Pos	Ht	Wt	College	G
Basing, Myrt	B	6-0	200	Lawrence	3
Bross, Marty	B	5-9	170	Gonzaga	2
Cahoon, Ivan (Tiny)	T	6-2	235	Gonzaga	8
Darling, Bernard (Boob)	C	6-3	216	Beloit	2
Dilweg, LaVern (Lavvie)	E	6-3	202	Marquette	10
Dunn, Joseph (Red)	B	6-0	178	Marquette	10
Earp, Francis (Jug)	C	6-1	235	Monmouth	10
Enright, Rex	B	5-11	195	Notre Dame	9
Hearden, Thomas	B	5-9	175	Notre Dame	4
Jones, Bruce	G	6-0	215	Alabama	9
Kotal, Eddie	B	5-10	165	Lawrence	8
Lambeau, Earl (Curly)	B	6-0	190	Notre Dame	10
Lewellen, Verne	B	6-2	181	Nebraska	10
Mayer, Frank	G/T	6-0	215	Notre Dame	10
O'Donnell, Dick	E	5-10	196	Minnesota	9
Perry, Claude	T	6-1	211	Alabama	9
Purdy, Everett (Pid)	B	5-10	175	Beloit	6
Rosatti, Roman	T	6-2	210	Michigan	6
Skeate, Gil	B	5-10	190	Gonzaga	2
Smith, Richard (Red)	G/E	5-10	225	Notre Dame	5
Tuttle, George	E	6-0	178	Minnesota	1
Woodin, Howard (Whitey)	G	5-11	206	Marquette	7

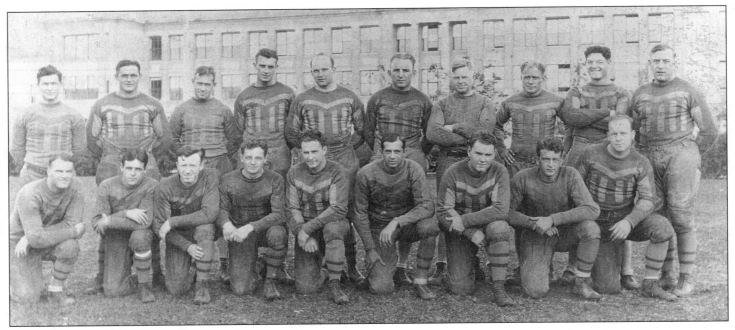

FRONT ROW: Roger Ashmore, Harry O'Boyle, Red Dunn, Eddie Kotal, Dick O'Donnell, Verne Lewellen, John Lollar, Bernard Darling, Paul Minick.
BACK ROW: (L-R) Curly Lambeau, James Bowdoin, Larry Marks, Lavvie Dilweg, Ivan Cahoon, Claude Perry, Whitey Woodin, Roy Baker, Bruce Jones, Jug Earp.

6-4-3   1928   6-4-3

Green Bay's slow start in 1928 didn't end its run for a first-ever league title. Though the 0-2-1 getaway was cause for concern, the team rebounded and settled into third place by the third week in November.

Rather, it was the club's poor play as the season wound down—its failure to beat the two league leaders combined with an unforgivable slip against one of the circuit's weakest members—that led to a 6-4-3 record and an end to title aspirations for another year.

For only the second time in its brief existence, Green Bay failed to garner a win in its first three games. A tie with the Bears, sandwiched between losses to Frankford and the Giants, dropped the Packers into a tie for last place in early October.

That the skid occurred at City Stadium was a bit disconcerting. Green Bay was tough on its home field, having earned a 16-2-2 record there from 1925 through 1927.

James Bowdoin, Bo Molenda, and Tom Nash were Curly Lambeau's top additions in 1928. Bowdoin, a guard, and Nash, an end, were rookies out of Alabama and Georgia, respectively. Molenda, a second-year man, played eight games with the Yankees before starting three of the Packers' final four games at fullback.

Green Bay fell into a hole of its own making in its season-opening, 19-9 loss to Frankford. A short punt by Verne Lewellen, a pass interference call on Dick O'Donnell, and a fumble and pass interference penalty on Red Dunn all proved costly as the Yellow Jackets opened a 19-3 lead early in the second quarter.

In Week 2, the Packers tied the Bears 12-12. Harry O'Boyle had a shot to win it, but his 25-yard field goal missed by inches and the game ended two plays later.

The slow start culminated in a 6-0 loss to the defending-champion Giants a week later. Green Bay's two best scoring threats fizzled after an apparent second-quarter touchdown by Lewellen was disallowed and Dunn's third-quarter pass from the New York 14 sailed incomplete into the end zone. The Giants' touchdown was set up by a Faye Wilson's 40-yard run.

Green Bay bounced back, winning five of its next six games. The resurgence started with a 20-0 decision over the Cardinals and ended with a 7-0 victory over the Giants in the Polo Grounds.

Perhaps the most satisfying encounter in the run occurred on Oct. 21 in Chicago. There, Green Bay defeated the Bears 16-6 for the first time in the Windy City. Bruce Jones sealed the verdict with an interception return for a touchdown on the last offensive play of the game.

Pottsville, winners of but one game in eight tries, sent the Packers into their late-season funk. The Maroons' Johnny Blood sparked a 26-0 upset with two touchdowns.

On Thanksgiving Day, second-place Frankford edged Green Bay 2-0 after a snap from center went over Lewellen's head and out of the end zone. Three days later, the Packers could manage no more than a 7-7 tie with Providence, who went on to win the championship. Eddie Kotal and O'Boyle blocked Gus Sonneberg's fourth-quarter field goal attempt to preserve the tie.

1928

TEAM STATISTICS

Regular Season   6-4-3

Date	GB		OPP
9/23	9	Frankford Yellow Jackets	19
9/30	12	Chicago Bears	12
10/7	0	New York Giants	6
10/14	20	Chicago Cardinals	0
10/21	16	at Chicago Bears	6
10/28	17	Dayton Triangles	0
11/4	26	Pottsville Maroons	14
11/11	0	New York Yankees	0
11/18	7	at New York Giants	0
11/25	0	at Pottsville Maroons	26
11/29	0	at Frankford Yellow Jackets	2
12/2	7	at Providence Steam Roller	7
12/9	6	at Chicago Bears	0

Score By Periods

	1	2	3	4	Total
Packers	15	53	13	39	120
Opponents	26	20	26	20	92

INDIVIDUAL STATISTICS

Touchdown Passes

	No
Lambeau	4
Kotal	1
Lambeau	1
Lewellen	1
Packers	**7**
Opponents	6

Scoring

	TDr	TDp	TDrt	PAT	FG	S	TP
Lewellen	6	3	0	0	0	0	54
O'Boyle	1	0	0	8	3	0	23
Kotal	2	1	0	0	0	0	18
Marks	0	2	0	0	0	0	12
Bruce Jones	0	0	1	0	0	0	6
O'Donnell	0	1	0	0	0	0	6
Dunn	0	0	0	1	0	0	1
Packers	**9**	**7**	**1**	**9**	**3**	**0**	**120**
Opponents	6	6	2	6	0	1	92

NFL STANDINGS

	W	L	T	Pct	PF	PA
Providence Steam Roller	8	1	2	.889	128	42
Frankford Yellow Jackets	11	3	2	.786	175	84
Detroit Wolverines	7	2	1	.778	189	76
Green Bay Packers	**6**	**4**	**3**	**.600**	**120**	**92**
Chicago Bears	7	5	1	.583	182	85
New York Giants	4	7	2	.364	79	136
New York Yankees	4	8	1	.333	103	179
Pottsville Maroons	2	8	0	.200	74	134
Chicago Cardinals	1	5	0	.167	7	107
Dayton Triangles	0	7	0	.000	9	131

ROSTER

Name	Pos	Ht	Wt	College	G
Ashmore, Roger	T	6-1	212	Gonzaga	13
Baker, Roy (Bullet)	B	6-0	177	USC	12
Bowdoin, James	G	6-2	220	Alabama	11
Cahoon, Ivan (Tiny)	T	6-2	235	Gonzaga	10
Darling, Bernard (Boob)	C	6-3	216	Beloit	7
Dilweg, LaVern (Lavvie)	E	6-3	202	Marquette	12
Dunn, Joseph (Red)	B	6-0	178	Marquette	12
Earp, Francis (Jug)	C/T	6-1	235	Monmouth	13
Griffen, Harold	C	6-3	238	Iowa	5
Hearden, Thomas	B	5-9	175	Notre Dame	1
Jones, Bruce	G	6-0	215	Alabama	13
Kotal, Eddie	B	5-10	165	Lawrence	12
Lambeau, Earl (Curly)	B/E	6-0	190	Notre Dame	8
Lewellen, Verne	B	6-2	181	Nebraska	13
Lollar, John	B	6-0	200	Samford	3
Marks, Larry	B	5-11	185	Indiana	11
Minick, Paul	G	5-11	210	Iowa	
Molenda, John (Bo)	B	5-11	208	Michigan	4
Nash, Tom	E	6-3	210	Georgia	8
O'Boyle, Harry	B	6-1	180	Notre Dame	11
O'Donnell, Dick	E	5-10	196	Minnesota	13
Perry, Claude	T	6-1	211	Alabama	13
Webber, Howard	E	6-0	185	Kansas State	3
Woodin, Howard (Whitey)	G	5-11	206	Marquette	10

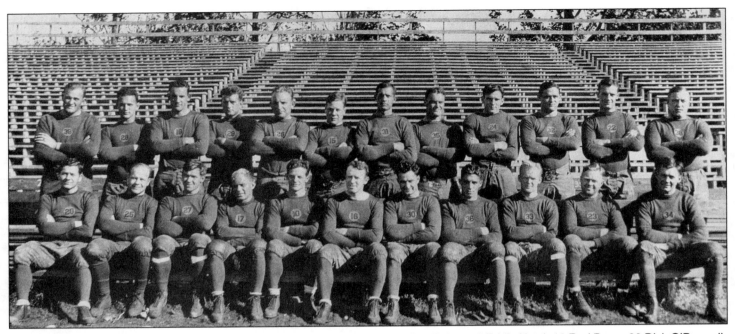

FRONT ROW: (L-R) 20 Curly Lambeau, 25 Paul Minick, 27 Bo Molenda, 17 Roy Baker, 10 Eddie Kotal, 16 Red Dunn, 30 Dick O'Donnell, 36 Mike Michalske, 33 William Kern, 23 Whitey Woodin, 34 Carl Lidberg.
BACK ROW: (L-R) 39 Cal Hubbard, 28 Hurdis McCrary, 19 Tom Nash, 29 Bernard Darling, 26 Claude Perry, 15 Red Smith, 31 Verne Lewellen, 35 Roger Ashmore, 24 Johnny Blood, 32 James Bowdoin, 22 Lavvie Dilweg, 38 Jug Earp.

12-0-1   1929   12-0-1

Imagine having the good fortune to land three future Hall of Famers during one offseason. A windfall such as that could turn a good team into a champion.

That's precisely what happened to Curly Lambeau and the Packers in the fall of 1929. With his knack for recognizing and obtaining talent reaching new heights, Lambeau added Mike Michalske, Cal Hubbard, and Johnny Blood to a club that had finished among the top five teams in the league three years running.

Michalske, a guard from Penn State, had played with the Yankees before they folded following the 1928 season. Hubbard, a Giant since 1927, wanted out of New York. Blood, the most colorful of the trio, had played with three teams before joining the Packers.

Blood, whose off-the-field exploits sometimes overshadowed his production on the field, could run, pass, and punt with the best of them. He started nine games and emerged as the best pass-catching back in the league.

Michalske and Hubbard solidified an already powerful line. Michalske started the last 11 games at left guard while Hubbard played right tackle or right end as needed. The two became mainstays on a defense that had no equal.

In 1929, the Packers allowed only 22 points in 13 games and pitched eight shutouts. Opponents came within 20 yards of the team's goal line on 17 occasions but cashed in just three times. More often than not, players like Bo Molenda (interception), Hubbard or Michalske (fourth-down stops), Lavvie Dilweg (blocked field goal), or others rose up to snuff out the threat.

That defense, and an offense second only to the Giants, paved the way for an undefeated season (12-0-1) and the team's first-ever championship. A scoreless tie with the Yellow Jackets in late November was the only blemish on the record.

Packers' power reached epic proportions in the fourth quarter of a battle for first place with the Giants in Week 10. In 15 minutes of domination, Green Bay ran 26 plays to New York's two and outscored the Giants 13-0. Molenda and Blood capped drives of 15 and 11 plays, respectively, as the Packers (10-0) knocked New York (8-1-1) from the unbeaten ranks with a 20-6 whipping.

After that monumental encounter in the Polo Grounds, the Packers could manage no more than a tie with Frankford four days later. That game ended with the Green and Gold perched at the Yellow Jackets' 9-yard line, the result of a 19-yard Blood-to-Eddie Kotal pass.

Green Bay wrapped up its season by pounding the Steam Roller and Bears by identical 25-0 scores.

The Packers trailed only once all year. In Week 3, the Cardinals went up 2-0 after a bad pass from center resulted in a safety. Green Bay rallied to post a 9-2 victory after a Red Dunn field goal and a Verne Lewellen touchdown.

For Lambeau, 1929 also meant an end to his playing days. The 31-year-old's only appearance occurred in a 12-0 win over the Cardinals. A week later, Lambeau remained on the sidelines as the little town team from the Midwest proved it could compete with the big boys from the nation's largest city.

TEAM STATISTICS

Regular Season 12-0-1

Date	GB		OPP
9/22	9	Dayton Triangles	0
9/29	23	Chicago Bears	0
10/6	9	Chicago Cardinals	2
10/13	14	Frankford Yellow Jackets	2
10/20	24	Minneapolis Red Jackets	0
10/27	7	at Chicago Cardinals	6
11/3	16	at Minneapolis Red Jackets	6
11/10	14	at Chicago Bears	0
11/17	12	at Chicago Cardinals	0
11/24	20	at New York Giants	6
11/28	0	at Frankford Yellow Jackets	0
12/1	25	at Providence Steam Roller	0
12/8	25	at Chicago Bears	0

Score By Periods

	1	2	3	4	Total
Packers	38	33	66	61	198
Opponents	2	0	14	6	22

INDIVIDUAL STATISTICS

Touchdown Passes

	No
Dunn	5
Lewellen	4
Blood	1
McCrary	1
Molenda	1
Packers	**12**
Opponents	2

Scoring

	TDr	TDp	TDrt	PAT	FG	S	TP
Lewellen	6	1	1	0	0	0	48
Blood	3	2	0	0	0	0	30
McCrary	1	2	1	0	0	0	24
Molenda	3	0	0	3	0	0	21
L. Dilweg	0	3	0	0	0	0	18
Kotal	0	3	0	0	0	0	18
Dunn	0	0	0	11	2	0	17
Lidberg	2	0	0	0	0	0	12
Nash	0	1	0	0	0	0	6
team	0	0	0	0	0	2	4
Packers	**15**	**12**	**2**	**14**	**2**	**2**	**198**
Opponents	1	2	0	0	0	2	22

NFL STANDINGS

	W	L	T	Pct	PF	PA
Green Bay Packers	**12**	**0**	**1**	**1.000**	**198**	**22**
New York Giants	13	1	1	.929	312	86
Frankford Yellow Jackets	9	4	5	.692	129	128
Chicago Cardinals	6	6	1	.500	154	83
Boston Bulldogs	4	4	0	.500	98	73
Orange Tornadoes	3	4	4	.429	35	80
Staten Island Stapletons	3	4	3	.429	89	65
Providence Steam Roller	4	6	2	.400	107	117
Chicago Bears	4	9	2	.308	119	227
Buffalo Bisons	1	7	1	.125	48	142
Minneapolis Red Jackets	1	9	0	.100	48	185
Dayton Triangles	0	6	0	.000	7	136

ROSTER

Name	Pos	Ht	Wt	College	G
Ashmore, Roger	T	6-1	212	Gonzaga	8
Baker, Roy (Bullet)	B	6-0	177	USC	2
Bowdoin, James	G	6-2	220	Alabama	12
Cahoon, Ivan (Tiny)	T	6-2	235	Gonzaga	2
Darling, Bernard (Boob)	C	6-3	216	Beloit	11
Dilweg, LaVern (Lavvie)	E	6-3	202	Marquette	13
Dunn, Joseph (Red)	B	6-0	178	Marquette	11
Earp, Francis (Jug)	C	6-1	235	Monmouth	11
Evans, Jack	B	6-0	195	California	
Hill, Don	B	5-11	190	Stanford	3
Hubbard, Robert (Cal)	T/E	6-5	250	Geneva	12
Kern, William	T	6-0	187	Pittsburgh	
Kotal, Eddie	B	5-10	165	Lawrence	11
Lambeau, Earl (Curly)	B	6-0	190	Notre Dame	1
Lewellen, Verne	B	6-2	181	Nebraska	13
Lidberg, Carl (Cully)	B	6-0	200	Minnesota	
McCrary, Hurdis	B	6-2	205	Georgia	13
McNally (Blood), Johnny	B	6-0	190	St. John's	12
Michalske, August (Mike)	G	6-1	215	Penn State	13
Minick, Paul	G	5-11	210	Iowa	6
Molenda, John (Bo)	B	5-11	208	Michigan	12
Nash, Tom	E	6-3	210	Georgia	10
O'Donnell, Dick	E	5-10	196	Minnesota	10
Perry, Claude	T	6-1	211	Alabama	12
Smith, Richard (Red)	B	5-10	225	Notre Dame	5
Woodin, Howard (Whitey)	G	5-11	206	Marquette	6
Young, Bill	G	6-1	200	Ohio State	2
Zuidmulder, Dave	B	6-1	184	St. Ambrose	1

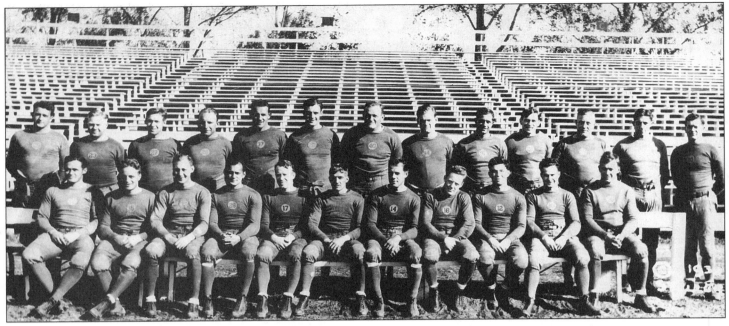

FRONT ROW: (L-R) 32 James Bowdoin, 35 Ken Radick, 33 Wuert Engelmann, 28 Hurdis McCrary, 17 Red Dunn, Dave Zuidmulder, 14 Merle Zuver, 18 Paul Fitzgibbons, 12 Arnie Herber, 30 Dick O'Donnell, 38 Carl Lidberg.
BACK ROW: (L-R) 29 Bernard Darling, 23 Whitey Woodin, 27 Bo Molenda, 26 Claude Perry, 37 Tom Nash, 22 Lavvie Dilweg, 40 Cal Hubbard, 34 Elmer Sleight, 31 Verne Lewellen, 24 Johnny Blood, 39 Jug Earp, 36 Mike Michalske, 20 Curly Lambeau.

10-3-1   1930   10-3-1

A strong offense and losses by its closest challenger in the late going helped Green Bay (10-3-1) secure a second consecutive championship in 1930. The Packers became just the second team—Canton (1922-23) was the first—to win back-to-back titles.

Gone was the stalwart defense. After allowing 22 points in 1929, the Packers surrendered 111, a four-fold increase.

Whereas Green Bay rolled over any and all comers the year previous, the 1930 aggregation wound up 3-2 in games against the best in the league. The Packers prevailed in two of three meetings with the Bears and split with the Giants.

As was the case a year earlier, New York was the team to beat. Green Bay drew first blood with a 14-7 win in early October. The Giants gained revenge and sole possession of first place after they trampled the Packers 13-6 in the rematch on Nov. 24.

Ten of the 28 players on the 1929 championship team did not return. The biggest names among those departed were Eddie Kotal, a five-year veteran of the backfield, and Lambeau, who turned his focus to coaching.

Eleven newcomers were added, most notably, Arnie Herber, one of the best football players to come out of Green Bay West High School. Herber started at quarterback in the opener. In the third quarter, he launched the first touchdown pass of his career—a 50-yarder to Lavvie Dilweg that finished off the Cardinals 14-0.

The 1929 championship pennant was on display in that game. Packers President Leland H. Joannes, Dr. David Jones of the Cardinals, and Green Bay Mayor John V. Diener were among those present at the ceremony.

Green Bay blanked the Bears 7-0 in Week 2 then ran smack into the Giants. Red Dunn hit Johnny Blood with a 55-yard, fourth-quarter scoring pass to seal a 14-7 win.

The Packers then reeled off five more wins to improve to 8-0. They defeated Frankford, Minneapolis (twice), and Portsmouth by an average of 20 points before edging the Bears 13-12.

The club's first misstep occurred against the Cardinals in Chicago. Ernie Nevers spearheaded a fourth-quarter offensive onslaught—capped by his short touchdown run—that sent Green Bay packing 13-6.

Emotion got the better of Dunn a week later in New York. With about five minutes to play in a 13-6 loss, Dunn took a swing at referee Tommy Hughitt. The back was upset because Bo Molenda's touchdown had been recalled due to offsetting penalties. Molenda got two more chances but twice failed to score from the one. Dale Burnett ended Green Bay's last gasp with an interception a series later.

Both New York (11-2) and the Packers (8-2) had four games remaining. Fortunately for Green Bay, the Giants stumbled twice at the same time the Packers downed Frankford and Staten Island. That turn of events pushed Green Bay back on top with room to spare. Despite losing 21-0 to the Bears and managing only a tie with the Spartans in the final two weeks, the Packers (10-3-1) edged the Giants (13-4) by .004 of a percentage point and clinched a second straight championship.

1930

TEAM STATISTICS

Regular Season   10-3-1

Date	GB		OPP
9/21	14	Chicago Cardinals	0
9/28	7	Chicago Bears	0
10/5	14	New York Giants	7
10/12	27	Frankford Yellow Jackets	12
10/19	13	at Minneapolis Red Jackets	0
10/26	19	Minneapolis Red Jackets	0
11/2	47	Portsmouth Spartans	13
11/9	13	at Chicago Bears	12
11/16	6	at Chicago Cardinals	13
11/23	6	at New York Giants	13
11/27	25	at Frankford Yellow Jackets	7
11/30	37	at Staten Island Stapletons	7
12/7	0	at Chicago Bears	21
12/14	6	at Portsmouth Spartans	6

Score By Periods

	1	2	3	4	Total
Packers	58	64	52	60	234
Opponents	0	40	31	40	111

INDIVIDUAL STATISTICS

Touchdown Passes

	No
Dunn	11
Herber	3
Lewellen	3
Packers	**17**
Opponents	9

Scoring

	TDr	TDp	TDrt	PAT	FG	S	TP
Lewellen	8	1	0	0	0	0	54
McCrary	4	2	0	0	0	0	36
Blood	0	5	0	0	0	0	30
Molenda	3	0	0	4	0	0	22
L. Dilweg	0	2	1	0	0	0	18
Engelmann	1	2	0	0	0	0	18
Fitzgibbons	1	2	0	0	0	0	18
Dunn	0	0	0	14	0	0	14
Herber	0	1	0	0	0	0	6
Hubbard	0	1	0	0	0	0	6
Lidberg	1	0	0	0	0	0	6
Nash	0	1	0	0	0	0	6
Packers	**18**	**17**	**1**	**18**	**0**	**0**	**234**
Opponents	8	9	0	9	0	0	111

NFL STANDINGS

	W	L	T	Pct	PF	PA
Green Bay Packers	10	3	1	.769	234	111
New York Giants	13	4	0	.765	308	98
Chicago Bears	9	4	1	.692	169	71
Brooklyn Dodgers	7	4	1	.636	154	59
Providence Steam Roller	6	4	1	.600	90	125
Staten Island Stapletons	5	5	2	.500	95	112
Chicago Cardinals	5	6	2	.455	128	132
Portsmouth Spartans	5	6	3	.455	176	161
Frankford Yellow Jackets	4	13	1	.222	113	321
Minneapolis Red Jackets	1	7	1	.125	27	165
Newark Tornadoes	1	10	1	.091	51	190

ROSTER

Name	Pos	Ht	Wt	College	G
Bloodgood, Elbert	B	6-1	175	Nebraska	
Bowdoin, James	G	6-2	220	Alabama	9
Darling, Bernard (Boob)	C	6-3	216	Beloit	
Dilweg, LaVern (Lavvie)	E	6-3	202	Marquette	12
Dunn, Joseph (Red)	B	6-0	178	Marquette	13
Earp, Francis (Jug)	C/T	6-1	235	Monmouth	13
Engelmann, Wuert	B	6-2	191	South Dakota State	9
Fitzgibbons, Paul	B	5-10	174	Creighton	9
Franta, Herb	G	6-0	220	St. Thomas (MN)	2
Hanny, Frank	T	6-0	200	Indiana	2
Haycraft, Ken	E	5-11	190	Minnesota	1
Herber, Arnie	B	5-11	208	Regis	10
Hubbard, Robert (Cal)	T/E	6-5	250	Geneva	14
Kern, William	T	6-0	187	Pittsburgh	6
Lewellen, Verne	B	6-2	181	Nebraska	14
Lidberg, Carl (Cully)	B	6-0	200	Minnesota	5
McCrary, Hurdis	B	6-2	205	Georgia	14
McNally (Blood), Johnny	B	6-0	190	St. John's	10
Michalske, August (Mike)	G	6-1	215	Penn State	14
Molenda, John (Bo)	B	5-11	208	Michigan	13
Nash, Tom	E	6-3	210	Georgia	12
O'Donnell, Dick	E	5-10	196	Minnesota	10
Pape, Oran	B	6-0	205	Iowa	2
Perry, Claude	T/G	6-1	211	Alabama	9
Radick, Ken	E/T	6-0	210	Marquette	4
Sleight, Elmer (Red)	T	6-2	228	Purdue	13
Woodin, Howard (Whitey)	G	5-11	206	Marquette	10
Zuidmulder, Dave	B	6-1	184	St. Ambrose	4
Zuver, Merle	G/C	6-2	198	Nebraska	10

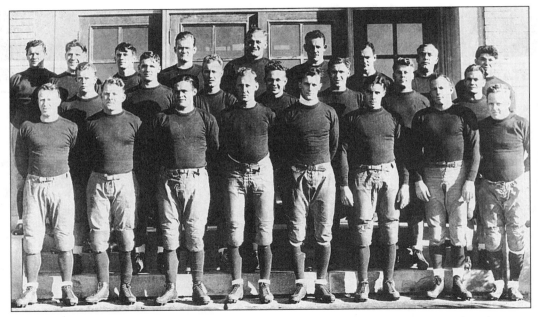

FRONT ROW: (L-R) Red Dunn, Nate Barragar, James Bowdoin, Wuert Engelmann, Lavvie Dilweg, Mike Michalske, Faye Wilson, Paul Fitzgibbons.
MIDDLE ROW: (L-R) Roger Grove, Waldo DonCarlos, Hank Bruder, Milt Gantenbein, Bo Molenda, Rudy Comstock, Russell Saunders.
BACK ROW: (L-R) Curly Lambeau, Dick Stahlman, Johnny Blood, Elmer Sleight, Cal Hubbard, Tom Nash, Hurdis McCrary, Jug Earp, Arnie Herber.

12-2-0   1931   12-2-0

The Packers opened with nine straight wins and never fell out of first place in garnering an unprecedented third straight NFL championship in 1931. The road to the top wasn't without its bumps, however.

In mid-October, league president Joe Carr threatened to fine Green Bay $500 and toss out all games played by the team after Week 3. The Giants and Cardinals, the Packers' opponents in Weeks 4 and 5, had complained to Carr that Green Bay had more than 22 players under contract, which was forbidden after the third week of the season. To gain compliance, Curly Lambeau released Whitey Woodin, Bernard Darling, Kenneth Radick and Arnie Herber, and lent Claude Perry to the Cardinals.

In Week 2, a fan fell from the bleachers at City Stadium and sued for $25,000. The impact of that action wasn't fully realized until a settlement was reached in 1933.

And finally, a bit of controversy with the Portsmouth Spartans unfolded at season's end. After a 7-6 loss to the Bears on Dec. 6, Green Bay's 12-2 record was a game better than that of the second-place Spartans (11-3). But the Spartans claimed the Packers owed them a game in Portsmouth on Dec. 13. Green Bay countered that it was not obligated to play, since the game had been penciled in after the league schedule was finalized, and, therefore, was not official. Carr concurred, and the Packers were crowned champions without ever having played the Spartans.

Despite winning titles in 1929 and 1930, Lambeau resisted the urge to leave his roster alone. Nine veterans from the previous year did not return, and 13 new names joined the ranks. Lambeau fine-tuned his line by adding former Giants Rudy Comstock and Dick Stahlman prior to opening day and center Nate Barragar in late October after an injury to Verne Lewellen. Rookies of note included Hank Bruder, Roger Grove, and Milt Gantenbein.

Green Bay was the undisputed offensive machine of 1931. Its 291 points dwarfed by more than 100 the output of any other team. The Packers' 44 touchdowns remained a team record for 30 years until the 1961 club scored 49.

Johnny Blood led the team in scoring with 78 points. His 10 receiving touchdowns by a running back remains the franchise record.

The Packers won seven of their first nine games by more than two touchdowns. The two exceptions: 7-0 and 6-2 squeakers over the Bears. Lavvie Dilweg's recovery of Joe Lintzenich's fumble set up Lewellen's lone touchdown run in the first, and Mike Michalske's 80-yard interception return proved the difference in the second.

Green Bay's two losses occurred in the final five games. On Nov. 15, Ernie Nevers ran wild, passing for two touchdowns and kicking three extra points in a 21-13 Cardinals' win. In the season finale, Lintzenich atoned for his earlier mistake with a 30-yard touchdown reception in the Bears' 7-6 triumph.

Though the controversy with Portsmouth eventually faded, the Spartans didn't go away. The team dealt Green Bay a costly blow in 1932, then changed its name and location in 1934, re-emerging as the Detroit Lions.

1931

TEAM STATISTICS

Regular Season 12-2-0

Date	GB		OPP
9/13	26	Cleveland Indians	0
9/20	32	Brooklyn Dodgers	6
9/27	7	Chicago Bears	0
10/4	27	New York Giants	7
10/11	26	Chicago Cardinals	7
10/18	15	Frankford Yellow Jackets	0
10/25	48	Providence Steam Roller	20
11/1	6	at Chicago Bears	2
11/8	26	Staten Island Stapletons	0
11/15	13	at Chicago Cardinals	21
11/22	14	at New York Giants	10
11/26	38	at Providence Steam Roller	7
11/29	7	at Brooklyn Dodgers	0
12/6	6	at Chicago Bears	7

Score By Periods

	1	2	3	4	Total
Packers	78	87	47	79	291
Opponents	28	24	22	13	87

INDIVIDUAL STATISTICS

Touchdown Passes

	No
Dunn	8
Fitzgibbons	4
Molenda	4
Grove	2
Bruder	1
Saunders	1
F. Wilson	1
Packers	**21**
Opponents	7

Scoring

	TDr	TDp	TDrt	PAT	FG	S	TP
Blood	2	10	1	0	0	0	78
Lewellen	6	0	0	0	0	0	36
L. Dilweg	0	4	0	1	0	0	25
Engelmann	1	2	1	0	0	0	24
Molenda	3	0	0	3	0	0	21
Bruder	1	2	0	0	0	0	18
Dunn	0	0	0	15	0	0	15
F. Wilson	2	0	0	0	0	0	12
Woodin	0	0	1	3	0	0	9
Grove	0	1	0	2	0	0	8
F. Baker	0	1	0	0	0	0	6
Herber	1	0	0	0	0	0	6
Gantenbein	0	1	0	0	0	0	6
McCrary	1	0	0	0	0	0	6
Michalske	0	0	1	0	0	0	6
Nash	0	1	0	0	0	0	6
Saunders	1	0	0	0	0	0	6
team	0	0	0	0	0	1	2
Fitzgibbons	0	0	0	1	0	0	1
Packers	**18**	**21**	**5**	**25**	**0**	**1**	**291**
Opponents	4	7	1	10	1	1	87

NFL STANDINGS

	W	L	T	Pct	PF	PA
Green Bay Packers	12	2	0	857	291	87
Portsmouth Spartans	11	3	0	786	175	77
Chicago Bears	8	5	0	615	145	92
Chicago Cardinals	5	4	0	556	120	128
New York Giants	7	6	1	538	154	100
Providence Steam Roller	4	4	3	500	78	127
Staten Island Stapletons	4	6	1	400	79	118
Cleveland Indians	2	8	0	200	45	137
Brooklyn Dodgers	2	12	0	143	64	199
Frankford Yellow Jackets	1	6	1	143	13	99

ROSTER

Name	Pos	Ht	Wt	College	G
Baker, Frank	E	6-2	182	Northwestern	2
Barragar, Nate	C/G	6-0	210	USC	7
Bowdoin, James	G	6-2	220	Alabama	13
Bruder, Hank	B	6-0	190	Northwestern	13
Comstock, Rudy	G	5-11	198	Georgetown	14
Darling, Bernard (Boob)	C	6-3	216	Beloit	4
Davenport, Wayne	B	6-4	185	Hardin-Simmons	2
Dilweg, LaVern (Lavvie)	E	6-3	202	Marquette	14
DonCarlos, Waldo	C	6-2	190	Drake	
Dunn, Joseph (Red)	B	6-0	178	Marquette	12
Earp, Francis (Jug)	C/T	6-1	235	Monmouth	12
Engelmann, Wuert	B	6-2	191	South Dakota State	14
Fitzgibbons, Paul	B	5-10	174	Creighton	14
Gantenbein, Milt	E	6-0	199	Wisconsin	14
Grove, Roger	B	6-0	175	Michigan State	14
Herber, Arnie	B	5-11	208	Regis	3
Hubbard, Robert (Cal)	T/E	6-5	250	Geneva	12
Jenison, Ray	T	6-2	220	South Dakota State	2
Johnston, Chester (Swede)	B	5-10	200	Marquette	2
Lewellen, Verne	B	6-2	181	Nebraska	7
McCrary, Hurdis	B	6-2	205	Georgia	12
McNally (Blood), Johnny	B	6-0	190	St. John's	13
Michalske, August (Mike)	G	6-1	215	Penn State	
Molenda, John (Bo)	B	5-11	208	Michigan	14
Nash, Tom	E	6-3	210	Georgia	13
Perry, Claude	T	6-1	211	Alabama	5
Radick, Ken	E	6-0	210	Marquette	1
Saunders, Russell	B	5-10	175	USC	9
Sleight, Elmer (Red)	T	6-2	228	Purdue	13
Stahlman, Dick	T	6-3	221	DePaul	14
Wilson, Faye (Mule)	B	5-11	190	Texas A&M	12
Woodin, Howard (Whitey)	G	5-11	206	Marquette	2
Zuidmulder, Dave	B	6-1	184	St. Ambrose	2

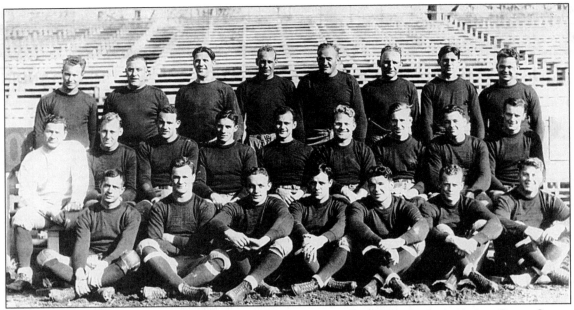

FRONT ROW: (L-R) Verne Lewellen, Joe Zeller, Clarke Hinkle, Harry O'Boyle, Arnie Herber, Roger Grove, Rudy Comstock.
MIDDLE ROW: (L-R) Coach Curly Lambeau, Wuert Engelmann, Tom Nash, Mike Michalske, Hurdis McCrary, Nate Barragar, Arthur Bultman, Lester Peterson, Lavvie Dilweg.
BACK ROW: (L-R) Hank Bruder, Jug Earp, Dick Stahlman, Al Rose, Cal Hubbard, Claude Perry, Johnny Blood, Milt Gantenbein.

10-3-1   1932   10-3-1

Had the season ended in November, the Packers of 1932 would have won a fourth straight NFL title. At the end of that month, Green Bay's 10-1-1 record was good enough for first place ahead of the Spartans (5-1-4) and the Bears (4-1-6).

But the schedule consisted of 14 games and not 12, so the Packers traveled to Portsmouth and Chicago on the first two weekends of December. They could have saved themselves a trip. An aroused Spartans team knocked them into third place with a 19-0 drubbing, and the always troublesome Bears then blanked them 9-0.

Against Portsmouth, the Packers' passing game failed to materialize. Arnie Herber, the NFL's leading passer, completed just one throw in better than a dozen attempts and was intercepted three times. The Spartans capitalized on two partially blocked Packers punts to open a 13-0 halftime lead and allowed their visitors to cross midfield but once.

With the loss, Green Bay (10-2-1) fell behind Portsmouth (6-1-4) and the Bears (5-1-6) who defeated the Giants 6-0. [Ties were thrown out when figuring the standings.] With Portsmouth having completed its schedule, the Packers had no chance to catch the Spartans even by winning their finale in Chicago against the Bears.

The idea of finishing on a positive note fizzled at snow-covered Wrigley Field. Green Bay squandered two scoring opportunities in the second quarter. First, Herber lost a fumble at the Bears' 1-yard line. Then, on the team's next possession, he reached the Chicago 8, only to have his gain erased by penalty. The Packers went backwards after that, and Paul Engebretsen and Bronko Nagurski closed the door with nine fourth-quarter points on a field goal and a 56-yard touchdown excursion.

By winning, Chicago (6-1-6) moved into a tie with Portsmouth (6-1-4). The two then met in a playoff game to determine the league champion. Chicago won, the game was added to the regular-season standings, and Green Bay (with a better winning percentage than the Spartans) moved into second place with its 10-3-1 record.

The Packers relied heavily on their defense. After having scored 44 touchdowns in 1931, Green Bay tallied only half that number in 1932. The defense, meanwhile, surrendered only 63 points, its lowest total since 1929.

Two young faces showed promise in the backfield. Herber, released in 1931 to avoid Joe Carr's wrath, didn't miss a game and tossed nine touchdown passes. Clarke Hinkle, a rookie fullback from Bucknell, led the team in rushing with 331 yards.

Green Bay started fast, winning eight of its first nine games. The exception: a scoreless tie with the Bears in Week 2 that ended a 20-game home winning streak that dated back to 1929.

New York dealt the Packers their first loss. Butch Gibson recovered Roger Grove's fumble at midfield. Five plays later, Ray Flaherty passed 31 yards to Jack McBride for the only touchdown in a 6-0 decision.

Green Bay rallied with wins over Brooklyn (7-0) and Staten Island (21-3), but its December swoon left it out of first place at season's end for the first time in four years.

1932

TEAM STATISTICS

Regular Season 10-3-1

Date	GB		OPP
9/18	15	Chicago Cardinals	7
9/25	0	Chicago Bears	0
10/2	13	New York Giants	0
10/9	15	Portsmouth Spartans	10
10/16	2	at Chicago Bears	0
10/23	13	Brooklyn Dodgers	0
10/30	26	Staten Island Stapletons	0
11/6	19	at Chicago Cardinals	9
11/13	21	at Boston Braves	0
11/20	0	at New York Giants	6
11/24	7	at Brooklyn Dodgers	0
11/27	21	at Staten Island Stapletons	3
12/4	0	at Portsmouth Spartans	19
12/11	0	at Chicago Bears	9

Score By Periods

	1	2	3	4	Total
Packers	36	35	34	47	152
Opponents	7	22	10	24	63

INDIVIDUAL STATISTICS

Rushing

	Att	Yds	Avg	TD
Hinkle	95	331	3.5	3
Blood	27	130	4.8	0

Receiving

	No	Yds	Avg	TD
Blood	14	168	12.0	3

Passing

	Att	Com	Yds	Pct	TD	In	Rate
Herber	101	37	639	36.6	9	9	51.5

Scoring

	TDr	TDp	TDrt	PAT	FG	S	TP
Blood	0	3	1	0	0	0	24
Bruder	2	2	0	0	0	0	24
Grove	0	3	0	4	0	0	22
Hinkle	3	0	0	1	0	0	19
Herber	1	0	1	0	0	0	12
A. Rose	0	0	2	0	0	0	12
O'Boyle	0	0	0	8	0	0	8
Engelmann	0	0	1	0	0	0	6
Lewellen	0	1	0	0	0	0	6
McCrary	1	0	0	0	0	0	6
Michalske	0	0	1	0	0	0	6
Nash	0	0	0	0	0	2	4
team	0	0	0	0	0	1	2
L. Dilweg	0	0	0	1	0	0	1
Packers	7	9	6	14	0	3	152
Opponents	4	3	1	4	3	1	63

NFL STANDINGS

	W	L	T	Pct	PF	PA
Chicago Bears	7	1	6	.875	160	44
Green Bay Packers	10	3	1	.769	152	63
Portsmouth Spartans	6	2	4	.750	116	71
Boston Braves	4	4	2	.500	55	79
New York Giants	4	6	2	.400	93	113
Brooklyn Dodgers	3	9	0	.250	63	131
Chicago Cardinals	2	6	2	.250	72	114
Staten Island Stapletons	2	7	3	.222	77	173

ROSTER

Name	Pos	Ht	Wt	College	G
Apsit, Marger	B	5-11	202	USC	2
Barragar, Nate	C/G	6-0	210	USC	
Bruder, Hank	B	6-0	190	Northwestern	14
Bultman, Arthur (Red)	C	6-2	199	Marquette	13
Comstock, Rudy	G/T	5-11	198	Georgetown	13
Culver, Al	T	6-2	212	Notre Dame	1
Dilweg, LaVern (Lavvie)	E	6-3	202	Marquette	14
Earp, Francis (Jug)	T/G/C	6-1	235	Monmouth	10
Engelmann, Wuert	B/E	6-2	191	South Dakota State	12
Fitzgibbons, Paul	B	5-10	174	Creighton	4
Gantenbein, Milt	E	6-0	199	Wisconsin	9
Grove, Roger	B	6-0	175	Michigan State	11
Herber, Arnie	B	5-11	208	Regis	14
Hinkle, Clarke	FB	5-11	200	Bucknell	13
Hubbard, Robert (Cal)	T	6-5	250	Geneva	13
Lewellen, Verne	B	6-2	181	Nebraska	14
McCrary, Hurdis	B	6-2	205	Georgia	11
McNally (Blood), Johnny	B	6-0	190	St. John's	13
Michalske, August (Mike)	G	6-1	215	Penn State	13
Molenda, John (Bo)	B	5-11	208	Michigan	2
Nash, Tom	E	6-3	210	Georgia	10
O'Boyle, Harry	B	5-9	180	Notre Dame	11
Perry, Claude	T	6-1	211	Alabama	13
Peterson, Lester	E	6-2	195	Texas	9
Rose, Al	E	6-3	195	Texas	13
Shelly, Dexter	B	5-11	192	Texas	2
Stahlman, Dick	T	6-3	221	DePaul	13
Van Sickle, Clyde	G	6-2	224	Arkansas	1
Zeller, Joe	G	6-1	198	Indiana	14

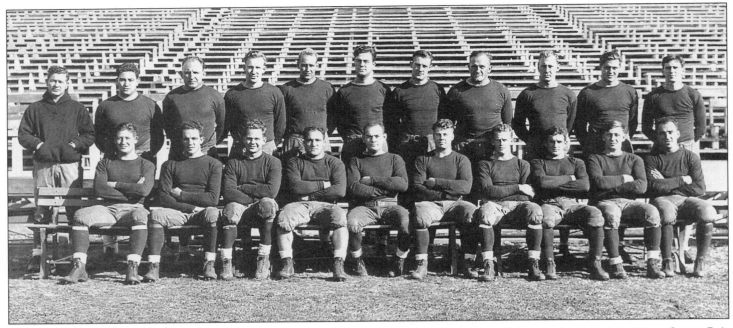

FRONT ROW: (L-R) Lon Evans, Joe Kurth, Milt Gantenbein, Buckets Goldenberg, Clyde Van Sickle, Rudy Comstock, Roger Grove, Bob Monnett, Norm Greeney, Larry Bettencourt.
BACK ROW: (L-R) Coach Curly Lambeau, Jess Quatse, Claude Perry, Arthur Bultman, Al Rose, Ben Smith, Lavvie Dilweg, Cal Hubbard, Wuert Engelmann, Al Sarafiny, Johnny Blood.

5-7-1   1933   5-7-1

Green Bay posted its first losing season in 1933 and as the losses mounted, Curly Lambeau became sick enough to seek out a New York physician. The visit proved beneficial to the coach, but not the team, as it never awoke from a season-long funk. The club's condition worsened near season's end when four losses in the final five games left the Packers out of contention with a 5-7-1 record.

The Packers of 1933 bore but a faint resemblance to their predecessors, who had won more games (50) than any other team in the NFL from 1928 through 1932. Unlike previous years, Green Bay struggled against the league's best with five of its losses coming against the Bears and Giants, who met in the first championship game.

In November, Green Bay dropped three in a row for the first time ever. After the third loss, a 17-6 setback to the Giants, Lambeau, who feared he might be suffering an attack of appendicitis, saw a doctor. The diagnosis, as reported in the Green Bay Press-Gazette, was "a stomach disorder brought on by nervousness." The remedy: medication and a strict diet.

The Packers struggles weren't confined to the playing field. The team had lost money two years running and took an additional $5,200 hit when the fan who had fallen from the bleachers in 1931 was granted that as compensation. Worse, the club's insurance company had gone bankrupt and refused to pay the claim.

Enter Lee Joannes and Frank J. Jonet. The Packers' corporate president loaned the organization $6,000 to help pay its bills and asked that a receiver be appointed by the courts

to act "in behalf of all creditors." Jonet, a CPA and Packers' stockholder, was given that duty.

Changes swept the NFL. The league was split into two divisions (Eastern and Western) and a playoff game between division winners was held to determine a champion. Rule changes, such as making the forward pass legal from anywhere behind the line of scrimmage and the moving of the goal posts to the goal line, helped the pros forge an identity distinct from that of the college ranks.

For the first time, the Packers played a home game in Milwaukee. On Oct. 1, Green Bay hosted the Giants at State Fair Park. From 1933 through 1994, the Packers played more than 300 home games in that city.

Green Bay had no luck with the Bears in 1933. The Packers lost three times to their rival by a combined 11 points. Chicago twice rallied late in the fourth quarter, then held on for a one-point victory in the season finale. The 14-7 setback administered in Week 2 ended Green Bay's home unbeaten streak at 30—an NFL record.

The Packers accounted for nearly half of their season's scoring output in two October blowouts. Rookie Bob Monnett rushed for 93 yards and two touchdowns in a 47-0 drubbing of the Pirates, and fellow freshman Buckets Goldenberg scored via three different means (run, pass, and blocked punt return) in a 35-9 pasting of Philadelphia.

The Bears made sure Green Bay went out as losers. Monnett's 88-yard punt return pulled the Packers to within a point, but Joe Zeller—a Packer in 1932—blocked Roger Grove's extra point try and Green Bay lost 7-6.

TEAM STATISTICS

	GB	OPP
Rushes	487	443
Yards Gained	1,513	1,226
Average Gain	3.11	2.77
Average Yards per Game	116.4	94.3
Passes Attempted	209	179
Completed	89	48
% Completed	42.58	26.82
Total Yards Gained	1,186	711
Yards Gained per Completion	13.33	14.81
Average Yards per Game	91.2	54.7
Laterals Attempted	9	7
Completed	3	6
Yards Gained	3	-8
Combined Yards Gained	2,702	1,929
Total Plays	705	629
Average Yards per Play	3.83	3.07
Average Yards per Game	207.8	148.4
Intercepted By	31	18
Total Points Scored	170	107
Total Touchdowns	24	14
Touchdowns Rushing	13	4
Touchdowns Passing	7	7
Touchdowns on Returns & Recoveries	4	3
Extra Points	20	12
Safeties	0	1
Field Goals Made	2	3

Regular Season   5-7-1

Date	GB		OPP
9/17	7	Boston Redskins	7
9/24	7	Chicago Bears	14
10/1	7	New York Giants (M)	10
10/8	17	Portsmouth Spartans	0
10/15	47	Pittsburgh Pirates	0
10/22	7	at Chicago Bears	10
10/29	35	Philadelphia Eagles	9
11/5	14	at Chicago Cardinals	6
11/12	0	at Portsmouth Spartans	7
11/19	7	at Boston Redskins	20
11/26	6	at New York Giants	17
12/3	10	at Philadelphia Eagles	0
12/10	6	at Chicago Bears	7

Score By Periods

	1	2	3	4	Total
Packers	28	30	44	68	170
Opponents	10	27	32	38	107

INDIVIDUAL STATISTICS

Rushing

	Att	Yds	Avg	TD
Monnett	108	413	3.8	3
Hinkle	139	413	3.0	3
Bruder	77	250	3.2	3
Goldenberg	52	213	4.1	4
Engelmann	23	79	3.4	0
Herber	62	77	1.2	0
Blood	14	41	2.9	0
Mott	5	13	2.6	0
McCrary	6	10	1.7	0
Grove	1	4	4.0	0
Packers	487	1,513	3.1	13
Opponents	443	1,226	2.8	4

Receiving

	No	Yds	Avg	LG	TD
Grove	18	215	11.9		0
L. Dilweg	17	225	13.2		0
Blood	10	215	21.5	t38	3
Gantenbein	8	144	18.0		1
A. Rose	7	89	12.7		1
Monnett	6	44	7.3		0
Hinkle	6	38	6.3		0
Bruder	4	69	17.3	40	0
Engelmann	4	54	13.5	23	1
Goldenberg	4	43	10.8	18	1
Herber	3	27	9.0	25	0
Ben Smith	2	23	11.5	13	0
Packers	89	1,186	13.3		7
Opponents	48	711	14.8	t40	7

Passing

	Att	Com	Yds	Pct	TD	In	Rate
Herber	124	50	656	40.3	4	12	28.9
Monnett	46	23	325	50.0	3	3	67.8
Hinkle	27	12	147	44.4	0	3	22.2
Bruder	7	3	14	42.9	0	0	—
Grove	3	1	44	33.3	0	0	—
Blood	2	0	0	00.0	0	0	—
Packers	209	89	1,186	42.6	7	18	36.5
Opponents	179	48	711	26.8	7	31	17.1

Scoring

	TDr	TDp	TDrt	PAT	FG	S	TP
Goldenberg	4	1	2	0	0	0	42
Monnett	3	0	1	10	0	0	34
Hinkle	3	0	0	0	2	0	24
Blood	0	3	0	1	0	0	19
Bruder	3	0	0	0	0	0	18
Engelmann	0	1	1	0	0	0	12
Grove	0	0	0	8	0	0	8
Gantenbein	0	1	0	0	0	0	6
A. Rose	0	1	0	0	0	0	6
Herber	0	0	0	1	0	0	1
Packers	13	7	4	20	2	0	170
Opponents	4	7	3	12	3	1	107

NFL STANDINGS

Western Division

	W	L	T	Pct	PF	PA
Chicago Bears	10	2	1	.833	133	82
Portsmouth Spartans	6	5	0	.545	128	87
Green Bay Packers	5	7	1	.417	170	107
Cincinnati Reds	3	6	1	.333	38	110
Chicago Cardinals	1	9	1	.100	52	101

Eastern Division

	W	L	T	Pct	PF	PA
New York Giants	11	3	0	.786	244	101
Brooklyn Dodgers	5	4	1	.556	93	54
Boston Redskins	5	5	2	.500	103	97
Philadelphia Eagles	3	5	1	.375	77	158
Pittsburgh Pirates	3	6	2	.333	67	208

ROSTER

Name	Pos	Ht	Wt	College	G
Bettencourt, Larry	C	6-3	215	St. Mary's (CA)	2
Bruder, Hank	B	6-0	190	Northwestern	9
Bultman, Arthur (Red)	C	6-2	199	Marquette	13
Comstock, Rudy	G	5-11	198	Georgetown	13
Dilweg, LaVern (Lavvie)	E	6-3	202	Marquette	11
Engelmann, Wuert	B	6-2	191	South Dakota State	9
Evans, Lon	G/T	6-2	225	TCU	12
Gantenbein, Milt	E	6-0	199	Wisconsin	12
Goldenberg, Charles (Buckets)	FB	5-10	220	Wisconsin	11
Greeney, Norm	G	6-0	215	Notre Dame	7
Grove, Roger	B	6-0	175	Michigan State	13
Herber, Arnie	B	5-11	208	Regis	11
Hinkle, Clarke	FB	5-11	200	Bucknell	13
Hubbard, Robert (Cal)	T	6-5	250	Geneva	
Kurth, Joe	T	6-3	202	Notre Dame	13
McCrary, Hurdis	B	6-2	205	Georgia	2
McNally (Blood), Johnny	B	6-0	190	St. John's	9
Michalske, August (Mike)	G	6-1	215	Penn State	13
Monnett, Bob	B	5-9	180	Michigan State	10
Mott, Norm (Buster)	B	5-11	190	Georgia	3
Perry, Claude	T	6-1	211	Alabama	11
Quatse, Jess	T	5-11	230	Pittsburgh	
Rose, Al	E	6-3	195	Texas	12
Sarafiny, Al	C	6-3	240	St. Edward's	
Smith, Ben	E	6-0	200	Alabama	9
Van Sickle, Clyde	G	6-2	224	Arkansas	9
Young, Paul	C	6-4	195	Oklahoma	2

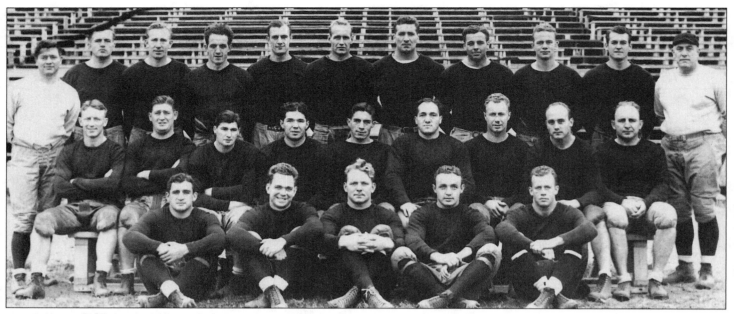

FRONT ROW: (L-R) Bob Monnett, Milt Gantenbein, Nate Barragar, Clarke Hinkle, Roger Grove.
MIDDLE ROW: (L-R) Coach Curly Lambeau, Al Norgard, Lon Evans, Joe Laws, Arnie Herber, Mike Michalske, Buckets Goldenberg, Hank Bruder, Ade Schwammel, Claude Perry, Jug Earp.
BACK ROW: (L-R) Frank Butler, Red Bultman, Joe Kurth, Lavvie Dilweg, Carl Jorgensen, Champ Seibold, Lester Peterson, Robert Jones, Earl Witte.

5-7-1   1934   5-7-1

Green Bay's post-championship slump entered a second year in 1934, and the team quickly fell behind the fast-charging Bears and Lions. A late-November upset of unbeaten Detroit was a positive, but the immediate impact of the win was to give Chicago the inside track to a second straight Western Division crown.

The Packers were eliminated fairly early from the playoff race. Chicago and Detroit each won their first 10 games and the Bears finished the regular season unbeaten (13-0). A 17-3 loss to New York on Nov. 11 left Green Bay (4-5) too far back to challenge the frontrunners.

The Packers' troubles came on two fronts: a running game that averaged an all-time franchise low 2.6 yards per carry and a passing attack that, while the best in the league, lacked a genuine playmaker. As a result, Green Bay's offense ranked sixth out of the nine teams that played at least 10 games.

The loss of Cal Hubbard and Johnny Blood hampered the offense. Hubbard took a coaching position with Texas A&M and Blood, who was suspended late in 1933 for "breaking training rules," was sold to Pittsburgh.

Both Bob Monnett and Clarke Hinkle, who had each gained 413 yards rushing in 1933, had off years. The pair combined for just 488 yards and three touchdowns, approximately half their output from the previous year.

Hinkle, a fullback, led all receivers with 12 catches but averaged fewer than 10 yards a pop. Lavvie Dilweg could still get open deep, but caught just five passes in his final year as a Packer.

Green Bay beat two of the league's elite teams, something it could not do in 1933. The Packers bounced the Giants 20-6 in Week 3 and squeaked past Detroit 3-0 in Week 11.

Hinkle and Roger Grove keyed a 163-yard rushing output to down the Giants. Monnett kicked two field goals, and Grove and Buckets Goldenberg ran for scores as Green Bay improved to 2-1.

The second upset was even bigger. In its first 10 games, Detroit had outscored its opposition 215 to 27. But 60-minute players like Bruce Jones, Ade Schwammel, Milt Gantenbein, Nate Barragar, and Mike Michalske kept the Lions off the scoreboard. Hinkle's 47-yard field goal early in the fourth quarter gave Green Bay a 3-0 victory.

As they had done the previous year, the Packers couldn't solve the Bears. In the first meeting, a 24-10 Bears' triumph, Bronko Nagurski rushed for 90 yards and two touchdowns. In the second affair, Beattie Feathers piled up 155 yards to spark a 339-yard ground assault that overwhelmed the Packers 27-14.

Teams like the Cincinnati Reds and St. Louis Gunners were more to the Packers' liking. Arnie Herber enjoyed his finest outing of the year against the Reds when he threw three touchdowns in a 41-0 rout. When the Reds folded after eight games, the Gunners, an independent pro team, finished out Cincinnati's schedule. Green Bay trampled them as well, 21-14 in the season finale at Sportsman's Park in St. Louis, to finish 7-6 and avoid a second straight losing season.

TEAM STATISTICS

	GB	OPP
Rushes	456	517
Yards Gained	1,183	1,564
Average Gain	2.59	3.03
Average Yards per Game	91.0	120.3
Passes Attempted	197	173
Completed	74	56
% Completed	37.56	32.37
Total Yards Gained	1,165	676
Yards Gained per Completion	15.74	12.07
Average Yards per Game	89.6	52.0
Laterals Attempted	1	9
Completed	1	9
Yards Gained	-8	94
Combined Yards Gained	2,340	2,334
Total Plays	654	699
Average Yards per Play	3.58	3.34
Average Yards per Game	180.0	179.5
Intercepted By	25	19
Total Points Scored	156	112
Total Touchdowns	19	14
Touchdowns Rushing	8	8
Touchdowns Passing	10	3
Touchdowns on Returns & Recoveries	1	3
Extra Points	16	10
Safeties	1	0
Field Goals Made	8	6

Regular Season 7-6-0

Date	GB		OPP
9/16	19	Philadelphia Eagles	6
9/23	10	Chicago Bears	24
9/30	20	New York Giants (M)	6
10/7	0	Detroit Lions	3
10/14	41	Cincinnati Reds	0
10/21	15	Chicago Cardinals	0
10/28	14	at Chicago Bears	27
11/4	10	at Boston Redskins	0
11/11	3	at New York Giants	17
11/18	3	Chicago Cardinals (M)	9
11/25	3	at Detroit Lions	0
11/29	0	at Chicago Cardinals	6
12/2	21	at St. Louis Gunners	14

Score By Periods

	1	2	3	4	Total
Packers	27	43	33	53	156
Opponents	19	6	47	40	112

INDIVIDUAL STATISTICS

Rushing

	Att	Yds	Avg	TD
Hinkle	144	359	2.5	1
Grove	62	262	4.2	1
Laws	46	155	3.4	1
Monnett	68	129	1.9	2
Bruder	48	106	2.2	1
Goldenberg	30	73	2.4	2
Herber	37	33	0.9	0
Johnston	7	23	3.3	0
Witte	8	22	2.8	0
Casper	4	19	4.8	0
Perry	1	2	2.0	0
L. Peterson	1	0	0.0	0
Packers	456	1,183	2.6	8
Opponents	517	1,564	3.0	8

Receiving

	No	Yds	Avg	LG	TD
Hinkle	12	113	9.4	t69	1
Gantenbein	11	155	14.1		0
Laws	9	165	18.3	61	1
L. Peterson	8	139	17.4		0
Bruder	7	104	14.9		1
Grove	6	125	20.8	37	3
A. Rose	6	117	19.5	36	2
L. Dilweg	5	135	27.0	39	2
Goldenberg	4	26	6.5	9	0
Norgard	3	29	9.7	22	0
Monnett	2	27	13.5	26	0
Unaccounted for	1	30	30.0	30	0
Packers	74	1,165	15.7	t69	10
Opponents	56	676	12.1	35	3

Passing

	Att	Com	Yds	Pct	TD	In	Rate
Herber	115	42	799	36.5	8	12	45.1
Monnett	43	16	223	37.2	2	4	31.4
Hinkle	19	9	87	47.4	0	2	21.1
Grove	10	5	34	50.0	0	0	57.9
Bruder	6	2	22	33.3	0	0	—
Blood	4	0	0	00.0	0	1	—
Packers	197	74	1,165	37.6	10	19	35.4
Opponents	173	56	676	32.4	3	25	11.5

Scoring

	TDr	TDp	TDrt	PAT	FG	S	TP
Monnett	2	0	0	6	4	0	30
Hinkle	1	1	0	5	3	0	26
Grove	1	3	0	1	0	0	25
Bruder	1	1	1	4	0	0	22
L. Dilweg	0	2	0	0	0	0	12
Goldenberg	2	0	0	0	0	0	12
Laws	1	1	0	0	0	0	12
A. Rose	0	2	0	0	0	0	12
Schwammel	0	0	0	0	1	0	3
team	0	0	0	0	0	1	2
Packers	8	10	1	16	8	1	156
Opponents	8	3	3	10	6	0	112

NFL STANDINGS

Western Division

	W	L	T	Pct	PF	PA
Chicago Bears	13	0	0	1.000	286	86
Detroit Lions	10	3	0	.769	238	59
Green Bay Packers	**7**	**6**	**0**	**.538**	**156**	**112**
Chicago Cardinals	5	6	0	.455	80	84
St. Louis Gunners	1	2	0	.333	27	61
Cincinnati Reds	0	8	0	.000	10	243

Eastern Division

	W	L	T	Pct	PF	PA
New York Giants	8	5	0	.615	147	107
Boston Redskins	6	6	0	.500	107	94
Brooklyn Dodgers	4	7	0	.364	61	153
Philadelphia Eagles	4	7	0	.364	127	85
Pittsburgh Pirates	2	10	0	.167	51	206

ROSTER

Name	Pos	Ht	Wt	College	G
Barragar, Nate	C	6-0	210	USC	12
Bruder, Hank	B	6-0	190	Northwestern	13
Bultman, Arthur (Red)	C	6-2	199	Marquette	
Butler, Frank	C	6-3	246	Michigan State	3
Casper, Charles	B	6-0	195	TCU	1
Dilweg, LaVern (Lavvie)	E	6-3	202	Marquette	12
Engebretsen, Paul (Tiny)	G/T	6-1	235	Northwestern	
Evans, Lon	T/G	6-2	225	TCU	12
Gantenbein, Milt	E	6-0	199	Wisconsin	10
Goldenberg, Charles (Buckets)	B	5-10	220	Wisconsin	10
Grove, Roger	B	6-0	175	Michigan State	11
Herber, Arnie	B	5-11	208	Regis	12
Hinkle, Clarke	FB	5-11	200	Bucknell	12
Johnston, Chester (Swede)	B	5-10	200	Marquette	1
Jones, Robert	G	6-0	216	Indiana	12
Jorgensen, Carl	T/G	6-2	200	St. Mary's (CA)	10
Kurth, Joe	T	6-3	202	Notre Dame	7
Laws, Joe	B	5-9	180	Iowa	13
Michalske, August (Mike)	G	6-1	215	Penn State	13
Monnett, Bob	B	5-9	180	Michigan State	11
Norgard, Al	E	6-0	193	Stanford	10
Perry, Claude	T	6-1	211	Alabama	13
Peterson, Lester	E	6-0	211	Texas	11
Rose, Al	E	6-3	195	Texas	10
Schwammel, Ade	T	6-2	230	Oregon State	13
Seibold, Champ	G	6-4	240	Wisconsin	1
Witte, Earl	B	6-1	187	Gustavus-Adolphus	5
Wunsch, Harry	G	5-11	210	Notre Dame	2

FRONT ROW: (L-R) 33 Mike Michalske, 36 Bob Tenner, 31 Nate Barragar, 50 Ade Schwammel, 43 George Svendsen, 46 Lon Evans, 25 George Sauer, 24 Bob O'Connor, 12 Bob Monnett, Trainer Dave Woodward.
MIDDLE ROW: (L-R) 44 Buckets Goldenberg, 29 Joe Laws, 34 Paul Engebretsen, 30 Clarke Hinkle, 38 Arnie Herber, 11 Roger Grove, 27 Hank Bruder, 22 Milt Gantenbein, 4 Herm Schneidman, 15 Swede Johnston.
BACK ROW: (L-R) Coach Curly Lambeau, 26 Johnny Blood McNally, 47 Al Rose, 48 Frank Butler, 52 Champ Seibold, 51 Cal Hubbard, 49 Walt Kiesling, 32 Claude Perry, 14 Don Hutson, 45 Ernie Smith.

8-4-0 · 1935 · 8-4-0

The Don Hutson era arrived with an impact that was felt throughout the league. In Week 2, the fleet-footed end out of Alabama turned a bomb from Arnie Herber into an 83-yard touchdown reception that beat the Bears 7-0 and signaled the arrival of a new breed of receiver.

The 6-foot-1, 185-pounder more than fulfilled the Packers' need for a playmaker at end. The rookie also put an end to the team's struggles against the Bears. In the rematch in Chicago, Hutson snagged two touchdown passes in the closing minutes to rally Green Bay to a 17-14 victory.

For the year, Hutson caught 18 passes for a team-high 420 yards and six touchdowns. His totals would have been higher had he not missed two of the last three games with an appendicitis.

Hutson's play and that of the team in general had Curly Lambeau in rare form. Despite a 20-10 loss in Detroit in Week 9, Lambeau was confident. "The toughest part of the season is just ahead of us, but we're sitting in the driver's seat now, and I don't think anyone will catch us."

Brash talk considering his team was just clinging to the Western Division lead with three games remaining. Green Bay (6-3) was essentially tied with the Cardinals (4-2-1) and only slightly ahead of the Bears (5-3) and Lions (5-3-1). It could ill afford a misstep.

But stumble it did, falling 9-7 to the Cardinals on the last weekend of November. Green Bay was without three of its top players because of injury: Herber (hand), Hutson (appendicitis), and George Sauer (torn muscle). With 55

seconds to go, Ade Schwammel missed a 16-yard field goal that essentially ended the Packers' season.

Now a longshot, Green Bay (7-4) needed to win its final game against the Eagles, have Brooklyn upset Detroit (6-3-2) and have the Cardinals (6-3-1) lose at least one of their last two games. Chicago cooperated, but the Lions did not, routing the Dodgers 28-0. Thus, the Packers (8-4) settled for second place behind Detroit (7-3-2).

While Green Bay rebounded against the Bears, it could not handle the other team from Chicago. The Cardinals beat the Packers three times by a combined six points.

Clarke Hinkle, Sauer, and Roger Grove missed the season opener with injuries. Herber, also banged up, threw only one pass, an interception that came on the last play of the game. With its backfield just a shadow of itself, Green Bay bowed out to the Cardinals 7-6.

After winning three straight, the Packers again tangled with the Cardinals. Green Bay was intercepted six times and lost 3-0 on a 12-yard Paul Pardonner field goal. Lost also, for two weeks, was Johnny Blood, who left the stadium in an ambulance with a "brain concussion."

The setback plunged the Packers (3-2) into last place in the division behind the Cardinals (2-0-1), Lions (2-1-1), and Bears (2-1). But Green Bay rang up three more wins, beating the Lions (twice) and Bears to regain the lead.

Hutson caught scoring passes of 69 and 3 yards in the final two-and-a-half minutes of that second Bears game. The victory gave Green Bay a sweep of its archrivals, a feat it would not accomplish again for 26 years.

TEAM STATISTICS

	GB	OPP
First Downs	130	96
Rushes	447	448
Yards Gained	1,562	1,219
Average Gain	3.49	2.72
Average Yards per Game	130.2	101.6
Passes Attempted	230	191
Completed	93	61
% Completed	40.43	31.94
Total Yards Gained	1,449	837
Yards Gained per Completion	15.58	13.72
Average Yards per Game	120.8	69.8
Laterals Attempted	5	10
Completed	2	10
Yards Gained	10	35
Combined Yards Gained	3,021	2,091
Total Plays	682	649
Average Yards per Play	4.43	3.22
Average Yards per Game	251.8	174.3
Intercepted By	26	27
Yards Penalized	295	190
Fumbles	29	27
Recovered	21	24
Total Points Scored	181	96
Total Touchdowns	23	13
Touchdowns Rushing	7	5
Touchdowns Passing	11	7
Touchdowns on Returns & Recoveries	5	1
Extra Points	19	9
Safeties	0	0
Field Goals Made	8	3

Regular Season 8-4-0

Date	GB		OPP
9/15	6	Chicago Cardinals	7
9/22	7	Chicago Bears	0
9/29	16	New York Giants	7
10/6	27	Pittsburgh Pirates	0
10/13	0	Chicago Cardinals (M)	3
10/20	13	Detroit Lions (M)	9
10/27	17	at Chicago Bears	14
11/10	31	Detroit Lions	7
11/17	10	at Detroit Lions	20
11/24	34	at Pittsburgh Pirates	14
11/28	7	at Chicago Cardinals	9
12/8	13	at Philadelphia Eagles	6

Score By Periods

	1	2	3	4	Total
Packers	26	53	37	65	181
Opponents	13	42	14	27	96

INDIVIDUAL STATISTICS

Rushing

	Att	Yds	Avg	TD
Monnett	68	336	4.9	1
Sauer	89	334	3.8	3
Hinkle	77	273	3.5	2
Johnston	52	176	3.4	0
Bruder	44	158	3.6	0
Blood	42	115	2.7	0
Laws	24	63	2.6	1
Goldenberg	15	52	3.5	0
Hutson	6	22	3.7	0
Grove	7	21	3.0	0
Schneidman	4	12	3.0	0
Herber	19			
Packers	447	1,562	3.5	7
Opponents	448	1,219	2.7	5

Receiving

	No	Yds	Avg	LG	TD
Blood	25	404	16.2	t70	3
Hutson	18	420	23.3	t83	6
Gantenbein	13	168	12.9		1
A. Rose	8	91	11.4		0
Johnston	6	59	9.8		1
Laws	4	82	20.5	41	0
Bruder	4	67	16.8	30	0
Goldenberg	3	42	14.0	21	0
Tenner	3	38	12.7	29	0
Sauer	3	32	10.7	14	0
Herber	2	36	13.0	17	0
Schneidman	2	16	8.0	8	0
Monnett	1	8	8.0	8	0
Hinkle	1	-4	-4.0	-4	0
Packers	93	1,449	15.6	t83	11
Opponents	61	837	13.7	t44	7

Passing

	Att	Com	Yds	Pct	TD	In	Rate
Herber	106	40	729	37.7	8	14	47.8
Monnett	65	31	354	47.7	2	5	42.7
Sauer	21	9	177	42.9	1	5	49.2
Blood	33	11	164	33.3	0	3	12.7
Bruder	1	1	17	100.0	0	0	—
Laws	4	1	8	25.0	0	0	—
Packers	230	93	1,449	40.4	11	27	38.4
Opponents	191	61	837	31.9	7	26	19.6

Scoring

	TDr	TDp	TDrt	PAT	FG	S	TP
Hutson	0	6	1	1	0	0	43
Blood	0	3	1	0	0	0	24
Sauer	3	0	1	0	0	0	24
Hinkle	2	0	0	1	2	0	19
Schwammel	0	0	0	2	4	0	14
Ernie Smith	0	0	0	11	1	0	14
Monnett	1	0	0	2	1	0	11
Bruder	0	0	1	0	0	0	6
Gantenbein	0	1	0	0	0	0	6
Hubbard	0	0	1	0	0	0	6
Johnston	0	1	0	0	0	0	6
Laws	1	0	0	0	0	0	6
Engebretsen	0	0	0	1	0	0	1
Herber	0	0	0	1	0	0	1
Packers	7	11	5	19	8	0	181
Opponents	5	7	1	9	3	0	96

NFL STANDINGS

Western Division

	W	L	T	Pct	PF	PA
Detroit Lions	7	3	2	.700	191	111
Green Bay Packers	8	4	0	.667	181	96
Chicago Bears	6	4	2	.600	192	106
Chicago Cardinals	6	4	2	.600	99	97

Eastern Division

	W	L	T	Pct	PF	PA
New York Giants	9	3	0	.750	180	96
Brooklyn Dodgers	5	6	1	.455	90	141
Pittsburgh Pirates	4	8	0	.333	100	209
Boston Redskins	2	8	1	.200	65	123
Philadelphia Eagles	2	9	0	.182	60	179

ROSTER

No	Name	Pos	Ht	Wt	DOB	College	G
31	Barragar, Nate	C	6-0	210		USC	11
27	Bruder, Hank	B	6-0	197	11/22/07	Northwestern	10
48	Butler, Frank	C	6-3	230	05/03/09	Michigan State	6
34	Engebretsen, Paul (Tiny)	G	6-1	235	07/27/10	Northwestern	9
46	Evans, Lon	G	6-2	219	12/25/11	TCU	12
22	Gantenbein, Milt	E	6-0	193	05/31/10	Wisconsin	12
44	Goldenberg, Charles (Buckets)	B	5-10	215	03/10/11	Wisconsin	12
11	Grove, Roger	B	6-0	184	06/19/08	Michigan State	
38	Herber, Arnie	B	5-11	203	04/02/10	Regis	11
30	Hinkle, Clarke	FB	5-11	205	04/10/09	Bucknell	9
51	Hubbard, Robert (Cal)	T/E	6-5	265	10/11/00	Geneva	11
14	Hutson, Don	E	6-1	189	01/31/13	Alabama	10
15	Johnston, Chester (Swede)	B	5-10	200	03/07/10	Marquette	11
49	Kiesling, Walt	G	6-3	260	05/27/03	St. Thomas (MN)	10
29	Laws, Joe	B	5-9	185	06/16/11	Iowa	12
28	Maddox, George (Buster)	T	6-3	240	11/04/11	Kansas State	1
42	McDonald, Dustin	G	5-4	202	10/03/08	Indiana	1
26	McNally (Blood), Johnny	B	6-0	190	11/27/03	St. John's	10
33	Michalske, August (Mike)	G	6-0	200	04/24/03	Penn State	10
3/12	Monnett, Bob	B	5-9	181	02/27/10	Michigan State	11
24	O'Connor, Bob	G	6-1	220	01/27/10	Stanford	7
32	Perry, Claude	T	6-1	211	10/31/01	Alabama	8
47	Rose, Al	E	6-3	195	01/26/07	Texas	12
25	Sauer, George	B	6-2	204	12/11/10	Nebraska	10
4	Schneidman, Herm	B	5-10	205	11/22/13	Iowa	11
33/50	Schwammel, Ade	T	6-2	230	10/14/08	Oregon State	11
37	Seibold, Champ	T	6-4	240	12/05/12	Wisconsin	6
45	Smith, Ernie	T	6-2	234	11/26/09	USC	12
43	Svendsen, George	C	6-4	214	03/22/13	Minnesota	11
36	Tenner, Bob	E	6-0	212	06/01/13	Minnesota	11
35	Vairo, Dominic	E	6-2	203	11/02/12	Notre Dame	1

FRONT ROW: (L-R) 39 Tony Paulekas, 52 Paul Engebretsen, 51 Lon Evans, 57 Ade Schwammel, 58 Champ Seibold, 59 Frank Butler, 25 George Sauer, 33 Cal Clemens, 44 Buckets Goldenberg.
MIDDLE ROW: (L-R) Coach Curly Lambeau, 40 Bernie Scherer, 18 Hank Bruder, 53 Lou Gordon, 43 George Svendsen, 60 Walt Kiesling, 55 Johnny Blood McNally, 61 Ernie Smith, 54 Swede Johnston, Assistant Coach Richard (Red) Smith.
BACK ROW: (L-R) 29 Joe Laws, 38 Arnie Herber, 41 Herm Schneidman, 62 Russ Letlow, 32 Wayland Becker, 3 Paul Miller, 41 Clarke Hinkle, 14 Don Hutson, 22 Milt Gantenbein, 5 Bob Monnett.

10-1-1   1936   10-1-1

A record-setting passing attack helped Green Bay overcome an early-season misadventure and capture its first NFL championship in five years. Piloted by record-breakers Arnie Herber and Don Hutson, the Packers' aerial assault accounted for 1,629 yards, 17 touchdowns, and was key in producing a league-best record (10-1-1) and point total (248).

Playing a full-season for just the second time in his career, Herber became the first NFL player to throw for 1,000 yards (1,239) in a single season. He also tossed a career-best 11 touchdown passes and led the league in passing for the third time in five years (1932, 1934, 1936).

Hutson, who took the league by storm as a rookie, established league marks for catches (34) and yards (534). Green Bay was 8-0 in games in which he caught at least one pass, and 2-1-1 in games where he was shut out.

Despite losing just once all season, the Packers did not lock up the Western Division title until they beat the Lions 26-17 in Week 11. In that game, Herber passed for 212 yards with Hutson making six catches for 97 yards and a touchdown. The sophomore sensation also recovered a blocked punt for a touchdown.

Green Bay looked like anything but champions in Week 2 against the Bears. Chicago lit up City Stadium with 20 second-half points and administered a 30-3 licking. For the next month and a half, the Packers maintained second place in the standings behind their arch rivals before a nicely executed rally at Wrigley Field in Week 7 pulled them even with the Bears.

One of Curly Lambeau's early concerns was finding replacements for departed linemen Mike Michalske, Cal Hubbard, Claude Perry, and Nate Barragar. The coach turned to Paul Engebretsen, Ernie Smith, Lou Gordon, George

UNCHAMPIONSHIP-LIKE CONDUCT

The Packers have won a record 12 NFL championships. During the course of those dozen seasons, however, the team didn't always play as though it was the best team in the league.

In 1936, Green Bay was dealt its most lopsided defeat in a season in which it won the league title. The Bears roared into City Stadium and drubbed them 30-3. Chicago forced four turnovers and rushed for 184 yards on 40 carries.

Ade Schwammel missed three field goals that would have given the Packers a 12-3 second-quarter lead had he made them all.

Below are the biggest losses Green Bay has suffered in seasons in which it won an NFL championship:

Margin of Defeat	Opponent	Date
27 points (30-3)	Bears	9-20-1936
24 points (24-0)	Giants	11-19-1944
24 points (45-21)	Colts	11-5-1961
21 points (21-0)	Bears	12-7-1930
21 points (21-0)	Bears	11-5-1944
21 points (31-10)	Bears	10-31-1965

TEAM STATISTICS

	GB	OPP
First Downs	148	136
Rushes	490	479
Yards Gained	1,664	1,494
Average Gain	3.40	3.12
Average Yards per Game	138.7	124.5
Passes Attempted	255	227
Completed	108	81
% Completed	42.35	35.68
Total Yards Gained	1,629	1,170
Yards Gained per Completion	15.08	14.44
Average Yards per Game	135.5	97.5
Laterals Attempted	5	7
Completed	5	6
Yards Gained	30	0
Combined Net Yards Gained	3,323	2,664
Total Plays	750	713
Average Yards per Play	4.43	3.74
Average Net Yards per Game	276.9	222.0
Intercepted By	31	19
Yards Penalized	478	386
Fumbles	23	29
Recovered	19	28
Total Points Scored	248	118
Total Touchdowns	31	14
Touchdowns Rushing	11	5
Touchdowns Passing	17	7
Touchdowns on Returns & Recoveries	3	2
Extra Points	30	12
Safeties	1	2
Field Goals Made	10	6

Regular Season 10-1-1

Date	GB		OPP	Att.
9/13	10	Chicago Cardinals	7	(8,900)
9/20	3	Chicago Bears	30	(14,312)
10/4	24	Chicago Cardinals (M)	0	(11,000)
10/11	31	Boston Redskins	2	(6,100)
10/18	20	Detroit Lions	18	(13,500)
10/25	42	Pittsburgh Pirates (M)	10	(10,000)
11/1	21	at Chicago Bears	10	(31,346)
11/8	7	at Boston Redskins	3	(11,220)
11/15	38	at Brooklyn Dodgers	7	(25,325)
11/22	26	at New York Giants	14	(20,000)
11/29	26	at Detroit Lions	17	(22,000)
12/6	0	at Chicago Cardinals	0	(4,793)

Postseason 1-0

12/13	21	Boston Redskins (at NY)	6	(29,545)

Score By Periods

	1	2	3	4	Total
Packers	40	86	76	46	248
Opponents	26	21	27	44	118

INDIVIDUAL STATISTICS

Rushing

	Att	Yds	Avg	TD
Hinkle	100	476	4.8	5
Sauer	94	305	3.2	3
Laws	50	296	5.9	1
P. Miller	52	227	4.4	1
Monnett	104	224	2.2	0
Johnston	42	110	2.6	1
Blood	13	65	5.0	0
Goldenberg	6	9	1.5	0
Mattos	1	2	2.0	0
Hutson	1	-3	-3.0	0
Bruder	4	-7	-1.7	0
Clemens	3	-8	-2.7	0
Herber	20	-32	-1.6	0
Packers	490	1,664	3.4	11
Opponents	479	1,494	3.1	5

Receiving

	No	Yds	Avg	LG	TD
Hutson	34	526	15.5	t58	8
Gantenbein	15	221	14.7	28	1
Monnett	13	169	13.0		0
Laws	10	132	13.2		2
P. Miller	8	113	14.1	34	2
Blood	7	147	21.0	t46	2
Sauer	6	110	18.3		0
Becker	5	66	13.2		1
Schneidman	3	68	22.7	t46	1
Bruder	2	25	12.5	23	0
Johnston	2	11	5.5		0
Clemens	1	18	18.0	18	0
Packers	108	1,629	15.1	t58	17
Opponents	81	1,170	14.4	52	7

Passing

	Att	Com	Yds	Pct	TD	In	Rate
Herber	173	77	1,239	44.5	11	13	58.9
Monnett	52	20	280	38.5	4	2	66.2
Mattos	12	4	32	33.3	0	2	2.8
Sauer	4	2	26	50.0	0	1	—
Laws	4	1	22	25.0	1	0	—
Blood	6	3	20	50.0	1	0	—
Hinkle	2	1	10	50.0	0	0	—
Clemens	1	0	0	0.00	0	0	—
P. Miller	1	0	0	0.00	0	1	—
Packers	255	108	1,629	42.4	17	19	60.7
Opponents	227	81	1,170	35.7	7	31	24.0

Scoring

	TDr	TDp	TDrt	PAT	FG	S	TP
Hutson	0	8	1	0	0	0	54
Hinkle	5	0	0	1	0	0	31
Ernie Smith	0	0	0	17	4	0	29
Blood	0	2	1	1	0	0	19
Laws	1	2	0	0	0	0	18
P. Miller	1	2	0	0	0	0	18
Engebretsen	0	0	0	2	5	0	17
Schwammel	0	0	0	5	1	0	8
Becker	0	1	0	0	0	0	6
Gantenbein	0	1	0	0	0	0	6
Johnston	1	0	0	0	0	0	6
Scherer	0	0	1	0	0	0	6
Schneidman	0	1	0	0	0	0	6
Monnett	0	0	0	3	0	0	3
team	0	0	0	0	0	1	2
Clemens	0	0	0	1	0	0	1
Packers	11	17	3	30	10	1	248
Opponents	5	7	2	12	6	2	118

NFL STANDINGS

Western Division

	W	L	T	Pct	PF	PA
Green Bay Packers	10	1	1	.909	248	118
Chicago Bears	9	3	0	.750	222	94
Detroit Lions	8	4	0	.667	235	102
Chicago Cardinals	3	8	1	.273	74	143

Eastern Division

	W	L	T	Pct	PF	PA
Boston Redskins	7	5	0	.583	149	110
Pittsburgh Pirates	6	6	0	.500	98	187
New York Giants	5	6	1	.455	115	163
Brooklyn Dodgers	3	8	1	.273	92	161
Philadelphia Eagles	1	11	0	.083	51	206

Svendsen, Frank Butler, and others. Evans and Smith didn't miss a game and both were named All-Pro at season's end.

Another concern—more of a headache, actually—was the status of Johnny Blood. The 12-year veteran staged what was probably the first contract holdout to drag on into the regular season in team history. Not until after the first Bears game did Blood and the Packers come to terms. In his last season with the Packers, the Vagabond Halfback gained but 65 yards rushing.

Green Bay opened against the Cardinals on Sept. 13. Ernie Smith's 23-yard field goal midway through the fourth quarter proved the difference in a 10-7 win.

After the Bears' fiasco, the Packers righted themselves against the Cardinals. Joe Laws' 41-yard scoring run put the finishing touches on a 24-0 rout.

Green Bay grabbed its second win in a row when it scored in every period to down Boston 31-2. Herber, Laws, and Bob Monnett each threw a touchdown pass.

The defending champion Lions (3-0) were next in line. Engebretsen, who hit a 40-yarder to start the game, made an 18-yard field goal to give Green Bay a 20-18 win.

After flogging Pittsburgh 42-10, the Packers (5-1) squared off against the Bears (6-0). Clark Hinkle (13 carries, 109 yards) keyed Green Bay's best rushing output of the year (219 yards) as he and his teammates erased a 10-point deficit to win going away 21-10.

A stubborn Boston team held the Packers to 20 yards rushing in Week 8. Green Bay escaped with a 7-3 win on the strength of a 19-yard Herber-to-Hutson pass.

Green Bay then dispensed with the Dodgers (38-7) and Giants (26-14) before downing the Lions a second time. Having wrapped up the division title, the Packers closed with a 0-0 tie against the Cardinals.

On Dec. 13, Green Bay earned its first-ever postseason win and fourth championship overall by dropping Boston 21-6 at New York's Polo Grounds.

ROSTER

No	Name	Pos	Ht	Wt	DOB	College	G
32	Becker, Wayland	E	6-0	183	11/02/10	Marquette	11
27/18	Bruder, Hank	B	6-0	197	11/22/07	Northwestern	11
48/59	Butler, Frank	C	6-3	246	05/03/09	Michigan State	11
33	Clemens, Cal	B	6-1	195	07/07/09	USC	9
34/52	Engebretsen, Paul (Tiny)	G	6-1	238	07/27/10	Northwestern	12
51	Evans, Lon	G	6-2	223	12/25/11	TCU	12
22	Gantenbein, Milt	E	6-0	208	05/31/10	Wisconsin	9
44	Goldenberg, Charles (Buckets)	G/B	5-10	212	03/10/11	Wisconsin	7
53	Gordon, Lou	T	6-5	235	07/15/06	Illinois	12
38	Herber, Arnie	B	5-11	195	04/02/10	Regis	12
41	Hinkle, Clarke	FB	5-11	202	04/10/09	Bucknell	12
14	Hutson, Don	E	6-1	180	01/31/13	Alabama	12
15/54	Johnston, Chester (Swede)	B	5-10	192	03/07/10	Marquette	10
49/60	Kiesling, Walt	G	6-3	248	05/27/03	St. Thomas (MN)	9
29	Laws, Joe	B	5-9	186	06/16/11	Iowa	12
46/62	Letlow, Russ	G	6-0	203	10/05/13	San Francisco	10
23	Mattos, Harry	B	6-0	201	04/07/11	St. Mary's (CA)	2
55	McNally, Johnny (Blood)	B	6-0	190	11/27/03	St. John's	8
3	Miller, Paul	B	5-10	175	01/23/13	South Dakota State	12
12/5	Monnett, Bob	B	5-9	181	02/27/10	Michigan State	12
39	Paulekas, Tony	C/G	5-10	207	08/09/12	Washington-Jefferson	11
47	Rose, Al	E	6-3	195	01/26/07	Texas	2
25	Sauer, George	B	6-2	208	12/11/10	Nebraska	10
40	Scherer, Bernie	E	6-1	183	01/28/13	Nebraska	10
4	Schneidman, Herm	B/E	5-10	205	11/22/13	Iowa	7
50/57	Schwammel, Ade	T	6-2	232	10/14/08	Oregon State	12
37/58	Seibold, Champ	T	6-4	230	12/05/12	Wisconsin	12
45/61	Smith, Ernie	T	6-2	221	11/26/09	USC	12
43	Svendsen, George	C	6-4	224	03/22/13	Minnesota	11

DRAFT

Rnd	Name	Pos	College
1	Russ Letlow	G	San Francisco
2	J.W. Wheeler	T	Oklahoma
3	Bernie Scherer	E	Nebraska
4	Theron Ward	B	Idaho
5	Darrell Lester	C	TCU
6	Bob Reynolds	T	Stanford
7	Wally Fromhart	B	Notre Dame
8	Wally Cruice	B	Northwestern
9	J.C. Wetsel	G	SMU

FRONT ROW: (L-R) Trainer Dave Woodward, 25 Ed Jankowski, 5 Bob Monnett, 22 Milt Gantenbein, 38 Arnie Herber, 3 Paul Miller, 45 Ernie Smith, 37 Francis Schammel, 39 Lon Evans, 34 Paul Engebretsen, Assistant Trainer Carl (Bud) Jorgensen.
SECOND ROW: (L-R) Coach Curly Lambeau, 30 Clarke Hinkle, 44 Buckets Goldenberg, 24 Joe Laws, 18 Hank Bruder, 11 Bernie Scherer, 46 Russ Letlow, 29 Darrell Lester, 17 George Sauer, 14 Don Hutson.
BACK ROW: (L-R) 47 Lou Gordon, 26 Lyle Sturgeon, 21 Herb Banet, 41 Champ Seibold, 40 Bill Lee, 43 George Svendsen, 4 Herm Schneidman, 7 Earl Svendsen, 32 Wayland Becker, Assistant Coach Richard (Red) Smith.

7-4-0   1937   7-4-0

To the defending champions go the spoils. Unfortunately for Green Bay, one of the rewards for scaling the NFL mountaintop in 1936 may have contributed to its slow start in 1937.

Beginning in 1934, the NFL champion from the previous year played in the College All-Star Game in Chicago. The matchup pitted the top professional team against the best players in the college ranks.

Green Bay's turn in the marquee event proved costly. On Sept. 1, the Packers became the first pro team to lose to the collegians 6-0. Further, they lost the services of Arnie Herber and Bob Monnett to shoulder injuries.

Herber was the more seriously injured. Both he and Monnett missed the season opener, but Herber sat out the Bears game as well. The long-ball specialist didn't throw a pass until Week 4 and didn't regain his form until a 35-10 thrashing of Cleveland a week later.

With the likes of Joe Laws, Herb Banet, Hank Bruder, Ray Peterson, Don Hutson, and Ed Smith taking turns passing, Green Bay dropped its first two games. After regaining its top passers, the team embarked on a seven-game winning streak to pull to within a game of the league-leading Bears. But losses in the final two weeks left the Packers out in the cold with a 7-4 mark.

City Stadium was enlarged by approximately 6,000 seats. A record 16,658 fans attended the Bears game on Sept. 19, and that total was surpassed two weeks later when 17,553 saw the Packers and Lions do battle.

With Herber and Monnett out, Green Bay turned to the run. Clarke Hinkle gained 72 of the team's 246 rushing yards in the season opener. But a meager four completions in 19 attempts—including just two for eight yards to Hutson—stymied the offense and the Packers fell 14-7.

GORDON'S GRAB

Chances are few Packers fans have heard of Lou Gordon. But the tackle, who played in Green Bay from 1936 to 1937, had a game to remember in the 1937 season opener.

Fumble recoveries were first compiled by the NFL in 1945. The record of three in a single game is shared by more than a dozen players. Gordon's name should be on that list.

Gordon recovered three fumbles by the Cardinals on Sept. 12. If the Packers had turned his recoveries into more than seven points, they might have won the game.

Gordon pounced on two fumbles by George Grosvenor and one by rookie Bill Crass. Crass fumbled first, and the Packers moved 66 yards in 10 plays to record their only score of the game.

Grosvenor's first bobble occurred on the opening kick-off of the second half. Four plays later, Ernie Smith missed a 22-yard field goal attempt.

Grosvenor's second fumble happened late in the fourth quarter. Gordon recovered at the Cardinals' 48-yard line. The Packers managed just two yards on two runs before a pair of passes by Joe Laws fell incomplete.

Chicago ran out the clock to escape with a 14-7 win.

1937

TEAM STATISTICS

	GB	OPP
First Downs	140	110
Rushes	483	400
Yards Gained	1,786	1,184
Average Gain	3.70	2.96
Average Yards per Game	162.4	107.6
Passes Attempted	216	197
Completed	95	70
% Completed	43.98	35.53
Total Yards Gained	1,398	1,115
Yards Gained per Completion	14.72	15.93
Average Yards per Game	127.1	101.4
Laterals Attempted	3	6
Completed	3	6
Yards Gained	17	0
Combined Yards Gained	3,201	2,299
Total Plays	702	603
Average Yards per Play	4.60	3.81
Average Yards per Game	291.0	209.0
Intercepted By	21	26
Yards Penalized	291	286
Fumbles	18	18
Recovered	11	9
Total Points Scored	220	122
Total Touchdowns	30	17
Touchdowns Rushing	10	8
Touchdowns Passing	17	7
Touchdowns on Returns & Recoveries	3	2
Extra Points	26	14
Safeties	1	0
Field Goals Made	4	2

Regular Season   7-4-0

Date	GB		OPP	Att.
9/12	7	Chicago Cardinals	14	(10,000)
9/19	2	Chicago Bears	14	(16,658)
10/3	26	Detroit Lions	6	(17,553)
10/10	34	Chicago Cardinals (M)	13	(16,181)
10/17	35	at Cleveland Rams	10	(12,100)
10/24	35	Cleveland Rams	7	(8,600)
10/31	14	at Detroit Lions	13	(21,311)
11/7	24	at Chicago Bears	14	(44,977)
11/14	37	Philadelphia Eagles (M)	7	(13,340)
11/21	0	at New York Giants	10	(38,965)
11/28	6	at Washington Redskins	14	(30,000)

Score By Periods

	1	2	3	4	Total
Packers	35	75	33	77	220
Opponents	7	26	62	27	122

INDIVIDUAL STATISTICS

Rushing

	Att	Yds	Avg	TD
Hinkle	129	552	4.3	5
Jankowski	61	324	5.3	2
Laws	74	310	4.2	1
P. Miller	71	262	3.7	0
Monnett	87	161	1.9	1
Bruder	15	56	3.7	1
Banet	9	29	3.2	0
Hutson	14	26	1.9	0
Goldenberg	4	18	4.5	0
Schneidman	5	17	3.4	0
Sauer	7	17	2.4	0
Herber	5	9	1.8	0
Becker	2	5	2.5	0
Packers	483	1,786	3.7	10
Opponents	400	1,184	3.0	8

Receiving

	No	Yds	Avg	LG	TD
Hutson	41	552	13.5	t78	7
Gantenbein	12	237	19.8	t77	2
Laws	10	121	12.1	19	1
Hinkle	8	116	14.5	t49	2
Scherer	6	149	24.8	t78	2
P. Miller	6	66	11.0	16	1
Monnett	4	32	8.0	13	0
Jankowski	2	60	30.0	46	1
Schneidman	2	35	17.5	23	1
Becker	2	13	6.5	11	0
G. Svendsen	1	11	11.0	11	0
Banet	1	6	6.0	6	0
Packers	95	1,398	14.7	t78	17
Opponents	70	1,115	15.9	t86	7

Passing

	Att	Com	Yds	Pct	TD	In	Rate
Herber	104	47	684	45.2	7	10	50.0
Monnett	73	37	580	50.7	9	8	77.4
R. Peterson	6	3	47	50.0	0	0	—
Hinkle	3	2	43	66.7	0	0	—
Laws	11	5	42	45.5	1	2	46.6
Banet	7	1	2	14.3	0	2	—
Bruder	6	0	0	00.0	0	2	—
Hutson	4	0	0	00.0	0	1	—
Ed Smith	2	0	0	00.0	0	1	—
Packers	216	95	1,398	44.0	17	26	52.4
Opponents	197	70	1,115	35.5	7	21	27.5

Scoring

	TDr	TDp	TDrt	PAT	FG	S	TP
Hinkle	5	2	0	8	2	0	56
Hutson	0	7	0	0	0	0	42
Jankowski	2	1	1	1	0	0	25
Ernie Smith	0	0	0	12	1	0	15
Gantenbein	0	2	0	0	0	0	12
Laws	1	1	0	0	0	0	12
Scherer	0	2	0	0	0	0	12
Engebretsen	0	0	0	5	1	0	8
Bruder	1	0	0	0	0	0	6
Goldenberg	0	0	1	0	0	0	6
P. Miller	0	1	0	0	0	0	6
Monnett	1	0	0	0	0	0	6
Schammel	0	0	1	0	0	0	6
Schneidman	0	1	0	0	0	0	6
team	0	0	0	0	0	1	2
Packers	10	17	3	26	4	1	220
Opponents	8	7	2	14	2	0	122

NFL STANDINGS

Western Division

	W	L	T	Pct	PF	PA
Chicago Bears	9	1	1	.900	201	100
Green Bay Packers	7	4	0	.636	220	122
Detroit Lions	7	4	0	.636	180	105
Chicago Cardinals	5	5	1	.500	135	165
Cleveland Rams	1	10	0	.091	75	207

Eastern Division

	W	L	T	Pct	PF	PA
Washington Redskins	8	3	0	.727	195	120
New York Giants	6	3	2	.667	128	109
Pittsburgh Pirates	4	7	0	.364	122	145
Brooklyn Dodgers	3	7	1	.300	82	174
Philadelphia Eagles	2	8	1	.200	86	177

In Week 2, the Bears pushed across 14 second-quarter points. Any comeback the Packers might have mustered died with four fourth-quarter interceptions, and Chicago won its first game of the season 14-2.

Green Bay enjoyed a 14-day break between that game and its contest with the Lions on Oct. 3. The extra rest helped Herber, Monnett and others recover.

The Packers notched their first win (26-6) at the expense of Detroit. Milt Gantenbein provided the highlight with a 77-yard touchdown pass from Monnett.

The team evened its record the following week with a 34-13 triumph over the Cardinals at State Fair Park. Eddie Jankowski, the club's top draft choice, led the way with 96 yards rushing on 13 carries.

In Week 5, Hutson registered the first three-touchdown outing of his career. He snagged two scoring passes from Herber and one from Monnett as Green Bay thumped Cleveland by 25 points in League Park.

A week later, the Rams traveled to City Stadium where they fared no better in falling 35-7. Clarke Hinkle cut loose for 146 yards (84 rushing; 62 receiving) including a 49-yard scoring collaboration with Monnett early in the game.

Hinkle's 2-yard, fourth-down run late in the fourth quarter allowed Green Bay to squeak past the Lions 14-13 in Detroit in Week 7. Dutch Clark missed a 31-yard dropkick with seconds left.

The Packers then blasted the Bears 24-14 before capping their run of seven straight with a 37-7 win over Philadelphia. Herber fired three touchdown passes including a 78-yarder to Bernie Scherer in the Eagles skirmish.

With a 7-2 record, Green Bay needed to win its last two games and have the Bears (6-1-1) lose at least once. Wishful thinking. The Packers flopped on their Eastern swing, falling 10-0 to New York and 14-6 to Washington, while the Bears wrapped up the Western Division crown by closing out with three straight wins.

ROSTER

No	Name	Pos	Ht	Wt	DOB	College	G
21	Banet, Herb	B	6-2	200	10/17/13	Manchester	
32	Becker, Wayland	E	6-0	205	11/02/10	Marquette	10
18	Bruder, Hank	B	6-0	200	11/22/07	Northwestern	10
23	Daniell, Averell	T	6-3	210	11/06/14	Pittsburgh	6
34	Engebretsen, Paul (Tiny)	G	6-1	240	07/27/10	Northwestern	10
39	Evans, Lon	G	6-2	230	12/25/11	TCU	11
22	Gantenbein, Milt	E	6-0	200	05/31/10	Wisconsin	11
44	Goldenberg, Charles (Buckets)	G/QB	5-10	220	03/10/11	Wisconsin	8
47	Gordon, Lou	T	6-5	230	07/15/06	Illinois	10
19/38	Herber, Arnie	B	5-11	195	04/02/10	Regis	9
30	Hinkle, Clarke	FB	5-11	205	04/10/09	Bucknell	11
14	Hutson, Don	E	6-1	180	01/31/13	Alabama	11
25	Jankowski, Ed	B	5-10	205	06/23/13	Wisconsin	11
15	Johnston, Chester (Swede)	B	5-10	195	03/07/10	Marquette	2
24	Laws, Joe	B	5-9	185	06/16/11	Iowa	11
40	Lee, Bill	T	6-3	225	10/19/11	Alabama	4
29	Lester, Darrell	C	6-3	220	04/29/14	TCU	8
46	Letlow, Russ	G	6-0	210	10/05/13	San Francisco	11
36	Michalske, August (Mike)	G	6-0	210	04/24/03	Penn State	6
3	Miller, Paul	B	5-10	180	01/23/13	South Dakota State	10
5	Monnett, Bob	B	5-9	180	02/27/10	Michigan State	10
33	Peterson, Ray	B	6-0	190	06/27/13	San Francisco	2
17	Sauer, George	B	6-2	208	12/11/10	Nebraska	2
37	Schammel, Francis (Zud)	G/T	6-2	235	08/26/10	Iowa	11
11	Scherer, Bernie	E	6-1	190	01/28/13	Nebraska	11
4	Schneidman, Herm	B	5-10	200	11/22/13	Iowa	11
41	Seibold, Champ	T	6-4	235	12/05/12	Wisconsin	10
28	Smith, Ed	B	6-2	205	06/17/13	New York	
45	Smith, Ernie	T	6-2	222	11/26/09	USC	11
26	Sturgeon, Lyle	T	6-3	250	02/07/15	North Dakota State	8
7	Svendsen, Earl	C	6-1	195	02/07/15	Minnesota	11
43	Svendsen, George	C	6-4	230	03/22/13	Minnesota	11

DRAFT

Rnd	Name	Pos	College
1	Ed Jankowski	B	Wisconsin
2	Averell Daniell	T	Pittsburgh
3	Charles (Bud) Wilkinson	B	Minnesota
4	Earl Svendsen	C	Minnesota
5	Dave Gavin	T	Holy Cross
6	Merle Wendt	E	Ohio State
7	Dick Dahlgren	G	Michigan State
8	Dick Chapman	T	Tulsa
9	Marv Baldwin	G	TCU
10	Gibson DeWitt	T	Northwestern

FRONT ROW: (L-R) Trainer Dave Woodward, 30 Clarke Hinkle, 50 Bob Monnett, 22 Milt Gantenbein, 36 Bernie Scherer, 35 Frank Butler, 19 Carl Mulleneaux, 40 Bill Lee, 51 Herm Schneidman, 48 Ookie Miller, 41 Champ Seibold, 18 Lee Mulleneaux, Assistant Trainer Carl (Bud) Jorgensen.
MIDDLE ROW: (L-R) Coach Curly Lambeau, 3 Paul Miller, 24 Joe Laws, 7 Ed Jankowski, 34 Paul Engebretsen, 37 Tom Jones, 14 Don Hutson, 5 Hank Bruder, 32 Wayland Becker, 11 Leo Katalinas, Assistant Coach Richard (Red) Smith.
BACK ROW: (L-R) 33 Dick Weisgerber, 8 Andy Uram, 38 Arnie Herber, 46 Russ Letlow, 49 John Howell, 20 Baby Ray, 29 Darrell Lester, 9 Tony Borak, 17 Cecil Isbell, 43 Buckets Goldenberg, 21 Pete Tinsley.

8-3-0   1938   8-3-0

The 1938 NFL draft produced only one future Hall of Famer: the Lions' Alex Wojciechowicz. But that number could have been doubled had Cecil Isbell, the Packers first-round choice, played more than five years.

Isbell, the seventh selection overall, led Green Bay in passing and rushing in 1938. He would go on to lead the team in passing four times, and was the league's leading passer two years in a row (1941-42). The halfback retired while still in his prime, departing after becoming the first player in league history to throw for more than 2,000 yards in a season.

Green Bay added three other players of note: Andy Uram, Pete Tinsley, and Baby Ray. Tinsley and Ray became mainstays on the line, enjoying 8- and 11-year careers, respectively. Uram, who reeled off a 97-yard run in 1939, was also a gifted receiver and return man.

The play of these newcomers, along with contributions from veterans such as Arnie Herber, Don Hutson, Clarke Hinkle, and a host of others, returned the Packers to championship play. With help from the Eagles (who defeated the Lions on the final weekend of the season), Green Bay won the Western Division with an 8-3 record. Unfortunately, the team's try for a fifth NFL title was spoiled by the Giants, who prevailed in the championship game 23-17.

For the second year in a row, Green Bay had the most potent offense in the circuit, and for a third year running, it scored the most points. Isbell's 5.2 yards per run, Bob Monnett's 54.4 completion percentage, and Don Hutson's 9 receiving touchdowns were all league season bests.

City Stadium was again renovated. The east end was filled in with new seats, the press box was enlarged, and a clock was placed near the field. Overall, 6,554 seats were added, which increased capacity from around 18,000 to more than 24,000.

A MONNETT TO REMEMBER

Green Bay was well stocked with passers in 1938. They had Arnie Herber, Cecil Isbell and Bob Monnett.

Bob Monnett? Yes, Bob Monnett. The six-year veteran had a better season than either Herber or Isbell. In fact, Monnett's season was the best in the league to that point.

Working primarily with second-teamers—Monnett hooked up with Hutson just six times—the 28-year-old completed 31 of 57 passes for 465 yards, nine touchdowns, and just four interceptions. That's a passer rating of 91.7.

By late October, Monnett had become the team's primary passer. He threw three touchdown passes in a 28-7 win in Cleveland and followed with two more in a 24-17 victory at Wrigley Field where, unfortunately, an injury ended his season.

Listed below are the best seasons by a passer (based on rating points, minimum 50 attempts) from 1932-38.

Rate	Passer	Team	Year
91.7	Bob Monnett	Packers	1938
72.8	Ed Danowski	Giants	1937
69.7	Ed Danowski	Giants	1935

TEAM STATISTICS

	GB	OPP
First Downs	134	118
Rushes	454	372
Yards Gained	1,571	1,206
Average Gain	3.46	3.24
Average Yards per Game	142.8	109.6
Passes Attempted	210	232
Completed	91	92
% Completed	43.33	39.66
Total Yards Gained	1,466	1,343
Yards Gained per Completion	16.11	14.60
Average Yards per Game	133.3	122.1
Laterals Attempted	1	9
Completed	1	9
Yards Gained	0	45
Combined Yards Gained	3,037	2,594
Total Plays	665	613
Average Yards per Play	4.57	4.23
Average Yards per Game	276.1	235.8
Intercepted By	21	20
Yards Penalized	250	334
Fumbles	18	27
Lost	11	12
Own Recovered for TD	0	0
Opponent's Recovered by	12	11
Opponent's Recovered for TD	0	0
Total Points Scored	223	118
Total Touchdowns	30	15
Touchdowns Rushing	9	7
Touchdowns Passing	20	6
Touchdowns on Returns & Recoveries	1	2
Extra Points	28	12
Safeties	0	2
Field Goals Attempted	14	10
Field Goals Made	5	4
% Successful	35.71	40.00

Regular Season   8-3-0

Date	GB		OPP	Att.
9/11	26	Cleveland Rams	17	(8,247)
9/18	0	Chicago Bears	2	(15,172)
9/25	28	Chicago Cardinals (M)	7	(18,000)
9/28	24	Chicago Cardinals at Buffalo	22	(10,678)
10/9	7	Detroit Lions	17	(21,968)
10/16	35	Brooklyn Dodgers (M)	7	(11,892)
10/23	20	Pittsburgh Pirates	0	(12,142)
10/30	28	at Cleveland Rams	7	(18,843)
11/6	24	at Chicago Bears	17	(40,208)
11/13	28	at Detroit Lions	7	(45,139)
11/20	3	at New York Giants	15	(48,279)

Postseason   0-1-0

12/11	17	at New York Giants	23	(48,120)

Score By Periods

	1	2	3	4	Total
Packers	45	87	61	30	223
Opponents	16	27	44	31	118

INDIVIDUAL STATISTICS

Rushing

	Att	Yds	Avg	TD
Isbell	85	445	5.2	2
Hinkle	114	299	2.6	3
Laws	60	253	4.2	0
Monnett	75	225	3.0	0
Uram	28	145	5.2	2
Jankowski	44	124	2.8	2
P. Miller	20	48	2.4	0
Weisgerber	6	13	2.2	0
Schneidman	4	8	2.0	0
Howell	7	7	1.0	0
Bruder	2	6	3.0	0
Hutson	3	-1	-0.3	0
Herber	6	-1	-0.2	0
Packers	**454**	**1,571**	**3.5**	**9**
Opponents	372	1,206	3.2	7

Receiving

	No	Yds	Avg	LG	TD
Hutson	32	548	17.1	54	9
Gantenbein	12	164	13.7	29	1
Becker	7	166	23.7	49	0
Hinkle	7	98	14.0	32	4
Laws	6	55	9.2	17	1
Isbell	5	104	20.8	49	0
Herber	5	84	16.8	20	2
C. Mulleneaux	4	97	24.3	36	2
Uram	4	46	11.5		0
P. Miller	4	36	9.0	12	0
Scherer	2	31	15.5	16	1
Bruder	2	14	7.0	9	0
Monnett	1	23	23.0	23	0
Packers	**91**	**1,466**	**16.1**	**54**	**20**
Opponents	92	1,343	14.6	63	6

Passing

	Att	Com	Yds	Pct	TD	In	Rate
Isbell	91	37	659	40.7	7	10	52.2
Monnett	57	31	465	54.4	9	4	91.7
Herber	55	22	336	40.0	4	4	54.8
Hinkle	2	1	6	50.0	0	0	—
Laws	5	0	0	00.0	0	2	—
Packers	**210**	**91**	**1,466**	**43.3**	**20**	**20**	**59.4**
Opponents	232	92	1,343	39.7	6	21	30.2

Scoring

	TDr	TDp	TDrt	PAT	FG	S	TP
Hinkle	3	4	0	7/8	3/9	0	58
Hutson	0	9	0	3/3	0/0	0	57
Engebretsen	0	0	0	9/9	2/4	0	15
Jankowski	2	0	0	2/3	0/0	0	14
Herber	0	2	0	0/0	0/1	0	12
Isbell	2	0	0	0/0	0/0	0	12
Laws	0	1	1	0/0	0/0	0	12
C. Mulleneaux	0	2	0	0/0	0/0	0	12
Uram	2	0	0	0/0	0/0	0	12
Monnett	0	0	0	7/7	0/0	0	7
Gantenbein	0	1	0	0/0	0/0	0	6
Scherer	0	1	0	0/0	0/0	0	6
Packers	**9**	**20**	**1**	**28/30**	**5/14**	**0**	**223**
Opponents	7	6	2	12/15	4/10	0	118

NFL STANDINGS

Western Division

	W	L	T	Pct	PF	PA
Green Bay Packers	8	3	0	.727	223	118
Detroit Lions	7	4	0	.636	119	108
Chicago Bears	6	5	0	.545	194	148
Cleveland Rams	4	7	0	.364	131	215
Chicago Cardinals	2	9	0	.182	111	168

Eastern Division

	W	L	T	Pct	PF	PA
New York Giants	8	2	1	.800	194	79
Washington Redskins	6	3	2	.667	148	154
Brooklyn Dodgers	4	4	3	.500	131	161
Philadelphia Eagles	5	6	0	.455	154	164
Pittsburgh Pirates	2	9	0	.182	79	169

An improved field didn't guarantee bigger crowds, as the team found out in the season opener. Only 8,247 turned out to see Herber throw three touchdown passes to Hutson as Green Bay beat Cleveland 26-17.

Nearly twice as many (15,172) braved heavy rains to watch the Packers drop a 2-0 decision to the Bears in Week 2. A bad snap from center Darrell Lester in punt formation early in the fourth quarter led to the safety. Herber grabbed the loose ball and threw up a pass that bounced off the Bears' Dick Plasman. Chicago was awarded two points after Tom Jones recovered in the end zone for the Packers.

Green Bay ended the month by playing the Cardinals twice in four days. In a 28-7 win in Milwaukee, Isbell caught three passes for 89 yards from Herber, who in turn caught a 15-yarder for a touchdown from Isbell. The following Wednesday, Paul Engebretsen kicked a 22-yard field goal in the fourth quarter as the Packers prevailed 24-22 at Civic Stadium in Buffalo.

Detroit dumped Green Bay into third place in Week 5. The Lions rushed for 188 yards in a 17-7 win. The loss left the Packers (3-2) behind the Bears (3-1) and Lions (2-1).

Green Bay then won its next five games, the last two against the Bears and Lions. In Chicago, John Howell batted away Ray Buivid's fourth-down pass with less than a minute remaining to preserve a 24-17 count. And in Detroit, Uram's 70-yard touchdown scamper highlighted a 217-yard rushing outburst in a 28-7 blowout.

A sixth win in a row would have clinched the Western Division title for Green Bay (8-2), for it would have eliminated the Lions (5-3) from the race. But Isbell, working without Hutson (knee), threw five interceptions and New York triumphed 15-3.

Fortunately, Detroit also dropped its season closer. The Eagles beat the Lions 21-7 on Dec. 4, giving Green Bay its second division title in three years.

ROSTER

No	Name	Pos	Ht	Wt	DOB	College	G
32	Becker, Wayland	E	6-0	205	11/02/10	Marquette	11
9	Borak, Fred (Fritz)	E	6-1	190	05/14/13	Creighton	1
18/5	Bruder, Hank	B	6-0	200	11/22/07	Northwestern	11
35	Butler, Frank	T	6-3	246	05/03/09	Michigan State	9
34	Engebretsen, Paul (Tiny)	G	6-1	240	07/27/10	Northwestern	10
22	Gantenbein, Milt	E	6-0	200	05/31/10	Wisconsin	11
43	Goldenberg, Charles (Buckets)	G	5-10	225	03/10/11	Wisconsin	11
38	Herber, Arnie	B	5-11	200	04/02/10	Regis	
30	Hinkle, Clarke	FB	5-11	205	04/10/09	Bucknell	11
49	Howell, John	B	5-11	185	12/04/15	Nebraska	8
14	Hutson, Don	E	6-1	185	01/31/13	Alabama	10
17	Isbell, Cecil	B	6-1	190	07/11/15	Purdue	11
7	Jankowski, Ed	B	5-10	195	06/23/13	Wisconsin	11
15	Johnston, Chester (Swede)	B	5-10	200	03/07/10	Marquette	
37	Jones, Tom	G	5-11	230	10/15/09	Bucknell	
11	Katalinas, Leo	T	6-2	240	02/04/15	Catholic University	8
24	Laws, Joe	B	5-9	185	06/16/11	Iowa	10
40	Lee, Bill	T	6-3	225	10/19/11	Alabama	11
29	Lester, Darrell	C	6-3	220	04/29/14	TCU	10
46	Letlow, Russ	G	6-0	212	10/05/13	San Francisco	11
48	Miller, Charles (Ookie)	C	6-1	215	11/11/09	Purdue	11
3	Miller, Paul	B	5-10	185	01/23/13	South Dakota State	10
50	Monnett, Bob	B	5-9	180	02/27/10	Michigan State	9
19	Mulleneaux, Carl (Moose)	E	6-4	210	04/01/17	Utah State	10
18	Mulleneaux, Lee	C	6-2	225	09/16/14	Northern Arizona	5
44	Ray, Buford (Baby)	T	6-6	250	09/30/15	Vanderbilt	11
36	Scherer, Bernie	E	6-1	193	01/28/13	Nebraska	10
51	Schneidman, Herm	B	5-10	200	11/22/13	Iowa	10
42	Schoemann, Roy	C	6-1	195	08/30/14	Marquette	3
41	Seibold, Champ	T	6-4	240	12/05/12	Wisconsin	11
21	Tinsley, Pete	G	5-8	205	03/16/13	Georgia	9
8	Uram, Andy	B	5-10	187	03/22/15	Minnesota	
33	Weisgerber, Dick	B	5-10	205	02/19/15	Williamette	4

DRAFT

Rnd	Name	Pos	College
1	Cecil Isbell	B	Purdue
3	Marty Schreyer	T	Purdue
5	Chuck Sweeney	E	Notre Dame
6	Andy Uram	B	Minnesota
7	John Kovatch	E	Northwestern
8	Phil Ragazzo	T	Case Western Reserve
9	John Howell	B	Nebraska
10	Frank Barnhart	G	Northern Colorado
11	Pete Tinsley	G	Georgia
12	Tony Falkenstein	B	St. Mary's (CA)

FRONT ROW: (L-R) Coach Curly Lambeau, 22 Milt Gantenbein, 42 Andy Uram, 14 Don Hutson, 17 Cecil Isbell, 43 Buckets Goldenberg, 24 Joe Laws, 29 Charley Brock, 34 Paul Engebretsen, 5 Hank Bruder, 51 Herm Schneidman, 7 Ed Jankowski.
MIDDLE ROW: (L-R) 54 Larry Craig, 38 Arnie Herber, 30, Clarke Hinkle, 33 Dick Weisgerber, 21 Pete Tinsley, 52 Larry Buhler, 56 Tom Greenfield, 46 Russ Letlow, 18 Lee Mulleneaux, 40 Bill Lee, 63 Gus Zarnas, Assistant Coach Richard (Red) Smith.
BACK ROW: (L-R) Trainer Dave Woodward, 53 Earl Svendsen, 41 Paul Kell, 60 Charles Schultz, 19 Carl Mulleneaux, 44 Baby Ray, 55 Allen Moore, 48 Harry Jacunski, 45 Ernie Smith, 35 Frank Balazs, Assistant Trainer Carl (Bud) Jorgensen.

9-2-0   1939   9-2-0

The Packers of 1939 rarely overwhelmed anyone on the scoreboard. But when it mattered most—the NFL championship game—the team sprang to life, grabbed its fifth NFL title and a gained a measure of revenge with a dominating 27-0 victory over the Giants, the team that had denied them in the title game the previous year.

In October, Green Bay defeated the Lions by 19 points. A month later, the club shut out the Dodgers 28-0. But none of its seven other wins came by more than 10 points.

Aside from Don Hutson, the Packers had no league leaders in any category. Offensively, the team ranked third. Defensively, it was fifth best among the 10 teams.

Green Bay was outscored 59-46 in the fourth quarter. It held on for wins against the Cardinals (twice), Bears, and Eagles despite being outscored 32-9 in that period in those four games.

The Packers were not as fortunate in Week 3 and Week 7. Both the Rams and Bears staged fourth-quarter rallies to defeat the Packers by three points in each case.

The Bears loss, a 30-27 setback, dropped Green Bay (5-2) behind the Lions (6-1) in the standings. Fortunately, it regrouped to win its final four games, including a Western Division clinching 12-7 decision over Detroit on the final weekend of play.

Curly Lambeau added two rookies of note via the draft. He selected center Charley Brock in the second round and end Larry Craig in the fourth. Brock enjoyed a nine-year career in Green Bay while Craig lasted two years longer, playing through the 1949 campaign.

With Craig, Lambeau made a decision that added years to Hutson's career. The head coach had the rookie play at end on

DEEP THREAT DON

With Don Hutson, the threat of going deep was always there. In 1939, the crafty veteran stretched the field like no Packers receiver before or since.

Starting with his first catch of the season (a 43-yard bomb from Arnie Herber), Hutson made serious inroads into opposing secondaries all year long. He burned the Lions with scores of 51 and 60 yards in Week 5. He had gains of 69 and 53 yards in Brooklyn a month later.

Against the Cardinals, the speedster recorded the longest gain of his career—a 92-yard collaboration with Herber.

All told, Hutson averaged 24.9 yards on 34 catches. In other words, he moved the ball nearly a quarter of the length of the field every time he touched it.

Below are the highest average gains by Packers receivers in a single season (minimum 24 receptions).

Average	Receiver	Year	No./Yards
24.88	Don Hutson	1939	(34-846)
23.68	Carroll Dale	1966	(37-876)
23.22	Bill Howton	1952	(53-1,231)
23.17	Max McGee	1959	(30-695)

1939

TEAM STATISTICS

	GB	OPP
First Downs	147	113
Rushing	73	40
Passing	66	64
Penalty	8	9
Rushes	500	333
Yards Gained	1,574	1,165
Average Gain	3.15	3.50
Average Yards per Game	143.1	105.9
Passes Attempted	248	239
Completed	101	106
% Completed	40.73	44.35
Total Yards Gained	1,871	1,602
Yards Gained per Completion	18.52	15.11
Average Yards per Game	170.1	145.6
Laterals Attempted	0	3
Completed	0	3
Yards Gained	0	3
Combined Yards Gained	3,445	2,770
Total Plays	748	575
Average Yards per Play	4.61	4.82
Average Yards per Game	313.2	251.8
Intercepted By	26	15
Punts	72	81
Yards Punted	2,866	3,263
Average Yards per Punt	39.81	40.28
Yards Penalized	259	315
Fumbles	16	27
Lost	7	9
Own Recovered for Touchdown	0	0
Opponent's Recovered by	9	7
Opponent's Recovered for Touchdown	2	0
Total Points Scored	233	153
Total Touchdowns	31	21
Touchdowns Rushing	13	12
Touchdowns Passing	14	9
Touchdowns on Returns & Recoveries	4	0
Extra Points	28	15
Safeties	2	0
Field Goals Attempted	18	10
Field Goals Made	5	4
% Successful	27.78	40.00

Regular Season 9-2-0

Date	GB		OPP	Att.
9/17	14	Chicago Cardinals	10	(11,792)
9/24	21	Chicago Bears	16	(19,192)
10/1	24	Cleveland Rams	27	(9,888)
10/8	27	Chicago Cardinals (M)	20	(18,965)
10/22	26	Detroit Lions	7	(22,558)
10/29	24	Washington Redskins (M)	14	(24,308)
11/5	27	at Chicago Bears	30	(40,537)
11/12	23	at Philadelphia Eagles	16	(23,000)
11/19	28	at Brooklyn Dodgers	0	(19,843)
11/26	7	at Cleveland Rams	6	(30,691)
12/3	12	at Detroit Lions	7	(30,699)

Postseason 1-0-0

12/10	27	New York Giants (M)	0	(32,279)

Score By Periods

	1	2	3	4	Total
Packers	51	78	58	46	233
Opponents	17	44	33	59	153

INDIVIDUAL STATISTICS

Rushing

	Att	Yds	Avg	TD
Isbell	132	407	3.1	2
Hinkle	135	381	2.8	5
Jankowski	75	278	3.7	2
Uram	52	272	5.2	1
Laws	55	162	2.9	2
Balazs	11	41	3.7	0
Hutson	5	26	5.2	0
C. Thompson	6	9	1.5	0
Craig	2	6	3.0	0
Buhler	5	3	0.6	0
Lawrence	4	0	0.0	0
Herber	18	-11	-0.6	1
Packers	**500**	**1,574**	**3.1**	**13**
Opponents	333	1,165	3.5	12

Receiving

	No	Yds	Avg	LG	TD
Hutson	34	846	24.9	t92	6
C. Mulleneaux	12	218	18.2	48	1
Laws	11	177	16.1	31	1
Isbell	9	71	7.9	20	0
Gantenbein	7	127	18.1	t32	1
Uram	7	93	13.3	t21	2
Jacunski	5	104	20.8	t29	2
Hinkle	4	70	17.5	25	0
Bruder	4	65	16.3	22	1
Craig	3	44	14.7	28	0
Lawrence	1	21	21.0	21	0
Herber	1	18	18.0	18	0
Balazs	1	11	11.0	11	0
Jankowski	1	5	5.0	5	0
C. Thompson	1	1	1.0	1	0
Packers	**101**	**1,871**	**18.5**	**t92**	**14**
Opponents	106	1,602	15.1	t61	9

Passing

	Att	Com	Yds	Pct	TD	In	Rate
Herber	139	57	1,107	41.0	8	9	61.6
Isbell	103	43	749	41.7	6	5	66.4
Lawrence	4	1	15	25.0	0	1	—
Laws	1	0	0	0.0	0	0	—
Uram	1	0	0	00.0	0	0	—
Packers	**248**	**101**	**1,871**	**40.7**	**14**	**15**	**61.1**
Opponents	239	106	1,602	44.4	9	26	39.9

Punting

	No	Yds	Avg	LG	HB
Hinkle	43	1,751	40.7	65	0
Herber	24	957	39.9	74	2
Isbell	4	123	30.8	39	0
Balazs	1	35	35.0	35	0
Packers	**72**	**2,866**	**39.8**	**74**	**2**
Opponents	81	3,263	40.3	70	0

Scoring

	TDr	TDp	TDrt	PAT	FG	S	TP
Hutson	0	6	0	2/2	0/0	0	38
Hinkle	5	0	0	2/3	1/10	0	35
Engebretsen	0	0	0	18/19	4/8	0	30
Laws	2	1	1	0/0	0/0	0	24
Uram	1	2	0	0/0	0/0	0	19
Isbell	2	0	0	3/3	0/0	0	15
Jacunski	0	2	0	0/0	0/0	0	12
Jankowski	2	0	0	0/0	0/0	0	12
C. Brock	0	0	1	0/0	0/0	0	6
Bruder	0	1	0	0/0	0/0	0	6
Gantenbein	0	1	0	0/0	0/0	0	6
Greenfield	0	0	1	0/0	0/0	0	6
Herber	1	0	0	0/0	0/0	0	6
C. Mulleneaux	0	1	0	0/0	0/0	0	6
E. Svendsen	0	0	1	0/0	0/0	0	6
team	0	0	0	0/0	0/0	2	4
Ernie Smith	0	0	0	3/4	0/0	0	3
Packers	**13**	**14**	**4**	**28/31**	**5/18**	**2**	**233**
Opponents	12	9	0	15/21	4/10	0	153

NFL STANDINGS

Western Division

	W	L	T	Pct	PF	PA
Green Bay Packers	9	2	0	.818	233	153
Chicago Bears	8	3	0	.727	298	157
Detroit Lions	6	5	0	.545	145	150
Cleveland Rams	5	5	1	.500	195	164
Chicago Cardinals	1	10	1	.091	84	254

Eastern Division

	W	L	T	Pct	PF	PA
New York Giants	9	1	1	.900	168	85
Washington Redskins	8	2	1	.800	242	92
Brooklyn Dodgers	4	6	1	.400	108	219
Philadelphia Eagles	1	9	1	.100	105	200
Pittsburgh Pirates	1	9	1	.100	114	216

---

defense in place of Hutson, who moved to safety. Freed from the constant collisions of the trenches, Hutson flourished and led the NFL in interceptions in 1940.

Hutson's throwing mate, Herber, received a $100 bonus when he weighed in at 199 pounds on Aug. 12. The halfback had been promised the money on July 3 (at which time he weighed a hefty 227) if he could slim down to 200 pounds or less by mid-August. Herber's weight had been a concern for years. In 1941, Herber himself suggested he forfeit $50 if he weighed more than 200 pounds on any Saturday before a game.

Two losses in its first seven games kept Green Bay from sole possession of first place until it clobbered Brooklyn 28-0 on Nov. 19. Until then, the Packers were locked in a race with the Bears and Lions for supremacy in the West.

Cleveland handed Green Bay its first loss. Parker Hall was superb, hitting 13 of 20 passes for 192 yards and a touch-down. His throws set up two fourth-quarter scores as the Rams rallied 27-24.

Chicago dealt the Packers its other setback. Rookie Sid Luckman hit Bob MacLeod with a 45-yard pass, and Bill Osmanski scored from four yards out two plays later for the decisive touchdown.

With the season hanging in the balance, Green Bay buckled down. The team piled up 376 yards to edge Philadelphia 23-16, then blanked the Dodgers 28-0. With Detroit losing in successive weeks, the Packers claimed first place with two weeks to go.

Cleveland and Detroit, Green Bay's final two opponents, proved stubborn. Both teams effectively neutralized Hutson. Fortunately, others picked up the slack. Cecil Isbell's 18-yard touchdown pass to Joe Laws late in the fourth quarter beat the Rams 7-6 on Nov. 26. A week later, Clarke Hinkle's fourth-quarter plunge resulted in a 12-7 win in Detroit.

ROSTER

No	Name	Pos	Ht	Wt	DOB	College	G
35	Balazs, Frank	B	6-2	215	01/23/18	Iowa	5
32	Biolo, John	G	5-10	191	02/08/16	Lake Forest	1
37	Brennan, John	G	6-1	204	08/28/13	Michigan	3
29	Brock, Charley	C	6-1	195	03/15/16	Nebraska	10
5	Bruder, Hank	B	6-0	200	11/22/07	Northwestern	10
52	Buhler, Larry	B	6-2	204	05/28/17	Minnesota	3
54	Craig, Larry	E	6-0	205	06/27/16	South Carolina	11
34	Engebretsen, Paul (Tiny)	G	6-1	240	07/27/10	Northwestern	11
22	Gantenbein, Milt	E	6-0	195	05/31/10	Wisconsin	11
43	Goldenberg, Charles (Buckets)	G	5-10	222	03/10/11	Wisconsin	9
56	Greenfield, Tom	C	6-4	209	11/10/17	Arizona	8
38	Herber, Arnie	B	5-11	200	04/02/10	Regis	10
30	Hinkle, Clarke	FB	5-11	195	04/10/09	Bucknell	11
14	Hutson, Don	E	6-1	185	01/31/13	Alabama	11
17	Isbell, Cecil	B	6-1	190	07/11/15	Purdue	11
48	Jacunski, Harry	E	6-2	197	10/20/15	Fordham	
7	Jankowski, Ed	B	5-10	200	06/23/13	Wisconsin	11
41	Kell, Paul	T	6-2	217	07/18/15	Notre Dame	10
58	Kilbourne, Warren	T	6-3	240	06/20/16	Minnesota	4
51	Lawrence, Jim	B	5-10	190	03/14/15	TCU	5
24	Laws, Joe	B	5-9	185	06/16/11	Iowa	11
40	Lee, Bill	T	6-3	225	10/19/11	Alabama	11
46	Letlow, Russ	G	6-0	212	10/05/13	San Francisco	11
55	Moore, Allen	E	6-2	218	03/12/09	Texas A&M	5
19	Mulleneaux, Carl (Moose)	E	6-4	206	04/01/17	Utah State	11
44	Ray, Buford (Baby)	T	6-6	240	09/30/15	Vanderbilt	11
51	Schneidman, Herm	B	5-10	200	11/22/13	Iowa	1
60	Schultz, Charles	T	6-3	230	10/08/16	Minnesota	10
45	Smith, Ernie	T	6-2	220	11/26/09	USC	6
36	Steen, Frank	E	6-1	190	10/05/13	Rice	3
53	Svendsen, Earl	C	6-1	185	02/07/15	Minnesota	10
50	Thompson, Clarence	B	5-11	170	09/28/14	Minnesota	2
21	Tinsley, Pete	G	5-8	205	03/16/13	Georgia	10
62	Twedell, Francis	G	5-11	220	05/29/17	Minnesota	
42	Uram, Andy	B	5-10	187	03/22/15	Minnesota	11
33	Weisgerber, Dick	B	5-10	205	02/19/15	Williamette	4
63	Zarnas, Gus	G	5-10	225	12/16/13	Ohio State	
57	Zoll, Dick	G	6-1	223	12/10/13	Indiana	1

DRAFT

Rnd	Name	Pos	College	Rnd	Name	Pos	College
1	Larry Buhler	B	Minnesota	13	Dan Elmer	C	Minnesota
3	Charley Brock	C	Nebraska	14	Bill Badgett	T	Georgia
5	Lynn Hovland	G	Wisconsin	15	Tom Greenfield	C	Arizona
6	Larry Craig	E	South Carolina	16	Roy Bellin	B	Wisconsin
7	Francis Twedell	T	Minnesota	17	John Yerby	E	Oregon
8	Paul Kell	T	Notre Dame	18	Frank Balazs	B	Iowa
9	John Hall	B	TCU	19	John Brennan	G	Michigan
10	Vince Gavre	B	Wisconsin	20	Charles Schultz	T	Minnesota
11	Charley Sprague	E	SMU	21	Willard Hofer	B	Notre Dame
12	(Choice to Dodgers)			22	Bill Gunther	B	Santa Clara

A demoralizing, 31-point loss to the Bears in the second week of the season had some trying to downplay the significance of the 41-10 loss by harking back to 1936. That year, the Packers were also clobbered by Chicago (30-3) in Week 2, yet regrouped to win the NFL title.

While the comparison was understandable, it couldn't alter the facts. The Packers of 1940 were not championship material. That the team remained in contention until the final weekend was more a testament to the shortcomings of the Bears than to the power of the Packers.

Green Bay failed to win more than six games for the first time since 1933, and its 6-4-1 record placed it second behind the Bears (8-3) in the Western Division.

While the team's passing attack remained strong, too many throws wound up in the hands of the enemy. Cecil Isbell, Arnie Herber, Hal Van Every and Frank Balasz threw a combined 26 interceptions, 11 more than the previous year. Nineteen of the 26 occurred in the team's four losses.

The Packers kicked off their 20th season in the professional ranks by hosting the Eagles. A stifling defense held Philadelphia to minus-7 yards rushing, so little Davey O'Brien (5-foot-7, 150 pounds) lit up the skies with 40 passes for 225 yards. Don Hutson's late interception stopped the Eagles' last serious threat and put an end to the visitors' 14-point, fourth-quarter rally.

Little went right in Week 2. Chicago turned nine Green Bay turnovers into 20 points and added another 14 on kickoff returns as they rolled to a 41-10 win. The Packers outgained the Bears (333 yards to 290) and had more first downs (19 to 5), but couldn't muster more than a Tiny Engebretsen field goal and a Herber-to-Hutson touchdown.

The Bears then dropped their next game to the Cardinals by 14 points. That opened the door for Green Bay to regain first place in Week 3 when it routed the very same Cardinals 31-6. The Packers intercepted six passes that led to 17 points in the win.

Joe Laws scored the last touchdown in the victory on a pass from Van Every. Shortly thereafter, he injured his knee and was carried from the field, his season ended.

In Week 4, Carl Mulleneaux registered the only 100-yard receiving day of his career. The 6-foot-4 end caught four passes for 111 yards and two scores as Green Bay won an aerial duel with the Rams. Isbell and Herber combined for 327 yards passing without an interception.

The Packers again fell from the top of the division after the Lions downed them 23-14 in Week 5. Detroit scored the last 16 points of the game, with Alex Wojciechowicz's 10-yard interception return for a touchdown capping the onslaught.

A week later, Green Bay took apart the lowly (1-4-2) Steelers 24-3.

With six weeks gone, the Bears (5-1) and Packers (4-2)

met in Wrigley Field. Joe Maniaci's 3-yard run gave Chicago a 7-0 lead, but Herber and Hutson tied the game on a 7-yard hookup early in the second period.

Scooter McLean (who would become the Packers' head coach in 1958), set up the winning drive with a 49-yard kickoff return. Eight plays later, Gary Famiglietti counted from seven yards out as the Bears won 14-7 to put the Packers two games behind them.

But as had happened earlier, Chicago couldn't handle success. A week after its win over Green Bay, the team lost to Detroit. Meanwhile, the Packers again found the Cardinals to their liking 28-7. Hinkle scored three times and Isbell romped for 118 yards in the 21-point blowout.

A week later, Green Bay became the first professional football team to travel by air to a game. The team boarded two planes in Chicago and flew to New York for its engagement with the Giants in the Polo Grounds.

While the flight may have been enjoyable, the game was not. Larry Buhler fumbled the opening kickoff and New York converted with Len Barnum passing to Leland Shaffer for the game's only touchdown. The Giants hung on 7-3 to serve Green Bay its fourth loss.

But the Bears (6-3) also stumbled to keep the Packers (5-4) mathematically alive with two games remaining. Green Bay hit stride in Week 10 by punishing the Lions 50-7, then finished with a 13-13 tie in Cleveland.

Chicago, meanwhile, won its final two games to sew up the division.

2.69 YARDS AND A CLOUD OF DUST

Green Bay didn't give up yards on the ground without a fight in 1940. The Packers allowed opponents an average of only 2.69 yards per rushing attempt, a franchise record low.

The stinginess started in the season opener. Green Bay swarmed all over the Eagles, holding them to minus-7 yards on 24 carries. Five Packers were credited with having at least one solo tackle for a loss on a running play, and Larry Craig and Russ Letlow each had two.

Green Bay held all of its opponents to fewer than four yards per carry. Not surprisingly, the Bears enjoyed the most success by churning out 187 yards on 50 carries (3.74 average) in their 14-7 win on Nov. 3.

Listed below are the seasons in which the Packers permitted the lowest average rushing gain by opponents:

Avg.	Year	Att.-Yds.	Record
2.69	1940	387-1,040	6-4-1
2.72	1935	448-1,219	8-4-0
2.77	1933	443-1,226	5-7-1
2.96	1937	400-1,184	7-4-0

TEAM STATISTICS

	GB	OPP
First Downs	154	120
Rushing	82	61
Passing	66	53
Penalty	6	6
Rushes	463	387
Yards Gained	1,604	1,040
Average Gain	3.46	2.69
Average Yards per Game	145.8	94.5
Passes Attempted	283	252
Completed	118	98
% Completed	41.70	38.89
Total Yards Gained	1,796	1,492
Yards Gained per Completion	15.22	15.22
Average Yards per Game	163.3	135.6
Laterals Attempted	0	0
Completed	0	0
Yards Gained	0	0
Combined Yards Gained	3,400	2,532
Total Plays	746	639
Average Yards per Play	4.56	3.96
Average Yards per Game	313.2	251.8
Intercepted By	40	26
Yards Returned	414	290
Returned for TD	1	1
Punts	57	76
Yards Punted	2,131	2,994
Average Yards per Punt	37.39	39.39
Yards Punt Returns	494	231
Returned for TD	0	0
Yards Kickoff Returns	381	995
Returned for TD	0	2
Yards Penalized	295	342
Fumbles	21	15
Lost	12	7
Own Recovered for Touchdown	0	0
Opponent's Recovered by	7	12
Opponent's Recovered for Touchdown	1	0
Total Points Scored	238	155
Total Touchdowns	30	22
Touchdowns Rushing	10	9
Touchdowns Passing	18	10
Touchdowns on Returns & Recoveries	2	3
Extra Points	28	17
Safeties	0	0
Field Goals Attempted	20	3
Field Goals Made	10	2
% Successful	50.00	66.67

Regular Season 6-4-1

Date	GB		OPP	Att.
9/15	27	Philadelphia Eagles	20	(11,657)
9/22	10	Chicago Bears	41	(22,557)
9/29	31	Chicago Cardinals (M)	6	(20,234)
10/13	31	Cleveland Rams	14	(16,299)
10/20	14	Detroit Lions	23	(21,001)
10/27	24	Pittsburgh Steelers (M)	3	(13,703)
11/3	7	at Chicago Bears	14	(45,434)
11/10	28	at Chicago Cardinals	7	(11,364)
11/17	3	at New York Giants	7	(28,262)
11/24	50	at Detroit Lions	7	(26,019)
12/1	13	at Cleveland Rams	13	(16,249)

Score By Periods

	1	2	3	4	Total
Packers	74	52	44	68	238
Opponents	24	54	30	47	155

INDIVIDUAL STATISTICS

Rushing

	Att	Yds	Avg	TD
Hinkle	109	383	3.5	2
Uram	71	270	3.8	1
Isbell	97	270	2.8	4
Jankowski	48	211	4.4	2
Van Every	38	154	4.1	0
Buhler	36	118	3.3	0
Balazs	25	107	4.3	1
L. Brock	18	60	3.3	0
Laws	7	21	3.0	0
Feathers	4	19	4.8	0
Craig	3	9	3.0	0
Adkins	1	5	5.0	0
Herber	6	-23	-3.8	0
Packers	463	1,604	3.5	10
Opponents	387	1,040	2.7	9

Receiving

	No	Yds	Avg	LG	TD
Hutson	45	664	14.8	t36	7
C. Mulleneaux	16	288	18.0	t47	6
Riddick	11	148	13.5		0
Uram	10	188	18.8	44	2
Craig	6	67	11.2	24	0
L. Brock	5	97	19.4	33	0
Laws	5	60	12.0	24	1
Adkins	4	73	18.3	t55	1
Van Every	4	41	10.3	23	0
Hinkle	4	28	7.0	t12	1
D. Evans	2	40	20.0	30	0
Jacunski	2	29	14.5	17	0
Weisgerber	1	37	37.0	37	0
C. Berry	1	17	17.0	17	0
Gantenbein	1	12	12.0	12	0
Balazs	1	7	7.0	7	0
Packers	118	1,796	15.2	t55	18
Opponents	98	1,492	15.2	74	10

Passing

	Att	Com	Yds	Pct	TD	In	Rate
Isbell	150	68	1,037	45.3	9	12	55.3
Herber	89	38	560	42.7	5	7	49.8
Van Every	41	12	199	29.3	4	6	40.2
L. Brock	2	0	0	00.0	0	0	—
Balazs	1	0	0	00.0	0	1	—
Packers	283	118	1,796	41.7	18	26	46.2
Opponents	252	98	1,492	38.9	10	40	32.8

Punting

	No	Yds	Avg	LG	HB
Hinkle	22	819	37.2	59	0
Van Every	17	620	36.5	50	0
Herber	13	504	38.8	55	0
L. Brock	3	125	41.7	52	0
Isbell	2	63	31.5	37	0
Packers	57	2,131	37.4	59	0
Opponents	76	2,994	39.4	75	0

Interceptions

	No	Yds	Avg	LG	TD
Hutson	6	24	4.0		0
L. Brock	5	116	23.2	74	0
Weisgerber	4	51	12.8	24	0
Van Every	3	30	10.0		0
Uram	3	27	9.0	15	0
C. Brock	3	7	2.3	6	0
Buhler	2	58	29.0	32	0
Adkins	2	35	17.5	t35	1
Isbell	2	14	7.0	14	0
Hinkle	2	11	5.5	8	0
Herber	2	0	0.0	0	0
B. Lee	1	14	14.0	14	0
Balazs	1	11	11.0	11	0
G. Svendsen	1	6	6.0	6	0
Goldenberg	1	5	5.0	5	0
Greenfield	1	5	5.0	5	0
Craig	1	0	0.0	0	0
Packers	40	414	10.4	74	1
Opponents	26	290	11.2	28	1

Scoring

	TDr	TDp	TDrt	PAT	FG	S	TP
Hutson	0	7	0	15/16	0/0	0	57
Hinkle	2	1	0	3/3	9/14	0	48
C. Mulleneaux	0	6	1	0/0	0/0	0	42
Isbell	4	0	0	0/0	0/0	0	24
Uram	1	2	0	1/2	0/0	0	19
Adkins	0	1	1	1/1	0/1	0	13
Jankowski	2	0	0	0/0	0/0	0	12
Engebretsen	0	0	0	8/8	1/5	0	11
Balazs	1	0	0	0/0	0/0	0	6
Laws	0	1	0	0/0	0/0	0	6
Packers	10	18	2	28/30	10/20	0	238
Opponents	9	10	3	17/22	2/3	0	155

NFL STANDINGS

Western Division

	W	L	T	Pct	PF	PA
Chicago Bears	8	3	0	.727	238	152
Green Bay Packers	6	4	1	.600	238	155
Detroit Lions	5	5	1	.500	138	153
Cleveland Rams	4	6	1	.400	171	191
Chicago Cardinals	2	7	2	.222	139	222

Eastern Division

	W	L	T	Pct	PF	PA
Washington Redskins	9	2	0	.818	245	142
Brooklyn Dodgers	8	3	0	.727	186	120
New York Giants	6	4	1	.600	131	133
Pittsburgh Steelers	2	7	2	.222	60	178
Philadelphia Eagles	1	10	0	.091	111	211

ROSTER

No	Name	Pos	Ht	Wt	DOB	College	G
55	Adkins, Robert	E	6-0	211	02/07/17	Marshall	11
35	Balazs, Frank	B	6-2	215	01/23/18	Iowa	7
37	Berry, Connie	E	6-3	210	04/19/15	North Carolina State	1
29	Brock, Charley	C	6-1	205	03/15/16	Nebraska	11
15	Brock, Lou	B	6-0	195	12/09/17	Purdue	11
52	Buhler, Larry	B	6-2	210	05/28/17	Minnesota	8
54	Craig, Larry	E	6-0	205	06/27/16	South Carolina	11
18	Disend, Leo	T	6-2	225	11/07/15	Albright	5
34	Engebretsen, Paul (Tiny)	G	6-1	245	07/27/10	Northwestern	
53	Evans, Dick	E	6-3	195	05/31/18	Iowa	
3	Feathers, Beattie	B	5-11	180	08/04/08	Tennessee	1
22	Gantenbein, Milt	E	6-0	200	05/31/10	Wisconsin	5
43	Goldenberg, Charles (Buckets)	G	5-10	225	03/10/11	Wisconsin	11
56	Greenfield, Tom	C	6-4	218	11/10/17	Arizona	9
38	Herber, Arnie	B	5-11	208	04/02/10	Regis	10
30	Hinkle, Clarke	FB	5-11	200	04/10/12	Bucknell	11
14	Hutson, Don	E	6-1	185	01/31/13	Alabama	11
17	Isbell, Cecil	B	6-1	191	07/11/15	Purdue	10
48	Jacunski, Harry	E	6-2	198	10/20/15	Fordham	10
7	Jankowski, Ed	B	5-10	205	06/23/13	Wisconsin	7
64	Johnson, Howard (Smiley)	G	5-10	200	09/22/16	Georgia	11
41	Kell, Paul	T	6-2	217	07/18/15	Notre Dame	11
24	Laws, Joe	B	5-9	186	06/16/11	Iowa	3
40	Lee, Bill	T	6-3	235	10/19/11	Alabama	11
46	Letlow, Russ	G	6-0	215	10/05/13	San Francisco	11
27	Midler, Lou	T/G	6-1	220	07/21/15	Minnesota	7
19	Mulleneaux, Carl (Moose)	E	6-4	205	04/01/17	Utah State	10
44	Ray, Buford (Baby)	T	6-6	248	09/30/15	Vanderbilt	11
5	Riddick, Ray	E	6-0	225	10/17/17	Fordham	10
60	Schultz, Charles	T	6-3	230	10/08/16	Minnesota	2
68	Seeman, George	E	6-0	194	04/03/16	Nebraska	1
57	Seibold, Champ	T	6-4	246	12/05/12	Wisconsin	1
18	Shirey, Fred	T	6-2	220	01/12/16	Nebraska	10
66	Svendsen, George	C	6-4	240	03/22/13	Minnesota	3
21	Tinsley, Pete	G	5-8	205	03/16/13	Georgia	7
42	Uram, Andy	B	5-10	188	03/22/15	Minnesota	11
36	Van Every, Hal	B	6-0	195	02/10/18	Minnesota	10
33	Weisgerber, Dick	B	5-10	194	02/19/15	Williamette	10
29	Wood, Bobby	T	6-1	235	01/14/16	Alabama	2
63	Zarnas, Gus	G	5-10	225	12/16/13	Ohio State	9

DRAFT

Rnd	Name	Pos	College
1	Hal Van Every	B	Minnesota
3	Lou Brock	B	Purdue
5	Esco Sarkkinen	E	Ohio State
6	Dick Cassiano	B	Pittsburgh
7	Millard White	T	Tulane
8	George Seeman	E	Nebraska
9	J.R. Manley	G	Oklahoma
10	Jack Brown	B	Purdue
11	Don Guritz	G	Northwestern
12	Phil Gaspar	B	USC
13	Ambrose Schindler	B	USC
14	Bill Kerr	E	Notre Dame
15	Mel Brewer	G	Illinois
16	Ray Andrus	B	Vanderbilt
17	Archie Kodros	C	Michigan
18	Jim Gillette	B	Virginia
19	Al Matuza	C	Georgetown
20	Jim Reeder	T	Illinois
21	Vince Eichler	B	Cornell
22	Henry Luebcke	T	Iowa

FRONT ROW: (L-R) 5 Ray Riddick, 63 Gus Zarnas, 40 Bill Lee, 42 Andy Uram, 33 Dick Weisgerber, 7 Ed Jankowski, 38 Arnie Herber, 54 Larry Craig, 19 Carl (Moose) Mulleneaux, 29 Charley Brock.

SECOND ROW: (L-R) Coach Curly Lambeau, 43 Buckets Goldenberg, 24 Joe Laws, 3 Beattie Feathers, 48 Harry Jacunski, 66 George Svendsen, 44 Baby Ray, 34 Paul Engebretsen, 37 Connie Berry, Assistant Coach Richard (Red) Smith.

THIRD ROW: (L-R) 68 George Seeman, 22 Milt Gantenbein, 64 Howard Johnson, 21 Pete Tinsley, 30 Clarke Hinkle, 14 Don Hutson, 55 Robert Adkins, 46 Russ Letlow, 17 Cecil Isbell, 15 Lou Brock.

BACK ROW: (L-R) 53 Dick Evans, 41 Paul Kell, 56 Tom Greenfield, 27 Lou Midler, 60 Charles Schultz, 52 Larry Buhler, 18 Leo Disend, 57 Champ Seibold, 36 Hal Van Every.

The Teams: 1940   **A Measure of Greatness**   57

Curly Lambeau had heard all about the supposed invincibility of the Chicago Bears. But unlike some, he was a nonbeliever. To prove his point, the Packers' mentor concocted a seven-man defensive front that exposed the Monsters of the Midway as mere mortals in an early-November showdown at Wrigley Field.

The Bears had stunned the world of professional football with a 73-0 thrashing of the Redskins in the 1940 NFL championship game. They continued on a roll in 1941, ringing up five wins by a combined 209-52 margin. Among the victories was a 25-17 mauling of the Packers in late September in which the Bears rushed for 258 yards and averaged better than six yards a clip.

But on Nov. 2, an aroused Packer defense gave up just 60 yards rushing and 154 yards overall in a 16-14 thriller in which the stubborn Bears rallied for 14 fourth-quarter points. Ed Frutig and Pete Tinsley provided the final big play at the Packers' 36-yard line with two-and-a-half minutes remaining. Frutig belted Sid Luckman who fumbled, and Tinsley recovered.

The loss was the only suffered by the Bears (10-1). Green Bay also finished 10-1, and a Western Division playoff game (the first ever) was played in Chicago on Dec. 14. The Packers were no match for the Bears that day, falling 33-14. Chicago then romped to a second straight NFL title by crushing the Giants 37-9 a week later.

Green Bay's resurgence was achieved without the services of Arnie Herber. Herber, who threw the deep pass like no other, was released just before the beginning of the regular season. He exited having thrown for 6,749 yards, more than any other player at that time.

Cecil Isbell, who led the team in passing in 1940, took control of the passing game and flourished. The four-year veteran led the league in attempts, yards, completions, and touchdown passes. He threw at least one touchdown pass in each of the team's 11 regular-season games and one in the playoff with the Bears.

Green Bay added one rookie of note. Tony Canadeo was selected in the seventh round of the draft and led the team in kickoff returns. The Grey Ghost of Gonzaga (he had prematurely gray hair) rushed for three touchdowns and intercepted two passes in 1941.

The Packers opened against the Lions. Hutson scored on a pass from Isbell, Canadeo counted on a 7-yard run, and Paul Engebretsen, Clarke Hinkle and Ed Jankowski each added a field goal as Green Bay prevailed 23-0. Hinkle became the NFL's all-time leading rusher on the eighth play of the game when he bettered Ace Gutowsky's previous record (3,478) by a yard.

Green Bay erupted for 17 fourth-quarter points against the Rams a week later. Even though Don Hutson was held without a reception for the first time since the 1936 season finale, the Packers emerged a 24-7 winner on the strength of 235 yards rushing on 62 carries.

The Bears then overran Green Bay in Week 3.

Green Bay nearly lost a second game a week later against the Cardinals in Milwaukee. Isbell hit Lou Brock with a 14-yard touchdown pass in the fourth quarter and Ernie Pannell blocked Lou Zontini's 43-yard field goal attempt in the final minute to preserve a 14-13 win.

Hutson caught eight passes for 126 yards against the Dodgers in Week 5. Isbell was hot as well, completing 12 of 15 passes for 141 yards and a touchdown (to Hutson). Green Bay won 30-7.

Hutson's first field goal in a league game came in Week 6. With just over a minute left, the receiving ace split the uprights with a 13-yard kick to down the Rams 17-14.

In Detroit, Isbell fired three touchdown passes and Andy Uram added 103 yards rushing in a 24-7 Green Bay romp.

The Packers then gained a share of first place in the West with their 16-14 triumph at Wrigley Field. The Cardinals and Steelers fell in the subsequent weeks.

Green Bay needed to win its finale in Washington to keep the pressure on the Bears. But Sammy Baugh and the Redskins didn't cooperate, taking a 17-0 halftime lead.

Isbell, who had thrown two interceptions in the first half, came back with three touchdown passes—all to Hutson—following intermission. Washington's Ray Hare was then tackled in the end zone for a safety. The final result: a 22-17 come-from-behind win and a playoff date with the Chicago Bears.

ROAD TO PERFECTION

While Green Bay's inspiring 16-14 win in Chicago proved the Bears were human after all, it also was a great example of how the Packers thrived on the road in 1941. With wins at Municipal Stadium (Cleveland), Briggs Stadium (Detroit), Wrigley Field, Forbes Field (Pittsburgh), and Griffith Stadium (Washington), the team forged its best ever record (5-0) away from home.

Going unbeaten and untied on the road is never easy. The Packers did it twice—1923 and 1941—but the 1923 team only played three games away from Green Bay and only once left the state of Wisconsin.

Listed below are the Packers' five best road records for a given season.

Record	Pct.	Year	PF	PA
5-0-0	1.000	1941	133	59
3-0-0	1.000	1923	29	7
7-0-1	1.000	1929	119	18
5-0-1	1.000	1936	118	51
6-1-0	(accomplished 3 times—1962, 1966, 1972)			

TEAM STATISTICS

	GB	OPP
First Downs	166	124
Rushing	82	78
Passing	69	49
Penalty	15	11
Rushes	467	356
Yards Gained	1,550	1,221
Average Gain	3.32	3.43
Average Yards per Game	140.9	111.0
Passes Attempted	253	233
Completed	133	104
% Completed	52.57	44.64
Total Yards Gained	1,731	1,343
Yards Gained per Completion	13.02	12.91
Average Yards per Game	157.4	122.1
Laterals Attempted	1	15
Completed	1	14
Yards Gained	13	22
Combined Yards Gained	3,294	2,586
Total Plays	721	604
Average Yards per Play	4.57	4.28
Average Yards per Game	299.5	235.1
Intercepted By	25	13
Yards Returned	455	170
Returned for TD	1	0
Punts	53	58
Yards Punted	2,232	2,367
Average Yards per Punt	42.11	40.81
Punt Returns	41	31
Yards Returned	487	432
Average Yards per Return	11.88	13.94
Returned for TD	1	1
Kickoff Returns	28	39
Yards Returned	567	880
Average Yards per Return	20.25	22.56
Returned for TD	0	0
Penalties	47	63
Yards Penalized	509	539
Fumbles	20	41
Lost	11	23
Own Recovered for Touchdown	0	0
Opponent's Recovered by	23	11
Opponent's Recovered for Touchdown	1	0
Total Points Scored	258	120
Total Touchdowns	33	16
Touchdowns Rushing	13	7
Touchdowns Passing	17	8
Touchdowns on Returns & Recoveries	3	1
Extra Points	28	12
Safeties	1	0
Field Goals Attempted	20	12
Field Goals Made	10	4
% Successful	50.00	33.33

Regular Season   10-1-0

Date	GB		OPP	Att.
9/14	23	Detroit Lions	0	(16,734)
9/21	24	Cleveland Rams (M)	7	(18,463)
9/28	17	Chicago Bears	25	(24,876)
10/5	14	Chicago Cardinals (M)	13	(10,000)
10/12	30	Brooklyn Dodgers (M)	7	(15,621)
10/19	17	at Cleveland Rams	14	(13,086)
10/26	24	at Detroit Lions	7	(30,269)
11/2	16	at Chicago Bears	14	(46,484)
11/16	17	Chicago Cardinals	9	(15,495)
11/23	54	at Pittsburgh Steelers	7	(15,202)
11/30	22	at Washington Redskins	17	(35,594)

Postseason   0-1-0

12/14	14	at Chicago Bears	33	(43,425)

Score By Periods

	1	2	3	4	Total
Packers	54	58	54	92	258
Opponents	39	23	20	38	120

INDIVIDUAL STATISTICS

Rushing

	Att	Yds	Avg	LG	TD
Hinkle	129	393	3.0	20	5
Isbell	72	317	4.4	24	1
Uram	49	258	5.3	61	0
Canadeo	43	137	3.2	16	3
Van Every	25	127	5.1	t31	2
Paskvan	38	116	3.1	12	0
Jankowski	47	65	1.4	13	0
Laws	21	58	2.8	10	0
L. Brock	14	44	3.1	14	0
Hutson	4	22	5.5	t18	2
Frutig	1	11	11.0	11	0
Rohrig	21	2	0.1	18	0
Craig	1	1	1.0	1	0
Balazs	2	-1	-0.5	1	0
Packers	**467**	**1,550**	**3.3**	**61**	**13**
Opponents	356	1,221	3.4	31	7

Receiving

	No	Yds	Avg	LG	TD
Hutson	58	738	12.7	t45	10
L. Brock	22	307	14.0	t36	2
Rohrig	11	58	5.3	19	0
C. Mulleneaux	9	216	24.0	56	2
Hinkle	8	78	9.8	28	1
Uram	6	124	20.7	44	0
Jacunski	4	48	12.0	27	0
Laws	4	48	12.0	t18	1
Riddick	3	33	11.0	16	0
Frutig	2	40	20.0	34	0
Urban	2	26	13.0	14	1
Craig	2	13	6.5	12	0
Van Every	1	3	3.0	3	0
Isbell	1	-1	-1.0	-1	0
Packers	**133**	**1,731**	**13.0**	**56**	**17**
Opponents	104	1,343	12.9	t80	8

Passing

	Att	Com	Yds	Pct	TD	In	Rate
Isbell	206	117	1,479	56.8	15	11	81.4
Van Every	30	11	195	36.7	0	2	31.9
Canadeo	16	4	54	25.0	2	0	80.7
Rohrig	1	1	3	100.0	0	0	—
Packers	**253**	**133**	**1,731**	**52.6**	**17**	**13**	**75.4**
Opponents	233	104	1,343	44.6	8	25	35.2

Punting

	No	Yds	Avg	LG	HB
Hinkle	22	980	44.5	63	0
Van Every	13	505	38.8	65	0
Canadeo	10	405	40.5	62	0
Rohrig	5	214	42.8	52	0
L. Brock	3	128	42.7	48	0
Packers	**53**	**2,232**	**42.1**	**65**	**0**
Opponents	58	2,367	40.8	74	1

Kickoff Returns

	No	Yds	Avg	LG	TD
Canadeo	4	110	27.5	55	0
Van Every	4	99	24.8	31	0
L. Brock	4	94	23.5	36	0
Laws	3	75	25.0	26	0
Rohrig	3	60	20.0	29	0
Hinkle	3	38	12.7	16	0
Isbell	2	32	16.0	20	0
Uram	2	27	13.5	14	0
Riddick	1	14	14.0	14	0
Buhler	1	10	10.0	10	0
Hutson	1	8	8.0	8	0
Packers	**28**	**567**	**20.3**	**55**	**0**
Opponents	39	880	22.6	51	0

Punt Returns

	No	Yds	Avg	LG	TD
L. Brock	15	153	10.2	45	0
Uram	7	121	17.3	t90	1
Van Every	4	58	14.5	20	0
Rohrig	4	46	11.5	14	0
Canadeo	4	26	6.5	10	0
Isbell	3	19	6.3	7	0
Hinkle	2	61	30.5	36	0
Laws	2	3	1.5	3	0
Packers	**41**	**487**	**11.9**	**t90**	**1**
Opponents	31	432	13.9	t77	1

Interceptions

	No	Yds	Avg	LG	TD
Van Every	3	104	34.7	t91	1
Adkins	2	79	39.5	54	0
Uram	2	37	18.5	28	0
Laws	2	36	18.0	36	0
Canadeo	2	30	15.0	22	0
Paskvan	2	6	3.0	4	0
L. Brock	2	3	1.5	3	0
G. Svendsen	1	42	42.0	42	0
Jankowski	1	33	33.0	33	0
Hutson	1	32	32.0	32	0
Tinsley	1	24	24.0	24	0
Rohrig	1	17	17.0	17	0
H. Johnson	1	10	10.0	10	0
Hinkle	1	2	2.0	2	0
Goldenberg	1	0	0.0	0	0
Isbell	1	0	0.0	0	0
Pannell	1	0	0.0	0	0
Packers	**25**	**455**	**18.2**	**t91**	**1**
Opponents	13	170	13.1	56	0

Scoring

	TDr	TDp	TDrt	PAT	FG	S	TP
Hutson	2	10	0	20/24	1/1	0	95
Hinkle	5	1	0	2/2	6/14	0	56
Canadeo	3	6	0	0/0	0/0	0	18
Van Every	2	0	1	0/0	0/0	0	18
L. Brock	0	2	0	0/0	0/0	0	12
C. Mulleneaux	0	2	0	0/0	0/0	0	12
Isbell	1	0	0	0/0	0/0	0	6
Laws	0	1	0	0/0	0/0	0	6
Pannell	0	0	1	0/0	0/0	0	6
Uram	0	0	1	0/0	0/0	0	6
Urban	0	1	0	0/0	0/0	0	6
Rohrig	0	0	0	1/1	1/1	0	4
Jankowski	0	0	0	1/2	1/1	0	4
Adkins	0	0	0	3/3	0/0	0	3
Engebretsen	0	0	0	0/0	1/3	0	3
team	0	0	0	0/0	0/0	1	2
Balazs	0	0	0	1/1	0/0	0	1
Packers	**13**	**17**	**3**	**28/33**	**10/20**	**1**	**258**
Opponents	7	8	1	12/16	4/12	0	120

NFL STANDINGS

Western Division

	W	L	T	Pct	PF	PA
Chicago Bears	10	1	0	.909	396	147
Green Bay Packers	**10**	**1**	**0**	**.909**	**258**	**120**
Detroit Lions	4	6	1	.400	121	195
Chicago Cardinals	3	7	1	.300	127	197
Cleveland Rams	2	9	0	.182	116	244

Eastern Division

	W	L	T	Pct	PF	PA
New York Giants	9	3	0	.727	238	114
Brooklyn Dodgers	7	4	0	.636	158	127
Washington Redskins	6	5	0	.545	176	174
Philadelphia Eagles	2	8	1	.200	119	218
Pittsburgh Steelers	1	9	1	.100	103	276

1941

ROSTER

No	Name	Pos	Ht	Wt	DOB	College	G
55	Adkins, Robert	E	6-0	211	02/07/17	Marshall	7
35	Balazs, Frank	FB	6-2	205	01/23/18	Iowa	1
29	Brock, Charley	C	6-1	207	03/15/16	Nebraska	11
16	Brock, Lou	HB	6-0	196	12/09/17	Purdue	11
33	Bucchianeri, Amadeo (Mike)	G	5-10	210	09/01/17	Indiana	1
52	Buhler, Larry	HB	6-2	210	05/28/17	Minnesota	11
3	Canadeo, Tony	HB	6-0	190	05/05/19	Gonzaga	9
54	Craig, Larry	E	6-0	210	06/27/16	South Carolina	11
34	Engebretsen, Paul (Tiny)	G	6-1	245	07/27/10	Northwestern	1
51	Frutig, Ed	E	6-1	190	08/19/20	Michigan	8
43	Goldenberg, Charles (Buckets)	G	5-10	230	03/10/11	Wisconsin	9
56	Greenfield, Tom	C	6-4	219	11/10/17	Arizona	5
30	Hinkle, Clarke	FB	5-11	205	04/10/12	Bucknell	11
14	Hutson, Don	E	6-1	180	01/31/13	Alabama	11
17	Isbell, Cecil	HB	6-1	190	07/11/15	Purdue	11
48	Jacunski, Harry	E	6-2	202	10/20/15	Fordham	11
7	Jankowski, Ed	FB	5-10	195	06/23/13	Wisconsin	11
50	Johnson, Bill	E	6-1	195	10/04/16	Minnesota	6
64	Johnson, Howard (Smiley)	G	5-10	195	09/22/16	Georgia	11
45	Kuusisto, William	G	6-0	235	04/26/18	Minnesota	10
24	Laws, Joe	HB	5-9	190	06/16/11	Iowa	11
40	Lee, Bill	T	6-3	240	10/19/11	Alabama	11
46	Letlow, Russ	G	6-0	220	10/05/13	San Francisco	4
15	Lyman, Del	T	6-2	225	07/09/18	UCLA	5
37	McLaughlin, Lee	G	6-1	225	02/28/17	Virginia	9
19	Mulleneaux, Carl (Moose)	E	6-4	205	04/01/17	Utah State	10
22	Pannell, Ernie	T	6-3	215	02/02/17	Texas A&M	11
68	Paskvan, George	FB	6-0	190	04/01/18	Wisconsin	
44	Ray, Buford (Baby)	T	6-6	250	09/30/15	Vanderbilt	11
5	Riddick, Ray	E	6-0	220	10/17/17	Fordham	11
8	Rohrig, Herman	HB	5-9	187	03/19/18	Nebraska	10
60	Schultz, Charles	T	6-3	235	10/08/16	Minnesota	11
66	Svendsen, George	C	6-4	240	03/22/13	Minnesota	11
21	Tinsley, Pete	G	5-8	200	03/16/13	Georgia	9
42	Uram, Andy	HB	5-10	188	03/22/15	Minnesota	11
23	Urban, Alex	E	6-3	199	07/16/17	South Carolina	7
36	Van Every, Hal	HB	6-0	195	02/10/18	Minnesota	11

DRAFT

Rnd	Name	Pos	College	Rnd	Name	Pos	College
1	George Paskvan	B	Wisconsin	13	Ed Heffernan	B	St. Mary's (CA)
3	Robert Paffrath	B	Minnesota	14	Del Lyman	T	UCLA
5	Ed Frutig	E	Michigan	15	John Frieberger	E	Arkansas
6	Herman Rohrig	B	Nebraska	16	Ernie Pannell	T	Texas A&M
7	Bill Telesmanic	E	San Francisco	17	Bob Saggau	B	Notre Dame
8	William Kuusisto	G	Minnesota	18	Heige Pukema	G	Minnesota
9	Tony Canadeo	B	Gonzaga	19	Robert Hayes	E	Toledo
10	Mike Byelene	B	Purdue	20	James Strasbaugh	B	Ohio State
11	Paul Hiemenz	C	Northwestern	21	Joe Bailey	C	Kentucky
12	Mike Enich	T	Iowa	22	Bruno Malinowski	B	Holy Cross

1941 GREEN BAY PACKERS

FRONT ROW: (L-R) 8 Herman Rohrig, 54 Larry Craig, 30 Clarke Hinkle, 42 Andy Uram, 7 Ed Jankowski, 24 Joe Laws, 33 Mike Bucchianeri, 40 Bill Lee, 14 Don Hutson.
SECOND ROW: (L-R) 51 Ed Frutig, 3 Tony Canadeo, 34 Paul Engebretsen, 64 Howard Johnson, 55 Bob Adkins, 60 Charles Schultz, 17 Cecil Isbell, 5 Ray Riddick, 29 Charley Brock, 43 Buckets Goldenberg.
THIRD ROW: (L-R) 68 George Paskvan, Lou Brock, 50 Bill Johnson, 36 Hal Van Every, 56 Tom Greenfield, 48 Harry Jacunski, 23 Alex Urban, 52 Larry Buhler, 21 Pete Tinsley, 45 William Kuusisto.
BACK ROW: (L-R) 15 Del Lyman, 35 Frank Balazs, 19 Carl Mulleneaux, 66 George Svendsen, 44 Baby Ray, 22 Ernie Pannell, 37 Lee McLaughlin.

From their earliest days, the Packers had embraced the forward pass as an offensive weapon. In 1942, they rewrote the record manual with a passing attack so powerful it offset a mediocre defense and powered the team to within two games of first place in the Western Division.

Cecil Isbell guided the assault. The halfback became the first 2,000-yard passer (2,021) in league history and bettered his NFL-record 15 touchdown passes in 1941 by nine. He again threw at least one touchdown in each of the Packers' 11 regular-season games.

Don Hutson was Isbell's favorite target and he set season records for most catches (74), yards (1,211), and touchdowns (17). He twice surpassed 200 yards receiving and caught at least two touchdown passes in six games.

Like 1927, Green Bay lost only twice all year. And like that season 15 years distant, those losses both came compliments of the Chicago Bears.

The Bears of 1942 were just one of three teams in NFL history to complete the regular season unbeaten and untied. (The 1934 Bears and 1972 Dolphins were the others.) The Bears staged a 17-point, fourth-quarter rally to knock off Green Bay 44-28 in the season opener, then crushed them 38-7 in the return engagement in Chicago. Those losses and a tie in the Polo Grounds left the Packers in second place in the West with an 8-2-1 mark.

Green Bay, like the other clubs in the league, saw many of its players called up to aid in the war effort. Fifteen players from 1941 did not return to the Packers in 1942 because of military commitments. Ten of those 15 never resumed their careers in Green Bay, and one, guard Howard (Smiley) Johnson, lost his life on the ninth day of the Iwo Jima invasion.

Clarke Hinkle was one of the 15 called. The veteran became a commissioned officer in the Coast Guard. He left as the NFL's all-time leading rusher (3,860 yards).

With Hinkle gone, rookie Ted Fritsch emerged as the team's top fullback. Curly Lambeau signed the undrafted Fritsch on the recommendation of backfield coach Eddie Kotal, and the rookie led the team in rushing with 323 yards.

Green Bay's eighth-ranked defense gave up more than 300 yards five times, including a season-high 394 yards to the Steelers on the last weekend of the season.

It was this defense that allowed the Bears to amass 228 yards rushing in Week 1, and this defense and two crucial turnovers that allowed Chicago to score 17 points in the closing six minutes. A fumble by Andy Uram and an Isbell interception were turned into a pair of touchdowns as the Bears prevailed 44-28.

Charley Brock turned pickpocket in Green Bay's first victory, a 17-13 decision over the Cardinals. Brock stole the ball from John Morrow and raced 20 yards for the deciding touchdown. The wily Brock recovered a second fumble a short time later to preserve the victory.

Green Bay then beat up on winless Detroit, 38-7.

The Packers exploded for a season-high 541 yards in earning their third win, a 45-28 triumph over Cleveland. Isbell completed 23 of 33 passes for 277 yards and Hutson gained 209 yards receiving on 13 catches.

Uram's 98-yard kickoff return highlighted Week 5, which saw the Packers down Detroit 28-7.

The Packers improved to 5-1 by overpowering the Cardinals 55-24 in City Stadium. Hutson and Uram each caught two touchdown passes of more than 60 yards.

Green Bay notched its sixth win by beating Cleveland 30-12. Isbell, Hutson, and Buckets Goldenberg each intercepted two passes, and Canadeo added a seventh theft.

The Packers (6-1) then got a second crack at the Bears (7-0). Bulldog Turner scored on a 45-yard fumble return and Sid Luckman on a 54-yard interception return. Chicago tacked on 17 more points before the Packers finally tallied on a 6-yard, Isbell-to-Hutson strike. It was much too little, much too late as the Bruins won easily 38-7.

The Giants then eliminated Green Bay from playoff consideration with a 21-21 tie at the Polo Grounds.

Green Bay rebounded to win its final two games. The Packers concluded with a 24-21 win over Pittsburgh in frigid Milwaukee. In a move the league wouldn't allow today, Curly Lambeau stationed his reserves in the warmth of the dressing room while the Steelers backups stood on the sidelines in subfreezing temperatures.

A 300 GAME IN 10 QUICK STRIKES

Although Don Hutson enjoyed a record-setting season, his numbers wouldn't have been nearly as great had Cecil Isbell not been at his finest.

Not only did Isbell become the first player to throw for 2,000 yards in a season, he became the first Packer to pass for more than 300 yards in a game. Further, he needed but 10 completions to reach that milestone, fewer than any other Packer in history.

On Nov. 1, Isbell threw 21 passes and completed 10 for 333 yards. Five of his completions went to Hutson for 207 yards (three touchdowns) and another three went to Andy Uram for 112 yards (two touchdowns).

Listed below are the completions on which 300 yards were accumulated the quickest in Packers history:

Com.	Passer	Date	Yards
10	Cecil Isbell	11-1-1942	333
13	Bart Starr	9-17-1967	308
15	Bart Starr	10-17-65	301
15	Brett Favre	11-16-97	304

TEAM STATISTICS

	GB	OPP
First Downs	176	147
Rushing	65	79
Passing	97	59
Penalty	14	9
Rushes	422	376
Yards Gained	1,374	1,549
Average Gain	3.26	4.12
Average Yards per Game	124.9	140.8
Passes Attempted	330	242
Completed	172	100
% Completed	52.12	41.32
Total Yards Gained	2,407	1,471
Yards Gained per Completion	13.99	14.71
Average Yards per Game	218.8	133.7
Laterals Attempted	3	4
Completed	3	4
Yards Gained	9	56
Combined Yards Gained	3,790	3,076
Total Plays	755	622
Average Yards per Play	5.02	4.95
Average Yards per Game	344.5	279.6
Intercepted By	33	18
Yards Returned	352	282
Returned for TD	1	2
Punts	58	56
Yards Punted	2,175	2,088
Average Yards per Punt	37.50	37.29
Punt Returns	32	38
Yards Returned	327	396
Average Yards per Return	10.22	10.42
Returned for TD	0	0
Kickoff Returns	37	45
Yards Returned	789	1,044
Average Yards per Return	21.32	23.20
Returned for TD	1	1
Penalties	38	63
Yards Penalized	312	539
Fumbles	13	22
Lost	8	15
Own Recovered for Touchdown	0	0
Opponent's Recovered by	15	8
Opponent's Recovered for Touchdown	1	2
Total Points Scored	300	215
Total Touchdowns	41	28
Touchdowns Rushing	10	14
Touchdowns Passing	28	8
Touchdowns on Returns & Recoveries	3	6
Extra Points	39	27
Safeties	0	1
Field Goals Attempted	10	7
Field Goals Made	5	6
% Successful	50.00	85.71

Regular Season 8-2-1

Date	GB		OPP	Att.
9/27	28	Chicago Bears	44	(20,007)
10/4	17	at Chicago Cardinals	13	(24,897)
10/11	38	Detroit Lions (M)	7	(19,500)
10/18	45	Cleveland Rams	28	(12,847)
10/25	28	at Detroit Lions	7	(19,097)
11/1	55	Chicago Cardinals	24	(14,782)
11/8	30	at Cleveland Rams	12	(16,473)
11/15	7	at Chicago Bears	38	(42,787)
11/22	21	at New York Giants	21	(30,246)
11/29	7	at Philadelphia Eagles	0	(13,700)
12/6	24	Pittsburgh Steelers (M)	21	(5,138)

Score By Periods

	1	2	3	4	Total
Packers	57	90	48	105	300
Opponents	45	61	43	66	215

INDIVIDUAL STATISTICS

Rushing

	Att	Yds	Avg	LG	TD
Fritsch	74	323	4.4	55	0
Canadeo	89	272	3.1	t50	3
Sample	57	255	4.5	31	4
L. Brock	95	237	2.5	24	2
Laws	29	100	3.4	17	0
Isbell	36	83	2.3	32	1
Uram	24	75	3.1	8	0
Weisgerber	5	21	4.2	6	0
Hutson	3	4	1.3	9	0
Bob Kahler	8	4	0.5	13	0
Craig	2	0	0	4	0
Packers	**422**	**1,374**	**3.3**	**55**	**10**
Opponents	376	1,549	4.1	54	14

Receiving

	No	Yds	Avg	LG	TD
Hutson	74	1,211	16.4	t73	17
Uram	21	420	20.0	t64	4
L. Brock	20	139	7.0	29	1
Canadeo	10	66	6.6	15	0
Fritsch	9	60	6.7	21	0
Jacunski	8	125	15.6	t49	1
J. Mason	7	86	12.3	19	0
Riddick	6	104	17.3	t24	1
Laws	6	96	16.0	28	1
Sample	6	35	5.8	t10	1
Bob Kahler	2	21	10.5	12	0
Joe Carter	2	19	9.5	t10	1
Ranspot	1	25	25.0	t25	1
Packers	**172**	**2,407**	**14.0**	**t73**	**28**
Opponents	100	1,471	14.7	t67	8

Passing

	Att	Com	Yds	Pct	TD	In	Rate
Isbell	268	146	2,021	54.5	24	14	87.0
Canadeo	59	24	310	40.7	3	4	46.6
Laws	3	2	76	66.7	1	0	—
Packers	**330**	**172**	**2,407**	**52.1**	**28**	**18**	**81.5**
Opponents	242	100	1,471	41.3	8	33	33.3

Punting

	No	Yds	Avg	LG	HB
L. Brock	32	1,226	38.3	52	2
Canadeo	18	643	35.7	47	0
Isbell	4	141	35.3	46	0
Fritsch	3	122	40.7	54	0
Starret	1	43	43.0	43	0
Packers	**58**	**2,175**	**37.5**	**54**	**2**
Opponents	56	2,088	37.3	67	1

Kickoff Returns

	No	Yds	Avg	LG	TD
L. Brock	9	179	19.9	26	0
Uram	8	208	26.0	t98	1
Canadeo	6	137	22.8	35	0
Isbell	4	64	16.0	20	0
Sample	3	91	30.3	35	0
Fritsch	2	43	21.5	23	0
Laws	2	36	18.0	18	0
Craig	2	24	12.0	16	0
Berezney	1	7	7.0	7	0
Packers	**37**	**789**	**21.3**	**t98**	**1**
Opponents	45	1,044	23.2	t95	1

Punt Returns

	No	Yds	Avg	LG	TD
L. Brock	8	86	10.8	22	0
Canadeo	7	76	10.9	26	0
Laws	7	56	8.0	15	0
Uram	7	50	7.1	24	0
Fritsch	1	31	31.0	31	0
Isbell	1	14	14.0	14	0
Bob Kahler	1	14	14.0	14	0
Packers	**32**	**327**	**10.2**	**31**	**0**
Opponents	38	396	10.4	44	0

Interceptions

	No	Yds	Avg	LG	TD
Hutson	7	71	10.1	27	0
Isbell	6	47	7.8	19	0
C. Brock	6	25	4.2	16	0
Goldenberg	4	31	7.8	15	0
Laws	3	67	22.3	38	0
L. Brock	2	32	16.0	19	0
Uram	2	18	9.0	18	0
Canadeo	1	35	35.0	35	0
Ingalls	1	23	23.0	t23	1
Tinsley	1	3	3.0	3	0
Packers	**33**	**352**	**10.7**	**38**	**1**
Opponents	18	282	15.7	t54	2

Scoring

	TDr	TDp	TDrt	PAT	FG	S	TP
Hutson	0	17	0	33/34	1/4	0	138
Uram	0	4	1	0/0	0/0	0	31
Sample	4	1	0	0/0	0/0	0	30
L. Brock	2	1	0	2/2	0/1	0	20
Canadeo	3	0	0	0/0	0/0	0	18
Fritsch	0	0	0	1/1	4/5	0	13
C. Brock	0	0	1	0/0	0/0	0	6
Joe Carter	0	1	0	0/0	0/0	0	6
Ingalls	0	0	1	0/0	0/0	0	6
Jacunski	0	1	0	0/0	0/0	0	6
Laws	0	1	0	0/0	0/0	0	6
Ranspot	0	1	0	0/0	0/0	0	6
Riddick	0	1	0	0/0	0/0	0	6
Weisgerber	0	0	0	2/2	0/0	0	2
Packers	**10**	**28**	**3**	**39/41**	**5/10**	**0**	**300**
Opponents	14	8	6	27/28	6/7	1	215

NFL STANDINGS

Western Division

	W	L	T	Pct	PF	PA
Chicago Bears	11	0	0	1.000	376	84
Green Bay Packers	8	2	1	.800	300	215
Cleveland Rams	5	6	0	.455	150	207
Chicago Cardinals	3	8	0	.273	98	209
Detroit Lions	0	11	0	.000	38	263

Eastern Division

	W	L	T	Pct	PF	PA
Washington Redskins	10	1	0	.909	227	102
Pittsburgh Steelers	7	4	0	.636	167	119
New York Giants	5	5	1	.500	155	139
Brooklyn Dodgers	3	8	0	.273	100	168
Philadelphia Eagles	2	9	0	.182	134	239

1942

ROSTER

No	Name	Pos	Ht	Wt	DOB	College	G
47	Berezney, Paul	T	6-2	220	09/25/16	Fordham	11
29	Brock, Charley	C	6-1	209	03/15/16	Nebraska	11
16	Brock, Lou	HB	6-0	192	12/09/17	Purdue	11
3	Canadeo, Tony	HB	6-0	195	05/05/19	Gonzaga	11
58	Carter, Joe	E	6-1	200	07/23/12	SMU	11
54	Craig, Larry	E	6-0	205	06/27/16	South Carolina	11
75	Croft, Milburn (Tiny)	T	6-4	300	11/07/20	Ripon	8
35	Flowers, Bob	C	6-1	205	08/06/17	Texas Tech	
64	Fritsch, Ted	FB	5-10	205	10/31/20	Stevens Point	11
43	Goldenberg, Charles (Buckets)	G	5-10	220	03/10/11	Wisconsin	11
15	Hinte, Harold	E	6-1	195	01/25/20	Pittsburgh	1
14	Hutson, Don	E	6-1	178	01/31/13	Alabama	11
53	Ingalls, Bob	C	6-3	200	01/17/19	Michigan	11
17	Isbell, Cecil	HB	6-1	190	07/11/15	Purdue	11
48	Jacunski, Harry	E	6-2	202	10/20/15	Fordham	6
8	Kahler, Bob	HB	6-3	200	02/13/17	Nebraska	7
72	Kahler, Royal	T	6-3	225	03/22/18	Nebraska	9
45	Kuusisto, William	G	6-0	225	04/26/18	Minnesota	10
24	Laws, Joe	HB	5-9	182	06/16/11	Iowa	10
40	Lee, Bill	T	6-3	240	10/19/11	Alabama	1
46	Letlow, Russ	G	6-0	220	10/05/13	San Francisco	11
7	Mason, Joel	E	6-0	198	03/12/13	Western Michigan	11
23	Ohlgren, Earl	E	6-3	210	02/21/18	Minnesota	
22	Pannell, Ernie	T	6-3	220	02/02/17	Texas A&M	5
27	Ranspot, Keith	E	6-0	190	12/11/14	SMU	5
44	Ray, Buford (Baby)	T	6-6	245	09/30/15	Vanderbilt	11
5	Riddick, Ray	E	6-0	220	10/17/17	Fordham	3
38	Sample, Chuck	FB	5-9	202	01/05/20	Toledo	9
63	Starret, Ben	B	5-11	210	11/19/17	St. Mary's (CA)	5
51	Stonebreaker, John	E	6-3	200	04/25/18	USC	9
21	Tinsley, Pete	G	5-8	200	03/16/13	Georgia	11
42	Uram, Andy	HB	5-10	188	03/22/15	Minnesota	11
18	Vant Hull, Fred	T/G	6-0	213	08/21/20	Minnesota	10
33	Weisgerber, Dick	HB	5-10	198	02/19/15	Williamette	9

DRAFT

Rnd	Name	Pos	College
1	Urban Odson	T	Minnesota
3	Ray Frankowski	G	Washington
5	Bill Green	B	Iowa
6	Joe Krivonak	G	South Carolina
7	Preston Johnson	B	SMU
8	Joe Rogers	E	Michigan
9	Phil Langdale	T	Alabama
10	Gene Flick	C	Minnesota
11	Tom Farris	B	Wisconsin
12	Jimmy Richardson	B	Marquette
13	Bruce Smith	B	Minnesota
14	Bill Applegate	G	South Carolina
15	Jim Trimble	T	Indiana
16	Tom Kinkade	B	Ohio State
17	Fred Preston	E	Nebraska
18	Bob Ingalls	C	Michigan
19	George Benson	B	Northwestern
20	Horace Young	B	SMU
21	Henry Woronicz	E	Boston College
22	Woody Adams	T	TCU

1942 GREEN BAY PACKERS

FRONT ROW: (L-R) Coach Curly Lambeau, Assistant Coach Richard (Red) Smith, 30 Tony Canadeo, 23 Earl Ohlgren, 40 Bill Lee, 43 Buckets Goldenberg, 29 Charley Brock, 46 Russ Letlow, 44 Baby Ray, 14 Don Hutson, 47 Paul Berezney, Trainer Carl (Bud) Jorgensen.

MIDDLE ROW: (L-R) 24 Joe Laws, 53 Bob Ingalls, 17 Cecil Isbell, 58 Joe Carter, 15 Tex Hinte, 27 Don Miller, 18 Fred Vant Hull, 7 Joel Mason, 54 Larry Craig, 42 Andy Uram, 21 Pete Tinsley, Assistant Coach Eddie Kotal.

BACK ROW: (L-R) 16 Lou Brock, 19 Art Albrecht, 22 Ernie Pannell, 35 Bob Flowers, 51 John Stonebreaker, 75 Tiny Croft, 8 Bob Kahler, 45 William Kuusisto, 64 Ted Fritsch, 63 Ben Starrett, 38 Chuck Sample, 72 James Finley.

Since 1936, the road to the Western Division Conference title had gone through either Green Bay or Chicago. That again was the case in 1943.

From 1936 through 1942, the Bears (1937, 1940, 1942) and Packers (1936, 1938-39) had each worn the crown three times. The two were co-champions in 1941.

In 1943, the rivalry produced a 21-21 opening day tie and a 21-7 Bears' triumph in the return engagement at Wrigley Field. Those games, and an earlier loss to the Redskins, added up to a 7-2-1 record for the Packers and a second-place finish behind the Bears (8-1-1).

That the rivalry continued another year was not a given. World War II raged overseas and many players were called upon to serve their country. NFL owners fretted that rosters might go unfilled and the season might be lost.

Changes were in order. The draft was moved back four months to April 1943. At a league meeting early that month, Dan Reeves withdrew his Rams from the NFL and the players were divided among the remaining clubs. Two months later, the Philadelphia and Pittsburgh franchises merged to form the "Steagles." That left eight teams to compete in a schedule shortened to 10 games.

In Green Bay, Don Hutson and Cecil Isbell announced their retirements. Hutson reconsidered, signed a contract in early August, and didn't miss a game despite learning of the deaths of his brother (killed in action in the South Pacific) and father less than a week before the season opener. Isbell stayed true to his word and became backfield coach at Purdue University, his alma mater.

Isbell's departure left a huge hole in the Packers passing game. Tony Canadeo, rookie Irv Comp and, to a lesser extent, Lou Brock filled the void. Green Bay's aerial attack slipped to second behind that of the Bears.

The Packers kicked off the season on Sept. 26. Canadeo threw a 26-yard touchdown pass to Hutson with about seven minutes remaining to tie the score at 21. Bob Snyder's last-minute, 42-yard field goal attempt was deflected and the game went into the books as a tie.

Joel Mason caught the only two touchdown passes of his career in Week 2 as the Packers downed the Cardinals 28-7. Ted Fritsch (2-yard run) and Harry Jacunski (35-yard reception) accounted for the other touchdowns.

Green Bay won its third straight, 35-14 over the Lions. Canadeo keyed a season-best 239-yard rushing output with 71 yards on 12 carries. The third-year player also threw three touchdown passes for the only time in his career.

The defending-champion Redskins then abruptly brought the Packers down to earth 33-7.

Green Bay rebounded in Detroit by intercepting an NFL-record nine passes. Eight different players had at least one steal, with Hutson getting two, in the 27-6 decision.

The Packers notched their fifth win in New York on Halloween. Canadeo rushed for 122 yards, and both Jacunski and Hutson went over 100 yards receiving. The team was without Charley Brock, who underwent an appendectomy just days before the game. Brock, who returned for the season finale, was replaced by Bob Flowers and Forrest McPherson.

On Nov. 7, the Packers (4-1-1) and Bears (5-0-1) squared off in rain-soaked Wrigley Field. The ankle-deep mud didn't stop the Bears from grabbing three touchdowns and the game 21-7.

For the Packers to catch the Bears, Chicago had to lose at least two of its last three games. The Bears did stumble against the Redskins, but clobbered New York by 49 points and the Cardinals by 11 to secure a playoff berth.

Green Bay, meanwhile, won its last three games. First up were the Cardinals, whom the Packers pounded 35-14 at State Fair Park. Comp, Canadeo and Lou Brock each threw a touchdown pass.

A week later, Hutson tore up Ebbets Field with eight receptions for a then-league-record 237 yards. Comp picked off three passes and scored on a 13-yard return in the fourth quarter.

After an exhibition victory (62-14) over the New London Diesels at Bristol, Conn., on Nov. 29, the Packers closed with a 38-28 win over the "Steagles." Green Bay forced eight Phil-Pitt turnovers, and Hutson scored the last touchdown of the year on a 24-yard pass from Comp.

IRV COMP AND HIS MERRY BAND OF THIEVES

Rookie Irv Comp, the Packers' second-round draft choice, touched off an avalanche of interceptions by picking off a team-record 10 in 1943.

Comp and a dozen of his teammates combined to steal 42 passes, the most in team history. Except for their game with the Giants, the Packers intercepted at least one pass in every game.

On Oct. 24, Green Bay set an NFL record by pilfering nine Detroit passes. Poor Frank Sinkwich was victimized seven times in just 26 pass attempts.

The Packers intercepted at least five passes in five other games. They snared five in the first game with the Lions to give them 14 in one season against Detroit.

Below is a list of the most passes Green Bay has intercepted in one season:

No.	Year	Yards	Leading Interceptor
42	1943	616	Irv Comp (10)
40	1940	414	Don Hutson (6)
33	1942	352	Don Hutson (7)

TEAM STATISTICS

	GB	OPP
First Downs	134	122
Rushing	60	62
Passing	66	56
Penalty	8	4
Rushes	397	350
Yards Gained	1,442	1,112
Average Gain	3.63	3.18
Average Yards per Game	144.2	111.2
Passes Attempted	253	242
Completed	114	111
% Completed	45.06	45.87
Total Yards Gained	1,909	1,420
Yards Gained per Completion	16.75	12.79
Average Yards per Game	190.9	142.0
Laterals Attempted	2	15
Completed	1	14
Yards Gained	0	175
Combined Yards Gained	3,351	2,707
Total Plays	652	607
Average Yards per Play	5.14	4.46
Average Yards per Game	335.1	270.7
Intercepted By	42	19
Yards Returned	616	188
Returned for TD	2	0
Punts	52	55
Yards Punted	1,870	2,017
Average Yards per Punt	35.96	36.67
Punt Returns	32	28
Yards Returned	371	330
Average Yards per Return	11.59	11.79
Returned for TD	0	0
Kickoff Returns	28	31
Yards Returned	661	606
Average Yards per Return	23.61	19.55
Returned for TD	0	0
Penalties	52	51
Yards Penalized	403	391
Fumbles	15	22
Lost	6	9
Own Recovered for Touchdown	0	0
Opponent's Recovered by	9	6
Opponent's Recovered for Touchdown	0	0
Total Points Scored	264	172
Total Touchdowns	36	25
Touchdowns Rushing	13	9
Touchdowns Passing	21	15
Touchdowns on Returns & Recoveries	2	1
Extra Points	36	22
Safeties	0	0
Field Goals Attempted	15	3
Field Goals Made	4	0
% Successful	26.67	00.00

Regular Season 7-2-1

Date	GB		OPP	Att.
9/26	21	Chicago Bears	21	(23,675)
10/3	28	at Chicago Cardinals	7	(15,563)
10/10	35	Detroit Lions	14	(21,396)
10/17	7	Washington Redskins (M)	33	(23,058)
10/24	27	at Detroit Lions	6	(41,463)
10/31	35	at New York Giants	21	(46,208)
11/7	7	at Chicago Bears	21	(43,425)
11/14	35	Chicago Cardinals (M)	14	(10,831)
11/21	31	at Brooklyn Dodgers	7	(18,992)
12/5	38	at Phil-Pitt Steagles	28	(34,294)

Score By Periods

	1	2	3	4	Total
Packers	80	62	56	66	264
Opponents	47	28	34	63	172

INDIVIDUAL STATISTICS

Rushing

	Att	Yds	Avg	LG	TD
Canadeo	94	489	5.2	t35	3
Laws	43	232	5.4	31	0
Falkenstein	58	198	3.4	59	1
Comp	77	182	2.4	27	3
Fritsch	54	169	3.1	14	4
L. Brock	45	67	1.5	9	2
Uram	15	53	3.5	9	0
Hutson	6	41	6.8	16	0
Bob Kahler	1	5	5.0	5	0
Craig	1	3	3.0	3	0
Lankas	2	2	1.0	1	0
Starret	1	1	1.0	1	0
Packers	397	1,442	3.6	59	13
Opponents	350	1,112	3.2	47	9

Receiving

	No	Yds	Avg	LG	TD
Hutson	47	776	16.5	t79	11
Jacunski	24	528	22.0	t86	3
Uram	10	212	21.2	51	2
J. Mason	8	107	13.4	21	2
D. Evans	8	71	8.9	13	0
Laws	5	33	6.6	22	0
L. Brock	4	57	14.3	32	1
Falkenstein	3	39	13.0	18	0
Canadeo	3	31	10.3	t13	2
Fritsch	2	55	27.5	32	0
Packers	114	1,909	16.7	t86	21
Opponents	111	1,420	12.8	t66	15

Passing

	Att	Com	Yds	Pct	TD	In	Rate
Canadeo	129	56	875	43.4	9	12	51.0
Comp	92	46	662	50.0	7	4	81.0
L. Brock	22	9	274	40.9	3	1	108.7
Uram	6	2	60	33.3	1	1	—
Hutson	4	1	38	25.0	1	1	—
Packers	253	114	1,909	45.1	21	19	67.4
Opponents	242	111	1,420	45.9	15	42	45.8

Punting

	No	Yds	Avg	LG	HB
L. Brock	32	1,164	36.4	72	1
Comp	12	453	37.8	46	0
Fritsch	5	151	30.2	47	0
Canadeo	3	102	34.0	39	0
Packers	52	1,870	36.0	72	1
Opponents	55	2,017	36.7	60	1

Kickoff Returns

	No	Yds	Avg	LG	TD
Canadeo	10	242	24.2	43	0
L. Brock	5	112	22.4	40	0
Fritsch	4	99	24.8	32	0
Comp	4	81	20.3	24	0
Falkenstein	2	47	23.5	24	0
Laws	2	47	23.5	24	0
Jacunski	1	33	33.0	33	0
Packers	28	661	23.6	43	0
Opponents	31	606	19.5	37	0

Punt Returns

	No	Yds	Avg	LG	TD
Laws	10	84	8.4	19	0
L. Brock	8	126	15.8	32	0
Canadeo	8	93	11.6	22	0
Uram	5	48	9.6	17	0
Comp	1	20	20.0	20	0
Packers	32	371	11.6	32	0
Opponents	28	330	11.8	22	0

Interceptions

	No	Yds	Avg	LG	TD
Comp	10	149	14.9	35	1
Hutson	8	197	24.6	t84	1
Laws	7	67	9.6	17	0
C. Brock	4	61	15.3	41	0
Uram	2	56	28.0	22	0
Goldenberg	2	37	18.5	30	0
Canadeo	2	15	7.5	15	0
Fries	2	6	3.0	4	0
L. Brock	1	9	9.0	9	0
Tinsley	1	8	8.0	8	0
Jacunski	1	7	7.0	7	0
Starret	1	4	4.0	4	0
Flowers	1	0	0.0	0	0
Packers	42	616	14.7	t84	2
Opponents	19	188	9.9	24	0

Scoring

	TDr	TDp	TDrt	PAT	FG	S	TP
Hutson	0	11	1	36/36	3/5	0	117
Canadeo	3	2	0	0/0	0/0	0	30
Comp	3	0	1	0/0	0/0	0	24
Fritsch	4	0	0	0/0	0/2	0	24
L. Brock	2	1	0	0/0	0/0	0	18
Jacunski	0	3	0	0/0	0/0	0	18
J. Mason	0	2	0	0/0	0/0	0	12
Uram	0	2	0	0/0	0/0	0	12
Falkenstein	1	0	0	0/0	0/0	0	6
Adams	0	0	0	0/0	1/6	0	3
Sorenson	0	0	0	0/0	0/2	0	0
Packers	13	21	2	36/36	4/15	0	264
Opponents	9	15	1	22/25	0/3	0	172

NFL STANDINGS

Western Division

	W	L	T	Pct	PF	PA
Chicago Bears	8	1	1	889	303	157
Green Bay Packers	7	2	1	778	264	172
Detroit Lions	3	6	1	333	178	218
Chicago Cardinals	0	10	0	000	95	238

Eastern Division

	W	L	T	Pct	PF	PA
Washington Redskins	6	3	1	667	229	137
New York Giants	6	3	1	667	197	170
Phil-Pitt Steagles	5	4	1	556	225	230
Brooklyn Dodgers	2	8	0	200	65	234

ROSTER

No	Name	Pos	Ht	Wt	DOB	College	G
27	Adams, Chet	T	6-3	240	10/24/16	Ohio State	10
47	Berezney, Paul	T	6-2	220	09/25/16	Fordham	10
29	Brock, Charley	C	6-1	210	03/15/16	Nebraska	6
16	Brock, Lou	HB	6-0	195	12/09/17	Purdue	10
3	Canadeo, Tony	HB	6-0	195	05/05/19	Gonzaga	10
51	Comp, Irv	HB	6-3	192	05/17/19	St. Benedict	9
54	Craig, Larry	E	6-0	208	06/27/16	South Carolina	10
75	Croft, Milburn (Tiny)	T	6-4	298	11/07/20	Ripon	
22	Evans, Dick	E	6-3	210	05/31/18	Iowa	10
18	Falkenstein, Tony	FB	5-10	210	02/16/15	St. Mary's (CA)	10
35	Flowers, Bob	C	6-1	215	08/06/17	Texas Tech	8
46	Fries, Sherwood	G	6-1	238	11/24/20	Colorado State	5
64	Fritsch, Ted	FB	5-10	205	10/31/20	Stevens Point	10
43	Goldenberg, Charles (Buckets)	G	5-10	220	03/10/11	Wisconsin	10
14	Hutson, Don	E	6-1	178	01/31/13	Alabama	10
48	Jacunski, Harry	E	6-2	198	10/20/15	Fordham	10
8	Kahler, Bob	HB	6-3	200	02/13/17	Nebraska	
45	Kuusisto, William	G	6-0	230	04/26/18	Minnesota	10
23	Lankas, Jim	FB	6-2	215	08/26/18	St. Mary's (CA)	3
24	Laws, Joe	HB	5-9	188	06/16/11	Iowa	10
7	Mason, Joel	E	6-0	198	03/12/13	Western Michigan	10
72	McPherson, Forrest	T/C	5-11	248	10/22/11	Nebraska	5
44	Ray, Buford (Baby)	T	6-6	250	09/30/15	Vanderbilt	8
40	Schwammel, Ade	T	6-2	215	10/14/08	Oregon State	2
33	Sorenson, Glen	G	6-0	225	02/29/20	Utah State	7
63	Starret, Ben	B	5-11	215	11/19/17	St. Mary's (CA)	7
21	Tinsley, Pete	G	5-8	200	03/16/13	Georgia	10
42	Uram, Andy	HB	5-10	190	03/22/15	Minnesota	8

DRAFT

Rnd	Name	Pos	College
1	Dick Wildung	T	Minnesota
3	Irv Comp	B	St. Benedict
5	Roy McKay	B	Texas
6	Nick Susseoff	E	Washington State
7	Ken Snelling	B	UCLA
8	Lester Gatewood	C	Baylor
9	Norm Verry	T	USC
10	Solon Barnett	G	Baylor
11	Bob Forte	B	Arkansas
12	Van Davis	E	Georgia
13	Tom Brock	C	Notre Dame
14	Ralph Tate	B	Oklahoma A&M
15	Don Carlson	T	Denver
16	Mike Welch	B	Minnesota
17	Ron Thomas	G	USC
18	James Powers	T	St. Mary's (CA)
19	Harold (Ace) Prescott	E	Hardin-Simmons
20	Ed Forrest	C	Santa Clara
21	Lloyd Wasserbach	T	Wisconsin
22	Mark Hoskins	B	Wisconsin
23	Earl Bennett	G	Hardin-Simmons
24	George Zellick	E	Oregon State
25	Gene Bierhaus	E	Minnesota
26	George Makris	G	Wisconsin
27	Pete Susick	B	Washington
28	Bud Hasse	E	Northwestern
29	Dick Thornally	T	Wisconsin
30	Bob Ray	B	Wisconsin
31	Brunnel Christensen	T	California
32	Ken Roskie	B	USC

1943 GREEN BAY PACKERS

FRONT ROW: (L-R) 72 Forrest McPherson, 24 Joe Laws, 42 Andy Uram, 43 Buckets Goldenberg, 21 Pete Tinsley, 18 Tony Falkenstein, 16 Lou Brock, 3 Tony Canadeo, 14 Don Hutson.
MIDDLE ROW: (L-R) Coach Curly Lambeau, 33 Glen Sorenson, 8 Bob Kahler, 48 Harry Jacunski, 27 Chet Adams, 44 Baby Ray, 75 Tiny Croft, 46 Sherwood Fries, 7 Joel Mason, 45 William Kuusisto, Assistant Coach Richard (Red) Smith.
BACK ROW: (L-R) Trainer Gust Seaburg, 23 Jim Lankas, 35 Bob Flowers, 50 Ade Schwammel, 22 Dick Evans, 47 Paul Berezney, 51 Irv Comp, 54 Larry Craig, 63 Ben Starret, 64 Ted Fritsch, Trainer Carl (Bud) Jorgensen.

Green Bay won its sixth and final championship under Curly Lambeau in 1944. But the manner in which they clinched the crown was anything but characteristic of a team at the top of its form.

The Packers were shut out twice in the same season for the first time in a decade. The Bears mauled them 21-0 in Week 7 and, two weeks later, the Giants followed suit 24-0. The losses were significant, considering Chicago and New York were the teams Green Bay would have to overcome—the Bears in the Western Conference standings, and should that happen, the Giants in the title game—if it wanted to win a sixth NFL championship.

Fortunately, Chicago started slowly (1-2-1) in part because of a 42-28 setback to Green Bay on Sept. 24. Even after being blanked five weeks later, the Packers (6-1) had a small cushion over the Bears (3-2-1). On the same day the Giants handed the Packers their second loss, Chicago absorbed its third and the stage was set for Green Bay to take revenge on the Giants in the title game on Dec. 17.

World War II continued to impact pro football. Hundreds of players were overseas and Green Bay had ties to at least 35 of them. One of the 35, Tony Canadeo, was granted a short leave and played in three games in midseason. Others such as Carl Mulleneaux, Herman Rohrig, and Russ Letlow wouldn't return until 1946. Still others, such as Ed Jankowski, never resumed their careers.

The league expanded from eight teams to 10. The Cleveland Rams returned and the Boston Yanks were added. The Eagles again were a separate franchise while the Steelers merged with the Cardinals for a year.

On paper, Green Bay appeared little better than average. Its running and passing game each ranked fourth, and its defense was fifth.

But the Packers still had Don Hutson, the NFL's top receiver and scorer. Hutson hauled in 58 passes and scored 85 points. No one else on the team caught even 10 passes.

Hutson again threatened retirement and didn't sign until Sept. 1. His teammate and Milwaukee restaurant owner, Buckets Goldenberg, waited a bit longer. The 11-year veteran missed the opener, but joined the team in time for the first meeting with the Bears in Week 2.

For the first time ever, Green Bay opened its season in Milwaukee. The city had become a great second home for the Packers, who were 18-4 there since 1933, including their season-opening, 14-7 win over the Tigers.

The Bears and Packers clashed on the final weekend in September. Chicago overcame a four-touchdown deficit to forge a 28-28 tie in the fourth quarter. But Lou Brock's 42-yard touchdown run and Ted Fritsch's 50-yard interception return for a score re-ignited the Packers, who escaped 42-28.

A goal-line stand spurred Green Bay on in Week 3. Down 6-0 to the Lions, the Packers struck back for 27 unanswered points after turning back Detroit on three straight plays from the 1-yard line.

A week later, Green Bay cast aside Card-Pitt 34-7. Irv Comp enjoyed one of his best days passing, completing 13 of 20 passes for 220 yards. His favorite target, Hutson, finished with 11 receptions for 207 yards and two scores.

Canadeo returned for a three-game stint in Week 5. The Army corporal came to play, picking up 107 yards. He also threw four passes and punted twice in a 30-21 victory over the Rams that pushed the Packers' record to 5-0.

Green Bay notched its sixth win by downing Detroit 14-0. A short plunge by Fritsch and a pass from Comp to Joe Laws accounted for the game's only touchdowns.

The Packers absorbed their first loss on Nov. 5. The Bears held them to a season-low 146 yards. Comp threw four interceptions and Green Bay fell 21-0.

Seven interceptions—three by Ted Fritsch—helped the Pack get back on track in Week 8. Laws scored twice on the ground and Hutson twice through the air as Green Bay dominated the Rams 42-7.

In Week 9, the Giants piled up 221 yards rushing in a 24-0 win. Former Packer Arnie Herber completed just one pass, a 36-yard scoring strike to Frank Liebel.

Green Bay then beat Card-Pitt 35-20 to clinch the Western Division title.

PENALTIES AND MISDEMEANORS

The season opener between the Packers and Brooklyn Tigers was the most penalty-filled game in NFL history.

Brooklyn was flagged 22 times and the Packers were whistled for 11 infractions. The 33 combined penalties remains an NFL record.

Referee Tom Dowd and his crew cited both teams for a wide range of violations, from being offside to holding to illegal use of hands to unsportsmanlike conduct.

Green Bay won 14-7. Surprisingly, perhaps, only two penalties occurred on the three touchdown drives. It was a blocked punt—not a rules violation—that set up Lou Brock's game-winning run.

Below is a list of the most penalty-filled games in Packers history:

Pen.	Teams	Date
33	Green Bay (11), Tigers (22)	9-17-44
28	Green Bay (11), Seahawks (17)	10-21-84
27	Green Bay (17), Yanks (10)	10-21-45
26	Green Bay (13), Raiders (13)	10-24-76

TEAM STATISTICS

	GB	OPP
First Downs	147	114
Rushing	70	56
Passing	63	49
Penalty	14	9
Rushes	395	357
Yards Gained	1,517	1,130
Average Gain	3.84	3.17
Average Yards per Game	151.7	113.0
Passes Attempted	253	227
Completed	105	89
% Completed	41.50	39.21
Total Yards Gained	1,471	1,229
Yards Gained per Completion	14.01	13.81
Average Yards per Game	147.1	122.9
Laterals Attempted	3	8
Completed	3	6
Yards Gained	36	58
Combined Yards Gained	3,024	2,417
Total Plays	651	592
Average Yards per Play	4.65	4.08
Average Yards per Game	302.4	241.7
Intercepted By	29	24
Yards Returned	454	344
Returned for TD	3	1
Punts	48	56
Yards Punted	1,774	2,083
Average Yards per Punt	36.96	37.20
Punt Returns	27	18
Yards Returned	241	192
Average Yards per Return	8.93	10.67
Returned for TD	0	0
Kickoff Returns	30	35
Yards Returned	610	828
Average Yards per Return	20.33	23.66
Returned for TD	0	0
Penalties	62	88
Yards Penalized	558	700
Fumbles	11	25
Lost	7	12
Own Recovered for Touchdown	0	0
Opponent's Recovered by	12	7
Opponent's Recovered for Touchdown	0	0
Total Points Scored	238	141
Total Touchdowns	34	20
Touchdowns Rushing	16	9
Touchdowns Passing	15	11
Touchdowns on Returns & Recoveries	3	1
Extra Points	32	18
Safeties	1	0
Field Goals Attempted	5	2
Field Goals Made	0	1
% Successful	.00.00	50.00

Regular Season   8-2-0

Date	GB		OPP	Att.
9/17	14	Brooklyn Tigers (M)	7	(12,994)
9/24	42	Chicago Bears	28	(24,362)
10/1	27	Detroit Lions (M)	6	(18,556)
10/8	34	Card-Pitt Carpets	7	(16,535)
10/22	30	Cleveland Rams	21	(18,780)
10/29	14	at Detroit Lions	0	(30,844)
11/5	0	at Chicago Bears	21	(45,553)
11/12	42	at Cleveland Rams	7	(17,166)
11/19	0	at New York Giants	24	(56,481)
11/26	35	at Card-Pitt Carpets	20	(7,158)

Postseason   1-0-0

12/17	14	at New York Giants	7	(46,016)

Score By Periods

	1	2	3	4	Total
Packers	56	77	41	64	238
Opponents	34	27	38	42	141

INDIVIDUAL STATISTICS

Rushing

	Att	Yds	Avg	LG	TD
Fritsch	94	322	3.4	18	4
Perkins	58	207	3.6	26	0
L. Brock	36	200	5.6	t42	3
Laws	45	200	4.4	20	3
Duhart	51	183	3.6	16	2
Canadeo	31	149	4.8	34	0
Comp	52	134	2.6	28	2
Hutson	12	87	7.3	27	0
Starret	10	21	2.1	8	2
McKay	5	12	2.4	11	0
Urban	1	2	2.0	2	0
Packers	395	1,517	3.8	t42	16
Opponents	357	1,130	3.2	t75	8

Receiving

	No	Yds	Avg	LG	TD
Hutson	58	866	14.9	t55	9
Duhart	9	176	19.6	32	2
Jacunski	9	151	16.8	48	0
Laws	7	61	8.7	t29	1
Wehba	6	67	11.2	17	0
L. Brock	4	74	18.5	t52	2
Fritsch	3	5	1.7	13	0
Craig	2	17	8.5	9	0
Comp	2	16	8.0	t11	1
Canadeo	1	12	12.0	12	0
Urban	1	10	10.0	10	0
J. Mason	1	9	9.0	9	0
Starret	1	6	6.0	6	0
Perkins	1	1	1.0	1	0
Packers	105	1,471	14.0	t55	15
Opponents	89	1,229	13.8	t72	11

Passing

	Att	Com	Yds	Pct	TD	In	Rate
Comp	177	80	1,159	45.2	12	21	50.0
L. Brock	21	5	94	23.8	2	0	77.5
Canadeo	20	9	89	45.0	0	0	58.1
McKay	14	6	72	42.9	1	2	43.5
Duhart	13	4	42	30.8	0	0	41.2
Laws	4	1	15	25.0	0	1	—
Hutson	3	0	0	00.0	0	0	—
Bilda	1	0	0	00.0	0	0	—
Packers	253	105	1,471	41.5	15	24	41.1
Opponents	227	89	1,229	39.2	11	29	33.9

Punting

	No	Yds	Avg	LG	HB
L. Brock	14	494	35.3	50	0
Canadeo	13	479	36.8	46	0
Fritsch	10	408	40.8	54	0
McKay	8	297	37.1	55	0
Starret	2	65	32.5	43	0
Perkins	1	31	31.0	31	0
Packers	48	1,774	37.0	55	0
Opponents	56	2,083	37.2	73	0

Kickoff Returns

	No	Yds	Avg	LG	TD
Fritsch	11	288	26.2	44	0
Laws	8	132	16.5	25	0
L. Brock	2	41	20.5	21	0
Comp	2	35	17.5	18	0
Perkins	2	34	17.0	18	0
Urban	1	20	20.0	20	0
Duhart	1	18	18.0	18	0
Craig	1	17	17.0	17	0
Starret	1	13	13.0	13	0
Canadeo	1	12	12.0	12	0
Packers	30	610	20.3	44	0
Opponents	35	828	23.7	44	0

Punt Returns

	No	Yds	Avg	LG	TD
Laws	15	118	7.9	23	0
L. Brock	4	36	9.0	22	0
Duhart	3	32	10.7	18	0
Comp	2	32	16.0	18	0
McKay	2	19	9.5	17	0
Canadeo	1	4	4.0	4	0
Packers	27	241	8.9	23	0
Opponents	18	192	10.7	20	0

Interceptions

	No	Yds	Avg	LG	TD
Fritsch	6	115	19.2	t50	1
Comp	6	54	9.0	43	0
Hutson	4	50	12.5	43	0
Duhart	4	23	5.8	14	0
Laws	3	36	12.0	16	0
Perkins	2	123	61.5	t83	2
Bilda	1	25	25.0	25	0
Craig	1	20	20.0	20	0
Wehba	1	7	7.0	7	0
C. Brock	1	1	1.0	1	0
Packers	29	454	15.7	t83	3
Opponents	24	344	14.3	48	1

Scoring

	TDr	TDp	TDrt	PAT	FG	S	TP
Hutson	0	9	0	31/33	0/3	0	85*
L. Brock	3	2	0	0/0	0/0	0	30
Fritsch	4	0	1	0/0	0/0	0	30
Duhart	2	2	0	0/0	0/0	0	24
Laws	3	1	0	0/0	0/0	0	24
Comp	2	1	0	0/0	0/0	0	18
Perkins	0	0	2	0/0	0/0	0	12
Starret	2	0	0	0/0	0/0	0	12
team	0	0	0	0/0	0/0	1	2
Sorenson	0	0	0	1/1	0/2	0	1
Packers	16	15	3	32/34	0/5	1	238
Opponents	8	11	1	18/20	1/2	0	141

NFL STANDINGS

Western Division

	W	L	T	Pct	PF	PA
Green Bay Packers	8	2	0	.800	238	141
Chicago Bears	6	3	1	.667	258	172
Detroit Lions	6	3	1	.667	216	151
Cleveland Rams	4	6	0	.400	188	224
Card-Pitt Carpets	0	10	0	.000	108	328

Eastern Division

	W	L	T	Pct	PF	PA
New York Giants	8	1	1	.889	206	75
Philadelphia Eagles	7	1	2	.875	267	131
Washington Redskins	6	3	1	.667	169	180
Boston Yanks	2	8	0	.200	82	233
Brooklyn Tigers	0	10	0	.000	69	166

ROSTER

No	Name	Pos	Ht	Wt	DOB	College	G
47	Berezney, Paul	T	6-2	220	09/25/16	Fordham	10
22	Bilda, Dick	HB	6-1	200	05/17/19	Marquette	
29	Brock, Charley	C	6-1	210	03/15/16	Nebraska	10
16	Brock, Lou	HB	6-0	195	12/09/17	Purdue	5
19	Bucchianeri, Amadeo (Mike)	G	5-10	215	09/01/17	Indiana	8
3	Canadeo, Tony	HB	6-0	195	05/05/19	Gonzaga	3
51	Comp, Irv	HB	6-3	192	05/17/19	St. Benedict	10
54	Craig, Larry	E	6-0	208	06/27/16	South Carolina	10
75	Croft, Milburn (Tiny)	T	6-4	298	11/07/20	Ripon	10
42	Duhart, Paul	HB	6-0	180	12/30/20	Florida	8
35	Flowers, Bob	C	6-1	215	08/06/17	Texas Tech	10
64	Fritsch, Ted	FB	5-10	205	10/31/20	Stevens Point	9
43	Goldenberg, Charles (Buckets)	G	5-10	220	03/10/11	Wisconsin	9
14	Hutson, Don	E	6-1	180	01/31/13	Alabama	10
48	Jacunski, Harry	E	6-2	198	10/20/15	Fordham	9
8	Kahler, Bob	HB	6-3	200	02/13/17	Nebraska	
18	Kercher, Bob	E	6-2	195	01/14/19	Georgetown	
45	Kuusisto, William	G	6-0	230	04/26/18	Minnesota	10
24	Laws, Joe	HB	5-9	188	06/16/11	Iowa	10
7	Mason, Joel	E	6-0	200	03/12/13	Western Michigan	10
3	McKay, Roy	HB	6-0	195	02/02/20	Texas	3
72	McPherson, Forrest	C	5-11	248	10/22/11	Nebraska	
23	Perkins, Don	FB	6-0	195	09/18/17	Platteville	10
44	Ray, Buford (Baby)	T	6-6	250	09/30/15	Vanderbilt	9
58	Schwammel, Ade	T	6-2	215	10/14/08	Oregon State	9
33	Sorenson, Glen	G	6-0	225	02/29/20	Utah State	10
63	Starret, Ben	B	5-11	215	11/19/17	St. Mary's (CA)	
21	Tinsley, Pete	G	5-8	200	03/16/13	Georgia	10
46	Tollefson, Charles	G	6-0	218	02/28/16	Iowa	7
18	Urban, Alex	E	6-2	200	07/16/17	South Carolina	3
17	Wehba, Ray	E	6-0	210	08/16/16	USC	10

DRAFT

Rnd	Name	Pos	College	Rnd	Name	Pos	College
1	Merv Pregulman	G	Michigan	18	Hugh Cox	B	North Carolina
3	Tom Kuzma	B	Michigan	19	Kermit Davis	E	Mississippi State
5	Bill McPartland	T	St. Mary's (CA)	20	Bob Johnson	C	Purdue
6	Mickey McCardle	B	USC	21	Jim Cox	T	Stanford
7	Jack Tracy	E	Washington	22	Cliff Anderson	E	Minnesota
8	Alex Agase	G	Illinois	23	John Perry	B	Duke
9	Don Whitmire	T	Alabama	24	Pete DeMaria	G	Purdue
10	Bob Koch	B	Oregon	25	Len Liss	T	Marquette
11	Virgil Johnson	E	Arkansas	26	Ray Jordan	B	North Carolina
12	Roy Giusti	B	St. Mary's (CA)	27	Al Grubaugh	T	Nebraska
13	Bill Baughman	C	Alabama	28	O.B. Howard	E	Mississippi State
14	Don Griffin	B	Illinois	29	Paul Paladino	G	Arkansas
15	Bert Gissler	E	Nebraska	30	Bob Butchofsky	B	Texas A&M
16	Lou Shelton	B	Oregon State	31	Russ Deal	G	Indiana
17	Charles Cusick	G	Oregon	32	Abel Gonzales	B	SMU

1944 GREEN BAY PACKERS

FRONT ROW: (L-R) 43 Buckets Goldenberg, 42 Paul Duhart, 63 Ben Starret, 21 Pete Tinsley, 72 Forrest McPherson, 54 Larry Craig, 29 Charley Brock, 16 Lou Brock, 3 Roy McKay, 24 Joe Laws.
MIDDLE ROW: (L-R) Trainer Carl (Bud) Jorgensen, 45 William Kuusisto, 17 Ray Wehba, 33 Glen Sorenson, 35 Bob Flowers, 48 Harry Jacunski, 64 Ted Fritsch, 23 Don Perkins, 46 Charles Tollefson, 7 Joel Mason, Trainer Gust Seaburg.
BACK ROW: (L-R) Coach Curly Lambeau, 14 Don Hutson, 47 Paul Berezney, 58 Ade Schwammel, 51 Irv Comp, 75 Tiny Croft, 18 Bob Kercher, 8 Bob Kahler, 44 Baby Ray, Mike Bucchianeri, Assistant Coach George (Brute) Trafton.

An era ended in 1945 when the last three players to have contributed to each of the Packers' three championships earned under the playoff system took to the field for the last time. Don Hutson, Joe Laws, and Buckets Goldenberg—with 36 total years of experience—played their final downs as autumn turned to winter.

Goldenberg was the first to depart. The 13-year guard, who had entered the league as a fullback, called it a career on Nov. 14 after sustaining a foot injury against the Bears 10 days earlier.

Laws waited until season's end before announcing his decision. The versatile, 12-year veteran played running back longer than any other in Packers history.

With Hutson, it wasn't so easy. Having reneged on retirement a number of times, the NFL's all-time leading receiver didn't officially retire in the minds of Packers' fans until he failed to suit up for the 1946 season opener.

Unfortunately for the trio, a championship sendoff was not in the cards. The Packers (6-4) finished third for the first time since 1934, behind Cleveland (9-1) and Detroit (7-3). Three of the team's four losses came at the expense of those two clubs.

Even with Hutson in uniform in 1945, the Packers' passing game slipped in touchdown production as it had every year since 1942. The 1942 team threw 28 touchdown passes; the 1945 club managed just half that total.

The running game was far from spectacular. Ted Fritsch led the way with 282 yards. The club sorely missed Tony Canadeo, who spent the entire season in the Army.

Green Bay remained in the running for the Western Division title throughout the first half of the season. A 33-14 win over the Cardinals on Oct. 28 drew them into a first-place tie with the Bears (4-1) and Lions (4-1).

But consecutive losses to the Bears and Rams on the first two weekends of November seriously damaged the Packers' chances. They were officially eliminated after the Rams carved up the Lions 28-21 on Thanksgiving.

The Packers opened their 25th season of professional football by playing turnover-free ball against the Bears. Fritsch (two scores), Roy McKay, and Don Perkins combined for four touchdowns rushing in a 31-21 victory.

A week later, Green Bay registered its highest single-game point total ever. Hutson and McKay worked some second-quarter magic, hooking up six times for 144 yards and four touchdowns, to stun the Lions 57-21.

A fourth-quarter meltdown cost the Packers their first game. The Rams scored 21 points in the final 15 minutes to slide past Green Bay 27-14 and into sole possession of first place in the West.

The Packers took out their frustrations a week later on the Boston Yanks. Green Bay amassed a season-high 456 yards,

with 277 coming on the ground, in the 38-14 win.

Hutson's final 100-yard receiving effort—seven catches for 141 yards and two touchdowns—was too much for the Cardinals in Week 5. The 33-14 loss had Chicago coach Phil Handler remarking: "It was just too much Hutson, that's about all I can say."

After catching eight touchdown passes in the first five games, Hutson caught just one touchdown pass in the second half of the season. No wonder the team lost three times in the final five weeks.

In Week 6, the Bears handed the Packers their second loss 28-24.

A week later, the Rams engineered their first-ever sweep of the Packers by turning in some big plays in a 20-7 win in League Park. Fred Gehrke counted first on runs of 72 and 42 yards before Jim Benton capped a wild first quarter with an 84-yard touchdown reception from Bob Waterfield. Neither team scored in the final 45 minutes.

Green Bay notched its fifth win with a 28-0 shutout of the Yanks. Hutson caught the last touchdown pass of his career—a 14-yarder from Comp—in the second quarter.

Charley Brock set up two short touchdown runs by Fritsch with an interception and a fumble recovery as the Packers beat the Giants 23-14 in the Polo Grounds.

The Lions exacted a measure of revenge on the final weekend of the season when they dropped the Packers 14-3. Hutson caught four passes for 40 yards and Laws ran twice for 20 yards in their last game in the NFL.

LIGHTNING IN A BOTTLE

On Oct. 7 in Milwaukee, lightning in the form of Don Hutson struck not once, but four times, precipitating a shower of points never seen before or since in the NFL.

Hutson dazzled by scoring a league-record 29 points in the second quarter of Green Bay's 57-21 rout of the Lions. The incomparable veteran caught four touchdown passes (all from Roy McKay) and kicked five extra points in a 41-point, second-quarter explosion by Green Bay.

The end finished the afternoon with 31 points.

Hutson had a knack for scoring. From 1935 to 1945 he caught 99 touchdown passes, six more than all other Packers receivers over that span combined.

Listed below are the best single-quarter scoring outputs by an individual in Green Bay's history:

Points	Name	Date
29	Don Hutson	10-7-45
18	Wuert Engelmann	10-25-31
18	Hal Van Every	11-23-41
17	Paul Hornung	11-26-59
16	Paul Hornung	11-12-61

TEAM STATISTICS

	GB	OPP
First Downs	131	137
Rushing	73	65
Passing	44	57
Penalty	14	15
Rushes	377	388
Yards Gained	1,325	1,349
Average Gain	3.51	3.48
Average Yards per Game	132.5	134.9
Passes Attempted	218	231
Completed	81	111
% Completed	37.16	48.05
Total Yards Gained	1,536	1,708
Yards Gained per Completion	18.96	15.39
Average Yards per Game	153.6	170.8
Laterals Attempted	1	9
Completed	1	9
Yards Gained	8	59
Combined Yards Gained	2,869	3,116
Total Plays	596	628
Average Yards per Play	4.81	4.96
Average Yards per Game	286.9	311.6
Intercepted By	24	24
Yards Returned	464	376
Returned for TD	5	0
Punts	46	59
Yards Punted	1,839	2,210
Average Yards per Punt	39.98	37.46
Punt Returns	35	25
Yards Returned	317	284
Average Yards per Return	9.06	11.36
Returned for TD	0	0
Kickoff Returns	33	39
Yards Returned	670	737
Average Yards per Return	20.30	18.90
Returned for TD	0	0
Penalties	69	68
Yards Penalized	723	701
Fumbles	21	31
Lost	8	17
Own Recovered for Touchdown	0	0
Opponent's Recovered by	17	8
Opponent's Recovered for Touchdown	1	0
Total Points Scored	258	173
Total Touchdowns	35	25
Touchdowns Rushing	15	16
Touchdowns Passing	14	9
Touchdowns on Returns & Recoveries	6	0
Extra Points	31	23
Safeties	1	0
Field Goals Attempted	13	2
Field Goals Made	5	0
% Successful	38.46	00.00

Regular Season   6-4-0

Date	GB		OPP	Att.
9/30	31	Chicago Bears	21	(24,525)
10/7	57	Detroit Lions (M)	21	(23,500)
10/14	14	Cleveland Rams	27	(24,607)
10/21	38	Boston Yanks (M)	14	(20,846)
10/28	33	Chicago Cardinals	14	(19,122)
11/4	24	at Chicago Bears	28	(45,527)
11/11	7	at Cleveland Rams	20	(28,686)
11/18	28	at Boston Yanks	0	(33,748)
11/25	23	at New York Giants	14	(52,681)
12/2	3	at Detroit Lions	14	(23,468)

Score By Periods

	1	2	3	4	Total
Packers	52	116	56	34	258
Opponents	40	42	35	56	173

INDIVIDUAL STATISTICS

Rushing

	Att	Yds	Avg	LG	TD
Fritsch	88	282	3.2	31	7
McKay	71	231	3.3	41	2
L. Brock	46	196	4.3	28	3
Perkins	36	192	5.3	49	1
Bruce Smith	21	94	4.5	27	0
Laws	16	82	5.1	20	0
Comp	57	75	1.3	18	1
Hutson	8	60	7.5	18	1
Mosley	16	49	3.1	9	0
Starret	5	26	5.2	13	0
Goodnight	8	26	3.3	12	0
Snelling	3	10	3.3	8	0
Sample	2	2	1.0	3	0
Packers	**377**	**1,325**	**3.5**	**49**	**15**
Opponents	388	1,349	3.5	t72	16

Receiving

	No	Yds	Avg	LG	TD
Hutson	47	834	17.7	t75	9
Luhn	10	151	15.1	t44	1
Goodnight	7	283	40.4	t75	3
L. Brock	4	87	21.8	46	0
C. Mulleneaux	3	31	10.3	13	0
Fritsch	3	13	4.3	9	0
Laws	2	11	5.5	7	0
Perkins	2	11	5.5	10	0
Urban	1	55	55.0	55	0
Comp	1	50	50.0	t50	1
Mosley	1	10	10.0	10	0
Packers	**81**	**1,536**	**19.0**	**t75**	**14**
Opponents	111	1,708	15.4	t84	9

Passing

	Att	Com	Yds	Pct	TD	In	Rate
Comp	106	44	865	41.5	7	11	53.1
McKay	89	32	520	36.0	5	9	35.5
L. Brock	22	5	151	22.7	2	4	46.4
Mosley	1	0	0	00.0	0	0	—
Packers	**218**	**81**	**1,536**	**37.2**	**14**	**24**	**44.2**
Opponents	231	111	1,708	48.1	9	24	46.3

Punting

	No	Yds	Avg	LG	HB
McKay	44	1,814	41.2	73	0
Perkins	1	13	13.0	13	0
Keuper	1	12	12.0	12	0
Packers	**46**	**1,839**	**40.0**	**73**	**0**
Opponents	59	2,210	37.5	56	0

Kickoff Returns

	No	Yds	Avg	LG	TD
Fritsch	8	279	34.9	79	0
Comp	5	110	22.0	31	0
Laws	4	72	18.0	29	0
McKay	4	67	16.8	26	0
Hutson	4	37	9.3	12	0
Bruce Smith	2	46	23.0	26	0
J. Mason	1	15	15.0	15	0
L. Brock	1	12	12.0	12	0
Craig	1	11	11.0	11	0
Pannell	1	10	10.0	10	0
Goodnight	1	8	8.0	8	0
Starret	1	3	3.0	3	0
Packers	**33**	**670**	**20.3**	**79**	**0**
Opponents	39	737	18.9	36	0

Punt Returns

	No	Yds	Avg	LG	TD
Laws	12	78	6.5	21	0
McKay	7	66	9.4	17	0
Bruce Smith	6	67	11.2	20	0
L. Brock	4	37	9.3	18	0
Comp	4	36	9.0	15	0
J. Mason	1	20	20.0	20	0
Mosley	1	13	13.0	13	0
Packers	**35**	**317**	**9.1**	**21**	**0**
Opponents	25	284	11.4	32	0

Interceptions

	No	Yds	Avg	LG	TD
C. Brock	4	122	30.5	38	2
Hutson	4	15	3.8	15	0
Laws	3	60	20.0	35	0
L. Brock	3	33	11.0	33	0
McKay	3	33	11.0	18	0
Comp	2	67	33.5	t54	1
Fritsch	1	69	69.0	t69	1
Starret	1	27	27.0	27	0
Mosley	1	20	20.0	20	0
Crimmins	1	12	12.0	t12	1
Tinsley	1	6	6.0	6	0
Packers	**24**	**464**	**19.3**	**t69**	**5**
Opponents	24	376	15.7	55	0

Scoring

	TDr	TDp	TDrt	PAT	FG	S	TP
Hutson	1	9	0	31/35	2/4	0	97
Fritsch	7	0	1	0/0	3/8	0	57
L. Brock	3	0	0	0/0	0/0	0	18
Comp	1	1	1	0/0	0/0	0	18
Goodnight	0	3	0	0/0	0/0	0	18
C. Brock	0	0	2	0/0	0/0	0	12
McKay	2	0	0	0/0	0/0	0	12
Craig	0	0	1	0/0	0/0	0	6
Crimmins	0	0	1	0/0	0/0	0	6
Luhn	0	1	0	0/0	0/0	0	6
Perkins	1	0	0	0/0	0/0	0	6
team	0	0	0	0/0	0/0	1	2
Sorenson	0	0	0	0/0	0/1	0	4
Packers	**15**	**14**	**6**	**31/35**	**5/13**	**1**	**258**
Opponents	16	9	0	23/25	0/2	0	173

Fumbles

	Fum	Ow	Op	Yds	Tot
Adkins	1	1	0	0	1
C. Brock	0	0	5	52	5
L. Brock	1	0	0	0	0
Comp	5	3	1	-1	4
Craig	0	0	2	18	2
Fritsch	2	1	1	0	2
Goodnight	1	1	0	8	1
Hutson	1	0	0	0	0
Keuper	0	0	1	0	1
Laws	2	1	0	2	1
Lipscomb	0	0	3	0	3
J. Mason	0	0	1	0	1
McKay	4	3	0	12	3
Perkins	1	0	0	15	1
Ray	0	0	1	0	1
Snelling	1	0	0	0	0
Bruce Smith	2	1	0	-2	1
Sorenson	0	0	1	0	1
Starret	1	1	0	0	1
Packers	**21**	**12**	**17**	**104**	**29**

NFL STANDINGS

Western Division

	W	L	T	Pct	PF	PA
Cleveland Rams	9	1	0	.900	244	136
Detroit Lions	7	3	0	.700	195	194
Green Bay Packers	**6**	**4**	**0**	**.600**	**258**	**173**
Chicago Bears	3	7	0	.300	192	235
Chicago Cardinals	1	9	0	.100	98	228

Eastern Division

	W	L	T	Pct	PF	PA
Washington Redskins	8	2	0	.800	209	121
Philadelphia Eagles	7	3	0	.700	272	133
New York Giants	3	6	1	.333	179	198
Boston Yanks	3	6	1	.333	123	211
Pittsburgh Steelers	2	8	0	.200	79	220

1945

ROSTER

No	Name	Pos	Ht	Wt	DOB	College	G
79	Adkins, Bob	B	6-0	220	02/07/17	Marshall	4
72	Barnett, Solon	T	6-1	235	03/30/21	Baylor	4
29	Brock, Charley	C	6-1	210	03/15/16	Nebraska	10
16	Brock, Lou	HB	6-0	195	12/09/17	Purdue	10
19	Bucchianeri, Amadeo (Mike)	G	5-10	210	09/01/17	Indiana	5
51	Comp, Irv	HB	6-3	192	05/17/19	St. Benedict	9
54	Craig, Larry	E	6-0	215	06/27/16	South Carolina	10
76	Crimmins, Bernard	G	5-11	195	04/14/19	Notre Dame	6
75	Croft, Milburn (Tiny)	T	6-4	285	11/07/20	Ripon	9
35	Flowers, Bob	C	6-1	210	08/06/17	Texas Tech	10
15	Frankowski, Ray	G	5-11	220	09/14/19	Washington	2
64	Fritsch, Ted	FB	5-10	210	10/31/20	Stevens Point	10
51	Frutig, Ed	E	6-1	185	08/19/20	Michigan	1
43	Goldenberg, Charles (Buckets)	G	5-10	220	03/10/11	Wisconsin	4
23	Goodnight, Clyde	E	6-1	195	03/03/24	Tulsa	10
14	Hutson, Don	E	6-1	180	01/31/13	Alabama	10
18	Keuper, Ken	HB	6-0	215	11/14/18	Georgia	9
45	Kuusisto, William	G	6-0	230	04/26/18	Minnesota	10
24	Laws, Joe	HB	5-9	185	06/16/11	Iowa	10
47	Lipscomb, Paul	T	6-5	230	01/13/23	Tennessee	10
38	Luhn, Nolan	E	6-3	200	07/27/21	Tulsa	9
7	Mason, Joel	E	6-0	200	03/12/13	Western Michigan	10
3	McKay, Roy	HB	6-0	195	02/02/20	Texas	10
72	McPherson, Forrest	C	5-11	240	10/22/11	Nebraska	5
8	Mosley, Russ	HB	5-10	170	07/22/18	Alabama	6
19	Mulleneaux, Carl (Moose)	E	6-4	210	04/01/17	Utah State	5
58	Neal, Ed	T	6-4	287	12/31/18	Tulane	9
22	Pannell, Ernie	T	6-3	220	02/02/17	Texas A&M	7
48	Perkins, Don	FB	6-0	198	09/18/17	Platteville	7
44	Ray, Buford (Baby)	T	6-6	256	09/30/15	Vanderbilt	10
38	Sample, Chuck	FB	5-9	210	01/05/20	Toledo	1
42	Smith, Bruce	HB	6-0	197	02/08/20	Minnesota	3
52	Snelling, Ken	FB	6-0	210	12/11/18	UCLA	2
33	Sorenson, Glen	G	6-0	210	02/29/20	Utah State	10
63	Starret, Ben	B	5-11	220	11/19/17	St. Mary's (CA)	8
21	Tinsley, Pete	G	5-8	205	03/16/13	Georgia	10
46	Tollefson, Charles	G	6-0	215	02/28/16	Iowa	9
79	Urban, Alex	E	6-2	210	07/16/17	South Carolina	1

DRAFT

Rnd	Name	Pos	College	Rnd	Name	Pos	College
1	Walt Schlinkman	B	Texas Tech	18	Frank Hazard	G	Nebraska
3	Clyde Goodnight	E	Tulsa	19	Ed Jeffers	T	Oklahoma State
5	Joseph Graham	E	Florida	20	William Prentice	B	Santa Clara
6	Don Wells	T	Georgia	21	Warren Fuller	E	Fordham
7	Casey Stephenson	B	Tennessee	22	Fred Neilsen	T	San Francisco
8	Wilder Collins	T	Tulsa	23	Robert Gilmore	B	Washington
9	Lamar Dingler	E	Arkansas	24	Lloyd Baxter	C	SMU
10	Harold Helscher	B	LSU	25	Nolan Luhn	E	Tulsa
11	Ralph Hammond	C	Pittsburgh	26	Nestor Blanco	G	Colorado Mines
12	Edward Podgorski	T	Lafayette	27	Bill Chestnut	B	Kansas
13	William Hackett	G	Ohio State	28	Jim Thompson	B	Washington State
14	Marvin Lindsey	B	Arkansas	29	John Evans	E	Idaho
15	Bob McClure	T	Nevada	30	Hamilton Nichols	G	Rice
16	Harry Pieper	C	California	31	John Friday	B	Ohio State
17	Robert Kula	B	Minnesota	32	Billy Joe Aldridge	B	Oklahoma State

FRONT ROW: (L-R) 14 Don Hutson, 42 Bruce Smith, 23 Clyde Goodnight, 17 Mike Bucchianeri, 8 Russ Mosley, 21 Pete Tinsley, 72 Forrest McPherson, 29 Charley Brock, 16 Lou Brock, 3 Roy McKay, 54 Larry Craig, 43 Buckets Goldenberg, 63 Ben Starret, 24 Joe Laws.

MIDDLE ROW: (L-R) Coach Curly Lambeau, 76 Bernie Crimmins, 35 Bob Flowers, 79 Bob Adkins, 19 Carl Mulleneaux, 58 Ed Neal, 75 Tiny Croft, 44 Baby Ray, 22 Ernie Pannell, 48 Don Perkins, 46 Charles Tollefson, 27 Solon Barnett, 7 Joel Mason, Assistant Coach Walt Kiesling.

BACK ROW: (L-R) Trainer Carl (Bud) Jorgensen, 33 Glen Sorenson, 52 Ken Snelling, 38 Nolan Luhn, Johnny (Blood) McNally, 47 Paul Lipscomb, 51 Irv Comp, 64 Ted Fritsch, 45 William Kuusisto, 18 Ken Keuper, 15 Ray Frankowski, Trainer John Proski.

This time, Don Hutson stayed on the sidelines. Hutson, perhaps the greatest receiver in NFL history, had been threatening to retire for years. But each time he reconsidered and was in the lineup in time for the start of the season.

Not so in 1946. When Green Bay entertained the Chicago Bears on Sept. 29, Hutson donned a coat, tie, and hat. Instead of hauling in passes, No. 14 settled into his role as the team's ends and backfield coach.

Without Hutson, the Packers passing attack sank to last in the league. Green Bay completed fewer passes for fewer yards and fewer first downs than any team in the NFL. The Rams' Jim Benton caught more passes for more yards and more scores than did the entire Packers team.

Irv Comp, Cliff Aberson and Tony Canadeo took turns throwing. None impressed, as the trio combined for a mere two touchdowns against 16 interceptions. Not once in 11 games did a Green Bay player break 100 yards passing.

As a result of its anemic passing game, Green Bay struggled to score. The Packers managed 148 points, eighth best among the 10 teams.

With half of its offense neutralized, the Packers emphasized the run as never before. The team led the league with 1,765 yards on a franchise-record 560 attempts. Canadeo, Ted Fritsch and Walt Schlinkman paved the way with 1,299 yards between them. Fritsch's nine rushing touchdowns was an NFL best.

Green Bay was fortunate to count Fritsch among its players in 1946. A rival league (the All-American Football Conference) lured established NFL stars to its ranks with the promise of big money. During the winter, Fritsch signed with the Cleveland Browns. Only after some maneuvering on the part of the Packers and the Los Angeles Rams did the veteran fullback return to Green Bay.

The Packers remained in the playoff hunt for the first half of the year. Not until a second unsuccessful meeting with the Bears did the team begin to fade as a contender.

Signs of a declining passing attack were evident in Green Bay's brutal, 30-7 season-opening loss to the Bears. The team completed only two passes, but that shortcoming took a back seat to the afternoon's rough play. Injured in the fray were Irv Comp (torn lip), Nolan Luhn (nose), and Herman Rohrig (cracked rib).

Those three recovered enough to play the following week against the Rams. Carl Mulleneaux did not. Bears center John Schiechl knocked Mulleneaux out with a vicious hit to the face during a punt return in the third quarter. For 10 minutes, the lanky end lay motionless on the field. The hit was so devastating, it ended Mulleneaux's playing career.

"I have nothing to say," said Curly Lambeau after the most lopsided opening day loss of his Packers career.

A week later, Green Bay came up short in a 21-17 last-second loss to the Rams.

The Packers rebounded against two teams it had never lost to. They beat the Eagles and Steelers 19-7 and 17-7, respectively.

In Week 5, Green Bay caught a break. At the same time the Packers defeated the Lions 10-7, the Bears lost to the Giants. That combination put Green Bay (3-2) in second place and set up a showdown for first place with the Bears in Chicago in Week 6.

The midseason matchup turned into a defensive battle. Green Bay gained only 125 yards and the Bears got 159. The Packers couldn't find the end zone until Fritsch rumbled in with 58 seconds left. Chicago held on for a 10-7 win.

In three of the four games that followed, Green Bay's running game hit full throttle. Against the Cardinals, the Packers piled up 220 yards. A week later, the team amassed 224 yards. After dropping the pace in a rematch with the Cardinals, Green Bay exploded for a season-high 301 yards on a team-record 64 rushing attempts in a 20-7 dismantling of the Washington Redskins.

In Week 9, the Bears eliminated the Packers from the Western Conference race. Chicago clinched first place for good with a 42-6 pounding of the Lions.

In the season's final week, the Packers (6-4) headed into Los Angeles (5-4-1) seeking to clinch second place. But Lambeau's team couldn't contain Bob Waterfield, who threw for three touchdowns. The 38-17 loss dropped the Packers into a third-place tie with the Cardinals. Not until 1960 would the team finish any higher in the standings.

CARRYING THE SCORING LOAD

Paul Hornung scored an NFL record 176 points in 1960, but no Packer ever accounted for a greater percentage of his team's scoring than did Ted Fritsch in 1946.

Fritsch scored 100 of Green Bay's 148 points (67.6 percent). He kicked nine field goals, booted 13 extra points, recorded an NFL-best 10 touchdowns, and led the league in scoring. He scored in every game but the season-opener.

Inexplicably, Curly Lambeau turned over much of the kicking game to Ward Cuff in 1947. Fritsch, though, continued in that capacity to some extent throughout the remainder of his career. He retired in 1950 with more points (380) at that time than any Packer except Don Hutson.

Listed below are the Packers who accounted for the greatest percentage of the team's scoring in a single year:

Pct.	Name	Year
67.57	Ted Fritsch (100 of 148)	1946
53.01	Paul Hornung (176 of 332)	1960
46.00	Don Hutson (138 of 300)	1942
45.00	Verne Lewellen (54 of 120)	1928

TEAM STATISTICS

	GB	OPP
First Downs	160	158
Rushing	112	84
Passing	34	59
Penalty	14	15
Rushes	560	367
Yards Gained	1,765	1,372
Average Gain	3.15	3.74
Average Yards per Game	160.5	124.7
Passes Attempted	178	214
Completed	54	94
% Completed	30.34	43.93
Total Yards Gained	841	1,288
Yards Gained per Completion	15.57	13.70
Average Yards per Game	76.5	117.1
Laterals Attempted	3	7
Completed	3	5
Yards Gained	12	1
Combined Yards Gained	2,618	2,661
Total Plays	741	588
Average Yards per Play	3.53	4.53
Average Yards per Game	238.0	241.9
Intercepted By	24	18
Yards Returned	399	275
Returned for TD	0	1
Punts	65	60
Yards Punted	2,787	2,513
Average Yards per Punt	42.88	41.88
Punt Returns	28	35
Yards Returned	284	414
Average Yards per Return	10.14	11.83
Returned for TD	0	0
Kickoff Returns	34	28
Yards Returned	740	683
Average Yards per Return	21.76	24.39
Returned for TD	0	0
Penalties	82	76
Yards Penalized	693	628
Fumbles	24	45
Lost	11	28
Own Recovered for Touchdown	0	0
Opponent's Recovered by	28	11
Opponent's Recovered for Touchdown	0	2
Total Points Scored	148	158
Total Touchdowns	17	21
Touchdowns Rushing	13	12
Touchdowns Passing	4	6
Touchdowns on Returns & Recoveries	0	3
Extra Points	15	20
Safeties	2	0
Field Goals Attempted	17	7
Field Goals Made	9	4
% Successful	52.94	57.14

Regular Season 6-5-0

Date	GB		OPP	Att.
9/29	7	Chicago Bears	30	(25,049)
10/6	17	Los Angeles Rams (M)	21	(27,049)
10/13	19	at Philadelphia Eagles	7	(36,127)
10/20	17	Pittsburgh Steelers	7	(22,588)
10/27	10	Detroit Lions (M)	7	(23,564)
11/3	7	at Chicago Bears	10	(46,321)
11/10	19	at Chicago Cardinals	7	(30,681)
11/17	9	at Detroit Lions	0	(22,950)
11/24	6	Chicago Cardinals	24	(16,150)
12/1	20	at Washington Redskins	7	(33,691)
12/8	17	at Los Angeles Rams	38	(46,838)

Score By Periods

	1	2	3	4	Total
Packers	13	47	33	55	148
Opponents	24	38	45	51	158

INDIVIDUAL STATISTICS

Rushing

	Att	Yds	Avg	LG	TD
Canadeo	122	476	3.9	27	0
Fritsch	128	444	3.5	32	9
Schlinkman	97	379	3.9	44	2
Aberson	48	161	3.4	13	0
Bruce Smith	22	119	5.4	36	0
B. Forte	17	73	4.3	20	0
Comp	61	62	1.0	29	1
Nussbaumer	29	43	1.5	16	0
McKay	21	34	1.6	9	1
Craig	1	-3	-3.0	-3	0
Rohrig	14	-23	-1.6	15	0
Packers	560	1,765	3.2	44	13
Opponents	367	1,372	3.7	t61	12

Receiving

	No	Yds	Avg	LG	TD
Goodnight	16	308	19.8	t51	1
Luhn	16	224	14.0	36	2
Nussbaumer	10	143	14.3	35	0
D. Wells	2	74	37.0	65	0
Rohrig	2	36	18.0	21	0
Canadeo	2	25	12.5	15	0
Fritsch	2	13	6.5	t12	1
B. Forte	2	5	2.5	4	0
Prescott	1	8	8.0	8	0
Schlinkman	1	5	5.0	5	0
Packers	54	841	15.6	65	4
Opponents	94	1,288	13.7	54	6

Passing

	Att	Com	Yds	Pct	TD	In	Rate
Comp	94	27	333	28.7	1	8	9.9
Aberson	41	14	184	34.1	0	5	9.7
Canadeo	27	7	189	25.9	1	3	29.0
Rohrig	8	2	97	25.0	1	1	—
B. Forte	7	3	28	42.9	1	1	—
Nussbaumer	1	1	10	100.0	0	0	—
Packers	178	54	841	30.3	4	18	15.0
Opponents	214	94	1,288	43.9	6	24	33.5

Punting

	No	Yds	Avg	LG	HB
McKay	64	2,735	42.7	64	1
Fritsch	1	52	52.0	52	0
Packers	65	2,787	42.9	64	1
Opponents	60	2,513	41.9	69	0

Kickoff Returns

	No	Yds	Avg	LG	TD
Canadeo	6	163	27.2	38	0
Nussbaumer	6	148	24.7	44	0
Rohrig	5	106	21.2	27	0
Aberson	3	69	23.0	26	0
Fritsch	3	68	22.7	37	0
Schlinkman	2	43	21.5	23	0
McKay	2	41	20.5	22	0
Luhn	2	28	14.0	17	0
Craig	2	18	9.0	11	0
Comp	1	29	29.0	29	0
Bruce Smith	1	21	21.0	21	0
Keuper	1	6	6.0	6	0
Packers	34	740	21.8	44	0
Opponents	28	683	24.4	51	0

Punt Returns

	No	Yds	Avg	LG	TD
Nussbaumer	12	98	8.2	21	0
Rohrig	8	98	12.3	18	0
Canadeo	6	76	12.7	22	0
Bruce Smith	2	12	6.0	8	0
Packers	28	284	10.1	22	0
Opponents	35	414	11.8	70	0

Interceptions

	No	Yds	Avg	LG	TD
Rohrig	5	134	26.8	51	0
Aberson	3	53	17.7	33	0
Nussbaumer	3	31	10.3	16	0
Keuper	3	22	7.3	10	0
Comp	2	38	19.0	21	0
B. Forte	2	23	11.5	16	0
Canadeo	1	23	23.0	23	0
McKay	1	20	20.0	20	0
Mosley	1	20	20.0	20	0
Mitchell	1	18	18.0	18	0
Fritsch	1	15	15.0	15	0
Ray	1	2	2.0	2	0
Packers	24	399	16.6	51	0
Opponents	18	275	15.3	t85	1

Scoring

	TDr	TDp	TDrt	PAT	FG	S	TP
Fritsch	9	1	0	13/15	9/17	0	100
Luhn	0	2	0	0/0	0/0	0	12
Schlinkman	2	0	0	0/0	0/0	0	12
McKay	1	0	0	2/2	0/0	0	8
Comp	1	0	0	0/0	0/0	0	6
Goodnight	0	1	0	0/0	0/0	0	6
Odson	0	0	0	0/0	0/0	1	2
team	0	0	0	0/0	0/0	1	2
Packers	13	4	0	15/17	9/17	2	148
Opponents	12	6	3	20/21	4/7	0	158

Fumbles

	Fum	Ow	Op	Yds	Tot
Aberson	2	0	1	0	1
C. Brock	0	1	5	31	6
Canadeo	3	0	0	0	0
Comp	6	4	0	0	4
Craig	0	2	4	3	6
Croft	0	0	3	16	3
B. Forte	1	0	0	0	1
Fritsch	3	3	0	-9	3
Keuper	0	0	1	0	1
Lipscomb	0	0	5	0	5
Luhn	1	0	0	0	1
McKay	2	1	0	-2	1
Nussbaumer	1	1	0	0	1
Odson	0	0	1	0	1
Ray	0	0	2	0	2
Rohrig	2	0	0	0	1
Schlinkman	2	1	0	0	1
Bruce Smith	1	0	0	0	1
D. Wells	0	0	3	47	3
Wildung	0	0	1	0	1
Packers	24	13	28	86	41

NFL STANDINGS

Western Division

	W	L	T	Pct	PF	PA
Chicago Bears	8	2	1	800	289	193
Los Angeles Rams	6	4	1	600	277	257
Green Bay Packers	6	5	0	545	148	158
Chicago Cardinals	6	5	0	545	260	198
Detroit Lions	1	10	0	091	142	310

Eastern Division

	W	L	T	Pct	PF	PA
New York Giants	7	3	1	700	236	162
Philadelphia Eagles	6	5	0	545	231	220
Washington Redskins	5	5	1	500	171	191
Pittsburgh Steelers	5	5	1	500	136	117
Boston Yanks	2	8	1	200	189	273

ROSTER

No	Name	Pos	Ht	Wt	DOB	College	G
78	Aberson, Cliff	HB	6-1	195	08/28/21	No college	10
72	Barnett, Solon	T	6-1	235	03/30/21	Baylor	1
15	Bennett, Earl	G	5-8	190	02/27/20	Hardin-Simmons	3
29	Brock, Charley	C	6-1	210	03/15/16	Nebraska	11
3	Canadeo, Tony	HB	6-0	190	05/05/19	Gonzaga	11
51	Comp, Irv	HB	6-3	205	05/17/19	St. Benedict	11
54	Craig, Larry	E	6-0	218	06/27/16	South Carolina	11
75	Croft, Milburn (Tiny)	T	6-4	285	11/07/20	Ripon	11
35	Flowers, Bob	C	6-1	210	08/06/17	Texas Tech	10
8	Forte, Bob	HB	6-0	195	07/15/22	Arkansas	9
64	Fritsch, Ted	FB	5-10	210	10/31/20	Stevens Point	11
33	Gatewood, Lester	C	6-2	195	05/30/21	Baylor	11
23	Goodnight, Clyde	E	6-1	195	03/03/24	Tulsa	8
18	Keuper, Ken	HB	6-0	205	11/14/18	Georgia	10
52	Kuusisto, William	G	6-0	225	04/26/18	Minnesota	4
40	Lee, Bill	T	6-3	225	10/19/11	Alabama	4
46	Letlow, Russ	G	6-0	218	10/05/13	San Francisco	5
47	Lipscomb, Paul	T	6-5	240	01/13/23	Tennessee	11
38	Luhn, Nolan	E	6-3	200	07/27/21	Tulsa	11
3	McKay, Roy	HB	6-0	195	02/02/20	Texas	11
76	Miller, Tom	E	6-2	208	05/23/18	Hampden-Sydney	9
16	Mitchell, Charles	HB	6-0	190	12/28/20	Tulsa	2
8	Mosley, Russ	HB	5-10	170	07/22/18	Alabama	2
19	Mulleneaux, Carl (Moose)	E	6-4	210	04/01/17	Utah State	1
58	Neal, Ed	T	6-4	290	12/31/18	Tulane	10
48	Nussbaumer, Bob	HB	5-11	175	04/23/24	Michigan	10
63	Odson, Urban	T	6-3	255	11/17/18	Minnesota	6
17	Pregulman, Merv	G	6-3	215	10/10/22	Michigan	11
31	Prescott, Harold (Ace)	E	6-2	210	10/18/20	Hardin-Simmons	2
44	Ray, Buford (Baby)	T	6-6	250	09/30/15	Vanderbilt	11
19	Riddick, Ray	E	6-0	220	10/17/17	Fordham	2
80	Rohrig, Herman	HB	5-9	190	03/19/18	Nebraska	8
7	Schlinkman, Walt	FB	5-9	190	05/02/22	Texas Tech	11
42	Smith, Bruce	HB	6-0	197	02/08/20	Minnesota	6
21	Sparlis, Al	G	5-11	185	05/20/20	UCLA	3
27	Tollefson, Charles	G	6-0	215	02/28/16	Iowa	2
43	Wells, Don	E	6-2	200	07/12/22	Georgia	11
45	Wildung, Dick	G	6-0	220	08/16/21	Minnesota	11
25	Zupek, Al	B	6-1	205	01/12/23	Lawrence	3

DRAFT

Rnd	Name	Pos	College	Rnd	Name	Pos	College
1	Johnny Strzykalski	B	Marquette	18	Boyd Morse	E	Arizona
3	Bob Nussbaumer	B	Michigan	19	Joe Bradford	C	USC
5	Ed Cody	B	Purdue	20	Bill DeRosa	B	Boston College
6	John Ferraro	T	USC	21	Ralph Grant	B	Bucknell
7	Art Renner	E	Michigan	22	Howard Brown	G	Indiana
8	Bert Cole	T	Oklahoma State	23	Andy Kosmac	C	LSU
9	Grant Darnell	G	Texas A&M	24	Maurice Stacy	B	Washington
10	Joe McAfee	B	Holy Cross	25	Chick Davidson	T	Cornell
11	Steve Conroy	B	Holy Cross	26	John Norton	B	Washington
12	Bill Hildebrand	E	Mississippi	27	Ed Holtsinger	B	Georgia Tech
13	Tom Hand	C	Iowa	28	Joe Campbell	E	Holy Cross
14	George Hills	G	Georgia Tech	29	Francis Saunders	T	Clemson
15	Jim Hough	B	Clemson	30	Al Sparlis	G	UCLA
16	Dean Gaines	T	Georgia Tech	31	Ralph Clymer	G	Purdue
17	J.P. Miller	G	Georgia	32	Joervin Henderson	C	Missouri

1946 GREEN BAY PACKERS

FRONT ROW: (L-R) 8 Bob Forte, 76 Tom Miller, 42 Bruce Smith, 29 Charley Brock, 15 Earl Bennett, 48 Bob Nussbaumer, 22 Roy McKay, 3 Tony Canadeo, 80 Herman Rohrig, 7 Walt Schlinkman, 46 Russ Letlow, 54 Larry Craig, 38 Nolan Luhn.

MIDDLE ROW: (L-R) Coach Curly Lambeau, 19 Ray Riddick, 78 Cliff Aberson, 40 Bill Lee, 43 Don Wells, 79 Bob Adkins, 17 Marv Pregulman, 58 Ed Neal, 47 Paul Lipscomb, 35 Bob Flowers, 21 Al Sparlis, 16 Charles Mitchell, 23 Clyde Goodnight, Assistant Coaches Walt Kiesling, Don Hutson.

BACK ROW: (L-R) Trainer Carl (Bud) Jorgensen, Assistant Trainer Tim O'Brien, 64 Ted Fritsch, 33 Lester Gatewood, 51 Irv Comp, 63 Urban Odson, 75 Tiny Croft, 44 Baby Ray, 25 Al Zupek, 52 William Kuusisto, 18 Ken Keuper, 45 Dick Wildung.

On the surface, the Packers of 1947 were nothing more than an average club that couldn't beat the NFL's elite. In reality, this was a talented group that saw its playoff aspirations take a hit during a rough, three-game stretch.

The Packers opened November with a heartbreaking three-game run. The Steelers and Cardinals both beat them by a point, and in between, the Bears topped them by a field goal. Those three losses—by a combined five points—dropped Green Bay from first place into third, a spot the team occupied for the remainder of the season.

The back-to-back setbacks in Chicago hurt, but both could have gone the other way. In Wrigley Field, Irv Comp failed to score from a yard out on fourth down in the third quarter, and Ward Cuff saw his 29-yard field goal attempt blocked by Noah Mullins with 20 seconds left. A week later in Comiskey Park, Cuff's last-second, 23-yard effort sailed wide. Had the Packers, who finished 6-5-1, prevailed in both those contests, they, and not the Bears, might have entertained the Eagles in the championship game.

The Packers' five losses came courtesy of the top two teams in each division—Cardinals (twice), Bears, Eagles, and Steelers. Even so, the talent level between those four and Green Bay was not all that great.

Green Bay's defense gave up fewer yards, fewer touchdowns, and fewer points than any other. The Packers also intercepted a league-high 30 passes.

On offense, the running game was second only to that of the Rams. Clyde Goodnight (42 catches) and Nolan Luhn (38) were among the top receiving duos in the league. And Jack Jacobs, acquired in an off-season trade that sent Bob Nussbaumer to Washington, enjoyed the finest season of his career.

Tony Canadeo and Walt Schlinkman headed a cast that amassed 2,149 rushing yards. The team ran for a franchise-record 366 yards against the Lions on Oct. 26.

Much of the offensive improvement resulted from solid performances by veterans like those mentioned. But part of the success also came as the result of Curly Lambeau's decision to finally employ the T formation; that is, with the quarterback up under center.

In March, Lambeau fired long-time publicity director George Whitney Calhoun and replaced him with George Strickler, who had been the director of public relations for the NFL. On July 23, Packers president Lee Joannes resigned, having served the team in that capacity since 1930.

Two touchdown passes from Jacobs gave Green Bay the lead for good in its opening 29-20 win over the Bears. Jacobs hit Luhn with a 25-yard scoring strike and Bruce Smith with a 36-yarder to put the Packers out front 17-7.

In State Fair Park a week later, big Ed Neal blocked a punt by Bob Waterfield then recovered the ball in the end zone for a 14-0 Packers lead. However, not until Waterfield missed a 43-yard field goal on the last play of the game did Green Bay triumph 17-14.

In Week 3, the Packers lost 14-10 to the Cardinals.

Green Bay improved to 3-1 by pulling away from Washington in the fourth quarter. Canadeo passed 26 yards to Luhn, Ted Fritsch booted a 49-yard field goal, and Forte returned an interception 68 yards as the Packers outscored the Redskins 17-0 in the period and 27-10 overall.

A week later, Ed Cody (111 yards on nine carries) spearheaded a rushing assault that gashed the Lions to the tune of 366 yards. Green Bay uncorked 10 runs of 10 or more yards and buried Detroit 34-17.

After five weeks, Green Bay (4-1) shared first place with the Cardinals (4-1). But three close losses and a tie with the Giants dropped the Packers (4-4-1) into third place behind the Bears (7-2) and Cardinals (7-2).

The Green and Gold rallied to win two of their last three games. On Nov. 30, Canadeo and Fritsch accounted for 159 yards rushing and three touchdowns in Green Bay's 30-10 win in Los Angeles. In Briggs Stadium a week later, Forte intercepted three passes and Green Bay toppled Detroit 35-14.

In the finale, a 28-14 setback in Philadelphia, the Packers came face to face with the NFL's leading rusher, Steve Van Buren. Van Buren ripped off 96 yards and three touchdowns and became only the second player in NFL history to gain 1,000 yards rushing (1,008).

THE TULSA TWINS

Clyde Goodnight and Nolan Luhn were rookies during Don Hutson's last season with the Packers. Though neither was Hutson's equal on the field, the two receivers teamed up in 1947 to have a better year than the Hall of Famer ever did.

Goodnight (38 catches) and Luhn (42) caught a combined 80 passes for 1,289 yards and 13 touchdowns. Together they were responsible for more than 70 percent of Green Bay's passing offense.

The tandem got better as the season wore on. In the last four games, the two grabbed 30 passes and scored eight touchdowns.

Luhn and Goodnight were both drafted out of Tulsa University in 1945.

Below are the Packers' duos who accounted for the greatest percentage of the teams receptions in a single season:

Pct.	Receivers	Year
.714	Nolan Luhn (42)/Clyde Goodnight (38)	1947
.704	Don Hutson (47)/Nolan Luhn (10)	1945
.638	Don Hutson (58)/two others (9 each)	1944

TEAM STATISTICS

	GB	OPP
First Downs	206	193
Rushing	105	96
Passing	82	71
Penalty	19	26
Rushes	510	433
Yards Gained	2,149	1,606
Average Gain	4.21	3.71
Average Yards per Game	179.1	133.8
Passes Attempted	253	277
Completed	112	122
% Completed	44.27	44.04
Total Yards Gained	1,724	1,790
Yards Lost	104	190
Net Yards Gained	1,620	1,600
Yards Gained per Completion	15.39	14.67
Average Yards per Game	143.6	149.2
Laterals Attempted	0	2
Completed	0	1
Yards Gained	0	0
Combined Yards Gained	3,873	3,396
Total Plays	763	712
Average Yards per Play	5.08	4.77
Average Yards per Game	322.8	283.0
Intercepted By	30	19
Yards Returned	428	293
Returned for TD	1	1
Punts	65	65
Yards Punted	2,831	2,830
Average Yards per Punt	43.55	43.54
Punt Returns	45	44
Yards Returned	563	483
Average Yards per Return	12.51	10.98
Returned for TD	0	0
Kickoff Returns	42	48
Yards Returned	888	1,034
Average Yards per Return	21.14	21.54
Returned for TD	0	0
Penalties	104	88
Yards Penalized	1,019	759
Fumbles	24	41
Lost	13	20
Own Recovered for Touchdown	0	0
Opponent's Recovered by	20	13
Opponent's Recovered for Touchdown	0	0
Total Points Scored	274	210
Total Touchdowns	33	28
Touchdowns Rushing	14	13
Touchdowns Passing	17	14
Touchdowns on Returns & Recoveries	2	1
Extra Points	33	25
Safeties	2	1
Field Goals Attempted	29	11
Field Goals Made	13	5
% Successful	44.83	45.45

Regular Season   6-5-1

Date	GB		OPP	Att.
9/28	29	Chicago Bears	20	(25,461)
10/5	17	Los Angeles Rams (M)	14	(31,613)
10/12	10	Chicago Cardinals	14	(25,502)
10/19	27	Washington Redskins (M)	10	(28,572)
10/26	34	Detroit Lions	17	(25,179)
11/2	17	Pittsburgh Steelers (M)	18	(30,073)
11/9	17	at Chicago Bears	20	(46,112)
11/16	20	at Chicago Cardinals	21	(40,086)
11/23	24	at New York Giants	24	(27,939)
11/30	30	at Los Angeles Rams	10	(31,040)
12/7	35	at Detroit Lions	14	(14,055)
12/14	14	at Philadelphia Eagles	28	(24,216)

Score By Periods

	1	2	3	4	Total
Packers	49	61	85	79	274
Opponents	37	57	58	58	210

INDIVIDUAL STATISTICS

Rushing

	Att	Yds	Avg	LG	TD
Canadeo	103	464	4.5	35	2
Schlinkman	115	439	3.8	20	2
Bruce Smith	47	288	7.0	37	1
Cody	56	263	4.7	51	2
Fritsch	68	247	3.6	48	6
Gillette	50	207	4.1	26	0
B. Forte	29	80	2.4	12	0
J. Jacobs	18	64	3.6	115	1
Comp	5	46	9.2	34	0
Rohrig	7	22	3.1	6	0
Keuper	6	14	2.3	8	0
McKay	3	11	3.7	5	0
Cuff	1	7	7.0	7	0
Goodnight	1	-1	-1.0	-1	0
G. Wilson	1	-2	-2.0	-2	0
Packers	**510**	**2,149**	**4.2**	**51**	**14**
Opponents	433	1,606	3.7	41	13

Receiving

	No	Yds	Avg	LG	TD
Luhn	42	696	16.5	44	7
Goodnight	38	593	15.6	t69	6
Gillette	12	224	18.6	50	1
B. Forte	7	80	11.4	t22	2
Bruce Smith	4	50	12.5	t36	1
G. Wilson	3	34	11.3	15	0
Keuper	2	37	18.5	26	0
Schlinkman	2	-6	-3.0	-1	0
Craig	1	14	14.0	14	0
Cody	1	2	2.0	2	0
Packers	**112**	**1,724**	**15.4**	**t69**	**17**
Opponents	122	1,790	14.7	t66	14

Passing

	Att	Com	Yds	Pct	TD	In	YL	Rate
J. Jacobs	242	108	1,615	44.6	16	17	104	59.8
Canadeo	8	3	101	37.5	1	1	0	—
B. Forte	2	1	8	50.0	0	0	0	—
Comp	1	0	0	00.0	0	1	0	—
Packers	**253**	**112**	**1,724**	**44.3**	**17**	**19**	**104**	**58.5**
Opponents	277	122	1,790	44.0	14	30	190	43.0

Punting

	No	Yds	Avg	LG	HB
J. Jacobs	57	2,481	43.5	74	1
McKay	8	350	43.8	54	0
Packers	**65**	**2,831**	**43.5**	**74**	**1**
Opponents	65	2,830	43.5	86	0

Kickoff Returns

	No	Yds	Avg	LG	TD
Canadeo	15	312	20.8	35	0
Cody	10	269	26.9	39	0
Fritsch	5	100	20.0	25	0
Gillette	3	66	22.0	29	0
Bruce Smith	3	61	20.3	23	0
Luhn	2	30	15.0	18	0
B. Forte	2	28	14.0	23	0
Rohrig	1	15	15.0	15	0
Goodnight	1	7	7.0	7	0
Packers	**42**	**888**	**21.1**	**39**	**0**
Opponents	48	1,034	21.5	40	0

Punt Returns

	No	Yds	Avg	LG	TD
Rohrig	18	213	11.8	28	0
Gillette	11	168	15.3	26	0
Canadeo	10	111	11.1	24	0
Cody	2	30	15.0	20	0
Bruce Smith	1	22	22.0	22	0
B. Forte	1	15	15.0	15	0
J. Jacobs	1	4	4.0	4	0
Comp	1	0	0.0	0	0
Packers	**45**	**563**	**12.5**	**28**	**0**
Opponents	44	483	11.0	35	0

Interceptions

	No	Yds	Avg	LG	TD
B. Forte	9	140	15.6	t68	1
Comp	6	65	10.8	30	0
Rohrig	5	80	16.0	28	0
J. Jacobs	4	64	16.0	29	0
Keuper	2	41	20.5	26	0
C. Brock	2	14	7.0	7	0
Flowers	1	12	12.0	12	0
Fritsch	1	12	12.0	12	0
Packers	**30**	**428**	**14.3**	**t68**	**1**
Opponents	19	293	15.4	t63	1

Scoring

	TDr	TDp	TDrt	PAT	FG	S	TP
Fritsch	6	0	0	2/2	6/13	0	56
Cuff	0	0	0	30/30	7/16	0	51
Luhn	0	7	0	0/0	0/0	0	42
Goodnight	0	6	0	0/0	0/0	0	36
B. Forte	0	2	1	0/0	0/0	0	18
Bruce Smith	1	1	0	0/0	0/0	1	14
Canadeo	2	0	0	0/0	0/0	0	12
Cody	2	0	0	0/0	0/0	0	12
Schlinkman	2	0	0	0/0	0/0	0	12
Gillette	0	1	0	0/0	0/0	0	6
J. Jacobs	1	0	0	0/0	0/0	0	6
E. Neal	0	0	1	0/0	0/0	0	6
Wildung	0	0	0	0/0	0/0	1	2
McKay	0	0	0	1/1	0/0	0	1
Packers	**14**	**17**	**2**	**33/33**	**13/29**	**2**	**274**
Opponents	13	14	1	25/28	5/11	1	210

Fumbles

	Fum	Ow	Op	Yds	Tot
C. Brock	0	1	1	0	2
Canadeo	0	1	0	2	1
Cody	2	1	0	0	1
Comp	2	1	1	-5	2
Craig	0	0	1	0	1
Flowers	0	0	1	0	1
A. Forte	0	0	2	0	2
B. Forte	1	0	2	0	2
Fritsch	1	0	0	0	0
Gatewood	0	1	1	0	2
Gillette	2	0	0	0	0
J. Jacobs	5	1	0	0	1
Keuper	0	0	1	0	1
Lipscomb	0	0	1	1	1
Luhn	1	0	1	4	1
Ray	0	0	3	5	3
Rohrig	2	2	1	-2	3
Schlinkman	8	2	0	10	2
Skoglund	0	0	2	0	2
D. Wells	0	0	1	0	1
Wildung	0	0	3	1	3
Packers	**24**	**11**	**21**	**17**	**32**

NFL STANDINGS

Western Division

	W	L	T	Pct	PF	PA
Chicago Cardinals	9	3	0	.750	306	231
Chicago Bears	8	4	0	.667	363	241
Green Bay Packers	6	5	1	.545	274	210
Los Angeles Rams	6	6	0	.500	259	214
Detroit Lions	3	9	0	.250	231	305

Eastern Division

	W	L	T	Pct	PF	PA
Philadelphia Eagles	8	4	0	.667	308	242
Pittsburgh Steelers	8	4	0	.667	240	259
Boston Yanks	4	7	1	.364	168	256
Washington Redskins	4	8	0	.333	295	367
New York Giants	2	8	2	.200	190	309

ROSTER

No	Name	Pos	Ht	Wt	DOB	College	G
82	Bell, Edward	G	6-1	233	09/20/21	Indiana	11
29	Brock, Charley	C	6-1	210	03/15/16	Nebraska	12
3	Canadeo, Tony	HB	6-0	190	05/05/19	Gonzaga	12
46	Clemons, Raymond	G	5-10	200	04/02/21	St. Mary's (CA)	9
17	Cody, Ed	FB	5-9	190	02/27/23	Purdue	10
51	Comp, Irv	HB	6-3	205	05/17/19	St. Benedict	12
54	Craig, Larry	E	6-0	218	06/27/16	South Carolina	12
75	Croft, Milburn (Tiny)	T	6-4	280	11/07/20	Ripon	10
21	Cuff, Ward	HB	6-1	192	08/13/14	Marquette	10
66	Davis, Ralph	G	5-11	205	05/30/22	Wisconsin	11
35	Flowers, Bob	C	6-1	210	08/06/17	Texas Tech	12
40	Forte, Aldo	G	6-0	215	01/20/18	Montana	10
8	Forte, Bob	HB	6-0	195	07/15/22	Arkansas	12
64	Fritsch, Ted	FB	5-10	210	10/31/20	Stevens Point	12
33	Gatewood, Lester	C	6-2	200	05/30/21	Baylor	12
16	Gillette, Jim	HB	6-1	185	12/19/17	Virginia	10
23	Goodnight, Clyde	E	6-1	195	03/03/24	Tulsa	11
27	Jacobs, Jack	QB	6-2	190	08/07/19	Oklahoma	12
18	Keuper, Ken	HB	6-0	205	11/14/18	Georgia	12
76	Kovatch, John	E	6-3	200	07/21/20	Notre Dame	3
47	Lipscomb, Paul	T	6-5	245	01/13/23	Tennessee	12
38	Luhn, Nolan	E	6-3	200	07/27/21	Tulsa	12
19	McDougal, Robert	FB	6-2	205	03/19/21	Miami (FL)	1
22	McKay, Roy	HB	6-0	195	02/02/20	Texas	11
58	Neal, Ed	T	6-4	290	12/31/18	Tulane	12
63	Odson, Urban	T	6-3	250	11/17/18	Minnesota	11
44	Ray, Buford (Baby)	T	6-6	250	09/30/15	Vanderbilt	11
80	Rohrig, Herman	HB	5-9	190	03/19/18	Nebraska	7
7	Schlinkman, Walt	FB	5-9	190	05/02/22	Texas Tech	12
52	Skoglund, Robert	E	6-1	198	07/29/25	Notre Dame	9
42	Smith, Bruce	HB	6-0	197	02/08/20	Minnesota	10
15	Tassos, Damon	G	6-1	225	12/05/23	Texas A&M	3
43	Wells, Don	E	6-2	200	07/12/22	Georgia	12
45	Wildung, Dick	G	6-0	220	08/16/21	Minnesota	3
65	Wilson, Gene	E	5-10	175	06/24/26	SMU	9

DRAFT

Rnd	Name	Pos	College	Rnd	Name	Pos	College
1	Ernie Case	B	UCLA	18	Jim Goodman	T	Indiana
3	Burr Baldwin	E	UCLA	19	Dick Miller	G	Lawrence
5	Paul (Buddy) Burris	G	Oklahoma	20	Brad Ecklund	C	Oregon
6	Gene Wilson	E	SMU	21	Bob West	B	Colorado
7	Dick Connors	B	Northwestern	22	Tex Reilly	B	Colorado
8	Monte Moncrief	T	Texas A&M	23	Ron Sockolov	T	California
9	Robert McDougal	B	Miami	24	Herb St. John	G	Georgia
10	Bob Kelly	B	Notre Dame	25	Fred Redeker	B	Cincinnati
11	Tom Moulton	C	Oklahoma State	26	Herm Lubker	E	Arkansas
12	George Hills	G	Georgia Tech	27	Bob Palladino	B	Notre Dame
13	Bob Skoglund	E	Notre Dame	28	Jerrell Baxter	T	North Carolina
14	Jack Mitchell	B	Oklahoma	29	Ray Sellers	E	Georgia
15	Denver Crawford	T	Tennessee	30	Jerry Carle	B	Northwestern
16	Jim Callahan	E	USC	31	Bill Hogan	B	Kansas
17	Ted Scalissi	B	Ripon	32	Ralph Olsen	E	Utah

1947 GREEN BAY PACKERS

FRONT ROW: (L-R) Assistant Trainer Tim O'Brien, 22 Roy McKay, 65 Gene Wilson, 3 Tony Canadeo, 17 Ed Cody, 80 Herman Rohrig, 29 Charley Brock, 7 Walt Schlinkman, 43 Don Wells, 23 Clyde Goodnight, 54 Larry Craig, Trainer Carl (Bud) Jorgensen.
MIDDLE ROW: (L-R) 46 Bill McPartland, 66 Ralph Davis, 64 Ted Fritsch, 8 Bob Forte, 18 Ken Keuper, 35 Bob Flowers, 38 Nolan Luhn, 33 Lester Gatewood, 40 Aldo Forte, 16 Jim Gillette, 27 Jack Jacobs, 15 Damon Tassos, Assistant Coach Don Hutson.
BACK ROW: (L-R) Assistant Coach Walt Kiesling, 42 Bruce Smith, 52 Robert Skoglund, 75 Tiny Croft, 58 Ed Neal, 47 Paul Lipscomb, 44 Baby Ray, 63 Urban Odson, 51 Irv Comp, 82 Edward Bell, 45 Dick Wildung, Coach Curly Lambeau.

For more than a quarter century, the Packers had enjoyed life as one of the brightest stars in the NFL: more than 200 wins, 26 winning seasons, and 6 world championships. In 1948, the glow dimmed as a 3-9 record and seven-game losing streak jettisoned the team into a 12-year period in which it never won more games than it lost.

Curly Lambeau often received much of the credit for the team's success. He was an innovator, a great judge of talent, and he could motivate a team like few others.

By the late 1940s, he was no longer at the top of his game.

Where once Lambeau lured the likes of Johnny Blood, Cal Hubbard, and Lavvie Dilweg to Green Bay, he was now landing players such as Don Deeks, Ted Cremer, and Ken Roskie. And though a motivational stunt —withholding players' pay—appeared to work in the short term with a 16-0 win over the Rams, the coach's refusal to return the wages after the shutout contributed to the team's subsequent seven-game slide.

Going into 1948, just six players remained from the 1944 championship team. Losing such talent was problem enough. Replacing it proved virtually impossible.

Lambeau's drafts in 1946 and 1947 yielded little talent. Though he got contributions from a number of his picks in 1948, the team still needed to upgrade.

That being the case, Lambeau sought players wherever he could find them. He signed castoffs Cremer and Ted Cook from Detroit, Deeks from Washington, James Kekeris from Philadelphia, and Pat West from Los Angeles. He even gave Roskie, last of the AAFC's 49ers, a shot at fullback. Of those six, only Cook went on to play for Green Bay in 1949.

The season's turning point came after the Packers knocked off the Rams 16-0 in Week 5. The win elevated Green Bay (3-2) into third place in the Western Division standings behind the Bears (4-0) and Cardinals (3-1).

Buoyed by the turn of events, the players fully expected Lambeau to return the half-game's pay he had withheld as a "salary adjustment" following the team's 17-7 loss to the Cardinals a week earlier. But instead, Lambeau held on to the money and morale plummeted. Only after the season was over did Lambeau relent, and by then Green Bay was among the worst teams in the league.

The Packers opened with a Friday game against the Boston Yanks at Fenway Park. Green Bay won easily 31-0, highlighted by Ralph Earhart's 72-yard touchdown run.

The Bears then whipped the Packers 45-7 on Sept. 26. Chicago rushed for 240 yards and forced six turnovers.

A week later, Canadeo racked up 118 yards rushing as Detroit fell 33-21. The Packers posted season highs in yards (423), yards rushing (268), and first downs (23).

Green Bay hosted the defending champion Cardinals in Milwaukee on Oct. 10. Chicago piled up 320 rushing yards in a 17-7 win. Afterward, Lambeau was livid.

"I'm not feeling bad, I'm mad," said the frustrated coach who added, "Salary adjustments will be made until we begin to play the brand of ball we're capable of."

Lambeau's outburst had the desired effect. At least for the fifth game of the season.

Six players intercepted seven passes and Canadeo had his second 100-yard rushing day of the season as the Packers shut out the Rams. Earhart kicked off the scoring on a 64-yard pass from Jacobs in the opening quarter.

"The boys tried for 60 minutes today. Everybody tried hard all the time and we feel pretty good about it," said Lambeau who made no comment on the previous week's fines.

A week later, Washington put Lambeau and the Packers back in a foul mood. The Redskins used 14 plays to drive 97 yards for their final touchdown in a 23-7 win.

Green Bay's best showing in the season's second half came in Chicago on Nov. 14. The Packers held the Bears to 199 yards and threatened to tie the game after Jacobs hit Luhn with a 14-yard pass late in the game. But Ed Cody missed the extra point and the Bears escaped 7-6.

The Packers closed with three more losses. After falling 49-3 to the Giants in Milwaukee, Lambeau remarked: "Of this one thing I'm sure. There won't be a repetition of this next season."

He couldn't have been more wrong. Packers fans were in for more of the same in 1949.

GONE FISHING

Somewhere in his later years as coach of the Packers, Curly Lambeau was said to have "Gone Hollywood" as he increasingly spent more time in California. In 1948, his team could well have hung out a "Gone Fishing" sign, as it did little to indicate it was present in four blowout losses.

The Bears, Steelers, Giants, and Cardinals all defeated the Packers by more than 30 points. Those four teams combined to outscore Green Bay 174 to 24. The Giants administered the worst beating, 49-3 in Milwaukee.

Clearly, Lambeau wasn't getting through to his team. In the 29 years from 1919 through 1947, the Packers had suffered just three such losses combined.

Though he probably didn't realize it at the time, Lambeau was soon to be "Gone from Green Bay."

Below are the seasons in which the Packers endured the most losses by more than 30 points:

Year	Number of Losses	Record
1948	4	3-9-0
1950	3	3-9-0
1986	2	4-12-0

TEAM STATISTICS

	GB	OPP
First Downs	172	222
Rushing	89	132
Passing	58	74
Penalty	25	16
Rushes	446	537
Yards Gained	1,759	2,153
Average Gain	3.94	4.01
Average Yards per Game	146.6	179.4
Passes Attempted	274	260
Completed	109	134
% Completed	39.78	51.54
Total Yards Gained	1,364	1,626
Yards Lost	293	150
Net Yards Gained	1,071	1,514
Yards Gained per Completion	12.51	12.13
Average Yards per Game	113.7	135.5
Laterals Attempted	1	5
Completed	1	5
Yards Gained	12	69
Combined Yards Gained	3,135	3,848
Total Plays	721	802
Average Yards per Play	4.35	4.80
Average Yards per Game	261.3	320.7
Intercepted By	29	29
Yards Returned	405	457
Returned for TD	0	2
Punts	78	70
Yards Punted	3,140	3,029
Average Yards per Punt	40.26	43.27
Punt Returns	47	38
Yards Returned	527	473
Average Yards per Return	11.21	12.45
Returned for TD	0	1
Kickoff Returns	47	22
Yards Returned	926	611
Average Yards per Return	19.70	27.77
Returned for TD	0	1
Penalties	104	91
Yards Penalized	941	771
Fumbles	30	23
Lost	19	15
Own Recovered for Touchdown	0	0
Opponent's Recovered by	15	19
Opponent's Recovered for Touchdown	1	0
Total Points Scored	154	290
Total Touchdowns	20	39
Touchdowns Rushing	11	21
Touchdowns Passing	8	13
Touchdowns on Returns & Recoveries	1	5
Extra Points	16	38
Safeties	0	0
Field Goals Attempted	16	14
Field Goals Made	6	6
% Successful	37.50	42.86

Regular Season   3-9-0

Date	GB		OPP	Att.
9/17	31	at Boston Yanks	0	(15,443)
9/26	7	Chicago Bears	45	(25,546)
10/3	33	Detroit Lions	21	(24,206)
10/10	7	Chicago Cardinals (M)	17	(34,369)
10/17	16	Los Angeles Rams	0	(25,119)
10/24	7	Washington Redskins (M)	23	(13,433)
10/31	20	at Detroit Lions	24	(16,174)
11/7	7	at Pittsburgh Steelers	38	(26,058)
11/14	6	at Chicago Bears	7	(48,113)
11/21	3	New York Giants (M)	49	(12,639)
11/28	10	at Los Angeles Rams	24	(23,874)
12/5	7	at Chicago Cardinals	42	(26,072)

Score By Periods

	1	2	3	4	Total
Packers	40	44	20	50	154
Opponents	55	90	59	86	290

INDIVIDUAL STATISTICS

Rushing

	Att	Yds	Avg	LG	TD
Canadeo	123	589	4.8	49	4
Schlinkman	106	441	4.2	19	4
Fritsch	37	173	4.7	30	0
Earhart	30	140	4.7	t72	1
Provo	29	90	3.1	28	0
O.E. Smith	27	85	3.1	10	0
J. Jacobs	24	73	3.0	23	1
Cody	26	58	2.2	10	0
B. Forte	12	30	2.5	9	0
Roskie	5	28	5.6	9	1
Girard	13	26	2.0	7	0
Bruce Smith	6	21	3.5	20	0
Comp	3	3	1.0	2	0
Moss	5	2	0.4	3	0
Packers	**446**	**1,759**	**3.9**	**t72**	**11**
Opponents	537	2,153	4.0	t72	21

Receiving

	No	Yds	Avg	LG	TD
Goodnight	28	448	16.0	57	3
Luhn	17	285	16.8	40	2
Earhart	17	194	11.4	t64	2
T. Cook	13	156	12.0	23	0
O.E. Smith	12	121	10.1	49	0
Canadeo	9	81	9.0	32	0
B. Forte	6	63	10.5	19	1
Provo	4	-9	-2.3	3	0
G. Wilson	2	23	11.5	14	0
Girard	1	2	2.0	2	0
Packers	**109**	**1,364**	**12.5**	**t64**	**8**
Opponents	134	1,626	12.1	t61	13

Passing

	Att	Com	Yds	Pct	TD	In	YL	Rate
J. Jacobs	184	82	848	44.6	5	21	169	27.9
Comp	49	16	335	32.7	1	7	76	25.0
Girard	14	4	117	28.6	1	1	29	56.0
Canadeo	8	2	24	25.0	0	0	0	—
Moss	17	4	20	23.5	0	0	19	39.6
Provo	1	1	20	100.0	1	0	0	—
Bruce Smith	1	0	0	00.0	0	0	0	—
Packers	**274**	**109**	**1,364**	**39.8**	**8**	**29**	**293**	**26.1**
Opponents	260	134	1,626	51.5	13	29	150	48.2

Punting

	No	Yds	Avg	LG	HB
J. Jacobs	69	2,782	40.3	78	1
Girard	8	320	40.0	49	0
Canadeo	1	38	38.0	38	0
Packers	**78**	**3,140**	**40.3**	**78**	**1**
Opponents	70	3,029	43.3	88	0

Kickoff Returns

	No	Yds	Avg	LG	TD
O.E. Smith	12	287	23.9	36	0
Provo	10	205	20.5	28	0
Canadeo	9	166	18.4	28	0
Schlinkman	4	89	22.3	34	0
Luhn	3	18	6.0	11	0
Earhart	2	51	25.5	27	0
Cody	2	31	15.5	20	0
B. Forte	2	30	15.0	17	0
Girard	1	20	20.0	20	0
Fritsch	1	17	17.0	17	0
Goodnight	1	12	12.0	12	0
Packers	**47**	**926**	**19.7**	**36**	**0**
Opponents	22	611	27.8	t96	1

Punt Returns

	No	Yds	Avg	LG	TD
Provo	18	208	11.6	40	0
Earhart	11	137	12.5	27	0
O.E. Smith	8	71	8.9	27	0
Canadeo	4	55	13.8	20	0
Comp	3	35	11.7	16	0
T. Cook	2	18	9.0	14	0
J. Jacobs	1	3	3.0	3	0
Packers	**47**	**527**	**11.2**	**40**	**0**
Opponents	38	473	12.5	t49	1

Interceptions

	No	Yds	Avg	LG	TD
T. Cook	6	81	13.5	27	0
Comp	5	86	17.2	28	0
B. Forte	5	56	11.2	40	0
Flowers	4	21	5.3	19	0
Canadeo	3	26	8.7	25	0
G. Wilson	2	13	6.5	13	0
Fritsch	1	52	52.0	52	0
Girard	1	34	34.0	34	0
Rhodemyre	1	24	24.0	24	0
Roskie	1	12	12.0	12	0
Packers	**29**	**405**	**14.0**	**52**	**0**
Opponents	29	457	15.8	t82	2

Scoring

	TDr	TDp	TDrt	PAT	FG	S	TP
Fritsch	0	0	1	5/6	6/16	0	29
Canadeo	4	0	0	0/0	0/0	0	24
Schlinkman	4	0	0	0/0	0/0	0	24
Earhart	1	2	0	0/0	0/0	0	18
Goodnight	0	3	0	0/0	0/0	0	18
Luhn	0	2	0	0/0	0/0	0	12
Cody	0	0	0	11/13	0/0	0	11
B. Forte	0	1	0	0/0	0/0	0	6
J. Jacobs	1	0	0	0/0	0/0	0	6
Roskie	1	0	0	0/0	0/0	0	6
Packers	**11**	**8**	**1**	**16/20**	**6/16**	**0**	**154**
Opponents	21	13	5	38/39	6/14	0	290

Fumbles

	Fum	Ow	Op	Yds	Tot
Baxter	0	0	1	0	1
Canadeo	5	0	0	0	0
Cody	2	0	0	0	0
Comp	3	1	2	5	3
T. Cook	1	0	0	0	0
Craig	0	0	1	0	1
Cremer	0	0	1	0	1
Earhart	0	1	0	0	1
Flowers	0	0	1	1	1
B. Forte	1	0	1	0	1
Fritsch	2	0	4	8	4
Girard	2	0	0	0	0
Goodnight	2	0	0	0	1
J. Jacobs	1	1	0	-3	1
Lipscomb	0	1	1	0	2
Moss	3	1	0	-1	1
E. Neal	0	0	1	0	1
Olsonoski	0	2	0	0	2
Provo	1	0	1	0	1
Schlinkman	4	0	0	0	0
Bruce Smith	1	0	0	0	0
O.E. Smith	2	0	0	0	0
Vogds	0	0	1	0	1
Wildung	0	1	1	5	2
G. Wilson	0	0	1	0	1
Packers	**30**	**11**	**15**	**15**	**26**

NFL STANDINGS

Western Division

	W	L	T	Pct	PF	PA
Chicago Cardinals	11	1	0	.917	395	226
Chicago Bears	10	2	0	.833	375	151
Los Angeles Rams	6	5	1	.545	327	269
Green Bay Packers	**3**	**9**	**0**	**.250**	**154**	**290**
Detroit Lions	2	10	0	.167	200	407

Eastern Division

	W	L	T	Pct	PF	PA
Philadelphia Eagles	9	2	1	.818	376	156
Washington Redskins	7	5	0	.583	291	287
New York Giants	4	8	0	.333	297	388
Pittsburgh Steelers	4	8	0	.333	200	243
Boston Yanks	3	9	0	.250	174	372

ROSTER

No	Name	Pos	Ht	Wt	DOB	College	G
33	Baxter, Lloyd	C	6-2	210	01/18/23	SMU	11
82	Bell, Edward	G	6-1	233	09/20/21	Indiana	12
3	Canadeo, Tony	HB	6-0	190	05/05/19	Gonzaga	12
17	Cody, Ed	FB	5-9	190	02/27/23	Purdue	10
51	Comp, Irv	HB	6-3	205	05/17/19	St. Benedict	11
48	Cook, Ted	E	6-2	195	02/06/22	Alabama	12
54	Craig, Larry	E	6-0	218	06/27/16	South Carolina	12
18	Cremer, Ted	E	6-2	210	03/16/19	Auburn	3
66	Davis, Ralph	G	5-11	205	05/30/22	Wisconsin	11
85	Deeks, Donald	G	6-4	245	02/10/23	Washington	8
41	Earhart, Ralph	HB	5-10	165	03/29/23	Texas Tech	12
35	Flowers, Bob	C	6-1	210	08/06/17	Texas Tech	11
8	Forte, Bob	HB	6-0	195	07/15/22	Arkansas	12
64	Fritsch, Ted	FB	5-10	210	10/31/20	Stevens Point	12
36	Girard, Earl (Jug)	HB	5-11	175	01/25/27	Wisconsin	10
23	Goodnight, Clyde	E	6-1	195	03/03/24	Tulsa	9
27	Jacobs, Jack	QB	6-2	190	08/07/19	Oklahoma	12
72	Kekeris, James	T	6-1	257	10/17/23	Missouri	5
47	Lipscomb, Paul	T	6-5	245	01/13/23	Tennessee	12
38	Luhn, Nolan	E	6-3	200	07/27/21	Tulsa	12
10	Moss, Perry	QB	5-10	170	08/04/26	Illinois	6
58	Neal, Ed	T	6-4	290	12/31/18	Tulane	12
63	Odson, Urban	T	6-3	250	11/17/18	Minnesota	12
46	Olsonoski, Larry	G	6-2	215	09/10/25	Minnesota	12
80	Provo, Fred	HB	5-9	185	04/17/22	Washington	9
44	Ray, Buford (Baby)	T	6-6	250	09/30/15	Vanderbilt	12
22	Rhodemyre, Jay	C	6-1	210	12/16/22	Kentucky	9
34	Roskie, Ken	FB	6-1	220	11/29/21	South Carolina	6
7	Schlinkman, Walt	FB	5-9	190	05/02/22	Texas Tech	11
42	Smith, Bruce	HB	6-0	197	02/08/20	Minnesota	4
21	Smith, Oscar E.	HB	6-0	185	07/20/23	Texas-El Paso	12
15	Tassos, Damon	G	6-1	225	12/05/23	Texas A&M	11
79	Vogds, Evan	G	5-10	215	02/10/23	Wisconsin	12
43	Wells, Don	E	6-2	200	07/12/22	Georgia	12
25	West, Pat	FB	6-0	201	02/21/23	USC	3
45	Wildung, Dick	G	6-0	220	08/16/21	Minnesota	12
65	Wilson, Gene	E	5-10	180	06/24/26	SMU	12

DRAFT

Rnd	Name	Pos	Ht	Wt	College
1	Earl (Jug) Girard	B	5-11	180	Wisconsin
3	Oscar E. Smith	B	6-0	190	Texas-El Paso
5a	Don Richards	T	6-2	245	Arkansas
	(Choice from Lions)				
5b	Wayman Sellers	E	6-1	190	Georgia
6	Larry Olsonoski	G	6-2	215	Minnesota
7	Jay Rhodemyre	C	6-1	210	Kentucky
8	Bob Cunz	T	5-10	220	Illinois
9	(Choice to Giants)				
10	George Walmsley	B	5-8	170	Rice
11	Bob Hodges	T	6-2	230	Bradley
12	Bob Rennebohm	E	6-0	195	Wisconsin
13	Perry Moss	B	5-10	190	Illinois
14	Fred Provo	B	5-9	185	Washington
15	Lou Agase	E-T	6-1	198	Illinois
16	Travis Raven	B	5-11	190	Texas
17	(Choice to Redskins)				
18	Ken Balge	E	6-2	210	Michigan State
19	Charley Tatom	T	6-5	236	Texas
20	Floyd Thomas	C	6-3	205	Arkansas
21	Herb St. John	G	5-10	210	Georgia
22	Don Anderson	B	5-11	190	Rice
23	Fred Kling	B	6-2	190	Missouri
24	Clyde Biggers	T	6-6	240	Catawba
25	Stan Heath	B	6-1	190	Nevada-Reno
26	Aubrey Allen	T	6-1	246	Colorado
27	Stan Gorski	E	6-2	193	Northwestern
28	Don Sharp	C	6-3	228	Tulsa
29	John Panelli	B	5-11	198	Notre Dame
30	Clarence McGeary	T	6-5	250	N. Dakota State
31	Mike Mills	E	6-1	200	Brigham Young
32	Ralph Earhart	B	5-10	165	Texas Tech

1948 GREEN BAY PACKERS

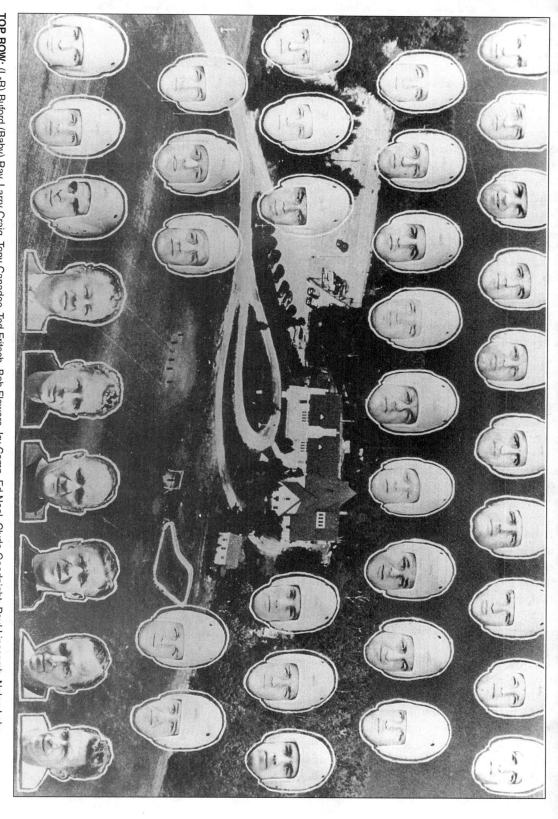

TOP ROW: (L–R) Buford (Baby) Ray, Larry Craig, Tony Canadeo, Ted Fritsch, Bob Flowers, Irv Comp, Ed Neal, Clyde Goodnight, Paul Lipscomb, Nolan Luhn.
SECOND ROW: (L–R) Dick Wildung, Don Wells, Bob Forte, Urban Odson, Walt Schlinkman, Gene Wilson, Damon Tassos, Edward Bell, Ed Cody.
THIRD ROW: (L–R) Ralph Davis, Robert Skoglund, Jack Jacobs, Fred Provo, Ted Cook, Jug Girard.
FOURTH ROW: (L–R) Lloyd Baxter, Perry Moss, Larry Olsonoski, Oscar E. Smith, Donald Deeks.
BOTTOM ROW: (L–R) Evan Vogds, Ralph Earhart, Jay Rhodemyre, Coach Curly Lambeau, Assistant Coach Don Hutson, Line Coach Walt Kiesling, Backfield Coach Bo Molenda, Trainer Carl (Bud) Jorgensen, Assistant Trainer Tim O'Brien.

For the second year in a row, Green Bay posted one of the worst records in the NFL. As disconcerting as that may have been, of greater concern was the financial health of the club, which had deteriorated to the point that only a successful "$50,000 Drive to Save the Packers" prevented the last remaining town team from going belly up.

More than any other, 1949 was a year of disarray. The team dropped 10 games, battled bankruptcy, lost its head coach, and nervously awaited word as to whether or not it would have a home in the NFL once the league completed its merger with the All-American Football Conference.

Curly Lambeau was the lightning rod for much of the controversy. It started with his announcement—following a 17-0 season-opening loss to the Bears—that all on-the-field coaching duties would be handled by his assistants Tom Stidham, Bob Snyder, and Charley Brock. Lambeau would remain as an advisory coach with his focus on rebuilding the club.

Some of Lambeau's moves toward that end were questionable. He released Clyde Goodnight, second only to Don Hutson in career receptions as a Packer, and eight-year veteran Bob Flowers after the opening setback. Then with one game to go, he waived Ted Cook, the team's leading receiver and interceptor.

The city was divided as to whether or not Lambeau should stay. The board of directors renewed his contract for another two years in late November. The pact was never presented to Lambeau, who resigned on Jan. 31, 1950, to become head coach of the Chicago Cardinals.

The Packers fought to stay alive financially. In mid-November, a "$50,000 Drive to Save the Packers" was launched. It included an intrasquad game slated for Thanksgiving.

By the time that holiday rolled around, $42,174 in cash and nearly $8,000 more in pledges had been raised. A crowd of about 15,000 watched the Veteran Blues, quarterbacked by Jug Girard, defeat the Newcomer Golds 35-31. In addition, the game served as a homecoming with many of the members of the 1919 team in attendance.

Shortly after the game, a new sale of stock (20,000 shares at $10 each) was authorized. The sale began in March 1950, when 9,500 shares were offered at $25 apiece.

On the field, the news wasn't as good. Green Bay won two of its first six games to move into a third-place tie with the Cardinals. But six straight losses dropped the Packers (2-10) into last place in the Western Division and ahead of only the New York Bulldogs (1-10-1) in the league overall.

The Packers failed to complete a pass in 13 attempts when they hosted the Bears on Sept. 25. Girard, Jack Jacobs and Stan Heath did complete four throws to the opposition as Chicago won easily 17-0.

The Rams pounded Green Bay 48-7 in Week 2. Los Angeles ripped off 247 yards rushing and scored four times on the ground.

Green Bay grabbed its first win against the hapless New York Bulldogs on Oct. 7. Tony Canadeo picked up 100 yards rushing as he and his mates amassed a season-best 385 yards in a 19-0 shutout.

Nine days later, the Cardinals dealt Green Bay its third loss 39-17.

Green Bay won for the second time in Week 6. After Wally Triplett ran 80 yards to pay dirt, the Lions recovered an onside kick and moved in for a field goal try. Bill Dudley botched the attempt and the Packers prevailed 16-14.

The Green and Gold then lost their last six games. Only once in that span—the season finale in Detroit—did the team not get blown out by at least 20 points.

The Bears were the first to whip them 24-3. Then in Week 8, Charley Conerly of the Giants scorched the Packers with 357 passing yards in a 30-10 rout. A week later, Jerry Nuzum rumbled for 168 yards rushing as the Steelers cruised 30-7.

In the final three weeks, other opponents put up big numbers as well.

While Green Bay struggled, the NFL and All-American Football Conference agreed to merge. On Dec. 9, the two leagues announced their decision. The realigned league called for a 13-team setup in 1950 that included the Packers. Once again, the pro team with the college spirit survived to play another day.

DECISIVELY OUTSCORED

Aside from Tony Canadeo gaining 1,000 yards rushing, there was little to cheer if you were a Packers fan in 1949. In 12 games, Green Bay was outscored by a whopping 215 points.

The Packers scored just 14 touchdowns and gave up 42. Canadeo and Steve Pritko were the only players to score more than one touchdown all season.

Conversely, every team with the exception of the Bulldogs scored at least two touchdowns on the Packers.

Two players, Gene Roberts of the Giants and Pat Harder of the Cardinals, each amassed nearly as many points (102) as did the entire Packers team (114).

Listed below are the seasons in which Green Bay was outscored by the most points:

Points	Year	Record
215	1949 (114-329)	2-10-0
189	1958 (193-382)	1-10-1
164	1986 (254-418)	4-12-0
162	1950 (244-406)	3-9-0

1949

TEAM STATISTICS

	GB	OPP
First Downs	182	218
Rushing	99	110
Passing	68	89
Penalty	15	19
Rushes	503	501
Yards Gained	2,061	2,077
Average Gain	4.10	4.15
Average Yards per Game	171.8	173.1
Passes Attempted	299	292
Completed	91	138
% Completed	30.43	47.26
Total Yards Gained	1,291	2,123
Yards Lost	233	244
Net Yards Gained	1,058	1,879
Yards Gained per Completion	14.19	15.38
Average Yards per Game	107.6	176.9
Laterals Attempted	0	7
Completed	0	6
Yards Gained	0	43
Combined Yards Gained	3,352	4,243
Total Plays	802	800
Average Yards per Play	4.18	5.30
Average Yards per Game	279.3	353.6
Intercepted By	20	29
Yards Returned	187	406
Returned for TD	0	4
Punts	87	68
Yards Punted	3,500	2,708
Average Yards per Punt	40.23	39.82
Punt Returns	37	50
Yards Returned	310	932
Average Yards per Return	8.38	18.64
Returned for TD	1	3
Kickoff Returns	42	29
Yards Returned	815	583
Average Yards per Return	19.40	20.10
Returned for TD	0	0
Penalties	76	91
Yards Penalized	722	836
Fumbles	32	23
Lost	16	15
Own Recovered for Touchdown	0	0
Opponent's Recovered by	15	16
Opponent's Recovered for Touchdown	0	0
Total Points Scored	114	329
Total Touchdowns	14	42
Touchdowns Rushing	7	20
Touchdowns Passing	5	15
Touchdowns on Returns & Recoveries	2	7
Extra Points	12	40
Safeties	0	2
Field Goals Attempted	22	26
Field Goals Made	6	11
% Successful	27.27	42.31

Regular Season 2-10-0

Date	GB		OPP	Att.
9/25	0	Chicago Bears	17	(25,571)
10/2	7	Los Angeles Rams	48	(24,308)
10/7	19	at New York Bulldogs	0	(5,099)
10/16	17	Chicago Cardinals (M)	39	(18,464)
10/23	7	at Los Angeles Rams	35	(37,546)
10/30	16	Detroit Lions (M)	14	(10,855)
11/6	3	at Chicago Bears	24	(47,218)
11/13	10	New York Giants	30	(20,151)
11/20	7	Pittsburgh Steelers (M)	30	(5,483)
11/27	21	at Chicago Cardinals	41	(16,787)
12/4	0	at Washington Redskins	30	(23,200)
12/11	7	at Detroit Lions	21	(12,576)

Score By Periods

	1	2	3	4	Total
Packers	6	47	26	35	114
Opponents	95	47	83	104	329

INDIVIDUAL STATISTICS

Rushing

	Att	Yds	Avg	LG	TD
Canadeo	208	1,052	5.1	54	4
Fritsch	69	227	3.3	27	1
Girard	45	198	4.4	35	1
Schlinkman	47	196	4.2	37	0
B. Forte	40	135	3.4	25	0
Summerhays	29	101	3.5	14	0
Earhart	20	54	2.7	14	0
Cifers	23	52	2.3	19	0
Heath	10	25	2.5	18	1
O.E. Smith	9	15	1.7	11	0
Kirby	3	6	2.0	8	0
Packers	503	2,061	4.1	54	7
Opponents	501	2,077	4.2	t80	20

Receiving

	No	Yds	Avg	LG	TD
T. Cook	25	442	17.7	50	1
Kelley	17	222	13.1	32	1
Luhn	15	169	11.3	30	1
B. Forte	7	85	12.1	28	0
Pritko	6	94	15.7	24	2
Fritsch	6	81	13.5	35	0
Earhart	5	109	21.8	50	0
Orlich	4	39	9.8	12	0
Canadeo	3	-2	-0.7	3	0
Summerhays	1	34	34.0	34	0
Girard	1	13	13.0	13	0
Cifers	1	5	5.0	5	0
Packers	91	1,291	14.2	50	5
Opponents	138	2,123	15.4	t64	15

Passing

	Att	Com	Yds	Pct	TD	In	YL	Rate
Girard	175	62	881	35.4	4	12	193	31.6
Heath	106	26	355	24.5	1	14	40	4.6
J. Jacobs	16	3	55	18.8	0	3	0	1.8
B. Forte	1	0	0	0.0	0	0	0	—
Fritsch	1	0	0	00.0	0	0	0	—
Packers	299	91	1,291	30.4	5	29	233	11.4
Opponents	292	138	2,123	47.3	15	20	244	60.3

Punting

	No	Yds	Avg	LG	HB
Girard	69	2,694	39.0	72	3
J. Jacobs	17	757	44.5	58	0
Cifers	1	49	49.0	49	0
Packers	87	3,500	40.2	72	3
Opponents	68	2,708	39.8	82	1

Kickoff Returns

	No	Yds	Avg	LG	TD
Kirby	14	315	22.5	34	0
Earhart	11	187	17.0	30	0
B. Forte	7	159	22.7	36	0
Girard	2	45	22.5	24	0
O.E. Smith	2	36	18.0	21	0
Canadeo	2	20	10.0	12	0
Fritsch	1	23	23.0	23	0
Schlinkman	1	23	23.0	23	0
T. Cook	1	7	7.0	7	0
Vogds	1	0	0.0	0	0
Packers	42	815	19.4	36	0
Opponents	29	583	20.1	48	0

Punt Returns

	No	Yds	Avg	LG	TD
Earhart	14	161	11.5	t57	1
Girard	11	70	6.4	11	0
Kirby	8	48	6.0	13	0
O.E. Smith	2	9	4.5	9	0
B. Forte	1	13	13.0	13	0
J. Jacobs	1	9	9.0	9	0
Packers	37	310	8.4	t57	1
Opponents	50	932	18.6	85	3

Interceptions

	No	Yds	Avg	LG	TD
T. Cook	5	52	10.4	30	0
Rhodemyre	4	12	3.0	9	0
Comp	3	24	8.0	14	0
J. Jacobs	2	26	13.0	26	0
B. Forte	2	17	8.5	17	0
Girard	1	41	41.0	41	0
Tassos	1	10	10.0	10	0
Harding	1	5	5.0	5	0
Burris	1	0	0.0	0	0
Packers	20	187	9.4	41	0
Opponents	29	406	14.0	68	4

Scoring

	TDr	TDp	TDrt	PAT	FG	S	TP
Fritsch	1	0	0	11/13	5/20	0	32
Canadeo	4	0	0	0/0	0/0	0	24
Pritko	0	2	0	0/0	0/0	0	12
T. Cook	0	1	0	0/0	0/0	0	6
Earhart	0	0	1	0/0	0/0	0	6
Girard	1	0	0	0/0	0/0	0	6
Heath	1	0	0	0/0	0/0	0	6
G. Johnson	0	0	1	0/0	0/0	0	6
Kelley	0	1	0	0/0	0/0	0	6
Luhn	0	1	0	0/0	0/0	0	6
Ethridge	0	0	0	1/1	1/2	0	4
Packers	7	5	2	12/14	6/22	0	114
Opponents	20	15	7	40/42	11/26	2	329

Fumbles

	Fum	Ow	Op	Yds	Tot
E. Bell	0	1	0	0	1
Burris	0	0	1	0	1
Canadeo	6	1	0	0	1
Cifers	0	1	0	5	1
T. Cook	0	0	1	2	1
Craig	0	0	1	0	1
Earhart	5	1	0	0	1
Ethridge	0	1	0	0	1
Ferry	0	0	2	0	2
B. Forte	1	1	1	3	2
Fritsch	2	0	0	0	0
Girard	4	2	0	5	2
Harding	0	0	1	0	1
Heath	2	1	0	0	0
J. Jacobs	1	0	1	0	1
Kelley	1	0	0	0	0
Kirby	3	0	0	0	0
Kranz	0	0	1	7	1
Luhn	0	0	1	0	1
E. Neal	1	2	1	0	3
Odson	0	0	2	0	2
Olsen	0	0	1	0	1
Rhodemyre	0	0	1	0	1
Schlinkman	6	2	0	0	2
Summerhays	1	0	0	0	0
Tassos	0	0	2	0	2
D. Wells	0	0	1	0	1
Wildung	0	1	0	0	1
Packers	32	16	15	22	31

NFL STANDINGS

Western Division

	W	L	T	Pct	PF	PA
Los Angeles Rams	8	2	2	.800	360	239
Chicago Bears	9	3	0	.750	332	218
Chicago Cardinals	6	5	1	.545	360	301
Detroit Lions	4	8	0	.333	237	259
Green Bay Packers	2	10	0	.167	114	329

Eastern Division

	W	L	T	Pct	PF	PA
Philadelphia Eagles	11	1	0	.917	364	134
Pittsburgh Steelers	6	5	1	.545	224	214
New York Giants	6	6	0	.500	287	298
Washington Redskins	4	7	1	.364	268	339
New York Bulldogs	1	10	1	.091	153	365

The Teams: 1949   A Measure of Greatness

ROSTER

No	Name	Pos	Ht	Wt	DOB	College	G
82	Bell, Edward	G	6-1	233	09/20/21	Indiana	12
33	Burris, Paul (Buddy)	G	5-11	215	01/20/23	Oklahoma	10
3	Canadeo, Tony	HB	6-0	190	05/05/19	Gonzaga	12
16	Cifers, Bob	HB	5-11	210	09/05/20	Tennessee	9
51	Comp, Irv	HB	6-3	205	05/17/19	St. Benedict	7
48	Cook, Ted	E	6-2	195	02/06/22	Alabama	11
54	Craig, Larry	E	6-0	218	06/27/16	South Carolina	12
41	Earhart, Ralph	HB	5-10	165	03/29/23	Texas Tech	12
40	Eason, Roger	G	6-2	230	07/31/18	Oklahoma	12
85	Ethridge, Joe	T	6-0	230	04/15/28	SMU	12
18	Ferry, Louis	T	6-2	233	12/01/27	Villanova	12
35	Flowers, Bob	C	6-1	210	08/06/17	Texas Tech	1
8	Forte, Bob	HB	6-0	195	07/15/22	Arkansas	12
64	Fritsch, Ted	FB	5-10	210	10/31/20	Stevens Point	12
36	Girard, Earl (Jug)	HB	5-11	175	01/25/27	Wisconsin	12
23	Clyde Goodnight	E	6-1	195	03/03/24	Tulsa	1
31	Harding, Roger	C	6-2	215	06/11/23	California	6
39	Heath, Stan	QB	6-1	190	03/05/27	Nevada-Reno	12
27	Jacobs, Jack	QB	6-2	190	08/07/19	Oklahoma	12
35	Johnson, Glenn	T	6-4	265	06/28/22	Temple Tech	8
26	Kelley, Bill	E	6-2	195	08/23/26	Texas Tech	12
43	Kirby, Jack	HB	5-11	185	09/21/22	USC	6
42	Kranz, Kenneth	HB	5-11	187	09/12/23	Wisconsin-Milwaukee	7
47	Lipscomb, Paul	T	6-5	245	01/13/23	Tennessee	12
38	Luhn, Nolan	E	6-3	200	07/27/21	Tulsa	12
58	Neal, Ed	T	6-4	290	12/31/18	Tulane	12
63	Odson, Urban	T	6-3	250	11/17/18	Minnesota	10
46	Olsonoski, Larry	G	6-2	215	09/10/25	Minnesota	4
19	Olsen, Ralph	E	6-4	220	04/10/24	Utah	4
49	Orlich, Dan	E	6-5	215	12/21/24	Nevada-Reno	12
23	Pritko, Steve	E	6-2	215	12/25/21	Villanova	8
22	Rhodemyre, Jay	C	6-1	210	12/16/22	Kentucky	12
7	Schlinkman, Walt	FB	5-9	190	05/02/22	Texas Tech	12
21	Smith, Oscar E.	HB	6-0	185	07/20/23	Texas-El Paso	2
77	Summerhays, Bob	FB	6-1	207	03/19/27	Utah	12
15	Tassos, Damon	G	6-1	225	12/05/23	Texas A&M	12
79	Vogds, Evan	G	5-10	215	02/10/23	Wisconsin	12
43	Wells, Don	E	6-2	200	07/12/22	Georgia	2
45	Wildung, Dick	G	6-0	220	08/16/21	Minnesota	12

DRAFT

Rnd	Name	Pos	Ht	Wt	College
1	Stan Heath	B	6-1	190	Nevada-Reno
2	Dan Dworsky	C	6-0	205	Michigan
3	Louis Ferry	T	6-2	232	Villanova
4	Bob Summerhays	B	6-1	207	Utah
5	Glenn Lewis	B	5-11	190	Texas Tech
6	Joe Ethridge	T	6-0	230	SMU
7	(Choice to Rams)				
8	Dan Orlich	E	6-5	215	Nevada-Reno
9	Everett Faunce	B	5-11	178	Minnesota
10	(Choice to Rams through Lions)				
11	Harry Larche	T	6-1	220	Arkansas State
12	Rebel Steiner	E	6-0	190	Alabama
13	Al Mastrangeli	C	6-1	202	Illinois
14	Bobby Williams	C	6-2	202	Texas Tech
15	Ken Cooper	G	6-0	205	Vanderbilt
16	Gene Remenar	T	6-2	225	West Virginia
17	Paul Devine	B	5-11	185	Heidelberg
18	Floyd Lewis	G	5-11	210	SMU
19	Bobby Folsom	E	6-1	190	SMU
20	Larry Cooney	B	5-11	185	Penn State
21	Kenneth Kranz	B	5-11	187	Wis.-Milwaukee
22	John Kordick	B	5-11	190	USC
23	Bill Kelley	E	6-2	195	Texas Tech
24	Jimmy Ford	B	5-8	158	Tulsa
25	Frank Lambright	G	5-11	205	Arkansas

1949 GREEN BAY PACKERS

LEFT GROUP KNEELING: (L–R) 38 Nolan Luhn, 47 Paul Lipscomb, 15 Damon Tassos, 33 Paul Burris, 45 Dick Wildung, 44 Baby Ray, 23 Clyde Goodnight.
LEFT GROUP STANDING: (L–R) 21 Oscar E. Smith, 64 Ted Fritsch, 42 Kenneth Kranz, 27 Jack Jacobs.
MIDDLE GROUP STANDING: (L–R) 85 Joe Ethridge, 79 Evan Vogds, 77 Bob Summerhays, 66 Ralph Davis, unidentified, 16 Bob Cifers, 8 Bob Forte, 3 Tony Canadeo, 48 Ted Cook, 28 unidentified, 22 Jay Rhodemyre, 82 Edward Bell.
RIGHT GROUP KNEELING: (L–R) 43 Don Wells, 63 Urban Odson, 40 Roger Eason, 35 Bob Flowers, 58 Ed Neal, 75 Tiny Croft, 25 Eugene Canada.
RIGHT GROUP STANDING: (L–R) 18 Louis Ferry, 80 Glenn Lewis, 7 Walt Schlinkman, 51 Irv Comp.

For the first time in more than 30 years, the Packers took to the field without Curly Lambeau. Gene Ronzani, hired in early February, called the shots. The Iron Mountain, Mich., native and former Bears player and assistant coach shook up the roster like never before. Only about a third of the 35 players that suited up for at least one game in 1950 had ties to the Lambeau era. The other 23 were newcomers, added through the draft or by other means.

Finding a capable quarterback was one or Ronzani's early concerns. Jack Jacobs and Stan Heath had departed for Canada, leaving Jug Girard as the only holdover. To bolster the position, Ronzani drafted Tobin Rote out of Rice University in the second round and traded a draft choice to the Browns for Tom O'Malley. Rote, a 6-foot-3, 200-pounder, could run as well as pass and never missed a game in seven years in Green Bay. O'Malley threw a team-record six interceptions in his only appearance as a Packer. That was a 45-7 season-opening disaster against the Lions, a game in which Rote injured his shoulder.

With Rote ailing and O'Malley sent packing, Ronzani traded for the Cardinals' Paul Christman. Christman had led Chicago to the NFL title in 1947, but his stock had declined. In his final year in the NFL, the 32-year-old Christman tied Rote for the team lead in touchdown passes with seven.

Green Bay's defense presented Ronzani with problems all season long. The unit surrendered a staggering 406 points and gave up nearly 400 yards a game. It had the distinction of being the first in franchise history to allow opponents 50 touchdowns in one season.

Lambeau offered his take on the situation during Green Bay's 38-7 loss to the Browns in a preseason game on Aug. 12. Lambeau was on hand because his Cardinals were to meet the Packers that Wednesday. "Just like 1949—no effort," the coach said of his former team.

Playing off that remark, Green Bay silenced the Cardinals and Lambeau 17-14 in midweek. But by season's end, when the 3-9 Packers limped home ahead of only the lowly Baltimore Colts, Lambeau's assessment appeared on the mark.

A contingent of fans from Iron Mountain dubbed the season opener "Gene Ronzani Day" and presented the coach with a set of luggage just prior to kickoff. It was downhill from there as the Lions intercepted O'Malley and Rote seven times in a 45-7 drubbing.

Green Bay regrouped to win its next two games and climb into a five-way tie for first place. In the first, the Packers pushed aside Washington 35-21. In the second, Larry Coutre and Breezy Reid combined for 150 yards rushing in a 31-21 taming of the Bears.

The Packers wasted a 312-yard rushing effort in Week 4. Billy Grimes spearheaded the attack with 167 yards on just 10 carries, but the Yanks came out on top 44-31.

A week later, the Bears avenged their earlier loss with a 28-14 victory in Wrigley Field. Johnny Lujack scored on runs of 25, 1, and 8 yards.

Green Bay closed out the first half of the season with a 35-17 loss to the Yanks. One of the highlights was an 85-yard scoring pass from Rote to Al Baldwin.

The winless Colts then humbled the Packers. The first-year team exploded for 506 yards and six touchdowns in 41-21 affair. Jimmie Spavital pushed across three touchdowns, including a 96-yard romp.

The Rams were just as deadly in a racking up a 45-14 win on Nov. 14.

The Packers dropped their sixth straight in Detroit on Nov. 19. Fred Enke passed to Doak Walker with less than two minutes left to give the Lions a 24-21 victory.

Green Bay staged a fourth-quarter rally amid blustery conditions at City Stadium in Week 10. Ignoring winds that gusted up to 28 miles per hour, the Packers posted 12 points in the final period to defeat San Francisco 25-21. The winning touchdown was engineered by Christman on a 44-yard pass to Reid with three minutes remaining.

The Green and Gold wrapped up its season by traveling to California for two early-December games. The change in the weather did them no good.

On Dec. 3, Tom Fears caught a then-record 18 passes for 189 yards and two touchdowns as the Rams throttled Green Bay 51-14. A week later the season mercifully ended in San Francisco, where the 49ers notched their third win of the year 30-14.

A TORRENT OF TURNOVERS

On the Packers' 13th offensive play of the season, Tobin Rote's pass was intercepted by the Lions' Don Doll. It was the first of a team-record 57 turnovers committed by Green Bay in 1950.

Green Bay passers were intercepted a league-high 37 times. The team also lost 20 fumbles. Only the Steelers (58) had more turnovers than did the Packers.

The Packers were guilty of at least two turnovers in every game except one. They had a clean slate in a 35-21 win over the Redskins in Week 2.

Surprisingly, the Packers' eight turnovers in the season opener was not the team high. They coughed up the ball nine times to the Rams who trounced them 45-14 in Week 8.

Most Turnovers, Season

No.	Year	Record
57	1950	3-9-0
56	1952	6-6-0
50	1983, 1988	8-8-0, 4-12-0
48	1948, 1953	3-9-0, 2-9-1

TEAM STATISTICS

	GB	OPP
First Downs	174	220
Rushing	82	91
Passing	70	110
Penalty	22	19
Rushes	398	422
Yards Gained	1,706	1,885
Average Gain	4.29	4.47
Average Yards per Game	142.2	157.1
Passes Attempted	367	379
Completed	140	185
% Completed	38.15	48.81
Total Yards Gained	1,831	2,818
Yards Lost	327	230
Net Yards Gained	1,504	2,588
Yards Gained per Completion	13.08	15.23
Average Net Yards per Game	152.6	234.8
Combined Net Yards Gained	3,537	4,703
Total Plays	765	801
Average Yards per Play	4.62	5.87
Average Net Yards per Game	294.8	391.9
Intercepted By	27	37
Yards Returned	337	575
Returned for TD	2	5
Punts	74	72
Yards Punted	2,822	2,891
Average Yards per Punt	38.14	40.15
Punt Returns	44	49
Yards Returned	729	372
Average Yards per Return	16.57	7.59
Returned for TD	2	0
Kickoff Returns	56	41
Yards Returned	1,233	845
Average Yards per Return	22.02	20.61
Returned for TD	0	0
Penalties	85	95
Yards Penalized	757	919
Fumbles	35	34
Lost	20	15
Own Recovered for Touchdown	0	1
Opponent's Recovered by	15	20
Opponent's Recovered for Touchdown	1	3
Total Points Scored	244	406
Total Touchdowns	34	56
Touchdowns Rushing	15	24
Touchdowns Passing	14	24
Touchdowns on Returns & Recoveries	5	8
Extra Points	31	50
Safeties	0	1
Field Goals Attempted	17	13
Field Goals Made	3	6
% Successful	17.65	46.15

Regular Season   3-9-0

Date	GB		OPP	Att.
9/17	7	Detroit Lions	45	(22,096)
9/24	35	Washington Redskins (M)	21	(14,109)
10/1	31	Chicago Bears	21	(24,893)
10/8	31	New York Yank	44	(23,871)
10/15	14	at Chicago Bears	28	(51,065)
10/19	17	at New York Yank	35	(13,661)
11/5	21	at Baltimore Colts	41	(12,971)
11/12	14	Los Angeles Rams (M)	45	(20,456)
11/19	21	at Detroit Lions	24	(17,752)
11/26	25	San Francisco 49ers	21	(13,196)
12/3	14	at Los Angeles Rams	51	(39,323)
12/10	14	at San Francisco 49ers	30	(20,797)

Score By Periods

	1	2	3	4	Total
Packers	41	58	77	68	244
Opponents	53	123	127	103	406

INDIVIDUAL STATISTICS

Rushing

	Att	Yds	Avg	LG	TD
Grimes	84	480	5.7	t73	5
Reid	87	394	4.5	57	1
Coutre	41	283	6.9	53	1
Canadeo	93	247	2.7	15	4
Rote	27	158	5.9	29	1
Cloud	18	52	2.9	13	3
Girard	14	39	2.8	11	0
Christman	7	18	2.6	4	1
Boedecker	8	16	2.0	8	0
Fritsch	7	13	1.9	5	0
B. Forte	9	13	1.4	11	0
Cannava	1	2	2.0	2	0
Dreyer	1	0	0.0	0	0
O'Malley	1	-9	-9.0	-9	0
Packers	398	1,706	4.3	t73	15
Opponents	422	1,885	4.5	t96	24

Receiving

	No	Yds	Avg	LG	TD
Baldwin	28	555	19.8	t85	3
Grimes	17	261	15.4	t96	1
Coutre	17	206	12.1	t77	2
Pritko	17	125	7.4	14	2
T. Cook	16	182	11.4	t21	3
Reid	11	120	10.9	t44	2
Canadeo	10	54	5.4	20	0
B. Mann	6	89	14.8	40	1
Manley	5	66	13.2	18	0
Girard	4	89	22.3	55	0
Cloud	3	19	6.3	13	0
Wimberly	2	18	9.0	10	0
B. Forte	2	9	4.5	10	0
Cannava	1	28	28.0	28	0
Boedecker	1	10	10.0	10	0
Packers	140	1,831	13.1	t96	14
Opponents	185	2,818	15.2	t74	24

Passing

	Att	Com	Yds	Pct	TD	In	Yds	Rate
Rote	224	83	1,231	37.1	7	24	153	26.7
Christman	126	51	545	40.5	7	7	132	49.2
O'Malley	15	4	31	26.7	0	6	42	0.0
B. Forte	2	2	24	100.0	0	0	0	—
Packers	367	140	1,831	38.2	14	37	327	27.8
Opponents	379	185	2,818	48.8	24	27	230	65.2

Punting

	No	Yds	Avg	LG	HB
Girard	71	2,715	38.2	63	2
B. Forte	3	107	35.7	39	0
Packers	74	2,822	38.1	63	2
Opponents	72	2,891	40.2	65	1

Kickoff Returns

	No	Yds	Avg	LG	TD
Grimes	26	600	23.1	36	0
Canadeo	16	411	25.7	48	0
B. Forte	3	73	24.3	34	0
DiPierro	3	42	14.0	26	0
Burris	3	18	6.0	11	0
Fritsch	2	34	17.0	19	0
Girard	1	25	25.0	25	0
Boedecker	1	20	20.0	20	0
Cannava	1	10	10.0	10	0
Packers	56	1,233	22.0	48	0
Opponents	41	845	20.6	50	0

Punt Returns

	No	Yds	Avg	LG	TD
Grimes	29	555	19.1	t85	2
Canadeo	5	68	13.6	21	0
Boedecker	5	49	9.8	12	0
Dreyer	3	48	16.0	22	0
Cannava	2	9	4.5	9	0
Packers	44	729	16.6	t85	2
Opponents	49	372	7.6	29	0

Interceptions

	No	Yds	Avg	LG	TD
Steiner	7	190	27.1	t94	1
Dreyer	5	62	12.4	34	1
Baldwin	5	35	7.0	22	0
Wizbicki	2	38	19.0	34	0
Girard	1	6	6.0	6	0
B. Forte	1	5	5.0	5	0
Tonnemaker	1	1	1.0	1	0
Orlich	1	0	0.0	0	0
Schuette	1	0	0.0	0	0
J. Spencer	1	0	0.0	0	0
Summerhays	1	0	0.0	0	0
Wimberly	1	0	0.0	0	0
Packers	27	337	12.5	t94	2
Opponents	37	575	15.5	t56	5

Scoring

	TDr	TDp	TDrt	PAT	FG	S	TP
Grimes	5	1	2	0/0	0/0	0	48
Fritsch	0	0	0	30/33	3/17	0	39
Canadeo	4	0	0	0/0	0/0	0	24
Baldwin	0	3	0	0/0	0/0	0	18
Cloud	3	0	0	0/0	0/0	0	18
T. Cook	0	3	0	0/0	0/0	0	18
Coutre	1	2	0	0/0	0/0	0	18
Reid	1	2	0	0/0	0/0	0	18
Pritko	0	2	0	0/0	0/0	0	12
Christman	1	0	0	0/0	0/0	0	6
Dreyer	0	0	1	0/0	0/0	0	6
B. Mann	0	1	0	0/0	0/0	0	6
Orlich	0	0	1	0/0	0/0	0	6
Steiner	0	0	1	0/0	0/0	0	6
Tonnemaker	0	0	0	0/1	0/0	1	1
Packers	15	14	5	31/34	3/17	0	244
Opponents	24	24	8	50/56	6/13	1	406

Fumbles

	Fum	Ow	Op	Yds	Tot
Baldwin	3	1	0	-3	1
Canadeo	4	2	0	0	2
Cannava	1	0	0	0	0
Christman	2	0	0	0	0
Cloud	1	0	0	0	0
T. Cook	1	0	0	0	0
Coutre	1	0	0	0	0
Girard	1	0	0	0	0
Grimes	8	3	0	0	3
McGeary	0	0	1	0	1
E. Neal	0	0	1	0	1
Orlich	0	0	3	37	3
Pritko	1	0	0	0	0
Reid	3	0	0	0	0
Rote	9	3	0	-21	3
Schuette	0	0	3	0	3
J. Spencer	0	1	1	0	2
Stansauk	0	0	2	0	2
Summerhays	0	0	1	0	1
Szarfaryn	0	1	1	0	2
Wildung	0	2	0	1	2
Wimberly	0	0	2	0	2
Wizbicki	0	0	2	12	2
Packers	35	15	15	34	30

NFL STANDINGS

National Conference

	W	L	T	Pct	PF	PA
Los Angeles Rams	9	3	0	.750	466	309
Chicago Bears	9	3	0	.750	279	207
New York Yanks	7	5	0	.583	366	367
Detroit Lions	6	6	0	.500	321	285
Green Bay Packers	3	9	0	.250	244	406
San Francisco 49ers	3	9	0	.250	213	300
Baltimore Colts	1	11	0	.083	213	462

American Conference

	W	L	T	Pct	PF	PA
Cleveland Browns	10	2	0	.833	310	144
New York Giants	10	2	0	.833	268	150
Philadelphia Eagles	6	6	0	.500	254	141
Pittsburgh Steelers	6	6	0	.500	180	195
Chicago Cardinals	5	7	0	.417	233	287
Washington Redskins	3	9	0	.250	232	326

1950

ROSTER

No	Name	Pos	Ht	Wt	DOB	College	G
19	Baldwin, Al	E	6-2	210	02/21/25	Arkansas	12
31	Boedecker, Bill	HB	5-11	195	03/07/24	Kalamazoo	9
33	Burris, Paul (Buddy)	G	5-11	215	01/20/23	Oklahoma	12
3	Canadeo, Tony	HB	6-0	190	05/05/19	Gonzaga	12
42	Cannava, Al	HB	5-10	180	05/24/24	Boston College	1
28	Christman, Paul	QB	6-0	200	03/05/18	Missouri	11
82	Cloud, Jack	FB	5-10	220	01/01/25	William and Mary	9
48	Cook, Ted	E	6-2	195	02/06/22	Alabama	12
27	Coutre, Larry	HB	5-10	175	04/11/28	Notre Dame	12
21	DiPierro, Ray	G	5-11	210	08/22/26	Ohio State	12
42	Dryer, Wally	HB	5-10	170	02/25/23	Wisconsin	12
18	Drulis, Charles	G	5-10	220	03/08/18	Temple	11
55	Ecker, Ed	T	6-7	270	01/21/23	John Carroll	12
8	Forte, Bob	HB	6-0	205	07/15/22	Arkansas	12
64	Fritsch, Ted	FB	5-10	210	10/31/20	Stevens Point	12
36	Girard, Earl (Jug)	HB	5-11	175	01/25/27	Wisconsin	12
22	Grimes, Billy	HB	6-1	197	07/27/27	Oklahoma State	12
90	Manley, Leon	G/T	6-2	210	05/20/26	Oklahoma	12
31	Mann, Bob	E	5-11	175	04/08/24	Michigan	3
44	McGeary, Clarence	T	6-5	250	08/08/26	North Dakota	12
58	Neal, Ed	T	6-4	275	12/31/18	Tulane	12
76	O'Malley, Tom	QB	5-11	185	07/23/25	Cincinnati	1
49	Orlich, Dan	E	6-5	215	12/21/24	Nevada-Reno	12
23	Pritko, Steve	E	6-2	210	12/25/21	Villanova	12
80	Reid, Floyd (Breezy)	HB	5-10	187	09/04/27	Georgia	11
38	Rote, Tobin	QB	6-3	200	01/18/28	Rice	12
25	Wizbicki, Alex	B	5-11	188	10/06/21	Holy Cross	11
17	Schuette, Carl	C	6-1	210	04/04/22	Marquette	12
34	Spencer, Joe	T	6-3	240	08/15/23	Oklahoma State	12
63	Stansauk, Don	T	6-2	255	03/16/26	Denver	11
74	Steiner, Rebel	DB	6-0	185	08/27/27	Alabama	12
77	Summerhays, Bob	FB	6-1	207	03/19/27	Utah	11
51	Szafaryn, Len	G	6-2	229	01/19/28	North Carolina	12
35	Tonnemaker, Clayton	C	6-2	235	08/08/28	Minnesota	12
45	Wildung, Dick	T	6-0	220	08/16/21	Minnesota	12
16	Wimberly, Abner	E	6-1	210	05/04/26	LSU	11

DRAFT

Rnd	Name	Pos	Ht	Wt	College
1	Clayton Tonnemaker	C	6-2	235	Minnesota
2	Tobin Rote	QB	6-3	200	Rice
3	Gordy Soltau	E	6-2	215	Minnesota
4	Larry Coutre	RB	5-10	175	Notre Dame
5	(Choice to Steelers)				
6	Jack Cloud	B	5-10	220	William and Mary
7	Leon Manley	T	6-2	220	Oklahoma
8	Harry Szulborski	B	5-10	175	Purdue
9	Roger Wilson	E	6-1	210	South Carolina
10	Bob Mealey	T	6-2	225	Minnesota
11	Gene Lorendo	E	6-0	205	Georgia
12	Andy Pavich	E	6-0	196	Denver
13	Carlton Elliott	E	6-4	215	Virginia
14	Fred Leon	T	6-0	220	Nevada-Reno
15	Gene Huebner	C	6-4	230	Baylor
16	Frank Kuzma	B	6-0	200	Minnesota
17	Hal Otterback	G	6-2	210	Wisconsin
18	Arnold Galiffa	QB	6-2	190	Army
19	Earl T. Rowan	T	5-11	240	Hardin-Simmons
20	Jim Howe	B	6-2	190	Kentucky
21	Gene Evans	B	5-7	165	Wisconsin
22	Chuck Beatty	C	6-1	215	Penn State
23	George Mattey	G	5-10	225	Ohio State
24	Don Delph	B	6-0	190	Dayton
25	Frank Waters	B	6-0	202	Michigan State
26	Claude Radtke	E	6-3	196	Lawrence
27	Bill Osbourne	B	6-1	205	Nevada-Reno
28	Herm Hering	B	6-2	195	Rutgers
29	Ben Zaranka	E	6-4	191	Kentucky
30	Ray Mallouf	B	6-0	185	SMU

1950 GREEN BAY PACKERS

FRONT ROW: (L-R) 18 Charles Drulis, 16 Abner Wimberly, 21 Ray DiPierro, 63 Don Stansauk, 36 Earl (Jug) Girard, 22 Billy Grimes, 82 Jack Cloud, 58 Ed Neal, 64 Ted Fritsch, 3 Tony Canadeo.
SECOND ROW: (L-R) 17 Carl Schuette, 44 Clarence McGeary, 33 Paul Burris, 74 Rebel Steiner, 25 Alex Wizbicki, 31 Bill Boedecker, 35 Clayton Tonnemaker, 27 Larry Coutre, 42 Wally Dreyer.
THIRD ROW: (L-R) 55 Ed Ecker, 77 Bob Summerhays, 51 Len Szafaryn, 49 Dan Orlich, 90 Leon Manley, 38 Tobin Rote, 19 Al Baldwin, 34 Joe Spencer.
FOURTH ROW: (L-R) Property Man Dick Geniesse, 23 Steve Pritko, 28 Paul Christman, 8 Bob Forte, 45 Dick Wildung, 48 Ted Cook, 80 Breezy Reid, Trainer Carl (Bud) Jorgensen.
BACK ROW: (L-R) Head Coach Gene Ronzani, Backfield Coach Ray Nolting, End Coach Dick Plasman, Line Coach John (Tarzan) Taylor.

The Packers of 1951 were a pass-happy bunch that threw more often than any other, finishing second only to the vaunted aerial attack of the Rams in yards gained. Passes by Tobin Rote and Bobby Thomason accounted for more than two-thirds of the team's offensive production. The club attempted 478 passes and completed 231 for 2,846 yards—single-season team records that wouldn't be broken until the 16-game schedules of the late 1970s.

Seventeen players caught at least one pass. Heading the list were Bob Mann, Ray Pelfrey, and Carlton Elliott.

Mann caught 50 passes for 696 yards and eight touchdowns. He joined the Packers for the last three games of 1950 and became the first African-American to play in a regular-season game for the team. As a Lion in 1949, Mann led the NFL in receiving yards (1,014).

Elliott and Pelfrey arrived via the draft. Elliott, who failed to make the team as a 13th-round pick in 1950, caught 35 passes. Pelfrey, a 17th-round selection in 1951, hauled in 38 passes. Both reached the end zone five times.

With such an emphasis on the pass, Green Bay's running game lagged. The team failed to average 100 yards rushing per game (99.7) for the first time since 1934. Green Bay's eight rushing touchdowns was a league low.

The Korean War entered its second year in 1951 and many players were called to duty. Green Bay lost Bob Forte, Larry Coutre, Wally Dreyer, Clayton Tonnemaker and Len Szafaryn to the war effort.

The war also affected how the Packers drafted. Going into the selection process, the team targeted players who were either 4-F or who had already fulfilled their service obligations. This approach—taking available bodies over talent—produced only four draftees that made the team: Fred Cone, Rip Collins, Dick Afflis and Pelfrey.

Gene Ronzani didn't rely solely on the draft. He obtained Thomason from the Rams and sent Ted Cook to Washington in exchange for defensive end John Martinkovic. The coach also pulled off a trade with Cleveland, getting Dom Moselle, Ace Loomis, Charley Schroll, Walt Michaels and Dan Orlich. The Browns picked up the rights to sign the Green Bay's top pick, Bob Gain, who was playing in Canada, and a draft choice in 1952.

The Packers severed ties with one of the last players remaining from the 1944 championship team. Ted Fritsch, a rookie in 1942, was released on the final cutdown. That left Tony Canadeo as the only holdover from that era.

Green Bay unveiled a new one-back offense in opening against the Bears. Ronzani kept only the fullback (either Jack Cloud or Fred Cone) in the backfield with Rote. He sent his halfbacks (Canadeo, Billy Grimes or Jug Girard) out wide. The effect of this new look was debateable as the Bears won easily 31-20.

Green Bay blew a 28-point lead in Week 2 only to regain the upper hand in the last five minutes when Rote's 16-yard touchdown pass to Mann edged Pittsburgh 35-33.

As they had done in 1950, the Packers won again in Week 3 to create a five-way tie for first place. Mann caught three touchdown passes to beat the Eagles 37-24.

The Rams again proved troublesome. Dan Towler rushed for 144 yards and Elroy Hirsch snagged three passes for 111 yards in a 28-0 shutout.

In Week 5, Thomason had his finest game as a Packer. The 23-year-old launched three touchdown passes in the fourth quarter and presided over the final scoring drive that resulted in Fred Cone's 16-yard field goal with 11 seconds left. Thomason completed 15 passes in 22 attempts for 214 yards and three scores.

The win was the last of the year. Green Bay blew its last seven games to fall completely out of the race and finish the year with the same record (3-9) it had in 1950.

On Nov. 22, the team began its annual rite of playing in Detroit on Thanksgiving, a tradition that ran through the 1963 season. The Packers had little luck on this initial outing, dropping a 52-35 decision that featured two long punt returns for touchdowns by Jack Christiansen.

The Packers returned home to celebrate their past with Don Hutson Day. The record-setting end had his number officially retired at halftime. His presence had little effect on the outcome, as Green Bay fell to the Yanks 31-28.

Green Bay then closed with two losses on the West Coast: 31-19 at San Francisco and 42-14 in Los Angeles.

A PASSING FANCY

Just how pass-happy was Green Bay in 1951? No team in Packers history attempted more passes per game than did the club piloted by Tobin Rote and Bobby Thomason.

That the team would emphasize this method of attack was evident from the start. In the season opener, Green Bay unveiled a two-man backfield consisting of a quarterback and fullback. The halfbacks played out wide. The Packers threw 41 passes at the Bears that day.

In the rematch, Rote often lined up as the only back behind center. He threw 33 passes and rushed for 150 yards on 14 carries. His teammates gained 23 yards on 10 tries.

The Packers threw 40 or more passes in 8 different games. In the season finale, Rote and Thomason combined for 56 throws and 379 yards of passing offense.

Most Pass Attempts per Game, Season

Atts.	Year	Att./Games
39.83	1951	(478/12)
38.06	1994	(609/16)
37.81	1999	(605/16)
37.50	2000	(600/16)

TEAM STATISTICS

	GB	OPP
First Downs	218	236
Rushing	75	127
Passing	115	95
Penalty	28	14
Rushes	313	496
Yards Gained	1,196	2,152
Average Gain	3.82	4.34
Average Yards per Game	99.7	179.3
Passes Attempted	478	313
Completed	231	157
% Completed	48.33	50.16
Total Yards Gained	2,846	2,535
Yards Lost	289	212
Net Yards Gained	2,557	2,318
Yards Gained per Completion	12.32	16.15
Average Net Yards per Game	237.2	211.3
Combined Net Yards Gained	4,042	4,687
Total Plays	791	809
Average Yards per Play	5.11	5.79
Average Net Yards per Game	336.8	390.6
Intercepted By	22	29
Yards Returned	292	387
Returned for TD	1	1
Punts	61	62
Yards Punted	2,504	2,333
Average Yards per Punt	41.05	37.63
Punt Returns	29	38
Yards Returned	213	564
Average Yards per Return	7.34	14.84
Returned for TD	0	2
Kickoff Returns	60	40
Yards Returned	1,449	741
Average Yards per Return	24.15	18.53
Returned for TD	0	0
Penalties	90	99
Yards Penalized	790	924
Fumbles	23	23
Lost	15	13
Own Recovered for Touchdown	0	0
Opponent's Recovered by	13	15
Opponent's Recovered for Touchdown	0	0
Total Points Scored	254	375
Total Touchdowns	35	50
Touchdowns Rushing	8	22
Touchdowns Passing	26	25
Touchdowns on Returns & Recoveries	1	3
Extra Points	29	49
Safeties	0	1
Field Goals Attempted	8	17
Field Goals Made	5	8
% Successful	62.50	47.06

Regular Season   3-9-0

Date	GB		OPP	Att.
9/30	20	Chicago Bears	31	(24,666)
10/7	35	Pittsburgh Steelers (M)	33	(8,324)
10/14	37	Philadelphia Eagles	24	(18,489)
10/21	31	Los Angeles Rams (M)	28	(21,393)
10/28	29	at New York Yanks	27	(7,351)
11/4	17	Detroit Lions	24	(18,800)
11/11	7	at Pittsburgh Steelers	28	(20,080)
11/18	13	at Chicago Bears	24	(36,771)
11/22	35	at Detroit Lions	52	(33,452)
12/2	28	New York Yanks	31	(14,297)
12/9	19	at San Francisco 49ers	31	(18,681)
12/16	14	at Los Angeles Rams	42	(23,698)

Score By Periods

	1	2	3	4	Total
Packers	62	56	37	99	254
Opponents	68	96	86	125	375

INDIVIDUAL STATISTICS

Rushing

	Att	Yds	Avg	LG	TD
Rote	76	523	6.9	t55	3
Cone	56	190	3.4	16	1
Canadeo	54	131	2.4	15	1
Grimes	44	123	2.8	t18	1
Reid	23	73	3.2	33	0
Cloud	29	61	2.1	19	1
Pelfrey	3	44	14.7	24	0
Moselle	12	23	1.9	7	1
Girard	4	20	5.0	32	0
B. Mann	2	9	4.5	9	0
A. Collins	5	4	0.8	6	0
Thomason	5	-5	-1.0	10	0
Packers	**313**	**1,196**	**3.8**	**t55**	**8**
Opponents	496	2,152	4.3	t85	22

Receiving

	No	Yds	Avg	LG	TD
B. Mann	50	696	13.9	52	8
Pelfrey	38	462	12.2	49	5
Elliott	35	317	9.1	33	5
Cone	28	315	11.3	49	0
Canadeo	22	226	10.3	46	2
Grimes	15	170	11.3	t38	1
Moselle	14	233	16.6	85	2
Girard	10	220	22.0	t75	2
Reid	9	115	12.8	29	0
Cloud	3	16	5.3	t6	1
H. Davis	1	15	15.0	15	0
Moje	1	11	11.0	11	0
Wimberly	1	10	10.0	10	0
Loomis	1	9	9.0	9	0
Orlich	1	9	9.0	9	0
Jansante	1	6	6.0	6	0
A. Collins	1	5	5.0	5	0
Rote	0	11	—	11	0
Packers	**231**	**2,846**	**12.3**	**85**	**26**
Opponents	157	2,535	16.2	t81	25

Passing

	Att	Com	Yds	Pct	TD	In	Yds	Rate
Rote	256	106	1,540	41.4	15	20	143	48.6
Thomason	221	125	1,306	56.6	11	9	146	73.5
Reid	1	0	0	00.0	0	0	0	—
Packers	**478**	**231**	**2,846**	**48.3**	**26**	**29**	**289**	**60.0**
Opponents	313	157	2,535	50.2	25	22	212	75.0

Punting

	No	Yds	Avg	LG	HB
Girard	52	2,101	40.4	66	0
Pelfrey	5	220	44.0	46	0
A. Collins	2	81	40.5	49	0
Rote	1	55	55.0	55	0
Cone	1	47	47.0	47	0
Packers	**61**	**2,504**	**41.1**	**66**	**0**
Opponents	62	2,333	37.6	72	0

Kickoff Returns

	No	Yds	Avg	LG	TD
Grimes	23	582	25.3	47	0
Moselle	20	547	27.4	44	0
W. Michaels	5	86	17.2	26	0
Canadeo	4	101	25.3	48	0
Martinkovic	2	34	17.0	31	0
Wimberly	2	4	2.0	3	0
A. Collins	1	40	40.0	40	0
Summerhays	1	21	21.0	21	0
Cone	1	20	20.0	20	0
Elliott	1	14	14.0	14	0
Packers	**60**	**1,449**	**24.2**	**48**	**0**
Opponents	40	741	18.5	41	0

Punt Returns

	No	Yds	Avg	LG	TD
Grimes	16	100	6.3	26	0
Moselle	9	80	8.9	17	0
H. Davis	2	21	10.5	17	0
Girard	1	9	9.0	9	0
Nussbaumer	1	3	3.0	3	0
Packers	**29**	**213**	**7.3**	**26**	**0**
Opponents	38	564	14.8	t89	2

Interceptions

	No	Yds	Avg	LG	TD
Girard	5	25	5.0	15	0
Loomis	4	103	25.8	66	0
H. Davis	4	37	9.3	25	0
Steiner	3	4	1.3	3	0
Summerhays	2	112	56.0	t88	1
A. Collins	2	0	0.0	0	0
Ruetz	1	11	11.0	11	0
Moselle	1	0	0.0	0	0
Packers	**22**	**292**	**13.3**	**t88**	**1**
Opponents	29	387	13.3	40	1

Scoring

	TDr	TDp	TDrt	PAT	FG	S	TP
Cone	1	0	0	29/35	5/7	0	50
B. Mann	0	8	0	0/0	0/0	0	48
Elliott	0	5	0	0/0	0/0	0	30
Pelfrey	0	5	0	0/0	0/0	0	30
Canadeo	1	2	0	0/0	0/0	0	18
Moselle	1	2	0	0/0	0/0	0	18
Rote	3	0	0	0/0	0/0	0	18
Cloud	1	1	0	0/0	0/0	0	12
Girard	0	2	0	0/0	0/0	0	12
Grimes	1	1	0	0/0	0/0	0	12
Summerhays	0	0	1	0/0	0/0	0	6
W. Michaels	0	0	0	0/0	0/0	0	0
Packers	**8**	**26**	**1**	**29/35**	**5/8**	**0**	**254**
Opponents	22	25	3	49/50	8/17	1	375

Fumbles

	Fum	Ow	Op	Yds	Tot
Burris	0	1	0	0	1
Canadeo	2	0	0	0	0
Cloud	2	1	0	0	1
Cone	1	0	1	0	1
H. Davis	0	1	0	0	1
Girard	1	1	0	0	2
Grimes	5	0	0	0	0
Loomis	0	0	2	0	2
Martinkovic	0	0	2	10	2
Moselle	4	1	0	0	2
Orlich	0	0	1	31	1
Reid	1	0	0	0	0
Rhodemyre	0	0	1	0	1
Rote	4	1	0	0	1
Ruetz	0	0	1	0	1
Summerhays	0	0	2	0	2
Thomason	2	0	0	0	0
Wildung	0	0	2	0	2
Wimberly	1	1	0	0	1
Packers	**23**	**8**	**13**	**41**	**21**

NFL STANDINGS

National Conference

	W	L	T	Pct	PF	PA
Los Angeles Rams	8	4	0	.667	392	261
Detroit Lions	7	4	1	.636	336	259
San Francisco 49ers	7	4	1	.636	255	205
Chicago Bears	7	5	0	.583	286	282
Green Bay Packers	**3**	**9**	**0**	**.250**	**254**	**375**
New York Yanks	1	9	2	.100	241	382

American Conference

	W	L	T	Pct	PF	PA
Cleveland Browns	11	1	0	.917	331	152
New York Giants	9	2	1	.818	254	161
Washington Redskins	5	7	0	.417	183	296
Pittsburgh Steelers	4	7	1	.364	183	235
Philadelphia Eagles	4	8	0	.333	234	264
Chicago Cardinals	3	9	0	.250	210	287

1951

ROSTER

No	Name	Pos	Ht	Wt	DOB	College	G
15	Afflis, Dick	G	6-0	252	06/27/29	Nevada	12
33	Burris, Paul (Buddy)	G	5-11	215	01/20/23	Oklahoma	7
3	Canadeo, Tony	HB	6-0	190	05/05/19	Gonzaga	12
82	Cloud, Jack	FB	5-10	220	01/01/25	William and Mary	4
65	Collins, Albin (Rip)	HB	5-11	190	09/27/27	LSU	7
66	Cone, Fred	FB	5-11	197	06/21/26	Clemson	12
25	Davis, Harper	HB	5-11	172	12/11/25	Mississippi State	12
21	DiPierro, Ray	G	5-11	210	08/22/26	Ohio State	6
55	Ecker, Ed	T	6-7	270	01/21/23	John Carroll	7
40	Elliott, Carlton	E	6-4	215	11/12/27	Virginia	12
36	Girard, Earl (Jug)	HB	5-11	175	01/25/27	Wisconsin	12
22	Grimes, Billy	HB	6-1	197	07/27/27	Oklahoma State	12
23	Jansante, Val	E	6-1	190	09/27/21	Duquesne	3
7	Loomis, Ace	HB	6-1	190	06/12/28	Wisconsin-LaCrosse	12
90	Manley, Leon	G/T	6-2	225	05/20/26	Oklahoma	12
31	Mann, Bob	E	5-11	175	04/08/24	Michigan	11
39	Martinkovic, John	DE	6-3	235	02/04/27	Xavier	12
35	Michaels, Walt	G	6-0	225	10/16/29	Washington and Lee	12
79	Moje, Dick	E	6-3	210	05/08/27	Loyola (Los Angeles)	2
93	Moselle, Dom	HB	6-0	192	06/03/26	Wisconsin-Superior	12
58	Neal, Ed	T	6-4	275	12/31/18	Tulane	1
46	Nichols, Hamilton	G	5-11	215	10/18/24	Rice	9
23	Nussbaumer, Bob	HB	5-11	175	04/23/24	Michigan	4
49	Orlich, Dan	E	6-5	215	12/21/24	Nevada-Reno	12
8	Pelfrey, Ray	E	6-0	190	01/11/28	Eastern Kentucky	12
80	Reid, Floyd (Breezy)	HB	5-10	187	09/04/27	Georgia	12
85	Rhodemyre, Jay	C	6-1	210	12/16/22	Kentucky	12
18	Robinson, Charley	G	5-11	240	05/30/27	Morgan State	2
38	Rote, Tobin	QB	6-3	200	01/18/28	Rice	12
75	Ruetz, Howard	T	6-3	265	08/18/27	Loras	12
86	Schroll, Charles	G	6-0	218	01/24/26	LSU	12
17	Schuette, Carl	C	6-1	210	04/04/22	Marquette	12
34	Spencer, Joe	T	6-3	240	08/15/23	Oklahoma State	12
63	Stansauk, Don	T	6-2	255	03/16/26	Denver	4
74	Steiner, Rebel	DB	6-0	185	08/27/27	Alabama	12
44	Stephenson, Dave	G	6-2	235	10/22/25	West Virginia	12
77	Summerhays, Bob	FB	6-1	215	03/19/27	Utah	12
28	Thomason, Bobby	QB	6-1	197	03/26/28	Virginia Military	11
45	Wildung, Dick	T	6-0	220	08/16/21	Minnesota	12
16	Wimberly, Abner	E	6-1	210	05/04/26	LSU	12

DRAFT

Rnd	Name	Pos	Ht	Wt	College
1	Bob Gain	T	6-3	235	Kentucky
2	Albin (Rip) Collins	HB	5-11	190	LSU
3	Fred Cone	FB	5-10	197	Clemson
4	(Choice to Browns)				
5	Wade Stinson	HB	5-11	180	Kansas
6	Sidmund Holowenko	T	6-3	240	John Carroll
7	Bill Sutherland	E	6-2	210	St. Vincent
8	(Choice to Browns)				
9	Dick McWilliams	T	6-3	242	Michigan
10	Bob Noppinger	E	6-3	215	Georgetown
11	George Rooks	FB	6-0	215	Morgan State
12	Carl Kreager	C	6-1	215	Michigan
13	Ed Stephens	HB	5-11	182	Missouri
14	Ray Bauer	E	6-1	190	Montana
15	Joe Ernst	QB	6-0	185	Tulane
16	Dick Afflis	T	5-11	252	Nevada
17	Ray Pelfrey	HB	6-0	190	Eastern Kentucky
18	Ed Petela	FB	5-10	200	Boston College
19	Jim Liber	HB	5-8	175	Xavier
20	Dick Johnson	T	6-1	225	Virginia
21	Art Edling	E	6-2	200	Minnesota
22	Art Felker	E	6-2	205	Marquette
23	Tubba Chamberlain	T	6-3	285	Wis.-Eau Claire
24	Dick Christie	FB	5-11	190	Nevada-Omaha
25	Charles Monte	HB	6-1	195	Hillsdale
26	Bill Miller	T	6-1	225	Ohio State
27	Bob Bossons	C	6-0	198	Georgia Tech
28	Bill Ayre	HB	5-11	192	Abilene Christian
29	Ralph Fieler	E	6-5	230	Miami (FL)
30	Ed Withers	HB	6-0	188	Wisconsin

1951 GREEN BAY PACKERS

FRONT ROW: (L-R) 66 Fred Cone, 21 Ray DiPierro, 36 Jug Girard, 93 Dom Moselle, 8 Ray Pelfrey, 3 Tony Canadeo, 74 Rebel Steiner, 65 Rip Collins, 31 Bob Mann, 25 Harper Davis, 80 Breezy Reid.

MIDDLE ROW: (L-R) Tubby Bero, 7 Ace Loomis, 85 Jay Rhodemyre, 17 Carl Schuette, 16 Abner Wimberly, 77 Bob Summerhays, 86 Charles Schroll, 28 Bobby Thomason, 22 Billy Grimes, 23 Val Jansante, 35 Walt Michaels, 15 Dick Afflis, Line Coach Charles Drulis.

BACK ROW: (L-R) Head Coach Gene Ronzani, Line Coach John (Tarzan) Taylor, Backfield Coach Ray (Scooter) McLean, 45 Dick Wildung, 44 Dave Stephenson, 90 Leon Manley, 34 Joe Spencer, 19 Dan Orlich, 55 Ed Ecker, 40 Carlton Elliott, 38 Tobin Rote, 39 John Martinkovic, 75 Howard Ruetz, End Coach Dick Plasman, Trainer Carl (Bud) Jorgensen, Assistant Trainer John Proski.

Swept along by a four-game winning streak, the Packers of 1952 ascended to first place in the National Conference with three weeks remaining. Not since the championship year of 1944 had the team controlled its own playoff destiny so late in a season.

After nine weeks, the Packers, Lions, Rams, and 49ers all had six wins and three losses. The schedule made the situation even better for Green Bay, which, in order, finished at Detroit, Los Angeles, and San Francisco.

The mission was simple. Win all three and win the conference title outright. Even one win (as long as it wasn't against Detroit) opened possibilities (however remote) in which Green Bay could have tied for the conference lead.

Unfortunately, the stretch run did little more than confirm the team did not belong among the elite. Green Bay dropped its final three games by a combined score of 65 to 117 to finish in fourth place with a 6-6 record.

The early resurgence was due in part to the efforts of a talented rookie class, the likes of which hadn't been seen in Green Bay in a long time. A change in drafting philosophy—taking the best player available—resulted in the Packers nabbing Babe Parilli, Bill Howton, Bobby Dillon, Dave Hanner and Deral Teteak all within the first nine rounds. Each of the five reached the Pro Bowl at least once in his career, with all but Parilli doing so as a Packer.

All five made an immediate impact. Howton led the league with 1,231 receiving yards, breaking Don Hutson's team single-season mark in the process. Parilli led the club in passing yardage. Dillon grabbed four interceptions, and Hanner and Teteak bolstered a defense that improved from 10th in 1951 to fifth overall in 1952.

As the defense went, so did Green Bay. The Packers held six opponents to fewer than 300 yards and won all six times. During a four-game winning streak in November—the longest since 1944—the Green and Gold held each of its adversaries to fewer than 200 yards.

The Packers opened against the Bears. The game was the first at City Stadium in which yard line numbers (4 1/2 feet tall) were painted on the field.

Curly Lambeau returned to Milwaukee in Week 2. Lambeau had been fired as coach of the Cardinals with two games remaining in 1951. In 1952, he was chosen by owner George Preston Marshall to lead the Redskins.

The Packers did little to make Lambeau feel welcome. Parilli threw for 248 yards and two touchdowns and Howton caught three passes for 128 yards and a score as Green Bay knocked off Washington 35-20.

"The Packer team outplayed us and outgained us all the way," said Lambeau, who added. "I have no alibis."

A week later, Green Bay was on the verge of a second straight win until it suffered the worst collapse in team history. Parilli and Bob Mann put the team ahead 28-6 late in the third quarter. But Bob Waterfield, who had replaced Norm Van Brocklin in the second half, guided the Rams to four scores as Los Angeles came back 30-28.

"I'd rather get beat 100 to 0 than lose like that," said a dejected Bobby Jack Floyd.

In Week 4, Green Bay evened its record by turning two interceptions and three fumbles by the Texans into 24 points in staging a 24-14 win in the Cotton Bowl.

Demonstrating that they could give as well as receive, the Packers coughed up the ball nine times in getting routed 52-17 by Detroit in Week 5.

Teteak and John Martinkovic got the Packers back on track. Teteak blocked an Adrian Burk punt that Martinkovic returned seven yards for a touchdown as Green Bay slipped past Philadelphia 12-10.

A week later, the Packers beat the Bears in Chicago for the first time in 11 years.

"Well, I said we were going to beat 'em today—my first year and my last year," said Tony Canadeo, who was given the game ball.

Canadeo was honored two weeks later when the team celebrated Tony Canadeo Day at City Stadium. The veteran scored twice as the Packers won their fourth straight, 42-14 over the Texans.

That high was short-lived. The Rams eliminated Green Bay from contention with a 45-27 drubbing on Dec. 7. The following week, Canadeo lost four yards on his final carry, and his team did little better in losing 24-14 to the 49ers.

THE NEXT HUTSON?

Rookie Bill Howton made such a splash in 1952 that comparisons to the legendary Don Hutson were all but inevitable. In 12 games, Howton caught 53 passes for 1,231 yards and 13 touchdowns, all rookie records at the time.

The Packers selected the 6-foot-2 end in the second round of the draft. Howton caught a 40-yard scoring pass in the season opener and only got better as the weeks went by.

Howton had six 100-yard receiving games. He caught at least one touchdown pass in nine games. In the final three weeks, he caught 21 passes for 485 yards and five scores.

Howton again topped 1,000 yards receiving in 1956. He was traded to the Browns in 1959 and finished his career with the Cowboys, where he broke Hutson's record for most receptions in a career.

Most Yards Receiving, Rookie, Season

Yards	Name	Year
1,231	Bill Howton	1952
818	James Lofton	1978
791	Sterling Sharpe	1988
614	Max McGee	1954

TEAM STATISTICS

	GB	OPP
First Downs	197	202
Rushing	84	87
Passing	95	97
Penalty	18	18
Rushes	405	415
Yards Gained	1,485	1,507
Average Gain	3.67	3.63
Average Yards per Game	123.8	125.6
Passes Attempted	337	340
Completed	161	162
% Completed	47.77	47.65
Total Yards Gained	2,688	2,205
Yards Lost	314	443
Net Yards Gained	2,374	1,762
Yards Gained per Completion	16.70	13.61
Average Net Yards per Game	197.8	146.8
Combined Net Yards Gained	3,859	3,269
Total Plays	742	755
Average Yards per Play	5.20	4.33
Average Net Yards per Game	321.6	272.4
Intercepted By	22	25
Yards Returned	254	339
Returned for TD	1	3
Punts	65	72
Yards Punted	2,645	2,808
Average Yards per Punt	40.69	39.00
Punt Returns	38	36
Yards Returned	370	281
Average Yards per Return	9.74	7.81
Returned for TD	0	1
Kickoff Returns	52	51
Yards Returned	1,085	1,312
Average Yards per Return	20.87	25.73
Returned for TD	0	2
Penalties	83	96
Yards Penalized	739	752
Fumbles	40	28
Lost	31	19
Own Recovered for Touchdown	0	1
Opponent's Recovered by	19	31
Opponent's Recovered for Touchdown	0	1
Total Points Scored	295	312
Total Touchdowns	40	40
Touchdowns Rushing	11	16
Touchdowns Passing	26	17
Touchdowns on Returns & Recoveries	3	7
Extra Points	37	39
Safeties	0	0
Field Goals Attempted	21	20
Field Goals Made	6	11
% Successful	28.57	55.00

Regular Season 6-6-0

Date	GB		OPP	Att.
9/28	14	Chicago Bears	24	(24,656)
10/5	35	Washington Redskins (M)	20	(9,657)
10/12	28	Los Angeles Rams (M)	30	(21,693)
10/18	24	at Dallas Texans	14	(14,000)
10/26	17	Detroit Lions	52	(24,656)
11/2	12	Philadelphia Eagles (M)	10	(10,149)
11/9	41	at Chicago Bears	28	(41,751)
11/16	17	at New York Giants	3	(26,723)
11/23	42	Dallas Texans	14	(16,340)
11/27	24	at Detroit Lions	48	(39,101)
12/7	27	at Los Angeles Rams	45	(49,822)
12/14	14	at San Francisco 49ers	24	(18,086)

Score By Periods

	1	2	3	4	Total
Packers	51	97	80	67	295
Opponents	58	75	77	102	312

INDIVIDUAL STATISTICS

Rushing

	Att	Yds	Avg	LG	TD
Rote	58	313	5.4	30	2
Cone	70	276	3.9	t30	2
Floyd	61	236	3.9	17	1
Canadeo	65	191	2.9	35	2
Reid	58	156	2.7	14	2
Reichardt	39	121	3.1	14	1
Parilli	32	106	3.3	19	1
Grimes	17	59	3.5	31	0
B. Robinson	3	4	1.3	4	0
Pearson	2	2	1.0	2	0
Self	0	21	—	21	0
Packers	**405**	**1,485**	**3.7**	**35**	**11**
Opponents	415	1,507	3.6	74	16

Receiving

	No	Yds	Avg	LG	TD
Howton	53	1,231	23.2	t90	13
B. Mann	30	517	17.2	42	6
Keane	18	191	10.6	t29	1
Reid	12	250	20.8	t81	2
Elliott	12	114	9.5	15	1
Floyd	11	129	11.7	44	0
Canadeo	9	86	9.6	t21	1
Cone	8	98	12.3	37	1
Reichardt	5	18	3.6	12	0
Rote	1	28	28.0	t28	1
Pearson	1	16	16.0	16	0
Pelfrey	1	10	10.0	10	0
Packers	**161**	**2,688**	**16.7**	**t90**	**26**
Opponents	162	2,205	13.6	t78	17

Passing

	Att	Com	Yds	Pct	TD	In	Yds	Rate
Parilli	177	77	1,416	43.5	13	17	127	56.6
Rote	157	82	1,268	52.2	13	8	187	85.6
B. Forte	2	2	4	100.0	0	0	0	—
Canadeo	1	0	0	00.0	0	0	0	—
Packers	**337**	**161**	**2,688**	**47.8**	**26**	**25**	**314**	**69.9**
Opponents	340	162	2,205	47.7	17	22	443	58.5

Punting

	No	Yds	Avg	LG	HB
Parilli	65	2,645	40.7	63	0
Packers	**65**	**2,645**	**40.7**	**63**	**0**
Opponents	72	2,808	39.0	68	2

Kickoff Returns

	No	Yds	Avg	LG	TD
Grimes	18	422	23.4	34	0
Loomis	10	207	20.7	34	0
Moselle	5	83	16.6	26	0
Floyd	5	75	15.0	26	0
Self	3	85	28.3	33	0
Canadeo	2	62	31.0	40	0
B. Robinson	2	49	24.5	26	0
Cone	2	23	11.5	13	0
Pelfrey	1	26	26.0	26	0
Dees	1	20	20.0	20	0
Reichardt	1	19	19.0	19	0
Schmidt	1	14	14.0	14	0
Martinkovic	1	0	0.0	0	0
Packers	**52**	**1,085**	**20.9**	**40**	**0**
Opponents	51	1,312	25.7	t89	2

Punt Returns

	No	Yds	Avg	LG	TD
Grimes	18	179	9.9	72	0
Loomis	8	83	10.4	31	0
Moselle	7	77	11.0	24	0
Dillon	2	22	11.0	13	0
Sandifer	2	5	2.5	5	0
Canadeo	1	4	4.0	4	0
Packers	**38**	**370**	**9.7**	**72**	**0**
Opponents	36	281	7.8	t65	1

Interceptions

	No	Yds	Avg	LG	TD
Loomis	4	115	28.8	t45	1
B. Forte	4	50	12.5	25	0
Dillon	4	35	8.8	17	0
Moselle	3	2	0.7	2	0
Sandifer	2	25	12.5	17	0
M. Johnson	2	22	11.0	22	0
Wimberly	1	5	5.0	5	0
Self	1	0	0.0	0	0
Teteak	1	0	0.0	0	0
Packers	**22**	**254**	**11.5**	**t45**	**1**
Opponents	25	339	13.6	t80	3

Scoring

	TDr	TDp	TDrt	PAT	FG	S	TP
Howton	0	13	0	0/0	0/0	0	78
Cone	2	1	0	32/34	1/1	0	53
B. Mann	0	6	0	0/0	0/0	0	36
Reichardt	1	0	0	5/5	5/20	0	26
Reid	2	2	0	0/0	0/0	0	24
Canadeo	2	1	0	0/0	0/0	0	18
Rote	2	1	0	0/0	0/0	0	18
Martinkovic	0	0	2	0/0	0/0	0	12
Elliott	0	1	0	0/0	0/0	0	6
Floyd	1	0	0	0/0	0/0	0	6
Keane	0	1	0	0/0	0/0	0	6
Loomis	0	0	1	0/0	0/0	0	6
Parilli	1	0	0	0/0	0/0	0	6
Packers	**11**	**26**	**3**	**37/39**	**6/21**	**0**	**295**
Opponents	16	17	7	39/40	11/20	0	312

Fumbles

	Fum	Ow	Op	Yds	Tot
Canadeo	3	1	0	0	1
Cone	6	1	0	0	1
Faverty	0	0	3	0	3
Floyd	5	1	0	0	1
B. Forte	0	0	4	0	4
Grimes	5	2	0	0	2
Howton	1	0	0	0	0
Loomis	2	0	0	0	0
Martinkovic	0	0	4	19	4
Parilli	4	0	0	0	0
Pelfrey	1	0	0	0	0
Reichardt	1	0	0	0	0
Reid	1	0	0	0	0
Rote	10	1	0	0	1
Ruetz	0	0	1	0	1
Ruzich	0	0	2	0	2
Self	0	0	3	10	3
Serini	0	0	3	0	3
Wimberly	0	0	2	0	2
Packers	**40**	**9**	**19**	**29**	**28**

NFL STANDINGS

National Conference

	W	L	T	Pct	PF	PA
Detroit Lions	9	3	0	750	344	192
Los Angeles Rams	9	3	0	750	349	234
San Francisco 49ers	7	5	0	583	285	221
Green Bay Packers	**6**	**6**	**0**	**500**	**295**	**312**
Chicago Bears	5	7	0	417	245	326
Dallas Texans	1	11	0	083	182	427

American Conference

	W	L	T	Pct	PF	PA
Cleveland Browns	8	4	0	667	310	213
New York Giants	7	5	0	583	234	231
Philadelphia Eagles	7	5	0	583	252	271
Pittsburgh Steelers	5	7	0	417	300	273
Chicago Cardinals	4	8	0	333	172	221
Washington Redskins	4	8	0	333	240	287

1952

ROSTER

No	Name	Pos	Ht	Wt	DOB	College	G
62	Afflis, Dick	G	6-0	252	06/27/29	Nevada	12
81	Berrang, Ed	E	6-2	205	10/14/22	Villanova	1
65	Boerio, Chuck	LB	6-0	205	03/09/30	Wisconsin	1
63	Bray, Ray	G	6-0	240	02/01/17	Western Michigan	12
3	Canadeo, Tony	HB	6-0	190	05/05/19	Gonzaga	12
31	Cone, Fred	FB	5-11	197	06/21/26	Clemson	10
76	Dees, Robert	T	6-4	245	09/26/29	Southwest Missouri State	9
44	Dillon, Bobby	DB	6-1	185	02/23/30	Texas	12
70	Dowden, Steve	T	6-2	235	02/24/29	Baylor	12
80	Elliott, Carlton	E	6-4	215	11/12/27	Virginia	12
51	Faverty, Hal	DE	6-2	220	09/26/27	Wisconsin	11
33	Floyd, Bobby Jack	FB	6-0	210	12/08/29	TCU	12
8	Forte, Bob	LB	6-0	205	07/15/22	Arkansas	12
22	Grimes, Billy	HB	6-1	195	07/27/27	Oklahoma State	12
77	Hanner, Joel (Dave)	DT	6-2	245	05/20/30	Arkansas	12
86	Howton, Bill	E	6-2	185	07/05/30	Rice	12
41	Johnson, Marvin	DB	5-11	185	04/13/27	San Jose State	5
72	Johnson, Tom	DT	6-2	230	01/19/31	Michigan	8
81	Keane, Jim	E	6-4	215	01/11/24	Iowa	11
67	Logan, Dick	DT	6-2	225	05/04/30	Ohio State	7
43	Loomis, Ace	DB	6-1	190	06/12/28	Wisconsin-LaCrosse	11
87	Mann, Bob	E	5-11	175	04/08/24	Michigan	12
83	Martinkovic, John	DE	6-3	235	02/04/27	Xavier	12
47	Moselle, Dom	HB	6-0	192	06/03/26	Wisconsin-Superior	8
15	Parilli, Vito (Babe)	QB	6-1	190	05/07/30	Kentucky	12
26	Pearson, Lindell	HB	6-0	200	03/06/29	Oklahoma	2
8	Pelfrey, Ray	E	6-0	190	01/11/28	Eastern Kentucky	1
37	Reichardt, Bill	FB	5-11	210	06/24/30	Iowa	12
24	Reid, Floyd (Breezy)	HB	5-10	187	09/04/27	Georgia	12
50	Rhodemyre, Jay	C	6-1	210	12/16/22	Kentucky	12
41	Robinson, Bill	HB	6-0	190	09/09/29	Lincoln	2
18	Rote, Tobin	QB	6-3	200	01/18/28	Rice	12
75	Ruetz, Howard	T	6-3	265	08/18/27	Loras	3
61	Ruzich, Steve	G	6-2	225	12/24/28	Ohio State	12
20	Sandifer, Dan	DB	6-2	190	03/01/29	LSU	12
54	Schmidt, George	C	6-2	220	10/28/27	Lewis	7
28	Self, Clarence	HB	5-9	180	10/10/25	Wisconsin	12
73	Serini, Washington	DT	6-2	240	03/09/24	Kentucky	11
69	Stephenson, Dave	G	6-2	235	10/22/25	West Virginia	11
66	Teteak, Deral	LB	5-10	210	12/11/29	Wisconsin	12
85	Wimberly, Abner	E	6-1	215	05/04/26	LSU	12

DRAFT

Rnd	Name	Pos	Ht	Wt	College
1	Vito (Babe) Parilli	QB	6-1	190	Kentucky
2	Bill Howton	E	6-2	185	Rice
3	Bobby Dillon	DB	6-1	185	Texas
4	(Choice to Browns)				
5	Joel (Dave) Hanner	DT	6-2	245	Arkansas
6	Tom Johnson	T	6-2	230	Michigan
7	Bill Reichardt	FB	5-11	210	Iowa
8	Mel Becket	C	6-3	220	Indiana
9	Deral Teteak	G	5-10	210	Wisconsin
10a	Art Kleinschmidt	G	6-1	230	Tulane
10b	Bud Roffler	HB	6-1	185	Washington State
	(Choice from Bears)				
11	Bill Burkhalter	HB	5-10	180	Rice
12	Bill Wilson	E	6-2	205	Texas
13	Billy Hair	HB	6-0	178	Clemson
14	Jack Morgan	T	6-2	235	Michigan State
15	Bobby Jack Floyd	FB	6-0	210	TCU
16	Johnny Coatta	QB	5-11	180	Wisconsin
17	Don Peterson	HB	5-11	180	Michigan
18	Howard Tisdale	T	6-3	250	Stephen A. Austin
19	John Pont	HB	5-8	170	Miami (OH)
20	Charles Boerio	C	6-0	205	Illinois
21	Herb Zimmerman	G	6-0	220	TCU
22	Karl Kluckhorn	E	6-2	195	Colgate
23	Frank Kapral	G	5-10	210	Michigan State
24	John Schuetzner	E	6-3	220	North Carolina
25	Charles LaPradd	T	6-3	222	Florida
26	Charles Stokes	C	6-2	210	Tennessee
27	I.D. Russell	B	6-1	210	SMU
28	Bill Barrett	HB	5-9	180	Notre Dame
29	Bill Stratton	B	6-2	210	Lewis
30	Jack Fulkerson	T	6-2	230	Mississippi Southern

1952 GREEN BAY PACKERS

FRONT ROW: (L-R) Line Coach John (Tarzan) Taylor, Line Coach Charles Drulis, Head Coach Gene Ronzani, Backfield Coach Ray (Scooter) McLean, End Coach Dick Plasman.
SECOND ROW: (L-R) Trainer Carl (Bud) Jorgensen, 86 Bill Howton, 72 Tom Johnson, 8 Bob Forte, 83 John Martinkovic, 73 Washington Serini, 80 Carlton Elliott, 81 Jim Keane, 54 George Schmidt, 41 Bill Robinson, 76 Robert Dees, 77 Dave Hanner, Assistant Trainer John Proski.
THIRD ROW: (L-R) 70 Steve Dowden, 51 Hal Faverty, 61 Steve Ruzich, 67 Dick Logan, 18 Tobin Rote, 85 Abner Wimberly, 20 Dan Sandifer, 22 Billy Grimes, 69 Dave Stephenson, 63 Ray Bray, 50 Jay Rhodemyre, 43 Ace Loomis.
BACK ROW: (L-R) 15 Babe Parilli, 37 Bill Reichardt, 62 Dick Afflis, 24 Breezy Reid, 3 Tony Canadeo, 66 Deral Teteak, 87 Bob Mann, 47 Dom Moselle, 31 Fred Cone, 44 Bobby Dillon, 28 Clarence Self, 33 Bobby Jack Floyd.

The Teams: 1952   A Measure of Greatness

In their long and storied history, the Packers have fired only one head coach before season's end. Gene Ronzani earned that dubious honor in 1953 when his club took a marked turn for the worse after generating such promise only a year earlier.

So pathetic were the Packers (2-9-1) that the only team they could beat was the Colts—back after a two-year hiatus—yet still finish a half game behind Baltimore (3-9) at the bottom of the Western Conference standings.

Green Bay's passing attack, one of the top in the league in 1951 and 1952, misfired badly. Tobin Rote and Babe Parilli threw just nine touchdown passes (fewest in the league) while tossing a league-high 34 interceptions.

The attack was hindered early after Bill Howton suffered cracked ribs in the preseason and missed the first four regular-season contests. In those games, Green Bay managed one touchdown pass against 11 interceptions.

The defense, fifth in 1952, slipped to ninth in 1953. Only the Colts allowed more points (350) than did the Packers (338).

A collapse on Thanksgiving Day precipitated Ronzani's exit. The Packers let the Lions score 27 unanswered points in blowing a 15-7 lead in a nationally televised game.

The next day, Ronzani was let go. Three of his assistants—Hugh Devore, Scooter McLean, and Chuck Drulis were named to replace him, although Drulis was dropped from the group a few days later.

Green Bay then traveled to the West Coast for its closing swing against the 49ers and Rams, getting blasted 48-14 in San Francisco and 33-17 in Los Angeles.

Good news arrived in the form of a television contract the NFL signed with ABC and the Dumont networks. The $1.3 million deal called for a game a week to be played and televised on Saturday nights. With the growing popularity of the medium and the sport, fans could now watch two out-of-town teams go at it Saturday night, then catch their home team in person on Sunday.

Green Bay followed up its strong draft in 1952 with another good showing in 1953. In addition to top pick Al Carmichael, the Packers selected Bill Forester, Roger Zatkoff, and Jim Ringo within the first seven rounds. Carmichael became one of the top kick returners of the decade, Forester enjoyed 11 solid seasons in Green Bay, Zatkoff played in three Pro Bowls (1955-57), and Ringo wound up in the Pro Football Hall of Fame.

The Packers kicked off their season in County Stadium in Milwaukee. Otto Graham completed 18 of 24 passes for 292 yards and ran for two touchdowns as Cleveland won convincingly 27-0.

George Blanda and Jim Dooley applied the knockout punch for the Bears in Week 2. The duo collaborated on a 16-yard scoring pass with 3:35 remaining to sink Green Bay 17-13.

The Rams then continued their mastery in Week 3. Norm Van Brocklin passed for 250 yards and a touchdown in a 38-20 win.

Green Bay picked up its first win in Week 4. Carmichael and Howie Ferguson combined for 126 yards rushing in a 303-yard outpouring that overwhelmed the Colts 37-14.

Howton returned a week later and caught eight passes in Pittsburgh. It mattered little as Green Bay generated a season-low 125 yards in a 31-14 setback.

The Packers capped the season's first half with a 35-24 win in Baltimore on Halloween. Breezy Reid raced for 120 yards rushing and Howton scored two touchdowns.

Howton figured prominently in Week 7 as well. The end caught a touchdown pass from Parilli with less than two minutes remaining to forge a 21-21 tie with the Bears.

In Week 9, San Francisco cashed in on six Packers turnovers, pounding them 37-7.

The Ronzani regime lasted one more game, an affair in which the Lions converted six Packers turnovers into 31 points. With that, Ronzani was gone.

"The Packers will always be a credit to Green Bay and the National Football League wherever they play," Ronzani said in his first interview after resigning. "I know they'll always give 100 percent and I hope it's good enough to win; so far, it hasn't been."

For the Packers, giving 100 percent meant throwing nine interceptions in two games on the West Coast. In both, the Packers fell behind early and never recovered.

A PAIR OF PICKED-OFF PACKERS

Babe Parilli and Tobin Rote had thrown 25 interceptions in their first year sharing the Packers' quarterbacking duties. But in 1953, they outdid themselves as 34 of their throws wound up in the hands of the opposition. Only the Giants could match that prolific pace.

The pair was intercepted at least once in every game, and seven times they combined for at least three interceptions. The team was 0-7 in those games.

Parilli threw 19 interceptions; Rote tossed 15. Twenty-four players from the opposition feasted on the duo's throws. The Rams' Woodley Lewis led that group with four interceptions while Don Kindt of the Bears and Rex Berry of the 49ers each returned one for a touchdown.

Most Interceptions by Two Quarterbacks, Season

No	Year	Duo
34	1953	Babe Parilli 19, Tobin Rote 15
31	1950	Tobin Rote 24, Paul Christman 7
31	1983	Lynn Dickey 29, David Whitehurst 2
29	1951	Tobin Rote 20, Bobby Thomason 9

TEAM STATISTICS

	GB	OPP
First Downs	189	199
Rushing	93	95
Passing	79	91
Penalty	17	13
Rushes	424	407
Yards Gained	1,665	1,746
Average Gain	3.93	4.29
Average Yards per Game	138.8	145.5
Passes Attempted	352	312
Completed	147	144
% Completed	41.76	46.15
Total Yards Gained	1,833	2,341
Yards Lost	278	236
Net Yards Gained	1,555	2,105
Yards Gained per Completion	12.47	16.26
Average Net Yards per Game	129.6	175.4
Combined Net Yards Gained	3,220	3,851
Total Plays	776	719
Average Yards per Play	4.15	5.36
Average Net Yards per Game	268.3	320.9
Intercepted By	28	34
Yards Returned	351	407
Returned for TD	2	2
Punts	80	66
Yards Punted	3,005	2,750
Average Yards per Punt	37.56	41.67
Punt Returns	39	41
Yards Returned	348	232
Average Yards per Return	8.92	5.66
Returned for TD	1	1
Kickoff Returns	56	40
Yards Returned	1,197	851
Average Yards per Return	21.38	21.28
Returned for TD	0	0
Penalties	67	84
Yards Penalized	624	617
Fumbles	29	28
Lost	14	19
Own Recovered for Touchdown	0	0
Opponent's Recovered by	19	14
Opponent's Recovered for Touchdown	0	0
Total Points Scored	200	338
Total Touchdowns	27	44
Touchdowns Rushing	14	24
Touchdowns Passing	9	15
Touchdowns on Returns & Recoveries	4	5
Extra Points	23	41
Safeties	0	0
Field Goals Attempted	16	22
Field Goals Made	5	11
% Successful	31.25	50.00

Regular Season   2-9-1

Date	GB		OPP	Att.
9/27	0	Cleveland Browns (M)	27	(22,604)
10/4	13	Chicago Bears	17	(24,835)
10/11	20	Los Angeles Rams (M)	38	(23,352)
10/18	37	Baltimore Colts	14	(18,713)
10/24	14	at Pittsburgh Steelers	31	(22,918)
10/31	35	at Baltimore Colts	24	(33,797)
11/8	21	at Chicago Bears	21	(39,889)
11/15	7	Detroit Lions	14	(20,834)
11/22	7	San Francisco 49ers (M)	37	(16,378)
11/26	15	at Detroit Lions	34	(52,607)
12/6	14	at San Francisco 49ers	48	(33,887)
12/12	17	at Los Angeles Rams	33	(23,069)

Score By Periods

	1	2	3	4	Total
Packers	52	62	31	55	200
Opponents	98	76	92	72	338

INDIVIDUAL STATISTICS

Rushing

	Att	Yds	Avg	LG	TD
Reid	95	492	5.2	43	3
Cone	92	201	3.3	t41	5
Carmichael	49	199	4.1	t41	1
Rote	33	180	5.5	21	0
Parilli	42	171	4.1	19	4
Ferguson	52	134	2.6	12	0
Papit	6	44	7.3	21	1
Barton	7	40	5.7	14	0
Coutre	22	39	1.8	8	0
Bailey	13	29	2.2	13	0
Boone	7	24	3.4	24	0
G. Dawson	5	18	3.6	18	0
Rush	1	-6	-6.0	-6.0	0
Packers	**424**	**1,665**	**3.9**	**43**	**14**
Opponents	407	1,746	4.3	58	24

Receiving

	No	Yds	Avg	LG	TD
Howton	25	463	18.5	t80	4
B. Mann	23	327	14.2	42	2
Cone	18	165	9.2	30	1
Ferguson	15	86	5.7	23	0
Rush	14	190	13.6	24	0
Elliott	13	150	11.5	19	0
Carmichael	12	131	10.9	52	0
Reid	10	100	10.0	26	0
Bailey	8	119	14.9	50	0
Boone	6	55	9.2	18	1
Barton	2	51	25.5	t42	1
Coutre	1	-4	-4.0	-4	0
Packers	**147**	**1,833**	**12.5**	**t80**	**9**
Opponents	144	2,341	16.3	t97	15

Passing

	Att	Com	Yds	Pct	TD	In	Yds	Rate
Rote	185	72	1,005	38.9	5	15	117	32.4
Parilli	166	74	830	44.6	4	19	161	28.5
Boone	1	1	-2	100.0	0	0	0	—
Packers	**352**	**147**	**1,833**	**41.8**	**9**	**34**	**278**	**27.5**
Opponents	312	144	2,341	46.2	15	28	236	50.4

Punting

	No	Yds	Avg	LG	HB
Rush	60	2,262	37.7	60	0
Parilli	19	686	36.1	58	0
Rote	1	57	57.0	57	0
Packers	**80**	**3,005**	**37.6**	**60**	**0**
Opponents	66	2,750	41.7	60	1

Kickoff Returns

	No	Yds	Avg	LG	TD
Carmichael	26	641	24.7	43	0
Ferguson	7	123	17.6	30	0
G. Dawson	4	102	25.5	33	0
Reid	4	82	20.5	23	0
Coutre	3	52	17.3	27	0
Teteak	2	62	31.0	47	0
Papit	2	38	19.0	21	0
Bailey	2	34	17.0	21	0
Martinkovic	2	12	6.0	8	0
Loomis	1	19	19.0	19	0
Barton	1	14	14.0	14	0
Forester	1	12	12.0	12	0
Wildung	1	6	6.0	6	0
Packers	**56**	**1,197**	**21.4**	**47**	**0**
Opponents	40	851	21.3	47	0

Punt Returns

	No	Yds	Avg	LG	TD
Carmichael	20	199	10.0	52	0
G. Dawson	7	72	10.3	t60	1
Boone	5	24	4.8	9	0
Sandifer	3	35	11.7	23	0
Barton	2	13	6.5	9	0
Coutre	1	5	5.0	5	0
B. Aldridge	1	0	0.0	0	0
Packers	**39**	**348**	**8.9**	**t60**	**1**
Opponents	41	232	5.7	t71	1

Interceptions

	No	Yds	Avg	LG	TD
Dillon	9	112	12.4	t49	1
B. Aldridge	5	85	17.0	34	0
V.J. Walker	4	74	18.5	t54	1
M. Johnson	4	39	9.8	36	0
Loomis	4	39	9.8	27	0
Hanner	1	2	2.0	2	0
Forester	1	0	0.0	0	0
Packers	**28**	**351**	**12.5**	**t54**	**2**
Opponents	34	407	12.0	t67	2

Scoring

	TDr	TDp	TDrt	PAT	FG	S	TP
Cone	5	1	0	23/25	5/16	0	74
Howton	0	4	0	0/0	0/0	0	24
Parilli	4	0	0	0/0	0/0	0	24
Reid	3	0	0	0/0	0/0	0	18
B. Mann	0	2	0	0/0	0/0	0	12
Barton	0	1	0	0/0	0/0	0	6
Boone	0	1	0	0/0	0/0	0	6
Carmichael	1	0	0	0/0	0/0	0	6
G. Dawson	0	0	1	0/0	0/0	0	6
Dillon	0	0	1	0/0	0/0	0	6
Elliott	0	1	0	0/0	0/0	0	6
Papit	1	0	0	0/0	0/0	0	6
V.J. Walker	0	0	1	0/0	0/0	0	6
Packers	**14**	**9**	**4**	**23/25**	**5/16**	**0**	**200**
Opponents	24	15	5	41/44	11/22	0	338

Fumbles

	Fum	Ow	Op	Yds	Tot
B. Aldridge	0	0	2	0	2
Bailey	1	0	0	0	1
Boone	1	1	0	0	1
Bill Brown	0	1	1	0	2
Carmichael	3	0	0	0	0
Cifelli	0	0	1	0	1
Cone	2	2	0	5	2
G. Dawson	1	0	0	0	0
Dillon	0	0	1	0	1
Elliott	0	0	1	17	1
Ferguson	4	1	0	0	1
Forester	0	0	2	0	2
B. Forte	0	0	1	0	1
Howton	1	0	0	0	0
M. Johnson	0	0	1	0	1
Dick Logan	0	0	1	0	1
Loomis	0	0	3	0	3
Martinkovic	0	0	1	3	1
Parilli	8	3	0	0	3
Reid	5	4	0	2	4
Rote	2	0	0	0	0
Ruetz	0	0	1	13	1
Rush	1	0	0	0	0
Ruzich	0	0	1	0	1
Szafaryn	0	0	1	0	1
V.J. Walker	0	0	3	0	3
Zatkoff	0	0	1	0	1
Packers	**29**	**15**	**19**	**40**	**34**

NFL STANDINGS

Western Conference

	W	L	T	Pct	PF	PA
Detroit Lions	10	2	0	.833	271	205
San Francisco 49ers	9	3	0	.750	372	237
Los Angeles Rams	8	3	1	.727	366	236
Chicago Bears	3	8	1	.273	218	262
Baltimore Colts	3	9	0	.250	182	350
Green Bay Packers	**2**	**9**	**1**	**.182**	**200**	**338**

Eastern Conference

	W	L	T	Pct	PF	PA
Cleveland Browns	11	1	0	.917	348	162
Philadelphia Eagles	7	4	1	.636	352	215
Washington Redskins	6	5	1	.545	208	215
Pittsburgh Steelers	6	6	0	.500	211	263
New York Giants	3	9	0	.250	179	277
Chicago Cardinals	1	10	1	.091	190	337

1953

ROSTER

No	Name	Pos	Ht	Wt	DOB	College	G
72	Afflis, Dick	G	6-0	250	06/27/29	Nevada	12
40	Aldridge, Ben	DB	6-1	195	10/24/26	Oklahoma State	8
20	Bailey, Byron	HB	5-11	198	10/12/30	Washington State	9
43	Barton, Don	HB	5-11	175	05/29/30	Texas	5
22	Boone, J.R.	HB	5-9	167	07/28/25	Tulsa	8
62	Brown, Bill (Buddy)	G	6-1	220	10/19/26	Arkansas	11
42	Carmichael, Al	HB	6-1	190	11/10/28	USC	12
73	Cifelli, Gus	T	6-4	250	02/03/26	Notre Dame	12
31	Cone, Fred	FB	5-11	197	06/21/26	Clemson	12
27	Coutre, Larry	HB	5-10	180	04/11/28	Notre Dame	7
26	Dawson, Gib	HB	5-11	180	08/27/30	Texas	7
44	Dillon, Bobby	DB	6-1	185	02/23/30	Texas	10
80	Elliott, Carlton	E	6-4	220	11/12/27	Virginia	12
37	Ferguson, Howie	FB	6-2	210	08/05/30	No college	11
69	Forester, Bill	DT	6-3	230	08/09/32	SMU	12
8	Forte, Bob	LB	6-0	205	07/15/22	Arkansas	11
77	Hanner, Joel (Dave)	DT	6-2	250	05/20/30	Arkansas	12
88	Hays, George	DE	6-2	215	08/29/25	St. Bonaventure	9
86	Howton, Bill	E	6-2	185	07/05/30	Rice	8
41	Johnson, Marvin	DB	5-11	185	04/13/27	San Jose State	7
67	Logan, Dick	DT	6-2	230	05/04/30	Ohio State	12
48	Loomis, Ace	DB	6-1	190	06/12/28	Wisconsin-LaCrosse	10
87	Mann, Bob	E	5-11	175	04/08/24	Michigan	10
83	Martinkovic, John	DE	6-3	240	02/04/27	Xavier	12
22	Papit, Johnny	HB	6-0	190	07/25/28	Virginia	4
15	Parilli, Vito (Babe)	QB	6-1	190	05/07/30	Kentucky	12
24	Reid, Floyd (Breezy)	HB	5-10	185	09/04/27	Georgia	12
51	Ringo, Jim	C	6-1	225	11/21/32	Syracuse	5
18	Rote, Tobin	QB	6-3	200	01/18/28	Rice	12
75	Ruetz, Howard	T	6-3	250	08/18/27	Loras	5
81	Rush, Clive	E	6-2	197	02/14/31	Miami (OH)	11
61	Ruzich, Steve	G	6-2	225	12/24/28	Ohio State	12
23	Sandifer, Dan	DB	6-2	190	03/01/29	LSU	1
53	Stephenson, Dave	G	6-2	225	10/22/25	West Virginia	12
68	Szafaryn, Len	G	6-2	230	01/19/28	North Carolina	7
66	Teteak, Deral	LB	5-10	210	12/11/29	Wisconsin	7
58	Tonnemaker, Clayton	LB	6-2	235	06/08/28	Minnesota	12
47	Walker, Val Joe	DB	6-1	179	01/07/30	SMU	12
70	Wildung, Dick	T	6-0	230	08/16/21	Minnesota	12
74	Zatkoff, Roger	T	6-2	215	03/25/31	Michigan	12

DRAFT

Rnd	Name	Pos	Ht	Wt	College
1	Al Carmichael	HB	6-1	190	USC
2	Gil Reich	HB	6-0	188	Kansas
3	Bill Forester	DT	6-3	235	SMU
4	Gib Dawson	HB	5-11	175	Texas
5	Roger Zatkoff	T	6-2	201	Michigan
6	Bob Kennedy	G	5-11	225	Wisconsin
7	Jim Ringo	C	6-1	225	Syracuse
8	Lauren Hargrove	HB	6-1	193	Georgia
9	Floyd Harrawood	T	6-4	240	Tulsa
10	Victor Rimkus	G	6-1	220	Holy Cross
*11	Joe Johnson	HB	6-0	185	Boston College
*12	Dick Curran	HB	6-0	185	Arizona State
*13	Bob Orders	C	6-3	230	West Virginia
*14	Charles Wrenn	T	6-3	250	TCU
15	Gene Helwig	G	6-1	190	Tulsa
16	John Hlay	FB	6-1	218	Ohio State
17	Bill Georges	E	6-1	195	Texas
18	Jim Philbee	HB	6-2	185	Bradley
*19	Bill Lucky	T	6-3	230	Baylor
20	John Harville	HB	6-2	200	TCU
21	Bob Conway	HB	6-0	185	Alabama
22	Bill Turnbeaugh	T	6-3	265	Auburn
23	Bill Murray	E	6-2	215	Am. International
24	Jim Haslam	T	6-3	210	Tennessee
25	Ike Jones	E	5-11	185	UCLA
*26	George Bozanic	HB	6-2	210	USC
27	James McConaughey	E	6-3	215	Houston
28	Zack Jordan	HB	6-1	190	Colorado
29	Henry O'Brien	G	6-1	240	Boston College
30	Al Barry	G	6-2	222	USC

* denotes juniors

1953 GREEN BAY PACKERS

FRONT ROW: (L-R) Property Man Toby Sylvester, 88 George Hays, 69 Bill Forester, 43 Don Barton, 47 Val Joe Walker, 53 Dave Stephenson, 26 Gib Dawson, 27 Larry Coutre, 67 Dick Logan, Trainer Carl (Bud) Jorgensen.

SECOND ROW: (L-R) 83 John Martinkovic, 74 Roger Zatkoff, 41 Marvin Johnson, 61 Steve Ruzich, 72 Dick Afflis, 87 Bob Mann, 15 Babe Parilli, 42 Al Carmichael, 20 Byron Bailey, 37 Howie Ferguson, 40 Ben Aldridge, 58 Clayton Tonnemaker.

THIRD ROW: (L-R) 81 Clive Rush, 62 Bill (Buddy) Brown, 75 Dave Hanner, 51 Jim Ringo, 18 Tobin Rote, 68 Len Szafaryn, 80 Carlton Elliott, 73 Gus Cifelli, 23 Dan Sandifer, 86 Bill Howton, 48 Ace Loomis, 44 Bobby Dillon, 70 Dick Wildung, 8 Bob Forte.

BACK ROW: (L-R) Head Coach Gene Ronzani, Backfield Coach Ray (Scooter) McLean, 22 J.R. Boone, 24 Breezy Reid, 31 Fred Cone, 66 Deral Teteak, End Coach Hugh Devore, Line Coach Charles Drulis.

Lisle Blackbourn, former head coach at Marquette University, assumed command of the Packers on-the-field fortunes in 1954. If he and his staff accomplished anything in their inaugural year, it was to keep the team within striking distance in all but a couple of games.

Green Bay's record of 4-8 was only slightly better than that of a year before. But aside from a 35-0 misstep in San Francisco in early December, the blowouts of years past all but disappeared. Seven of eight losses were by eight points or less, and the Packers led at one time or another in all but two games.

Of course, coming tantalizingly close only to fall short can be frustrating in its own right. The Packers blew fourth-quarter leads in each of their first three games. Jim Finks passed 38 yards to Ray Matthews with five minutes left to give Pittsburgh a 21-20 win. A week later, George Blanda lofted a 5-yard scoring toss to Billy Stone then added an insurance field goal in a 10-3 victory for the Bears. And Joe Perry and Y.A. Tittle each ran for touchdowns in a 23-17 triumph by the 49ers. Green Bay was outscored 30-0 in the fourth quarter during that span.

Said Blackbourn: "Nobody realizes any more than I do that we've lost our three league games by a total of 14 points. It drains you, and it was the same thing during the exhibition season. That's slicing 'em about as thin as you can slice 'em."

The Packers squandered one other fourth-quarter lead. Blanda again led a come-from-behind effort, this time in Wrigley Field on Nov. 7.

Training camp wasn't quite two weeks old when Blackbourn pulled off a blockbuster trade. On Aug. 6, the Packers traded Babe Parilli and second-round pick Bob Fleck to the Browns. In return, Green Bay got quarterback Bob Garrett, guard John Bauer, defensive back Don Miller and tackle Chester Giarola.

On paper, the trade looked good. Garrett was the Browns' bonus pick and Bauer its first-round selection. Plus Green Bay had already lost Parilli to the Air Force for two years in July. But Giarola never reported, Bauer failed to make the squad, Miller played but one game and Garrett did little in the nine games in which he participated.

The draft in 1954 did not yield many impact players, but Blackbourn did acquire Veryl Switzer and Max McGee in the first and fifth rounds, respectively. Switzer led the league in punt return average. McGee hit his stride after Bob Mann was waived on Oct. 22, making 30 of his 36 receptions in the eight games following Mann's departure.

Mann was injured in the preseason. He returned for the first Bears game and saw some action in two other games. At the time he was let go, his 109 catches were second only to Don Hutson's 488 in team history.

Green Bay got its first win on Oct. 17 by defeating the Rams for the first time in six years. Tobin Rote passed for three touchdowns and 284 yards in the 35-17 victory.

Breezy Reid's 3-yard run and Fred Cone's subsequent extra point edged Baltimore 7-6 in Week 5. Reid led all runners with 77 yards and Bill Howton added 147 yards receiving on 11 catches.

McGee caught three passes for three touchdowns and 104 yards as the Packers (3-3) evened their record with a 37-14 win in Philadelphia.

The Bears frustrated Green Bay in Week 7. Blanda connected with Jack Hoffman from seven yards out with 2:05 left to earn a 28-23 decision. Ignoring a broken nose, Rote led the Packers to the Chicago 16-yard line in the closing minutes, only to be sacked on the game's last play.

Ferguson rushed for 112 yards and Rote scored on three short runs as the Packers roared back from a 13-point deficit to beat the Colts 24-13 in Milwaukee.

Two close games with the Lions followed. Detroit escaped 21-17 in the first after Ferguson fumbled away the Packers' last chance late in the game. The Lions then prevailed 28-24 on Thanksgiving after Green Bay failed to score on any of its three fourth-quarter possessions.

As usual, the Packers wrapped up their season on the West Coast. And as had become custom, Green Bay failed to secure a win in December. Not since Dec. 7, 1947, (a 35-14 win in Detroit) had the team won in the final month of the year, and San Francisco and Los Angeles again made sure that streak continued.

MCGEE MAXES OUT

When quarterback Tobin Rote looked to throw a touchdown pass in 1954, more often than not he turned to rookie Max McGee. McGee, Green Bay's fifth-round draft choice, was on the receiving end of 9 of the team's 14 touchdown passes (64.3 percent). No other Packers rookie ever accounted for a higher percentage.

On the year, McGee snagged 36 passes for 614 yards and nine touchdowns. He caught scoring passes in six different games, and seven of his touchdowns came after veteran Bob Mann was waived on Oct. 22.

McGee, who also punted 72 times, was lost to military service for two years beginning in 1955. He returned in 1957 and played 11 more seasons before retiring in 1967.

Rookies With Greatest Percentage of Team's TD Catches

Pct.	Name	Year
64.3	Max McGee	1954 (9 of 14)
54.5	Don Hutson	1935 (6 of 11)
54.5	James Lofton	1978 (6 of 11)
50.0	Bill Howton	1952 (13 of 26)

TEAM STATISTICS

	GB	OPP
First Downs	207	228
Rushing	79	101
Passing	112	119
Penalty	16	8
Rushes	321	403
Yards Gained	1,328	1,871
Average Gain	4.14	4.64
Average Yards per Game	110.7	155.9
Passes Attempted	412	374
Completed	195	208
% Completed	47.33	55.61
Total Yards Gained	2,454	2,690
Yards Lost	295	211
Net Yards Gained	2,159	2,479
Yards Gained per Completion	12.58	12.93
Average Net Yards per Game	179.9	206.6
Combined Net Yards Gained	3,487	4,350
Total Plays	733	777
Average Yards per Play	4.76	5.60
Average Net Yards per Game	290.6	362.5
Third Down Efficiency	62/173	54/162
Percentage	35.84	33.33
Fourth Down Efficiency	5/17	3/15
Percentage	29.41	20.00
Intercepted By	19	19
Yards Returned	285	380
Returned for TD	1	1
Punts	72	64
Yards Punted	2,999	2,568
Average Yards per Punt	41.65	40.13
Punt Returns	40	43
Yards Returned	394	290
Average Yards per Return	9.85	6.74
Returned for TD	1	1
Kickoff Returns	49	45
Yards Returned	1,193	832
Average Yards per Return	24.35	18.49
Returned for TD	0	0
Penalties	57	72
Yards Penalized	522	666
Fumbles	21	22
Lost	12	14
Own Recovered for Touchdown	0	0
Opponent's Recovered by	14	12
Opponent's Recovered for Touchdown	1	1
Total Points Scored	234	251
Total Touchdowns	30	33
Touchdowns Rushing	13	13
Touchdowns Passing	14	17
Touchdowns on Returns & Recoveries	3	3
Extra Points	27	32
Safeties	0	0
Field Goals Attempted	16	14
Field Goals Made	9	7
% Successful	56.25	50.00

Regular Season 4-8-0

Date	GB		OPP	Att.
9/26	20	Pittsburgh Steelers	21	(20,675)
10/3	3	Chicago Bears	10	(24,414)
10/10	17	San Francisco 49ers (M)	23	(15,571)
10/17	35	Los Angeles Rams (M)	17	(17,455)
10/24	7	at Baltimore Colts	6	(28,680)
10/30	37	at Philadelphia Eagles	14	(25,378)
11/7	23	at Chicago Bears	28	(47,038)
11/13	24	Baltimore Colts	13	(19,786)
11/21	17	Detroit Lions	21	(20,767)
11/25	24	at Detroit Lions	28	(55,532)
12/5	0	at San Francisco 49ers	35	(33,712)
12/12	27	at Los Angeles Rams	35	(38,839)

Score By Periods

	1	2	3	4	Total
Packers	38	70	77	49	234
Opponents	72	73	34	72	251

INDIVIDUAL STATISTICS

Rushing

	Att	Yds	Avg	LG	TD
Reid	99	507	5.1	t69	5
Rote	67	301	4.5	30	8
Ferguson	83	276	3.3	25	0
Carmichael	33	130	3.9	23	0
Switzer	15	59	3.9	33	0
J. Johnson	7	31	4.4	10	0
Cone	15	18	1.2	11	0
McGee	1	9	9.0	9	0
B. Garrett	1	-3	-3.0	-3	0
Packers	**321**	**1,328**	**4.1**	**t69**	**13**
Opponents	403	1,871	4.6	44	13

Receiving

	No	Yds	Avg	LG	TD
Howton	52	768	14.8	59	2
Ferguson	41	398	9.7	49	0
McGee	36	614	17.1	t82	9
Carmichael	18	251	13.9	45	0
Switzer	17	166	9.8	28	2
Reid	14	129	9.2	25	0
J. Johnson	10	72	7.2	17	1
Cone	4	19	4.8	13	0
Knafelc	3	37	12.3	15	0
Packers	**195**	**2,454**	**12.6**	**t82**	**14**
Opponents	208	2,690	12.9	t71	17

Passing

	Att	Com	Yds	Pct	TD	In	Yds	Rate
Rote	382	180	2,311	47.1	14	18	295	59.1
B. Garrett	30	15	143	50.0	0	1	0	49.7
Packers	**412**	**195**	**2,454**	**47.3**	**14**	**19**	**295**	**58.5**
Opponents	374	208	2,690	55.6	17	19	211	72.4

Punting

	No	Yds	Avg	Net	TB	In20	LG	HB
McGee	72	2,999	41.7	35.4	8	15	63	0
Packers	**72**	**2,999**	**41.7**	**35.4**	**8**	**15**	**63**	**0**
Opponents	64	2,568	40.1	34.0	0	15	72	0

Kickoff Returns

	No	Yds	Avg	LG	TD
Carmichael	20	531	26.6	49	0
Switzer	20	500	25.0	88	0
J. Johnson	4	91	22.8	28	0
Ferguson	2	31	15.5	22	0
Cone	1	22	22.0	22	0
Forester	1	18	18.0	18	0
Bill Brown	1	0	0.0	0	0
Packers	**49**	**1,193**	**24.3**	**88**	**0**
Opponents	45	832	18.5	35	0

Punt Returns

	No	Yds	Avg	LG	TD
Switzer	24	306	12.8	t93	1
Carmichael	9	43	4.8	14	0
J. Johnson	5	38	7.6	9	0
Dillon	1	7	7.0	7	0
Psaltis	1	0	0.0	0	0
Packers	**40**	**394**	**9.9**	**t93**	**1**
Opponents	43	290	6.7	t61	1

Interceptions

	No	Yds	Avg	LG	TD
Dillon	7	111	15.9	t59	1
V.J. Walker	4	83	20.8	44	0
Self	2	23	11.5	23	0
Teteak	1	23	23.0	23	0
Forester	1	21	21.0	21	0
G. White	1	20	20.0	20	0
Afflis	1	3	3.0	3	0
Tonnemaker	1	1	1.0	1	0
Zatkoff	1	0	0.0	0	0
Packers	**19**	**285**	**15.0**	**t59**	**1**
Opponents	19	380	20.0	57	1

Scoring

	TDr	TDp	TDrt	PAT	FG	S	TP
Cone	0	0	0	27/29	9/16	0	54
McGee	0	9	0	0/0	0/0	0	54
Rote	8	0	0	0/0	0/0	0	48
Reid	5	0	0	0/0	0/0	0	30
Switzer	0	2	2	0/0	0/0	0	24
Howton	0	2	0	0/0	0/0	0	12
Dillon	0	0	1	0/0	0/0	0	6
J. Johnson	0	1	0	0/0	0/0	0	6
Packers	**13**	**14**	**3**	**27/30**	**9/16**	**0**	**234**
Opponents	13	17	3	32/33	7/14	0	251

Fumbles

	Fum	Ow	Op	Yds	Tot
Carmichael	2	1	0	0	1
Cone	1	0	0	0	0
Dillon	1	0	0	0	0
Elliott	0	0	1	0	1
Ferguson	8	1	0	0	1
B. Garrett	2	1	0	0	1
Hanner	0	0	1	0	1
Helluin	0	0	2	0	2
Howton	0	0	1	0	1
A. Hunter	0	0	1	0	1
G. Knutson	0	0	1	0	1
Martinkovic	0	0	1	0	1
Psaltis	0	0	1	0	1
Reid	0	1	0	0	1
Rote	4	2	0	0	2
Self	0	0	1	0	1
Switzer	3	1	1	0	2
V.J. Walker	0	0	1	3	1
G. White	0	0	1	0	1
Zatkoff	0	0	3	0	3
Packers	**21**	**9**	**14**	**3**	**23**

NFL STANDINGS

Western Conference

	W	L	T	Pct	PF	PA
Detroit Lions	9	2	1	.818	337	189
Chicago Bears	8	4	0	.667	301	279
San Francisco 49ers	7	4	1	.636	313	251
Los Angeles Rams	6	5	1	.545	314	285
Green Bay Packers	**4**	**8**	**0**	**.333**	**234**	**251**
New York Yanks	3	9	0	.250	131	279

Eastern Conference

	W	L	T	Pct	PF	PA
Cleveland Browns	9	3	0	.750	336	162
Philadelphia Eagles	7	4	1	.636	284	230
New York Giants	7	5	0	.583	293	184
Pittsburgh Steelers	5	7	0	.417	219	263
Washington Redskins	3	9	0	.250	207	432
Chicago Cardinals	2	10	0	.167	183	347

ROSTER

No	Name	Pos	Ht	Wt	DOB	College	G
75	Afflis, Dick	G	6-0	250	06/27/29	Nevada	12
63	Barry, Al	G	6-2	225	12/24/30	USC	12
62	Brown, Bill (Buddy)	G	6-1	225	10/19/26	Arkansas	12
42	Carmichael, Al	HB	6-1	190	11/10/28	USC	10
31	Cone, Fred	FB	5-11	200	06/21/26	Clemson	12
44	Dillon, Bobby	DB	6-1	180	02/23/30	Texas	12
80	Elliott, Carlton	E	6-4	230	11/12/27	Virginia	12
37	Ferguson, Howie	FB	6-2	210	08/05/30	No college	12
69	Forester, Bill	DT	6-3	235	08/09/32	SMU	12
15	Garrett, Bob	QB	6-1	198	08/16/32	Stanford	9
77	Hanner, Joel (Dave)	DT	6-2	260	05/20/30	Arkansas	12
72	Helluin, Jerry	DT	6-2	280	08/08/29	Tulane	12
86	Howton, Bill	E	6-2	190	07/05/30	Rice	12
70	Hunter, Art	T	6-4	240	04/24/33	Notre Dame	12
40	Johnson, Joe	HB	6-0	185	11/03/29	Boston College	12
84	Knafelc, Gary	E	6-4	205	01/02/32	Colorado	8
81	Knutson, Gene	E	6-2	205	11/10/32	Michigan	12
87	Mann, Bob	E	5-11	175	04/08/24	Michigan	3
83	Martinkovic, John	DE	6-3	245	02/04/27	Xavier	12
85	McGee, Max	E	6-3	203	07/16/32	Tulane	12
41	Mihajlovich, Lou	E	5-11	175	02/19/25	Indiana	3
20	Miller, Don	DB	6-2	195	05/24/32	SMU	1
48	Psaltis, Jim	HB	6-1	190	12/14/27	USC	11
24	Reid, Floyd (Breezy)	HB	5-10	190	09/04/27	Georgia	12
51	Ringo, Jim	C	6-1	230	11/21/32	Syracuse	12
18	Rote, Tobin	QB	6-3	205	01/18/28	Rice	12
61	Ruzich, Steve	G	6-2	230	12/24/28	Ohio State	12
28	Self, Clarence	DB	5-9	185	10/25/25	Wisconsin	12
53	Stephenson, Dave	G	6-2	225	10/22/25	West Virginia	12
27	Switzer, Veryl	HB	5-11	190	08/06/32	Kansas State	12
68	Szafaryn, Len	G	6-2	225	01/19/28	North Carolina	12
66	Teteak, Deral	LB	5-10	210	12/11/29	Wisconsin	6
58	Tonnemaker, Clayton	LB	6-2	240	06/08/28	Minnesota	12
47	Walker, Val Joe	DB	6-1	179	01/07/30	SMU	10
88	White, Gene	DB	6-2	205	06/21/30	Georgia	8
74	Zatkoff, Roger	T	6-2	215	03/25/31	Michigan	12

DRAFT

Rnd	Name	Pos	Ht	Wt	College
1a	Art Hunter	T	6-2	240	Notre Dame
1b	Veryl Switzer	HB	5-11	190	Kansas State
	(Choice from Giants)				
2	Bob Fleck	T	6-2	260	Syracuse
3	George Timberlake	G	6-1	220	USC
4a	(Choice to Redskins for Johnny Papit)				
4b	Tom Allman	FB	6-0	210	West Virginia
	(Choice from Colts)				
5	Max McGee	E	6-3	203	Tulane
6	(Choice to Lions for Gus Cifelli)				
7	Sam Marshall	T	6-2	240	Florida A&M
8	Jimmie Williams	T	6-3	220	Texas Tech
9	Dave Davis	E	6-4	210	Georgia Tech
10	Gene Knutson	E	6-2	205	Michigan
11	Ken Hall	E	6-1	200	North Texas State
12	Bill Oliver	HB	6-2	190	Alabama
13	Mike Takacs	G	6-0	240	Ohio State
14	Dave Johnson (Kosse)	HB	6-0	180	Rice

Rnd	Name	Pos	Ht	Wt	College
15	(Choice to 49ers for Ben Aldridge)				
16	Desmond Koch	HB	6-0	205	USC
17	J.D. Roberts	G	5-10	210	Oklahoma
18	Emery Barnes	E	6-6	215	Oregon
19	Ken Hall	C	6-0	220	Springfield
20	Herbert Lowell	G	5-11	215	Pacific
21	Art Liebscher	HB	5-11	180	Pacific
22	Bill Buford	T	6-1	235	Morgan State
23	Clint Sathrum	QB	6-1	195	St. Olaf
24	Marvin Tennefoss	E	6-2	210	Stanford
25	Jack Smalley	T	6-3	225	Alabama
*26	Ralph Baierl	T	6-3	220	Maryland
27	Hosea Sims	E	6-0	192	Marquette
28	Evan Slonac	FB	5-8	175	Michigan State
29	Jerry Dufek	T	6-3	210	St. Norbert
30	Terry Campbell	QB	6-2	172	Washington State

* denotes juniors

1954 GREEN BAY PACKERS

FRONT ROW: (L-R) 84 Gary Knafelc, 69 Bill Forester, 37 Howie Ferguson, 61 Steve Ruzich, 68 Len Szafaryn, 88 Gene White, 40 Joe Johnson, Property Man Toby Sylvester.
SECOND ROW: (L-R) 42 Al Carmichael, 70 Art Hunter, 74 Roger Zatkoff, 66 Deral Teteak, 24 Floyd (Breezy) Reid, 47 Val Joe Walker, 28 Clarence Self, 44 Bobby Dillon, 27 Veryl Switzer, 41 Lou Mihajlovich, Trainer Carl (Bud) Jorgensen.
THIRD ROW: (L-R) Head Coach Lisle Blackbourn, Line Coach Lou Rymkus, 83 John Martinkovic, 86 Bill Howton, 15 Bob Garrett, 53 Dave Stephenson, 75 Dick Afflis, 31 Fred Cone, 63 Al Barry, End Coach Tom Hearden.
BACK ROW: (L-R) 79 Dave Hanner, 62 Bill (Buddy) Brown, 81 Gene Knutson, 85 Max McGee, 80 Carlton Elliott, 72 Jerry Helluin, 58 Clayton Tonnemaker, 18 Tobin Rote, 51 Jim Ringo, 48 Jim Psaltis, Backfield Coach Ray (Scooter) McLean.

With one bullet-like pass, Tobin Rote capped an electrifying, last-minute comeback never before staged in a Packers opener. His 18-yard strike to Gary Knafelc with 20 seconds left did more than merely topple the defending Western Conference champion Lions 20-17. It triggered a release of emotion rarely seen in City Stadium.

Before the extra point could be kicked, fans spilled onto the field. They hoisted Rote and Knafelc upon their shoulders. The friendly mob then carried Knafelc to the sidelines before order was restored.

"Finally, we won a game in Green Bay," said coach Lisle Blackbourn, whose teams had been 0-for-5 in the city, counting regular and preseason games, dating to 1954.

Knafelc eluded defensive backs Karl Karilivacz and Jack Christiansen on the winning play.

"I got hit just about two feet out," said the end, who was acquired early in 1954 after the Cardinals released him. "I turned around and saw the goal line and dived over."

The early-season euphoria continued through the first third of the schedule as the Packers won two of their next three games. They pounded the Bears 24-3 in Week 2, and surged past the Rams 30-28 in Week 4 thanks to Fred Cone's 25-yard field goal with 24 seconds left.

From there, Green Bay's fortunes headed south. By early November, the team settled into third place, a position it nailed down with a 6-6 record.

A number of veterans had good years. Howie Ferguson rushed for 859 yards, second best in the league behind Alan Ameche. Rote fired 17 touchdown passes to tie Y.A. Tittle for the NFL lead. Bobby Dillon, Val Joe Walker and others intercepted a league-best 31 passes. Al Carmichael's kickoff return average of 29.9 yards was second to none.

With Max McGee in the Air Force, Dick Deschaine, who had not played football in college, became the team's punter. Though he was also an end, Deschaine was the Packers' first kicking specialist.

Another change brought the game closer to its modern counterpart. Hash marks were added to City Stadium's playing field. The stripes aided ball placement and made keeping a statistical play-by-play easier.

The Packers took apart the Bears 24-3 in Week 2. Ferguson plowed for 153 yards, and Rote threw two touchdown passes and no interceptions. Green Bay piled up 386 yards and forced four second-half turnovers to prevent a Chicago comeback.

"It was a team win all the way," said Blackbourn.

Green Bay missed securing a third victory in a row by inches. That's the distance by which Rote's last pass missed Howton in the end zone with no time remaining. The incompletion left Baltimore a 24-20 winner in a Saturday night contest at County Stadium.

Cone's last-second field goal in Week 4 pushed Green Bay into a three-way tie for first place in the Western Conference. The Packers, Colts, and Rams all stood atop the standings with 3-1 records.

Green Bay traveled to Cleveland and was overwhelmed by the Browns 41-10. Rote completed but one pass in nine attempts for three yards in the second half.

Charlie Brackins, the team's 16th-round draft choice, directed three offensive plays. He became the first African American to play quarterback in a regular-season game for the Packers. Brackins, who also handled the team's kickoff duties, was waived on Nov. 8 to make room for quarterback Paul Held.

Rematches with the Colts and Bears followed. Green Bay lost 14-10 and 52-31, respectively. Baltimore gained 202 yards rushing; Chicago an astonishing 406 yards. The Bears didn't punt once all afternoon.

Green Bay won three of its last five games, including a 31-14 decision over the Cardinals that brought the Packers to within a game of first place. With Rote throwing three touchdown passes, the Packers evened their record (4-4), and trailed only the Bears (5-3) and Rams (5-3).

A week later, Knafelc and Ferguson each scored to cap a 27-21 come-from-behind win against the 49ers. After a 24-10 loss to the Lions on Thanksgiving, Green Bay beat the 49ers 28-7 to earn its first win in San Francisco.

The Packers closed their season down the coast in Los Angeles, where the Rams finished them off 31-17.

MAULED

Give the Chicago Bears an inch and they'll take a yard. Four hundred six yards to be precise.

Bobby Watkins, Rick Casares, Chick Jagade and five other Bears rushed 54 times for 406 yards against the Packers on Nov. 6. They reeled off 16 runs of 10 or more yards. Officially, they piled up 19 rushing first downs, but in examining the play-by-play, that total should have been 20.

Watkins, who rushed for 115 yards, scored two of Chicago's five rushing touchdowns. Casares also gained 115 yards, as the Packers were trampled by two 100-yard rushers in the same game for the first time.

In 1954, Chicago rushed for the fewest yards in the NFL. In 1955, the Bears led the league in that category, thanks in part to the woeful defensive performance of Green Bay.

Most Yards Rushing by a Packers Opponent, Game

Yards	Team	FDs	TDs	Date
406	Bears	19	5	Nov. 6, 1955
375	Bears	19	3	Oct. 30, 1977
323	Rams	16	2	Oct. 21, 1951

1955

TEAM STATISTICS

	GB	OPP
First Downs	213	196
Rushing	106	118
Passing	95	71
Penalty	12	7
Rushes	433	475
Yards Gained	1,883	2,174
Average Gain	4.35	4.58
Average Yards per Game	156.9	181.2
Passes Attempted	348	259
Completed	159	118
% Completed	45.69	45.56
Total Yards Gained	2,004	1,768
Yards Lost	225	80
Net Yards Gained	1,779	1,688
Yards Gained per Completion	12.60	14.98
Average Net Yards per Game	148.3	140.7
Combined Net Yards Gained	3,662	3,862
Total Plays	781	734
Average Yards per Play	4.69	5.26
Average Net Yards per Game	305.2	321.8
Third Down Efficiency	62/171	53/154
Percentage	36.26	34.42
Fourth Down Efficiency	10/18	7/12
Percentage	55.56	58.33
Intercepted By	31	19
Yards Returned	400	268
Returned for TD	0	1
Punts	56	52
Yards Punted	2,420	2,174
Average Yards per Punt	43.21	41.81
Punt Returns	35	36
Yards Returned	252	223
Average Yards per Return	7.20	6.19
Returned for TD	0	1
Kickoff Returns	39	48
Yards Returned	1,002	1,157
Average Yards per Return	25.69	24.10
Returned for TD	1	0
Penalties	41	56
Yards Penalized	401	490
Fumbles	37	27
Lost	25	18
Own Recovered for Touchdown	0	0
Opponent's Recovered by	18	25
Opponent's Recovered for Touchdown	0	3
Total Points Scored	258	276
Total Touchdowns	30	36
Touchdowns Rushing	11	18
Touchdowns Passing	17	13
Touchdowns on Returns & Recoveries	2	5
Extra Points	30	36
Safeties	0	0
Field Goals Attempted	24	17
Field Goals Made	16	8
% Successful	66.67	47.06

Regular Season 6-6-0

Date	GB		OPP	Att.
9/25	20	Detroit Lions	17	(22,217)
10/2	24	Chicago Bears	3	(24,662)
10/8	20	Baltimore Colts (M)	24	(40,199)
10/16	30	Los Angeles Rams (M)	28	(26,960)
10/23	10	at Cleveland Browns	41	(51,482)
10/29	10	at Baltimore Colts	14	(34,411)
11/6	31	at Chicago Bears	52	(48,890)
11/13	31	Chicago Cardinals	14	(20,104)
11/20	27	San Francisco 49ers (M)	21	(19,099)
11/24	10	at Detroit Lions	24	(51,685)
12/4	28	at San Francisco 49ers	7	(34,527)
12/11	17	at Los Angeles Rams	31	(90,535)

Score By Periods

	1	2	3	4	Total
Packers	40	101	45	72	258
Opponents	77	59	58	82	276

INDIVIDUAL STATISTICS

Rushing

	Att	Yds	Avg	LG	TD
Ferguson	192	859	4.5	57	4
Rote	74	332	4.5	49	5
Reid	83	303	3.7	28	2
J. Johnson	49	210	4.3	21	0
Switzer	16	101	6.3	38	0
Carmichael	6	45	7.5	20	0
Cone	12	25	2.1	14	0
Held	1	8	8.0	8	0
Packers	**433**	**1,883**	**4.4**	**57**	**11**
Opponents	475	2,174	4.6	t55	18

Receiving

	No	Yds	Avg	LG	TD
Howton	44	697	15.8	60	5
Knafelc	40	613	15.3	48	8
Ferguson	22	153	7.0	16	0
Carmichael	16	222	13.9	32	1
Switzer	14	103	7.4	22	1
Reid	13	138	10.6	t60	1
J. Johnson	9	71	7.9	30	1
Cone	1	7	7.0	7	0
Packers	**159**	**2,004**	**12.6**	**t60**	**17**
Opponents	118	1,768	15.0	t98	13

Passing

	Att	Com	Yds	Pct	TD	In	Yds	Rate
Rote	342	157	1,977	45.9	17	19	218	57.8
Held	4	2	27	50.0	0	0	0	—
Brackins	2	0	0	00.0	0	0	7	—
Packers	**348**	**159**	**2,004**	**45.7**	**17**	**19**	**225**	**57.7**
Opponents	259	118	1,768	45.6	13	31	80	45.6

Punting

	No	Yds	Avg	Net	TB	In20	LG	HB
Deschaine	56	2,420	43.2	37.8	4	19	73	0
Packers	**56**	**2,420**	**43.2**	**37.8**	**4**	**19**	**73**	**0**
Opponents	52	2,174	41.8	36.2	2	11	55	1

Kickoff Returns

	No	Yds	Avg	LG	TD
Switzer	17	445	26.2	57	0
Carmichael	14	418	29.9	t100	1
Forester	3	52	17.3	20	0
J. Johnson	2	46	23.0	27	0
Reid	2	21	10.5	17	0
Ferguson	1	20	20.0	20	0
Packers	**39**	**1,002**	**25.7**	**t100**	**1**
Opponents	48	1,157	24.1	81	0

Punt Returns

	No	Yds	Avg	LG	TD
Switzer	24	158	6.6	38	0
Carmichael	10	89	8.9	40	0
J. Johnson	1	5	5.0	5	0
Packers	**35**	**252**	**7.2**	**40**	**0**
Opponents	36	223	6.2	t55	1

Interceptions

	No	Yds	Avg	LG	TD
Dillon	9	153	17.0	61	0
V.J. Walker	6	77	12.8	36	0
Nix	5	33	6.6	12	0
Forester	4	32	8.0	17	0
Zatkoff	3	25	8.3	15	0
Teteak	2	41	20.5	32	0
Bookout	2	39	19.5	27	0
Packers	**31**	**400**	**12.9**	**61**	**0**
Opponents	19	268	14.1	36	1

Scoring

	TDr	TDp	TDrt	PAT	FG	S	TP
Cone	0	0	0	30/30	16/24	0	78
Knafelc	0	8	0	0/0	0/0	0	48
Howton	0	5	0	0/0	0/0	0	30
Rote	5	0	0	0/0	0/0	0	30
Ferguson	4	0	0	0/0	0/0	0	24
Reid	2	1	0	0/0	0/0	0	18
Carmichael	0	1	1	0/0	0/0	0	12
J. Johnson	0	1	0	0/0	0/0	0	6
Switzer	0	1	0	0/0	0/0	0	6
Szafaryn	0	0	1	0/0	0/0	0	6
Packers	**11**	**17**	**2**	**30/30**	**16/24**	**0**	**258**
Opponents	18	13	5	36/36	8/17	0	276

Fumbles

	Fum	Ow	Op	Yds	Tot
Bookout	0	1	2	0	3
Borden	0	0	3	0	3
Bill Brown	0	1	0	0	1
Cone	0	0	1	0	1
Dillon	0	0	1	0	1
Ferguson	8	0	0	0	8
Forester	1	0	0	0	0
Helluin	0	0	1	0	1
Howton	2	0	1	0	1
Jennings	0	0	1	0	1
J. Johnson	4	0	0	0	0
Martinkovic	0	0	1	0	1
Nix	0	0	1	0	1
Reid	4	2	0	0	2
Ringo	0	1	0	0	1
Rote	10	2	0	0	2
Switzer	6	3	0	0	3
Teteak	0	0	3	0	3
V.J. Walker	1	0	3	0	3
Zatkoff	1	0	0	0	1
Packers	**37**	**12**	**18**	**0**	**30**

NFL STANDINGS

Western Conference

	W	L	T	Pct	PF	PA
Los Angeles Rams	8	3	1	.727	260	231
Chicago Bears	8	4	0	.667	294	251
Green Bay Packers	6	6	0	.500	258	276
Baltimore Colts	5	6	1	.455	214	239
San Francisco 49ers	4	8	0	.333	216	298
Detroit Lions	3	9	0	.250	230	275

Eastern Conference

	W	L	T	Pct	PF	PA
Cleveland Browns	9	2	1	.818	349	218
Washington Redskins	8	4	0	.667	246	222
New York Giants	6	5	1	.545	267	223
Chicago Cardinals	4	7	1	.364	224	252
Philadelphia Eagles	4	7	1	.364	248	231
Pittsburgh Steelers	4	8	0	.333	195	285

ROSTER

No	Name	Pos	Ht	Wt	DOB	College	G
58	Bettis, Tom	LB	6-2	225	03/17/33	Purdue	12
20	Bookout, Billy	DB	5-11	180	06/01/32	Austin	12
87	Borden, Nate	DE	6-0	205	09/22/32	Indiana	12
15	Brackins, Charles	QB	6-2	202	01/12/32	Prairie View A&M	7
62	Brown, Bill (Buddy)	G	6-1	225	10/19/26	Arkansas	12
67	Bullough, Hank	G	6-0	220	01/24/34	Michigan State	12
23	Capuzzi, Jim	DB	6-0	190	03/12/32	Cincinnati	3
48	Carmichael, Al	HB	6-1	190	11/10/28	USC	12
33	Clemens, Bob	FB	6-2	200	08/03/33	Georgia	2
31	Cone, Fred	FB	5-11	200	06/21/26	Clemson	12
78	Dahms, Tom	T	6-5	240	04/19/27	San Diego	12
80	Deschaine, Dick	P	6-0	190	04/28/32	No college	12
44	Dillon, Bobby	DB	6-1	180	02/23/30	Texas	12
37	Ferguson, Howie	FB	6-2	212	08/05/30	No college	12
69	Forester, Bill	DT	6-3	235	08/09/32	SMU	12
77	Hanner, Joel (Dave)	DT	6-2	250	05/20/30	Arkansas	12
15	Held, Paul	QB	6-2	194	10/20/28	San Diego	5
72	Helluin, Jerry	DT	6-2	280	08/08/29	Tulane	12
86	Howton, Bill	E	6-2	190	07/05/30	Rice	12
85	Jennings, Jim	E	6-3	205	11/14/33	Missouri	6
40	Johnson, Joe	HB	6-0	180	11/03/29	Boston College	12
84	Knafelc, Gary	E	6-4	215	01/02/32	Colorado	12
71	Lucky, Bill	DT	6-3	250	08/24/31	Baylor	12
83	Martinkovic, John	DE	6-3	245	02/04/27	Xavier	12
41	Nix, Doyle	DB	6-1	188	05/30/33	SMU	12
81	O'Donahue, Pat	DE	6-2	215	10/07/30	Wisconsin	12
24	Reid, Floyd (Breezy)	HB	5-10	190	09/04/27	Georgia	12
51	Ringo, Jim	C	6-1	230	11/21/32	Syracuse	12
23	Romine, Al	HB	6-2	190	03/10/32	North Alabama	4
18	Rote, Tobin	QB	6-3	215	01/18/28	Rice	12
28	Self, Clarence	DB	5-9	180	10/25/25	Wisconsin	2
63	Skibinski, Joe	G	5-11	228	12/23/28	Purdue	12
61	Spinks, Jack	G	6-1	240	02/04/30	Alcorn State	6
53	Stephenson, Dave	G	6-2	230	10/22/25	West Virginia	2
27	Switzer, Veryl	HB	5-11	190	08/06/32	Kansas State	12
68	Szafaryn, Len	G	6-2	230	01/19/28	North Carolina	12
66	Teteak, Deral	LB	5-10	210	12/11/29	Wisconsin	12
53	Timberlake, George	G	6-1	220	11/03/32	USC	6
47	Walker, Val Joe	DB	6-1	179	01/07/30	SMU	12
74	Zatkoff, Roger	T	6-2	215	03/25/31	Michigan	12

DRAFT

Rnd	Name	Pos	Ht	Wt	College
1	Tom Bettis	LB	6-2	225	Purdue
2	Jim Temp	DE	6-4	230	Wisconsin
3	John Leake	HB	6-0	185	Oklahoma
4	(Choice to Browns for Jerry Helluin)				
5	Hank Bullough	G	6-0	220	Michigan State
6	Norm Amundsen	G	5-11	222	Wisconsin
7	Bob Clemens	FB	6-2	200	Georgia
8	John Crouch	HB	6-2	195	TCU
9	Ed Culpepper	T	6-1	245	Alabama
*10	George Rogers	T	6-5	247	Auburn
11	Ron Clark	HB	5-11	180	Nebraska
12	Art Walker	T	5-11	220	Michigan
13	Ed Adams	FG	6-2	225	North Carolina
14	Fred Baer	HB	5-11	190	Michigan
15	George Machoukas	C	6-2	220	Toledo
16	Charles Brackins	QB	6-2	202	Prairie View A&M
*17	Ed Beightol	QB	6-1	185	Maryland
18	Doyle Nix	DB	6-1	188	SMU
19	Robert Carter	T	6-3	250	Grambling
20a	Carl Bolt	HB	6-1	185	So. Mississippi
20b	Bob Antkowiak	T	6-5	240	Bucknell
	(Choice from Giants for John Bauer)				
*21	Lavell Isbell	T	6-3	220	Houston
*22	Bill Brunner	FB	6-3	220	Arkansas Tech
*23	Elton Shaw	T	6-3	225	LSU
24	Charles Bryant	G	6-0	197	Nebraska
25	Nate Borden	DE	6-0	205	Indiana
26	Jim Jennings	E	6-3	205	Missouri
27	Bob Peringer	E	6-3	195	Washington State
28	Jack Spears	T	6-4	230	Tenn.-Chattanooga
29	Sam Pino	FB	5-8	197	Boston U.
*30	Bob Sala	FB	6-0	195	Tulane

* denotes juniors

1955 GREEN BAY PACKERS

FRONT ROW: (L–R) 84 Gary Knafelc, 40 Joe Johnson, 23 Jim Capuzzi, 15 Paul Held, 86 Bill Howton, 41 Doyle Nix, 31 Fred Cone, 80 Dick Deschaine.
SECOND ROW: (L–R) 48 Al Carmichael, 37 Howie Ferguson, 24 Floyd (Breezy) Reid, 47 Val Joe Walker, 44 Bobby Dillon, 62 Bill (Buddy) Brown, 74 Roger Zatkoff, 20 Billy Bookout, 27 Veryl Switzer, 66 Deral Teteak.
THIRD ROW: (L–R) Backfield Coach Ray (Scooter) McLean, Line Coach Lou Rymkus, 83 John Martinkovic, 87 Nate Borden, 78 Tom Dahms, 71 Bill Lucky, 72 Jerry Helluin, 81 Pat O'Donahue, End Coach Tom Hearden, Head Coach Lisle Blackbourn.
BACK ROW: (L–R) 68 Len Szafaryn, 61 Jack Spinks, 58 Tom Bettis, 63 Joe Skibinski, 67 Hank Bullough, 69 Bill Forester, 51 Jim Ringo, 79 Dave Hanner, Trainer Carl (Bud) Jorgensen, Equipment Manager Toby Sylvester.

City Stadium was 31 years old and a year away from being replaced by a new, larger structure on the city's west side. An appropriate sendoff would have included a win. But unlike a year earlier when the team went unbeaten in Green Bay, the 1956 Packers floundered there and instead bid farewell with a trio of losses.

The team's struggles at home merely increased frustrations in a year that began with high hopes. Green Bay breezed through its exhibition season with a 4-1 record that included a 21-20 win over the defending NFL champion Browns. That record and the team's improved showing in 1955 had many fans looking for a winning record.

The Packers, however, didn't deliver. While wins against the Rams and Colts in Weeks 3 and 4 kept the team (2-2) within sight of the Lions (4-0) and Bears (3-1), an ensuing four-game losing streak eliminated them from the playoff race by Thanksgiving. When the season ended in mid-December, Green Bay (4-8) sat alongside the Rams in the cellar of the Western Conference standings.

Green Bay's defense, or lack of thereof, was its undoing. The unit, ranked sixth the year previous, dropped to last place. No team gave up more first downs, total yardage, or rushing yardage than did the Packers. Opponents staked out turf at the rate of nearly 400 yards (392.5) a game. On Dec. 16, the lowly Rams exploded for 611 yards, the most ever surrendered by the Green and Gold.

As a result, the Packers only won when they outgained their opponents. That happened but four times, despite the presence of two of the best playmakers in football. Tobin Rote led the league in passing yards (2,203) and touchdowns (18). Bill Howton set the NFL pace in yards receiving (1,188) and touchdown receptions (12).

Rote left his stamp on the running game as well. The seven-year veteran scrambled for a team-high 398 yards and accounted for 11 of the team's 13 rushing touchdowns. Fred Cone was the only other back to score on the ground.

Cone, the NFL's leading field goal kicker in 1955, had announced his retirement in the off-season. When finding a reliable kicker proved impossible, Blackbourn convinced Cone to return in early August and the fullback went on to tie Howton for scoring honors with 72 points.

Television wasn't new to the Packers (Milwaukee games had been broadcast as far back as 1948), but it was becoming more pervasive. In 1956, CBS announced it would televise all Green Bay home games. The team would also appear in the national spotlight twice—in Detroit on Thanksgiving and at the 49ers in early December.

The Packers opened against the Lions in Green Bay for a second straight year. For the second year in a row, Rote connected on a touchdown pass late in the fourth quarter. But this time the throw—an 8-yarder to Howton—wasn't enough as the Packers came up short 20-16.

Al Carmichael's NFL-record, 106-yard kickoff return spiced Week 2. Unfortunately his score—and two by Howton—couldn't stop the Bears 37-21.

Two Bobby Dillon interceptions helped Green Bay upend the Colts 38-33 in Milwaukee.

In Week 4, Green Bay produced a season-high 498 yards and beat the Rams 42-17. Rote passed for 279 yards and three touchdowns, and first-round draft choice John Losch tossed a 63-yard bomb. Howton established a team record with 257 receiving yards on seven catches.

Lenny Moore ran wild in Week 5, gaining 185 yards including scoring runs of 72 and 79 yards. Green Bay, as a team, managed just 20 rushing yards in falling 28-21 to the Colts.

After a 38-14 misstep in Wrigley Field, Green Bay (2-5) returned home for its final league game in City Stadium. Bart Starr got his first-ever start at quarterback. The rookie completed three of six passes for 63 yards and a touchdown before giving way to Rote in the second quarter. Carmichael, Ferguson, and Rote all lost fumbles in the final six minutes to ensure a 17-16 loss to the 49ers.

During halftime, the Packers honored former team publicist George Whitney Calhoun for his many years of service.

Now out of the playoff race, Green Bay rose up to smite the Lions 24-20 for its first win on Thanksgiving in Detroit. Rote hit Howton with a 13-yard pass for the deciding score with just over a minute-and-a-half remaining, and Dillon intercepted Bobby Layne with 38 seconds left to end Detroit's final threat.

TRAMPLED UNDERFOOT

Only once in Packers history has the team given up an average of more than 200 yards rushing in a single season. The defenders of 1956 earned that unenviable honor.

It didn't take long for the opposition to discover that Green Bay couldn't stop the run. The Lions picked up 175 yards in the opener and the Bears followed with 278 yards a week later. Both the Colts and Rams surpassed the 300-yard mark, and the Cardinals were the only team to fail to amass at least 100 yards on the ground.

The competition got a great return for its investment. The Packers allowed an average of 5.12 yards per rush, the only time in club history it surrendered more than five yards a carry over the course of an entire season.

Most Yards Rushing per Game, Opponents, Season

Avg./Game	Season	Avg./Carry
218.3	1956 (2,619/12)	5.12
181.2	1955 (2,174/12)	4.58
180.3	1979 (2,885/16)	4.51
179.9	1957 (2,159/12)	4.67

TEAM STATISTICS

	GB	OPP
First Downs	212	246
Rushing	86	129
Passing	112	104
Penalty	14	13
Rushes	337	512
Yards Gained	1,421	2,619
Average Gain	4.22	5.12
Average Yards per Game	118.4	218.3
Passes Attempted	353	260
Completed	171	144
% Completed	48.44	55.38
Total Yards Gained	2,591	2,166
Yards Lost	193	75
Net Yards Gained	2,398	2,091
Yards Gained per Completion	15.15	15.04
Average Net Yards per Game	199.8	174.3
Combined Net Yards Gained	3,819	4,710
Total Plays	690	772
Average Yards per Play	5.53	6.10
Average Net Yards per Game	318.3	392.5
Third Down Efficiency	62/157	67/149
Percentage	39.49	44.97
Fourth Down Efficiency	10/18	11/17
Percentage	55.56	64.71
Intercepted By	21	18
Yards Returned	406	312
Returned for TD	1	3
Punts	62	50
Yards Punted	2,649	2,040
Average Yards per Punt	42.73	40.80
Punt Returns	30	49
Yards Returned	239	280
Average Yards per Return	7.97	5.71
Returned for TD	0	1
Kickoff Returns	59	48
Yards Returned	1,442	924
Average Yards per Return	24.44	19.25
Returned for TD	1	0
Penalties	42	52
Yards Penalized	393	493
Fumbles	24	17
Lost	11	8
Own Recovered for Touchdown	0	0
Opponent's Recovered by	8	11
Opponent's Recovered for Touchdown	0	2
Total Points Scored	264	342
Total Touchdowns	36	44
Touchdowns Rushing	13	21
Touchdowns Passing	21	17
Touchdowns on Returns & Recoveries	2	6
Extra Points	33	42
Safeties	0	0
Field Goals Attempted	8	18
Field Goals Made	5	12
% Successful	62.50	66.67

Regular Season 4-8-0

Date	GB		OPP	Att.
9/30	16	Detroit Lions	20	(24,668)
10/7	21	Chicago Bears	37	(24,668)
10/14	38	Baltimore Colts (M)	33	(24,214)
10/21	42	Los Angeles Rams (M)	17	(24,200)
10/28	21	at Baltimore Colts	28	(40,086)
11/4	7	Cleveland Browns (M)	24	(28,590)
11/11	14	at Chicago Bears	38	(49,172)
11/18	16	San Francisco 49ers	17	(17,986)
11/22	24	at Detroit Lions	20	(54,087)
12/2	24	at Chicago Cardinals	21	(22,620)
12/8	20	at San Francisco 49ers	38	(32,436)
12/16	21	at Los Angeles Rams	49	(45,209)

Score By Periods

	1	2	3	4	Total
Packers	51	61	62	90	264
Opponents	78	125	54	85	342

INDIVIDUAL STATISTICS

Rushing

	Att	Yds	Avg	LG	TD
Rote	84	398	4.7	39	11
Ferguson	99	367	3.7	24	0
Cone	49	211	4.3	21	2
Carmichael	32	199	6.2	35	0
J. Johnson	35	129	3.7	14	0
Losch	19	43	2.3	8	0
Reid	14	39	2.8	11	0
Starr	5	35	7.0	14	0
Packers	**337**	**1,421**	**4.2**	**39**	**13**
Opponents	512	2,619	5.1	t86	21

Receiving

	No	Yds	Avg	LG	TD
Howton	55	1,188	21.6	t66	12
Knafelc	30	418	13.9	38	6
J. Johnson	28	258	9.2	20	0
Ferguson	22	214	9.7	25	0
Carmichael	13	180	13.8	63	1
Cone	12	218	18.2	t69	2
Losch	7	85	12.1	43	0
Reid	3	16	5.3	12	0
Roberts	1	14	14.0	14	0
Packers	**171**	**2,591**	**15.2**	**t69**	**21**
Opponents	144	2,166	15.0	t70	17

Passing

	Att	Com	Yds	Pct	TD	In	Yds	Rate
Rote	308	146	2,203	47.4	18	15	177	70.6
Starr	44	24	325	54.5	2	3	16	65.1
Losch	1	1	63	100.0	1	0	0	—
Packers	**353**	**171**	**2,591**	**48.4**	**21**	**18**	**193**	**71.6**
Opponents	260	144	2,166	55.4	17	21	75	71.1

Punting

	No	Yds	Avg	Net	TB	In20	LG	HB
Deschaine	62	2,649	42.7	37.2	3	16	57	0
Packers	**62**	**2,649**	**42.7**	**37.2**	**3**	**16**	**57**	**0**
Opponents	50	2,040	40.8	35.2	2	10	56	0

Kickoff Returns

	No	Yds	Avg	LG	TD
Carmichael	33	927	28.1	t106	1
Losch	15	390	26.0	51	0
Ferguson	5	83	16.6	34	0
Forester	4	36	9.0	17	0
Gremminger	1	6	6.0	6	0
Borden	1	0	0.0	0	0
Packers	**59**	**1,442**	**24.4**	**t106**	**1**
Opponents	48	924	19.3	45	0

Punt Returns

	No	Yds	Avg	LG	TD
Carmichael	21	165	7.9	22	0
Losch	8	74	9.3	58	0
Reid	1	0	0.0	0	0
Packers	**39**	**239**	**8.0**	**58**	**0**
Opponents	49	280	5.7	t90	1

Interceptions

	No	Yds	Avg	LG	TD
Dillon	7	244	34.9	45	1
Forester	4	35	8.8	13	0
Capuzzi	2	65	32.5	65	0
Gremminger	2	36	18.0	21	0
Teteak	2	20	10.0	18	0
Gorgal	2	2	1.0	2	0
Bookout	1	4	4.0	4	0
V.J. Walker	1	0	0.0	0	0
Packers	**21**	**406**	**19.3**	**65**	**1**
Opponents	18	312	17.3	t95	3

Scoring

	TDr	TDp	TDrt	PAT	FG	S	TP
Cone	0	0	0	33/35	5/8	0	72
Howton	0	12	0	0/0	0/0	0	72
Rote	11	0	0	0/0	0/0	0	66
Knafelc	0	6	0	0/0	0/0	0	36
Carmichael	0	1	1	0/0	0/0	0	12
Dillon	0	0	1	0/0	0/0	0	6
Packers	**13**	**21**	**2**	**33/36**	**5/8**	**0**	**264**
Opponents	21	17	6	42/44	12/18	0	342

Fumbles

	Fum	Ow	Op	Yds	Tot
Capuzzi	0	0	1	0	1
Carmichael	6	0	0	0	1
Cone	2	1	1	0	2
Dillon	0	0	1	0	1
Ferguson	6	3	0	0	1
Forester	0	0	1	0	1
Hanner	0	1	0	0	1
J. Johnson	1	0	0	0	0
Losch	3	3	0	0	3
Martinkovic	0	0	1	0	1
Reid	1	0	0	0	0
Ringo	0	2	0	0	1
Rote	5	2	0	0	1
Szafaryn	0	1	0	0	1
Teteak	0	0	2	0	2
Zatkoff	0	0	1	0	1
Packers	**24**	**13**	**8**		**21**

NFL STANDINGS

Western Conference

	W	L	T	Pct	PF	PA
Chicago Bears	9	2	1	.818	363	246
Detroit Lions	9	3	0	.750	300	188
San Francisco 49ers	5	6	1	.455	233	284
Baltimore Colts	5	7	0	.417	270	322
Green Bay Packers	**4**	**8**	**0**	**.333**	**264**	**342**
Los Angeles Rams	4	8	0	.333	291	307

Eastern Conference

	W	L	T	Pct	PF	PA
New York Giants	8	3	1	.727	264	197
Chicago Cardinals	7	5	0	.583	240	182
Washington Redskins	6	6	0	.500	183	225
Cleveland Browns	5	7	0	.417	167	177
Pittsburgh Steelers	5	7	0	.417	217	250
Philadelphia Eagles	3	8	1	.273	143	215

ROSTER

No	Name	Pos	Ht	Wt	DOB	College	G
85	Barnes, Emery	DE	6-6	235	12/15/29	Oregon	2
65	Bettis, Tom	LB	6-2	230	03/17/33	Purdue	12
20	Bookout, Billy	DB	5-11	180	06/01/32	Austin	7
87	Borden, Nate	DE	6-0	225	09/22/32	Indiana	12
62	Brown, Bill (Buddy)	G	6-1	225	10/19/26	Arkansas	12
67	Bullough, Hank	G	6-0	220	01/24/34	Michigan State	12
26	Capuzzi, Jim	DB	6-0	190	03/12/32	Cincinnati	7
48	Carmichael, Al	HB	6-1	190	11/10/28	USC	12
31	Cone, Fred	FB	5-11	200	06/21/26	Clemson	12
80	Deschaine, Dick	P	6-0	210	04/28/32	No college	12
44	Dillon, Bobby	DB	6-1	180	02/23/30	Texas	12
37	Ferguson, Howie	FB	6-2	215	08/05/30	No college	11
69	Forester, Bill	DT	6-3	235	08/09/32	SMU	12
26/27	Gorgal, Ken	DB	6-2	210	02/13/29	Purdue	5
75	Gregg, Alvis (Forrest)	T	6-4	240	10/18/33	SMU	11
46	Gremminger, Hank	DB	6-1	195	09/01/33	Baylor	12
79	Hanner, Joel (Dave)	DT	6-2	255	05/20/30	Arkansas	12
72	Helluin, Jerry	DT	6-2	265	08/08/29	Tulane	12
86	Howton, Bill	E	6-2	190	07/05/30	Rice	12
40	Johnson, Joe	HB	6-0	180	11/03/29	Boston College	11
70	King, Don	DT	6-3	265	03/11/29	Kentucky	6
84	Knafelc, Gary	E	6-4	215	01/02/32	Colorado	12
81	Knutson, Gene	E	6-2	230	11/20/32	Michigan	6
58	Lauer, Larry	C	6-3	265	08/27/29	Alabama	6
25	Losch, John	HB	6-1	205	08/13/34	Miami (FL)	12
83	Martinkovic, John	DE	6-3	245	02/04/27	Xavier	12
24	Reid, Floyd (Breezy)	HB	5-10	190	09/04/27	Georgia	7
51	Ringo, Jim	C	6-1	235	11/21/32	Syracuse	12
22	Roberts, Bill	HB	6-0	200	09/11/29	Dartmouth	4
18	Rote, Tobin	QB	6-3	215	01/18/28	Rice	12
77	Sandusky, John	DT	6-1	250	12/28/25	Villanova	12
63	Skibinski, Joe	G	5-11	230	12/23/28	Purdue	12
76	Skoronski, Bob	T	6-3	250	03/05/34	Indiana	12
61	Smith, Jerry	G	6-0	230	09/09/30	Wisconsin	3
61	Spinks, Jack	G	6-1	240	02/04/30	Alcorn State	1
15	Starr, Bryan (Bart)	QB	6-1	200	01/09/34	Alabama	9
68	Szafaryn, Len	G	6-2	225	01/19/28	North Carolina	12
66	Teteak, Deral	LB	5-10	210	12/11/29	Wisconsin	12
47	Walker, Val Joe	DB	6-1	180	01/07/30	SMU	12
23	Young, Glenn	DB	6-2	205	12/22/30	Purdue	4
74	Zatkoff, Roger	T	6-2	215	03/25/31	Michigan	12

DRAFT

Rnd	Name	Pos	Ht	Wt	College
1	John Losch	HB	6-1	205	Miami (FL)
2	Forrest Gregg	T	6-4	240	SMU
3	(Choice to Rams in Tom Dahms deal)				
4	Cecil Morris	G	6-2	230	Oklahoma
5	Bob Skoronski	T	6-3	250	Indiana
6	Bob Burris	HB	6-0	190	Oklahoma
7	Hank Gremminger	E	6-1	195	Baylor
8	Russ Dennis	E	6-3	215	Maryland
9	Gordon Duvall	FB	6-0	200	USC
10	Bob Laugherty	FB	6-0	210	Maryland
*11	Mike Hudock	C	6-2	220	Miami (FL)
12	Max Burnett	HB	6-0	190	Arizona
13	James Mense	C	6-1	220	Notre Dame
14	Charlie Thomas	FB	5-11	217	Wisconsin
15	Buddy Allison Vaughn	G	6-0	210	Mississippi
16	Curtis Lynch	T	6-3	230	Alabama
17	Bart Starr	QB	6-1	200	Alabama
18	Stan Intihar	E	6-3	220	Cornell
*19	Ken Vakey	E	6-3	200	Texas Tech
*20	Clyde Letbetter	G	6-2	225	Baylor
21	Hal O'Brien	FB	6-0	200	SMU
22	John Popson	HB	6-1	195	Furman
*23	Jesse Birchfield	G	6-2	220	Duke
24	Don Wilson	C	6-3	215	Rice
25	Franz Koeneke	E	6-2	220	Minnesota
26	Dick Goehe	T	6-4	225	Mississippi
27	Dick Kolian	E	6-2	212	Wisconsin
28	Bob Lance	QB	6-1	185	Florida
29	Vester Newcomb	C	6-2	200	SW Jr. College
30	Rod Hermes	QB	6-2	202	Beloit

* denotes juniors

1956 GREEN BAY PACKERS

FRONT ROW: (L-R) 83 John Martinkovic, 69 Bill Forester, 26 Jim Capuzzi, 80 Dick Deschaine, 84 Gary Knafelc, 86 Bill Howton, 66 Deral Teteak, 47 Val Joe Walker, 44 Bobby Dillon, 37 Howie Ferguson, 24 Breezy Reid, 61 Jerry Smith, 58 Larry Lauer.

MIDDLE ROW: (L-R) Propertyman Gerald (Dad) Braisher, Head Coach Lisle Blackbourn, Defensive Line Coach Earl Klapstein, 74 Roger Zatkoff, 68 Len Szafaryn, 48 Al Carmichael, 31 Fred Cone, 46 Hank Gremminger, 25 John Losch, 63 Joe Skibinski, 40 Joe Johnson, 22 Bill Roberts, Backfield Coach Ray (Scooter) McLean, Offensive Line Coach Lou Rymkus, Trainer Carl (Bud) Jorgensen.

BACK ROW: (L-R) Defensive Backfield Coach Emmett (Abe) Stuber, 51 Jim Ringo, 79 Dave Hanner, 62 Bill (Buddy) Brown, 81 Gene Knutson, 72 Jerry Helluin, 15 Bart Starr, 18 Tobin Rote, 77 John Sandusky, 23 Glenn Young, 65 Tom Bettis, 87 Nate Borden, 76 Bob Skoronski.

The Packers had hosted season-openers before, but none with the pomp and pageantry of the kickoff to the 1957 season.

On the last weekend of September, Green Bay celebrated the opening of New City Stadium. Miss America (Marilyn Van Derbur) and television's Matt Dillon (James Arness) presided at a farewell ceremony to the old stadium on Saturday. On Sunday, the two were joined by Vice President Richard Nixon and other dignitaries as Green Bay disposed of the Bears 21-17 in front of 32,150 fans.

The victory capped a weekend that included speeches, a parade, and a Venetian night with fireworks and a flotilla of 22 yachts on the Fox River. That the win came against the Packers' fiercest and oldest adversary only made the whole affair all the more satisfying.

As usual, the Packers-Bears game was a battle. Green Bay lost Howie Ferguson to a leg injury on the second play of the game. Ollie Spencer and Bears defensive back Stan Wallace were ejected for fighting. And the contest wasn't decided until the fourth quarter, when the Packers forced two turnovers and made a key fourth-down stop.

Green Bay twice had to come from behind before Vito (Babe) Parilli threw a 6-yard scoring pass to Gary Knafelc with 8:21 left in the game. Early in the quarter, the Packers stuffed Bobby Watkins on fourth-down near midfield, and Bobby Dillon's interception and Larry Lauer's recovery of a Perry Jeter fumble then sealed the verdict.

The season-opening euphoria quickly faded as Green Bay lost six of its next seven games. The Packers won only twice more all season and wound up alone in the Western Conference cellar for the first time since 1953.

Green Bay seemingly never ran out of creative ways to lose. In Week 2, Lions' punter Yale Lary picked up 32 yards on fourth-and-22 from the Detroit 45. Five plays later, former Packer Tobin Rote scooted in from two yards out and the Lions never looked back in winning 24-14.

A week later, Green Bay gave up a team-record 38 second-half points in a 45-17 loss to the Colts. The following Sunday, Ron Kramer's only career passing attempt was intercepted by the 49ers, who went on to post 21 unanswered points in a 24-14 win in Milwaukee.

The Packers won just once in the seven weeks following the season opener. That victory occurred in Baltimore in late October. Parilli delivered a 75-yard scoring pass to Bill Howton with 29 seconds left to cap the team's 24-point fourth-quarter explosion and secure a 24-21 decision.

Any momentum the win may have generated quickly evaporated in the three weeks that followed. The Packers stumbled 31-17 against the Giants, a game in which Emlen Tunnell returned a Bart Starr interception 52 yards for a touchdown. In a 21-14 loss to the Bears, officials at Wrigley Field ruled that halfback Joe Johnson failed to hold on to an apparent touchdown pass from Starr. And the Rams overcame a 21-point deficit to post a 31-27 victory.

By the time Green Bay garnered its third win (27-10 in Pittsburgh), it was three games back of front-running Baltimore (6-3) with just three weeks left. In those final weeks, the Lions, Rams, and 49ers each beat the Packers.

In early January 1958, Lisle Blackbourn was fired.

Blackbourn, who had begun his stay in Green Bay with a large trade, worked three major deals in his final year. In April, he sent Roger Zatkoff and Bobby Garrett to Cleveland for Carlton Massey, John Macerelli, Sam Palumbo, Parilli, John Petitbon and Billy Kinard. In July, Rote and Val Joe Walker were dealt to the Lions for Spencer, Norm Masters, Jim Salsbury and Don McIlhenny. In September, Blackbourn traded John Martinkovic to the Giants for a third-round pick that was used to select Ray Nitschke in 1958.

Green Bay landed two key players in the draft. Paul Hornung, the bonus pick, finished second to McIlhenny in rushing, and his 72-yard gallop against the Giants was a season-best. Kramer, whose ill-fated pass hurt in the 49ers game, caught 28 passes, second best on the team.

The Packers could hardly use injuries as an excuse for their 3-9 record. Aside from a knee injury that forced Knafelc to miss the final nine games, Green Bay coasted through the season relatively free of injury.

Green Bay endured its ninth and final loss in San Francisco. With his team trailing by a touchdown, Blackbourn replaced Starr with Parilli midway through the fourth quarter. The hero of September's opener failed this time out. He tossed interceptions on each of his first two passes. Then, on the final snap of the season, Parilli was unceremoniously dumped for an 8-yard loss, a symbol of just how far the team had fallen in the months since it opened with such promise and fanfare against the Bears.

THE THUD QUARTER

If third-quarter scoring is a gauge of how well a team uses halftime to make adjustments, then the Packers of 1957 failed in that regard while their opponents prospered.

Green Bay scored just one touchdown in the third quarter all season long. The opposition posted 84 points in the 15 minutes following intermission.

The Packers had 35 drives that fell completely within the bounds of the third quarter. Sixteen ended in punts, seven in interceptions, five on fumbles, three on downs, two on missed field goals, one in a safety, and one on Don McIlhenny's 40-yard touchdown run against the Giants. Never before or since has the team been outscored so badly in that period.

Most Points Outscored by Opponents, Third Quarter

Difference	Season
-77	1957 Green Bay (7), Opponents (84)
-65	1983 Green Bay (44), Opponents (109)
-61	1953 Green Bay (31), Opponents (92)
-57	1948 Green Bay (26), Opponents (83)

TEAM STATISTICS

	GB	OPP
First Downs	179	226
Rushing	72	117
Passing	90	97
Penalty	17	12
Rushes	380	462
Yards Gained	1,441	2,159
Average Gain	3.79	4.67
Average Yards per Game	120.1	179.9
Passes Attempted	325	314
Completed	157	153
% Completed	48.31	48.73
Total Yards Gained	2,157	2,185
Yards Lost	366	147
Net Yards Gained	1,791	2,038
Yards Gained per Completion	13.74	14.28
Average Net Yards per Game	149.3	169.8
Combined Net Yards Gained	3,232	4,197
Total Plays	705	776
Average Yards per Play	4.58	5.41
Average Net Yards per Game	269.3	349.8
Third Down Efficiency	51/165	64/159
Percentage	30.91	40.25
Fourth Down Efficiency	10/22	8/12
Percentage	45.45	66.67
Intercepted By	30	23
Yards Returned	561	252
Returned for TD	1	2
Punts	63	50
Yards Punted	2,645	2,151
Average Yards per Punt	41.98	43.02
Punt Returns	36	40
Yards Returned	256	149
Average Yards per Return	7.11	3.73
Returned for TD	0	0
Kickoff Returns	58	42
Yards Returned	1,261	897
Average Yards per Return	21.74	21.36
Returned for TD	0	0
Penalties	43	75
Yards Penalized	516	709
Fumbles	28	26
Lost	18	17
Own Recovered for Touchdown	0	0
Opponent's Recovered by	17	18
Opponent's Recovered for Touchdown	0	0
Total Points Scored	218	311
Total Touchdowns	26	39
Touchdowns Rushing	13	18
Touchdowns Passing	12	18
Touchdowns on Returns & Recoveries	1	3
Extra Points	26	39
Safeties	0	1
Field Goals Attempted	21	22
Field Goals Made	12	12
% Successful	57.14	54.55

Regular Season   3-9-0

Date	GB		OPP	Att.
9/29	21	Chicago Bears	17	(32,132)
10/6	14	Detroit Lions	24	(32,120)
10/13	17	Baltimore Colts (M)	45	(26,322)
10/20	14	San Francisco 49ers (M)	24	(18,919)
10/27	24	at Baltimore Colts	21	(48,510)
11/3	17	New York Giants	31	(32,070)
11/10	14	at Chicago Bears	21	(47,183)
11/17	27	Los Angeles Rams (M)	31	(19,540)
11/24	27	at Pittsburgh Steelers	10	(29,701)
11/28	6	at Detroit Lions	18	(54,301)
12/8	17	at Los Angeles Rams	42	(70,572)
12/15	20	at San Francisco 49ers	27	(59,522)

Score By Periods

	1	2	3	4	Total
Packers	30	99	7	82	218
Opponents	72	61	84	94	311

INDIVIDUAL STATISTICS

Rushing

	Att	Yds	Avg	LG	TD
McIlhenny	100	384	3.8	t40	1
Hornung	60	319	5.3	72	3
Ferguson	59	216	3.7	t40	1
Cone	53	135	2.5	t26	2
Carmichael	37	118	3.2	10	1
Starr	31	98	3.2	16	3
Parilli	24	83	3.5	20	2
McGee	5	40	8.0	24	0
Purnell	5	22	4.4	7	0
Howton	4	20	5.0	11	0
J. Johnson	2	6	3.0	3	0
Packers	**380**	**1,441**	**3.8**	**72**	**13**
Opponents	462	2,159	4.7	76	18

Receiving

	No	Yds	Avg	LG	TD
Howton	38	727	19.1	t77	5
R. Kramer	28	337	12.0	31	0
McIlhenny	18	210	11.7	t28	2
McGee	17	273	16.1	49	1
Ferguson	15	107	7.1	17	1
Carmichael	13	184	14.2	39	0
Knafelc	9	164	18.2	53	2
J. Johnson	7	75	10.7	14	1
Hornung	6	34	5.7	16	0
Cone	4	30	7.5	10	0
Purnell	2	16	8.0	15	0
Packers	**157**	**2,157**	**13.7**	**t77**	**12**
Opponents	153	2,185	14.3	t61	18

Passing

	Att	Com	Yds	Pct	TD	In	Tk/Yds	Rate
Starr	215	117	1,489	54.4	8	10	25/231	69.3
Parilli	102	39	669	38.2	4	12	14/125	34.8
Hornung	6	1	-1	16.7	0	0	1/10	—
Ferguson	1	0	0	00.0	0	0	0/0	—
R. Kramer	1	0	0	00.0	0	0	0/0	—
Packers	**325**	**157**	**2,157**	**48.3**	**12**	**23**	**40/366**	**52.8**
Opponents	314	153	2,185	48.7	18	30	19/147	51.2

Punting

	No	Yds	Avg	Net	TB	In20	LG	HB
Deschaine	63	2,645	42.0	38.0	5	18	71	2
Packers	**63**	**2,645**	**42.0**	**38.0**	**5**	**18**	**71**	**2**
Opponents	50	2,151	43.0	37.9	0	11	66	0

Kickoff Returns

	No	Yds	Avg	LG	TD
Carmichael	31	690	22.3	33	0
McIlhenny	14	362	25.9	53	0
Cone	5	83	16.6	25	0
McGee	4	69	17.3	32	0
Forester	4	57	14.3	27	0
Packers	**58**	**1,261**	**21.7**	**53**	**0**
Opponents	42	897	21.4	46	0

Punt Returns

	No	Yds	Avg	LG	TD
Carmichael	25	190	7.6	48	0
J. Johnson	4	39	9.8	13	0
Kinard	3	19	6.3	19	0
Symank	3	0	0.0	0	0
Dillon	1	8	8.0	8	0
Packers	**36**	**256**	**7.1**	**48**	**0**
Opponents	40	149	3.7	22	0

Interceptions

	No	Yds	Avg	LG	TD
Symank	9	198	22.0	36	0
Dillon	9	180	20.0	t55	1
Gremminger	5	93	18.6	45	0
Forester	4	79	19.8	37	0
Palumbo	1	11	11.0	11	0
Helluin	1	0	0.0	0	0
Petitbon	1	0	0.0	0	0
Packers	**30**	**561**	**18.7**	**t55**	**1**
Opponents	23	252	11.0	t52	2

Scoring

	TDr	TDp	TDrt	PAT	FG	S	TP
Cone	2	0	0	26/26	12/17	0	74
Howton	0	5	0	0/0	0/0	0	30
Hornung	3	0	0	0/0	0/4	0	18
McIlhenny	1	2	0	0/0	0/0	0	18
Starr	3	0	0	0/0	0/0	0	18
Ferguson	1	1	0	0/0	0/0	0	12
Knafelc	0	2	0	0/0	0/0	0	12
Parilli	2	0	0	0/0	0/0	0	12
Carmichael	1	0	0	0/0	0/0	0	6
Dillon	0	0	1	0/0	0/0	0	6
J. Johnson	0	1	0	0/0	0/0	0	6
McGee	0	1	0	0/0	0/0	0	6
Packers	**13**	**12**	**1**	**26/26**	**12/21**	**0**	**218**
Opponents	18	18	3	39/39	12/22	1	311

Fumbles

	Fum	Ow	Op	Yds	Tot
Bettis	0	0	1	0	1
Borden	0	0	2	0	2
Carmichael	3	1	0	0	1
Cone	2	1	0	0	1
Danjean	0	0	1	0	1
Ferguson	2	0	0	0	0
Forester	1	1	3	45	4
Gremminger	1	0	0	0	0
Helluin	0	0	3	0	3
Hornung	2	0	0	0	0
Howton	1	0	0	0	0
Kinard	2	0	1	0	1
R. Kramer	0	0	1	0	1
Lauer	0	0	1	0	1
Masters	0	0	1	0	1
McIlhenny	4	0	0	0	0
Parilli	3	0	0	0	0
Petitbon	0	0	1	0	1
Purnell	1	0	0	0	0
Salsbury	0	0	1	0	1
O. Spencer	0	0	1	0	1
Starr	4	1	0	0	1
Symank	1	0	2	0	2
Temp	0	1	1	4	2
Packers	**28**	**10**	**17**	**52**	**27**

NFL STANDINGS

Western Conference

	W	L	T	Pct	PF	PA
Detroit Lions	8	4	0	.667	251	231
San Francisco 49ers	8	4	0	.667	260	264
Baltimore Colts	7	5	0	.583	303	235
Los Angeles Rams	6	6	0	.500	307	278
Chicago Bears	5	7	0	.417	203	211
Green Bay Packers	**3**	**9**	**0**	**.250**	**218**	**311**

Eastern Conference

	W	L	T	Pct	PF	PA
Cleveland Browns	9	2	1	.818	269	172
New York Giants	7	5	0	.583	254	211
Pittsburgh Steelers	5	6	1	.455	251	230
Philadelphia Eagles	4	8	0	.333	173	230
Chicago Cardinals	3	9	0	.250	200	299

ROSTER

No	Name	Pos	Ht	Wt	DOB	College	G
62	Amundsen, Norm	G	5-11	245	09/28/32	Wisconsin	12
66	Barry, Al	G	6-2	235	12/24/30	USC	12
65	Bettis, Tom	LB	6-2	235	03/17/33	Purdue	12
87	Borden, Nate	DE	6-0	235	09/22/32	Indiana	9
48	Carmichael, Al	HB	6-1	190	11/10/28	USC	12
31	Cone, Fred	FB	5-11	205	06/21/26	Clemson	12
64	Danjean, Ernest	LB	6-0	230	03/05/34	Auburn	12
80	Deschaine, Dick	P	6-0	215	04/28/32	No college	12
44	Dillon, Bobby	DB	6-1	180	02/23/30	Texas	12
37	Ferguson, Howie	FB	6-2	220	08/05/30	No college	12
71	Finnin, Tom	DT	6-2	262	09/28/27	Detroit Mercy	3
69	Forester, Bill	LB	6-3	235	08/09/32	SMU	12
46	Gremminger, Hank	DB	6-1	195	09/01/33	Baylor	12
79	Hanner, Dave	DT	6-2	250	05/20/30	Arkansas	12
72	Helluin, Jerry	DT	6-2	265	08/08/29	Tulane	12
5	Hornung, Paul	HB	6-2	215	12/23/35	Notre Dame	12
86	Howton, Bill	E	6-2	190	07/05/30	Rice	12
40	Johnson, Joe	HB	6-0	180	11/03/29	Boston College	12
25	Kinard, Billy	DB	6-0	185	12/16/33	Mississippi	12
84	Knafelc, Gary	E	6-4	215	01/02/32	Colorado	3
88	Kramer, Ron	E	6-3	220	06/24/35	Michigan	11
58	Lauer, Larry	C	6-3	235	08/27/29	Alabama	12
81	Massey, Carlton	DE	6-4	225	01/17/30	Texas	12
78	Masters, Norm	T	6-2	240	09/19/33	Michigan State	12
85	McGee, Max	E	6-3	205	07/16/32	Tulane	12
42	McIlhenny, Don	HB	6-0	200	11/22/34	SMU	12
53	Palumbo, Sam	LB	6-2	230	06/07/32	Notre Dame	9
10	Parilli, Vito (Babe)	QB	6-1	190	05/07/30	Kentucky	12
20	Petitbon, John	DB	5-11	190	06/04/31	Notre Dame	12
33	Purnell, Frank	FB	5-11	230	04/05/33	Alcorn State	9
51	Ringo, Jim	C	6-1	230	11/21/32	Syracuse	12
67	Salsbury, Jim	G	6-0	235	08/08/32	UCLA	12
77	Spencer, Ollie	T	6-2	250	04/17/31	Kansas	12
15	Starr, Bryan (Bart)	QB	6-1	200	01/09/34	Alabama	12
27	Symank, John	DB	5-11	180	08/31/35	Florida	12
82	Temp, Jim	DE	6-4	230	10/14/33	Wisconsin	12
74	Vereen, Carl	T	6-2	247	01/27/36	Georgia Tech	12

DRAFT

Rnd	Name	Pos	Ht	Wt	College
**	Paul Hornung	HB	6-2	215	Notre Dame
1	Ron Kramer	E	6-3	220	Michigan
2	Joel Wells	HB	6-1	198	Clemson
3	Dalton Truax	T	6-2	230	Tulane
4	Carl Vereen	T	6-2	247	Georgia Tech
5	(Choice to Browns for Don King)				
6a	(Choice to Browns for John Sandusky)				
6b	Jack Nisby	G	6-0	230	Pacific
	(Choice from Cardinals for Tom Dahms)				
7	Frank Gilliam	HB	6-2	185	Iowa
8	George Belotti	T	6-3	240	USC
9	Ken Wineburg	HB	5-11	185	TCU
10	Gary Gustafson	HB	6-1	193	Gust.- Adolph.
11	Jim Roseboro	HB	5-11	180	Ohio State
*12a	Ed Sullivan	C	6-1	190	Notre Dame
12b	Glenn Bestor	B	6-2	215	Wisconsin
	(Choice from Giants for Jack Spinks)				
13	Jim Morse	HB	5-11	185	Notre Dame
14	Rudy Schoendorf	T	6-1	245	Miami (OH)
15	Pat Hinton	G	6-2	230	Louisiana Tech
16	Ed Buckingham	T	6-4	250	Minnesota
*17	Don Boudreaux	T	6-3	220	Houston
18	Credell Grenn	HB	5-10	200	Washington
19	Ernest Danjean	G	6-0	230	Auburn
20	Percy Oliver	G	6-1	205	Illinois
21	Charles Mehrer	T	6-3	230	Missouri
22	Ron Quillian	QB	6-2	205	Tulane
23	John Symank	DB	5-11	180	Florida
24	Charles Leyendecker	T	6-2	220	SMU
*25	Jerry Johnson	T	6-3	250	St. Norbert
26	Buddy Bass	B	6-1	190	Duke
27	Martin Booher	T	6-1	240	Wisconsin
*28	Dave Herbold	G	5-10	225	Minnesota
*29	Howard Dare	RB	6-1	180	Maryland

* denotes juniors
** bonus choice

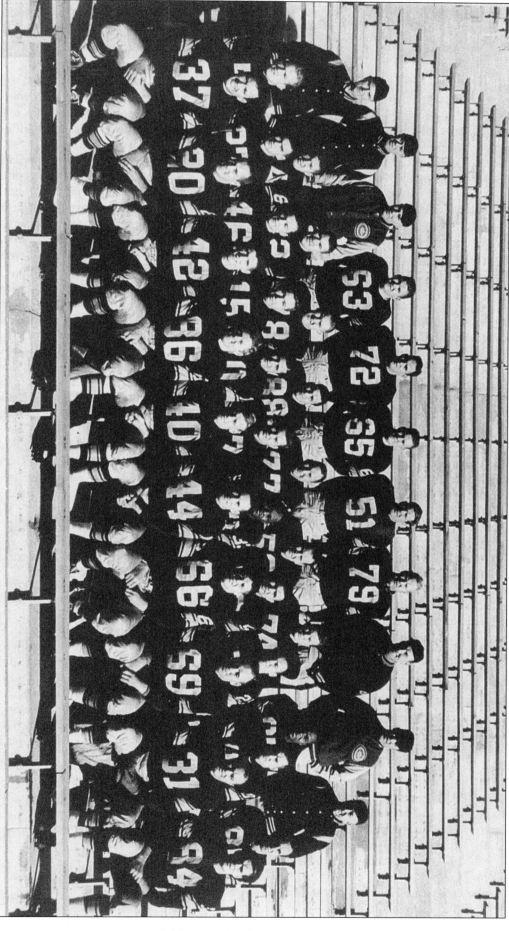

FRONT ROW: (L–R) 37 Howie Ferguson, 20 Billy Bookout, 42 Don McIlhenny, 86 Bill Howton, 40 Joe Johnson, 44 Bobby Dillon, 66 Al Barry, 69 Bill Forester, 31 Fred Cone, 84 Gary Knafelc.

SECOND ROW: (L–R) 5 Paul Hornung, 27 John Symank, 46 Hank Gremminger, 15 Bart Starr, 10 Babe Parilli, 67 Jim Salsbury, 33 Frank Purnell, 53 Sam Palumbo, 25 Billy Kinard, 81 Carlton Massey, 85 Max McGee.

THIRD ROW: (L–R) Trainer Carl (Bud) Jorgensen, 64 Ernest Danjean, 62 Norm Amundsen, 78 Norm Masters, 88 Ron Kramer, 77 Ollie Spencer, 58 Larry Lauer, 74 Carl Vereen, 87 Nate Borden, Assistant Trainer Gerald (Dad) Braisher.

BACK ROW: (L–R) Backfield Coach Ray (Scooter) McLean, Head Coach Lisle Blackbourn, 63 Joe Skibinski, 72 Jerry Helluin, 65 Tom Bettis, 51 Jim Ringo, 79 Dave Hanner, Offensive Line Coach Lou Rymkus, Defensive Line Coach Jack Morton.

ow bad were the Packers of 1958? The ineptness of Scooter McLean's team extended beyond just posting the worst record (1-10-1) in franchise history. Only the Lions gained fewer yards. Only the Cardinals gave up more. And for the first and only time in its history, Green Bay not only scored the fewest points, but it also gave up the most points of any team in the league.

The Packers did not lack for imaginative ways to hinder their cause. They could blow leads (wasting a 17-0 advantage in a 24-17 loss to the Colts), squander opportunity (scoring only three points off three first-quarter Bears turnovers in a 24-10 setback in Chicago) and fail to protect the football (the 49ers intercepted Green Bay's first three pass attempts in Week 11).

They could also be overpowered. The Redskins and 49ers rolled to 34-point leads before allowing the Packers to score. The Colts pummeled them 56-0 on Nov. 2.

McLean insisted the effort was there. After falling to the Colts 24-17, he said, "They (the Packers) were hustling at all times." After losing to the Bears for a second time, McLean opined, "There were 35 boys out there trying. I was satisfied with their effort." A week later, following a 20-7 setback to the Rams, he insisted, "They were all trying. There's no question about that."

Though the doormat of the league, Green Bay wasn't entirely lacking for talent. Seventeen of the players who would help secure the 1961 NFL championship were already in place. Six of the 17 would wind up in the Pro Football Hall of Fame.

What the team lacked was motivation and discipline. McLean, who had been the team's backfield coach since 1951, put the players on an honor system.

"They've set up a committee and will have their own system of fines for discipline," said McLean.

Such a system invited trouble. Coupled with McLean's easygoing manner, the team never had the strong leadership it desperately needed.

Green Bay opened against the Bears and got good performances from a pair of newcomers. Nitschke, a third-round pick, forced a fumble, blocked a field goal attempt and pressured quarterback Ed Brown into an interception. Veteran Len Ford, obtained from the Browns, blocked a try for extra point and registered the team's only sack.

Green Bay lost 34-20.

A week later, the Packers tied the defending world champion Lions 13-13.

Even the two most prolific passing outings of the season couldn't stop Green Bay from dropping its next two games. Starr threw for 320 yards in a 24-17 loss to the Colts. Babe Parilli followed with 297 yards against the Redskins, who trounced the Packers 37-21.

Green Bay had to endure a furious rally by the Eagles to earn its only win. Parilli again was hot, throwing four touchdown passes in helping the Packers to a 38-14 lead. But Philadelphia scored 21 fourth-quarter points and closed to 38-35 with 54 seconds left. Only after Nitschke recovered Dick Bielski's onside kick and Parilli ran a final play could the Green and Gold relax.

The Packers (1-3-1) were tied with the Lions for last place. By dropping its final seven games (including a nationally-televised Thanksgiving matchup with Detroit), Green Bay ensured itself of a last-place finish.

Two injuries added to the misery. Howie Ferguson was lost for the year after suffering a shoulder separation in the rematch with the Bears. Gary Knafelc, who missed nine games in 1957 after undergoing surgery on his left knee, was lost for the final six games with "pinched cartilage" in his right knee. McLean brought in linebacker Marv Matuszak and halfback Joe Johnson to replace the two.

As the losses mounted, so too did the pressure on McLean. Three days after his team was dumped 34-20 by the Rams in the season finale, the former Bears' halfback resigned to become backfield coach of the Lions.

Bright spots were hard to find. One player who rated a second look was rookie Jim Taylor, who broke into the starting lineup in the final two weeks. Taylor opened the team's annual trip to the West Coast at right halfback and piled up a season-high 137 yards rushing against the 49ers. A week later in Los Angeles, he amassed 99 yards playing fullback, a position at which he'd excel in the coming decade.

LOSING BIG

The Packers have played in hundreds of games over the years, often with less than desired results. Never was that more evident than on the afternoon of Nov. 2, 1958, when the Colts humbled Green Bay 56-0. The margin of defeat remains the largest in team history.

A steady rain fell throughout the game. But the rain, and the loss of starting quarterback Johnny Unitas to a rib injury late in the first half, didn't faze the Colts. After struggling early, Baltimore exploded for seven touchdowns on its final eight drives. Backup George Shaw threw three touchdown passes and directed the Colts to 35 second-half points. Green Bay's lone scoring opportunity fizzled when Paul Hornung missed a 50-yard field goal attempt to open the second quarter.

Greatest Margin of Defeat

Margin of Defeat	Opponent	Date
56 points (56-0)	Colts	11-2-1958
54 points (61-7)	Bears	12-7-1980
46 points (49-3)	Giants	11-21-48
41 points (48-7)	Rams	10-2-49

TEAM STATISTICS

	GB	OPP
First Downs	177	236
Rushing	76	109
Passing	87	111
Penalty	14	16
Rushes	345	427
Yards Gained	1,421	2,040
Average Gain	4.12	4.78
Average Yards per Game	118.4	170.0
Passes Attempted	348	336
Completed	161	175
% Completed	46.26	52.08
Total Yards Gained	2,118	2,653
Yards Lost	298	78
Net Yards Gained	1,820	2,575
Yards Gained per Completion	13.16	15.16
Average Net Yards per Game	151.7	214.6
Combined Net Yards Gained	3,241	4,615
Total Plays	693	763
Average Yards per Play	4.68	6.05
Average Net Yards per Game	270.1	384.6
Third Down Efficiency	58/171	68/155
Percentage	33.92	43.87
Fourth Down Efficiency	5/14	7/14
Percentage	35.71	50.00
Intercepted By	13	27
Yards Returned	174	371
Returned for TD	1	1
Punts	62	42
Yards Punted	2,625	1,747
Average Yards per Punt	42.34	41.60
Punt Returns	33	46
Yards Returned	179	268
Average Yards per Return	5.42	5.83
Returned for TD	0	0
Kickoff Returns	60	32
Yards Returned	1,309	710
Average Yards per Return	21.82	22.19
Returned for TD	0	0
Penalties	52	72
Yards Penalized	545	657
Fumbles	26	31
Lost	17	19
Own Recovered for Touchdown	0	0
Opponent's Recovered by	19	17
Opponent's Recovered for Touchdown	0	1
Total Points Scored	193	382
Total Touchdowns	23	50
Touchdowns Rushing	7	24
Touchdowns Passing	15	24
Touchdowns on Returns & Recoveries	1	2
Extra Points	22	46
Safeties	0	0
Field Goals Attempted	21	25
Field Goals Made	11	12
% Successful	52.38	48.00

Regular Season   1-10-1

Date	GB		OPP	Att.
9/28	20	Chicago Bears	34	(32,150)
10/5	13	Detroit Lions	13	(32,053)
10/12	17	Baltimore Colts (M)	24	(24,553)
10/19	21	at Washington Redskins	37	(25,228)
10/26	38	Philadelphia Eagles	35	(31,043)
11/2	0	at Baltimore Colts	56	(51,333)
11/9	10	at Chicago Bears	24	(48,424)
11/16	7	Los Angeles Rams	20	(28,051)
11/23	12	San Francisco 49ers (M)	33	(19,786)
11/27	14	at Detroit Lions	24	(50,971)
12/7	21	at San Francisco 49ers	48	(50,792)
12/14	20	at Los Angeles Rams	34	(54,634)

Score By Periods

	1	2	3	4	Total
Packers	63	44	41	45	193
Opponents	77	113	93	99	382

INDIVIDUAL STATISTICS

Rushing

	Att	Yds	Avg	LG	TD
Hornung	69	310	4.5	55	2
Ferguson	59	268	4.5	29	1
J. Taylor	52	247	4.8	25	1
McIlhenny	74	239	3.2	36	1
Francis	24	153	6.4	20	1
Starr	25	113	4.5	20	1
Shanley	23	30	1.3	5	0
Carmichael	9	21	2.3	8	0
Parilli	8	15	1.9	5	0
Ringo	0	13	—	13	0
McGee	1	9	9.0	9	0
Salsbury	0	3	—	3	0
Romine	1	0	0.0	0	0
Packers	**345**	**1,421**	**4.1**	**55**	**7**
Opponents	427	2,040	4.8	t80	24

Receiving

	No	Yds	Avg	LG	TD
McGee	37	655	17.7	t80	7
Howton	36	507	14.1	50	2
McIlhenny	20	154	7.7	t55	1
Hornung	15	137	9.1	39	0
Meilinger	13	139	10.7	19	1
Ferguson	12	121	10.1	27	0
J. Johnson	10	176	17.6	61	1
Knafelc	8	118	14.8	40	1
J. Taylor	4	72	18.0	t31	1
Carmichael	3	26	8.7	t14	1
Shanley	3	13	4.3	7	0
Packers	**161**	**2,118**	**13.2**	**t80**	**15**
Opponents	175	2,653	15.2	t93	24

Passing

	Att	Com	Yds	Pct	TD	In	Tk/Yds	Rate
Parilli	157	68	1,068	43.3	10	13	10/89	53.3
Starr	157	78	875	49.7	3	12	19/147	41.2
Francis	31	15	175	48.4	2	2	7/62	60.6
Ferguson	1	0	0	00.0	0	0	0/0	—
Hornung	1	0	0	00.0	0	0	0/0	—
McGee	1	0	0	00.0	0	0	0/0	—
Packers	**348**	**161**	**2,118**	**46.3**	**15**	**27**	**36/298**	**48.0**
Opponents	336	175	2,653	52.1	24	13	10/78	86.1

Punting

	No	Yds	Avg	Net	TB	In20	LG	HB
McGee	62	2,625	42.3	36.7	4	15	61	0
Packers	**62**	**2,625**	**42.3**	**36.7**	**4**	**15**	**61**	**0**
Opponents	42	1,747	41.6	37.3	0	15	61	0

Kickoff Returns

	No	Yds	Avg	LG	TD
Carmichael	29	700	24.1	60	0
Hornung	10	248	24.8	39	0
J. Taylor	7	185	26.4	47	0
McIlhenny	7	146	20.9	45	0
Currie	2	14	7.0	7	0
Massey	1	10	10.0	10	0
Forester	1	6	6.0	6	0
J. Kramer	1	0	0.0	0	0
Nitschke	1	0	0.0	0	0
Temp	1	0	0.0	0	0
Packers	**60**	**1,309**	**21.8**	**60**	**0**
Opponents	32	710	22.2	50	0

Punt Returns

	No	Yds	Avg	LG	TD
Carmichael	15	67	4.5	51	0
Shanley	14	105	7.5	26	0
Romine	2	7	3.5	7	0
McIlhenny	1	0	0.0	0	0
Symank	1	0	0.0	0	0
Packers	**33**	**179**	**5.4**	**51**	**0**
Opponents	46	268	5.8	38	0

Interceptions

	No	Yds	Avg	LG	TD
Dillon	6	134	22.3	46	1
Gremminger	3	15	5.0	14	0
Symank	1	23	23.0	23	0
Nitschke	1	2	2.0	2	0
Romine	1	0	0.0	0	0
Whittenton	1	0	0.0	0	0
Packers	**13**	**174**	**13.4**	**46**	**1**
Opponents	27	371	13.7	69	1

Scoring

	TDr	TDp	TDrt	PAT	FG	S	TP
Hornung	2	0	0	22/23	11/21	0	67
McGee	0	7	0	0/0	0/0	0	42
Howton	0	2	0	0/0	0/0	0	12
McIlhenny	1	1	0	0/0	0/0	0	12
J. Taylor	1	1	0	0/0	0/0	0	12
Carmichael	0	1	0	0/0	0/0	0	6
Dillon	0	0	1	0/0	0/0	0	6
Ferguson	1	0	0	0/0	0/0	0	6
Francis	1	0	0	0/0	0/0	0	6
J. Johnson	0	1	0	0/0	0/0	0	6
Knafelc	0	1	0	0/0	0/0	0	6
Meilinger	0	1	0	0/0	0/0	0	6
Starr	1	0	0	0/0	0/0	0	6
Packers	**7**	**15**	**1**	**22/23**	**11/21**	**0**	**193**
Opponents	24	24	2	46/50	12/25	0	382

Fumbles

	Fum	Ow	Op	Yds	Tot
Bettis	0	0	2	0	2
Borden	0	0	1	0	1
Bullough	0	0	1	0	1
Carmichael	2	0	0	0	0
Ferguson	1	1	0	0	1
Ford	0	0	1	5	1
Forester	0	1	0	0	1
Francis	3	0	0	0	0
Gregg	0	1	0	0	1
Hanner	0	0	2	0	2
Hornung	1	1	1	0	2
J. Johnson	1	0	0	0	0
Kimmel	0	0	1	0	1
Kinard	0	0	1	11	1
Massey	0	0	1	0	1
McGee	1	0	0	0	0
McIlhenny	8	2	0	0	2
Nitschke	0	0	2	0	2
Parilli	4	0	0	0	0
Ringo	0	2	0	1	2
Salsbury	0	0	1	0	1
Shanley	1	1	0	0	1
Starr	2	0	0	0	0
Symank	1	0	3	37	3
J. Taylor	1	0	0	0	0
Whittenton	0	0	2	2	2
Packers	**26**	**9**	**19**	**56**	**28**

NFL STANDINGS

Western Conference

	W	L	T	Pct	PF	PA
Baltimore Colts	9	3	0	.750	381	203
Chicago Bears	8	4	0	.667	298	230
Los Angeles Rams	8	4	0	.667	344	278
San Francisco 49ers	6	6	0	.500	257	324
Detroit Lions	4	7	1	.364	261	276
Green Bay Packers	**1**	**10**	**1**	**.091**	**193**	**382**

Eastern Conference

	W	L	T	Pct	PF	PA
New York Giants	9	3	0	.750	246	183
Cleveland Browns	9	3	0	.750	302	217
Pittsburgh Steelers	7	4	1	.636	261	230
Washington Redskins	4	7	1	.364	214	268
Chicago Cardinals	2	9	1	.182	261	356
Philadelphia Eagles	2	9	1	.182	235	306

1958

ROSTER

No	Name	Pos	Ht	Wt	DOB	College	G
65	Bettis, Tom	LB	6-2	225	03/17/33	Purdue	12
87	Borden, Nate	DE	6-0	240	09/22/32	Indiana	12
61	Bullough, Hank	G	6-0	240	01/24/34	Michigan State	8
48	Carmichael, Al	HB	6-1	195	11/10/28	USC	12
58	Currie, Dan	LB	6-3	235	06/27/35	Michigan State	12
44	Dillon, Bobby	DB	6-1	189	02/23/30	Texas	12
37	Ferguson, Howie	FB	6-2	213	08/05/30	No college	7
83	Ford, Len	DE	6-5	251	02/18/26	Michigan	11
69	Forester, Bill	LB	6-3	240	08/09/32	SMU	12
20	Francis, Joe	QB	6-1	194	04/21/36	Oregon State	12
75	Gregg, Forrest	G	6-4	245	10/18/33	SMU	12
46	Gremminger, Hank	DB	6-1	201	09/01/33	Baylor	12
79	Hanner, Dave	DT	6-2	266	05/20/30	Arkansas	12
5	Hornung, Paul	HB	6-2	211	12/23/35	Notre Dame	12
86	Howton, Bill	E	6-2	195	07/05/30	Rice	12
40	Johnson, Joe	HB	6-0	188	11/03/29	Boston College	6
72	Kimmel, J.D.	DT	6-4	250	09/30/29	Houston	12
25	Kinard, Billy	DB	6-0	202	12/16/33	Mississippi	12
84	Knafelc, Gary	E	6-4	217	01/02/32	Colorado	6
64	Kramer, Jerry	G	6-3	235	01/23/36	Idaho	12
81	Massey, Carlton	DE	6-4	225	01/17/30	Texas	2
78	Masters, Norm	T	6-2	250	09/19/33	Michigan State	12
63	Matuszak, Marv	LB	6-3	235	09/12/31	Tulsa	3
85	McGee, Max	E	6-3	196	07/16/32	Tulane	12
42	McIlhenny, Don	HB	6-0	200	11/22/34	SMU	12
80	Meilinger, Steve	E	6-2	230	12/12/30	Kentucky	12
33	Nitschke, Ray	LB	6-3	220	12/29/36	Illinois	12
10	Parilli, Vito (Babe)	QB	6-1	196	05/07/30	Kentucky	12
51	Ringo, Jim	C	6-1	236	11/21/32	Syracuse	12
23	Romine, Al	HB	6-2	184	03/10/32	North Alabama	12
67	Salsbury, Jim	G	6-0	241	08/08/32	UCLA	12
22	Shanley, Jim	HB	5-9	174	07/27/36	Oregon	12
77	Spencer, Ollie	T	6-2	245	04/17/31	Kansas	12
15	Starr, Bryan (Bart)	QB	6-1	200	01/09/34	Alabama	12
27	Symank, John	DB	5-11	180	08/31/35	Florida	12
31	Taylor, Jim	FB	6-0	205	09/20/35	LSU	12
82	Temp, Jim	DE	6-4	250	10/14/33	Wisconsin	12
47	Whittenton, Jesse	DB	6-0	195	05/09/34	Texas-El Paso	8

DRAFT

Rnd	Name	Pos	Ht	Wt	College
1	Dan Currie	C	6-3	240	Michigan State
2	Jim Taylor	FB	6-0	205	LSU
3a	Dick Christy	HB	5-10	190	No. Carolina St.
3b	Ray Nitschke	LB	6-3	220	Illinois
	(Choice from Giants for John Martinkovic)				
4	Jerry Kramer	G	6-3	235	Idaho
5	Joe Francis	QB	6-1	194	Oregon State
6	Ken Gray	T	6-2	235	Howard Payne
7	Doug Maison	QB	6-3	200	Hillsdale
8	Mike Bill	C	6-3	225	Syracuse
9	Norm Jarock	HB	6-0	195	St. Norbert
*10	Carl Johnson	T	6-3	230	Illinois
11	Harry Horton	E	6-3	220	Wichita
12	Wayne Miller	E	6-2	195	Baylor
13	Gene Cook	E	6-2	205	Toledo
14	Harry Hauffe	T	6-4	240	South Dakota
*15	Tom Newell	HB	6-2	195	Drake
*16	Arley Finley	T	6-4	240	Georgia Tech
17	Joe Reese	E	6-3	197	Arkansas Tech
18	Charles Strid	G	6-1	225	Syracuse
19	(Choice to Bears for Lee Hermsen)				
20	John Duboise	HB	6-0	150	Trinity (TX)
21	Jerry Kershner	T	6-4	220	Oregon
22	Dick Maggard	HB	5-11	205	College of Idaho
**23	Jack Ashton	G	6-1	220	South Carolina
**24	John Jereck	T	6-4	250	Detroit
25	Larry Plenty	HB	6-1	210	Boston College
26	Esker Harris	G	6-1	210	UCLA
27	Neil Habig	C	6-0	210	Purdue
**28	Dave Crowell	G	6-3	225	Washington State
29	Robert Haynes	T	6-3	240	Sam Houston State
30	John Peters	G	6-2	240	Houston

*   denotes juniors
**   denotes sophomores

1958 GREEN BAY PACKERS

FRONT ROW: (L-R) Head Coach Ray (Scooter) McLean, 46 Hank Gremminger, 80 Steve Meilinger, 86 Bill Howton, 84 Gary Knafelc, 44 Bobby Dillon, 27 John Symank, 25 Billy Kinard, Backfield Coach Floyd (Breezy) Reid.

SECOND ROW: (L-R) Offensive Line Coach Nick Skorich, 48 Al Carmichael, 58 Dan Currie, 47 Jesse Whittenton, 85 Max McGee, 5 Paul Hornung, 37 Howie Ferguson, 22 Jim Shanley, 42 Don McIlhenny, 31 Jim Taylor, 69 Bill Forester, Defense Coach Ray Richards.

THIRD ROW: (L-R) Trainer Carl (Bud) Jorgensen, 83 Len Ford, 23 Al Romine, 77 Ollie Spencer, 64 Jerry Kramer, 10 Babe Parilli, 15 Bart Starr, 20 Joe Francis, 33 Ray Nitschke, 40 Joe Johnson, Defensive Line Coach Jack Morton.

BACK ROW: (L-R) Assistant Trainer Gerald (Dad) Braisher, 81 Carlton Massey, 61 Hank Bullough, 72 J.D. Kimmel, 65 Tom Bettis, 78 Norm Masters, 82 Jim Temp, 75 Forrest Gregg, 67 Jim Salsbury, 79 Dave Hanner, 51 Jim Ringo, 87 Nate Borden.

"**I**'ve never been associated with a loser, and I don't expect to be now."

So spoke Vincent Thomas Lombardi days after he became the Packers' fifth head coach on Feb. 2. In the months following that pronouncement, the former Giants assistant coach directed his energies toward transforming a perennial loser into a winner.

From the start, Lombardi made it clear he was in charge. On April 24, he traded Bill Howton, the team's best receiver of the decade, to Cleveland for halfback Lew Carpenter and defensive end Bill Quinlan. A month later, he acquired quarterback Lamar McHan from the Cardinals for a third-round draft choice. After Bobby Dillon announced his retirement, Lombardi obtained defensive back Emlen Tunnell from the Giants. He also picked up guard Fuzzy Thurston from the Colts in exchange for Marv Matuszak, and defensive tackle Henry Jordan from Cleveland for a fourth-round pick.

Lombardi was organized and demanding. He filmed practices, simplified the team's playbook, and expected players to conduct themselves in a professional manner.

In June, he held a non-throwing quarterbacks camp in which he unveiled his offense. In July, he took conditioning to new heights in a strenuous training camp that had players shedding pounds daily.

In addition to Howton, three other big names didn't last the year. Howie Ferguson, bothered by shoulder, back, and leg problems, retired. Al Carmichael and Babe Parilli, former first-round picks, were waived in August and September, respectively. In all, 16 veterans from the previous season were sent packing.

Through it all, Lombardi set about to end the attitude of defeatism that had settled upon an organization accustomed to losing. From 1948 to 1958, the Packers had finished last or second-to-last in their respective conference or division nine times, and their 37 wins over that stretch were by far the fewest of any of the nine teams that played in every one of those 11 seasons.

The results of Lombardi's approach were dramatic. The team posted its first winning record (7-5) in 12 years and vaulted into third place in the conference behind the Colts (9-3) and Bears (8-4). The running game, powered by Paul Hornung, Jim Taylor, and others, climbed from 10th to third. The defense made a similar jump (11th to third).

The passing attack improved. McHan was the starter for the first seven weeks. Bart Starr took over for the final five games and closed with four straight victories.

Green Bay opened against the Bears in dramatic fashion. Taylor scored from five yards out to give the Packers a 7-6 lead with 7:15 remaining. Dave Hanner then sacked quarterback Ed Brown in the end zone with 44 seconds left to clinch a 9-6 win. Tunnell and Carpenter hoisted Lombardi onto their shoulders and gave him a victory ride.

"It's just like I told you when I first came here, you have to have a defense to win in this game," said Lombardi whose team held the Bears to 164 yards and 10 first downs.

In Week 2, McHan threw four touchdown passes, including two to Max McGee, as the Packers pounded the Lions 28-10. McGee had three receptions for 124 yards.

A week later, Green Bay beat the 49ers 21-20 and found itself the only unbeaten team in the NFL.

The Packers then suffered five straight losses. The Rams, Colts (twice), Giants, and Bears combined to drop Green Bay into fourth place with a 3-5 record.

Starr got his first start in the fifth loss, a 28-24 setback to the Colts in Milwaukee. The four-year veteran completed 14 of 40 passes for 242 yards with three interceptions.

The following week, he tossed a pair of touchdown passes as the Packers blanked the Redskins 21-0.

The Packers evened their record (5-5) on Thanksgiving, beating the Lions 24-17 behind 18 points from Hornung.

The West Coast posed no problem for Lombardi and his team. Hornung hit rookie Boyd Dowler with two touchdown passes as the Packers romped 38-20 over the Rams.

A week later, Green Bay closed with a season-high 479 yards in San Francisco. Starr completed 20 of 25 passes for 249 yards, Carpenter pounded out 113 yards rushing, and Hornung posted 22 points in a 36-14 rout.

"This is the first time since I've been in Green Bay that the guys are talking about next year," said veteran center Jim Ringo.

INCREASING THE PERCENTAGES

Improvement under the gruff and demanding Vince Lombardi was evident in nearly every facet of the Packers' game. The running attack picked up, the defense tightened, and the team won six more games than it had a year earlier.

The additional wins meant that the team's winning percentage rose from .091 in 1958 to .583 in 1959. Never before or since has a Packers team enjoyed such a dramatic upswing from one season to the next.

The turnaround could have been even greater had the club not suffered through a five-game losing streak in mid-season. In those games, Green Bay committed 19 turnovers (compared to just 14 in the other seven games), and threw only three touchdown passes.

Greatest Percentage Increase, One Season to Another

Increase	Years
.492	1958 (.091) to 1959 (.583)
.400	1928 (.600) to 1929 (1.000)
.381	1971 (.333) to 1972 (.714)
.375	1988 (.250) to 1989 (.625)

TEAM STATISTICS

	GB	OPP
First Downs	212	215
Rushing	109	101
Passing	87	102
Penalty	16	12
Rushes	421	430
Yards Gained	1,907	1,770
Average Gain	4.53	4.12
Average Yards per Game	158.9	147.5
Passes Attempted	268	329
Completed	128	169
% Completed	47.76	51.37
Total Yards Gained	1,963	2,030
Yards Lost	131	248
Net Yards Gained	1,832	1,782
Yards Gained per Completion	15.34	12.01
Average Net Yards per Game	152.7	148.5
Combined Net Yards Gained	3,739	3,552
Total Plays	689	759
Average Yards per Play	5.43	4.68
Average Net Yards per Game	311.6	296.0
Third Down Efficiency	48/145	60/163
Percentage	33.10	36.81
Fourth Down Efficiency	3/5	8/19
Percentage	60.00	42.11
Intercepted By	14	17
Yards Returned	231	227
Returned for TD	0	1
Punts	64	56
Yards Punted	2,716	2,481
Average Yards per Punt	42.44	44.30
Punt Returns	33	40
Yards Returned	316	291
Average Yards per Return	9.58	7.28
Returned for TD	1	1
Kickoff Returns	43	40
Yards Returned	949	917
Average Yards per Return	22.07	22.93
Returned for TD	0	0
Penalties	49	51
Yards Penalized	435	450
Fumbles	24	28
Lost	16	15
Own Recovered for Touchdown	0	0
Opponent's Recovered by	15	16
Opponent's Recovered for Touchdown	0	0
Total Points Scored	248	246
Total Touchdowns	32	30
Touchdowns Rushing	15	14
Touchdowns Passing	16	14
Touchdowns on Returns & Recoveries	1	2
Extra Points	31	28
Safeties	2	1
Field Goals Attempted	17	22
Field Goals Made	7	12
% Successful	41.18	54.55

Regular Season   7-5-0

Date	GB		OPP	Att.
9/27	9	Chicago Bears	6	(32,150)
10/4	28	Detroit Lions	10	(32,150)
10/11	21	San Francisco 49ers	20	(32,150)
10/18	6	Los Angeles Rams (M)	45	(36,194)
10/25	21	at Baltimore Colts	38	(57,557)
11/1	3	at New York Giants	20	(68,837)
11/8	17	at Chicago Bears	28	(46,205)
11/15	24	Baltimore Colts (M)	28	(25,521)
11/22	21	Washington Redskins	0	(31,853)
11/26	24	at Detroit Lions	17	(49,221)
12/6	38	at Los Angeles Rams	20	(61,044)
12/13	36	at San Francisco 49ers	14	(55,997)

Score By Periods

	1	2	3	4	Total
Packers	55	82	44	67	248
Opponents	66	68	75	37	246

INDIVIDUAL STATISTICS

Rushing

	Att	Yds	Avg	LG	TD
Hornung	152	681	4.5	63	7
J. Taylor	120	452	3.8	21	6
Carpenter	60	322	5.4	t55	1
McIlhenny	47	231	4.9	46	1
Starr	16	83	5.2	39	0
McHan	16	64	4.0	19	0
B. Butler	7	49	7.0	16	0
Dowler	1	20	20.0	20	0
Francis	2	5	2.5	8	0
Packers	**421**	**1,907**	**4.5**	**63**	**15**
Opponents	430	1,770	4.1	t49	14

Receiving

	No	Yds	Avg	LG	TD
Dowler	32	549	17.2	35	4
McGee	30	695	23.2	t81	5
Knafelc	27	384	14.2	38	4
Hornung	15	113	7.5	19	0
J. Taylor	9	71	7.9	t20	2
McIlhenny	8	95	11.9	30	1
Carpenter	5	47	9.4	23	0
A. D. Williams	1	11	11.0	11	0
B. Butler	1	-2	-2.0	-2	0
Packers	**128**	**1,963**	**15.3**	**t81**	**16**
Opponents	169	2,030	12.0	t75	14

Passing

	Att	Com	Yds	Pct	TD	In	Yds	Rate
Starr	134	70	972	52.2	6	7	30	69.0
McHan	108	48	805	44.4	8	9	94	60.1
Francis	18	5	91	27.8	0	1	7	25.0
Hornung	8	5	95	62.5	2	0	0	—
Packers	**268**	**128**	**1,963**	**47.8**	**16**	**17**	**131**	**65.9**
Opponents	329	169	2,030	51.4	14	14	248	67.1

Punting

	No	Yds	Avg	Net	TB	In20	LG	HB
McGee	64	2,716	42.4	36.3	5	10	61	1
Packers	**64**	**2,716**	**42.4**	**36.3**	**5**	**10**	**61**	**1**
Opponents	56	2,481	44.3	36.2	7	14	61	0

Kickoff Returns

	No	Yds	Avg	LG	TD
B. Butler	21	472	22.5	35	0
Symank	14	338	24.1	39	0
McIlhenny	3	50	16.7	24	0
Francis	2	52	26.0	28	0
Nitschke	2	13	6.5	10	0
Carpenter	1	24	24.0	24	0
Packers	**43**	**949**	**22.1**	**39**	**0**
Opponents	40	917	22.9	85	0

Punt Returns

	No	Yds	Avg	LG	TD
B. Butler	18	163	9.1	t61	1
Carpenter	13	150	11.5	51	0
Tunnell	1	3	3.0	3	0
Symank	1	0	0.0	0	0
Packers	**33**	**316**	**9.6**	**t61**	**1**
Opponents	40	291	7.3	t71	1

Interceptions

	No	Yds	Avg	LG	TD
Forester	2	48	24.0	34	0
Symank	2	46	23.0	25	0
Freeman	2	22	11.0	22	0
Tunnell	2	20	10.0	18	0
Gremminger	1	45	45.0	45	0
Currie	1	25	25.0	25	0
Temp	1	13	13.0	13	0
Dillon	1	7	7.0	7	0
Quinlan	1	5	5.0	5	0
Bettis	1	0	0.0	0	0
Packers	**14**	**231**	**16.5**	**45**	**0**
Opponents	17	227	13.4	49	1

Scoring

	TDr	TDp	TDrt	PAT	FG	S	TP
Hornung	7	0	0	31/32	7/17	0	94
J. Taylor	6	2	0	0/0	0/0	0	48
McGee	0	5	0	0/0	0/0	0	30
Dowler	0	4	0	0/0	0/0	0	24
Knafelc	0	4	0	0/0	0/0	0	24
McIlhenny	1	1	0	0/0	0/0	0	12
B. Butler	0	0	1	0/0	0/0	0	6
Carpenter	1	0	0	0/0	0/0	0	6
Forester	0	0	0	0/0	0/0	1	2
Hanner	0	0	0	0/0	0/0	1	2
Packers	**15**	**16**	**1**	**31/32**	**7/17**	**2**	**248**
Opponents	14	14	2	28/30	12/22	1	246

Fumbles

	Fum	Ow	Op	Yds	Tot
Bettis	0	0	1	0	1
Borden	0	0	1	0	1
B. Butler	1	1	0	0	1
Carpenter	3	0	0	0	0
Dittrich	0	0	1	0	1
Forester	0	0	3	0	3
Hanner	0	0	1	0	1
Hornung	7	0	0	0	0
H. Jordan	0	0	2	0	2
Knafelc	0	1	0	0	1
McHan	3	0	0	0	0
McIlhenny	1	1	0	0	1
Nitschke	0	1	1	10	2
Ringo	0	0	1	0	1
Starr	2	2	0	-8	2
Symank	4	1	2	0	3
J. Taylor	2	1	0	0	1
Whittenton	0	0	2	45	2
Packers	**24**	**8**	**15**	**47**	**23**

NFL STANDINGS

Western Conference

	W	L	T	Pct	PF	PA
Baltimore Colts	9	3	0	750	374	251
Chicago Bears	8	4	0	667	252	196
Green Bay Packers	7	5	0	583	248	246
San Francisco 49ers	7	5	0	583	255	237
Detroit Lions	3	8	1	273	203	275
Los Angeles Rams	2	10	0	167	242	315

Eastern Conference

	W	L	T	Pct	PF	PA
New York Giants	10	2	0	833	284	170
Cleveland Browns	7	5	0	583	270	214
Philadelphia Eagles	7	5	0	583	268	278
Pittsburgh Steelers	6	5	1	545	257	216
Washington Redskins	3	9	0	250	185	350
Chicago Cardinals	2	10	0	167	234	324

ROSTER

No	Name	Pos	Ht	Wt	DOB	College	G
73	Beck, Ken	DT	6-2	240	09/03/35	Texas A&M	12
65	Bettis, Tom	LB	6-2	225	03/17/33	Purdue	12
87	Borden, Nate	DE	6-0	240	09/22/32	Indiana	12
25	Brown, Tim	HB	5-10	195	05/24/37	Ball State	1
22	Butler, Bill	HB	5-10	180	07/10/37	Chattanooga	11
33	Carpenter, Lew	FB	6-2	210	01/12/32	Arkansas	12
58	Currie, Dan	LB	6-3	235	06/27/35	Michigan State	12
44	Dillon, Bobby	DB	6-1	180	02/23/30	Texas	12
68	Dittrich, John	G	6-1	235	05/07/33	Wisconsin	12
86	Dowler, Boyd	E	6-5	225	10/18/37	Colorado	12
69	Forester, Bill	LB	6-3	240	08/09/32	SMU	12
20	Francis, Joe	QB	6-1	195	04/21/36	Oregon State	12
41	Freeman, Bob	DB	6-1	205	10/19/32	Auburn	12
75	Gregg, Alvis (Forrest)	G	6-4	245	10/18/33	SMU	12
46	Gremminger, Hank	DB	6-1	205	09/01/33	Baylor	12
79	Hanner, Joel (Dave)	DT	6-2	260	05/20/30	Arkansas	12
5	Hornung, Paul	HB	6-2	215	12/23/35	Notre Dame	12
74	Jordan, Henry	DT	6-3	250	01/26/35	Virginia	12
84	Knafelc, Gary	E	6-4	220	01/02/32	Colorado	12
64	Kramer, Jerry	G	6-3	245	01/23/36	Idaho	12
88	Kramer, Ron	E	6-3	230	06/24/35	Michigan	12
78	Masters, Norm	T	6-2	250	09/19/33	Michigan State	12
85	McGee, Max	E	6-3	205	07/16/32	Tulane	12
17	McHan, Lamar	QB	6-1	205	12/16/32	Arkansas	12
42	McIlhenny, Don	HB	6-0	200	11/22/34	SMU	12
66	Nitschke, Ray	LB	6-3	230	12/29/36	Illinois	12
83	Quinlan, Bill	DE	6-3	250	06/19/32	Michigan State	12
51	Ringo, Jim	C	6-1	230	11/21/32	Syracuse	12
76	Skoronski, Bob	T	6-3	250	03/05/34	Indiana	12
15	Starr, Bryan (Bart)	QB	6-1	200	01/09/34	Alabama	12
27	Symank, John	DB	5-11	180	08/31/35	Florida	12
31	Taylor, Jim	FB	6-0	212	09/20/35	LSU	12
82	Temp, Jim	DE	6-4	250	10/14/33	Wisconsin	12
63	Thurston, Fred (Fuzzy)	G	6-1	245	05/07/35	Valparaiso	12
45	Tunnell, Emlen	DB	6-1	215	03/29/25	Iowa	12
47	Whittenton, Jesse	DB	6-0	195	05/09/34	Texas-El Paso	12
81	Williams, A.D.	E	6-2	210	11/21/33	Pacific	12

DRAFT

Rnd	Name	Pos	Ht	Wt	College
1	Randy Duncan	QB	6-0	190	Iowa
2	Alex Hawkins	HB	6-1	195	South Carolina
3	Boyd Dowler	E	6-5	225	Colorado
4	(Choice to Browns for Len Ford)				
5a	(Choice to Redskins for J.D. Kimmel)				
5b	Andy Cvercko	G	6-0	235	Northwestern
	(Choice to Steelers for Dick Christy)				
6	Willie Taylor	C	6-0	232	Florida A&M
7a	Bobby Jackson	HB	6-1	185	Alabama
7b	Gary Raid	T	6-2	255	Williamette
	(Choice from Giants for Al Barry)				
8a	Buddy Mayfield	E	6-2	190	South Carolina
8b	Bob Laraba	HB	6-2	190	Texas-El Paso
	(Choice from Browns for Dick Deschaine)				
9	George Dixon	HB	6-1	195	Bridgeport
10	Sam Tuccio	G/T	6-2	248	So. Mississippi
11	Bob Webb	QB	6-0	204	St. Ambrose
12	Larry Hall	G	6-0	235	Missouri Valley
*13	Jim Hurd	FB	6-1	220	Albion
14	Jim Kerr	G	6-2	265	Arizona State
15	Dick Teteak	C	6-0	212	Wisconsin
16	Dan Edgington	E	6-2	191	Florida
17	Tom Secules	HB	6-3	200	William and Mary
18	Dick Nearents	T	6-2	265	Eastern Washington
19	Bill Butler	HB	5-10	180	Chattanooga
*20	Chuck Sample	FB	6-3	208	Arkansas
21	Dave Smith	FB	6-1	201	Ripon
22	Charles Anderson	E	6-5	235	Drake
*23	Orville Lawver	T	6-3	280	Lewis and Clark
24	Joe Hergert	C	6-2	215	Florida
25	Leroy Hardee	HB	6-0	180	Florida A&M
*26	Tom Higginbotham	E	6-3	201	Trinity (TX)
27	Tim Brown	HB	5-10	195	Ball State
28	Jerry Epps	G	6-1	230	West Texas State
29	John Flara	HB	5-11	182	Pittsburgh
30	Dick Emerich	T	6-2	230	West Chester

* denotes juniors

FRONT ROW: (L-R) 66 Ray Nitschke, 74 Henry Jordan, 81 A.D. Williams, 41 Bob Freeman, 47 Jesse Whittenton, 27 John Symank, 25 Tim Brown.
SECOND ROW: (L-R) 67 Andy Cvercko, 15 Bart Starr, 42 Don McIlhenny, 69 Bill Forester, 44 Bobby Dillon, 33 Lew Carpenter, 84 Gary Knafelc, 88 Ron Kramer, 46 Hank Gremminger.
THIRD ROW: (L-R) 75 Forrest Gregg, 45 Emlen Tunnell, 20 Joe Francis, 68 John Dittrich, 17 Lamar McHan, 86 Boyd Dowler, 58 Dan Currie, 83 Bill Quinlan, 63 Fuzzy Thurston, 31 Jim Taylor.
BACK ROW: (L-R) 64 Jerry Kramer, 76 Bob Skoronski, 87 Nate Borden, 82 Jim Temp, 85 Max McGee, 5 Paul Hornung, 65 Tom Bettis, 78 Norm Masters, 51 Jim Ringo, 79 Dave Hanner.

The Packers returned to the championship game for the first time in 16 years. They did so with a powerful running attack, a record-setting halfback, and a quarterback who ranked last in the league just two years earlier.

Reaching the title game didn't come easily. Losses to the Rams and Lions in late November dropped the Packers (5-4) behind the Colts (6-2) and Bears (4-3-1). Instead of folding, Green Bay reeled off three convincing wins that, coupled with the collapse of the Colts (0-4 down the stretch) and Bears (1-3), paved the way for 8-4 season and a championship date with the Eagles on Dec. 26.

Gone was the defeatist attitude. In its place was an eagerness to get the season rolling. Bart Starr, Henry Jordan, Max McGee, and others reported more than a week earlier than required.

"This is very unusual," admitted business manager Jack Vainisi who had been with the club since 1950. "Even some of our rookies, who are due in two days before the veterans, want to come in now."

The team, when assembled, had the look of a winner. Jim Taylor, the league's busiest back (230 carries), rushed for 1,101 yards and broke Tony Canadeo's club record. Paul Hornung tallied an NFL record 176 points. Starr, 15th among the 15 quarterbacks with enough attempts to be ranked in 1958, became the starter for good in Week 6.

Vince Lombardi added three players of note. He selected halfback Tom Moore—who went on to lead the league in kickoff return average (33.1)—in the first round of the draft. He obtained cat-quick defensive end Willie Davis from Cleveland in a trade for A.D. Williams. He signed free agent Willie Wood, a hard-hitting safety from Southern Cal, to back up Emlen Tunnell.

Three men who played key roles in the development of the franchise passed away in 1960. Andrew Turnbull, the team's first president, died on Oct. 17 at age 76. Thirteen days later, the club's physician from 1945 to 1959, H.S. Atkinson, died. On Nov. 27, the 33-year-old Vainisi succumbed to rheumatic fever. The team's business manager and chief talent scout had been instrumental in discovering and acquiring many of the players who would go on to win five championships in the 1960s.

The American Football League inaugurated play on Sept. 9 when the Denver Broncos beat the Boston Patriots 13-10 in a night game. As had been the case with the AAFC, the AFL lured away established players, competed for draft choices and drove up salaries.

A bold gamble by the Bears ignited a 17-point fourth quarter that doomed Green Bay 17-14 in the opener. Coach George Halas, his team down 14-0, elected to go for it on fourth-and-one from his own 30-yard line. Rick Casares converted and the comeback was on.

Starr, who had started the opener, was pulled in favor of Lamar McHan. McHan guided Green Bay to four straight wins, including lopsided victories over the Lions (28-9) and 49ers (41-14).

But McHan struggled in the fourth game, a 19-13 squeaker in Pittsburgh. After completing just four passes in 16 tries, he gave way to Starr, who directed a game-winning 66-yard drive capped by Taylor's plunge with 1:03 left.

Lombardi stuck it out with Starr, even though the five-year pro struggled in the four weeks after the Steelers' game. He threw four interceptions in a 38-24 loss to the Colts. He tossed another interception that led to seven points in a 33-31 setback to the Rams. And he was sacked five times on Thanksgiving as the Lions prevailed 23-10.

But with the season on the line, the quarterback came through. In Wrigley Field, Starr exacted revenge on the Bears, completing 17 of 23 passes for 227 yards and two touchdowns. The game was dedicated to Vainisi, who had died a week earlier.

"He (Vainisi) won it for us," said Hornung who broke Don Hutson's single-season scoring record (138 points) with a 23-point outing.

A week later, Green Bay clinched at least a share of the conference title by downing the 49ers 13-0 in a mudbath in Kezar Stadium. Jim Taylor slogged his way to 161 yards rushing and Hornung added 86 more in a 251-yard output.

Starr was at his efficient best in the finale in the Coliseum. He completed bombs of 57 yards to McGee and 91 yards to Boyd Dowler as the Packers fought off the Rams 35-21 to reach the championship game.

A RISING STARR

Vince Lombardi became head coach of the Packers in 1959. But Bart Starr didn't become the clear-cut starter at quarterback until the second half of the 1960 season.

Lamar McHan opened at quarterback 11 times in the first 17 games under Lombardi. Starr got the nod on Nov. 6 and from that point forward—except when injured—he started every game for the rest of the decade.

Green Bay needed to defeat the Rams in Los Angeles on Dec. 17 to clinch the Western Conference title outright. Starr—his running game choked off (30 carries, 58 yards)—rose to the occasion completing 8 of 9 passes for 201 yards and two touchdowns. His passer rating was a perfect 158.3.

Listed below are the only Packers to have a perfect passer rating (minimum 3 pass attempts).

Player	Att	Com	Yds	TD	Date
Bart Starr	9	8	201	2	12-17-60
Cecil Isbell	9	7	170	3	10-11-42
Paul Christman	4	4	67	1	11-26-50
Bob Monnett	3	3	54	1	10-23-38

TEAM STATISTICS

	GB	OPP
First Downs	237	199
Rushing	135	74
Passing	86	110
Penalty	16	15
Rushes	463	350
Yards Gained	2,150	1,285
Average Gain	4.64	3.67
Average Yards per Game	179.2	107.1
Passes Attempted	279	365
Completed	137	192
% Completed	49.10	52.60
Total Yards Gained	1,993	2,432
Yards Lost	118	275
Net Yards Gained	1,875	2,157
Yards Gained per Completion	14.55	12.67
Average Net Yards per Game	156.3	179.8
Combined Net Yards Gained	4,025	3,442
Total Plays	742	715
Average Yards per Play	5.42	4.81
Average Yards per Game	335.4	286.8
Third Down Efficiency	62/153	51/152
Percentage	40.52	33.55
Fourth Down Efficiency	4/8	9/13
Percentage	50.00	69.23
Intercepted By	22	13
Yards Returned	358	185
Returned for TD	1	0
Punts	49	66
Yards Punted	2,020	2,600
Average Yards per Punt	41.22	39.39
Punt Returns	26	22
Yards Returned	172	144
Average Yards per Return	6.62	6.55
Returned for TD	0	0
Kickoff Returns	35	57
Yards Returned	852	1,158
Average Yards per Return	24.34	20.32
Returned for TD	0	0
Penalties	64	61
Yards Penalized	578	636
Fumbles	18	23
Lost	12	15
Own Recovered for Touchdown	0	0
Opponent's Recovered by	15	12
Opponent's Recovered for Touchdown	0	0
Total Points Scored	332	209
Total Touchdowns	41	26
Touchdowns Rushing	29	7
Touchdowns Passing	9	19
Touchdowns on Returns & Recoveries	3	0
Extra Points	41	24
Safeties	0	1
Field Goals Attempted	28	13
Field Goals Made	15	9
% Successful	53.57	69.23

Regular Season 8-4-0

Date	GB		OPP	Att.
9/25	14	Chicago Bears	17	(32,150)
10/2	28	Detroit Lions	9	(32,150)
10/9	35	Baltimore Colts	21	(32,150)
10/23	41	San Francisco 49ers (M)	14	(39,914)
10/30	19	at Pittsburgh Steelers	13	(30,155)
11/6	24	at Baltimore Colts	38	(57,808)
11/13	41	Dallas Cowboys	7	(32,294)
11/20	31	Los Angeles Rams (M)	33	(35,763)
11/24	10	at Detroit Lions	23	(51,123)
12/4	41	at Chicago Bears	13	(46,406)
12/10	13	at San Francisco 49ers	0	(53,612)
12/17	35	at Los Angeles Rams	21	(53,445)

Postseason 0-1-0

12/26	13	at Philadelphia Eagles	17	(67,325)

Score By Periods

	1	2	3	4	Total
Packers	47	98	69	118	332
Opponents	40	53	34	82	209

INDIVIDUAL STATISTICS

Rushing

	Att	Yds	Avg	LG	TD
J. Taylor	230	1,101	4.8	32	11
Hornung	160	671	4.2	37	13
T. Moore	45	237	5.3	t59	4
McHan	8	67	8.4	t35	1
Carpenter	1	24	24.0	24	0
Hickman	7	22	3.1	4	0
Starr	7	12	1.7	13	0
McGee	2	11	5.5	16	0
Dowler	1	8	8.0	8	0
Winslow	2	-3	-1.5	3	0
Packers	**463**	**2,150**	**4.6**	**t59**	**29**
Opponents	350	1,285	3.7	35	7

Receiving

	No	Yds	Avg	LG	TD
McGee	38	787	20.7	t57	4
Dowler	30	505	16.8	t91	2
Hornung	28	257	9.2	33	2
J. Taylor	15	121	8.1	27	0
Knafelc	14	164	11.7	23	0
T. Moore	5	40	8.0	t12	1
R. Kramer	4	55	13.8	18	0
Meilinger	2	43	21.5	23	0
Carpenter	1	21	21.0	21	0
Packers	**137**	**1,993**	**14.6**	**t91**	**9**
Opponents	192	2,432	12.7	58	19

Passing

	Att	Com	Yds	Pct	TD	In	YL	Rate
Starr	172	98	1,358	57.0	4	8	78	70.8
McHan	91	33	517	36.3	3	5	33	44.1
Hornung	16	6	118	37.5	2	0	7	103.6
Packers	**279**	**137**	**1,993**	**49.1**	**9**	**13**	**118**	**64.1**
Opponents	365	192	2,432	52.6	19	22	275	65.9

Punting

	No	Yds	Avg	Net	TB	In20	LG	HB
McGee	31	1,291	41.6	37.4	12	3	58	1
Dowler	18	729	40.5	35.4	4	1	61	2
Packers	**49**	**2,020**	**41.2**	**36.7**	**16**	**4**	**61**	**3**
Opponents	66	2,600	39.4	35.6	11	4	59	2

Kickoff Returns

	No	Yds	Avg	LG	TD
T. Moore	12	397	33.1	84	0
Carpenter	12	249	20.8	29	0
Symank	4	103	25.8	32	0
Hickman	3	54	18.0	27	0
Nitschke	2	33	16.5	17	0
Temp	1	16	16.0	16	0
Meilinger	1	0	0.0	0	0
Packers	**35**	**852**	**24.3**	**84**	**0**
Opponents	57	1,158	20.3	42	0

Punt Returns

	No	Yds	Avg	LG	TD
Wood	16	106	6.6	33	0
Carpenter	9	59	6.6	12	0
Forester	1	7	7.0	7	0
Packers	**26**	**172**	**6.6**	**33**	**0**
Opponents	22	144	6.6	15	0

Interceptions

	No	Yds	Avg	LG	TD
Whitteton	6	101	16.8	52	0
Currie	4	75	18.8	33	0
Nitschke	3	90	30.0	t43	1
Gremminger	3	52	17.3	21	0
Tunnell	3	22	7.3	22	0
Forester	2	18	9.0	15	0
Symank	1	0	0.0	0	0
Packers	**22**	**358**	**16.3**	**52**	**1**
Opponents	13	185	14.2	44	0

Scoring

	TDr	TDp	TDrt	PAT	FG	S	TP
Hornung	13	2	0	41/41	15/28	0	176
J. Taylor	11	0	0	0/0	0/0	0	66
T. Moore	4	1	0	0/0	0/0	0	30
McGee	0	4	0	0/0	0/0	0	24
Dowler	0	2	0	0/0	0/0	0	12
W. Davis	0	0	1	0/0	0/0	0	6
McHan	1	0	0	0/0	0/0	0	6
Nitschke	0	0	1	0/0	0/0	0	6
Winslow	0	0	1	0/0	0/0	0	6
Packers	**29**	**9**	**3**	**41/41**	**15/28**	**0**	**332**
Opponents	7	19	0	24/26	9/13	1	209

Fumbles

	Fum	Ow	Op	Yds	Tot
Bettis	0	0	1	4	1
Carpenter	4	0	0	0	0
Currie	0	0	1	0	1
W. Davis	0	0	1	0	1
Gremminger	0	0	2	0	2
Hornung	3	0	0	0	0
H. Jordan	0	1	4	0	5
McGee	1	0	0	0	0
T. Moore	0	1	0	0	1
Nitschke	0	0	1	0	1
Starr	3	2	0	0	2
Symank	0	0	2	13	2
J. Taylor	5	2	0	1	2
Tunnell	0	0	1	0	1
Whitteton	0	0	2	0	2
Wood	2	0	0	0	0
Packers	**18**	**6**	**15**	**18**	**21**

NFL STANDINGS

Western Conference

	W	L	T	Pct	PF	PA
Green Bay Packers	8	4	0	.667	332	209
Detroit Lions	7	5	0	.583	239	212
San Francisco 49ers	7	5	0	.583	208	205
Baltimore Colts	6	6	0	.500	288	234
Chicago Bears	5	6	1	.455	194	299
Los Angeles Rams	4	7	1	.364	265	297
Dallas Cowboys	0	11	1	.000	177	369

Eastern Conference

	W	L	T	Pct	PF	PA
Philadelphia Eagles	10	2	0	.833	321	246
Cleveland Browns	8	3	1	.727	362	217
New York Giants	6	4	2	.600	271	261
St. Louis Cardinals	6	5	1	.545	288	230
Pittsburgh Steelers	5	6	1	.455	240	275
Washington Redskins	1	9	2	.100	178	309

ROSTER

No	Name	Pos	Ht	Wt	DOB	College	G
73	Beck, Ken	DT	6-2	250	09/03/35	Texas A&M	12
65	Bettis, Tom	LB	6-2	225	03/17/33	Purdue	12
33	Carpenter, Lew	FB	6-2	215	01/12/32	Arkansas	12
58	Currie, Dan	LB	6-3	240	06/27/35	Michigan State	12
62	Cvercko, Andy	G	6-0	240	11/06/37	Northwestern	12
87	Davis, Willie	DE	6-3	240	07/24/34	Grambling	12
86	Dowler, Boyd	E	6-5	220	10/18/37	Colorado	12
71	Forester, Bill	LB	6-3	240	08/09/32	SMU	12
75	Gregg, Alvis (Forrest)	G	6-4	250	10/18/33	SMU	12
46	Gremminger, Hank	DB	6-1	205	09/01/33	Baylor	12
40	Hackbart, Dale	DB	6-3	200	07/21/38	Wisconsin	12
79	Hanner, Joel (Dave)	DT	6-2	260	05/20/30	Arkansas	12
37	Hickman, Larry	FB	6-1	230	10/10/35	Baylor	12
5	Hornung, Paul	HB	6-2	215	12/23/35	Notre Dame	12
53	Iman, Ken	C	6-1	230	02/08/39	Southeast Missouri State	12
74	Jordan, Henry	DT	6-3	250	01/26/35	Virginia	12
84	Knafelc, Gary	E	6-4	220	01/02/32	Colorado	12
64	Kramer, Jerry	G	6-3	250	01/23/36	Idaho	12
88	Kramer, Ron	E	6-3	230	06/24/35	Michigan	12
78	Masters, Norm	T	6-2	250	09/19/33	Michigan State	12
85	McGee, Max	E	6-3	205	07/16/32	Tulane	12
17	McHan, Lamar	QB	6-1	210	12/16/32	Arkansas	12
80	Meilinger, Steve	E	6-2	230	12/12/30	Kentucky	12
72	Miller, John	T	6-5	260	02/01/34	Boston College	5
25	Moore, Tom	HB	6-2	215	07/17/38	Vanderbilt	12
66	Nitschke, Ray	LB	6-3	235	12/29/36	Illinois	12
48	Pesonen, Dick	DB	6-0	190	06/10/38	Minnesota-Duluth	12
83	Quinlan, Bill	DE	6-3	250	06/19/32	Michigan State	12
51	Ringo, Jim	C	6-1	235	11/21/32	Syracuse	12
76	Skoronski, Bob	T	6-3	250	03/05/34	Indiana	12
15	Starr, Bryan (Bart)	QB	6-1	200	01/09/34	Alabama	12
27	Symank, John	DB	5-11	180	08/31/35	Florida	12
31	Taylor, Jim	FB	6-0	215	09/20/35	LSU	12
82	Temp, Jim	DE	6-4	250	10/14/33	Wisconsin	7
63	Thurston, Fred (Fuzzy)	G	6-1	250	05/07/35	Valparaiso	12
45	Tunnell, Emlen	DB	6-1	210	03/29/25	Iowa	12
47	Whittenton, Jesse	DB	6-0	195	05/09/34	Texas-El Paso	12
23	Winslow, Paul	HB	5-11	200	02/28/38	North Carolina Central	12
24	Wood, Willie	DB	5-10	185	12/23/36	USC	12

DRAFT

Rnd	Name	Pos	Ht	Wt	College
1	Tom Moore	HB	6-2	212	Vanderbilt
2	Bob Jeter	HB	6-1	185	Iowa
3	(Choice to Cardinals for Lamar McHan)				
4	(Choice to Browns for Henry Jordan)				
5a	Dale Hackbart	DB	6-3	200	Wisconsin
	(Choice from Lions for Ollie Spencer)				
5b	(Choice to Browns for Bob Freeman)				
6	Mike Wright	T	6-3	235	Minnesota
7	Kirk Phares	G	6-2	235	South Carolina
8	Don Hitt	C	6-3	235	Oklahoma State
*9	Frank Brixius	T	6-5	265	Minnesota
10	(Choice to Cardinals for Ken Beck)				
11	Ron Ray	T	6-4	234	Howard Payne
12	Harry Hall	T	6-1	235	Boston College
13	Paul Winslow	HB	5-11	200	North Carolina Central
14	Jon Gilliam	C	6-2	210	East Texas State
15	Garney Henley	HB	5-11	177	Huron
*16	John Littlejohn	HB	6-1	190	Kansas State
17	Joe Gomes	HB	6-1	200	South Carolina
18	Royce Whittington	T	6-2	265	SW Louisiana
19	Rich Brooks	E	6-3	195	Purdue
20	Gilmer Lewis	T	6-4	215	Oklahoma

* denotes juniors

FRONT ROW: (L-R) 67 Andy Cvercko, 53 Ken Iman, 40 Dale Hackbart, 23 Paul Winslow, 48 Dick Pesonen, 24 Willie Wood, 25 Tom Moore.
SECOND ROW: (L-R) 71 Bill Forester, 27 John Symank, 64 Jerry Kramer, 63 Fred (Fuzzy) Thurston, 46 Hank Gremminger, 47 Jesse Whittenton, 31 Jim Taylor, 58 Dan Currie, 33 Lew Carpenter, 88 Ron Kramer, 80 Steve Meilinger.
THIRD ROW: (L-R) Equipment Manager Gerald (Dad) Braisher, 15 Bart Starr, 76 Bob Skoronski, 84 Gary Knafelc, 51 Jim Ringo, 82 Jim Temp, 78 Norm Masters, 74 Henry Jordan, 79 Dave Hanner, 72 John Miller, 86 Boyd Dowler, 37 Larry Hickman, Trainer Carl (Bud) Jorgensen.
BACK ROW: (L-R) 75 Forrest Gregg, 45 Emlen Tunnell, 66 Ray Nitschke, 73 Ken Beck, 20 Joe Francis, 17 Lamar McHan, 83 Bill Quinlan, 65 Tom Bettis, 5 Paul Hornung, 85 Max McGee.

The Teams: 1960   A Measure of Greatness

An expanded schedule, Uncle Sam and the opposition all failed to stop the Packers from earning a championship in 1961.

Green Bay steamrolled the competition with the league's most dominant running game and a highly accurate passing attack. Jim Taylor, Paul Hornung, Tom Moore and others piled up more yards (2,350), more first downs (142), and more touchdowns (27) than any other ground-gaining group. Bart Starr threw for a then-club record 2,418 yards and completed better than 58 percent of his passes.

The defense, while ranked sixth, gave up fewer points (223) than all but the Giants (220). The club pilfered 29 balls to tie Detroit for second place in that category.

Green Bay bolted to a 6-1 record in the first half of a 14-game schedule. Then, despite having to contend with the U. S. government and a key injury to one of its top linemen, the team had enough in reserve to notch five victories, including a conference clinching, 20-17 win over the Giants in Milwaukee on Dec. 3. At season's end, the Packers' 11-3 record was the best in the NFL.

Events on the world stage made achieving that record more difficult. Thousands of military reservists and National Guardsmen were called to active duty in response to the building of the Berlin wall. On Oct. 17, Hornung and Ray Nitschke got word to report. Nine days later, Boyd Dowler was notified as well.

Weekend passes helped minimize the losses. Though rarely able to practice, Hornung and Nitschke missed only two games. Dowler got away to play in all 14. Still, the uncertainty regarding player availability had to impact the team's weekly preparations.

Jerry Kramer was lost as well, but not to military duty. The veteran guard shattered his ankle in the second Vikings game and was lost for the season.

The Packers took a major step to ensure their long-term success when they signed Vince Lombardi to a new five-year contract in August. The new pact and the Giants' hiring of Allie Sherman as head coach ended speculation that Lombardi might leave Green Bay for New York.

The NFL and CBS also signed a contract—a two-year, $9.3 million deal in which the network agreed to broadcast the league's entire 98-game schedule. The package deal—a first for the league—placed more than $664,000 in the coffers of each of the NFL's 14 teams.

Green Bay fell 17-13 to the Lions in the opener. Nick Pietrosante scored twice and Jim Martin kicked a 44-yard field goal. Night Train Lane sealed the Packers' fate by intercepting Starr with 1:32 remaining.

The Green and Gold then won its next six games by at least 18 points each.

After beating the 49ers 30-10 in Week 2, the Packers shut out the Bears 24-0 for the first time in 26 years. Defensive tackle Dave Hanner, who had undergone an appendectomy just 10 days earlier, suited up and played.

In Week 4, the Packers crushed the Colts 45-7. The game marked the first appearance by Lamar McHan in Green Bay since the quarterback was traded to Baltimore for a fifth-round draft choice in March. McHan threw five passes after relieving Johnny Unitas late in the contest.

The Packers clobbered Cleveland 49-17 in Week 5. Taylor rushed for 158 yards and four touchdowns.

Green Bay stretched its winning streak to six with back-to-back wins over the Vikings.

"They just nickel and dime you to death," pouted rookie head coach Norm Van Brocklin after the first loss.

The Packers lost to the Colts 45-21 on Nov. 5, then withstood a 21-point rally and a 9-catch, 190-yard effort by Mike Ditka to nip the Bears 31-28 in Wrigley Field.

Wins over the Rams (35-17) and Lions (17-9) followed. Herb Adderley, the Packers' first-round draft choice, debuted at defensive back when he replaced Hank Gremminger in the third quarter on Thanksgiving. He set up Taylor's go-ahead score with the first interception of his career, a 9-yarder off Jim Ninowski.

Green Bay clinched its second consecutive Western Conference crown by edging the Giants 20-17. Taylor pounded out a then-team record 186 yards rushing and scored the winning touchdown early in the fourth quarter.

Players carried both Lombardi and defensive assistant Phil Bengtson off the field.

RUNNING TO DAYLIGHT

Green Bay not only rushed for more yards (2,350) than any other team in 1961, it averaged more yards per carry (4.96) than any of the other 13 clubs.

The Packers hit top gear in October. Beginning with the Colts game on Oct. 8, Green Bay rushed for more than 200 yards in each of three consecutive games, the only time in its history it has done so.

Paul Hornung set the pace against Baltimore, picking up 111 of Green Bay's 211 yards rushing. A week later, Jim Taylor led the charge, accouting for 158 of the club's 216-yard output. On Oct. 22, Tom Moore stormed to a career-best 159 yards, as the Packers amassed 241 yards in Minnesota.

"Lombardi doesn't try to be cute," Vikings coach Norm Van Brocklin said. "He just keeps hitting you and pretty soon something comes out. It's as simple as that."

During the three-game stretch, the Packers rushed 100 times for 668 yards and 11 touchdowns. They outscored their opponents 127 to 31.

The streak ended on Oct. 29, when the Vikings held Green Bay to 157 yards rushing in a 28-10 Packers win.

TEAM STATISTICS

	GB	OPP
First Downs	274	245
Rushing	142	110
Passing	115	117
Penalty	17	18
Rushes	474	412
Yards Gained	2,350	1,694
Average Gain	4.96	4.11
Average Yards per Game	167.9	121.0
Passes Attempted	306	414
Completed	177	218
% Completed	57.84	52.66
Total Yards Gained	2,502	2,630
Yards Lost	138	273
Net Yards Gained	2,364	2,357
Yards Gained per Completion	14.14	12.06
Average Net Yards per Game	168.9	168.4
Combined Net Yards Gained	4,714	4,051
Total Plays	780	826
Average Yards per Play	6.04	4.90
Average Net Yards per Game	336.7	289.4
Third Down Efficiency	60/148	63/177
Percentage	40.54	35.59
Fourth Down Efficiency	4/5	10/23
Percentage	80.00	43.48
Intercepted By	29	16
Yards Returned	446	238
Returned for TD	2	0
Punts	51	49
Yards Punted	2,194	1,851
Average Yards per Punt	43.02	37.78
Punt Returns	20	25
Yards Returned	355	313
Average Yards per Return	17.75	12.52
Returned for TD	2	1
Kickoff Returns	41	69
Yards Returned	1,077	1,597
Average Yards per Return	26.27	23.14
Returned for TD	0	0
Penalties	66	52
Yards Penalized	647	609
Fumbles	18	30
Lost	10	17
Own Recovered for Touchdown	0	0
Opponent's Recovered by	17	10
Opponent's Recovered for Touchdown	0	0
Total Points Scored	391	223
Total Touchdowns	49	26
Touchdowns Rushing	27	12
Touchdowns Passing	18	13
Touchdowns on Returns & Recoveries	4	1
Extra Points	49	26
Safeties	0	1
Field Goals Attempted	24	21
Field Goals Made	16	13
% Successful	66.67	61.90

Regular Season   11-3-0

Date	GB		OPP	Att.
9/17	13	Detroit Lions (M)	17	(44,307)
9/24	30	San Francisco 49ers	10	(38,669)
10/1	24	Chicago Bears	0	(38,669)
10/8	45	Baltimore Colts	7	(38,669)
10/15	49	at Cleveland Browns	17	(75,042)
10/22	33	at Minnesota Vikings	7	(42,007)
10/29	28	Minnesota Vikings (M)	10	(44,116)
11/5	21	at Baltimore Colts	45	(57,641)
11/12	31	at Chicago Bears	28	(49,711)
11/19	35	Los Angeles Rams	17	(38,669)
11/23	17	at Detroit Lions	9	(55,662)
12/3	20	New York Giants (M)	17	(47,012)
12/10	21	at San Francisco 49ers	22	(55,722)
12/17	24	at Los Angeles Rams	17	(49,169)

Postseason   1-0-0

12/31	37	New York Giants	0	(39,029)

Score By Periods

	1	2	3	4	Total
Packers	100	123	44	124	391
Opponents	45	81	39	58	223

INDIVIDUAL STATISTICS

Rushing

	Att	Yds	Avg	LG	TD
J. Taylor	243	1,307	5.4	53	15
Hornung	127	597	4.7	t54	8
T. Moore	61	302	5.0	69	1
E. Pitts	23	75	3.3	t17	1
Starr	12	56	4.7	t21	1
R. Kramer	5	13	2.6	12	0
Carpenter	1	5	5.0	5	0
Roach	2	-5	-2.5	t1	1
Packers	**474**	**2,350**	**5.0**	**69**	**27**
Opponents	412	1,694	4.1	t55	12

Receiving

	No	Yds	Avg	LG	TD
McGee	51	883	17.3	53	7
Dowler	36	633	17.6	t78	1
R. Kramer	35	559	16.0	t53	4
J. Taylor	25	175	7.0	18	1
Hornung	15	145	9.7	t34	2
T. Moore	8	41	5.1	11	1
Knafelc	3	32	10.7	13	0
Carpenter	3	29	9.7	16	0
E. Pitts	1	5	5.0	5	0
Packers	**177**	**2,502**	**14.1**	**t78**	**18**
Opponents	218	2,630	12.1	t51	13

Passing

	Att	Com	Yds	Pct	TD	In	YL	Rate
Starr	295	172	2,418	58.3	16	16	138	80.3
Hornung	5	3	42	60.0	1	0	0	—
T. Moore	2	2	42	100.0	1	0	0	—
Roach	4	0	0	00.0	0	0	0	—
Packers	**306**	**177**	**2,502**	**57.8**	**18**	**16**	**138**	**82.2**
Opponents	414	218	2,630	52.7	13	29	273	53.7

Punting

	No	Yds	Avg	Net	TB	In20	LG	HB
Dowler	38	1,674	44.1	32.3	9	4	75	0
McGee	13	520	40.0	34.9	1	3	51	0
Packers	**51**	**2,194**	**43.0**	**33.0**	**10**	**7**	**75**	**0**
Opponents	49	1,851	37.8	29.7	2	9	61	0

Kickoff Returns

	No	Yds	Avg	LG	TD
Adderley	18	478	26.6	61	0
T. Moore	15	409	27.3	60	0
Symank	4	121	30.3	38	0
Forester	3	55	18.3	20	0
E. Pitts	1	14	14.0	14	0
Packers	**41**	**1,077**	**26.3**	**61**	**0**
Opponents	69	1,597	23.1	64	0

Punt Returns

	No	Yds	Avg	FC	LG	TD
Wood	14	225	16.1	11	t72	2
Carpenter	6	130	21.7	5	48	0
Packers	**20**	**355**	**17.8**	**16**	**t72**	**2**
Opponents	25	313	12.5	4	t90	1

Interceptions

	No	Yds	Avg	LG	TD
Symank	5	99	19.8	41	0
Whittenton	5	98	19.6	t41	1
Gremminger	5	54	10.8	41	0
Wood	5	52	10.4	21	0
Currie	3	59	19.7	t21	1
Nitschke	2	41	20.5	27	0
Forester	2	33	16.5	33	0
Adderley	1	9	9.0	9	0
Hanner	1	1	1.0	1	0
Packers	**29**	**446**	**15.4**	**t41**	**2**
Opponents	16	238	14.9	63	0

Scoring

	TDr	TDp	TDrt	PAT	FG	S	TP
Hornung	8	2	0	41/41	15/22	0	146
J. Taylor	15	1	0	0/0	0/0	0	96
McGee	0	7	0	0/0	0/0	0	42
R. Kramer	0	4	0	0/0	0/0	0	24
Dowler	0	3	0	0/0	0/0	0	18
T. Moore	1	1	0	0/0	0/0	0	12
Wood	0	0	2	0/0	0/0	0	12
Agajanian	0	0	0	8/8	1/2	0	11
Currie	0	0	1	0/0	0/0	0	6
E. Pitts	1	0	0	0/0	0/0	0	6
Roach	1	0	0	0/0	0/0	0	6
Starr	1	0	0	0/0	0/0	0	6
Whittenton	0	0	1	0/0	0/0	0	6
Packers	**27**	**18**	**4**	**49/49**	**16/24**	**0**	**391**
Opponents	12	13	1	26/26	13/21	1	223

Fumbles

	Fum	Ow	Op	Yds	Tot
Adderley	1	0	0	0	0
Currie	0	0	2	0	2
W. Davis	0	0	3	0	3
Gremminger	0	0	1	0	1
Hanner	0	0	2	0	2
Hornung	0	0	0	0	0
Masters	0	2	0	0	2
McGee	1	0	0	0	0
T. Moore	2	1	0	2	1
Nitschke	0	0	1	0	1
Quinlan	0	0	1	0	1
Roach	1	0	0	0	0
Starr	8	0	0	0	2
Symank	1	0	2	0	2
J. Taylor	2	1	0	0	1
Toburen	0	0	1	0	1
Whittenton	0	0	1	0	1
Wood	1	1	4	2	5
Packers	**18**	**8**	**17**	**2**	**25**

NFL STANDINGS

Western Conference

	W	L	T	Pct	PF	PA
Green Bay Packers	**11**	**3**	**0**	**786**	**391**	**223**
Detroit Lions	8	5	1	615	270	258
Baltimore Colts	8	6	0	571	302	307
Chicago Bears	8	6	0	571	326	302
San Francisco 49ers	7	6	1	538	346	272
Los Angeles Rams	4	10	0	286	263	333
Minnesota Vikings	3	11	0	214	285	407

Eastern Conference

	W	L	T	Pct	PF	PA
New York Giants	10	3	1	769	368	220
Philadelphia Eagles	10	4	0	714	361	297
Cleveland Browns	8	5	1	615	319	270
St. Louis Cardinals	7	7	0	500	279	267
Pittsburgh Steelers	6	8	0	429	295	287
Dallas Cowboys	4	9	1	308	236	380
Washington Redskins	1	12	1	077	174	392

1961

ROSTER

No	Name	Pos	Ht	Wt	DOB	College	G
26	Adderley, Herb	CB	6-1	205	06/08/39	Michigan State	14
3	Agajanian, Ben	K	6-0	220	08/28/19	New Mexico	3
65	Bettis, Tom	LB	6-2	225	03/17/33	Purdue	12
33	Carpenter, Lew	FB	6-2	215	01/12/32	Arkansas	14
58	Currie, Dan	LB	6-3	240	06/27/35	Michigan State	14
72	Davidson, Ben	DE	6-8	275	06/14/40	Washington	14
87	Davis, Willie	DE	6-3	240	07/24/34	Grambling	14
86	Dowler, Boyd	E	6-5	220	10/18/37	Colorado	14
81	Folkins, Lee	DE	6-5	220	07/04/39	Washington	14
71	Forester, Bill	LB	6-3	240	08/09/32	SMU	14
75	Gregg, Alvis (Forrest)	T	6-4	250	10/18/33	SMU	14
46	Gremminger, Hank	DB	6-1	205	09/01/33	Baylor	14
40	Hackbart, Dale	DB	6-3	200	07/21/38	Wisconsin	2
79	Hanner, Joel (Dave)	DT	6-2	260	05/20/30	Arkansas	13
5	Hornung, Paul	HB	6-2	215	12/23/35	Notre Dame	12
53	Iman, Ken	C	6-1	230	02/08/39	Southeast Missouri State	14
74	Jordan, Henry	DT	6-3	250	01/26/35	Virginia	14
84	Knafelc, Gary	E	6-4	220	01/02/32	Colorado	13
77	Kostelnik, Ron	DT	6-4	260	01/14/40	Cincinnati	14
64	Kramer, Jerry	G	6-3	250	01/23/36	Idaho	7
88	Kramer, Ron	E	6-3	230	06/24/35	Michigan	14
78	Masters, Norm	T	6-2	250	09/19/33	Michigan State	14
85	McGee, Max	E	6-3	205	07/16/32	Tulane	13
25	Moore, Tom	HB	6-2	215	07/17/38	Vanderbilt	13
66	Nitschke, Ray	LB	6-3	235	12/29/36	Illinois	12
22	Pitts, Elijah	HB	6-1	200	02/03/39	Philander Smith	14
83	Quinlan, Bill	DE	6-3	250	06/19/32	Michigan State	14
51	Ringo, Jim	C	6-1	235	11/21/32	Syracuse	14
10	Roach, John	QB	6-4	200	03/26/33	SMU	7
76	Skoronski, Bob	T	6-3	250	03/05/34	Indiana	13
15	Starr, Bryan (Bart)	QB	6-1	200	01/09/34	Alabama	14
27	Symank, John	DB	5-11	180	08/31/35	Florida	14
31	Taylor, Jim	FB	6-0	215	09/20/35	LSU	14
63	Thurston, Fred (Fuzzy)	G	6-1	250	05/07/35	Valparaiso	14
61	Toburen, Nelson	LB	6-3	235	11/24/38	Wichita	14
45	Tunnell, Emlen	DB	6-1	210	03/29/25	Iowa	13
47	Whittenton, Jesse	DB	6-0	195	05/09/34	Texas-El Paso	14
24	Wood, Willie	DB	5-10	185	12/23/36	USC	14

DRAFT

Rnd	Name	Pos	Ht	Wt	College
1	Herb Adderley	DB	6-1	205	Michigan State
2	Ron Kostelnik	T	6-4	260	Cincinnati
3	Phil Nugent	QB	6-1	192	Tulane
*4a	Paul Dudley	HB	6-0	195	Arkansas
4b	Joe LeSage	G	6-2	235	Tulane
	(Choice from Eagles for Bob Freeman)				
5	Jack Novak	G	6-2	225	Miami (FL)
6	Lee Folkins	DE	6-5	220	Washington
7	Lewis Johnson	HB	6-1	195	Florida A&M
8	(Choice to Browns for Bob Jarus)				
9	Vester Flanagan	T	6-4	250	Humboldt
10a	Roger Hagberg	FB	6-1	212	Minnesota
	(Choice from Cowboys for Fred Cone)				
10b	Terry McLeod	T	6-3	230	Baylor
11	Val Keckin	QB	6-3	210	Southern Mississippi
*12	John Denvir	T	6-2	230	Colorado
13	Elijah Pitts	HB	6-1	200	Philander Smith
14	Nelson Toburen	LB	6-3	230	Wichita
*15	Ray Lardani	T	6-3	265	Miami (FL)
16	Clarence Mason	E	6-2	185	Bowling Green
17	Jim Brewington	T	6-5	270	No. Carolina Central
18	Randy Sims	B	6-0	190	Texas A&M
19	Leland Bondhus	T	6-3	230	South Dakota State
20	Ray Ratkowski	HB	6-1	185	Notre Dame

* denotes juniors

FRONT ROW: (L-R) 26 Herb Adderley, 72 Ben Davidson, 22 Elijah Pitts, 81 Lee Folkins, 77 Ron Kostelnik, 61 Nelson Toburen.
SECOND ROW: (L-R) 53 Ken Iman, 24 Willie Wood, 46 Hank Gremminger, 25 Tom Moore, 64 Jerry Kramer, 63 Fred (Fuzzy) Thurston, 47 Jesse Whittenton, 27 John Symank, 65 Tom Bettis.
THIRD ROW: (L-R) Trainer Carl (Bud) Jorgensen, 76 Bob Skoronski, 15 Bart Starr, 84 Gary Knafelc, 51 Jim Ringo, 78 Norm Masters, 58 Dan Currie, 87 Willie Davis, 10 John Roach, 33 Lew Carpenter, Equipment Manager Gerald (Dad) Braisher.
BACK ROW: (L-R) 83 Bill Quinlan, 75 Forrest Gregg, 45 Emlen Tunnell, 66 Ray Nitschke, 79 Dave Hanner, 74 Henry Jordan, 86 Boyd Dowler, 31 Jim Taylor, 88 Ron Kramer, 71 Bill Forester, 5 Paul Hornung, 85 Max McGee.

Vince Lombardi preached perfection. Of all his teams, the 1962 edition came the closest to attaining it. From start to finish, the Packers perched themselves atop the Western Conference and were never seriously threatened. The team reeled off 10 straight wins to start the season, then ran off three more to close with a flourish. Only a 26-14 setback to the Lions on Thanksgiving kept the Green and Gold from an unbeaten season.

If the Packers were good in 1961, they dominated in 1962. Green Bay scored a league-best 415 points while holding opponents to a league-low 148. The running game exploded for an NFL-record 36 touchdowns. The defense, led by ball-hawking Herb Adderley and Willie Wood, intercepted more passes (31) than any other.

As the victories piled up, so too did speculation as to whether or not the team could finish undefeated. "They'll get beat—and they'll lose more than one," insisted head coach Norm Van Brocklin after his Vikings were flattened 48-21. The Colts' Gino Marchetti conceded the Packers "were good, but somebody's going to knock them off."

Even Lombardi felt going unbeaten was near impossible. "I think it's highly improbable. Let's put it that way."

In any case, Green Bay earned rave reviews as it ripped through the competition. Even a knee injury to Paul Hornung, the league's top scorer from 1959 through 1961, couldn't slow the Packers. Hornung suffered ligament damage to his right knee in Week 5 when tackled by the Vikings' Cliff Livingston and missed five of the team's next six games. Jerry Kramer handled Hornung's kicking duties and Tom Moore subbed at halfback in Hornung's absence.

The Packers faced their toughest tests in the Lions and Colts. In three of those four contests, Green Bay was outrushed and outgained. Twice it had to rally in the fourth quarter in order to prevail.

Green Bay kicked off with a 34-7 thrashing of the Vikings. Adderley, Wood and Hank Gremminger intercepted Fran Tarkenton five times. The defense also sacked the slippery scrambler on five occasions for 52 yards in losses.

The Cardinals provided the next challenge. Green Bay held St. Louis to 16 yards rushing. Bart Starr engineered a 12-play drive in the third quarter that consumed almost eight minutes and netted the Packers their first touchdown.

The Bears traveled to City Stadium in Week 3. Minus Bill George, Charlie Bivins, and Willie Galimore, Chicago offered little resistance in falling 49-0. Jim Taylor rushed for three touchdowns and Adderley closed the scoring with a 50-yard interception return for a touchdown.

Green Bay (3-0) played host to the unbeaten Lions. With 1:25 to go, Detroit clung to a 7-6 lead. On third-and-eight, Adderley intercepted a Milt Plum pass intended for Terry Barr and returned it 40 yards to set up Hornung's game-winning, 21-yard field goal with 33 seconds left.

The Packers grabbed their fifth win in Minnesota. Starr completed his first 10 passes on the way to a sterling 20-for-28 performance that was good for 297 yards.

In Week 6, Green Bay downed the 49ers 31-13 and moved two games ahead of the Lions. It completed the season's first half by stopping the Colts three times on fourth down in a 17-6 win.

In the next two weeks, the Packers easily overpowered the Bears (38-7) and Eagles (49-0). They picked up their 10th win in a rematch with the Colts. The game also marked the end of linebacker Nelson Toburen's playing days. The second-year defender broke his neck tackling John Unitas in the fourth quarter.

Green Bay then traveled to Detroit for its holiday tilt with the Lions. Led by Roger Brown, Detroit sacked Starr nine times for 93 yards in losses. The Lions (9-2) forced five turnovers and moved to within a game of first place.

"From now on, we'll be a lot better ball club for it (the loss). I think we're all a little relieved," said Lombardi as the pressure of being an unbeaten team lifted.

Green Bay rebounded with a 41-10 pounding of the Rams, but was far from dominant in its last two games on the West Coast. A 14-point fourth quarter earned them a 31-21 win at San Francisco and the team then held on for a 20-17 victory in Los Angeles.

"We're a tired ball club, a very tired ball club," said Lombardi. Not so tired, however, that the club couldn't deliver another championship in New York on Dec. 30.

OUTGAINED BUT NOT OUTSCORED

Detroit handed Green Bay its only loss of 1962 in an infamous 26-14 ambush on Thanksgiving Day. In hindsight, the loss was hardly surprising given the team's struggles with the Colts four days earlier.

Against Baltimore on Nov. 18, Green Bay could muster no more than 116 yards of offense. The Colts, on the other hand, ran roughshod to the tune of 382 yards. Despite the 266-yard imbalance, the Packers emerged victorious 17-13.

Two goal-line stands saved the day. Bill Forester capped one with a sack of John Unitas, and Herb Adderley ended the other with a knockdown of a pass intended for Jimmy Orr.

The 266-yard differential is the most yards by which Green Bay has been outgained in a game it won. A list of the top five such games is presented below:

Yds. Outgained	Game	Final
266	11-18-62 vs. Colts	won 17-13
202	9-24-50 vs. Redskins	won 35-21
192	10-9-60 vs. Colts	won 35-21
191	10-8-78 vs. Bears	won 24-14
172	12-13-92 vs. Oilers	won 16-14

1962

TEAM STATISTICS

	GB	OPP
First Downs	281	191
Rushing	145	88
Passing	120	94
Penalty	16	9
Rushes	518	404
Yards Gained	2,460	1,531
Average Gain	4.75	3.79
Average Yards per Game	175.7	109.4
Passes Attempted	311	355
Completed	187	187
% Completed	60.13	52.68
Total Yards Gained	2,621	2,084
Yards Lost	290	338
Net Yards Gained	2,331	1,746
Yards Gained per Completion	14.02	11.14
Average Net Yards per Game	166.5	124.7
Combined Net Yards Gained	4,791	3,277
Total Plays	829	759
Average Yards per Play	5.78	4.32
Average Net Yards per Game	342.2	234.1
Third Down Efficiency	70/164	49/173
Percentage	42.68	28.32
Fourth Down Efficiency	11/15	13/28
Percentage	73.33	46.43
Intercepted By	31	13
Yards Returned	452	122
Returned for TD	1	1
Punts	50	58
Yards Punted	2,046	2,506
Average Yards per Punt	40.92	43.21
Punt Returns	31	20
Yards Returned	290	183
Average Yards per Return	9.35	9.15
Returned for TD	0	1
Kickoff Returns	30	76
Yards Returned	716	1,524
Average Yards per Return	23.87	20.05
Returned for TD	1	0
Penalties	59	54
Yards Penalized	617	611
Fumbles	29	28
Lost	15	19
Own Recovered for Touchdown	1	0
Opponent's Recovered by	19	15
Opponent's Recovered for Touchdown	0	1
Total Points Scored	415	148
Total Touchdowns	53	17
Touchdowns Rushing	36	4
Touchdowns Passing	14	10
Touchdowns on Returns & Recoveries	3	3
Extra Points	52	17
Safeties	0	1
Field Goals Attempted	21	22
Field Goals Made	15	9
% Successful	71.43	40.91

Regular Season   13-1-0

Date	GB		OPP	Att.
9/16	34	Minnesota Vikings	7	(38,669)
9/23	17	St. Louis Cardinals (M)	0	(44,885)
9/30	49	Chicago Bears	0	(38,669)
10/7	9	Detroit Lions	7	(38,669)
10/14	48	at Minnesota Vikings	21	(41,475)
10/21	31	San Francisco 49ers (M)	13	(46,010)
10/28	17	at Baltimore Colts	6	(57,966)
11/4	38	at Chicago Bears	7	(48,753)
11/11	49	at Philadelphia Eagles	0	(60,671)
11/18	17	Baltimore Colts	13	(38,669)
11/22	14	at Detroit Lions	26	(57,578)
12/2	41	Los Angeles Rams (M)	10	(46,833)
12/9	31	at San Francisco 49ers	21	(53,769)
12/16	20	at Los Angeles Rams	17	(60,353)

Postseason   1-0-0

12/30	16	at New York Giants	7	(64,892)

Score By Periods

	1	2	3	4	Total
Packers	71	115	93	136	415
Opponents	26	71	16	35	148

INDIVIDUAL STATISTICS

Rushing

	Att	Yds	Avg	LG	TD
J. Taylor	272	1,474	5.4	51	19
T. Moore	112	377	3.4	t32	7
Hornung	57	219	3.8	t37	5
Gros	29	155	5.3	26	2
E. Pitts	22	110	5.0	t26	2
Starr	21	72	3.4	18	1
McGee	3	52	17.3	36	0
Roach	1	5	5.0	5	0
R. Kramer	1	-4	-4.0	-4	0
Packers	518	2,460	4.8	51	36
Opponents	404	1,531	3.8	40	4

Receiving

	No	Yds	Avg	LG	TD
McGee	49	820	16.7	64	3
Dowler	49	724	14.8	41	2
R. Kramer	37	555	15.0	t54	7
J. Taylor	22	106	4.8	25	0
T. Moore	11	100	9.1	34	0
Hornung	9	168	18.7	t83	2
Carpenter	7	104	14.9	22	0
E. Pitts	3	44	14.7	29	0
Packers	187	2,621	14.0	t83	14
Opponents	187	2,084	11.1	63	10

Passing

	Att	Com	Yds	Pct	TD	In	YL	Rate
Starr	285	178	2,438	62.5	12	9	286	90.7
Hornung	6	4	80	66.7	0	2	0	—
T. Moore	5	2	70	40.0	2	1	0	—
Hornung	12	3	33	25.0	0	4	4	39.6
E. Pitts	2	0	0	00.0	0	0	0	—
McGee	1	0	0	00.0	0	1	0	—
Packers	311	187	2,621	60.1	14	13	290	84.9
Opponents	355	187	2,084	52.7	10	31	338	43.4

Punting

	No	Yds	Avg	Net	TB	In20	LG	HB
Dowler	36	1,550	43.1	37.5	2	6	75	0
McGee	14	496	35.4	32.3	1	6	56	0
Packers	50	2,046	40.9	36.1	3	12	75	0
Opponents	58	2,506	43.2	37.2	3	15	80	1

Kickoff Returns

	No	Yds	Avg	LG	TD
Adderley	15	418	27.9	t103	1
T. Moore	13	284	21.8	28	0
Gros	1	7	7.0	7	0
Nitschke	1	7	7.0	7	0
Packers	30	716	23.9	t103	1
Opponents	76	1,524	20.1	47	0

Punt Returns

	No	Yds	Avg	FC	LG	TD
Wood	23	273	11.9	9	65	0
E. Pitts	7	17	2.4	3	7	0
Kostelnik	1	0	0.0	0	0	0
Packers	31	290	9.4	12	65	0
Opponents	20	183	9.2	6	t85	1

Interceptions

	No	Yds	Avg	LG	TD
Wood	9	132	14.7	37	0
Adderley	7	132	18.9	t50	1
Gremminger	5	88	17.6	35	0
Nitschke	4	56	14.0	28	0
Whittenton	3	40	13.3	36	0
Quinlan	1	4	4.0	4	0
Hanner	1	0	0.0	0	0
H. Jordan	1	0	0.0	0	0
Packers	31	452	14.6	t50	1
Opponents	13	122	9.4	35	1

Scoring

	TDr	TDp	TDrt	PAT	FG	S	TP
J. Taylor	19	0	0	0/0	0/0	0	114
Hornung	5	2	0	14/14	6/10	0	74
J. Kramer	0	0	0	38/39	9/11	0	65
R. Kramer	0	7	0	0/0	0/0	0	42
T. Moore	7	0	0	0/0	0/0	0	42
McGee	0	3	0	0/0	0/0	0	18
Adderley	0	0	2	0/0	0/0	0	12
Dowler	0	2	0	0/0	0/0	0	12
Gros	2	0	0	0/0	0/0	0	12
E. Pitts	2	0	0	0/0	0/0	0	12
W. Davis	0	0	1	0/0	0/0	0	6
Starr	1	0	0	0/0	0/0	0	6
Packers	36	14	3	52/53	15/21	0	415
Opponents	4	10	3	17/17	9/22	1	148

Fumbles

	Fum	Ow	Op	Yds	Tot
Adderley	2	3	1	15	4
Carpenter	0	0	1	0	1
Currie	0	0	1	0	1
W. Davis	0	1	2	0	3
Dowler	1	0	0	0	0
Forester	0	0	2	0	2
Gremminger	0	0	1	0	1
Gros	1	0	0	0	1
Hanner	0	0	1	0	1
Hornung	1	0	0	0	0
Iman	0	1	0	0	1
H. Jordan	0	0	1	7	1
J. Kramer	0	2	0	13	2
McGee	2	1	0	16	3
T. Moore	4	2	0	0	2
Nitschke	1	1	3	0	4
E. Pitts	2	0	0	0	0
Quinlan	1	0	1	0	1
Ringo	0	0	1	0	1
Roach	1	0	0	0	0
Starr	8	0	0	0	1
J. Taylor	5	0	0	0	1
Whittenton	0	0	2	0	0
Wood	0	0	0	36	0
Packers	29	14	19	87	33

NFL STANDINGS

Western Conference

	W	L	T	Pct	PF	PA
Green Bay Packers	13	1	0	929	415	148
Detroit Lions	11	3	0	786	315	177
Chicago Bears	9	5	0	643	321	287
Baltimore Colts	7	7	0	500	293	288
San Francisco 49ers	6	8	0	429	282	331
Minnesota Vikings	2	11	1	154	254	410
Los Angeles Rams	1	12	1	077	220	334

Eastern Conference

	W	L	T	Pct	PF	PA
New York Giants	12	2	0	857	398	283
Pittsburgh Steelers	9	5	0	643	312	363
Cleveland Browns	7	6	1	538	291	257
Washington Redskins	5	7	2	417	305	376
Dallas Cowboys	5	8	1	385	398	402
St. Louis Cardinals	4	9	1	308	287	361
Philadelphia Eagles	3	10	1	231	282	356

ROSTER

No	Name	Pos	Ht	Wt	DOB	College	G
26	Adderley, Herb	CB	6-1	205	06/08/39	Michigan State	14
80	Barnes, Gary	E	6-4	210	09/13/39	Clemson	13
60	Blaine, Ed	G	6-2	240	01/30/40	Missouri	14
33	Carpenter, Lew	FB	6-2	215	01/12/32	Arkansas	14
58	Currie, Dan	LB	6-3	240	06/27/35	Michigan State	12
87	Davis, Willie	DE	6-3	240	07/24/34	Grambling	14
86	Dowler, Boyd	E	6-5	225	10/18/37	Colorado	14
71	Forester, Bill	LB	6-3	240	08/09/32	SMU	14
73	Gassert, Ron	DT	6-3	260	07/22/40	Virginia	11
75	Gregg, Alvis (Forrest)	T	6-4	250	10/18/33	SMU	14
46	Gremminger, Hank	DB	6-1	205	09/01/33	Baylor	14
40	Gros, Earl	FB	6-3	230	08/29/40	Louisiana	14
79	Hanner, Joel (Dave)	DT	6-2	260	05/20/30	Arkansas	14
5	Hornung, Paul	HB	6-2	215	12/23/35	Notre Dame	9
53	Iman, Ken	C	6-1	230	02/08/39	Southeast Missouri State	14
74	Jordan, Henry	DT	6-3	250	01/26/35	Virginia	14
84	Knafelc, Gary	E	6-4	220	01/02/32	Colorado	11
77	Kostelnik, Ron	DT	6-4	260	01/14/40	Cincinnati	14
64	Kramer, Jerry	G	6-3	255	01/23/36	Idaho	14
88	Kramer, Ron	E	6-3	240	06/24/35	Michigan	14
78	Masters, Norm	T	6-2	250	09/19/33	Michigan State	14
85	McGee, Max	E	6-3	205	07/16/32	Tulane	14
25	Moore, Tom	HB	6-2	215	07/17/38	Vanderbilt	14
66	Nitschke, Ray	LB	6-3	235	12/29/36	Illinois	14
22	Pitts, Elijah	HB	6-1	200	02/03/39	Philander Smith	14
83	Quinlan, Bill	DE	6-3	250	06/19/32	Michigan State	14
51	Ringo, Jim	C	6-1	235	11/21/32	Syracuse	14
10	Roach, John	QB	6-4	200	03/26/33	SMU	8
76	Skoronski, Bob	T	6-3	250	03/05/34	Indiana	13
15	Starr, Bryan (Bart)	QB	6-1	200	01/09/34	Alabama	14
27	Symank, John	DB	5-11	180	08/31/35	Florida	14
31	Taylor, Jim	FB	6-0	215	09/20/35	LSU	14
63	Thurston, Fred (Fuzzy)	G	6-1	250	05/07/35	Valparaiso	14
61	Toburen, Nelson	LB	6-3	235	11/24/38	Wichita	10
47	Whittenton, Jesse	DB	6-0	195	05/09/34	Texas-El Paso	14
29	Williams, Howard	DB	6-1	190	12/04/37	Howard J.C.	3
24	Wood, Willie	DB	5-10	185	12/23/36	USC	14

DRAFT

Rnd	Name	Pos	Ht	Wt	College
1	Earl Gros	FB	6-3	230	LSU
2	Ed Blaine	G	6-2	240	Missouri
3a	Gary Barnes	E	6-4	210	Clemson
	(Choice from Giants for Joel Wells)				
3b	(Choice to Browns for John Roach)				
4	Ron Gassert	DT	6-3	260	Virginia
*5a	Chuck Morris	HB	6-1	195	Mississippi
	(Choice from Colts for Lamar McHan)				
5b	Jon Schopf	G	6-2	240	Michigan
6a	John Sutro	T	6-4	250	San Jose State
	(Choice from Redskins for Dale Hackbart)				
6b	Oscar Donahue	E	6-3	205	San Jose State
7	Gary Cutsinger	T	6-4	230	Oklahoma State
*8	James Tulis	HB	6-3	195	Florida A&M
9	Pete Schenk	DB	6-2	200	Washington State
10	Gale Weidener	QB	6-1	195	Colorado

Rnd	Name	Pos	Ht	Wt	College
*11	Jim Thrush	E	6-4	230	Xavier
12a State	Joe Thorne	HB	6-1	195	South Dakota
	(Choice from Cowboys for Steve Meilinger)				
12b	Tom Pennington	K	6-2	210	Georgia
13	Tom Kepner	T	6-3	245	Villanova
14	Ernest Green	HB	6-2	205	Louisville
15	Roger Holdinsky	HB	5-11	185	West Virginia
*16	James Field	DB	6-1	190	LSU
17	Junias Buchanon	T	6-5	246	Grambling
18	Bob Joiner	QB	6-1	205	Presbyterian
19	Jerry Scatini	DB	6-2	200	California
20	Mike Snodgrass	C	6-2	220	Western Michigan
*	denotes juniors				

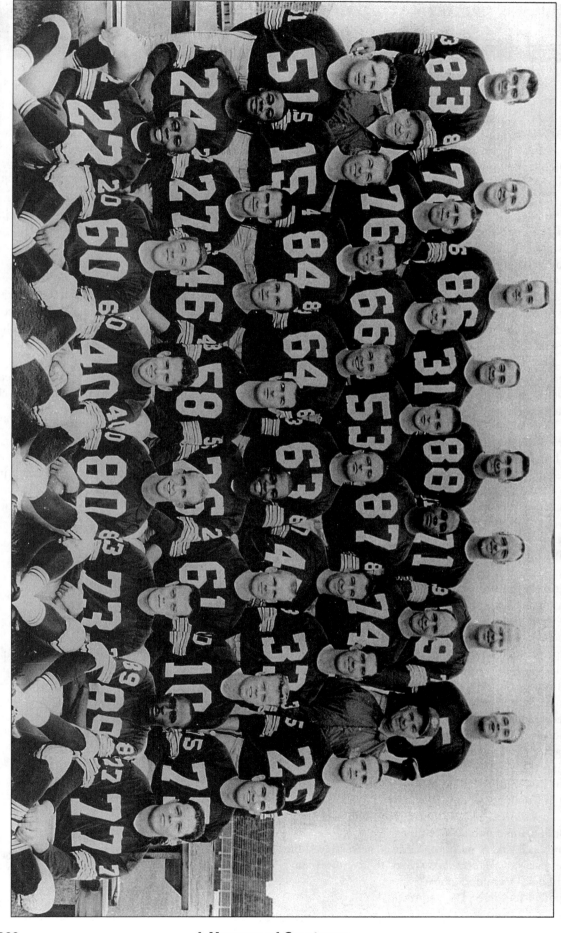

FRONT ROW: (L-R) 22 Elijah Pitts, 60 Ed Blaine, 40 Earl Gros, 80 Gary Barnes, 73 Ron Gassert, 89 Oscar Donahue, 77 Ron Kostelnik.
SECOND ROW: (L-R) 24 Willie Wood, 27 John Symank, 46 Hank Gremminger, 58 Dan Currie, 26 Herb Adderley, 61 Nelson Toburen, 10 John Roach, 75 Forrest Gregg.
THIRD ROW: (L-R) 51 Jim Ringo, 15 Bart Starr, 84 Gary Knafelc, 64 Jerry Kramer, 63 Fred (Fuzzy) Thurston, 47 Jesse Whittenton, 33 Lew Carpenter, 25 Tom Moore.
FOURTH ROW: (L-R) Property Manager Gerald (Dad) Braisher, 76 Bob Skoronski, 66 Ray Nitschke, 53 Ken Iman, 87 Willie Davis, 74 Henry Jordan, Trainer Carl (Bud) Jorgensen.
BACK ROW: (L-R) 83 Bill Quinlan, 78 Norm Masters, 86 Boyd Dowler, 31 Jim Taylor, 88 Ron Kramer, 71 Bill Forester, 79 Dave Hanner, 5 Paul Hornung.

One team kept the Packers from a fourth straight Western Conference title and a shot at a third consecutive NFL championship: the Chicago Bears.

Green Bay lost only twice all year; both times to the Bears. Still, that was double the number of losses endured by Chicago, which came up short just once to the 49ers. At season's end, the 11-2-1 Packers had to settle for second place behind the 11-1-2 Bears.

Defense ruled in the first Packers-Bears clash. Green Bay never crossed the Bears 30-yard line and only three times had the ball past midfield. Those three occasions ended in a 41-yard field goal and two interceptions.

Bart Starr and his offensive mates gained but 150 yards. Chicago was held to 231. Joe Marconi's 1-yard run in the third quarter lifted the Bears to a 10-3 win.

Green Bay fared no better in the rematch at Wrigley Field. With Starr out of action, John Roach and Zeke Bratkowski combined to throw five interceptions. With Herb Adderley and Roach also losing fumbles, the Packers were guilty of seven turnovers, which the Bears converted into 17 points. Chicago also piled up 248 yards rushing and won easily 26-7.

Aside from those missteps, the Packers were as impressive as they had been in 1961 and 1962. Their rushing attack slipped to second (behind the Browns), but their 22 rushing touchdowns ranked first. Defensively, Green Bay was second (Bears) and allowed a league-low nine touchdown passes. Only the Giants scored more points and only the Bears allowed fewer.

On April 17, NFL commissioner Pete Rozelle suspended Paul Hornung and the Lions' Alex Karras indefinitely for gambling. Hornung and Karras had placed bets, ranging from $50 to $200, on a number of NFL games over the years. Five other Lions were fined $2,000 apiece for placing one-time wagers on the 1962 championship game. In all cases, the men did not bet against their teams, and no evidence of point-shaving was found.

With Hornung out, Green Bay looked to Tom Moore, Elijah Pitts and Earl Gros to pick up the slack. Jerry Kramer again handled the kicking duties.

After the opener against the Bears, Starr vowed: "We'll give you a better performance next week." The team did just that by routing the Lions in Week 2. Moore and Jim Taylor combined for 204 yards rushing as Green Bay bounced the Lions 31-10 in County Stadium.

A week later, Green Bay and the Colts combined for 12 turnovers. Both teams fumbled five times.

"Ten fumbles," said Vince Lombardi as he reviewed the statistics afterwards. "We recovered five of theirs, they recovered three of ours. Holy good gravy."

Good enough for Green Bay to prevail 31-14.

In Week 4, Green Bay routed the Rams 42-10 as temperatures soared into the mid-80s.

A stubborn Vikings squad awaited in Week 5. With less than two minutes to play, Fred Cox attempted a 10-yard field goal that Adderley blocked. Hank Gremminger returned the block 80 yards for a touchdown as Green Bay escaped 37-28.

The Packers rolled to their fifth win in St. Louis (30-7), but not without a price. In the third quarter, defensive back Jimmy Hill shoved Starr out of bounds with his forearm, then punched the quarterback in the face. Hill was ejected and Starr was out for the next four weeks with a broken passing hand, having injured it in the collision.

John Roach filled in and presided over three straight wins. Nevertheless, Lombardi obtained Zeke Bratkowski on waivers for $100 from the Rams as insurance.

Roach got the call in the Bears' rematch. Neither he nor Bratkowski (in just his second game with the Packers) could stop the onslaught.

"This is our greatest victory since we beat the Giants for the world championship in 1946," said an ebullient George Halas.

Starr returned in Week 11. The eight-year veteran threw seven touchdown passes and no interceptions in the last four games.

The Packers suffered a tie (and Ray Nitschke a broken arm) on Thanksgiving when the Lions drove 78 yards in 17 plays to knot the score at 13 on Nick Pietrosante's run with 16 seconds left.

NO PLAYOFF PAYOFF

In 1963, Green Bay surged to an impressive 11-2-1 record —a winning percentage of .846. Despite the impeccable credentials, the Packers missed out on postseason play for the first time in four years.

Never before or since has the Green and Gold produced such a glittering record and not secured a playoff berth. Since the playoff system was first adopted by the NFL in 1933, only two teams with better records than the 1963 Packers failed to make the playoffs: the 1944 Eagles (7-1-2; .875) and the 1967 Colts (11-1-2; .917).

In 1963, the Packers had the Bears to thank for their misfortune. Chicago defeated Green Bay twice and won the Western Conference crown with an 11-1-2 mark (.917).

Below is a list of the best Packers teams (based on winning percentage) that did not qualify for the playoffs:

Year	W	L	T	Pct.	Conference Winner
1963	11	2	1	.846	Bears (11-1-2; .917)
1942	8	2	1	.800	Bears (11-0-0; 1.000)
1943	7	2	1	.778	Bears (8-1-1; .889)
1935	8	4	0	.667	Lions (7-3-2; .700)

TEAM STATISTICS

	GB	OPP
First Downs	258	193
Rushing	114	92
Passing	126	87
Penalty	18	14
Rushes	504	428
Yards Gained	2,248	1,586
Average Gain	4.46	3.71
Average Yards per Game	160.6	113.3
Passes Attempted	345	378
Completed	179	180
% Completed	51.88	47.62
Total Yards Gained	2,711	2,340
Times Sacked	20	39
Yards Lost	178	327
Net Yards Gained	2,533	2,013
Yards Gained per Completion	15.15	13.00
Net Yards per Attempt	6.94	4.83
Average Net Yards per Game	180.9	143.8
Combined Net Yards Gained	4,781	3,599
Total Plays	869	845
Average Yards per Play	5.50	4.26
Average Net Yards per Game	341.5	257.1
Third Down Efficiency	76/182	50/183
Percentage	41.76	27.32
Fourth Down Efficiency	7/12	9/25
Percentage	58.33	36.00
Intercepted By	22	21
Yards Returned	312	297
Returned for TD	0	1
Punts	51	59
Yards Punted	2,279	2,558
Average Yards per Punt	44.69	43.36
Punt Returns	26	29
Yards Returned	229	220
Average Yards per Return	8.81	7.59
Returned for TD	0	0
Kickoff Returns	46	69
Yards Returned	1,122	1,331
Average Yards per Return	24.39	19.29
Returned for TD	1	0
Penalties	53	59
Yards Penalized	517	568
Fumbles	30	31
Lost	20	21
Own Recovered for Touchdown	0	0
Opponent's Recovered by	21	20
Opponent's Recovered for Touchdown	0	2
Total Points Scored	369	206
Total Touchdowns	46	23
Touchdowns Rushing	22	11
Touchdowns Passing	22	9
Touchdowns on Returns & Recoveries	2	3
Extra Points	43	23
Safeties	1	0
Field Goals Attempted	34	33
Field Goals Made	16	15
% Successful	47.06	45.45

Regular Season 11-2-1

Date	GB		OPP	Att.
9/15	3	Chicago Bears	10	(42,327)
9/22	31	Detroit Lions (M)	10	(45,912)
9/29	31	Baltimore Colts	20	(42,327)
10/6	42	Los Angeles Rams	10	(42,327)
10/13	37	at Minnesota Vikings	28	(42,567)
10/20	30	at St. Louis Cardinals	7	(32,224)
10/27	34	at Baltimore Colts	20	(60,065)
11/3	33	Pittsburgh Steelers (M)	14	(46,293)
11/10	28	Minnesota Vikings	7	(42,327)
11/17	7	at Chicago Bears	26	(49,166)
11/24	28	San Francisco 49ers (M)	10	(45,905)
11/28	13	at Detroit Lions	13	(54,016)
12/7	31	at Los Angeles Rams	14	(52,357)
12/14	21	at San Francisco 49ers	17	(31,031)

Score By Periods

	1	2	3	4	Total
Packers	66	97	92	114	369
Opponents	47	47	44	68	206

INDIVIDUAL STATISTICS

Rushing

	Att	Yds	Avg	LG	TD
J. Taylor	248	1,018	4.1	t40	9
T. Moore	132	658	5.0	t77	6
E. Pitts	54	212	3.9	t34	5
Gros	48	203	4.2	t19	2
Starr	13	116	8.9	20	0
Roach	3	31	10.3	22	0
Carpenter	2	8	4.0	5	0
Mestnik	1	4	4.0	4	0
J. Norton	2	0	0.0	4	0
Bratkowski	1	-2	-2.0	-2	0
Packers	**504**	**2,248**	**4.5**	**177**	**22**
Opponents	428	1,586	3.7	t52	11

Receiving

	No	Yds	Avg	LG	TD
Dowler	53	901	17.0	t53	6
McGee	39	749	19.2	64	6
R. Kramer	32	537	16.8	49	4
T. Moore	23	237	10.3	t45	2
J. Taylor	13	68	5.2	t27	1
E. Pitts	9	54	6.0	21	1
Fleming	7	132	18.9	33	2
Gros	1	19	19.0	19	0
Carpenter	1	12	12.0	12	0
Jeter	1	2	2.0	2	0
Packers	**179**	**2,711**	**15.1**	**64**	**22**
Opponents	180	2,340	13.0	62	9

Passing

	Att	Com	Yds	Pct	TD	In	Tk/Yds	Rate
Starr	244	132	1,855	54.1	15	10	11/109	82.3
Roach	84	38	620	45.2	4	8	7/53	46.8
T. Moore	4	3	99	75.0	1	0	1/6	—
Bratkowski	11	4	96	36.4	1	3	0/0	59.5
E. Pitts	2	2	41	100.0	1	0	0/0	—
J. Taylor	0	0	0	0.0	0	0	1/10	—
Packers	**345**	**179**	**2,711**	**51.9**	**22**	**21**	**20/178**	**74.0**
Opponents	378	180	2,340	47.6	9	22	39/327	51.2

Punting

	No	Yds	Avg	Net	TB	In20	LG	HB
J. Norton	51	2,279	44.7	39.2	3	12	61	0
Packers	**51**	**2,279**	**44.7**	**39.2**	**3**	**12**	**61**	**0**
Opponents	59	2,558	43.4	38.1	4	19	68	0

Kickoff Returns

	No	Yds	Avg	LG	TD
Adderley	20	597	29.9	t98	1
Gros	17	430	25.3	51	0
Carpenter	5	75	15.0	24	0
Wood	1	20	20.0	20	0
Fleming	1	0	0.0	0	0
J. Kramer	1	0	0.0	0	0
Mestnik	1	0	0.0	0	0
Packers	**46**	**1,122**	**24.4**	**t98**	**1**
Opponents	69	1,331	19.3	93	0

Punt Returns

	No	Yds	Avg	FC	LG	TD
Wood	19	169	8.9	9	41	0
E. Pitts	7	60	8.6	7	20	0
Packers	**26**	**229**	**8.8**	**16**	**41**	**0**
Opponents	29	220	7.6	10	32	0

Interceptions

	No	Yds	Avg	LG	TD
Adderley	5	86	17.2	35	0
Wood	5	67	13.4	22	0
Whittenton	4	90	22.5	33	0
Gremminger	3	25	8.3	16	0
Nitschke	2	8	4.0	5	0
Currie	1	23	23.0	23	0
Forester	1	13	13.0	13	0
Hanner	1	0	0.0	0	0
Packers	**22**	**312**	**14.2**	**35**	**0**
Opponents	21	297	14.1	t47	1

Scoring

	TDr	TDp	TDrt	PAT	FG	S	TP
J. Kramer	0	0	0	43/46	16/34	0	91
J. Taylor	9	1	0	0/0	0/0	0	60
T. Moore	6	2	0	0/0	0/0	0	48
Dowler	0	6	0	0/0	0/0	0	36
McGee	0	6	0	0/0	0/0	0	36
E. Pitts	5	1	0	0/0	0/0	0	36
R. Kramer	0	4	0	0/0	0/0	0	24
Fleming	0	2	0	0/0	0/0	0	12
Gros	2	0	0	0/0	0/0	0	12
Adderley	0	0	1	0/0	0/0	0	6
Gremminger	0	0	1	0/0	0/0	0	6
W. Davis	0	0	0	0/0	0/0	1	2
Packers	**22**	**22**	**2**	**43/46**	**16/34**	**1**	**369**
Opponents	11	9	3	23/23	15/33	0	206

Fumbles

	Fum	Ow	Op	Yds	Tot
Adderley	1	0	0	0	0
L. Aldridge	0	0	1	0	1
Carpenter	0	0	1	0	1
Currie	0	0	1	0	1
W. Davis	0	0	4	10	4
Dowler	4	0	0	0	0
Fleming	1	0	0	0	1
Forester	0	0	2	0	2
Gregg	2	2	0	0	2
Gremminger	0	0	1	0	1
Gros	6	1	0	0	1
H. Jordan	0	0	4	0	4
R. Kramer	1	1	0	0	1
Mestnik	0	0	1	0	1
T. Moore	2	0	0	0	0
Nitschke	1	1	0	0	1
E. Pitts	2	0	0	0	0
Roach	2	0	0	0	1
Starr	5	3	0	0	3
J. Taylor	5	1	0	0	0
Whittenton	0	0	1	0	1
Wood	0	0	4	0	4
Packers	**30**	**10**	**20**	**10**	**30**

NFL STANDINGS

Western Conference

	W	L	T	Pct	PF	PA
Chicago Bears	11	1	2	917	301	144
Green Bay Packers	**11**	**2**	**1**	**846**	**369**	**206**
Baltimore Colts	8	6	0	571	316	285
Detroit Lions	5	8	1	385	326	265
Minnesota Vikings	5	8	1	385	309	390
Los Angeles Rams	5	9	0	357	210	350
San Francisco 49ers	2	12	0	143	198	391

Eastern Conference

	W	L	T	Pct	PF	PA
New York Giants	11	3	0	786	448	280
Cleveland Browns	10	4	0	714	343	262
St. Louis Cardinals	9	5	0	643	341	283
Pittsburgh Steelers	7	4	3	636	321	295
Dallas Cowboys	4	10	0	286	305	378
Washington Redskins	3	11	0	214	279	398
Philadelphia Eagles	2	10	2	167	242	381

ROSTER

No	Name	Pos	Ht	Wt	DOB	College	G
26	Adderley, Herb	CB	6-1	210	06/08/39	Michigan State	14
62	Aldridge, Lionel	DE	6-4	245	02/18/41	Utah State	14
82	Barrett, Jan	E	6-3	230	11/13/39	Fresno State	3
12	Bratkowski, Zeke	QB	6-3	200	10/20/31	Georgia	2
33	Carpenter, Lew	FB	6-2	215	01/12/32	Arkansas	14
58	Currie, Dan	LB	6-3	240	06/27/35	Michigan State	14
87	Davis, Willie	DE	6-3	245	07/24/34	Grambling	14
86	Dowler, Boyd	E	6-5	225	10/18/37	Colorado	14
81	Fleming, Marv	TE	6-4	230	01/02/42	Utah	14
71	Forester, Bill	LB	6-3	240	08/09/32	SMU	14
75	Gregg, Alvis (Forrest)	T	6-4	250	10/18/33	SMU	14
46	Gremminger, Hank	DB	6-1	200	09/01/33	Baylor	14
67	Grimm, Dan	G	6-3	245	02/07/41	Colorado	14
40	Gros, Earl	FB	6-3	230	08/29/40	Louisiana	13
79	Hanner, Joel (Dave)	DT	6-2	260	05/20/30	Arkansas	14
83	Henry, Urban	DE-DT	6-4	265	06/07/35	Georgia Tech	14
65	Holler, Ed	LB	6-2	235	01/23/40	South Carolina	2
53	Iman, Ken	C	6-1	230	02/08/39	Southeast Missouri State	14
21	Jeter, Bob	E	6-1	205	05/09/37	Iowa	13
74	Jordan, Henry	DT	6-3	250	01/26/35	Virginia	14
77	Kostelnik, Ron	DT	6-4	260	01/14/40	Cincinnati	13
64	Kramer, Jerry	G	6-3	245	01/23/36	Idaho	14
88	Kramer, Ron	E	6-3	240	06/24/35	Michigan	12
78	Masters, Norm	T	6-2	250	09/19/33	Michigan State	14
85	McGee, Max	E	6-3	205	07/16/32	Tulane	14
35	Mestnik, Frank	FB	6-2	220	02/23/38	Marquette	11
25	Moore, Tom	HB	6-2	210	07/17/38	Vanderbilt	12
66	Nitschke, Ray	LB	6-3	240	12/29/36	Illinois	12
23	Norton, Jerry	P	5-11	195	05/16/31	SMU	14
22	Pitts, Elijah	HB	6-1	205	02/03/39	Philander Smith	14
51	Ringo, Jim	C	6-1	235	11/21/32	Syracuse	14
10	Roach, John	QB	6-4	200	03/26/33	SMU	8
89	Robinson, Dave	LB	6-3	245	05/03/41	Penn State	14
76	Skoronski, Bob	T	6-3	250	03/05/34	Indiana	14
15	Starr, Bryan (Bart)	QB	6-1	200	01/09/34	Alabama	13
31	Taylor, Jim	FB	6-0	215	09/20/35	LSU	14
63	Thurston, Fred (Fuzzy)	G	6-1	245	05/07/35	Valparaiso	14
47	Whittenton, Jesse	DB	6-0	195	05/09/34	Texas-El Paso	14
29	Williams, Howard	DB	6-1	190	12/04/37	Howard J.C.	7
24	Wood, Willie	DB	5-10	190	12/23/36	USC	14

DRAFT

Rnd	Name	Pos	Ht	Wt	College
1	Dave Robinson	DE	6-3	245	Penn State
2	Tom Brown	DB	6-1	195	Maryland
*3a	Dennis Claridge	QB	6-3	210	Nebraska
	(Choice from Steelers for Tom Bettis)				
3b	Tony Liscio	T	6-4	250	Tulsa
4a	Lionel Aldridge	G	6-4	245	Utah State
	(Choice from Giants for Paul Dudley)				
4b	Carlton Simons	C	6-2	230	Stanford
*5a	Jack Cverko	G	6-1	240	Northwestern
	(Choice from Redskins for Ben Davidson)				
5b	Dan Grimm	T	6-3	240	Colorado
*6a	John Simmons	E	6-3	205	Tulsa
	(Choice from Cowboys)				
6b	Jan Barrett	E	6-3	230	Fresno State
7a	Gary Kroner	HB	6-1	198	Wisconsin
	(Choice from Browns for Ernie Green)				
7b	Olin Hill	T	6-4	240	Furman
	(Choice from Steelers)				

Rnd	Name	Pos	Ht	Wt	College
*7c	Turnley Todd	LB	6-2	225	Virginia
8a	Keith Kinderman	HB	6-0	210	Florida State
	(Choice from Cowboys)				
8b	Louis Rettino	FB	6-1	225	Villanova
*9	Bill Freeman	T	6-4	225	Miss. Southern
10	Earl McQuiston	G	6-2	240	Iowa
11	Marv Fleming	E	6-4	230	Utah
12	Daryle Lamonica	QB	6-2	205	Notre Dame
*13	Bill Kellum	T	6-4	237	Tulane
14	Ed Holler	LB	6-2	235	South Carolina
*15	Gene Breen	LB	6-2	215	Virginia Tech
16	Coolidge Hunt	FB	6-2	215	Texas Tech
17	Thurman Walker	E	6-2	200	Illinois
18	Louis Hernandez	G	6-1	255	Texas-El Paso
*19	Herman Hamp	HB	5-11	195	Fresno State
20	Bobby Brezina	HB	6-1	205	Houston

* denotes futures

FRONT ROW: (L–R) Property Manager Gerald (Dad) Braisher, 62 Lionel Aldridge, 21 Bob Jeter, 81 Marv Fleming, 67 Dan Grimm, 82 Jan Barrett, 89 Dave Robinson, Trainer Carl (Bud) Jorgensen.
SECOND ROW: (L–R) 26 Herb Adderley, 74 Henry Jordan, 77 Ron Kostelnik, 51 Jim Ringo, 71 Bill Forester, 58 Dan Currie, 23 Jerry Norton, 46 Hank Gremminger, 47 Jesse Whittenton, 40 Earl Gros, 24 Willie Wood.
THIRD ROW: (L–R) 76 Bob Skoronski, 15 Bart Starr, 78 Norm Masters, 53 Ken Iman, 87 Willie Davis, 63 Fred (Fuzzy) Thurston, 64 Jerry Kramer, 10 John Roach, 33 Lew Carpenter, 25 Tom Moore.
BACK ROW: (L–R) 29 Howard Williams, 22 Elijah Pitts, 66 Ray Nitschke, 75 Forrest Gregg, 86 Boyd Dowler, 31 Jim Taylor, 88 Ron Kramer, 83 Urban Henry, 79 Dave Hanner, 85 Max McGee.

Mediocre, a word not found in Vince Lombardi's vocabulary, summed up the Packers' first half of 1964. Two one-point losses, nagging injuries, the loss of Jerry Kramer and Paul Hornung's kicking struggles left Green Bay at 3-4 and only a game out of last place at mid-season.

Emotions boiled over in Week 7 after the Packers blew a 17-0 lead against the Rams. After the 27-17 loss, Lombardi closed the locker room to all but himself and his players. After seven minutes he permitted his assistant coaches, trainers, and equipment men to enter. He didn't let the media in until another three minutes had passed.

"I don't think Coach Lombardi has ever said anything to this ball club that didn't need saying," said defensive end Willie Davis when asked what took place.

Green Bay turned itself around in its last seven games. It posted a 5-1-1 record to close the season and finished in a second place tie with the Vikings at 8-5-1.

Even in a down year, Green Bay was not to be taken lightly. It owned the best defense—and best pass defense—in the circuit. The club forced 34 fumbles and recovered a league-high 25. Jim Taylor, Hornung, and Tom Moore fueled the NFL's No. 1 ground game and Bart Starr refused to throw an interception in the last 11 games.

Hornung was reinstated, but his kicking left much to be desired. The halfback botched extra point tries in one-point losses to the Colts and Vikings. He missed four field goals in a 10-point setback in San Francisco. His worst performance was an 0-for-5 display in the rematch with Baltimore that prompted Lombardi to hire Ben Agajanian (a Packer in 1961) to tutor the beleaguered kicker.

Jerry Kramer missed most of the year. He pulled himself out of the lineup early in the first quarter of Week 2 and never returned. Exploratory surgery after the game revealed an abscess beneath his abdomen. When his condition worsened, he had more surgery. Three wooden splinters, there since a childhood accident years ago, were removed. Kramer, who had come back before from numerous injuries, was fortunate to escape with his life.

"We'll sink or swim with Hornung," said Lombardi before the season began. But Hornung and his kicking woes were not solely to blame for the subpar season. In the first loss to the Colts, Starr threw two fourth-quarter interceptions in Baltimore territory. In the Minnesota setback, the defense let the Vikings waltz 61 yards in the final two minutes to set up the winning field goal. In the rematch in Baltimore, a pass interference call against Herb Adderley set up Lenny Moore's game-winning touchdown run.

Green Bay gained revenge over the Bears 23-12 in the opener. Chicago managed just 130 total yards and Hornung booted a 52-yard field goal on a free kick just before halftime.

In Week 2, Starr, who had not been intercepted in more than 150 pass attempts, threw three interceptions against Baltimore in a 21-20 loss.

Green Bay then edged the Lions 14-10. Starr re-injured the shoulder he had hurt in the preseason and missed most of the second half. Hank Gremminger's recovery of a Pat Studstill fumble in the closing minutes sealed the victory.

In Week 4, the Vikings' Fred Cox connected on a 27-yard field goal with 18 seconds left to top the Packers 24-23. Fran Tarkenton's 44-yard pass to Gordy Smith overcame a fourth-and-22 and set up Cox's game-winner.

In Week 6, Green Bay absorbed a 24-21 loss in Baltimore. The Packers then squandered a 17-point lead and fell to the Rams 27-17 to close the first half of the season.

"We'll just have to regroup our forces and our thoughts. I think we can come out of it," Lombardi said.

Green Bay rolled over Minnesota 42-13 and Detroit 30-7. Starr threw four touchdown passes in the first win and Taylor blasted for 145 yards rushing in the second.

The 49ers halted the Packers' 24-14 in Kezar Stadium. They knocked Starr from the game in the second quarter with a concussion. The loss knocked Green Bay (5-5) four games behind the Colts (9-1) with four games to play.

Despite being all but eliminated from the playoff race, the Packers triumphed in three of their final four contests. The lone exception was a 24-24 with the Rams.

Because Green Bay (8-5-1) had outscored Minnesota (8-5-1) in head-to-head competition, it earned a spot in the Playoff Bowl against the Cardinals.

"We don't put as much emphasis on second place as some teams do," said an unimpressed Lombardi.

MISSING IN ACTION

Commissioner Pete Rozelle reinstated Paul Hornung for the 1964 season. The emotional lift that move gave the Packers was offset by the kicking struggles the halfback endured throughout the season.

Except when injured, Hornung had been Green Bay's kicker since 1958. In that time, he had missed just two extra point attempts and owned a field goal percentage of better than 55 percent.

In 1964, Hornung missed two extra points and failed to connect on 26 of his 38 field goal attempts. No other kicker in NFL history missed 26 field goal tries in a single season.

Below is a list of kickers who missed the most field goal attempts in a single season:

No.	Kicker	Att./Made
26	Paul Hornung, 1963	12/38
23	John Aveni, 1961	5/28
	Bruce Gossett, 1967	20/43
21	Tommy Davis, 1963	10/31
	Bruce Gossett, 1966	28/49
	Roy Gerela, 1969	19/40

TEAM STATISTICS

	GB	OPP
First Downs	250	197
Rushing	133	95
Passing	106	91
Penalty	11	11
Rushes	495	417
Yards Gained	2,276	1,532
Average Gain	4.60	3.67
Average Yards per Game	162.6	109.4
Passes Attempted	321	318
Completed	186	173
% Completed	57.94	54.40
Total Yards Gained	2,474	1,980
Times Sacked	47	45
Yards Lost	369	333
Net Yards Gained	2,105	1,647
Yards Gained per Completion	13.30	11.45
Net Yards per Attempt	5.72	4.54
Average Net Yards per Game	150.4	117.6
Combined Net Yards Gained	4,381	3,179
Total Plays	863	780
Average Yards per Play	5.08	4.08
Average Net Yards per Game	312.9	227.1
Third Down Efficiency	66/177	63/175
Percentage	37.29	36.00
Fourth Down Efficiency	5/7	4/8
Percentage	71.43	50.00
Intercepted By	16	6
Yards Returned	263	58
Returned for TD	1	0
Punts	56	72
Yards Punted	2,365	3,131
Average Yards per Punt	42.23	43.49
Punt Returns	34	31
Yards Returned	443	397
Average Yards per Return	13.03	12.81
Returned for TD	1	2
Kickoff Returns	45	60
Yards Returned	1,160	1,320
Average Yards per Return	25.78	22.00
Returned for TD	0	0
Penalties	50	56
Yards Penalized	576	521
Fumbles	25	34
Lost	17	25
Own Recovered for Touchdown	1	0
Opponent's Recovered by	25	17
Opponent's Recovered for Touchdown	2	1
Total Points Scored	342	245
Total Touchdowns	44	30
Touchdowns Rushing	23	15
Touchdowns Passing	16	11
Touchdowns on Returns & Recoveries	5	4
Extra Points	42	29
Safeties	0	0
Field Goals Attempted	39	23
Field Goals Made	12	12
% Successful	30.77	52.17

Regular Season   8-5-1

Date	GB		OPP	Att.
9/13	23	Chicago Bears	12	(42,327)
9/20	20	Baltimore Colts	21	(42,327)
9/28	14	at Detroit Lions	10	(59,203)
10/4	23	Minnesota Vikings	24	(42,327)
10/11	24	San Francisco 49ers (M)	14	(47,380)
10/18	21	at Baltimore Colts	24	(60,213)
10/25	17	Los Angeles Rams (M)	27	(46,617)
11/1	42	at Minnesota Vikings	13	(44,278)
11/8	30	Detroit Lions	7	(42,327)
11/15	14	at San Francisco 49ers	24	(38,483)
11/22	28	Cleveland Browns (M)	21	(48,065)
11/29	45	at Dallas Cowboys	21	(44,975)
12/5	17	at Chicago Bears	3	(43,636)
12/13	24	at Los Angeles Rams	24	(40,735)

Score By Periods

	1	2	3	4	Total
Packers	63	132	65	82	342
Opponents	49	92	57	47	245

INDIVIDUAL STATISTICS

Rushing

	Att	Yds	Avg	LG	TD
J. Taylor	235	1,169	5.0	t84	12
Hornung	103	415	4.0	40	5
T. Moore	102	371	3.6	35	2
Starr	24	165	6.9	28	3
E. Pitts	27	127	4.7	27	1
J. Norton	1	24	24.0	24	0
Crutcher	1	5	5.0	5	0
Bratkowski	2	0	0.0	0	0
Packers	**495**	**2,276**	**4.6**	**184**	**23**
Opponents	417	1,532	3.7	t53	11

Receiving

	No	Yds	Avg	LG	TD
Dowler	45	623	13.8	t50	5
J. Taylor	38	354	9.3	t35	3
R. Kramer	34	551	16.2	55	0
McGee	31	592	19.1	55	6
T. Moore	17	140	8.2	t33	2
Hornung	9	98	10.9	40	0
E. Pitts	6	38	6.3	22	0
Fleming	4	36	9.0	10	0
Jeter	1	23	23.0	23	0
Long	1	19	19.0	19	0
Packers	**186**	**2,474**	**13.3**	**55**	**16**
Opponents	173	1,980	11.4	t95	11

Passing

	Att	Com	Yds	Pct	TD	In	Tk/Yds	Rate
Starr	272	163	2,144	59.9	15	4	42/323	97.1
Bratkowski	36	19	277	52.8	1	1	5/46	75.8
Hornung	10	3	25	30.0	0	1	0/0	0.0
T. Moore	3	1	28	33.3	0	0	0/0	—
Packers	**321**	**186**	**2,474**	**57.9**	**16**	**6**	**47/369**	**91.3**
Opponents	318	173	1,980	54.4	11	16	45/333	63.9

Punting

	No	Yds	Avg	Net	TB	In20	LG	HB
J. Norton	56	2,365	42.2	33.0	6	13	61	0
Packers	**56**	**2,365**	**42.2**	**33.0**	**6**	**13**	**61**	**0**
Opponents	72	3,131	43.5	36.2	4	22	66	0

Kickoff Returns

	No	Yds	Avg	LG	TD
Adderley	19	508	26.7	43	0
T. Moore	16	431	26.9	55	0
T. Brown	7	167	23.9	34	0
Crutcher	2	54	27.0	37	0
Caffey	1	0	0.0	0	0
Packers	**45**	**1,160**	**25.8**	**55**	**0**
Opponents	60	1,320	22.0	53	0

Punt Returns

	No	Yds	Avg	FC	LG	TD
Wood	19	252	13.3	11	64	0
E. Pitts	15	191	12.7	7	t65	1
Packers	**34**	**443**	**13.0**	**18**	**t65**	**1**
Opponents	31	397	12.8	9	t70	2

Interceptions

	No	Yds	Avg	LG	TD
Adderley	4	56	14.0	35	0
Wood	3	73	24.3	t42	1
Nitschke	2	36	18.0	18	0
Currie	2	11	5.5	10	0
Caffey	1	44	44.0	44	0
T. Brown	1	30	30.0	30	0
Gremminger	1	13	13.0	13	0
Hart	1	0	0.0	0	0
Whittenton	1	0	0.0	0	0
Packers	**16**	**263**	**16.4**	**44**	**1**
Opponents	6	58	9.7	23	0

Scoring

	TDr	TDp	TDrt	PAT	FG	S	TP
Hornung	5	0	0	41/43	12/38	0	107
J. Taylor	12	3	0	0/0	0/0	0	90
McGee	0	6	1	0/0	0/0	0	42
Dowler	0	5	0	0/0	0/0	0	30
T. Moore	2	2	0	0/0	0/0	0	24
Starr	3	0	0	0/0	0/0	0	18
E. Pitts	1	0	1	0/0	0/0	0	12
Wood	0	0	1	1/1	0/1	0	7
L. Aldridge	0	0	1	0/0	0/0	0	6
H. Jordan	0	0	1	0/0	0/0	0	6
Packers	**23**	**16**	**5**	**42/44**	**12/39**	**0**	**342**
Opponents	15	11	4	29/30	12/23	0	245

Fumbles

	Fum	Ow	Op	Yds	Tot
Adderley	1	0	1	18	1
L. Aldridge	0	0	5	29	5
Bowman	0	1	0	0	1
Bratkowski	2	1	0	0	1
Caffey	0	0	1	0	1
Currie	0	0	1	0	1
W. Davis	0	0	2	0	2
Dowler	1	0	0	0	0
Gremminger	0	0	2	0	2
Hanner	0	0	1	0	1
Hart	0	0	1	0	1
Hornung	4	1	0	0	1
H. Jordan	0	0	3	60	3
Kostelnik	0	0	3	0	3
R. Kramer	1	0	0	0	0
Masters	0	1	0	0	1
McDowell	0	0	1	0	1
McGee	1	1	0	27	1
Nitschke	0	0	2	0	2
E. Pitts	1	0	1	0	1
Starr	7	2	0	0	0
J. Taylor	6	0	0	0	0
Wood	1	0	1	0	2
Packers	**25**	**8**	**25**	**134**	**33**

NFL STANDINGS

Western Conference

	W	L	T	Pct	PF	PA
Baltimore Colts	12	2	0	.857	428	225
Green Bay Packers	8	5	1	.615	342	245
Minnesota Vikings	8	5	1	.615	355	296
Detroit Lions	7	5	2	.583	280	260
Los Angeles Rams	5	7	2	.417	283	339
Chicago Bears	5	9	0	.357	260	379
San Francisco 49ers	4	10	0	.286	236	330

Eastern Conference

	W	L	T	Pct	PF	PA
Cleveland Browns	10	3	1	.769	415	293
St. Louis Cardinals	9	3	2	.750	357	331
Philadelphia Eagles	6	8	0	.429	312	313
Washington Redskins	6	8	0	.429	307	305
Dallas Cowboys	5	8	1	.385	250	289
Pittsburgh Steelers	5	9	0	.357	253	315
New York Giants	2	10	2	.167	241	399

1964

ROSTER

No	Name	Pos	Ht	Wt	DOB	College	G
26	Adderley, Herb	CB	6-1	210	06/08/39	Michigan State	13
82	Aldridge, Lionel	DE	6-4	245	02/18/41	Utah State	14
57	Bowman, Ken	C	6-3	230	12/15/42	Wisconsin	14
12	Bratkowski, Zeke	QB	6-3	200	10/20/31	Georgia	5
61	Breen, Gene	LB	6-2	230	06/21/41	Virginia Tech	6
40	Brown, Tom	DB	6-1	190	12/12/40	Maryland	14
60	Caffey, Lee Roy	LB	6-3	250	06/03/41	Texas A&M	14
37	Crutcher, Tommy	LB	6-3	230	08/10/41	TCU	14
58	Currie, Dan	LB	6-3	240	06/27/35	Michigan State	14
87	Davis, Willie	DE	6-3	245	07/24/34	Grambling	14
86	Dowler, Boyd	WR	6-5	225	10/18/37	Colorado	14
81	Fleming, Marv	TE	6-4	235	01/02/42	Utah	14
75	Gregg, Alvis (Forrest)	T	6-4	250	10/18/33	SMU	14
46	Gremminger, Hank	DB	6-1	200	09/01/33	Baylor	13
67	Grimm, Dan	G	6-3	245	02/07/41	Colorado	14
79	Hanner, Joel (Dave)	DT	6-2	260	05/20/30	Arkansas	11
43	Hart, Doug	DB	6-0	190	06/03/39	Arlington State	14
5	Hornung, Paul	HB	6-2	215	12/23/35	Notre Dame	14
21	Jeter, Bob	WR	6-1	205	05/09/37	Iowa	13
74	Jordan, Henry	DT	6-3	250	01/26/35	Virginia	12
77	Kostelnik, Ron	DT	6-4	260	01/14/40	Cincinnati	14
64	Kramer, Jerry	G	6-3	245	01/23/36	Idaho	2
88	Kramer, Ron	E	6-3	240	06/24/35	Michigan	14
80	Long, Bob	WR	6-3	190	06/16/42	Wichita	7
78	Masters, Norm	T	6-2	250	09/19/33	Michigan State	14
73	McDowell, John	G-T	6-3	260	02/12/42	St. John's (MN)	12
85	McGee, Max	E	6-3	205	07/16/32	Tulane	13
25	Moore, Tom	HB	6-2	210	07/17/38	Vanderbilt	14
66	Nitschke, Ray	LB	6-3	240	12/29/36	Illinois	14
23	Norton, Jerry	P	5-11	195	05/16/31	SMU	14
22	Pitts, Elijah	HB	6-1	205	02/03/39	Philander Smith	14
89	Robinson, Dave	LB	6-3	245	05/03/41	Penn State	11
76	Skoronski, Bob	T	6-3	250	03/05/34	Indiana	14
15	Starr, Bryan (Bart)	QB	6-1	200	01/09/34	Alabama	14
31	Taylor, Jim	FB	6-0	215	09/20/35	LSU	13
63	Thurston, Fred (Fuzzy)	G	6-1	245	05/07/35	Valparaiso	11
71	Voss, Lloyd	T	6-4	260	02/13/42	Nebraska	14
47	Whittenton, Jesse	DB	6-0	195	05/09/34	Texas-El Paso	14
24	Wood, Willie	DB	5-10	190	12/23/36	USC	14
72	Wright, Steve	T	6-6	250	07/18/42	Alabama	14

DRAFT

Rnd	Name	Pos	Ht	Wt	College
1	Lloyd Voss	T	6-4	245	Nebraska
2	Jon Morris	C	6-3	228	Holy Cross
3a	Ode Burrell (Choice from Colts)	HB	6-0	180	Mississippi State
3b	Joe O'Donnell (Choice from Giants as part of Bill Quinlan, John Symank deal)	G	6-2	250	Michigan
3c	Tommy Crutcher	LB	6-3	230	TCU
4a	Bob Long (Choice from Eagles for Ed Blaine)	WR	6-3	190	Wichita
*4b	Paul Costa	HB	6-4	232	Notre Dame
5a	Duke Carlisle (Choice from Cowboys for Gary Barnes)	HB	6-1	180	Texas
5b	Steve Wright	T	6-6	250	Alabama
6	(Choice to Cowboys for Jerry Norton)				
*7	Dick Herzing	T	6-4	250	Drake

Rnd	Name	Pos	Ht	Wt	College
8	Ken Bowman	C	6-3	230	Wisconsin
9	John McDowell	T	6-3	260	St. John's (MN)
*10	Allen Jacobs	HB	6-1	210	Utah
11	Jack Peterson	T	6-6	275	Omaha
12	Dwaine Bean	HB	6-0	205	Texas State
13	Jack Mauro	T	6-2	247	Northern Michigan
14	Tom O'Grady	WR	6-4	205	Northwestern
*15	Alex Zenko	T	6-5	250	Kent State
*16	Andrew Ireland	HB	6-1	195	Utah
17	Leonard St. Jean	E	6-0	240	Northern Michigan
18	Mike Hicks	G	6-3	235	Marshall
19	John Baker	E	6-4	235	Virginia Union
*20	Bill Curry	C	6-2	225	Georgia Tech
*	denotes futures				

1964 GREEN BAY PACKERS

FRONT ROW: (L-R) 82 Lionel Aldridge, 78 Norm Masters, 23 Jerry Norton, 43 Doug Hart, 46 Hank Gremminger, 76 Bob Skoronski, 37 Tommy Crutcher, 47 Jesse Whittenton, 21 Bob Jeter, 81 Marv Fleming.

SECOND ROW: (L-R) Equipment Manager Gerald (Dad) Braisher, Jerry Kramer, 89 Dave Robinson, 15 Bart Starr, 22 Elijah Pitts, 58 Dan Currie, 87 Willie Davis, 74 Henry Jordan, 25 Tom Moore, 26 Herb Adderley, 24 Willie Wood, Trainer Carl (Bud) Jorgensen.

THIRD ROW: (L-R) Assistant Trainer Domenic Gentile, 73 John McDowell, 40 Tom Brown, 57 Ken Bowman, 66 Ray Nitschke, 63 Fred (Fuzzy) Thurston, 67 Dan Grimm, 60 Lee Roy Caffey, 79 Dave Hanner, 72 Steve Wright, 80 Bob Long.

BACK ROW: (L-R) 10 Dennis Claridge, 71 Lloyd Voss, 12 Zeke Bratkowski, 77 Ron Kostelnik, 86 Boyd Dowler, 75 Forrest Gregg, 31 Jim Taylor, 88 Ron Kramer, 5 Paul Hornung, 85 Max McGee.

"I think I marked this team pretty well," said Vince Lombardi after the Packers of 1965 wrapped up their first championship in three years. "I said this may not be the best team I've had, but it has the most character."

Lombardi might well have tossed in resilient and resourceful among the adjectives he used to describe his team. Often outgained and occasionally outplayed, the Packers relied on savvy and experience to stay in the Western Conference race. During a four-game stretch in midseason, the Packers scored just 36 points, yet managed to post wins over Dallas and the Rams.

The running game, so vital to Lombardi's offense, produced its worst showing since the days of Scooter McLean. Jim Taylor failed to gain 1,000 yards for the first time since 1959. Paul Hornung added another 299, but the team's average per gain of 3.4 yards was its lowest since 1946.

With its running attack sputtering, the Packers' offense finished 12th, ahead of only the Lions and Steelers. The team was outgained in nine of its 14 games, yet managed to win five of those and tie another.

Defensively, Green Bay ranked third. It boasted the league's top pass defense and recorded 44 sacks (third best) and 27 interceptions (tied for first).

Securing the conference crown was no cakewalk. The team lost a key game to the lowly Rams, righted itself in a classic showdown in Baltimore, then tied the 49ers on the season's final weekend when a win would have given them the title outright. Instead, the Packers (10-3-1) had to engage the Colts (10-3-1) for a third time, in a playoff game that Green Bay won 13-10 in overtime.

Frustrated by the kicking game in 1964, Lombardi obtained Don Chandler from the Giants. Chandler was successful on 17 of 26 field goal attempts, including a last-second boot that beat the Rams 6-3 in Week 9.

Green Bay opened on the road for the first time since 1948 and ripped the Steelers 41-9. Bart Starr completed 17 of 23 passes for 226 yards and two scores.

The Packers edged the Colts 20-17 in Week 2 despite being outgained by 125 yards. Green Bay turned Baltimore turnovers into 17 points. Max McGee scored the game-winning touchdown on a 37-yard pass from Zeke Bratkowski with 2:48 left. Herb Adderley recovered Tom Matte's fumble on the Colts' final drive.

Green Bay then beat the Bears 23-14. Max McGee and Bob Long started at split end and flanker, respectively, because of injuries to Boyd Dowler and Carroll Dale.

The Packers won their fourth straight by downing the 49ers 27-10. Starr, who threw two touchdown passes, was intercepted for the first time in more than a year. Jim Johnson got the steal, ending Starr's run of 294 passes attempted without an interception.

The quarterback played a major role in the team's comeback at Tiger Stadium a week later. Down 21-3 at halftime, Starr threw three touchdown passes in the third quarter to lead Green Bay to a 31-21 win over the Lions.

The Packers then slipped into an offensive funk that lasted four weeks. In that time, Green Bay passers were sacked 23 times, completed only one pass of more than 25 yards, and failed to throw even one touchdown pass.

The Packers broke loose in a 38-13 win in Minnesota.

In Week 11, the 1-9 Rams surprised Green Bay 21-10. Roman Gabriel passed for 255 yards and Los Angeles allowed the Packers just 22 yards rushing.

The Packers (8-3) trailed the Colts (9-1-1) and needed Baltimore to lose at least twice. The resurgent Bears couldn't have been more helpful. While the Packers got past the Vikings 24-19, Chicago blanked the Colts 13-0 and knocked Johnny Unitas out for the rest of the season.

On Dec. 12, Hornung led Green Bay past Baltimore 42-27 by scoring a team-record five touchdowns. Hornung gained 61 yards rushing and caught touchdown passes of 50 and 65 yards.

Green Bay tied the 49ers on Dec. 19 to creat the need for the playoff game with the Colts.

In November, Lombardi signed a contract extension through January 1974 as the team addressed its future.

On June 1, the team lost a prominent figure from its past when Curly Lambeau died of a heart attack in Sturgeon Bay, Wis. In his honor, City Stadium was renamed Lambeau Field prior to the first preseason game with the Giants on Aug. 14.

WINNING ON CHARACTER (AND DEFENSE)

Green Bay won its third championship under Vince Lombardi in 1965. But unlike the two previous title-holding teams, the 1965 club had to work overtime for just about everything it got.

On Oct. 24, the Packers defeated the Cowboys 13-3 in Milwaukee despite gaining only 63 yards on 53 offensive plays. That average of 1.2 yard per play is the lowest ever in a game in which Green Bay emerged victorious.

Defense saved the day. Willie Davis and his unit sacked Craig Morton nine times and held Dallas to 192 yards. Green Bay forced five turnovers and turned them into 13 points.

The Packers won twice more when held to fewer than 200 yards.

Listed below are the lowest average gains per offensive play the Packers have had in winning efforts.

Avg.	Plays-Yds.	Date	Result
1.19	53-63	10-24-65	beat Cowboys 13-3
1.74	35-61	11-4-34	beat Redskins 10-0
2.23	71-158	10-27-46	beat Lions 10-7
2.23	57-127	9-24-78	beat Chargers 24-3

1965

TEAM STATISTICS

	GB	OPP
First Downs	201	240
Rushing	85	115
Passing	103	111
Penalty	13	14
Rushes	432	480
Yards Gained	1,488	1,988
Average Gain	3.44	4.14
Average Yards per Game	106.3	142.0
Passes Attempted	306	383
Completed	166	187
% Completed	54.25	48.83
Total Yards Gained	2,508	2,316
Times Sacked	43	44
Yards Lost	395	335
Net Yards Gained	2,113	1,981
Yards Gained per Completion	15.11	12.39
Net Yards per Attempt	6.05	4.64
Average Net Yards per Game	150.9	141.5
Combined Net Yards Gained	3,601	3,969
Total Plays	781	907
Average Yards per Play	4.61	4.38
Average Net Yards per Game	257.2	283.5
Third Down Efficiency	50/166	65/192
Percentage	30.12	33.85
Fourth Down Efficiency	6/9	6/15
Percentage	66.67	40.00
Intercepted By	27	14
Yards Returned	561	209
Returned for TD	4	1
Punts	74	60
Yards Punted	3,176	2,523
Average Yards per Punt	42.92	42.05
Punt Returns	22	36
Yards Returned	65	290
Average Yards per Return	2.95	8.06
Returned for TD	0	0
Kickoff Returns	50	52
Yards Returned	1,040	1,216
Average Yards per Return	20.80	23.38
Returned for TD	0	0
Penalties	48	67
Yards Penalized	529	677
Fumbles	18	37
Lost	12	23
Own Recovered for Touchdown	0	0
Opponent's Recovered by	23	12
Opponent's Recovered for Touchdown	1	0
Total Points Scored	316	224
Total Touchdowns	38	22
Touchdowns Rushing	14	10
Touchdowns Passing	19	11
Touchdowns on Returns & Recoveries	5	1
Extra Points	37	22
Safeties	0	2
Field Goals Attempted	26	33
Field Goals Made	17	22
% Successful	65.38	66.67

Regular Season   10-3-1

Date	GB		OPP	Att.
9/19	41	at Pittsburgh Steelers	9	(38,383)
9/26	20	Baltimore Colts (M)	17	(48,130)
10/3	23	Chicago Bears	14	(50,852)
10/10	27	San Francisco 49ers	10	(50,852)
10/17	31	at Detroit Lions	21	(56,712)
10/24	13	Dallas Cowboys (M)	3	(48,311)
10/31	10	at Chicago Bears	31	(45,664)
11/7	7	Detroit Lions	12	(50,852)
11/14	6	Los Angeles Rams (M)	3	(48,485)
11/21	38	at Minnesota Vikings	13	(47,426)
11/28	10	at Los Angeles Rams	21	(39,733)
12/5	24	Minnesota Vikings	19	(50,852)
12/12	42	at Baltimore Colts	27	(60,238)
12/19	24	at San Francisco 49ers	24	(45,710)

Postseason   2-0

Date	GB		OPP	Att.
12/26	13	Baltimore Colts (OT)	10	(50,484)
1/2	23	Cleveland Browns	12	(50,777)

Score By Periods

	1	2	3	4	Total
Packers	65	66	82	103	316
Opponents	40	85	37	62	224

INDIVIDUAL STATISTICS

Rushing

	Att	Yds	Avg	LG	TD
J. Taylor	207	734	3.5	35	4
Hornung	89	299	3.4	17	5
Starr	18	169	9.4	38	1
T. Moore	51	124	2.4	13	0
E. Pitts	54	122	2.3	12	4
Chandler	1	27	27.0	27	0
Coffey	3	12	4.0	10	0
A. Jacobs	3	5	1.7	2	0
Bratkowski	4	-1	-0.3	1	0
Claridge	2	-3	-1.5	1	0
Packers	**432**	**1,488**	**3.4**	**38**	**14**
Opponents	480	1,988	4.1	43	10

Receiving

	No	Yds	Avg	LG	TD
Dowler	44	610	13.9	t47	4
Dale	20	382	19.1	t77	2
J. Taylor	20	207	10.4	41	0
Hornung	19	336	17.7	t65	3
Fleming	14	141	10.1	t31	2
Long	13	304	23.4	t62	4
E. Pitts	11	182	16.5	t80	1
McGee	10	154	15.4	t37	1
B. Anderson	8	105	13.1	t27	1
T. Moore	7	87	12.4	t31	1
Packers	**166**	**2,508**	**15.1**	**t80**	**19**
Opponents	187	2,316	12.4	t65	11

Passing

	Att	Com	Yds	Pct	TD	In	Tk/Yds	Rate
Starr	251	140	2,055	55.8	16	9	34/303	89.0
Bratkowski	48	21	348	43.8	3	4	8/79	54.9
E. Pitts	2	1	51	50.0	0	0	0/0	—
T. Moore	2	2	22	100.0	0	0	0/0	—
Hornung	2	1	19	50.0	0	1	1/13	—
Claridge	1	1	13	100.0	0	0	0/0	—
Packers	**306**	**166**	**2,508**	**54.2**	**19**	**14**	**43/395**	**83.1**
Opponents	383	187	2,316	48.8	11	27	44/335	48.2

Punting

	No	Yds	Avg	Net	TB	In20	LG	HB
Chandler	74	3,176	42.9	35.5	13	9	90	0
Packers	**74**	**3,176**	**42.9**	**35.5**	**13**	**9**	**90**	**0**
Opponents	60	2,523	42.1	39.0	6	15	63	0

Kickoff Returns

	No	Yds	Avg	LG	TD
E. Pitts	20	396	19.8	29	0
T. Moore	15	361	24.1	52	0
Adderley	10	221	22.1	33	0
Crutcher	3	53	17.7	21	0
Coffey	1	9	9.0	9	0
Grimm	1	0	0.0	0	0
Packers	**50**	**1,040**	**20.8**	**52**	**0**
Opponents	52	1,216	23.4	68	0

Punt Returns

	No	Yds	Avg	FC	LG	TD
Wood	13	38	2.9	10	14	0
E. Pitts	8	27	3.4	6	12	0
Adderley	1	0	0.0	0	0	0
T. Brown	0	0	0.0	1	0	0
Packers	**22**	**65**	**3.0**	**17**	**14**	**0**
Opponents	36	290	8.1	11	62	0

Interceptions

	No	Yds	Avg	LG	TD
Adderley	6	175	29.2	t44	3
Wood	6	65	10.8	28	0
Hart	4	29	7.3	24	0
D. Robinson	3	141	47.0	87	0
T. Brown	3	42	14.0	27	0
Caffey	1	42	42.0	42	1
W. Davis	1	21	21.0	21	0
Jeter	1	21	21.0	21	0
Nitschke	1	21	21.0	21	0
Crutcher	1	4	4.0	4	0
Packers	**27**	**561**	**20.8**	**87**	**4**
Opponents	14	209	14.9	t36	1

Scoring

	TDr	TDp	TDrt	PAT	FG	S	TP
Chandler	0	0	0	37/38	17/26	0	88
Hornung	5	3	0	0/0	0/0	0	48
E. Pitts	4	1	0	0/0	0/0	0	30
Dowler	0	4	0	0/0	0/0	0	24
Long	0	4	0	0/0	0/0	0	24
J. Taylor	4	0	0	0/0	0/0	0	24
Adderley	0	0	3	0/0	0/0	0	18
Dale	0	2	0	0/0	0/0	0	12
Fleming	0	2	0	0/0	0/0	0	12
B. Anderson	0	1	0	0/0	0/0	0	6
Caffey	0	0	1	0/0	0/0	0	6
Hart	0	0	1	0/0	0/0	0	6
McGee	0	1	0	0/0	0/0	0	6
T. Moore	0	1	0	0/0	0/0	0	6
Starr	1	0	0	0/0	0/0	0	6
Packers	**14**	**19**	**5**	**37/38**	**17/26**	**0**	**316**
Opponents	10	11	1	22/22	22/33	2	224

Fumbles

	Fum	Ow	Op	Yds	Tot
Adderley	1	0	3	2	3
L. Aldridge	0	0	2	0	1
Bratkowski	1	1	0	0	1
T. Brown	0	0	1	0	1
Claridge	1	0	0	0	1
Coffey	0	0	1	0	1
Curry	0	1	0	0	1
Dale	1	0	0	0	1
W. Davis	0	0	2	0	2
Dowler	1	0	0	0	1
Gregg	0	1	0	0	1
Grimm	0	0	1	0	1
Hart	0	0	1	20	1
Hornung	2	0	0	0	1
H. Jordan	0	0	3	0	3
Kostelnik	0	0	1	0	1
Marshall	0	0	1	0	1
T. Moore	4	0	0	0	0
Nitschke	0	0	3	18	3
E. Pitts	2	1	0	0	1
D. Robinson	0	0	2	2	2
Starr	1	0	0	0	0
J. Taylor	3	1	0	0	1
Wood	0	0	2	0	2
S. Wright	0	1	0	0	1
Packers	**18**	**6**	**23**	**42**	**29**

NFL STANDINGS

Western Conference

	W	L	T	Pct	PF	PA
Green Bay Packers	10	3	1	769	316	224
Baltimore Colts	10	3	1	769	389	284
Chicago Bears	9	5	0	643	409	275
San Francisco 49ers	7	6	1	538	421	402
Minnesota Vikings	7	7	0	500	383	403
Detroit Lions	6	7	1	462	257	295
Los Angeles Rams	4	10	0	286	269	328

Eastern Conference

	W	L	T	Pct	PF	PA
Cleveland Browns	11	3	0	786	363	325
Dallas Cowboys	7	7	0	500	325	280
New York Giants	7	7	0	500	270	338
Washington Redskins	6	8	0	429	257	301
Philadelphia Eagles	5	9	0	357	363	359
St. Louis Cardinals	5	9	0	357	296	309
Pittsburgh Steelers	2	12	0	143	202	397

ROSTER

No	Name	Pos	Ht	Wt	DOB	College	G
26	Adderley, Herb	CB	6-1	210	06/08/39	Michigan State	14
82	Aldridge, Lionel	DE	6-4	245	02/18/41	Utah State	14
88	Anderson, Bill	TE	6-3	216	07/16/36	Tennessee	14
57	Bowman, Ken	C	6-3	230	12/15/42	Wisconsin	14
12	Bratkowski, Zeke	QB	6-3	200	10/20/31	Georgia	6
40	Brown, Tom	DB	6-1	190	12/12/40	Maryland	14
60	Caffey, Lee Roy	LB	6-3	250	06/03/41	Texas A&M	14
34	Chandler, Don	K	6-2	210	09/05/34	Florida	14
10	Claridge, Dennis	QB	6-3	225	08/18/41	Nebraska	1
41	Coffey, Junior	HB	6-1	210	03/21/42	Washington	13
56	Crutcher, Tommy	LB	6-3	230	08/10/41	TCU	14
50	Curry, Bill	C	6-2	235	10/21/42	Georgia Tech	14
84	Dale, Carroll	WR	6-2	200	04/24/38	Virginia Tech	13
87	Davis, Willie	DE	6-3	245	07/24/34	Grambling	14
86	Dowler, Boyd	WR	6-5	225	10/18/37	Colorado	14
81	Fleming, Marv	TE	6-4	235	01/02/42	Utah	13
75	Gregg, Alvis (Forrest)	T	6-4	250	10/18/33	SMU	14
46	Gremminger, Hank	DB	6-1	200	09/01/33	Baylor	8
67	Grimm, Dan	G	6-3	245	02/07/41	Colorado	14
43	Hart, Doug	DB	6-0	190	06/03/39	Arlington State	14
5	Hornung, Paul	HB	6-2	215	12/23/35	Notre Dame	12
35	Jacobs, Allen	HB	6-1	215	05/19/41	Utah	14
21	Jeter, Bob	DB	6-1	205	05/09/37	Iowa	13
74	Jordan, Henry	DT	6-3	250	01/26/35	Virginia	14
77	Kostelnik, Ron	DT	6-4	260	01/14/40	Cincinnati	14
64	Kramer, Jerry	G	6-3	245	01/23/36	Idaho	14
80	Long, Bob	WR	6-3	190	06/16/42	Wichita	13
70	Marshall, Rich	DT	6-5	270	09/12/41	Stephen A. Austin	14
85	McGee, Max	E	6-3	205	07/16/32	Tulane	12
25	Moore, Tom	HB	6-2	210	07/17/38	Vanderbilt	13
66	Nitschke, Ray	LB	6-3	240	12/29/36	Illinois	12
22	Pitts, Elijah	HB	6-1	205	02/03/39	Philander Smith	14
89	Robinson, Dave	LB	6-3	245	05/03/41	Penn State	14
76	Skoronski, Bob	T	6-3	250	03/05/34	Indiana	14
15	Starr, Bryan (Bart)	QB	6-1	200	01/09/34	Alabama	14
31	Taylor, Jim	FB	6-0	215	09/20/35	LSU	13
63	Thurston, Fred (Fuzzy)	G	6-1	245	05/07/35	Valparaiso	14
71	Voss, Lloyd	T	6-4	260	02/13/42	Nebraska	14
24	Wood, Willie	DB	5-10	190	12/23/36	USC	14
72	Wright, Steve	T	6-6	250	07/18/42	Alabama	14

DRAFT

Rnd	Name	Pos	Ht	Wt	College
*1a	Donny Anderson	HB	6-3	210	Texas Tech
	(Choice from Eagles as part of Jim Ringo, Earl Gros, Lee Roy Caffey deal)				
1b	Larry Elkins	WR	6-1	190	Baylor
2	Alphonse Dotson	T	6-4	260	Grambling
3a	(Choice to Giants)				
3b	Allen Brown	E	6-4	230	Mississippi
4	Wally Mahle	HB	6-3	195	Syracuse
*5a	James Harvey	T	6-4	240	Mississippi
	(Choice from Steelers)				
5b	Doug Goodwin	FB	6-3	220	Maryland State
6a	Rick Koeper	T	6-4	245	Oregon State
	(Choice from Steelers)				
6b	Bill Symons	HB	6-1	196	Colorado
7a	Jerry Roberts	E	6-4	205	Baldwin-Wallace
	(Choice from Giants for Turnley Todd)				
7b	Roger Jacobazzi	T	6-3	250	Wisconsin
	(Choice from 49ers)				
7c	Junior Coffey	HB	6-1	210	Washington
*8	Mike Shinn	E	6-3	220	Kansas
9	Larry Bulaich	HB	6-2	200	TCU
10	Rick Marshall	T	6-5	270	Stephen A. Austin
*11	Jim Weatherwax	T	6-7	260	Los Angeles State
12	Eugene Jeter	HB	6-3	200	Arkansas-Pine Bluff
*13	Roy Schmidt	G	6-3	240	Long Beach State
14	John Putman	FB	6-3	234	Drake
15	Chuck Hurston	T	6-5	220	Auburn
*16	Phil Vandersea	FB	6-3	225	Massachusetts
17	Steve Clark	K	6-2	210	Oregon State
*18	Jeff White	E	6-3	185	Texas Tech
*19	Len Sears	T	6-5	240	South Carolina
20	James Chandler	HB	6-4	206	Benedict

* denotes futures

FRONT ROW: (L-R) 89 Dave Robinson, 34 Don Chandler, 82 Lionel Aldridge, 43 Doug Hart, 46 Hank Gremminger, 77 Ron Kostelnik, 24 Willie Wood, 26 Herb Adderley, 21 Bob Jeter, 81 Marv Fleming.

SECOND ROW: (L-R) Trainer Carl (Bud) Jorgensen, 71 Lloyd Voss, 84 Carroll Dale, 15 Bart Starr, 22 Elijah Pitts, 88 Bill Anderson, 12 Zeke Bratkowski, 67 Dan Grimm, 25 Tom Moore, 80 Bob Long, 40 Tom Brown, Equipment Manager Gerald (Dad) Braisher.

THIRD ROW: (L-R) Assistant Trainer Domenic Gentile, 50 Bill Curry, 56 Tommy Crutcher, 41 Junior Coffey, 60 Lee Roy Caffey, 74 Henry Jordan, 64 Jerry Kramer, 63 Fred (Fuzzy) Thurston, 76 Bob Skoronski, 87 Willie Davis, 66 Ray Nitschke, Assistant Equipment Manager Bob Noel.

BACK ROW: (L-R) 35 Allen Jacobs, 70 Rich Marshall, 10 Dennis Claridge, 57 Ken Bowman, 86 Boyd Dowler, 75 Forrest Gregg, 72 Steve Wright, 31 Jim Taylor, 5 Paul Hornung, 85 Max McGee.

On June 8, 1966, the NFL and AFL announced they had put aside their differences and would become one league in time for the 1970 season. The two would participate in common drafts beginning in 1967, and would inaugurate interleague preseason play that year as well.

The announcement that a world championship game between the leagues would take place at season's end piqued the Packers' interest. Anything championship interested Green Bay, and the club decided in training camp it wanted in on that game.

A one-point loss to the 49ers and a three-point setback to the Vikings kept the Packers from a perfect season. Green Bay held down the top spot in the West from the get-go and finished 12-2. After outscoring the Cowboys 34-27 in the NFL Championship Game, the Packers dismantled Kansas City 35-10 in the first AFL-NFL World Championship game, now known as the Super Bowl.

Bart Starr enjoyed perhaps his finest season. He led the league in passing and was voted league MVP. The efficient leader completed 62.2 percent of his passes and was intercepted only three times all year.

Jim Taylor and Paul Hornung were near the end of their careers. Taylor's 705 yards rushing was his lowest output since 1959 and Hornung didn't have a run of 10 yards or more all season. The two last lined up together in the second half of the season finale in Los Angeles.

In looking to replace that valuable tandem, the Packers shelled out approximately $1 million to sign all-America running backs Donny Anderson and Jim Grabowski. Anderson, who received about $600,000, was a junior eligible selected in 1965. Grabowski, a 225-pound fullback, was taken using the first-round draft pick Green Bay obtained from the Lions for tight end Ron Kramer.

Defensively, the Packers ranked third. They gave up just 17 touchdowns, one fewer than the highly publicized Bears defense of 1963.

Green Bay led the NFL in pass defense. Henry Jordan, Willie Davis and others sacked enemy quarterbacks 47 times. Herb Adderley, Willie Wood and others intercepted 28 passes, second behind the 30 of Cleveland.

Green Bay opened 1966 against the two teams it had defeated for the 1965 NFL crown. First up were the Colts. Lee Roy Caffey and Bob Jeter both returned interceptions for touchdowns as the Packers prevailed 24-3.

Next in line were the Browns, who proved more troublesome. It took a 9-yard Starr-to-Taylor touchdown pass with 2:34 left to put away Cleveland 21-20.

The Packers won their next two games also. They beat the Rams 24-13 as Starr passed 80 yards to Elijah Pitts for a score, and they knocked off the Lions 23-14 with the help of three Don Chandler field goals.

A week later, Chandler failed in the clutch. Dave Robinson intercepted a George Mira pass and returned it to the 49ers' 9-yard line, but Chandler missed a 26-yard field goal attempt with 6:57 remaining. San Francisco slipped by 21-20.

Green Bay rebounded with a 17-0 shutout of the Bears in Chicago. The Packers held Gale Sayers to 29 yards rushing in 15 attempts and the Bears to 94 yards overall.

The Packers then closed out the first half of the season with a 56-3 rout of the expansion Atlanta Falcons. Starr threw for 217 yards on just eight completions while the defense dumped Atlanta passers eight times.

Green Bay pushed its record to 7-1 by crushing the Lions 31-7 in Tiger Stadium. Pitts tallied 130 yards from scrimmage (99 rushing) and scored three touchdowns.

Minnesota rallied for 10 points in the fourth quarter to hand the Packers their second loss. The Vikings controlled the ball for 36 of the final 48 plays from scrimmage.

In Week 10, Zeke Bratkowski came on in relief of Starr, who pulled a hamstring. Super Sub threw two touchdown passes and guided Green Bay past the Bears 13-6.

On Dec. 4, the Packers edged the 49ers 20-7 to clinch at least a share of the Western Conference title. They took the title outright a week later after Davis forced a John Unitas fumble that Robinson recovered to preserve a 14-10 win with only minutes remaining.

"I guess that might have been the biggest tackle I ever made," Davis said.

Green Bay then edged the Rams 27-23 before heading into the postseason, where it made history for the NFL.

THE FRIENDLY SKIES

In 1966, the Packers gained more yards passing than in any other year under head coach Vince Lombardi. But the additional yards the ball spent in the air did not translate into more passes being intercepted.

Green Bay passers were intercepted only five times. Bart Starr tossed three and Zeke Bratkowski threw two. Every other team in the league threw at least 14.

Starr was intercepted three times in his first 125 attempts and not at all in his last 126 tries. Bratkowski's errant throws came against the Bears on Nov. 20 and in Los Angeles on Dec. 18.

Opponents converted the five interceptions into 20 points. The Packers, on the other hand, turned the 28 interceptions they made into 89 points.

Below is a list of the fewest interceptions the Packers have thrown in a season:

No.	Year	Passers
5	1966	Starr (3), Bratkowski (2)
6	1964	Starr (4), Bratkowski (1), Hornung (1)
9	1972	Hunter (9)

TEAM STATISTICS

	GB	OPP
First Downs	231	211
Rushing	98	90
Passing	115	106
Penalty	18	15
Rushes	475	446
Yards Gained	1,673	1,644
Average Gain	3.52	3.69
Average Yards per Game	119.5	117.4
Passes Attempted	318	390
Completed	193	202
% Completed	60.69	51.79
Total Yards Gained	2,831	2,316
Times Sacked	31	47
Yards Lost	229	357
Net Yards Gained	2,602	1,959
Yards Gained per Completion	14.67	11.47
Net Yards per Attempt	7.46	4.48
Average Net Yards per Game	185.9	139.9
Combined Net Yards Gained	4,275	3,603
Total Plays	824	883
Average Yards per Play	5.19	4.08
Average Net Yards per Game	305.4	257.4
Third Down Efficiency	65/172	65/200
Percentage	37.79	32.50
Fourth Down Efficiency	4/8	11/19
Percentage	50.00	57.89
Intercepted By	28	5
Yards Returned	547	75
Returned for TD	6	0
Punts	62	69
Yards Punted	2,541	2,850
Average Yards per Punt	40.98	41.30
Punt Returns	37	30
Yards Returned	215	171
Average Yards per Return	5.81	5.70
Returned for TD	1	0
Kickoff Returns	42	52
Yards Returned	903	1,213
Average Yards per Return	21.50	23.33
Returned for TD	0	0
Penalties	57	67
Yards Penalized	544	745
Fumbles	23	26
Lost	19	14
Own Recovered for Touchdown	0	0
Opponent's Recovered by	14	19
Opponent's Recovered for Touchdown	0	1
Total Points Scored	335	163
Total Touchdowns	43	17
Touchdowns Rushing	18	9
Touchdowns Passing	18	7
Touchdowns on Returns & Recoveries	7	1
Extra Points	41	16
Safeties	0	0
Field Goals Attempted	28	27
Field Goals Made	12	15
% Successful	42.86	55.56

Regular Season 12-2-0

Date	GB		OPP	Att.
9/10	24	Baltimore Colts (M)	3	(48,650)
9/18	21	at Cleveland Browns	20	(83,943)
9/25	24	Los Angeles Rams	13	(50,861)
10/2	23	Detroit Lions	14	(50,861)
10/9	20	at San Francisco 49ers	21	(39,290)
10/16	17	at Chicago Bears	0	(48,573)
10/23	56	Atlanta Falcons (M)	3	(48,623)
10/30	31	at Detroit Lions	7	(56,954)
11/6	17	Minnesota Vikings	20	(50,861)
11/20	13	Chicago Bears	6	(50,861)
11/27	28	at Minnesota Vikings	16	(47,426)
12/4	20	San Francisco 49ers	7	(48,725)
12/10	14	at Baltimore Colts	10	(60,238)
12/18	27	at Los Angeles Rams	23	(72,416)

Postseason 2-0

1/1	34	at Dallas Cowboys	27	(74,152)
1/15	35	Chiefs at LA Coliseum	10	(61,946)

Score By Periods

	1	2	3	4	Total
Packers	62	117	54	102	335
Opponents	13	66	23	61	163

INDIVIDUAL STATISTICS

Rushing

	Att	Yds	Avg	LG	TD
J. Taylor	204	705	3.5	19	4
E. Pitts	115	393	3.4	20	7
Hornung	76	200	2.6	9	2
Grabowski	29	127	4.4	t36	1
Starr	21	104	5.0	21	2
D. Anderson	25	104	4.2	15	2
Chandler	1	33	33.0	33	0
Bratkowski	4	7	1.8	4	0
Packers	475	1,673	3.5	t36	18
Opponents	446	1,644	3.7	38	9

Receiving

	No	Yds	Avg	LG	TD
J. Taylor	41	331	8.1	21	2
Dale	37	876	23.7	t83	7
Fleming	31	361	11.6	t53	2
Dowler	29	392	13.5	40	0
E. Pitts	26	460	17.7	t80	3
Hornung	14	192	13.7	t44	3
McGee	4	91	22.8	29	1
Grabowski	4	13	3.3	7	0
Long	3	68	22.7	42	0
D. Anderson	2	33	16.5	22	0
B. Anderson	2	14	7.0	8	0
Packers	193	2,831	14.7	t83	18
Opponents	202	2,316	11.5	t65	7

Passing

	Att	Com	Yds	Pct	TD	In	Tk/Yds	Rate
Starr	251	156	2,257	62.2	14	3	26/183	105.0
Bratkowski	64	36	569	56.3	4	2	5/46	93.8
Hornung	1	1	5	100.0	0	0	0/0	—
E. Pitts	2	0	0	00.0	0	0	0/0	—
Packers	318	193	2,831	60.7	18	5	31/229	102.1
Opponents	390	202	2,316	51.8	7	28	47/357	46.1

Punting

	No	Yds	Avg	Net	TB	In20	LG	HB
Chandler	60	2,452	40.9	36.4	5	15	58	0
D. Anderson	2	89	44.5	44.0	0	0	49	0
Packers	62	2,541	41.0	36.6	5	15	58	0
Opponents	69	2,850	41.3	36.7	5	15	58	1

Kickoff Returns

	No	Yds	Avg	LG	TD
D. Anderson	23	533	23.2	61	0
Adderley	14	320	22.9	65	0
Vandersea	3	50	16.7	21	0
E. Pitts	1	0	0.0	0	0
Wood	1	0	0.0	0	0
Packers	42	903	21.5	65	0
Opponents	52	1,213	23.3	51	0

Punt Returns

	No	Yds	Avg	FC	LG	TD
Wood	22	82	3.7	9	13	0
E. Pitts	7	9	1.3	4	6	0
D. Anderson	6	124	20.7	1	t77	1
T. Brown	2	0	0.0	1	0	0
Packers	37	215	5.8	15	t77	1
Opponents	30	171	5.7	15	29	0

Interceptions

	No	Yds	Avg	LG	TD
Jeter	5	142	28.4	t75	1
D. Robinson	5	60	12.0	23	0
Adderley	4	125	31.3	t68	1
T. Brown	4	21	5.3	15	0
Caffey	3	62	20.7	t52	1
Wood	3	38	12.7	t20	1
Nitschke	2	44	22.0	22	0
Hart	1	40	40.0	t40	1
Crutcher	1	15	15.0	15	0
Packers	28	547	19.5	t75	6
Opponents	5	75	15.0	44	0

Scoring

	TDr	TDp	TDrt	PAT	FG	S	TP
Chandler	0	0	0	41/43	12/28	0	77
E. Pitts	7	3	0	0/0	0/0	0	60
Dale	0	7	0	0/0	0/0	0	42
J. Taylor	4	2	0	0/0	0/0	0	36
Hornung	2	3	0	0/0	0/0	0	30
D. Anderson	2	0	1	0/0	0/0	0	18
Fleming	0	2	0	0/0	0/0	0	12
Jeter	0	0	2	0/0	0/0	0	12
Starr	2	0	0	0/0	0/0	0	12
Adderley	0	0	1	0/0	0/0	0	6
Caffey	0	0	1	0/0	0/0	0	6
Grabowski	1	0	0	0/0	0/0	0	6
Hart	0	0	1	0/0	0/0	0	6
McGee	0	1	0	0/0	0/0	0	6
Wood	0	0	1	0/0	0/0	0	6
Packers	18	18	7	41/43	12/28	0	335
Opponents	9	7	1	16/17	15/27	0	163

Fumbles

	Fum	Ow	Op	Yds	Tot
Adderley	1	1	1	0	2
L. Aldridge	0	0	2	3	2
D. Anderson	3	0	0	0	0
Bratkowski	0	1	0	0	1
T. Brown	0	0	2	5	2
Caffey	0	0	1	0	1
Dale	0	1	0	0	1
W. Davis	0	0	2	0	2
Dowler	1	0	0	0	1
Fleming	0	1	0	0	1
Grabowski	2	0	0	0	0
Hart	0	0	1	0	1
Hornung	1	0	0	0	0
Jeter	0	0	1	0	1
Kostelnik	0	0	2	0	2
E. Pitts	4	0	0	0	0
D. Robinson	0	0	2	7	2
Starr	7	0	0	0	0
J. Taylor	4	0	0	0	0
Packers	23	4	14	15	18

NFL STANDINGS

Western Conference

	W	L	T	Pct	PF	PA
Green Bay Packers	12	2	0	.857	335	163
Baltimore Colts	9	5	0	.643	314	226
Los Angeles Rams	8	6	0	.571	289	212
San Francisco 49ers	6	6	2	.500	320	325
Chicago Bears	5	7	2	.417	234	272
Detroit Lions	4	9	1	.308	206	317
Minnesota Vikings	4	9	1	.308	292	304

Eastern Conference

	W	L	T	Pct	PF	PA
Dallas Cowboys	10	3	1	.769	445	239
Cleveland Browns	9	5	0	.643	403	259
Philadelphia Eagles	9	5	0	.643	326	340
St. Louis Cardinals	8	5	1	.615	264	265
Washington Redskins	7	7	0	.500	351	355
Pittsburgh Steelers	5	8	1	.385	316	347
Atlanta Falcons	3	11	0	.214	204	437
New York Giants	1	12	1	.077	263	501

ROSTER

No	Name	Pos	Ht	Wt	DOB	College	G
26	Adderley, Herb	CB	6-1	200	06/08/39	Michigan State	14
82	Aldridge, Lionel	DE	6-4	245	02/18/41	Utah State	13
88	Anderson, Bill	TE	6-3	225	07/16/36	Tennessee	10
44	Anderson, Donny	RB	6-3	210	05/16/43	Texas Tech	14
57	Bowman, Ken	C	6-3	230	12/15/42	Wisconsin	4
12	Bratkowski, Zeke	QB	6-3	210	10/20/31	Georgia	8
83	Brown, Allen	TE	6-5	235	03/02/43	Mississippi	5
78	Brown, Bob	DE	6-5	260	02/23/40	Arkansas-Pine Bluff	14
40	Brown, Tom	DB	6-1	190	12/12/40	Maryland	14
60	Caffey, Lee Roy	LB	6-3	250	06/03/41	Texas A&M	14
34	Chandler, Don	K	6-2	210	09/05/34	Florida	14
56	Crutcher, Tommy	LB	6-3	230	08/10/41	TCU	14
50	Curry, Bill	C	6-2	235	10/21/42	Georgia Tech	14
84	Dale, Carroll	WR	6-2	200	04/24/38	Virginia Tech	14
87	Davis, Willie	DE	6-3	245	07/24/34	Grambling	14
86	Dowler, Boyd	WR	6-5	225	10/18/37	Colorado	14
81	Fleming, Marv	TE	6-4	235	01/02/42	Utah	14
68	Gillingham, Gale	G	6-3	255	02/03/44	Minnesota	14
33	Grabowski, Jim	RB	6-2	220	09/09/44	Illinois	14
75	Gregg, Alvis (Forrest)	T	6-4	250	10/18/33	SMU	14
43	Hart, Doug	DB	6-0	190	06/03/39	Arlington State	14
45	Hathcock, Dave	DB	6-0	195	07/20/43	Memphis State	14
5	Hornung, Paul	HB	6-2	215	12/23/35	Notre Dame	9
21	Jeter, Bob	DB	6-1	205	05/09/37	Iowa	14
74	Jordan, Henry	DT	6-3	250	01/26/35	Virginia	14
77	Kostelnik, Ron	DT	6-4	260	01/14/40	Cincinnati	14
64	Kramer, Jerry	G	6-3	245	01/23/36	Idaho	14
80	Long, Bob	WR	6-3	205	06/16/42	Wichita	5
27	Mack, Red	WR	5-10	185	06/19/37	Notre Dame	8
85	McGee, Max	E	6-3	210	07/16/32	Tulane	12
66	Nitschke, Ray	LB	6-3	240	12/29/36	Illinois	14
22	Pitts, Elijah	HB	6-1	205	02/03/39	Philander Smith	14
89	Robinson, Dave	LB	6-3	240	05/03/41	Penn State	14
76	Skoronski, Bob	T	6-3	245	03/05/34	Indiana	14
15	Starr, Bryan (Bart)	QB	6-1	190	01/09/34	Alabama	14
31	Taylor, Jim	FB	6-0	215	09/20/35	LSU	14
63	Thurston, Fred (Fuzzy)	G	6-1	245	05/07/35	Valparaiso	12
37	Vandersea, Phil	LB	6-3	235	02/25/43	Massachusetts	14
73	Weatherwax, Jim	DT	6-7	260	01/09/43	Cal State-Los Angeles	14
24	Wood, Willie	DB	5-10	190	12/23/36	USC	14
72	Wright, Steve	T	6-6	250	07/18/42	Alabama	14

DRAFT

Rnd	Name	Pos	Ht	Wt	College
1a	Jim Grabowski	FB	6-2	225	Illinois
	(Choice from Lions for Ron Kramer)				
1b	Gale Gillingham	T	6-3	250	Minnesota
*2	Tom Cichowski	T	6-4	238	Maryland
3a	Fred Heron	T	6-5	250	San Jose State
	(Choice from Browns)				
3b	Tony Jeter	E	6-4	238	Nebraska
*4	John Roderick	HB	6-1	171	SMU
5	(Choice to Rams)				
6	(Choice to Redskins for Bill Anderson)				
*7	Ray Miller	E	6-4	250	Idaho
8	Ken McLean	HB	6-0	191	Texas A&M
9	Ron Rector	HB	5-11	196	Northwestern

Rnd	Name	Pos	Ht	Wt	College
10	Sam Montgomery	HB	6-1	200	Southern
11	Ralph Wenzel	C	6-3	240	San Diego State
*12	Jim Mankins	FB	6-1	238	Florida State
*13	Ed King	LB	6-2	220	USC
14	Ron Hanson	E	6-3	200	North Dakota State
15	Grady Bolton	T	6-2	250	Mississippi State
16	Robert Schultz	T	6-3	255	Wis.-Stevens Point
17	Dave Hathcock	DB	6-0	195	Memphis State
18	Jim Jones	DT	6-3	260	Omaha
19	Dave Norton	TE	6-0	220	USC
20	Ed Maras	E	6-2	220	South Dakota State
*	denotes futures				

1966 GREEN BAY PACKERS

FRONT ROW: (L-R) 89 Dave Robinson, 22 Elijah Pitts, 82 Lionel Aldridge, 43 Doug Hart, 21 Bob Jeter, 87 Willie Davis, 76 Bob Skoronski, 26 Herb Adderley, 45 Dave Hathcock, 81 Marv Fleming.
SECOND ROW: (L-R) Trainer Carl (Bud) Jorgensen, 44 Donny Anderson, 12 Zeke Bratkowski, 84 Carroll Dale, 15 Bart Starr, 78 Bob Brown, 77 Ron Kostelnik, 74 Henry Jordan, 33 Jim Grabowski, 88 Bill Anderson, 68 Gale Gillingham, Equipment Manager Gerald (Dad) Braisher.
THIRD ROW: (L-R) 24 Willie Wood, 27 Red Mack, 66 Ray Nitschke, 50 Bill Curry, 56 Tommy Crutcher, 60 Lee Roy Caffey, 63 Fred (Fuzzy) Thurston, 64 Jerry Kramer, 57 Ken Bowman, 75 Forrest Gregg, 80 Bob Long, 37 Phil Vandersea, Assistant Equipment Manager Bob Noel.
BACK ROW: (L-R) 40 Tom Brown, 73 Jim Weatherwax, 34 Don Chandler, 83 Allen Brown, 86 Boyd Dowler, 72 Steve Wright, 31 Jim Taylor, 5 Paul Hornung, 85 Max McGee.

Three straight NFL championships. Only the Packers of 1929, 1930 and 1931 had accomplished that feat, and they did so before the league adopted a playoff format. In 1967, Vince Lombardi's team geared up for another run at three in a row. They had fallen short in 1963, the last time they had the opportunity to make such history.

The Packers, said Lombardi, "have the wherewithal to win a third straight National Football League championship." The coach made that comment at a Packers recognition luncheon at St. Norbert College in De Pere, Wis., in early September.

Four months later, his team delivered. Despite numerous injuries and an offense that was no better than average, Green Bay posted a 9-4-1 record, good enough for first place in the newly created Central Division. Wins over the Rams, Cowboys, and Raiders in the playoffs gave the Packers their third straight title.

For the first time in nearly a decade, the Packers were without Jim Taylor and Paul Hornung. Taylor played out his option and was traded to the New Orleans Saints in July. Hornung ended up there also, as the expansion team stocked itself by selecting unprotected players from lists provided by the other clubs.

Green Bay used six different running backs throughout the year. Fullback Jim Grabowski and halfback Elijah Pitts were tabbed as the starters. But Grabowski twisted a knee and missed five games, and Pitts tore his Achilles' tendon and was lost for the final six games.

With Pitts out and Grabowski ailing, Lombardi signed Chuck Mercein from the Redskins' taxi squad on Nov. 9. The Yale graduate backed up Ben Wilson (obtained from the Rams at the time Taylor was traded) who took over for Grabowski. Donny Anderson assumed the halfback duties ahead of rookie sensation Travis Williams, who averaged an NFL-record 41.1 yards per kickoff return.

Bart Starr took his lumps in 1967. Ailing from thumb and rib injuries suffered in the preseason, the quarterback was picked off nine times in the opening two games. In Week 3, the Falcons' Bob Riggle and Tommy Nobis injured Starr's shoulder on a sack early in the game. Zeke Bratkowski started the next two games. Not until Week 6, in a 48-20 rout of the Giants, did Starr get on track and throw his first touchdown pass.

The Packers had the NFL's top defense. Its pass defense gave up fewer than 100 yards a game.

Green Bay didn't look like a team on the verge of a third straight championship in the opening two weeks. They fell behind the Lions 17-0 in the opener and committed eight turnovers a week later against the Bears. The Packers came back to tie the Lions 17-17, and a 46-yard Don Chandler field goal lifted them past the Bears 13-10.

Boyd Dowler and Carroll Dale combined for 202 yards receiving and all 10 of Green Bay's passing first downs in a 23-0 win over Atlanta in Week 3.

Green Bay improved to 3-0-1 by coming back to nip the Lions 27-17 at Tiger Stadium. Ray Nitschke's limping, 20-yard return of a Milt Plum pass early in the fourth quarter highlighted the Packers' 17-point fourth quarter.

Bud Grant secured his first win in the NFL when his Vikings edged Green Bay 10-7 in Week 5.

On Oct. 22, Starr returned and Grabowski enjoyed his most productive day as a Packer. Starr threw for 151 yards with a touchdown pass to Grabowski, who gained 123 yards rushing. The fullback also scored on a 2-yard run.

The first half of the season ended with a bang. Williams zipped 93 yards for a touchdown on his third kickoff return of the afternoon in a 31-23 win over the Cardinals.

The rookie wasn't finished. Two weeks later, he returned two kickoffs for touchdowns as the Packers pounded the Browns 55-7. He nailed a fourth return for a touchdown on Dec. 9 in a 27-24 loss to the Rams.

On Nov. 26, the Packers traveled to Chicago, needing a win to sew up the Central Division title. Starr and Dowler led the way, hooking up six times for 105 yards and a touchdown. The Packers won 17-13 and improved to 8-2-1. The second-place Bears fell to 5-6.

The Packers closed out with losses to the Rams and Steelers. Green Bay hadn't lost its final two games since Scooter McLean's boys dropped their final seven in 1958. While no one expected the team to sink to that level, the Packers' great run in the 1960s was nearing its end.

PUNTS OF LOW RETURN

The Packers punt return coverage unit was pretty special in 1967. It surrendered just 22 yards on 13 returns and forced opponents into 27 fair catches.

It all started with Donny Anderson. The running back took the punting duties away from Don Chandler and dropped 22 punts inside the opponents' 20-yard line. Half of those weren't returned, another seven were fair caught, and the remaining four were returned for a loss of 4 yards.

Even when opponents had some room, the Packers shut them down. Seven of the returns were for no gain or a loss. The Steelers' Roy Jefferson was the only player to get 10 yards on a punt return against Green Bay.

Below is a list of the fewest punt returns yards that the Packers have given up in one season:

Yds.	Rets.	Avg.	FC	TD	Year
22	13	1.7	27	0	1967
62	18	3.4	25	0	1969
66	19	3.5	20	0	1968
144	22	6.6	--	0	1960

TEAM STATISTICS

	GB	OPP
First Downs	243	183
Rushing	115	98
Passing	112	78
Penalty	16	7
Rushes	474	443
Yards Gained	1,915	1,923
Average Gain	4.04	4.34
Average Yards per Game	136.8	137.4
Passes Attempted	331	337
Completed	182	155
% Completed	54.98	45.99
Total Yards Gained	2,758	1,644
Times Sacked	41	29
Yards Lost	394	267
Net Yards Gained	2,364	1,377
Yards Gained per Completion	15.15	10.61
Net Yards per Attempt	6.35	3.76
Average Net Yards per Game	168.9	98.4
Combined Net Yards Gained	4,279	3,300
Total Plays	846	809
Average Yards per Play	5.06	4.08
Average Yards per Game	305.6	235.7
Third Down Efficiency	66/179	55/183
Percentage	36.87	30.05
Fourth Down Efficiency	4/8	7/15
Percentage	50.00	46.67
Intercepted By	26	27
Yards Returned	284	370
Returned for TD	2	3
Punts	66	75
Yards Punted	2,409	3,119
Average Yards per Punt	36.50	41.59
Punt Returns	39	13
Yards Returned	157	22
Average Yards per Return	4.03	1.69
Returned for TD	0	0
Kickoff Returns	46	59
Yards Returned	1,241	1,276
Average Yards per Return	26.98	21.63
Returned for TD	4	0
Penalties	48	55
Yards Penalized	531	482
Fumbles	19	23
Lost	10	14
Own Recovered for Touchdown	0	0
Opponent's Recovered by	14	10
Opponent's Recovered for Touchdown	0	1
Total Points Scored	332	209
Total Touchdowns	39	24
Touchdowns Rushing	18	7
Touchdowns Passing	15	13
Touchdowns on Returns & Recoveries	6	4
Extra Points	39	23
Safeties	1	0
Field Goals Attempted	29	28
Field Goals Made	19	14
% Successful	65.52	50.00

Regular Season   9-4-1

Date	GB		OPP	Att.
9/17	17	Detroit Lions	17	(50,861)
9/24	13	Chicago Bears	10	(50,861)
10/1	23	Atlanta Falcons (M)	0	(49,467)
10/8	27	at Detroit Lions	17	(57,877)
10/15	7	Minnesota Vikings (M)	10	(49,601)
10/22	48	at New York Giants	21	(62,585)
10/30	31	at St. Louis Cardinals	23	(49,792)
11/5	10	at Baltimore Colts	13	(60,238)
11/12	55	Cleveland Browns (M)	7	(50,074)
11/19	13	San Francisco 49ers	0	(50,861)
11/26	17	at Chicago Bears	13	(47,513)
12/3	30	at Minnesota Vikings	27	(47,693)
12/9	24	at Los Angeles Rams	27	(76,637)
12/17	17	Pittsburgh Steelers	24	(50,861)

Postseason   3-0

12/23	28	Los Angeles Rams (M)	7	(49,861)
12/31	21	Dallas Cowboys	17	(50,861)
1/14	33	Raiders at Orange Bowl	14	(75,546)

Score By Periods

	1	2	3	4	Total
Packers	76	93	53	110	332
Opponents	40	69	30	70	209

INDIVIDUAL STATISTICS

Rushing

	Att	Yds	Avg	LG	TD
Grabowski	120	466	3.9	24	2
B. Wilson	103	453	4.4	40	2
D. Anderson	97	402	4.1	40	6
E. Pitts	77	247	3.2	30	6
T. Williams	35	188	5.4	37	1
Starr	21	90	4.3	23	0
Mercein	14	56	4.0	15	1
Dale	1	9	9.0	9	0
Bratkowski	5	6	1.2	4	0
Horn	1	-2	-2.0	-2	0
Packers	**474**	**1,915**	**4.0**	**40**	**18**
Opponents	443	1,923	4.3	t59	7

Receiving

	No	Yds	Avg	LG	TD
Dowler	54	836	15.5	t57	4
Dale	35	738	21.9	t86	5
D. Anderson	22	331	15.0	37	3
E. Pitts	15	210	14.0	84	0
B. Wilson	14	88	6.3	21	0
Grabowski	12	171	14.3	53	1
Fleming	10	126	12.6	19	1
Long	8	96	12.3	21	0
T. Williams	5	80	16.0	t29	1
Allen Brown	3	43	14.3	17	0
McGee	3	33	11.0	13	0
Mercein	1	6	6.0	6	0
Packers	**182**	**2,758**	**15.2**	**t86**	**15**
Opponents	155	1,644	10.6	t49	13

Passing

	Att	Com	Yds	Pct	TD	In	Tk/Yds	Rate
Starr	210	115	1,823	54.8	9	17	34/322	64.4
Bratkowski	94	53	724	56.4	5	9	6/64	59.3
Horn	24	12	171	50.0	1	1	1/8	70.0
E. Pitts	1	1	21	100.0	0	0	0/0	—
D. Anderson	2	1	19	50.0	0	0	0/0	—
Packers	**331**	**182**	**2,758**	**55.0**	**15**	**27**	**41/394**	**63.7**
Opponents	337	155	1,644	46.0	13	26	29/267	41.5

Punting

	No	Yds	Avg	Net	TB	In20	LG	HB
D. Anderson	65	2,378	36.6	35.9	1	22	63	1
Chandler	1	31	31.0	31.0	0	0	31	0
Packers	**66**	**2,409**	**36.5**	**35.9**	**1**	**22**	**63**	**1**
Opponents	75	3,119	41.6	38.4	4	21	78	0

Kickoff Returns

	No	Yds	Avg	LG	TD
T. Williams	18	739	41.1	t104	4
D. Anderson	11	226	20.5	30	0
Adderley	10	207	20.7	37	0
Crutcher	3	48	16.0	23	0
Allen Brown	1	13	13.0	13	0
Hart	1	8	8.0	8	0
D. Robinson	1	0	0.0	0	0
Wood	1	0	0.0	0	0
Packers	**46**	**1,241**	**27.0**	**t104**	**4**
Opponents	59	1,276	21.6	50	0

Punt Returns

	No	Yds	Avg	FC	LG	TD
Wood	12	3	0.3	6	8	0
D. Anderson	9	98	10.9	3	43	0
T. Brown	9	40	4.4	1	12	0
E. Pitts	9	16	1.8	3	10	0
Packers	**39**	**157**	**4.0**	**13**	**43**	**0**
Opponents	13	22	1.7	27	10	0

Interceptions

	No	Yds	Avg	LG	TD
Jeter	8	78	9.8	25	0
Wood	4	60	15.0	25	0
Adderley	4	16	4.0	t12	1
D. Robinson	4	16	4.0	12	0
Nitschke	3	35	11.7	t20	1
Caffey	2	28	14.0	24	0
T. Brown	1	51	51.0	51	0
Packers	**26**	**284**	**10.9**	**51**	**2**
Opponents	27	370	13.7	37	3

Scoring

	TDr	TDp	TDrt	PAT	FG	S	TP
Chandler	0	0	0	39/39	19/29	0	96
D. Anderson	6	3	0	0/0	0/0	0	54
E. Pitts	6	0	0	0/0	0/0	0	36
T. Williams	1	1	4	0/0	0/0	0	36
Dale	0	5	0	0/0	0/0	0	30
Dowler	0	4	0	0/0	0/0	0	24
Grabowski	2	1	0	0/0	0/0	0	18
B. Wilson	2	0	0	0/0	0/0	0	12
Adderley	0	0	1	0/0	0/0	0	6
Fleming	0	1	0	0/0	0/0	0	6
Mercein	1	0	0	0/0	0/0	0	6
Nitschke	0	0	1	0/0	0/0	0	6
W. Davis	0	0	0	0/0	0/0	1	2
Packers	**18**	**15**	**6**	**39/39**	**19/29**	**1**	**332**
Opponents	7	13	4	23/24	14/28	0	209

Fumbles

	Fum	Ow	Op	Yds	Tot
Adderley	0	1	0	0	1
L. Aldridge	0	0	1	0	1
D. Anderson	3	0	0	0	3
Bowman	0	1	0	0	1
Bratkowski	2	1	0	0	1
T. Brown	0	0	2	0	2
Flanigan	0	0	1	0	1
Grabowski	3	0	0	0	3
Gregg	0	1	0	0	1
Hart	0	0	1	0	1
Horn	1	0	0	0	0
Jeter	0	0	1	7	1
J. Kramer	0	1	0	0	1
Mercein	1	0	0	1	1
Nitschke	0	0	1	0	1
E. Pitts	1	0	0	0	0
D. Robinson	0	0	1	0	1
Rowser	0	0	1	0	1
Skoronski	0	1	0	0	1
Starr	3	1	0	0	1
Weatherwax	0	0	1	0	1
T. Williams	1	0	0	0	0
B. Wilson	4	2	0	0	2
S. Wright	0	0	3	0	3
Packers	**19**	**9**	**14**	**7**	**23**

NFL STANDINGS

Western Conference

Coastal Division

	W	L	T	Pct	PF	PA
Los Angeles Rams	11	1	2	.917	398	196
Baltimore Colts	11	1	2	.917	394	198
San Francisco 49ers	7	7	0	.500	273	337
Atlanta Falcons	1	12	1	.077	175	422

Central Division

	W	L	T	Pct	PF	PA
Green Bay Packers	9	4	1	.692	332	209
Chicago Bears	7	6	1	.538	239	218
Detroit Lions	5	7	2	.417	260	259
Minnesota Vikings	3	8	3	.273	233	294

Eastern Conference

Capitol Division

	W	L	T	Pct	PF	PA
Dallas Cowboys	9	5	0	.643	342	268
Philadelphia Eagles	6	7	1	.462	351	409
Washington Redskins	5	6	3	.455	347	353
New Orleans Saints	3	11	0	.214	233	379

Century Division

	W	L	T	Pct	PF	PA
Cleveland Browns	9	5	0	.643	334	297
New York Giants	7	7	0	.500	369	379
St. Louis Cardinals	6	7	1	.462	333	356
Pittsburgh Steelers	4	9	1	.308	281	320

1967

ROSTER

No	Name	Pos	Ht	Wt	DOB	College	G
26	Adderley, Herb	CB	6-1	200	06/08/39	Michigan State	14
82	Aldridge, Lionel	DE	6-4	245	02/18/41	Utah State	12
44	Anderson, Donny	RB	6-3	210	05/16/43	Texas Tech	14
57	Bowman, Ken	C	6-3	230	12/15/42	Wisconsin	13
12	Bratkowski, Zeke	QB	6-3	210	10/20/31	Georgia	6
83	Brown, Allen	TE	6-5	235	03/02/43	Mississippi	14
78	Brown, Bob	DE	6-5	260	02/23/40	Arkansas-Pine Bluff	14
40	Brown, Tom	DB	6-1	190	12/12/40	Maryland	14
60	Caffey, Lee Roy	LB	6-3	250	06/03/41	Texas A&M	13
88	Capp, Dick	TE	6-3	235	04/09/42	Boston College	2
34	Chandler, Don	K	6-2	210	09/05/34	Florida	14
56	Crutcher, Tommy	LB	6-3	230	08/10/41	TCU	14
84	Dale, Carroll	WR	6-2	200	04/24/38	Virginia Tech	14
87	Davis, Willie	DE	6-3	245	07/24/34	Grambling	14
86	Dowler, Boyd	WR	6-5	225	10/18/37	Colorado	14
55	Flanigan, Jim	LB	6-3	240	04/15/45	Pittsburgh	12
81	Fleming, Marv	TE	6-4	235	01/02/42	Utah	14
68	Gillingham, Gale	G	6-3	255	02/03/44	Minnesota	14
33	Grabowski, Jim	RB	6-2	220	09/09/44	Illinois	9
75	Gregg, Alvis (Forrest)	T	6-4	250	10/18/33	SMU	14
43	Hart, Doug	DB	6-0	190	06/03/39	Arlington State	14
13	Horn, Don	QB	6-2	195	03/09/45	San Diego State	3
50	Hyland, Bob	C-G	6-5	250	07/21/45	Boston College	14
27	James, Claudis	WR	6-2	190	11/07/43	Jackson State	1
21	Jeter, Bob	DB	6-1	205	05/09/37	Iowa	14
74	Jordan, Henry	DT	6-3	250	01/26/35	Virginia	14
77	Kostelnik, Ron	DT	6-4	260	01/14/40	Cincinnati	14
64	Kramer, Jerry	G	6-3	245	01/23/36	Idaho	14
80	Long, Bob	WR	6-3	205	06/16/42	Wichita	10
85	McGee, Max	WR	6-3	210	07/16/32	Tulane	10
30	Mercein, Chuck	RB	6-3	230	04/09/43	Yale	6
66	Nitschke, Ray	LB	6-3	240	12/29/36	Illinois	14
22	Pitts, Elijah	HB	6-1	205	02/03/39	Philander Smith	8
89	Robinson, Dave	LB	6-3	240	05/03/41	Penn State	14
45	Rowser, John	DB	6-1	180	04/24/44	Michigan	14
76	Skoronski, Bob	T	6-3	245	03/05/34	Indiana	14
15	Starr, Bryan (Bart)	QB	6-1	190	01/09/34	Alabama	14
63	Thurston, Fred (Fuzzy)	G	6-1	245	05/07/35	Valparaiso	9
73	Weatherwax, Jim	DT	6-7	260	01/09/43	Cal State-Los Angeles	14
23	Williams, Travis	RB	6-1	210	01/14/46	Arizona State	14
36	Wilson, Ben	RB	6-0	225	03/09/40	USC	14
24	Wood, Willie	DB	5-10	190	12/23/36	USC	14
72	Wright, Steve	T	6-6	250	07/18/42	Alabama	14

DRAFT

Rnd	Name	Pos	Ht	Wt	College
1a	Bob Hyland (9)	C-G	6-5	255	Boston College
	(Choice from Steelers as part of Tony Jeter, Lloyd Voss deal)				
1b	Don Horn (25)	QB	6-2	195	San Diego State
2a	Dave Dunaway (41)	WR	6-2	205	Duke
	(Choice from Rams for Tom Moore)				
2b	Jim Flanigan (51)	LB	6-3	240	Pittsburgh
3	John Rowser (78)	DB	6-1	180	Michigan
4a	Travis Williams (93)	RB	6-1	210	Arizona State
	(Choice from Redskins for Ron Rector)				
4b	(Choice (105) traded to Cardinals for Cardinals No. 3 in 1968)				
5a	Dwight Hood (116)	DE	6-5	240	Baylor
	(Choice from Steelers for Ron Smith)				
5b	Dick Tate (130)	DB	6-0	185	Utah
	(Choice from Cowboys for Hank Gremminger)				
5c	Jay Bachman (132)	C	6-3	240	Cincinnati
6	Stew Williams (158)	FB	6-1	240	Bowling Green
7a	Bob Ziolkowski (161)	T	6-5	270	Iowa
	(Choice from Giants for Allen Jacobs)				
7b	Bill Powell (184)	G-LB	6-1	240	Missouri
8	Clarence Mills (210)	DT	6-6	280	Trinity
9	Harland Reed (236)	TE	6-2	220	Mississippi State
10	Bill Shear (262)	K	5-10	175	Cortland State
11	Dave Bennett (287)	QB	6-4	200	Springfield
12	Mike Bass (314)	DB	6-0	190	Michigan
13	Keith Brown (340)	WR	6-5	215	Central Missouri
14	Claudis James (366)	HB	6-2	190	Jackson State
15	James Schneider (392)	DT	6-5	230	Colgate
16	Fred Cassidy (418)	HB	6-1	200	Miami (FL)
17	Jeff Elias (444)	TE	6-5	230	Kansas

1967 GREEN BAY PACKERS

FRONT ROW: (L-R) 89 Dave Robinson, 22 Elijah Pitts, 82 Lionel Aldridge, 43 Doug Hart, 21 Bob Jeter, 76 Bob Skoronski, 87 Willie Davis, 26 Herb Adderley, 24 Willie Wood, 81 Marv Fleming.

SECOND ROW: (L-R) Trainer Carl (Bud) Jorgensen, 40 Tom Brown, 66 Ray Nitschke, 12 Zeke Bratkowski, 84 Carroll Dale, 15 Bart Starr, 77 Ron Kostelnik, 34 Don Chandler, 13 Don Horn, 45 John Rowser, 80 Bob Long, Equipment Manager Gerald (Dad) Braisher.

THIRD ROW: (L-R) Assistant Trainer Domenic Gentile, 78 Bob Brown, 57 Ken Bowman, 33 Jim Grabowski, 64 Jerry Kramer, 63 Fred (Fuzzy) Thurston, 36 Ben Wilson, 68 Gale Gillingham, 50 Bob Hyland, 27 Claudis James, Assistant Equipment Manager Bob Noel.

BACK ROW: (L-R) 44 Donny Anderson, 73 Jim Weatherwax, 56 Tommy Crutcher, 55 Jim Flanigan, 83 Allen Brown, 86 Boyd Dowler, 75 Forrest Gregg, 60 Lee Roy Caffey, 72 Steve Wright, 88 Dick Capp, 23 Travis Williams, 85 Max McGee.

The Teams: 1967   **A Measure of Greatness**   165

When Green Bay hosted the Eagles to open the 1968 season, it marked the first time in a decade that Vince Lombardi was not on the sideline with the team. Instead, Phil Bengtson, Lombardi's defensive assistant for nine years, ran the show from the field. Lombardi watched the action from a soundproof room near the press box

Bengtson, the architect of the Packers' great defenses of the championship years, was handpicked by Lombardi to become the team's sixth head coach on Feb. 1. Lombardi remained the team's general manager.

"(Following a legend) really doesn't bother me," said the 54-year-old Bengtson. "Four in a row ... that's my ambition. I see no reason why we can't continue winning."

In the end, four in a row remained but a dream. In a season when a mere 8-6 record would have secured the NFC Central Division title, the Packers hovered near the .500 mark and finished in third place behind the Vikings (8-6) and Bears (7-7), with a 6-7-1 record.

The Packers were getting long in the tooth. The average age of the 11 offensive starters on opening day was almost 29 years. The defense averaged 29 1/2 years per starter. More than a dozen players were in their 30s.

The team was in need of a decent kicker. Jerry Kramer, Chuck Mercein, Errol Mann and Mike Mercer all tried, with little success. Mercer ended up as the only one to convert better than 50 percent of his field goal attempts.

Had the Green and Gold had a reliable kicker, its record in close games might have been better. Seven games were decided by a touchdown or less, and Green Bay won only one of those: a 28-27 squeaker at Chicago in Week 14 after it had already been eliminated from the playoff race.

Bart Starr led the league in completion percentage for the third time in his career. He completed 63.7 percent of his throws and averaged nearly 9.5 yards per attempt. But the 34-year-old also missed part or all of eight games due to injury and failed to attempt 200 passes for the first time since 1960.

Green Bay's defense remained steadfast. It ranked third in fewest yards given up and was No. 1 against the pass for an NFL record fifth time in succession.

The season got off to a flying start with a 30-13 triumph over the Eagles in Lambeau Field. Starr completed 14 of 18 passes for 220 yards and two scores. Boyd Dowler had five receptions for 110 yards and a touchdown.

A week later, the Vikings toppled the Packers 26-13. Joe Kapp's fourth-down sneak from his own 26-yard line in the third quarter broke the Packers' back.

"There's no way he (Kapp) penetrated," Lee Roy Caffey said. "Ray (Nitschke) hit him straight on and I came in from an angle and got him by the back of the shirt."

The officials gave Kapp a first down, and the Vikings continued on an 83-yard drive that put them ahead 23-6.

The Lions dropped the Packers to 1-2 when Bill Munson hooked up with Billy Gambrell on a 12-yard pass play with 1:55 left in a 23-17 win in Week 3. A week later, Green Bay blew out the Falcons 38-7.

A pass interference call on Herb Adderley in Week 5 helped the Rams to a 16-14 win. The veteran cornerback was penalized while covering Jack Snow. Four plays after the 18-yard infraction, Bruce Gossett hit the game-winning field goal from 27 yards out with 55 seconds left.

Green Bay played perhaps its finest game in Dallas in Week 7. Starr returned after a two-week absence (arm) and threw for 260 yards and four touchdowns in a 28-17 win. The defense intercepted Don Meredith three times.

The Packers then fell into a tie with the Lions for last place after close losses to the Bears and Vikings.

Green Bay rebounded with convincing wins over the Saints and Redskins to climb within a half game of the Vikings. Zeke Bratkowski engineered the second, a 27-7 win in the nation's capital after Starr couldn't go (ribs).

A collapse at Kezar prevented the Packers from winning three in a row. San Francisco scored on each of its four fourth-quarter possessions and won 27-20.

Green Bay (5-6-1) had to beat Baltimore and Chicago and hope Minnesota (6-6) lost at least once. It didn't happen. With the Packers trailing the Colts 16-13 at Lambeau Field, band director Wilner Burke approached the microphone. "For years these Packers have given some great thrills. How about a standing ovation for them?" With that, the crowd arose and paid tribute to the team that had delivered five championships in seven years.

ROAD WARRIORS

The Packers have had many losing seasons over the years. The 1968 club is the only one to fall into that category, yet still post a winning record on the road.

In 1968, Green Bay lost more games than it won for the first time in a decade. Surprisingly, the team put together a 4-2-1 record on the road.

In Atlanta, the club rolled up 470 yards and rolled over the Falcons 38-7. In Dallas, Bart Starr directed a 28-17 upset over the playoff-bound Cowboys. In the nation's capitol, the Packers held the Redskins to 167 yards in a 27-7 win. And in the only game he played in all season, Don Horn engineered a one-point, 28-27 win in Chicago.

Green Bay's two road losses came in Minnesota and San Francisco. The team played to a 14-14 tie in Detroit.

Listed below are the club's best road records in losing seasons.

On Road	Pct.	Year	Overall Record
4-2-1	.667	1968	6-7-1
3-4-0	.429	1987	5-9-1
3-5-0	.375	1986	4-12-0
3-5-0	.375	1990	6-10-0

TEAM STATISTICS

	GB	OPP
First Downs	240	213
Rushing	96	105
Passing	130	92
Penalty	14	16
Rushes	450	476
Yards Gained	1,749	1,800
Average Gain	3.89	3.78
Average Yards per Game	124.9	128.6
Passes Attempted	318	327
Completed	188	157
% Completed	59.12	48.01
Total Yards Gained	2,651	2,031
Times Sacked	41	28
Yards Lost	376	235
Net Yards Gained	2,275	1,796
Yards Gained per Completion	14.10	12.94
Net Yards per Attempt	6.34	5.06
Average Net Yards per Game	162.5	128.3
Combined Net Yards Gained	4,024	3,596
Total Plays	809	831
Average Yards per Play	4.97	4.33
Average Net Yards per Game	287.4	256.9
Third Down Efficiency	65/169	68/188
Percentage	38.46	36.17
Fourth Down Efficiency	3/8	6/9
Percentage	37.50	66.67
Intercepted By	17	15
Yards Returned	244	150
Returned for TD	0	0
Punts	59	77
Yards Punted	2,359	3,049
Average Yards per Punt	39.98	39.60
Punt Returns	43	19
Yards Returned	238	66
Average Yards per Return	5.53	3.47
Returned for TD	1	0
Kickoff Returns	48	56
Yards Returned	1,007	1,211
Average Yards per Return	20.98	21.63
Returned for TD	0	0
Penalties	64	60
Yards Penalized	653	541
Fumbles	31	28
Lost	18	17
Own Recovered for Touchdown	0	0
Opponent's Recovered by	17	18
Opponent's Recovered for Touchdown	1	0
Total Points Scored	281	227
Total Touchdowns	35	25
Touchdowns Rushing	12	11
Touchdowns Passing	21	14
Touchdowns on Returns & Recoveries	2	0
Extra Points	32	24
Safeties	0	1
Field Goals Attempted	29	26
Field Goals Made	13	17
% Successful	44.83	65.38

Regular Season 6-7-1

Date	GB		OPP	Att.
9/15	30	Philadelphia Eagles	13	(50,861)
9/22	13	Minnesota Vikings (M)	26	(49,346)
9/29	17	Detroit Lions	23	(50,861)
10/6	38	at Atlanta Falcons	7	(58,850)
10/13	14	Los Angeles Rams (M)	16	(49,646)
10/20	14	at Detroit Lions	14	(57,302)
10/28	28	at Dallas Cowboys	17	(74,604)
11/3	10	Chicago Bears	13	(50,861)
11/10	10	at Minnesota Vikings	14	(47,644)
11/17	29	New Orleans Saints	7	(49,644)
11/24	27	at Washington Redskins	7	(50,621)
12/1	20	at San Francisco 49ers	27	(47,218)
12/7	3	Baltimore Colts	16	(50,861)
12/15	28	at Chicago Bears	27	(46,435)

Score By Periods

	1	2	3	4	Total
Packers	68	61	95	57	281
Opponents	55	69	40	63	227

INDIVIDUAL STATISTICS

Rushing

	Att	Yds	Avg	LG	TD
D. Anderson	170	761	4.5	42	5
Grabowski	135	518	3.8	25	3
E. Pitts	72	264	3.7	14	2
T. Williams	33	63	1.9	9	0
Starr	11	62	5.6	15	1
Mercein	17	49	2.9	8	1
Bratkowski	8	24	3.0	13	0
James	1	15	15.0	15	0
Horn	3	-7	-2.3	1	0
Packers	**450**	**1,749**	**3.9**	**42**	**12**
Opponents	476	1,800	3.8	63	11

Receiving

	No	Yds	Avg	LG	TD
Dowler	45	668	14.8	t72	6
Dale	42	818	19.5	t63	8
D. Anderson	25	333	13.3	t47	1
Fleming	25	278	11.1	t32	3
Grabowski	18	210	11.7	t67	1
E. Pitts	17	142	8.4	19	0
James	8	148	18.5	24	2
T. Williams	5	48	9.6	17	0
Mercein	3	6	2.0	6	0
Packers	**188**	**2,651**	**14.1**	**t72**	**21**
Opponents	157	2,031	12.9	t60	14

Passing

	Att	Com	Yds	Pct	TD	In	Tk/Yds	Rate
Starr	171	109	1,617	63.7	15	8	29/261	104.3
Bratkowski	126	68	835	54.0	3	7	11/107	59.5
Horn	16	10	187	62.5	2	0	1/8	142.4
D. Anderson	3	1	12	33.3	1	0	0/0	—
Stevens	2	0	0	00.0	0	0	0/0	—
Packers	**318**	**188**	**2,651**	**59.1**	**21**	**15**	**41/376**	**88.4**
Opponents	327	157	2,031	48.0	14	17	28/235	60.6

Punting

	No	Yds	Avg	Net	TB	In20	LG	HB
D. Anderson	59	2,359	40.0	37.8	3	15	65	0
Packers	**59**	**2,359**	**40.0**	**37.8**	**3**	**15**	**65**	**0**
Opponents	77	3,049	39.6	34.9	6	9	62	0

Kickoff Returns

	No	Yds	Avg	LG	TD
T. Williams	28	599	21.4	60	0
Adderley	14	331	23.6	50	0
E. Pitts	2	40	20.0	27	0
D. Robinson	2	29	14.5	19	0
Vandersea	1	8	8.0	8	0
Winkler	1	0	0.0	0	0
Packers	**48**	**1,007**	**21.0**	**60**	**0**
Opponents	56	1,211	21.6	46	0

Punt Returns

	No	Yds	Avg	FC	LG	TD
Wood	26	126	4.8	11	16	0
T. Brown	16	111	6.9	5	t52	1
E. Pitts	1	1	1.0	1	1	0
Packers	**43**	**238**	**5.5**	**17**	**t52**	**1**
Opponents	19	66	3.5	20	16	0

Interceptions

	No	Yds	Avg	LG	TD
T. Brown	4	66	16.5	25	0
Jeter	3	35	11.7	29	0
Adderley	3	27	9.0	17	0
Wood	2	54	27.0	35	0
Nitschke	2	20	10.0	11	0
D. Robinson	2	18	9.0	18	0
Hart	1	24	24.0	24	0
Packers	**17**	**244**	**14.4**	**35**	**0**
Opponents	15	150	10.0	36	0

Scoring

	TDr	TDp	TDrt	PAT	FG	S	TP
Dale	0	8	0	0/0	0/0	0	48
D. Anderson	5	1	0	0/0	0/0	0	36
Dowler	0	6	0	0/0	0/0	0	36
Mercer	0	0	0	12/14	7/12	0	33
Grabowski	3	1	0	0/0	0/0	0	24
J. Kramer	0	0	0	9/9	4/9	0	21
Mercein	1	0	0	7/7	2/5	0	19
Fleming	0	3	0	0/0	0/0	0	18
T. Brown	0	0	2	0/0	0/0	0	12
James	0	2	0	0/0	0/0	0	12
E. Pitts	2	0	0	0/0	0/0	0	12
Starr	1	0	0	0/0	0/0	0	6
E. Mann	0	0	0	4/4	0/3	0	4
Packers	**12**	**21**	**2**	**32/35**	**13/29**	**0**	**281**
Opponents	11	14	0	24/25	17/26	1	227

Fumbles

	Fum	Ow	Op	Yds	Tot
Adderley	2	0	2	25	2
L. Aldridge	1	0	2	12	2
D. Anderson	7	0	0	0	0
Bowman	0	1	0	0	1
Bratkowski	4	1	0	0	1
T. Brown	0	0	1	22	1
Caffey	0	1	0	0	1
Carr	0	0	1	0	1
Carroll	0	0	1	0	1
Dale	1	0	0	0	0
W. Davis	0	0	3	9	3
Gillingham	0	1	0	0	1
Grabowski	6	1	0	0	1
Gregg	0	2	0	0	2
Horn	1	1	0	0	1
James	2	0	0	0	0
H. Jordan	0	1	1	0	2
Kostelnik	0	0	1	0	1
Nitschke	0	0	3	6	3
E. Pitts	1	0	0	0	1
D. Robinson	1	1	0	0	1
Starr	4	0	0	0	0
T. Williams	3	0	1	0	2
Winkler	0	0	1	0	1
Wood	1	0	0	0	0
Packers	**31**	**13**	**17**	**74**	**30**

NFL STANDINGS

Western Conference

Coastal Division

	W	L	T	Pct	PF	PA
Baltimore Colts	13	1	0	.929	402	144
Los Angeles Rams	10	3	1	.769	312	200
San Francisco 49ers	7	6	1	.538	303	310
Atlanta Falcons	2	12	0	.143	170	389

Central Division

	W	L	T	Pct	PF	PA
Minnesota Vikings	8	6	0	.571	282	242
Chicago Bears	7	7	0	.500	250	333
Green Bay Packers	**6**	**7**	**1**	**.462**	**281**	**227**
Detroit Lions	4	8	2	.333	207	241

Eastern Conference

Capitol Division

	W	L	T	Pct	PF	PA
Dallas Cowboys	12	2	0	.857	431	186
New York Giants	7	7	0	.500	294	325
Washington Redskins	5	9	0	.357	249	358
Philadelphia Eagles	2	12	0	.143	202	351

Century Division

	W	L	T	Pct	PF	PA
Cleveland Browns	10	4	0	.714	394	273
St. Louis Cardinals	9	4	1	.692	325	289
New Orleans Saints	4	9	1	.308	246	327
Pittsburgh Steelers	2	11	1	.154	244	397

ROSTER

No	Name	Pos	Ht	Wt	DOB	College	G
26	Adderley, Herb	CB	6-1	200	06/08/39	Michigan State	14
82	Aldridge, Lionel	DE	6-4	245	02/18/41	Utah State	14
44	Anderson, Donny	RB	6-3	210	05/16/43	Texas Tech	14
57	Bowman, Ken	C	6-3	230	12/15/42	Wisconsin	14
12	Bratkowski, Zeke	QB	6-3	210	10/20/31	Georgia	10
78	Brown, Bob	DE	6-5	260	02/23/40	Arkansas-Pine Bluff	6
40	Brown, Tom	DB	6-1	190	12/12/40	Maryland	14
60	Caffey, Lee Roy	LB	6-3	250	06/03/41	Texas A&M	14
53	Carr, Fred	LB	6-5	238	08/19/46	Texas-El Paso	14
67	Carroll, Leo	DE	6-7	250	02/16/44	San Diego State	6
70	Crenshaw, Leon	DT	6-6	280	07/14/43	Tuskegee	10
84	Dale, Carroll	WR	6-2	200	04/24/38	Virginia Tech	14
87	Davis, Willie	DE	6-3	245	07/24/34	Grambling	14
86	Dowler, Boyd	WR	6-5	225	10/18/37	Colorado	14
29	Dunaway, Dave	WR	6-2	205	01/19/45	Duke	2
55	Flanigan, Jim	LB	6-3	240	04/15/45	Pittsburgh	13
81	Fleming, Marv	TE	6-4	235	01/02/42	Utah	14
68	Gillingham, Gale	G	6-3	255	02/03/44	Minnesota	14
33	Grabowski, Jim	RB	6-2	220	09/09/44	Illinois	14
75	Gregg, Alvis (Forrest)	T	6-4	250	10/18/33	SMU	14
43	Hart, Doug	DB	6-0	190	06/03/39	Arlington State	14
72	Himes, Dick	T	6-4	244	05/25/46	Ohio State	14
13	Horn, Don	QB	6-2	195	03/09/45	San Diego State	1
50	Hyland, Bob	C-G	6-5	250	07/21/45	Boston College	14
27	James, Claudis	WR	6-2	190	11/07/43	Jackson State	14
21	Jeter, Bob	DB	6-1	205	05/09/37	Iowa	12
74	Jordan, Henry	DT	6-3	250	01/26/35	Virginia	14
77	Kostelnik, Ron	DT	6-4	260	01/14/40	Cincinnati	13
64	Kramer, Jerry	G	6-3	245	01/23/36	Idaho	14
62	Lueck, Bill	G	6-3	235	04/07/46	Arizona	11
39	Mann, Errol	K	6-0	203	06/27/41	North Dakota	2
30	Mercein, Chuck	RB	6-3	230	04/09/43	Yale	11
38	Mercer, Mike	K	6-0	217	11/21/35	Arizona State	6
66	Nitschke, Ray	LB	6-3	235	12/29/36	Illinois	14
71	Peay, Francis	T	6-5	250	05/23/44	Missouri	14
22	Pitts, Elijah	HB	6-1	205	02/03/39	Philander Smith	14
80	Pope, Bucky	WR	6-5	200	03/23/41	Catawba	3
89	Robinson, Dave	LB	6-3	240	05/03/41	Penn State	14
45	Rowser, John	CB	6-1	180	04/24/44	Michigan	14
47	Rule, Gordon	S	6-2	180	03/01/46	Dartmouth	1
76	Skoronski, Bob	T	6-3	245	03/05/34	Indiana	14
15	Starr, Bryan (Bart)	QB	6-1	190	01/09/34	Alabama	12
10	Stevens, Bill	QB	6-3	195	08/27/45	Texas-El Paso	1
83	Vandersea, Phil	LB	6-3	235	02/25/43	Massachusetts	10
23	Williams, Travis	RB	6-1	210	01/14/46	Arizona State	14
58	Winkler, Francis	DE	6-3	230	10/20/46	Memphis State	7
24	Wood, Willie	DB	5-10	190	12/23/36	USC	14

DRAFT

Rnd	Name	Pos	Ht	Wt	College
Rnd	Name	Pos	Ht	Wt	College
1a	Fred Carr (5)	LB	6-5	238	Texas-El Paso
	(Choice from Saints for Jim Taylor)				
1b	Bill Lueck (26)	G	6-3	235	Arizona
2	(Choice (53) to Rams in Ben Wilson deal)				
3a	Bill Stevens (67)	QB	6-3	195	Texas-El Paso
	(Choice from Cardinals for Fred Heron)				
3b	Dick Himes (81)	T	6-4	244	Ohio State
4a	Brendan McCarthy (92)	FB	6-3	217	Boston College
	(Choice from Steelers for Dick Arndt)				
4b	John Robinson (108)	WR	6-2	196	Tennessee State
5a	Steve Duich (121)	T	6-3	248	San Diego State
	(Choice from Steelers for Kent Nix)				
5b	Francis Winkler (137)	DE	6-3	230	Memphis State

Rnd	Name	Pos	Ht	Wt	College
6	Walter Chadwick (164)	HB	6-0	205	Tennessee
7	Andy Beath (191)	DB	6-2	192	Duke
8	Tom Owens (218)	G	6-3	240	Missouri-Rolla
9	Bob Apisa (245)	FB	6-2	225	Michigan State
10a	Richard Cash (260)	T	6-5	260	NE Missouri State
	(Choice from Giants for Dave Hathcock)				
10b	Ron Worthen (272)	C	6-5	235	Arkansas State
11	Gordon Rule (299)	DB	6-2	180	Dartmouth
12	Dennis Porter (325)	DT	6-4	242	Northern Michigan
13	Frank Geiselman (353)	WR	6-2	207	Rhode Island
14	John Farler (380)	WR	6-1	208	Colorado
15	Ridley Gibson (407)	DB	6-2	200	Baylor
16	Al Groves (434)	DT	6-4	270	St. Norbert
17	Ken Rota (461)	HB	6-2	200	North Dakota State

1968 GREEN BAY PACKERS

FRONT ROW: (L-R) 89 Dave Robinson, 82 Lionel Aldridge, 43 Doug Hart, 57 Ken Bowman, 21 Bob Jeter, 76 Bob Skoronski, 87 Willie Davis, 40 Tom Brown, 26 Herb Adderley, 24 Willie Wood, 81 Marv Fleming.

SECOND ROW: (L-R) Trainer Carl (Bud) Jorgensen, 15 Bart Starr, 84 Carroll Dale, 12 Zeke Bratkowski, 77 Ron Kostelnik, 74 Henry Jordan, 45 John Rowser, 83 Phil Vandersea, 27 Claudis James, 50 Bob Hyland, 22 Elijah Pitts, Equipment Manager Gerald (Dad) Braisher.

THIRD ROW: (L-R) Assistant Trainer Domenic Gentile, 66 Ray Nitschke, 36 Ben Wilson, 33 Jim Grabowski, 44 Donny Anderson, 68 Gale Gillingham, 64 Jerry Kramer, 30 Chuck Mercein, 29 Dave Dunaway, 67 Leo Carroll, 78 Bob Brown, 70 Leon Crenshaw, Assistant Equipment Manager Bob Noel.

BACK ROW: (L-R) 23 Travis Williams, 53 Fred Carr, 73 Jim Weatherwax, 60 Lee Roy Caffey, 86 Boyd Dowler, 75 Forrest Gregg, 55 Jim Flanigan, 71 Francis Peay, 58 Francis Winkler, 62 Bill Lueck, 72 Dick Himes.

"The Pack will be back!"

Those five words became the rallying cry of Packers fans everywhere shortly after the 1968 team finished with a losing record—the club's first in 10 years. Stickers with that slogan showed up everywhere during the offseason. The local newspaper—the Green Bay Press-Gazette—made reference to "Operation Pack Will Be Back" prior to the team's first preseason game. Everybody, it seemed, was eager for the team to return to its winning ways.

For half a season, that goal remained feasible. The Packers whipped the Bears 17-0, then edged the 49ers 14-7. Three wins in the next five games pulled Green Bay (5-2) to within a game of the Vikings (6-1).

But three consecutive losses (Colts, Vikings, and Lions) in November eliminated the Packers from the playoff chase. The last of those, a 16-10 setback to Detroit, dropped Green Bay (5-5) four games behind the Vikings (9-1) with four games to play.

By winning three of its last four games, Green Bay (8-6) finished third in the Central Division behind the Vikings (12-2) and Lions (9-4-1).

Six more players from the Lombardi era were scratched from the roster. Bob Skoronski, Jerry Kramer, Zeke Bratkowski and Forrest Gregg retired. Ron Kostelnik and Tom Brown were traded to the Colts and Redskins, respectively. Bratkowski and Gregg became Packers assistant coaches, but Gregg reconsidered and came out of retirement on Sept. 2. He played in all 14 games and ran his team-record string of consecutive games played to 173.

Vince Lombardi found himself in the nation's capital. The Packers' general manager was released from his contract and became head coach, executive vice president, and part owner of the Washington Redskins.

Phil Bengtson was named the Packers' general manager after meeting with team president Dominic Olejniczak on March 6.

Bengtson promised "a little tougher camp than what we had a year ago." For the first time, players were put through a rigorous series of physical tests to determine their condition prior to participating in training camp.

Quarterback and kicker remained areas of concern. Bart Starr again was plagued by injuries and threw only 148 passes, his lowest output in a decade. The kicking duties fell to Mike Mercer and Booth Lusteg, who connected on only six of 22 field goal attempts.

The Packers opened against the Bears. Green Bay gave up only 204 yards and won 17-0. At halftime, commissioner Pete Rozelle paid tribute to Packers fans and thanked them for their "help during the first 50 years of the National Football League."

Herb Adderley's interception of John Brodie with 17 seconds left preserved a 14-7 win over the 49ers in Week 2.

A week later, the Vikings sacked Starr eight times for 63 yards in losses. Minnesota also got four field goals from Fred Cox in posting a 19-7 triumph.

Starr and Carroll Dale carried the team offensively in Week 4. Starr threw for 234 yards and Dale had seven catches for 167 yards in a 28-17 win in Detroit.

A 34-21 loss to the Rams was followed by consecutive wins (Falcons and Steelers) that catapulted Green Bay into second place at midseason. Donny Anderson had his best rushing day (114 yards) as a Packer in the 28-10 win over Atlanta, and Dale went over 100 yards receiving (134) in a 38-34 nail-biter in Pittsburgh.

In Week 8, two plays helped the Colts to a 14-6 victory. Ray Nitschke and Doug Hart collided attempting to tackle Tom Mitchell, and the tight end rumbled 51 yards for a score. Tom Maxwell and Mike Curtis then blocked a Mercer field goal try to set up the Colts' other touchdown.

The following week, Bobby Bryant intercepted a pass intended for Dave Hampton with 1:47 left as the Vikings escaped with a 9-7 win in Milwaukee.

The Lions dealt the Packers a third straight loss 16-10. Errol Mann, a Packer in 1968, scored 10 points on three field goals and an extra point.

Starr did not attempt a pass in Green Bay's final four games. Don Horn started all four and emerged victorious on three occasions.

The third-year pro saved his best for last in a 45-28 rout of the Cardinals. On Dec. 21, he riddled the Cardinals for 410 yards and five touchdowns. The heir apparent to Starr completed 22 of 31 throws and led the team to scores on five of its first six possessions.

HORN APLENTY

Sometimes touted as the next "Bart Starr," Don Horn never lived up to those lofty expectations. The 25th pick overall in the 1967 draft did, however, pass for more yards in a single game (excluding overtime contests) than any other player in team annals.

On Dec. 21, Horn passed for 410 yards and five touchdowns in a 45-28 rout of St. Louis. He completed 22 of 31 throws and led the team to scores five of the first six times he got the ball.

"Horn did a tremendous job of locating receivers and holding his poise. He ought to lead them to a championship next year," said Cardinals coach Charlie Winner.

Winner was as off as was his team in that loss. Horn played one more season before being traded to the Denver Broncos.

Listed below are the most yards passing by a Packer in a non-overtime game:

Yards	Player	Date
410	Don Horn	12-21-69
402	Brett Favre	12-5-93
390	Brett Favre	10-10-99

TEAM STATISTICS

	GB	OPP
First Downs	242	224
Rushing	95	103
Passing	122	107
Penalty	25	14
Rushes	432	485
Yards Gained	1,692	1,982
Average Gain	3.92	4.09
Average Yards per Game	120.9	141.6
Passes Attempted	319	360
Completed	182	177
% Completed	57.05	49.17
Total Yards Gained	2,678	2,133
Times Sacked	34	36
Yards Lost	302	288
Net Yards Gained	2,376	1,845
Yards Gained per Completion	14.71	12.05
Net Yards per Attempt	6.73	4.66
Average Net Yards per Game	169.7	131.8
Combined Net Yards Gained	4,068	3,827
Total Plays	785	881
Average Yards per Play	5.18	4.34
Average Net Yards per Game	290.6	273.4
Third Down Efficiency	52/155	77/203
Percentage	33.55	37.93
Fourth Down Efficiency	5/8	5/13
Percentage	62.50	38.46
Intercepted By	19	17
Yards Returned	428	256
Returned for TD	2	1
Punts	59	72
Yards Punted	2,363	2,855
Average Yards per Punt	40.05	39.65
Punt Returns	32	18
Yards Returned	287	62
Average Yards per Return	8.97	3.44
Returned for TD	1	0
Kickoff Returns	50	51
Yards Returned	1,165	1,078
Average Yards per Return	23.30	21.14
Returned for TD	2	1
Penalties	63	65
Yards Penalized	602	733
Fumbles	31	23
Lost	21	7
Own Recovered for Touchdown	0	0
Opponent's Recovered by	7	21
Opponent's Recovered for Touchdown	0	1
Total Points Scored	269	221
Total Touchdowns	36	23
Touchdowns Rushing	11	7
Touchdowns Passing	20	13
Touchdowns on Returns & Recoveries	5	3
Extra Points	35	23
Safeties	0	0
Field Goals Attempted	22	34
Field Goals Made	6	20
% Successful	27.27	58.82

Regular Season 8-6-0

Date	GB		OPP	Att.
9/21	17	Chicago Bears	0	(50,861)
9/28	14	San Francisco 49ers (M)	7	(48,184)
10/5	7	at Minnesota Vikings	19	(60,740)
10/12	28	at Detroit Lions	17	(58,384)
10/19	21	at Los Angeles Rams	34	(78,947)
10/26	28	Atlanta Falcons	10	(50,861)
11/2	38	at Pittsburgh Steelers	34	(46,403)
11/9	6	at Baltimore Colts	14	(60,238)
11/16	7	Minnesota Vikings (M)	9	(48,321)
11/23	10	Detroit Lions	16	(50,861)
11/30	20	New York Giants (M)	10	(48,156)
12/7	7	at Cleveland Browns	20	(82,137)
12/14	21	at Chicago Bears	3	(45,216)
12/21	45	St. Louis Cardinals	28	(50,861)

Score By Periods

	1	2	3	4	Total
Packers	48	72	59	90	269
Opponents	53	87	55	26	221

INDIVIDUAL STATISTICS

Rushing

	Att	Yds	Avg	LG	TD
T. Williams	129	536	4.2	t39	4
Hampton	80	365	4.6	53	4
D. Anderson	87	288	3.3	t16	1
Grabowski	73	261	3.6	22	1
E. Pitts	35	134	3.8	13	0
Starr	7	60	8.6	18	0
P. Williams	18	55	3.1	13	0
Horn	3	-7	-2.3	t2	1
Packers	**432**	**1,692**	**3.9**	**53**	**11**
Opponents	485	1,982	4.1	52	7

Receiving

	No	Yds	Avg	LG	TD
Dale	45	879	19.5	48	6
Dowler	31	477	15.4	45	4
T. Williams	27	275	10.2	t60	3
Fleming	18	226	12.6	23	2
Hampton	15	216	14.4	50	2
D. Anderson	14	308	22.0	51	1
Grabowski	12	98	8.2	25	1
E. Pitts	9	47	5.2	t21	1
Spilis	7	89	12.7	16	0
P. Williams	4	63	15.8	24	0
Packers	**182**	**2,678**	**14.7**	**t60**	**20**
Opponents	177	2,133	12.1	t80	13

Passing

	Att	Com	Yds	Pct	TD	In	Tk/Yds	Rate
Horn	168	89	1,505	53.0	11	11	10/85	78.1
Starr	148	92	1,161	62.2	9	6	24/217	89.9
Stevens	3	1	12	33.3	0	0	0/0	—
Packers	**319**	**182**	**2,678**	**57.1**	**20**	**17**	**34/302**	**83.3**
Opponents	360	177	2,133	49.2	13	19	36/288	57.8

Punting

	No	Yds	Avg	Net	TB	In20	LG	HB
D. Anderson	58	2,329	40.2	38.5	2	21	58	0
Dowler	1	34	34.0	30.0	0	0	34	0
Packers	**59**	**2,363**	**40.1**	**38.3**	**2**	**21**	**58**	**0**
Opponents	72	2,855	39.7	33.7	7	12	66	0

Kickoff Returns

	No	Yds	Avg	LG	TD
Hampton	22	582	26.5	t87	1
T. Williams	21	517	24.6	t96	1
D. Robinson	3	31	10.3	15	0
E. Pitts	1	22	22.0	22	0
Gillingham	1	13	13.0	13	0
Hyland	1	0	0.0	0	0
P. Williams	1	0	0.0	0	0
Packers	**50**	**1,165**	**23.3**	**t96**	**2**
Opponents	51	1,078	21.1	t100	1

Punt Returns

	No	Yds	Avg	FC	LG	TD
E. Pitts	16	60	3.8	8	10	0
T. Williams	8	189	23.6	3	t83	1
Wood	8	38	4.8	6	13	0
Packers	**32**	**287**	**9.0**	**17**	**t83**	**1**
Opponents	18	62	3.4	25	15	0

Interceptions

	No	Yds	Avg	LG	TD
Adderley	5	169	33.8	t80	1
Hart	3	156	52.0	t85	1
Wood	3	40	13.3	21	0
Jeter	3	30	10.0	30	0
Nitschke	2	32	16.0	20	0
Caffey	2	1	0.5	1	0
W. Davis	1	0	0.0	0	0
Packers	**19**	**428**	**22.5**	**t85**	**2**
Opponents	17	256	15.1	44	1

Scoring

	TDr	TDp	TDrt	PAT	FG	S	TP
T. Williams	4	3	2	0/0	0/0	0	54
Hampton	4	2	1	0/0	0/0	0	42
Mercer	0	0	0	23/23	5/17	0	38
Dale	0	6	0	0/0	0/0	0	36
Dowler	0	4	0	0/0	0/0	0	24
Lusteg	0	0	0	12/12	1/5	0	15
D. Anderson	1	1	0	0/0	0/0	0	12
Fleming	0	2	0	0/0	0/0	0	12
Grabowski	1	1	0	0/0	0/0	0	12
Adderley	0	0	1	0/0	0/0	0	6
Hart	0	0	1	0/0	0/0	0	6
Horn	1	0	0	0/0	0/0	0	6
E. Pitts	0	1	0	0/0	0/0	0	6
Packers	**11**	**20**	**5**	**35/36**	**6/22**	**0**	**269**
Opponents	7	13	3	23/23	20/34	0	221

Fumbles

	Fum	Ow	Op	Yds	Tot
L. Aldridge	0	0	1	0	1
D. Anderson	4	2	0	0	2
Caffey	0	0	1	0	1
W. Davis	0	0	2	0	2
Fleming	0	1	0	0	1
Gillingham	0	0	1	0	1
Grabowski	2	0	0	0	0
Hampton	7	2	0	0	2
Horn	6	1	0	0	1
Lueck	0	0	1	0	1
R. Moore	0	0	1	0	1
E. Pitts	2	1	0	0	1
D. Robinson	0	0	1	0	1
Starr	4	0	0	0	0
P. Williams	1	0	0	0	0
T. Williams	5	1	0	0	1
Wood	0	0	1	0	1
Packers	**31**	**10**	**7**	**0**	**17**

NFL STANDINGS

Western Conference

Coastal Division

	W	L	T	Pct	PF	PA
Los Angeles Rams	11	3	0	.786	320	243
Baltimore Colts	8	5	1	.615	279	268
Atlanta Falcons	6	8	0	.429	276	268
San Francisco 49ers	4	8	2	.333	277	319

Central Division

	W	L	T	Pct	PF	PA
Minnesota Vikings	12	2	0	.857	379	133
Detroit Lions	9	4	1	.692	259	188
Green Bay Packers	**8**	**6**	**0**	**.571**	**269**	**221**
Chicago Bears	1	13	0	.071	210	339

Eastern Conference

Capitol Division

	W	L	T	Pct	PF	PA
Dallas Cowboys	11	2	1	.846	369	223
Washington Redskins	7	5	2	.583	307	319
New Orleans Saints	5	9	0	.357	311	393
Philadelphia Eagles	4	9	1	.308	279	377

Century Division

	W	L	T	Pct	PF	PA
Cleveland Browns	10	3	1	.769	351	300
New York Giants	6	8	0	.429	264	298
St. Louis Cardinals	4	9	1	.308	314	389
Pittsburgh Steelers	1	13	0	.071	218	404

ROSTER

No	Name	Pos	Ht	Wt	DOB	College	G
26	Adderley, Herb	CB	6-1	200	06/08/39	Michigan State	14
82	Aldridge, Lionel	DE	6-4	245	02/18/41	Utah State	14
44	Anderson, Donny	RB	6-3	210	05/16/43	Texas Tech	14
57	Bowman, Ken	C	6-3	230	12/15/42	Wisconsin	14
61	Bradley, Dave	G	6-4	245	02/13/47	Penn State	4
78	Brown, Bob	DE	6-5	260	02/23/40	Arkansas-Pine Bluff	14
60	Caffey, Lee Roy	LB	6-3	250	06/03/41	Texas A&M	14
53	Carr, Fred	LB	6-5	238	08/19/46	Texas-El Paso	14
84	Dale, Carroll	WR	6-2	200	04/24/38	Virginia Tech	14
87	Davis, Willie	DE	6-3	245	07/24/34	Grambling	14
86	Dowler, Boyd	WR	6-5	225	10/18/37	Colorado	14
55	Flanigan, Jim	LB	6-3	240	04/15/45	Pittsburgh	4
81	Fleming, Marv	TE	6-4	235	01/02/42	Utah	12
68	Gillingham, Gale	G	6-3	255	02/03/44	Minnesota	14
33	Grabowski, Jim	RB	6-2	220	09/04/44	Illinois	14
75	Gregg, Alvis (Forrest)	T	6-4	250	10/18/33	SMU	14
25	Hampton, Dave	RB	6-0	210	05/07/47	Wyoming	14
43	Hart, Doug	DB	6-0	190	06/03/39	Arlington State	14
77	Hayhoe, Bill	T	6-8	258	10/06/46	USC	14
72	Himes, Dick	T	6-4	244	05/25/46	Ohio State	14
13	Horn, Don	QB	6-2	195	03/09/45	San Diego State	9
50	Hyland, Bob	C-G	6-5	250	07/21/45	Boston College	14
21	Jeter, Bob	CB	6-1	205	05/09/37	Iowa	14
88	Jones, Ron	TE	6-3	220	07/17/47	Texas-El Paso	6
74	Jordan, Henry	DT	6-3	250	01/26/35	Virginia	5
62	Lueck, Bill	G	6-3	235	04/07/46	Arizona	14
32	Lusteg, Booth	K	5-11	190	05/08/39	Connecticut	4
30	Mercein, Chuck	RB	6-3	230	04/09/43	Yale	5
38	Mercer, Mike	K	6-0	217	11/21/35	Arizona State	10
70	Moore, Rich	DT	6-6	285	04/26/47	Villanova	14
66	Nitschke, Ray	LB	6-3	235	12/29/36	Illinois	14
71	Peay, Francis	T	6-5	250	05/23/44	Missouri	14
22	Pitts, Elijah	HB	6-1	205	02/03/39	Philander Smith	14
89	Robinson, Dave	LB	6-3	240	05/03/41	Penn State	14
45	Rowser, John	CB	6-1	180	04/24/44	Michigan	14
47	Rule, Gordon	S	6-2	180	03/01/46	Dartmouth	14
85	Spilis, John	WR	6-3	205	10/14/47	Northern Illinois	12
15	Starr, Bryan (Bart)	QB	6-1	190	01/09/34	Alabama	12
10	Stevens, Bill	QB	6-3	195	08/27/45	Texas-El Paso	1
83	Vandersea, Phil	LB	6-3	235	02/25/43	Massachusetts	14
73	Weatherwax, Jim	DT	6-7	260	01/09/43	Cal State-Los Angeles	6
31	Williams, Perry	RB	6-2	219	12/11/46	Purdue	14
23	Williams, Travis	RB	6-1	210	01/14/46	Arizona State	13
58	Winkler, Francis	DE	6-3	230	10/20/46	Memphis State	14
24	Wood, Willie	S	5-10	190	12/23/36	USC	14

DRAFT

Rnd	Name	Pos	Ht	Wt	College
1	Rich Moore (12)	DT	6-6	285	Villanova
2	Dave Bradley (38)	T	6-4	255	Penn State
3	John Spilis (64)	WR	6-3	205	Northern Illinois
4	Perry Williams (90)	FB	6-2	219	Purdue
5	Bill Hayhoe (116)	T	6-8	258	USC
6a	Ron Jones (134)	TE	6-3	220	Texas-El Paso
	(Choice from Cardinals through Steelers in Dick Capp trade)				
6b	Ken Vinyard (142)	K	5-10	180	Texas Tech
7	Larry Agajanian (168)	DT	6-3	250	UCLA
8	Doug Gosnell (194)	DT	6-4	250	Utah State
9	Dave Hampton (220)	RB	6-0	210	Wyoming
10	Bruce Nelson (246)	T	6-4	225	North Dakota State
11	Leon Harden (272)	DB	5-11	197	Texas-El Paso
12	Tom Buckman (298)	TE	6-4	230	Texas A&M
13	Craig Koinzan (324)	LB	6-4	238	Doane
14	Rich Voltzke (350)	HB	6-2	206	Minnesota
15	Dan Eckstein (376)	S	5-10	180	Presbyterian
16	Dick Hewins (402)	WR	6-1	180	Drake
17	John Mack (428)	RB	6-3	230	Cen. Missouri State

1969 GREEN BAY PACKERS

FRONT ROW: (L-R) 89 Dave Robinson, 22 Elijah Pitts, 82 Lionel Aldridge, 43 Doug Hart, 21 Bob Jeter, 57 Ken Bowman, 75 Forrest Gregg, 87 Willie Davis, 26 Herb Adderley, 24 Willie Wood, 74 Henry Jordan, 81 Marv Fleming.

SECOND ROW: (L-R) Assistant Trainer Domenic Gentile, 23 Travis Williams, 88 Ron Jones, 53 Fred Carr, 66 Ray Nitschke, 84 Carroll Dale, 15 Bart Starr, 45 John Rowser, 25 Dave Hampton, 38 Mike Mercer, 47 Gordon Rule, 50 Bob Hyland, 70 Rich Moore, Equipment Manager Gerald (Dad) Braisher.

THIRD ROW: (L-R) 71 Francis Peay, 73 Jim Weatherwax, 61 Dave Bradley, 78 Bob Brown, 44 Donny Anderson, 68 Gale Gillingham, 33 Jim Grabowski, 13 Don Horn, 30 Chuck Mercein, 83 Phil Vandersea, 55 Jim Flanigan, 56 Larry Agajanian, Assistant Equipment Manager Bob Noel.

BACK ROW: (L-R) Trainer Carl (Bud) Jorgensen, 85 John Spilis, 31 Perry Williams, 10 Bill Stevens, 60 Lee Roy Caffey, 86 Boyd Dowler, 77 Bill Hayhoe, 72 Dick Himes, 58 Francis Winkler, 27 Claudis James, 62 Bill Lueck, 28 Leon Harden.

The 1970 season opener left little doubt that the glory days of the previous decade were over. Green Bay hosted the Lions and was mauled 40-0. Not since 1958 had the team been subjected to such a trouncing and not since the late '40s had it been crushed so convincingly at home.

Head coach Phil Bengtson, whose ties to the game of football went back more than 40 years, called the game "the worst I've ever experienced."

The Packers converted only one of 12 third-down opportunities. They managed 114 yards while giving up 398. And, as a final ignominy, the Lions' Greg Landry galloped 76 yards on a quarterback sneak to set up the last score.

"The harder you try, sometimes the worse it gets," said Bart Starr who was bothered by a sore arm all season.

Little went right for the Packers in 1970. The team averaged just 243.5 yards per game, its poorest showing since 1946. The club surrendered 293 points, the most in 12 years. Green Bay's 6-8 record left it tied with the Bears at the bottom of the Central Division standings.

The National Football League Players Association and NFL management were at odds over a labor agreement. On July 9, the NFLPA asked its members not to report to training camp. Owners then locked out the veterans less than a week later.

NFLPA president John Mackey (Colts), Packers player representative Ken Bowman and others locked horns with owners over issues such as improved working conditions and pension pay. On July 29, owners ended the lockout and invited veterans to return. With no resolution in sight, the players stayed out, putting the preseason in jeopardy.

On Aug. 2, commissioner Pete Rozelle stepped in. In a marathon 22-hour session with the NFLPA and representatives from each team, he accomplished what federal mediators had been unable to do: reach an agreement, in this case, a four-year pact.

While the midsummer labor dispute dragged on, Vince Lombardi was in and out of Georgetown Hospital. On June 27, the Redskins coach had a tumor (thought to be nonmalignant) removed. A weakened Lombardi left the hospital on July 13 and attended NFL meetings and watched the Redskins' rookie game.

In late July, Lombardi underwent a second operation and his condition deteriorated. On Sept. 3, he died of cancer at the age of 57.

In February, the once-warring NFL and AFL officially completed their merger. Pittsburgh, Baltimore and Cleveland joined the 10 AFL teams to form the American Football Conference. The remaining 13 NFL teams made up the National Football Conference.

Green Bay shook off its dismal opener and reeled off three narrow victories to improve to 3-1.

On Oct. 18, Lambeau Field celebrated "Bart Starr Day," and the honoree almost pulled out a fourth-straight win. With less than a minute remaining, the 15-year veteran hit Travis Williams with a pass that pushed the Packers past midfield. But what could have been the game-winning drive ended after the Rams' Clancy Williams stole Starr's next pass and raced 65 yards for a touchdown.

The Packers closed out the first half of the season with a win over the Eagles and a loss to the 49ers.

After dropping a 13-10 decision to the Colts, the Packers grabbed their fifth win by squeaking past the Bears 20-19. Starr, who hadn't played against Baltimore, ran three yards for the winning touchdown with three seconds left.

Two consecutive losses then ended Green Bay's playoff hopes. The Vikings administered the first, 10-3, and the Cowboys followed with a 16-3 showing.

The Packers picked up their sixth win 20-12 in Pittsburgh, where they intercepted Terry Bradshaw four times. Afterwards, co-captains Gale Gillingham and Willie Wood presented Bengtson with the game ball.

"He stuck with us through two bad games and we felt he deserved it," Gillingham said.

Bengtson had two more bad games to get through. First, Jack Concannon threw for 338 yards and four touchdowns as the Bears romped 35-17. A week later, the Lions closed the season by pounding the Packers 20-0.

Queried after the loss as to whether he would be back in 1971 as coach, Bengtson replied: "I hope so."

Two days later, the architect of some of the league's best defenses of the 1960s changed his mind and retired.

A BLANKETY-BLANK START AND FINISH

Speechwriters know that audiences tend to remember the beginning and ending of a presentation. When it came to opening and closing the 1970 season, the Packers and their fans probably were hoping for a case of amnesia.

The Lions pounced on Green Bay 40-0 in the opener. The two met again three months later, and the Lions swatted the Packers 20-0 to close out the Phil Bengtson era.

Never before or since has the team been outscored so badly in the first and last games of a season.

In the two games combined, Green Bay punted 18 times, gained 238 yards, and committed eight turnovers. Quarterback Greg Landry gained more yards rushing (98) than did the Packers (96) as a team.

Listed below are the most points by which the Packers have been outscored at the start and end of a season:

Points	Year	Results
60	1970	Lost 40-0 to Lions; 20-0 to Lions
59	1986	Lost 31-3 to Oilers; 55-24 to Giants
54	1950	Lost 45-7 to Lions; 30-14 to 49ers
44	1946	Lost 30-7 to Bears; 38-17 to Rams

TEAM STATISTICS

	GB	OPP
First Downs	194	202
Rushing	69	88
Passing	110	102
Penalty	15	12
Rushes	453	453
Yards Gained	1,595	1,829
Average Gain	3.52	4.04
Average Yards per Game	113.9	130.6
Passes Attempted	351	369
Completed	177	177
% Completed	50.43	47.97
Total Yards Gained	2,196	2,496
Times Sacked	43	32
Yards Lost	382	270
Net Yards Gained	1,814	2,226
Yards Gained per Completion	12.41	14.10
Net Yards per Attempt	4.60	5.55
Average Net Yards per Game	129.6	159.0
Combined Net Yards Gained	3,409	4,055
Total Plays	847	854
Average Yards per Play	4.02	4.75
Average Net Yards per Game	243.5	289.6
Third Down Efficiency	59/199	57/193
Percentage	29.65	29.53
Fourth Down Efficiency	2/9	6/10
Percentage	22.22	60.00
Intercepted By	20	24
Yards Returned	398	421
Returned for TD	1	3
Punts	87	71
Yards Punted	3,501	2,845
Average Yards per Punt	40.24	40.07
Punt Returns	25	40
Yards Returned	98	338
Average Yards per Return	3.92	8.45
Returned for TD	0	0
Kickoff Returns	63	36
Yards Returned	1,422	888
Average Yards per Return	22.57	24.67
Returned for TD	2	0
Penalties	76	63
Yards Penalized	691	686
Fumbles	34	29
Lost	17	17
Own Recovered for Touchdown	0	0
Opponent's Recovered by	17	17
Opponent's Recovered for Touchdown	0	1
Total Points Scored	196	293
Total Touchdowns	22	30
Touchdowns Rushing	8	14
Touchdowns Passing	11	13
Touchdowns on Returns & Recoveries	3	3
Extra Points	19	29
Safeties	0	0
Field Goals Attempted	28	42
Field Goals Made	15	28
% Successful	53.57	66.67

Regular Season   6-8-0

Date	GB		OPP	Att.
9/20	0	Detroit Lions	40	(56,263)
9/27	27	Atlanta Falcons	24	(56,263)
10/4	13	Minnesota Vikings (M)	10	(47,967)
10/12	22	at San Diego Chargers	20	(53,064)
10/18	21	Los Angeles Rams	31	(56,263)
10/25	30	Philadelphia Eagles (M)	17	(48,022)
11/1	10	at San Francisco 49ers	26	(59,335)
11/9	10	Baltimore Colts	13	(48,063)
11/15	20	Chicago Bears	19	(56,263)
11/22	3	at Minnesota Vikings	10	(47,900)
11/26	3	at Dallas Cowboys	16	(67,182)
12/6	20	at Pittsburgh Steelers	12	(46,418)
12/13	17	at Chicago Bears	35	(44,957)
12/20	0	at Detroit Lions	20	(57,387)

Score By Periods

	1	2	3	4	Total
Packers	51	47	29	69	196
Opponents	47	49	73	124	293

INDIVIDUAL STATISTICS

Rushing

	Att	Yds	Avg	LG	TD
D. Anderson	222	853	3.8	54	5
T. Williams	74	276	3.7	37	1
Grabowski	67	210	3.1	17	1
Hampton	48	115	2.4	14	0
Starr	12	62	5.2	15	1
P. Williams	17	44	2.6	4	0
Krause	2	13	6.5	12	0
Dale	2	9	4.5	8	0
Patrick	2	5	2.5	3	0
Horn	5	4	0.8	4	0
McGeorge	1	3	3.0	3	0
Livingston	1	1	1.0	1	0
Packers	453	1,595	3.5	54	8
Opponents	453	1,829	4.0	76	14

Receiving

	No	Yds	Avg	LG	TD
Dale	49	814	16.6	t89	2
D. Anderson	36	414	11.5	34	0
Hilton	25	350	14.0	t65	4
Grabowski	19	83	4.4	19	0
Clancy	16	244	15.3	t33	2
T. Williams	12	127	10.6	t55	1
Hampton	7	23	3.3	12	0
Spilis	6	76	12.7	18	0
P. Williams	3	11	3.7	6	0
McGeorge	2	32	16.0	t16	2
Krause	2	22	11.0	11	0
Packers	177	2,196	12.4	t89	11
Opponents	177	2,496	14.1	t87	13

Passing

	Att	Com	Yds	Pct	TD	In	Tk/Yds	Rate
Starr	255	140	1,645	54.9	8	13	29/252	63.9
Horn	76	28	428	36.8	2	10	6/59	25.4
R. Norton	5	3	64	60.0	1	0	2/16	—
Patrick	14	6	59	42.9	0	1	6/55	25.6
D. Anderson	1	0	0	00.0	0	0	0/0	—
Packers	351	177	2,196	50.4	11	24	43/382	52.1
Opponents	369	177	2,496	48.0	13	20	32/270	59.4

Punting

	No	Yds	Avg	Net	TB	In20	LG	HB
D. Anderson	81	3,302	40.4	35.5	6	18	62	0
Livingston	6	199	33.2	27.8	0	0	52	0
Packers	87	3,501	40.2	35.0	6	18	62	0
Opponents	71	2,845	40.1	36.2	9	14	65	0

Kickoff Returns

	No	Yds	Avg	LG	TD
K. Ellis	22	451	20.5	48	0
Krause	18	513	28.5	t100	1
T. Williams	10	203	20.3	28	0
Hampton	6	188	31.3	t101	1
M.P. McCoy	3	22	7.3	10	0
Gregg	2	21	10.5	16	0
P. Williams	1	20	20.0	20	0
Himes	1	4	4.0	4	0
Packers	63	1,422	22.6	t101	2
Opponents	36	888	24.7	82	0

Punt Returns

	No	Yds	Avg	FC	LG	TD
Wood	11	58	5.3	18	12	0
K. Ellis	7	27	3.9	0	8	0
T. Williams	4	20	5.0	2	11	0
Harden	2	-7	-3.5	0	0	0
C. Williams	1	0	0.0	0	0	0
Packers	25	98	3.9	20	12	0
Opponents	40	338	8.5	11	65	0

Interceptions

	No	Yds	Avg	LG	TD
Wood	7	110	15.7	24	0
Hart	3	114	38.0	t76	1
K. Ellis	3	69	23.0	60	0
Jeter	3	27	9.0	18	0
Carr	2	45	22.5	28	0
D. Robinson	2	33	16.5	20	0
Packers	20	398	19.9	t76	1
Opponents	24	421	17.5	70	3

Scoring

	TDr	TDp	TDrt	PAT	FG	S	TP
Livingston	0	0	0	19/21	15/28	0	64
D. Anderson	5	0	0	0/0	0/0	0	30
Hilton	0	4	0	0/0	0/0	0	24
Clancy	0	2	0	0/0	0/0	0	12
Dale	0	2	0	0/0	0/0	0	12
McGeorge	0	2	0	0/0	0/0	0	12
T. Williams	1	1	0	0/0	0/0	0	12
Grabowski	1	0	0	0/0	0/0	0	6
Hampton	0	0	1	0/0	0/0	0	6
Hart	0	0	1	0/0	0/0	0	6
Krause	0	0	1	0/0	0/0	0	6
Starr	1	0	0	0/0	0/0	0	6
Packers	8	11	3	19/22	15/28	0	196
Opponents	14	13	3	29/30	28/42	0	293

Fumbles

	Fum	Ow	Op	Yds	Tot
L. Aldridge	0	0	1	0	1
D. Anderson	8	2	0	0	2
Bowman	1	0	0	-4	0
Bradley	0	0	1	0	1
Carr	0	0	3	0	3
Jim Carter	0	0	1	0	1
Dale	2	0	0	0	0
K. Ellis	3	1	1	5	2
Gregg	0	0	1	0	1
Hampton	3	1	0	0	1
L. Harden	1	1	0	0	0
Hart	0	0	1	0	1
Hilton	2	0	0	0	0
Horn	2	0	0	0	2
Krause	2	0	1	0	1
Al Matthews	0	0	1	0	1
M.P. McCoy	1	0	0	0	0
McGeorge	0	0	1	0	1
Nitschke	0	0	2	0	2
R. Norton	1	0	0	0	1
Peay	0	1	0	0	1
Starr	6	3	0	0	3
M. Walker	0	1	1	4	2
C. Williams	1	0	2	0	2
P. Williams	1	0	0	0	0
Wood	0	0	1	0	1
Packers	34	15	17	5	32

NFL STANDINGS

National Conference

Eastern Division

	W	L	T	Pct	PF	PA
Dallas Cowboys	10	4	0	.714	299	221
New York Giants	9	5	0	.643	301	270
St. Louis Cardinals	8	5	1	.615	325	228
Washington Redskins	6	8	0	.429	297	314
Philadelphia Eagles	3	10	1	.231	241	332

Central Division

	W	L	T	Pct	PF	PA
Minnesota Vikings	12	2	0	.857	335	143
Detroit Lions	10	4	0	.714	347	202
Chicago Bears	6	8	0	.429	256	261
Green Bay Packers	6	8	0	.429	196	293

Western Division

	W	L	T	Pct	PF	PA
San Francisco 49ers	10	3	1	.769	352	267
Los Angeles Rams	9	4	1	.692	325	202
Atlanta Falcons	4	8	2	.333	206	261
New Orleans Saints	2	11	1	.154	172	347

American Conference

Eastern Division

	W	L	T	Pct	PF	PA
Baltimore Colts	11	2	1	.846	321	234
Miami Dolphins	10	4	0	.714	297	228
New York Jets	4	10	0	.286	255	286
Buffalo Bills	3	10	1	.231	204	337
Boston Patriots	2	12	0	.143	149	361

Central Division

	W	L	T	Pct	PF	PA
Cincinnati Bengals	8	6	0	.571	312	255
Cleveland Browns	7	7	0	.500	286	265
Pittsburgh Steelers	5	9	0	.357	210	272
Houston Oilers	3	10	1	.231	217	352

Western Division

	W	L	T	Pct	PF	PA
Oakland Raiders	8	4	2	.667	300	293
Kansas City Chiefs	7	5	2	.583	272	244
San Diego Chargers	5	6	3	.455	282	278
Denver Broncos	5	8	1	.385	253	264

ROSTER

No	Name	Pos	Ht	Wt	DOB	College	G
82	Aldridge, Lionel	DE	6-4	245	02/18/41	Utah State	14
87	Amsler, Marty	DE	6-5	255	10/26/42	Evansville	9
44	Anderson, Donny	RB	6-3	210	05/16/43	Texas Tech	14
57	Bowman, Ken	C	6-3	230	12/15/42	Wisconsin	10
61	Bradley, Dave	G	6-4	245	02/13/47	Penn State	4
78	Brown, Bob	DT	6-5	260	02/23/40	Arkansas-Pine Bluff	14
53	Carr, Fred	LB	6-5	238	08/19/46	Texas-El Paso	14
50	Carter, Jim	LB	6-3	235	10/18/48	Minnesota	11
36	Carter, Mike	WR	6-1	210	02/18/48	Sacramento State	2
80	Clancy, Jack	WR	6-1	195	06/18/44	Michigan	14
84	Dale, Carroll	WR	6-2	200	04/24/38	Virginia Tech	14
48	Ellis, Ken	CB	5-10	190	09/27/47	Southern University	14
55	Flanigan, Jim	LB	6-3	240	04/15/45	Pittsburgh	11
68	Gillingham, Gale	G	6-3	255	02/03/44	Minnesota	14
33	Grabowski, Jim	RB	6-2	220	09/09/44	Illinois	14
75	Gregg, Alvis (Forrest)	T	6-4	250	10/18/33	SMU	14
25	Hampton, Dave	RB	6-0	210	05/07/47	Wyoming	6
28	Harden, Leon	DB	5-11	195	08/17/47	Texas-El Paso	8
73	Hardy, Kevin	DT	6-5	260	07/28/45	Notre Dame	14
43	Hart, Doug	DB	6-0	190	06/03/39	Arlington State	14
77	Hayhoe, Bill	T	6-8	258	10/06/46	USC	14
86	Hilton, John	TE	6-5	225	03/12/42	Richmond	14
72	Himes, Dick	T	6-4	244	05/25/46	Ohio State	11
13	Horn, Don	QB	6-2	195	03/09/45	San Diego State	9
45	Hunt, Ervin	DB	6-2	190	07/01/47	Fresno State	6
21	Jeter, Bob	CB	6-1	205	05/09/37	Iowa	14
30	Krause, Larry	RB	6-0	208	04/22/48	St. Norbert	14
59	Kuechenberg, Rudy	LB	6-2	215	02/07/43	Indiana	6
37	Livingston, Dale	K	6-1	210	03/12/45	Western Michigan	14
62	Lueck, Bill	G	6-3	235	04/07/46	Arizona	14
29	Matthews, Al	DB	5-11	190	11/07/47	Texas A&I	14
76	McCoy, Mike P.	DT	6-5	284	09/06/48	Notre Dame	14
81	McGeorge, Rich	TE	6-4	235	09/14/48	Elon	14
70	Moore, Rich	T	6-6	280	04/26/47	Villanova	6
66	Nitschke, Ray	LB	6-3	235	12/29/36	Illinois	14
11	Norton, Rick	QB	6-2	190	11/16/43	Kentucky	1
10	Patrick, Frank	QB	6-7	225	03/11/47	Nebraska	1
71	Peay, Francis	T	6-5	250	05/23/44	Missouri	14
89	Robinson, Dave	LB	6-3	245	05/03/41	Penn State	4
85	Spilis, John	WR	6-3	205	10/14/47	Northern Illinois	14
15	Starr, Bryan (Bart)	QB	6-1	190	01/09/34	Alabama	14
52	Walker, Cleo	LB	6-2	219	02/07/48	Louisville	12
54	Walker, Malcolm	C-T	6-4	250	05/24/43	Rice	11
83	Williams, Clarence	DE	6-5	255	09/03/46	Prairie View	14
31	Williams, Perry	RB	6-2	219	12/11/46	Purdue	13
23	Williams, Travis	RB	6-1	210	01/14/46	Arizona State	7
24	Wood, Willie	S	5-10	190	12/23/36	USC	14

DRAFT

Rnd	Name	Pos	Ht	Wt	College
1a	Mike P. McCoy (2)	DT	6-5	284	Notre Dame
	(Choice from Bears in Lee Roy Caffey, Elijah Pitts, Bob Hyland trade)				
1b	Rich McGeorge (16)	TE	6-4	235	Elon
2	Al Matthews (41)	DB	5-11	190	Texas A&I
3	Jim Carter (68)	LB	6-3	240	Minnesota
4a	Ken Ellis (93)	WR	5-10	190	Southern
4b	Skip Butler (96)	K	6-1	198	Texas-Arlington
	(Choice from Colts for Ron Kostelnik)				
5	Cecil Pryor (120)	DE	6-5	240	Michigan
6	Ervin Hunt (145)	DB	6-2	190	Fresno State
7	Cleo Walker (172)	C-LB	6-3	219	Louisville
8	Tim Mjos (197)	HB	6-2	205	North Dakota State
9	Bob Reinhard (224)	G	6-2	230	Stanford
10a	Russ Melby (248)	DT	6-4	250	Weber State
10b	Frank Patrick (251)	TE	6-7	225	Nebraska
	(Choice from Redskins for Leo Carroll)				
11	Dan Hook (276)	LB	6-3	215	Cal State-Humboldt
12	Frank Foreman (300)	WR	6-2	204	Michigan State
13	Dave Smith (328)	RB	6-1	210	Utah
14	Bob Lints (353)	G	6-3	250	Eastern Michigan
15	Mike Carter (380)	WR	6-1	208	Cal State-Sacramento
16	Jim Heacock (405)	DB	6-2	180	Muskingum
17	Larry Krause (432)	HB	6-0	208	St. Norbert

1970 GREEN BAY PACKERS

FRONT ROW: (L-R) 53 Fred Carr, 23 Travis Williams, 82 Lionel Aldridge, 43 Doug Hart, 21 Bob Jeter, 57 Ken Bowman, 24 Willie Wood, 68 Gale Gillingham, 78 Bob Brown, 48 Ken Ellis, 37 Dale Livingston, 75 Forrest Gregg.

SECOND ROW: (L-R) Trainer Domenic Gentile, 36 Mike Carter, 52 Cleo Walker, 66 Ray Nitschke, 15 Bart Starr, 84 Carroll Dale, 30 Larry Krause, 13 Don Horn, 62 Bill Lueck, 80 Jack Clancy, Equipment Manager Gerald (Dad) Braisher, Assistant Equipment Manager Bob Noel.

THIRD ROW: (L-R) 29 Al Matthews, 83 Clarence Williams, 71 Francis Peay, 85 John Spilis, 44 Donny Anderson, 33 Jim Grabowski, 86 John Hilton, 10 Frank Patrick, 31 Perry Williams, 61 Dave Bradley, 70 Rich Moore.

BACK ROW: (L-R) Trainer Carl (Bud) Jorgensen, 39 Jerry Warren, 45 Ervin Hunt, 81 Rich McGeorge, 73 Kevin Hardy, 77 Bill Hayhoe, 54 Malcolm Walker, 87 Marty Amsler, 72 Dick Himes, 55 Jim Flanigan, 76 Mike P. McCoy, 50 Jim Carter, 28 Leon Harden.

Dan Devine's first game as head coach of the Packers had him feeling literally run down. Besides losing to the Giants 42-40, the long-time college coach broke his leg midway through the fourth quarter in a sideline pileup following an interception by Doug Hart. Devine was taken to St. Vincent Hospital where he listened to the remainder of the game on radio.

Devine, who had posted winning records at both Arizona State and the University of Missouri, struggled in his first year in the professional ranks. Inconsistency, turnovers, and the lack of a passing game led to a 4-8-2 record.

Bart Starr, who underwent surgeries in late June and July to repair a shredded bicipital tendon in his passing arm, missed the opening 10 games. He started three of the last four games but was a shadow of his former self. The 16-year veteran was intercepted three times and did not throw a touchdown pass in 45 attempts.

Ray Nitschke was another veteran nearing the end. The intimidating middle linebacker, who had anchored the team's defense for much of the past decade, found himself backing up sophomore Jim Carter in all but two games. One of those starts came on Dec. 12, a day Wisconsin Gov. Patrick J. Lucey declared "Ray Nitschke Day."

The draft produced two rookies of note. John Brockington, the ninth selection overall, rushed for a then-rookie NFL record 1,105 yards. Only Larry Little (1,133 yards) gained more rushing yardage in 1971.

Brockington and Donny Anderson (757 yards rushing) formed the most productive running tandem in the league.

Scott Hunter, the team's sixth round pick, led the team in passing. He started 10 games, and his production was among the best of any rookie quarterback in team history.

Defensive line coach Dave Hanner took over for the sidelined Devine. Hanner took charge in the final minutes of the opener and conducted practice the following Tuesday. On Wednesday, Devine returned to the field in a golf-cart-like setup, but Hanner handled the on-the-field duties for the second game while Devine directed the team from the County Stadium press box. A week later, Devine returned to his customary spot, albeit on crutches.

The Giants turned seven Packers turnovers into 28 points as the season kicked off on Sept. 19. Fran Tarkenton threw four touchdown passes and the visitors scored twice on fumble recoveries to beat Green Bay 42-40.

Ken Ellis and the defense intercepted former teammate Don Horn six times in Week 2. Ellis had three of the steals against the Denver Broncos, which set up 20 points for the Packers.

A week later, Brockington ran for 120 yards as the Packers slipped past the Bengals 20-17.

Zeke Bratkowski, returning to the team for the first time since 1968, engineered a 14-point rally that came up just short in a 31-28 loss to the Lions. Super Sub ran for a third-quarter

touchdown and connected with Rich McGeorge from 5 yards out with 56 seconds remaining.

Gary Cuozzo and the Vikings dropped Green Bay's record to 2-3 with a 24-13 win in Week 5.

Roman Gabriel tossed three scoring passes in the Rams' 30-13 victory on Oct. 24. It marked the third week in a row that Packers opponents had thrown at least three touchdown passes.

Green Bay and Detroit played to a 14-14 tie on a rain-soaked Monday night in Milwaukee. Because of the weather, Hunter attempted only five passes and completed just one: a 9-yarder to Carroll Dale. A 17-yard strike to Dale was wiped out because of penalty.

Brockington, who had 111 yards rushing against Detroit, ripped off 142 in a 17-14 win at Chicago and 149 yards in a 3-0 loss in Minnesota a week later.

Starr returned to the lineup on Nov. 28. He threw for 116 yards but couldn't overcome six turnovers as the Saints triumphed 29-21 and dropped Green Bay to 3-7-1.

The Packers notched their last win on Ray Nitschke Day. Devine moved Carter to outside linebacker so that Nitschke could start in the middle. The 14-year veteran made at least six tackles and played most of the game.

"It felt great," Nitschke said. "It's easier to play than to be on the sidelines. I appreciate Coach Devine giving me the opportunity to play."

A week later, the Packers endured their worst loss of the season, a 27-6 setback in Miami. It was the last game for Bart Starr, who completed 13 of 22 passes for 126 yards.

BROCKINGTON'S GRAND ENTRANCE

The Packers traded up three spots to select running back John Brockington with the ninth pick overall in the draft. The team was rewarded, as the former Ohio State back rushed for a team rookie record 1,105 yards.

Brockington picked up 34 yards in the opener. He bettered that total in Week 2 with 85 yards, including a 52-yard dash for his first NFL touchdown.

He broke the 100-yard barrier on Oct. 3 against the Bengals with 120 yards on 19 carries. His three other 100-yard rushing days came in consecutive games, starting with a 111-yard effort against the Lions on Nov. 1.

Brockington's average of 5.1 yards per carry was second to Miami's Larry Csonka (5.4).

Listed below are the most yards gained by a rookie running back in Packers history:

Yards	Player	Year
1,105	John Brockington	1971
545	Gerry Ellis	1980
519	Kenneth Davis	1986
445	Cecil Isbell	1938

TEAM STATISTICS

	GB	OPP
First Downs	208	230
Rushing	115	104
Passing	87	110
Penalty	6	16
Rushes	500	489
Yards Gained	2,229	1,707
Average Gain	4.46	3.49
Average Yards per Game	159.2	121.9
Passes Attempted	254	353
Completed	121	186
% Completed	47.64	52.69
Total Yards Gained	1,842	2,469
Times Sacked	18	19
Yards Lost	157	168
Net Yards Gained	1,685	2,301
Yards Gained per Completion	15.22	13.27
Net Yards per Attempt	6.19	6.19
Average Net Yards per Game	120.4	164.4
Combined Net Yards Gained	3,914	4,008
Total Plays	772	861
Average Yards per Play	5.07	4.66
Average Net Yards per Game	279.6	286.3
Third Down Efficiency	62/171	82/200
Percentage	36.26	41.00
Fourth Down Efficiency	5/10	2/8
Percentage	50.00	25.00
Intercepted By	16	24
Yards Returned	205	449
Returned for TD	0	2
Punts	56	61
Yards Punted	2,238	2,448
Average Yards per Punt	39.96	40.13
Punt Returns	38	23
Yards Returned	177	169
Average Yards per Return	4.66	7.35
Returned for TD	0	0
Kickoff Returns	58	56
Yards Returned	1,546	1,248
Average Yards per Return	26.66	22.29
Returned for TD	1	0
Penalties	61	60
Yards Penalized	568	514
Fumbles	29	33
Lost	20	16
Own Recovered for Touchdown	0	0
Opponent's Recovered by	16	20
Opponent's Recovered for Touchdown	0	3
Total Points Scored	274	298
Total Touchdowns	33	34
Touchdowns Rushing	18	7
Touchdowns Passing	12	21
Touchdowns on Returns & Recoveries	3	6
Extra Points	32	32
Safeties	1	1
Field Goals Attempted	26	37
Field Goals Made	14	20
% Successful	53.85	54.05

Regular Season 4-8-2

Date	GB		OPP	Att.
9/19	40	New York Giants	42	(56,263)
9/26	34	Denver Broncos (M)	13	(47,957)
10/3	20	Cincinnati Bengals	17	(56,263)
10/10	28	at Detroit Lions	31	(54,418)
10/17	13	Minnesota Vikings	24	(56,263)
10/24	13	at Los Angeles Rams	30	(75,351)
11/1	14	Detroit Lions (M)	14	(47,961)
11/7	17	at Chicago Bears	14	(55,049)
11/14	0	at Minnesota Vikings	3	(49,784)
11/22	21	at Atlanta Falcons	28	(58,850)
11/28	21	New Orleans Saints (M)	29	(48,035)
12/5	16	at St. Louis Cardinals	16	(50,443)
12/12	31	Chicago Bears	10	(56,263)
12/19	6	at Miami Dolphins	27	(76,812)

Score By Periods

	1	2	3	4	Total
Packers	41	85	64	84	274
Opponents	57	72	78	91	298

INDIVIDUAL STATISTICS

Rushing

	Att	Yds	Avg	LG	TD
Brockington	216	1,105	5.1	t52	4
D. Anderson	186	757	4.1	31	5
Hampton	67	307	4.6	41	3
S. Hunter	21	50	2.4	16	4
Starr	3	11	3.7	9	1
P. Williams	3	4	1.3	3	0
Bratkowski	1	1	1.0	11	1
Krause	3	-6	-2.0	2	0
Packers	**500**	**2,229**	**4.5**	**t52**	**18**
Opponents	489	1,707	3.5	42	7

Receiving

	No	Yds	Avg	LG	TD
Dale	31	598	19.3	t77	4
McGeorge	27	463	17.1	50	4
D. Anderson	26	306	11.8	39	1
Spilis	14	281	20.1	39	1
Brockington	14	98	7.0	29	1
D. Davis	6	59	9.8	20	0
Hampton	3	37	12.3	t19	1
Packers	**121**	**1,842**	**15.2**	**t77**	**12**
Opponents	186	2,469	13.3	t81	21

Passing

	Att	Com	Yds	Pct	TD	In	Tk/Yds	Rate
S. Hunter	163	75	1,210	46.0	7	17	11/81	46.1
Starr	45	24	286	53.3	0	3	6/64	45.2
Bratkowski	37	19	298	51.4	4	3	1/12	80.7
Patrick	5	1	39	20.0	0	1	0/0	—
Packers	**254**	**121**	**1,842**	**47.6**	**12**	**24**	**18/157**	**48.4**
Opponents	353	186	2,469	52.7	21	16	19/168	76.1

Punting

	No	Yds	Avg	Net	TB	In20	LG	HB
D. Anderson	50	2,022	40.4	34.8	6	9	58	0
Duncan	6	216	36.0	31.5	1	1	47	0
Packers	**56**	**2,238**	**40.0**	**34.4**	**7**	**10**	**58**	**0**
Opponents	61	2,448	40.1	35.6	5	15	63	0

Kickoff Returns

	No	Yds	Avg	LG	TD
Hampton	46	1,314	28.6	t90	1
Krause	5	101	20.2	29	0
E. Pitts	2	41	20.5	22	0
P. Williams	2	41	20.5	21	0
D. Davis	1	22	22.0	22	0
K. Ellis	1	22	22.0	22	0
Jim Carter	1	5	5.0	5	0
Packers	**58**	**1,546**	**26.7**	**t90**	**1**
Opponents	56	1,248	22.3	82	0

Punt Returns

	No	Yds	Avg	FC	LG	TD
K. Ellis	22	107	4.9	1	30	0
D. Davis	6	36	6.0	0	19	0
E. Pitts	5	13	2.6	2	5	0
Wood	4	21	5.3	2	9	0
A. Randolph	1	0	0.0	0	0	0
Packers	**38**	**177**	**4.7**	**5**	**30**	**0**
Opponents	23	169	7.3	12	38	0

Interceptions

	No	Yds	Avg	LG	TD
K. Ellis	6	10	1.7	5	0
D. Robinson	3	44	14.7	23	0
Hart	2	73	36.5	69	0
A. Randolph	1	34	34.0	34	0
Al Matthews	1	20	20.0	20	0
Jim Carter	1	16	16.0	16	0
Wood	1	8	8.0	8	0
Nitschke	1	0	0.0	0	0
Packers	**16**	**205**	**12.8**	**69**	**0**
Opponents	24	449	18.7	t65	2

Scoring

	TDr	TDp	TDrt	PAT	FG	S	TP
L. Michaels	0	0	0	19/20	8/14	0	43
D. Anderson	5	1	0	0/0	0/0	0	36
Brockington	4	1	0	0/0	0/0	0	30
Hampton	3	1	1	0/0	0/0	0	30
Webster	0	0	0	8/8	6/11	0	26
Dale	0	4	0	0/0	0/0	0	24
S. Hunter	4	0	0	0/0	0/0	0	24
McGeorge	0	4	0	0/0	0/0	0	24
Hart	0	0	0	0/0	0/0	1	8
Bratkowski	1	0	0	0/0	0/0	0	6
K. Ellis	0	0	0	0/0	0/0	0	6
Spilis	0	1	0	0/0	0/0	0	6
Starr	1	0	0	0/0	0/0	0	6
Conway	0	0	0	5/5	0/1	0	5
Packers	**18**	**12**	**3**	**32/33**	**14/26**	**1**	**274**
Opponents	7	21	6	32/34	20/37	1	298

Fumbles

	Fum	Ow	Op	Yds	Tot
L. Aldridge	0	0	1	0	1
D. Anderson	6	1	0	-5	1
Bratkowski	1	0	0	0	0
Brockington	4	2	0	0	2
Carr	0	0	2	34	2
Jim Carter	0	0	1	0	1
D. Davis	1	1	0	18	1
Hampton	7	1	0	0	1
S. Hunter	7	0	0	-11	1
Krause	0	0	1	0	1
M.P. McCoy	0	0	2	17	2
McGeorge	0	1	0	0	1
Nitschke	0	0	1	0	1
A. Randolph	0	0	1	0	1
D. Robinson	0	0	1	0	1
Roche	0	0	2	0	2
Spilis	1	0	0	0	0
Starr	0	0	0	0	0
C. Williams	0	0	2	0	2
Wood	0	0	1	3	1
Packers	**29**	**7**	**16**	**56**	**23**

NFL STANDINGS

National Conference

Eastern Division

	W	L	T	Pct	PF	PA
Dallas Cowboys	11	3	0	.786	406	222
Washington Redskins	9	4	1	.692	276	190
Philadelphia Eagles	6	7	1	.462	221	302
St. Louis Cardinals	4	9	1	.308	231	279
New York Giants	4	10	0	.286	228	362

Central Division

	W	L	T	Pct	PF	PA
Minnesota Vikings	11	3	0	.786	245	139
Detroit Lions	7	6	1	.538	341	286
Chicago Bears	6	8	0	.429	185	276
Green Bay Packers	**4**	**8**	**2**	**.333**	**274**	**298**

Western Division

	W	L	T	Pct	PF	PA
San Francisco 49ers	9	5	0	.643	300	216
Los Angeles Rams	8	5	1	.615	313	260
Atlanta Falcons	7	6	1	.538	274	277
New Orleans Saints	4	8	2	.333	266	347

American Conference

Eastern Division

	W	L	T	Pct	PF	PA
Miami Dolphins	10	3	1	.769	315	174
Baltimore Colts	10	4	0	.714	313	140
New England Patriots	6	8	0	.429	238	325
New York Jets	6	8	0	.429	212	299
Buffalo Bills	1	13	0	.071	184	394

Central Division

	W	L	T	Pct	PF	PA
Cleveland Browns	9	5	0	.643	285	273
Pittsburgh Steelers	6	8	0	.429	246	292
Houston Oilers	4	9	1	.308	251	330
Cincinnati Bengals	4	10	0	.286	284	265

Western Division

	W	L	T	Pct	PF	PA
Kansas City Chiefs	10	3	1	.769	302	208
Oakland Raiders	8	4	2	.667	344	278
San Diego Chargers	6	8	0	.429	311	341
Denver Broncos	4	9	1	.308	203	275

ROSTER

No	Name	Pos	Ht	Wt	DOB	College	G
82	Aldridge, Lionel	DE	6-4	245	02/18/41	Utah State	14
44	Anderson, Donny	RB	6-3	210	05/16/43	Texas Tech	14
57	Bowman, Ken	C	6-3	230	12/15/42	Wisconsin	14
61	Bradley, Dave	G	6-4	245	02/13/47	Penn State	7
12	Bratkowski, Zeke	QB	6-3	210	10/20/31	Georgia	6
42	Brockington, John	RB	6-1	225	09/07/48	Ohio State	14
78	Brown, Bob	DT	6-5	260	02/23/40	Arkansas-Pine Bluff	14
53	Carr, Fred	LB	6-5	238	08/19/46	Texas-El Paso	14
50	Carter, Jim	LB	6-3	235	10/18/48	Minnesota	13
35	Conway, Dave	K	6-0	195	01/06/45	Texas	1
56	Crutcher, Tommy	LB	6-3	230	08/10/41	TCU	12
84	Dale, Carroll	WR	6-2	200	04/24/38	Virginia Tech	14
47	Davis, Dave	WR	6-0	175	07/05/48	Tennessee State	14
79	DeLisle, Jim	DT	6-4	255	01/20/49	Wisconsin	9
18	Duncan, Ken	P	6-2	200	02/28/46	Tulsa	2
48	Ellis, Ken	CB	5-10	190	09/27/47	Southern University	14
88	Garrett, Len	TE	6-3	225	12/18/47	New Mexico Highlands	14
68	Gillingham, Gale	G	6-3	255	02/03/44	Minnesota	14
21	Hall, Charlie	CB	6-1	195	03/31/48	Pittsburgh	14
25	Hampton, Dave	RB	6-0	210	05/07/47	Wyoming	13
43	Hart, Doug	DB	6-0	190	06/03/39	Arlington State	14
77	Hayhoe, Bill	T	6-8	258	10/06/46	USC	14
72	Himes, Dick	T	6-4	244	05/25/46	Ohio State	14
16	Hunter, Scott	QB	6-2	205	11/19/47	Alabama	13
30	Krause, Larry	RB	6-0	208	04/22/48	St. Norbert	9
62	Lueck, Bill	G	6-3	235	04/07/46	Arizona	14
29	Matthews, Al	DB	5-11	190	11/07/47	Texas A&I	14
76	McCoy, Mike P.	DT	6-5	284	09/06/48	Notre Dame	12
81	McGeorge, Rich	TE	6-4	235	09/14/48	Elon	14
75	Michaels, Lou	K	6-2	250	09/28/36	Kentucky	10
66	Nitschke, Ray	LB	6-3	235	12/29/36	Illinois	9
10	Patrick, Frank	QB	6-7	225	03/11/47	Nebraska	1
71	Peay, Francis	T	6-5	250	05/23/44	Missouri	14
22	Pitts, Elijah	RB	6-1	205	02/03/39	Philander Smith	6
27	Randolph, Al	S	6-2	205	07/08/44	Iowa	14
89	Robinson, Dave	LB	6-3	245	05/03/41	Penn State	14
87	Roche, Alden	DE	6-4	255	04/09/45	Southern University	14
74	Smith, Donnell	DE	6-4	245	05/25/49	Southern University	4
85	Spilis, John	WR	6-3	205	10/14/47	Northern Illinois	14
15	Starr, Bryan (Bart)	QB	6-1	190	01/09/34	Alabama	4
38	Webster, Tim	K	6-0	195	09/11/49	Arkansas	4
83	Williams, Clarence	DE	6-5	255	09/03/46	Prairie View	14
31	Williams, Perry	RB	6-2	219	12/11/46	Purdue	14
63	Winkler, Randy	G	6-4	260	07/18/43	Tarleton State	7
52	Winther, Wimpy	C	6-4	260	10/22/47	Mississippi	11
74	Withrow, Cal	C	6-0	240	08/04/45	Kentucky	14
24	Wood, Willie	S	5-10	190	12/23/36	USC	14

DRAFT

Rnd	Name	Pos	Ht	Wt	College
1a	John Brockington (9)	FB	6-1	225	Ohio State
	(Packers traded own choice (12) and Don Horn for Broncos (9) and Alden Roche)				
1b	(Choice (12) to Broncos in deal above)				
2a	(Choice (37) to 49ers for Kevin Hardy)				
2b	Virgil Robinson (46)	WR-CB	5-11	195	Grambling
	(Choice from Rams as part of Travis Williams deal)				
3	Charlie Hall (62)	CB	6-1	195	Pittsburgh
4	(Choice (90) to Rams as part of Travis Williams deal)				
5a	(Choice (115) to Chargers for Jacque MacKinnon)				
5b	Donnell Smith (116)	DE	6-4	245	Southern University
	(Choice from Redskins, deferred payment for Tom Brown)				
5c	Jim Stillwagon (124)	LB	6-0	230	Ohio State
	(Choice from Rams through Redskins for rights to Boyd Dowler)				
6	Scott Hunter (140)	QB	6-2	205	Alabama
7a	Dave Davis (168)	WR	6-0	175	Tennessee State
7b	James Johnson (175)	WR	5-10	175	Bishop
	(Choice from Raiders for Jacque MacKinnon)				
8	Win Headley (193)	C	6-3	255	Wake Forest
9	Barry Mayer (218)	RB	6-2	215	Minnesota
10	Kevin Hunt (246)	T	6-5	250	Doane
11	John Lanier (271)	RB-TE	6-2	235	Parsons
12	Greg Hendren (296)	G-C	6-2	240	California
13	Jack Martin (324)	RB	6-2	205	Angelo State
14	Leroy Spears (348)	DE	6-5	225	Moorhead State
15	Len Garrett (374)	TE	6-3	210	New Mex. Highlands
16	Jack O'Donnell (402)	G	6-1	245	Cent. Oklahoma State
17	Monty Johnson (427)	S	5-11	190	Oklahoma

1971 GREEN BAY PACKERS

FRONT ROW: (L-R) 89 Dave Robinson, 22 Elijah Pitts, 82 Lionel Aldridge, 43 Doug Hart, 57 Ken Bowman, 56 Tommy Crutcher, 68 Gale Gillingham, 24 Willie Wood, 78 Bob Brown, 48 Ken Ellis, 53 Fred Carr, 29 Al Matthews.

SECOND ROW: (L-R) 66 Ray Nitschke, 12 Zeke Bratkowski, 84 Carroll Dale, 15 Bart Starr, 21 Charlie Hall, 44 Donny Anderson, 47 Dave Davis, 87 Alden Roche, 54 Wimpy Winther, 75 Lou Michaels, 18 Ken Duncan.

THIRD ROW: (L-R) 61 Dave Bradley, 36 Mike Carter, 81 Rich McGeorge, 85 John Spilis, 42 John Brockington, 16 Scott Hunter, 25 Dave Hampton, 30 Larry Krause, 58 Cal Withrow, 62 Bill Lueck, 27 Al Randolph, 80 Sam Dickerson.

BACK ROW: (L-R) 71 Francis Peay, 83 Clarence Williams, 88 Len Garrett, 31 Perry Williams, 10 Frank Patrick, 63 Randy Winkler, 72 Dick Himes, 77 Bill Hayhoe, 74 Donnell Smith, 79 Jim DeLisle, 76 Mike P. McCoy, 50 Jim Carter.

Green Bay parlayed a strong running attack and a stifling defense into its first playoff berth in five years. From opening day to the regular-season wrap-up in New Orleans, the Packers never relinquished first place in the NFC Central Division, winning it with a 10-4 mark.

Getting there wasn't easy. The team's schedule was the fourth toughest in the league based on opponents' winning percentage (.579) from 1971. Green Bay also butted heads with five teams that made the playoffs in 1971—six if the Vikings were counted twice. The Packers won four of those six encounters, including close wins over NFC champion runner-up San Francisco and the defending Super Bowl champion Cowboys.

Devine did some reshuffling in his second year. Donny Anderson was traded to the Cardinals for running back MacArthur Lane. Lionel Aldridge was dealt to San Diego for safety Jim Hill. Dave Hampton was sent to Atlanta in return for guard Malcolm Snider.

Devine traded his second-round draft pick in 1973 for the Cowboys' kick-return specialist Ike Thomas and punter Ron Widby. He also claimed wide receiver Jon Staggers off waivers from the Steelers just before the opener.

The draft also yielded a couple of standouts. Top pick Willie Buchanon joined a secondary that permitted a league-low seven touchdown passes. Chester Marcol, a second-round selection, led the league in scoring with 128 points and won three games with his kicks.

A number of greats from the Lombardi era made their exit. Bart Starr announced his retirement in late July after playing a team-record 16 years. Zeke Bratkowski, Elijah Pitts, Willie Wood, and Doug Hart also hung up their cleats.

For a second year in a row, Brockington formed half of one of the best running tandems in the NFL. He and Lane rushed for 1,848 yards, second only to the 2,117 yards of Miami's Larry Csonka and Mercury Morris.

Rich McGeorge and Gale Gillingham both suffered season-ending knee injuries in Week 2. Gillingham, an offensive guard, had switched allegiances and was filling in for Mike McCoy after the defensive tackle broke a bone in his foot during the preseason.

Green Bay opened with a 26-10 win in Cleveland. Marcol kicked four field goals and McGeorge snared two touchdown passes from Scott Hunter as Green Bay romped.

A controversial call helped Oakland down the Packers 20-14 in Week 2. The Raiders' Jack Tatum returned a Lane fumble 104 yards for a touchdown. Later in the week, NFL supervisor of officials Art McNally confirmed what Packers fans already knew: the fumble was actually a muff and should not have been advanced.

Two second-half field goals by Marcol proved the difference as Green Bay slipped past the Cowboys 16-13 to improve to 2-1. Buchanon sealed the win with an interception of Craig Morton in the closing minute.

Marcol again provided the deciding field goal in a 20-17 squeaker over the Bears.

Hunter and Leland Glass handled the last second heroics the following week in a thrilling, 24-23 win in Detroit. The two hooked up on a 15-yard touchdown pass with just under two minutes remaining on "Monday Night Football."

Green Bay then dropped back-to-back games. Atlanta pulled out a 10-9 decision and the Vikings rallied for 17 fourth-quarter points to down the Packers 27-13.

Ken Ellis intercepted Steve Spurrier and reached pay dirt with 23 seconds left in a 34-24 win over the 49ers.

Jerry Tagge, former Green Bay West High School quarterback and the second of the team's two first-round draft picks, made his debut in relief of Hunter in Week 9. Tagge completed four passes in a 23-17 win in Chicago.

The Packers were handed their fourth loss by the Redskins. Bill Kilmer threw two touchdown passes, including one in the fourth quarter when Ellis (separated shoulder) was replaced by Thomas at cornerback.

"We needed to win this one," a frustrated Jim Carter said, "but if we win the last three, we're in anyway, no matter what else happens."

That's what Green Bay did. The Packers clinched the division title on a frigid afternoon in Minnesota on Dec. 10. Brockington and Lane rushed for 213 yards, and Buchanon and Ellis intercepted Fran Tarkenton three times in a 23-7 win over the four-time defending Central Division champion Vikings.

THE POLISH PRINCE

Czeslaw (Chester) Marcol was born in Poland and immigrated to the United States in 1965. A soccer star in his native land, he became one of the top kickers in the NFL from 1972 through 1974.

Marcol got a workout as a rookie. He kicked 33 field goals and scored 128 points to lead the league in both categories. He beat the Cowboys (field goal), Bears (field goal), and Lions (extra point) with fourth-quarter kicks.

Marcol had a strong leg. Twenty-nine of his 74 kickoffs (39 percent) resulted in opponents starting from their own 20-yard line. Marcol also kicked two field goals of 51 yards.

Bears coach Abe Gibron dubbed Marcol the "Polish Prince."

Listed below are the most field goals made by a rookie in Packers history:

No.	Player	Year
33	Chester Marcol	1972
24	Ryan Longwell	1997
22	Chris Jacke	1989
11	Joe Danelo	1975

TEAM STATISTICS

	GB	OPP
First Downs	195	209
Rushing	109	85
Passing	72	109
Penalty	14	15
Rushes	544	443
Yards Gained	2,127	1,517
Average Gain	3.91	3.42
Average Yards per Game	151.9	108.4
Passes Attempted	237	340
Completed	101	174
% Completed	42.62	51.18
Total Yards Gained	1,536	2,209
Times Sacked	17	29
Yards Lost	124	252
Net Yards Gained	1,412	1,957
Yards Gained per Completion	15.21	12.70
Net Yards per Attempt	5.56	5.30
Average Net Yards per Game	100.9	139.8
Combined Net Yards Gained	3,539	3,474
Total Plays	798	812
Average Yards per Play	4.43	4.28
Average Net Yards per Game	252.8	248.1
Third Down Efficiency	65/196	66/176
Percentage	33.16	37.50
Fourth Down Efficiency	4/4	4/9
Percentage	100.00	44.44
Intercepted By	17	9
Yards Returned	223	69
Returned for TD	1	2
Punts	65	66
Yards Punted	2,714	2,732
Average Yards per Punt	41.75	41.39
Punt Returns	25	32
Yards Returned	364	225
Average Yards per Return	14.56	7.03
Returned for TD	2	0
Kickoff Returns	49	46
Yards Returned	1,141	932
Average Yards per Return	23.29	20.26
Returned for TD	0	0
Penalties	63	50
Yards Penalized	610	446
Fumbles	22	35
Lost	10	19
Own Recovered for Touchdown	1	0
Opponent's Recovered by	19	10
Opponent's Recovered for Touchdown	1	1
Total Points Scored	304	226
Total Touchdowns	29	26
Touchdowns Rushing	17	14
Touchdowns Passing	7	7
Touchdowns on Returns & Recoveries	5	5
Extra Points	29	25
Safeties	1	0
Field Goals Attempted	48	27
Field Goals Made	33	15
% Successful	68.75	55.56

Regular Season 10-4-0

Date	GB		OPP	Att.
9/17	26	at Cleveland Browns	10	(75,771)
9/24	14	Oakland Raiders	20	(56,263)
10/1	16	Dallas Cowboys (M)	13	(47,103)
10/8	20	Chicago Bears	17	(56,263)
10/16	24	at Detroit Lions	23	(54,418)
10/22	9	Atlanta Falcons (M)	10	(47,967)
10/29	13	Minnesota Vikings	27	(56,263)
11/5	34	San Francisco 49ers (M)	24	(47,897)
11/12	23	at Chicago Bears	17	(55,701)
11/19	23	at Houston Oilers	10	(41,752)
11/26	16	at Washington Redskins	21	(53,039)
12/3	33	Detroit Lions	7	(56,263)
12/10	23	at Minnesota Vikings	7	(49,784)
12/17	30	at New Orleans Saints	20	(65,881)

Postseason 0-1-0

12/24	3	at Washington Redskins	16	(53,140)

Score By Periods

	1	2	3	4	Total
Packers	80	95	63	66	304
Opponents	37	68	49	72	226

INDIVIDUAL STATISTICS

Rushing

	Att	Yds	Avg	LG	TD
Brockington	274	1,027	3.7	t30	8
Lane	177	821	4.6	41	3
P. Williams	33	139	4.2	14	0
B. Hudson	15	62	4.1	17	0
Kopay	10	39	3.9	20	0
S. Hunter	22	37	1.7	15	5
Glass	2	13	6.5	13	0
D. Davis	2	0	0.0	7	0
Tagge	8	-3	-0.4	2	1
Staggers	1	-8	-8.0	-8	0
Packers	**544**	**2,127**	**3.9**	**41**	**17**
Opponents	443	1,517	3.4	26	14

Receiving

	No	Yds	Avg	LG	TD
Lane	26	285	11.0	49	0
Brockington	19	243	12.8	t48	1
Dale	16	317	19.8	48	1
Glass	15	261	17.4	31	1
Staggers	8	123	15.4	t48	1
D. Davis	4	119	29.8	t68	1
L. Garrett	4	66	16.5	21	0
McGeorge	4	50	12.5	t23	2
Kopay	3	19	6.3	8	0
Nitschke	1	34	34.0	34	0
Lammons	1	19	19.0	19	0
Packers	**101**	**1,536**	**15.2**	**t68**	**7**
Opponents	174	2,209	12.7	t62	7

Passing

	Att	Com	Yds	Pct	TD	In	Tk/Yds	Rate
S. Hunter	199	86	1,252	43.2	6	9	13/86	55.5
Tagge	29	10	154	34.5	0	0	3/27	52.9
Widby	2	2	102	100.0	1	0	0/0	—
Lane	2	2	19	100.0	0	0	0/0	—
Patrick	4	1	9	25.0	0	0	1/11	—
Staggers	1	0	0	0.0	0	0	0/0	—
Packers	**237**	**101**	**1,536**	**42.6**	**7**	**9**	**17/124**	**58.6**
Opponents	340	174	2,209	51.2	7	17	29/252	57.8

Punting

	No	Yds	Avg	Net	TB	In20	LG	HB
Widby	65	2,714	41.8	35.5	9	9	64	2
Packers	**65**	**2,714**	**41.8**	**35.5**	**9**	**9**	**64**	**2**
Opponents	66	2,732	41.4	34.1	6	16	61	0

Kickoff Returns

	No	Yds	Avg	LG	TD
I. Thomas	21	572	27.2	89	0
Staggers	11	260	23.6	39	0
B. Hudson	11	247	22.5	55	0
Kroll	1	23	23.0	23	0
D. Robinson	1	20	20.0	20	0
K. Ellis	1	10	10.0	10	0
P. Williams	1	9	9.0	9	0
L. Garrett	1	0	0.0	0	0
Wortman	1	0	0.0	0	0
Packers	**49**	**1,141**	**23.3**	**89**	**0**
Opponents	46	932	20.3	37	0

Punt Returns

	No	Yds	Avg	FC	LG	TD
K. Ellis	14	215	15.4	1	t80	1
Staggers	9	148	16.4	20	t85	1
Glass	1	1	1.0	0	1	0
B. Hudson	1	0	0.0	2	0	0
Packers	**25**	**364**	**14.6**	**23**	**t85**	**2**
Opponents	32	225	7.0	6	33	0

Interceptions

	No	Yds	Avg	LG	TD
K. Ellis	4	106	26.5	40	1
Buchanon	4	62	15.5	26	0
J. Hill	4	37	9.3	21	0
D. Robinson	2	10	5.0	7	0
Al Matthews	2	8	4.0	8	0
Jim Carter	1	0	0.0	0	0
Packers	**17**	**223**	**13.1**	**40**	**1**
Opponents	9	69	7.7	t32	2

Scoring

	TDr	TDp	TDrt	PAT	FG	S	TP
Marcol	0	0	0	29/29	33/48	0	128
Brockington	8	1	0	0/0	0/0	0	54
S. Hunter	5	0	0	0/0	0/0	0	30
Lane	3	0	0	0/0	0/0	0	18
K. Ellis	0	0	2	0/0	0/0	0	12
McGeorge	0	2	0	0/0	0/0	0	12
Staggers	0	1	1	0/0	0/0	0	12
Buchanon	0	0	1	0/0	0/0	0	6
Dale	0	1	0	0/0	0/0	0	6
D. Davis	0	1	0	0/0	0/0	0	6
Glass	0	1	0	0/0	0/0	0	6
Tagge	1	0	0	0/0	0/0	0	6
C. Williams	0	0	1	0/0	0/0	0	6
Bob Brown	0	0	0	0/0	0/0	1	2
Packers	**17**	**7**	**5**	**29/29**	**33/48**	**1**	**304**
Opponents	14	7	5	25/26	15/27	0	226

Fumbles

	Fum	Ow	Op	Yds	Tot
Brockington	4	0	0	0	0
Bob Brown	0	0	1	0	1
Buchanon	0	0	3	0	3
Carr	0	0	2	30	2
Jim Carter	0	0	1	0	1
K. Ellis	2	1	1	0	2
L. Garrett	0	0	1	0	1
Glass	0	1	0	0	1
Hayhoe	0	1	0	0	1
J. Hill	0	0	1	15	1
Himes	0	1	0	0	1
B. Hudson	1	1	0	0	0
S. Hunter	5	0	0	0	3
Kopay	1	0	0	0	1
Kroll	0	0	1	0	1
Lammons	0	1	0	0	1
Lane	6	0	0	0	1
Al Matthews	0	0	2	-7	2
M.P. McCoy	0	0	1	0	1
D. Robinson	0	0	1	14	1
Roche	0	1	0	0	1
Staggers	2	0	0	0	0
I. Thomas	0	1	0	0	1
C. Williams	0	0	2	21	2
P. Williams	1	0	0	0	0
Withrow	0	1	0	0	1
Packers	**22**	**11**	**19**	**74**	**30**

NFL STANDINGS

National Conference

Eastern Division

	W	L	T	Pct	PF	PA
Washington Redskins	11	3	0	.786	336	218
Dallas Cowboys	10	4	0	.714	319	240
New York Giants	8	6	0	.571	331	247
St. Louis Cardinals	4	9	1	.321	193	303
Philadelphia Eagles	2	11	1	.179	145	352

Central Division

	W	L	T	Pct	PF	PA
Green Bay Packers	10	4	0	.714	304	226
Detroit Lions	8	5	1	.607	339	290
Minnesota Vikings	7	7	0	.500	301	252
Chicago Bears	4	9	1	.321	225	275

Western Division

	W	L	T	Pct	PF	PA
San Francisco 49ers	8	5	1	.607	353	249
Atlanta Falcons	7	7	0	.500	269	274
Los Angeles Rams	6	7	1	.464	291	286
New Orleans Saints	2	11	1	.179	215	361

American Conference

Eastern Division

	W	L	T	Pct	PF	PA
Miami Dolphins	14	0	0	1.000	385	171
New York Jets	7	7	0	.500	367	324
Baltimore Colts	5	9	0	.357	235	252
Buffalo Bills	4	9	1	.321	257	377
New England Patriots	3	11	0	.214	192	446

Central Division

	W	L	T	Pct	PF	PA
Pittsburgh Steelers	11	3	0	.786	343	175
Cleveland Browns	10	4	0	.714	268	249
Cincinnati Bengals	8	6	0	.571	299	229
Houston Oilers	1	13	0	.071	164	380

Western Division

	W	L	T	Pct	PF	PA
Oakland Raiders	10	3	1	.750	365	248
Kansas City Chiefs	8	6	0	.571	287	254
Denver Broncos	5	9	0	.357	325	350
San Diego Chargers	4	9	1	.321	264	344

ROSTER

No	Name	Pos	Ht	Wt	DOB	College	G
57	Bowman, Ken	C	6-3	230	12/15/42	Wisconsin	14
42	Brockington, John	RB	6-1	225	09/07/48	Ohio State	14
78	Brown, Bob	DT	6-5	260	02/23/40	Arkansas-Pine Bluff	14
28	Buchanon, Willie	CB	6-0	190	11/04/50	San Diego State	14
53	Carr, Fred	LB	6-5	238	08/19/46	Texas-El Paso	14
50	Carter, Jim	LB	6-3	235	10/18/48	Minnesota	14
56	Crutcher, Tommy	LB	6-3	230	08/10/41	TCU	12
84	Dale, Carroll	WR	6-2	200	04/24/38	Virginia Tech	14
47	Davis, Dave	WR	6-0	175	07/05/48	Tennessee State	10
48	Ellis, Ken	CB	5-10	190	09/27/47	Southern University	14
88	Garrett, Len	TE	6-3	230	12/18/47	New Mexico Highlands	14
41	Gibson, Paul	S	6-2	195	06/20/48	Texas-El Paso	1
68	Gillingham, Gale	DT	6-3	255	02/03/44	Minnesota	2
46	Glass, Leland	WR	6-0	185	11/05/50	Oregon	14
21	Hall, Charlie	CB	6-1	195	03/31/48	Pittsburgh	14
77	Hayhoe, Bill	T	6-8	258	10/06/46	USC	14
51	Hefner, Larry	LB	6-2	215	08/02/49	Clemson	2
39	Hill, Jim	S	6-2	190	10/21/46	Texas A&I	14
72	Himes, Dick	T	6-4	244	05/25/46	Ohio State	14
23	Hudson, Bob	RB	5-11	210	03/21/48	Southeast Oklahoma	12
64	Hunt, Kevin	T	6-5	260	11/29/48	Doane	3
16	Hunter, Scott	QB	6-2	205	11/19/47	Alabama	14
40	Kopay, Dave	RB	6-0	218	06/28/42	Washington	14
44	Kroll, Bob	S	6-1	195	06/09/50	Northern Michigan	5
86	Lammons, Pete	TE	6-3	228	10/20/43	Texas	12
36	Lane, MacArthur	RB	6-1	220	03/16/42	Utah State	14
62	Lueck, Bill	G	6-3	235	04/07/46	Arizona	14
13	Marcol, Chester	K	6-0	190	10/24/49	Hillsdale	14
29	Matthews, Al	DB	5-11	190	11/07/47	Texas A&I	14
76	McCoy, Mike P.	DT	6-5	284	09/06/48	Notre Dame	12
81	McGeorge, Rich	TE	6-4	235	09/14/48	Elon	2
66	Nitschke, Ray	LB	6-3	235	12/29/36	Illinois	11
10	Patrick, Frank	QB	6-7	225	03/11/47	Nebraska	2
71	Peay, Francis	T	6-5	250	05/23/44	Missouri	6
75	Pureifory, Dave	DE	6-1	260	07/12/49	Eastern Michigan	14
89	Robinson, Dave	LB	6-3	245	05/03/41	Penn State	14
87	Roche, Alden	DE	6-4	255	04/09/45	Southern University	14
67	Snider, Malcolm	G	6-4	251	04/05/47	Stanford	14
22	Staggers, Jon	WR	5-10	180	12/14/48	Missouri	11
17	Tagge, Jerry	QB	6-2	220	04/12/50	Nebraska	4
37	Thomas, Ike	CB	6-2	193	11/04/47	Bishop	12
73	Vanoy, Vernon	DT	6-8	270	12/31/46	Kansas	13
26	Walsh, Ward	RB	6-0	208	11/21/49	Colorado	2
20	Widby, Ron	P	6-4	210	03/09/45	Tennessee	14
83	Williams, Clarence	DE	6-5	255	09/03/46	Prairie View	14
31	Williams, Perry	RB	6-2	219	12/11/46	Purdue	14
58	Withrow, Cal	C	6-0	240	08/04/45	Kentucky	14
65	Wortman, Keith	G	6-2	245	07/20/50	Nebraska	13

DRAFT

Rnd	Name	Pos	Ht	Wt	College
1a	Willie Buchanon (7)	CB	6-0	190	San Diego State
1b	Jerry Tagge (11)	QB	6-2	220	Nebraska
	(Choice from Chargers for Kevin Hardy)				
2	Chester Marcol (34)	K	6-0	190	Hillsdale
3	(Choice (59) to Vikings for Zeke Bratkowski)				
4	Eric Patton (86)	LB	6-3	240	Notre Dame
5	(Choice (111) to Saints for Wimpy Winther)				
6a	Nate Ross (138)	CB	6-1	195	Bethune-Cookman
6b	Dave Pureifory (142)	LB	6-1	240	Eastern Michigan
	(Choice from Bears for Bob Jeter)				
6c	Bob Hudson (147)	RB	5-11	210	NE Oklahoma
	(Choice from Rams as part of Travis Williams trade)				
7	Bill Bushong (163)	DT	6-3	250	Kentucky
8	Leland Glass (190)	WR	6-0	185	Oregon
9	(Choice (215) to Colts)				
10	Keith Wortman (242)	G	6-2	245	Nebraska
11	Dave Bailey (266)	WR	6-1	195	Alabama
12	Mike Rich (294)	RB	6-2	210	Florida
13	Jesse Lakes (319)	RB	5-11	195	Central Michigan
14	Larry Hefner (346)	LB	6-2	215	Clemson
15	Rick Thone (371)	S	6-1	200	Arkansas Tech
16	Charles Burrell (398)	DT	6-0	290	Arkansas-Pine Bluff
17	(Choice (423) to Chargers for Cal Withrow)				

FRONT ROW: (L-R) 57 Ken Bowman, 58 Cal Withrow, 62 Bill Lueck, 72 Dick Himes, 39 Jim Hill, 66 Ray Nitschke, 89 Dave Robinson, 68 Gale Gillingham, 29 Al Matthews, 48 Ken Ellis, 31 Perry Williams, 40 Dave Kopay, 53 Fred Carr.

SECOND ROW: (L-R) Trainer Domenic Gentile, Assistant Trainer Dan Davis, 17 Jerry Tagge, 20 Ron Widby, 78 Bob Brown, 36 MacArthur Lane, Offensive Line Coach Rollie Dotsch, Offensive Backfield Coach John (Red) Cochran, Quarterbacks Coach Bart Starr, Head Coach Dan Devine, Defensive Coordinator Dave Hanner, Receivers Coach John Polonchek, Defensive Backfield Coach Don Doll, 33 Charlie Pittman, 11 Charlie Napper, 44 Bob Kroll, Equipment Manager Gerald (Dad) Braisher, Assistant Equipment Manager Bob Noel.

THIRD ROW: (L-R) 88 Len Garrett, 71 Francis Peay, 81 Rich McGeorge, 56 Tommy Crutcher, 84 Carroll Dale, 16 Scott Hunter, 21 Charlie Hall, 42 John Brockington, 28 Willie Buchanon, 30 Larry Krause, 76 Mike P. McCoy, 47 Dave Davis, 22 Jon Staggers, 37 Ike Thomas.

BACK ROW: (L-R) 87 Alden Roche, 67 Malcolm Snider, 10 Frank Patrick, 64 Kevin Hunt, 73 Vernon Vanoy, 83 Clarence Williams, 77 Bill Hayhoe, 65 Keith Wortman, 75 Dave Pureifory, 13 Chester Marcol, 23 Bob Hudson, 46 Leland Glass, 51 Larry Hefner, 50 Jim Carter.

Any possibility that the Packers might claim a second straight Central Division title ended abruptly during a three-game stretch that left the team shaken and searching for answers. The club, unfortunately, failed to address many of its problems down the stretch and it stumbled to a 5-7-2 record and a third-place finish in the division.

After hovering in second place for most of the first five weeks, the Packers were thrashed by the Rams, Lions, and Bears in consecutive weeks. The Rams' Fred Dryer overpowered Malcolm Snider to register two fourth-quarter safeties in the Rams' 24-7 win, and quarterback Bobby Douglass ran for 100 yards and four touchdowns in the Bears' 31-17 triumph. In between, the Lions tossed in a 34-0 shutout for good measure.

"All the guys are bleeding inside," MacArthur Lane said on the heels of the Bears' loss.

"I don't have the answer and neither does Coach (Dan) Devine. He's frustrated," Jim Carter added.

The rough stretch pushed Green Bay (2-4-2) into the cellar, well behind the Vikings (8-0).

Unlike the previous year, Devine tinkered little with his team, the exception being at quarterback. In late August, he obtained Jim Del Gaizo from Miami for two second-round draft choices (1974 and 1975).

For eight weeks, Devine wavered between Hunter and Del Gaizo. Neither quarterback made more than two consecutive starts in that span and, in all but the opener, the starter was pulled because of injury or ineffectiveness.

Green Bay's 1,283 net passing yards was its lowest since 1946.

Ray Nitschke, who played in the opening preseason game against the Bears, announced his retirement on Aug. 28. The 15-year veteran had played in 190 regular-season games, second only to the 196 of Bart Starr. Veteran Carroll Dale was placed on waivers in September to clear room for defensive back Perry Smith.

In mid-September, Congress passed a bill that allowed home games to be televised locally if a game sold out 72 hours before it was to be played. The league opposed the legislation, fearing it would diminish ticket sales. Some fans with tickets did stay home, and for the first time the league kept track of "no show" counts.

In the opener, Green Bay turned three Jets' turnovers into 17 points and a 23-7 win at Milwaukee.

"I wasn't throwing the ball worth a damn," visiting quarterback Joe Namath said.

Del Gaizo replaced Hunter in the waning minutes against the Lions in Week 2 and directed the team to a 14-14 tie. The second-year pro completed three passes, including a 25-yarder to Jon Staggers on fourth-and-23 at the Packers' 38, to set up Chester Marcol's 24-yard field goal with 22 seconds left.

Three Fred Cox field goals and a safety led to the Packers first loss, as the Vikings rolled up 206 rushing yards in an 11-3 victory.

A 16-14 win over the Giants and a 10-10 tie with the Chiefs pushed the Packers' record to 2-1-2.

Three disastrous games followed. In the first, cornerback Willie Buchanon broke his left leg in two places while covering Jack Snow and was lost for the season. In the second, the Lions' Charlie Taylor erupted for 160 yards rushing and a touchdown. In the third, Green Bay finished with minus-12 passing yards as Hunter's 17 yards in completions were offset by 29 yards in sacks.

Eight-year veteran Gale Gillingham addressed the team prior to its engagement with the Cardinals. Green Bay responded with a 25-21 win.

"This is a helluva bunch of guys," said the guard. "They could have folded their tents awfully easy, but they didn't."

At halftime, Starr's No. 15 was officially retired.

The Packers then closed out November with two losses. They then beat the Saints 30-10.

A week later, the Vikings crushed the Packers 31-7 at Lambeau Field. A reporter asked Packers president Dominic Olejniczak about Devine's status.

"I never discuss such things during the season and I'm surprised that you would ask the question," he said.

Green Bay closed in Chicago. Brockington and Lane each surpassed 100 yards rushing in a 21-0 win. Brockington picked up 142 yards and Lane added 101 as the Packers churned out 298 yards on the ground.

A THREE-WEEK LEAVE OF ABSENCE

The Packers of 1973 experienced one of the worst offensive slumps in team history.

Green Bay failed to gain even 100 yards in three-game span that began on Oct. 21. In order, the Packers managed 63, 63, and 98 yards against the Rams, Lions, and Bears. Never before or since has the team gone more than one week without gaining 100 yards.

The passing game in particular was off. The Packers had a net of 19 yards passing in the three games combined. Scott Hunter, Jim Del Gaizo, and Jerry Tagge were sacked 10 times for 98 yards in losses. Green Bay attempted 47 passes and completed 14 for 117 yards.

Green Bay's opponents, meanwhile, each produced more than 300 yards, for a combined total of 1,044 yards.

Listed below are the seasons in which the Packers had the most sub-100-yard games:

No.	Year(s)
3	1973
2	1934, 1965
1	1935, 1976, 1981

TEAM STATISTICS

	GB	OPP
First Downs	187	230
Rushing	98	114
Passing	72	101
Penalty	17	15
Rushes	527	506
Yards Gained	1,973	1,999
Average Gain	3.74	3.95
Average Yards per Game	140.9	142.8
Passes Attempted	255	327
Completed	119	180
% Completed	46.67	55.05
Total Yards Gained	1,503	2,050
Times Sacked	27	25
Yards Lost	220	228
Net Yards Gained	1,283	1,822
Yards Gained per Completion	12.63	11.39
Net Yards per Attempt	4.55	5.18
Average Net Yards per Game	91.6	130.1
Combined Net Yards Gained	3,256	3,821
Total Plays	809	858
Average Yards per Play	4.02	4.45
Average Net Yards per Game	232.6	272.9
Third Down Efficiency	54/182	64/185
Percentage	29.67	34.59
Fourth Down Efficiency	7/15	10/19
Percentage	46.67	52.63
Intercepted By	15	17
Yards Returned	220	256
Returned for TD	3	1
Punts	68	67
Yards Punted	2,787	2,605
Average Yards per Punt	40.99	38.88
Punt Returns	30	41
Yards Returned	137	300
Average Yards per Return	4.57	7.32
Returned for TD	0	0
Kickoff Returns	53	40
Yards Returned	1,189	817
Average Yards per Return	22.43	20.43
Returned for TD	0	0
Penalties	68	54
Yards Penalized	653	483
Fumbles	23	34
Lost	12	18
Own Recovered for Touchdown	0	0
Opponent's Recovered by	18	12
Opponent's Recovered for Touchdown	0	0
Total Points Scored	202	259
Total Touchdowns	20	28
Touchdowns Rushing	10	13
Touchdowns Passing	7	14
Touchdowns on Returns & Recoveries	3	1
Extra Points	19	28
Safeties	0	3
Field Goals Attempted	35	27
Field Goals Made	21	19
% Successful	60.00	70.37

Regular Season   5-7-2

Date	GB		OPP	Att.
9/17	23	New York Jets (M)	7	(47,124)
9/23	13	Detroit Lions	13	(55,495)
9/30	3	at Minnesota Vikings	11	(48,176)
10/7	16	at New York Giants	14	(70,050)
10/14	10	Kansas City Chiefs (M)	10	(46,583)
10/21	7	at Los Angeles Rams	24	(80,558)
10/28	0	at Detroit Lions	34	(43,616)
11/4	17	Chicago Bears	31	(53,231)
11/11	25	St. Louis Cardinals	21	(52,922)
11/18	24	at New England Patriots	33	(60,525)
11/26	6	at San Francisco 49ers	20	(49,244)
12/2	30	New Orleans Saints	10	(46,092)
12/8	7	Minnesota Vikings	31	(53,830)
12/16	21	at Chicago Bears	0	(29,157)

Score By Periods

	1	2	3	4	Total
Packers	51	78	30	43	202
Opponents	52	64	40	103	259

INDIVIDUAL STATISTICS

Rushing

	Att	Yds	Avg	LG	TD
Brockington	265	1,144	4.3	53	3
Lane	170	528	3.1	20	1
Goodman	18	88	4.9	19	1
P. Williams	32	87	2.7	9	1
Tagge	15	62	4.1	t41	2
Staggers	4	33	8.3	t20	1
Staroba	1	11	11.0	11	0
Krause	1	8	8.0	8	0
Highsmith	7	7	1.0	4	0
Barry Smith	1	5	5.0	5	0
S. Hunter	8	3	0.4	6	1
Del Gaizo	4	1	0.3	1	0
D. Gordon	1	-4	-4.0	-4	0
Packers	**527**	**1,973**	**3.7**	**53**	**10**
Opponents	506	1,999	4.0	t50	13

Receiving

	No	Yds	Avg	LG	TD
Lane	27	255	9.4	30	1
Staggers	25	412	16.5	50	3
McGeorge	16	260	16.3	44	1
Brockington	16	128	8.0	37	0
Barry Smith	15	233	15.5	24	2
Glass	11	119	10.8	23	0
P. Williams	5	44	8.8	14	0
Goodman	2	19	9.5	12	0
Staroba	1	23	23.0	23	0
Donohoe	1	10	10.0	10	0
Packers	**119**	**1,503**	**12.6**	**50**	**7**
Opponents	180	2,050	11.4	t63	14

Passing

	Att	Com	Yds	Pct	TD	In	Tk/Yds	Rate
Tagge	106	56	720	52.8	2	7	9/54	53.2
Hunter	84	35	442	41.7	2	4	10/89	46.8
Del Gaizo	62	27	318	43.5	2	6	8/77	30.9
Lane	2	1	23	50.0	1	0	0/0	—
Brockington	1	0	0	0.0	0	0	0/0	—
Packers	**255**	**119**	**1,503**	**46.7**	**7**	**17**	**27/220**	**46.9**
Opponents	327	180	2,050	55.0	14	15	25/228	69.2

Punting

	No	Yds	Avg	Net	TB	In20	LG	HB
Widby	56	2,414	43.1	37.1	2	6	60	0
Staroba	12	373	31.1	27.7	2	1	49	0
Packers	**68**	**2,787**	**41.0**	**35.4**	**4**	**7**	**60**	**0**
Opponents	67	2,605	38.9	35.3	5	13	58	1

Kickoff Returns

	No	Yds	Avg	LG	TD
I. Thomas	23	527	22.9	34	0
K. Ellis	12	319	26.6	84	0
Krause	11	244	22.2	30	0
Aaron Brown	3	26	8.7	12	0
Lane	2	31	15.5	29	0
P. Williams	1	24	24.0	24	0
Highsmith	1	18	18.0	18	0
Packers	**53**	**1,189**	**22.4**	**84**	**0**
Opponents	40	817	20.4	45	0

Punt Returns

	No	Yds	Avg	FC	LG	TD
Staggers	19	90	4.7	12	26	0
K. Ellis	11	47	4.3	7	23	0
Packers	**30**	**137**	**4.6**	**19**	**26**	**0**
Opponents	41	300	7.3	13	72	0

Interceptions

	No	Yds	Avg	LG	TD
K. Ellis	3	53	17.7	t47	1
J. Hill	3	53	17.7	20	0
Jim Carter	3	44	14.7	t42	1
Al Matthews	2	58	29.0	t58	1
MacLeod	2	8	4.0	4	0
Hefner	1	3	3.0	3	0
Toner	1	1	1.0	1	0
Packers	**15**	**220**	**14.7**	**t58**	**3**
Opponents	17	256	15.1	t46	1

Scoring

	TDr	TDp	TDrt	PAT	FG	S	TP
Marcol	0	0	0	19/20	21/35	0	82
Staggers	1	3	0	0/0	0/0	0	24
Brockington	3	0	0	0/0	0/0	0	18
Lane	1	1	0	0/0	0/0	0	12
Barry Smith	0	2	0	0/0	0/0	0	12
Tagge	2	0	0	0/0	0/0	0	12
Jim Carter	0	0	1	0/0	0/0	0	6
K. Ellis	0	0	1	0/0	0/0	0	6
Goodman	1	0	0	0/0	0/0	0	6
S. Hunter	1	0	0	0/0	0/0	0	6
Al Matthews	0	0	1	0/0	0/0	0	6
McGeorge	0	1	0	0/0	0/0	0	6
P. Williams	1	0	0	0/0	0/0	0	6
Packers	**10**	**7**	**3**	**19/20**	**21/35**	**0**	**202**
Opponents	13	14	1	28/28	19/27	3	259

Fumbles

	Fum	Ow	Op	Yds	Tot
Bowman	1	0	0	-24	0
Brockington	4	2	0	0	2
Buchanon	0	0	1	0	1
Carr	0	0	2	0	2
Jim Carter	0	0	1	0	1
Del Gaizo	3	2	0	0	2
Donohoe	0	1	0	2	1
K. Ellis	0	0	2	0	2
Goodman	2	0	0	0	0
Hefner	0	0	1	4	1
Highsmith	1	0	0	0	0
J. Hill	0	0	4	0	4
S. Hunter	1	1	0	0	1
Krause	1	0	0	0	0
Lane	4	1	0	0	1
MacLeod	0	0	2	0	2
Al Matthews	0	0	2	0	2
M.P. McCoy	0	0	2	0	2
Roche	0	0	1	0	1
Staggers	1	1	0	0	1
Tagge	1	0	0	0	0
I. Thomas	2	2	0	0	2
C. Williams	0	0	1	0	1
P. Williams	1	0	0	0	0
Packers	**23**	**10**	**18**	**-18**	**28**

NFL STANDINGS

National Conference

Eastern Division

	W	L	T	Pct	PF	PA
Dallas Cowboys	10	4	0	.714	382	203
Washington Redskins	10	4	0	.714	325	198
Philadelphia Eagles	5	8	1	.393	310	393
St. Louis Cardinals	4	9	1	.321	286	365
New York Giants	2	11	1	.179	226	362

Central Division

	W	L	T	Pct	PF	PA
Minnesota Vikings	12	2	0	.857	296	168
Detroit Lions	6	7	1	.464	271	247
Green Bay Packers	**5**	**7**	**2**	**.429**	**202**	**259**
Chicago Bears	3	11	0	.214	195	334

Western Division

	W	L	T	Pct	PF	PA
Los Angeles Rams	12	2	0	.857	388	178
Atlanta Falcons	9	5	0	.643	318	224
New Orleans Saints	5	9	0	.357	163	312
San Francisco 49ers	5	9	0	.357	262	319

American Conference

Eastern Division

	W	L	T	Pct	PF	PA
Miami Dolphins	12	2	0	.857	343	150
Buffalo Bills	9	5	0	.643	259	230
New England Patriots	5	9	0	.357	258	300
Baltimore Colts	4	10	0	.286	226	341
New York Jets	4	10	0	.286	240	306

Central Division

	W	L	T	Pct	PF	PA
Cincinnati Bengals	10	4	0	.714	286	231
Pittsburgh Steelers	10	4	0	.714	347	210
Cleveland Browns	7	5	2	.571	234	255
Houston Oilers	1	13	0	.071	199	447

Western Division

	W	L	T	Pct	PF	PA
Oakland Raiders	9	4	1	.679	292	175
Denver Broncos	7	5	2	.571	354	296
Kansas City Chiefs	7	5	2	.571	231	192
San Diego Chargers	2	11	1	.179	188	386

ROSTER

No	Name	Pos	Ht	Wt	DOB	College	G
27	Austin, Hise	CB	6-4	195	09/08/50	Prairie View	9
57	Bowman, Ken	C	6-3	245	12/15/42	Wisconsin	14
71	Branstetter, Kent	T	6-3	260	02/03/49	Houston	9
42	Brockington, John	RB	6-1	230	09/07/48	Ohio State	14
74	Brown, Aaron	DE	6-5	270	11/16/43	Minnesota	8
78	Brown, Bob	DE	6-5	280	02/23/40	Arkansas-Pine Bluff	14
28	Buchanon, Willie	CB	6-0	190	11/04/50	San Diego State	6
53	Carr, Fred	LB	6-5	240	08/19/46	Texas-El Paso	14
50	Carter, Jim	LB	6-3	245	10/18/48	Minnesota	14
12	Del Gaizo, Jim	QB	6-1	198	05/31/47	Tampa	8
86	Donohoe, Mike	TE	6-3	230	05/06/45	San Francisco	13
48	Ellis, Ken	CB	5-10	195	09/27/47	Southern University	14
88	Garrett, Len	TE	6-3	230	12/18/47	New Mexico Highlands	2
68	Gillingham, Gale	G	6-3	265	02/03/44	Minnesota	14
46	Glass, Leland	WR	6-0	185	11/05/50	Oregon	12
25	Goodman, Les	RB	5-11	206	09/01/50	Yankton	6
85	Gordon, Dick	WR	5-11	190	01/01/44	Michigan State	2
21	Hall, Charlie	CB	6-1	190	03/31/48	Pittsburgh	13
77	Hayhoe, Bill	T	6-8	260	10/06/46	USC	6
51	Hefner, Larry	LB	6-2	230	08/02/49	Clemson	14
32	Highsmith, Don	RB	6-0	200	03/12/48	Michigan State	7
39	Hill, Jim	S	6-2	195	10/21/46	Texas A&I	13
72	Himes, Dick	T	6-4	260	05/25/46	Ohio State	14
16	Hunter, Scott	QB	6-2	210	11/19/47	Alabama	8
55	Jenke, Noel	LB	6-1	225	12/17/47	Minnesota	2
30	Krause, Larry	RB	6-0	208	04/22/48	St. Norbert	14
36	Lane, MacArthur	RB	6-1	220	03/16/42	Utah State	13
62	Lueck, Bill	G	6-3	235	04/07/46	Arizona	14
13	Marcol, Chester	K	6-0	190	10/24/49	Hillsdale	14
29	Matthews, Al	DB	5-11	190	11/07/47	Texas A&I	14
56	MacLeod, Tom	LB	6-3	225	01/10/51	Minnesota	11
24	McBride, Ron	RB	6-0	200	10/12/48	Missouri	1
54	McCarren, Larry	C	6-3	240	11/09/51	Illinois	5
76	McCoy, Mike P.	DT	6-5	285	09/06/48	Notre Dame	14
81	McGeorge, Rich	TE	6-4	230	09/14/48	Elon	14
73	Oats, Carleton	DT	6-3	260	04/24/42	Florida A&M	8
75	Pureifory, Dave	DE	6-1	250	07/12/49	Eastern Michigan	13
87	Roche, Alden	DE	6-4	255	04/09/45	Southern University	13
80	Smith, Barry	WR	6-1	190	01/15/51	Florida State	14
45	Smith, Perry	CB	6-1	195	03/29/51	Colorado State	8
67	Snider, Malcolm	G	6-4	250	04/05/47	Stanford	14
22	Staggers, Jon	WR	5-10	180	12/14/48	Missouri	14
85	Staroba, Paul	WR	6-3	204	01/20/49	Michigan	2
17	Tagge, Jerry	QB	6-2	215	04/12/50	Nebraska	7
37	Thomas, Ike	CB	6-2	195	11/04/47	Bishop	13
59	Toner, Tom	LB	6-3	235	01/25/50	Idaho State	14
20	Widby, Ron	P	6-4	220	03/09/45	Tennessee	12
83	Williams, Clarence	DE	6-5	255	09/03/46	Prairie View	14
31	Williams, Perry	RB	6-2	225	12/11/46	Purdue	14
58	Withrow, Cal	C	6-0	230	08/04/45	Kentucky	14
65	Wortman, Keith	G	6-2	250	07/20/50	Nebraska	8

DRAFT

Rnd	Name	Pos	Ht	Wt	College
1	Barry Smith (21)	WR	6-1	185	Florida State
2	(Choice (46) to Cowboys for Ike Thomas and Ron Widby)				
3	Tom MacLeod (74)	LB	6-3	221	Minnesota
4	(Choice (99) to Rams for Tommy Crutcher)				
5	(Choice (124) to Raiders as part of Carleton Oats trade)				
6	Tom Toner (152)	LB	6-3	225	Idaho State
7	John Muller (177)	G-T	6-3	260	Iowa
8	Hise Austin (202)	CB	6-4	187	Prairie View
9	Rick Brown (230)	LB	6-3	225	USC
10	Larry Allen (255)	S-LB	6-1	214	Illinois
11	Phil Engle (280)	G	6-2	270	South Dakota State
12	Larry McCarren (308)	C	6-3	242	Illinois
13	Tim Alderson (333)	S	6-2	193	Minnesota
14	Jim Anderson (358)	DT	6-5	250	Northwestern
15	Reggie Echols (386)	WR	6-2	185	UCLA
16	Keith Pretty (411)	TE	6-4	229	Western Michigan
17	Harold Sampson (436)	DT	6-5	268	Southern University

1973 GREEN BAY PACKERS

FRONT ROW: Equipment Manager Gerald (Dad) Braisher, Assistant Equipment Manager Bob Noel, 12 Jim Del Gaizo, 57 Ken Bowman, 58 Cal Withrow, 72 Dick Himes, 68 Gale Gillingham, 31 Perry Williams, 50 Jim Carter, 29 Al Matthews, 48 Ken Ellis, 39 Jim Hill, 28 Willie Buchanon, 53 Fred Carr, 51 Larry Hefner.

SECOND ROW: (L–R) Assistant Trainer Dan Davis, Trainer Domenic Gentile, 20 Ron Widby, 30 Larry Krause, 76 Mike P. McCoy, 78 Bob Brown, 36 MacArthur Lane, 59 Tom Toner,21 Charlie Hall, 16 Scott Hunter, 42 John Brockington, 87 Alden Roche, Offensive Backfield Coach John (Red) Cochran, Receivers Coach John Polonchek, Head Coach Dan Devine, Defensive Secondary Coach Don Doll, Defensive Coordinator Dave Hanner.

THIRD ROW: (L–R) Offensive Line Coach Rollie Dotsch, Linebackers Coach Burt Gustafson, 25 Les Goodman, 88 Len Garrett, 83 Clarence Williams, 81 Rich McGeorge, 32 Don Highsmith, 17 Jerry Tagge, 13 Chester Marcol, 80 Barry Smith, 22 Jon Staggers, 37 Ike Thomas, 46 Leland Glass, Special Teams Coach Hank Kuhlmann, Pro Scout Bill Tobin.

BACK ROW: (L–R) 86 Mike Donohoe, 54 Larry McCarren, 45 Perry Smith, 56 Tom MacLeod, 27 Hise Austin, 77 Bill Hayhoe, 67 Malcolm Snyder, 62 Bill Lueck, 65 Keith Wortman,75 Dave Pureifory, 74 Aaron Brown, 73 Carleton Oats.

Dan Devine's exit following the completion of the 1974 season was similar in at least one regard to his coaching debut in 1971: it came with a surprise.

Devine, realizing he was losing support with the team's executive committee as another unsuccessful season played out, put out feelers in a search for other positions. He met with an official from Notre Dame prior to a season-ending loss in Atlanta, then demanded to know his status with the Packers upon his return.

He met with Packers president Dominic Olejniczak Sunday night following the game. The next day, Devine resigned before any determination had been made as to whether or not he would return for the fifth and final year of his contract. The man who broke his leg in his first game as Packers coach also announced that he was leaving to become the head coach at Notre Dame.

"I want to thank the Green Bay Packers for giving me an opportunity to coach here for the last four years," Devine said at a farewell press conference. "And, particularly, I want to thank the players who never gave up."

Throughout his tenure, Devine struggled to find a reliable quarterback. The situation worsened in 1974. For the first time in 51 years, Packers' passers threw just one touchdown pass in the first seven games of a season.

Devine, who had given up two second-round draft picks for Jim Del Gaizo in 1973 and a fifth-round selection for Jack Concannon in July, pulled out all the stops. He traded two first-round picks (1975, 1976), two second-round choices (1975, 1976) and a third-rounder (1975) to the Rams for 34-year-old John Hadl.

Hadl threw all of three touchdown passes in the final seven games, and the team's record in that span (3-4) was no better than it had been in the opening seven weeks. For the second year in a row, Green Bay (6-8) finished ahead of only the Bears in the Central Division.

As they had done in 1970, NFL players went on strike. This time the work stoppage dragged into the preseason.

Free agency was the main issue of contention. Players wanted the freedom to sign with any team after their initial contract expired. Management disagreed, and veterans struck on July 1.

San Diego was the first team to open training camp and the first to have a picket line. Jim Hill and Willie Buchanon represented Green Bay at that site.

When the Packers opened camp, the assistant coaches arranged for draft choices to disembark on the runway at Austin Straubel Airport rather than enter the terminal. A chain-link fence prevented the veterans from approaching the newcomers, who were quickly taken to team headquarters in waiting cars. The team did permit one 50-minute meeting between the two groups.

On July 18, Packers veterans Jim Carter and Larry Hefner crossed the picket line. Five days later, Chester Marcol joined them. A handful more returned, but the first two preseason games were played with mostly rookies.

After the second weekend of preseason games, the NFL Players Association suspended its strike and entered a self-imposed 14-day cooling off period. Veterans reported to camp; however, a new collective bargaining agreement was not reached until February of 1977.

Of the three games the Packers won in the first five weeks, a 17-6 triumph over the Rams in Week 5 had to be the most satisfying. Green Bay atoned for its dismal showing of the previous year and handed Los Angeles just its fourth loss in its last 19 regular-season games. Hadl completed just six of 16 passes for the Rams and was pulled in favor of seldom-used James Harris.

"It's a bunch of bull," Hadl said, when asked if his passing arm wasn't what it used to be.

Three weeks later, Hadl was in a Packers uniform. After losing to the Bears, Green Bay whipped Minnesota 19-7 and trounced the Chargers 34-0 to improve to 6-5 and pull within a game of the front-running Vikings (7-4).

One week later, Philadelphia mauled Green Bay 36-14. Coupled with a Minnesota win, the loss eliminated the Packers from the playoff race.

Green Bay lost its last two games. First, the 49ers edged them 7-6 on Del Williams' 2-yard run with 9:23 left. Then, the lowly Falcons pulled out a 10-3 win in front of a mere 10,020 fans (48,830 no shows). The following day, the Packers began searching for a head coach.

THE STORK DELIVERS

At 6-feet-7 inches tall, Ted Hendricks was one of the tallest Packers to ever play the game. In 1974, he used his long frame to become the best kick blocker in team history.

Hendricks, nicknamed The Stork, arrived via a trade involving Tom MacLeod and a couple of draft choices. He started 14 games at MacLeod's old left linebacker position. As a special teamer, he blocked seven kicks.

In the opener, Hendricks blocked a Fred Cox extra point. A week later, he deflected a Toni Linhart field goal.

On Sept. 29, he slipped through and smothered a Herman Weaver punt, which rolled out of the end zone for a safety. Green Bay beat Detroit by two points, 21-19.

Hendricks registered his fourth block against Bears punter Bob Parsons on Oct. 21. He batted away an Errol Mann field goal attempt six days later.

On Dec. 8, Hendricks double dipped. He turned back a Bruce Gossett field goal, then blocked a Tom Wittum punt in the fourth quarter. Despite his efforts, the 49ers won 7-6.

In 1975, Hendricks played out his option and became a Raider. He played nine more seasons and was inducted into the Pro Football Hall of Fame in 1990.

1974

TEAM STATISTICS

	GB	OPP
First Downs	214	218
Rushing	87	93
Passing	108	106
Penalty	19	19
Rushes	482	465
Yards Gained	1,571	1,641
Average Gain	3.26	3.53
Average Yards per Game	112.2	117.2
Passes Attempted	385	383
Completed	187	188
% Completed	48.57	49.09
Total Yards Gained	2,162	2,254
Times Sacked	17	28
Yards Lost	126	254
Net Yards Gained	2,036	2,000
Yards Gained per Completion	11.56	11.99
Net Yards per Attempt	5.06	4.87
Average Net Yards per Game	145.4	142.9
Combined Net Yards Gained	3,607	3,641
Total Plays	884	876
Average Yards per Play	4.08	4.16
Average Net Yards per Game	257.6	260.1
Third Down Efficiency	70/206	75/204
Percentage	33.98	36.76
Fourth Down Efficiency	3/15	2/8
Percentage	20.00	25.00
Intercepted By	23	21
Yards Returned	278	289
Returned for TD	1	1
Punts	69	84
Yards Punted	2,648	3,074
Average Yards per Punt	38.38	36.60
Punt Returns	42	48
Yards Returned	416	356
Average Yards per Return	9.90	7.42
Returned for TD	2	0
Kickoff Returns	49	55
Yards Returned	1,022	1,156
Average Yards per Return	20.86	21.02
Returned for TD	0	0
Penalties	55	88
Yards Penalized	536	715
Fumbles	25	19
Lost	16	12
Own Recovered for Touchdown	0	0
Opponent's Recovered by	12	16
Opponent's Recovered for Touchdown	1	2
Total Points Scored	210	206
Total Touchdowns	19	23
Touchdowns Rushing	10	10
Touchdowns Passing	5	10
Touchdowns on Returns & Recoveries	4	3
Extra Points	19	17
Safeties	1	0
Field Goals Attempted	39	26
Field Goals Made	25	17
% Successful	64.10	65.38

Regular Season 6-8-0

Date	GB		OPP	Att.
9/15	17	Minnesota Vikings	32	(55,131)
9/22	20	at Baltimore Colts	13	(35,873)
9/29	21	Detroit Lions (M)	19	(45,970)
10/6	7	Buffalo Bills	27	(51,919)
10/13	17	Los Angeles Rams (M)	6	(45,938)
10/21	9	at Chicago Bears	10	(50,623)
10/27	17	at Detroit Lions	19	(51,775)
11/3	6	Washington Redskins	17	(55,288)
11/10	20	Chicago Bears (M)	3	(46,567)
11/17	19	at Minnesota Vikings	7	(47,924)
11/24	34	San Diego Chargers	0	(50,321)
12/1	14	at Philadelphia Eagles	36	(42,030)
12/8	6	at San Francisco 49ers	7	(47,475)
12/15	3	at Atlanta Falcons	10	(10,020)

Score By Periods

	1	2	3	4	Total
Packers	12	78	59	61	210
Opponents	48	61	40	57	206

INDIVIDUAL STATISTICS

Rushing

	Att	Yds	Avg	LG	TD
Brockington	266	883	3.3	33	5
Lane	137	362	2.6	20	3
Goodman	20	101	5.1	47	0
Odom	6	66	11.0	28	1
Torkelson	13	60	4.6	21	0
Tagge	18	58	3.2	12	0
Barty Smith	9	19	2.1	4	0
R. Walker	1	18	18.0	18	0
Concannon	3	7	2.3	6	1
Leigh	1	0	0.0	0	0
Hadl	8	-3	-0.4	6	0
Packers	**482**	**1,571**	**3.3**	**47**	**10**
Opponents	465	1,641	3.5	27	10

Receiving

	No	Yds	Avg	LG	TD
Brockington	43	314	7.3	29	0
Lane	34	315	9.3	t68	3
Staggers	32	450	14.1	63	0
McGeorge	30	440	14.7	51	0
Barry Smith	20	294	14.7	t27	1
Odom	15	249	16.6	57	1
Payne	5	63	12.6	18	0
Goodman	5	19	3.8	12	0
Torkelson	2	10	5.0	8	0
Donohoe	1	8	8.0	8	0
Packers	**187**	**2,162**	**11.6**	**t68**	**5**
Opponents	188	2,254	12.0	t57	10

Passing

	Att	Com	Yds	Pct	TD	In	Tk/Yds	Rate
Hadl	184	89	1,072	48.4	3	8	9/70	54.0
Tagge	146	70	709	47.9	1	10	5/35	36.0
Concannon	54	28	381	51.9	1	3	3/21	57.7
Lane	1	0	0	00.0	0	0	0/0	—
Packers	**385**	**187**	**2,162**	**48.6**	**5**	**21**	**17/126**	**47.6**
Opponents	383	188	2,254	49.1	10	23	28/254	51.2

Punting

	No	Yds	Avg	Net	TB	In20	LG	HB
R. Walker	69	2,648	38.4	31.5	6	14	58	0
Packers	**69**	**2,648**	**38.4**	**31.5**	**6**	**14**	**58**	**0**
Opponents	84	3,074	36.6	30.0	7	16	52	3

Kickoff Returns

	No	Yds	Avg	LG	TD
Odom	31	713	23.0	52	0
Leigh	9	201	22.3	30	0
Goodman	4	49	12.3	20	0
Okoniewski	2	11	5.5	11	0
Van Valkenburg	1	22	22.0	22	0
Torkelson	1	20	20.0	20	0
Krause	1	6	6.0	6	0
Packers	**49**	**1,022**	**20.9**	**52**	**0**
Opponents	55	1,156	21.0	43	0

Punt Returns

	No	Yds	Avg	FC	LG	TD
Staggers	22	222	10.1	6	t68	1
Odom	15	191	12.7	2	t95	1
K. Ellis	3	3	1.0	0	9	0
Hefner	1	0	0.0	0	0	0
Torkelson	1	0	0.0	0	0	0
Packers	**42**	**416**	**9.9**	**8**	**t95**	**2**
Opponents	48	356	7.4	2	26	0

Interceptions

	No	Yds	Avg	LG	TD
Hendricks	5	74	14.8	44	0
Buchanon	4	10	2.5	8	0
K. Ellis	3	36	18.7	t38	1
Al Matthews	3	41	13.7	32	0
J. Hill	2	47	23.5	24	0
C. Hall	2	22	11.0	19	0
C. Williams	1	23	23.0	23	0
M.P. McCoy	1	5	5.0	5	0
Carr	1	0	0.0	0	0
Jim Carter	1	0	0.0	0	0
Packers	**23**	**278**	**12.1**	**44**	**1**
Opponents	21	289	13.8	45	1

Scoring

	TDr	TDp	TDrt	PAT	FG	S	TP
Marcol	0	0	0	19/19	25/39	0	94
Lane	3	3	0	0/0	0/0	0	36
Brockington	5	0	0	0/0	0/0	0	30
Odom	1	1	1	0/0	0/0	0	18
Concannon	1	0	0	0/0	0/0	0	6
K. Ellis	0	0	1	0/0	0/0	0	6
Barry Smith	0	1	0	0/0	0/0	0	6
Staggers	0	0	1	0/0	0/0	0	6
Torkelson	0	0	1	0/0	0/0	0	6
Hendricks	0	0	0	0/0	0/0	1	2
Packers	**10**	**5**	**4**	**19/19**	**25/39**	**1**	**210**
Opponents	10	10	3	17/23	17/26	0	206

Fumbles

	Fum	Ow	Op	Yds	Tot
Brockington	6	0	0	0	0
Buchanon	0	0	1	0	1
Carr	0	0	2	0	1
Jim Carter	0	0	1	19	1
K. Ellis	0	0	1	0	0
Goodman	1	0	0	0	0
Hadl	4	0	0	0	0
Hefner	0	1	0	0	1
Hendricks	0	0	1	0	1
Himes	0	0	0	0	1
Lane	3	0	0	0	0
D. Mason	0	0	1	19	1
M.P. McCoy	0	0	1	0	2
McGeorge	0	1	0	0	1
Odom	5	0	0	0	2
Roche	0	0	1	0	1
H. Schuh	0	2	0	0	2
P. Smith	0	0	1	0	1
Tagge	5	0	0	-6	1
Torkelson	0	0	1	29	1
C. Williams	0	0	1	0	1
Packers	**25**	**8**	**12**	**61**	**20**

NFL STANDINGS

National Conference

Eastern Division

	W	L	T	Pct	PF	PA
St. Louis Cardinals	10	4	0	.714	285	218
Washington Redskins	10	4	0	.714	320	196
Dallas Cowboys	8	6	0	.571	297	235
Philadelphia Eagles	7	7	0	.500	242	217
New York Giants	2	12	0	.143	195	299

Central Division

	W	L	T	Pct	PF	PA
Minnesota Vikings	10	4	0	.714	310	195
Detroit Lions	7	7	0	.500	256	270
Green Bay Packers	**6**	**8**	**0**	**.429**	**210**	**206**
Chicago Bears	4	10	0	.286	152	279

Western Division

	W	L	T	Pct	PF	PA
Los Angeles Rams	10	4	0	.714	263	181
San Francisco 49ers	6	8	0	.429	226	236
New Orleans Saints	5	9	0	.357	166	263
Atlanta Falcons	3	11	0	.214	111	271

American Conference

Eastern Division

	W	L	T	Pct	PF	PA
Miami Dolphins	11	3	0	.786	327	216
Buffalo Bills	9	5	0	.643	264	244
New England Patriots	7	7	0	.500	348	289
New York Jets	7	7	0	.500	279	300
Baltimore Colts	2	12	0	.143	190	329

Central Division

	W	L	T	Pct	PF	PA
Pittsburgh Steelers	10	3	1	.750	305	189
Cincinnati Bengals	7	7	0	.500	283	259
Houston Oilers	7	7	0	.500	236	282
Cleveland Browns	4	10	0	.286	251	344

Western Division

	W	L	T	Pct	PF	PA
Oakland Raiders	12	2	0	.857	355	228
Denver Broncos	7	6	1	.536	302	294
Kansas City Chiefs	5	9	0	.357	233	293
San Diego Chargers	5	9	0	.357	212	285

1974

ROSTER

No	Name	Pos	Ht	Wt	DOB	College	G
52	Acks, Ron	LB	6-2	225	10/03/44	Illinois	13
71	Basinger, Mike	DE	6-3	258	12/11/51	California-Riverside	1
42	Brockington, John	RB	6-1	225	09/07/48	Ohio State	14
74	Brown, Aaron	DE	6-5	270	11/16/43	Minnesota	2
28	Buchanon, Willie	CB	6-0	190	11/04/50	San Diego State	14
53	Carr, Fred	LB	6-5	240	08/19/46	Texas-El Paso	14
50	Carter, Jim	LB	6-3	245	10/18/48	Minnesota	14
10	Concannon, Jack	QB	6-3	200	02/25/43	Boston College	14
58	Cooney, Mark	LB	6-4	222	06/02/51	Colorado	13
86	Donohoe, Mike	TE	6-3	230	05/06/45	San Francisco	14
48	Ellis, Ken	CB	5-10	195	09/27/47	Southern University	14
71	Fanucci, Mike	DE	6-4	242	09/25/49	Arizona State	13
68	Gillingham, Gale	G	6-3	265	02/03/44	Minnesota	14
25	Goodman, Les	RB	5-11	206	09/01/50	Yankton	13
12	Hadl, John	QB	6-1	214	02/15/40	Kansas	7
21	Hall, Charlie	CB	6-1	190	03/31/48	Pittsburgh	14
51	Hefner, Larry	LB	6-2	230	08/02/49	Clemson	14
56	Hendricks, Ted	LB	6-7	220	11/01/47	Miami	14
39	Hill, Jim	S	6-2	195	10/21/46	Texas A&I	14
72	Himes, Dick	T	6-4	260	05/25/46	Ohio State	14
55	Jenke, Noel	LB	6-1	225	12/17/47	Minnesota	8
30	Krause, Larry	RB	6-0	208	04/22/48	St. Norbert	14
36	Lane, MacArthur	RB	6-1	220	03/16/42	Utah State	14
23	Leigh, Charlie	RB	5-11	206	10/30/45	No college	11
62	Lueck, Bill	G	6-3	235	04/07/46	Arizona	9
13	Marcol, Chester	K	6-0	190	10/24/49	Hillsdale	14
43	Mason, Dave	DB	6-0	195	11/02/49	Nebraska	12
29	Matthews, Al	DB	5-11	190	11/07/47	Texas A&I	14
54	McCarren, Larry	C	6-3	240	11/09/51	Illinois	14
76	McCoy, Mike P.	DT	6-5	285	09/06/48	Notre Dame	14
81	McGeorge, Rich	TE	6-4	230	09/14/48	Elon	14
70	Nystrom, Lee	T	6-5	258	10/30/51	MacAlester	13
84	Odom, Steve	WR	5-8	165	09/05/52	Utah	14
73	Okoniewski, Steve	DT	6-4	252	08/22/49	Montana	14
85	Payne, Ken	WR	6-1	185	10/06/50	Langston	12
75	Pureifory, Dave	DE	6-1	250	07/12/49	Eastern Michigan	13
87	Roche, Alden	DE	6-4	255	04/09/45	Southern University	14
52	Schmitt, John	C	6-4	250	11/12/42	Hofstra	14
79	Schuh, Harry	T	6-3	260	09/25/42	Memphis State	14
80	Smith, Barry	WR	6-1	190	01/15/51	Florida State	14
33	Smith, Barty	FB	6-3	240	03/23/52	Richmond	8
45	Smith, Perry	CB	6-1	195	03/29/51	Colorado State	12
67	Snider, Malcolm	G	6-4	250	04/05/47	Stanford	14
22	Staggers, Jon	WR	5-10	180	12/14/48	Missouri	14
17	Tagge, Jerry	QB	6-2	215	04/12/50	Nebraska	6
26	Torkelson, Eric	RB	6-2	194	03/03/52	Connecticut	14
61	Van Dyke, Bruce	G	6-2	255	08/06/44	Missouri	1
40	Van Valkenburg, Pete	RB	6-2	205	05/19/50	BYU	6
78	Wafer, Carl	T	6-3	250	01/17/51	Tennessee State	2
18	Walker, Randy	P	5-10	177	08/29/51	Northwestern State (LA)	14
49	Wicks, Bob	WR	6-3	205	07/24/50	Utah State	1
83	Williams, Clarence	DE	6-5	255	09/03/46	Prairie View	14
65	Wortman, Keith	G	6-2	250	07/20/50	Nebraska	12

DRAFT

Rnd	Name	Pos	Ht	Wt	College
1	Barty Smith (12)	FB	6-3	240	Richmond
2	(Choice (38) to Dolphins in Jim Del Gaizo trade)				
3	(Choice (64) to Vikings through Chargers in Jim Hill trade)				
4	(Choice (90) to 49ers for Al Randolph)				
5	Steve Odom (116)	WR	5-8	165	Utah
6a	Don Woods (134)	RB	6-1	191	New Mexico
	(Choice from Bears for rights to Zeke Bratkowski)				
6b	Ken Payne (142)	WR	6-1	185	Langston
7	Bart Purvis (168)	G	6-4	240	Maryland
8a	Monte Doris (194)	LB	6-2	245	USC
8b	Ned Guillet (200)	S	6-1	183	Boston College
	(Choice from Falcons through Saints for Len Garrett)				
9	Harold Holton (220)	G	6-2	242	Texas-El Paso
10	Doug Troszak (246)	DT	6-3	248	Michigan
11	Eric Torkelson (272)	RB	6-2	194	Connecticut
12	Randy Walker (298)	P	5-10	177	Northwestern State (LA)
13	Emanuel Armstrong (324)	LB	6-3	222	San Jose State
14	Andy Neloms (350)	DT	6-4	260	Kentucky State
15	Dave Wannstedt (376)	T	6-4	245	Pittsburgh
16	Mark Cooney (402)	LB	6-4	222	Colorado
17	Randy Woodfield (428)	WR	6-0	170	Portland State

1974 GREEN BAY PACKERS

FRONT ROW: (L-R) 76 Mike P. McCoy, 30 Larry Krause, 80 Barry Smith, 51 Larry Hefner, 50 Jim Carter, 68 Gale Gillingham, 17 Jerry Tagge, 48 Ken Ellis, 39 Jim Hill, 29 Al Matthews, 28 Willie Buchanon, 53 Fred Carr.

SECOND ROW: (L-R) Assistant Trainer Dan Davis, Trainer Domenic Gentile, 36 MacArthur Lane, 10 Jack Concannon, 21 Charlie Hall, 42 John Brockington, 40 Pete Van Valkenburg, 57 Ron Acks, Assistant Equipment Manager Bob Noel, Equipment Manager Gerald (Dad) Braisher.

THIRD ROW: (L-R) 84 Steve Odom, 33 Barty Smith, 23 Charlie Leigh, 13 Chester Marcol, 45 Perry Smith, 43 Dave Mason, 18 Randy Walker, 25 Les Goodman, 75 Dave Pureifory, 22 Jon Staggers.

FOURTH ROW: (L-R) 62 Bill Lueck, 65 Keith Wortman, 52 John Schmitt, 78 Carl Wafer, 54 Larry McCarren, 73 Steve Okoniewski, 71 Mike Fanucci, 26 Eric Torkelson, 79 Harry Schuh.

BACK ROW: (L-R) 85 Ken Payne, 86 Mike Donohoe, 12 Dean Carlson, 87 Alden Roche, 58 Mark Cooney, 83 Clarence Williams, 56 Ted Hendricks, 67 Malcolm Snider, 70 Lee Nystrom, 81 Rich McGeorge, 72 Dick Himes.

On Christmas Eve 1974, Bart Starr, a five-time NFL champion as a player, was named Packers head coach and general manager with the hope he could lead the team to additional titles in his new role.

"I'm absolutely ecstatic about this opportunity," he said. "I'm extremely thrilled and honored ... but I'm not awed by it."

Starr admitted he had little coaching experience, and he asked fans for their prayers and patience. His resume consisted of a one-year stint (1972) as the team's quarterback coach.

Starr faced a number of challenges. Devine had traded away many of the team's top draft choices. All-Pro linebacker Ted Hendricks became a free agent after contract talks broke off in July. Four days later, cornerback Ken Ellis walked out of camp over a contract dispute. In August, offensive lineman Bill Lueck asked to be traded.

Despite the dearth of selections, the draft produced three players—guard Bill Bain, running back Willard Harrell, and safety Steve Luke—who contributed as rookies. Hendricks was sent to Oakland in return for two first-round draft choices (1976, 1977). Ellis was fined and suspended for a week, but returned to play. Lueck was shipped to the Eagles for a fourth-round pick in 1976.

The Packers lost their season opener 30-16 to the Lions, a game in which punter Steve Broussard had an NFL-record three punts blocked. Chester Marcol's season ended the same day when he tore a quadriceps muscle. A week later, Willie Buchanon went out with a broken leg in Denver. In addition, John Brockington's production dipped dramatically, John Hadl threw an NFC-high 21 interceptions and the team's run defense was the worst in the league.

Starr replaced Marcol with Joe Danelo, Broussard with David Beverly, and Buchanon with Perry Smith. He undoubtedly would have liked to replace the team's 0-4 start, the worst getaway in team history to that point.

"Packer Coach Bart Starr (0-4) is off to his worst start since 1955 when he helped quarterback Alabama to an 0-10 season," wrote Steve Harvey, who ranked Green Bay No. 1 for the week in his syndicated "Bottom Ten" column.

Green Bay wasn't about to remain winless all season. On Oct. 19, the Packers stunned the previously unbeaten Cowboys 19-17 in Dallas. Hadl fired a 26-yard touchdown pass to Rich McGeorge with 1:52 left to give the 17-point underdogs their first win.

Steve Luke set up the touchdown when he recovered Golden Richards' fumble at the Cowboys' 31-yard line.

"We're elated. We're about three feet off the ground right now," Starr said.

The reinvigorated Packers then went toe-to-toe with the defending Super Bowl champion Steelers in Milwaukee. Despite dominating on the ground (59 rushes, 248 yards), Pittsburgh didn't pull ahead for good until Roy Gerela's 29-yard goal with 1:04 left.

Green Bay closed out the first half of the season with a 28-17 loss to the Vikings at Lambeau Field. Barty Smith, the Packers' top draft choice in 1974, received the first significant playing time of his pro career when Brockington went out early with a thigh injury. Smith fought his way to 88 yards on 16 carries and scored twice.

Two more losses dropped the Packers' record to 1-8. The Bears dumped them 27-14 and the Lions edged them 13-10. Detroit drove 74 yards in 12 plays to set up Errol Mann's 23-yard game-winning field goal.

"It's frustrating," Brockington said. "I'm getting tired of saying we played well, but lost."

On Nov. 23, the Packers turned in their biggest offensive show. Hadl threw for a season-high 275 yards and his offensive mates tossed in another 210 on the ground as the Green and Gold romped 40-14 over the Giants.

"I don't think I've ever been associated with this bad of a game in all my years of football," Giants coach Bill Arnsparger said before boarding the team bus.

Green Bay followed up by thumping the Bears 28-7, then lost to the playoff-bound Vikings and Rams.

The Packers closed with a 22-13 win over the Falcons. Eric Torkelson gained 86 yards rushing and scored a touchdown. Afterwards, the fans tore down the goal posts.

"Our fans are sensational and without question the finest in the world," said Starr. "They're something special, I'll tell you."

PAYNE'S WORLD: END ZONE NOT INCLUDED

Ken Payne went from unknown rookie to one of the top receivers in the NFL in the short span of a year.

Payne, the second of Green Bay's two sixth-round draft choices in 1974, caught five passes as a rookie. A year later, he became quarterback John Hadl's go-to receiver, hauling in 58 passes, fourth best in the league.

Hadl and Payne developed a chemistry early. On a Monday night in Denver in Week 2, Payne caught 12 passes for 167 yards but did not reach the end zone.

Though Payne caught another 41 passes, he failed to score a touchdown. His 766 yards receiving without a touchdown are the most by a Packer in a single season.

Payne got his first six-pointer in October 1976. He was released the following year.

Most Yards Receiving, No Touchdowns, Season

Yards Rec.	Year		Player
766	58	1975	Ken Payne
620	48	1988	Perry Kemp
551	34	1964	Ron Kramer

TEAM STATISTICS

	GB	OPP
First Downs	210	262
Rushing	99	132
Passing	94	107
Penalty	17	23
Rushes	485	546
Yards Gained	1,722	2,288
Average Gain	3.55	4.19
Average Yards per Game	123.0	163.4
Passes Attempted	357	354
Completed	164	196
% Completed	45.94	55.37
Total Yards Gained	2,105	2,192
Times Sacked	41	43
Yards Lost	375	357
Net Yards Gained	1,730	1,835
Yards Gained per Completion	12.84	11.18
Net Yards per Attempt	4.35	4.62
Average Net Yards per Game	123.6	131.1
Combined Net Yards Gained	3,452	4,123
Total Plays	883	943
Average Yards per Play	3.91	4.37
Average Net Yards per Game	246.6	294.5
Third Down Efficiency	66/205	73/206
Percentage	32.43	35.44
Fourth Down Efficiency	13/19	8/13
Percentage	68.42	61.54
Intercepted By	11	22
Yards Returned	197	362
Returned for TD	2	3
Punts	84	77
Yards Punted	3,074	2,966
Average Yards per Punt	36.60	38.52
Punt Returns	40	48
Yards Returned	300	268
Average Yards per Return	7.50	5.58
Returned for TD	0	0
Kickoff Returns	65	44
Yards Returned	1,361	784
Average Yards per Return	20.94	17.82
Returned for TD	0	0
Penalties	87	104
Yards Penalized	791	914
Fumbles	37	27
Lost	23	15
Own Recovered for Touchdown	0	0
Opponent's Recovered by	15	23
Opponent's Recovered for Touchdown	0	0
Total Points Scored	218	299
Total Touchdowns	27	34
Touchdowns Rushing	15	17
Touchdowns Passing	10	13
Touchdowns on Returns & Recoveries	2	4
Extra Points	24	29
Safeties	1	0
Field Goals Attempted	19	33
Field Goals Made	10	22
% Successful	52.63	66.67

Regular Season 5-9-0

Date	GB		OPP	Att.
9/12	14	San Francisco 49ers	26	(54,628)
9/19	0	at St. Louis Cardinals	29	(48,842)
9/26	7	at Cincinnati Bengals	28	(44,103)
10/3	24	Detroit Lions	14	(54,758)
10/10	27	Seattle Seahawks (M)	20	(54,983)
10/17	28	Philadelphia Eagles	13	(55,115)
10/24	14	at Oakland Raiders	18	(52,232)
10/31	6	at Detroit Lions	27	(74,582)
11/7	32	New Orleans Saints (M)	27	(52,936)
11/14	13	at Chicago Bears	24	(52,907)
11/21	10	Minnesota Vikings (M)	17	(53,104)
11/28	10	Chicago Bears	16	(56,267)
12/5	9	at Minnesota Vikings	20	(43,700)
12/12	24	at Atlanta Falcons	20	(23,116)

Score By Periods

	1	2	3	4	Total
Packers	60	50	34	74	218
Opponents	46	128	60	65	299

INDIVIDUAL STATISTICS

Rushing

	Att	Yds	Avg	LG	TD
Harrell	130	435	3.3	56	3
Brockington	117	406	3.5	29	2
Barty Smith	97	355	3.7	16	5
Torkelson	88	289	3.3	15	2
Odom	4	78	19.5	28	0
C. Brown	12	49	4.1	21	0
C. Taylor	14	47	3.4	17	1
R. Johnson	5	25	5.0	11	1
Dickey	11	19	1.7	12	1
Osborn	6	16	2.7	6	0
Zimmerman	1	3	3.0	3	0
Packers	485	1,722	3.6	56	15
Opponents	546	2,288	4.2	59	17

Receiving

	No	Yds	Avg	LG	TD
Payne	33	467	14.2	t57	4
McGeorge	24	278	11.6	28	1
Odom	23	456	19.8	t66	2
O. Smith	20	364	18.2	47	1
Torkelson	19	140	7.4	31	0
Harrell	17	201	11.8	t69	1
Barty Smith	11	88	8.0	35	0
Brockington	11	49	4.5	20	0
C. Taylor	2	21	10.5	18	0
C. Hall	1	18	18.0	18	0
Zimmerman	1	13	13.0	13	0
M. Jackson	1	8	8.0	8	0
Askson	1	2	2.0	t2	1
Packers	164	2,105	12.8	t69	10
Opponents	196	2,192	11.2	t88	13

Passing

	Att	Com	Yds	Pct	TD	In	Tk/Yds	Rate
Dickey	243	115	1,465	47.3	7	14	28/279	52.2
C. Brown	74	26	333	35.1	2	6	10/66	25.3
R. Johnson	35	21	249	60.0	0	1	2/23	69.8
Harrell	4	1	40	25.0	1	1	1/7	—
Beverly	1	1	18	100.0	0	0	0/0	—
Packers	357	164	2,105	45.9	10	22	41/375	48.6
Opponents	354	196	2,192	55.4	13	11	43/357	73.3

	No	Yds	Avg	Net	TB	In20	LG	HB
Beverly	83	3,074	37.0	32.2	5	14	60	1
Packers	84	3,074	37.0	32.2	5	14	60	1
Opponents	77	2,966	38.5	31.5	12	13	57	0

Kickoff Returns

	No	Yds	Avg	LG	TD
Odom	29	610	21.0	88	0
M.C. McCoy	18	457	25.4	65	0
Torkelson	6	123	20.5	29	0
C. Taylor	3	59	19.7	23	0
Hyland	3	31	10.3	11	0
Osborn	3	19	6.3	10	0
S. Wagner	1	27	27.0	27	0
J. Gray	1	23	23.0	23	0
O. Smith	1	12	12.0	12	0
Packers	65	1,361	20.9	88	0
Opponents	44	784	17.8		0

Punt Returns

	No	Yds	Avg	FC	LG	TD
J. Gray	37	307	8.3	7	27	0
Harrell	3	-7	-2.3	1	1	0
Packers	40	300	7.5	8	27	0
Opponents	48	268	5.6	10	19	0

Interceptions

	No	Yds	Avg	LG	TD
J. Gray	4	101	20.3	67	1
Luke	2	30	15.0	15	0
Buchanon	2	28	14.0	22	0
Toner	1	28	28.0	28	0
Carr	1	10	10.0	t10	1
P. Smith	1	0	0.0	0	0
Packers	11	197	17.9	67	2
Opponents	22	362	16.5	t53	3

Scoring

	TDr	TDp	TDrt	PAT	FG	S	TP
Marcol	0	0	0	24/27	10/19	0	54
Barty Smith	5	0	0	0/0	0/0	0	30
Harrell	3	1	0	0/0	0/0	0	24
Payne	0	4	0	0/0	0/0	0	24
Brockington	2	0	0	0/0	0/0	0	12
Odom	0	2	0	0/0	0/0	0	12
Torkelson	2	0	0	0/0	0/0	0	12
Askson	0	1	0	0/0	0/0	0	6
Carr	0	0	1	0/0	0/0	0	6
Dickey	1	0	0	0/0	0/0	0	6
J. Gray	0	0	1	0/0	0/0	0	6
R. Johnson	1	0	0	0/0	0/0	0	6
McGeorge	0	1	0	0/0	0/0	0	6
O. Smith	0	1	0	0/0	0/0	0	6
C. Taylor	1	0	0	0/0	0/0	0	6
team	0	0	0	0/0	0/0	1	2
Packers	15	10	2	24/27	10/19	1	218
Opponents	17	13	4	29/34	22/33	0	299

Fumbles

	Fum	Ow	Op	Yds	Tot
Brockington	3	0	0	0	0
C. Brown	2	2	0	0	2
Carr	0	0	1	0	1
Dickey	7	3	0	-8	3
J. Gray	0	0	4	0	4
Gueno	0	1	1	0	2
Harrell	9	0	0	0	0
Hyland	1	0	0	0	0
R. Johnson	2	1	0	-4	1
M.C. McCoy	1	0	0	0	0
M.P. McCoy	0	0	3	0	3
McGeorge	0	1	0	0	1
Odom	2	1	0	0	1
Payne	1	1	0	0	1
Pureifory	0	0	1	0	1
Roller	0	0	2	-2	2
Barty Smith	4	1	0	0	1
O. Smith	2	0	0	0	0
Torkelson	3	2	0	0	2
Van Dyke	0	1	0	0	1
S. Wagner	0	0	2	0	2
Weaver	0	0	1	0	1
Packers	37	14	15	-14	29

NFL STANDINGS

National Conference

Eastern Division

	W	L	T	Pct	PF	PA
Dallas Cowboys	11	3	0	.786	296	194
Washington Redskins	10	4	0	.714	291	217
St. Louis Cardinals	10	4	0	.714	309	267
Philadelphia Eagles	4	10	0	.286	165	286
New York Giants	3	11	0	.214	170	250

Central Division

	W	L	T	Pct	PF	PA
Minnesota Vikings	11	2	1	.821	305	176
Chicago Bears	7	7	0	.500	253	216
Detroit Lions	6	8	0	.429	262	220
Green Bay Packers	5	9	0	.357	218	299

Western Division

	W	L	T	Pct	PF	PA
Los Angeles Rams	10	3	1	.750	351	190
San Francisco 49ers	8	6	0	.571	270	190
Atlanta Falcons	4	10	0	.286	172	312
New Orleans Saints	4	10	0	.286	253	346
Seattle Seahawks	2	12	0	.143	229	429

American Conference

Eastern Division

	W	L	T	Pct	PF	PA
Baltimore Colts	11	3	0	.786	417	246
New England Patriots	11	3	0	.786	376	236
Miami Dolphins	6	8	0	.429	263	264
New York Jets	3	11	0	.214	169	383
Buffalo Bills	2	12	0	.143	245	363

Central Division

	W	L	T	Pct	PF	PA
Pittsburgh Steelers	10	4	0	.714	342	138
Cincinnati Bengals	10	4	0	.714	335	210
Cleveland Browns	9	5	0	.643	267	287
Houston Oilers	5	9	0	.357	222	273

Western Division

	W	L	T	Pct	PF	PA
Oakland Raiders	13	1	0	.929	350	237
Denver Broncos	9	5	0	.643	315	206
San Diego Chargers	6	8	0	.429	248	285
Kansas City Chiefs	5	9	0	.357	290	376
Tampa Bay Buccaneers	0	14	0	.000	125	412

ROSTER

No	Name	Pos	Ht	Wt	DOB	College	G
57	Acks, Ron	LB	6-2	225	10/03/44	Illinois	13
88	Askson, Bert	TE	6-2	225	12/18/45	Texas Southern	14
70	Barber, Bob	DE	6-3	240	12/26/51	Grambling	14
11	Beverly, David	P	6-2	180	08/19/50	Auburn	14
42	Brockington, John	RB	6-1	225	09/07/48	Ohio State	14
19	Brown, Carlos	QB	6-3	210	07/31/52	Pacific	13
28	Buchanon, Willie	CB	6-0	190	11/04/50	San Diego State	14
41	Burrow, Jim	S	5-11	180	11/29/53	Montana	3
53	Carr, Fred	LB	6-5	240	08/19/46	Texas-El Paso	14
10	Dickey, Lynn	QB	6-4	210	10/19/49	Kansas State	10
67	Enderle, Dick	G	6-2	250	11/06/47	Minnesota	3
68	Gillingham, Gale	G	6-3	265	02/03/44	Minnesota	14
24	Gray, Johnnie	S	5-11	185	12/18/53	Cal State-Fullerton	14
86	Green, Jessie	WR	6-2	185	02/21/54	Tulsa	1
51	Gueno, Jim	LB	6-2	220	01/15/54	Tulane	14
44	Hall, Charlie	CB	6-1	190	03/31/48	Pittsburgh	14
58	Hansen, Don	LB	6-2	228	08/20/44	Illinois	12
40	Harrell, Willard	RB	5-9	182	09/16/52	Pacific	13
72	Himes, Dick	T	6-4	260	05/25/46	Ohio State	14
55	Hyland, Bob	C	6-5	255	07/25/45	Boston College	14
71	Jackson, Mel	G	6-1	267	05/05/54	USC	13
16	Johnson, Randy	QB	6-3	205	06/17/44	Texas A&I	3
60	Knutson, Steve	T	6-3	254	10/05/51	USC	12
79	Koncar, Mark	T	6-5	268	05/05/53	Colorado	14
58	Lally, Bob	LB	6-2	230	02/12/52	Cornell	2
46	Luke, Steve	S	6-2	205	09/04/53	Ohio State	14
13	Marcol, Chester	K	6-0	190	10/24/49	Hillsdale	14
54	McCarren, Larry	C	6-3	248	11/09/51	Illinois	14
29	McCoy, Mike C.	CB	5-11	183	08/16/53	Colorado	14
76	McCoy, Mike P.	DT	6-5	275	09/06/48	Notre Dame	14
81	McGeorge, Rich	TE	6-4	230	09/14/48	Elon	14
84	Odom, Steve	WR	5-8	174	09/05/52	Utah	12
41	Osborn, Dave	RB	6-0	208	03/18/43	North Dakota	6
85	Payne, Ken	WR	6-1	185	10/06/50	Langston	14
56	Perko, Tom	LB	6-3	233	06/17/54	Pittsburgh	14
75	Pureifory, Dave	DE	6-1	255	07/12/49	Eastern Michigan	12
87	Roche, Alden	DE	6-4	255	04/09/45	Southern University	14
74	Roller, Dave	DT	6-2	270	10/28/49	Kentucky	13
33	Smith, Barty	FB	6-3	240	03/23/52	Richmond	8
89	Smith, Ollie	WR	6-3	200	03/08/49	Tennessee State	13
45	Smith, Perry	CB	6-1	195	03/29/51	Colorado State	13
32	Starch, Ken	RB	5-11	219	03/05/54	Wisconsin	6
27	Taylor, Cliff	RB	6-0	195	05/10/52	Memphis State	7
59	Toner, Tom	LB	6-3	235	01/25/50	Idaho State	11
26	Torkelson, Eric	RB	6-2	194	03/02/52	Connecticut	14
61	Van Dyke, Bruce	G	6-2	255	08/06/44	Missouri	14
21	Wagner, Steve	S	6-2	208	04/18/54	Wisconsin	11
52	Weaver, Gary	LB	6-1	225	03/13/49	Fresno State	14
83	Williams, Clarence	DE	6-5	255	09/03/46	Prairie View	14
80	Zimmerman, Don	WR	6-3	195	11/22/49	Northeast Louisiana	2

DRAFT

Rnd	Name	Pos	Ht	Wt	College
1a	(Choice (8) to Rams for John Hadl)				
1b	Mark Koncar (23)	T	6-4	268	Colorado
	(Choice from Raiders for Ted Hendricks)				
2	(Choice (39) to Rams for John Hadl)				
3a	(Choice (70) to Steelers for Bruce Van Dyke)				
3b	Mike C. McCoy (72)	DB	5-11	183	Colorado
	(Choice from Chiefs for MacArthur Lane)				
3c	(Choice (74) from Giants for Jim Del Gaizo to Chiefs for Dean Carlson)				
4a	Tom Perko (101)	LB	6-3	233	Pittsburgh
4b	(Choice (117) from Eagles for Bill Lueck to Oilers for Lynn Dickey)				
5	Aundra Thompson (132)	RB	6-0	202	East Texas State
6	(Choice (166) to Oilers for Paul Robinson)				

Rnd	Name	Pos	Ht	Wt	College
7	(Choice (192) to Bengals for Pat Matson)				
8	Jim Burrow (218)	DB	5-11	181	Nebraska
9	Jim Gueno (245)	LB	6-2	220	Tulane
10	Jessie Green (274)	WR	6-2	185	Tulsa
11	Curtis Leak (301)	WR	5-11	180	Johnson C. Smith
12	Mel Jackson (328)	G	6-1	267	USC
13	Bradley Bowman (355)	DB	5-11	195	Southern Mississippi
14	John Henson (386)	RB	6-1	226	Cal Poly-SLO
15	Jerry Dandridge (413)	LB	6-1	222	Memphis State
16	Mike Timmermans (440)	G	6-1	240	Northern Iowa
17	Ray Hall (467)	TE	6-6	231	Cal Poly-SLO

1976 GREEN BAY PACKERS

FRONT ROW: (L-R) 19 Carlos Brown, 13 Chester Marcol, 84 Steve Odom, 53 Fred Carr, 40 Willard Harrell, 45 Perry Smith, 28 Willie Buchanon, 46 Steve Luke, 24 Johnnie Gray, 29 Mike C. McCoy.

SECOND ROW: (L-R) 57 Ron Acks, 71 Mel Jackson, 11 David Beverly, 52 Gary Weaver, 61 Bruce Van Dyke, 88 Bert Askson, 75 Dave Pureifory, 33 Barty Smith, 89 Ollie Smith, 10 Lynn Dickey, 85 Ken Payne, 51 Jim Gueno.

THIRD ROW: (L-R) Team Physician Dr. Eugene Brusky, Assistant Equipment Manager Bob Noel, Film Director Al Treml, Quarterbacks Coach Zeke Bratkowski, Offensive Coordinator Paul Roach, Offensive Line Coach Leon McLaughlin, Passing Game Coach Lew Carpenter, Head Coach Bart Starr, Assistant Head Coach/Defensive Coordinator Dave Hanner, Defensive Backfield Coach Dick LeBeau, Special Teams Coach Bob Lord, Linebackers Coach John Meyer, Equipment Assistant Jack Noel, Equipment Manager Gerald (Dad) Braisher.

FOURTH ROW: (L-R) Assistant Trainer Dan Davis, 87 Alden Roche, 58 Don Hansen, 54 Larry McCarren, 59 Tom Toner, 21 Steve Wagner, 74 Dave Roller, 44 Charlie Hall, 42 John Brockington, 27 Cliff Taylor, 26 Eric Torkelson, Pro Player Personnel Director Dick Corrick.

BACK ROW: (L-R) Jim Huxford, 55 Bob Hyland, 56 Tom Perko, 70 Bob Barber, 68 Gale Gillingham, 72 Dick Himes, 76 Mike P. McCoy, 81 Rich McGeorge, 79 Mark Koncar, 83 Clarence Williams, 60 Steve Knutson, Trainer Domenic Gentile.

The Packers offense in 1977 was a throwback to the low scoring early years of pro football. Green Bay ranked 27th in total yards and 27th in rushing yards. It scored an average of one touchdown per game. Its 134 points were the team's lowest output since 1949.

With such an unproductive attack, the team was fortunate to finish 4-10.

The offensive woes could be traced to the preseason. New England manhandled the Packers 38-3 in a game in which Bart Starr accused Patriots coach Chuck Fairbanks of running up the score. Tampa Bay, the doormat of the league, embarrassed Green Bay 10-7 on Aug. 20.

The year was difficult in other respects. In the offseason, Starr asked for and got the resignations of assistant coaches Paul Roach and Leon McLaughlin. John Brockington was put on waivers to make room for rookie back Jim Culbreath, after gaining just 25 yards on 11 carries in the opener. Wide receiver Ken Payne was fined for insubordination, suspended, and finally waived on Oct. 14 for his actions during the Bengals game of Oct. 9.

Other moves were made. Defensive lineman Alden Roche was traded to the Colts in early September. A few days later, defensive tackle Mike P. McCoy, who had been moved to left guard by Starr in an "experimental move" earlier in training camp, was shipped to the Raiders for Herb McMath and two draft choices.

With Roche and McCoy gone, the Packers' starting defensive front four consisted of top pick Mike Butler at left end, Dave Roller and David Pureifory at the tackles, and Bob Barber at right end. Except for four starts by Clarence Williams, the unit started every game together.

Lynn Dickey and Gary Weaver suffered season-ending injuries. Weaver banged up his knee in the first Lions game and was lost for the final nine games. Dickey broke his leg on the final play of the Rams' game and didn't return until the 1979 season.

The Packers scored more than 16 points only once and that was in the opener at New Orleans. Barty Smith, Willard Harrell, and Payne each notched a touchdown as Green Bay prevailed 24-20 after leading 24-0 at halftime. Roller was credited with four quarterback sacks.

The Packers missed going 2-0 when Dickey's pass near the Oilers' end zone was intercepted by Willie Alexander and returned 95 yards for the deciding touchdown in a 16-10 heartbreaker.

In Week 3, the Vikings rolled to a 19-7 victory.

The team's third loss, a 17-7 setback to the Bengals in Milwaukee, had both Starr and Dickey in a sour mood.

Said the coach: "For us to have stayed with them as long as we did, as well as we did; and you ask if we were flat—I think that's a ludicrous question."

Added the quarterback: "We lost. Nobody likes to lose. If

they do, I don't need it. If you expect me to be happy after we lost a game, you've got me figured wrong."

A week later, Green Bay lost for a fourth time. Greg Landry passed to Ray Jarvis early in the fourth quarter for the game's only touchdown in the Lions' 10-6 win.

The Packers improved to 2-4 as Eric Torkelson gained 73 yards rushing and a touchdown in a 13-0 win in Tampa.

"This is the bottom. This is a terrible blow to our whole team," Buccaneers coach John McKay said.

In Week 7, Walter Payton rushed for 205 yards and two scores in a 26-0 Bears' rout. Overall, Chicago amassed 375 yards rushing on 54 carries.

"We may have put him in the Hall of Fame," said linebacker Jim Carter who participated in nine tackles.

Dickey went down against the Rams in Milwaukee. Even though the Packers were trailing 24-6 with less than two minutes to play, Starr sent Dickey back out. The former Oiler broke his lower leg in two places after completing a 12-yard pass to Harrell on the game's final play.

David Whitehurst, the team's 10th-round draft choice, started the final five games, leading the team to two wins in its last three games. The first was a 10-9 squeaker over Detroit in which punter David Beverly intentionally took a safety in order to avoid a block in the closing moments. The second was a 16-14 effort that saw Whitehurst throw his first touchdown pass. The Furman graduate completed 17 of 22 passes for 219 yards.

"I think I can play in this league," Whitehurst said. "But I must take advantage of the experience I've gotten."

TD DIET: AVOID SECOND HELPINGS

The Packers scored more than one touchdown in just two games in 1977. The team had never put on such a pitiful display, even in the Stone Age of football (the '20s).

The Green and Gold scored three touchdowns in beating the Saints 24-20 in the opener. The team then scored no more than one touchdown in each of its next 12 games. It closed with two touchdowns in a 16-14 win over the 49ers.

Green Bay sorely lacked playmakers. Steve Odom came closest to fitting that description, but he didn't become a full-time starter until Week 8.

Barty Smith was the club's top rusher, plodding along at 3.3 yards per clip. He was also the leading receiver.

Fewest Games Scoring More Than one Touchdown, Season
(minimum 10 games played)

No.	Year(s)
2	1977
3	1923
4	1922, 1948, 1949

TEAM STATISTICS

	GB	OPP
First Downs	195	261
Rushing	81	140
Passing	91	105
Penalty	23	16
Rushes	469	582
Yards Gained	1,464	2,314
Average Gain	3.12	3.98
Average Yards per Game	104.6	165.3
Passes Attempted	327	319
Completed	164	186
% Completed	50.15	58.31
Total Yards Gained	2,013	2,042
Times Sacked	32	37
Yards Lost	265	323
Net Yards Gained	1,748	1,719
Yards Gained per Completion	12.27	10.98
Net Yards per Attempt	4.87	4.83
Average Net Yards per Game	124.9	122.8
Combined Net Yards Gained	3,212	4,033
Total Plays	828	938
Average Yards per Play	3.88	4.30
Average Net Yards per Game	229.4	288.1
Third Down Efficiency	66/209	89/211
Percentage	31.58	42.18
Fourth Down Efficiency	7/14	6/11
Percentage	50.00	54.55
Intercepted By	13	21
Yards Returned	89	349
Returned for TD	1	1
Punts	86	76
Yards Punted	3,391	2,776
Average Yards per Punt	39.43	36.53
Punt Returns	38	53
Yards Returned	321	311
Average Yards per Return	8.45	5.87
Returned for TD	1	0
Kickoff Returns	51	39
Yards Returned	947	786
Average Yards per Return	18.57	20.15
Returned for TD	1	0
Penalties	82	101
Yards Penalized	690	799
Fumbles	24	27
Lost	9	11
Own Recovered for Touchdown	0	0
Opponent's Recovered by	11	9
Opponent's Recovered for Touchdown	0	0
Total Points Scored	134	219
Total Touchdowns	14	27
Touchdowns Rushing	5	16
Touchdowns Passing	6	10
Touchdowns on Returns & Recoveries	3	1
Extra Points	11	22
Safeties	0	1
Field Goals Attempted	21	23
Field Goals Made	13	11
% Successful	61.90	47.83
Average Time of Possession	27:47	32:13

Regular Season   4-10-0

Date	GB		OPP	Att.
9/18	24	at New Orleans Saints	20	(56,250)
9/25	10	Houston Oilers	16	(55,071)
10/2	7	at Minnesota Vikings	19	(47,143)
10/9	7	Cincinnati Bengals (M)	17	(53,653)
10/16	6	at Detroit Lions	10	(78,087)
10/23	13	at Tampa Bay Buccaneers	0	(47,635)
10/30	0	Chicago Bears	26	(56,002)
11/6	10	at Kansas City Chiefs	20	(62,687)
11/13	6	Los Angeles Rams (M)	24	(52,948)
11/21	9	at Washington Redskins	10	(51,498)
11/27	6	Minnesota Vikings	13	(50,000)
12/4	10	Detroit Lions	9	(50,000)
12/11	10	at Chicago Bears	21	(33,557)
12/18	16	San Francisco 49ers (M)	14	(44,902)

Score By Periods

	1	2	3	4	Total
Packers	53	49	22	10	134
Opponents	44	76	21	78	219

INDIVIDUAL STATISTICS

Rushing

	Att	Yds	Avg	LG	TD
Barty Smith	166	554	3.3	11	2
Torkelson	103	309	3.0	29	1
N. Simpson	60	204	3.4	40	0
Harrell	60	140	2.3	9	1
Middleton	35	97	2.8	16	0
Whitehurst	14	55	3.9	19	1
Culbreath	12	53	4.4	18	0
Brockington	11	25	2.3	8	0
Dickey	5	24	4.8	10	0
Odom	1	6	6.0	6	0
Beverly	2	-3	-1.5		0
Packers	**469**	**1,464**	**3.1**	**40**	**5**
Opponents	582	2,314	4.0	58	16

Receiving

	No	Yds	Avg	LG	TD
Barty Smith	37	340	9.2	42	1
Odom	27	549	20.3	t95	3
O. Smith	22	357	16.2	41	0
Harrell	19	194	10.2	48	0
McGeorge	17	142	8.4	18	1
Torkelson	11	107	9.7	14	0
Vataha	10	109	10.9	20	0
Payne	7	99	14.1	45	1
N. Simpson	5	19	3.8	14	0
Askson	2	51	25.5	34	0
Aundra Thompson	2	12	6.0	14	0
Culbreath	2	6	3.0	5	0
Brockington	2	1	0.5	6	0
Middleton	1	27	27.0	27	0
Packers	**164**	**2,013**	**12.3**	**t95**	**6**
Opponents	186	2,042	11.0	t59	10

Passing

	Att	Com	Yds	Pct	TD	In	Tk/Yds	Rate
Dickey	220	113	1,346	51.4	5	14	21/187	51.4
Whitehurst	105	50	634	47.6	1	7	10/68	42.3
Harrell	1	1	33	100.0	0	0	1/10	—
Dowling	1	0	0	0.0	0	0	0/0	—
Packers	**327**	**164**	**2,013**	**50.2**	**6**	**21**	**32/265**	**48.9**
Opponents	319	186	2,042	58.3	10	13	37/323	70.8

Punting

	No	Yds	Avg	Net	TB	In20	LG	HB
Beverly	85	3,391	39.9	33.7	9	16	59	1
Packers	**86**	**3,391**	**39.4**	**33.7**	**9**	**16**	**59**	**1**
Opponents	76	2,776	36.5	31.3	4	17	57	2

Kickoff Returns

	No	Yds	Avg	LG	TD
Odom	23	468	20.3	37	0
S. Wagner	6	62	10.3	20	0
Culbreath	5	82	16.4	30	0
Middleton	4	141	35.3	t85	1
Aundra Thompson	4	82	20.5	30	0
Harrell	3	48	16.0	24	0
Torkelson	2	36	18.0	25	0
Moresco	1	15	15.0	15	0
Gofourth	1	13	13.0	13	0
Gueno	1	0	0.0	0	0
N. Simpson	1	0	0.0	0	0
Packers	**51**	**947**	**18.6**	**t96**	**1**
Opponents	39	786	20.2	68	0

Punt Returns

	No	Yds	Avg	FC	LG	TD
Harrell	28	253	9.0	10	t75	1
J. Gray	10	68	6.8	3	24	0
Packers	**38**	**321**	**8.4**	**13**	**t75**	**1**
Opponents	53	311	5.9	4	18	0

Interceptions

	No	Yds	Avg	LG	TD
Luke	4	9	2.3	7	0
M.C. McCoy	4	2	0.5	2	0
Buchanon	2	41	20.5	t29	1
Carr	1	15	15.0	15	0
J. Gray	1	12	12.0	12	0
Toner	1	10	10.0	10	0
Packers	**13**	**89**	**6.8**	**t29**	**1**
Opponents	21	349	16.6	t95	1

Scoring

	TDr	TDp	TDrt	PAT	FG	S	TP
Marcol	0	0	0	11/14	13/21	0	50
Odom	0	3	0	0/0	0/0	0	18
Barty Smith	2	1	0	0/0	0/0	0	18
Harrell	1	0	1	0/0	0/0	0	12
Buchanon	0	0	1	0/0	0/0	0	6
McGeorge	0	1	0	0/0	0/0	0	6
Middleton	0	0	1	0/0	0/0	0	6
Payne	0	1	0	0/0	0/0	0	6
Torkelson	1	0	0	0/0	0/0	0	6
Whitehurst	1	0	0	0/0	0/0	0	6
Packers	**5**	**6**	**3**	**11/14**	**13/21**	**0**	**134**
Opponents	16	10	1	22/27	11/23	1	219

Fumbles

	Fum	Ow	Op	Yds	Tot
Barber	0	0	2	0	2
Beverly	1	1	0	0	1
Buchanon	1	0	1	0	1
M. Butler	0	0	1	0	1
Culbreath	1	2	0	0	2
Dickey	1	0	0	0	1
J. Gray	0	0	2	0	2
Gueno	0	1	0	0	1
Harrell	3	0	0	0	0
Himes	0	1	0	0	1
E. Johnson	0	0	1	0	1
Koncar	0	1	0	0	1
Luke	0	0	1	0	1
McGeorge	1	0	0	0	1
Middleton	4	1	0	0	1
Pureifory	0	0	1	0	1
Roller	0	0	1	0	1
N. Simpson	4	1	0	0	1
Barty Smith	1	1	0	0	1
O. Smith	1	0	0	0	0
Torkelson	4	0	0	0	1
S. Wagner	0	0	1	0	1
Whitehurst	0	0	0	0	1
Packers	**24**	**12**	**11**	**0**	**23**

NFL STANDINGS

National Conference

Eastern Division

	W	L	T	Pct	PF	PA
Dallas Cowboys	12	2	0	.857	345	212
Washington Redskins	9	5	0	.643	196	189
St. Louis Cardinals	7	7	0	.500	272	287
Philadelphia Eagles	5	9	0	.357	220	207
New York Giants	5	9	0	.357	181	265

Central Division

	W	L	T	Pct	PF	PA
Minnesota Vikings	9	5	0	.643	231	227
Chicago Bears	9	5	0	.643	255	253
Detroit Lions	6	8	0	.429	183	252
Green Bay Packers	**4**	**10**	**0**	**.286**	**134**	**219**
Tampa Bay Buccaneers	2	12	0	.143	103	223

Western Division

	W	L	T	Pct	PF	PA
Los Angeles Rams	10	4	0	.714	302	146
Atlanta Falcons	7	7	0	.500	179	129
San Francisco 49ers	5	9	0	.357	220	260
New Orleans Saints	3	11	0	.214	232	336

American Conference

Eastern Division

	W	L	T	Pct	PF	PA
Baltimore Colts	10	4	0	.714	295	221
Miami Dolphins	10	4	0	.714	313	197
New England Patriots	9	5	0	.643	278	217
New York Jets	3	11	0	.214	191	300
Buffalo Bills	3	11	0	.214	160	313

Central Division

	W	L	T	Pct	PF	PA
Pittsburgh Steelers	9	5	0	.643	283	243
Houston Oilers	8	6	0	.571	299	230
Cincinnati Bengals	8	6	0	.571	238	235
Cleveland Browns	6	8	0	.429	269	267

Western Division

	W	L	T	Pct	PF	PA
Denver Broncos	12	2	0	.857	274	148
Oakland Raiders	11	3	0	.786	351	230
San Diego Chargers	7	7	0	.500	222	205
Seattle Seahawks	5	9	0	.357	282	373
Kansas City Chiefs	2	12	0	.143	225	349

ROSTER

No	Name	Pos	Ht	Wt	DOB	College	G
88	Askson, Bert	TE	6-2	225	12/18/45	Texas Southern	14
70	Barber, Bob	DE	6-3	240	12/26/51	Grambling	14
11	Beverly, David	P	6-2	180	08/19/50	Auburn	14
42	Brockington, John	RB	6-1	225	09/07/48	Ohio State	1
28	Buchanon, Willie	CB	6-0	190	11/04/50	San Diego State	14
77	Butler, Mike	DE	6-5	265	04/04/54	Kansas	14
53	Carr, Fred	LB	6-5	240	08/19/46	Texas-El Paso	14
50	Carter, Jim	LB	6-3	245	10/18/48	Minnesota	14
31	Culbreath, Jim	RB	6-0	210	10/21/52	Oklahoma	13
10	Dickey, Lynn	QB	6-4	210	10/19/49	Kansas State	9
12	Dowling, Brian	QB	6-2	200	04/01/47	Yale	2
57	Gofourth, Derrel	C	6-3	260	03/20/55	Oklahoma State	14
24	Gray, Johnnie	S	5-11	185	12/18/53	Cal State-Fullerton	14
51	Gueno, Jim	LB	6-2	220	01/15/54	Tulane	14
58	Hansen, Don	LB	6-2	228	08/20/44	Illinois	8
40	Harrell, Willard	RB	5-9	182	09/16/52	Pacific	13
82	Hartwig, Keith	WR	6-0	186	12/10/53	Arizona	4
62	Havig, Dennis	G	6-3	255	05/06/49	Colorado	7
72	Himes, Dick	T	6-4	260	05/25/46	Ohio State	13
71	Jackson, Mel	G	6-1	267	05/05/54	USC	13
90/78	Johnson, Ezra	DE	6-4	240	10/02/55	Morris Brown	14
60	Knutson, Steve	T	6-3	254	10/05/51	USC	13
68	Koch, Greg	T	6-4	265	06/14/55	Arkansas	14
79	Koncar, Mark	T	6-5	268	05/05/53	Colorado	13
67	Kowalkowski, Bob	G	6-3	245	11/05/43	Virginia	9
46	Luke, Steve	S	6-2	205	09/04/53	Ohio State	14
13	Marcol, Chester	K	6-0	190	10/24/49	Hillsdale	14
54	McCarren, Larry	C	6-3	248	11/09/51	Illinois	14
29	McCoy, Mike C.	CB	5-11	183	08/16/53	Colorado	14
81	McGeorge, Rich	TE	6-4	230	09/14/48	Elon	14
61	McMath, Herb	DT	6-4	250	09/06/54	Morningside	8
34	Middleton, Terdell	HB	6-0	195	04/08/55	Memphis State	14
37	Moresco, Tim	S	5-10	176	10/03/54	Syracuse	14
84	Odom, Steve	WR	5-8	174	09/05/52	Utah	14
85	Payne, Ken	WR	6-1	185	10/06/50	Langston	4
75	Pureifory, Dave	DE	6-1	255	07/12/49	Eastern Michigan	12
23	Randolph, Terry	CB	6-0	184	07/17/55	American International	14
74	Roller, Dave	DT	6-2	270	10/28/49	Kentucky	13
48	Simpson, Nate	RB	5-11	190	11/30/54	Tennessee State	12
33	Smith, Barty	FB	6-3	240	03/23/52	Richmond	14
56	Smith, Blane	G	6-3	238	07/13/54	Purdue	1
89	Smith, Ollie	WR	6-3	200	03/08/49	Tennessee State	12
43	Thompson, Aundra	WR	6-0	186	01/02/53	East Texas State	14
59	Toner, Tom	LB	6-3	235	01/25/50	Idaho State	14
26	Torkelson, Eric	RB	6-2	194	03/03/52	Connecticut	14
18	Vataha, Randy	WR	5-10	170	12/04/48	Stanford	6
21	Wagner, Steve	S	6-2	208	04/18/54	Wisconsin	14
52	Weaver, Gary	LB	6-1	225	03/13/49	Fresno State	5
17	Whitehurst, David	QB	6-2	204	04/27/55	Furman	7
83	Williams, Clarence	DE	6-5	255	09/03/46	Prairie View	13

DRAFT

Rnd	Name	Pos	Ht	Wt	College
1a	Mike Butler (9)	DE	6-5	265	Kansas
1b	Ezra Johnson (28)	DE	6-4	240	Morris Brown
	(Choice from Raiders for Ted Hendricks)				
2	Greg Koch (39)	G-T	6-4	265	Arkansas
3a	(Choice (66) to Oilers for Lynn Dickey)				
3b	Rick Scribner (74)	G	6-4	257	Idaho State
	(Choice from Broncos for Bill Bain)				
3c	Terdell Middleton (80)	RB	6-0	195	Memphis State
	(Choice from Cardinals for Perry Smith)				
4	(Choice (94) to Steelers for Bob Barber)				
5	Nate Simpson (122)	RB	5-10	190	Tennessee State
6	Tim Moresco (149)	DB	5-10	176	Syracuse
7a	Derrel Gofourth (172)	C	6-3	260	Oklahoma State
	(Choice from Giants for Joe Danelo)				
7b	Rell Tipton (176)	G	6-4	245	Baylor
8	David Whitehurst (206)	QB	6-2	204	Furman
9	Joel Mullins (233)	T	6-4	260	Arkansas State
10	Jim Culbreath (260)	RB	6-0	209	Oklahoma
11	Terry Randolph (290)	DB	6-0	184	Am. International
12	(Choice (317) to Raiders for Ollie Smith)				

1977 GREEN BAY PACKERS

FRONT ROW: (L-R) 24 Johnnie Gray, 46 Steve Luke, 29 Mike C. McCoy, 28 Willie Buchanon, 13 Chester Marcol, 40 Willard Harrell, 53 Fred Carr, 72 Dick Himes, 75 Dave Pureifory, 74 Dave Roller, 67 Bob Kowalkowski, 60 Steve Knutson, 84 Steve Odom.

SECOND ROW: (L-R) Groundskeeper Earl DuChateau, Film Director Al Treml, Equipment Assistant Jack Noel, Assistant Equipment Manager Bob Noel, Quarterbacks Coach Zeke Bratkowski, Passing Game Coach Lew Carpenter, Special Teams Coach Burt Gustafson, Head Coach Bart Starr, Assistant Head Coach/Defensive Coordinator Dave Hanner, Defensive Backfield Coach Dick LeBeau, Offensive Line Coach Bill Curry, Offensive Backfield Coach Bob Lord, Linebackers Coach John Meyer, Pro Player Personnel Director Dick Corrick.

THIRD ROW: (L-R) Team Physician Dr. Eugene Brusky, 52 Gary Weaver, 18 Randy Vataha, 59 Tom Toner, 34 Terdell Middleton, 43 Aundra Thompson, 88 Bert Askson, 11 David Beverly, 71 Mel Jackson, 89 Ollie Smith, 10 Lynn Dickey, 48 Nate Simpson, Jim Huxford.

FOURTH ROW: (L-R) Trainer Domenic Gentile, 51 Jim Gueno, 58 Don Hansen, 57 Derrel Gofourth, 77 Mike Butler, 23 Terry Randolph, 31 Jim Culbreath, 68 Greg Koch, 17 David Whitehurst, 37 Tim Moresco, Assistant Trainer Greg Vergamini.

BACK ROW: (L-R) 62 Dennis Havig, 54 Larry McCarren, 83 Clarence Williams, 81 Rich McGeorge, 33 Barty Smith, 26 Eric Torkelson, 78 Ezra Johnson, 21 Steve Wagner, 70 Bob Barber, 79 Mark Koncar, 50 Jim Carter.

Youth was served, and with it came an energy that catapulted the Packers to their best start in a dozen years. Green Bay raced to a 6-1 record and a three-game advantage in the NFC Central Division before costly mistakes led to a second-half slide that caused the club (8-7-1) to narrowly miss its first trip to the playoffs in six years.

Since Day One, coach Bart Starr had been rebuilding. The team in 1978 hardly resembled the group he had inherited in 1975. Only four starters from that club continued to start three years later: Larry McCarren, Rich McGeorge, Willie Buchanon, and Johnnie Gray. The 22 starters in 1978 averaged less than 25 years of age, the first time that had happened in more than a decade.

In fact, only 10 starters from the finale in 1977 found themselves still holding their jobs at the start of 1978.

A number of players had career years. Terdell Middleton rushed for 1,116 yards and 11 touchdowns. Ezra Johnson broke into the starting lineup and registered 20 1/2 sacks, second in the league behind the 22 of Detroit's Al "Bubba" Baker. Willie Buchanon intercepted nine passes, including an NFL-record-tying four against the Chargers. Rookie receiver James Lofton caught 46 passes.

Not all was right in Titletown. In May, the Packers forfeited their fourth-round draft choice because they had illegally worked out college prospects. Linebacker Fred Carr, who had played in 140 consecutive games, was waived in mid-August because, according to Starr, he "failed to honor verbal training programs" and had finished "dead last" in physical testing among players before training camp opened. And Starr had a run-in with four reporters who asked why back Duane Thomas was still on Packers property a week after his 24-hour tryout had ended.

Turnovers were one reason why the team started 6-1 and finished 2-6-1. In the first seven games, Green Bay created 30 turnovers and committed 16. In the final nine games, the team caused 17 turnovers but coughed up 26.

The Packers dumped quarterback Greg Landry eight times in their 13-7 opening win over the Lions. Ezra Johnson was credited with five of the sacks.

Lofton, the team's top pick, caught three passes for 107 yards—all touchdowns—against the Saints. Middleton added in 114 yards rushing in the 28-17 win.

In Week 3, Oakland rushed 58 times for 348 yards and dominated 28-3. Afterwards, Whitehurst wondered aloud about the Raiders' defense.

"I'm not saying they knew what we were doing, but it seemed like they knew what we were doing," he said.

Buchanon, who played collegiately at San Diego State, enjoyed a productive homecoming in Week 4 against the Chargers. The defensive back tied an NFL record with four interceptions and returned one 77 yards for a touchdown. Green Bay won 24-3.

The Packers took over sole possession of first place in the Central Division by sweeping the Lions 35-14. Middleton had 148 yards rushing on 11 carries and Aundra Thompson scored two touchdowns.

Green Bay improved to 5-1 with a 24-14 verdict over the Bears. The Packers forced five turnovers and turned the miscues into 17 points.

A 45-28 win over the Seahawks in Week 7 put Green Bay (6-1) three games ahead of the second-place Bears, Lions and Vikings who were all 3-4.

Minnesota made up some ground when it beat the Packers 21-7 in Week 8. Dave Roller was ejected for hitting Fran Tarkenton out of bounds.

Chester Marcol nailed a 48-yard field goal with 41 seconds left to push Green Bay past Tampa Bay 9-7 a week later. Whitehurst completed an 18-yard pass to Steve Odom on fourth-down to set up the kick.

The unraveling began in Philadelphia in Week 10. The Eagles prevailed 10-3 despite being outgained by more than 235 yards.

Three weeks later, the Packers and Vikings fought to a 10-10 standstill. Tarkenton passed to Ahmad Rashad for the touchdown that tied the game with 10 seconds left.

"This drains the (expletive) out of you," Roller said of the marathon that lasted more than three-and-a-half hours. "It psychologically hurts. But we're 7-5-1, they're 7-5-1, and we're still in the thick of it."

Green Bay dropped two of its last three games and failed to secure either the division title or a wildcard berth.

YARDS A MANY: TOUCHDOWNS NOT ANY

For the Packers, the beginning of the end may have occurred in Philadelphia on Nov. 5. That day, Green Bay lost despite outgunning the Eagles by more than 200 yards.

David Whitehurst and company generated 385 yards of offense to 148 for the Eagles. Even so, the Packers failed to find the end zone and lost 10-3. Never before or since has the team generated so many yards and failed to score at least one touchdown.

Green Bay got into Eagles territory eight times. For all its effort, the team had nothing but a 42-yard Chester Marcol field goal to show for it.

A 79-yard touchdown pass to James Lofton was called back because of holding late in the first period.

Most Yards Gained, No Touchdown, Game

Yards	Date	Result
385	11-5-78	GB 3, Eagles 10
380	9-7-97	GB 9, Eagles 10
367	12-7-86	GB 6, Vikings 32
363	12-12-83	GB 12, Buccaneers 9 (OT)

1978

TEAM STATISTICS

	GB	OPP
First Downs	226	302
Rushing	105	137
Passing	101	143
Penalty	20	22
Rushes	550	620
Yards Gained	2,023	2,439
Average Gain	3.68	3.93
Average Yards per Game	126.4	152.4
Passes Attempted	357	463
Completed	180	254
% Completed	50.42	54.86
Total Yards Gained	2,358	2,910
Times Sacked	37	48
Yards Lost	274	386
Net Yards Gained	2,084	2,524
Yards Gained per Completion	13.10	11.46
Net Yards per Attempt	5.29	4.94
Average Net Yards per Game	130.3	157.8
Combined Net Yards Gained	4,107	4,963
Total Plays	944	1,131
Average Yards per Play	4.35	4.39
Average Net Yards per Game	256.7	310.2
Third Down Efficiency	65/226	102/269
Percentage	28.76	37.92
Fourth Down Efficiency	8/16	10/23
Percentage	50.00	43.48
Intercepted By	27	18
Yards Returned	344	262
Returned for TD	2	1
Punts	106	90
Yards Punted	3,759	3,411
Average Yards per Punt	35.46	37.90
Punt Returns	46	51
Yards Returned	393	286
Average Yards per Return	8.54	5.61
Returned for TD	0	0
Kickoff Returns	52	52
Yards Returned	1,085	1,015
Average Yards per Return	20.87	19.52
Returned for TD	1	0
Penalties	99	116
Yards Penalized	776	949
Fumbles	35	40
Lost	24	20
Own Recovered for Touchdown	0	0
Opponent's Recovered by	20	24
Opponent's Recovered for Touchdown	0	0
Total Points Scored	249	269
Total Touchdowns	31	36
Touchdowns Rushing	16	19
Touchdowns Passing	11	16
Touchdowns on Returns & Recoveries	4	1
Extra Points	30	36
Safeties	0	1
Field Goals Attempted	19	18
Field Goals Made	11	5
% Successful	57.89	27.78
Average Time of Possession	28:16	31:44

Regular Season 8-7-1

Date	GB		OPP	Att.
9/3	13	at Detroit Lions	7	(51,187)
9/10	28	New Orleans Saints (M)	14	(52,646)
9/17	3	Oakland Raiders	28	(55,903)
9/24	24	at San Diego Chargers	3	(42,755)
10/1	35	Detroit Lions (M)	14	(54,606)
10/8	24	Chicago Bears	14	(55,352)
10/15	45	Seattle Seahawks (M)	28	(52,712)
10/22	7	at Minnesota Vikings	21	(47,411)
10/29	9	Tampa Bay Buccaneers	7	(55,108)
11/5	3	at Philadelphia Eagles	10	(64,214)
11/12	14	Dallas Cowboys (M)	42	(55,256)
11/19	3	at Denver Broncos	16	(74,743)
11/26	10	Minnesota Vikings (OT)	10	(51,354)
12/3	17	at Tampa Bay Buccaneers	7	(67,754)
12/10	0	at Chicago Bears	14	(34,306)
12/17	14	at Los Angeles Rams	31	(42,500)

Score By Periods

	1	2	3	4	Total
Packers	77	58	66	48	249
Opponents	20	84	83	82	269

INDIVIDUAL STATISTICS

Rushing

	Att	Yds	Avg	LG	TD
Middleton	284	1,116	3.9	t76	11
Barty Smith	154	567	3.7	33	4
Culbreath	30	92	3.1	15	0
Whitehurst	28	67	2.4	18	1
N. Simpson	27	58	2.1	11	0
Landers	7	40	5.7	10	0
B. Douglass	4	27	6.8	17	0
Aundra Thompson	4	25	6.3	13	0
Torkelson	6	18	3.0	6	0
Lofton	3	13	4.3	15	0
Beverly	1	0	0.0	—	0
Sproul	2	0	0.0	—	0
Packers	**550**	**2,023**	**3.7**	**t76**	**16**
Opponents	620	2,439	3.9	t33	19

Receiving

	No	Yds	Avg	LG	TD
Lofton	46	818	17.8	t58	6
Barty Smith	37	256	6.9	24	0
Middleton	34	332	9.8	50	1
Aundra Thompson	26	527	20.3	57	2
McGeorge	23	247	10.7	25	1
Culbreath	7	78	11.1	19	0
Odom	4	60	15.0	t18	1
Torkelson	2	36	18.0	31	0
N. Simpson	1	4	4.0	4	0
Packers	**180**	**2,358**	**13.1**	**t58**	**11**
Opponents	254	2,910	11.5	53	16

Passing

	Att	Com	Yds	Pct	TD	In	Tk/Yds	Rate
Whitehurst	328	168	2,093	51.2	10	17	35/258	59.9
B. Douglass	12	5	90	41.7	1	1	1/9	61.1
Beverly	2	2	88	100.0	0	0	0/0	—
Sproul	13	5	87	38.5	0	0	1/7	62.0
Lofton	2	0	0	00.0	0	0	0/0	—
Packers	**357**	**180**	**2,358**	**50.4**	**11**	**18**	**37/274**	**60.9**
Opponents	463	254	2,910	54.9	16	27	48/386	61.2

Punting

	No	Yds	Avg	Net	TB	In20	LG	HB
Beverly	106	3,759	35.5	31.1	9	20	57	0
Packers	**106**	**3,759**	**35.5**	**31.1**	**9**	**20**	**57**	**0**
Opponents	90	3,411	37.9	32.2	6	24	61	1

Kickoff Returns

	No	Yds	Avg	LG	TD
Odom	25	677	27.1	t95	1
Aundra Thompson	6	124	20.7	31	0
S. Wagner	6	84	14.0	17	0
Culbreath	4	58	14.5	20	0
Hood	3	74	24.7	33	0
Sampson	1	23	23.0	23	0
Middleton	1	22	22.0	22	0
E. Johnson	1	14	14.0	14	0
Gueno	1	9	9.0	9	0
Landers	1	0	0.0	0	0
Lofton	1	0	0.0	0	0
McGeorge	1	0	0.0	0	0
Barty Smith	1	0	0.0	0	0
Packers	**52**	**1,085**	**20.9**	**t95**	**1**
Opponents	52	1,015	19.5	32	0

Punt Returns

	No	Yds	Avg	FC	LG	TD
Odom	33	298	9.0	7	48	0
J. Gray	11	95	8.6	6	22	0
Sampson	1	0	0.0	0	0	0
Tullis	1	0	0.0	0	0	0
Packers	**46**	**393**	**8.5**	**13**	**48**	**0**
Opponents	51	286	5.6	22	16	0

Interceptions

	No	Yds	Avg	LG	TD
Buchanon	9	93	10.3	t77	1
J. Anderson	5	27	5.4	12	0
J. Gray	3	66	22.0	66	0
M.C. McCoy	3	34	11.3	23	0
Hood	3	18	6.0	18	0
Luke	2	91	45.5	t63	1
M. Hunt	1	10	10.0	10	0
Barzilauskas	1	5	5.0	5	0
Packers	**27**	**344**	**12.7**	**t77**	**2**
Opponents	18	262	14.6	t44	1

Scoring

	TDr	TDp	TDrt	PAT	FG	S	TP
Middleton	11	1	0	0/0	0/0	0	72
Marcol	0	0	0	30/30	11/19	0	63
Lofton	0	6	0	0/0	0/0	0	36
Barty Smith	4	0	0	0/0	0/0	0	24
Odom	0	1	1	0/0	0/0	0	12
Aundra Thompson	0	2	0	0/0	0/0	0	12
Buchanon	0	0	1	0/0	0/0	0	6
Landers	0	0	0	0/0	0/0	0	6
Luke	0	0	1	0/0	0/0	0	6
McGeorge	0	1	0	0/0	0/0	0	6
Whitehurst	1	0	0	0/0	0/0	0	6
Packers	**16**	**11**	**4**	**30/31**	**11/19**	**0**	**249**
Opponents	19	16	1	36/36	5/18	1	269

Fumbles

	Fum	Ow	Op	Yds	Tot
J. Anderson	0	0	1	0	1
Barber	0	0	1	0	1
Beverly	1	0	0	-11	0
Buchanon	0	0	1	0	1
Jim Carter	0	0	2	0	2
Culbreath	1	0	0	0	0
M. Douglass	0	0	2	0	2
J. Gray	1	0	0	0	1
Hood	0	0	1	0	1
M. Hunt	0	0	1	0	1
E. Johnson	0	0	2	0	2
Lofton	1	0	0	0	1
Luke	0	0	2	0	2
M.C. McCoy	2	0	0	0	1
Middleton	8	0	0	0	0
Nuzum	0	0	1	15	1
Odom	2	1	0	0	0
Roller	0	1	1	-2	2
Sampson	1	0	0	0	0
N. Simpson	1	0	0	0	0
Barty Smith	5	1	0	0	1
Sproul	2	1	0	-5	1
Aundra Thompson	1	0	0	0	1
Torkelson	0	0	1	0	1
Weaver	0	0	1	0	1
Whitehurst	8	2	0	-28	2
Packers	**35**	**7**	**20**	**-31**	**27**

NFL STANDINGS

National Conference

Eastern Division

	W	L	T	Pct	PF	PA
Dallas Cowboys	12	4	0	.750	384	208
Philadelphia Eagles	9	7	0	.563	270	250
Washington Redskins	8	8	0	.500	273	283
St. Louis Cardinals	6	10	0	.375	248	296
New York Giants	6	10	0	.375	264	298

Central Division

	W	L	T	Pct	PF	PA
Minnesota Vikings	8	7	1	.531	294	306
Green Bay Packers	8	7	1	.531	249	269
Detroit Lions	7	9	0	.438	290	300
Chicago Bears	7	9	0	.438	253	274
Tampa Bay Buccaneers	5	11	0	.313	241	259

Western Division

	W	L	T	Pct	PF	PA
Los Angeles Rams	12	4	0	.750	316	245
Atlanta Falcons	9	7	0	.563	240	290
New Orleans Saints	7	9	0	.438	281	298
San Francisco 49ers	2	14	0	.125	219	350

American Conference

Eastern Division

	W	L	T	Pct	PF	PA
New England Patriots	11	5	0	.688	358	286
Miami Dolphins	11	5	0	.688	372	254
New York Jets	8	8	0	.500	359	364
Buffalo Bills	5	11	0	.313	302	354
Baltimore Colts	5	11	0	.313	239	421

Central Division

	W	L	T	Pct	PF	PA
Pittsburgh Steelers	14	2	0	.875	356	195
Houston Oilers	10	6	0	.625	283	298
Cleveland Browns	8	8	0	.500	334	356
Cincinnati Bengals	4	12	0	.250	252	284

Western Division

	W	L	T	Pct	PF	PA
Denver Broncos	10	6	0	.625	282	198
Oakland Raiders	9	7	0	.563	311	283
Seattle Seahawks	9	7	0	.563	345	358
San Diego Chargers	9	7	0	.563	355	309
Kansas City Chiefs	4	12	0	.250	243	327

1978

ROSTER

No	Name	Pos	Ht	Wt	DOB	College	G
60	Anderson, John	LB	6-3	221	02/14/56	Michigan	13
70	Barber, Bob	DE	6-3	240	12/26/51	Grambling	16
75	Barzilauskas, Carl	DT	6-6	265	03/19/51	Indiana	16
11	Beverly, David	P	6-2	180	08/19/50	Auburn	16
85	Boyd, Elmo	WR	6-0	188	06/15/54	Eastern Kentucky	2
28	Buchanon, Willie	CB	6-0	190	11/04/50	San Diego State	16
77	Butler, Mike	DE	6-5	265	04/04/54	Kansas	16
50	Carter, Jim	LB	6-3	245	10/18/48	Minnesota	14
53	Chesley, Francis	LB	6-3	219	07/14/55	Wyoming	1
82	Coffman, Paul	TE	6-3	218	03/29/56	Kansas State	16
31	Culbreath, Jim	RB	6-0	210	10/21/52	Oklahoma	12
19	Douglass, Bobby	QB	6-4	225	06/22/48	Kansas	12
65	Douglass, Mike	LB	6-0	224	03/15/55	San Diego State	16
57	Gofourth, Derrel	C	6-3	260	03/20/55	Oklahoma State	16
24	Gray, Johnnie	S	5-11	185	12/18/53	Cal State-Fullerton	16
51	Gueno, Jim	LB	6-2	220	01/15/54	Tulane	15
69	Harris, Leotis	G	6-1	267	06/28/55	Arkansas	13
38	Hood, Estus	CB	5-11	180	11/14/55	Illinois State	16
55	Hunt, Mike	LB	6-2	240	10/06/56	Minnesota	16
71	Jackson, Mel	G	6-1	267	05/05/54	USC	16
58	Johnson, Danny	LB	6-1	216	05/07/55	Tennessee State	3
78	Johnson, Ezra	DE	6-4	240	10/02/55	Morris Brown	16
63	Jones, Terry	DT	6-2	259	11/08/56	Alabama	16
68	Koch, Greg	T	6-4	265	06/14/55	Arkansas	16
42	Landers, Walt	FB	6-0	214	07/04/53	Clark	4
80	Lofton, James	WR	6-3	187	07/05/56	Stanford	16
46	Luke, Steve	S	6-2	205	09/04/53	Ohio State	16
13	Marcol, Chester	K	6-0	190	10/24/49	Hillsdale	16
54	McCarren, Larry	C	6-3	248	11/09/51	Illinois	16
29	McCoy, Mike C.	CB	5-11	183	08/16/53	Colorado	16
81	McGeorge, Rich	TE	6-4	230	09/14/48	Elon	16
34	Middleton, Terdell	HB	6-0	195	04/08/55	Memphis State	16
56	Nuzum, Rick	C	6-4	238	06/30/52	Kentucky	16
84	Odom, Steve	WR	5-8	174	09/05/52	Utah	12
74	Roller, Dave	DT	6-2	270	10/28/49	Kentucky	16
66	Rudzinski, Paul	LB	6-1	220	07/28/56	Michigan State	16
36	Sampson, Howard	DB	5-10	185	07/07/56	Arkansas	15
48	Simpson, Nate	RB	5-11	190	11/30/54	Tennessee State	16
73	Skinner, Gerald	T	6-4	260	01/12/54	Arkansas	15
33	Smith, Barty	FB	6-3	240	03/23/52	Richmond	16
16	Sproul, Dennis	QB	6-2	210	07/17/56	Arizona	6
76	Stokes, Tim	T	6-5	252	03/16/50	Oregon	16
89	Taylor, Willie	WR	6-1	179	12/09/55	Pittsburgh	1
43	Thompson, Aundra	WR	6-0	186	01/02/53	East Texas State	16
26	Torkelson, Eric	RB	6-2	194	03/02/52	Connecticut	14
20	Tullis, Walter	WR	6-0	170	04/12/53	Delaware State	16
21	Wagner, Steve	S	6-2	208	04/18/54	Wisconsin	16
52	Weaver, Gary	LB	6-1	225	03/13/49	Fresno State	16
17	Whitehurst, David	QB	6-2	204	04/27/55	Furman	16

DRAFT

Rnd	Name	Pos	Ht	Wt	College
1a	James Lofton (6)	WR	6-3	187	Stanford
1b	John Anderson (26)	LB	6-3	221	Michigan
	(Choice from Raiders for Mike P. McCoy)				
2	Mike Hunt (34)	LB	6-2	240	Minnesota
3	Estus Hood (62)	DB	5-11	180	Illinois State
4	(Choice declared forfeit by commissioner Pete Rozelle for scouting violations)				
5a	Mike Douglass (116)	LB	6-0	224	San Diego State
5b	Willie Wilder (128)	RB	6-1	200	Florida
	(Choice from Steelers in Dave Pureifory trade)				
6	Leotis Harris (144)	G	6-1	267	Arkansas
7	George Plasketes (172)	LB	6-0	220	Mississippi
8	Dennis Sproul (200)	QB	6-2	210	Arizona State
9	Keith Myers (228)	QB	6-2	190	Utah State
10a	Larry Key (256)	RB	5-9	193	Florida State
10b	Mark Totten (259)	C	6-3	288	Florida
	(Choice from Giants in Joe Danelo deal)				
11	Terry Jones (284)	DT	6-2	259	Alabama
12	Eason Ramson (312)	TE	6-2	221	Washington State

FRONT ROW: (L-R) 38 Estus Hood, 29 Mike C. McCoy, 24 Johnnie Gray, 46 Steve Luke, 28 Willie Buchanon, 20 Walter Tullis, 11 David Beverly, 13 Chester Marcol, 84 Steve Odom, 43 Aundra Thompson, 48 Nate Simpson, 42 Walt Landers, 36 Howard Sampson.

SECOND ROW: (L-R) Equipment Assistant Jack Noel, Team Physician Dr. Eugene Brusky, Trainer Domenic Gentile, Equipment Manager Bob Noel, Quarterbacks Coach Zeke Bratkowski, Offensive Line Assistant Ernie McMillan, Head Coach Bart Starr, Assistant Head Coach/Defensive Coordinator Dave Hanner, Passing Game Coach Lew Carpenter, Defensive Backfield Coach Dick LeBeau, Linebackers Coach John Meyer, Offensive Line Coach Bill Curry, Offensive Backfield Coach Bob Lord.

THIRD ROW: (L-R) Film Director Al Treml, Groundskeeper Earl DuChateau, 71 Mel Jackson, 79 Mark Koncar, 54 Larry McCarren, 57 Derrel Gofourth, 65 Mike Douglass, 16 Dennis Sproul, 55 Mike Hunt, 19 Bobby Douglass, 17 David Whitehurst, Assistant Trainer Jim Popp, Special Teams Coach Burt Gustafson.

FOURTH ROW: (L-R) 69 Leotis Harris, 26 Eric Torkelson, 81 Rich McGeorge, 33 Barty Smith, 80 James Lofton, 74 Dave Roller, 66 Paul Rudzinski, 51 Jim Gueno, 21 Steve Wagner, 60 John Anderson, 63 Terry Jones.

BACK ROW: (L-R) 34 Terdell Middleton, 73 Gerald Skinner, 68 Greg Koch, 76 Tim Stokes, 78 Ezra Johnson, 77 Mike Butler, 75 Carl Barzilauskas, 70 Bob Barber, 56 Rick Nuzum, 82 Paul Coffman, 52 Gary Weaver, 50 Jim Carter.

The worst rushing defense in the league, the dismissal of a long-time member of the organization and a rash of injuries all factored into a disappointing 5-11 season that fell far short of expectations. For the first time, Bart Starr's job security was questioned.

On the bright side, Lynn Dickey returned, the Packers stunned the Patriots in a thriller on "Monday Night Football," and beat the Vikings for the first time in five years.

Green Bay's defense, particularly against the run, offered little resistance. The Packers gave up more than 150 yards rushing on 14 occasions and was 3-11 in those games. No other defense in the NFL was attacked as often on the ground (639 rushes) as was the Packers', and the resulting 2,885 yards surrendered was the fourth-most ever given up by an NFL team to that point.

Defensive coordinator Dave Hanner, with the team as either a player or coach for 28 years, paid the price for the defensive woes. In December, Starr fired him after he declined to tender his resignation.

First-round pick Eddie Lee Ivery suffered the first major injury of the regular season. The 15th overall selection sustained torn cartilage and damage to the anterior cruciate ligament of his left knee in the opener in Chicago.

Mike Hunt, Barty Smith, Bobby Kimball, and Steve Atkins also fell victim to season-ending knee injuries. Mark Koncar (ankle), John Anderson (broken arm) Terdell Middleton (separated shoulder), Ezra Johnson (ankle), and Mike Butler (dislocated elbow) also missed significant playing time with various ailments.

The fourth losing season in five years under Starr was not without its stressful moments. James Lofton threw his helmet and exchanged words with the coach after the team played it safe late in the fourth quarter and then lost to the Vikings in overtime. Weeks later, Lofton made an obscene gesture to the Lambeau Field crowd and told reporters the fans could "shove it as far as I'm concerned." David Whitehurst's comeback ability was questioned following an early-season loss to Tampa Bay. The Milwaukee Journal's Dave Begel wrote a piece that claimed Starr was unfeeling and out of touch with his players.

Rich McGeorge, a first-round draft choice in 1970, was let go in mid-August. He was replaced by undrafted Paul Coffman, who established a Packers single-season record for receptions by a tight end with 56.

Walter Payton rushed for 125 yards and Bob Thomas kicked two field goals as the Bears spoiled Green Bay's opener 6-3. Ivery was lost for the year on his third carry.

Two weeks later, the Packers lost 21-10 in Tampa. After the game, a reporter questioned Whitehurst's ability to lead the team from behind.

"What in the hell do you know about the comeback ability of anyone?" Starr fired back.

Tied with the Vikings at 21, the Packers ran three running plays from their own 25 with 1:41 left rather than drive for a field goal. In overtime, the Vikings' Tommy Kramer hit Ahmad Rashad with a 50-yard touchdown pass. Afterwards, Lofton threw his helmet and pads against a locker as the team knelt in prayer.

Green Bay's second win, 27-14 over the 1978 AFC Eastern Division champion Patriots in the first Monday night game at Lambeau Field, was its biggest of the year. The Packers sacked New England passers five times and intercepted them another five times.

The Packers notched their third win 24-16 at the expense of the Lions. Nate Simpson had 121 yards rushing.

Green Bay then lost three straight to fall to 3-7 and slip four games behind the surprising Buccaneers (7-3). The last in the series of losses was a 27-22 setback to the Jets at Lambeau Field. Lofton's drop of a second-quarter pass and his fumble on the next series had fans booing.

"I'm trying to play as hard as I can. It (expletive) me off," he said about the fans' behavior.

It was the last game of the season for Chester Marcol, who had been having trouble with his knee. Tom Birney handled the kicking duties in the final six games.

Green Bay won twice with Birney. It defeated the Vikings 19-7 and closed with an 18-13 win in Detroit.

In between those wins, the club welcomed back Dickey, who got his first start in more than two years. Dickey, who had come on in relief in two earlier games, threw for 212 yards in a 38-21 loss to the Redskins on Dec. 2.

150 YARD DASH

In 1979, Green Bay was an equal-opportunity enabler. Almost every Packers opponent, regardless of record or running ability, increased its rushing output by at least 150 yards after it got through playing the Green and Gold.

Green Bay surrendered more than 150 yards rushing a team-record 14 times. The 2-14 Lions rolled up 156 yards on Dec. 15. The Bills, who finished last in the league in rushing, piled up 187 yards in a 19-12 win on Nov. 18.

Good teams fared even better. The Buccaneers amassed 235 yards in the first meeting, then added 228 in the rematch. The Jets, the top rushing team in the NFL, gashed the Packers for 246 yards on Nov. 4.

The Lions (93 yards) and Vikings (117) were the only teams to fail to break the 150-yard mark.

Most Games, 150+ Yards Rushing Allowed, Season

No.	Year	Record in Those Games
14	1979	3-11
11	1956	3-8
10	1983	2-8

TEAM STATISTICS

	GB	OPP
First Downs	279	327
Rushing	121	162
Passing	133	146
Penalty	25	19
Rushes	483	639
Yards Gained	1,861	2,885
Average Gain	3.85	4.51
Average Yards per Game	116.3	180.3
Passes Attempted	444	440
Completed	240	249
% Completed	54.05	56.59
Total Yards Gained	3,057	3,041
Times Sacked	47	35
Yards Lost	376	279
Net Yards Gained	2,681	2,762
Yards Gained per Completion	12.74	12.21
Net Yards per Attempt	5.46	5.81
Average Net Yards per Game	167.6	172.6
Combined Net Yards Gained	4,542	5,647
Total Plays	974	1,114
Average Yards per Play	4.66	5.07
Average Net Yards per Game	283.9	352.9
Third Down Efficiency	85/224	114/248
Percentage	37.95	45.97
Fourth Down Efficiency	12/25	5/16
Percentage	48.00	31.25
Intercepted By	18	22
Yards Returned	243	247
Returned for TD	0	2
Punts	69	64
Yards Punted	2,785	2,516
Average Yards per Punt	40.36	39.31
Punt Returns	28	43
Yards Returned	141	305
Average Yards per Return	5.04	7.09
Returned for TD	0	0
Kickoff Returns	61	50
Yards Returned	1,295	999
Average Yards per Return	21.23	20.00
Returned for TD	1	0
Penalties	93	106
Yards Penalized	681	912
Fumbles	37	30
Lost	22	14
Own Recovered for Touchdown	0	0
Opponent's Recovered by	14	22
Opponent's Recovered for Touchdown	1	0
Total Points Scored	246	316
Total Touchdowns	31	37
Touchdowns Rushing	14	14
Touchdowns Passing	15	21
Touchdowns on Returns & Recoveries	2	2
Extra Points	24	32
Safeties	0	1
Field Goals Attempted	20	33
Field Goals Made	12	20
% Successful	60.00	60.60
Average Time of Possession	27:55	32:05

Regular Season   5-11-0

Date	GB		OPP	Att.
9/2	3	at Chicago Bears	6	(56,515)
9/9	28	New Orleans Saints (M)	19	(53,184)
9/16	10	Tampa Bay Buccaneers	21	(55,498)
9/23	21	at Minnesota Vikings (OT)	27	(46,524)
10/1	27	New England Patriots	14	(52,842)
10/7	7	at Atlanta Falcons	25	(56,184)
10/14	24	Detroit Lions (M)	16	(53,950)
10/21	3	at Tampa Bay Buccaneers	21	(67,186)
10/28	7	at Miami Dolphins	27	(47,741)
11/4	22	New York Jets	27	(54,201)
11/11	19	Minnesota Vikings (M)	7	(52,706)
11/18	12	at Buffalo Bills	19	(39,679)
11/25	10	Philadelphia Eagles	21	(50,023)
12/2	21	at Washington Redskins	38	(51,682)
12/9	14	Chicago Bears	15	(54,207)
12/15	18	at Detroit Lions	13	(57,376)

Score By Periods

	1	2	3	4	OT	Total
Packers	35	79	64	48	0	246
Opponents	61	90	68	91	6	316

INDIVIDUAL STATISTICS

Rushing

	Att	Yds	Avg	LG	TD
Middleton	131	495	3.8	28	2
Torkelson	98	401	4.1	15	3
Atkins	42	239	5.7	60	1
N. Simpson	66	235	3.6	22	1
Barty Smith	57	201	3.5	23	3
Patton	37	134	3.6	14	0
Whitehurst	18	73	4.1	17	4
Landers	17	41	2.4	14	0
Ivery	3	24	8.0	11	0
Wagner	1	16	16.0	16	0
Dickey	5	13	2.6	8	0
Culbreath	5	8	1.6	6	0
Lofton	1	-1	-1.0	-1	0
Aundra Thompson	2	-18	-9.0	-7	0
Packers	**483**	**1,861**	**3.9**	**60**	**14**
Opponents	639	2,885	4.5	80	14

Receiving

	No	Yds	Avg	LG	TD
Coffman	56	711	12.7	t78	4
Lofton	54	968	17.9	52	4
Aundra Thompson	25	395	15.8	50	3
Barty Smith	19	155	8.2	22	1
Torkelson	19	139	7.3	14	0
Middleton	18	155	8.6	29	1
N. Simpson	11	46	4.2	10	0
Tullis	10	173	17.3	t52	1
Atkins	10	89	8.9	19	0
Cassidy	6	102	17.0	23	0
Patton	6	41	6.8	9	0
Landers	5	60	12.0	t55	1
Gueno	1	23	23.0	23	0
Packers	**240**	**3,057**	**12.7**	**t78**	**15**
Opponents	249	3,041	12.2	t50	21

Passing

	Att	Com	Yds	Pct	TD	In	Tk/Yds	Rate
Whitehurst	322	179	2,247	55.6	10	18	32/256	64.5
Dickey	119	60	787	50.4	5	4	15/120	71.7
Beverly	2	1	23	50.0	0	0	0/0	—
Lofton	1	0	0	00.0	0	0	0/0	—
Packers	**444**	**240**	**3,057**	**54.1**	**15**	**22**	**47/376**	**66.4**
Opponents	440	249	3,041	56.6	21	18	35/279	76.9

Punting

	No	Yds	Avg	Net	TB	In20	LG	HB
Beverly	69	2,785	40.4	34.8	4	11	65	0
Packers	**69**	**2,785**	**40.4**	**34.8**	**4**	**11**	**65**	**0**
Opponents	64	2,516	39.3	34.0	10	21	68	0

Kickoff Returns

	No	Yds	Avg	LG	TD
Odom	29	622	21.4	31	0
Aundra Thompson	15	346	23.1	t100	1
M.C. McCoy	11	248	22.5	41	0
Sampson	4	61	15.3	21	0
Wellman	1	10	10.0	10	0
S. Wagner	1	8	8.0	8	0
Packers	61	1,295	21.2	t100	1
Opponents	50	999	20.0	69	0

Punt Returns

	No	Yds	Avg	FC	LG	TD
Odom	15	80	5.3	5	19	0
J. Gray	13	61	4.7	8	18	0
Packers	**28**	**141**	**5.0**	**13**	**19**	**0**
Opponents	43	305	7.1	7	19	0

Interceptions

	No	Yds	Avg	LG	TD
J. Gray	5	66	13.2	35	0
M. Douglass	3	73	24.3	46	0
M.C. McCoy	3	60	20.0	38	0
Wingo	2	13	6.5	13	0
Hood	2	8	4.0	6	0
M. Hunt	1	13	13.0	13	0
Luke	1	10	10.0	10	0
Charles Johnson	1	0	0.0	0	0
Packers	**18**	**243**	**13.5**	**46**	**0**
Opponents	22	247	11.2	66	2

Scoring

	TDr	TDp	TDrt	PAT	FG	S	TP
Birney	0	0	0	7/10	7/9	0	28
Marcol	0	0	0	16/18	4/10	0	28
Coffman	0	4	0	0/0	0/0	0	24
Lofton	0	4	0	0/0	0/0	0	24
Barty Smith	3	1	0	0/0	0/0	0	24
Aundra Thompson	0	3	1	0/0	0/0	0	24
Whitehurst	4	0	0	0/0	0/0	0	24
Middleton	2	1	0	0/0	0/0	0	18
Torkelson	3	0	0	0/0	0/0	0	18
Atkins	1	0	0	0/0	0/0	0	6
M. Butler	0	0	1	0/0	0/0	0	6
Landers	0	1	0	0/0	0/0	0	6
N. Simpson	1	0	0	0/0	0/0	0	6
Tullis	0	1	0	0/0	0/0	0	6
J. Anderson	0	0	0	1/2	1/1	0	4
Packers	**14**	**15**	**2**	**24/31**	**12/20**	**0**	**246**
Opponents	14	21	2	32/36	20/33	1	316

Fumbles

	Fum	Ow	Op	Yds	Tot
J. Anderson	0	0	1	0	1
Atkins	1	0	0	0	1
Barber	0	0	1	0	1
Barzilauskas	0	0	1	0	1
M. Butler	0	0	1	70	1
Coffman	4	0	0	0	4
Culbreath	0	1	0	0	1
Dickey	2	1	0	-1	1
J. Gray	0	1	3	0	4
L. Harris	0	0	1	0	1
Ivery	1	0	0	0	1
Charles Johnson	0	0	1	0	1
Terry Jones	0	0	1	0	1
Lathrop	0	0	1	0	1
Lofton	5	0	0	0	0
Luke	0	0	1	0	1
M.C. McCoy	1	0	2	0	2
Middleton	3	1	0	0	1
Odom	4	0	0	0	0
Patton	1	0	0	0	0
N. Simpson	2	1	0	0	1
Barty Smith	1	0	0	0	0
Aundra Thompson	3	1	0	0	1
J. Thompson	0	0	1	0	1
Torkelson	3	2	0	0	2
Weaver	0	0	1	0	1
Whitehurst	3	0	0	0	0
Wingo	0	0	1	0	1
Packers	**37**	**11**	**14**	**69**	**25**

NFL STANDINGS

National Conference

Eastern Division

	W	L	T	Pct	PF	PA
Dallas Cowboys	11	5	0	.688	371	313
Philadelphia Eagles	11	5	0	.688	339	282
Washington Redskins	10	6	0	.625	348	295
New York Giants	6	10	0	.375	237	323
St. Louis Cardinals	5	11	0	.313	307	358

Central Division

	W	L	T	Pct	PF	PA
Tampa Bay Buccaneers	10	6	0	.625	273	237
Chicago Bears	10	6	0	.625	306	249
Minnesota Vikings	7	9	0	.438	259	337
Green Bay Packers	**5**	**11**	**0**	**.313**	**246**	**316**
Detroit Lions	2	14	0	.125	219	365

Western Division

	W	L	T	Pct	PF	PA
Los Angeles Rams	9	7	0	.563	323	309
New Orleans Saints	8	8	0	.500	370	360
Atlanta Falcons	6	10	0	.375	300	388
San Francisco 49ers	2	14	0	.125	308	416

American Conference

Eastern Division

	W	L	T	Pct	PF	PA
Miami Dolphins	10	6	0	.625	341	257
New England Patriots	9	7	0	.563	411	326
New York Jets	8	8	0	.500	337	383
Buffalo Bills	7	9	0	.438	268	279
Baltimore Colts	5	11	0	.313	271	351

Central Division

	W	L	T	Pct	PF	PA
Pittsburgh Steelers	12	4	0	.750	416	262
Houston Oilers	11	5	0	.688	362	331
Cleveland Browns	9	7	0	.563	359	352
Cincinnati Bengals	4	12	0	.250	337	421

Western Division

	W	L	T	Pct	PF	PA
San Diego Chargers	12	4	0	.750	411	246
Denver Broncos	10	6	0	.625	289	262
Seattle Seahawks	9	7	0	.563	378	372
Oakland Raiders	9	7	0	.563	365	337
Kansas City Chiefs	7	9	0	.438	238	262

ROSTER

No	Name	Pos	Ht	Wt	DOB	College	G
59	Anderson, John	LB	6-3	221	02/14/56	Michigan	7
32	Atkins, Steve	RB	6-0	216	06/22/56	Maryland	7
70	Barber, Bob	DE	6-3	240	12/26/51	Grambling	16
75	Barzilauskas, Carl	DT	6-6	265	03/19/51	Indiana	5
11	Beverly, David	P	6-2	180	08/19/50	Auburn	16
19	Birney, Tom	K	6-4	220	08/11/56	Michigan	6
77	Butler, Mike	DE	6-5	265	04/04/54	Kansas	14
88	Cassidy, Ron	WR	6-0	175	07/23/57	Utah State	8
82	Coffman, Paul	TE	6-3	218	03/29/56	Kansas State	16
31	Culbreath, Jim	RB	6-0	210	10/21/52	Oklahoma	4
10	Dickey, Lynn	QB	6-4	220	10/19/49	Kansas State	5
53	Douglass, Mike	LB	6-0	224	03/15/55	San Diego State	16
73	Edwards, Earl	DT	6-6	260	03/17/46	Wichita State	9
57	Gofourth, Derrel	C	6-3	260	03/20/55	Oklahoma State	16
24	Gray, Johnnie	S	5-11	185	12/18/53	Cal State-Fullerton	16
51	Gueno, Jim	LB	6-2	220	01/15/54	Tulane	16
69	Harris, Leotis	G	6-1	267	06/28/55	Arkansas	15
38	Hood, Estus	CB	5-11	180	11/14/55	Illinois State	16
55	Hunt, Mike	LB	6-2	240	10/06/56	Minnesota	3
40	Ivery, Eddie Lee	RB	6-1	210	07/30/57	Georgia Tech	1
71	Jackson, Mel	G	6-1	267	05/05/54	USC	16
99	Johnson, Charles	DT	6-1	262	06/29/57	Maryland	16
90	Johnson, Ezra	DE	6-4	240	10/02/55	Morris Brown	11
39	Johnson, Sammy	RB	6-1	226	09/22/52	North Carolina	3
63	Jones, Terry	DT	6-2	259	11/08/56	Alabama	12
85	Kimball, Bobby	WR	6-1	190	03/12/57	Oklahoma	7
68	Koch, Greg	T	6-4	265	06/14/55	Arkansas	16
79	Koncar, Mark	T	6-5	268	05/05/53	Colorado	12
42	Landers, Walt	FB	6-0	214	07/04/53	Clark	9
72	Lathrop, Kit	DT	6-5	253	05/10/56	Arizona State	2
80	Lofton, James	WR	6-3	187	07/05/56	Stanford	16
46	Luke, Steve	S	6-2	205	09/04/53	Ohio State	16
13	Marcol, Chester	K	6-0	190	10/24/49	Hillsdale	10
54	McCarren, Larry	C	6-3	248	11/09/51	Illinois	16
29	McCoy, Mike C.	CB	5-11	183	08/16/53	Colorado	16
62	McLaughlin, Joe	LB	6-1	235	07/01/57	Massachusetts	3
78	Merrill, Casey	DE	6-4	255	07/16/57	California-Davis	13
34	Middleton, Terdell	HB	6-0	195	04/08/55	Memphis State	14
43	Monroe, Henry	DB	5-11	180	12/30/56	Mississippi State	3
84	Odom, Steve	WR	5-8	174	09/05/52	Utah	9
30	Patton, Ricky	RB	5-11	189	04/06/54	Jackson State	6
66	Rudzinski, Paul	LB	6-1	220	07/28/56	Michigan State	11
36	Sampson, Howard	CB	5-10	185	07/07/56	Arkansas	16
61	Simmons, Davie	LB	6-4	218	01/19/57	North Carolina	16
48	Simpson, Nate	RB	5-11	190	11/30/54	Tennessee State	15
33	Smith, Barty	FB	6-3	240	03/23/52	Richmond	6
58	Stewart, Steve	LB	6-3	215	05/01/56	Minnesota	3
76	Stokes, Tim	T	6-5	252	03/16/50	Oregon	16
89	Thompson, Aundra	WR	6-0	186	01/02/53	East Texas State	15
83	Thompson, John	TE	6-3	228	01/18/57	Utah State	16
26	Torkelson, Eric	RB	6-2	194	03/03/52	Connecticut	14
87	Tullis, Walter	WR	6-0	170	04/12/53	Delaware State	16
20	Turner, Wylie	CB	5-10	182	04/19/57	Angelo State	12
21	Wagner, Steve	S	6-2	208	04/18/54	Wisconsin	16
52	Weaver, Gary	LB	6-1	225	03/13/49	Fresno State	14
65	Wellman, Mike	C	6-3	253	07/15/56	Kansas	16
17	Whitehurst, David	QB	6-2	204	04/27/55	Furman	13
50	Wingo, Rich	LB	6-1	230	07/16/56	Alabama	16

DRAFT

Rnd	Name	Pos	Ht	Wt	College
1	Eddie Lee Ivery (15)	RB	6-0	210	Georgia Tech
2	Steve Atkins (44)	RB	6-0	216	Maryland
3	Charles Johnson (71)	DT	6-1	262	Maryland
4a	(Choice (98) to Jets as part of Carl Barzilauskas deal)				
4b	(Choice (103) from Raiders for Mike P. McCoy to Redskins for Tim Stokes)				
5	(Choice (125) to Jets as part of Carl Barzilauskas deal)				
6	Davie Simmons (153)	LB	6-4	218	North Carolina
7a	Henry Monroe (180)	DB	5-11	180	Mississippi State
7b	Rich Wingo (184)	LB	6-1	230	Alabama
	(Choice from Chargers as part of Willie Buchanon deal)				
8a	Ron Cassidy (193)	WR	6-0	175	Utah State
	(Choice from 49ers for Steve Knutson)				
8b	Rick Partridge (208)	P	6-1	175	Utah
9	John Thompson (235)	TE	6-3	228	Utah State
10	Frank Lockett (264)	WR	5-11	192	Nebraska
11	Mark Thorson (290)	DB	5-10	188	Ottawa
12	Bill Moats (318)	P	5-11	177	South Dakota

1979 GREEN BAY PACKERS

FRONT ROW: (L-R) 48 Nate Simpson, 71 Mel Jackson, 79 Mark Koncar, 77 Mike Butler, 55 Mike Hunt, 11 David Beverly, 34 Terdell Middleton, 58 Steve Stewart, 89 Aundra Thompson, 84 Steve Odom, 54 Larry McCarren, 33 Barty Smith, 26 Eric Torkelson, 13 Chester Marcol.

SECOND ROW: (L-R) Equipment Assistant Jack Noel, Equipment Manager Bob Noel, Offensive Backfield Coach Zeke Bratkowski, Special Assistant Dick Rehbein, Special Teams Coach Fred vonAppen, Passing Game Coach Lew Carpenter, Assistant Head Coach/Defensive Coordinator Dave Hanner, Head Coach Bart Starr, Linebackers Coach John Meyer, Offensive Line Assistant Ernie McMillan, Defensive Backfield Coach Dick LeBeau, Offensive Line Coach Bill Curry, Orthopedic Consultant Dr. James W. Nellen, Assistant Trainer Jim Popp.

THIRD ROW: (L-R) 46 Steve Luke, 38 Estus Hood, 29 Mike C. McCoy, 40 Eddie Lee Ivery 42 Walt Landers, 43 Henry Monroe, 36 Howard Sampson, 50 Rich Wingo, 85 Bobby Kimball, 24 Johnnie Gray, 82 Paul Coffman, 17 David Whitehurst, 52 Gary Weaver.

FOURTH ROW: (L-R) Groundskeeper Earl DuChateau, 31 Jim Culbreath, 88 Ron Cassidy, 65 Mike Wellman, 61 Davie Simmons, 63 Terry Jones, 87 Walter Tullis, 80 James Lofton, 53 Mike Douglass, 99 Charles Johnson, 51 Jim Gueno, 21 Steve Wagner, 59 John Anderson, 32 Steve Atkins, Film Director Al Treml.

BACK ROW: (L-R) Team Physician Dr. Eugene Brusky, 78 Casey Merrill, 57 Derrel Gofourth, 76 Tim Stokes, 68 Greg Koch, 10 Lynn Dickey, 90 Ezra Johnson, 75 Carl Barzilauskas, 69 Leotis Harris, 70 Bob Barber, 83 John Thompson, Trainer Domenic Gentile.

In professional sport, being given a public vote of confidence is often a sign that one's job is in jeopardy. The Green Bay Packers' board of directors provided Coach Bart Starr with such a gesture in Week 5, and although the six-year coaching veteran retained his job at season's end, he was stripped of his general manager title following a 5-10-1 season that was filled with more lows than highs.

The list of the unusual started early. First-round draft choice Bruce Clark bolted for the Canadian Football League. The Packers' first preseason game, the Hall of Fame Game, was suspended because of lightning. Earlier that day, former Packer Herb Adderley had his induction speech interrupted by a man who walked to the speaker's stand and said, "I want to protest."

Green Bay went winless in exhibition play for the first time since 1946, then endured a tumultuous week leading to its season opener. Under fire for an 0-4-1 preseason that ended with a 38-0 blasting by the Broncos, Starr vowed not to resign. Instead, defensive line coach Fred von Appen quit after one of his charges, Ezra Johnson, was seen eating a hot dog on the sidelines late in the second half of the Denver debacle. Johnson was fined.

The Packers again had their share of injuries. Linebacker George Cumby, the team's other first-round pick, underwent knee surgery on Aug. 1 and didn't return until midseason. David Whitehurst missed the first five games with ligament damage to his knee. As he had done in each of the previous two years, John Anderson broke his arm, this time against the Steelers. Mike Hunt, who complained of headaches throughout much of training camp, suffered a severe concussion against the Rams and never played in another regular-season game for the team.

John Meyer replaced Dave Hanner as defensive coordinator. The team employed the 3-4 defense as its primary front for the first time, with less-than-satisfactory results. Green Bay surrendered 5,782 yards, second most in franchise history.

The team ranked 14th in yards gained despite Lynn Dickey becoming the first Packer to throw for 3,000 yards (3,529) in a single season. Green Bay's 231 points were the fewest in the league.

The Packers regrouped to win their opener 12-6 over the Bears. A swarming defense held Walter Payton to 65 yards rushing on 31 carries. Larry McCarren went the distance at center despite undergoing a hernia operation just 3 1/2 weeks earlier. Chester Marcol scooted 25 yards for the game-winning touchdown after Alan Page blocked his field goal attempt in overtime.

Marcol, who was swarmed under by his teammates, didn't last the season.

The emotional high of week 1 quickly evaporated. In the three weeks that followed, the Packers were pummeled by the Lions (29-7), the Rams (51-21), and the Cowboys (28-7). Dickey was asking questions after the Rams debacle.

"I'm wondering if I'm the guy for the job," said Dickey, who threw three interceptions and was sacked six times. "I don't know if I can help this team."

On Oct. 12, Dickey set numerous single-game team records for passing in a 14-14 tie with the Buccaneers. Tom Birney missed three field goals in the Tampa Bay game. It was his first outing after he replaced Marcol, who was waived following a 14-9 win over Cincinnati.

Dickey threw fourth-quarter touchdown passes to Bill Larson and Paul Coffman to down the Vikings 16-3 on Oct. 26. Lofton played defense in an unorthodox 3-1-7 alignment in a 23-16 win over the 49ers. Eddie Lee Ivery and Gerry Ellis combined for 246 yards rushing in Minnesota as Green Bay (5-6-1) pulled to within 1 1/2 games of division-leading Detroit (7-5).

The Vikings game was the last for Birney, who had botched three extra point attempts and seven field goal attempts. Veteran Jan Stenerud took his place.

Green Bay closed with ugly losses to the Bears (61-7), Oilers (22-3), and Lions (24-3). Chicago gained 594 yards. Houston recorded a last-second touchdown that had Starr seething because he believed it should have been discounted due to an Oiler being offside. Detroit merely outperformed a listless opponent.

"I'm going to work tomorrow as though we've got 10 years to go on the (my) contract," Starr said after losing to the Lions.

UNBEARABLY PERFECT

The highest rating a passer can attain using the NFL's system is 158.3. The Bears' Vince Evans is the only opponent to garner such a rating in a game against the Packers (minimum 20 attempts).

On Dec. 7, the Bears crushed Green Bay 61-7. Chicago picked up 33 first downs and 594 yards. This wasn't the same team Green Bay beat 12-6 in the opener.

Mike Phipps started that day. Evans got the nod in December. In his 11th career start, the four-year veteran completed 18 of 22 passes for 316 yards and three touchdowns. After guiding the team to a 48-7 lead early in the fourth quarter, Evans retired for the day.

Evans started two more games against the Packers (both losses in 1981) and managed ratings of 64.6 and 16.2.

Listed below are the players with the highest passer ratings in a single game against the Packers (min. 20 atts.):

Rating	Player	Date	Result
158.3	Vince Evans	12-7-80	GB 7, Bears 61
158.1	Norm Van Brocklin	12-16-56	GB 21, Rams 49
145.8	Randall Cunningham	10-5-98	GB 24, Vikings 37

TEAM STATISTICS

	GB	OPP
First Downs	307	316
Rushing	119	136
Passing	164	166
Penalty	24	14
Rushes	493	565
Yards Gained	1,806	2,399
Average Gain	3.66	4.25
Average Yards per Game	112.9	149.9
Passes Attempted	511	460
Completed	289	259
% Completed	56.56	56.30
Total Yards Gained	3,651	3,617
Times Sacked	43	34
Yards Lost	360	234
Net Yards Gained	3,291	3,383
Yards Gained per Completion	12.63	13.97
Net Yards per Attempt	5.94	6.85
Average Net Yards per Game	205.7	211.4
Combined Net Yards Gained	5,097	5,782
Total Plays	1,047	1,059
Average Yards per Play	4.87	5.46
Average Net Yards per Game	318.6	361.4
Third Down Efficiency	91/234	102/237
Percentage	38.89	43.04
Fourth Down Efficiency	11/20	5/16
Percentage	55.00	31.25
Intercepted By	13	29
Yards Returned	92	483
Returned for TD	0	4
Punts	87	83
Yards Punted	3,327	3,247
Average Yards per Punt	38.24	39.12
Punt Returns	37	50
Yards Returned	297	342
Average Yards per Return	8.03	6.84
Returned for TD	0	0
Kickoff Returns	73	52
Yards Returned	1,415	902
Average Yards per Return	19.38	17.35
Returned for TD	0	0
Penalties	84	109
Yards Penalized	697	872
Fumbles	36	27
Lost	12	14
Own Recovered for Touchdown	0	0
Opponent's Recovered by	14	12
Opponent's Recovered for Touchdown	0	1
Total Points Scored	231	371
Total Touchdowns	29	43
Touchdowns Rushing	13	19
Touchdowns Passing	15	19
Touchdowns on Returns & Recoveries	1	5
Extra Points	24	36
Safeties	0	1
Field Goals Attempted	20	27
Field Goals Made	11	25
% Successful	55.00	92.59
Average Time of Possession	30:15	29:45

Regular Season   5-10-1

Date	GB		OPP	Att.
9/7	12	Chicago Bears (OT)	6	(54,381)
9/14	7	Detroit Lions (M)	29	(53,099)
9/21	21	at Los Angeles Rams	51	(63,850)
9/28	7	Dallas Cowboys (M)	28	(54,776)
10/5	14	Cincinnati Bengals	9	(55,006)
10/12	14	at TB Buccaneers (OT)	14	(64,854)
10/19	21	at Cleveland Browns	26	(75,548)
10/26	16	Minnesota Vikings	3	(55,361)
11/2	20	at Pittsburgh Steelers	22	(52,165)
11/9	23	San Francisco 49ers	16	(54,475)
11/16	21	at New York Giants	27	(72,368)
11/23	25	at Minnesota Vikings	13	(47,234)
11/30	17	Tampa Bay Buccaneers (M)	20	(54,225)
12/7	7	at Chicago Bears	61	(57,176)
12/14	3	Houston Oilers	22	(53,201)
12/21	3	at Detroit Lions	24	(75,111)

Score By Periods

	1	2	3	4	OT	Total
Packers	21	91	33	80	6	231
Opponents	64	135	65	107	0	371

INDIVIDUAL STATISTICS

Rushing

	Att	Yds	Avg	LG	TD
Ivery	202	831	4.1	t38	3
G. Ellis	126	545	4.3	22	5
Atkins	67	216	3.2	16	1
Middleton	56	155	2.8	15	2
Beverly	6	21	3.5	11	0
Huckleby	6	11	1.8	9	1
Dickey	19	11	0.6	t7	1
V. R. Anderson	4	5	1.3	4	0
Aundra Thompson	5	5	1.0	16	0
Coffman	1	3	3.0	3	0
Barty Smith	1	3	3.0	3	0
Packers	**493**	**1,806**	**3.7**	**38**	**13**
Opponents	565	2,399	4.2	48	19

Receiving

	No	Yds	Avg	LG	TD
Lofton	71	1,226	17.3	47	4
Ivery	50	481	9.6	t46	1
G. Ellis	48	496	10.3	t69	3
Coffman	42	496	11.8	25	3
Aundra Thompson	40	609	15.2	55	2
Middleton	13	59	4.5	17	0
Atkins	7	47	6.7	16	1
Cassidy	5	109	21.8	43	0
Nixon	4	78	19.5	32	0
B. Larson	4	37	9.3	21	1
Huckleby	3	11	3.7	8	0
V. R. Anderson	2	2	1.0	2	0
Packers	**289**	**3,651**	**12.6**	**t69**	**15**
Opponents	259	3,617	14.0	t87	19

Passing

	Att	Com	Yds	Pct	TD	In	Tk/Yds	Rate
Dickey	478	278	3,529	58.2	15	25	37/314	70.0
Whitehurst	15	5	55	33.3	0	1	3/19	17.4
Troup	12	4	48	33.3	0	3	2/20	6.9
Pisarkiewicz	5	2	19	40.0	0	0	1/7	—
Beverly	1	0	0.0	0	0	0	—	—
Packers	**511**	**289**	**3,651**	**56.6**	**15**	**29**	**43/360**	**65.1**
Opponents	460	259	3,617	56.3	19	13	34/234	83.8

Punting

	No	Yds	Avg	Net	TB	In20	LG	HB
Beverly	86	3,294	38.3	32.9	6	18	55	0
Marcol	1	33	33.0	13.0	1	0	33	0
Packers	**87**	**3,327**	**38.2**	**32.7**	**7**	**18**	**55**	**0**
Opponents	83	3,247	39.1	32.9	11	23	61	1

Kickoff Returns

	No	Yds	Avg	LG	TD
M. Lee	30	589	19.6	35	0
Aundra Thompson	15	283	18.9	57	0
M.C. McCoy	14	261	18.6	32	0
Nixon	6	160	26.7	54	0
J. Gray	5	63	12.6	18	0
Huckleby	3	59	19.7	21	0
Packers	**73**	**1,415**	**19.4**	**57**	**0**
Opponents	52	902	17.3	59	0

Punt Returns

	No	Yds	Avg	FC	LG	TD
Cassidy	17	139	8.2	5	20	0
Nixon	11	85	7.7	2	16	0
M. Lee	5	32	6.4	0	17	0
J. Gray	4	41	10.3	2	16	0
Packers	**37**	**297**	**8.0**	**9**	**20**	**0**
Opponents	50	342	6.8	12	21	0

Interceptions

	No	Yds	Avg	LG	TD
J. Gray	5	54	10.8	21	0
W. Turner	2	13	6.5	13	0
Jolly	2	2	1.0	2	0
Rudzinski	1	14	14.0	14	0
Luke	1	9	9.0	9	0
Hood	1	0	0.0	0	0
M.C. McCoy	1	0	0.0	0	0
Packers	**13**	**92**	**7.1**	**21**	**0**
Opponents	29	483	16.7	t99	4

Scoring

	TDr	TDp	TDrt	PAT	FG	S	TP
G. Ellis	5	3	0	0/0	0/0	0	48
Birney	0	0	0	14/18	6/12	0	32
Ivery	3	1	0	0/0	0/0	0	24
Lofton	0	4	0	0/0	0/0	0	24
Marcol	0	0	0	7/7	2/3	0	19
Coffman	0	3	0	0/0	0/0	0	18
Atkins	1	1	0	0/0	0/0	0	12
Middleton	2	0	0	0/0	0/0	0	12
Stenerud	0	0	0	3/3	3/5	0	12
Aundra Thompson	0	2	0	0/0	0/0	0	12
Dickey	1	0	0	0/0	0/0	0	6
Huckleby	1	0	0	0/0	0/0	0	6
B. Larson	0	1	0	0/0	0/0	0	6
Packers	**13**	**15**	**1**	**24/29**	**11/20**	**0**	**231**
Opponents	19	19	5	36/43	25/27	1	371

Fumbles

	Fum	Ow	Op	Yds	Tot
J. Anderson	0	0	1	0	1
V. R. Anderson	1	0	0	0	0
Atkins	1	1	0	0	1
Aydelette	1	0	0	-28	0
Beverly	1	0	0	-5	1
Ken Brown	1	0	0	-37	0
Cassidy	1	0	0	0	0
Dickey	13	5	0	-7	5
M. Douglass	0	0	2	0	2
G. Ellis	7	5	0	0	5
J. Gray	0	0	4	30	4
Gueno	0	0	1	0	1
L. Harris	0	1	0	0	1
Hood	0	0	1	0	1
Ivery	3	2	0	0	2
C. Johnson	0	0	1	0	1
Jolly	0	1	0	0	1
T. Jones	0	0	1	0	1
Lathrop	0	1	0	0	1
M. Lee	1	0	0	0	0
McCarren	0	1	0	0	1
M.C. McCoy	1	0	0	0	0
C. Merrill	0	0	1	0	1
Middleton	1	0	0	0	0
Nixon	1	0	0	0	0
E. O'Neil	0	0	2	26	2
Stokes	0	1	0	0	1
Aundra Thompson	2	2	0	5	2
Whitehurst	1	0	0	0	0
Packers	**36**	**22**	**14**	**-16**	**36**

NFL STANDINGS

National Conference

Eastern Division

	W	L	T	Pct	PF	PA
Philadelphia Eagles	12	4	0	.750	384	222
Dallas Cowboys	12	4	0	.750	454	311
Washington Redskins	6	10	0	.375	261	293
St. Louis Cardinals	5	11	1	.313	299	350
New York Giants	4	12	0	.250	249	425

Central Division

	W	L	T	Pct	PF	PA
Minnesota Vikings	9	7	0	.563	317	308
Detroit Lions	9	7	0	.563	334	272
Chicago Bears	7	9	0	.438	304	264
Tampa Bay Buccaneers	5	10	1	.344	271	341
Green Bay Packers	5	10	1	.344	231	371

Western Division

	W	L	T	Pct	PF	PA
Atlanta Falcons	12	4	0	.750	405	272
Los Angeles Rams	11	5	0	.688	424	289
San Francisco 49ers	6	10	0	.375	320	415
New Orleans Saints	1	15	0	.063	291	487

American Conference

Eastern Division

	W	L	T	Pct	PF	PA
Buffalo Bills	11	5	0	.688	320	260
New England Patriots	10	6	0	.625	441	325
Miami Dolphins	8	8	0	.500	266	305
Baltimore Colts	7	9	0	.438	355	387
New York Jets	4	12	0	.250	302	395

Central Division

	W	L	T	Pct	PF	PA
Cleveland Browns	11	5	0	.688	357	310
Houston Oilers	11	5	0	.688	295	251
Pittsburgh Steelers	9	7	0	.563	352	313
Cincinnati Bengals	6	10	0	.375	244	312

Western Division

	W	L	T	Pct	PF	PA
San Diego Chargers	11	5	0	.688	418	327
Oakland Raiders	11	5	0	.688	364	306
Kansas City Chiefs	8	8	0	.500	319	336
Denver Broncos	8	8	0	.500	310	323
Seattle Seahawks	4	12	0	.250	291	408

ROSTER

No	Name	Pos	Ht	Wt	DOB	College	G
60	Allerman, Kurt	LB	6-2	222	08/30/55	Penn State	13
59	Anderson, John	LB	6-3	221	02/14/56	Michigan	9
44	Anderson, Vickey Ray	HB	6-0	205	05/03/56	Oklahoma	7
32	Atkins, Steve	RB	6-0	216	06/22/56	Maryland	9
62	Aydelette, Buddy	T	6-4	250	08/19/56	Alabama	9
58	Beekley, Bruce	LB	6-2	225	12/15/56	Oregon	15
11	Beverly, David	P	6-2	180	08/19/50	Auburn	16
19	Birney, Tom	K	6-4	220	08/11/56	Michigan	7
74	Brown, Ken	C	6-1	245	04/19/54	New Mexico	6
77	Butler, Mike	DE	6-5	265	04/04/54	Kansas	16
65	Cabral, Brian	LB	6-1	224	06/23/56	Colorado	7
88	Cassidy, Ron	WR	6-0	185	07/23/57	Utah State	15
82	Coffman, Paul	TE	6-3	218	03/29/56	Kansas State	16
52	Cumby, George	LB	6-0	215	07/05/56	Oklahoma	9
12	Dickey, Lynn	QB	6-4	220	10/19/49	Kansas State	16
92	Dimler, Rich	DT	6-6	260	07/18/56	USC	3
53	Douglass, Mike	LB	6-0	224	03/15/55	San Diego State	16
31	Ellis, Gerry	FB	5-11	216	11/12/57	Missouri	15
57	Gofourth, Derrel	C	6-3	260	03/20/55	Oklahoma State	16
24	Gray, Johnnie	S	5-11	185	12/18/53	Cal State-Fullerton	16
51	Gueno, Jim	LB	6-2	220	01/15/54	Tulane	16
69	Harris, Leotis	G	6-1	267	06/28/55	Arkansas	16
38	Hood, Estus	CB	5-11	180	11/14/55	Illinois State	15
25	Huckleby, Harlan	HB	6-1	199	12/30/57	Michigan	16
55	Hunt, Mike	LB	6-2	240	10/06/56	Minnesota	3
40	Ivery, Eddie Lee	RB	6-1	210	07/30/57	Georgia Tech	16
71	Jackson, Mel	G	6-1	267	05/05/54	USC	6
99	Johnson, Charles	DT	6-1	262	06/29/57	Maryland	15
90	Johnson, Ezra	DE	6-4	240	10/02/55	Morris Brown	15
21	Jolly, Mike	S	6-3	185	03/19/58	Michigan	16
63	Jones, Terry	DT	6-2	259	11/08/56	Alabama	15
85	Kimball, Bobby	WR	6-1	190	03/12/57	Oklahoma	1
64	Kitson, Syd	G	6-4	252	09/27/58	Wake Forest	14
68	Koch, Greg	T	6-4	265	06/14/55	Arkansas	16
79	Koncar, Mark	T	6-5	268	05/05/53	Colorado	1
87	Larson, Bill	TE	6-4	225	10/07/53	Colorado State	9
72	Lathrop, Kit	DT	6-5	253	05/10/56	Arizona State	15
22	Lee, Mark	CB	5-11	187	03/20/58	Washington	15
66	Lewis, Mike	DT	6-4	260	07/14/49	Arkansas A&M	10
80	Lofton, James	WR	6-3	187	07/05/56	Stanford	16
46	Luke, Steve	S	6-2	205	09/04/53	Ohio State	16
13	Marcol, Chester	K	6-0	190	10/24/49	Hillsdale	5
54	McCarren, Larry	C	6-3	248	11/09/51	Illinois	16
29	McCoy, Mike C.	CB	5-11	183	08/16/53	Colorado	16
78	Merrill, Casey	DE	6-4	255	07/16/57	California-Davis	16
34	Middleton, Terdell	HB	6-0	195	04/08/55	Memphis State	13
37	Murphy, Mark	S	6-2	199	04/22/58	West Liberty State	1
84	Nixon, Fred	WR	5-11	191	09/22/58	Oklahoma	15
56	O'Neil, Ed	LB	6-3	235	09/08/52	Penn State	12
19	Pisarkewicz, Steve	QB	6-2	205	11/10/53	Missouri	1
70	Rudzinski, Paul	LB	6-1	220	07/28/56	Michigan State	6
33	Smith, Barty	FB	6-3	240	03/23/52	Richmond	1
10	Stenerud, Jan	K	6-2	190	11/26/43	Montana State	4
76	Stokes, Tim	T	6-5	252	03/16/50	Oregon	16
67	Swanke, Karl	T	6-6	251	12/29/57	Boston College	16
89	Thompson, Aundra	WR	6-0	186	01/02/53	East Texas State	15
83	Thompson, John	TE	6-3	228	01/18/57	Utah State	7
10	Troup, Bill	QB	6-5	215	04/02/51	South Carolina	2
20	Turner, Wylie	CB	5-10	182	04/19/57	Angelo State	16
65	Wellman, Mike	C	6-3	253	07/15/56	Kansas	4
17	Whitehurst, David	QB	6-2	204	04/27/55	Furman	2

DRAFT

Rnd	Name	Pos	Ht	Wt	College
1a	Bruce Clark (4)	DT	6-2	255	Penn State
1b	George Cumby (26)	LB	6-0	215	Oklahoma
	(Choice from Chargers in Willie Buchanon deal)				
2	Mark Lee (34)	DB	5-11	187	Washington
3	Syd Kitson (61)	G	6-4	252	Wake Forest
4	Fred Nixon (87)	WR	5-11	191	Oklahoma
5	(Choice (116) to Rams for Rick Nuzum)				
6	Karl Swanke (143)	T/C	6-6	251	Boston College
7	Buddy Aydelette (169)	T	6-4	250	Alabama
8	Tim Smith (199)	S	6-1	194	Oregon State
9	Kelly Saalfeld (226)	C	6-3	246	Nebraska
10	Jafus White (253)	S	6-2	195	Texas A&I
11	Ricky Skiles (283)	LB	6-3	220	Louisville
12	James Stewart (310)	DB	5-11	186	Memphis State

1980 GREEN BAY PACKERS

FRONT ROW: (L–R) 57 Derrel Gofourth, 79 Mark Koncar, 71 Mel Jackson, 29 Mike C. McCoy, 12 Lynn Dickey, 24 Johnnie Gray, 11 David Beverly, 89 Aundra Thompson, 34 Terdell Middleton, 55 Mike Hunt, 56 Ed O'Neil, 13 Chester Marcol, 54 Larry McCarren, 33 Barty Smith, 26 Eric Torkelson.

SECOND ROW: (L–R) Equipment Assistant Jack Noel, Equipment Manager Bob Noel, Trainer Domenic Gentile, Receivers Coach Lew Carpenter, Defensive Backfield Coach Ross Fichtner, Special Assistant Dick Rehbein, Linebackers/Special Teams Coach John Marshall, Offensive Backfield Coach Zeke Bratkowski, Head Coach Bart Starr, Offensive Line Coach Ernie McMillan, Defensive Coordinator John Meyer, Defensive Line Coach Jim Champion, Assistant Offensive Line Coach Tom Lovat, Director of Player Personnel Burt Gustafson.

THIRD ROW: (L–R) Film Director Al Treml, 50 Rich Wingo, 88 Ron Cassidy, 65 Mike Wellman, 20 Wylie Turner, 51 Jim Gueno, 59 John Anderson, 25 Harlan Huckleby, 31 Gerry Ellis, 69 Leotis Harris, 68 Greg Koch, 82 Paul Coffman, 17 David Whitehurst, Assistant Trainer Jim Popp.

FOURTH ROW: (L–R) 38 Estus Hood, 46 Steve Luke, 60 Kurt Allerman, 64 Syd Kitson, 62 Buddy Aydelette, 40 Eddie Lee Ivery, 58 Bruce Beekley, 83 John Thompson, 19 Steve Pisarkiewicz, 66 Mike Lewis, 99 Charles Johnson, 63 Terry Jones.

FIFTH ROW: (L–R) 72 Kit Lathrop, 76 Tim Stokes, 67 Karl Swanke, 84 Fred Nixon, 52 George Cumby, 53 Mike Douglass, 80 James Lofton, 32 Steve Atkins, 77 Mike Butler, 90 Ezra Johnson, 78 Casey Merrill, 96 Troy Thomas, 22 Mark Lee.

BACK ROW: (L–R) 85 Bobby Kimball, 21 Mike Jolly, 10 Bill Troup, 37 Mark Murphy, 44 Vickey Ray Anderson, 43 Calvin Perkins, 18 Mark Miller, 61 Davie Simmons.

Opening the first half of a season with a losing record as the Packers of 1981 did was nothing out of the ordinary for a Bart Starr-coached team. Only once since 1975 had the team owned a winning mark at midseason.

Rallying, however, as the club did by winning six of its last eight games was something not seen in nearly a decade. Unfortunately, the revival fell one game short of a return to the playoffs. The Jets ended the Packers' season 28-3 at Shea Stadium in week 16.

The Falcons kicked off Green Bay's early-season troubles in week 2. Atlanta overcame a 17-0 deficit by exploding for 31 points in the fourth quarter. The Lambeau Field crowd, which had earlier bestowed a standing ovation upon its team at the end of the third quarter, went home stunned.

The Packers didn't recover until November.

Eddie Lee Ivery went down with a knee injury in the season opener. Tackle Mark Koncar briefly left the team after being criticized by Starr in a team meeting. San Francisco running back and former Packer Ricky Patton said he was told Starr had shown the Packers a bullwhip joking, "This is a real motivator," a comment that upset some black players.

By the end of October, almost 90 percent of respondents in a poll conducted by the Racine Journal Times said Starr should be replaced as head coach.

The acquisition of Chargers wide receiver John Jefferson on Sept. 17 was a positive. The Packers swapped their first-round draft for that of the Chargers in 1982 and also gave up a second-round pick in 1982 and a first-round choice in 1983. Green Bay sent receiver Aundra Thompson to San Diego as part of the trade.

After the Packers fell to 2-6, Starr appealed to the team's fans. He asked them to rekindle the enthusiasm that had taken a hit in the loss to the Falcons.

Starr got his wish. For the Seattle game on Nov. 1, the Green Bay Area Visitor and Convention Bureau, with the help of business and civic leaders, organized a Packer Support Sunday. Pre-game festivities included performances by a number of bands and cheerleaders. The Packers defeated the Seahawks 34-24.

Green Bay traveled to Chicago to open the season. Matt Suhey's fumble on the one-foot line with 32 seconds left and Johnnie Gray's recovery served up a 16-9 victory. The collapse against the Falcons followed.

"Obviously, this is a kick in the butt," center Larry McCarren said. "It's depressing as hell. I think we have enough character to (bounce back). But we've got to prove that."

A trip to the West Coast didn't help as the Rams won 35-23. The two teams combined for 25 penalties.

Jefferson made his Packers debut in Week 4. No. 83 caught seven passes for 121 yards but did not reach the end zone in a 30-13 loss to the Vikings.

Harlan Huckleby's first start as a professional was a busy one. The former Michigan Wolverine rushed 30 times for 88 yards in Green Bay's 27-14 win over the Giants.

Two weeks later, Dickey went out with a neck injury as San Francisco triumphed 13-3. His replacement, David Whitehurst, was booed by the County Stadium crowd, who wanted to see first-round pick Rich Campbell in action.

Dickey's neck injury didn't keep him from starting against the Lions. But his afternoon ended early after he was speared in the back by defensive end William Gay on a late hit. Gay was fined $2,000.

Green Bay's second-half turnaround began with a 34-24 win over the Seahawks. Gerry Ellis rushed for 127 yards and Whitehurst tossed three touchdown passes.

Close wins over the Giants (26-24) and Bears (21-17) pushed the Packers' record to 5-6 and kept them—and a half dozen other teams—in the running for a wildcard spot.

Tampa Bay halted Green Bay's winning streak 37-3 in Week 12. Whitehurst went out with a groin injury late in the first quarter and Campbell was intercepted four times in his first 30 pass attempts as a professional.

Dickey started the final four games. In Week 15, he completed 19 of 21 passes for 218 yards and five scores against the Saints.

Green Bay (8-7) needed to beat the Jets to make the playoffs. It didn't happen. New York, which also needed a win to reach the postseason, sacked Dickey nine times and dominated 28-3.

AGED TO NEAR PERFECTION

Jan Stenerud, a 14-year veteran, came to rescue the Packers kicking game late in 1980. In 1981, he turned in the best performance by a field goal kicker in team history.

Stenerud missed the mark just twice on field goals. He was wide left on a 46-yarder in the first Vikings game and missed right on a 28-yard attempt against the 49ers.

Overall, he nailed 22 of 24 field goals, for a then NFL-record 91.7 percent. His accuracy was a far cry from the 55 percent the Packers had managed the previous year.

On Nov. 8, Stenerud's 23-yarder beat the Giants 26-24.

Stenerud, born in Norway and a Kansas City Chief for 13 years, played with the Packers through 1983. He closed out his career with the Vikings.

Highest Field Goal Percentage, Season

Pct.	Player, Year	Made/Att.
91.7	Jan Stenerud, 1981	22/24
87.8	Ryan Longwell, 1998	29/33
86.8	Ryan Longwell, 2000	33/38
84.2	Max Zendejas, 1987	16/19

TEAM STATISTICS

	GB	OPP
First Downs	308	326
Rushing	104	140
Passing	174	168
Penalty	30	18
Rushes	478	546
Yards Gained	1,670	2,098
Average Gain	3.49	3.84
Average Yards per Game	104.4	131.1
Passes Attempted	514	505
Completed	286	284
% Completed	55.64	56.24
Total Yards Gained	3,576	3,353
Times Sacked	52	36
Yards Lost	387	266
Net Yards Gained	3,189	3,087
Yards Gained per Completion	12.50	11.81
Net Yards per Attempt	5.63	5.71
Average Net Yards per Game	199.3	192.9
Combined Net Yards Gained	4,859	5,185
Total Plays	1,044	1,087
Average Yards per Play	4.65	4.77
Average Net Yards per Game	303.7	324.1
Third Down Efficiency	72/210	103/230
Percentage	34.29	44.78
Fourth Down Efficiency	3/12	11/14
Percentage	25.00	78.57
Intercepted By	30	24
Yards Returned	495	475
Returned for TD	1	3
Punts	84	69
Yards Punted	3,330	2,738
Average Yards per Punt	39.64	39.68
Punt Returns	40	50
Yards Returned	306	511
Average Yards per Return	7.65	10.22
Returned for TD	1	0
Kickoff Returns	58	70
Yards Returned	1,066	1,183
Average Yards per Return	18.38	16.90
Returned for TD	0	0
Penalties	84	108
Yards Penalized	687	907
Fumbles	31	42
Lost	17	24
Own Recovered for Touchdown	0	0
Opponent's Recovered by	24	17
Opponent's Recovered for Touchdown	0	3
Total Points Scored	324	361
Total Touchdowns	37	45
Touchdowns Rushing	11	21
Touchdowns Passing	24	18
Touchdowns on Returns & Recoveries	2	6
Extra Points	36	43
Safeties	0	0
Field Goals Attempted	24	24
Field Goals Made	22	16
% Successful	91.67	66.67
Average Time of Possession	29:23	30:37

Regular Season   8-8-0

Date	GB		OPP	Att.
9/6	16	at Chicago Bears	9	(62,411)
9/13	17	Atlanta Falcons	31	(55,382)
9/20	23	at Los Angeles Rams	35	(61,286)
9/27	13	Minnesota Vikings (M)	30	(55,012)
10/4	27	at New York Giants	14	(73,684)
10/11	10	Tampa Bay Buccaneers	21	(55,264)
10/18	3	San Francisco 49ers (M)	13	(50,171)
10/25	27	at Detroit Lions	31	(76,063)
11/1	34	Seattle Seahawks	24	(54,099)
11/8	26	New York Giants (M)	24	(54,138)
11/15	21	Chicago Bears	17	(55,338)
11/22	3	at Tampa Bay Buccaneers	37	(63,251)
11/29	35	at Minnesota Vikings	23	(46,025)
12/6	31	Detroit Lions	17	(54,481)
12/13	35	at New Orleans Saints	7	(45,518)
12/20	3	at New York Jets	28	(56,340)

Score By Periods

	1	2	3	4	OT	Total
Packers	89	108	64	63	0	324
Opponents	51	127	81	102	0	361

INDIVIDUAL STATISTICS

Rushing

	Att	Yds	Avg	LG	TD
G. Ellis	196	860	4.4	29	4
Huckleby	139	381	2.7	22	5
Middleton	53	181	3.4	34	0
J. Jensen	27	79	2.9	15	0
Ivery	14	72	5.1	28	1
Whitehurst	15	51	3.4	15	1
J. Jefferson	2	22	11.0	15	0
Atkins	11	12	1.1	15	0
Dickey	19	6	0.3	13	0
Torkelson	1	4	4.0	4	0
Aundra Thompson	1	2	2.0	2	0
Packers	478	1,670	3.5	34	11
Opponents	546	2,098	3.8	t35	21

Receiving

	No	Yds	Avg	LG	TD
Lofton	71	1,294	18.2	t75	8
G. Ellis	65	499	7.7	t46	3
Coffman	55	687	12.5	29	4
J. Jefferson	39	632	16.2	41	4
Huckleby	27	221	8.2	t39	3
Middleton	12	86	7.2	27	1
J. Jensen	5	49	9.8	16	0
G. Lewis	3	31	10.3	15	0
Aundra Thompson	2	30	15.0	25	0
Nixon	2	27	13.5	19	0
Ivery	2	10	5.0	8	0
Cassidy	1	6	6.0	6	0
Atkins	1	2	2.0	2	0
Swanke	1	2	2.0	t2	1
Packers	286	3,576	12.5	t75	24
Opponents	284	3,353	11.8	t50	18

Passing

	Att	Com	Yds	Pct	TD	In	Tk/Yds	Rate
Dickey	354	204	2,593	57.6	17	15	40/298	79.0
Whitehurst	128	66	792	51.6	7	5	10/78	72.8
Campbell	30	15	168	50.0	0	4	2/11	27.5
G. Ellis	2	1	23	50.0	0	0	0/0	—
Packers	514	286	3,576	55.6	24	24	52/387	73.5
Opponents	505	284	3,353	56.2	18	30	36/266	63.7

Punting

	No	Yds	Avg	Net	TB	In20	LG	HB
Stachowicz	82	3,330	40.6	31.4	9	16	72	2
Packers	84	3,330	39.6	31.4	9	16	72	2
Opponents	69	2,738	39.7	33.8	5	14	58	0

Kickoff Returns

	No	Yds	Avg	LG	TD
M. Lee	14	270	19.3	31	0
Nixon	12	222	18.5	25	0
M.C. McCoy	11	221	20.1	36	0
Huckleby	7	134	19.1	27	0
Middleton	6	100	16.7	30	0
Coffman	3	77	25.7	52	0
J. Gray	2	24	12.0	19	0
J. Jensen	1	15	15.0	15	0
J. Jefferson	1	3	3.0	3	0
Braggs	1	0	0.0	0	0
Packers	58	1,066	18.4	52	0
Opponents	70	1,183	16.9	42	0

Punt Returns

	No	Yds	Avg	FC	LG	TD
M. Lee	20	187	9.4	1	t94	1
Nixon	15	118	7.9	4	17	0
Whitaker	2	1	0.5	1	1	0
Cassidy	2	0	0.0	4	0	0
J. Gray	1	0	0.0	1	0	0
Packers	40	306	7.7	10	t94	1
Opponents	50	511	10.2	4	56	0

Interceptions

	No	Yds	Avg	LG	TD
Harvey	6	217	36.2	53	0
M. Lee	6	50	8.3	25	0
Hood	3	59	19.7	t41	1
M. Murphy	3	57	19.0	50	0
Cumby	3	22	7.3	17	0
M. Douglass	3	20	6.7	13	0
J. Anderson	3	12	4.0	8	0
M.C. McCoy	2	20	10.0	16	0
Wingo	1	38	38.0	38	0
Packers	30	495	16.5	53	1
Opponents	24	475	19.8	t81	3

Scoring

	TDr	TDp	TDrt	PAT	FG	S	TP
Stenerud	0	0	0	35/36	22/24	0	101
Huckleby	5	3	0	0/0	0/0	0	48
Lofton	0	8	0	0/0	0/0	0	48
G. Ellis	4	3	0	0/0	0/0	0	42
Coffman	0	4	0	0/0	0/0	0	24
J. Jefferson	0	4	0	0/0	0/0	0	24
Hood	0	0	1	0/0	0/0	0	6
Ivery	1	0	0	0/0	0/0	0	6
M. Lee	0	0	1	0/0	0/0	0	6
Middleton	0	1	0	0/0	0/0	0	6
Swanke	0	1	0	0/0	0/0	0	6
Whitehurst	1	0	0	0/0	0/0	0	6
Wingo	0	0	0	0/0	0/0	0	1
Packers	11	24	2	36/37	22/24	0	324
Opponents	21	18	6	43/45	16/24	0	361

Fumbles

	Fum	Ow	Op	Yds	Tot
Allerman	0	0	1	0	1
J. Anderson	0	0	4	22	4
Ane	0	1	1	0	2
Atkins	1	0	0	0	1
Cassidy	1	0	0	0	0
Coffman	1	0	1	0	1
Cumby	0	0	2	70	2
Dickey	8	3	0	-36	3
M. Douglass	0	0	3	0	3
G. Ellis	5	1	0	0	1
Gofourth	0	1	0	0	1
J. Gray	0	0	1	0	1
L. Harris	0	0	1	0	1
Harvey	1	1	2	0	3
Huckleby	3	0	0	0	0
J. Jensen	1	0	0	0	0
T. Jones	0	0	1	0	1
Koncar	0	1	0	0	1
M. Lee	0	0	1	0	1
Lofton	0	1	0	0	1
McCarren	1	0	0	0	0
M.C. McCoy	1	1	0	0	1
C. Merrill	0	0	3	0	3
Middleton	2	1	0	0	1
M. Murphy	0	0	2	0	2
Nixon	2	0	0	0	0
Arland Thompson	0	1	0	0	1
Whitaker	0	0	1	0	1
Whitehurst	1	0	0	-2	1
Packers	31	14	24	54	38

NFL STANDINGS

National Conference

Eastern Division

	W	L	T	Pct	PF	PA
Dallas Cowboys	12	4	0	.750	367	277
Philadelphia Eagles	10	6	0	.625	368	221
New York Giants	9	7	0	.563	295	257
Washington Redskins	8	8	0	.500	347	349
St. Louis Cardinals	7	9	0	.438	315	408

Central Division

	W	L	T	Pct	PF	PA
Tampa Bay Buccaneers	9	7	0	.563	315	268
Detroit Lions	8	8	0	.500	397	322
Green Bay Packers	8	8	0	.500	324	361
Minnesota Vikings	7	9	0	.438	325	369
Chicago Bears	6	10	0	.375	253	324

Western Division

	W	L	T	Pct	PF	PA
San Francisco 49ers	13	3	0	.813	357	250
Atlanta Falcons	7	9	0	.438	426	355
Los Angeles Rams	6	10	0	.375	303	351
New Orleans Saints	4	12	0	.250	207	378

American Conference

Eastern Division

	W	L	T	Pct	PF	PA
Miami Dolphins	11	4	1	.719	345	275
New York Jets	10	5	1	.656	355	287
Buffalo Bills	10	6	0	.625	311	276
Baltimore Colts	2	14	0	.125	259	533
New England Patriots	2	14	0	.125	322	370

Central Division

	W	L	T	Pct	PF	PA
Cincinnati Bengals	12	4	0	.750	421	304
Pittsburgh Steelers	8	8	0	.500	356	297
Houston Oilers	7	9	0	.438	281	355
Cleveland Browns	5	11	0	.313	276	375

Western Division

	W	L	T	Pct	PF	PA
San Diego Chargers	10	6	0	.625	478	390
Denver Broncos	10	6	0	.625	321	289
Kansas City Chiefs	9	7	0	.563	343	290
Oakland Raiders	7	9	0	.438	273	343
Seattle Seahawks	6	10	0	.375	322	388

ROSTER

No	Name	Pos	Ht	Wt	DOB	College	G
60	Allerman, Kurt	LB	6-2	222	08/30/55	Penn State	16
59	Anderson, John	LB	6-3	221	02/14/56	Michigan	16
61	Ane, Charlie	C	6-1	237	08/12/52	Michigan State	16
32	Atkins, Steve	RB	6-0	216	06/22/56	Maryland	3
73	Braggs, Byron	NT	6-4	290	10/10/59	Alabama	16
77	Butler, Mike	DE	6-5	265	04/04/54	Kansas	16
19	Campbell, Rich	QB	6-4	224	12/22/58	California	2
88	Cassidy, Ron	WR	6-0	185	07/23/57	Utah State	11
82	Coffman, Paul	TE	6-3	218	03/29/56	Kansas State	16
52	Cumby, George	LB	6-0	215	07/05/56	Oklahoma	16
12	Dickey, Lynn	QB	6-4	220	10/19/49	Kansas State	13
53	Douglass, Mike	LB	6-0	224	03/15/55	San Diego State	16
31	Ellis, Gerry	FB	5-11	216	11/12/57	Missouri	15
57	Gofourth, Derrel	C	6-3	260	03/20/55	Oklahoma State	15
24	Gray, Johnnie	S	5-11	185	12/18/53	Cal State-Fullerton	9
69	Harris, Leotis	G	6-1	267	06/28/55	Arkansas	16
23	Harvey, Maurice	S	5-10	190	01/14/56	Ball State	16
38	Hood, Estus	CB	5-11	180	11/14/55	Illinois State	16
25	Huckleby, Harlan	HB	6-1	199	12/30/57	Michigan	16
74	Huffman, Tim	T	6-5	277	08/31/59	Notre Dame	4
40	Ivery, Eddie Lee	RB	6-1	210	07/30/57	Georgia Tech	1
83	Jefferson, John	WR	6-1	198	02/03/56	Arizona State	13
33	Jensen, Jim	RB	6-3	235	11/28/53	Iowa	15
90	Johnson, Ezra	DE	6-4	240	10/02/55	Morris Brown	16
63	Jones, Terry	NT	6-2	259	11/08/56	Alabama	16
64	Kitson, Syd	G	6-4	252	09/27/58	Wake Forest	11
68	Koch, Greg	T	6-4	265	06/14/55	Arkansas	16
79	Koncar, Mark	T	6-5	268	05/05/53	Colorado	14
22	Lee, Mark	CB	5-11	187	03/20/58	Washington	16
56	Lewis, Cliff	LB	6-1	226	11/09/59	Southern Mississippi	16
81	Lewis, Gary	TE	6-5	234	12/30/58	Texas-Arlington	16
80	Lofton, James	WR	6-3	187	07/05/56	Stanford	16
54	McCarren, Larry	C	6-3	248	11/09/51	Illinois	16
29	McCoy, Mike C.	CB	5-11	183	08/16/53	Colorado	16
78	Merrill, Casey	DE	6-4	255	07/16/57	California-Davis	16
34	Middleton, Terdell	HB	6-0	195	04/08/55	Memphis State	12
37	Murphy, Mark	S	6-2	199	04/22/58	West Liberty State	16
84	Nixon, Fred	WR	5-11	191	09/22/56	Oklahoma	8
72	Oats, Brad	T	6-6	270	09/30/53	BYU	1
47	Petway, David	S	6-2	207	10/17/55	Northern Illinois	5
51	Prather, Guy	LB	6-2	230	03/28/58	Grambling	16
55	Scott, Randy	LB	6-1	220	01/31/59	Alabama	16
16	Stachowicz, Ray	P	5-11	185	03/06/59	Michigan State	16
10	Stenerud, Jan	K	6-2	190	11/26/43	Montana State	16
76	Stokes, Tim	T	6-5	252	03/16/50	Oregon	7
67	Swanke, Karl	T	6-6	251	12/29/57	Boston College	4
71	Thompson, Arland	G	6-4	265	09/19/57	Baylor	10
89	Thompson, Aundra	WR	6-0	186	01/02/53	East Texas State	3
87	Thompson, John	TE	6-3	228	01/18/57	Utah State	2
26	Torkelson, Eric	RB	6-2	210	03/03/52	Connecticut	8
75	Turner, Rich	NT	6-2	260	02/14/59	Oklahoma	16
30	Whitaker, Bill	S	6-0	182	11/18/59	Missouri	16
17	Whitehurst, David	QB	6-2	204	04/27/55	Furman	2
20	William, Delvin	RB	6-0	195	04/17/51	Kansas	1
50	Wingo, Rich	LB	6-1	230	07/16/56	Alabama	16

DRAFT

Rnd	Name	Pos	Ht	Wt	College
1	Rich Campbell (6)	QB	6-4	224	California
2	Gary Lewis (35)	TE	6-5	234	Texas-Arlington
3	Ray Stachowicz (62)	P	5-11	185	Michigan State
4a	(Choice (90) traded to Redskins for Redskins' 4th round pick (105) and 5th round pick (117))				
4b	Richard Turner (105)	DT	6-2	260	Oklahoma
	(Choice from Redskins through the Rams in draft pick exchange)				
5	Byron Braggs (117)	DT	6-4	290	Alabama
	(Choice (117) to Rams for Mike Wellman, subsequently traded through a separate deal by the Rams to the Redskins, who turned choice back to Green Bay for position exchange)				
6	(Choice (145) to Giants for Randy Dean)				
7	Bill Whitaker (182)	DB	6-0	182	Missouri
8	Larry Werts (200)	LB	6-2	231	Jackson State
9	Tim Huffman (227)	T	6-5	277	Notre Dame
10	Nickie Hall (255)	QB	6-4	205	Tulane
11	Forrest Valora (282)	LB	6-0	236	Oklahoma
12	Cliff Lewis (311)	LB	6-1	226	Southern Mississippi

FRONT ROW: (L–R) 79 Mark Koncar, 57 Derrel Gofourth, 24 Johnnie Gray, 29 Mike C. McCoy, 83 John Jefferson, 84 Fred Nixon, 34 Terdell Middleton, 78 Casey Merrill, 33 Jim Jensen, 12 Lynn Dickey, 26 Eric Torkelson, 54 Larry McCarren.

SECOND ROW: (L–R) Equipment Assistant Dick Zoll, Equipment Manager Bob Noel, Director of Player Personnel Burt Gustafson, Defensive Backfield Coach Ross Fichtner, Special Teams Coach Dick Rehbein, Offensive Backfield Coach Zeke Bratkowski, Receivers Coach Lew Carpenter, Head Coach Bart Starr, Special Assistant Pete Kettela, Defensive Coordinator John Meyer, Linebackers Coach John Marshall, Offensive Line Coach Ernie McMillan, Defensive Line Coach Richard (Doc) Urich, Trainer Domenic Gentile.

THIRD ROW: (L–R) 67 Karl Swanke, 40 Eddie Lee Ivery, 62 Buddy Aydelette, 64 Syd Kitson, 37 Mark Murphy, 55 Randy Scott, 48 Willard Reaves, 60 Kurt Allerman, 59 John Anderson, 25 Harlan Huckleby, 75 Richard Turner, 98 Chris Godfrey, 23 Maurice Harvey, 63 Terry Jones.

FOURTH ROW: (L–R) Groundskeeper Earl DuChateau, 10 Jan Stenerud, 61 Charlie Ane, 74 Tim Huffman, 19 Rich Campbell, 16 Ray Stachowicz, 51 Guy Prather, 52 George Cumby, 80 James Lofton, 53 Mike Douglass, 69 Leotis Harris, 68 Greg Koch, 82 Paul Coffman, 17 David Whitehurst, 71 Arland Thompson, Assistant Trainer Jim Popp, 38 Estus Hood, Equipment Assistant Jack Noel.

BACK ROW: (L–R) Film Director Al Treml, 30 Bill Whitaker, 88 Ron Cassidy, 50 Rich Wingo, 58 Paul Rudzinski, 21 Mike Jolly, 56 Cliff Lewis, 11 Nickie Hall, 31 Gerry Ellis, 77 Mike Butler, 90 Ezra Johnson, 81 Gary Lewis, 76 Tim Stokes, 87 John Thompson, 22 Mark Lee, 73 Byron Braggs.

A 57-day long strike by NFL players shortened the 1982 season to nine games, but otherwise had minimal impact on the Packers, who romped to a 5-3-1 record and their first playoff berth in a decade.

The NFL Players Association called for a work stoppage on the Tuesday following the Packers-Giants Monday night game of Sept. 20. That a last-minute agreement might be reached faded as the stadium in East Rutherford went dark.

The players' union had a number of demands, including free agency, but the focus centered on revenue sharing. In March, the NFL announced a new $2.1 billion contract with CBS, NBC, and ABC. Led by executive director Ed Garvey and president Gene Upshaw, the players' union called for owners to set aside 55 percent of gross revenues from all sources for players' salaries.

For eight consecutive weekends, the nation went cold turkey. A pair of all-star games sponsored by the union were played the weekend of Oct. 17-18, but drew little interest. Aside from that, fans turned to Canada and the college ranks to get their fill of football.

Finally, on Nov. 16, the league and the NFLPA reached a tentative agreement. Even though the actual contract was not signed until Dec. 11, play resumed on Sunday, Nov. 21. The season was cut to nine games and the playoffs expanded to include 16 teams.

Green Bay was in good position to make a run. It had posted two come-from-behind wins prior to the strike and, unlike some teams, its players held informal practices at St. Norbert College in De Pere during the layoff.

In February, coach Bart Starr hired Bob Schnelker as offensive coordinator. Schnelker had held the same position with the Lions for four years and had been an assistant coach with the Packers from 1965 to 1971.

A month later, assistant coach Zeke Bratkowski left Green Bay to become offensive coordinator of the Colts. His departure left receivers coach Lew Carpenter and defensive coordinator John Meyer as the only two assistants who had been with Starr from the start in 1975.

The Packers Executive Committee elected Judge Robert J. Parins to the corporation's presidency. Parins, a Brown County judge since 1967 and a member of the team's board of directors since 1966, became the team's eighth president on May 3. He replaced Dominic Olejniczak, who had held the position since 1958.

Green Bay pulled off two comebacks to start the season. It overcame a 23-0 deficit to beat the Rams 35-23 in Milwaukee, then rallied past the Giants 27-19 after trailing by as many as 12 points.

When play resumed in November, Green Bay looked sharp in routing the Vikings 26-7 at County Stadium. Dickey threw for 244 yards and a touchdown as the Packers outgained Minnesota 359 yards to 184.

On Nov. 28, Phillip Epps caught his first two touchdown passes as a pro, but the Jets' Pat Leahy's kicked a 25-yard field goal late in the third quarter to sink Green Bay 15-13. In addition to the loss, Starr was also upset about a forearm shot that linebacker Stan Blinka delivered to the head of John Jefferson.

"That type of act is the act of a hoodlum and hoodlums shouldn't have the privilege of being in our game," said Starr of Blinka, who was penalized but not ejected.

Jefferson, his jaw intact, came back to catch three passes against Buffalo in a quagmire that bore only a slight resemblance to the field at County Stadium.

"It was murder," said Bills coach Chuck Knox, whose team came up short 33-21. "In this day and age you shouldn't have to play a game under these conditions."

A 20-point loss to the Lions and a tie with the winless Colts dropped Green Bay's record to 4-2-1.

The Packers rebounded to tear apart the Falcons 38-7. Lofton caught three passes for 146 yards and two touchdowns and Ivery rushed for two first-half scores.

"Yes, this is the biggest win we've had to date," said Starr of the game that clinched a date with the playoffs.

Green Bay closed the regular season in Detroit. Rookie tight end Rob Rubick scored on a 1-yard run with just under six minutes left as the Lions battled back 27-24.

"We're disappointed," Starr said. "I want to make that very clear. But the regular season is over. There is no need to spend too much time worrying about this one. It's gone."

THE GREATEST COMEBACK

"This is the greatest comeback I've ever witnessed," said head coach Bart Starr after his team erased a 23-point Rams lead to win 35-23 in the season opener. "I am at a loss for words to tell you how proud I am of this football team."

The 23 points were the most the Packers had ever overcome in a single game, surpassing the 18-point deficit against the Lions that Starr and his teammates surmounted in October 1965.

In rallying, the Packers shook off five first-half turnovers with a 234-yard second-half performance in which they held the Rams to half that total. Lynn Dickey threw a pair of touchdown passes to Paul Coffman and another to James Lofton. Eddie Lee Ivery gained 63 of his game-high 109 yards rushing and scored twice in the final two quarters.

Most points overcome to win game

Pts.	Opponent	Date	Result
23	Rams	9-12-82	Down 0-23, won 35-23
21	Saints	9-17-89	Down 0-21, won 35-34
18	Lions	10-17-65	Down 3-21, won 31-21

TEAM STATISTICS

	GB	OPP
First Downs	175	164
Rushing	59	58
Passing	97	96
Penalty	19	10
Rushes	283	275
Yards Gained	1,081	932
Average Gain	3.82	3.39
Average Yards per Game	120.1	103.6
Passes Attempted	267	327
Completed	143	177
% Completed	53.56	54.13
Total Yards Gained	2,068	1,950
Times Sacked	32	20
Yards Lost	239	175
Net Yards Gained	1,829	1,775
Yards Gained per Completion	14.46	11.02
Net Yards per Attempt	6.12	5.12
Average Net Yards per Game	203.2	197.2
Combined Net Yards Gained	2,910	2,707
Total Plays	582	622
Average Yards per Play	5.00	4.35
Average Net Yards per Game	323.3	300.8
Third Down Efficiency	50/121	53/138
Percentage	41.32	38.41
Fourth Down Efficiency	1/4	4/15
Percentage	25.00	26.67
Intercepted By	12	15
Yards Returned	174	146
Returned for TD	0	0
Punts	42	46
Yards Punted	1,687	1,925
Average Yards per Punt	40.17	41.85
Punt Returns	26	27
Yards Returned	198	286
Average Yards per Return	7.62	10.59
Returned for TD	0	0
Kickoff Returns	34	45
Yards Returned	664	875
Average Yards per Return	19.53	19.44
Returned for TD	0	1
Penalties	42	72
Yards Penalized	343	629
Fumbles	20	26
Lost	11	11
Own Recovered for Touchdown	2	0
Opponent's Recovered by	11	11
Opponent's Recovered for Touchdown	1	0
Total Points Scored	226	169
Total Touchdowns	27	19
Touchdowns Rushing	12	9
Touchdowns Passing	12	9
Touchdowns on Returns & Recoveries	3	1
Extra Points	25	17
Safeties	0	1
Field Goals Attempted	18	18
Field Goals Made	13	12
% Successful	72.22	66.67
Average Time of Possession	29:40	30:20

Regular Season 5-3-1

Date	GB		OPP	Att.
9/12	35	Los Angeles Rams (M)	23	(53,694)
9/20	27	at New York Giants	19	(68,405)
9/26	*	Miami Dolphins		
10/3	*	Philadelphia Eagles (M)		
10/10	*	at Chicago Bears		
10/17	*	Tampa Bay Buccaneers		
10/24	*	at Minnesota Vikings		
10/31	*	Chicago Bears		
11/7	*	at Tampa Bay Buccaneers		
11/14	**	at Detroit Lions		
11/21	26	Minnesota Vikings (M)	7	(44,681)
11/28	13	at New York Jets	15	(53,872)
12/5	33	Buffalo Bills (M)	21	(46,655)
12/12	10	Detroit Lions	30	(51,875)
12/19	20	at Baltimore Colts (OT)	20	(25,920)
12/26	38	at Atlanta Falcons	7	(50,245)
1/2	24	at Detroit Lions	27	(64,377)

* game cancelled because of players' strike
** game played on January 2

Postseason 1-1-0

1/8	41	St. Louis Cardinals	16	(54,282)
1/16	26	at Dallas Cowboys	37	(63,972)

Score By Periods

	1	2	3	4	OT	Total
Packers	26	65	64	71	0	226
Opponents	59	46	29	35	0	169

INDIVIDUAL STATISTICS

Rushing

	Att	Yds	Avg	LG	TD
Ivery	127	453	3.6	32	9
G. Ellis	62	228	3.7	29	1
Rodgers	46	175	3.8	13	1
Lofton	4	101	25.3	t83	1
Meade	14	42	3.0	19	0
J. Jensen	9	28	3.1	10	0
Dickey	13	19	1.5	11	0
Huckleby	4	19	4.8	7	0
J. Jefferson	2	16	8.0	11	0
Stachowicz	2	0	0.0	0	0
Packers	**283**	**1,081**	**3.8**	**t83**	**12**
Opponents	275	932	3.4	36	9

Receiving

	No	Yds	Avg	LG	TD
Lofton	35	696	19.9	t80	4
J. Jefferson	27	452	16.7	50	0
Coffman	23	287	12.5	42	2
G. Ellis	18	140	7.8	20	0
Ivery	16	186	11.6	62	1
Epps	10	226	22.6	50	2
Rodgers	3	23	7.7	16	0
G. Lewis	3	21	7.0	12	0
J. Jensen	3	18	6.0	11	1
Meade	3	-5	-1.7	-1	0
J. Thompson	2	24	12.0	t23	2
Packers	**143**	**2,068**	**14.5**	**t80**	**12**
Opponents	177	1,950	11.0	44	9

Passing

	Att	Com	Yds	Pct	TD	In	Tk/Yds	Rate
Dickey	218	124	1,790	56.9	12	14	25/196	75.3
Whitehurst	47	18	235	38.3	0	1	7/43	46.0
Lofton	1	1	43	100.0	0	0	0/0	—
Ivery	1	0	0	00.0	0	0	0/0	—
Packers	**267**	**143**	**2,068**	**53.6**	**12**	**15**	**32/239**	**70.6**
Opponents	327	177	1,950	44.1	9	12	20/175	65.9

Punting

	No	Yds	Avg	Net	TB	In20	LG	HB
Stachowicz	42	1,687	40.2	32.4	2	7	53	0
Packers	**42**	**1,687**	**40.2**	**32.4**	**2**	**7**	**53**	**0**
Opponents	46	1,925	41.8	35.8	4	11	55	0

Kickoff Returns

	No	Yds	Avg	LG	TD
Rodgers	20	436	21.8	76	0
Huckleby	5	89	17.8	26	0
A. Clark	4	75	18.8	30	0
Meade	2	31	15.5	17	0
J. Gray	2	29	14.5	25	0
C. Lewis	1	4	4.0	4	0
Packers	**34**	**664**	**19.5**	**76**	**0**
Opponents	45	875	19.4	t96	1

Punt Returns

	No	Yds	Avg	FC	LG	TD
Epps	20	150	7.5	5	35	0
J. Gray	6	48	8.0	1	15	0
Packers	**26**	**198**	**7.6**	**6**	**35**	**0**
Opponents	27	286	10.6	3	58	0

Interceptions

	No	Yds	Avg	LG	TD
J. Anderson	3	22	7.3	9	0
M. Douglass	2	55	27.5	30	0
Harvey	2	32	16.0	17	0
M. Lee	1	40	40.0	40	0
J. Gray	1	21	21.0	21	0
Cumby	1	4	4.0	4	0
Hood	1	0	0.0	0	0
Wingo	1	0	0.0	0	0
Packers	**12**	**174**	**14.5**	**40**	**0**
Opponents	15	146	9.7	36	0

Scoring

	TDr	TDp	TDrt	PAT	FG	S	TP
Stenerud	0	0	0	25/27	13/18	0	64
Ivery	9	1	0	0/0	0/0	0	60
Lofton	1	4	0	0/0	0/0	0	30
Rodgers	1	0	0	0/0	0/0	0	18
Coffman	0	2	0	0/0	0/0	0	12
Epps	0	2	0	0/0	0/0	0	12
J. Thompson	0	2	0	0/0	0/0	0	12
G. Ellis	1	0	0	0/0	0/0	0	6
Harvey	0	0	1	0/0	0/0	0	6
J. Jensen	0	1	0	0/0	0/0	0	6
Packers	**12**	**12**	**3**	**25/27**	**13/18**	**0**	**226**
Opponents	9	9	1	17/19	12/18	1	169

Fumbles

	Fum	Ow	Op	Yds	Tot
J. Anderson	0	0	2	0	2
R. Brown	0	0	1	0	1
M. Butler	0	0	1	0	1
Cumby	0	0	1	0	1
Dickey	5	2	0	-1	2
M. Douglass	0	0	1	6	1
G. Ellis	6	6	0	0	0
Epps	1	0	0	0	0
Gofourth	0	1	0	0	1
Harvey	0	0	3	25	3
Ivery	2	0	0	0	0
J. Jensen	1	0	0	0	0
M.C. McCoy	0	0	1	0	1
Prather	0	0	1	0	1
Rodgers	2	2	0	0	2
Rubens	1	0	0	-15	0
Stachowicz	0	0	0	-10	0
Stokes	0	1	0	0	1
Swanke	0	1	0	0	1
A. Clark	1	1	0	0	0
Packers	**20**	**8**	**11**	**5**	**19**

Quarterback Sacks

	No
E. Johnson	5.5
C. Merrill	4.0
M. Douglass	3.0
T. Jones	3.0
M. Butler	2.0
Harvey	1.0
Wingo	1.0
J. Anderson	0.5
Packers	**20.0**
Opponents	32.0

NFL STANDINGS

National Conference

	W	L	T	Pct	PF	PA
Washington Redskins	8	1	0	.889	190	128
Dallas Cowboys	6	3	0	.667	226	145
Green Bay Packers	**5**	**3**	**1**	**.611**	**226**	**169**
Minnesota Vikings	5	4	0	.556	187	198
Atlanta Falcons	5	4	0	.556	183	199
St. Louis Cardinals	5	4	0	.556	135	170
Tampa Bay Buccaneers	5	4	0	.556	158	178
Detroit Lions	4	5	0	.444	181	176
New Orleans Saints	4	5	0	.444	129	160
New York Giants	4	5	0	.444	164	160
San Francisco 49ers	3	6	0	.333	209	206
Chicago Bears	3	6	0	.333	141	174
Philadelphia Eagles	3	6	0	.333	191	195
Los Angeles Rams	2	7	0	.222	200	250

American Conference

	W	L	T	Pct	PF	PA
Los Angeles Raiders	8	1	0	.889	260	200
Miami Dolphins	7	2	0	.778	198	131
Cincinnati Bengals	7	2	0	.778	232	177
Pittsburgh Steelers	6	3	0	.667	204	146
San Diego Chargers	6	3	0	.667	288	221
New York Jets	6	3	0	.667	245	166
New England Patriots	5	4	0	.556	143	157
Cleveland Browns	4	5	0	.444	140	182
Buffalo Bills	4	5	0	.444	150	154
Seattle Seahawks	4	5	0	.444	127	147
Kansas City Chiefs	3	6	0	.333	176	184
Denver Broncos	2	7	0	.222	148	226
Houston Oilers	1	8	0	.111	136	245
Baltimore Colts	0	8	1	.056	113	236

ROSTER

No	Name	Pos	Ht	Wt	DOB	College	G
59	Anderson, John	LB	6-3	221	02/14/56	Michigan	9
73	Braggs, Byron	NT	6-4	290	10/10/59	Alabama	9
93	Brown, Robert	DE	6-2	238	05/21/60	Virginia Tech	9
77	Butler, Mike	DE	6-5	265	04/04/54	Kansas	9
19	Campbell, Rich	QB	6-4	224	12/22/58	California	1
34	Clark, Allan	RB	5-10	186	06/08/57	Northern Arizona	4
82	Coffman, Paul	TE	6-3	218	03/29/56	Kansas State	9
52	Cumby, George	LB	6-0	215	07/05/56	Oklahoma	9
12	Dickey, Lynn	QB	6-4	220	10/19/49	Kansas State	9
53	Douglass, Mike	LB	6-0	224	03/15/55	San Diego State	9
31	Ellis, Gerry	FB	5-11	216	11/12/57	Missouri	9
85	Epps, Phillip	WR	5-10	165	11/11/58	TCU	9
57	Gofourth, Derrel	C	6-3	260	03/20/55	Oklahoma State	9
24	Gray, Johnnie	S	5-11	185	12/18/53	Cal State-Fullerton	9
65	Hallstrom, Ron	G	6-6	286	06/11/59	Iowa	6
69	Harris, Leotis	G	6-1	267	06/28/55	Arkansas	9
23	Harvey, Maurice	S	5-10	190	01/14/56	Ball State	9
38	Hood, Estus	CB	5-11	180	11/14/55	Illinois State	9
25	Huckleby, Harlan	HB	6-1	199	12/30/57	Michigan	9
74	Huffman, Tim	T	6-5	277	08/31/59	Notre Dame	9
40	Ivery, Eddie Lee	RB	6-1	210	07/30/57	Georgia Tech	9
83	Jefferson, John	WR	6-1	198	02/03/56	Arizona State	8
33	Jensen, Jim	RB	6-3	235	11/28/53	Iowa	8
90	Johnson, Ezra	DE	6-4	240	10/02/55	Morris Brown	9
21	Jolly, Mike	S	6-3	185	03/19/58	Michigan	7
63	Jones, Terry	NT	6-2	259	11/08/56	Alabama	9
68	Koch, Greg	T	6-4	265	06/14/55	Arkansas	9
60	Laslavic, Jim	LB	6-2	236	10/24/51	Penn State	6
22	Lee, Mark	CB	5-11	187	03/20/58	Washington	9
56	Lewis, Cliff	LB	6-1	226	11/09/59	Southern Mississippi	9
81	Lewis, Gary	TE	6-5	234	12/30/58	Texas-Arlington	9
80	Lofton, James	WR	6-3	187	07/05/56	Stanford	9
54	McCarren, Larry	C	6-3	248	11/09/51	Illinois	9
29	McCoy, Mike C.	CB	5-11	183	08/16/53	Colorado	9
39	Meade, Mike	RB	5-10	228	02/12/60	Penn State	2
78	Merrill, Casey	DE	6-4	255	07/16/57	California-Davis	9
62	Merrill, Mark	LB	6-3	234	05/05/55	Minnesota	2
37	Murphy, Mark	S	6-2	199	04/22/58	West Liberty State	9
51	Prather, Guy	LB	6-2	230	03/28/58	Grambling	9
35	Rodgers, Del	RB	5-10	197	06/22/60	Utah	9
58	Rubens, Larry	C	6-1	253	01/25/59	Montana State	9
55	Scott, Randy	LB	6-1	220	01/31/59	Alabama	9
16	Stachowicz, Ray	P	5-11	185	03/06/59	Michigan State	9
10	Stenerud, Jan	K	6-2	190	11/26/43	Montana State	9
76	Stokes, Tim	T	6-5	252	03/16/50	Oregon	9
67	Swanke, Karl	T	6-6	251	12/29/57	Boston College	8
87	Thompson, John	TE	6-3	228	01/18/57	Utah State	9
75	Turner, Rich	NT	6-2	260	02/14/59	Oklahoma	9
30	Whitaker, Bill	S	6-0	182	11/18/59	Missouri	9
17	Whitehurst, David	QB	6-2	204	04/27/55	Furman	3
50	Wingo, Rich	LB	6-1	230	07/16/56	Alabama	5

DRAFT

Rnd	Name	Pos	Ht	Wt	College
1a	(Choice (13) to Chargers in John Jefferson trade)				
1b	Ron Hallstrom (22)	G	6-6	286	Iowa
	(Choice from Chargers in John Jefferson trade)				
2	(Choice (40) to Chargers in John Jefferson trade)				
3	Del Rodgers (71)	RB	5-10	197	Utah
4	Robert Brown (98)	LB	6-2	238	Virginia Tech
5	Mike Meade (126)	RB	5-10	228	Penn State
6	Chet Parlavecchio (152)	LB	6-2	225	Penn State
7	Joe Whitley (183)	DB	5-11	177	Texas-El Paso
8	Thomas Boyd (210)	LB	6-2	210	Alabama
9	Charles Riggins (237)	DE	6-3	245	Bethune-Cookman
10	Eddie Garcia (264)	K	5-8	188	SMU
11	John Macaulay (294)	C	6-3	254	Stanford
12	Phillip Epps (321)	WR	5-10	165	TCU

1982 GREEN BAY PACKERS

FRONT ROW: (L-R) 24 Johnnie Gray, 29 Mike C. McCoy, 34 Allan Clark, 22 Mark Lee, 85 Phillip Epps, 31 Gerry Ellis, 12 Lynn Dickey, 30 Bill Whitaker, 78 Casey Merrill, 54 Larry McCarren.

SECOND ROW: (L-R) Administrative Assistant Paul Rudzinski, Defensive Secondary Coach Ross Fichtner, Special Teams Coach Dick Rehbein, Offensive Backfield Coach Pete Kettela, Receivers Coach Lew Carpenter, Offensive Line Assistant Bill Meyers, Head Coach Bart Starr, Offensive Coordinator Bob Schnelker, Offensive Line Coach Ernie McMillan, Linebackers Coach John Marshall, Defensive Line Coach Richard (Doc) Urich, Defensive Coordinator John Meyer, Director of Pro Personnel Burt Gustafson.

THIRD ROW: (L-R) 51 Guy Prather, 23 Maurice Harvey, 35 Del Rodgers, 33 Jim Jensen, 25 Harlan Huckleby, 80 James Lofton, 53 Mike Douglass, 40 Eddie Lee Ivery, 79 Angelo Fields, 87 John Thompson, 63 Terry Jones.

FOURTH ROW: (L-R) 39 Mike Meade, 57 Derrel Gofourth, 58 Larry Rubens, 62 Mark Merrill, 60 Jim Laslavic, 59 John Anderson, 55 Randy Scott, 50 Rich Wingo, 16 Ray Stachowicz, 10 Jan Stenerud.

FIFTH ROW: (L-R) 38 Estus Hood, 56 Cliff Lewis, 65 Ron Hallstrom, 19 Rich Campbell, 67 Karl Swanke, 76 Tim Stokes, 69 Leotis Harris, 68 Greg Koch, 82 Paul Coffman, 17 David Whitehurst.

SIXTH ROW: (L-R) 74 Tim Huffman, 93 Robert Brown, 90 Ezra Johnson, 77 Mike Butler, 81 Gary Lewis, 75 Richard Turner, 37 Mark Murphy, 21 Mike Jolly, 73 Byron Braggs.

BACK ROW: (L-R) Film Director Al Treml, Team Physician Dr. Eugene Brusky, Equipment Assistant Dick Zoll, Head Trainer Domenic Gentile, Equipment Manager Bob Noel, Groundskeeper Earl DuChateau, Assistant Film Director Bob Eckberg, Equipment Assistant Jack Noel, Assistant Trainer Jim Popp.

The Packers offense in 1983 was high octane, able to explode at a moment's notice. Unfortunately, the team's defense misfired to such a degree that it sometimes hindered Green Bay more than it did the opposition.

Lynn Dickey, James Lofton, John Jefferson, Paul Coffman, and Gerry Ellis were key cogs on a team that tallied 6,172 yards, 52 touchdowns and 429 points. Dickey set a franchise record with 4,458 yards passing, Lofton averaged a league-leading 22.4 yards per reception, Coffman snared a team-best 11 touchdown passes, and Ellis became the first Packer to surpass 500 yards in a single season in both rushing and receiving.

The numbers were just as scary on defense: 6,403 yards, 50 touchdowns and 439 points. It all added up to an 8-8 season and numerous high-scoring games.

Green Bay gained more than 300 yards in all but three games. It amassed more than 400 yards on six occasions, with a season-high 519 against Tampa Bay on Oct. 2.

Conversely, the team gave up more than 300 yards 14 times and more than 400 yards eight times. The Redskins did the most damage with 552 yards on Oct. 17.

With the exception of Mike Butler, who jumped to the USFL, Green Bay opened with the same starters on defense as it had at the close of 1982. In 1983, 22 players started at least one game on defense, nine on the line alone. Only four—Ezra Johnson, John Anderson, Mark Lee and Johnnie Gray—started all 16 games on defense.

Injuries didn't help. Linebacker Randy Scott (knee) and Rich Turner (knee) both missed 10 games, cornerback Mike McCoy (torn quadriceps muscle) missed seven, and Terry Jones (Achilles tendon) played in only the opener. Jones was the starting nose tackle and Turner his backup.

In addition, starting defensive back Maurice Harvey was released on Sept. 30 for what Starr said was "a lousy attitude" and linebacker Mike Douglass was suspended for the first Bears game because he walked out of a meeting and missed a practice.

Eddie Lee Ivery missed the final eight games after he took a leave of absence to battle chemical dependency.

In February, Bart Starr was given a one-year contract extension to Jan. 31, 1985. Though he was hoping for more, Starr said "It will allow us to continue our program."

Starr's ninth year began in stunning fashion at Houston. Despite suffering from a severe headache that forced him to the sidelines in the fourth quarter, Dickey threw for 333 yards and five touchdowns. He completed his first 18 passes in a row. David Whitehurst replaced him and Jan Stenerud won the game 41-38 in overtime with a 42-yard field goal.

In Week 2, Dickey and James Lofton hooked up for three touchdowns, but the Steelers rushed for 285 yards in beating Green Bay 25-21 at Lambeau Field.

Eric Dickerson's last-minute fumble allowed the Packers to slip past the Rams 27-24 in Week 3. Byron Braggs recovered the rookie running back's fumble at the Rams' 19-yard line to set up Stenerud's game-winning field goal.

A week later, the Giants embarrassed Green Bay 27-3 on Monday night. Packers' fumbles, penalties, and an interception helped the Giants to a 17-point third quarter.

In Week 5, Green Bay crushed Tampa Bay 55-14. The Packers scored seven first-half touchdowns.

Detroit pounded the Packers 38-14 the following Sunday even without star running back Billy Sims.

On Oct. 17, Green Bay and Washington met in a shootout. The Packers won 48-47 after Mark Moseley's 39-yard field goal sailed wide right as time expired. The two teams combined for 1,025 yards and 95 points in the highest scoring "Monday Night Football" game ever.

After falling to the Vikings and Bengals, the Packers beat Cleveland and Minnesota. Dickey directed a late, 12-play touchdown drive that finished off the Vikings 29-21.

Ray Nitschke's No. 66 jersey was formally retired on Dec. 4 as the Packers beat the Bears 31-28. The Packers then edged Tampa Bay 12-9 to improve to 8-7.

With a playoff berth on the line in Chicago, Starr and the Packers stumbled. With his team ahead 21-20 and the Bears driving for a last-minute field goal, Starr declined to use his remaining timeouts. As a result, the Packers had only 10 seconds left—instead of a minute or more—to attempt to retake the lead after Bob Thomas kicked a 22-yard field goal to put the Bears ahead 23-21.

Starr was fired the next day.

THE 400 CLUB

Only the Baltimore Colts of 1981 kept the Packers from the NFL record for most yards given up in a single season.

Green Bay surrendered 6,403 yards for an average of just over 400 yards per game. Two years earlier, the Colts were overrun for 6,793 yards.

From mid-October to mid-November, the defense was at its most porous. Five clubs—the Redskins, Vikings, Bengals, Browns, and Vikings a second time—each gained more than 400 yards at the expense of the Packers. That's the only time Green Bay has given up 400 or more yards in five straight games.

Amazingly, the Green and Gold won three times in that span.

Most Yards Given Up On Average, Season

Avg.	Year	Yards/Games	Record
400.2	1983	6,403/16	8-8
392.5	1956	4,710/12	4-8
391.9	1950	4,703/12	3-9
390.6	1951	4,687/12	3-9

TEAM STATISTICS

	GB	OPP
First Downs	340	366
Rushing	99	171
Passing	214	187
Penalty	27	8
Rushes	439	597
Yards Gained	1,807	2,641
Average Gain	4.12	4.42
Average Yards per Game	112.9	165.1
Passes Attempted	526	518
Completed	311	300
% Completed	59.13	57.92
Total Yards Gained	4,688	4,033
Times Sacked	42	41
Yards Lost	323	271
Net Yards Gained	4,365	3,762
Yards Gained per Completion	15.07	13.44
Net Yards per Attempt	7.68	6.73
Average Net Yards per Game	272.8	235.1
Combined Net Yards Gained	6,172	6,403
Total Plays	1,007	1,156
Average Yards per Play	6.13	5.54
Average Net Yards per Game	385.8	400.2
Third Down Efficiency	72/189	111/239
Percentage	38.10	46.44
Fourth Down Efficiency	2/8	5/10
Percentage	25.00	50.00
Intercepted By	19	32
Yards Returned	227	337
Returned for TD	1	4
Punts	70	78
Yards Punted	2,869	3,052
Average Yards per Punt	40.99	39.13
Punt Returns	41	43
Yards Returned	329	384
Average Yards per Return	8.02	8.93
Returned for TD	1	1
Kickoff Returns	79	78
Yards Returned	1,339	1,429
Average Yards per Return	16.95	18.32
Returned for TD	0	0
Penalties	80	110
Yards Penalized	648	965
Fumbles	37	32
Lost	18	12
Own Recovered for Touchdown	0	1
Opponent's Recovered by	12	18
Opponent's Recovered for Touchdown	2	1
Total Points Scored	429	439
Total Touchdowns	52	55
Touchdowns Rushing	15	28
Touchdowns Passing	33	20
Touchdowns on Returns & Recoveries	4	7
Extra Points	52	50
Safeties	1	1
Field Goals Attempted	26	29
Field Goals Made	21	19
% Successful	80.77	65.52
Average Time of Possession	27:01	32:59

Regular Season 8-8-0

Date	GB		OPP	Att.
9/4	41	at Houston Oilers (OT)	38	(44,073)
9/11	21	Pittsburgh Steelers	25	(55,154)
9/18	27	Los Angeles Rams (M)	24	(54,037)
9/26	3	at New York Giants	27	(75,308)
10/2	55	Tampa Bay Buccaneers	14	(54,272)
10/9	14	at Detroit Lions	38	(67,738)
10/17	48	Washington Redskins	47	(55,255)
10/23	17	Minnesota Vikings (OT)	20	(55,236)
10/30	14	at Cincinnati Bengals	34	(53,349)
11/6	35	Cleveland Browns (M)	21	(54,089)
11/13	29	at Minnesota Vikings	21	(60,113)
11/20	20	Detroit Lions (M) (OT)	23	(50,050)
11/27	41	at Atlanta Falcons (OT)	47	(35,688)
12/4	31	Chicago Bears	28	(51,147)
12/12	12	at Tampa Bay Buccaneers (OT) 9		(50,763)
12/18	21	at Chicago Bears	23	(35,807)

Score By Periods

	1	2	3	4	OT	Total
Packers	120	147	44	112	6	429
Opponents	74	105	109	139	12	439

INDIVIDUAL STATISTICS

Rushing

	Att	Yds	Avg	LG	TD
G. Ellis	141	696	4.9	71	4
Ivery	86	340	4.0	21	2
J. Clark	71	328	4.6	42	0
Meade	55	201	3.7	15	1
Huckleby	50	182	3.6	20	4
Lofton	9	36	4.0	13	0
G. Lewis	4	16	4.0	11	1
Dickey	21	12	0.6	4	3
Whitehurst	2	-4	-2.0	0	0
Packers	**439**	**1,807**	**4.1**	**71**	**15**
Opponents	597	2,641	4.4	43	28

Receiving

	No	Yds	Avg	LG	TD
Lofton	58	1,300	22.4	t74	8
J. Jefferson	57	830	14.6	36	7
Coffman	54	814	15.1	74	11
G. Ellis	52	603	11.6	56	2
Epps	18	313	17.4	45	0
J. Clark	18	279	15.5	t75	1
Ivery	16	139	8.7	17	1
Meade	16	110	6.9	t31	2
G. Lewis	11	204	18.5	49	1
Huckleby	10	87	8.7	14	0
Kitson	1	9	9.0	9	0
Packers	**311**	**4,688**	**15.1**	**t75**	**33**
Opponents	300	4,033	13.4	t87	20

Passing

	Att	Com	Yds	Pct	TD	In	Tk/Yds	Rate
Dickey	484	289	4,458	59.7	32	29	40/307	87.3
Whitehurst	35	18	149	51.4	0	2	2/16	38.9
Ivery	2	2	50	100.0	0	0	0/0	—
G. Ellis	5	2	31	40.0	1	1	0/0	—
Packers	**526**	**311**	**4,688**	**59.1**	**33**	**32**	**42/323**	**84.1**
Opponents	518	300	4,033	57.9	20	19	41/271	80.4

Punting

	No	Yds	Avg	Net	TB	In20	LG	HB
Scribner	69	2,869	41.6	33.5	7	11	70	1
Packers	**70**	**2,869**	**41.0**	**33.5**	**7**	**11**	**70**	**1**
Opponents	78	3,052	39.1	33.1	7	19	59	0

Kickoff Returns

	No	Yds	Avg	LG	TD
Huckleby	41	757	18.5	57	0
T. Lewis	20	358	17.9	30	0
J. Gray	11	178	16.2	26	0
Winters	3	28	9.3	12	0
Ivery	1	17	17.0	17	0
Drechsler	1	1	1.0	1	0
Kitson	1	0	0.0	0	0
M. Lee	1	0	0.0	0	0
Packers	**79**	**1,339**	**16.9**	**57**	**0**
Opponents	78	1,429	18.3	41	0

Punt Returns

	No	Yds	Avg	FC	LG	TD
Epps	36	324	9.0	13	t90	1
J. Gray	2	9	4.5	0	5	0
Hood	1	0	0.0	0	0	0
C. Lewis	1	0	0.0	0	0	0
M. Lee	1	-4	-4.0	0	-4	0
Packers	**41**	**329**	**8.0**	**13**	**t90**	**1**
Opponents	43	384	8.9	8	t59	1

Interceptions

	No	Yds	Avg	LG	TD
T. Lewis	5	111	22.2	46	0
J. Anderson	5	54	10.8	t27	1
M. Lee	4	23	5.8	15	0
J. Gray	2	5	2.5	5	0
Laughlin	1	22	22.0	22	0
R. Scott	1	12	12.0	12	0
Jolly	1	0	0.0	0	0
Packers	**19**	**227**	**11.9**	**46**	**1**
Opponents	32	337	10.5	58	4

Scoring

	TDr	TDp	TDrt	PAT	FG	S	TP
Stenerud	0	0	0	52/52	21/26	0	115
Coffman	0	11	0	0/0	0/0	0	66
Lofton	0	8	0	0/0	0/0	0	48
J. Jefferson	0	7	0	0/0	0/0	0	42
G. Ellis	4	2	0	0/0	0/0	0	36
Huckleby	4	0	0	0/0	0/0	0	24
Dickey	3	0	0	0/0	0/0	0	18
Ivery	2	1	0	0/0	0/0	0	18
Meade	1	2	0	0/0	0/0	0	18
M. Douglass	0	0	0	0/0	0/0	0	12
G. Lewis	1	1	0	0/0	0/0	0	12
J. Anderson	0	0	1	0/0	0/0	0	6
J. Clark	0	1	0	0/0	0/0	0	6
Epps	0	0	1	0/0	0/0	0	6
G. Boyd	0	0	0	0/0	0/0	1	2
Packers	**15**	**33**	**4**	**52/52**	**21/26**	**1**	**429**
Opponents	28	20	7	50/55	19/29	1	439

Fumbles

	Fum	Ow	Op	Yds	Tot
J. Anderson	0	0	1	0	1
Braggs	0	0	2	0	2
J. Clark	2	1	0	0	0
Coffman	1	0	0	0	0
Dickey	9	6	0	0	6
M. Douglass	0	0	4	57	4
G. Ellis	7	1	0	0	1
Epps	2	0	0	0	0
J. Gray	2	1	1	0	1
Huckleby	4	1	0	0	1
Ivery	1	0	0	0	0
J. Jefferson	1	1	0	0	0
E. Johnson	0	0	2	0	0
M. Lee	0	0	1	15	1
G. Lewis	1	0	0	0	0
T. Lewis	3	1	0	0	1
Meade	2	1	0	0	1
M. Murphy	0	0	1	0	1
Rubens	0	0	1	0	1
Swanke	0	0	0	0	2
Whitehurst	2	1	0	0	1
Packers	**37**	**16**	**12**	**72**	**28**

Quarterback Sacks

	No
E. Johnson	14.5
Braggs	5.5
M. Douglass	5.5
J. Anderson	4.5
C. Johnson	3.5
G. Boyd	2.0
Cumby	2.0
C. Lewis	2.0
R. Turner	1.0
Spears	0.5
Packers	**41.0**
Opponents	42.0

NFL STANDINGS

National Conference

Eastern Division

	W	L	T	Pct	PF	PA
Washington Redskins	14	2	0	.875	541	332
Dallas Cowboys	12	4	0	.750	479	360
St. Louis Cardinals	8	7	1	.531	374	428
Philadelphia Eagles	5	11	0	.313	233	322
New York Giants	3	12	1	.219	267	347

Central Division

	W	L	T	Pct	PF	PA
Detroit Lions	9	7	0	.563	347	286
Green Bay Packers	8	8	0	.500	429	439
Chicago Bears	8	8	0	.500	311	301
Minnesota Vikings	8	8	0	.500	316	348
Tampa Bay Buccaneers	2	14	0	.125	241	380

Western Division

	W	L	T	Pct	PF	PA
San Francisco 49ers	10	6	0	.625	432	293
Los Angeles Rams	9	7	0	.563	361	344
New Orleans Saints	8	8	0	.500	319	337
Atlanta Falcons	7	9	0	.438	370	389

American Conference

Eastern Division

	W	L	T	Pct	PF	PA
Miami Dolphins	12	4	0	.750	389	250
New England Patriots	8	8	0	.500	274	289
Buffalo Bills	8	8	0	.500	283	351
Baltimore Colts	7	9	0	.438	264	354
New York Jets	7	9	0	.438	313	331

Central Division

	W	L	T	Pct	PF	PA
Pittsburgh Steelers	10	6	0	.625	355	303
Cleveland Browns	9	7	0	.563	356	342
Cincinnati Bengals	7	9	0	.438	346	302
Houston Oilers	2	14	0	.125	288	460

Western Division

	W	L	T	Pct	PF	PA
Los Angeles Raiders	12	4	0	.750	442	338
Seattle Seahawks	9	7	0	.563	403	397
Denver Broncos	9	7	0	.563	302	327
San Diego Chargers	6	10	0	.375	358	462
Kansas City Chiefs	6	10	0	.375	386	367

1983

ROSTER

No	Name	Pos	Ht	Wt	DOB	College	G
59	Anderson, John	LB	6-3	229	02/14/56	Michigan	16
72	Boyd, Greg	DE	6-6	280	09/15/53	San Diego State	12
73	Braggs, Byron	NT	6-4	270	10/10/59	Alabama	16
93	Brown, Robert	DE	6-2	250	05/21/60	Virginia Tech	1
19	Campbell, Rich	QB	6-4	219	12/22/58	California	1
88	Cassidy, Ron	WR	6-0	180	07/23/57	Utah State	16
33	Clark, Jessie	FB	6-0	233	01/03/60	Arkansas	16
82	Coffman, Paul	TE	6-3	225	03/29/56	Kansas State	16
52	Cumby, George	LB	6-0	224	07/05/56	Oklahoma	15
57	Curcio, Mike	LB	6-1	232	01/24/57	Temple	14
12	Dickey, Lynn	QB	6-4	203	10/19/49	Kansas State	16
53	Douglass, Mike	LB	6-0	214	03/15/55	San Diego State	15
61	Drechsler, Dave	G	6-3	264	07/18/60	North Carolina	16
31	Ellis, Gerry	FB	5-11	225	11/12/57	Missouri	15
85	Epps, Phillip	WR	5-10	165	11/11/58	TCU	16
11	Garcia, Eddie	K	5-8	178	04/15/59	SMU	12
77	Getty, Charlie	T	6-4	270	07/24/52	Penn State	16
24	Gray, Johnnie	S	5-11	202	12/18/53	Cal State-Fullerton	16
65	Hallstrom, Ron	G	6-6	283	06/11/59	Iowa	16
69	Harris, Leotis	G	6-1	265	06/28/55	Arkansas	6
23	Harvey, Maurice	S	5-10	190	01/14/56	Ball State	4
38	Hood, Estus	CB	5-11	189	11/14/55	Illinois State	16
25	Huckleby, Harlan	HB	6-1	201	12/30/57	Michigan	16
74	Huffman, Tim	T	6-5	282	08/31/59	Notre Dame	15
40	Ivery, Eddie Lee	RB	6-1	214	07/30/57	Georgia Tech	8
83	Jefferson, John	WR	6-1	204	02/03/56	Arizona State	16
99	Johnson, Charles	NT	6-2	265	06/29/57	Maryland	15
90	Johnson, Ezra	DE	6-4	259	10/02/55	Morris Brown	16
21	Jolly, Mike	S	6-3	185	03/19/58	Michigan	12
63	Jones, Terry	NT	6-2	253	11/08/56	Alabama	1
64	Kitson, Syd	G	6-4	264	09/27/58	Wake Forest	14
68	Koch, Greg	T	6-4	276	06/14/55	Arkansas	15
62	Laughlin, Jim	LB	6-1	222	07/05/58	Ohio State	15
22	Lee, Mark	CB	5-11	188	03/20/58	Washington	16
56	Lewis, Cliff	LB	6-1	224	11/09/59	Southern Mississippi	16
81	Lewis, Gary	TE	6-5	234	12/30/58	Texas-Arlington	16
26	Lewis, Tim	CB	5-11	191	12/18/61	Pittsburgh	16
80	Lofton, James	WR	6-3	197	07/05/56	Stanford	16
54	McCarren, Larry	C	6-3	251	11/09/51	Illinois	16
29	McCoy, Mike C.	CB	5-11	190	08/16/53	Colorado	9
39	Meade, Mike	RB	5-10	224	02/12/60	Penn State	16
78	Merrill, Casey	DE	6-4	255	07/16/57	California-Davis	5
37	Murphy, Mark	S	6-2	201	04/22/58	West Liberty State	16
44	O'Steen, Dwayne	CB	6-1	195	12/20/54	San Jose State	7
57	Parlavecchio, Chet	LB	6-2	225	02/14/60	Penn State	3
51	Prather, Guy	LB	6-2	229	03/28/58	Grambling	16
58	Rubens, Larry	C	6-1	250	01/25/59	Montana State	16
70	Sams, Ron	G	6-3	269	04/12/61	Pittsburgh	5
55	Scott, Randy	LB	6-1	222	01/31/59	Alabama	6
13	Scribner, Bucky	P	6-0	202	07/11/60	Kansas	16
91	Skaugstad, Daryle	NT	6-5	268	04/08/57	California	9
79	Spears, Ron	DE	6-6	255	11/23/59	San Diego State	13
10	Stenerud, Jan	K	6-2	190	11/26/43	Montana State	16
67	Swanke, Karl	T	6-6	262	12/29/57	Boston College	16
75	Turner, Rich	NT	6-2	261	02/14/59	Oklahoma	6
17	Whitehurst, David	QB	6-2	205	04/27/55	Furman	4
50	Wingo, Rich	LB	6-1	227	07/16/56	Alabama	16
20	Winters, Chet	RB	5-11	204	10/22/61	Oklahoma	4

DRAFT

Rnd	Name	Pos	Ht	Wt	College
1a	Tim Lewis (11)	DB	5-11	192	Pittsburgh
	(Choice from Saints for Bruce Clark)				
1b	(Choice (20) to Chargers in John Jefferson trade)				
2	Dave Drechsler (48)	G	6-3	264	North Carolina
3	(Choice (76) to Oilers for Angelo Fields)				
4	Mike Miller (104)	WR	5-11	182	Tennessee
5	Bryan Thomas (132)	RB	5-10	198	Pittsburgh
6	Ron Sams (160)	G	6-3	265	Pittsburgh
7	Jessie Clark (188)	RB	6-0	226	Arkansas
8	Carlton Briscoe (216)	DB	6-0	180	McNeese State
9	Robin Ham (243)	C	6-2	252	West Texas State
10a	Byron Williams (253)	WR	6-1	180	Texas-Arlington
	(Choice from Oilers in Mark Koncar trade)				
10b	Jimmy Thomas (271)	DB	6-3	190	Indiana
11	Bucky Scribner (299)	P	6-0	203	Kansas
12	John Harvey (327)	LB	6-2	236	USC

1983 GREEN BAY PACKERS

FRONT ROW: (L-R) 29 Mike C. McCoy, 88 Ron Cassidy, 19 Rich Campbell, 12 Lynn Dickey, 85 Phillip Epps, 31 Gerry Ellis, 10 Jan Stenerud, 59 John Anderson, 38 Estus Hood, 54 Larry McCarren.
SECOND ROW: (L-R) 79 Ron Spears, 91 Daryle Skaugstad, 65 Ron Hallstrom, 74 Tim Huffman, 81 Gary Lewis, 75 Rich Turner, 26 Tim Lewis, 83 John Jefferson, 22 Mark Lee, 35 Del Rodgers, 40 Eddie Lee Ivery, 69 Leotis Harris.
THIRD ROW: (L-R) 51 Guy Prather, 57 Mike Curcio, 93 Robert Brown, 77 Charlie Getty, 80 James Lofton, 53 Mike Douglass, 67 Karl Swanke, 64 Syd Kitson, 21 Mike Jolly, 37 Mark Murphy, 55 Randy Scott, 63 Terry Jones.
FOURTH ROW: (L-R) 56 Cliff Lewis, 99 Charles Johnson, 13 Bucky Scribner, 90 Ezra Johnson, 52 George Cumby, 50 Rich Wingo, 58 Larry Rubens, 70 Ron Sams, 68 Greg Koch, 82 Paul Coffman, 17 David Whitehurst.
FIFTH ROW: (L-R) 11 Eddie Garcia, 62 Jim McLaughlin, 39 Mike Meade, 33 Jessie Clark, 25 Harlan Huckleby, 61 Dave Drechsler, 24 Johnnie Gray, 20 Chet Winters, 72 Greg Boyd, 73 Byron Braggs.
SIXTH ROW: (L-R) Offensive Backfield Coach John Brunner, Receivers Coach Lew Carpenter, Pro Player Personnel Director Burt Gustafson, Special Teams Coach Dick Rehbein, Defensive Backfield Coach Ross Fichtner, Defensive Line Coach Richard (Doc) Urich, Offensive Line Coach Bill Meyers, Head Coach Bart Starr, Offensive Coordinator Bob Schnelker, Offensive Line Coach Ernie McMillan, Defensive Coordinator John Meyer, Linebackers Coach Monte Kiffin.
BACK ROW: (L-R) Film Director Al Treml, Head Trainer Domenic Gentile, Assistant Film Director Bob Eckberg, Team Physician Dr. Eugene Brusky; Dr. H.A. Tressler, Equipment Manager Bob Noel, Equipment Assistant Jack Noel, Assistant Trainer Jim Popp, Groundskeeper Earl DuChateau.

As they had done nine years earlier, the Packers selected a former player to fill their head coaching vacancy. This time, however, they hired someone with more than a year's worth of coaching experience.

Forrest Gregg was named the ninth head coach in Packers history on Dec. 26, 1983. The former offensive lineman had been the head coach at Cleveland (1975-77) and Cincinnati (1980-83). In 1981, Gregg's Bengals made it to the Super Bowl, where they lost 26-21 to the 49ers.

Gregg's team started slowly but awoke in the season's second half. Green Bay downed the Cardinals 24-23 on opening day, then lost seven straight. The team recovered and went 7-1 in the last eight weeks.

The turnaround was the result of a resurgent running game, changes in the offensive line and kicking game, a better turnover ratio, and an improved defense.

Eddie Lee Ivery, who missed the first six games with a recurring knee problem, rushed for 552 yards in the second half of the season. The team averaged more than 158 yards rushing per game with Ivery back in action.

Gregg pulled guards Dave Dreschler and Syd Kitson from the starting lineup in favor of the larger Ron Hallstrom and Tim Huffman after the team managed just 31 yards rushing against Chicago in Week 3. Kitson was released on Oct. 23 to make room for guard Keith Uecker and Dreschler lasted the year as a backup. The line allowed just 11 sacks in the last eight weeks, down from 31 in the first eight weeks.

Gregg also tinkered with the kicking game. In the offseason, Gregg traded Jan Stenerud to Minnesota and kept second year Eddie Garcia. But after two missed field goals in Denver dropped Garcia's success rate to 33 percent, Gregg brought in rookie Al Del Greco, who connected on nine of 12 attempts.

Green Bay forced 29 turnovers during its second-half drive. Eight of those came courtesy of rookie Tom Flynn, who led the NFC with nine interceptions. The Packers' turnover differential in the season's second half was a plus-14 compared with a minus-9 in the opening eight weeks.

Hank Bullough was slated to rebuild the defense. But when he departed in May to the USFL, Dick Modzelewski took over and his unit climbed to 16th in yards allowed. The club gave up 130 fewer points than it did in 1983.

Gregg was given the game ball after the Packers beat the Cardinals 24-23 to start the season.

"I thought our offensive line did a great job against an exceptional pass rushing team," Gregg said.

The following week, the world champion Raiders battered them 28-7. Los Angeles knocked Lynn Dickey from the game with a back injury after just six plays. Rookie Randy Wright and Rich Campbell filled in, but completed just 14 passes in 32 attempts for 104 yards.

In Week 3, Green Bay picked up just 154 yards in a 9-7 loss to the Bears. Garcia missed a 47-yard field goal with just under five minutes left.

The Packers' struggles continued in Texas Stadium against the Cowboys. After the game, Dickey, who completed just five passes in 16 attempts and couldn't go in the third quarter, revealed he had broken three transverse processes in his back in the Raiders game.

"I couldn't do things physically that I felt I had to do after I got hit a couple more times," Dickey said. "I was more of a hindrance than a help."

Green Bay lost four more games, the last a 30-24 setback to Seattle that left it with a 1-7 record

"Sure it's possible (to turn around the season)," Gregg said. "All we have to do is play with some intensity and cut out some of the mental mistakes."

Green Bay did not commit a turnover and blew past Detroit 41-9 in Week 9. Ivery piled up 109 yards rushing.

Three weeks later, Green Bay won for a fourth straight time when it toppled the Rams 31-6 to move into second place in the Central Division standings.

Detroit quashed the Packers' playoff hopes on Thanksgiving. The Lions came back from a 21-7 deficit to register a 31-28 win and eliminate Green Bay from contention.

The contest also was the first time in 162 games that the Packers were without Larry McCarren. A pinched nerve in his neck kept the center out of the final four games.

"I would have liked to (maintain the streak)," he said. "But not if it would have taken going in for a token play."

McCarren attempted to come back in 1985 but retired in August. "The Rock" anchored the line longer than Charley Brock, Jim Ringo or Ken Bowman, a select group of centers in whose company he belonged.

FORGET FUMBLING

On a snowy Monday night in Denver, fumbles by Gerry Ellis and Jessie Clark on back-to-back kickoff returns put the Packers in a 14-0 hole within the first minute of their game with the Broncos. Green Bay fumbled seven times that night.

That game was an aberration. The Green and Gold fumbled 17 times in 1984, an average of just over one per game. That's the lowest rate in team history.

In seven games, the Packers did not fumble. They had only one in six other contests. In the second half of the season, the team fumbled just five times, losing two.

In contrast, the team had 37 fumbles in 1983.

Green Bay and the Giants tied for the fewest fumbles in the league. Every other team had more than 20.

Fewest Fumbles on Average, Season

Avg.	Year	No./Games	Record
1.06	1984	17/16	8-8
1.10	1944	11/10	8-2
1.18	1942	13/11	8-2-1

TEAM STATISTICS

	GB	OPP
First Downs	315	323
Rushing	120	136
Passing	168	166
Penalty	27	21
Rushes	461	545
Yards Gained	2,019	2,145
Average Gain	4.38	3.94
Average Yards per Game	126.2	134.1
Passes Attempted	506	551
Completed	281	315
% Completed	55.53	57.17
Total Yards Gained	3,740	3,470
Times Sacked	42	44
Yards Lost	310	324
Net Yards Gained	3,430	3,146
Yards Gained per Completion	13.31	11.02
Net Yards per Attempt	6.26	5.29
Average Net Yards per Game	214.4	196.6
Combined Net Yards Gained	5,449	5,291
Total Plays	1,009	1,140
Average Yards per Play	5.40	4.64
Average Net Yards per Game	340.6	330.7
Third Down Efficiency	75/205	89/243
Percentage	36.59	36.63
Fourth Down Efficiency	4/13	12/18
Percentage	30.77	66.67
Intercepted By	27	30
Yards Returned	338	317
Returned for TD	2	2
Punts	85	89
Yards Punted	3,596	3,643
Average Yards per Punt	42.31	40.93
Punt Returns	48	46
Yards Returned	351	368
Average Yards per Return	7.31	8.00
Returned for TD	0	0
Kickoff Returns	67	73
Yards Returned	1,362	1,171
Average Yards per Return	20.33	16.04
Returned for TD	1	0
Penalties	110	145
Yards Penalized	915	1,129
Fumbles	17	33
Lost	7	15
Own Recovered for Touchdown	0	0
Opponent's Recovered by	15	7
Opponent's Recovered for Touchdown	0	2
Total Points Scored	390	309
Total Touchdowns	51	34
Touchdowns Rushing	18	14
Touchdowns Passing	30	16
Touchdowns on Returns & Recoveries	3	4
Extra Points	48	33
Safeties	0	0
Field Goals Attempted	21	31
Field Goals Made	12	24
% Successful	57.14	77.42
Average Time of Possession	26:48	33:12

Regular Season   8-8-0

Date	GB		OPP	Att.
9/2	24	St. Louis Cardinals	23	(53,738)
9/9	7	at Los Angeles Raiders	28	(46,269)
9/16	7	Chicago Bears	9	(55,942)
9/23	6	at Dallas Cowboys	20	(64,222)
9/30	27	at TB Buccaneers (OT)	30	(47,487)
10/7	28	San Diego Chargers	34	(54,045)
10/15	14	at Denver Broncos	17	(62,546)
10/21	24	Seattle Seahawks (M)	30	(52,286)
10/28	41	Detroit Lions	9	(54,289)
11/4	23	at New Orleans Saints	13	(57,426)
11/11	45	Minnesota Vikings	17	(52,931)
11/18	31	Los Angeles Rams (M)	6	(52,031)
11/22	28	at Detroit Lions	31	(63,698)
12/2	27	Tampa Bay Buccaneers	14	(46,800)
12/9	20	at Chicago Bears	14	(59,374)
12/16	38	at Minnesota Vikings	14	(51,197)

Score By Periods

	1	2	3	4	OT	Total
Packers	79	121	108	82	0	390
Opponents	72	88	65	81	3	309

INDIVIDUAL STATISTICS

Rushing

	Att	Yds	Avg	LG	TD
G. Ellis	123	581	4.7	50	4
Ivery	99	552	5.6	49	6
J. Clark	87	375	4.3	t43	4
Crouse	53	169	3.2	14	0
Huckleby	35	145	4.1	23	0
Rodgers	25	94	3.8	15	0
Lofton	10	82	8.2	26	0
R. Wright	8	11	1.4	5	0
Dickey	18	6	0.3	9	3
Campbell	2	2	1.0	5	0
E. West	1	2	2.0	t2	1
Packers	**461**	**2,019**	**4.4**	**50**	**18**
Opponents	545	2,145	3.9	39	14

Receiving

	No	Yds	Avg	LG	TD
Lofton	62	1,361	22.0	t79	7
Coffman	43	562	13.1	t44	9
G. Ellis	36	312	8.7	22	2
J. Clark	29	234	8.1	20	2
Epps	26	435	16.7	56	3
J. Jefferson	26	339	13.0	33	0
Ivery	19	141	7.4	18	1
Crouse	9	93	10.3	25	1
Huckleby	8	65	8.1	13	0
E. West	6	54	9.0	t29	4
Rodgers	5	56	11.2	22	0
Childs	4	32	8.0	17	0
G. Lewis	4	29	7.3	15	0
Cassidy	2	16	8.0	10	0
L. Taylor	1	8	8.0	8	0
Blake Moore	1	3	3.0	t3	1
Packers	**281**	**3,740**	**13.3**	**t79**	**30**
Opponents	315	3,470	11.0	50	16

Passing

	Att	Com	Yds	Pct	TD	In	Tk/Yds	Rate
Dickey	401	237	3,195	59.1	25	19	32/244	85.6
R. Wright	62	27	310	43.5	2	6	4/17	30.4
R. Campbell	38	16	218	42.1	3	5	5/46	47.8
G. Ellis	4	1	17	25.0	0	0	1/3	—
Scribner	1	0	0	00.0	0	0	0/0	—
Packers	**506**	**281**	**3,740**	**55.5**	**30**	**30**	**42/310**	**74.2**
Opponents	551	315	3,470	57.2	16	27	44/324	65.2

Punting

	No	Yds	Avg	Net	TB	In20	LG	HB
Scribner	85	3,596	42.3	35.2	12	18	61	0
Packers	**85**	**3,596**	**42.3**	**35.2**	**12**	**18**	**61**	**0**
Opponents	89	3,643	40.9	36.1	4	13	63	0

Kickoff Returns

	No	Yds	Avg	LG	TD
Rodgers	39	843	21.6	t97	1
Huckleby	14	261	18.6	54	0
Epps	12	232	19.3	47	0
D. Jones	1	19	19.0	19	0
Prather	1	7	7.0	7	0
Packers	**67**	**1,362**	**20.3**	**t97**	**1**
Opponents	73	1,171	16.0	51	0

Punt Returns

	No	Yds	Avg	FC	LG	TD
Epps	29	199	6.9	10	39	0
Flynn	15	128	8.5	4	20	0
G. Hayes	4	24	6.0	0	10	0
M. Murphy	0	0	0.0	2	0	0
Packers	**48**	**351**	**7.3**	**16**	**39**	**0**
Opponents	46	368	8.0	5	22	0

Interceptions

	No	Yds	Avg	LG	TD
Flynn	9	106	11.8	31	0
T. Lewis	7	151	21.6	t99	1
M. Lee	3	33	11.0	14	0
J. Anderson	3	24	8.0	22	0
Hood	1	8	8.0	8	0
Cumby	1	7	7.0	7	0
R. Brown	1	5	5.0	t5	1
M. Murphy	1	4	4.0	4	0
McLeod	1	0	0.0	0	0
Packers	**27**	**338**	**12.5**	**t99**	**2**
Opponents	30	317	10.6	t53	2

Scoring

	TDr	TDp	TDrt	PAT	FG	S	TP
Del Greco	0	0	0	34/34	9/12	0	61
Coffman	0	9	0	0/0	0/0	0	54
Ivery	6	1	0	0/0	0/0	0	42
Lofton	0	7	0	0/0	0/0	0	42
J. Clark	4	2	0	0/0	0/0	0	36
G. Ellis	4	2	0	0/0	0/0	0	36
E. West	1	4	0	0/0	0/0	0	30
Garcia	0	0	0	14/15	3/9	0	23
Dickey	3	0	0	0/0	0/0	0	18
Epps	0	3	0	0/0	0/0	0	18
R. Brown	0	0	1	0/0	0/0	0	6
Crouse	0	1	0	0/0	0/0	0	6
T. Lewis	0	0	1	0/0	0/0	0	6
Blake Moore	0	1	0	0/0	0/0	0	6
Rodgers	0	0	1	0/0	0/0	0	6
Packers	**18**	**30**	**3**	**48/51**	**12/21**	**0**	**390**
Opponents	14	16	4	33/34	24/31	0	309

Fumbles

	Fum	Ow	Op	Yds	Tot
J. Anderson	0	0	1	0	1
R. Campbell	1	0	0	0	0
J. Clark	2	0	0	0	0
Coffman	1	1	0	0	1
Cumby	0	0	2	0	2
Dickey	3	1	0	-11	1
M. Douglass	0	1	1	0	2
G. Ellis	2	0	0	0	0
Epps	1	1	0	0	1
Flynn	1	0	3	3	3
Hallstrom	0	2	0	1	2
Huckleby	1	1	0	0	1
Ivery	1	0	0	0	0
D. Jones	0	1	2	0	3
T. Jones	0	0	1	0	1
M. Lee	0	0	2	0	2
Lofton	1	0	0	0	0
McLeod	0	0	1	0	1
M. Murphy	1	0	1	2	1
Prather	0	0	1	0	1
Rodgers	1	0	0	0	0
E. West	0	1	0	0	1
R. Wright	0	1	0	0	1
Packers	**17**	**10**	**15**	**-5**	**25**

Quarterback Sacks

	No
M. Douglass	9.0
E. Johnson	7.0
R. Brown	5.0
T. Jones	4.0
J. Anderson	3.5
Carreker	3.0
C. Martin	3.0
R. Scott	3.0
Cumby	2.5
M. Murphy	2.0
Humphrey	1.0
Neill	1.0
Packers	**44.0**
Opponents	42.0

NFL STANDINGS

National Conference

Eastern Division

	W	L	T	Pct	PF	PA
Washington Redskins	11	5	0	.688	426	310
New York Giants	9	7	0	.563	299	301
St. Louis Cardinals	9	7	0	.563	423	345
Dallas Cowboys	9	7	0	.563	308	308
Philadelphia Eagles	6	9	1	.406	278	320

Central Division

	W	L	T	Pct	PF	PA
Chicago Bears	10	6	0	.625	325	248
Green Bay Packers	8	8	0	.500	390	309
Tampa Bay Buccaneers	6	10	0	.375	335	380
Detroit Lions	4	11	1	.281	283	408
Minnesota Vikings	3	13	0	.188	276	484

Western Division

	W	L	T	Pct	PF	PA
San Francisco 49ers	15	1	0	.938	475	227
Los Angeles Rams	10	6	0	.625	346	316
New Orleans Saints	7	9	0	.438	298	361
Atlanta Falcons	4	12	0	.250	281	382

American Conference

Eastern Division

	W	L	T	Pct	PF	PA
Miami Dolphins	14	2	0	.875	513	298
New England Patriots	9	7	0	.563	362	352
New York Jets	7	9	0	.438	332	364
Indianapolis Colts	4	12	0	.250	239	414
Buffalo Bills	2	14	0	.125	250	454

Central Division

	W	L	T	Pct	PF	PA
Pittsburgh Steelers	9	7	0	.563	387	310
Cincinnati Bengals	8	8	0	.500	339	339
Cleveland Browns	5	11	0	.313	250	297
Houston Oilers	3	13	0	.188	240	437

Western Division

	W	L	T	Pct	PF	PA
Denver Broncos	13	3	0	.813	353	241
Seattle Seahawks	12	4	0	.750	418	282
Los Angeles Raiders	11	5	0	.688	368	278
Kansas City Chiefs	8	8	0	.500	314	324
San Diego Chargers	7	9	0	.438	394	413

ROSTER

No	Name	Pos	Ht	Wt	DOB	College	G
59	Anderson, John	LB	6-3	229	02/14/56	Michigan	16
93	Brown, Robert	DE	6-2	250	05/21/60	Virginia Tech	16
19	Campbell, Rich	QB	6-4	219	12/22/58	California	3
58	Cannon, Mark	C	6-3	258	06/14/62	Texas-Arlington	16
76	Carreker, Alphonso	DE	6-6	260	05/25/62	Florida State	14
88	Cassidy, Ron	WR	6-0	180	07/23/57	Utah State	15
89	Childs, Henry	TE	6-2	220	04/16/51	Kansas State	3
33	Clark, Jessie	FB	6-0	233	01/03/60	Arkansas	11
82	Coffman, Paul	TE	6-3	225	03/29/56	Kansas State	14
21	Crouse, Ray	RB	5-11	214	03/16/59	Nevada-Las Vegas	16
52	Cumby, George	LB	6-0	224	07/05/56	Oklahoma	16
10	Del Greco, Al	K	5-10	195	03/02/62	Auburn	9
98	DeLuca, Tony	NT	6-4	250	11/16/60	Rhode Island	1
12	Dickey, Lynn	QB	6-4	203	10/19/49	Kansas State	15
99	Dorsey, John	LB	6-2	235	08/31/60	Connecticut	16
53	Douglass, Mike	LB	6-0	214	03/15/55	San Diego State	16
61	Drechsler, Dave	G	6-3	264	07/18/60	North Carolina	16
31	Ellis, Gerry	FB	5-11	225	11/12/57	Missouri	16
85	Epps, Phillip	WR	5-10	165	11/11/58	TCU	16
41	Flynn, Tom	S	6-0	195	03/24/62	Pittsburgh	15
11	Garcia, Eddie	K	5-8	178	04/15/59	SMU	7
65	Hallstrom, Ron	G	6-6	283	06/11/59	Iowa	16
27	Hayes, Gary	CB	5-10	180	08/19/57	Fresno State	16
78	Hoffman, Gary	T	6-7	282	09/28/61	Santa Clara	1
38	Hood, Estus	CB	5-11	189	11/14/55	Illinois State	16
25	Huckleby, Harlan	HB	6-1	201	12/30/57	Michigan	16
74	Huffman, Tim	T	6-5	282	08/31/59	Notre Dame	16
79	Humphrey, Donnie	DE	6-3	275	04/20/61	Auburn	16
40	Ivery, Eddie Lee	RB	6-1	214	07/30/57	Georgia Tech	10
83	Jefferson, John	WR	6-1	204	02/03/56	Arizona State	13
90	Johnson, Ezra	DE	6-4	259	10/02/55	Morris Brown	13
71	Jones, Boyd	T	6-3	272	05/30/61	Texas Southern	2
43	Jones, Daryll	S	6-0	190	03/23/62	Georgia	16
63	Jones, Terry	NT	6-2	253	11/08/56	Alabama	16
64	Kitson, Syd	G	6-4	264	09/27/58	Wake Forest	8
68	Koch, Greg	T	6-4	276	06/14/55	Arkansas	15
22	Lee, Mark	CB	5-11	188	03/20/58	Washington	16
56	Lewis, Cliff	LB	6-1	224	11/09/59	Southern Mississippi	16
81	Lewis, Gary	TE	6-5	234	12/30/58	Texas-Arlington	3
26	Lewis, Tim	CB	5-11	191	12/18/61	Pittsburgh	16
80	Lofton, James	WR	6-3	197	07/05/56	Stanford	16
94	Martin, Charles	DE	6-4	270	08/31/59	Livingston	16
54	McCarren, Larry	C	6-3	263	11/09/51	Illinois	12
28	McLeod, Mike	S	6-0	180	05/04/58	Montana State	11
60	Moore, Blake	C	6-5	272	05/08/58	Wooster	11
37	Murphy, Mark	S	6-2	201	04/22/58	West Liberty State	16
77	Neill, Bill	NT	6-4	255	03/15/59	Pittsburgh	16
44	O'Steen, Dwayne	CB	6-1	195	12/20/54	San Jose State	4
51	Prather, Guy	LB	6-2	229	03/28/58	Grambling	16
35	Rodgers, Del	RB	5-10	202	06/22/60	Utah	14
55	Scott, Randy	LB	6-1	222	01/31/59	Alabama	16
13	Scribner, Bucky	P	6-0	202	07/11/60	Kansas	16
67	Swanke, Karl	T	6-6	262	12/29/57	Boston College	15
84	Taylor, Lenny	WR	5-10	179	02/15/61	Tennessee	2
70	Uecker, Keith	G	6-5	270	06/29/60	Auburn	6
49/86	West, Ed	TE	6-1	242	08/02/61	Auburn	16
50	Wingo, Rich	LB	6-1	227	07/16/56	Alabama	16
16	Wright, Randy	QB	6-2	194	01/12/61	Wisconsin	8

DRAFT

Rnd	Name	Pos	Ht	Wt	College
1	Alphonso Carreker (12)	DE	6-6	260	Florida State
2	(Choice (39) to Chargers in John Jefferson trade)				
3	Donnie Humphrey (72)	DE	6-3	275	Auburn
4	John Dorsey (99)	LB	6-2	235	Connecticut
5	Tom Flynn (126)	S	6-0	195	Pittsburgh
6	Randy Wright (153)	QB	6-2	194	Wisconsin
7	Daryll Jones (181)	DB	6-0	190	Georgia
8	(Choice (207) to Broncos for Greg Boyd)				
9	(Choice (240) to Chiefs for Charlie Getty)				
10	Gary Hoffman (267)	T	6-7	282	Santa Clara
11	Mark Cannon (294)	C	6-3	258	Texas-Arlington
12a	Lenny Taylor (313)	WR	5-10	179	Tennessee
	(Choice from Chargers for Derrel Gofourth)				
12b	Mark Emans (323)	LB	6-3	223	Bowling Green

1984 GREEN BAY PACKERS

FRONT ROW: (L-R) 11 Eddie Garcia, 12 Lynn Dickey, 13 Bucky Scribner, 16 Randy Wright, 19 Rich Campbell, 21 Ray Crouse, 22 Mark Lee, 24 Johnnie Gray, 25 Harlan Huckleby.
SECOND ROW: (L-R) 26 Tim Lewis, 27 Gary Hayes, 29 Mike C. McCoy, 31 Gerry Ellis, 33 Jessie Clark, 35 Del Rodgers, 37 Mark Murphy, 38 Estus Hood, 40 Eddie Lee Ivery, 41 Tom Flynn.
THIRD ROW: (L-R) 42 Lenny Taylor, 43 Daryll Jones, 44 Dwayne O'Steen, 50 Rich Wingo, 51 Guy Prather, 52 George Cumby, 53 Mike Douglass, 54 Larry McCarren, 55 Randy Scott.
FOURTH ROW: (L-R) 56 Cliff Lewis, 58 Mark Cannon, 59 John Anderson, 61 Dave Drechsler, 63 Terry Jones, 64 Syd Kitson, 65 Ron Hallstrom, 67 Karl Swanke, 68 Greg Koch, 69 Leotis Harris.
FIFTH ROW: (L-R) 74 Tim Huffman, 76 Alphonso Carreker, 77 Bill Neill, 78 Gary Hoffman, 79 Donnie Humphrey, 80 James Lofton, 81 Gary Lewis, 82 Paul Coffman, 83 John Jefferson, 85 Phillip Epps.
SIXTH ROW: (L-R) Equipment Manager Bob Noel, 86 Ed West, 88 Ron Cassidy, 89 Henry Childs, 90 Ezra Johnson, 93 Robert Brown, 94 Charles Martin, 95 Ken Walter, 99 John Dorsey, Equipment Assistant Jack Noel.
BACK ROW: (L-R) Special Teams/Linebackers Coach Chuck Priefer, Trainer Domenic Gentile, Receivers Coach Lew Carpenter, Offensive Line Coach Jerry Wampfler, Linebackers/Special Teams Coach Herb Paterra, Offensive Coordinator Bob Schnelker, Head Coach Forrest Gregg, Strength-Conditioning Coach Virgil Knight, Secondary Coach Ken Riley, Defensive Coordinator/Line Coach Dick Modzelewski, Offensive Backfield Coach George Sefcik, Director of Pro Personnel Burt Gustafson.

Green Bay Packers football without Lynn Dickey? That notion, always a possibility with a quarterback as oft-injured as Dickey, turned into reality late in 1985. For the seventh time since joining the team in 1976, Dickey failed to play a complete season. An injury sidelined him in Week 14, but in a concession to the future, coach Forrest Gregg kept a healthy Dickey on the bench in the final two games in order to get a better read on backups Jim Zorn and Randy Wright.

Zorn, who signed in September, directed a come-from-behind, 26-23 win in Detroit in Week 15. Wright relieved Zorn in the finale at Tampa Bay and produced a 20-17 victory by driving the team 73 yards to the winning score.

With the wins, Green Bay finished 8-8 for the third year in a row and the fourth time since 1981.

For Dickey, it was another challenging year. The former Oiler started the first three games, but was pulled in a 24-3 loss to the Jets in Week 3. Two days later, he asked for a demotion and Wright opened against the Cardinals. When Wright floundered, Dickey led the Packers to 28 second-half points.

Dickey then started seven of the next nine games. Despite not playing in the last three weeks, the 36-year-old expected to return the following year. However, he and the Packers could not agree on a contract, and in June 1986, Dickey and the team parted company.

Not surprisingly, Green Bay's average of 197.7 net yards passing per game was its lowest since 1979, when David Whitehurst was the primary starter at quarterback. The trade of John Jefferson to Cleveland further weakened the Packers' passing game.

Eddie Lee Ivery, Jessie Clark and Gerry Ellis formed a three-headed running threat that piled up yardage at a pace not seen since the days of John Brockington. Green Bay's average of 138 yards rushing per game was its highest since 1973.

Lambeau Field had a new look. Seventy-two luxury boxes were added and its seating capacity increased from 56,263 to 56,926.

Green Bay opened its season on the road against the Patriots. Paul Coffman and Clark registered two fourth-quarter touchdowns, but New England prevailed 26-20.

Green Bay improved to 1-1 with a 23-20 win over the Giants. Ivery's 1-yard touchdown run with 4:07 left capped a 75-yard drive and provided the margin of victory.

In Week 3, Gregg replaced Dickey with Wright with three minutes left in the third quarter. The change had little impact on the outcome as the Jets dominated 24-3.

St. Louis followed and the Cardinals jumped to a 26-0 lead. Dickey came on in relief of Wright and threw three touchdown passes in a 43-28 loss.

James Lofton caught 10 passes for 151 yards in a 43-10 rout of the Lions, spiced by 512 yards of offense.

A week later, Al Del Greco's 22-yard field goal with seven seconds left sank the Vikings 20-17.

Chicago unveiled a new offensive weapon in defensive tackle William "The Refrigerator" Perry on a Monday night in October. Perry participated in five offensive plays, and the first three resulted in touchdowns. He was the lead blocker on two scores by Walter Payton and reached the end zone himself on a short plunge.

If the Packers thought their 23-7 setback to the Bears was going to the season's low point, they were mistaken. In Week 8, the lowly Colts (2-5) embarrassed them 37-10, and the visitors' locker room was kept closed to the media for an unusually long time. Players were heard shouting and were apparently restraining one another.

"It's personal and private," said Gregg after emerging from the dressing room. "You probably heard me yelling."

Emotions continued to run high the following week in Lambeau Field, where the Bears outslugged the Packers 16-10. Five unsportsmanlike conduct or unnecessary roughness penalties were called. Mark Lee was ejected.

Battered, bruised, and 3-6, the Packers rallied to win five of their last seven games and even have a little fun in the process. On Dec. 1, amid more than a foot of snow, Green Bay overwhelmed the Buccaneers 21-0 in what was termed a "meteorological mismatch" by one reporter. Dickey threw for 299 yards with 106 going to Lofton. Ivery and Ellis both surpassed 100 yards rushing as the Packers sledded to 512 yards while holding Tampa Bay to 65 in the game that came to be known as The Snow Bowl.

BETTER THAN AVERAGE

On Dec. 1, Gerry Ellis gained 101 yards rushing despite carrying just nine times. His performance on that snowy afternoon was the high point in a year in which he set the team record for the highest average per carry in a season.

Ellis, Eddie Lee Ivery and Jessie Clark teamed up to gain 1,840 yards rushing. Ellis' average of 5.49 yards per carry was easily the best of the three and broke Jim Taylor's previous record of 5.42 set in 1962.

Ellis, who started seven games, came within a whisker of leading the league. The Cardinals' Stump Mitchell edged him by seven one-thousands of a yard.

A rookie in 1980, Ellis played through 1986. His career average of 4.58 yards per carry is second highest in team annals behind the 5.26 of Tobin Rote (min. 400 carries).

Highest average gain, season (min. 100 carries)

Avg.	Player	Year
5.49	Gerry Ellis	1985
5.42	Jim Taylor	1962
5.38	Jim Taylor	1961

TEAM STATISTICS

	GB	OPP
First Downs	318	310
Rushing	114	111
Passing	172	178
Penalty	32	21
Rushes	470	494
Yards Gained	2,208	2,047
Average Gain	4.70	4.14
Average Yards per Game	138.0	127.9
Passes Attempted	513	509
Completed	267	295
% Completed	52.05	57.96
Total Yards Gained	3,552	3,509
Times Sacked	50	48
Yards Lost	389	383
Net Yards Gained	3,163	3,126
Yards Gained per Completion	13.30	11.89
Net Yards per Attempt	5.62	5.61
Average Net Yards per Game	197.7	195.4
Combined Net Yards Gained	5,371	5,173
Total Plays	1,033	1,051
Average Yards per Play	5.20	4.92
Average Net Yards per Game	335.7	323.3
Third Down Efficiency	66/200	80/213
Percentage	33.00	37.56
Fourth Down Efficiency	6/12	6/15
Percentage	50.00	40.00
Intercepted By	15	27
Yards Returned	262	326
Returned for TD	2	1
Punts	82	77
Yards Punted	3,262	3,290
Average Yards per Punt	39.78	42.73
Punt Returns	38	46
Yards Returned	370	411
Average Yards per Return	9.74	8.93
Returned for TD	0	0
Kickoff Returns	67	71
Yards Returned	1,318	1,570
Average Yards per Return	19.67	22.11
Returned for TD	0	2
Penalties	101	102
Yards Penalized	798	797
Fumbles	39	44
Lost	18	25
Own Recovered for Touchdown	0	0
Opponent's Recovered by	25	18
Opponent's Recovered for Touchdown	1	1
Total Points Scored	337	355
Total Touchdowns	40	43
Touchdowns Rushing	16	17
Touchdowns Passing	21	22
Touchdowns on Returns & Recoveries	3	4
Extra Points	38	41
Safeties	1	4
Field Goals Attempted	26	31
Field Goals Made	19	16
% Successful	73.08	51.61
Average Time of Possession	28:59	31:01

Regular Season 8-8-0

Date	GB		OPP	Att.
9/8	20	at New England Patriots	26	(49,488)
9/15	23	New York Giants	20	(56,149)
9/22	3	New York Jets (M)	24	(53,667)
9/29	28	at St. Louis Cardinals	43	(48,598)
10/6	43	Detroit Lions	10	(55,914)
10/13	20	Minnesota Vikings (M)	17	(54,674)
10/21	7	at Chicago Bears	23	(65,095)
10/27	10	at Indianapolis Colts	37	(59,708)
11/3	10	Chicago Bears	16	(56,895)
11/10	27	at Minnesota Vikings	17	(59,970)
11/17	38	New Orleans Saints (M)	14	(52,104)
11/24	17	at Los Angeles Rams	34	(52,710)
12/1	21	Tampa Bay Buccaneers	0	(19,856)
12/8	24	Miami Dolphins	34	(52,671)
12/15	26	at Detroit Lions	23	(49,379)
12/22	20	at Tampa Bay Buccaneers	17	(33,992)

Score By Periods

	1	2	3	4	OT	Total
Packers	50	82	89	116	0	337
Opponents	68	109	66	112	0	355

INDIVIDUAL STATISTICS

Rushing

	Att	Yds	Avg	LG	TD
Ivery	132	636	4.8	34	2
J. Clark	147	633	4.3	t80	5
G. Ellis	104	571	5.5	t39	5
Ellerson	32	205	6.4	t37	2
Epps	5	103	20.6	34	1
Huckleby	8	41	5.1	15	0
Lofton	4	14	3.5	21	0
Zorn	10	9	0.9	8	0
R. Wright	8	8	1.0	8	0
Prather	1	0	0.0	0	0
E. West	1	0	0.0	0	0
Dickey	18	-12	-0.7	3	1
Packers	**470**	**2,208**	**4.7**	**80**	**16**
Opponents	494	2,047	4.1	t65	17

Receiving

	No	Yds	Avg	LG	TD
Lofton	69	1,153	16.7	t56	4
Coffman	49	666	13.6	32	6
Epps	44	683	15.5	63	3
Ivery	28	270	9.6	24	2
J. Clark	24	252	10.5	t55	2
G. Ellis	24	206	8.6	35	0
Dennard	13	182	14.0	34	2
E. West	8	95	11.9	30	1
Huckleby	5	27	5.4	8	0
Ellerson	2	15	7.5	11	0
Blake Moore	1	3	3.0	t3	1
Packers	**267**	**3,552**	**13.3**	**63**	**21**
Opponents	295	3,509	11.9	t61	22

Passing

	Att	Com	Yds	Pct	TD	In	Tk/Yds	Rate
Dickey	314	172	2,206	54.8	15	17	30/226	70.4
Zorn	123	56	794	45.5	4	6	11/89	57.4
R. Wright	74	39	552	52.7	2	4	8/67	63.6
G. Ellis	1	0	0	0.0	0	0	0/0	—
Ivery	1	0	0	00.0	0	0	1/7	—
Packers	**513**	**267**	**3,552**	**52.0**	**21**	**27**	**50/389**	**66.0**
Opponents	509	295	3,509	58.0	22	15	48/383	81.2

Punting

	No	Yds	Avg	Net	TB	In20	LG	HB
Prokop	56	2,210	39.5	32.6	6	9	66	0
Bracken	26	1,052	40.5	33.3	2	1	54	0
Packers	**82**	**3,262**	**39.8**	**32.8**	**8**	**10**	**66**	**0**
Opponents	77	3,290	42.7	35.1	11	24	68	0

Kickoff Returns

	No	Yds	Avg	LG	TD
Ellerson	29	521	18.0	32	0
G. Ellis	13	247	19.0	40	0
Epps	12	279	23.3	48	0
Stanley	9	212	23.6	36	0
Flynn	1	20	20.0	20	0
J. Anderson	1	14	14.0	14	0
Stills	1	14	14.0	14	0
D. Jones	1	11	11.0	11	0
Packers	**67**	**1,318**	**19.7**	**48**	**0**
Opponents	71	1,570	22.1	t98	2

Punt Returns

	No	Yds	Avg	FC	LG	TD
Epps	15	146	9.7	3	46	0
Stanley	14	179	12.8	3	27	0
Flynn	7	41	5.9	4	13	0
M. Murphy	1	4	4.0	—	4	0
G. Hayes	1	0	0.0	—	0	0
Packers	**38**	**370**	**9.7**	**10**	**46**	**0**
Opponents	46	411	8.9	10	47	0

Interceptions

	No	Yds	Avg	LG	TD
T. Lewis	4	4	1.0	4	0
M. Douglass	2	126	63.0	t80	1
M. Murphy	2	50	25.0	t50	1
R. Scott	2	50	25.0	30	0
J. Anderson	2	2	1.0	2	0
M. Lee	1	23	23.0	23	0
Flynn	1	7	7.0	7	0
Cade	1	0	0.0	0	0
Packers	**15**	**262**	**17.5**	**t80**	**2**
Opponents	27	326	12.1	67	1

Scoring

	TDr	TDp	TDrt	PAT	FG	S	TP
Del Greco	0	0	0	38/40	19/26	0	95
J. Clark	5	2	0	0/0	0/0	0	42
Coffman	0	6	0	0/0	0/0	0	36
G. Ellis	5	0	0	0/0	0/0	0	30
Epps	1	3	0	0/0	0/0	0	24
Ivery	2	2	0	0/0	0/0	0	24
Lofton	0	4	0	0/0	0/0	0	24
Dennard	0	2	0	0/0	0/0	0	12
Ellerson	2	0	0	0/0	0/0	0	12
Dickey	1	0	0	0/0	0/0	0	6
M. Douglass	0	0	1	0/0	0/0	0	6
T. Lewis	0	0	1	0/0	0/0	0	6
Blake Moore	0	1	0	0/0	0/0	0	6
M. Murphy	0	0	1	0/0	0/0	0	6
E. West	0	1	0	0/0	0/0	0	6
R. Brown	0	0	0	0/0	0/0	1	2
Packers	**16**	**21**	**3**	**38/40**	**19/26**	**1**	**337**
Opponents	17	22	4	41/43	16/31	4	355

Fumbles

	Fum	Ow	Op	Yds	Tot
J. Anderson	0	0	1	0	1
R. Brown	0	0	4	0	4
Cade	0	0	1	0	1
Cannon	0	0	2	0	2
J. Clark	4	2	0	0	2
Coffman	1	0	0	0	0
Dennard	1	0	0	0	0
Dickey	8	5	0	-18	5
J. Dorsey	0	0	2	0	2
M. Douglass	1	0	1	0	1
Ellerson	3	2	1	0	3
G. Ellis	2	1	0	0	1
Epps	1	0	0	0	0
Flynn	0	0	1	0	1
Hallstrom	0	1	0	0	1
G. Hayes	1	1	2	0	3
Ivery	1	1	0	0	1
E. Johnson	0	0	2	0	2
Koch	0	1	0	0	1
T. Lewis	0	0	1	6	1
Lofton	3	0	0	0	0
C. Martin	0	0	1	0	1
Blake Moore	1	0	0	0	0
M. Murphy	0	0	1	0	1
Prather	1	0	0	0	0
R. Scott	0	0	5	31	5
Stanley	2	0	0	0	0
Uecker	0	0	1	0	1
E. West	1	0	0	0	0
R. Wright	5	2	0	-6	2
Zorn	3	2	0	-1	2
Packers	**39**	**20**	**25**	**12**	**45**

Quarterback Sacks

	No
E. Johnson	9.5
Carreker	9.0
J. Anderson	6.0
M. Murphy	4.0
R. Brown	3.0
C. Martin	3.0
Noble	3.0
R. Scott	3.0
M. Butler	2.0
Humphrey	2.0
Prather	2.0
M. Douglass	1.5
Packers	**48.0**
Opponents	50.0

NFL STANDINGS

National Conference

Eastern Division

	W	L	T	Pct	PF	PA
Dallas Cowboys	10	6	0	.625	357	333
New York Giants	10	6	0	.625	399	283
Washington Redskins	10	6	0	.625	297	312
Philadelphia Eagles	7	9	0	.438	286	310
St. Louis Cardinals	5	11	0	.313	278	414

Central Division

	W	L	T	Pct	PF	PA
Chicago Bears	15	1	0	.938	456	198
Green Bay Packers	8	8	0	.500	337	355
Minnesota Vikings	7	9	0	.438	346	359
Detroit Lions	7	9	0	.438	307	366
Tampa Bay Buccaneers	2	14	0	.125	294	448

Western Division

	W	L	T	Pct	PF	PA
Los Angeles Rams	11	5	0	.688	340	277
San Francisco 49ers	10	6	0	.625	411	263
New Orleans Saints	5	11	0	.313	294	401
Atlanta Falcons	4	12	0	.250	282	452

American Conference

Eastern Division

	W	L	T	Pct	PF	PA
Miami Dolphins	12	4	0	.750	428	320
New York Jets	11	5	0	.688	393	264
New England Patriots	11	5	0	.688	362	290
Indianapolis Colts	5	11	0	.313	320	386
Buffalo Bills	2	14	0	.125	200	381

Central Division

	W	L	T	Pct	PF	PA
Cleveland Browns	8	8	0	.500	287	294
Cincinnati Bengals	7	9	0	.438	441	437
Pittsburgh Steelers	7	9	0	.438	379	355
Houston Oilers	5	11	0	.313	284	412

Western Division

	W	L	T	Pct	PF	PA
Los Angeles Raiders	12	4	0	.750	354	308
Denver Broncos	11	5	0	.688	380	329
Seattle Seahawks	8	8	0	.500	349	303
San Diego Chargers	8	8	0	.500	467	435
Kansas City Chiefs	6	10	0	.375	317	360

ROSTER

No	Name	Pos	Ht	Wt	DOB	College	G
59	Anderson, John	LB	6-3	229	02/14/56	Michigan	16
17	Bracken, Don	P	6-0	205	02/16/62	Michigan	7
93	Brown, Robert	DE	6-2	270	05/21/60	Virginia Tech	16
39	Burgess, Ronnie	DB	5-11	175	03/07/63	Wake Forest	11
77	Butler, Mike	DE	6-5	269	04/04/54	Kansas	12
24	Cade, Mossy	CB	6-1	195	12/26/61	Texas	14
58	Cannon, Mark	C	6-3	268	06/14/62	Texas-Arlington	16
76	Carreker, Alphonso	DE	6-6	270	05/25/62	Florida State	16
23	Clanton, Chuck	DB	5-11	192	05/15/62	Auburn	3
33	Clark, Jessie	FB	6-0	233	01/03/60	Arkansas	16
82	Coffman, Paul	TE	6-3	225	03/29/56	Kansas State	16
52	Cumby, George	LB	6-0	224	07/05/56	Oklahoma	16
95	Degrate, Tony	DE	6-3	280	04/25/62	Texas	1
10	Del Greco, Al	K	5-10	195	03/02/62	Auburn	16
88	Dennard, Preston	WR	6-1	183	11/28/55	New Mexico	16
12	Dickey, Lynn	QB	6-4	210	10/19/49	Kansas State	12
99	Dorsey, John	LB	6-2	235	08/31/60	Connecticut	16
53	Douglass, Mike	LB	6-0	214	03/15/55	San Diego State	16
42	Ellerson, Gary	RB	5-11	220	07/17/63	Wisconsin	15
31	Ellis, Gerry	FB	5-11	225	11/12/57	Missouri	16
85	Epps, Phillip	WR	5-10	165	11/11/58	TCU	16
41	Flynn, Tom	S	6-0	195	03/24/62	Pittsburgh	15
65	Hallstrom, Ron	G	6-6	289	06/11/59	Iowa	16
27	Hayes, Gary	CB	5-10	180	08/19/57	Fresno State	16
25	Huckleby, Harlan	HB	6-1	201	12/30/57	Michigan	11
74	Huffman, Tim	T	6-5	280	08/31/59	Notre Dame	2
79	Humphrey, Donnie	DE	6-3	275	04/20/61	Auburn	16
40	Ivery, Eddie Lee	RB	6-1	210	07/30/57	Georgia Tech	15
90	Johnson, Ezra	DE	6-4	259	10/02/55	Morris Brown	16
43	Jones, Daryll	S	6-0	195	03/23/62	Georgia	8
68	Koch, Greg	T	6-4	276	06/14/55	Arkansas	16
22	Lee, Mark	CB	5-11	188	03/20/58	Washington	14
89	Lewis, Mark	TE	6-2	237	05/05/61	Texas A&M	1
26	Lewis, Tim	CB	5-11	191	12/18/61	Pittsburgh	16
80	Lofton, James	WR	6-3	197	07/05/56	Stanford	16
94	Martin, Charles	DE	6-4	282	08/31/59	Livingston	16
28	McLeod, Mike	S	6-0	180	05/04/58	Montana State	8
60	Moore, Blake	C	6-5	272	05/08/58	Wooster	16
57	Moran, Rich	G	6-2	272	03/19/62	San Diego State	16
37	Murphy, Mark	S	6-2	201	04/22/58	West Liberty State	14
91	Noble, Brian	LB	6-3	237	09/06/62	Arizona State	16
51	Prather, Guy	LB	6-2	229	03/28/58	Grambling	16
11	Prokop, Joe	P	6-3	225	07/07/60	Cal Poly-Pomona	9
75	Ruettgers, Ken	T	6-5	267	08/20/62	USC	16
55	Scott, Randy	LB	6-1	228	01/31/59	Alabama	16
71	Shumate, Mark	NT	6-5	265	03/30/60	Wisconsin	3
87	Stanley, Walter	WR	5-9	180	11/05/62	Mesa	14
29	Stills, Ken	S	5-10	185	09/06/63	Wisconsin	8
67	Swanke, Karl	T	6-6	275	12/29/57	Boston College	15
20	Turner, Maurice	RB	5-11	199	09/10/60	Utah State	13
70	Uecker, Keith	G	6-5	270	06/29/60	Auburn	8
86	West, Ed	TE	6-1	236	08/02/61	Auburn	16
61	Wingle, Blake	G	6-2	260	04/17/60	UCLA	2
16	Wright, Randy	QB	6-2	194	01/12/61	Wisconsin	7
18	Zorn, Jim	QB	6-2	200	05/10/53	Cal Poly-Pomona	13

DRAFT

Rnd	Name	Pos	Ht	Wt	College
1	Ken Ruettgers (7)	T	6-5	267	USC
	(Traded positions with Bills, 14th choice to 7th)				
2	(Choice (42) to Bills for position switch)				
3	Rich Moran (71)	G	6-2	272	San Diego State
4	Walter Stanley (98)	WR	5-9	180	Mesa (CO)
5	Brian Noble (125)	LB	6-3	237	Arizona State
6	Mark Lewis (155)	TE	6-2	237	Texas A&M
7a	Eric Wilson (171)	LB	6-1	247	Maryland
	(Choice from Vikings for Jan Stenerud)				
7b	Gary Ellerson (182)	RB	5-11	220	Wisconsin
8	Ken Stills (209)	DB	5-10	185	Wisconsin
9	Morris Johnson (239)	G	6-3	317	Alabama A&M
10	Ronnie Burgess (266)	CB	5-11	174	Wake Forest
11	Joe Shield (294)	QB	6-1	185	Trinity (CT)
12	Jim Meyer (323)	P	6-4	204	Arizona State

1985 GREEN BAY PACKERS

FRONT ROW: 10 Al Del Greco, 11 Joe Prokop, 12 Lynn Dickey, 16 Randy Wright, 17 Joe Shield, 22 Mark Lee, 24 Mossy Cade, 25 Harlan Huckleby.

SECOND ROW: (L-R) 26 Tim Lewis, 27 Gary Hayes, 28 Mike McLeod, 31 Gerry Ellis, 33 Jessie Clark, 35 Del Rodgers, 37 Mark Murphy, 39 Ronnie Burgess, 40 Eddie Lee Ivery.

THIRD ROW: (L-R) 41 Tom Flynn, 42 Gary Ellerson, 43 Daryll Jones, 50 Rich Wingo, 51 Guy Prather, 52 George Cumby, 53 Mike Douglass, 55 Randy Scott, 57 Rich Moran, 58 Mark Cannon.

FOURTH ROW: (L-R) 59 John Anderson, 60 Blake Moore, 63 Terry Jones, 65 Ron Hallstrom, 67 Karl Swanke, 68 Greg Koch, 70 Keith Uecker, 74 Tim Huffman, 75 Ken Ruettgers.

FIFTH ROW: (L-R) 76 Alphonso Carreker, 77 Mike Butler, 79 Donnie Humphrey, 80 James Lofton, 82 Paul Coffman, 85 Phillip Epps, 86 Ed West, 87 Walter Stanley, 88 Preston Dennard, 89 Mark Lewis.

SIXTH ROW: (L-R) Equipment Assistant Jack Noel, Trainer Domenic Gentile, 90 Ezra Johnson, 91 Brian Noble, 93 Robert Brown, 94 Charles Martin, 99 John Dorsey, Administrative Assistant Burt Gustafson, Equipment Manager Bob Noel.

BACK ROW: (L-R) Special Teams Coach Chuck Priefer, Offensive Coordinator Bob Schnelker, Linebackers Coach Herb Paterra, Receivers Coach Lew Carpenter, Head Coach Forrest Gregg, Strength-Conditioning Coach Virgil Knight, Offensive Line Coach Jerry Wampfler, Defensive Coordinator/Line Coach Dick Modzelewski, Offensive Backfield George Sefcik, Secondary Coach Ken Riley.

Having failed to produce a winner in his first two seasons, Packers head coach Forrest Gregg looked to do a little housecleaning. The highly competitive Texan released more than a half dozen veterans, some fan favorites and offensive coordinator Bob Schnelker in a shakeup the magnitude of which had not been seen in years.

"This team's been sitting on high center for a long time," said Gregg. "We reached the conclusion that we're making changes and it was time to make a change."

The result: the club dropped its first six games (the worst start in franchise history) and tied the Chargers and Bills for the third worst record in the NFL at 4-12.

Long-time veterans who received pink slips were defensive end Mike Butler, tight end Paul Coffman, linebackers Mike Douglass and George Cumby and tackle Greg Koch. In their place, Gregg turned to less experienced but younger players such as Alphonso Carreker, Ed West, Brian Noble, Burnell Dent and Alan Veingrad.

Green Bay had its share of injuries. Cornerback Tim Lewis suffered a career-ending neck injury when tackling the Bears' Willie Gault on Sept. 22. John Anderson missed 12 games and Phillip Epps four after they broke fibulas in their left legs. Guard Rich Moran partially tore the medial collateral ligament in his left knee and missed 11 games. Punter Don Bracken dislocated his left elbow on an icy practice field. His replacement, Bill Renner, had three punts blocked in the last three games.

Events on and off the field tarnished the Packers' image. Defensive end Charles Martin was suspended for two games by NFL commissioner Pete Rozelle after body slamming Bears quarterback Jim McMahon. James Lofton saw his Packers career end after second-degree sexual assault charges were filed against him following an alleged incident at a local nightclub.

With Lynn Dickey and the Packers unable to agree on a contract in June, Randy Wright became the team's starting quarterback. Though he became just the second player in club history to throw for 3,000 or more yards in a single season, the Packers were interested in trading for Jim Everett or Doug Flutie at different points in the season.

The lowly Houston Oilers pummeled the Packers in the season opener at Lambeau Field. Houston rolled up 375 yards and held the ball for just over 39 minutes in administering a 31-3 whipping.

Two weeks later, Green Bay fell 25-12 to the more talented Chicago Bears. Before the game, Walter Payton summed up the rivalry for ESPN by saying: "It's like two old roosters when they meet in a barnyard walking around with their chests stuck out."

Tommy Kramer and the Vikings dropped Green Bay to 0-4. Kramer threw for 241 yards and six touchdowns in a game plan designed by Schnelker, the Packers' former offensive coordinator who accepted the same position with Minnesota after his release in Green Bay.

Don Hutson's Packers career reception record fell in Milwaukee on Oct. 5. Lofton caught seven passes against the Bengals, giving him 489 in his nine-year career, or one more than Hutson snagged in his 11 years with the team.

The Lions then handed Green Bay its sixth straight loss 21-14.

The Packers' first win came against the Browns, a 13-point favorite, on Oct. 19. Wright completed 21 of 27 throws for 277 yards and a touchdown. The game also marked the first start by linebacker Tim Harris.

A week later, Green Bay outgained San Francisco 464 yards to 222. But two fourth-quarter interception returns for touchdowns by Ronnie Lott and Tory Nixon cost the Packers in a 31-17 loss.

Green Bay discovered the winning formula three times in its last six games thanks in no small measure to the Buccaneers. The Packers beat them 31-17 on Nov. 16 and 21-7 nearly a month later.

Walter Stanley provided the highlights in Green Bay's other win. The second-year kick returner/wide receiver gained 287 all-purpose yards in Detroit on Thanksgiving. His electrifying, 83-yard punt return for a touchdown with 41 seconds left lifted the Packers past the Lions 44-40.

Stanley said: "I just didn't feel like fair-catching. I felt, 'Hey, this is a game to take chances. Something's going to happen big or something isn't going to happen big.'

"I went for it."

DELAY OF VICTORY

"Somehow it's just slipping away from us, and I don't know why," Charles Martin said after the Packers fell to 0-6 on Oct.12. The defensive end was far from alone in his frustration.

In 1986, Green Bay went winless in its first six games. It's the most consecutive losses the Packers have had to start a season.

Two of the losses were blowouts: 31-3 to Houston and 42-7 to Minnesota. Two others could have been, but second-half rallies kept the final score within reason.

In the other two losses, Green Bay battled valiantly against a more talented Bears team and stayed close to a Lions team that finished one game ahead of the Packers in the Central Division standings.

Most consecutive games lost, start of season

No.	Year	Final Record
6	1986	4-12
5	1988	4-12
4	1975	4-10

TEAM STATISTICS

	GB	OPP
First Downs	286	313
Rushing	96	135
Passing	172	151
Penalty	18	27
Rushes	424	565
Yards Gained	1,614	2,095
Average Gain	3.81	3.71
Average Yards per Game	100.9	130.9
Passes Attempted	565	448
Completed	305	267
% Completed	53.98	59.60
Total Yards Gained	3,708	3,142
Times Sacked	37	28
Yards Lost	261	222
Net Yards Gained	3,447	2,920
Yards Gained per Completion	12.16	11.77
Net Yards per Attempt	5.73	6.13
Average Net Yards per Game	215.4	182.5
Combined Net Yards Gained	5,061	5,015
Total Plays	1,026	1,041
Average Yards per Play	4.93	4.82
Average Yards per Game	316.3	313.4
Third Down Efficiency	79/222	94/217
Percentage	35.59	43.32
Fourth Down Efficiency	13/25	7/14
Percentage	52.00	50.00
Intercepted By	20	27
Yards Returned	147	357
Returned for TD	1	3
Punts	75	70
Yards Punted	2,825	2,769
Average Yards per Punt	37.67	39.56
Punt Returns	33	44
Yards Returned	316	287
Average Yards per Return	9.58	6.52
Returned for TD	1	0
Kickoff Returns	76	62
Yards Returned	1,470	1,181
Average Yards per Return	19.34	19.05
Returned for TD	0	0
Penalties	128	79
Yards Penalized	949	657
Fumbles	35	32
Lost	18	12
Own Recovered for Touchdown	0	0
Opponent's Recovered by	12	18
Opponent's Recovered for Touchdown	0	0
Total Points Scored	254	418
Total Touchdowns	29	52
Touchdowns Rushing	8	16
Touchdowns Passing	18	31
Touchdowns on Returns & Recoveries	3	5
Extra Points	29	48
Safeties	0	2
Field Goals Attempted	27	25
Field Goals Made	17	18
% Successful	62.96	72.00
Average Time of Possession	28:11	31:49

Regular Season 4-12-0

Date	GB		OPP	Att.
9/7	3	Houston Oilers	31	(54,065)
9/14	10	at New Orleans Saints	24	(46,383)
9/22	12	Chicago Bears	25	(55,527)
9/28	7	at Minnesota Vikings	42	(60,478)
10/5	28	Cincinnati Bengals (M)	34	(51,230)
10/12	14	Detroit Lions	21	(52,290)
10/19	17	at Cleveland Browns	14	(76,438)
10/26	17	San Francisco 49ers (M)	31	(50,557)
11/2	3	at Pittsburgh Steelers	27	(52,831)
11/9	7	Washington Redskins	16	(47,728)
11/16	31	Tampa Bay Buccaneers (M)	7	(48,271)
11/23	10	at Chicago Bears	12	(59,291)
11/27	44	at Detroit Lions	40	(61,199)
12/7	6	Minnesota Vikings	32	(47,637)
12/14	21	at Tampa Bay Buccaneers	7	(30,099)
12/20	24	at New York Giants	55	(71,351)

Score By Periods

	1	2	3	4	OT	Total
Packers	57	80	65	52	0	254
Opponents	124	106	78	110	0	418

INDIVIDUAL STATISTICS

Rushing

	Att	Yds	Avg	LG	TD
K. Davis	114	519	4.6	50	0
G. Ellis	84	345	4.1	24	2
Carruth	81	308	3.8	42	2
Ellerson	90	287	3.2	18	3
J. Clark	18	41	2.3	9	0
R. Wright	18	41	2.3	18	1
Ivery	4	25	6.3	15	0
Stanley	1	19	19.0	19	0
Epps	4	18	4.5	20	0
Fusina	7	11	1.6	6	0
Ferragamo	1	0	0.0	0	0
Renner	1	0	0.0	0	0
Swanke	1	0	0.0	0	0
Packers	**424**	**1,614**	**3.8**	**50**	**8**
Opponents	565	2,095	3.7	t41	16

Receiving

	No	Yds	Avg	LG	TD
Lofton	64	840	13.1	36	4
Epps	49	612	12.5	t53	4
Stanley	35	723	20.7	62	2
Ivery	31	385	12.4	42	1
G. Ellis	24	258	10.8	29	0
Carruth	24	134	5.6	19	2
K. Davis	21	142	6.8	18	1
Ross	17	143	8.4	16	1
E. West	15	199	13.3	t46	1
Ellerson	12	130	10.8	32	0
J. Clark	6	41	6.8	12	0
Moffitt	4	87	21.8	34	0
M. Lewis	2	7	3.5	t4	2
Franz	1	7	7.0	7	0
Packers	**305**	**3,708**	**12.2**	**62**	**18**
Opponents	267	3,142	11.8	84	31

Passing

	Att	Com	Yds	Pct	TD	In	Tk/Yds	Rate
R. Wright	492	263	3,247	53.5	17	23	33/243	66.2
Ferragamo	40	23	283	57.5	1	3	3/15	56.6
Fusina	32	19	178	59.4	0	1	1/3	61.7
Lofton	1	0	0	00.0	0	0	0/0	—
Packers	**565**	**305**	**3,708**	**54.0**	**18**	**27**	**37/261**	**65.1**
Opponents	448	267	3,142	59.6	31	20	28/222	85.4

Punting

	No	Yds	Avg	Net	TB	In20	LG	HB
Bracken	55	2,203	40.1	32.8	5	6	63	2
Renner	15	622	41.5	30.6	1	2	50	3
Packers	**75**	**2,825**	**37.7**	**32.2**	**6**	**8**	**63**	**5**
Opponents	70	2,769	39.6	31.3	13	16	61	2

Kickoff Returns

	No	Yds	Avg	LG	TD
Stanley	28	559	20.0	55	0
Watts	12	239	19.9	40	0
K. Davis	12	231	19.3	35	0
Stills	10	209	20.9	38	0
Ellerson	7	154	22.0	57	0
Carruth	4	40	10.0	20	0
Epps	1	21	21.0	21	0
E. Berry	1	16	16.0	16	0
Noble	1	1	1.0	1	0
Packers	**76**	**1,470**	**19.3**	**57**	**0**
Opponents	62	1,181	19.0	64	0

Punt Returns

	No	Yds	Avg	FC	LG	TD
Stanley	33	316	9.6	7	t83	1
Packers	**33**	**316**	**9.6**	**7**	**t83**	**1**
Opponents	44	287	6.5	5	17	0

Interceptions

	No	Yds	Avg	LG	TD
M. Lee	9	33	3.7	11	0
Cade	4	26	6.5	18	0
Greene	2	0	0.0	0	0
Stills	1	58	58.0	t58	1
Leopold	1	21	21.0	21	0
Watts	1	6	6.0	6	0
J. Anderson	1	3	3.0	3	0
Flynn	1	0	0.0	0	0
Packers	**20**	**147**	**7.4**	**t58**	**1**
Opponents	27	357	13.2	t88	3

Scoring

	TDr	TDp	TDrt	PAT	FG	S	TP
Del Greco	0	0	0	29/29	17/27	0	80
Carruth	2	2	0	0/0	0/0	0	24
Epps	0	4	0	0/0	0/0	0	24
Lofton	0	4	0	0/0	0/0	0	24
Ellerson	3	0	0	0/0	0/0	0	18
Stanley	0	2	1	0/0	0/0	0	18
G. Ellis	2	0	0	0/0	0/0	0	12
M. Lewis	0	2	0	0/0	0/0	0	12
K. Davis	0	1	0	0/0	0/0	0	6
Ivery	0	1	0	0/0	0/0	0	6
Ross	0	1	0	0/0	0/0	0	6
Simmons	0	0	1	0/0	0/0	0	6
Stills	0	0	1	0/0	0/0	0	6
E. West	0	1	0	0/0	0/0	0	6
R. Wright	1	0	0	0/0	0/0	0	6
Packers	**8**	**18**	**3**	**29/29**	**17/27**	**0**	**254**
Opponents	16	31	5	48/52	18/25	2	418

Fumbles

	Fum	Ow	Op	Yds	Tot
E. Berry	0	1	0	0	1
R. Brown	0	0	1	0	1
Carreker	0	0	2	0	2
Carruth	1	0	0	0	0
Cherry	0	0	0	-23	0
J. Clark	1	0	0	0	0
K. Davis	2	0	0	0	0
J. Dorsey	0	0	1	0	1
Ellerson	3	0	0	0	0
G. Ellis	4	1	0	0	1
Ferragamo	3	0	0	-8	0
Fusina	4	4	0	-1	4
T. Harris	0	0	1	0	1
Humphrey	0	0	1	0	1
Ivery	0	0	0	0	1
Koart	0	0	1	0	1
M. Lee	0	0	1	0	1
Lofton	3	2	0	8	2
C. Martin	0	0	1	0	1
Ruettgers	0	1	0	0	1
R. Scott	0	0	1	0	1
Stanley	1	0	0	0	0
Stills	1	0	0	0	0
Swanke	0	0	0	-4	0
Veingrad	0	1	0	0	1
E. West	0	0	1	0	1
R. Wright	8	3	0	-4	3
Packers	**35**	**14**	**12**	**-32**	**26**

Quarterback Sacks

	No
T. Harris	8.0
Greenwood	3.0
E. Johnson	3.0
Carreker	2.5
R. Brown	2.0
Noble	2.0
Leopold	1.5
Cade	1.0
Greene	1.0
C. Martin	1.0
R. Scott	1.0
B. Thomas	1.0
Watts	1.0
Packers	**28.0**
Opponents	37.0

NFL STANDINGS

National Conference

Eastern Division

	W	L	T	Pct	PF	PA
New York Giants	14	2	0	.875	371	236
Washington Redskins	12	4	0	.750	368	296
Dallas Cowboys	7	9	0	.438	346	337
Philadelphia Eagles	5	10	1	.344	256	312
St. Louis Cardinals	4	11	1	.281	218	351

Central Division

	W	L	T	Pct	PF	PA
Chicago Bears	14	2	0	.875	352	187
Minnesota Vikings	9	7	0	.563	398	273
Detroit Lions	5	11	0	.313	277	326
Green Bay Packers	**4**	**12**	**0**	**.250**	**254**	**418**
Tampa Bay Buccaneers	2	14	0	.125	239	473

Western Division

	W	L	T	Pct	PF	PA
San Francisco 49ers	10	5	1	.656	374	247
Los Angeles Rams	10	6	0	.625	309	267
Atlanta Falcons	7	8	1	.469	280	280
New Orleans Saints	7	9	0	.438	288	287

American Conference

Eastern Division

	W	L	T	Pct	PF	PA
New England Patriots	11	5	0	.688	412	307
New York Jets	10	6	0	.625	364	386
Miami Dolphins	8	8	0	.500	430	405
Buffalo Bills	4	12	0	.250	287	348
Indianapolis Colts	3	13	0	.188	229	400

Central Division

	W	L	T	Pct	PF	PA
Cleveland Browns	12	4	0	.750	391	310
Cincinnati Bengals	10	6	0	.625	409	394
Pittsburgh Steelers	6	10	0	.375	307	336
Houston Oilers	5	11	0	.313	274	329

Western Division

	W	L	T	Pct	PF	PA
Denver Broncos	11	5	0	.688	378	327
Kansas City Chiefs	10	6	0	.625	358	326
Seattle Seahawks	10	6	0	.625	366	293
Los Angeles Raiders	8	8	0	.500	323	346
San Diego Chargers	4	12	0	.250	335	396

ROSTER

No	Name	Pos	Ht	Wt	DOB	College	G
59	Anderson, John	LB	6-3	228	02/14/56	Michigan	4
20	Berry, Ed	DB	5-10	183	09/28/63	Utah State	16
61	Boyarsky, Jerry	NT	6-3	290	05/15/59	Pittsburgh	2
17	Bracken, Don	P	6-0	211	02/16/62	Michigan	13
93	Brown, Robert	DE	6-2	267	05/21/60	Virginia Tech	16
24	Cade, Mossy	CB	6-1	198	12/26/61	Texas	16
58	Cannon, Mark	C	6-3	268	06/14/62	Texas-Arlington	7
76	Carreker, Alphonso	DE	6-6	271	05/25/62	Florida State	16
30	Carruth, Paul Ott	RB	6-1	220	07/22/61	Alabama	16
69	Cherry, Bill	C	6-4	277	01/05/61	Mid Tenn. State	16
33	Clark, Jessie	FB	6-0	228	01/03/60	Arkansas	5
36	Davis, Kenneth	RB	5-10	209	04/16/62	TCU	16
10	Del Greco, Al	K	5-10	191	03/02/62	Auburn	16
56	Dent, Burnell	LB	6-1	236	03/16/63	Tulane	16
99	Dorsey, John	LB	6-2	243	08/31/60	Connecticut	16
42	Ellerson, Gary	RB	5-11	219	07/17/63	Wisconsin	16
31	Ellis, Gerry	FB	5-11	235	11/12/57	Missouri	16
85	Epps, Phillip	WR	5-10	165	11/11/58	TCU	12
77	Feasel, Greg	T	6-7	301	11/07/58	Abilene Christian	15
5	Ferragamo, Vince	QB	6-3	217	04/24/54	Nebraska	3
41	Flynn, Tom	S	6-0	195	03/24/62	Pittsburgh	7
84	Franz, Nolan	WR	6-2	183	09/11/59	Tulane	1
4	Fusina, Chuck	QB	6-1	195	05/31/57	Penn State	7
23	Greene, George (Tiger)	DB	6-0	194	02/15/62	Western Carolina	13
49	Greenwood, David	S	6-3	210	03/25/60	Wisconsin	9
65	Hallstrom, Ron	G	6-6	290	06/11/59	Iowa	16
97	Harris, Tim	LB	6-5	235	09/10/64	Memphis State	16
27	Hayes, Gary	CB	5-10	180	08/19/57	Fresno State	10
79	Humphrey, Donnie	DE	6-3	295	04/20/61	Auburn	16
40	Ivery, Eddie Lee	RB	6-1	206	07/30/57	Georgia Tech	12
90	Johnson, Ezra	DE	6-4	264	10/02/55	Morris Brown	16
92	Koart, Matt	DE	6-5	256	09/28/63	USC	6
22	Lee, Mark	CB	5-11	189	03/20/58	Washington	16
53	Leopold, Bobby	LB	6-1	224	10/18/57	Notre Dame	12
89	Lewis, Mark	TE	6-2	237	05/05/61	Texas A&M	16
26	Lewis, Tim	CB	5-11	191	12/18/61	Pittsburgh	3
80	Lofton, James	WR	6-3	197	07/05/56	Stanford	15
44	Mandeville, Chris	S	6-1	213	02/01/65	California-Davis	2
94	Martin, Charles	DE	6-4	280	08/31/59	Livingston	14
88	McConkey, Phil	WR	5-10	170	02/24/57	Navy	4
62	Mendoza, Ruben	G	6-3	278	05/10/63	Wayne State	6
82	Moffitt, Mike	WR	6-4	211	07/28/63	Fresno State	4
57	Moran, Rich	G	6-2	275	03/19/62	San Diego State	5
72	Neville, Tom	G	6-5	306	09/04/61	Fresno State	16
91	Noble, Brian	LB	6-3	252	09/06/62	Arizona State	16
71	Ploeger, Kurt	DE	6-5	260	12/01/62	Gustavus Adolphus	1
13	Renner, Bill	P	6-0	198	05/23/59	Virginia Tech	3
81	Ross, Dan	TE	6-4	240	02/09/57	Northeastern	15
75	Ruettgers, Ken	T	6-5	280	08/20/62	USC	16
54	Schuh, Jeff	LB	6-3	234	05/22/58	Minnesota	12
55	Scott, Randy	LB	6-1	228	01/31/59	Alabama	15
18	Shield, Joe	QB	6-1	185	06/26/62	Trinity College	3
32	Simmons, John	CB	5-11	192	12/01/58	SMU	6
87	Stanley, Walter	WR	5-9	179	11/05/62	Mesa	16
29	Stills, Ken	S	5-10	186	09/06/63	Wisconsin	16
38	Sullivan, John	S	6-1	190	10/15/61	California	6
67	Swanke, Karl	T	6-6	280	12/29/57	Boston College	10
92	Thomas, Ben	DE	6-4	275	07/02/61	Auburn	9
53	Turpin, Mike	LB	6-4	230	05/15/64	California	1
73	Veingrad, Alan	T	6-5	277	07/24/63	E. Texas State	9
28	Watts, Elbert	CB	6-1	205	03/20/63	USC	9
52	Weddington, Mike	LB	6-4	245	10/09/60	Oklahoma	3
86	West, Ed	TE	6-1	243	08/02/61	Auburn	16
16	Wright, Randy	QB	6-2	203	01/12/61	Wisconsin	16

DRAFT

Rnd	Name	Pos	Ht	Wt	College
1	(Choice (14) to Chargers for Mossy Cade)				
2	Kenneth Davis (41)	RB	5-10	209	TCU
3	Robbie Bosco (72)	QB	6-3	200	Brigham Young
4a	Tim Harris (84)	LB	6-5	235	Memphis State
	(Choice from Bills in first round switch of 1985)				
4b	Dan Knight (98)	T	6-5	280	San Diego State
5	Matt Koart (125)	DT	6-5	256	USC
6a	Burnell Dent (143)	LB	6-1	230	Tulane
	(Choice from Cardinals for Scott Brunner)				
6b	(Choice (151) to Broncos for Scott Brunner)				
7	Ed Berry (183)	DB	5-10	176	Utah State
8	Michael Cline (210)	NT	6-3	265	Arkansas State
9	Brent Moore (236)	LB	6-5	242	USC
10	Gary Spann (263)	LB	6-2	220	TCU
11	(Choice (294) to Bengals for Mike Obrovac)				
12	(Choice (331) to Bills for Preston Dennard)				

FRONT ROW: (L-R) 5 Vince Ferragamo, 10 Al Del Greco, 11 Robbie Bosco, 16 Randy Wright, 17 Don Bracken, 20 Ed Berry, 22 Mark Lee, 24 Mossy Cade, 26 Tim Lewis, 27 Gary Hayes.

SECOND ROW: (L-R) 29 Ken Stills, 30 Paul Ott Carruth, 31 Gerry Ellis, 33 Jessie Clark, 34 Mike Moffitt, 36 Kenneth Davis, 37 Mark Murphy, 38 John Sullivan, 39 Freddie Parker, 40 Eddie Lee Ivery, 41 Tom Flynn.

THIRD ROW: (L-R) 42 Gary Ellerson, 52 Mike Weddington, 54 Jeff Schuh, 55 Randy Scott, 56 Burnell Dent, 57 Rich Moran, 58 Mark Cannon, 59 John Anderson, 62 Ruben Mendoza, 65 Ron Hallstrom.

FOURTH ROW: (L-R) 67 Karl Swanke, 69 Bill Cherry, 70 Keith Uecker, 72 Tom Neville, 73 Alan Veingrad, 74 Dan Knight, 75 Ken Ruettgers, 76 Alphonso Carreker, 77 Greg Feasel, 79 Donnie Humphrey, 80 James Lofton.

FIFTH ROW: (L-R) 81 Dan Ross, 84 Nolan Franz, 85 Phillip Epps, 86 Ed West, 87 Walter Stanley, 88 Phil McConkey, 89 Mark Lewis, 90 Ezra Johnson, 91 Brian Noble, 92 Matt Koart.

SIXTH ROW: (L-R) 81 Medical Assistant Derick Brook, Trainer Domenic Gentile, 93 Robert Brown, 94 Charles Martin, 97 Tim Harris, 98 Brent Moore, 99 John Dorsey, Equipment Manager Bob Noel, Equipment Assistant Jack Noel, Assistant Equipment Manager Bryan Nehring.

BACK ROW: (L-R) Passing Game/Receivers Coach Tom Coughlin, Administrative Assistant Forrest Gregg, Jr., Defensive Backfield Coach Dick Jauron, Strength-Conditioning/Offensive Line Coach Virgil Knight, Linebackers Coach Dale Lindsey, Head Coach Forrest Gregg, Special Teams/Offensive Backfield Coach John Hilton, Offensive Line Coach Jerry Wampfler, Defensive Coordinator/Line Coach Dick Modzelewski, Quarterbacks Coach George Sefcik.

The Packers' desire to get off to a quick start in 1987 was interrupted by a players' strike, the second in five years. But unlike 1982, when the team rallied to clinch its first playoff berth in a decade, the Packers of this abbreviated season stumbled to a 5-9-1 record.

Two teams took the field for Green Bay in 1987. In addition to its regular team, the Packers fielded a B Team, or replacement team. That team was assembled after NFL players went on strike following the conclusion of the Jets-Patriots game of Monday, Sept. 21. For three weeks in October, the nation was treated to replacement football. The union ended its 24-day walkout on Oct. 15, and those who had been striking were back in uniform for games played on the final weekend of the month.

On Jan. 31, the Packers created the position of executive vice president of football operations and hired Tom Braatz from the Atlanta Falcons to fill it. Some of Braatz's duties included conducting the draft in conjunction with the head coach, making trades and waiver acquisitions and negotiating players' contracts. Braatz's appointment marked the first time since 1958 that control of the team was divided between two men.

Eddie Lee Ivery, Gerry Ellis, Karl Swanke, and Randy Scott saw their careers come to an end. Ivery, converted to wide receiver in 1986, missed the entire season after undergoing surgery to repair a disc problem in his lower back. Ellis ruptured an Achilles' tendon in the offseason, had surgery, failed his physical, and was waived in early August. Swanke retired, and Scott was cut just before the season opener.

Contract holdouts were in vogue. Randy Wright held out for 15 days before signing in mid-August and looked rusty in the season opener. First-round draft pick Brent Fullwood missed 12 days before inking a deal, then failed to live up to expectations by gaining just 274 yards over the course of the season. Even Patrick Scott, the team's 11th-round pick, held out into August for more money.

Off-the-field incidents further tarnished the Packers' reputation. Charles Martin, who admitted to a drinking problem, was waived Sept. 23 after fighting in a bar. Cornerback Mossy Cade was sentenced to two years in prison on Aug. 3 after being found guilty of sexually assaulting a woman in November 1985.

"Operation: Quickstart" became the team's motto as it sought to avoid the slow starts of the recent past. Green Bay did little toward that end when it bungled its opener 20-0 against the Raiders. Wright threw three interceptions and conceded his holdout affected his performance.

Rookie Don Majkowski started at quarterback the following week. The team's 10th-round draft choice presided over a 17-17 tie with Denver.

"I met my expectations," Majkowski said.

Games in Week 3 were canceled due to the strike. For Green Bay, that meant it did not travel to Tampa Bay for an engagement with the Buccaneers on Sept. 27.

When the strike ended, the Packers and Lions met in the Silverdome. Al Del Greco's 45-yard field goal proved the difference in a 34-33 Green Bay win.

The win put the Packers (3-2-1) a game-and-a-half behind the division leading Bears (5-1). But consecutive losses to Tampa Bay, Chicago, and Seattle knocked the team out of second place.

Frankie Neal helped snap that three-game losing streak by catching two touchdown passes in a 23-3 triumph in Kansas City. Green Bay surrendered a season-low 201 yards to the Chiefs.

Walter Payton gained only 22 yards in his final game against the Packers on Nov. 29, a 23-10 Bears win. Joe Montana then completed his first 17 passes in a row as the 49ers outmaneuvered Green Bay 23-12 on Dec. 6.

The Green and Gold notched its last win of 1987 against the Vikings in Milwaukee. Kenneth Davis' 7-yard run with 1:14 left gave the Packers a 16-10 win.

After the season wrapped, Gregg predicted a winning season was just around the corner.

"Maybe we won't make the playoffs, but I think we'll have a winning team," he said.

Maybe with Gregg at the helm, the team would have. But the point became moot, for Gregg resigned on Jan. 15, 1988, to become head coach at his alma mater, Southern Methodist University.

A PROPENSITY FOR PENALTIES

Forrest Gregg's Packers were penalized more than 100 times in each of his four seasons as coach. In 1987, the team was penalized a team-record 135 times.

On opening day, the team had 12 penalties. It had at least 10 on five other occasions.

The two worst outings came during the first two Sundays in November. On Nov. 1, the club had 14 penalties against the Buccaneers in Tampa Bay. On Nov. 8, it had 16 penalties against the Bears in Lambeau Field.

Green Bay and the Jets tied for the most penalties in the league. The Packers, however, lost more yards (1,103) because of penalties than any other team in the NFL.

Even the replacement team was affected. It had 27 penalties in three games, an average of nine per game.

Most penalties, season

No.	Year	Record
135	1987	5-9-1
128	1986	4-12-0
110	1984	8-8-0

TEAM STATISTICS

	GB	OPP
First Downs	248	296
Rushing	97	118
Passing	133	152
Penalty	18	26
Rushes	464	521
Yards Gained	1,801	1,920
Average Gain	3.88	3.69
Average Yards per Game	120.1	128.0
Passes Attempted	455	469
Completed	234	279
% Completed	51.43	59.49
Total Yards Gained	2,977	3,200
Times Sacked	45	34
Yards Lost	296	197
Net Yards Gained	2,681	3,003
Yards Gained per Completion	12.72	11.47
Net Yards per Attempt	5.36	5.97
Average Net Yards per Game	178.7	200.2
Combined Net Yards Gained	4,482	4,923
Total Plays	964	1,024
Average Yards per Play	4.65	4.81
Average Net Yards per Game	298.8	328.2
Third Down Efficiency	68/217	86/220
Percentage	31.34	39.09
Fourth Down Efficiency	2/8	10/14
Percentage	25.00	71.43
Intercepted By	18	17
Yards Returned	220	115
Returned for TD	0	1
Punts	93	77
Yards Punted	3,659	3,084
Average Yards per Punt	39.34	40.05
Punt Returns	35	54
Yards Returned	245	422
Average Yards per Return	7.00	7.81
Returned for TD	0	0
Kickoff Returns	59	61
Yards Returned	1,032	1,140
Average Yards per Return	17.49	18.69
Returned for TD	0	0
Penalties	135	104
Yards Penalized	1,103	852
Fumbles	35	42
Lost	18	24
Own Recovered for Touchdown	0	0
Opponent's Recovered by	24	18
Opponent's Recovered for Touchdown	0	0
Total Points Scored	255	300
Total Touchdowns	28	31
Touchdowns Rushing	13	15
Touchdowns Passing	15	14
Touchdowns on Returns & Recoveries	0	2
Extra Points	24	29
Safeties	0	2
Field Goals Attempted	29	36
Field Goals Made	21	27
% Successful	72.41	75.00
Average Time of Possession	29:02	30:58

Regular Season   5-9-1

Date	GB		OPP	Att.
9/13	0	Los Angeles Raiders	20	(54,983)
9/20	17	Denver Broncos (M) (OT)	17	(50,624)
9/27	**	at Tampa Bay Buccaneers		
10/4	*23	at Minnesota Vikings	16	(13,911)
10/11	*16	Detroit Lions (OT)	19	(35,779)
10/18	*16	Philadelphia Eagles (OT)	10	(35,842)
10/25	34	at Detroit Lions	33	(27,278)
11/1	17	Tampa Bay Buccaneers (M)	23	(50,308)
11/8	24	Chicago Bears	26	(53,320)
11/15	13	at Seattle Seahawks	24	(60,963)
11/22	23	at Kansas City Chiefs	3	(34,611)
11/29	10	at Chicago Bears	23	(61,638)
12/6	12	San Francisco 49ers	23	(51,118)
12/13	16	Minnesota Vikings (M)	10	(47,059)
12/19	10	at New York Giants	20	(51,013)
12/27	24	at New Orleans Saints	33	(68,364)

*   replacement games
**   game cancelled because of players' strike

Score By Periods

	1	2	3	4	OT	Total
Packers	80	75	42	52	6	255
Opponents	40	98	71	88	3	300

INDIVIDUAL STATISTICS

Rushing

	Att	Yds	Avg	LG	TD
K. Davis	109	413	3.8	t39	3
Fullwood	84	274	3.3	18	5
Willhite	53	251	4.7	61	0
J. Clark	56	211	3.8	57	0
Carruth	64	192	3.0	23	3
Majkowski	15	127	8.5	33	0
R. Wright	13	70	5.4	27	0
Risher	11	64	5.8	15	1
Hargrove	11	38	3.5	7	1
Stanley	4	38	9.5	24	0
Parker	8	33	4.1	17	0
Weigel	10	26	2.6	7	0
Sterling	5	20	4.0	9	0
L. Thomas	5	19	3.8	5	0
Larry Morris	8	18	2.3	10	0
K. Cook	2	3	1.5	2	0
P. Scott	1	2	2.0	2	0
Lee Morris	2	2	1.0	4	0
Epps	1	0	0.0	0	0
T. Hunter	1	0	0.0	0	0
F. Neal	1	0	0.0	0	0
Packers	**464**	**1,801**	**3.9**	**61**	**13**
Opponents	521	1,920	3.7	t57	15

Receiving

	No	Yds	Avg	LG	TD
Stanley	38	672	17.7	t70	3
F. Neal	36	420	11.7	38	3
Epps	34	516	15.2	40	2
J. Clark	22	119	5.4	19	1
E. West	19	261	13.7	40	1
Lee Morris	16	259	16.2	t46	1
K. Davis	14	110	7.9	35	0
Paskett	12	188	15.7	t47	1
Carruth	10	78	7.8	19	1
P. Scott	8	79	9.9	16	0
Summers	7	83	11.9	17	1
Willhite	6	37	6.2	12	0
Parker	3	22	7.3	13	0
L. Thomas	2	52	26.0	t30	1
D. Harden	2	29	14.5	15	0
Fullwood	2	11	5.5	12	0
Redick	1	18	18.0	18	0
Weigel	1	17	17.0	17	0
Hargrove	1	6	6.0	6	0
Packers	**234**	**2,977**	**12.7**	**t70**	**15**
Opponents	279	3,200	11.5	t63	14

Passing

	Att	Com	Yds	Pct	TD	In	Tk/Yds	Rate
R. Wright	247	132	1,507	53.4	6	11	20/128	61.6
Majkowski	127	55	875	43.3	5	3	10/77	70.2
Risher	74	44	564	59.5	3	3	12/77	80.0
Gillus	5	2	28	40.0	0	0	3/14	—
Carruth	1	1	3	100.0	1	0	0/0	—
F. Neal	1	0	0	00.0	0	0	0/0	—
Packers	**455**	**234**	**2,977**	**51.4**	**15**	**17**	**45/296**	**67.6**
Opponents	469	279	3,200	59.5	14	18	34/197	74.0

Punting

	No	Yds	Avg	Net	TB	In20	LG	HB
Bracken	72	2,947	40.9	34.2	5	13	65	1
Renner	20	712	35.6	31.2	1	4	49	0
Packers	**93**	**3,659**	**39.3**	**33.5**	**6**	**17**	**65**	**1**
Opponents	77	3,084	40.1	35.3	11	22	71	0

Kickoff Returns

	No	Yds	Avg	LG	TD
Fullwood	24	510	21.3	46	0
K. Cook	10	147	14.7	38	0
Lee Morris	6	104	17.3	28	0
D. Harden	4	72	18.0	20	0
F. Neal	4	44	11.0	18	0
Stanley	3	47	15.7	29	0
N. Jefferson	2	30	15.0	18	0
P. Scott	2	32	16.0	23	0
Carruth	1	8	8.0	8	0
Weishuhn	1	1	1.0	1	0
Cherry	1	0	0.0	0	0
Sterling	1	0	0.0	0	0
Willhite	0	37	—	37	0
Packers	**59**	**1,032**	**17.5**	**46**	**0**
Opponents	61	1,140	18.7	74	0

Punt Returns

	No	Yds	Avg	FC	LG	TD
Stanley	28	173	6.2	4	48	0
P. Scott	6	71	11.8	2	36	0
Lee Morris	1	1	1.0	0	1	0
Packers	**35**	**245**	**7.0**	**6**	**48**	**0**
Opponents	54	422	7.8	8	37	0

Interceptions

	No	Yds	Avg	LG	TD
J.B. Morris	3	135	45.0	73	0
D. Brown	3	16	5.3	11	0
J. Anderson	2	22	11.0	13	0
Holland	2	4	2.0	4	0
Mansfield	1	14	14.0	14	0
Greene	1	11	11.0	11	0
Noble	1	10	10.0	10	0
Carreker	1	6	6.0	6	0
K. Johnson	1	2	2.0	2	0
A. Harrison	1	0	0.0	0	0
M. Lee	1	0	0.0	0	0
Melka	1	0	0.0	0	0
Packers	**18**	**220**	**12.2**	**73**	**0**
Opponents	17	115	6.8	t35	1

Scoring

	TDr	TDp	TDrt	PAT	FG	S	TP
Zendejas	0	0	0	13/15	16/19	0	61
Fullwood	5	0	0	0/0	0/0	0	30
Del Greco	0	0	0	11/11	5/10	0	26
Carruth	3	1	0	0/0	0/0	0	24
K. Davis	3	0	0	0/0	0/0	0	18
F. Neal	0	3	0	0/0	0/0	0	18
Stanley	0	3	0	0/0	0/0	0	18
Epps	0	2	0	0/0	0/0	0	12
J. Clark	0	1	0	0/0	0/0	0	6
Hargrove	1	0	0	0/0	0/0	0	6
Lee Morris	0	1	0	0/0	0/0	0	6
Paskett	0	1	0	0/0	0/0	0	6
Risher	1	0	0	0/0	0/0	0	6
Summers	0	1	0	0/0	0/0	0	6
L. Thomas	0	1	0	0/0	0/0	0	6
E. West	0	1	0	0/0	0/0	0	6
Packers	**13**	**15**	**0**	**24/27**	**21/29**	**0**	**255**
Opponents	15	14	2	29/31	27/36	2	300

Quarterback Sacks

	No
T. Harris	7.0
J. Anderson	4.0
Carreker	4.0
R. Brown	3.0
Boyarsky	2.0
Drost	2.0
E. Johnson	2.0
M. Murphy	2.0
Browner	1.0
Holland	1.0
K. Johnson	1.0
K. Jordan	1.0
C. Martin	1.0
J.B. Morris	1.0
Noble	1.0
Caldwell	0.5
C. Sullivan	0.5
Packers	**34.0**
Opponents	45.0

NFL STANDINGS

National Conference

Eastern Division

	W	L	T	Pct	PF	PA
Washington Redskins	11	4	0	.733	379	285
Dallas Cowboys	7	8	0	.467	340	348
St. Louis Cardinals	7	8	0	.467	362	368
Philadelphia Eagles	7	8	0	.467	337	380
New York Giants	6	9	0	.400	280	312

Central Division

	W	L	T	Pct	PF	PA
Chicago Bears	11	4	0	.733	356	282
Minnesota Vikings	8	7	0	.533	336	335
Green Bay Packers	5	9	1	.367	255	300
Tampa Bay Buccaneers	4	11	0	.267	286	360
Detroit Lions	4	11	0	.267	269	384

Western Division

	W	L	T	Pct	PF	PA
San Francisco 49ers	13	2	0	.867	459	253
New Orleans Saints	12	3	0	.800	422	283
Los Angeles Rams	6	9	0	.400	317	361
Atlanta Falcons	3	12	0	.200	205	436

American Conference

Eastern Division

	W	L	T	Pct	PF	PA
Indianapolis Colts	9	6	0	.600	300	238
New England Patriots	8	7	0	.533	320	293
Miami Dolphins	8	7	0	.533	362	335
Buffalo Bills	7	8	0	.467	270	305
New York Jets	6	9	0	.400	334	360

Central Division

	W	L	T	Pct	PF	PA
Cleveland Browns	10	5	0	.667	390	239
Houston Oilers	9	6	0	.600	345	349
Pittsburgh Steelers	8	7	0	.533	285	299
Cincinnati Bengals	4	11	0	.267	285	370

Western Division

	W	L	T	Pct	PF	PA
Denver Broncos	10	4	1	.700	379	288
Seattle Seahawks	9	6	0	.600	371	314
San Diego Chargers	8	7	0	.533	253	317
Los Angeles Raiders	5	10	0	.333	301	289
Kansas City Chiefs	4	11	0	.267	273	388

"UNION" ROSTER

No	Name	Pos	Ht	Wt	DOB	College	G
59	Anderson, John	LB	6-3	228	02/14/56	Michigan	12
61	Boyarsky, Jerry	NT	6-3	290	05/15/59	Pittsburgh	12
17	Bracken, Don	P	6-0	211	02/16/62	Michigan	12
32	Brown, Dave	CB	6-1	197	01/16/53	Michigan	12
93	Brown, Robert	DE	6-2	267	05/21/60	Virginia Tech	12
79	Browner, Ross	DE	6-3	265	03/22/54	Notre Dame	11
58	Cannon, Mark	C	6-3	270	06/14/62	Texas-Arlington	12
76	Carreker, Alphonso	DE	6-6	271	05/25/62	Florida State	12
30	Carruth, Paul Ott	RB	6-1	220	07/22/61	Alabama	12
69	Cherry, Bill	C	6-4	277	01/05/61	Middle Tennessee State	12
33	Clark, Jessie	FB	6-0	228	01/03/60	Arkansas	12
64	Collier, Steve*	T	6-7	342	04/19/63	Bethune-Cookman	7
20	Cook, Kelly	RB	5-10	225	08/20/62	Oklahoma State	11
36	Davis, Kenneth	RB	5-10	209	04/16/62	TCU	10
10	Del Greco, Al	K	5-10	191	03/02/62	Auburn	5
56	Dent, Burnell	LB	6-1	236	03/16/63	Tulane	9
99	Dorsey, John	LB	6-2	243	08/31/60	Connecticut	12
85	Epps, Phillip	WR	5-10	165	11/11/58	TCU	10
21	Fullwood, Brent	FB	5-11	209	10/10/63	Auburn	11
23	Greene, George (Tiger)	DB	6-0	194	02/15/62	Western Carolina	11
89	Hackett, Joey	TE	6-5	267	09/29/58	Elon	11
65	Hallstrom, Ron	G	6-6	290	06/11/59	Iowa	12
97	Harris, Tim	LB	6-5	235	09/10/64	Memphis State	12
50	Holland, Johnny	LB	6-2	221	03/11/65	Texas A&M	12
38	Jefferson, Norman	DB	5-10	183	08/07/64	LSU	12
90	Johnson, Ezra	DE	6-4	264	10/02/55	Morris Brown	6
39	Johnson, Kenneth	CB	6-0	185	12/28/63	Mississippi State	12
22	Lee, Mark	CB	5-11	189	03/20/58	Washington	12
89	Lewis, Mark	TE	6-2	237	05/05/61	Texas A&M	1
94	Logan, Dave	NT	6-2	250	10/25/56	Pittsburgh	2
5	Majkowski, Don	QB	6-2	197	02/25/64	Virginia	7
44	Mandeville, Chris	S	6-1	213	02/01/65	California-Davis	4
94	Martin, Charles	DE	6-4	280	08/31/59	Livingston	2
98	Moore, Brent	LB	6-5	242	01/09/63	USC	4
57	Moran, Rich	G	6-2	275	03/19/62	San Diego State	12
47	Morris, Jim Bob*	S	6-3	211	05/17/61	Kansas State	8
81	Morris, Lee*	WR	5-10	180	07/14/64	Oklahoma	2
37	Murphy, Mark	S	6-2	201	04/22/58	West Liberty	12
80	Neal, Frankie	WR	6-1	202	10/01/65	Fort Hays State	12
72	Neville, Tom	G	6-5	306	09/04/61	Fresno State	12
91	Noble, Brian	LB	6-3	252	09/06/62	Arizona State	12
82	Paskett, Keith	WR	5-11	180	12/07/64	Western Kentucky	12
77	Robison, Tommy	G	6-4	290	11/17/61	Texas A&M	3
75	Ruettgers, Ken	T	6-5	280	08/20/62	USC	12
83	Scott, Patrick*	WR	5-10	170	09/13/64	Grambling	5
87	Stanley, Walter	WR	5-9	179	11/05/62	Mesa	12
54	Stephen, Scott	LB	6-2	232	06/18/64	Arizona State	8
29	Stills, Ken	S	5-10	186	09/06/63	Wisconsin	11
70	Uecker, Keith*	G	6-5	284	06/29/60	Auburn	7
73	Veingrad, Alan	T	6-5	277	07/24/63	East Texas State	11
52	Weddington, Mike	LB	6-4	245	10/09/60	Oklahoma	12
51	Weishuhn, Clayton	LB	6-1	218	10/07/59	Angelo State	9
86	West, Ed	TE	6-1	243	08/02/61	Auburn	12
16	Wright, Randy	QB	6-2	203	01/12/61	Wisconsin	9
8	Zendejas, Max*	K	5-11	184	09/02/63	Arizona	7

* also played in replacement games

DRAFT

Rnd	Name	Pos	Ht	Wt	College
1	Brent Fullwood (4)	RB	5-11	209	Auburn
2a	(Traded positions with Falcons, 31st choice to 41st and an extra 3rd round selection)				
2b	Johnny Holland (41)	LB	6-2	221	Texas A&M
	(Choice from Falcons for position switch)				
3a	Dave Croston (61)	T	6-5	280	Iowa
3b	Scott Stephen (69)	LB	6-2	232	Arizona State
	(Choice from Falcons for position switch)				
3c	Frankie Neal (71)	WR	6-1	202	Fort Hays State
	(Choice from Raiders in James Lofton trade)				
4	Lorenzo Freeman (89)	DT	6-5	255	Pittsburgh
5	(Choice (115) to Chargers for Mossy Cade)				
6	Willie Marshall (145)	WR	6-1	190	Temple
7a	Tony Leiker (172)	DT	6-5	250	Stanford
7b	Bill Smith (191)	P	6-3	222	Mississippi
	(Choice from Browns for John Jefferson)				
8	Jeff Drost (198)	DT	6-5	286	Iowa
9	Gregg Harris (228)	G	6-4	279	Wake Forest
10	Don Majkowski (255)	QB	6-2	197	Virginia
11	Patrick Scott (282)	WR	5-10	170	Grambling
12a	(Choice (312) to Seahawks for Dan Ross)				
12b	Norman Jefferson (335).	DB	5-10	183	LSU
	(Choice from Giants in Phil McConkey trade)				

"REPLACEMENT" ROSTER

No	Name	Pos	Ht	Wt	DOB	College	G
53	Anderson, Aric	LB	6-2	220	04/09/65	Iona	3
72/98	Auer, Todd	LB	6-1	230	01/08/65	Western Illinois	3
72	Bone, Warren	DE	6-4	265	11/04/64	Texas Southern	1
73	Caldwell, David	NT	6-1	261	02/28/65	TCU	3
57	Choate, Putt	LB	6-0	225	12/11/56	SMU	2
92/70/74	Collier, Steve*	T	6-7	342	04/19/63	Bethune-Cookman	3
41	Compton, Chuck	DB	5-10	190	01/13/65	Boise State	2
71	Drost, Jeff	DT	6-5	286	01/27/64	Iowa	2
27	Elliott, Tony	DB	5-10	195	01/10/64	Central Michigan	1
79	Estep, Mike	G	6-4	265	12/29/63	Bowling Green	1
89	Fitzgerald, Kevin	TE	6-3	235	06/30/64	Wisconsin-Eau Claire	1
5	Gillus, Willie	QB	6-4	215	09/01/63	Norfolk State	1
69	Gruber, Bob	T	6-5	280	06/07/58	Pittsburgh	1
82	Harden, Derrick	WR	6-1	175	04/21/64	East New Mexico	3
20	Hargrove, James	RB	6-2	232	11/13/58	Wake Forest	2
46	Harrison, Anthony	DB	6-1	195	09/26/65	Georgia Tech	3
63	Hartnett, Perry	G	6-5	285	04/28/60	SMU	1
78	Hobbins, Jim	T	6-6	275	06/04/64	Minnesota	3
31	Hunter, Tony	RB	5-9	215	02/24/63	Minnesota	1
26/81	Jay, Craig	TE	6-4	257	02/05/63	Mt. Senario	3
54/60	Jensen, Greg	OL	6-3	266	01/23/62	No college	1
55	Jordan, Kenneth	LB	6-2	235	04/29/64	Tuskegee	3
40	King, David	DB	5-9	175	05/19/63	Auburn	3
17/32	King, Don	DB	6-0	200	02/10/64	SMU	1
68	Konopasek, Ed	T	6-6	289	04/12/64	Ball State	3
96	Leiker, Tony	DT	6-4	250	09/26/64	Stanford	1
60/54	Malancon, Rydell	LB	6-2	230	01/10/62	LSU	3
44	Mansfield, Von	DB	5-11	183	07/12/60	Wisconsin	3
94	Mataele, Stan	DL	6-2	278	06/24/63	Arizona	2
61	McGarry, John	OL	6-5	288	11/24/63	St. Joseph's	2
77	McGrew, Sylvester	DE	6-4	257	02/27/60	Tulane	3
52	Melka, James	LB	6-1	235	01/15/62	Wisconsin	1
62	Meyer, Jim	T	6-5	290	06/09/63	Illinois State	2
97	Miller, John	LB	6-2	218		Mississippi State	1
51	Monaco, Ron	LB	6-2	240	05/03/63	South Carolina	2
47	Morris, Jim Bob*	DB	6-3	211	05/17/61	Kansas State	3
43	Morris, Larry	RB	5-7	207	02/27/62	Syracuse	2
48/85	Morris, Lee*	WR	5-10	180	07/14/64	Oklahoma	3
39	Parker, Freddie	RB	5-10	215	07/06/62	Mississippi Valley	1
56	Pointer, John	LB	6-2	225	01/16/58	Vanderbilt	3
50	Rafferty, Vince	C-G	6-4	285	08/06/61	Colorado	3
34	Rash, Lou	DB	5-10	190	06/05/60	Mississippi Valley State	3
87	Redick, Cornelius	WR	6-0	185	01/07/64	Cal State Fullerton	1
13	Renner, Bill	P	6-0	198	05/23/59	Virginia Tech	3
11	Risher, Alan	QB	6-2	190	05/06/61	LSU	3
83	Scott, Patrick*	WR	5-10	170	09/13/64	Grambling	3
67	Simpson, Travis	OL	6-3	272	11/19/63	Oklahoma	3
84	Smith, Wes	WR	6-0	190	06/24/63	East Texas	1
33	Sterling, John	RB	6-2	203	09/15/64	Central State Oklahoma	2
95	Sullivan, Carl	DE	6-4	248	04/30/62	San Jose State	3
86	Summer, Don	TE	6-4	235	02/22/61	Boise State	3
45	Thomas, Lavale	RB	6-0	205	12/12/63	Fresno State	1
70	Uecker, Keith*	G	6-5	284	06/29/60	Auburn	1
64	Villanucci, Vince	NT	6-2	265	05/30/64	Bowling Green	2
93	Wallace, Calvin	DE	6-2	230	04/17/65	West VA Tech	1
18/38	Washington, Chuck	DB	5-11	186	01/09/64	Arkansas	3
25	Weigel, Lee	RB	5-11	220	11/15/63	Wisconsin-Eau Claire	2
35	Willhite, Kevin	RB	5-11	208	05/04/63	Oregon	3
8	Zendejas, Max*	K	5-11	184	09/02/63	Arizona	3

* also played in union games

Fumbles

	Fum	Ow	Op	Yds	Tot
J. Anderson	0	0	3	0	3
R. Brown	0	0	4	0	4
Cannon	1	0	0	-8	0
Choate	0	0	1	4	1
K. Davis	2	0	0	0	0
Epps	1	0	0	0	0
Fullwood	2	1	0	0	1
Greene	0	0	2	0	2
Hallstrom	0	0	1	0	1
D. Harden	1	0	0	0	0
A. Harrison	0	0	1	0	1
Hobbins	0	1	0	0	1

	Fum	Ow	Op	Yds	Tot
Holland	0	0	1	0	1
N. Jefferson	2	0	1	0	1
Majkowski	5	0	0	0	0
V. Mansfield	1	0	0	0	0
Moran	1	1	0	3	1
Lee Morris	1	2	0	0	2
M. Murphy	0	0	2	0	2
F. Neal	1	0	0	0	0
Neville	0	1	0	0	1
Noble	0	0	5	0	5
Pointer	0	0	1	0	1
Risher	4	1	0	0	1

	Fum	Ow	Op	Yds	Tot
P. Scott	2	2	0	0	2
Stanley	5	3	0	0	3
Stills	0	1	0	0	1
L. Thomas	0	1	1	3	2
C. Washington	0	0	1	0	1
Weddington	0	0	1	0	1
Willhite	2	0	0	0	0
R. Wright	3	1	0	-4	1
Sterling	0	0	1	0	0
Packers	**35**	**16**	**24**	**-2**	**40**

On Monday, Sept. 21, players' union leader Gene Upshaw announced that NFL players would strike following the completion of the Jets/Patriots game. New York pounded New England 43-24 and the NFL was hit with a work stoppage for the second time in six years.

In 1982, the main issue of contention had been revenue sharing. In 1987, the sticking point was free agency. Players wanted unlimited freedom after their fourth year.

Owners were determined to carry on. Though the games of Sept. 27 were wiped out, the games of Oct. 4-5 were played primarily with replacement players.

The Packers had prepared for a possible walkout. They offered a $1,000 bonus to players cut during the preseason who agreed to play for the team in the case of a strike.

On Sept. 24, Green Bay conducted practice with the strikebreakers. Packers veterans, stationed outside the fences that surrounded the practice field, hurled verbal insults at the B Team.

About half of the new faces had been with the team in training camp. Others had played in the United States Football League and/or had limited NFL experience.

Quarterback Alan Risher had been working as a stockbroker before getting the call. Linebacker Jim Bob Morris had been selling real estate in Kansas City.

On Oct. 4, the Packers and Vikings met in the Metrodome. Green Bay won 23-16, aided in no small part by three field goals from Max Zendejas.

"Basically, we looked like we knew what we were doing," said Risher, who completed 12 passes for 164 yards.

A week later, Mike Prindle kicked a 31-yard field goal in overtime in a 19-16 Lions win at Lambeau Field.

From the start, union solidarity was not as strong as it could have been. Regulars such as the Jets' Mark Gastineau, and the Cowboys' Ed Jones and Randy White played in the first week of replacement games.

More crossed the picket line. On Oct. 15, Upshaw ordered an end to the 24-day walkout even though no new collective bargaining agreement had been reached.

During the strike, owners had set a deadline of 1 p.m. on Wednesdays for regulars to declare whether or not they were going to play in the game on Sunday. Because Upshaw's decision came on Thursday, owners played the games of Oct. 18-19 with replacement players.

Green Bay beat Philadelphia 16-10 in overtime on Oct. 18. James Hargrove's 5-yard run capped a 10-play, 76-yard drive.

In a farewell letter to B Team players, Packers coach Forrest Gregg wrote: "I have enjoyed coaching this football team as much as any I have coached, and every bit as much as I enjoyed coaching the championship team I had with the Cincinnati Bengals in 1981."

REPLACEMENT TEAM RECORDS

National Conference

Eastern Division

	W	L	T	Pct	PF	PA
Washington Redskins	3	0	0	1.000	79	40
Dallas Cowboys	2	1	0	.667	86	59
St. Louis Cardinals	1	2	0	.333	73	81
New York Giants	0	3	0	.000	36	85
Philadelphia Eagles	0	3	0	.000	35	92

Central Division

	W	L	T	Pct	PF	PA
Chicago Bears	2	1	0	.667	79	29
Green Bay Packers	2	1	0	.667	55	45
Tampa Bay Buccaneers	2	1	0	.667	64	54
Detroit Lions	1	2	0	.333	60	84
Minnesota Vikings	0	3	0	.000	33	70

Western Division

	W	L	T	Pct	PF	PA
San Francisco 49ers	3	0	0	1.000	100	66
New Orleans Saints	2	1	0	.667	75	51
Atlanta Falcons	1	2	0	.333	53	73
Los Angeles Rams	1	2	0	.333	61	82

American Conference

Eastern Division

	W	L	T	Pct	PF	PA
Indianapolis Colts	2	1	0	.667	60	27
New England Patriots	2	1	0	.667	45	34
Buffalo Bills	1	2	0	.333	19	64
Miami Dolphins	1	2	0	.333	93	61
New York Jets	1	2	0	.333	61	75

Central Division

	W	L	T	Pct	PF	PA
Cleveland Browns	2	1	0	.667	64	25
Pittsburgh Steelers	2	1	0	.667	70	50
Houston Oilers	2	1	0	.667	62	41
Cincinnati Bengals	1	2	0	.333	26	54

Western Division

	W	L	T	Pct	PF	PA
San Diego Chargers	3	0	0	1.000	50	39
Denver Broncos	2	1	0	.667	66	71
Seattle Seahawks	2	1	0	.667	71	51
Los Angeles Raiders	1	2	0	.333	66	70
Kansas City Chiefs	0	3	0	.000	34	103

THE LONGEST GAME

The replacement Packers and replacement Lions made history on a 45-degree day at Lambeau Field on Oct. 11. The two went at it for four hours and nine minutes, the longest game in Packers history.

Penalties and injuries slowed the game considerably. The two teams were flagged for 29 infractions, although just 17 were accepted. Injured Packers included guards Perry Hartnett (hamstring) and John McGarry (knee), defensive lineman Jeff Drost (knee), and safety Anthony Harrison (neck).

Max Zendejas kicked a 45-yard field goal as time expired to send the game into overtime. Mike Prindle mercifully ended the marathon with a 31-yard field goal after 12 minutes and 26 seconds of overtime had been played.

Longest games in packers history

Length	Date	Result
4:09	10-11-87	GB 16, Lions 19 (OT)
4:02	9-30-84	GB 27, Buccaneers 30 (OT)
3:48	9-20-87	GB 17, Broncos 17 (OT)

1987 GREEN BAY PACKERS

FRONT ROW: (L-R) 5 Don Majkowski, 6 Robbie Bosco, 8 Max Zendejas, 10 Al Del Greco, 16 Randy Wright, 17 Don Bracken, 20 Kelly Cook, 21 Brent Fullwood, 22 Mark Lee, 23 George (Tiger) Greene, 28 Elbert Watts, 29 Ken Stills.

SECOND ROW: (L-R) 30 Paul Ott Carruth, 32 Dave Brown, 33 Jessie Clark, 35 Kevin Willhite, 36 Kenneth Davis, 37 Mark Murphy, 38 Norman Jefferson, 39 Kenneth Johnson, 44 Chris Mandeville, 45 Lavale Thomas, 47 Jim Bob Morris, 48 Don Summers.

THIRD ROW: (L-R) 49 David Greenwood, 50 Johnny Holland, 51 Clayton Weishuhn, 52 Mike Weddington, 54 Scott Stephen, 56 Burnell Dent, 57 Rich Moran, 58 Mark Cannon, 59 John Anderson, 60 Dave Croston, 61 Jerry Boyarsky.

FOURTH ROW: (L-R) 63 Gregg Harris, 64 Steve Collier, 65 Ron Hallstrom, 69 Bill Cherry, 70 Keith Uecker, 72 Tom Neville, 73 Alan Veingrad, 75 Ken Ruettgers, 76 Alphonso Carreker, 77 Tommy Robison.

FIFTH ROW: (L-R) 79 Ross Browner, 80 Frankie Neal, 81 Lee Morris, 82 Keith Paskett, 83 Patrick Scott, 85 Phillip Epps, 86 Ed West, 87 Walter Stanley, 89 Joey Hackett, 90 Ezra Johnson.

BACK ROW: (L-R) Team Physician Eugene Brusky, Medical Assistant Bob Kunz, Medical Assistant Larry Lemberger, 91 Brian Noble, 93 Robert Brown, 97 Tim Harris, 98 Brent Moore, 99 John Dorsey, Administrative Assistant Burt Gustafson, Equipment Manager Bob Noel, Trainer Domenic Gentile, Equipment Assistant Jack Noel, Assistant Equipment Manager Bryan Nehring.

Lindy Infante, regarded as an offensive innovator, became the 10th coach in Packers history on Feb. 3, 1988. A native of Florida, Infante was the Bengals' quarterback/receiver coach in 1981 when the team reached the Super Bowl. In 1986, he was offensive coordinator when the Browns set numerous team records on offense and came within an eyelash of the Super Bowl.

The Packers and Infante did not reach such lofty heights in 1988. Less than satisfactory kicking, injuries, an anemic running attack and contract holdouts contributed to a 4-12 finish. As had become the script in recent years, Green Bay dropped its opener (34-7 to the Rams), got off to a poor start (0-5), then showed signs of improvement with victories over Minnesota and Phoenix late in the season.

Infante brought with him a passing game different than the one used by Forrest Gregg. He looked at a half-dozen quarterbacks, including former Raider Marc Wilson, Randy Wright, and Don Majkowski, before deciding Wright would open as his starter.

The Packers employed four kickers. Max Zendejas, so accurate in 1987, was released after blowing a 24-yard field goal attempt against Washington that would have sent the game into overtime. In the second half of the season, Dale Dawson, Dean Dorsey and Curtis Burrow combined to make four of nine field goals and six of 10 extra points.

First-round draft choice Sterling Sharpe and free agent Perry Kemp emerged as the Packers' leading receivers. Veterans Phillip Epps (broken wrist, hamstring) and Walter Stanley (separated shoulder) lagged behind, missing a combined 19 games because of injuries.

Brent Fullwood was the only player beside Majkowski to gain more than 200 yards rushing. Green Bay failed to gain 100 yards rushing in 12 of the 16 games it played. For the first time ever, the Packers averaged less than 90 yards rushing (86.2) per game. Only against New England (207 yards, five touchdowns) did the running game truly click.

As July turned into August, six veterans remained unsigned: Rich Moran, Ron Hallstrom, Mark Cannon, Epps, Stanley and Brian Noble. All but Noble signed before the opener. The fourth-year linebacker sat out the first four regular-season games before coming to terms.

Another linebacker, Tim Harris, led the Packers in sacks with 13.5. He also recorded two safeties and blocked a punt, which he returned for a touchdown.

Green Bay broke out of its early-season slump by piling on the Patriots 45-3 in Milwaukee on Oct. 9. Fullwood gained 118 yards rushing and scored three times.

The Packers improved to 2-5 the following week by upsetting the Vikings 34-14 in Minnesota. Harris had two sacks in addition to his blocked punt.

Majkowski was the starter at quarterback in both wins.

He replaced Wright, who pulled a groin muscle in Tampa.

After coming close against Washington in Week 8, the Packers' offense went into hiding as both Buffalo and Atlanta blanked the team. Green Bay hadn't been shut out in consecutive games in the same season since 1925.

Green Bay was held scoreless for a third time on Nov. 27 when the Bears whipped them 16-0.

Wright returned to the starting lineup the following week. He threw for 284 yards in a 30-14 loss in Detroit. For the Packers, it was their seventh consecutive loss.

Green Bay closed with two wins. Perry Kemp caught six passes for 108 yards and Larry Mason rushed for 65 yards as the Packers swept the series with Minnesota 18-6 and ended any chance the Vikings had of winning the Central Division title.

Majkowski, back in the starting lineup after Wright aggravated his injury in the Vikings gave, led Green Bay to a 26-17 win in the windup in Arizona. The victory meant Dallas (3-13) and not the Packers (4-12) earned the first spot in the 1989 college draft.

"We're in this business to win," Infante said. "This victory means a heck of a lot more to us than having the first pick."

Noble added: "Hey, if we're going to go out and lose a football game for the first pick, tell me before, because I don't want to play."

Dallas used its pick to select quarterback Troy Aikman. The Packers drafted tackle Tony Mandarich second.

A STERLING BEGINNING

The Packers drafted Sterling Sharpe with the seventh pick overall in the 1988 draft. The wide receiver established the club record for most receptions by a rookie with 55.

Sharpe started all 16 games. His debut was mostly forgettable. He ran a reverse for no gain and had two passes thrown in his direction. One of the two was intercepted by the Rams' Jerry Gray and returned 47 yards for a touchdown.

Sharpe caught his first pass in Week 2. He was shut out the following week, but hit the big time with seven catches for 137 yards in a 24-6 loss to the Bears.

Once in the mix, Sharpe had a tough time finding the end zone. His first and only touchdown reception didn't occur until Dec. 4, when he caught a 24-yard pass from Randy Wright in Detroit.

Most pass receptions by a rookie, season

No.	Player	Year
55	Sterling Sharpe	1988
53	Bill Howton	1952
48	Gerry Ellis	1980

TEAM STATISTICS

	GB	OPP
First Downs	280	281
Rushing	77	130
Passing	176	136
Penalty	27	15
Rushes	385	514
Yards Gained	1,379	2,110
Average Gain	3.58	4.11
Average Yards per Game	86.2	131.9
Passes Attempted	582	474
Completed	319	256
% Completed	54.81	54.01
Total Yards Gained	3,609	2,949
Times Sacked	51	30
Yards Lost	324	216
Net Yards Gained	3,285	2,733
Yards Gained per Completion	11.31	11.52
Net Yards per Attempt	5.19	5.42
Average Net Yards per Game	205.3	170.8
Combined Net Yards Gained	4,664	4,843
Total Plays	1,018	1,018
Average Net Yards per Play	4.58	4.76
Average Net Yards per Game	291.5	302.7
Third Down Efficiency	77/215	76/215
Percentage	35.81	35.35
Fourth Down Efficiency	7/14	8/16
Percentage	50.00	50.00
Intercepted By	20	24
Yards Returned	224	386
Returned for TD	0	4
Punts	86	76
Yards Punted	3,287	2,859
Average Yards per Punt	38.22	37.62
Punt Returns	35	39
Yards Returned	208	314
Average Yards per Return	5.94	8.05
Returned for TD	1	0
Kickoff Returns	64	49
Yards Returned	1,181	966
Average Yards per Return	18.45	19.71
Returned for TD	0	0
Penalties	94	112
Yards Penalized	785	903
Fumbles	44	33
Lost	26	21
Own Recovered for Touchdown	0	0
Opponent's Recovered by	21	26
Opponent's Recovered for Touchdown	0	1
Total Points Scored	240	315
Total Touchdowns	29	34
Touchdowns Rushing	14	17
Touchdowns Passing	13	12
Touchdowns on Returns & Recoveries	2	5
Extra Points	23	34
Safeties	2	1
Field Goals Attempted	25	35
Field Goals Made	13	25
% Successful	52.00	71.43
Average Time of Possession	29:16	30:44

Regular Season 4-12-0

Date	GB		OPP	Att.
9/4	7	Los Angeles Rams	34	(53,769)
9/11	10	Tampa Bay Buccaneers	13	(52,984)
9/18	17	at Miami Dolphins	24	(54,409)
9/25	6	Chicago Bears	24	(56,492)
10/2	24	at Tampa Bay Buccaneers	27	(40,003)
10/9	45	New England Patriots (M)	3	(51,932)
10/16	34	at Minnesota Vikings	14	(59,053)
10/23	17	Washington Redskins (M)	20	(51,767)
10/30	0	at Buffalo Bills	28	(79,176)
11/6	0	at Atlanta Falcons	20	(29,952)
11/13	13	Indianapolis Colts	20	(53,942)
11/20	9	Detroit Lions (M)	19	(44,327)
11/27	0	at Chicago Bears	16	(62,026)
12/4	14	at Detroit Lions	30	(28,124)
12/11	18	Minnesota Vikings	6	(48,892)
12/18	26	at Phoenix Cardinals	17	(44,586)

Score By Periods

	1	2	3	4	OT	Total
Packers	58	58	47	77	0	240
Opponents	78	131	38	68	0	315

INDIVIDUAL STATISTICS

Rushing

	Att	Yds	Avg	LG	TD
Fullwood	101	483	4.8	t33	7
Majkowski	47	225	4.8	24	1
Woodside	83	195	2.3	10	3
L. Mason	48	194	4.0	17	0
K. Davis	39	121	3.1	27	1
Carruth	49	114	2.3	14	0
R. Wright	8	43	5.4	19	2
Aubrey Matthews	3	3	1.0	4	0
P. Collins	2	2	1.0	2	0
Stanley	1	1	1.0	1	0
Sharpe	4	-2	-0.5	5	0
Packers	**385**	**1,379**	**3.6**	**t33**	**14**
Opponents	514	2,110	4.1	t80	17

Receiving

	No	Yds	Avg	LG	TD
Sharpe	55	791	14.4	51	1
Kemp	48	620	12.9	36	0
Woodside	39	352	9.0	t49	2
E. West	30	276	9.2	35	3
Stanley	28	436	15.6	56	0
Carruth	24	211	8.8	31	0
P. Scott	20	275	13.8	41	1
Fullwood	20	128	6.4	t30	1
Aubrey Matthews	15	167	11.1	25	2
Epps	11	99	9.0	25	0
K. Davis	11	81	7.4	11	0
L. Mason	8	84	10.5	39	1
Didier	5	37	7.4	15	1
Bolton	2	33	16.5	18	0
P. Collins	2	17	8.5	9	0
Hackett	1	2	2.0	t2	1
Packers	**319**	**3,609**	**11.3**	**56**	**13**
Opponents	256	2,949	11.5	t46	12

Passing

	Att	Com	Yds	Pct	TD	In	Tk/Yds	Rate
Majkowski	336	178	2,119	53.0	9	11	31/176	67.8
R. Wright	244	141	1,490	57.8	4	13	20/148	58.9
Carruth	2	0	0	0.0	0	0	0/0	—
Packers	**582**	**319**	**3,609**	**54.8**	**13**	**24**	**51/324**	**63.9**
Opponents	474	256	2,949	54.0	12	20	30/216	63.9

Punting

	No	Yds	Avg	Net	TB	In20	LG	HB
Bracken	85	3,287	38.7	31.8	12	20	62	1
Packers	**86**	**3,287**	**38.2**	**31.8**	**12**	**20**	**62**	**1**
Opponents	76	2,859	37.6	33.6	5	22	69	1

Kickoff Returns

	No	Yds	Avg	LG	TD
Fullwood	21	421	20.0	31	0
Woodside	19	343	18.1	29	0
P. Scott	12	207	17.3	27	0
N. Jefferson	4	116	29.0	46	0
Stanley	2	39	19.5	22	0
R. Pitts	1	17	17.0	17	0
Sharpe	1	17	17.0	17	0
Hackett	1	9	9.0	9	0
Winter	1	7	7.0	7	0
Stills	1	4	4.0	4	0
N. Hill	1	1	1.0	1	0
Packers	**64**	**1,181**	**18.5**	**46**	**0**
Opponents	49	966	19.7	37	0

Punt Returns

	No	Yds	Avg	FC	LG	TD
Stanley	12	52	4.3	3	15	0
R. Pitts	9	93	10.3	6	t63	1
Sharpe	9	48	5.3	7	14	0
N. Jefferson	5	15	3.0	2	9	0
Packers	**35**	**208**	**5.9**	**18**	**t63**	**1**
Opponents	39	314	8.1	14	46	0

Interceptions

	No	Yds	Avg	LG	TD
M. Murphy	5	19	3.8	9	0
Cecil	4	56	14.0	33	0
M. Lee	3	37	12.3	27	0
Stills	3	29	9.7	17	0
D. Brown	3	27	9.0	15	0
R. Pitts	2	56	28.0	31	0
Packers	**20**	**224**	**11.2**	**33**	**0**
Opponents	24	386	16.1	t90	4

Scoring

	TDr	TDp	TDrt	PAT	FG	S	TP
Fullwood	7	1	0	0/0	0/0	0	48
Zendejas	0	0	0	17/19	9/16	0	44
Woodside	3	2	0	0/0	0/0	0	30
E. West	0	3	0	0/0	0/0	0	18
Aubrey Matthews	0	2	0	0/0	0/0	0	12
R. Wright	2	0	0	0/0	0/0	0	12
D. Dawson	0	0	0	1/2	3/5	0	10
T. Harris	0	0	1	0/0	0/0	2	10
K. Davis	1	0	0	0/0	0/0	0	6
Didier	0	1	0	0/0	0/0	0	6
D. Dorsey	0	0	0	3/4	1/3	0	6
Hackett	0	1	0	0/0	0/0	0	6
Majkowski	1	0	0	0/0	0/0	0	6
L. Mason	0	1	0	0/0	0/0	0	6
R. Pitts	0	0	1	0/0	0/0	0	6
P. Scott	0	1	0	0/0	0/0	0	6
Sharpe	0	1	0	0/0	0/0	0	6
C. Burrow	0	0	0	2/4	0/1	0	2
Packers	**14**	**13**	**2**	**23/29**	**13/25**	**2**	**240**
Opponents	17	12	5	34/34	25/35	1	315

Fumbles

	Fum	Ow	Op	Yds	Tot
Cannon	2	0	0	-31	0
Carreker	0	0	1	0	1
Carruth	4	0	0	0	0
Cecil	0	0	1	0	1
Dent	0	0	1	0	1
Didier	1	0	1	4	1
Fullwood	6	1	0	0	1
Holland	0	0	1	0	1
N. Jefferson	0	0	1	0	1
Kemp	3	0	0	0	0
M. Lee	0	0	1	0	1
Majkowski	8	3	0	0	3
M. Murphy	0	0	4	0	4
Noble	0	0	1	0	1
Patterson	0	0	1	0	1
R. Pitts	1	2	2	0	4
Ruettgers	0	1	0	0	1
Sharpe	3	1	0	0	1
Stanley	3	1	0	0	1
Stills	0	1	2	4	3
Uecker	0	1	1	0	2
Weddington	0	0	2	0	2
E. West	1	0	0	0	0
Winter	0	0	2	0	2
Woodside	3	1	0	0	1
R. Wright	6	3	0	-5	3
Packers	**44**	**16**	**21**	**-28**	**37**

Quarterback Sacks

	No
T. Harris	13.5
Winter	5.0
Patterson	4.0
R. Brown	1.5
J. Anderson	1.0
Dent	1.0
Greene	1.0
Stephens	1.0
Stills	1.0
Boyarsky	0.5
Noble	0.5
Packers	**30.0**
Opponents	51.0

NFL STANDINGS

National Conference

Eastern Division

	W	L	T	Pct	PF	PA
Philadelphia Eagles	10	6	0	.625	379	319
New York Giants	10	6	0	.625	359	387
Washington Redskins	7	9	0	.438	345	387
Phoenix Cardinals	7	9	0	.438	344	398
Dallas Cowboys	3	13	0	.188	265	381

Central Division

	W	L	T	Pct	PF	PA
Chicago Bears	12	4	0	.750	312	215
Minnesota Vikings	11	5	0	.688	406	233
Tampa Bay Buccaneers	5	11	0	.313	261	350
Detroit Lions	4	12	0	.250	220	313
Green Bay Packers	**4**	**12**	**0**	**.250**	**240**	**315**

Western Division

	W	L	T	Pct	PF	PA
San Francisco 49ers	10	6	0	.625	369	294
Los Angeles Rams	10	6	0	.625	407	293
New Orleans Saints	10	6	0	.625	312	283
Atlanta Falcons	5	11	0	.313	244	315

American Conference

Eastern Division

	W	L	T	Pct	PF	PA
Buffalo Bills	12	4	0	.750	329	237
Indianapolis Colts	9	7	0	.563	354	315
New England Patriots	9	7	0	.563	250	284
New York Jets	8	7	1	.531	372	354
Miami Dolphins	6	10	0	.375	319	380

Central Division

	W	L	T	Pct	PF	PA
Cincinnati Bengals	12	4	0	.750	448	329
Cleveland Browns	10	6	0	.625	304	288
Houston Oilers	10	6	0	.625	424	365
Pittsburgh Steelers	5	11	0	.313	336	421

Western Division

	W	L	T	Pct	PF	PA
Seattle Seahawks	9	7	0	.563	339	329
Denver Broncos	8	8	0	.500	327	352
Los Angeles Raiders	7	9	0	.438	325	369
San Diego Chargers	6	10	0	.375	231	332
Kansas City Chiefs	4	11	1	.281	254	320

ROSTER

No	Name	Pos	Ht	Wt	DOB	College	G
59	Anderson, John	LB	6-3	228	02/14/56	Michigan	14
88	Bell, Albert	WR	6-0	170	04/23/64	Alabama	5
82	Bolton, Scott	WR	6-0	188	01/04/65	Auburn	4
61	Boyarsky, Jerry	NT	6-3	290	05/15/59	Pittsburgh	2
17	Bracken, Don	P	6-0	205	02/16/62	Michigan	16
32	Brown, Dave	CB	6-1	197	01/16/53	Michigan	16
93	Brown, Robert	DE	6-2	267	05/21/60	Virginia Tech	16
5	Burrow, Curtis	K	5-11	185	12/11/62	Central Arkansas	1
58	Cannon, Mark	C	6-3	270	06/14/62	Texas-Arlington	16
76	Carreker, Alphonso	DE	6-6	271	05/25/62	Florida State	14
30	Carruth, Paul Ott	RB	6-1	220	07/22/61	Alabama	15
26	Cecil, Chuck	S	6-0	184	11/08/64	Arizona	16
25	Collins, Pat	RB	5-9	188	08/04/66	Oklahoma	6
53	Corker, John	LB	6-5	240	12/29/58	Oklahoma State	2
60	Croston, Dave	T	6-5	280	11/10/63	Iowa	16
36	Davis, Kenneth	RB	5-10	209	04/16/62	TCU	9
4	Dawson, Dale	K	6-1	212	11/02/64	Eastern Kentucky	4
56	Dent, Burnell	LB	6-1	236	03/16/63	Tulane	10
80	Didier, Clint	TE	6-5	240	04/04/59	Portland State	15
9	Dorsey, Dean	K	5-11	195	03/15/57	Toronto	3
99	Dorsey, John	LB	6-2	243	08/31/60	Connecticut	16
85	Epps, Phillip	WR	5-10	165	11/11/58	TCU	6
21	Fullwood, Brent	FB	5-11	209	10/10/63	Auburn	14
23	Greene, George (Tiger)	DB	6-0	194	02/15/62	Western Carolina	16
89	Hackett, Joey	TE	6-5	267	09/29/58	Elon	9
74	Haley, Darryl	T	6-5	265	02/16/61	Utah	13
65	Hallstrom, Ron	G	6-6	290	06/11/59	Iowa	16
97	Harris, Tim	LB	6-5	235	09/10/64	Memphis State	16
90	Hill, Nate	DE	6-4	273	02/22/66	Auburn	3
50	Holland, Johnny	LB	6-2	221	03/11/65	Texas A&M	13
38	Jefferson, Norman	DB	5-10	183	08/07/64	LSU	2
62	Kauahi, Kani	C	6-2	271	09/06/59	Hawaii	16
81	Kemp, Perry	WR	5-11	170	12/31/61	California State (PA)	16
22	Lee, Mark	CB	5-11	189	03/20/58	Washington	15
7	Majkowski, Don	QB	6-2	197	02/25/64	Virginia	13
34	Mason, Larry	RB	5-11	205	05/21/61	Troy State	15
88	Matthews, Aubrey	WR	5-7	165	09/15/62	Delta State	7
57	Moran, Rich	G	6-2	275	03/19/62	San Diego State	16
37	Murphy, Mark	S	6-2	201	04/22/58	West Liberty	14
79	Nelson, Bob	NT	6-4	275	03/03/59	Miami	14
72	Neville, Tom	G	6-5	300	09/04/61	Fresno State	2
91	Noble, Brian	LB	6-3	252	09/06/62	Arizona State	12
96	Patterson, Shawn	DE	6-5	261	04/06/65	Arizona State	15
28	Pitts, Ron	DB	5-10	175	10/14/62	UCLA	14
46	Richard, Gary	CB	5-9	171	10/09/65	Pittsburgh	10
75	Ruettgers, Ken	T	6-5	280	08/20/62	USC	15
83	Scott, Patrick	WR	5-10	170	09/13/64	Grambling	16
84	Sharpe, Sterling	WR	5-11	202	04/06/65	South Carolina	16
51	Simpkins, Ron	LB	6-1	234	04/02/58	Michigan	7
87	Stanley, Walter	WR	5-9	179	11/05/62	Mesa	7
54	Stephen, Scott	LB	6-2	232	06/18/64	Arizona State	8
29	Stills, Ken	S	5-10	186	09/06/63	Wisconsin	14
45	Thomas, Lavale	RB	6-0	205	12/12/63	Fresno State	1
70	Uecker, Keith	G	6-5	284	06/29/60	Auburn	16
52	Weddington, Mike	LB	6-4	245	10/09/60	Oklahoma	16
86	West, Ed	TE	6-1	243	08/02/61	Auburn	16
68	Winter, Blaise	DE	6-3	275	01/31/62	Syracuse	16
33	Woodside, Keith	RB	5-11	203	07/29/64	Texas A&M	16
16	Wright, Randy	QB	6-2	203	01/12/61	Wisconsin	8
8	Zendejas, Max	K	5-11	184	09/02/63	Arizona	8

DRAFT

Rnd	Name	Pos	Ht	Wt	College
1	Sterling Sharpe (7)	WR	5-11	202	South Carolina
2	Shawn Patterson (34)	DT	6-5	261	Arizona State
3	Keith Woodside (61)	RB	5-11	203	Texas A&M
4a	Rollin Putzier (88)	NT	6-4	279	Oregon
	(Choice from Raiders in James Lofton trade)				
4b	Chuck Cecil (89)	FS	6-0	184	Arizona
5	Darrell Reed (116)	LB	6-1	225	Oklahoma

Rnd	Name	Pos	Ht	Wt	College
6	Nate Hill (144)	DE	6-4	273	Auburn
7	Gary Richard (173)	CB	5-9	172	Pittsburgh
8	Patrick Collins (200)	HB	5-9	188	Oklahoma
9	Neal Wilkinson (228)	TE	6-5	226	James Madison
10	Bud Keyes (256)	QB	6-2	211	Wisconsin
11	(Choice (284) to Seahawks in Dave Brown trade)				
12	Scott Bolton (312)	WR	6-0	188	Auburn

1988 GREEN BAY PACKERS

FRONT ROW: (L-R) 7 Don Majkowski, 8 Max Zendejas, 16 Randy Wright, 17 Don Bracken, 20 Kelly Cook, 21 Brent Fullwood, 22 Mark Lee, 23 George (Tiger) Greene, 25 Pat Collins, 26 Chuck Cecil, 27 Tony Elliott.
SECOND ROW: (L-R) 28 Ron Pitts, 29 Ken Stills, 30 Paul Ott Carruth, 31 Joe Armentrout, 32 Dave Brown, 33 Keith Woodside, 34 Larry Mason, 36 Kenneth Davis, 37 Mark Murphy, 38 Norman Jefferson, 39 Kenneth Johnson.
THIRD ROW: (L-R) 42 Scott Bolton, 45 Lavale Thomas, 46 Gary Richard, 50 Johnny Holland, 51 Ron Simpkins, 52 Mike Weddington, 54 Scott Stephen, 56 Burnell Dent, 57 Rich Moran, 58 Mark Cannon, 59 John Anderson.
FOURTH ROW: (L-R) 60 Dave Croston, 61 Jerry Boyarsky, 62 Kani Kauahi, 64 Steve Collier, 65 Ron Hallstrom, 68 Blaise Winter, 70 Keith Uecker, 74 Darryl Haley, 75 Ken Ruettgers, 76 Alphonso Carreker, 77 Tommy Robison.
FIFTH ROW: (L-R) 79 Bob Nelson, 80 Clint Didier, 81 Perry Kemp, 82 Keith Paskett, 83 Patrick Scott, 84 Sterling Sharpe, 85 Phillip Epps, 86 Ed West, 87 Walter Stanley, 88 Albert Bell, 89 Joey Hackett.
SIXTH ROW: (L-R) Assistant Video Director Bob Eckberg, Training Room Assistant Tim Wall, Training Room Assistant Kurt Fielding, Trainer Domenic Gentile, 93 Robert Brown, 96 Shawn Patterson, 97 Tim Harris, 99 John Dorsey, Team Physician Dr. Eugene Brusky, Equipment Manager Bob Noel, Equipment Assistant Jack Noel, Assistant Equipment Manager Bryan Nehring.
BACK ROW: (L-R) Defensive Line Coach Greg Blache, Outside Linebackers Coach Dick Moseley, Receivers Coach Wayne (Buddy) Geis, Defensive Backfield Coach Dick Jauron, Strength-Conditioning/Tight Ends Coach Virgil Knight, Offensive Backfield Coach Willie Peete, Head Coach Lindy Infante, Special Teams Coach Howard Tippett, Offensive Line Coach Charlie Davis, Defensive Coordinator Hank Bullough, Administrative Assistant Burt Gustafson, Video Director Al Treml.

The Packers of 1989 were not for the faint of heart. For one exhilarating season, Green Bay transformed itself into the "Cardiac Pack." The year was one of "Majik," of excitement, of comebacks and close games galore. Those who jumped on the bandwagon needed nerves of steel and a never-say-die attitude as the Green and Gold came from behind to win seven times and set an NFL record with four 1-point wins.

The dizzying ride came to an end on Christmas Day when the Vikings edged the Bengals 29-21. With the two wild card spots already locked up by the Rams and Eagles, winning the Central Division title was the last chance the Pack had to qualify for the postseason. But when Minnesota prevailed and matched Green Bay's 10-6 record, it was awarded that honor because it had a better division record (6-2) than did the Packers (5-3).

Swept along by a high-powered offense, Green Bay wasted little time in putting fans on the edge of their seats. In Week 2, Don "Majik" Majkowski erased a 17-point halftime deficit against the Saints by clicking on 20 of 22 passes for 273 yards and three touchdowns. Two weeks later, the Packers rallied from 15 down in the fourth quarter to shoot down the Falcons.

In between, the team just missed staging what would have been the greatest comeback in NFL history to that point. Had Brent Fullwood not lost a fumble at the Rams' 1-yard line, the Packers might have beaten Los Angeles despite trailing by 31 points at halftime.

Green Bay became a legitimate playoff contender after it downed the Bears 14-13 and upset the defending Super Bowl champion 49ers 21-17 in San Francisco. Both were dramatic affairs, with the outcome of the Chicago clash resting in the hands of a replay official for what—to Packers fans at least—must have seemed an interminable amount of time.

Majkowski, Sterling Sharpe, Tim Harris, Fullwood, and Chris Jacke played key roles in Green Bay's 6-game turnaround from the previous year. Majkowski established single-season team records for most pass attempts (599) and completions (353). Sharpe had 90 catches and became the first Packer since Don Hutson to lead the NFL in receptions. Fullwood gained 821 yards rushing, Harris garnered 19 1/2 sacks. Jacke, a rookie, won five games in the last two minutes with his kicks.

Plan B was established by the NFL. It granted free agency to some players. Green Bay signed a league-high 20 players through Plan B, and four of them—Carl Bland, Blair Bush, Michael Haddix and Van Jakes—played in all 16 games.

On June 5, Bob Harlan was elected Packers president and chief executive officer. Harlan replaced Judge Robert J. Parins, who was elected honorary chairman of the board.

Green Bay swept the Bears for the first time since 1983. In the first meeting, Majkowski tossed what looked like a 14-yard touchdown pass to Sharpe with 32 seconds left. But an official on the field ruled the ball had crossed the line of scrimmage before being released by Majkowski.

Bill Parkinson, the replay official, reviewed the play in the press box. He took several minutes, but he eventually overruled the call. Green Bay won 14-13.

In the rematch, the Packers rolled up 217 yards rushing and 456 yards overall. Keith Woodside ripped off 116 yards on 10 carries and Scott Stephen returned a fumble 76 yards to set up the final points in a 40-28 romp.

The Lions proved a troublesome adversary. A 38-yard field goal by Jacke got the team past them 23-20 in Milwaukee. In the second meeting, Majkowski threw 59 passes but the Packers came up short 31-22 to a Detroit club that had won but one game.

"We had a good thing rolling," linebacker Brian Noble said. "To lose to a 1-8 football team is definitely not something we can expect to do if we're going to be in the playoffs."

For the most part, Green Bay looked like a playoff team down the stretch as it won five of its last six games. That one loss, however, proved costly. Kansas City, with the best defense in the AFC, held Green Bay to a season-low 98 yards passing in forging a 21-3 win.

That setback, and the events that unfolded in the season's final two weeks, had the Packers and their fans rooting for the Bengals on Christmas.

TOO CLOSE FOR COMFORT

The Packers set a league record in 1989 by winning four games by a single point.

Most of the Packers' 10 victories were close affairs. The team won seven games by fewer than five points.

On Sept. 17, Don Majkowski passed to Sterling Sharpe with 1:26 left to earn a 35-34 win over the Saints. On Nov. 5, the Packers beat the Bears 14-13 on a controversial pass from Majkowski to Sharpe with 32 seconds remaining. Three weeks later, Dave Brown intercepted two Wade Wilson passes in the final minutes to preserve a 20-19 victory over the Vikings in Milwaukee. And on Dec. 3, Chris Jacke booted a 47-yard field goal as time ran out in a 17-16 squeaker in Tampa.

The Packers might have won a fifth game by one point in the opener had Majkowski not thrown an interception from the Buccaneers' 16-yard line with 5:32 left in the game. A field goal would have given Green Bay a 24-23 lead. Instead, Tampa Bay ran off 13 plays to kill the clock.

Aside from 1989, the Packers have never won more than one game by one point in a single season.

1989

TEAM STATISTICS

	GB	OPP
First Downs	342	307
Rushing	114	116
Passing	207	179
Penalty	21	12
Rushes	397	460
Yards Gained	1,732	2,008
Average Gain	4.36	4.37
Average Yards per Game	108.3	125.5
Passes Attempted	600	476
Completed	354	302
% Completed	59.00	63.45
Total Yards Gained	4,325	3,553
Times Sacked	48	34
Yards Lost	277	214
Net Yards Gained	4,048	3,339
Yards Gained per Completion	12.22	11.76
Net Yards per Attempt	6.25	6.55
Average Net Yards per Game	253.0	208.7
Combined Net Yards Gained	5,780	5,347
Total Plays	1,045	970
Average Net Yards per Play	5.53	5.51
Average Net Yards per Game	361.3	334.2
Third Down Efficiency	93/204	86/191
Percentage	45.59	45.03
Fourth Down Efficiency	8/12	5/6
Percentage	66.67	83.33
Intercepted By	25	20
Yards Returned	232	321
Returned for TD	0	2
Punts	66	65
Yards Punted	2,682	2,644
Average Yards per Punt	40.64	40.68
Punt Returns	35	30
Yards Returned	289	416
Average Yards per Return	8.26	13.87
Returned for TD	0	0
Kickoff Returns	69	63
Yards Returned	1,239	1,389
Average Yards per Return	17.96	22.05
Returned for TD	0	0
Penalties	81	105
Yards Penalized	666	851
Fumbles	35	28
Lost	13	15
Own Recovered for Touchdown	2	0
Opponent's Recovered by	15	13
Opponent's Recovered for Touchdown	0	2
Total Points Scored	362	356
Total Touchdowns	42	41
Touchdowns Rushing	13	15
Touchdowns Passing	27	22
Touchdowns on Returns & Recoveries	2	4
Extra Points	42	39
Safeties	1	1
Field Goals Attempted	28	30
Field Goals Made	22	23
% Successful	78.57	76.67
Average Time of Possession	30:21	29:39

Regular Season 10-6-0

Date	GB		OPP	Att.
9/10	21	Tampa Bay Buccaneers	23	(55,650)
9/17	35	New Orleans Saints	34	(55,809)
9/24	38	at Los Angeles Rams	41	(57,701)
10/1	23	Atlanta Falcons (M)	21	(54,647)
10/8	31	Dallas Cowboys	13	(56,656)
10/15	14	at Minnesota Vikings	26	(62,075)
10/22	20	at Miami Dolphins	23	(56,624)
10/29	23	Detroit Lions (M) (OT)	20	(53,731)
11/5	14	Chicago Bears	13	(56,556)
11/12	22	at Detroit Lions	31	(44,324)
11/19	21	at San Francisco 49ers	17	(62,219)
11/26	20	Minnesota Vikings (M)	19	(55,592)
12/3	17	at Tampa Bay Buccaneers	16	(58,120)
12/10	3	Kansas City Chiefs	21	(56,694)
12/17	40	at Chicago Bears	28	(44,781)
12/24	20	at Dallas Cowboys	10	(41,265)

Score By Periods

	1	2	3	4	OT	Total
Packers	71	74	89	125	3	362
Opponents	77	157	70	52	0	356

INDIVIDUAL STATISTICS

Rushing

	Att	Yds	Avg	LG	TD
Fullwood	204	821	4.0	38	5
Majkowski	75	358	4.8	20	5
Woodside	46	273	5.9	t68	1
Haddix	44	135	3.1	10	0
Fontenot	17	69	4.1	19	1
Kemp	5	43	8.6	14	0
Sharpe	2	25	12.5	26	0
Workman	4	8	2.0	3	1
Packers	397	1,732	4.4	t68	13
Opponents	460	2,008	4.4	73	15

Receiving

	No	Yds	Avg	LG	TD
Sharpe	90	1,423	15.8	t79	12
Woodside	59	527	8.9	33	0
Kemp	48	611	12.7	39	2
Fontenot	40	372	9.3	t38	3
Query	23	350	15.2	45	2
E. West	22	269	12.2	31	5
Fullwood	19	214	11.3	67	0
Aubrey Matthews	18	200	11.1	25	0
Haddix	15	111	7.4	23	1
Bland	11	164	14.9	t46	1
Didier	7	71	10.1	t24	1
Spagnola	2	13	6.5	14	0
Packers	354	4,325	12.2	t79	27
Opponents	302	3,553	11.8	61	22

Passing

	Att	Com	Yds	Pct	TD	In	Tk/Yds	Rate
Majkowski	599	353	4,318	58.9	27	20	47/268	82.3
A. Dilweg	1	1	7	100.0	0	0	0/0	—
Fontenot	0	0	0	—	0	0	1/9	—
Packers	600	354	4,325	59.0	27	20	48/277	82.4
Opponents	476	302	3,553	63.4	22	25	34/214	79.6

Punting

	No	Yds	Avg	Net	TB	In20	LG	HB
Bracken	66	2,682	40.6	31.0	11	17	63	0
Packers	66	2,682	40.6	31.0	11	17	63	0
Opponents	65	2,644	40.7	35.9	1	16	55	0

Kickoff Returns

	No	Yds	Avg	LG	TD
Workman	33	547	16.6	46	0
Bland	13	256	19.7	37	0
Fullwood	11	243	22.1	35	0
Query	6	125	20.8	28	0
Woodside	2	38	19.0	23	0
Fontenot	2	30	15.0	20	0
Didier	1	0	0.0	0	0
Mandarich	1	0	0.0	0	0
Packers	69	1,239	18.0	46	0
Opponents	63	1,389	22.0	90	0

Punt Returns

	No	Yds	Avg	FC	LG	TD
Query	30	247	8.2	7	15	0
Sutton	5	42	8.4	1	17	0
R. Pitts	0	0	0.0	1	0	0
Packers	35	289	8.3	9	17	0
Opponents	30	416	13.9	11	74	0

Interceptions

	No	Yds	Avg	LG	TD
D. Brown	6	12	2.0	12	0
M. Murphy	3	31	10.3	20	0
Stills	3	20	6.7	12	0
Stephen	2	16	8.0	8	0
M. Lee	2	10	5.0	10	0
Noble	2	10	5.0	10	0
Dent	1	53	53.0	53	0
R. Pitts	1	37	37.0	37	0
Holland	1	26	26.0	26	0
Cecil	1	16	16.0	16	0
J. Anderson	1	1	1.0	1	0
Greene	1	0	0.0	0	0
Jakes	1	0	0.0	0	0
Packers	25	232	9.3	53	0
Opponents	20	321	16.1	t81	2

Scoring

	TDr	TDp	TDrt	PAT	FG	S	TP
Jacke	0	0	0	42/42	22/28	0	108
Sharpe	0	12	1	0/0	0/0	0	78
Fullwood	5	0	0	0/0	0/0	0	30
Majkowski	5	0	0	0/0	0/0	0	30
E. West	0	5	0	0/0	0/0	0	30
Fontenot	1	3	0	0/0	0/0	0	24
Bland	0	1	1	0/0	0/0	0	12
Kemp	0	2	0	0/0	0/0	0	12
Query	0	2	0	0/0	0/0	0	12
Didier	0	1	0	0/0	0/0	0	6
Haddix	0	1	0	0/0	0/0	0	6
Woodside	1	0	0	0/0	0/0	0	6
Workman	1	0	0	0/0	0/0	0	6
team	0	0	0	0/0	0/0	1	2
Packers	13	27	2	42/42	22/28	1	362
Opponents	15	22	4	39/41	23/30	1	356

Fumbles

	Fum	Ow	Op	Yds	Tot
Bland	0	2	1	4	3
Bush	0	1	0	0	1
Fontenot	0	1	1	0	2
Fullwood	6	1	0	0	1
Greene	1	0	1	0	1
Haddix	2	0	0	0	0
T. Harris	0	0	3	0	3
Holland	0	0	3	0	3
Kemp	3	1	0	0	1
Majkowski	15	6	0	-13	6
McGruder	0	1	0	0	1
Moran	0	1	0	0	1
M. Murphy	0	0	1	0	1
B. Nelson	0	0	1	0	1
Noble	0	0	1	0	1
Query	1	0	0	0	1
Ruettgers	0	2	0	0	2
Sharpe	1	1	0	5	1
Stephen	0	0	1	76	1
Sutton	1	0	0	0	0
Weddington	0	0	1	0	1
Woodside	4	1	0	0	1
Workman	1	1	0	0	1
Packers	35	19	15	72	34

Quarterback Sacks

	No
T. Harris	19.5
R. Brown	3.0
Greene	2.0
Noble	2.0
Winter	2.0
M. Hall	1.0
M. Murphy	1.0
B. Nelson	1.0
Stephen	1.0
Weddington	1.0
Patterson	0.5
Packers	34.0
Opponents	48.0

NFL STANDINGS

National Conference

Eastern Division

	W	L	T	Pct	PF	PA
New York Giants	12	4	0	.750	348	252
Philadelphia Eagles	11	5	0	.688	342	274
Washington Redskins	10	6	0	.625	386	308
Phoenix Cardinals	5	11	0	.313	258	377
Dallas Cowboys	1	15	0	.063	204	393

Central Division

	W	L	T	Pct	PF	PA
Minnesota Vikings	10	6	0	.625	351	275
Green Bay Packers	10	6	0	.625	362	356
Detroit Lions	7	9	0	.438	312	364
Chicago Bears	6	10	0	.375	358	377
Tampa Bay Buccaneers	5	11	0	.313	320	419

Western Division

	W	L	T	Pct	PF	PA
San Francisco 49ers	14	2	0	.875	442	253
Los Angeles Rams	11	5	0	.688	426	344
New Orleans Saints	9	7	0	.563	386	301
Atlanta Falcons	3	13	0	.188	279	437

American Conference

Eastern Division

	W	L	T	Pct	PF	PA
Buffalo Bills	9	7	0	.563	409	317
Indianapolis Colts	8	8	0	.500	298	301
Miami Dolphins	8	8	0	.500	331	379
New England Patriots	5	11	0	.313	297	391
New York Jets	4	12	0	.250	253	411

Central Division

	W	L	T	Pct	PF	PA
Cleveland Browns	9	6	1	.594	334	254
Houston Oilers	9	7	0	.563	365	412
Pittsburgh Steelers	9	7	0	.563	265	326
Cincinnati Bengals	8	8	0	.500	404	285

Western Division

	W	L	T	Pct	PF	PA
Denver Broncos	11	5	0	.688	362	226
Kansas City Chiefs	8	7	1	.531	318	286
Los Angeles Raiders	8	8	0	.500	315	297
Seattle Seahawks	7	9	0	.438	241	327
San Diego Chargers	6	10	0	.375	266	290

ROSTER

No	Name	Pos	Ht	Wt	DOB	College	G
59	Anderson, John	LB	6-3	228	02/14/56	Michigan	14
67	Ard, Billy	G	6-3	270	03/12/59	Wake Forest	15
76	Ariey, Mike	T	6-5	285	03/12/64	San Diego State	1
83	Bland, Carl	WR	5-11	182	08/17/61	Virginia Union	16
61	Boyarsky, Jerry	NT	6-3	290	05/15/59	Pittsburgh	13
17	Bracken, Don	P	6-0	211	02/16/62	Michigan	16
62	Brock, Matt	DE	6-4	267	01/14/66	Oregon	7
32	Brown, Dave	CB	6-1	197	01/16/53	Michigan	16
93	Brown, Robert	DE	6-2	270	05/21/60	Virginia Tech	16
51	Bush, Blair	C	6-3	272	11/25/56	Washington	16
63	Campen, James	C	6-3	270	06/11/64	Tulane	15
58	Cannon, Mark	C	6-3	270	06/14/62	Texas-Arlington	15
26	Cecil, Chuck	S	6-0	184	11/08/64	Arizona	9
56	Dent, Burnell	LB	6-1	236	03/16/63	Tulane	16
80	Didier, Clint	TE	6-5	240	04/04/59	Portland State	16
8	Dilweg, Anthony	QB	6-3	215	03/28/65	Duke	1
27	Fontenot, Herman	RB	6-0	206	09/12/63	LSU	16
21	Fullwood, Brent	FB	5-11	209	10/10/63	Auburn	15
23	Greene, George (Tiger)	DB	6-0	194	02/15/62	Western Carolina	16
35	Haddix, Michael	RB	6-1	227	12/27/61	Mississippi State	16
72	Hall, Mark	DE	6-4	285	08/21/65	Southwestern Louisiana	7
65	Hallstrom, Ron	G	6-6	290	06/11/59	Iowa	16
97	Harris, Tim	LB	6-5	235	09/10/64	Memphis State	16
50	Holland, Johnny	LB	6-2	221	03/11/65	Texas A&M	16
13	Jacke, Chris	K	6-0	197	03/12/66	Texas-El Paso	16
24	Jakes, Van	CB	6-0	190	05/10/61	Kent State	16
81	Kemp, Perry	WR	5-11	170	12/31/61	California State (PA)	14
22	Lee, Mark	CB	5-11	189	03/20/58	Washington	12
7	Majkowski, Don	QB	6-2	197	02/25/64	Virginia	16
77	Mandarich, Tony	T	6-5	315	09/23/66	Michigan State	14
88	Matthews, Aubrey	WR	5-7	165	09/15/62	Delta State	13
20	McGruder, Michael	DB	5-11	180	08/25/64	Kent State	2
57	Moran, Rich	G	6-2	275	03/19/62	San Diego State	16
37	Murphy, Mark	S	6-2	201	04/22/58	West Liberty	16
79	Nelson, Bob	NT	6-4	275	03/03/59	Miami	16
91	Noble, Brian	LB	6-3	252	09/06/62	Arizona State	16
96	Patterson, Shawn	DE	6-5	261	04/06/65	Arizona State	6
28	Pitts, Ron	DB	5-10	175	10/14/62	UCLA	14
85	Query, Jeff	WR	5-11	165	03/07/67	Millikin	16
75	Ruettgers, Ken	T	6-5	280	08/20/62	USC	16
84	Sharpe, Sterling	WR	5-11	202	04/06/65	South Carolina	16
89	Spagnola, John	TE	6-4	242	08/01/57	Yale	6
54	Stephen, Scott	LB	6-2	232	06/18/64	Arizona State	16
29	Stills, Ken	S	5-10	186	09/06/63	Wisconsin	16
49	Sutton, Mickey	CB	5-9	172	08/28/60	Montana	3
73	Veingrad, Alan	T	6-5	277	07/24/63	East Texas State	16
52	Weddington, Mike	LB	6-4	245	10/09/60	Oklahoma	15
86	West, Ed	TE	6-1	243	08/02/61	Auburn	13
68	Winter, Blaise	DE	6-3	275	01/31/62	Syracuse	16
33	Woodside, Keith	RB	5-11	213	07/29/64	Texas A&M	16
46	Workman, Vince	RB	5-10	193	05/09/68	Ohio State	15

DRAFT

Rnd	Name	Pos	Ht	Wt	College
1	Tony Mandarich (2)	T	6-5	315	Michigan State
2	(Packers traded 2nd round choice (31) and 5th round selection (114) to Browns for Browns' No. 1 pick in 1990 and Browns' 3rd and 5th round choices in 1989 plus Herman Fontenot)				
3a	Matt Brock (58)	DE	6-4	267	Oregon
3b	Anthony Dilweg (74)	QB	6-3	215	Duke
	(Choice from Browns in deal mentioned above)				
4	Jeff Graham (87)	QB	6-4	205	Long Beach State
	(Packers then traded Graham to Redskins for Erik Affholter plus Redskins' 5th and 8th round choices in 1989)				
5a	(Choice (114) to Browns in deal mentioned above)				
5b	Jeff Query (124)	WR	5-11	167	Millikin
	(Choice from Redskins in deal mentioned above)				
5c	Vince Workman (127)	RB	5-10	195	Ohio State
	(Choice from Browns in deal mentioned above)				
6	Chris Jacke (142)	K	6-0	197	Texas-El Paso
7	Mark Hall (169)	DT	6-4	285	SW Louisiana
8a	Thomas King (198)	DB	6-1	198	SW Louisiana
8b	Brian Shulman (206)	P	5-10	185	Auburn
	(Choice from Redskins in deal mentioned above)				
9	Scott Kirby (225)	T	6-6	290	Arizona State
10	Ben Jessie (254)	DB	6-0	205	SW Texas State
11	Cedric Stallworth (281)	DB	6-0	180	Georgia Tech
12	Stan Shiver (310)	DB	6-1	208	Florida State

1989 GREEN BAY PACKERS

FRONT ROW: (L-R) 7 Don Majkowski, 8 Anthony Dilweg, 10 Blair Kiel, 13 Chris Jacke, 17 Don Bracken, 20 Michael McGruder, 21 Brent Fullwood, 22 Mark Lee, 23 George (Tiger) Greene, 24 Van Jakes, 26 Chuck Cecil.

SECOND ROW: (L-R) 27 Herman Fontenot, 28 Ron Pitts, 29 Ken Stills, 32 Dave Brown, 33 Keith Woodside, 35 Michael Haddix, 36 George Cooper, 37 Mark Murphy, 38 Stan Shiver, 40 Cedric Gordon, 46 Vince Workman, 50 Johnny Holland.

THIRD ROW: (L-R) 51 Blair Bush, 52 Mike Weddington, 54 Scott Stephen, 56 Burnell Dent, 57 Rich Moran, 58 Mark Cannon, 59 John Anderson, 60 Dave Croston, 61 Jerry Boyarsky, 62 Matt Brock, 63 James Campen.

FOURTH ROW: (L-R) Team Physician Dr. Eugene Brusky, 64 Scott Kirby, 65 Ron Hallstrom, 67 Billy Ard, 68 Blaise Winter, 70 Keith Uecker, 72 Mark Hall, 73 Alan Veingrad, 75 Ken Ruettgers, 76 Mike Ariey, 77 Tony Mandarich, Trainer Domenic Gentile.

FIFTH ROW: (L-R) Equipment Assistant Jack Noel, Equipment Manager Bob Noel, 79 Bob Nelson, 80 Clint Didier, 81 Perry Kemp, 82 Erik Affholter, 83 Carl Bland, 84 Sterling Sharpe, 85 Jeff Query, Assistant Video Director Bob Eckberg, Video Director Al Treml.

SIXTH ROW: (L-R) Trainer Intern Larry Lemberger, Assistant Equipment Manager Bryan Nehring, 86 Ed West, 88 Aubrey Matthews, 89 John Spagnola, 91 Brian Noble, 93 Robert Brown, 96 Shawn Patterson, 97 Tim Harris, 99 John Dorsey, Trainer Intern Greg Everts, Trainer Intern John Bray.

BACK ROW: (L-R) Defensive Line Coach Greg Blache, Defensive Backs Coach Dick Jauron, Offensive Backfield Coach Willie Peete, Outside Linebackers Coach Dick Moseley, Strength-Conditioning/Tight Ends Coach Virgil Knight, Head Coach Lindy Infante, Special Teams Coach Howard Tippett, Defensive Coordinator Hank Bullough, Receivers Coach Wayne (Buddy) Geis, Offensive Line Coach Charlie Davis, General Offensive Assistant Joe Clark, Administrative Assistant Jesse Kaye.

Just how vital Don Majkowski had been to the Packers' resurgence of the previous year became painfully obvious in 1990. A torn rotator cuff ended the quarterback's season in Game 10, and the team responded by dropping its final five games to finish a disappointing 6-10.

The loss of Majkowski was huge, but other factors contributed to the swoon as well. Contract problems, a weak running game, and turnovers hindered the team.

Eighteen players, most of them starters, missed the first day of training camp because of contract problems. Four of the five starting offensive linemen—Alan Veingrad (15 practices), Ken Ruettgers (25), Rich Moran (29) and Ron Hallstrom (32)—missed a combined 101 practices because they could not come to terms.

Majkowski held out almost until the opener and his absence didn't help him on the field. He ended a 45-day holdout by signing a 1-year, $1.5 million deal on Sept. 5. He regained his starter status in Game 3, but not until he orchestrated a 24-21 come-from-behind win at Detroit in Game 4 did he completely get back in sync.

Because of the holdouts, head coach Lindy Infante made changes to his offensive line. He replaced Moran and Hallstrom with Billy Ard and Keith Uecker, respectively, for most of the season. Tony Mandarich, the team's top draft choice in 1989, moved ahead of Veingrad but did little to distinguish himself. Only Ruettgers and center James Campen started the season in their usual spots.

Michael Haddix was Green Bay's leading rusher with 311 yards, the only time in team history that the leader failed to average at least 20 yards a game. The Packers' average of 85.6 rushing yards per game was its worst ever, and the club scored just five rushing touchdowns.

Brent Fullwood aptly summed up just how tough the Packers were on the ground. The team's first-round pick in 1987 told the team's medical staff he was too ill to come out for the second half of the second Bears game on Oct. 7. That evening he was spotted dancing at a local nightclub. He was promptly traded to Cleveland three days later.

Green Bay surrendered a team record 62 sacks. The Packers gave up at least one sack in all 16 games and multiple sacks in 14 games.

A third wild card in each conference was added to the NFL's playoff format. Had such a setup existed in 1989, the Packers would have reached the postseason. In 1990, Green Bay could have gotten in as the third wild card if only it could have beaten the lowly Lions and Broncos on the final two weeks of the season.

Anthony Dilweg made his first NFL start at quarterback for the Packers in the season opener against the Rams. The second-year player completed 20 of 32 passes for 248 yards and three touchdowns in a 36-24 victory.

In the fourth quarter of the Bears game a week later, Infante replaced Dilweg with Majkowski. The switch had no bearing on the outcome and Green Bay lost 31-13.

Majkowski regained his starting status in Game 3. A week later, his impeccable fourth quarter (two touchdown passes, 10 completions in 11 attempts, and 32 yards rushing) rallied the Packers to a 24-21 win in Detroit.

A three-game winning streak in the heart of November pushed Green Bay into the wild card race. Chris Jacke kicked five field goals in a 29-16 win at Oakland, Dilweg did his best Majkowski imitation and rallied the Packers past the Cardinals 24-21 and the defense held the Buccaneers to 61 yards rushing in a workmanlike, 20-10 victory in Milwaukee. Aside from the division leaders (49ers, Giants, and Bears), Green Bay (6-5) trailed only Philadelphia (7-3) in the quest for a playoff berth.

Majkowski banged up his shoulder in the Cardinals' contest. He was flushed from the pocket and sacked by defensive end Freddie Joe Nunn in the second quarter. Expected to miss only one game initially, Majkowski sought a second opinion after the soreness persisted. Dr. Gary Losse of San Diego discovered a torn rotator cuff and surgically repaired it on Dec. 13.

Dilweg and Blair Kiel, inactive for almost three years, presided over the five-game slide. Kiel came close to victory on two occasions. He led the team into the red zone in the final two minutes against both Seattle and Detroit, but was stymied by a fourth-down incompletion and an interception, respectively.

PACK A SACKED

The Packers gave up a team-record 62 sacks in 1990, to finish last in the league in that category.

Ken Ruettgers (left tackle; 11 starts), Billy Ard (left guard; 15), James Campen (center; 16), Keith Uecker (right guard; 13), and Tony Mandarich (right tackle; 16) started most of the games on the line. Alan Veingrad (4 starts), Ron Hallstrom (4) and Rich Moran (1) were the others.

Green Bay surrendered at least three sacks in 11 games. Its worst performance came against the Raiders. Majkowski was dumped eight times for 40 yards in losses in a 29-16 win.

The Packers allowed just one sack on two occasions. The team lost both games, 27-13 to the Bears on Oct. 7 and 24-17 to the Lions on Dec. 22.

Most times sacked, season

No.	Year	Record
62	1990	6-10-0
52	1981	8-8-0
51	1988	4-12-0

TEAM STATISTICS

	GB	OPP
First Downs	276	286
Rushing	72	113
Passing	183	160
Penalty	21	13
Rushes	350	475
Yards Gained	1,369	2,059
Average Gain	3.91	4.33
Average Yards per Game	85.6	128.7
Passes Attempted	541	479
Completed	302	256
% Completed	55.82	53.44
Total Yards Gained	3,696	3,555
Times Sacked	62	27
Yards Lost	390	172
Net Yards Gained	3,306	3,383
Yards Gained per Completion	12.24	13.89
Net Yards per Attempt	5.48	6.69
Average Net Yards per Game	206.6	211.4
Combined Net Yards Gained	4,675	5,442
Total Plays	953	981
Average Net Yards per Play	4.91	5.55
Average Net Yards per Game	292.2	340.1
Third Down Efficiency	76/196	85/210
Percentage	38.78	40.48
Fourth Down Efficiency	5/14	3/9
Percentage	35.71	33.33
Intercepted By	16	21
Yards Returned	154	293
Returned for TD	1	2
Punts	65	69
Yards Punted	2,431	2,698
Average Yards per Punt	37.40	39.10
Punt Returns	32	34
Yards Returned	308	266
Average Yards per Return	9.63	7.82
Returned for TD	0	0
Kickoff Returns	63	56
Yards Returned	1,303	1,125
Average Yards per Return	20.68	20.09
Returned for TD	1	0
Penalties	84	109
Yards Penalized	674	854
Fumbles	37	26
Lost	22	14
Own Recovered for Touchdown	0	0
Opponent's Recovered by	14	22
Opponent's Recovered for Touchdown	1	2
Total Points Scored	271	347
Total Touchdowns	29	40
Touchdowns Rushing	5	16
Touchdowns Passing	20	20
Touchdowns on Returns & Recoveries	4	4
Extra Points	28	39
Safeties	0	1
Field Goals Attempted	30	34
Field Goals Made	23	22
% Successful	76.67	64.71
Average Time of Possession	29:34	30:26

Regular Season 6-10-0

Date	GB		OPP		Att.
9/9	36	Los Angeles Rams	24		(57,685)
9/16	13	Chicago Bears	31		(58,938)
9/23	3	Kansas City Chiefs	17		(58,817)
9/30	24	at Detroit Lions	21		(64,509)
10/7	13	at Chicago Bears	27		(59,929)
10/14	14	at Tampa Bay Buccaneers	26		(67,472)
10/28	24	Minnesota Vikings (M)	10		(55,125)
11/4	20	San Francisco 49ers	24		(58,835)
11/11	29	at Los Angeles Raiders	16		(50,855)
11/18	24	at Phoenix Cardinals	21		(46,878)
11/25	20	Tampa Bay Buccaneers (M)	10		(53,677)
12/2	7	at Minnesota Vikings	23		(62,058)
12/9	14	Seattle Seahawks (M)	20		(52,015)
12/16	0	at Philadelphia Eagles	31		(65,627)
12/22	17	Detroit Lions	24		(46,700)
12/30	13	at Denver Broncos	22		(46,943)

Score By Periods

	1	2	3	4	OT	Total
Packers	36	76	57	102	0	271
Opponents	64	103	88	92	0	347

INDIVIDUAL STATISTICS

Rushing

	Att	Yds	Avg	LG	TD
Haddix	98	311	3.2	13	0
D. Thompson	76	264	3.5	37	1
Majkowski	29	186	6.4	24	1
Woodside	46	182	4.0	21	1
Fullwood	44	124	2.8	16	1
A. Dilweg	21	114	5.4	22	0
Fontenot	17	76	4.5	18	0
Workman	8	51	6.4	31	0
Query	3	39	13.0	18	0
Sharpe	2	14	7.0	10	0
Kiel	5	9	1.8	4	1
Kemp	1	-1	-1.0	-1	0
Packers	350	1,369	3.9	37	5
Opponents	475	2,059	4.3	52	16

Receiving

	No	Yds	Avg	LG	TD
Sharpe	67	1,105	16.5	t76	6
Kemp	44	527	12.0	29	2
Query	34	458	13.5	t47	2
Weathers	33	390	11.8	29	1
Fontenot	31	293	9.5	59	1
E. West	27	356	13.2	50	5
Woodside	24	184	7.7	25	0
Haddix	13	94	7.2	28	2
J. Harris	12	157	13.1	26	0
C. Wilson	7	84	12.0	18	0
Workman	4	30	7.5	9	1
Fullwood	3	17	5.7	10	0
D. Thompson	3	1	0.3	1	0
Packers	302	3,696	12.2	t76	20
Opponents	256	3,555	13.9	74	20

Passing

	Att	Com	Yds	Pct	TD	In	Tk/Yds	Rate
Majkowski	264	150	1,925	56.8	10	12	32/178	73.5
A. Dilweg	192	101	1,267	52.6	8	7	22/150	72.1
Kiel	85	51	504	60.0	2	2	8/62	74.8
Packers	541	302	3,696	55.8	20	21	62/390	73.2
Opponents	479	256	3,555	53.4	20	16	27/172	77.5

Punting

	No	Yds	Avg	Net	TB	In20	LG	HB
Bracken	64	2,431	38.0	32.7	2	17	59	1
Packers	65	2,431	38.0	32.7	2	17	59	1
Opponents	69	2,698	39.1	31.7	10	16	61	2

Kickoff Returns

	No	Yds	Avg	LG	TD
C. Wilson	35	798	22.8	36	0
Workman	14	210	15.0	26	0
Bland	7	104	14.9	24	0
D. Thompson	3	103	34.3	t76	1
Fontenot	3	88	29.3	50	0
E. West	1	0	0.0	0	0
Packers	63	1,303	20.7	t76	1
Opponents	56	1,125	20.1	87	0

Punt Returns

	No	Yds	Avg	FC	LG	TD
Query	32	308	9.6	9	25	0
R. Pitts	0	0	—	2	0	0
Packers	32	308	9.6	9	25	0
Opponents	34	266	7.8	13	30	0

Interceptions

	No	Yds	Avg	LG	TD
L. Butler	3	42	14.0	28	0
Holmes	3	39	13.0	24	0
M. Murphy	3	6	2.0	4	0
Stephen	2	26	13.0	26	0
Holland	1	32	32.0	32	0
Patterson	1	9	9.0	t9	1
Cecil	1	0	0.0	0	0
M. Lee	1	0	0.0	0	0
R. Pitts	1	0	0.0	0	0
Packers	16	154	9.6	32	1
Opponents	21	293	14.0	47	2

Scoring

	TDr	TDp	TDrt	PAT	FG	S	TP
Jacke	0	0	0	28/29	23/30	0	97
Sharpe	0	6	0	0/0	0/0	0	36
E. West	0	5	0	0/0	0/0	0	30
Query	0	2	1	0/0	0/0	0	18
Haddix	0	2	0	0/0	0/0	0	12
Kemp	0	2	0	0/0	0/0	0	12
D. Thompson	1	0	1	0/0	0/0	0	12
Fontenot	0	1	0	0/0	0/0	0	6
Fullwood	1	0	0	0/0	0/0	0	6
Greene	0	0	1	0/0	0/0	0	6
Kiel	1	0	0	0/0	0/0	0	6
Majkowski	1	0	0	0/0	0/0	0	6
Patterson	0	0	1	0/0	0/0	0	6
Weathers	0	1	0	0/0	0/0	0	6
Woodside	1	0	0	0/0	0/0	0	6
Workman	0	1	0	0/0	0/0	0	6
Packers	5	20	4	28/29	23/30	0	271
Opponents	16	20	4	39/40	22/34	1	347

Fumbles

	Fum	Ow	Op	Yds	Tot
T. Bennett	0	0	1	0	1
Bland	0	0	1	0	1
R. Brown	0	0	1	0	1
Campen	2	0	0	-21	0
A. Dilweg	10	4	0	-9	4
Fontenot	1	0	1	0	1
Fullwood	1	0	0	0	0
Haddix	3	0	0	0	0
T. Harris	0	0	2	28	2
Holland	0	0	1	0	1
Holmes	0	0	3	44	3
Kemp	2	0	0	0	0
Kiel	0	0	0	0	0
Majkowski	6	3	0	-10	3
Mandarich	0	1	0	0	1
Pitts	0	0	1	0	1
Query	3	2	1	0	3
Ruettgers	0	1	0	0	1
Stephen	1	0	2	15	2
D. Thompson	1	0	0	0	0
E. West	3	0	0	0	0
Woodside	2	0	0	0	0
Packers	37	12	14	47	26

Quarterback Sacks

	No
T. Harris	7.0
M. Brock	4.0
Patterson	4.0
Bennett	3.0
R. Brown	3.0
Dent	1.0
Holmes	1.0
M. Murphy	1.0
B. Nelson	1.0
Noble	1.0
Stephen	1.0
Packers	27.0
Opponents	62.0

NFL STANDINGS

National Conference

Eastern Division

	W	L	T	Pct	PF	PA
New York Giants	13	3	0	.813	335	211
Philadelphia Eagles	10	6	0	.625	396	299
Washington Redskins	10	6	0	.625	381	301
Dallas Cowboys	7	9	0	.438	244	308
Phoenix Cardinals	5	11	0	.313	268	396

Central Division

	W	L	T	Pct	PF	PA
Chicago Bears	11	5	0	.688	348	280
Tampa Bay Buccaneers	6	10	0	.375	264	367
Detroit Lions	6	10	0	.375	373	413
Green Bay Packers	6	10	0	.375	271	347
Minnesota Vikings	6	10	0	.375	351	326

Western Division

	W	L	T	Pct	PF	PA
San Francisco 49ers	14	2	0	.875	353	239
New Orleans Saints	8	8	0	.500	274	275
Los Angeles Rams	5	11	0	.313	345	412
Atlanta Falcons	5	11	0	.313	348	365

American Conference

Eastern Division

	W	L	T	Pct	PF	PA
Buffalo Bills	13	3	0	.813	428	263
Miami Dolphins	12	4	0	.750	336	242
Indianapolis Colts	7	9	0	.438	281	353
New York Jets	6	10	0	.375	295	345
New England Patriots	1	15	0	.063	181	446

Central Division

	W	L	T	Pct	PF	PA
Cincinnati Bengals	9	7	0	.563	360	352
Houston Oilers	9	7	0	.563	405	307
Pittsburgh Steelers	9	7	0	.563	292	240
Cleveland Browns	3	13	0	.188	228	462

Western Division

	W	L	T	Pct	PF	PA
Los Angeles Raiders	12	4	0	.750	337	268
Kansas City Chiefs	11	5	0	.688	369	257
Seattle Seahawks	9	7	0	.563	306	286
San Diego Chargers	6	10	0	.375	315	281
Denver Broncos	5	11	0	.313	331	374

ROSTER

No	Name	Pos	Ht	Wt	DOB	College	G
74	Archambeau, Lester	DE	6-4	270	06/27/67	Stanford	4
67	Ard, Billy	G	6-3	273	03/12/59	Wake Forest	15
90	Bennett, Tony	LB	6-2	233	07/01/67	Mississippi	14
83	Bland, Carl	WR	5-11	179	08/17/61	Virginia Union	14
17	Bracken, Don	P	6-0	218	02/16/62	Michigan	16
62	Brock, Matt	DE	6-4	285	01/14/66	Oregon	16
93	Brown, Robert	DE	6-2	270	05/21/60	Virginia Tech	16
51	Bush, Blair	C	6-3	273	11/25/56	Washington	16
36	Butler, LeRoy	CB	6-0	192	07/19/68	Florida State	16
63	Campen, James	C	6-3	275	06/11/64	Tulane	16
26	Cecil, Chuck	S	6-0	188	11/08/64	Arizona	9
56	Dent, Burnell	LB	6-1	234	03/16/63	Tulane	15
8	Dilweg, Anthony	QB	6-3	198	03/28/65	Duke	9
27	Fontenot, Herman	RB	6-0	205	09/12/63	LSU	14
21	Fullwood, Brent	FB	5-11	209	10/10/63	Auburn	5
23	Greene, George (Tiger)	DB	6-0	192	02/15/62	Western Carolina	16
35	Haddix, Michael	RB	6-1	230	12/27/61	Mississippi State	16
72	Hall, Mark	DE	6-4	280	08/21/65	Southwestern Louisiana	3
65	Hallstrom, Ron	G	6-6	297	06/11/59	Iowa	16
80	Harris, Jackie	TE	6-3	240	01/04/68	Northeast Louisiana	16
97	Harris, Tim	LB	6-5	258	09/10/64	Memphis State	16
89	Harris, William	TE	6-5	255	02/10/65	Bishop	4
50	Holland, Johnny	LB	6-2	233	03/11/65	Texas A&M	16
44	Holmes, Jerry	CB	6-1	176	12/22/57	West Virginia	16
60	Houston, Bobby	LB	6-2	234	10/26/67	North Carolina State	1
13	Jacke, Chris	K	6-0	197	03/12/66	Texas-El Paso	16
81	Kemp, Perry	WR	5-11	170	12/31/61	California State (PA)	16
10	Kiel, Blair	QB	6-0	205	11/29/61	Notre Dame	3
22	Lee, Mark	CB	5-11	189	03/20/58	Washington	16
7	Majkowski, Don	QB	6-2	208	02/25/64	Virginia	9
77	Mandarich, Tony	T	6-5	295	09/23/66	Michigan State	16
57	Moran, Rich	G	6-2	283	03/19/62	San Diego State	16
37	Murphy, Mark	S	6-2	203	04/22/58	West Liberty	16
79	Nelson, Bob	NT	6-4	275	03/03/59	Miami	16
91	Noble, Brian	LB	6-3	243	09/06/62	Arizona State	14
96	Patterson, Shawn	DE	6-5	265	04/06/65	Arizona State	11
95	Paup, Bryce	LB	6-4	245	02/29/68	Northern Iowa	5
28	Pitts, Ron	DB	5-10	183	10/14/62	UCLA	16
85	Query, Jeff	WR	5-11	167	03/07/67	Millikin	16
75	Ruettgers, Ken	T	6-5	288	08/20/62	USC	11
84	Sharpe, Sterling	WR	5-11	202	04/06/65	South Carolina	16
54	Stephen, Scott	LB	6-2	243	06/18/64	Arizona State	16
39	Thompson, Darrell	FB	6-0	215	11/23/67	Minnesota	16
70	Uecker, Keith	G	6-5	295	06/29/60	Auburn	13
73	Veingrad, Alan	T	6-5	281	07/24/63	East Texas State	16
87	Weathers, Clarence	WR	5-8	182	01/10/62	Delaware State	14
52	Weddington, Mike	LB	6-4	243	10/09/60	Oklahoma	6
86	West, Ed	TE	6-1	240	08/02/61	Auburn	16
88	Wilson, Charles	WR	5-9	174	0701/68	Memphis State	15
68	Winter, Blaise	DE	6-3	282	01/31/62	Syracuse	13
29	Woods, Jerry	S	5-8	193	02/13/66	Northern Michigan	16
33	Woodside, Keith	RB	5-11	200	07/29/64	Texas A&M	16
46	Workman, Vince	RB	5-10	195	05/09/68	Ohio State	15

DRAFT

Rnd	Name	Pos	Ht	Wt	College
1a	Tony Bennett (18)	LB	6-2	233	Mississippi
	(Choice from Browns completing 1989 trade involving draft choices and Herman Fontenot)				
1b	Darrell Thompson (19)	FB	6-0	215	Minnesota
2	LeRoy Butler (48)	CB	5-11	192	Florida State
3	Bobby Houston (75)	LB	6-2	234	North Carolina State
4	Jackie Harris (102)	TE	6-3	240	Northeast Louisiana
5	Charles Wilson (132)	WR	5-9	174	Memphis State
6	Bryce Paup (154)	LB	6-4	245	Northern Iowa
7	Lester Archambeau (186)	DE	6-4	270	Stanford
8	Roger Brown (215)	CB	6-0	196	Virginia Tech
9	Kirk Baumgartner (242)	QB	6-3	210	Wis.-Stevens Point
10	Jerome Martin (269)	S	6-0	222	Western Kentucky
11	Harry Jackson (299)	FB	5-11	220	St. Cloud State
12	Kirk Maggio (325)	P	5-11	157	UCLA

1990 GREEN BAY PACKERS

FRONT ROW: (L-R) 7 Don Majkowski, 8 Anthony Dilweg, 10 Blair Kiel, 13 Chris Jacke, 17 Don Bracken, 21 Brent Fullwood, 22 Mark Lee, 23 George (Tiger) Greene, 26 Chuck Cecil, 27 Herman Fontenot.
SECOND ROW: (L-R) 28 Ron Pitts, 29 Jerry Woods, 32 Dave Brown, 33 Keith Woodside, 35 Michael Haddix, 36 LeRoy Butler, 37 Mark Murphy, 39 Darrell Thompson, 44 Jerry Holmes, 46 Vince Workman, 50 Johnny Holland.
THIRD ROW: (L-R) 51 Blair Bush, 52 Mike Weddington, 54 Scott Stephen, 56 Burnell Dent, 57 Rich Moran, 60 Bobby Houston, 62 Matt Brock, 63 James Campen, 65 Ron Hallstrom, 67 Billy Ard.
FOURTH ROW: (L-R) Trainer Domenic Gentile, 68 Blaise Winter, 70 Keith Uecker, 72 Mark Hall, 73 Alan Veingrad, 74 Lester Archambeau, 75 Ken Ruettgers, 77 Tony Mandarich, 79 Bob Nelson, 80 Jackie Harris.
FIFTH ROW: (L-R) Dr. Eugene Brusky, 81 Perry Kemp, 82 Erik Affholter, 83 Carl Bland, 84 Sterling Sharpe, 85 Jeff Query, 86 Ed West, 87 Clarence Weathers, 88 Charles Wilson, Assistant Video Director Bob Eckberg,
Video Director Al Treml.
SIXTH ROW: (L-R) Equipment Assistant Jack Noel, Assistant Equipment Manager Bryan Nehring, Equipment Manager Bob Noel, 90 Tony Bennett, 91 Brian Noble, 93 Robert Brown, 95 Bryce Paup, 96 Shawn Patterson, 97 Tim Harris, Trainer Intern Kurt Fielding,
Trainer Intern Michael Van Veghel, Trainer Intern Larry Lemberger.
BACK ROW: (L-R) Defensive Backfield Coach Dick Jauron, Defensive Coordinator Hank Bullough, Defensive Line Coach Greg Blache, Outside Linebackers Coach Dick Moseley, Receivers Coach Wayne (Buddy) Geis,
Head Coach Lindy Infante, Special Teams Coach Howard Tippett, Offensive Line Coach Charlie Davis, Strength-Conditioning/Tight Ends Coach Virgil Knight, Offensive Backfield Coach Willie Peete, Assistant Offensive Line Coach Joe Clark, Administrative
Assistant/Pro Scout Jesse Kaye.

Losing can be frustrating.

Just two years removed from one of the more exciting seasons in team history, the Packers and their fans had to come to grips with the fact that Green Bay was no longer a good football team. Don Majkowski dinged an ambulance with his helmet after an early-season loss in Detroit. Tim Harris fired parting shots at the city after he was traded to San Francisco in October. A larger-than-usual number of Packers faithful were arrested after a dismal 10-0 loss at home to the Bears on national television.

Green Bay finished 4-12. Three of its wins came against the hapless Buccaneers (twice) and Colts. Not until the season finale against the Vikings (8-7 at the time) did the Packers defeat a team with a winning record.

As the losses mounted, the spotlight shined brightest on vice president of football operations Tom Braatz and head coach Lindy Infante. Packers president Bob Harlan fired Braatz on Nov. 20. Infante lasted the year, but was dismissed by Braatz's replacement the day after the season finale.

Ranked sixth in yards gained in 1989, the Packers offense slid to 20th in 1990 and 24th in 1991. Darrell Thompson, Keith Woodside and Vince Workman were the main cogs in a running game that produced just 20 more yards than the previous year. On the passing front, Majkowski again missed a major portion of the season (seven games) due to a hamstring injury. Former Bear and Plan B acquisition Mike Tomczak led the team in passing.

A solid defense kept Green Bay in most games. Eight of its losses were by 10 or fewer points. Even without Tim Harris, traded to the 49ers on Sept. 30, the unit finished 10th overall. The Packers permitted opponents just 3.38 yards per carry (second best to the Eagles' 2.97) and 96.6 yards rushing per game, lowest since the 1940 club yielded 94.5 yards per game.

Jim McMahon and the Eagles beat up on Green Bay 20-3 in the season opener. The former Bear passed for 257 yards and two touchdowns, including a 75-yard connection with Fred Barnett for the game's final points.

The Lions roared past Green Bay 23-14 in Game 2. Robert Clark caught 10 passes for 143 yards. Though he didn't reach the end zone, nine of his receptions were good for first downs.

Chris Jacke's 22-yard field goal with 22 seconds left got the Packers past the Buccaneers 15-13 in Game 3. Earlier in the fourth quarter, Majkowski hit Vince Workman with an 8-yard scoring pass to start the 10-point rally.

In the three weeks that followed their first win, the Packers were at their gift-giving best. Nose tackle Chuck Klingbeil recovered a Majkowski fumble in the end zone to spur a rally that secured coach Don Shula's 300th career win. A week later, the Rams turned two Packers' fumbles into 14 points in a span of seven seconds. The Cowboys then followed

suit, needing but 37 seconds to convert a pair of Green Bay fumbles into touchdowns.

The Green and Gold sank even lower in a 10-0 loss to the Bears. The team generated a measly 138 yards and five first downs.

"I don't have the answers," Infante said. "I wish I did. All I can do is apologize for our performance offensively."

A trip to Tampa Bay provided some relief. Defensively, Green Bay dominated, forcing eight turnovers and inflicting six sacks on the hapless Buccaneers. Brian Noble started the Packers on their 27-0 rout with a fumble return for a touchdown in the first quarter.

Three straight losses followed. Braatz was fired after the third, a 35-21 setback to the Vikings.

A week later, the Packers made the Jets' Ron Wolf their new general manager. Wolf was given total control of football operations, a luxury Braatz never enjoyed.

Wolf closely observed the team over its final four games, a span in which it won just once. One day after Infante was given the game ball by his players in the Metrodome, Wolf brought the Infante era to a close.

Wolf needed to "feel comfortable in doing what I know how to do, and who I can direct to do it with. I didn't particularly feel comfortable. That's the reason for the move."

Three weeks later, Wolf signed Infante's replacement, Mike Holmgren. The move would prove to be a comfortable fit in the years ahead.

RUNNING ON EMPTY

Lindy Infante's Packers were never going to be mistaken for a power running team. Green Bay failed to gain 100 yards rushing in 41 of the 64 games that Infante coached.

But in 1991, the team reached a new low. The club failed to gain 100 yards rushing in each of its first 11 games, the longest such run in a single season in team history.

Darrell Thompson, Vince Workman, Keith Woodside, and Allen Rice all gave it a try at running back. The numbers through 11 games were discouraging. Thompson (189 yards; 2.8 average), Woodside (166; 3.6), Workman (150; 3.3) and Rice (100; 3.3).

The team couldn't muster even 50 yards in three of the 11 games.

Green Bay finally broke out on Nov. 24. Led by Thompson's 63 yards, the Packers amassed 164 yards rushing in defeating the Colts 14-10. A week later, Thompson turned in the season's best performance by an individual when he gained 93 yards on 18 carries in a 35-31 loss to the Falcons.

Thompson led the club with 471 yards rushing for the season.

TEAM STATISTICS

	GB	OPP
First Downs	259	298
Rushing	88	99
Passing	150	177
Penalty	21	22
Rushes	381	457
Yards Gained	1,389	1,546
Average Gain	3.65	3.38
Average Yards per Game	86.8	96.6
Passes Attempted	514	531
Completed	272	305
% Completed	52.92	57.44
Total Yards Gained	3,213	3,573
Times Sacked	45	45
Yards Lost	270	307
Net Yards Gained	2,943	3,266
Yards Gained per Completion	11.81	11.71
Net Yards per Attempt	5.26	5.67
Average Net Yards per Game	183.9	204.1
Combined Net Yards Gained	4,332	4,812
Total Plays	940	1,033
Average Yards per Play	4.61	4.66
Average Net Yards per Game	270.8	300.8
Third Down Efficiency	77/207	85/220
Percentage	37.20	38.64
Fourth Down Efficiency	8/14	10/19
Percentage	57.14	52.63
Intercepted By	15	19
Yards Returned	234	185
Returned for TD	0	1
Punts	86	76
Yards Punted	3,473	3,199
Average Yards per Punt	40.38	42.09
Punt Returns	41	35
Yards Returned	396	375
Average Yards per Return	9.66	10.71
Returned for TD	0	1
Kickoff Returns	60	46
Yards Returned	1,197	942
Average Yards per Return	19.96	20.48
Returned for TD	1	0
Penalties	98	106
Yards Penalized	834	777
Fumbles	41	31
Lost	17	14
Own Recovered for Touchdown	0	0
Opponent's Recovered by	14	17
Opponent's Recovered for Touchdown	1	3
Total Points Scored	273	313
Total Touchdowns	31	35
Touchdowns Rushing	12	10
Touchdowns Passing	17	20
Touchdowns on Returns & Recoveries	2	5
Extra Points	31	35
Safeties	1	0
Field Goals Attempted	24	31
Field Goals Made	18	23
% Successful	75.00	74.19
Average Time of Possession	28:15	31:45

Regular Season   4-12-0

Date	GB		OPP	Att.
9/1	3	Philadelphia Eagles	20	(58,991)
9/8	14	at Detroit Lions	23	(43,132)
9/15	15	Tampa Bay Buccaneers	13	(58,114)
9/22	13	at Miami Dolphins	16	(56,583)
9/29	21	at Los Angeles Rams	23	(54,736)
10/6	17	Dallas Cowboys (M)	20	(53,695)
10/17	0	Chicago Bears	10	(58,435)
10/27	24	at Tampa Bay Buccaneers	27	(40,275)
11/3	16	at New York Jets (OT)	19	(67,435)
11/10	24	Buffalo Bills (M)	34	(52,175)
11/17	14	Minnesota Vikings	35	(57,614)
11/24	14	Indianapolis Colts (M)	10	(42,132)
12/1	31	at Atlanta Falcons	35	(43,270)
12/8	13	at Chicago Bears	27	(62,353)
12/15	17	Detroit Lions	21	(43,881)
12/21	27	at Minnesota Vikings	7	(52,860)

Score By Periods

	1	2	3	4	OT	Total
Packers	68	78	55	72	0	273
Opponents	47	102	49	112	3	313

INDIVIDUAL STATISTICS

Rushing

	Att	Yds	Avg	LG	TD
D. Thompson	141	471	3.3	t40	1
Woodside	84	326	3.9	29	1
Workman	71	237	3.3	t30	7
Majkowski	25	108	4.3	15	2
Rice	30	100	3.3	21	0
Tomczak	17	93	5.5	48	1
Kiel	4	46	11.5	26	0
Sharpe	4	4	1.0	12	0
C. Wilson	3	3	1.0	5	0
J. Harris	1	1	1.0	1	0
McJulien	1	0	0.0	0	0
Packers	**381**	**1,389**	**3.6**	**48**	**12**
Opponents	457	1,546	3.4	27	10

Receiving

	No	Yds	Avg	LG	TD
Sharpe	69	961	13.9	t58	4
Workman	46	371	8.1	25	4
Kemp	42	583	13.9	39	2
J. Harris	24	264	11.0	35	3
Woodside	22	185	8.4	28	0
C. Wilson	19	305	16.1	t75	1
E. West	15	151	10.1	21	3
Weathers	12	150	12.5	22	0
Query	7	94	13.4	26	0
D. Thompson	7	71	10.1	18	0
Affholter	7	68	9.7	20	0
Rice	2	10	5.0	7	0
Packers	**272**	**3,213**	**11.8**	**t75**	**17**
Opponents	305	3,573	11.7	t87	20

Passing

	Att	Com	Yds	Pct	TD	In	Tk/Yds	Rate
Tomczak	238	128	1,490	53.8	11	9	13/105	72.6
Majkowski	226	115	1,362	50.9	3	8	30/152	59.3
Kiel	50	29	361	58.0	3	2	2/13	83.8
Packers	**514**	**272**	**3,213**	**52.9**	**17**	**19**	**45/270**	**67.9**
Opponents	531	305	3,573	57.4	20	15	45/307	78.8

Punting

	No	Yds	Avg	Net	TB	In20	LG	HB
McJulien	86	3,473	40.4	34.4	7	22	62	0
Packers	**86**	**3,473**	**40.4**	**34.4**	**7**	**22**	**62**	**0**
Opponents	76	3,199	42.1	34.5	9	19	61	0

Kickoff Returns

	No	Yds	Avg	LG	TD
C. Wilson	23	522	22.7	t82	1
Sikahema	15	325	21.7	35	0
Workman	8	139	17.4	26	0
D. Thompson	7	127	18.1	30	0
Rice	3	36	12.0	15	0
Webb	2	40	20.0	23	0
Davey	1	8	8.0	8	0
Dean	1	0	0.0	0	0
Packers	**60**	**1,197**	**20.0**	**t82**	**1**
Opponents	46	942	20.5	56	0

Punt Returns

	No	Yds	Avg	FC	LG	TD
Sikahema	26	239	9.2	4	62	0
Query	14	157	11.2	3	28	0
Workman	1	0	0.0	0	0	0
Packers	**41**	**396**	**9.7**	**7**	**62**	**0**
Opponents	35	375	10.7	24	t78	1

Interceptions

	No	Yds	Avg	LG	TD
Cecil	3	76	25.3	32	0
Murphy	3	27	9.0	16	0
L. Butler	3	6	2.0	6	0
V. Clark	2	42	21.0	22	0
R. Brown	1	37	37.0	37	0
Stephen	1	23	23.0	23	0
Tuaolo	1	23	23.0	23	0
Holmes	1	0	0.0	0	0
Packers	**15**	**234**	**15.6**	**37**	**0**
Opponents	19	185	9.7	t65	1

Scoring

	TDr	TDp	TDrt	PAT	FG	S	TP
Jacke	0	0	0	31/31	18/24	0	85
Workman	7	4	0	0/0	0/0	0	66
Sharpe	0	4	0	0/0	0/0	0	24
J. Harris	0	3	0	0/0	0/0	0	18
E. West	0	3	0	0/0	0/0	0	18
Kemp	0	2	0	0/0	0/0	0	12
Majkowski	2	0	0	0/0	0/0	0	12
C. Wilson	0	1	1	0/0	0/0	0	12
Noble	0	0	1	0/0	0/0	0	6
D. Thompson	1	0	0	0/0	0/0	0	6
Tomczak	1	0	0	0/0	0/0	0	6
Woodside	1	0	0	0/0	0/0	0	6
Paup	0	0	0	0/0	0/0	1	2
Packers	**12**	**17**	**2**	**31/31**	**18/24**	**1**	**273**
Opponents	10	20	5	34/35	23/31	0	313

Fumbles

	Fum	Ow	Op	Yds	Tot
Ard	0	2	0	0	2
R. Brown	0	0	1	0	1
Bush	0	0	1	0	1
L. Butler	0	0	1	0	1
Dean	1	0	0	0	0
Dent	0	0	1	0	1
Hallstrom	1	0	0	0	0
J. Harris	1	0	0	0	1
Hauck	1	0	0	0	0
Holland	0	0	4	3	4
Holmes	0	0	1	12	1
Kemp	2	0	0	0	0
Kiel	2	1	0	0	1
Majkowski	10	4	0	-3	4
McJulien	1	1	0	-2	1
Murphy	0	0	1	0	1
Noble	0	0	1	1	1
Query	1	1	0	0	1
Rice	2	0	0	0	0
Ruettgers	0	1	0	0	1
Sharpe	1	2	0	0	2
Sikahema	3	0	0	0	0
Stephen	0	0	1	1	1
D. Thompson	1	1	0	0	1
Tomczak	5	2	0	-1	2
Weathers	1	0	0	0	0
C. Wilson	4	1	0	0	1
Woodside	3	1	0	0	1
Workman	3	4	0	9	4
Packers	**41**	**22**	**14**	**19**	**36**

Quarterback Sacks

	No
Bennett	13.0
Paup	7.5
Archambeau	4.5
D. Brown	4.0
Tuaolo	3.5
M. Brock	2.5
Noble	2.5
Dent	1.5
Patterson	1.5
Stephen	1.5
R. Mitchell	1.0
Murphy	1.0
team	1.0
Packers	**45.0**
Opponents	45.0

NFL STANDINGS

National Conference

Eastern Division

	W	L	T	Pct	PF	PA
Washington Redskins	14	2	0	.875	485	224
Dallas Cowboys	11	5	0	.688	342	310
Philadelphia Eagles	10	6	0	.625	285	244
New York Giants	8	8	0	.500	281	297
Phoenix Cardinals	4	12	0	.250	196	344

Central Division

	W	L	T	Pct	PF	PA
Detroit Lions	12	4	0	.750	339	295
Chicago Bears	11	5	0	.688	299	269
Minnesota Vikings	8	8	0	.500	301	306
Green Bay Packers	4	12	0	.250	273	313
Tampa Bay Buccaneers	3	13	0	.188	199	365

Western Division

	W	L	T	Pct	PF	PA
New Orleans Saints	11	5	0	.688	341	211
Atlanta Falcons	10	6	0	.625	361	338
San Francisco 49ers	10	6	0	.625	393	239
Los Angeles Rams	3	13	0	.188	234	390

American Conference

Eastern Division

	W	L	T	Pct	PF	PA
Buffalo Bills	13	3	0	.813	458	318
New York Jets	8	8	0	.500	314	293
Miami Dolphins	8	8	0	.500	343	349
New England Patriots	6	10	0	.375	211	305
Indianapolis Colts	1	15	0	.063	143	381

Central Division

	W	L	T	Pct	PF	PA
Houston Oilers	11	5	0	.688	386	251
Pittsburgh Steelers	7	9	0	.438	292	344
Cleveland Browns	6	10	0	.375	293	298
Cincinnati Bengals	3	13	0	.188	263	435

Western Division

	W	L	T	Pct	PF	PA
Denver Broncos	12	4	0	.750	304	235
Kansas City Chiefs	10	6	0	.625	322	252
Los Angeles Raiders	9	7	0	.563	298	297
Seattle Seahawks	7	9	0	.438	276	261
San Diego Chargers	4	12	0	.250	274	342

ROSTER

No	Name	Pos	Ht	Wt	DOB	College	G
82	Affholter, Erik	WR	6-0	187	04/10/66	USC	4
74	Archambeau, Lester	DE	6-4	270	06/27/67	Stanford	16
67	Ard, Billy	G	6-3	273	03/12/59	Wake Forest	5
32	Avery, Steve	FB	6-1	225	08/18/66	Northern Michigan	1
90	Bennett, Tony	LB	6-2	233	07/01/67	Mississippi	16
62	Brock, Matt	DE	6-4	285	01/14/66	Oregon	16
93	Brown, Robert	DE	6-2	270	05/21/60	Virginia Tech	16
55	Burnette, Reggie	LB	6-1	240	10/04/68	Houston	3
51	Bush, Blair	C	6-3	273	11/25/56	Washington	16
36	Butler, LeRoy	CB	6-0	192	07/19/68	Florida State	16
63	Campen, James	C	6-3	275	06/11/64	Tulane	13
26	Cecil, Chuck	S	6-0	188	11/08/64	Arizona	16
78	Cheek, Louis	G/T	6-7	286	10/06/64	Texas A&M	12
55	Clark, Greg	LB	6-0	226	03/05/65	Arizona State	2
25	Clark, Vinnie	CB	6-0	194	01/22/69	Ohio State	16
99	Davey, Don	DE	6-4	273	04/08/68	Wisconsin	16
42	Dean, Walter	FB	5-10	216	05/01/68	Grambling	9
56	Dent, Burnell	LB	6-1	234	03/16/63	Tulane	14
21	Fuller, Joe	CB	5-10	186	09/25/64	Northern Iowa	16
72	Gabbard, Steve	G/T	6-3	290	07/19/66	Florida State	4
65	Hallstrom, Ron	G	6-6	297	06/11/59	Iowa	16
80	Harris, Jackie	TE	6-3	240	01/04/68	Northeast Louisiana	16
24	Hauck, Tim	S	5-10	181	12/20/66	Montana	16
50	Holland, Johnny	LB	6-2	233	03/11/65	Texas A&M	16
44	Holmes, Jerry	CB	6-1	176	12/22/57	West Virginia	13
13	Jacke, Chris	K	6-0	197	03/12/66	Texas-El Paso	16
71	Jones, Scott	T	6-6	284	03/20/66	Washington	2
92	Jurkovic, John	NT	6-2	297	08/18/67	Eastern Illinois	4
81	Kemp, Perry	WR	5-11	170	12/31/61	California State (PA)	16
10	Kiel, Blair	QB	6-0	205	11/29/61	Notre Dame	4
59	Larson, Kurt	LB	6-4	241	02/25/66	Michigan State	13
7	Majkowski, Don	QB	6-2	208	02/25/64	Virginia	9
77	Mandarich, Tony	T	6-5	295	09/23/66	Michigan State	15
16	McJulien, Paul	P	5-10	210	02-24-65	Jackson State	16
47	Mitchell, Roland	CB	5-11	198	03/15/64	Texas Tech	16
57	Moran, Rich	G	6-2	283	03/19/62	San Diego State	16
37	Murphy, Mark	S	6-2	203	04/22/58	West Liberty	16
91	Noble, Brian	LB	6-3	243	09/06/62	Arizona State	16
96	Patterson, Shawn	DE	6-5	265	04/06/65	Arizona State	12
95	Paup, Bryce	LB	6-4	245	02/29/68	Northern Iowa	12
85	Query, Jeff	WR	5-11	167	03/07/67	Millikin	16
31	Rice, Allen	RB	5-10	206	04/05/62	Baylor	6
75	Ruettgers, Ken	T	6-5	288	08/20/62	USC	4
84	Sharpe, Sterling	WR	5-11	202	04/06/65	South Carolina	16
45	Sikahema, Vai	RB/KR	5-8	196	08/29/62	BYU	11
54	Stephen, Scott	LB	6-2	243	06/18/64	Arizona State	16
39	Thompson, Darrell	FB	6-0	215	11/23/67	Minnesota	13
18	Tomczak, Mike	QB	6-1	204	10/23/62	Ohio State	12
98	Tuaolo, Esera	NT	6-2	284	07/11/68	Oregon State	16
70	Uecker, Keith	G	6-5	295	06/29/60	Auburn	14
87	Weathers, Clarence	WR	5-8	182	01/10/62	Delaware State	14
30	Webb, Chuck	FB	5-9	201	11/17/69	Tennessee	2
86	West, Ed	TE	6-1	240	08/02/61	Auburn	16
88	Wilson, Charles	WR	5-9	174	0701/68	Memphis State	15
33	Woodside, Keith	RB	5-11	200	07/29/64	Texas A&M	16
46	Workman, Vince	RB	5-10	195	05/09/68	Ohio State	16

DRAFT

Rnd	Name	Pos	Ht	Wt	College
1b	Vinnie Clark (19)	CB	6-0	194	Ohio State

(Traded positions with Eagles, 8th choice for 19th and Eagles' 1st round pick in 1992)

Rnd	Name	Pos	Ht	Wt	College
2	Esera Tuaolo	NT	6-2	284	Oregon State
3a	Don Davey (67)	DE	6-4	273	Wisconsin

(Traded 3rd round pick (63) to Jets for Jets' 3rd (67) and 5th (121) round picks)

Rnd	Name	Pos	Ht	Wt	College
3b	Chuck Webb (81)	FB	5-9	201	Tennessee

(Traded 4th (95) and 5th (122) round picks to 49ers for 3rd (81) round pick)

4 (Choice (95) to 49ers for 49ers 3rd (81) round pick)

5a (Choice (121) from Jets to Dolphins for Dolphins 5th (135) and 6th (164) round picks)

5b (Choice (122) to 49ers for 49ers 3rd (81) round pick)

Rnd	Name	Pos	Ht	Wt	College
5c	Jeff Fite (135)	P	6-0	206	Memphis State

(Choice from Miami for Packers 5th (121) round pick from Jets)

Rnd	Name	Pos	Ht	Wt	College
6a	Walter Dean (149)	FB	5-10	216	Grambling
6b	Joe Garten (164)	C/G	6-2	286	Colorado

(Choice from Miami for Packers 5th (121) round pick from Jets)

Rnd	Name	Pos	Ht	Wt	College
7a	Frank Blevins (169)	LB	6-4	232	Oklahoma

(Choice from Browns for Brent Fullwood)

Rnd	Name	Pos	Ht	Wt	College
7b	Reggie Burnette (176)	LB	6-1	240	Houston
8	Johnny Walker (203)	WR	5-11	188	Texas
9	Dean Witkowski (229)	LB	6-1	238	North Dakota
10	Rapier Porter (262)	TE	6-3	275	AK-Pine Bluff
11	J.J. Wierenga (289)	DE	6-3	276	Central Michigan
12	Linzy Collins (316)	WR	6-0	185	Missouri

1991 GREEN BAY PACKERS

FRONT ROW: (L-R) 7 Don Majkowski, 10 Blair Kiel, 13 Chris Jacke, 16 Paul McJulien, 18 Mike Tomczak, 21 Joe Fuller, 24 Tim Hauck, 25 Vinnie Clark, 26 Chuck Cecil, 30 Chuck Webb, 31 Allen Rice.

SECOND ROW: (L-R) 33 Keith Woodside, 36 LeRoy Butler, 37 Mark Murphy, 39 Darrell Thompson, 42 Walter Dean, 44 Jerry Holmes, 45 Vai Sikahema, 46 Vince Workman, 47 Roland Mitchell, 49 Ray Porter, 50 Johnny Holland, 51 Blair Bush.

THIRD ROW: (L-R) 54 Scott Stephen, 55 Greg Clark, 56 Burnell Dent, 57 Rich Moran, 59 Kurt Larson, 62 Matt Brock, 63 James Campen, 65 Ron Hallstrom, 67 Billy Ard, 69 Reggie Burnette, 70 Keith Uecker.

FOURTH ROW: (L-R) 71 Scott Jones, 72 Steve Gabbard, 74 Lester Archambeau, 75 Ken Ruettgers, 77 Tony Mandarich, 78 Louis Cheek, 80 Jackie Harris, 81 Perry Kemp, 82 Erik Affholter, 83 Johnny Walker, 84 Sterling Sharpe.

FIFTH ROW: (L-R) 85 Jeff Query, 86 Ed West, 87 Clarence Weathers, 88 Charles Wilson, 90 Tony Bennett, 91 Brian Noble, 92 John Jurkovic, Assistant Video Director Bob Eckberg, Video Director Al Treml.

SIXTH ROW: (L-R) Assistant Equipment Manager Bryan Nehring, Equipment Assistant Jack Noel, Equipment Assistant Bob Noel, 93 Robert Brown, 95 Bryce Paup, 96 Shawn Patterson, 98 Esera Tuaolo, 99 Don Davey, Trainer Domenic Gentile, Team Physician Dr. Clarence Novotny, Assistant Trainer Kurt Fielding, Assistant Trainer Larry Lemberger.

BACK ROW: (L-R) Defensive Backfield Coach Dick Jauron, Outside Linebackers Coach Dick Moseley, Defensive Coordinator Hank Bullough, Defensive Line Coach Greg Blache, Receivers Coach Buddy Geis, Special Teams Coach Howard Tippett, Head Coach Lindy Infante, Offensive Line Coach Charlie Davis, Tight Ends Coach Virgil Knight, Strength and Conditioning Coach Russ Riederer, Offensive Backfield Coach Willie Peete, Assistant Offensive Line Coach Joe Clark.

Ageneration and a half after Vince Lombardi set out to end the Packers' "attitude of defeatism," Mike Holmgren, the 11th head coach in team annals, ventured forth on a similar mission. The former 49ers assistant declared a need "to establish a winning attitude" for his new charges and, as had happened with Lombardi in 1959, the Packers of 1992 responded with a winning season, going 9-7.

Holmgren was named coach on Jan. 11. He was sought after by at least six other NFL teams before being hired by the Packers. In order to complete the deal, Green Bay returned to the 49ers the second-round pick it had received in exchange for linebacker Tim Harris.

Holmgren didn't waste time assembling a staff. He hired Sherman Lewis and Ray Rhodes from the 49ers to be his offensive and defensive coordinators, respectively. Then, in just over a week's time, he landed Steve Mariucci (quarterbacks), Andy Reid (tight ends/assistant offensive line), and Jon Gruden (offensive assistant/quality control). All three were 36 years of age or younger and all three would go on to become successful NFL coaches.

Wolf, too, was busy. He replaced half the scouting team and dismissed nearly half the roster from the previous year. He bolstered the offensive line and defensive backfield by drafting Terrell Buckley with the fifth pick in the draft and by acquiring veteran tackle Tootie Robbins from Phoenix for a sixth-round choice.

In February, Wolf traded a first-round draft choice to the Falcons for quarterback Brett Favre. Denver and Kansas City also put in offers. In Game 3, Favre relieved an injured Don Majkowski and never looked back.

Holmgren installed his version of the 49ers' West Coast Offense. He also scripted the first 15 offensive plays of each game, a practice his mentor, Bill Walsh, had introduced by scripting the first 20 offensive plays when he was head coach of the 49ers.

The players responded. Favre passed his way to the Pro Bowl. Sterling Sharpe caught a then NFL-record 108 passes and joined his quarterback in Hawaii. Jackie Harris emerged at tight end and snagged 55 passes. And Vince Workman was headed for 1,000 yards rushing before a shoulder injury knocked him out in Game 10.

Defensively, Chuck Cecil, Johnny Holland and Tony Bennett played well. Cecil led the team with four interceptions and also made the Pro Bowl. Holland led all tacklers with 122 stops, despite missing the final two games after sustaining a neck injury that ended his career. Bennett racked up 13 1/2 sacks and forced three fumbles.

Majkowski started the first three games at quarterback. Torn ankle ligaments sent the veteran to the sidelines in the first quarter of Game 3 against Cincinnati. Favre, who had thrown 14 passes in a dismal 31-3 loss to Tampa the week before, engineered a 24-23 comeback win over the Bengals. He hit Kitrick Taylor with the game-winner, a 35-yard pass

with 13 seconds left.

"I made enough mistakes in this first half to last the whole year," said Favre, who threw for 289 yards and two scores. "And I was wondering if they were going to run me out of town."

Far from being run off, Favre settled in as the starter. He and the team reeled off six straight wins beginning in mid-November.

Green Bay sneaked past the Eagles 27-24 in Milwaukee on the strength of two Chris Jacke fourth-quarter field goals. Rookie Edgar Bennett followed with 107 yards rushing on 29 carries in a 17-3 win over the Bears. Favre and Jackie Harris then sank the Buccaneers 19-14 with a 9-yard, fourth-quarter pass and catch.

Back to even at 6-6, the Packers continued to roll. Favre threw three touchdown passes in a 38-10 rout of the Lions. A week later, the team controlled the ball for more than 20 minutes in the second half and earned a hard-fought, 16-14 decision in Houston. Green Bay then notched its sixth win in a row by pounding the Rams 28-13.

"It would be nice to finish up strong and get into the play-offs," Jackie Harris said. "But we killed ourselves early in the season."

The Packers had to beat the Vikings in the season finale and get outside help in order to make the playoffs. But Minnesota refused to cooperate, instead racking up 447 yards in a one-sided, 27-7 affair that ran Green Bay's string of seasons without a playoff appearance to 10.

ON THE MARK, GET BRETT, GO!

That Brett Favre had a strong arm was a given. That he would become the Packers most accurate passer in a single season was unexpected.

Favre completed 302 of 471 passes in his first year as a starter. His completion percentage of 64.1 broke Bart Starr's record of 63.7 set in 1968.

Favre bettered 50 percent in each of the 15 games he played. He was above 60 percent 11 times.

On Dec. 6, Favre was at his most accurate best. The 23-year-old completed 15 of 19 passes (78.9 percent) for 214 yards and three touchdowns. That's a passer rating of 153.2.

Over the next 10 years, Favre would surpass 60 percent in six different seasons, but never exceed the 64.1 percent of his first season in Green Bay.

Highest completion percentage, season

Pct.	Player	Year
65.4	Brett Favre	2003
64.12	Brett Favre	1992
63.74	Bart Starr	1968

TEAM STATISTICS

	GB	OPP
First Downs	291	277
Rushing	101	89
Passing	171	170
Penalty	19	18
Rushes	420	406
Yards Gained	1,556	1,821
Average Gain	3.70	4.49
Average Yards per Game	97.3	113.8
Passes Attempted	527	483
Completed	340	277
% Completed	64.52	57.35
Total Yards Gained	3,498	3,496
Times Sacked	43	34
Yards Lost	268	219
Net Yards Gained	3,230	3,277
Yards Gained per Completion	10.29	12.62
Net Yards per Attempt	5.67	6.34
Average Net Yards per Game	201.9	204.8
Combined Net Yards Gained	4,786	5,098
Total Plays	990	923
Average Yards per Play	4.83	5.52
Average Yards per Game	299.1	318.6
Third Down Efficiency	91/214	71/189
Percentage	42.52	37.57
Fourth Down Efficiency	6/11	7/16
Percentage	54.54	43.75
Intercepted By	15	15
Yards Returned	222	198
Returned for TD	1	1
Punts	68	68
Yards Punted	2,608	2,941
Average Yards per Punt	38.35	43.25
Punt Returns	35	26
Yards Returned	315	230
Average Yards per Return	9.00	8.85
Returned for TD	1	1
Kickoff Returns	54	57
Yards Returned	1,017	901
Average Yards per Return	18.83	15.81
Returned for TD	0	0
Penalties	88	98
Yards Penalized	749	830
Fumbles	42	32
Lost	21	19
Own Recovered for Touchdown	0	0
Opponent's Recovered by	19	21
Opponent's Recovered for Touchdown	1	1
Total Points Scored	276	296
Total Touchdowns	30	32
Touchdowns Rushing	7	12
Touchdowns Passing	20	16
Touchdowns on Returns & Recoveries	3	4
Extra Points	30	32
Safeties	0	0
Field Goals Attempted	29	27
Field Goals Made	22	24
% Successful	75.86	88.89
Average Time of Possession	32:30	27:30

Regular Season 9-7-0

Date	GB		OPP	Att.
9/6	20	Minnesota Vikings (OT)	23	(58,617)
9/13	3	at Tampa Bay Buccaneers	31	(50,051)
9/20	24	Cincinnati Bengals	23	(57,272)
9/27	17	Pittsburgh Steelers	3	(58,724)
10/4	10	at Atlanta Falcons	24	(63,769)
10/18	6	at Cleveland Browns	17	(69,268)
10/25	10	Chicago Bears	30	(59,435)
11/01	27	at Detroit Lions	13	(60,594)
11/08	7	at New York Giants	27	(72,038)
11/15	27	Philadelphia Eagles (M)	24	(52,689)
11/22	17	at Chicago Bears	3	(56,170)
11/29	19	Tampa Bay Buccaneers (M)	14	(52,347)
12/6	38	Detroit Lions (M)	10	(49,469)
12/13	16	at Houston Oilers	14	(57,285)
12/20	28	Los Angeles Rams	13	(57,796)
12/27	7	at Minnesota Vikings	27	(61,461)

Score By Periods

	1	2	3	4	OT	Total
Packers	48	115	25	88	0	276
Opponents	73	73	71	76	3	296

INDIVIDUAL STATISTICS

Rushing

	Att	Yds	Avg	LG	TD
Workman	159	631	4.0	44	2
D. Thompson	76	255	3.4	33	2
E. Bennett	61	214	3.5	18	0
Favre	47	198	4.2	19	1
Sydney	51	163	3.2	19	2
Majkowski	8	33	4.1	8	0
B. McGee	8	19	2.4	4	0
R. Brooks	2	14	7.0	8	0
McNabb	2	11	5.5	8	0
C. Harris	2	10	5.0	7	0
Sharpe	4	8	2.0	14	0
Packers	**420**	**1,556**	**3.7**	**44**	**7**
Opponents	406	1,821	4.5	71	12

Receiving

	No	Yds	Avg	LG	TD
Sharpe	108	1,461	13.5	t76	13
J. Harris	55	595	10.8	40	2
Sydney	49	384	7.8	20	1
Workman	47	290	6.2	21	0
Beach	17	122	7.2	20	1
R. Lewis	13	152	11.7	27	0
D. Thompson	13	129	9.9	43	1
E. Bennett	13	93	7.2	22	0
R. Brooks	12	126	10.5	18	1
B. McGee	6	60	10.0	15	0
E. West	4	30	7.5	10	0
K. Taylor	2	63	31.5	t35	1
Favre	1	-7	-7	-7.0	0
Packers	**340**	**3,498**	**10.3**	**t76**	**20**
Opponents	277	3,496	12.6	t75	16

Passing

	Att	Com	Yds	Pct	TD	In	Tk/Yds	Rate
Favre	471	302	3,227	64.1	18	13	34/208	85.3
Majkowski	55	38	271	69.1	2	2	9/60	77.2
McJulien	1	0	0	0.00	0	0	0/0	39.6
Packers	**527**	**340**	**3,498**	**64.5**	**20**	**15**	**43/268**	**84.3**
Opponents	483	277	3,496	57.3	16	15	34/219	78.1

Punting

	No	Yds	Avg	Net	TB	In20	LG	HB
McJulien	36	1,386	38.5	30.2	4	8	67	2
B. Wagner	30	1,222	40.7	35.0	5	10	52	0
Packers	**66**	**2,608**	**38.4**	**32.3**	**9**	**18**	**67**	**2**
Opponents	68	2,941	43.3	33.9	16	14	71	0

Kickoff Returns

	No	Yds	Avg	LG	TD
C. Harris	23	485	21.1	50	0
R. Brooks	18	338	18.8	30	0
E. Bennett	5	104	20.8	33	0
Jurkovic	3	39	13.0	14	0
Workman	1	17	17.0	17	0
McNabb	1	15	15.0	15	0
Sims	1	11	11.0	11	0
Davey	1	8	8.0	8	0
E. West	1	0	0.0	0	0
Packers	**54**	**1,017**	**18.8**	**50**	**0**
Opponents	57	901	15.8	48	0

Punt Returns

	No	Yds	Avg	FC	LG	TD
Buckley	21	211	10.0	5	t58	1
R. Brooks	11	102	9.3	1	22	0
Hauck	1	2	2.0	0	2	0
Cecil	1	0	0.0	0	0	0
V. Clark	1	0	0.0	0	0	0
Packers	**35**	**315**	**9.0**	**6**	**t58**	**1**
Opponents	26	230	8.8	10	t95	1

Interceptions

	No	Yds	Avg	LG	TD
Cecil	4	52	13.0	29	0
Buckley	3	33	11.0	t33	1
Holland	3	27	9.0	22	0
V. Clark	2	70	35.0	43	0
R. Mitchell	2	40	20.0	35	0
L. Butler	1	0	0.0	0	0
Packers	**15**	**222**	**14.8**	**43**	**1**
Opponents	15	198	13.2	t69	1

Scoring

	TDr	TDp	TDrt	PAT	FG	S	TP
Jacke	0	0	0	30/30	22/29	0	96
Sharpe	0	13	0	0/0	0/0	0	78
Sydney	2	1	0	0/0	0/0	0	18
D. Thompson	2	1	0	0/0	0/0	0	18
Buckley	0	0	2	0/0	0/0	0	12
J. Harris	0	2	0	0/0	0/0	0	12
Workman	2	0	0	0/0	0/0	0	12
Beach	0	1	0	0/0	0/0	0	6
T. Bennett	0	0	1	0/0	0/0	0	6
R. Brooks	0	1	0	0/0	0/0	0	6
Favre	1	0	0	0/0	0/0	0	6
K. Taylor	0	1	0	0/0	0/0	0	6
Packers	**7**	**20**	**3**	**30/30**	**22/29**	**0**	**276**
Opponents	12	16	4	32/32	24/27	0	296

Fumbles

	Fum	Ow	Op	Yds	Tot
Beach	1	0	1	0	1
E. Bennett	2	0	0	0	0
T. Bennett	0	0	3	18	3
Billups	0	0	1	0	1
M. Brock	0	0	2	34	2
R. Brown	0	0	1	0	1
Buckley	7	3	1	0	4
L. Butler	0	0	1	17	1
Campen	0	1	0	0	1
Cecil	1	0	0	0	0
Favre	12	3	0	-12	3
J. Harris	1	0	0	0	0
Holland	2	1	2	0	3
Koonce	0	0	1	0	1
Majkowski	4	3	0	0	3
McJulien	0	1	0	0	1
Millard	0	0	1	0	1
R. Mitchell	0	0	1	0	1
Moran	0	1	0	0	1
Noble	0	0	2	0	2
Paup	0	0	2	0	2
Sharpe	2	1	0	0	1
Sydney	2	2	0	0	2
D. Thompson	2	0	0	0	0
Winters	1	0	0	0	0
Workman	4	2	0	0	2
Packers	**41**	**18**	**19**	**57**	**37**

Quarterback Sacks

	No
T. Bennett	13.5
Paup	6.5
M. Brock	4.0
Jurkovic	2.0
Noble	2.0
Koonce	1.5
Archambeau	1.0
R. Brown	1.0
Dent	1.0
Tuaolo	1.0
Holland	0.5
Packers	**34.0**
Opponents	43.0

NFL STANDINGS

National Conference

Eastern Division

	W	L	T	Pct	PF	PA
Dallas Cowboys	13	3	0	.813	409	243
Philadelphia Eagles	11	5	0	.688	354	245
Washington Redskins	9	7	0	.563	300	255
N.Y. Giants	6	10	0	.375	306	367
Phoenix Cardinals	4	12	0	.250	243	332

Central Division

	W	L	T	Pct	PF	PA
Minnesota Vikings	11	5	0	.688	374	249
Green Bay Packers	**9**	**7**	**0**	**.563**	**276**	**296**
Tampa Bay Buccaneers	5	11	0	.313	267	365
Chicago Bears	5	11	0	.313	295	361
Detroit Lions	5	11	0	.313	273	332

Western Division

	W	L	T	Pct	PF	PA
San Francisco 49ers	14	2	0	.875	431	236
New Orleans Saints	12	4	0	.750	330	202
Atlanta Falcons	6	10	0	.375	327	414
Los Angeles Rams	6	10	0	.375	313	383

American Conference

Eastern Division

	W	L	T	Pct	PF	PA
Miami Dolphins	11	5	0	.688	340	281
Buffalo Bills	11	5	0	.688	381	283
Indianapolis Colts	9	7	0	.563	216	302
New York Jets	4	12	0	.250	220	315
New England Patriots	2	14	0	.125	205	363

Central Division

	W	L	T	Pct	PF	PA
Pittsburgh Steelers	11	5	0	.688	299	225
Houston Oilers	10	6	0	.625	352	258
Cleveland Browns	7	9	0	.438	272	275
Cincinnati Bengals	5	11	0	.313	274	364

Western Division

	W	L	T	Pct	PF	PA
San Diego Chargers	11	5	0	.688	335	241
Kansas City Chiefs	10	6	0	.625	348	282
Denver Broncos	8	8	0	.500	262	329
Los Angeles Raiders	7	9	0	.438	249	281
Seattle Seahawks	2	14	0	.125	140	312

ROSTER

No	Name	Pos	Ht	Wt	DOB	College	G
74	Archambeau, Lester	DE	6-4	270	06/27/67	Stanford	16
67	Barrie, Sebastian	DE	6-2	270	05/26/70	Liberty University	3
82	Beach, Sanjay	WR	6-1	194	02/21/66	Colorado State	16
34	Bennett, Edgar	RB	6-0	223	02/15/69	Florida State	16
90	Bennett, Tony	LB	6-2	243	07/01/67	Mississippi	16
22	Billups, Lewis	CB	5-11	182	10/10/63	North Alabama	5
51	Brady, Jeff	LB	6-1	235	11/09/68	Kentucky	8
62	Brock, Matt	DE	6-4	290	01/14/66	Oregon	16
87	Brooks, Robert	WR	6-0	171	06/23/70	South Carolina	16
93	Brown, Robert	DE	6-2	280	05/21/60	Virginia Tech	16
27	Buckley, Terrell	CB	5-9	174	06/07/71	Florida State	14
36	Butler, LeRoy	S	6-0	200	07/19/68	Florida State	15
63	Campen, James	C	6-3	280	06/11/64	Tulane	13
21	Carter, Carl	CB	5-11	190	03/07/64	Texas Tech	7
26	Cecil, Chuck	S	6-0	190	11/08/64	Arizona	16
25	Clark, Vinnie	CB	6-0	194	01/22/69	Ohio State	16
55	Collins, Brett	LB	6-1	226	10/08/68	Washington	11
99	Davey, Don	DE	6-4	280	04/08/68	Wisconsin	9
56	Dent, Burnell	LB	6-1	238	03/16/63	Tulane	15
58	D'Onofrio, Mark	LB	6-2	235	03/17/69	Penn State	2
4	Favre, Brett	QB	6-2	220	10/10/69	Southern Mississippi	15
71	Gray, Cecil	T	6-4	292	02/16/68	North Carolina	2
65	Hallstrom, Ron	G	6-6	310	06/11/59	Iowa	16
81	Harris, Corey	WR	5-11	195	10/25/69	Vanderbilt	10
80	Harris, Jackie	TE	6-3	243	01/04/68	North Louisiana	16
24	Hauck, Tim	S	5-10	181	12/20/66	Montana	16
50	Holland, Johnny	LB	6-2	235	03/11/65	Texas A&M	14
88	Ingram, Darryl	TE	6-3	250	05/02/66	California	16
13	Jacke, Chris	K	6-0	197	03/12/66	Texas-El Paso	16
40	Jackson, Johnnie	S	6-1	204	01/11/67	Houston	1
92	Jurkovic, John	NT	6-2	300	08/18/67	Eastern Illinois	16
53	Koonce, George	LB	6-1	238	10/15/68	East Carolina	16
85	Lewis, Ron	WR	5-11	180	03/25/68	Florida State	6
7	Majkowski, Don	QB	6-2	203	02/25/64	Virginia	14
23	McCloughan, Dave	CB	6-1	185	11/20/66	Colorado	5
31	McGee, Buford	RB	6-0	210	08/16/60	Mississippi	4
16	McJulien, Paul	P	5-10	210	02/24/65	Jackson State	9
45	McNabb, Dexter	FB	6-1	245	07/09/69	Florida	16
77	Millard, Keith	DT	6-5	268	03/18/62	Washington State	2
47	Mitchell, Roland	CB	5-11	195	03/15/64	Texas Tech	15
57	Moran, Rich	G	6-2	280	03/19/62	San Diego State	8
61	Neville, Tom	G	6-5	288	09/04/61	Fresno State	8
91	Noble, Brian	LB	6-3	250	09/06/62	Arizona State	13
97	Noonan, Danny	NT	6-4	275	07/14/65	Nebraska	6
98	Oglesby, Alfred	NT	6-3	285	01/27/67	Houston	7
95	Paup, Bryce	LB	6-4	247	02/29/68	Northern Iowa	16
73	Robbins, Tootie	T	6-5	315	06/02/58	East Carolina	15
75	Ruettgers, Ken	T	6-5	286	08/20/62	USC	16
72	Salem, Harvey	T	6-6	289	01/15/61	California	4
84	Sharpe, Sterling	WR	5-11	205	04/06/65	South Carolina	16
68	Sims, Joe	OL	6-3	294	03/01/69	Nebraska	15
42	Sydney, Harry	FB	6-0	217	06/29/59	Kansas	16
85	Taylor, Kitrick	WR	5-11	189	07/22/64	Washington State	10
39	Thompson, Darrell	RB	6-0	222	11/23/67	Minnesota	7
98	Tuaolo, Esera	NT	6-2	284	07/11/68	Oregon State	4
76	Viaene, David	OL	6-5	300	07/14/65	Minnesota-Duluth	1
9	Wagner, Bryan	P	6-2	200	03/28/62	Cal State-Northridge	7
86	West, Ed	TE	6-1	244	08/02/61	Auburn	16
38	White, Adrian	S	6-0	205	04/06/64	Florida	15
29	Wilson, Marcus	RB	6-1	210	04/16/68	Virginia	6
52	Winters, Frank	C	6-3	290	01/23/64	West Illinois	16
46	Workman, Vince	RB	5-10	205	05/09/68	Ohio State	10

DRAFT

Rnd	Name	Pos	Ht	Wt	College
1a	Terrell Buckley (5)	DB	5-9	174	Florida State
1b	(Choice (17) from Eagles in 1991 position exchange. Choice traded to Falcons for Brett Favre)				
2a	Mark D'Onofrio (34)	LB	6-2	235	Penn State
2b	(Choice (45) from 49ers for Tim Harris. Choice returned to 49ers for right to hire Mike Holmgren)				
3	Robert Brooks (62)	WR	6-0	171	South Carolina
4a	(Choice (89) and 8th round pick (203) to 49ers for 49ers' 4th round pick (103), 5th round pick (130) and 6th round pick (157))				
4b	Edgar Bennett (103)	RB	6-0	223	Florida State
	(Choice from 49ers in exchange mentioned above)				
5a	Dexter McNabb (119)	FB	6-1	245	Florida
5b	Orlando McKay (130)	WR	5-10	175	Washington
	(Choice from 49ers in exchange mentioned above)				
6a	(Choice (146) to Phoenix for Tootie Robbins)				
6b	Mark Chmura (157)	TE	6-5	240	Boston College
	(Choice from 49ers in exchange mentioned above)				
7a	(Choice (173) to the Raiders for Raiders' 7th round choice (190) and 9th round choice (240))				
7b	Chris Holder (190)	WR	6-0	182	Tuskegee
	(Choice from Raiders in exchange mentioned above)				
8	(Choice (203) to 49ers in exchange mentioned above)				
9a	Ty Detmer (230)	QB	5-9	183	BYU
9b	Shazzon Bradley (240)	NT	6-1	272	Tennessee
	(Choice from Raiders in exchange mentioned above)				
10	Andrew Oberg (257)	T	6-6	300	North Carolina
11	Gabe Mokwuah (287)	LB	6-1	254	Am. International
12	Brett Collins (314)	LB	6-1	226	Washington

1992 GREEN BAY PACKERS

FRONT ROW: (L–R) 4 Brett Favre, 7 Don Majkowski, 11 Ty Detmer, 13 Chris Jacke, 16 Paul McJulien, 22 Lewis Billups, 23 Dave McCloughan, 24 Tim Hauck, 25 Vinnie Clark, 26 Chuck Cecil, 27 Terrell Buckley.

SECOND ROW: (L–R) 29 Marcus Wilson, 31 Buford McGee, 34 Edgar Bennett, 36 LeRoy Butler, 38 Adrian White, 39 Darrell Thompson, 42 Harry Sydney, 45 Dexter McNabb, 46 Vince Workman, 47 Roland Mitchell, 50 Johnny Holland, 51 Jeff Brady.

THIRD ROW: (L–R) 52 Frank Winters, 53 George Koonce, 55 Brett Collins, 56 Burnell Dent, 57 Rich Moran, 62 Matt Brock, 63 James Campen, 65 Ron Hallstrom, 69 Joe Sims, 72 Harvey Salem.

FOURTH ROW: (L–R) 73 Tootie Robbins, 74 Lester Archambeau, 75 Ken Ruettgers, 79 Tony Mandarich, 80 Jackie Harris, 82 Orlando McKay, 84 Sterling Sharpe, 85 Kitrick Taylor, 86 Ed West, 87 Robert Brooks.

FIFTH ROW: (L–R) 88 Darryl Ingram, 89 Mark Chmura, 90 Tony Bennett, 91 Brian Noble, 92 John Jurkovic, 93 Robert Brown, 94 Mark D'Onofrio, 95 Bryce Paup, 96 Shawn Patterson, 97 Danny Noonan, 98 Esera Tuaolo.

SIXTH ROW: (L–R) Defensive Assistant/Quality Control Jim Lind, Tight Ends/Assistant Offensive Line Coach Andy Reid, Offensive Line Coach Tom Lovat, Quarterbacks Coach Steve Mariucci, Special Teams Coach Nolan Cromwell, Offensive Coordinator Sherman Lewis, Head Coach Mike Holmgren, Defensive Coordinator Ray Rhodes, Defensive Line Coach Greg Blache, Linebackers Coach Bob Valesente, Offensive Assistant/Quality Control Jon Gruden, Strength and Conditioning Kent Johnston, Defensive Backs Coach Dick Jauron, Running Backs Coach Gil Haskell.

BACK ROW: (L–R) Equipment Assistant Jack Noel, Assistant Equipment Manager Bryan Nehring, Equipment Manager Bob Noel, Administrative Assistant John Johnson, Head Trainer Domenic Gentile, Assistant Trainer Kurt Fielding, Assistant Trainer Jay Davide, Training Room Intern Sam Ramsden, Staff Orthopedist Dr. Patrick J. McKenzie, Team Physician Dr. Clarence G. Novotny, Assistant Video Director Bob Eckberg, Video Director Al Treml.

Free agency, long a staple of major-league baseball, entered the NFL in 1993. The biggest name on the open market belonged to Reggie White.

At least a dozen teams expressed an interest in signing White, a 7-time Pro Bowler while with the Eagles. He spent more than a month touring the NFL as teams eagerly courted his services.

In April, the Packers did what many thought impossible. They signed the highly coveted defensive end to a 4-year, $17-million deal.

White's signing ended the notion that Green Bay couldn't compete successfully on the open market. His presence also helped the team to a 9-7 record and its first playoff berth in 11 years.

With White in the fold, the Packers defensive ranking rose from 23rd in 1992 to 2nd, its highest finish since the 1972 club also finished in that position. For the first time since the 16-game season was instituted, Green Bay held opponents to an average of less than 300 yards per game.

On offense, Favre remained the quarterback, but the honeymoon was over. The third-year player threw a league-leading 24 interceptions, with a bad habit of forcing passes into coverage rather than throwing them away.

Sterling Sharpe again was Favre's favorite receiver. He broke his NFL single-season record with 112 catches.

White was not the only new face in 1993. The Packers obtained guard Harry Galbreath and safety Mike Prior through free agency and traded for receiver Mark Clayton and running back John Stephens.

For the second year in a row, Green Bay lost one of its top linebackers to a career-ending injury. Brian Noble saw his 9-year Packers career come to an end after he suffered a knee injury in Game 2 against the Eagles.

The offensive line was also beset by injury. Center James Campen (hamstring) and guard Rich Moran (knee) missed a combined 25 games and Tootie Robbins (torn triceps muscle) was lost for the final four games.

Frank Winters filled in for Campen, Doug Widell replaced Moran and Joe Sims relieved Robbins.

Green Bay pounced on the Rams 36-6 in the opener, holding them to 228 yards. Bryce Paup and George Koonce opened the scoring by tackling running back Cleveland Gary in the end zone for a first-quarter safety.

Three losses followed. The Eagles held Green Bay to a season-low 159 yards in winning 20-17 on Sept. 12, Fuad Reveiz kicked five field goals to give Minnesota a 15-13 victory on Sept. 26, and Troy Aikman lit up Texas Stadium with 317 yards passing in a 36-14 laugher on Oct. 3.

Tied with the Buccaneers for last place, the Packers righted themselves with three straight wins. White sacked John Elway three times—twice in the closing minutes—to preserve a 30-27 win over the Broncos. Sharpe caught four touchdown passes in a 37-14 rout in Tampa, and a late, 12-play, 91-yard drive put away the Bears 17-3.

Green Bay closed out the first half of the season with six turnovers and a 23-16 loss in Kansas City.

A come-from-behind 19-17 win over the NFC Western Division leading Saints followed. Favre and Sharpe collaborated on a 54-yard pass play to set up Jacke's game-winning, 36-yard field goal with three seconds left.

"It was a real heartbuster," Saints cornerback Toi Cook said. "Don't ask me how Sterling got through the seam, but he did."

Victories over the Lions (26-17) and Buccaneers (13-10) pushed Green Bay (7-4) into a first-place tie with the Lions in the Central Division. A week later, a three-way tie ensued as the Bears moved into a share of the lead with a 30-17 dismantling of the Packers.

Green Bay won two of its next three games. It beat San Diego 20-13, thanks to last-minute interceptions by Buckley and Prior. After losing to the Vikings 21-17, the Packers clinched their first playoff berth in 11 years by icing the Raiders 28-0 at Lambeau Field where the wind chill bottomed out at 22 below.

Green Bay (9-6) and the Lions (9-6) then met in the Silverdome in the last regular-season game of the season with the Central Division title at stake. Jacke's 47-yard field goal near the end of the third quarter put the Green and Gold ahead 20-16. But Detroit responded with touchdowns from Eric Lynch and Rodney Holman to squeeze out a 30-20 win and force the Packers to return to the Silverdome for a playoff showdown just six days later.

AREA CODE 112

Sterling Sharpe believed his job was to catch footballs. In 1993, he caught more in a single season than any Packer player in history.

In 1992, Sharpe broke Art Monk's NFL record of 106 catches by hauling in 108 passes. A year later, Sharpe broke his own record with 112 catches. Sharpe was the only player to hit the century mark in either 1992 or 1993 and was just the sixth player to do so in any year.

Sharpe caught at least six passes in 14 games. He had five 100-yard receiving games. His most productive day came in Tampa where he caught 10 passes for 147 yards and four touchdowns.

Sharpe's NFL record for most catches in a season has since been broken.

Most Catches, Season

No.	Player	Year
112	Sterling Sharpe	1993
108	Sterling Sharpe	1992
102	Robert Brooks	1995

TEAM STATISTICS

	GB	OPP
First Downs	282	261
Rushing	98	88
Passing	166	157
Penalty	18	16
Rushes	448	424
Yards Gained	1,619	1,582
Average Gain	3.61	3.73
Average Yards per Game	101.2	98.9
Passes Attempted	528	529
Completed	322	290
% Completed	60.98	54.82
Total Yards Gained	3,330	3,201
Times Sacked	30	46
Yards Lost	199	301
Net Yards Gained	3,131	2,900
Yards Gained per Completion	10.34	11.04
Net Yards per Attempt	5.61	5.04
Average Net Yards per Game	195.7	181.3
Combined Net Yards Gained	4,750	4,482
Total Plays	1,006	999
Average Yards per Play	4.72	4.49
Average Net Yards per Game	296.9	280.1
Third Down Efficiency	81/218	70/217
Percentage	37.16	32.26
Fourth Down Efficiency	9/16	3/19
Percentage	56.25	15.79
Intercepted By	18	24
Yards Returned	255	437
Returned for TD	0	3
Punts	74	79
Yards Punted	3,174	3,176
Average Yards per Punt	42.89	40.20
Punt Returns	45	38
Yards Returned	404	350
Average Yards per Return	8.98	9.21
Returned for TD	0	0
Kickoff Returns	60	70
Yards Returned	1,483	1,407
Average Yards per Return	24.72	20.10
Returned for TD	1	0
Penalties	85	85
Yards Penalized	734	712
Fumbles	26	33
Lost	10	15
Own Recovered for Touchdown	0	0
Opponent's Recovered by	15	10
Opponent's Recovered for Touchdown	1	2
Total Points Scored	340	282
Total Touchdowns	35	27
Touchdowns Rushing	14	6
Touchdowns Passing	19	16
Touchdowns on Returns & Recoveries	2	5
Extra Points	35	27
Safeties	1	0
Field Goals Attempted	37	40
Field Goals Made	31	31
% Successful	83.78	77.50
Average Time of Possession	30:53	29:07

Regular Season 9-7-0

Date	GB		OPP	Att.
9/5	36	Los Angeles Rams (M)	6	(54,648)
9/12	17	Philadelphia Eagles	20	(59,061)
9/26	13	at Minnesota Vikings	15	(61,077)
10/3	14	at Dallas Cowboys	36	(63,568)
10/10	30	Denver Broncos	27	(58,943)
10/24	37	at Tampa Bay Buccaneers	14	(47,354)
10/31	17	Chicago Bears	3	(58,945)
11/8	16	at Kansas City Chiefs	23	(76,742)
11/14	19	at New Orleans Saints	17	(69,043)
11/21	26	Detroit Lions (M)	17	(55,119)
11/28	13	Tampa Bay Buccaneers	10	(56,995)
12/5	17	at Chicago Bears	30	(62,236)
12/12	20	at San Diego Chargers	13	(57,930)
12/19	17	Minnesota Vikings (M)	21	(54,773)
12/26	28	Los Angeles Raiders	0	(54,482)
1/2	20	at Detroit Lions	30	(77,510)

Postseason 1-1-0

1/8	28	at Detroit Lions	24	(68,479)
1/16	17	at Dallas Cowboys	27	(64,790)

Score By Periods

	1	2	3	4	OT	Total
Packers	97	95	77	71	0	340
Opponents	29	76	90	87	0	282

INDIVIDUAL STATISTICS

Rushing

	Att	Yds	Avg	LG	TD
D. Thompson	169	654	3.9	t60	3
E. Bennett	159	550	3.5	19	9
Favre	58	216	3.7	27	1
J. Stephens	48	173	3.6	22	1
R. Brooks	3	17	5.7	21	0
Sharpe	4	8	2.0	5	0
M. Wilson	6	3	0.5	5	0
Detmer	1	-2	-2.0		0
Packers	**448**	**1,619**	**3.6**	**t60**	**14**
Opponents	424	1,582	3.7	60	6

Receiving

	No	Yds	Avg	LG	TD
Sharpe	112	1,274	11.4	54	11
E. Bennett	59	457	7.7	t39	1
J. Harris	42	604	14.4	t66	4
Clayton	32	331	10.3	32	3
E. West	25	253	10.1	24	0
R. Brooks	20	180	9.0	25	0
D. Thompson	18	129	7.2	34	0
J. Stephens	5	31	6.2	10	0
R. Lewis	2	21	10.5	17	0
M. Wilson	2	18	9.0	11	0
Chmura	2	13	6.5	7	0
C. Harris	2	11	5.5	6	0
Morgan	1	8	8.0	8	0
Packers	**322**	**3,330**	**10.3**	**t66**	**19**
Opponents	290	3,201	11.0	t67	16

Passing

	Att	Com	Yds	Pct	TD	In	Tk/Yds	Rate
Favre	522	318	3,303	60.9	19	24	30/199	72.2
Detmer	5	3	26	60.0	0	0	0/0	73.8
Sharpe	1	1	1	100.0	0	0	0/0	79.2
Packers	**528**	**322**	**3,330**	**61.0**	**19**	**24**	**30/199**	**72.2**
Opponents	529	290	3,201	54.8	16	18	46/301	68.9

Punting

	No	Yds	Avg	Net	TB	In20	LG	HB
B. Wagner	74	3,174	42.9	36.3	7	19	60	0
Packers	**74**	**3,174**	**42.9**	**36.3**	**7**	**19**	**60**	**0**
Opponents	79	3,176	40.2	34.3	3	20	58	0

Kickoff Returns

	No	Yds	Avg	LG	TD
R. Brooks	23	611	26.6	t95	1
C. Harris	16	482	30.1	65	0
M. Wilson	9	197	21.9	37	0
D. Thompson	9	171	19.0	42	0
Jurkovic	2	22	11.0	13	0
Chmura	1	0	0.0	0	0
Packers	**60**	**1,483**	**24.7**	**t95**	**1**
Opponents	70	1,407	20.1	68	0

Punt Returns

	No	Yds	Avg	FC	LG	TD
Prior	17	194	11.4	3	24	0
R. Brooks	16	135	8.4	4	35	0
Buckley	11	76	6.9	5	39	0
Teague	1	-1	-1.0	0	-1	0
Packers	**45**	**404**	**9.0**	**12**	**39**	**0**
Opponents	38	350	9.2	12	35	0

Interceptions

	No	Yds	Avg	LG	TD
L. Butler	6	131	21.8	39	0
Holland	2	41	20.5	30	0
Buckley	2	31	15.5	31	0
Simmons	2	21	10.5	19	0
Teague	1	22	22.0	22	0
Paup	1	8	8.0	8	0
Prior	1	1	1.0	1	0
M. Brock	1	0	0.0	0	0
D. Evans	1	0	0.0	0	0
R. Mitchell	1	0	0.0	0	0
Packers	**18**	**255**	**14.2**	**39**	**0**
Opponents	24	437	18.2	t86	3

Scoring

	TDr	TDp	TDrt	PAT	FG	S	TP
Jacke	0	0	0	35/35	31/37	0	128
Sharpe	0	11	0	0/0	0/0	0	66
E. Bennett	9	1	0	0/0	0/0	0	60
J. Harris	0	4	0	0/0	0/0	0	24
Clayton	0	3	0	0/0	0/0	0	18
D. Thompson	3	0	0	0/0	0/0	0	18
R. Brooks	0	0	1	0/0	0/0	0	6
L. Butler	0	0	1	0/0	0/0	0	6
Favre	1	0	0	0/0	0/0	0	6
J. Stephens	1	0	0	0/0	0/0	0	6
team	0	0	0	0/0	0/0	1	2
Packers	**14**	**19**	**2**	**35/35**	**31/37**	**1**	**340**
Opponents	6	16	5	27/27	31/40	0	282

Fumbles

	Fum	Ow	Op	Yds	Tot
E. Bennett	0	1	0	0	1
M. Brock	0	0	1	0	1
R. Brooks	1	1	0	0	1
Buckley	0	0	0	0	0
L. Butler	0	0	1	25	1
Campen	0	1	0	0	1
Chmura	1	1	0	0	1
Coleman	0	0	1	0	1
D. Evans	0	0	2	0	2
Favre	14	2	0	-1	2
Hauck	0	0	1	0	1
Holland	2	0	0	0	2
Koonce	0	0	1	0	1
Morrissey	0	0	1	0	1
Noble	0	0	1	0	1
Prior	3	2	0	0	2
Ruettgers	0	2	0	0	2
Sharpe	1	0	0	0	0
Simmons	0	0	1	0	1
J. Stephens	0	0	0	0	2
Teague	0	0	1	0	2
D. Thompson	2	1	0	0	1
R. White	0	1	1	10	2
Willis	0	1	0	0	1
M. Wilson	1	0	0	0	1
Packers	**26**	**15**	**15**	**34**	**30**

Quarterback Sacks

	No
R. White	13.0
Paup	11.0
T. Bennett	6.5
Jurkovic	5.5
Koonce	3.0
M. Brock	2.0
Holland	2.0
L. Butler	1.0
Patterson	1.0
Simmons	1.0
Packers	**46.0**
Opponents	30.0

NFL STANDINGS

National Conference

Eastern Division

	W	L	T	Pct	PF	PA
Dallas Cowboys	12	4	0	.750	376	229
New York Giants	11	5	0	.688	288	205
Philadelphia Eagles	8	8	0	.500	293	315
Phoenix Cardinals	7	9	0	.438	326	269
Washington Redskins	4	12	0	.250	230	345

Central Division

	W	L	T	Pct	PF	PA
Detroit Lions	10	6	0	.625	298	292
Minnesota Vikings	9	7	0	.563	277	290
Green Bay Packers	9	7	0	.563	340	282
Chicago Bears	7	9	0	.438	234	230
Tampa Bay Buccaneers	5	11	0	.313	237	376

Western Division

	W	L	T	Pct	PF	PA
San Francisco 49ers	10	6	0	.625	473	295
New Orleans Saints	8	8	0	.500	317	343
Atlanta Falcons	6	10	0	.375	316	385
Los Angeles Rams	5	11	0	.313	221	367

American Conference

Eastern Division

	W	L	T	Pct	PF	PA
Buffalo Bills	12	4	0	.750	329	242
Miami Dolphins	9	7	0	.563	349	351
New York Jets	8	8	0	.500	270	247
New England Patriots	5	11	0	.313	238	286
Indianapolis Colts	4	12	0	.250	189	378

Central Division

	W	L	T	Pct	PF	PA
Houston Oilers	12	4	0	.750	368	238
Pittsburgh Steelers	9	7	0	.563	308	281
Cleveland Browns	7	9	0	.438	304	307
Cincinnati Bengals	3	13	0	.188	187	319

Western Division

	W	L	T	Pct	PF	PA
Kansas City Chiefs	11	5	0	.688	328	291
Los Angeles Raiders	10	6	0	.625	306	326
Denver Broncos	9	7	0	.563	373	284
San Diego Chargers	8	8	0	.500	322	290
Seattle Seahawks	6	10	0	.375	280	314

ROSTER

No	Name	Pos	Ht	Wt	DOB	College	G
34	Bennett, Edgar	RB	6-0	224	02/15/69	Florida State	16
90	Bennett, Tony	LB	6-2	243	07/01/67	Mississippi	10
62	Brock, Matt	DE	6-4	290	01/14/66	Oregon	16
87	Brooks, Robert	WR	6-0	175	06/23/70	South Carolina	14
93	Brown, Gilbert	NT	6-2	330	02/22/71	Kansas	2
27	Buckley, Terrell	CB	5-9	176	06/07/71	Florida State	16
36	Butler, LeRoy	S	6-0	197	07/19/68	Florida State	16
63	Campen, James	C	6-3	280	06/11/64	Tulane	4
89	Chmura, Mark	TE	6-5	245	02/22/69	Boston College	14
83	Clayton, Mark	WR	5-9	185	04/08/61	Louisville	16
54	Coleman, Keo	LB	6-1	245	05/01/70	Mississippi State	12
55	Collins, Brett	LB	6-1	234	10/08/68	Washington	4
81	Collins, Shawn	WR	6-2	205	02/20/67	Northern Arizona	4
99	Davey, Don	DE	6-4	270	04/08/68	Wisconsin	9
11	Detmer, Ty	QB	6-0	186	10/30/67	BYU	3
72	Dotson, Earl	T	6-3	310	12/17/70	Texas A&I	13
33	Evans, Doug	CB	6-1	188	05/13/70	Louisiana Tech	16
4	Favre, Brett	QB	6-2	222	10/10/69	Southern Mississippi	16
76	Galbreath, Harry	G	6-1	285	01/01/65	Tennessee	16
70	Grant, David	NT	6-4	275	09/17/65	West Virginia	7
30	Harris, Corey	CB	5-11	195	10/25/69	Vanderbilt	11
80	Harris, Jackie	TE	6-3	243	01/04/68	North Louisiana	12
24	Hauck, Tim	S	5-10	187	12/20/66	Montana	13
50	Holland, Johnny	LB	6-2	235	03/11/65	Texas A&M	16
67	Hutchins, Paul	T	6-4	335	02/11/70	Western Michigan	1
79	Ilkin, Tunch	T	6-3	272	09/23/57	Indiana State	1
88	Ingram, Darryl	TE	6-3	245	05/02/66	California	2
13	Jacke, Chris	K	6-0	200	03/12/66	Texas-El Paso	16
64	Jurkovic, John	NT	6-2	290	08/18/67	Eastern Illinois	16
53	Koonce, George	LB	6-1	240	10/15/68	East Carolina	15
85	Lewis, Ron	WR	5-11	192	03/25/68	Florida State	9
77	Maas, Bill	NT	6-5	282	03/02/62	Pittsburgh	14
45	McNabb, Dexter	FB	6-1	245	07/09/69	Florida	16
47	Mitchell, Roland	CB	5-11	195	03/15/64	Texas Tech	16
57	Moran, Rich	G	6-2	280	03/19/62	San Diego State	3
81	Morgan, Anthony	WR	6-1	195	11/15/67	Tennessee	2
51	Morrissey, Jim	LB	6-3	225	12/24/62	Michigan State	6
55	Mott, Joe	LB	6-4	255	10/06/65	Iowa	2
91	Noble, Brian	LB	6-3	245	09/06/62	Arizona State	2
25	Oliver, Muhammad	CB	5-11	180	03/12/69	Oregon	2
96	Patterson, Shawn	DE	6-5	270	06/13/64	Arizona State	5
95	Paup, Bryce	LB	6-4	247	02/29/68	Northern Iowa	15
38	Pickens, Bruce	CB	5-11	190	05/09/68	Nebraska	2
45	Prior, Mike	S	6-0	215	11/14/63	Illinois State	16
73	Robbins, Tootie	T	6-5	315	06/02/58	East Carolina	12
75	Ruettgers, Ken	T	6-5	290	08/20/62	USC	16
84	Sharpe, Sterling	WR	5-11	210	04/06/65	South Carolina	16
59	Simmons, Wayne	LB	6-2	245	12/15/69	Clemson	14
68	Sims, Joe	OL	6-3	310	03/01/69	Nebraska	13
32	Stephens, John	RB	6-1	215	02/23/66	Northwestern (LA) State	5
31	Teague, George	S	6-1	187	02/18/71	Alabama	16
39	Thompson, Darrell	RB	6-0	217	11/23/67	Minnesota	16
97	Traylor, Keith	DE	6-2	290	09/03/69	Central Oklahoma	5
9	Wagner, Bryan	P	6-2	200	03/28/62	Cal State-Northridge	16
23	Walker, Sammy	CB	5-11	200	01/20/69	Texas Tech	8
86	West, Ed	TE	6-1	245	08/02/61	Auburn	16
92	White, Reggie	DE	6-5	295	12/19/61	Tennessee	16
74	Widell, Doug	G	6-4	287	09/23/66	Boston College	16
20	Williams, Kevin	RB	6-1	215	02/17/70	UCLA	3
56	Willis, James	LB	6-1	238	09/02/72	Auburn	13
29	Wilson, Marcus	RB	6-1	210	04/16/68	Virginia	16
52	Winters, Frank	C	6-3	290	01/23/64	West Illinois	16
60	Zeno, Lance	C	6-4	279	04/15/67	UCLA	5

DRAFT

Rnd	Name	Pos	Ht	Wt	College
1a	Wayne Simmons (15)	LB	6-2	236	Louisiana Tech
1b	George Teague (29)	DB	6-1	185	Alabama

(Packers traded two 2nd-round choices (46 & 54), a 4th-round pick (94) and an 8th-round pick (213) to the Cowboys for the Cowboys' 1st-round choice (29) and 4th-round pick (112))

2a	(Choice (46) traded to the Cowboys in deal mentioned above)				
2b	(Choice (54) from 49ers for Tim Harris; to Cowboys in deal mentioned above)				
3a	(Choice (72) to Raiders for Raiders' 3rd-round pick (81) and 6th-round pick (152))				
3b	Earl Dotson (81)	T	6-3	318	Texas A&I

(Choice from Raiders in deal mentioned above)

4a	(Choice (94) from Falcons for Vinnie Clark; to Cowboys in deal mentioned above)				
4b	(Choice (99) to Patriots for John Stephens)				
4c	(Choice (112) from Cowboys in deal mentioned above; to Bears for Bears' 5th-round pick (118) and 6th-round pick (156))				

Rnd	Name	Pos	Ht	Wt	College
5a	Mark Brunell (118)	QB	6-1	206	Washington

(Choice from Bears in deal mentioned above)

5b	James Willis (119)	LB	6-1	230	Auburn

(Choice from Buccaneers for signing Vince Workman)

5c	(Choice (129) to Jets for Ken O'Brien)				
6a	Doug Evans (141)	CB	6-1	186	Louisiana Tech

(Choice from Seahawks for Doug McCloughan)

6b	Paul Hutchins (152)	T	6-4	347	Western Michigan

(Choice from Raiders in deal mentioned above)

6c	Tim Watson (156)	SS	6-2	215	Howard

(Choice (156) traded to Colts for Dave McCloughan. Colts traded choice to Bears who traded it back to Packers in the deal mentioned above)

7	Robert Kuberski (183)	DT	6-4	281	Naval Academy
8	(Choice (213) to Cowboys in deal mentioned above)				

1993 GREEN BAY PACKERS

FRONT ROW: (L-R) 4 Brett Favre, 8 Mark Brunell, 11 Ty Detmer, 13 Chris Jacke, 24 Tim Hauck, 25 Tim Watson, 27 Terrell Buckley, 29 Marcus Wilson, 30 Corey Harris, 31 George Teague.

SECOND ROW: (L-R) Tight Ends/Assistant Offensive Line Coach Andy Reid, Offensive Line Coach Tom Lovat, Wide Receivers Coach Jon Gruden, Running Backs Coach Gil Haskell, Quarterbacks Coach Steve Mariucci, Offensive Coordinator Sherman Lewis, Head Coach Mike Holmgren, Defensive Coordinator Ray Rhodes, Defensive Line Coach Greg Blache, Linebackers Coach Bob Valesente, Defensive Backs Coach Dick Jauron, Defensive Assistant/Quality Control Jim Lind, Strength and Conditioning Kent Johnston, Special Teams Coach Nolan Cromwell.

THIRD ROW: (L-R) 32 John Stephens, 33 Doug Evans, 34 Edgar Bennett, 36 LeRoy Butler, 39 Darrell Thompson, 44 Dexter McNabb, 45 Mike Prior, 47 Roland Mitchell, 50 Johnny Holland, 52 Frank Winters, 53 George Koonce, 54 Keo Coleman.

FOURTH ROW: (L-R) 55 Brett Collins, 56 James Willis, 57 Rich Moran, 59 Wayne Simmons, 62 Matt Brock, 63 James Campen, 64 John Jurkovic, 68 Joe Sims, 71 Gilbert Brown.

FIFTH ROW: (L-R) 72 Earl Dotson, 73 Tootie Robbins, 74 Doug Widell, 75 Ken Ruettgers, 76 Harry Galbreath, 77 Bill Maas, 79 Tunch Ilkin, 80 Jackie Harris, 81 Shawn Collins, 82 Sanjay Beach.

SIXTH ROW: (L-R) 83 Mark Clayton, 84 Sterling Sharpe, 86 Ed West, 87 Robert Brooks, 89 Mark Chmura, 91 Brian Noble, 92 Reggie White, 95 Bryce Paup, 96 Shawn Patterson, 98 David Grant, 99 Don Davey.

BACK ROW: (L-R) Corporate Security Officer Jerry Parins, Strength/Conditioning Intern Craig Kodanko, Assoc. Team Physician Dr. John Gray, Team Physician Dr. Patrick J. McKenzie, Head Trainer Pepper Burruss, Assistant Trainer Sam Ramsden, Assistant Trainer Kurt Fielding, Training Room Intern Geoff Kaplan, Equipment Manager Bob Noel, Assistant Equipment Manager Bryan Nehring, Equipment Assistant Jack Noel, Assistant to Head Coach Gary Reynolds, Video Assistant Chris Kirby, Assistant Video Director Bob Eckberg, Video Director Al Treml.

If one play can salvage a season, for the Packers in 1994 that play came on a sunny December day in Milwaukee's County Stadium. With the season hanging in the balance, the team faced a third-and-two at the Falcons' 9-yard line. Twenty-one seconds remained and the club had just burned its last timeout.

What Green Bay did have was Brett Favre. The highly competitive Mississippian had already thrown for 321 yards and two touchdowns. But on this occasion, Favre turned to his feet, sprinting the remaining distance to deliver a 21-17 victory and keep alive the team's playoff hopes.

A week later, Favre fired three touchdown passes to Sterling Sharpe in a 34-19 romp in Tampa Bay. The win clinched a third consecutive winning season (9-7) and a second straight trip to the playoffs.

For half a season, the Packers owned the best defense in the NFL. Through eight games, Green Bay had given up only 2,082 yards, or 22 fewer than the next-best team team: the defending Super Bowl champion Cowboys.

The final eight games were a different story. Opponents averaged just over 335 yards and 23 points a game (up from the 260 yards and 13 points it had been permitting). By season's end, Green Bay's defense ranked sixth.

On the other side of the ball, Favre broke by one Lynn Dickey's team record for most touchdown passes in a season (32). Sterling Sharpe caught 18 of the touchdown throws to break Don Hutson's club record of 17 set in 1942.

On the eve of the season opener, Sharpe threatened to sit out if his contract was not reworked. A deal was quickly done and Sharpe went on to catch 94 passes for 1,119 yards.

The season was Sharpe's last. He experienced numbness and lay on the field in each of the last two regular-season games. An examination revealed that the receiver had a looseness in the ligaments that held together the two vertebrae directly below his skull. Because the ligaments couldn't be repaired, the two vertebrae were fused together. He was released by the Packers on Feb. 28, 1995.

Sharpe wasn't the only player to suffer injury. In a June minicamp, top draft pick Aaron Taylor was lost for the year after he ruptured a patellar tendon in a one-on-one blocking drill. The team's other top pick, running back LeShon Johnson, tore his ACL just days after the regular-season ended. Guard Guy McIntyre missed six weeks with a blood clot and safety LeRoy Butler sat out three games with pneumonia.

All wasn't doom and gloom. Favre signed a long-term contract prior to training camp and both Holmgren and general manager Ron Wolf agreed to contract extensions that ran through the 1999 season.

In October, the club announced it was pulling out of Milwaukee. With additional luxury boxes being readied for use at Lambeau Field in 1995, the team stood to lose millions of dollars if it continued to play in Milwaukee.

The Packers were 0-for-4 against the Vikings in Holmgren's first two years. They put an end to that drought with a 16-10 victory in the season opener.

Minnesota returned the favor in a defensive battle on Oct. 20. Fuad Reveiz's 27-yard field goal in overtime dropped Green Bay to 3-4.

The Packers rebounded by winning three straight games. On Halloween night, amid monsoon-like conditions at Soldier Field, Edgar Bennett (105 yards) led a 223-yard rushing onslaught that tamed the Bears 33-6. A week later, Green Bay held on to beat the Lions 38-30. The Packers then edged the Jets 17-10 to pull to within a game of the division-leading Vikings (7-5).

A brutal, three-game road stretch threatened to derail a promising season. The Bills, Cowboys, and Lions teamed up for 105 points and 1,278 yards in dishing out the losses to the Packers.

Whatever ailed the Packers was cured when the team returned to Lambeau Field to face the Bears on Dec. 11. Bennett again excelled (106 yards) as he and his running mates amassed 257 yards on the ground. After Chicago took a 3-0 lead on a Kevin Butler field goal, Green Bay responded with 40 unanswered points.

The Falcons were up next and a Bobby Hebert-to-Terance Mathis touchdown put Atlanta out front 17-14 with five minutes and 53 seconds left. Just 1:59 remained when Favre embarked upon what turned out to be a 67-yard march that he capped with his season-saving 9-yard run in the final seconds.

PASS HAPPY

With an offensive system that favored the pass and a young quarterback who liked to sling the ball downfield, it is not surprising that the Packers of 1994 attempted a team-record 609 passes.

The Packers threw more passes in 1994 than all but six teams. Brett Favre accounted for 582 of the throws; Mark Brunell was responsible for the other 27.

Despite all the dropbacks, the team's net passing total of 3,773 yards was just third best at the time. It trailed the 4,365 of 1983 and the 4,048 of 1989.

Favre surpassed 300 yards passing four times. A year later, he would set the franchise single-season record with seven such games.

Most Pass Attempts, Season

No.	Year	Record
609	1994	9-7-0
605	1999	8-8-0
600	1989	10-6-0
600	2000	9-7-0
593	1995	11-5-0

TEAM STATISTICS

	GB	OPP
First Downs	314	281
Rushing	88	82
Passing	205	182
Penalty	21	17
Rushes	417	381
Yards Gained	1,543	1,363
Average Gain	3.70	3.58
Average Yards per Game	96.4	85.2
Passes Attempted	609	605
Completed	375	337
% Completed	61.58	55.70
Total Yards Gained	3,977	3,677
Times Sacked	33	37
Yards Lost	204	276
Net Yards Gained	3,773	3,401
Yards Gained per Completion	10.61	10.91
Net Yards per Attempt	5.88	5.30
Average Net Yards per Game	235.8	212.6
Combined Net Yards Gained	5,316	4,764
Total Plays	1,059	1,023
Average Yards per Play	5.02	4.66
Average Net Yards per Game	332.3	297.8
Third Down Efficiency	97/225	79/222
Percentage	43.11	35.59
Fourth Down Efficiency	6/14	9/18
Percentage	42.86	50.00
Intercepted By	21	14
Yards Returned	232	193
Returned for TD	1	0
Punts	81	88
Yards Punted	3,351	3,491
Average Yards per Punt	41.37	39.67
Punt Returns	49	36
Yards Returned	414	272
Average Yards per Return	8.45	7.56
Returned for TD	1	0
Kickoff Returns	56	75
Yards Returned	1,168	1,380
Average Yards per Return	20.86	18.40
Returned for TD	1	1
Penalties	85	82
Yards Penalized	760	675
Fumbles	25	32
Lost	8	12
Own Recovered for Touchdown	0	1
Opponent's Recovered by	12	8
Opponent's Recovered for Touchdown	0	1
Total Points Scored	382	287
Total Touchdowns	47	32
Touchdowns Rushing	11	9
Touchdowns Passing	33	20
Touchdowns on Returns & Recoveries	3	3
Extra Points	41	24
Safeties	0	1
Field Goals Attempted	26	25
Field Goals Made	19	21
% Successful	73.08	84.00
Average Time of Possession	30:56	29:04

Regular Season 9-7-0

Date	GB		OPP	Att.
9/4	16	Minnesota Vikings	10	(59,487)
9/11	14	Miami Dolphins (M)	24	(55,011)
9/18	7	at Philadelphia Eagles	13	(63,922)
9/25	30	Tampa Bay Buccaneers	3	(58,551)
10/2	16	at New England Patriots	17	(57,522)
10/9	24	Los Angeles Rams	17	(58,911)
10/20	10	at Minnesota Vikings (OT)	13	(63,041)
10/31	33	at Chicago Bears	6	(47,381)
11/6	38	Detroit Lions (M)	30	(54,995)
11/13	17	New York Jets1	10	(58,307)
11/20	20	at Buffalo Bills	29	(79,029)
11/24	31	at Dallas Cowboys	42	(64,597)
12/4	31	at Detroit Lions	34	(76,338)
12/11	40	Chicago Bears	3	(57,927)
12/18	21	Atlanta Falcons (M)	17	(54,885)
12/24	34	at Tampa Bay Buccaneers	19	(65,076)

Postseason 1-1-0

12/31	16	Detroit Lions	12	(58,125)
1/8	9	at Dallas Cowboys	35	(64,745)

Score By Periods

	1	2	3	4	OT	Total
Packers	89	129	92	72	0	382
Opponents	40	96	65	83	3	287

INDIVIDUAL STATISTICS

Rushing

	Att	Yds	Avg	LG	TD
E. Bennett	178	623	3.5	t39	5
Cobb	153	579	3.8	30	3
Favre	42	202	4.8	t36	2
L. Johnson	26	99	3.8	43	0
Levens	5	15	3.0	5	0
Sharpe	3	15	5.0	8	0
Brunell	6	7	1.2	t5	1
C. Jordan	1	5	5.0	5	0
R. Brooks	1	0	0.0	0	0
D. Thompson	2	-2	-1.0	2	0
Packers	**417**	**1,543**	**3.7**	**43**	**11**
Opponents	381	1,363	3.6	63	9

Receiving

	No	Yds	Avg	LG	TD
Sharpe	94	1,119	11.9	49	18
E. Bennett	78	546	7.0	40	4
R. Brooks	58	648	11.2	35	4
Cobb	35	299	8.5	t37	1
E. West	31	377	12.2	26	2
Morgan	28	397	14.2	t47	4
Chmura	14	165	11.8	27	0
L. Johnson	13	168	12.9	33	0
R. Lewis	7	108	15.4	38	0
Reg. Johnson	7	79	11.3	24	0
Wilner	5	31	6.2	9	0
Mickens	4	31	7.8	11	0
Levens	1	9	9.0	9	0
Packers	**375**	**3,977**	**10.6**	**49**	**33**
Opponents	337	3,677	10.9	68	20

Passing

	Att	Com	Yds	Pct	TD	In	Tk/Yds	Rate
Favre	582	363	3,882	62.4	33	14	31/188	90.7
Brunell	27	12	95	44.4	0	0	2/16	53.8
Packers	**609**	**375**	**3,977**	**61.6**	**33**	**14**	**33/204**	**89.1**
Opponents	605	337	3,677	55.7	20	21	37/276	70.4

Punting

	No	Yds	Avg	Net	TB	In20	LG	HB
Hentrich	81	3,351	41.4	35.5	10	24	70	0
Packers	**81**	**3,351**	**41.4**	**35.5**	**10**	**24**	**70**	**0**
Opponents	88	3,491	39.7	33.8	5	21	60	0

Kickoff Returns

	No	Yds	Avg	LG	TD
C. Harris	29	618	21.3	59	0
R. Brooks	9	260	28.9	t96	1
C. Jordan	5	115	23.0	33	0
D. Thompson	4	67	16.8	19	0
Jurkovic	4	57	14.3	16	0
Levens	2	31	15.5	16	0
M. Wilson	2	14	7.0	14	0
Davey	1	6	6.0	6	0
Packers	**56**	**1,168**	**20.9**	**t96**	**1**
Opponents	75	1,380	18.4	t91	1

Punt Returns

	No	Yds	Avg	FC	LG	TD
R. Brooks	40	352	8.8	13	t85	1
Prior	8	62	7.8	4	16	0
C. Jordan	1	0	0.0	1	0	0
Packers	**49**	**414**	**8.4**	**18**	**t85**	**1**
Opponents	36	272	7.6	10	25	0

Interceptions

	No	Yds	Avg	LG	TD
Buckley	5	38	7.6	26	0
L. Butler	3	68	22.7	51	0
Paup	3	47	15.7	30	1
Teague	3	33	11.0	16	0
Willis	2	20	10.0	17	0
McGill	2	16	8.0	16	0
Strickland	1	7	7.0	7	0
KeShon Johnson	1	3	3.0	3	0
D. Evans	1	0	0.0	0	0
Packers	**21**	**232**	**11.0**	**51**	**1**
Opponents	14	193	13.8	36	0

Scoring

	TDr	TDp	TDrt	PAT	2pt	FG	S	TP
Sharpe	0	18	0	0/0	0	0	0	108
Jacke	0	0	0	41/43	0	19/26	0	98
E. Bennett	5	4	0	0/0	0	0/0	0	54
R. Brooks	0	4	2	0/0	0	0/0	0	36
Cobb	3	1	0	0/0	0	0/0	0	24
Morgan	0	4	0	0/0	0	0/0	0	24
E. West	0	2	0	0/0	0	0/0	0	14
Favre	2	0	0	0/0	0	0/0	0	12
Brunell	1	0	0	0/0	0	0/0	0	6
Paup	0	0	1	0/0	0	0/0	0	6
Packers	**11**	**33**	**3**	**41/43**	**1**	**19/26**	**0**	**382**
Opponents	9	20	3	24/24	3	21/25	0	287

2-point conversions: Packers (1-4); Opponents (3-8)

Fumbles

	Fum	Ow	Op	Yds	Tot
E. Bennett	1	1	0	0	1
R. Brooks	4	1	0	0	1
Brunell	1	0	0	-2	0
Buckley	0	0	1	0	1
Cobb	1	0	0	0	0
D. Evans	0	0	1	3	1
Favre	7	1	0	-2	1
C. Harris	1	1	0	0	1
KeShon Johnson	0	0	1	0	1
S. Jones	0	0	3	0	3
C. Jordan	1	0	0	0	0
Koonce	0	0	2	0	2
McMichael	0	0	1	0	1
Morgan	1	0	0	0	0
Paup	0	1	1	0	2
Prior	3	2	0	0	2
Ruettgers	0	1	0	0	1
Sharpe	1	0	0	0	0
Sims	0	0	1	0	1
Strickland	0	0	1	0	1
E. West	1	0	0	0	0
R. White	0	0	1	0	1
M. Williams	0	1	0	0	1
Willis	1	1	0	0	1
M. Wilson	0	0	1	0	1
Winters	1	1	0	-2	1
Packers	**25**	**12**	**12**	**-3**	**24**

Quarterback Sacks

	No
S. Jones	10.5
R. White	8.0
Paup	7.5
Gi. Brown	3.0
McMichael	2.5
Davey	1.5
L. Butler	1.0
D. Evans	1.0
Koonce	1.0
Wilkins	1.0
Packers	**37.0**
Opponents	33.0

NFL STANDINGS

National Conference

Eastern Division

	W	L	T	Pct	PF	PA
Dallas Cowboys	12	4	0	.750	414	248
New York Giants	9	7	0	.563	279	305
Arizona Cardinals	8	8	0	.500	235	267
Philadelphia Eagles	7	9	0	.438	308	308
Washington Redskins	3	13	0	.188	320	412

Central Division

	W	L	T	Pct	PF	PA
Minnesota Vikings	10	6	0	.625	356	314
Green Bay Packers	**9**	**7**	**0**	**.563**	**382**	**287**
Detroit Lions	9	7	0	.563	357	342
Chicago Bears	9	7	0	.563	271	307
Tampa Bay Buccaneers	6	10	0	.375	251	351

Western Division

	W	L	T	Pct	PF	PA
San Francisco 49ers	13	3	0	.813	505	296
New Orleans Saints	7	9	0	.438	348	407
Atlanta Falcons	7	9	0	.438	317	385
Los Angeles Rams	4	12	0	.250	286	365

American Conference

Eastern Division

	W	L	T	Pct	PF	PA
Miami Dolphins	10	6	0	.625	389	327
New England Patriots	10	6	0	.625	351	312
Indianapolis Colts	8	8	0	.500	307	320
Buffalo Bills	7	9	0	.438	340	356
New York Jets	6	10	0	.375	264	320

Central Division

	W	L	T	Pct	PF	PA
Pittsburgh Steelers	12	4	0	.750	316	234
Cleveland Browns	11	5	0	.688	340	204
Cincinnati Bengals	3	13	0	.188	276	406
Houston Oilers	2	14	0	.125	226	352

Western Division

	W	L	T	Pct	PF	PA
San Diego Chargers	11	5	0	.688	381	306
Kansas City Chiefs	9	7	0	.563	319	298
Los Angeles Raiders	9	7	0	.563	303	327
Denver Broncos	7	9	0	.438	347	396
Seattle Seahawks	6	10	0	.375	287	323

1994

ROSTER

No	Name	Pos	Ht	Wt	DOB	College	G
34	Bennett, Edgar	RB	6-0	224	02/15/69	Florida State	16
94	Brock, Matt	DE	6-4	290	01/14/66	Oregon	5
87	Brooks, Robert	WR	6-0	175	06/23/70	South Carolina	16
71	Brown, Gary	T	6-4	288	06/25/71	Georgia Tech	1
93	Brown, Gilbert	NT	6-2	330	02/22/71	Kansas	13
8	Brunell, Mark	QB	6-1	208	09/17/70	Washington	2
27	Buckley, Terrell	CB	5-9	176	06/07/71	Florida State	16
36	Butler, LeRoy	S	6-0	197	07/19/68	Florida State	13
89	Chmura, Mark	TE	6-5	245	02/22/69	Boston College	14
32	Cobb, Reggie	RB	6-0	215	07/07/68	Tennessee	16
99	Davey, Don	DE	6-4	270	04/08/68	Wisconsin	16
72	Dotson, Earl	T	6-3	310	12/17/70	Texas A&I	4
21	Duckett, Forey	CB	6-3	195	02/05/70	Nevada-Reno	3
63	Dukes, Jamie	C	6-1	295	06/14/64	Florida State	6
33	Evans, Doug	CB	6-1	188	05/13/70	Louisiana Tech	16
4	Favre, Brett	QB	6-2	222	10/10/69	Southern Mississippi	16
76	Galbreath, Harry	G	6-1	285	01/01/65	Tennessee	16
58	Hamilton, Ruffin	LB	6-1	230	03/02/71	Tulane	5
30	Harris, Corey	CB	5-11	195	10/25/69	Vanderbilt	16
24	Hauck, Tim	S	5-10	187	12/20/66	Montana	13
17	Hentrich, Craig	P	6-3	200	05/18/71	Notre Dame	16
70	Hope, Charles	G	6-3	303	03/12/70	Central State	6
67	Hutchins, Paul	T	6-4	335	02/11/70	Western Michigan	16
13	Jacke, Chris	K	6-0	200	03/12/66	Texas-El Paso	16
37	Johnson, KeShon	CB	5-10	179	07/17/70	Arizona	7
42	Johnson, LeShon	RB	5-11	200	01/15/71	Northern Illinois	12
82	Johnson, Reggie	TE	6-2	256	01/27/68	Florida State	9
96	Jones, Sean	DE	6-7	275	12/19/62	Northeastern	16
80	Jordan, Charles	WR	5-10	175	10/09/69	Long Beach City College	10
64	Jurkovic, John	NT	6-2	290	08/18/67	Eastern Illinois	16
53	Koonce, George	LB	6-1	240	10/15/68	East Carolina	16
25	Levens, Dorsey	RB	6-1	235	05/21/70	Georgia Tech	14
85	Lewis, Ron	WR	5-11	192	03/25/68	Florida State	6
22	McGill, Lenny	CB	6-1	194	05/31/71	Arizona State	6
62	McIntyre, Guy	G	6-3	265	02/17/61	Georgia	10
90	McMichael, Steve	DT	6-2	270	10/17/57	Texas	16
88	Mickens, Terry	WR	6-0	200	02/21/71	Florida A&M	12
47	Mitchell, Roland	CB	5-11	195	03/15/64	Texas Tech	1
81	Morgan, Anthony	WR	6-1	195	11/15/67	Tennessee	16
95	Paup, Bryce	LB	6-4	247	02/29/68	Northern Iowa	16
39	Prior, Mike	S	6-0	215	11/14/63	Illinois State	16
75	Ruettgers, Ken	T	6-5	290	08/20/62	USC	16
84	Sharpe, Sterling	WR	5-11	210	04/06/65	South Carolina	16
59	Simmons, Wayne	LB	6-2	245	12/15/69	Clemson	12
68	Sims, Joe	OL	6-3	310	03/01/69	Nebraska	15
55	Strickland, Fred	LB	6-2	250	08/15/66	Purdue	16
31	Teague, George	S	6-1	187	02/18/71	Alabama	16
26	Thompson, Darrell	RB	6-0	217	11/23/67	Minnesota	8
86	West, Ed	TE	6-1	245	08/02/61	Auburn	14
92	White, Reggie	DE	6-5	295	12/19/61	Tennessee	16
98	Wilkins, Gabe	DE	6-4	300	09/01/71	Gardner-Webb	15
51	Williams, Mark	LB	6-3	240	05/17/71	Ohio State	16
56	Willis, James	LB	6-1	238	09/02/72	Auburn	12
83	Wilner, Jeff	TE	6-4	250	12/31/71	Wesleyan	11
29	Wilson, Marcus	RB	6-1	210	04/16/68	Virginia	12
35	Wilson, Ray	S	6-2	202	08/26/71	New Mexico	3
52	Winters, Frank	C	6-3	290	01/23/64	West Illinois	16

DRAFT

Rnd	Name	Pos	Ht	Wt	College
1a	Aaron Taylor (16)	G	6-4	300	Notre Dame
	(Packers traded 1st-round (20) and 3rd-round (89) picks to Dolphins for Dolphins' 1st-round pick (16))				
1b	(Choice (20) to Dolphins in deal mentioned above)				
2	(Choice (53) to 49ers for 49ers' 3rd-round (84), 5th-round (149), and two 6th-round picks (175) and (190))				
3a	LeShon Johnson (84)	RB	5-11	200	Northern Illinois
	(Choice from 49ers in deal mentioned above)				
3b	(Choice (89) to Dolphins in deal mentioned above)				
4a	(Choice (120) to Raiders for Raiders' 4th-round (126) and 6th-round (169) picks)				
4b	Gabe Wilkins (126)	DE	6-4	300	Gardner-Webb
	(Choice from Raiders in deal mentioned above)				
5a	Terry Mickens (146)	WR	6-0	200	Florida A&M
5b	Dorsey Levens (149)	RB	6-1	235	Georgia Tech
	(Choice from 49ers in deal mentioned above)				
6a	Jay Kearney (169)	WR	6-1	195	West Virginia
	(Choice from Raiders in deal mentioned above)				
6b	Ruffin Hamilton (175)	LB	6-1	230	Tulane
	(Choice from 49ers in deal mentioned above)				
6c	Bill Schroeder (181)	WR	6-1	195	UW-La Crosse
6d	Paul Duckworth (190)	LB	6-1	245	Connecticut
	(Choice from 49ers in deal mentioned above)				
7	(Choice (212) to Broncos for Doug Widell)				

1994 GREEN BAY PACKERS

FRONT ROW: (L-R) 4 Brett Favre, 8 Mark Brunell, 11 Ty Detmer, 13 Chris Jacke, 22 Lenny McGill, 24 Tim Hauck, 25 Dorsey Levens, 26 Darrell Thompson, 27 Terrell Buckley, 29 Marcus Wilson.

SECOND ROW: (L-R) Special Teams Coach Nolan Cromwell, Tight Ends/Assistant Offensive Line Coach Andy Reid, Offensive Line Coach Tom Lovat, Wide Receivers Coach Jon Gruden, Quarterbacks Coach Steve Mariucci, Running Backs Coach Gil Haskell, Offensive Coordinator Sherman Lewis, Head Coach Mike Holmgren, Defensive Coordinator Fritz Shurmur, Defensive Line Coach Larry Brooks, Linebackers Coach Bob Valesente, Defensive Backs Coach Dick Jauron, Defensive Assistant/Quality Control Jim Lind, Strength and Conditioning Kent Johnston, General Assistant Harry Sydney.

THIRD ROW: (L-R) 30 Corey Harris, 31 George Teague, 32 Reggie Cobb, 33 Doug Evans, 34 LeRoy Butler, 39 Mike Prior, 42 LeShon Johnson, 47 Roland Mitchell, 51 Mark Williams, 52 Frank Winters.

FOURTH ROW: (L-R) 53 George Koonce, 55 Fred Strickland, 56 James Willis, 58 Ruffin Hamilton, 59 Wayne Simmons, 62 Guy McIntyre, 63 Jamie Dukes, 64 John Jurkovic, 67 Paul Hutchins, 68 Joe Sims.

FIFTH ROW: (L-R) 71 Gary Brown, 72 Earl Dotson, 75 Ken Ruettgers, 76 Harry Galbreath, 79 Aaron Taylor, 80 Charles Jordan, 81 Anthony Morgan, 83 Jeff Wilner, 85 Ron Lewis, 86 Ed West, 87 Robert Brooks.

SIXTH ROW: (L-R) 88 Terry Mickens, 89 Mark Chmura, 90 Reggie White, 93 Gilbert Brown, 94 Matt Brock, 95 Bryce Paup, 96 Sean Jones, 98 Gabe Wilkins, 99 Don Davey.

BACK ROW: (L-R) Corporate Security Officer Jerry Parins, Administrative Assistant to Head Coach Gary Reynolds, Training Room Intern Omar Ross, Assistant Trainer Sam Ramsden, Assistant Trainer Kurt Fielding, Head Trainer Pepper Burruss, Associate Team Physician Dr. John Gray, Team Physician Dr. Patrick J. McKenzie, Administrative Assistant Bryan Nehring, Assistant Equipment Manager Tom Bakken, Equipment Assistant Gary Poels, Video Assistant Chris Kirby, Assistant Video Director Bob Eckberg, Video Director Al Treml.

Yancey Thigpen dropped the ball and with his failure, the Packers secured their first outright Central Division championship in 23 years.

The scene: Lambeau Field on Christmas Eve. Sixteen seconds remained. On fourth and goal from the 6-yard line, Steelers' quarterback Neil O'Donnell threw for Thigpen in the left corner of the end zone. The receiver bobbled the ball, then saw it pop free as it hit his knee.

"Merry Christmas, Green Bay," Thigpen said after Pittsburgh's 24-19 loss. "That's my Christmas present right there to Green Bay."

The Packers (11-5) edged the Lions (10-6) to claim the Central Division title. Not since 1972 had the team found itself alone in such a lofty position.

Brett Favre was another key player that day. He suffered a bruised chest after a hit from strong safety Myron Bell in the third quarter, then had to sit for two plays after being hit in the head by linebacker Kevin Greene in the fourth period. The tough-as-nails quarterback finished the day with 301 yards passing and two touchdowns.

It wasn't the first time he played in pain. He tore ligaments in his ankle against the Vikings on Nov. 5, but came back the following week to throw five touchdown passes and lead the Packers past the Bears 35-28.

Favre threw 38 touchdown passes. He earned All-Pro honors and was named the league's most valuable player.

Favre wasn't the only player to suffer injury. Reggie White tore a hamstring against the Bengals on Dec. 3 and was thought to be lost for the season. But after missing the first game in his 11-year career against Tampa, the defensive end returned for Green Bay's 34-23 win in New Orleans.

Sterling Sharpe's career with the Packers officially came to an end when he was released on Feb. 28. In trying to find a replacement, Green Bay traded for tight end Keith Jackson and offered to make Andre Rison the highest-paid receiver in the NFL. Rison signed with the Browns instead and Jackson didn't report until Oct. 20, nearly seven months after the trade.

The Packers also sent a fourth-round draft choice to Miami for receiver Mark Ingram.

Robert Brooks, on the roster since being drafted in the third round in 1992, showed he was the best choice to replace Sharpe. Brooks caught 102 passes for a team-record 1,497 yards.

Running back Edgar Bennett also surpassed the 1,000-yard milestone. His 1,067 yards rushing were the most by a Packer since Terdell Middleton in 1978.

After dropping an opener for the first time in three years, Green Bay slipped past Chicago 27-24. White sacked Bears' quarterback Erik Kramer, causing him to fumble. Wayne Simmons recovered with 1:59 left.

On Oct. 8, the Packers tangled with one of the league's best. The Cowboys piled up 448 yards in casting aside Green Bay 34-24. Troy Aikman passed for 316 yards and was not intercepted.

The Packers closed out the first half of the season on a sour note. Lions' receiver Herman Moore became the first player to catch three touchdown passes against Green Bay in a single half as Detroit came out on top 24-16.

Green Bay hit bottom a week later at the Metrodome. With Favre (ankle) and backup Ty Detmer (torn thumb ligaments) out, third-string quarterback T. J. Rubley called an audible on third-and-one at the Vikings' 38. His pass was intercepted by linebacker Jeff Brady to set up Fuad Reveiz's game-winning field goal.

"I made a poor decision," Rubley said of his forced throw. "That's what it comes down to."

The Packers (5-4) then rallied to win six of their final seven games. The lone exception was a 13-10 setback to the Buccaneers on Dec. 10. Chris Jacke missed a 45-yard field goal with nine seconds left, and Michael Husted won it with a 47-yard kick in overtime.

A week later, Green Bay clinched a playoff berth. Favre enjoyed a near-perfect day, passing for 308 yards and four touchdowns as the Packers toppled the Saints 34-23.

"I want Lambeau Field rocking like it has never rocked before," coach Mike Holmgren said prior to the finale with the Steelers. Even he couldn't have foreseen the exciting finish that transpired.

"Regardless of how far we go, this has been my most memorable year coaching, because this is really an unselfish group," Holmgren said afterwards.

A RARE RECOVERY

Green Bay won 11 games in 1995 for the first time in 29 years. That the team did so by forcing just 16 turnovers is all the more remarkable.

In 75 previous NFL seasons, just 17 teams had forced fewer than 20 turnovers in one season. Sixteen posted losing records. Only one, the 1982 Cardinals (5-4), managed more wins than losses.

The Packers were terrible at recovering opponents' fumbles. They grabbed just three, to tie the NFL record for fewest in a season set by the 1974 Rams. Sean Jones, Wayne Simmons and George Teague had the recoveries.

The Packers failed to force a turnover on six occasions. The team was 3-3 in those games.

Fewest Turnovers by Opponents, Season

No.	Year	Record
16	1995	11-5-0
23	1982	5-3-1
23	1998	11-5-0
24	1939	9-2-0
24	1977	4-10-0
26	1969	8-6-0
26	1976	5-9-0

TEAM STATISTICS

	GB	OPP
First Downs	339	303
Rushing	84	99
Passing	235	188
Penalty	20	16
Rushes	410	374
Yards Gained	1,428	1,515
Average Gain	3.48	4.05
Average Yards per Game	89.3	94.7
Passes Attempted	593	616
Completed	372	351
% Completed	62.73	56.98
Total Yards Gained	4,539	3,915
Times Sacked	33	39
Yards Lost	217	275
Net Yards Gained	4,322	3,640
Yards Gained per Completion	12.20	11.15
Net Yards per Pass Play	6.90	5.56
Average Net Yards per Game	270.1	227.5
Combined Net Yards Gained	5,750	5,155
Total Plays	1,036	1,029
Average Yards per Play	5.55	5.01
Average Net Yards per Game	359.4	322.2
Third Down Efficiency	108/220	75/214
Percentage	49.09	35.05
Fourth Down Efficiency	5/8	12/26
Percentage	62.50	46.15
Intercepted By	13	15
Yards Returned	253	243
Returned for TD	0	0
Punts	67	88
Yards Punted	2,740	3,746
Average Yards per Punt	40.90	42.57
Punt Returns	61	36
Yards Returned	515	279
Average Yards per Return	8.44	7.75
Returned for TD	0	0
Kickoff Returns	61	74
Yards Returned	1,282	1,581
Average Yards per Return	21.02	21.36
Returned for TD	0	0
Penalties	85	98
Yards Penalized	604	738
Fumbles	22	12
Lost	6	3
Own Recovered for Touchdown	0	0
Opponent's Recovered by	3	6
Opponent's Recovered for Touchdown	1	0
Total Points Scored	404	314
Total Touchdowns	49	39
Touchdowns Rushing	9	12
Touchdowns Passing	39	25
Touchdowns on Returns & Recoveries	1	0
Extra Points (Kicking)	48	35
Two-Point Conversions	1/1	0/2
Safeties	0	0
Field Goals Attempted	28	21
Field Goals Made	20	19
% Successful	71.42	90.48
Average Time of Possession	31:12	28:48

Regular Season 11-5-0

Date	GB		OPP	Att.
9/3	14	St. Louis Rams	17	(60,104)
9/11	27	at Chicago Bears	24	(64,855)
9/17	14	New York Giants	6	(60,117)
9/24	24	at Jacksonville Jaguars	14	(66,744)
10/8	24	at Dallas Cowboys	34	(64,806)
10/15	30	Detroit Lions	21	(60,302)
10/22	38	Minnesota Vikings	21	(60,332)
10/29	16	at Detroit Lions	24	(73,462)
11/5	24	at Minnesota Vikings	27	(62,839)
11/12	35	Chicago Bears	28	(59,996)
11/19	31	at Cleveland Browns	20	(55,388)
11/26	35	Tampa Bay Buccaneers	13	(59,218)
12/3	24	Cincinnati Bengals	10	(60,318)
12/10	10	at Tampa Bay Buccaneers(OT)	13	(67,557)
12/16	34	at New Orleans Saints	23	(50,132)
12/24	24	Pittsburgh Steelers	19	(60,649)

Postseason 2-1-0

Date	GB		OPP	Att.
12/31	37	Atlanta Falcons	20	(60,453)
1/6	27	at San Francisco 49ers	17	(69,311)
1/14	27	at Dallas Cowboys	38	(65,135)

Score By Periods

	1	2	3	4	OT	Total
Packers	83	146	81	94	0	404
Opponents	41	106	72	92	3	314

INDIVIDUAL STATISTICS

Rushing

	Att	Yds	Avg	LG	TD
E. Bennett	316	1,067	3.4	23	3
Favre	39	181	4.6	40	3
Levens	36	120	3.3	22	3
Henderson	7	35	5.0	17	0
R. Brooks	4	21	5.3	21	0
Rubley	2	6	3.0	6	0
Detmer	3	3	1.0	5	0
L. Johnson	2	-2	-1.0	0	0
Ingram	1	-3	-3.0	-3	0
Packers	**410**	**1,428**	**3.5**	**40**	**9**
Opponents	374	1,515	4.1	37	12

Receiving

	No	Yds	Avg	LG	TD
R. Brooks	102	1,497	14.7	t99	13
E. Bennett	61	648	10.6	35	4
Chmura	54	679	12.6	33	7
Levens	48	434	9.0	27	4
Ingram	39	469	12.0	29	3
Morgan	31	344	11.1	t29	4
K. Jackson	13	142	10.9	22	1
Freeman	8	106	13.3	28	1
C. Jordan	7	117	16.7	35	2
Mickens	3	50	16.7	24	0
Thomason	3	32	10.7	15	0
Henderson	3	21	7.0	9	0
Packers	**372**	**4,539**	**12.2**	**t99**	**39**
Opponents	351	3,915	11.2	t69	25

Passing

	Att	Com	Yds	Pct	TD	In	Tk/Yds	Rate
Favre	570	359	4,413	63.0	38	13	33/217	99.5
Detmer	16	8	81	50.0	1	1	0/0	59.6
Rubley	6	4	39	66.7	0	1	0/0	45.1
McMahon	1	1	6	100.0	0	0	0/0	91.7
Packers	**593**	**372**	**4,539**	**62.7**	**39**	**15**	**33/217**	**97.6**
Opponents	616	351	3,915	57.0	25	13	39/275	80.8

Punting

	No	Yds	Avg	Net	TB	In20	LG	HB
Hentrich	65	2,740	42.2	34.6	7	26	61	2
Packers	**67**	**2,740**	**40.9**	**34.6**	**7**	**26**	**61**	**2**
Opponents	88	3,746	42.6	35.6	5	17	58	0

Kickoff Returns

	No	Yds	Avg	LG	TD
Freeman	24	556	23.2	45	0
C. Jordan	21	444	21.1	33	0
Jervey	8	165	20.6	28	0
Morgan	3	46	15.3	20	0
R. Brooks	1	28	28.0	28	0
Jurkovic	1	17	17.0	17	0
Thomason	1	16	16.0	16	0
Arthur	1	10	10.0	10	0
Mickens	1	0	0.0	0	0
Packers	**61**	**1,282**	**21.0**	**45**	**0**
Opponents	74	1,581	21.4	46	0

Punt Returns

	No	Yds	Avg	FC	LG	TD
Freeman	37	292	7.9	3	26	0
C. Jordan	21	213	10.1	2	18	0
Prior	1	10	10.0	2	10	0
D. Evans	1	0	0.0	0	0	0
Ingram	1	0	0.0	0	0	0
Packers	**61**	**515**	**8.4**	**7**	**26**	**0**
Opponents	36	279	7.8	11	40	0

Interceptions

	No	Yds	Avg	LG	TD
L. Butler	5	105	21.0	76	0
Teague	2	100	50.0	74	0
D. Evans	2	24	12.0	24	0
Koonce	1	12	12.0	12	0
Prior	1	9	9.0	9	0
Newsome	1	3	3.0	3	0
Kelly	1	0	0.0	0	0
Packers	**13**	**253**	**19.5**	**76**	**0**
Opponents	15	243	16.2	61	0

Scoring

	TDr	TDp	TDrt	PAT	2pt	FG	S	TP
Jacke	0	0	0	43/43	0	17/23	0	94
R. Brooks	0	13	0	0/0	0	0/0	0	78
Chmura	0	7	0	0/0	1	0/0	0	44
E. Bennett	3	4	0	0/0	0	0/0	0	42
Levens	3	4	0	0/0	0	0/0	0	42
Morgan	0	4	0	0/0	0	0/0	0	24
Favre	3	0	0	0/0	0	0/0	0	18
Ingram	0	3	0	0/0	0	0/0	0	18
Hentrich	0	0	0	5/5	0	3/5	0	14
C. Jordan	0	2	0	0/0	0	0/0	0	12
Freeman	0	1	0	0/0	0	0/0	0	6
K. Jackson	0	1	0	0/0	0	0/0	0	6
S. Jones	0	0	1	0/0	0	0/0	0	6
Packers	**9**	**39**	**1**	**48/48**	**1**	**20/28**	**0**	**404**
Opponents	12	25	0	35/35	0	19/21	0	314

2-point conversions: Packers (1-1); Opponents (0-2)

Fumbles

	Fum	Ow	Op	Yds	Tot
E. Bennett	2	1	0	0	1
Detmer	1	1	0	0	1
D. Evans	1	0	0	0	0
Favre	8	0	0	0	0
Freeman	7	4	0	0	4
Ingram	1	0	0	0	0
Jervey	0	1	0	0	1
S. Jones	0	0	1	0	1
C. Jordan	1	1	0	0	1
McGill	0	0	1	0	1
Prior	0	1	0	0	1
Rubley	1	0	0	0	0
Ruettgers	0	0	1	0	1
Simmons	0	0	1	0	1
A. Taylor	0	0	1	0	2
Teague	0	0	1	4	1
Thomason	0	1	0	0	1
Packers	**22**	**15**	**3**	**4**	**18**

Quarterback Sacks

	No.
R. White	12.0
S. Jones	9.0
Simmons	4.0
LaBounty	3.0
Wilkins	3.0
Kuberski	2.0
D. Holland	1.5
Prior	1.5
L. Butler	1.0
D. Evans	1.0
Koonce	1.0
Packers	**39.0**
Opponents	33.0

NFL STANDINGS

National Conference

Eastern Division

	W	L	T	Pct	PF	PA
Dallas Cowboys	12	4	0	.750	435	291
Philadelphia Eagles	10	6	0	.625	318	338
Washington Redskins	6	10	0	.375	326	359
New York Giants	5	11	0	.313	290	340
Arizona Cardinals	4	12	0	.250	275	422

Central Division

	W	L	T	Pct	PF	PA
Green Bay Packers	11	5	0	.688	404	314
Detroit Lions	10	6	0	.625	436	336
Chicago Bears	9	7	0	.563	392	360
Minnesota Vikings	8	8	0	.500	412	385
Tampa Bay Buccaneers	7	9	0	.438	238	335

Western Division

	W	L	T	Pct	PF	PA
San Francisco 49ers	11	5	0	.688	457	258
Atlanta Falcons	9	7	0	.563	362	349
St. Louis Rams	7	9	0	.438	309	418
Carolina Panthers	7	9	0	.438	289	325
New Orleans Saints	7	9	0	.438	319	348

American Conference

Eastern Division

	W	L	T	Pct	PF	PA
Buffalo Bills	10	6	0	.625	350	335
Indianapolis Colts	9	7	0	.563	331	316
Miami Dolphins	9	7	0	.563	398	332
New England Patriots	6	10	0	.375	294	377
New York Jets	3	13	0	.188	233	384

Central Division

	W	L	T	Pct	PF	PA
Pittsburgh Steelers	11	5	0	.688	407	327
Cincinnati Bengals	7	9	0	.438	349	374
Houston Oilers	7	9	0	.438	348	324
Cleveland Browns	5	11	0	.313	289	356
Jacksonville Jaguars	4	12	0	.250	275	404

Western Division

	W	L	T	Pct	PF	PA
Kansas City Chiefs	13	3	0	.813	358	241
San Diego Chargers	9	7	0	.563	321	323
Seattle Seahawks	8	8	0	.500	363	366
Denver Broncos	8	8	0	.500	388	345
Oakland Raiders	8	8	0	.500	348	332

ROSTER

No	Name	Pos	Ht	Wt	DOB	College	G
50	Arthur, Mike	C	6-3	280	05/07/68	Texas A&M	11
48	Bartrum, Mike	TE	6-4	245	06/23/70	Marshall	4
34	Bennett, Edgar	RB	6-0	217	02/15/69	Florida State	16
9	Borgognone, Dirk	K	6-2	221	01/09/68	Pacific	2
87	Brooks, Robert	WR	6-0	180	06/23/70	South Carolina	16
71	Brown, Gary	T	6-4	315	06/25/71	Georgia Tech	16
93	Brown, Gilbert	NT	6-2	325	02/22/71	Kansas	13
36	Butler, LeRoy	S	6-0	200	07/19/68	Florida State	16
89	Chmura, Mark	TE	6-5	250	02/22/69	Boston College	16
91	Clavelle, Shannon	DE	6-2	287	10/12/72	Colorado	1
45	Crawford, Keith	CB	6-2	198	11/21/70	Howard Payne	13
11	Detmer, Ty	QB	6-0	190	10/30/67	BYU	4
23	Dorsett, Matthew	CB	5-11	187	08/23/73	Southern	10
72	Dotson, Earl	T	6-3	310	12/17/70	Texas A&I	16
33	Evans, Doug	CB	6-1	190	05/13/70	Louisiana Tech	16
4	Favre, Brett	QB	6-2	220	10/10/69	Southern Mississippi	16
86	Freeman, Antonio	WR	6-0?	187	05/27/72	Virginia Tech	11
76	Galbreath, Harry	G	6-1	295	01/01/65	Tennessee	16
54	Harris, Bernardo	LB	6-2	243	10/15/71	North Carolina	11
30	Henderson, William	FB	6-1	248	02/19/71	North Carolina	15
17	Hentrich, Craig	P	6-3	200	05/18/71	Notre Dame	16
90	Holland, Darius	DT	6-4	305	11/10/73	Colorado	14
82	Ingram, Mark	WR	5-11	194	08/23/65	Michigan State	16
13	Jacke, Chris	K	6-0	205	03/12/66	Texas-El Paso	14
88	Jackson, Keith	TE	6-2	258	04/19/65	Oklahoma	9
32	Jervey, Travis	RB	5-11?	225	05/05/72	The Citadel	16
42	Johnson, LeShon	RB	5-11	200	01/15/71	Northern Illinois	2
96	Jones, Sean	DE	6-7	283	12/19/62	Northeastern	16
80	Jordan, Charles	WR	5-10	183	10/09/69	Long Beach City College	8
64	Jurkovic, John	NT	6-2	295	08/18/67	Eastern Illinois	16
57	Kelly, Joe	LB	6-2	235	12/11/64	Washington	13
53	Koonce, George	LB	6-1	243	10/15/68	East Carolina	16
94	Kuberski, Bob	NT	6-4	300	04/05/71	Navy	9
97	LaBounty, Matt	DE	6-3	278	01/03/69	Oregon	14
25	Levens, Dorsey	RB	6-1	240	05/21/70	Georgia Tech	15
22	McGill, Lenny	CB	6-1	198	05/31/71	Arizona State	15
9	McMahon, Jim	QB	6-1	195	08/21/59	BYU	1
85	Mickens, Terry	WR	6-0	198	02/21/71	Florida A&M	16
81	Morgan, Anthony	WR	6-1	200	11/15/67	Tennessee	16
28	Mullen, Roderick	CB	6-1	204	12/05/72	Grambling State	8
21	Newsome, Craig	CB	6-0	188	08/10/71	Arizona State	16
39	Prior, Mike	S	6-0	208	11/14/63	Illinois State	16
12	Rubley, T.J.	QB	6-3	205	11/29/68	Tulsa	1
75	Ruettgers, Ken	T	6-5	292	08/20/62	USC	15
59	Simmons, Wayne	LB	6-2	248	12/15/69	Clemson	16
68	Sims, Joe	OL	6-3	310	03/01/69	Nebraska	4
55	Strickland, Fred	LB	6-2	250	08/15/66	Purdue	14
73	Taylor, Aaron	G	6-4	305	11/14/72	Notre Dame	16
31	Teague, George	S	6-1	195	02/18/71	Alabama	15
83	Thomason, Jeff	TE	6-4	250	12/30/69	Oregon	16
63	Timmerman, Adam	G	6-4	288	08/14/71	South Dakota State	13
92	White, Reggie	DE	6-5	300	12/19/61	Tennessee	15
98	Wilkins, Gabe	DE	6-4	300	09/01/71	Gardner-Webb	13
51	Williams, Brian	LB	6-1	240	12/17/72	USC	13
83	Wilner, Jeff	TE	6-4	250	12/31/71	Wesleyan	2
29	Wilson, Marcus	RB	6-1	215	04/16/68	Virginia	14
52	Winters, Frank	C	6-3	295	01/23/64	West Illinois	16

DRAFT

Rnd	Name	Pos	Ht	Wt	College
1a	(Packers traded 1st-round pick (22) and 6th-round pick (188) to Panthers for Panthers' 1st-round (32), 3rd-round (65), and 6th-round (173) picks)				
1b	Craig Newsome (32) (Choice from Panthers in deal mentioned above)	DB	6-0	185	Arizona State
2	(Choice (53) traded to Dolphins for Keith Jackson)				
3a	Darius Holland (65) (Choice from Panthers in deal mentioned above)	DT	6-4	310	Colorado
3b	William Henderson (66) (Choice from Jaguars for Mark Brunell)	FB	6-1	246	North Carolina
3c	Brian Williams (73) (Compensation from Seahawks for Corey Harris)	LB	6-1	238	USC
3d	(Choice (84) to Browns for Browns' 3rd-round (90) and 5th-round (160) picks)				
3e	Antonio Freeman (90) (Choice from Browns in deal mentioned above)	WR	6-0?	185	Virginia Tech
4	Jeff Miller (117)	T	6-3	303	Mississippi
5a	Jay Barker (160) (Choice from Browns in deal mentioned above)	QB	6-2	212	Alabama
5b	Travis Jervey (170) (Choice to Raiders for Charles Jordan; from Jaguars for Mark Brunell)	RB	6-1	210	The Citadel
6a	Charlie Simmons (173) (Choice from Panthers in deal mentioned above)	WR	6-3	202	Georgia Tech
6b	(Choice (188) to Panthers in deal mentioned above)				
7	Adam Timmerman (230)	G	6-4	289	So. Dakota State

1995 GREEN BAY PACKERS

FRONT ROW: (L-R) 4 Brett Favre, 11 Ty Detmer, 12 T.J. Rubley, 13 Chris Jacke, 17 Craig Hentrich, 21 Craig Newsome, 22 Matthew Dorsett, 24 Russell White, 25 Dorsey Levens, 29 Marcus Wilson, 30 William Henderson.

SECOND ROW: (L-R) Tight Ends/Assistant Offensive Line Coach Andy Reid, Offensive Line Coach Tom Lovat, Offensive Assistant/Quality Control Marty Mornhinweg, Running Backs Coach Harry Sydney, Quarterbacks Coach Steve Mariucci, Wide Receivers Coach Gil Haskell, Offensive Coordinator Sherman Lewis, Head Coach Mike Holmgren, Defensive Coordinator Fritz Shurmur, Defensive Line Coach Larry Brooks, Linebackers Coach Jim Lind, Defensive Backs Coach Bob Valesente, Defensive Assistant/Quality Control Johnny Holland, Strength and Conditioning Coach Kent Johnston, Special Teams Coach Nolan Cromwell.

THIRD ROW: (L-R) 31 George Teague, 32 Travis Jervey, 33 Doug Evans, 34 Edgar Bennett, 36 LeRoy Butler, 39 Mike Prior, 42 LeShon Johnson, 45 Keith Crawford, 48 Mike Bartrum, 50 Mike Arthur, 51 Brian Williams.

FOURTH ROW: (L-R) 52 Frank Winters, 53 George Koonce, 54 Bernardo Harris, 55 Fred Strickland, 56 James Willis, 57 Joe Kelly, 59 Wayne Simmons, 63 Adam Timmerman, 64 John Jurkovic, 65 Lindsay Knapp, 68 Joe Sims.

FIFTH ROW: (L-R) 70 Jeff Miller, 71 Gary Brown, 72 Earl Dotson, 73 Aaron Taylor, 75 Ken Ruettgers, 76 Harry Galbreath, 80 Charles Jordan, 81 Anthony Morgan, 82 Mark Ingram, 83 Jeff Thomason, 85 Terry Mickens.

SIXTH ROW: (L-R) 86 Antonio Freeman, 87 Robert Brooks, 89 Mark Chmura, 90 Darius Holland, 92 Reggie White, 93 Gilbert Brown, 94 Bob Kuberski, 96 Sean Jones, 97 Matt LaBounty, 98 Gabe Wilkins.

BACK ROW: (L-R) Strength and Conditioning Assistant Barry Rubin, Administrative Assistant/Football Gary Reynolds, Corporate Security Officer Jerry Parins, Training Room Intern Andre Daniel, Assistant Trainer Sam Ramsden, Assistant Trainer Kurt Fielding, Head Trainer Pepper Burruss, Associate Team Physician Dr. John Gray, Team Physician Dr. Patrick J. McKenzie, Equipment Manager Gordon (Red) Batty, Assistant Equipment Manager Bryan Nehring, Assistant Equipment Assistant Tim O'Neill, Video Assistant Chris Kirby, Assistant Video Director Bob Eckberg, Video Director Al Treml.

"What a moment! Oh, man. Is this good? Is this heaven or what?"

Twenty-nine often frustrating years of less than championship-caliber football came to an end in 1996 when Green Bay won its first Super Bowl in nearly three decades. As the rhetorical questions of the Packers' longtime radio play-by-play announcer Jim Irwin implied, it was indeed paradise on earth for many long-suffering fans.

Green Bay was capable of dominating opponents. It outscored its first three opponents 115-26. Then after overcoming a rough stretch in November, it won its last four games by a combined score of 138-36.

The Packers scored more points than any team—a team record 456—and gave up the fewest. The club boasted the No. 1 defense and its offense ranked fifth.

Brett Favre was named league MVP for a second consecutive year. He threw a franchise-record and NFL-best 39 touchdown passes.

In May, Favre dropped a bombshell. He announced he had become addicted to painkillers. He spent 46 days in a Kansas drug rehabilitation clinic.

At a press conference in July, Favre declared: "You know, I'm going to beat this thing. I'm going to win a Super Bowl. There's a lot of things I'm going to do. And all I can tell people if they don't believe me is, 'Just bet against me.'"

Injuries threatened to wipe out Favre's gifted receiving corps. Robert Brooks tore the anterior cruciate ligament and patellar tendon in his right knee against the 49ers on Oct. 14 and was lost for the season. Antonio Freeman missed four games after he broke his left forearm on Oct. 27. And tight end Mark Chmura was out for three games with a sprained arch suffered in a 27-20 loss at Kansas City on Nov. 10.

Key off-season acquisitions included Don Beebe, Santana Dotson, Desmond Howard, Bruce Wilkerson (all free agents), Andre Rison (waivers) and Eugene Robinson (trade for defensive end Matt LaBounty). Beebe averaged a team-high 17.9 yards per catch, Dotson made 38 tackles (third among defensive linemen), Howard established numerous punt return records, Wilkerson solidified the left tackle spot late in the season, Rison added a deep threat at receiver, and Robinson had a club-best six interceptions.

The Packers overwhelmed Tampa Bay, Philadelphia, and San Diego to start the season. Favre had passer ratings of 141.5, 115.1, and 104.5 in the three games.

Minnesota had also started strong. In Game 4, the Vikings brought Green Bay back to earth 30-21. Linebacker Dixon Edwards was motivated by the large number of Packers fans in attendance in Minneapolis.

"They told me it was going to be like that, that more people would be cheering for the Packers than the Vikings," he said. "If anything, it helped us. You know what I'm saying?

There was an emotional factor."

The Metrodome wasn't the only stadium to be visited by Packers fans in droves. The team had a large, loyal following on the road throughout the year.

Green Bay blew out Seattle (31-10) and the Bears (37-6) before a Monday night showdown with the 49ers. Beebe stepped up in Brooks' absence and caught 11 passes for 220 yards and a touchdown. Chris Jacke's 53-yard field goal in overtime delivered a 23-20 victory.

Wins over Tampa Bay and Detroit followed and propelled the Packers to an 8-1 record.

Its receivers ailing, Green Bay dropped consecutive games to the Chiefs and Cowboys. Doug Evans' interception return for a touchdown a week later in St. Louis awoke the slumbering Pack, sparked a 24-9 win and returned the team to form for its stretch run.

The final four games also saw the emergence of Dorsey Levens. He gained 267 yards rushing and scored three rushing touchdowns.

On Dec. 8, the Packers clinched their second straight Central Division title by beating up on the John Elway-less Broncos 41-6. Two weeks later, they ensured themselves of home-field advantage throughout the playoffs by crushing the Vikings 38-10.

That win also gave Green Bay a perfect 8-0 record at home and prompted general manager Ron Wolf to say: "I think everyone's scared to death to come in here and play. And that's the way we want it."

MANY HAPPY RETURNS

On July 11, the Packers signed unrestricted free agent Desmond Howard to a one-year contract. The acquisition was arguably the best the team made in 1996, as the wide receiver/kick returner set an NFL record with 875 yards on 58 punt returns.

Howard set a Packers record by returning three punts for touchdowns: 65 yards with a Darren Bennett punt on Sept. 15, 75 yards with a Todd Sauerbrun boot on Dec. 1, and 92 yards with a Mark Royals punt on Dec. 15.

Howard was just as good in the postseason. He returned a punt for a touchdown against the 49ers in Green Bay and took a kickoff back 99 yards for a score in the Super Bowl. He was voted the game's most valuable player.

Listed below are the three individuals with the most punt return yardage in a single season in NFL history:

Yds	Player, Team	Year
875	Desmond Howard, Packers	1996
692	Fulton Walker, Dolphins-Raiders	1985
666	Greg Pruitt, Raiders	1983

TEAM STATISTICS

	GB	OPP
First Downs	338	248
Rushing	118	74
Passing	197	151
Penalty	23	23
Rushes	465	400
Yards Gained	1,838	1,416
Average Gain	3.95	3.54
Average Yards per Game	114.9	88.5
Passes Attempted	548	544
Completed	328	283
% Completed	59.85	52.02
Total Yards Gained	3,938	2,942
Times Sacked	40	37
Yards Lost	241	202
Net Yards Gained	3,697	2,740
Yards Gained per Completion	12.01	10.40
Net Yards per Pass Play	6.29	4.72
Average Net Yards per Game	231.1	171.3
Combined Net Yards Gained	5,535	4,156
Total Plays	1,053	981
Average Yards per Play	5.26	4.24
Average Net Yards per Game	345.9	259.8
Third Down Efficiency	97/219	74/226
Percentage	44.29	32.74
Fourth Down Efficiency	5/11	14/22
Percentage	45.45	63.63
Intercepted By	26	13
Yards Returned	524	98
Returned for TD	3	0
Punts	68	90
Yards Punted	2,886	3,876
Average Yards per Punt	42.44	43.07
Punt Returns	58	29
Yards Returned	875	237
Average Yards per Return	15.09	8.17
Returned for TD	3	0
Kickoff Returns	47	76
Yards Returned	1,038	1,649
Average Yards per Return	22.09	21.70
Returned for TD	1	0
Penalties	92	107
Yards Penalized	714	797
Fumbles	33	25
Lost	11	13
Own Recovered for Touchdown	1	0
Opponent's Recovered by	12	11
Opponent's Recovered for Touchdown	0	0
Total Points Scored	456	210
Total Touchdowns	56	19
Touchdowns Rushing	9	7
Touchdowns Passing	39	12
Touchdowns on Returns & Recoveries	8	0
Extra Points (Kicking)	51	17
Two-Point Conversions	2/3	1/2
Safeties	1	1
Field Goals Attempted	27	27
Field Goals Made	21	25
% Successful	77.78	92.59
Average Time of Possession	31:44	28:16

Regular Season   13-3-0

Date	GB		OPP	Att.
9/1	34	at Tampa Bay Buccaneers	3	(54,102)
9/9	39	Philadelphia Eagles	13	(60,666)
9/15	42	San Diego Chargers	10	(60,584)
9/22	21	at Minnesota Vikings	30	(64,168)
9/29	31	at Seattle Seahawks	10	(59,973)
10/6	37	at Chicago Bears	6	(65,480)
10/14	23	San Francisco 49ers (OT)	20	(60,716)
10/27	13	Tampa Bay Buccaneers	7	(60,627)
11/3	28	Detroit Lions	18	(60,695)
11/10	20	at Kansas City Chiefs	27	(79,281)
11/18	6	at Dallas Cowboys	21	(65,032)
11/24	24	at St. Louis Rams	9	(61,499)
12/1	28	Chicago Bears	17	(59,682)
12/8	41	Denver Broncos	6	(60,712)
12/15	31	at Detroit Lions	3	(73,214)
12/22	38	Minnesota Vikings	10	(59,306)

Postseason   3-0-0

1/4	35	San Francisco 49ers	14	(60,787)
1/12	30	Carolina Panthers	13	(60,215)
1/26	35	Patriots (Super Bowl)	21	(72,301)

Score By Periods

	1	2	3	4	OT	Total
Packers	76	125	136	116	3	456
Opponents	32	96	25	57	0	210

INDIVIDUAL STATISTICS

Rushing	Att	Yds	Avg	LG	TD
E. Bennett	222	899	4.0	23	2
Levens	121	566	4.7	24	5
Favre	49	136	2.8	23	2
Henderson	39	130	3.3	14	0
Jervey	26	106	4.1	12	0
R. Brooks	4	2	0.5	6	0
McMahon	4	-1	-0.3	2	0
Packers	**465**	**1,838**	**4.0**	**24**	**9**
Opponents	400	1,416	3.5	t37	7

Receiving	No	Yds	Avg	LG	TD
Freeman	56	933	16.7	t51	9
K. Jackson	40	505	12.6	t51	10
Beebe	39	699	17.9	t80	4
Levens	31	226	7.3	49	5
E. Bennett	31	176	5.7	t25	1
Chmura	28	370	13.2	29	0
Henderson	27	203	7.5	27	1
R. Brooks	23	344	15.0	38	4
Mickens	18	161	8.9	19	2
Rison	13	135	10.4	t22	1
D. Howard	13	95	7.3	12	0
Mayes	6	46	7.7	12	2
Thomason	3	45	15.0	24	0
Packers	**328**	**3,938**	**12.0**	**t80**	**39**
Opponents	283	2,942	10.4	69	12

Passing	Att	Com	Yds	Pct	TD	In	Tk/Yds	Rate
Favre	543	325	3,899	59.9	39	13	40/241	95.8
McMahon	4	3	39	75.0	0	0	0/0	105.2
Hentrich	1	0	0	00.0	0	0	0/0	39.6
Packers	**548**	**328**	**3,938**	**59.9**	**39**	**13**	**40/241**	**95.7**
Opponents	544	283	2,942	52.0	12	26	37/202	55.4

Punting	No	Yds	Avg	Net	TB	In20	LG	HB
Hentrich	68	2,886	42.4	36.3	9	28	65	0
Packers	**68**	**2,886**	**42.4**	**36.3**	**9**	**28**	**65**	**0**
Opponents	90	3,876	43.1	32.5	4	15	63	1

Kickoff Returns	No	Yds	Avg	LG	TD
D. Howard	22	460	20.9	40	0
Beebe	15	403	26.9	t90	1
Levens	5	84	16.8	29	0
Henderson	2	38	19.0	23	0
Thomason	1	20	20.0	20	0
Jervey	1	17	17.0	17	0
Freeman	1	16	16.0	16	0
Packers	**47**	**1,038**	**22.1**	**t90**	**1**
Opponents	76	1,649	21.7	45	0

Punt Returns	No	Yds	Avg	FC	LG	TD
D. Howard	58	875	15.1	16	t92	3
Prior	0	0	0.0	1	0	0
Packers	**58**	**875**	**15.1**	**17**	**t92**	**3**
Opponents	29	237	8.2	15	26	0

Interceptions	No	Yds	Avg	LG	TD
E. Robinson	6	107	17.8	39	0
L. Butler	5	149	29.8	t90	1
D. Evans	5	102	20.4	63	1
Koonce	3	84	28.0	t75	1
Newsome	2	22	11.0	20	0
R. White	1	46	46.0	46	0
Prior	1	7	7.0	7	0
Dowden	1	5	5.0	5	0
Hollinquest	1	2	2.0	2	0
Simmons	1	0	0.0	0	0
Packers	**26**	**524**	**20.2**	**t90**	**3**
Opponents	13	98	7.5	41	0

Scoring	TDr	TDp	TDrt	PAT	2pt	FG	S	TP
Jacke	0	0	0	51/53	0	21/27	0	114
K. Jackson	0	10	0	0/0	0	0/0	0	60
Levens	5	5	0	0/0	0	0/0	0	60
Freeman	0	9	0	0/0	0	0/0	0	54
Beebe	0	4	2	0/0	0	0/0	0	36
R. Brooks	0	4	0	0/0	0	0/0	0	24
E. Bennett	2	1	0	0/0	0	0/0	0	22
D. Howard	0	0	3	0/0	0	0/0	0	18
Favre	0	0	0	0/0	0	0/0	0	12
Mayes	0	2	0	0/0	0	0/0	0	12
Mickens	0	2	0	0/0	0	0/0	0	12
L. Butler	0	0	1	0/0	0	0/0	0	6
D. Evans	0	0	1	0/0	0	0/0	0	6
Henderson	0	1	0	0/0	0	0/0	0	6
Koonce	0	0	1	0/0	0	0/0	0	6
Rison	0	1	0	0/0	0	0/0	0	6
Packers	**9**	**39**	**8**	**51/53**	**2**	**21/27**	**1**	**456**
Opponents	7	12	0	17/17	1	25/27	1	210

2-point conversions: Packers (2-3); Opponents (1-2)

Fumbles	Fum	Ow	Op	Yds	Tot
Arthur	1	0	0	0	0
Beebe	1	1	0	0	1
E. Bennett	2	1	0	0	1
L. Butler	0	1	1	2	2
E. Dotson	0	1	0	0	1
S. Dotson	0	0	1	8	1
D. Evans	0	1	1	2	1
Favre	11	5	0	-10	5
Freeman	3	1	0	14	1
Henderson	1	0	0	0	0
Hentrich	0	0	1	0	1
D. Howard	2	1	0	0	1
Jervey	4	1	0	0	1
S. Jones	0	0	1	0	1
Koonce	0	0	1	0	1
Levens	0	0	1	0	1
McMahon	1	0	0	0	1
Mickens	1	1	0	0	1
Newsome	0	1	0	0	1
Rison	1	0	0	0	0
A. Taylor	0	0	1	0	1
R. White	2	0	3	2	3
B. Williams	0	0	3	0	3
T. Williams	0	0	1	0	1
Winters	0	1	0	0	1
Packers	**33**	**19**	**12**	**18**	**31**

Quarterback Sacks	No.
R. White	8.5
L. Butler	6.5
S. Dotson	5.5
S. Jones	5.0
D. Evans	3.0
Wilkins	3.0
Simmons	2.5
G. Brown	1.0
K. McKenzie	1.0
Clavelle	0.5
B. Williams	0.5
Packers	**37.0**
Opponents	40.0

NFL STANDINGS

National Conference

Eastern Division	W	L	T	Pct	PF	PA
Dallas Cowboys	10	6	0	625	286	250
Philadelphia Eagles	10	6	0	625	363	341
Washington Redskins	9	7	0	563	364	312
Arizona Cardinals	7	9	0	438	300	397
New York Giants	6	10	0	375	242	297

Central Division	W	L	T	Pct	PF	PA
Green Bay Packers	**13**	**3**	**0**	**813**	**456**	**210**
Minnesota Vikings	9	7	0	563	298	315
Chicago Bears	7	9	0	438	283	305
Tampa Bay Buccaneers	6	10	0	375	221	293
Detroit Lions	5	11	0	313	302	368

Western Division	W	L	T	Pct	PF	PA
Carolina Panthers	12	4	0	750	367	218
San Francisco 49ers	12	4	0	750	398	257
St. Louis Rams	6	10	0	375	303	409
Atlanta Falcons	3	13	0	188	309	461
New Orleans Saints	3	13	0	188	229	339

American Conference

Eastern Division	W	L	T	Pct	PF	PA
New England Patriots	11	5	0	688	418	313
Buffalo Bills	10	6	0	625	319	266
Indianapolis Colts	9	7	0	563	317	334
Miami Dolphins	8	8	0	500	339	325
New York Jets	1	15	0	063	279	454

Central Division	W	L	T	Pct	PF	PA
Pittsburgh Steelers	10	6	0	625	344	257
Jacksonville Jaguars	9	7	0	563	325	335
Cincinnati Bengals	8	8	0	500	372	369
Houston Oilers	8	8	0	500	345	319
Baltimore Ravens	4	12	0	250	371	441

Western Division	W	L	T	Pct	PF	PA
Denver Broncos	13	3	0	813	391	275
Kansas City Chiefs	9	7	0	563	297	300
San Diego Chargers	8	8	0	500	310	376
Oakland Raiders	7	9	0	438	340	293
Seattle Seahawks	7	9	0	438	317	376

ROSTER

No	Name	Pos	Ht	Wt	DOB	College	G
50	Arthur, Mike	C	6-3	280	05/07/68	Texas A&M	5
82	Beebe, Don	WR	5-11	183	12/18/64	Chadron State	16
34	Bennett, Edgar	RB	6-0	217	02/15/69	Florida State	16
22	Brooks, Bucky	CB	6-0	195	01/22/71	North Carolina	2
87	Brooks, Robert	WR	6-0	180	06/23/70	South Carolina	7
68	Brown, Gary	T	6-4	315	06/25/71	Georgia Tech	8
93	Brown, Gilbert	NT	6-2	325	02/22/71	Kansas	16
36	Butler, LeRoy	S	6-0	200	07/19/68	Florida State	16
89	Chmura, Mark	TE	6-5	250	02/22/69	Boston College	13
91	Clavelle, Shannon	DE	6-2	287	10/12/72	Colorado	8
54	Cox, Ron	LB	6-2	235	03/29/68	Fresno State	16
67	Dellenbach, Jeff	C	6-6	300	02/14/63	Wisconsin	3
72	Dotson, Earl	T	6-3	315	12/17/70	Texas A&I	15
71	Dotson, Santana	DT	6-5	285	12/19/69	Baylor	16
42	Dowden, Corey	CB	5-11	190	10/18/68	Tulane	9
33	Evans, Doug	CB	6-1	190	05/13/70	Louisiana Tech	16
4	Favre, Brett	QB	6-2	225	10/10/69	Southern Mississippi	16
86	Freeman, Antonio	WR	6-0?	190	05/27/72	Virginia Tech	12
55	Harris, Bernardo	LB	6-2	243	10/15/71	North Carolina	16
40	Hayes, Chris	S	6-0	200	05/07/72	Washington State	2
30	Henderson, William	FB	6-1	248	02/19/71	North Carolina	16
17	Hentrich, Craig	P	6-3	200	05/18/71	Notre Dame	16
90	Holland, Darius	DT	6-4	310	11/10/73	Colorado	16
56	Hollinquest, Lamont	LB	6-3	243	10/24/70	USC	16
81	Howard, Desmond	WR	5-10	180	05/15/70	Michigan	16
13	Jacke, Chris	K	6-0	205	03/12/66	Texas-El Paso	16
88	Jackson, Keith	TE	6-2	258	04/19/65	Oklahoma	16
32	Jervey, Travis	RB	5-11?	225	05/05/72	The Citadel	16
27	Jones, Calvin	RB	5-11	205	11/27/70	Nebraska	1
96	Jones, Sean	DE	6-7	283	12/19/62	Northeastern	15
65	Knapp, Lindsey	G	6-6	300	02/25/70	Notre Dame	9
53	Koonce, George	LB	6-1	243	10/15/68	East Carolina	16
94	Kuberski, Bob	NT	6-4	295	04/05/71	Navy	1
25	Levens, Dorsey	RB	6-1	235	05/21/70	Georgia Tech	16
80	Mayes, Derrick	WR	6-0	200	01/28/74	Notre Dame	7
60	McGuire, Gene	C	6-2	285	07/17/70	Notre Dame	8
95	McKenzie, Keith	DE	6-3	242	10/17/73	Ball State	10
9	McMahon, Jim	QB	6-1	195	08/21/59	BYU	5
77	Michels, John	T	6-7	290	03/19/73	USC	15
85	Mickens, Terry	WR	6-0	198	02/21/71	Florida A&M	8
81	Morgan, Anthony	WR	6-1	200	11/15/67	Tennessee	3
28	Mullen, Roderick	CB	6-1	204	12/05/72	Grambling State	14
21	Newsome, Craig	CB	6-0	190	08/10/71	Arizona State	16
18	Pederson, Doug	QB	6-3	215	01/31/68	Northeast Louisiana	1
39	Prior, Mike	S	6-0	208	11/14/63	Illinois State	16
84	Rison, Andre	WR	6-1	195	03/18/67	Michigan State	5
41	Robinson, Eugene	S	6-0	195	05/28/63	Colgate	16
46	Robinson, Michael	CB	6-1	192	06/24/73	Hampton	6
75	Ruettgers, Ken	T	6-5	292	08/20/62	USC	4
38	Satterfield, Brian	FB	6-0	225	12/22/69	North Alabama	1
59	Simmons, Wayne	LB	6-2	248	12/15/69	Clemson	16
49	Smith, Kevin	TE	6-4	255	07/25/69	UCLA	1
73	Taylor, Aaron	G	6-4	305	11/14/72	Notre Dame	16
83	Thomason, Jeff	TE	6-4	250	12/30/69	Oregon	16
63	Timmerman, Adam	G	6-4	295	08/14/71	South Dakota State	16
92	White, Reggie	DE	6-5	300	12/19/61	Tennessee	16
64	Wilkerson, Bruce	T	6-5	305	07/28/64	Tennessee	14
98	Wilkins, Gabe	DE	6-4	305	09/01/71	Gardner-Webb	16
51	Williams, Brian	LB	6-1	235	12/17/72	USC	16
37	Williams, Tyrone	CB	5-11	195	05/31/73	Nebraska	16
52	Winters, Frank	C	6-3	295	01/23/64	West Illinois	16

DRAFT

Rnd	Name	Pos	Ht	Wt	College
1	John Michels (27)	T	6-7	282	USC
2	Derrick Mayes (56)	WR	6-0	204	Notre Dame
3a	Mike Flanagan (90)	C	6-5	290	UCLA
3b	Tyrone Williams (93)	DB	5-11	195	Nebraska
	(Free agent compensatory pick)				
4	Chris Darkins (123)	RB	6-0	215	Minnesota
5	(Choice (161) to Chiefs for Lindsay Knapp)				

Rnd	Name	Pos	Ht	Wt	College
6a	(Choice (197) to Eagles for Joe Sims)				
6b	Marco Rivera (208)	G	6-4	295	Penn State
	(Free agent compensatory pick)				
7a	Kyle Wachholtz (240)	QB	6-4	235	USC
7b	Keith McKenzie (252)	LB	6-3	238	Ball State
	(Free agent compensatory pick)				

FRONT ROW: (L-R) 4 Brett Favre, 9 Jim McMahon, 13 Chris Jacke, 17 Craig Hentrich, 18 Doug Pederson, 21 Craig Newsome, 25 Dorsey Levens, 28 Roderick Mullen, 30 William Henderson, 32 Travis Jervey.

SECOND ROW: (L-R) Tight Ends/Assistant Offensive Line Coach Andy Reid, Offensive Line Coach Tom Lovat, Quarterbacks Coach Marty Mornhinweg, Running Backs Coach Harry Sydney, Wide Receivers Coach Gil Haskell, Offensive Coordinator Sherman Lewis, Head Coach Mike Holmgren, Defensive Coordinator Fritz Shurmur, Defensive Line Coach Larry Brooks, Linebackers Coach Jim Lind, Defensive Assistant/Quality Control Johnny Holland, Defensive Backs Coach Bob Valesente, Strength and Conditioning Coach Kent Johnston, Special Teams Coach Nolan Cromwell.

THIRD ROW: (L-R) 33 Doug Evans, 34 Edgar Bennett, 36 LeRoy Butler, 37 Tyrone Williams, 39 Mike Prior, 41 Eugene Robinson, 42 Corey Dowden, 49 Kevin Smith, 50 Mike Arthur, 51 Brian Williams, 52 Frank Winters.

FOURTH ROW: (L-R) 53 George Koonce, 54 Ron Cox, 55 Bernardo Harris, 56 Lamont Hollinquest, 59 Wayne Simmons, 62 Marco Rivera, 63 Adam Timmerman, 64 Bruce Wilkerson, 65 Lindsay Knapp, 68 Gary Brown.

FIFTH ROW: (L-R) 71 Santana Dotson, 72 Earl Dotson, 73 Aaron Taylor, 75 Ken Ruettgers, 77 John Michels, 80 Derrick Mayes, 81 Desmond Howard, 82 Don Beebe, 83 Jeff Thomason, 85 Terry Mickens, 86 Antonio Freeman.

SIXTH ROW: (L-R) 87 Robert Brooks, 88 Keith Jackson, 89 Mark Chmura, 90 Darius Holland, 91 Shannon Clavelle, 92 Reggie White, 93 Gilbert Brown, 94 Bob Kuberski, 95 Keith McKenzie, 96 Sean Jones, 98 Gabe Wilkins.

BACK ROW: (L-R) Strength and Conditioning Assistant Barry Rubin, Offensive Assistant/Quality Control Gary Reynolds, Corporate Security Officer Jerry Parins, Training Room Intern Andre Daniel, Assistant Trainer Sam Ramsden, Assistant Trainer Kurt Fielding, Head Trainer Pepper Burruss, Associate Team Physician Dr. John Gray, Team Physician Dr. Patrick J. McKenzie, Equipment Manager Gordon (Red) Batty, Assistant Equipment Manager Bryan Nehring, Assistant Equipment Manager Tom Bakken, Equipment Assistant Tim O'Neill, Video Assistant Chris Kirby, Assistant Video Director Bob Eckberg, Video Director Al Treml.

LeRoy Butler's exuberance was understandable. He just wasn't being realistic.

During the preseason, the Packers' strong safety predicted his team would go unbeaten in 1997. A Super Bowl win and a spotless exhibition record can do that to a player.

There was no question Green Bay was again an elite team. But these Packers were not the Miami Dolphins of 1972. It took only two weeks' time and the Philadelphia Eagles to make Butler's prediction go awry.

Green Bay won five of its first seven games, but none were blowouts as had been the case the previous year. The team hit stride after the bye week by defeating the Patriots 28-10 in a rematch of the Super Bowl. Then, aside from an embarrassing loss to winless Indianapolis, the team couldn't be stopped as it rolled to a 13-3 record and made up for past indignities with a pair of sweet, decisive wins over the Cowboys and Vikings.

Head coach Mike Holmgren sent a message to his team and fans alike when he dropped all of his paid television and radio commitments for the season. His mission was clear: Get the Packers back to the Super Bowl.

The team experienced relatively little turnover. Sean Jones, Keith Jackson, and Jim McMahon retired. Desmond Howard and Andre Rison took their services elsewhere. Chris Jacke was not re-signed in favor of third-round pick Brett Conway.

Linebacker Seth Joyner (free agent), running back Aaron Hayden (waivers) and long snapper Rob Davis (free agent) were notable players signed by the Packers. Joyner was a disappointment (34 tackles, 10th on the team), but Hayden provided depth, and Davis played quietly but efficiently into the next decade.

Brett Favre was named league MVP for a third consecutive year, sharing the honor with the Lions' Barry Sanders. The durable quarterback ran his streak of regular-season starts to 93 (106 counting playoffs).

While Favre didn't miss a beat, others were not as fortunate. Running back Edgar Bennett tore the Achilles' tendon in his left foot in the preseason opener and was placed on injured reserve. George Koonce remained on the physically unable to perform list until the final five games, as he rehabilitated the knee he injured a year earlier against the 49ers in the playoffs.

Green Bay dropped from the ranks of the unbeaten in Week 2 in Philadelphia. Rookie kicker Ryan Longwell, who took over for Conway after he suffered a season-ending quadriceps injury in training camp, missed a 28-yard field goal with 11 seconds left in a 10-9 loss.

Three weeks later, the Packers were dealt their second loss 26-15 in Detroit. Don Beebe was knocked unconscious after taking a hit from safety Mark Carrier and Favre threw three interceptions, including one from his knees that linebacker Reggie Brown returned for a score.

Gabe Wilkins' 77-yard interception return against the Buccaneers and Bears coach Dave Wannestedt's decision to go for a 2-point conversion attempt that failed helped Green Bay squeeze out wins over Tampa Bay 21-16 and Chicago 24-23.

His team 5-2, Holmgren made excellent use of the bye week. He gave his players an entire week off to recharge and added a hurry-up, no huddle offense that served to revive the club in its 28-10 win over New England on Monday night.

"We played tonight like champions are supposed to play," Packers general manager Ron Wolf said.

Green Bay clamped down on the Lions (256 total yards) and Rams (269) to improve to 8-2. But for reasons unknown, the Green and Gold lost a 41-38 shootout in Indianapolis against a winless Colts team headed by former Packers coach Lindy Infante.

"I'd be lying if I said this wasn't really special," Infante said. "I'm human like anybody else. It's especially gratifying."

Green Bay closed out with five wins, the most satisfying coming at the expense of the Cowboys and Vikings. Dorsey Levens rushed for a franchise-record 190 yards on 33 carries in a 45-17 ambush of the Cowboys at Lambeau Field. Eight days later, he churned out 108 yards on 31 carries in a 27-11 win in the Metrodome.

"I don't want to be too premature and say we're back," safety Eugene Robinson said. "But I think we are."

THE 100-YARD DAY PARADE

Marshall Faulk, Barry Sanders, Terry Glenn, and a host of other players had big offensive showings against the Packers in 1997. Thirteen players combined to post 15 100-yard days, the most Green Bay has given up in one season.

The Packers' defense slipped from first in 1996 to seventh in 1997. Its run defense dropped from fourth to 20th.

With the exception of Games 12-14, Green Bay allowed at least one individual 100-yard effort every week. The parade started with the Bears' Raymont Harris (122 yards rushing) in Week 1 and ended with the Bills' Quinn Early (120 yards receiving) in the season finale.

Terry Glenn of the Patriots had the best outing in terms of yards. The wide receiver caught seven passes for 163 yards in a 28-10 loss on Oct. 27.

Listed below are the years in which the Packers gave up the most individual 100-yard rushing/receiving performances:

No.	Year	Rushing/Receiving
15	1997	8/7
13	1983	9/4
12	1985	7/5
12	1990	5/7
12	1995	4/8

1997

TEAM STATISTICS

	GB	OPP
First Downs	325	288
Rushing	103	105
Passing	191	156
Penalty	31	27
Rushes	459	443
Yards Gained	1,909	1,876
Average Gain	4.16	4.23
Average Yards per Game	119.3	117.3
Passes Attempted	523	563
Completed	309	288
% Completed	59.08	51.15
Total Yards Gained	3,896	3,225
Times Sacked	26	41
Yards Lost	191	274
Net Yards Gained	3,705	2,951
Yards Gained per Completion	12.61	11.20
Net Yards per Pass Play	6.75	4.89
Average Net Yards per Game	231.6	184.4
Combined Net Yards Gained	5,614	4,827
Total Plays	1,008	1,047
Average Yards per Play	5.57	4.61
Average Net Yards per Game	350.9	301.7
Third Down Efficiency	80/202	77/232
Percentage	39.60	33.19
Fourth Down Efficiency	5/5	12/24
Percentage	100.0	50.0
Intercepted By	21	16
Yards Returned	329	305
Returned for TD	3	3
Punts	75	90
Yards Punted	3,378	3,828
Average Yards per Punt	45.04	42.53
Punt Returns	56	32
Yards Returned	515	255
Average Yards per Return	9.20	7.97
Returned for TD	0	0
Kickoff Returns	49	78
Yards Returned	1,119	1,599
Average Yards per Return	22.84	20.50
Returned for TD	0	0
Penalties	93	114
Yards Penalized	718	945
Fumbles	24	25
Lost	16	11
Own Recovered for Touchdown	0	0
Opponent's Recovered by	11	16
Opponent's Recovered for Touchdown	3	1
Total Points Scored	422	282
Total Touchdowns	50	30
Touchdowns Rushing	9	16
Touchdowns Passing	35	10
Touchdowns on Returns & Recoveries	6	4
Extra Points (Kicking)	48	18
Two-Point Conversions	1/2	6/12
Safeties	0	0
Field Goals Attempted	30	30
Field Goals Made	24	24
% Successful	80.00	80.00
Average Time of Possession	30:05	29:55

Regular Season   13-3-0

Date	GB		OPP	Att.
9/1	38	Chicago Bears	24	(60,766)
9/7	9	at Philadelphia Eagles	10	(66,803)
9/14	23	Miami Dolphins	18	(60,075)
9/21	38	Minnesota Vikings	32	(60,115)
9/28	15	at Detroit Lions	26	(78,110)
10/5	21	Tampa Bay Buccaneers	16	(60,100)
10/12	24	at Chicago Bears	23	(62,212)
10/27	28	at New England Patriots	10	(59,972)
11/2	20	Detroit Lions	10	(60,126)
11/9	17	St. Louis Rams	7	(60,093)
11/16	38	at Indianapolis Colts	41	(60,928)
11/23	45	Dallas Cowboys	17	(60,111)
12/1	27	at Minnesota Vikings	11	(64,001)
12/7	17	at Tampa Bay Buccaneers	6	(73,523)
12/14	31	at Carolina Panthers	10	(70,887)
12/20	31	Buffalo Bills	21	(60,108)

Postseason   2-1-0

1/4	21	Tampa Bay Buccaneers	7	(60,327)
1/11	23	at San Francisco 49ers	10	(68,987)
1/25	24	Broncos at Qualcomm Stadium	31	(68,912)

Score By Periods

	1	2	3	4	OT	Total
Packers	82	151	87	102	0	422
Opponents	48	78	56	100	0	282

INDIVIDUAL STATISTICS

Rushing

	Att	Yds	Avg	LG	TD
Levens	329	1,435	4.4	t52	7
Favre	58	187	3.2	16	1
Hayden	32	148	4.6	21	1
Henderson	31	113	3.6	15	0
R. Brooks	2	19	9.5	15	0
Freeman	1	14	14.0	14	0
Bono	3	-3	-1.0	-1	0
Pederson	3	-4	-1.3	-1	0
Packers	**459**	**1,909**	**4.2**	**t52**	**9**
Opponents	443	1,876	4.2	t68	16

Receiving

	No	Yds	Avg	LG	TD
Freeman	81	1,243	15.3	t58	12
R. Brooks	60	1,010	16.8	48	7
Levens	53	370	7.0	56	5
Henderson	41	367	9.0	25	1
Chmura	38	417	11.0	t32	6
Mayes	18	290	16.1	74	0
Thomason	9	115	12.8	27	1
Beebe	2	28	14.0	23	0
T. Davis	2	28	14.0	26	1
Schroeder	2	15	7.5	8	1
Hayden	2	11	5.5	7	0
Mickens	1	2	2.0	t2	1
Packers	**309**	**3,896**	**12.6**	**74**	**35**
Opponents	288	3,225	11.2	62	10

Passing

	Att	Com	Yds	Pct	TD	In	Tk/Yds	Rate
Favre	513	304	3,867	59.3	35	16	25/176	92.6
Bono	10	5	29	50.0	0	0	1/15	56.3
Packers	**523**	**309**	**3,896**	**59.1**	**35**	**16**	**26/191**	**91.9**
Opponents	563	288	3,225	51.2	10	21	41/274	59.0

Punting

	No	Yds	Avg	Net	TB	In20	LG	HB
Hentrich	75	3,378	45.0	36.0	21	26	65	0
Packers	**75**	**3,378**	**45.0**	**36.0**	**21**	**26**	**65**	**0**
Opponents	90	3,828	42.5	36.6	1	29	59	1

Kickoff Returns

	No	Yds	Avg	LG	TD
Schroeder	24	562	23.4	40	0
Preston	7	211	30.1	43	0
Hayden	6	141	23.5	35	0
Beebe	6	134	22.3	39	0
Darkins	4	68	17.0	20	0
Sharper	1	3	3.0	3	0
Mickens	1	0	0.0	0	0
Packers	**49**	**1,119**	**22.8**	**43**	**0**
Opponents	78	1,599	20.5	49	0

Punt Returns

	No	Yds	Avg	FC	LG	TD
Schroeder	33	342	10.4	8	46	0
Mayes	14	141	10.1	3	26	0
Sharper	7	32	4.6	3	23	0
Preston	1	0	0.0	1	0	0
Prior	1	0	0.0	3	0	0
Packers	**56**	**515**	**9.2**	**17**	**46**	**0**
Opponents	32	255	8.0	15	38	0

Interceptions

	No	Yds	Avg	LG	TD
L. Butler	5	4	0.8	2	0
Prior	4	72	18.0	49	0
D. Evans	3	33	11.0	27	0
Sharper	2	70	35.0	t50	2
B. Williams	2	30	15.0	25	0
Wilkins	1	77	77.0	t77	1
E. Robinson	1	26	26.0	26	0
Mullen	1	17	17.0	17	0
B. Harris	1	0	0.0	0	0
T. Williams	1	0	0.0	0	0
Packers	**21**	**329**	**15.7**	**t77**	**3**
Opponents	16	305	19.1	t52	3

Scoring

	TDr	TDp	TDrt	PAT	2pt	FG	S	TP
Longwell	0	0	0	48/48	0	24/30	0	120
Levens	7	5	0	0/0	1	0/0	0	74
Freeman	0	12	0	0/0	0	0/0	0	72
R. Brooks	0	7	0	0/0	0	0/0	0	42
Chmura	0	6	0	0/0	0	0/0	0	36
Sharper	0	0	3	0/0	0	0/0	0	18
T. Davis	0	1	0	0/0	0	0/0	0	12
Wilkins	0	0	2	0/0	0	0/0	0	12
Favre	1	0	0	0/0	0	0/0	0	6
Hayden	1	0	0	0/0	0	0/0	0	6
Henderson	0	1	0	0/0	0	0/0	0	6
Mickens	0	1	0	0/0	0	0/0	0	6
Schroeder	0	1	0	0/0	0	0/0	0	6
Thomason	0	1	0	0/0	0	0/0	0	6
Packers	**9**	**35**	**6**	**48/48**	**1**	**24/30**	**0**	**422**
Opponents	16	10	4	18/18	6	24/30	0	282

2-point conversions: Packers (1-2); Opponents (6-12)

Fumbles

	Fum	Ow	Op	Yds	Tot
Bono	1	0	0	0	0
L. Butler	0	1	0	0	1
Chmura	1	0	0	0	0
T. Davis	0	0	1	0	1
E. Dotson	0	1	0	0	1
Favre	7	1	0	-10	1
Freeman	1	0	0	0	0
Henderson	1	2	0	0	2
Levens	5	1	0	-7	1
Mullen	0	0	1	1	1
Prior	1	0	0	0	0
E. Robinson	1	0	2	0	2
Schroeder	1	0	0	0	0
Sharper	1	0	1	34	1
Thomason	1	0	0	0	0
R. White	0	0	2	0	2
Wilkins	0	0	3	1	3
B. Williams	0	0	1	0	1
Packers	**24**	**7**	**11**	**19**	**18**

Quarterback Sacks

	No.
R. White	11.0
S. Dotson	5.5
Wilkins	5.5
G. Brown	3.0
L. Butler	3.0
Joyner	3.0
E. Robinson	2.5
K. McKenzie	1.5
D. Evans	1.0
B. Harris	1.0
J. Smith	1.0
B. Williams	1.0
team	2.0
Packers	**41.0**
Opponents	26.0

NFL STANDINGS

National Conference

Eastern Division	W	L	T	Pct	PF	PA
New York Giants	10	5	1	656	307	265
Washington Redskins	8	7	1	531	327	289
Philadelphia Eagles	6	9	1	406	317	372
Dallas Cowboys	6	10	0	375	304	314
Arizona Cardinals	4	12	0	250	283	379

Central Division	W	L	T	Pct	PF	PA
Green Bay Packers	13	3	0	813	422	282
Tampa Bay Buccaneers	10	6	0	625	299	263
Detroit Lions	9	7	0	563	379	306
Minnesota Vikings	9	7	0	563	354	359
Chicago Bears	4	12	0	250	263	421

Western Division	W	L	T	Pct	PF	PA
San Francisco 49ers	13	3	0	813	375	265
Carolina Panthers	7	9	0	438	265	314
Atlanta Falcons	7	9	0	438	320	361
New Orleans Saints	6	10	0	375	237	327
St. Louis Rams	5	11	0	313	299	359

American Conference

Eastern Division	W	L	T	Pct	PF	PA
New England Patriots	10	6	0	625	369	289
Miami Dolphins	9	7	0	563	339	327
New York Jets	9	7	0	563	348	287
Buffalo Bills	6	10	0	375	255	367
Indianapolis Colts	3	13	0	188	313	401

Central Division	W	L	T	Pct	PF	PA
Pittsburgh Steelers	11	5	0	688	372	307
Jacksonville Jaguars	11	5	0	688	394	318
Tennessee Oilers	8	8	0	500	333	310
Cincinnati Bengals	7	9	0	438	355	405
Baltimore Ravens	6	9	1	406	326	345

Western Division	W	L	T	Pct	PF	PA
Kansas City Chiefs	13	3	0	813	375	232
Denver Broncos	12	4	0	750	472	287
Seattle Seahawks	8	8	0	500	365	362
Oakland Raiders	4	12	0	250	324	419
San Diego Chargers	4	12	0	250	266	425

ROSTER

No	Name	Pos	Ht	Wt	DOB	College	G
82	Beebe, Don	WR	5-11	185	12/18/64	Chadron State	10
13	Bono, Steve	QB	6-4	212	05/11/62	UCLA	2
22	Brooks, Bucky	CB	6-0	195	01/22/71	North Carolina	3
87	Brooks, Robert	WR	6-0	180	06/23/70	South Carolina	15
93	Brown, Gilbert	NT	6-2	345	02/22/71	Kansas	12
36	Butler, LeRoy	S	6-0	200	07/19/68	Florida State	16
89	Chmura, Mark	TE	6-5	253	02/22/69	Boston College	15
91	Clavelle, Shannon	DE	6-2	287	10/12/72	Colorado	6
26	Collins, Mark	CB	5-10	202	01/16/64	Cal State-Fullerton	1
44	Darkins, Chris	RB	6-0	210	04/30/74	Minnesota	14
60	Davis, Rob	LS	6-3	288	12/10/68	Shippensburg	7
81	Davis, Tyrone	TE	6-4	245	06/30/72	Virginia	13
67	Dellenbach, Jeff	C	6-6	300	02/14/63	Wisconsin	14
72	Dotson, Earl	T	6-3	315	12/17/70	Texas A&I	13
71	Dotson, Santana	DT	6-5	285	12/19/69	Baylor	16
33	Evans, Doug	CB	6-1	190	05/13/70	Louisiana Tech	15
4	Favre, Brett	QB	6-2	225	10/10/69	Southern Mississippi	16
97	Frase, Paul	DE	6-5	267	05/06/65	Syracuse	8
86	Freeman, Antonio	WR	6-0?	190	05/27/72	Virginia Tech	16
55	Harris, Bernardo	LB	6-2	243	10/15/71	North Carolina	16
24	Hayden, Aaron	RB	6-0	216	04/13/73	Tennessee	14
30	Henderson, William	FB	6-1	248	02/19/71	North Carolina	16
17	Hentrich, Craig	P	6-3	200	05/18/71	Notre Dame	16
90	Holland, Darius	DT	6-4	320	11/10/73	Colorado	12
56	Hollinquest, Lamont	LB	6-3	250	10/24/70	USC	16
32	Jervey, Travis	RB	5-11?	222	05/05/72	The Citadel	16
88	Johnson, Reggie	TE	6-2	256	01/27/68	Florida State	4
54	Joyner, Seth	LB	6-2	245	11/18/64	Texas-El Paso	11
43	Kinder, Randy	CB	6-1	213	04/04/75	Notre Dame	6
53	Koonce, George	LB	6-1	243	10/15/68	East Carolina	4
94	Kuberski, Bob	NT	6-4	295	04/05/71	Navy	11
25	Levens, Dorsey	RB	6-1	230	05/21/70	Georgia Tech	16
8	Longwell, Ryan	K	6-0	185	08/16/74	California	16
80	Mayes, Derrick	WR	6-0	205	01/28/74	Notre Dame	12
38	McElmurry, Blaine	S	6-0	187	10/23/73	Montana	1
95	McKenzie, Keith	DE	6-3	255	10/17/73	Ball State	16
77	Michels, John	T	6-7	304	03/19/73	USC	9
85	Mickens, Terry	WR	6-0	201	02/21/71	Florida A&M	11
28	Mullen, Roderick	CB	6-1	204	12/05/72	Grambling State	16
21	Newsome, Craig	CB	6-0	190	08/10/71	Arizona State	1
18	Pederson, Doug	QB	6-3	215	01/31/68	Northeast Louisiana	1
88	Preston, Roell	WR	5-10	195	06/23/72	Mississippi	1
39	Prior, Mike	S	6-0	208	11/14/63	Illinois State	16
62	Rivera, Marco	G	6-4	295	04/26/72	Penn State	14
41	Robinson, Eugene	S	6-0	197	05/28/63	Colgate	16
84	Schroeder, Bill	WR	6-2	198	01/09/71	Wisconsin-La Crosse	15
42	Sharper, Darren	DB	6-2	205	11/03/75	William & Mary	14
59	Simmons, Wayne	LB	6-2	248	12/15/69	Clemson	6
99	Smith, Jermaine	DT	6-3	289	02/03/72	Georgia	9
73	Taylor, Aaron	G	6-4	305	11/14/72	Notre Dame	14
83	Thomason, Jeff	TE	6-4	250	12/30/69	Oregon	13
63	Timmerman, Adam	G	6-4	295	08/14/71	South Dakota State	16
78	Verba, Ross	T	6-4	299	10/31/73	Iowa	16
92	White, Reggie	DE	6-5	304	12/19/61	Tennessee	16
64	Wilkerson, Bruce	T	6-5	310	07/28/64	Tennessee	16
98	Wilkins, Gabe	DE	6-4	295	09/01/71	Gardner-Webb	16
51	Williams, Brian	LB	6-1	240	12/17/72	USC	16
96	Williams, Gerald	DL	6-3	290	09/08/63	Auburn	4
37	Williams, Tyrone	CB	5-11	195	05/31/73	Nebraska	16
52	Winters, Frank	C	6-3	300	01/23/64	West Illinois	13

DRAFT

Rnd	Name	Pos	Ht	Wt	College
1	Ross Verba (30)	T	6-4	299	Iowa
2	Darren Sharper (60)	DB	6-2	205	William & Mary
3	Brett Conway (90)	K	6-2	192	Penn State
4	Jermaine Smith (126)	DT	6-3	290	Georgia
5	Anthony Hicks (160)	LB	6-1	242	Arkansas
6	(Choice (193) to Raiders for Raiders' 7th-round pick (213))				

Rnd	Name	Pos	Ht	Wt	College
7a	Chris Miller (213)	WR	5-10	192	USC
	(Choice from Raiders in deal mentioned above)				
7b	Jerald Sowell (231)	RB	6-0	246	Tulane
7c	Ronnie McAda (240)	QB	6-3	202	Army
	(Free agent compensatory pick)				

FRONT ROW: (L-R) 4 Brett Favre, 8 Ryan Longwell, 10 Brett Conway, 13 Steve Bono, 17 Craig Hentrich, 18 Doug Pederson, 21 Craig Newsome, 24 Aaron Hayden, 25 Dorsey Levens, 28 Roderick Mullen, 30 William Henderson.

SECOND ROW: (L-R) Special Teams Coach Nolan Cromwell, Quarterbacks Coach Andy Reid, Tight Ends/Assistant Offensive Line Coach Mike Sherman, Offensive Line Coach Tom Lovat, Running Backs Coach Harry Sydney, Wide Receivers Coach Gil Haskell, Offensive Coordinator Sherman Lewis, Head Coach Mike Holmgren, Defensive Coordinator Fritz Shurmur, Defensive Line Coach Larry Brooks, Linebackers Coach Jim Lind, Defensive Assistant/Quality Control Johnny Holland, Defensive Backs Coach Bob Valesente, Strength and Conditioning Kent Johnston, Strength and Conditioning Assistant Barry Rubin.

THIRD ROW: (L-R) 32 Travis Jervey, 33 Doug Evans, 34 Edgar Bennett, 36 LeRoy Butler, 37 Tyrone Williams, 39 Mike Prior, 41 Eugene Robinson, 42 Darren Sharper, 44 Chris Darkins, 50 Anthony Hicks, 51 Brian Williams, 52 Frank Winters.

FOURTH ROW: (L-R) 53 George Koonce, 54 Seth Joyner, 55 Bernardo Harris, 56 Lamont Hollinquest, 58 Mike Flanagan, 59 Wayne Simmons, 62 Marco Rivera, 63 Adam Timmerman, 64 Bruce Wilkerson, 67 Jeff Dellenbach, 70 Joe Andruzzi.

FIFTH ROW: (L-R) 71 Santana Dotson, 72 Earl Dotson, 73 Aaron Taylor, 77 John Michels, 78 Ross Verba, 80 Derrick Mayes, 81 Tyrone Davis, 82 Don Beebe, 83 Jeff Thomason, 84 Bill Schroeder, 85 Terry Mickens, 86 Antonio Freeman.

SIXTH ROW: (L-R) 87 Robert Brooks, 89 Mark Chmura, 90 Darius Holland, 91 Shannon Clavelle, 92 Reggie White, 93 Gilbert Brown, 94 Bob Kuberski, 95 Keith McKenzie, 97 Paul Frase, 98 Gabe Wilkins, 99 Jermaine Smith.

BACK ROW: (L-R) Administrative Assistant/Football Bill Nayes, Offensive Assistant/Quality Control Gary Reynolds, Corporate Security Officer Jerry Parins, Training Room Intern Bryan Engle, Assistant Trainer Sam Ramsden, Assistant Trainer Kurt Fielding, Head Trainer Pepper Burruss, Associate Team Physician Dr. John Gray, Team Physician Dr. Patrick J. McKenzie, Equipment Manager Gordon (Red) Batty, Assistant Equipment Manager Bryan Nehring, Assistant Equipment Manager Tom Bakken, Equipment Assistant Tim O'Neill, Video Assistant Chris Kirby, Assistant Video Director Bob Eckberg, Video Director Al Treml.

An injured Dorsey Levens, Reggie White's retirement/unretirement, speculation about Mike Holmgren's future, and an abrupt end to one of the longest home-winning streaks in NFL history were all elements of the Packers' 1998 campaign, a season in which they went 11-5 and made the playoffs for a sixth consecutive year.

On Sept. 3, Levens, after holding out the entire preseason, signed a five-year, $25 million contract. Ten days later, he broke his fibula and suffered a severe ankle sprain. He missed nine games.

Raymont Harris and then Travis Jervey replaced Levens. After Jervey was lost for the year with an ankle injury on Nov. 9, Harris and then Darick Holmes took over. Holmes led the team in rushing with just 386 yards, and Green Bay's running attack dropped from 12th in 1997 to 25th in 1998.

On April 19, the NFL's all-time sack leader announced he was retiring. Two days later, White changed his mind. In his final season with the Packers, White recorded 16 sacks and was named defensive player of the year by the Associated Press.

In the week before the Super Bowl with Denver, Seattle reportedly contacted Holmgren about possibly becoming the Seahawks' head coach and general manager. While the reports were inaccurate, Holmgren's future became a topic of discussion.

In November, Packers general manager Ron Wolf predicted there was an 80 percent chance Holmgren would leave at season's end. After the Eagles game, Holmgren cursed at a fan who suggested the coach concentrate on his current job rather than the next one.

The Packers opened with four straight wins for the first time in 32 years. But that success was quickly overshadowed by a 37-24 setback to the Vikings on a rainy Monday night at Lambeau Field. The loss ended Green Bay's run of 25 consecutive regular-season wins at home, second only to Miami's string of 27 in a row (1971-74).

For the first time since 1994, Brett Favre was not the league MVP. The honor went to the Broncos' Terrell Davis.

Favre's receivers suffered their share of injuries. Nagging back and hamstring injuries hindered Robert Brooks. Bill Schroeder broke his collarbone in Tampa (Dec. 7), and hamstring injuries caused Corey Bradford and Tyrone Davis to be inactive for the final three weeks, although both returned for a playoff game with the 49ers.

Antonio Freeman became Favre's favorite target. He caught 84 passes for 1,424 yards and 14 touchdowns.

In November 1997, the Packers issued new stock for the first time since 1950. The shares sold for $200 each. The sale ended March 16 and raised more than $24 million.

On Oct. 5, the Packers (4-0) hosted the Vikings (4-0) in an early-season Central Division showdown. Randall Cunningham passed for 442 yards and rookie Randy Moss and veteran Cris Carter combined for 309 yards receiving.

Moss (190 yards) caught two of Cunningham's four touchdown throws.

The team's bye week followed. Unlike 1996 and 1997, the team did not come out of the bye with a win. Favre threw three interceptions and Barry Sanders rushed for 155 yards in a 27-20 Detroit win on Oct. 15.

Green Bay rebounded with wins over Baltimore and San Francisco to improve to 6-2. The Packers held the Ravens to 56 yards rushing (233 overall) and sacked 49ers quarterback Steve Young nine times.

After stumbling 27-20 in Pittsburgh, Green Bay put on a dominating performance in New York. Offensively, the Packers ran 81 plays to the Giants' 49, they outgained them 433 yards to 127, and they won easily 37-3.

On Nov. 22, Green Bay (7-3) traveled to Minnesota (9-1) where Moss caught eight passes for 153 yards in a 28-14 Vikings' win.

Tampa Bay dealt Green Bay its fifth loss on Dec. 7.

The Packers closed out with three straight wins. But unlike the strong finishes of 1996 and 1997, none were blowouts. Ryan Longwell's 18-yard, fourth-quarter field goal edged the Bears 16-13 in the finale.

"We're going into the San Francisco (playoff) game on a real positive note," Santana Dotson said.

Once on the coast, Green Bay lost 30-27. Five days later, Holmgren resigned to become the executive vice president of football operations/general manager/head coach of the Seattle Seahawks.

MORE HAPPY RETURNS

Roell Preston played only one game with the Packers in 1997, but set a team record by returning kickoffs for 211 yards in a 41-38 loss in Indianapolis. A year later, the kick returner played in all 16 games and not only broke his own record, but established a number of other records as well.

Preston returned 57 kickoffs for 1,497 yards. Both were team records. He also brought back 44 punts for another 398 yards.

Originally a Falcon, Preston returned three kicks for touchdowns: a 100-yard kickoff return in the opener, a 101-yard kickoff return against the Vikings on Oct. 5, and a 71-yard punt return against the Ravens on Oct. 25.

Preston played with the Titans, Dolphins and 49ers in 1999 before getting out of football.

Most Combined Kick Returns, Season

No	Player, Year	Punt Rets/KO Rets
101	Roell Preston, 1998	44/57
80	Desmond Howard, 1996	58/22
79	Allen Rossum, 2000	29/50

TEAM STATISTICS

	GB	OPP
First Downs	329	246
Rushing	93	67
Passing	210	166
Penalty	26	13
Rushes	447	390
Yards Gained	1,526	1,442
Average Gain	3.41	3.70
Average Yards per Game	95.4	90.1
Passes Attempted	575	540
Completed	361	296
% Completed	62.78	54.81
Total Yards Gained	4,340	3,401
Times Sacked	39	50
Yards Lost	230	336
Net Yards Gained	4,110	3,065
Yards Gained per Completion	12.02	11.49
Net Yards per Pass Play	6.69	5.19
Average Net Yards per Game	256.9	191.6
Combined Net Yards Gained	5,636	4,507
Total Plays	1,061	980
Average Yards per Play	5.31	4.60
Average Net Yards per Game	352.3	281.7
Third Down Efficiency	99/218	92/233
Percentage	45.41	39.48
Fourth Down Efficiency	5/13	5/17
Percentage	38.46	29.41
Intercepted By	13	23
Yards Returned	111	312
Returned for TD	1	3
Punts	65	90
Yards Punted	2,788	3,920
Average Yards per Punt	42.89	43.56
Punt Returns	48	27
Yards Returned	412	237
Average Yards per Return	8.58	8.78
Returned for TD	1	1
Kickoff Returns	60	74
Yards Returned	1,547	1,807
Average Yards per Return	25.78	24.42
Returned for TD	2	2
Penalties	88	94
Yards Penalized	681	828
Fumbles	27	20
Lost	11	10
Own Recovered for Touchdown	0	0
Opponent's Recovered by	10	11
Opponent's Recovered for Touchdown	2	0
Total Points Scored	408	319
Total Touchdowns	46	36
Touchdowns Rushing	7	7
Touchdowns Passing	33	23
Touchdowns on Returns & Recoveries	6	6
Extra Points (Kicking)	41	28
Two-Point Conversions	1/3	3/6
Safeties	1	0
Field Goals Attempted	33	27
Field Goals Made	29	23
% Successful	87.88	65.19
Average Time of Possession	31:37	28:23

Regular Season 11-5-0

Date	GB		OPP	Att.
9/6	38	Detroit Lions	19	(60,102)
9/13	23	Tampa Bay Buccaneers	15	(60,124)
9/20	13	at Cincinnati Bengals	6	(56,346)
9/27	37	at Carolina Panthers	30	(69,723)
10/5	24	Minnesota Vikings	37	(59,849)
10/15	20	at Detroit Lions	27	(77,932)
10/25	28	Baltimore Ravens	10	(59,860)
11/1	36	San Francisco 49ers	22	(59,794)
11/9	20	at Pittsburgh Steelers	27	(60,507)
11/15	37	at New York Giants	3	(76,272)
11/22	14	at Minnesota Vikings	28	(64,471)
11/29	24	Philadelphia Eagles	16	(59,862)
12/7	22	at Tampa Bay Buccaneers	24	(65,497)
12/13	26	Chicago Bears	20	(59,813)
12/20	30	Tennessee Oilers	22	(59,888)
12/27	16	at Chicago Bears	13	(58,393)

Postseason 0-1-0

1/3	27	at San Francisco 49ers	30	(66,506)

Score By Periods

	1	2	3	4	OT	Total
Packers	107	89	73	139	0	408
Opponents	70	100	57	92	0	319

INDIVIDUAL STATISTICS

Rushing	Att	Yds	Avg	LG	TD
Holmes	93	386	4.2	13	1
Levens	115	378	3.3	50	1
Jervey	83	325	3.9	16	1
R. Harris	79	228	2.9	14	1
Favre	40	133	3.3	35	1
Henderson	23	70	3.0	9	2
Freeman	3	5	1.7	10	0
Blair	2	3	1.5	2	0
Brooks	1	2	2.0	2	0
Pederson	8	-4	-0.5	1	0
Packers	**447**	**1,526**	**3.4**	**50**	**7**
Opponents	390	1,442	3.7	t73	7

Receiving	No	Yds	Avg	LG	TD
Freeman	84	1,424	17.0	t84	14
Chmura	47	554	11.8	t25	4
Henderson	37	241	6.5	15	1
Schroeder	31	452	14.6	46	1
R. Brooks	31	420	13.5	t30	3
Mayes	30	394	13.1	t33	3
Levens	27	162	6.0	17	0
Holmes	19	179	9.4	24	0
T. Davis	18	250	13.9	t60	7
R. Harris	10	68	6.8	12	0
Thomason	9	89	9.9	22	0
Jervey	9	33	3.7	11	0
Bradford	3	27	9.0	18	0
Preston	2	23	11.5	13	0
Blair	2	13	6.5	10	0
Copeland	1	5	5.5	12	0
Packers	**361**	**4,340**	**12.0**	**t84**	**33**
Opponents	296	3,401	11.5	t68	23

Passing	Att	Com	Yds	Pct	TD	In	Tk/Yds	Rate
Favre	551	347	4,212	63.0	31	23	38/223	87.8
Pederson	24	14	128	58.3	2	0	1/7	100.7
Packers	**575**	**361**	**4,340**	**62.8**	**33**	**23**	**39/230**	**88.3**
Opponents	540	296	3,401	54.8	23	13	50/336	78.2

Punting	No	Yds	Avg	Net	TB	In20	LG	HB
Landeta	65	2,788	42.9	37.1	7	30	72	0
Packers	**65**	**2,788**	**42.9**	**37.1**	**7**	**30**	**72**	**0**
Opponents	90	3,920	43.6	37.2	8	17	62	0

Kickoff Returns	No	Yds	Avg	LG	TD
Preston	57	1,497	26.3	t101	2
Bradford	2	33	16.5	24	0
K. McKenzie	1	17	17.0	17	0
Packers	**60**	**1,547**	**25.8**	**t101**	**2**
Opponents	74	1,807	24.4	t101	2

Punt Returns	No	Yds	Avg	FC	LG	TD
Preston	44	398	9.0	17	t71	1
Schroeder	2	5	2.5	0	3	0
Mayes	1	9	9.0	0	9	0
Prior	1	0	0.0	4	0	0
Packers	**48**	**412**	**8.6**	**21**	**t71**	**1**
Opponents	27	237	8.8	14	t95	1

Interceptions	No	Yds	Avg	LG	TD
T. Williams	5	40	8.0	15	0
L. Butler	3	3	1.0	3	0
K. McKenzie	1	33	33.0	33	0
Newsome	1	26	26.0	26	0
Terrell	1	9	9.0	9	0
Prior	1	0	0.0	0	0
R. Smith	1	0	0.0	0	0
Packers	**13**	**111**	**8.5**	**t33**	**1**
Opponents	23	312	13.6	t58	3

Scoring	TDr	TDp	TDrt	PAT	2pt	FG	S	TP
Longwell	0	0	0	41/43	0	29/33	0	128
Freeman	0	14	0	0/0	1	0/0	0	86
T. Davis	0	7	0	0/0	0	0/0	0	42
Chmura	0	4	0	0/0	0	0/0	0	24
R. Brooks	0	3	0	0/0	0	0/0	0	18
Henderson	2	1	0	0/0	0	0/0	0	18
Mayes	0	3	0	0/0	0	0/0	0	18
Preston	0	0	3	0/0	0	0/0	0	18
K. McKenzie	0	0	2	0/0	0	0/0	0	12
L. Butler	0	0	1	0/0	0	0/0	0	6
Favre	1	0	0	0/0	0	0/0	0	6
R. Harris	1	0	0	0/0	0	0/0	0	6
Holmes	1	0	0	0/0	0	0/0	0	6
Jervey	1	0	0	0/0	0	0/0	0	6
Levens	1	0	0	0/0	0	0/0	0	6
Schroeder	0	1	0	0/0	0	0/0	0	6
Packers	**7**	**33**	**6**	**41/43**	**1**	**29/33**	**1**	**408**
Opponents	7	23	6	28/30	3	23/27	0	319

2-point conversions: Packers (1-3); Opponents (3-6)

Fumbles	Fum	Ow	Op	Yds	Tot
Andruzzi	0	1	0	0	1
Bradford	1	0	0	0	0
L. Butler	0	0	2	32	2
Chmura	1	0	0	0	0
K. Cooks	0	1	0	0	1
T. Davis	1	0	0	0	0
Dellenbach	0	2	0	0	1
S. Dotson	0	0	1	0	1
Favre	8	3	0	-1	3
R. Harris	3	0	0	0	0
Henderson	1	0	0	0	0
Holliday	0	0	2	0	2
Holmes	1	1	0	0	1
Koonce	0	0	1	4	1
Mayes	1	0	0	0	0
K. McKenzie	0	0	3	88	3
Pederson	1	0	0	-2	0
Preston	7	1	0	0	1
Prior	1	0	0	0	0
Schroeder	1	0	0	0	0
Terrell	0	0	1	6	1
Willig	0	1	0	0	1
Packers	**27**	**10**	**10**	**127**	**20**

Quarterback Sacks	No.
R. White	16.0
Holliday	8.0
K. McKenzie	8.0
L. Butler	4.0
Booker	3.0
S. Dotson	3.0
B. Harris	2.0
B. Williams	2.0
Koonce	1.0
Lyon	1.0
Terrell	1.0
Waddy	1.0
Packers	**50.0**
Opponents	39.0

NFL STANDINGS

National Conference

Eastern Division	W	L	T	Pct	PF	PA
Dallas Cowboys	10	6	0	.625	381	275
Arizona Cardinals	9	7	0	.563	325	378
New York Giants	8	8	0	.500	287	309
Washington Redskins	6	10	0	.375	319	421
Philadelphia Eagles	3	13	0	.188	161	344

Central Division	W	L	T	Pct	PF	PA
Minnesota Vikings	15	1	0	.938	556	296
Green Bay Packers	**11**	**5**	**0**	**.688**	**408**	**319**
Tampa Bay Buccaneers	8	8	0	.500	314	295
Detroit Lions	5	11	0	.313	306	378
Chicago Bears	4	12	0	.250	276	368

Western Division	W	L	T	Pct	PF	PA
Atlanta Falcons	14	2	0	.875	442	289
San Francisco 49ers	12	4	0	.750	479	328
New Orleans Saints	6	10	0	.375	305	359
Carolina Panthers	4	12	0	.250	336	413
St. Louis Rams	4	12	0	.250	285	378

American Conference

Eastern Division	W	L	T	Pct	PF	PA
New York Jets	12	4	0	.750	416	266
Miami Dolphins	10	6	0	.625	321	265
Buffalo Bills	10	6	0	.625	400	333
New England Patriots	9	7	0	.563	337	329
Indianapolis Colts	3	13	0	.188	310	444

Central Division	W	L	T	Pct	PF	PA
Jacksonville Jaguars	11	5	0	.688	392	338
Tennessee Titans	8	8	0	.500	330	320
Pittsburgh Steelers	7	9	0	.438	263	303
Baltimore Ravens	6	10	0	.375	269	335
Cincinnati Bengals	3	13	0	.188	268	452

Western Division	W	L	T	Pct	PF	PA
Denver Broncos	14	2	0	.875	501	309
Oakland Raiders	8	8	0	.500	288	356
Seattle Seahawks	8	8	0	.500	372	310
Kansas City Chiefs	7	9	0	.438	327	363
San Diego Chargers	5	11	0	.313	241	342

ROSTER

No	Name	Pos	Ht	Wt	DOB	College	G
70	Andruzzi, Joe	G	6-3	310	08/23/75	Southern Connecticut State	15
23	Blackmon, Roosevelt	CB	6-1	185	09/10/74	Morris Brown	3
27	Blair, Michael	RB	5-11	245	11/26/74	Ball State	11
46	Bolden, Juran	CB	6-2	201	06/27/74	Mississippi Delta Community College	3
96	Booker, Vaughn	DE/DT	6-5	300	02/24/68	Cincinnati	16
85	Bradford, Corey	WR	6-1	197	12/08/75	Jackson State	8
87	Brooks, Robert	WR	6-0	180	06/23/70	South Carolina	12
93	Brown, Gilbert	NT	6-2	350	02/22/71	Kansas	16
91	Brown, Jonathan	DE	6-4	265	11/28/75	Tennessee	4
36	Butler, LeRoy	S	6-0	198	07/19/68	Florida State	16
89	Chmura, Mark	TE	6-5	255	02/22/69	Boston College	15
45	Cooks, Kerry	S	5-11	202	03/28/74	Iowa	9
16	Copeland, Russell	WR	6-0	200	11/04/71	Memphis State	3
60	Davis, Rob	LS	6-3	290	12/10/68	Shippensburg	16
81	Davis, Tyrone	TE	6-4	252	06/30/72	Virginia	13
67	Dellenbach, Jeff	C	6-6	300	02/14/63	Wisconsin	16
72	Dotson, Earl	T	6-3	315	12/17/70	Texas A&I	16
71	Dotson, Santana	DT	6-5	285	12/19/69	Baylor	16
4	Favre, Brett	QB	6-2	230	10/10/69	Southern Mississippi	16
58	Flanagan, Mike	C	6-5	290	11/10/73	UCLA	2
86	Freeman, Antonio	WR	6-0?	198	05/27/72	Virginia Tech	15
47	Galbraith, Scott	TE	6-2	254	01/07/67	USC	1
55	Harris, Bernardo	LB	6-2	248	10/15/71	North Carolina	16
29	Harris, Raymont	RB	6-0	225	06/13/69	Ohio State	8
33	Henderson, William	FB	6-1	245	02/19/71	North Carolina	16
90	Holliday, Vonnie	DE	6-5	296	12/11/75	North Carolina	12
56	Hollinquest, Lamont	LB	6-3	250	10/24/70	USC	14
22	Holmes, Darick	RB	6-0	226	07/01/71	Portland State	11
32	Jervey, Travis	RB	5-11?	222	05/05/72	The Citadel	8
48	Kitts, Jim	FB	6-1	245	12/28/72	Ferrum	2
53	Koonce, George	LB	6-1	245	10/15/68	East Carolina	14
94	Kuberski, Bob	NT	6-4	298	04/05/71	Navy	16
7	Landeta, Sean	P	6-0	200	01/06/62	Towson State	16
25	Levens, Dorsey	RB	6-1	228	05/21/70	Georgia Tech	7
57	London, Antonio	LB	6-2	238	04/14/71	Alabama	1
8	Longwell, Ryan	K	6-0	192	08/16/74	California	16
98	Lyon, Billy	DT	6-5	295	12/10/73	Marshall	4
82	Manning, Brian	WR	5-11	186	04/22/75	Stanford	3
80	Mayes, Derrick	WR	6-0	205	01/28/74	Notre Dame	10
43	McGarrahan, Scott	S	6-1	197	02/12/74	New Mexico	15
95	McKenzie, Keith	DE	6-3	264	10/17/73	Ball State	16
21	Newsome, Craig	CB	6-0	190	08/10/71	Arizona State	13
18	Pederson, Doug	QB	6-3	215	01/31/68	Northeast Louisiana	12
88	Preston, Roell	WR	5-10	195	06/23/72	Mississippi	16
39	Prior, Mike	S	6-0	208	11/14/63	Illinois State	16
62	Rivera, Marco	G	6-4	305	04/26/72	Penn State	15
84	Schroeder, Bill	WR	6-2	198	01/09/71	Wisconsin-La Crosse	13
42	Sharper, Darren	DB	6-2	210	11/03/75	William & Mary	16
31	Smith, Rod	CB	5-11	187	03/12/70	Notre Dame	8
40	Terrell, Pat	S	6-1	208	03/18/68	Notre Dame	16
83	Thomason, Jeff	TE	6-4	255	12/30/69	Oregon	16
63	Timmerman, Adam	G	6-4	300	08/14/71	South Dakota State	16
78	Verba, Ross	T	6-4	302	10/31/73	Iowa	16
54	Waddy, Jude	LB	6-2	220	09/12/75	William & Mary	14
68	Wahle, Mike	G	6-6	306	03/29/77	Navy	1
92	White, Reggie	DE	6-5	300	12/19/61	Tennessee	16
51	Williams, Brian	LB	6-1	245	12/17/72	USC	16
37	Williams, Tyrone	CB	5-11	192	05/31/73	Nebraska	16
76	Willig, Matt	T	6-7	315	01/21/69	USC	16
52	Winters, Frank	C	6-3	300	01/23/64	West Illinois	13

DRAFT

Rnd	Name	Pos	Ht	Wt	College
1a	Vonnie Holliday (19)	DT	6-5	296	North Carolina

(Packers traded 1st-round (29) and 2nd-round (60) picks to Dolphins for Dolphins' 1st-round (19) pick)

1b	(Choice (29) to Dolphins in deal mentioned above)				
2	(Choice (60) to Dolphins in deal mentioned above)				
3	Jonathan Brown (90)	DE	6-4	268	Tennessee
4	Roosevelt Blackmon (121)	DB	6-1	185	Morris Brown
5a	Corey Bradford (150)	WR	6-1	197	Jackson State

(Choice from Chiefs for Wayne Simmons)

5b	(Choice (152) to Raiders for Raiders' 6th-round pick (156) and

Raiders' 6th-round pick (188) in 1999)

6a	Scott McGarrahan (156)	S	6-1	200	New Mexico

(Choice from Raiders in deal mentioned above)

6b	(Choice (182) to Jacksonville for Paul Frase)				
6c	Matt Hasselbeck (187)	QB	6-4	222	Boston College

(Free agency compensatory pick)

7	Edwin Watson (218)	RB	6-0	224	Purdue

1998 GREEN BAY PACKERS

FRONT ROW: (L-R) 4 Brett Favre, 7 Sean Landeta, 8 Ryan Longwell, 12 Rick Mirer, 18 Doug Pederson, 21 Craig Newsome, 23 Roosevelt Blackmon, 25 Dorsey Levens, 27 Michael Blair, 28 Roderick Mullen, 29 Raymont Harris, 32 Travis Jervey.

SECOND ROW: (L-R) Wide Receivers Coach Nolan Cromwell, Quarterbacks Coach Andy Reid, Tight Ends/Assistant Offensive Line Coach Mike Sherman, Offensive Assistant/Quality Control Gary Reynolds, Offensive Line Coach Tom Lovat, Running Backs Coach Harry Sydney, Offensive Coordinator Sherman Lewis, Head Coach Mike Holmgren, Defensive Coordinator Fritz Shurmur, Defensive Line Coach Larry Brooks, Linebackers Coach Jim Lind, Defensive Assistant/Quality Control Ken Flajole, Defensive Backs Coach Bob Valesente, Special Teams Coach Johnny Holland.

THIRD ROW: (L-R) 33 William Henderson, 36 LeRoy Butler, 37 Tyrone Williams, 39 Mike Prior, 40 Pat Terrell, 42 Darren Sharper, 43 Scott McGarrahan, 51 Brian Williams, 52 Frank Winters, 53 George Koonce, 54 Jude Waddy.

FOURTH ROW: (L-R) 55 Bernardo Harris, 56 Lamont Hollinquest, 57 Antonio London, 58 Mike Flanagan, 60 Rob Davis, 62 Marco Rivera, 63 Adam Timmerman, 67 Jeff Dellenbach, 68 Mike Wahle, 70 Joe Andruzzi, 71 Santana Dotson.

FIFTH ROW: (L-R) 72 Earl Dotson, 76 Matt Willig, 77 John Michels, 78 Ross Verba, 80 Derrick Mayes, 81 Tyrone Davis, 83 Jeff Thomason, 84 Bill Schroeder, 85 Corey Bradford, 86 Antonio Freeman, 87 Robert Brooks, 88 Roell Preston.

SIXTH ROW: (L-R) 89 Mark Chmura, 90 Vonnie Holliday, 91 Jonathan Brown, 92 Reggie White, 93 Gilbert Brown, 94 Bob Kuberski, 95 Keith McKenzie, 96 Vaughn Booker, 98 Billy Lyon, 99 Jermaine Smith, Strength and Conditioning Kent Johnston.

BACK ROW: (L-R) Administrative Assistant/Football Bill Nayes, Corporate Security Officer Jerry Parins, Training Room Intern Bryan Engle, Assistant Trainer Sam Ramsden, Assistant Trainer Kurt Fielding, Head Trainer Pepper Burruss, Associate Team Physician Dr. John Gray, Team Physician Dr. Patrick J. McKenzie, Equipment Manager Gordon (Red) Batty, Assistant Equipment Manager Bryan Nehring, Assistant Equipment Manager Tom Bakken, Equipment Assistant Tim O'Neill, Video Assistant Chris Kirby, Assistant Video Director Bob Eckberg, Video Director Al Treml.

Ray Rhodes sounded like a mechanic when he was introduced as the Packers' 12th head coach in January. "I think the key thing is to keep the machines running, keep the machine going. Be sure it stays fine-tuned."

Fine-tuned the Packers were not. A less-than-stellar defense, special teams woes, penalties, three losses at home, and a late-season slide added up to an 8-8 season. Rhodes became just the second head coach in Packers' history to be dismissed after only one season at the helm.

Green Bay's defense dropped from 4th in 1998 to 19th in 1999. With Reggie White retired, the team sacked opposing passers only 30 times to rank 29th in that department. The unit surrendered 5,309 yards, the most since the 1990 club gave up 5,442.

Special teams were an adventure. The team's punt return average (7.3), kickoff return average (18.8), and gross punting average (39.1) all ranked among the bottom five in the league. Three of Ryan Longwell's field goal attempts were blocked.

Green Bay's 100 penalties were the most since the club record of 135 was set in 1987.

The Packers lost three games at Lambeau Field from 1994 through 1998. Under Rhodes, the team lost three in one season and had to rally to avoid losing three others.

Also of concern was the Packers' December fade, coming as it did after the team had positioned itself to make a run for the Central Division title. Losses to Carolina, Minnesota, and Tampa Bay dropped Green Bay's record to 7-8. Not even a 49-24 blowout of the Cardinals in the finale could salvage a playoff berth as Detroit claimed the third wild card spot with a better conference record (7-5) than either the Packers (6-6) or Panthers (6-6).

Cognizant of what the Vikings' Randy Moss had done to the team in 1998, Green Bay drafted three defensive backs in the first three rounds of the draft: Antuan Edwards, Fred Vinson and Mike McKenzie. McKenzie had the best rookie year of the trio, starting 16 games at left cornerback.

In August, Robert Brooks retired and Antonio Freeman signed a 7-year, $42 million contract. Later that month, Fritz Shurmur, the Packers defensive coordinator from 1994-98 who had joined Holmgren's staff in Seattle, died just months after being diagnosed with cancer.

Brett Favre orchestrated three thrilling comeback wins in the first four games despite a badly bruised thumb on his passing hand. Favre's right hand and thumb were slammed against Raiders' helmets in separate incidents in the season opener, won by Green Bay 28-24.

In that game, Favre capped an 11-play, 82-yard drive with a 1-yard touchdown pass to Jeff Thomason in the final two minutes. Two weeks later, he hit Corey Bradford with a 23-yard touchdown pass on fourth down with 12 seconds left to beat the Vikings 23-20. On Oct. 10, he found Antonio Freeman open with 1:05 remaining to knock off Tampa Bay 26-23.

The Minister of Defense was honored at halftime of the Buccaneers game.

"I have been honored and privileged to have been a Packer and I always will be a Packer," White said.

Mike Holmgren returned to Lambeau Field on Nov. 1. The homecoming was painful for Packers fans as Seattle throttled Green Bay 27-7. Favre threw four interceptions and did not hold a post-game press conference.

That loss was followed by ugly performances against the Bears and Cowboys. Chicago's Bryan Robinson blocked Ryan Longwell's 28-yard field goal on the last play of the game as Chicago slipped by 14-13, and former Packer George Teague returned a Favre interception 95 yards for a touchdown in a 27-13 win by Dallas.

Green Bay rallied past the Lions 26-17 to end its three-game skid. Wins over San Francisco and Chicago put the Packers (7-5) within striking distance of division leaders Detroit (8-4) and Tampa Bay (8-4).

Under Holmgren, Green Bay had compiled one of the best December won-loss records. Not so with the Rhodes-coached Packers. Steve Beuerlein's quarterback draw as time ran out gave Carolina a 33-31 win. Leroy Hoard's 1-yard run early in the fourth quarter allowed Minnesota to escape 24-20. And Tampa Bay dominated from the outset in a resounding, 29-10 verdict on Dec. 26.

Green Bay's wild-card playoff hopes died as the Cowboys beat the Giants on Jan. 2.

"We have no one to blame but ourselves," Rhodes said.

THE IRONMAN

Brett Favre started his first game on Sept. 27, 1992, against the Steelers. On Nov. 7, 1999, he started his 117th consecutive game to break former Eagle Ron Jaworski's record for most consecutive starts by a quarterback.

As any player would over such a span, Favre was injured on a number of occasions. But No. 4 didn't let a shoulder separation (1993), severely sprained ankle (1995) or a badly injured thumb (1999) keep him from his work.

Favre put up some impressive numbers in his 117 starts. He threw for 28,496 yards and 223 touchdowns. His record was 78-39 (.667). In the 117 games prior to his first start, the Packers compiled a 45-71-1 record (.389).

"I feel very fortunate to have made it for 117 games, and I hope to make it for another 117. But I also like to win. That's why we play," Favre said about setting the record in a 14-13 loss to the Bears.

After Favre took the first snap from center Frank Winters, the game was stopped briefly. Favre and Jaworski embraced on the field, and Favre was presented with the ball that had just been snapped.

TEAM STATISTICS

	GB	OPP
First Downs	314	304
Rushing	87	103
Passing	196	177
Penalty	31	24
Rushes	386	472
Yards Gained	1,519	1,804
Average Gain	3.94	3.82
Average Yards per Game	94.9	112.8
Passes Attempted	605	538
Completed	344	304
% Completed	56.86	56.51
Total Yards Gained	4,132	3,690
Times Sacked	36	30
Yards Lost	232	185
Net Yards Gained	3,900	3,505
Yards Gained per Completion	12.01	12.14
Net Yards per Pass Play	6.08	6.17
Average Net Yards per Game	243.8	219.1
Combined Net Yards Gained	5,419	5,309
Total Plays	1,027	1,040
Average Yards per Play	5.28	5.10
Average Net Yards per Game	338.7	331.8
Third Down Efficiency	77/209	87/223
Percentage	36.84	39.01
Fourth Down Efficiency	2/9	8/20
Percentage	22.22	40.00
Intercepted By	26	23
Yards Returned	137	338
Returned for TD	1	2
Punts	80	69
Yards Punted	3,130	2,954
Average Yards per Punt	39.13	42.81
Punt Returns	29	39
Yards Returned	212	333
Average Yards per Return	7.31	8.54
Returned for TD	0	0
Kickoff Returns	66	72
Yards Returned	1,241	1,565
Average Yards per Return	18.80	21.74
Returned for TD	1	0
Penalties	100	99
Yards Penalized	808	993
Fumbles	28	36
Lost	13	15
Own Recovered for Touchdown	0	0
Opponent's Recovered by	15	13
Opponent's Recovered for Touchdown	2	0
Total Points Scored	357	341
Total Touchdowns	40	39
Touchdowns Rushing	13	16
Touchdowns Passing	23	20
Touchdowns on Returns & Recoveries	4	3
Extra Points (Kicking)	38	35
Two-Point Conversions	1/2	0/4
Safeties	1	0
Field Goals Attempted	30	31
Field Goals Made	25	24
% Successful	83.33	77.42
Average Time of Possession	29:13	30:47

Regular Season   8-8-0

Date	GB		OPP	Att.
9/12	28	Oakland Raiders	24	(59,872)
9/19	15	at Detroit Lions	23	(76,202)
9/26	23	Minnesota Vikings	20	(59,868)
10/10	26	Tampa Bay Buccaneers	23	(59,868)
10/17	10	at Denver Broncos	31	(73,352)
10/24	31	at San Diego Chargers	3	(68,274)
11/1	7	Seattle Seahawks	27	(59,869)
11/7	13	Chicago Bears	14	(59,867)
11/14	13	at Dallas Cowboys	27	(64,634)
11/21	26	Detroit Lions	17	(59,869)
11/29	20	at San Francisco 49ers	3	(68,304)
12/5	35	at Chicago Bears	19	(66,944)
12/12	31	Carolina Panthers	33	(59,869)
12/20	20	at Minnesota Vikings	24	(64,203)
12/26	10	at Tampa Bay Buccaneers	29	(65,273)
1/2	49	Arizona Cardinals	24	(59,818)

Score By Periods

	1	2	3	4	OT	Total
Packers	44	123	73	117	0	357
Opponents	54	95	93	99	0	341

INDIVIDUAL STATISTICS

Rushing	Att	Yds	Avg	LG	TD
Levens	279	1,034	3.7	36	9
Parker	36	184	5.1	26	2
Favre	28	142	5.1	20	0
Mitchell	29	117	4.0	15	0
Henderson	7	29	4.1	10	2
Hasselbeck	6	15	2.5	13	0
Freeman	1	-2	-2.0	-2	0
Packers	**386**	**1,519**	**3.9**	**36**	**13**
Opponents	472	1,804	3.8	51	16

Receiving	No	Yds	Avg	LG	TD
Freeman	74	1,074	14.5	51	6
Schroeder	74	1,051	14.2	51	5
Levens	71	573	8.1	53	1
Bradford	37	637	17.2	t74	5
Henderson	30	203	6.8	22	1
T. Davis	20	204	10.2	33	2
Thomason	14	140	10.0	22	2
Mitchell	6	48	8.0	20	0
Chmura	5	55	11.0	16	0
Parker	4	15	3.8	7	0
Hall	3	33	11.0	13	0
Driver	3	31	10.3	12	1
C. Jordan	2	54	27.0	43	0
Crawford	1	14	14.0	14	0
Packers	**344**	**4,132**	**12.0**	**t74**	**23**
Opponents	304	3,690	12.1	88	20

Passing	Att	Com	Yds	Pct	TD	In	Tk/Yds	Rate
Favre	595	341	4,091	57.3	22	23	35/223	74.7
Hasselbeck	10	3	41	30.0	1	0	1/9	77.5
Packers	**605**	**344**	**4,132**	**56.9**	**23**	**23**	**36/232**	**74.8**
Opponents	538	304	3,690	56.5	20	26	30/185	70.0

Punting	No	Yds	Avg	Net	TB	In20	LG	HB
Aguiar	75	2,954	39.4	33.9	4	20	64	0
Hanson	4	157	39.3	38.5	0	0	44	0
Longwell	1	19	19.0	19.0	0	1	19	0
Packers	**80**	**3,130**	**39.1**	**34.0**	**4**	**21**	**64**	**0**
Opponents	69	2,954	42.8	36.8	10	26	65	0

Kickoff Returns	No	Yds	Avg	LG	TD
Mitchell	21	464	22.1	t88	1
D. Howard	19	364	19.2	31	0
Parker	15	268	17.9	40	0
C. Jordan	6	95	15.8	22	0
Henderson	2	23	11.5	16	0
R. McKenzie	1	13	13.0	13	0
Schroeder	1	10	10.0	10	0
Sharper	1	4	4.0	4	0
Packers	**66**	**1,241**	**18.8**	**t88**	**1**
Opponents	72	1,565	21.7	91	0

Punt Returns	No	Yds	Avg	FC	LG	TD
D. Howard	12	93	7.8	7	20	0
Edwards	10	90	9.0	4	45	0
Jordan	5	29	5.8	2	13	0
Mitchell	2	0	0.0	0	0	0
Packers	**29**	**212**	**7.3**	**13**	**45**	**0**
Opponents	39	333	8.5	24	41	0

Interceptions	No	Yds	Avg	LG	TD
M. McKenzie	6	4	0.7	4	0
Edwards	4	26	6.5	t26	1
T. Williams	4	12	3.0	12	0
Sharper	3	12	4.0	9	0
B. Williams	2	60	30.0	60	0
Vinson	2	21	10.5	21	0
L. Butler	2	0	0.0	0	0
J. Smith	1	2	2.0	2	0
Lyon	1	0	0.0	0	0
Nelson	1	0	0.0	0	0
Packers	**26**	**137**	**5.3**	**60**	**1**
Opponents	23	338	14.7	t95	2

Scoring	TDr	TDp	TDrt	PAT	2pt	FG	S	TP
Longwell	0	0	0	38/38	0	25/30	0	113
Levens	9	1	0	0/0	0	0/0	0	60
Freeman	0	6	0	0/0	0	0/0	0	36
Bradford	0	5	0	0/0	1	0/0	0	32
Schroeder	0	5	0	0/0	0	0/0	0	30
Henderson	2	1	0	0/0	0	0/0	0	18
T. Davis	0	2	0	0/0	0	0/0	0	12
K. McKenzie	0	0	2	0/0	0	0/0	0	12
Parker	2	0	0	0/0	0	0/0	0	12
Thomason	0	2	0	0/0	0	0/0	0	12
Driver	0	1	0	0/0	0	0/0	0	6
Edwards	0	0	1	0/0	0	0/0	0	6
Mitchell	0	0	1	0/0	0	0/0	0	6
Packers	**13**	**23**	**4**	**38/38**	**1**	**25/30**	**1**	**357**
Opponents	16	20	3	35/35	0	24/31	0	341

2-point conversions: Packers (1-2); Opponents (0-4)

Fumbles	Fum	Ow	Op	Yds	Tot
Bradford	1	0	0	0	0
L. Butler	0	0	1	0	1
A. Edwards	1	0	0	0	0
Favre	9	1	0	-2	1
Freeman	1	1	0	0	1
B. Harris	0	0	1	0	1
Hasselbeck	1	1	0	-16	1
Henderson	1	0	0	0	0
Holliday	0	0	1	0	1
C. Hunt	0	0	1	0	1
C. Jordan	1	1	0	0	1
Levens	5	1	0	0	0
McBride	0	0	2	0	2
McGarrahan	0	1	0	0	1
K. McKenzie	0	0	4	63	4
Mitchell	2	1	1	0	2
Nelson	0	0	1	0	1
Parker	1	1	1	0	1
Rivera	0	0	1	0	1
Schroeder	3	0	0	0	0
Sharper	0	0	1	9	1
J. Smith	1	0	0	0	0
Verba	0	0	2	0	1
Wahle	0	0	1	0	1
B. Williams	0	0	1	0	1
T. Williams	1	0	2	12	2
Winters	0	1	0	0	1
Packers	**28**	**13**	**15**	**68**	**28**

Quarterback Sacks	No.
K. McKenzie	8.0
Holliday	6.0
Booker	3.5
S. Dotson	2.5
Lyon	2.0
B. Williams	2.0
L. Butler	1.0
Sharper	1.0
Vinson	1.0
Waddy	1.0
team	1.0
Hunt	0.5
J. Smith	0.5
Packers	**30.0**
Opponents	36.0

NFL STANDINGS

National Conference

Eastern Division	W	L	T	Pct	PF	PA
Washington Redskins	10	6	0	.625	443	377
Dallas Cowboys	8	8	0	.500	352	276
New York Giants	7	9	0	.438	299	358
Arizona Cardinals	6	10	0	.375	245	382
Philadelphia Eagles	5	11	0	.313	272	357

Central Division	W	L	T	Pct	PF	PA
Tampa Bay Buccaneers	11	5	0	.688	270	235
Minnesota Vikings	10	6	0	.625	399	335
Detroit Lions	8	8	0	.500	322	323
Green Bay Packers	8	8	0	.500	357	341
Chicago Bears	6	10	0	.375	272	341

Western Division	W	L	T	Pct	PF	PA
St. Louis Rams	13	3	0	.813	526	242
Carolina Panthers	8	8	0	.500	421	381
Atlanta Falcons	5	11	0	.313	285	380
San Francisco 49ers	4	12	0	.250	295	453
New Orleans Saints	3	13	0	.188	260	434

American Conference

Eastern Division	W	L	T	Pct	PF	PA
Indianapolis Colts	13	3	0	.813	423	333
Buffalo Bills	11	5	0	.688	320	229
Miami Dolphins	9	7	0	.563	326	336
New York Jets	8	8	0	.500	308	309
New England Patriots	8	8	0	.500	299	284

Central Division	W	L	T	Pct	PF	PA
Jacksonville Jaguars	14	2	0	.875	396	217
Tennessee Titans	13	3	0	.813	392	324
Baltimore Ravens	8	8	0	.500	324	277
Pittsburgh Steelers	6	10	0	.375	317	320
Cincinnati Bengals	4	12	0	.250	283	460
Cleveland Browns	2	14	0	.125	217	437

Western Division	W	L	T	Pct	PF	PA
Seattle Seahawks	9	7	0	.563	338	298
Kansas City Chiefs	9	7	0	.563	390	322
San Diego Chargers	8	8	0	.500	269	316
Oakland Raiders	8	8	0	.500	390	329
Denver Broncos	6	10	0	.375	314	318

ROSTER

No	Name	Pos	Ht	Wt	DOB	College	G
10	Aguiar, Louie	P	6-2	220	06/30/66	Utah State	15
70	Andruzzi, Joe	G	6-3	310	08/23/75	Southern Connecticut State	8
88	Arnold, Jahine	WR	6-0	180	06/19/73	Fresno State	1
46	Artmore, Rodney	S	6-0	210	06/14/74	Baylor	5
94	Barker, Roy	DE	6-5	290	02/24/69	North Carolina	1
47	Bell, Tyrone	CB	6-2	210	10/20/74	North Alabama	1
96	Booker, Vaughn	DE/DT	6-5	300	02/24/68	Cincinnati	14
85	Bradford, Corey	WR	6-1	205	12/08/75	Jackson State	16
93	Brown, Gilbert	NT	6-2	345	02/22/71	Kansas	16
36	Butler, LeRoy	S	6-0	203	07/19/68	Florida State	16
89	Chmura, Mark	TE	6-5	255	02/22/69	Boston College	2
45	Crawford, Keith	CB	6-2	198	11/21/70	Howard Payne	3
61	Curry, Scott	T	6-5	300	12/25/75	Montana	5
50	Davis, Anthony	LB	6-0	235	03/07/69	Utah	14
60	Davis, Rob	LS	6-3	285	12/10/68	Shippensburg	16
81	Davis, Tyrone	TE	6-4	255	06/30/72	Virginia	16
74	Dingle, Antonio	DT	6-2	315	10/07/76	Virginia	6
72	Dotson, Earl	T	6-3	310	12/17/70	Texas A&I	15
71	Dotson, Santana	DT	6-5	290	12/19/69	Baylor	12
80	Driver, Donald	WR	6-0	175	02/02/75	Alcorn State	6
24	Edwards, Antuan	CB	6-1	205	05/26/77	Clemson	16
4	Favre, Brett	QB	6-2	220	10/10/69	Southern Mississippi	16
58	Flanagan, Mike	C	6-5	295	11/10/73	UCLA	15
86	Freeman, Antonio	WR	6-0?	198	05/27/72	Virginia Tech	16
88	Hall, Lamont	TE	6-4	260	11/16/74	Clemson	14
7	Hanson, Chris	P	6-1	214	10/25/76	Marshall	1
55	Harris, Bernardo	LB	6-2	250	10/15/71	North Carolina	16
11	Hasselbeck, Matt	QB	6-4	220	09/25/75	Boston College	16
75	Heimburger, Craig	G/T	6-2	318	02/03/77	Missouri	2
33	Henderson, William	FB	6-1	250	02/19/71	North Carolina	16
90	Holliday, Vonnie	DE	6-5	300	12/11/75	North Carolina	16
82	Howard, Desmond	WR	5-10	180	05/15/70	Michigan	8
97	Hunt, Cletidus	DE	6-4	295	01/02/76	Kentucky State	11
82	Jordan, Charles	WR	5-10	175	10/09/69	Long Beach City College	4
53	Koonce, George	LB	6-1	245	10/15/68	East Carolina	15
25	Levens, Dorsey	RB	6-1	228	05/21/70	Georgia Tech	14
8	Longwell, Ryan	K	6-0	197	08/16/74	California	16
98	Lyon, Billy	DT	6-5	300	12/10/73	Marshall	16
56	Mays, Kivuusama	LB	6-3	248	01/07/75	North Carolina	3
27	McBride, Tod	DB	6-1	208	01/26/76	UCLA	15
43	McGarrahan, Scott	S	6-1	197	02/12/74	New Mexico	13
95	McKenzie, Keith	DE	6-3	266	10/17/73	Ball State	13
34	McKenzie, Mike	CB	6-0	190	04/26/76	Memphis	16
63	McKenzie, Raleigh	G	6-2	290	02/08/63	Tennessee	16
28	Mitchell, Basil	RB	5-10	200	09/07/75	Texas Christian	16
57	Nelson, Jim	LB	6-1	238	04/16/75	Penn State	16
22	Parker, De'Mond	RB	5-10	188	12/24/76	Oklahoma	11
62	Rivera, Marco	G	6-4	305	04/26/72	Penn State	16
84	Schroeder, Bill	WR	6-2	205	01/09/71	Wisconsin-La Crosse	16
42	Sharper, Darren	DB	6-2	210	11/03/75	William & Mary	16
99	Smith, Jermaine	DT	6-3	298	02/03/72	Georgia	10
38	Snider, Matt	FB	6-2	243	01/26/76	Richmond	8
83	Thomason, Jeff	TE	6-4	255	12/30/69	Oregon	14
78	Verba, Ross	T	6-4	308	10/31/73	Iowa	11
31	Vinson, Fred	CB	5-11	180	04/02/77	Vanderbilt	16
54	Waddy, Jude	LB	6-2	220	09/12/75	William & Mary	16
68	Wahle, Mike	G	6-6	306	03/29/77	Navy	16
51	Williams, Brian	LB	6-1	245	12/17/72	USC	7
37	Williams, Tyrone	CB	5-11	195	05/31/73	Nebraska	16
52	Winters, Frank	C	6-3	305	01/23/64	West Illinois	16

DRAFT

Rnd	Name	Pos	Ht	Wt	College
1	Antuan Edwards (25)	DB	6-1	205	Clemson
2a	Fred Vinson (47)	DB	5-11	180	Vanderbilt
	(Choice from Seahawks for Mike Holmgren)				
2b	(Choice exercised for Mike Wahle in 1998 supplemental draft)				
3a	Mike McKenzie (87)	DB	6-0	190	Memphis
3b	Cletidus Hunt (94)	DE	6-4	295	Kentucky State
	(Free agency compensatory pick)				
4a	(Choice (122) to Bills for Darick Holmes)				
4b	Aaron Brooks (131)	QB	6-4	205	Virginia
	(Free agency compensatory pick)				
4c	Josh Bidwell (133)	P	6-3	225	Oregon
	(Free agency compensatory pick)				
5a	De'Mond Parker (159)	RB	5-10	188	Oklahoma

Rnd	Name	Pos	Ht	Wt	College
5b	Craig Heimburger (163)	G	6-2	318	Missouri
	(Choice from Raiders for Packers' 6th round-pick (188))				
6a	(Choice (188) from Raiders in 1998 draft day trade; traded back to Raiders for Raiders' 5th round pick (163) in 1999)				
6b	Dee Miller (196)	WR	5-11	194	Ohio State
6c	Scott Curry (203)	T	6-5	295	Montana
	(Free agency compensatory pick)				
7a	Chris Akins (212)	S	5-11	194	Ark.-Pine Bluff
	(Choice from Rams for Steve Bono)				
7b	Donald Driver (213)	WR	6-0	180	Alcorn State
	(Choice from Bears for Glyn Milburn)				
7c	(Choice (232) to Lions for Glyn Milburn)				

1999 GREEN BAY PACKERS

FRONT ROW: (L–R) 2 Aaron Brooks, 4 Brett Favre, 8 Ryan Longwell, 10 Louie Aguiar, 11 Matt Hasselbeck, 22 DeMond Parker, 24 Antuan Edwards, 25 Dorsey Levens, 27 Tod McBride, 28 Basil Mitchell, 31 Fred Vinson.
SECOND ROW: (L–R) Strength and Conditioning Coach Barry Rubin, Special Teams Coach Steve Ortmayer, Defensive Assistant/Quality Control Chuck Knox, Assistant Defensive Backs Coach Lionel Washington, Defensive Backs Coach Joe Vitt, Linebackers Coach Johnny Holland, Defensive Line Coach Mike Trgovac, Defensive Coordinator Emmitt Thomas, Head Coach Ray Rhodes, Offensive Coordinator Sherman Lewis, Assistant Offensive Line Coach Larry Beightol, Quarterbacks Coach Mike McCarthy, Running Backs Coach Harry Sydney, Wide Receivers Coach Charlie Baggett, Tight Ends Coach Jeff Jagodzinski, Offensive Assistant/Quality Control Ken Zampese, Assistant Offensive Line Coach Irv Eatman.
THIRD ROW: (L–R) 33 William Henderson, 34 Mike McKenzie, 36 LeRoy Butler, 37 Tyrone Williams, 38 Matt Snider, 42 Darren Sharper, 43 Scott McGarrahan, 46 Rodney Artmore, 49 Lamont Hall, 50 Anthony Davis, 51 Brian Williams.
FOURTH ROW: (L–R) 52 Frank Winters, 53 George Koonce, 54 Jude Waddy, 55 Bernardo Harris, 57 Jim Nelson, 58 Mike Flanagan, 60 Rob Davis, 61 Scott Curry, 62 Marco Rivera, 63 Raleigh McKenzie.
FIFTH ROW: (L–R) 68 Mike Wahle, 70 Joe Andruzzi, 71 Santana Dotson, 72 Earl Dotson, 74 Antonio Dingle, 78 Ross Verba, 80 Donald Driver, 81 Tyrone Davis, 82 Desmond Howard, 83 Jeff Thomason, 84 Bill Schroeder.
SIXTH ROW: (L–R) 85 Corey Bradford, 86 Antonio Freeman, 88 Jahine Arnold, 89 Mark Chmura, 90 Vonnie Holliday, 93 Gilbert Brown, 95 Keith McKenzie, 96 Vaughn Booker, 97 Cletidus Hunt, 98 Billy Lyon, 99 Jermaine Smith.
BACK ROW: (L–R) Assistant Strength and Conditioning Coach Mark Lovat, Administrative Assistant/Football Matt Klein, Corporate Security Officer Jerry Parins, Training Room Intern Andre Daniel, Assistant Trainer Bryan Engel, Assistant Trainer Kurt Fielding, Head Trainer Pepper Burruss, Associate Team Physician Dr. John Gray, Team Physician Dr. Patrick J. McKenzie, Equipment Manager Gordon (Red) Batty, Assistant Equipment Manager Bryan Nehring, Assistant Equipment Manager Tom Bakken, Equipment Assistant Tim O'Neill, Equipment Intern Andy Ashenbrenner, Video Assistant Chris Kirby, Assistant Video Director Bob Eckberg, Video Director Al Treml.

Mike Sherman volunteered an answer even before reporters had a chance to ask questions at the press conference announcing his hiring.

"I'll answer your first question for you," he told the assembled members of the media. "Yes, I am ready to be the head coach of the Green Bay Packers."

A relative unknown, Sherman had never been a head coach at any level. He had just three years of NFL experience, having been the Packers' tight ends/assistant offensive line coach (1997-98) and the Seahawks' offensive coordinator (1999).

Organized, disciplined and focused were words often used to describe Sherman. In his first season, he restored the Packers' home-field advantage by winning five straight at Lambeau Field, and he had the team again playing its best football in December (4-0). Unfortunately, the club's 9-7 record didn't warrant a playoff berth as six teams in the NFC won at least 10 games.

The renovation of Lambeau Field was a hot topic. Packers president Bob Harlan spent much of the year touring the state to build support for the $295 million project. More than half of that total ($160 million) would come from residents of Brown County via a 0.5 percent sales tax, provided that measure passed in a binding referendum.

It did. On Sept. 12, the vote was 48,788 to 42,580 to enact the sales tax. As had happened five other times in the past, the community rallied to support the team.

"It's the best story in all of sports," Harlan said.

The renovation included increasing Lambeau Field's seating capacity to 71,000, adding an upper concourse and widening the lower one, and the construction of an atrium that would house team offices, the Packers' locker room, and more. The project was to be completed in time for the start of the 2003 season.

In June, Green Bay released two veterans from the Super Bowl years: George Koonce and Mark Chmura. Chmura, who had missed 14 games with a neck injury in 1999, was charged with sexual assault and child enticement for allegedly assaulting a 17-year-old at a party in April. He was acquitted in February 2001 in Waukesha County.

The Packers were relatively quiet in the free-agent market. Defensive linemen Russell Maryland and John Thierry were the team's biggest acquisitions in that arena.

Trades netted running back Ahman Green, linebacker Nate Wayne, defensive end David Bowens and kick returner Allen Rossum. Green rushed for 1,175 yards, Wayne finished second on the team in tackles (126), Bowens had 3.5 sacks and Rossum solidified the return game.

The Jets handed the Packers their first season-opening loss (20-16) in five years. Curtis Martin rushed for 110 yards and scored the game-winning touchdown on a 3-yard pass from Vinny Testaverde in the fourth quarter.

Green Bay secured its first win two weeks later in a 6-3 defensive battle with the Eagles. Two second-half field goals

by Ryan Longwell proved the difference.

A week later, Longwell tied the team record for most field goals in a game with five as the Packers downed Arizona 29-3.

The Bears won at Lambeau Field for a second year in a row on Oct. 1. Marcus Robinson scored on passes of 68 and 58 yards in Chicago's 27-24 triumph.

Green Bay closed out the first half of the season four weeks later in Miami where it blew a 17-0 lead. The Dolphins ripped off 28 straight points to win 28-20.

Antonio Freeman's spectacular 43-yard touchdown reception got the Packers past Minnesota 26-20 on a Monday night in early November. Freeman caught the ball on the ground after it bounced off his shoulder pad. Untouched, he got up and raced to the end zone.

For Freeman, the season was filled with more lows than highs. Over the course of the year, he missed a couple of meetings, returned late from the bye week and got a couple of speeding tickets. Sherman suspended him for the finale against the Buccaneers.

The Packers' perfect December started with a 28-6 mauling of the Bears. After taking care of Detroit 26-13, Green Bay won in the Metrodome for only the second time in nine years. In that game, Green rushed for 161 yards, and Favre threw three touchdowns and no interceptions.

On Christmas Eve, Longwell booted a 22-yard field goal in overtime to defeat the Buccaneers 17-14. De'Mond Parker set up the kick with a 21-yard run to the 4-yard line.

RUNNING DOWNHILL

Ahman Green ran the football in the second half of 2000 like no other back in Packers history.

Green, acquired in a trade that sent defensive back Fred Vinson to Seattle, gained more yards rushing (769) than any other Packers player in the final eight games of a season.

With various injuries limiting Dorsey Levens to just five starts, Green got an opportunity to shine. The newcomer became the full-time starter in Week 9 against the Vikings.

Green went over 100 yards rushing three times in the season's second half. His most productive afternoon came in the Metrodome, of all places, where he ripped off 161 yards on 25 carries and scored on a pass from Brett Favre.

A valuable receiver as well, Green led the team in rushing (1,175 yards) and receptions (73).

Most Rushing Yards, Final Eight Games of a Season

Yds	TD	Player	Year
769	7	Ahman Green	2000
756	3	John Brockington	1971
743	7	Jim Taylor	1961

TEAM STATISTICS

	GB	OPP
First Downs	315	284
Rushing	88	84
Passing	197	186
Penalty	30	14
Rushes	404	417
Yards Gained	1,643	1,618
Average Gain	4.07	3.88
Average Yards per Game	102.7	101.1
Passes Attempted	600	557
Completed	348	307
% Completed	58.00	55.12
Total Yards Gained	3,916	3,695
Times Sacked	34	38
Yards Lost	238	244
Net Yards Gained	3,678	3,451
Yards Gained per Completion	11.25	12.04
Net Yards per Pass Play	5.80	5.80
Average Net Yards per Game	229.9	215.7
Combined Net Yards Gained	5,321	5,069
Total Plays	1,038	1,012
Average Yards per Play	5.13	5.01
Average Net Yards per Game	332.6	316.8
Third Down Efficiency	85/218	82/224
Percentage	39.00	36.61
Fourth Down Efficiency	7/12	7/11
Percentage	58.33	63.64
Intercepted By	21	16
Yards Returned	315	201
Returned for TD	1	1
Punts	79	94
Yards Punted	3,033	3,888
Average Yards per Punt	38.39	41.36
Punt Returns	35	27
Yards Returned	300	205
Average Yards per Return	8.57	7.59
Returned for TD	0	1
Kickoff Returns	64	76
Yards Returned	1,570	1,639
Average Yards per Return	24.53	21.57
Returned for TD	1	0
Penalties	88	101
Yards Penalized	685	992
Fumbles	30	16
Lost	17	7
Own Recovered for Touchdown	0	0
Opponent's Recovered by	7	17
Opponent's Recovered for Touchdown	0	0
Total Points Scored	353	323
Total Touchdowns	36	37
Touchdowns Rushing	13	7
Touchdowns Passing	21	28
Touchdowns on Returns & Recoveries	2	2
Extra Points (Kicking)	32	36
Two-Point Conversions	2/3	1/1
Safeties	1	0
Field Goals Attempted	38	25
Field Goals Made	33	21
% Successful	86.84	84.00
Average Time of Possession	30:45	29:15

Regular Season 9-7-0

Date	GB		OPP	Att.
9/3	16	New York Jets	20	(59,870)
9/10	18	at Buffalo Bills	27	(72,722)
9/17	6	Philadelphia Eagles	3	(59,869)
9/24	29	at Arizona Cardinals	3	(69,568)
10/1	24	Chicago Bears	27	(59,869)
10/8	24	at Detroit Lions	31	(77,549)
10/15	31	San Francisco 49ers	28	(59,870)
10/29	20	at Miami Dolphins	28	(73,740)
11/6	26	Minnesota Vikings (OT)	20	(59,854)
11/12	15	at Tampa Bay Buccaneers	20	(65,621)
11/19	26	Indianapolis Colts	24	(59,869)
11/27	14	at Carolina Panthers	31	(73,295)
12/3	28	at Chicago Bears	6	(66,944)
12/10	26	Detroit Lions	13	(59,854)
12/17	33	at Minnesota Vikings	28	(64,183)
12/24	17	Tampa Bay Buccaneers (OT)	14	(59,692)

Score By Periods

	1	2	3	4	OT	Total
Packers	59	101	83	101	9	353
Opponents	51	91	82	99	0	323

INDIVIDUAL STATISTICS

Rushing	Att	Yds	Avg	LG	TD
Green	263	1,175	4.5	t39	10
Levens	77	224	2.9	17	3
Favre	27	108	4.0	18	0
Parker	18	85	4.7	24	0
Henderson	2	16	8.0	12	0
Rossum	1	16	16.0	16	0
Schroeder	2	11	5.5	12	0
Mitchell	2	8	4.0	4	0
Freeman	2	5	2.5	3	0
Driver	1	4	4.0	4	0
Goodman	3	-2	-0.7	3	0
Wuerffel	2	-2	-1.0	-1	0
Hasselbeck	4	-5	-1.3	-1	0
Packers	**404**	**1,643**	**4.1**	**t39**	**13**
Opponents	417	1,618	3.9	52	7

Receiving	No	Yds	Avg	LG	TD
Green	73	559	7.7	31	3
Schroeder	65	999	15.4	t55	4
Freeman	62	912	14.7	t67	9
Henderson	35	234	6.7	25	1
Franks	34	363	10.7	t27	1
Driver	21	322	15.3	49	1
T. Davis	19	177	9.3	41	2
Levens	16	146	9.1	37	0
Lee	10	134	13.4	38	0
Parker	9	50	5.6	10	0
Wetnight	3	20	6.7	9	0
Goodman	1	0	0.0	0	0
Packers	**348**	**3,916**	**11.3**	**t67**	**21**
Opponents	307	3,695	12.0	t78	28

Passing	Att	Com	Yds	Pct	TD	In	Tk/Yds	Rate
Favre	580	338	3,812	58.3	20	16	33/236	78.0
Hasselbeck	19	10	104	52.6	1	0	1/2	86.3
Green	1	0	0	0.0	0	0	0/0	--
Packers	**600**	**348**	**3,916**	**58.0**	**21**	**16**	**34/238**	**78.2**
Opponents	557	307	3,695	55.1	28	21	38/244	76.7

Punting	No	Yds	Avg	Net	TB	In20	LG	HB
Bidwell	78	3,003	38.5	34.6	5	22	53	0
Longwell	1	30	30.0	10.0	1	0	30	0
Packers	**79**	**3,033**	**38.4**	**34.3**	**6**	**22**	**53**	**0**
Opponents	94	3,888	41.4	34.6	17	25	60	0

Kickoff Returns	No	Yds	Avg	LG	TD
Rossum	50	1,288	25.8	t92	1
Henderson	5	80	16.0	22	0
Goodman	4	129	32.3	54	0
Mitchell	1	26	26.0	26	0
Berry	1	22	22.0	22	0
Morton	1	13	13.0	13	0
Bowens	1	12	12.0	12	0
Wetnight	1	0	0.0	0	0
Packers	**64**	**1,570**	**24.5**	**t92**	**1**
Opponents	76	1,639	21.6	40	0

Punt Returns	No	Yds	Avg	FC	LG	TD
Rossum	29	248	8.6	24	43	0
Lee	5	52	10.4	2	16	0
M. McKenzie	1	0	0.0	0	0	0
Packers	**35**	**300**	**8.6**	**26**	**43**	**0**
Opponents	27	205	7.6	27	t81	1

Interceptions	No	Yds	Avg	LG	TD
Sharper	9	109	12.1	47	0
T. Williams	4	105	26.3	46	1
McBride	2	43	21.5	43	0
L. Butler	2	25	12.5	22	0
Edwards	2	4	2.0	4	0
M. McKenzie	1	26	26.0	26	0
Holliday	1	3	3.0	3	0
Packers	**21**	**315**	**15.0**	**47**	**1**
Opponents	16	201	12.6	t42	1

Scoring	TDr	TDp	TDrt	PAT	2pt	FG	S	TP
Longwell	0	0	0	32/32	0	33/38	0	131
Green	10	3	0	0/0	0	0/0	0	78
Freeman	0	9	0	0/0	0	0/0	0	54
Schroeder	0	4	0	0/0	0	0/0	0	24
Levens	3	0	0	0/0	0	0/0	0	18
T. Davis	0	2	0	0/0	1	0/0	0	14
Driver	0	1	0	0/0	1	0/0	0	8
Franks	0	1	0	0/0	0	0/0	0	6
Henderson	0	1	0	0/0	0	0/0	0	6
Rossum	0	0	1	0/0	0	0/0	0	6
T. Williams	0	0	1	0/0	0	0/0	0	6
Maryland	0	0	0	0/0	0	0/0	1	2
Packers	**13**	**21**	**2**	**32/32**	**2**	**33/38**	**1**	**353**
Opponents	7	28	2	36/36	1	21/25	0	323

2-point conversions: Packers (2-3); Opponents (1-1)

Fumbles	Fum	Ow	Op	Yds	Tot
Bidwell	1	1	0	0	1
Bowens	0	0	1	0	1
L. Butler	0	0	1	0	1
R. Davis	0	0	1	0	1
T. Davis	2	0	0	0	0
Diggs	0	0	1	52	1
E. Dotson	0	0	1	0	1
Driver	0	0	1	0	1
Favre	9	2	0	-12	2
Franks	1	0	0	0	0
Freeman	1	0	0	0	0
Goodman	2	0	0	0	0
Green	6	1	0	0	1
Henderson	1	1	0	0	1
M. McKenzie	1	0	0	0	0
R. McKenzie	1	0	0	0	0
Mitchell	1	1	0	0	1
Rossum	4	3	0	0	3
Schroeder	1	0	0	0	0
Wayne	0	0	1	9	1
B. Williams	0	0	1	0	1
K.D. Williams	0	0	1	0	1
Packers	**30**	**12**	**7**	**49**	**19**

Quarterback Sacks	No.
Thierry	6.5
S. Dotson	6.0
Holliday	5.0
Hunt	5.0
Bowens	3.5
L. Butler	2.0
B. Harris	2.0
Wayne	2.0
Gbaja-Biamila	1.5
Lyon	1.0
Sharper	1.0
McGarrahan	0.5
B. Williams	0.5
K.D. Williams	0.5
team	1.0
Packers	**38.0**
Opponents	34.0

NFL STANDINGS

National Conference

Eastern Division	W	L	T	Pct	PF	PA
New York Giants	12	4	0	.750	328	246
Philadelphia Eagles	11	5	0	.688	351	245
Washington Redskins	8	8	0	.500	281	269
Dallas Cowboys	5	11	0	.313	294	361
Arizona Cardinals	3	13	0	.188	210	443

Central Division	W	L	T	Pct	PF	PA
Minnesota Vikings	11	5	0	.688	397	371
Tampa Bay Buccaneers	10	6	0	.625	388	269
Green Bay Packers	**9**	**7**	**0**	**.563**	**353**	**323**
Detroit Lions	9	7	0	.563	307	307
Chicago Bears	5	11	0	.313	216	355

Western Division	W	L	T	Pct	PF	PA
New Orleans	10	6	0	.625	354	305
St. Louis Rams	10	6	0	.625	540	471
Carolina Panthers	7	9	0	.438	310	310
San Francisco 49ers	6	10	0	.375	388	422
Atlanta Falcons	4	12	0	.250	252	413

American Conference

Eastern Division	W	L	T	Pct	PF	PA
Miami Dolphins	11	5	0	.688	323	226
Indianapolis Colts	10	6	0	.625	429	326
New York Jets	9	7	0	.563	322	321
Buffalo Bills	8	8	0	.500	315	350
New England Patriots	5	11	0	.313	276	338

Central Division	W	L	T	Pct	PF	PA
Tennessee Titans	13	3	0	.813	346	191
Baltimore Ravens	12	4	0	.750	333	165
Pittsburgh Steelers	9	7	0	.563	321	255
Jacksonville Jaguars	7	9	0	.438	367	327
Cincinnati Bengals	4	12	0	.250	185	359
Cleveland Browns	3	13	0	.188	161	419

Western Division	W	L	T	Pct	PF	PA
Oakland Raiders	12	4	0	.750	479	299
Denver Broncos	11	5	0	.688	485	369
Kansas City Chiefs	7	9	0	.438	355	354
Seattle Seahawks	6	10	0	.375	320	405
San Diego Chargers	1	15	0	.063	269	440

ROSTER

No	Name	Pos	Ht	Wt	DOB	College	G
31	Akins, Chris	S	5-11	195	11/29/76	Arkansas-Pine Bluff	2
21	Berry, Gary	S	5-11	193	10/24/77	Ohio State	4
9	Bidwell, Josh	P	6-3	222	03/13/76	Oregon	16
96	Bowens, David	DE	6-2	261	07/03/77	Western Illinois	14
85	Bradford, Corey	WR	6-1	205	12/08/75	Jackson State	2
36	Butler, LeRoy	S	6-0	203	07/19/68	Florida State	16
76	Clifton, Chad	T	6-5	325	06/26/76	Tennessee	13
60	Davis, Rob	LS	6-3	285	12/10/68	Shippensburg	16
81	Davis, Tyrone	TE	6-4	260	06/30/72	Virginia	14
59	Diggs, Na'il	LB	6-4	234	07/08/78	Ohio State	13
72	Dotson, Earl	T	6-3	317	12/17/70	Texas A&I	2
71	Dotson, Santana	DT	6-5	290	12/19/69	Baylor	12
80	Driver, Donald	WR	6-0	177	02/02/75	Alcorn State	16
24	Edwards, Antuan	CB	6-1	205	05/26/77	Clemson	12
4	Favre, Brett	QB	6-2	225	10/10/69	Southern Mississippi	16
58	Flanagan, Mike	C	6-5	297	11/10/73	UCLA	16
88	Franks, Bubba	TE	6-6	260	01/06/78	Miami (FL)	16
86	Freeman, Antonio	WR	6-0 1/2	198	05/27/72	Virginia Tech	15
94	Gbaja-Biamila, Kabeer	DE	6-4	245	09/24/77	San Diego State	7
57	Gizzi, Chris	LB	6-0	235	03/08/75	Air Force	11
29	Goodman, Herbert	RB	5-11	203	08/31/77	Graceland	5
30	Green, Ahman	RB	6-0	217	02/16/77	Nebraska	16
55	Harris, Bernardo	LB	6-2	246	10/15/71	North Carolina	16
11	Hasselbeck, Matt	QB	6-4	220	09/25/75	Boston College	16
33	Henderson, William	FB	6-1	253	02/19/71	North Carolina	16
90	Holliday, Vonnie	DE	6-5	290	12/11/75	North Carolina	12
97	Hunt, Cletidus	DE	6-4	299	01/02/76	Kentucky State	16
82	Lee, Charles	WR	6-2	202	11/19/77	Central Florida	15
25	Levens, Dorsey	RB	6-1	230	05/21/70	Georgia Tech	5
8	Longwell, Ryan	K	6-0	198	08/16/74	California	16
98	Lyon, Billy	DE/DT	6-5	295	12/10/73	Marshall	11
67	Maryland, Russell	DT	6-1	308	03/22/69	Miami (FL)	16
27	McBride, Tod	DB	6-1	207	01/26/76	UCLA	15
56	McCaslin, Eugene	LB	6-1	226	07/12/77	Florida	1
43	McGarrahan, Scott	S	6-1	198	02/12/74	New Mexico	16
34	McKenzie, Mike	CB	6-0	185	04/26/76	Memphis	10
63	McKenzie, Raleigh	G	6-2	290	02/08/63	Tennessee	3
28	Mitchell, Basil	RB	5-10	200	09/07/75	Texas Christian	1
40	Moore, Jason	S	5-10	191	01/15/76	San Diego State	3
53	Morton, Mike	LB	6-4	238	03/28/72	North Carolina	16
22	Parker, De'Mond	RB	5-10	185	12/24/76	Oklahoma	8
62	Rivera, Marco	G	6-4	310	04/26/72	Penn State	16
99	Robbins, Austin	DT	6-6	300	03/01/71	North Carolina	2
20	Rossum, Allen	CB/KR	5-8	178	10/22/75	Notre Dame	16
84	Schroeder, Bill	WR	6-2	205	01/09/71	Wisconsin-La Crosse	16
42	Sharper, Darren	DB	6-2	205	11/03/75	William & Mary	16
44	Snider, Matt	FB	6-2	240	01/26/76	Richmond	16
79	Stokes, Barry	G/T	6-4	310	12/20/73	Eastern Michigan	8
65	Tauscher, Mark	T	6-3	313	06/17/77	Wisconsin	16
91	Thierry, John	DE	6-4	262	09/04/71	Alcorn State	16
78	Verba, Ross	T	6-4	308	10/31/73	Iowa	16
68	Wahle, Mike	G	6-6	310	03/29/77	Navy	16
95	Warren, Steve	DT	6-1	298	01/22/78	Nebraska	13
54	Wayne, Nate	LB	6-0	230	01/12/75	Mississippi	16
83	Wetnight, Ryan	TE	6-2	230	11/05/70	Stanford	10
51	Williams, Brian	LB	6-1	245	12/17/72	USC	4
50	Williams, K.D.	LB	6-0	235	04/22/73	Henderson State	16
37	Williams, Tyrone	CB	5-11	193	05/31/73	Nebraska	16
52	Winters, Frank	C	6-3	305	01/23/64	West Illinois	14
7	Wuerffel, Danny	QB	6-1	212	05/27/74	Florida	1

DRAFT

Rnd	Name	Pos	Ht	Wt	College
1	Bubba Franks (14)	TE	6-6	260	Miami (FL)
2	Chad Clifton (44)	T	6-5	325	Tennessee
3	Steve Warren (74)	DT	6-1	298	Nebraska
4a	Na'il Diggs (98)	LB	6-4	234	Ohio State
	(Choice from 49ers for Packers' 4th-round (108) and 5th-round (132) picks)				
4b	(Choice (108) from Jets for Rick Mirer; to 49ers in deal mentioned above)				
4c	Anthony Lucas (114)	WR	6-2	197	Arkansas
4d	Gary Berry (126)	S	5-11	193	Ohio State
	(Free agent compensatory pick)				
5a	(Choice (132) from 49ers for Craig Newsome; to 49ers in deal mentioned above)				
5b	Kabeer Gbaja-Biamila (149)	DE	6-4	245	San Diego State
5c	Joey Jamison (151)	WR	5-9	167	Texas Southern
	(from Seahawks in Ahman Green/Fred Vinson trade)				
6	(Choice (185) to Seahawks in Ahman Green/Fred Vinson trade)				
7a	Mark Tauscher (224)	T	6-3	313	Wisconsin
7b	Ron Moore (229)	DT	6-4	295	NW Oklahoma
	(Choice from Seahawks for Derrick Mayes)				
7c	Charles Lee (242)	WR	6-2	200	Central Florida
	(Free agent compensatory pick)				
7d	Eugene McCaslin (249)	LB	6-1	225	Florida
	(Free agent compensatory pick)				
7e	Rondell Mealey (252)	RB	5-11	209	LSU
	(Free agency compensatory pick)				

2000 GREEN BAY PACKERS

FRONT ROW: (L-R) 4 Brett Favre, 7 Danny Wuerffel, 8 Ryan Longwell, 9 Josh Bidwell, 11 Matt Hasselbeck, 20 Allen Rossum, 21 Gary Berry, 22 De'Mond Parker, 24 Antuan Edwards, 25 Dorsey Levens, 27 Tod McBride.

SECOND ROW: (L-R) Strength and Conditioning Coach Barry Rubin, Special Teams Coach Frank Novak, Defensive Assistant/Quality Control Billy Davis, Assistant Defensive Backs Coach Lionel Washington, Defensive Backs Coach Bob Slowik, Linebackers Coach Bo Pelini, Defensive Line Coach Jethro Franklin, Defensive Coordinator Ed Donatell, Head Coach Mike Sherman, Offensive Coordinator Tom Rossley, Offensive Line Coach Larry Beightol, Running Backs Coach Kippy Brown, Wide Receivers Coach Ray Sherman, Tight Ends Coach Jeff Jagodzinski, Offensive Assistant/Quality Control Trent Miles, Offensive Assistant/Quality Control Darrell Bevell, Offensive Line Coach Rich McGeorge.

THIRD ROW: (L-R) 28 Basil Mitchell, 29 Herbert Goodman, 30 Ahman Green, 33 William Henderson, 34 Mike McKenzie, 36 LeRoy Butler, 37 Tyrone Williams, 42 Darren Sharper, 43 Scott McGarrahan, 44 Matt Snider, 50 K.D. Williams.

FOURTH ROW: (L-R) 51 Brian Williams, 52 Frank Winters, 53 Mike Morton, 54 Nate Wayne, 55 Bernardo Harris, 57 Chris Gizzi, 58 Mike Flanagan, 59 Na'il Diggs, 60 Rob Davis, 62 Marco Rivera.

FIFTH ROW: (L-R) 65 Mark Tauscher, 67 Russell Maryland, 68 Mike Wahle, 71 Santana Dotson, 72 Earl Dotson, 76 Chad Clifton, 78 Ross Verba, 79 Barry Stokes, 80 Donald Driver, 81 Tyrone Davis, 82 Charles Lee.

SIXTH ROW: (L-R) Director of Football Administration Bruce Warwick, 84 Bill Schroeder, 85 Corey Bradford, 86 Antonio Freeman, 88 Bubba Franks, 90 Vonnie Holliday, 91 John Thierry, 95 Steve Warren, 96 David Bowens, 97 Cletidus Hunt, 98 Billy Lyon, Administrative Assistant/Football Matt Klein.

BACK ROW: (L-R) Assistant Strength and Conditioning Coach Mark Lovat, Training Room Intern Brent Amble, Assistant Trainer Bryan Engel, Assistant Trainer Kurt Fielding, Head Trainer Pepper Burruss, Associate Team Physician Dr. John Gray, Equipment Manager Gordon (Red) Batty, Assistant Equipment Manager Bryan Nehring, Assistant Equipment Manager Tom Bakken, Equipment Assistant John Odea, Equipment Intern Andy Ashenbrenner, Corporate Security Officer Jerry Parins, Video Assistant Chris Kirby, Assistant Video Director Bob Eckberg, Video Director Al Treml.

The announcement that Ron Wolf would be stepping down as the Packers' general manager in June was big news. The kicker: head coach Mike Sherman would be replacing him.

Not since Bart Starr in 1980 had one man held down both positions within the Packers organization. The late Vince Lombardi stepped down as coach early in 1968, citing the difficulties associated with performing both roles.

"During the next four months, Ron and Mike will work in a dual capacity until Ron's subsequent departure," Packers president Bob Harlan said in February. "This will help facilitate the transitional process that will occur.

"Beginning June 1, Ron will continue to serve the organization as a consultant for the three years remaining on his contract."

One of Sherman's first moves was to restructure the football operations side of the organization. He expanded the roles of John Dorsey (director of college scouting) and Reggie McKenzie (director of pro personnel). In May, he hired executive Mark Hatley from the Bears to become the team's vice president of football operations.

Sherman didn't neglect his coaching duties. He guided the team to a 12-4 record and its first trip to the playoffs in three years.

Aside from defensive lineman Jim Flanigan and the return of Doug Pederson, Green Bay showed little interest in the free agency market. What the team did was re-sign its veterans—a number of them to long-term deals. The team locked up Ryan Longwell (five years, $7.5 million), Darren Sharper (six years, $30 million), Ahman Green (five years, $18.3 million), and Brett Favre (10 years, $100 million).

Favre threw more than 30 touchdown passes (32) for the first time since Mike Holmgren's last season in Green Bay. The team's passing game ranked third, its highest finish since 1998 as well.

Led by Kabeer Gbaja-Biamila, the Packers sacked opposing passers a club-record 52 times. Offensively, Green Bay gave up just 22 sacks.

The first 15 minutes of the season generated more offense than in any other season-opening first quarter in team history. Green, Favre, Bill Schroeder and the rest of the offense piled up 223 yards on 13 plays in going ahead of the Lions 21-0. The team tacked on another 201 yards in the final three periods to win 28-6.

Terrorists attacked the United States on Sept. 11. The league postponed the games it was to play in Week 2.

"We in the National Football League have decided that our priorities for this weekend are to pause, grieve and reflect," commissioner Paul Tagliabue said in a written statement. "It is a time to tend to families and neighbors and all those wounded by these horrific acts of terrorism."

On Sept. 24, the Packers trounced the Redskins 37-0 in an emotional return to football. Linebacker and Air Force reservist Chris Gizzi started the proceedings by sprinting out of the tunnel with an American flag in tow.

Tampa Bay bumped Green Bay from the unbeaten ranks on Oct. 8 with a 14-10 win. Mike Alstott got the game-winning score on a 39-yard run with 6:45 remaining.

The Packers rebounded with a 31-23 upset of the defending Super Bowl champion Ravens at Lambeau Field. Favre passed for 337 yards and three touchdowns.

Two weeks later, Allen Rossum returned a punt 55 yards for a touchdown to beat the Buccaneers 21-20. Green Bay then downed the Bears 20-12 to improve to 6-2 and move into a tie with Chicago for first place in the division.

Atlanta dropped Green Bay back into second place with a 23-20 win at Lambeau Field. It took three weeks and a 17-7 victory over the Bears on Dec. 9 for the Packers to again climb into a tie with Chicago for first place.

But as they had done with the Falcons, Green Bay tripped up, falling 26-20 to the Titans. Skip Hicks broke loose for 142 yards rushing on 17 carries.

"Sometimes I just question whether guys know how or believe enough in themselves to make it happen," said Favre, who led the team in rushing with a paltry 20 yards.

Green Bay clinched a playoff spot by crushing the Browns 30-7 on Dec. 23, a game in which Favre threw three touchdown passes and Green rushed for 150 yards. But the division title went to the Bears (13-3), who won their final four games.

SACKING UP NICELY

The Packers of 2001 did a nice job of sacking opposing passers while at the same time protecting Brett Favre.

Green Bay notched a team-record 52 sacks. Kabeer Gbaja-Biamila led all defenders with 13 1/2.

Favre dropped back to pass on 532 occasions, but was sacked only 22 times, the lowest total of his Packers career.

That Green Bay notched 30 more sacks than it gave up was unheard of in team annals. Since team sacks were first compiled in 1963, the club had never finished with a differential of greater than plus-20.

The Green and Gold dumped Lions quarterback Charlie Batch seven times in the opener. The team recorded at least one sack in every game except the second Bears game.

Listed below are the Packers' greatest differentials in sacks recorded versus sacks given up since 1963:

Diff.	Year	For/Against
+30	2001	52/22
+19	1963	39/20
+16	1966	47/31
+16	1993	46/30

TEAM STATISTICS

	GB	OPP
First Downs	282	278
Rushing	72	83
Passing	187	176
Penalty	23	19
Rushes	410	406
Yards Gained	1,693	1,769
Average Gain	4.13	4.36
Average Yards per Game	105.8	110.6
Passes Attempted	510	583
Completed	314	341
% Completed	61.57	58.49
Total Yards Gained	3,921	3,505
Times Sacked	22	52
Yards Lost	151	337
Net Yards Gained	3,770	3,168
Yards Gained per Completion	12.49	10.28
Net Yards per Pass Play	7.09	4.99
Average Net Yards per Game	235.6	198.0
Combined Net Yards Gained	5,463	4,937
Total Plays	942	1,041
Average Yards per Play	5.80	4.74
Average Net Yards per Game	341.4	308.6
Third Down Efficiency	72/197	93/238
Percentage	36.55	39.08
Fourth Down Efficiency	3/6	9/22
Percentage	50.00	40.91
Intercepted By	20	15
Yards Returned	344	252
Returned for TD	2	2
Punts	82	86
Yards Punted	3,485	3,644
Average Yards per Punt	42.50	42.37
Punt Returns	33	34
Yards Returned	251	288
Average Yards per Return	7.61	8.47
Returned for TD	1	0
Kickoff Returns	54	76
Yards Returned	1,008	1,520
Average Yards per Return	18.67	20.00
Returned for TD	0	0
Penalties	80	104
Yards Penalized	633	921
Fumbles	28	36
Lost	12	19
Own Recovered for Touchdown	0	0
Opponent's Recovered by	19	12
Opponent's Recovered for Touchdown	1	2
Total Points Scored	390	266
Total Touchdowns	47	28
Touchdowns Rushing	11	10
Touchdowns Passing	32	14
Touchdowns on Returns & Recoveries	4	4
Extra Points (Kicking)	44	20
Two-Point Conversions	1/2	5/8
Safeties	1	1
Field Goals Attempted	31	28
Field Goals Made	20	22
% Successful	64.52	78.57
Average Time of Possession	29:32	30:28

Regular Season 12-4-0

Date	GB		OPP	Att.
9/9	28	Detroit Lions	6	(59,523)
9/24	37	Washington Redskins	0	(59,771)
9/30	28	at Carolina Panthers	7	(73,120)
10/7	10	at Tampa Bay Buccaneers	14	(65,510)
10/14	31	Baltimore Ravens	23	(59,866)
10/21	13	at Minnesota Vikings	35	(64,165)
11/4	21	Tampa Bay Buccaneers	20	(59,861)
11/11	20	at Chicago Bears	12	(66,944)
11/18	20	Atlanta Falcons	23	(59,849)
11/22	29	at Detroit Lions	27	(77,730)
12/3	28	at Jacksonville Jaguars	21	(66,908)
12/9	17	Chicago Bears	7	(59,869)
12/16	20	at Tennessee Titans	26	(68,804)
12/23	30	Cleveland Browns	7	(59,824)
12/30	24	Minnesota Vikings	13	(59,870)
1/6	34	at New York Giants	25	(78,601)

Postseason 1-1-0

Date	GB		OPP	Att.
1/13	25	San Francisco 49ers	15	(59,825)
1/20	17	at St. Louis Rams	45	(66,338)

Score By Periods

	1	2	3	4	OT	Total
Packers	89	90	111	100	0	390
Opponents	37	106	34	89	0	266

INDIVIDUAL STATISTICS

Rushing	Att	Yds	Avg	LG	TD
Green	304	1,387	4.6	t83	9
Levens	44	165	3.8	40	0
Favre	38	56	1.5	14	1
Driver	3	38	12.7	t31	1
Mealey	11	37	3.4	9	0
Henderson	6	11	1.8	4	0
Schroeder	1	6	6.0	6	0
Goodman	1	-1	-1.0	-1	0
Pederson	1	-1	-1.0	-1	0
Freeman	1	-5	-5.0	-5	0
Packers	410	1,693	4.1	t83	11
Opponents	406	1,769	4.4	61	10

Receiving	No	Yds	Avg	LG	TD
Green	62	594	9.6	42	2
Schroeder	53	918	17.3	t67	9
Freeman	52	818	15.7	63	6
Franks	36	322	8.9	31	9
Bradford	31	526	17.0	56	2
Levens	24	159	6.6	19	1
Henderson	21	193	9.2	26	0
Driver	13	167	12.8	37	1
Martin	13	144	11.1	31	1
C. Lee	3	32	10.7	23	1
T. Davis	3	14	4.7	7	0
Mealey	2	31	15.5	19	0
B. Collins	1	3	3.0	3	0
Packers	314	3,921	12.5	t67	32
Opponents	341	3,505	10.3	t47	14

Passing	Att	Com	Yds	Pct	TD	In	Tk/Yds	Rate
Favre	510	314	3,921	61.6	32	15	22/151	94.1
Packers	510	314	3,921	61.6	32	15	22/151	94.1
Opponents	583	341	3,505	58.5	14	20	52/337	69.6

Punting	No	Yds	Avg	Net	TB	In20	LG	HB
Bidwell	82	3,485	42.5	36.5	10	21	68	0
Packers	82	3,485	42.5	36.5	10	21	68	0
Opponents	86	3,644	42.4	37.4	9	33	70	0

Kickoff Returns	No	Yds	Avg	LG	TD
Rossum	23	431	18.7	27	0
Levens	14	362	25.9	53	0
Henderson	6	62	10.3	14	0
Mealey	4	63	15.8	24	0
Ferguson	2	32	16.0	16	0
Freeman	2	28	14.0	24	0
Goodman	1	21	21.0	21	0
Flanigan	1	9	9.0	9	0
Akins	1	0	0.0	0	0
Packers	54	1,008	18.7	53	0
Opponents	76	1,520	20.0	43	0

Punt Returns	No	Yds	Avg	FC	LG	TD
Freeman	17	114	6.7	7	29	0
Rossum	11	109	9.9	8	t55	1
C. Lee	3	6	2.0	0	6	0
Sharper	1	18	18.0	3	18	0
Ferguson	1	4	4.0	2	4	0
Packers	33	251	7.6	20	t55	1
Opponents	34	288	8.5	19	37	0

Interceptions	No	Yds	Avg	LG	TD
Sharper	6	78	13.0	23	0
T. Williams	4	117	29.3	t69	1
Wayne	3	55	18.3	35	0
M. McKenzie	2	38	19.0	t38	1
Jue	2	35	17.5	35	0
B. Harris	2	12	6.0	8	0
Thibodeaux	1	9	9.0	9	0
Packers	20	344	17.2	t69	2
Opponents	15	252	16.8	t98	2

Scoring	TDr	TDp	TDrt	PAT	2pt	FG	S	TP
Longwell	0	0	0	44/45	0	20/31	0	104
Green	9	2	0	0/0	0	0/0	0	66
Franks	0	9	0	0/0	0	0/0	0	54
Schroeder	0	9	0	0/0	0	0/0	0	54
Freeman	0	6	0	0/0	1	0/0	0	38
Bradford	0	2	0	0/0	0	0/0	0	12
Driver	1	1	0	0/0	0	0/0	0	12
Favre	1	0	0	0/0	0	0/0	0	6
C. Lee	0	1	0	0/0	0	0/0	0	6
Levens	0	1	0	0/0	0	0/0	0	6
Martin	0	1	0	0/0	0	0/0	0	6
M. McKenzie	0	0	1	0/0	0	0/0	0	6
Mealey	0	0	1	0/0	0	0/0	0	6
Rossum	0	0	1	0/0	0	0/0	0	6
T. Williams	0	0	1	0/0	0	0/0	0	6
Thierry	0	0	0	0/0	0	0/0	1	2
Packers	11	32	4	44/45	1	20/31	1	390
Opponents	10	14	4	20/20	5	22/28	1	266

2-point conversions: Packers (1-2); Opponents (5-8)

Fumbles	Fum	Ow	Op	Yds	Tot
Akins	1	0	0	0	0
Bradford	1	0	0	0	0
Edwards	0	0	1	-2	1
Favre	16	6	0	-38	6
Flanagan	2	0	0	-18	0
Freeman	1	1	0	0	1
Gbaja-Biamila	0	0	1	0	1
Green	5	2	0	0	2
B. Harris	0	0	3	0	3
Henderson	0	2	0	0	2
Holliday	0	0	3	11	3
Hunt	0	0	1	0	1
Marshall	0	0	1	0	1
Mealey	0	0	1	27	1
A. O'Neal	0	0	1	0	1
Rivera	0	1	0	0	1
Schroeder	1	0	0	0	0
Sharper	0	0	1	17	1
Tauscher	0	1	0	0	1
Thierry	0	0	2	0	2
Wayne	0	0	2	0	2
K.D. Williams	0	0	1	0	1
T. Williams	0	0	1	0	1
Packers	28	13	19	-3	32

Quarterback Sacks	No.
Gbaja-Biamila	13.5
Holliday	7.0
Wayne	5.5
Flanigan	4.5
S. Dotson	3.5
Thierry	3.5
B. Harris	2.5
Diggs	2.0
Lyon	2.0
McBride	2.0
Reynolds	2.0
Sharper	2.0
L. Butler	1.0
team	1.0
Packers	52.0
Opponents	22.0

NFL STANDINGS

National Conference

Eastern Division	W	L	T	Pct	PF	PA
Philadelphia Eagles	11	5	0	.688	343	208
Washington Redskins	8	8	0	.500	256	303
New York Giants	7	9	0	.438	294	321
Arizona Cardinals	7	9	0	.438	295	343

Central Division	W	L	T	Pct	PF	PA
Chicago Bears	13	3	0	.813	338	203
Green Bay Packers	12	4	0	.750	390	266
Tampa Bay Buccaneers	9	7	0	.563	324	280
Minnesota Vikings	5	11	0	.313	290	390
Detroit Lions	2	14	0	.125	270	424

Western Division	W	L	T	Pct	PF	PA
St. Louis Rams	14	2	0	.875	503	273
San Francisco 49ers	12	4	0	.750	409	282
New Orleans Saints	7	9	0	.438	333	409
Atlanta Falcons	7	9	0	.438	291	377
Carolina Panthers	1	15	0	.063	253	410

American Conference

Eastern Division	W	L	T	Pct	PF	PA
New England Patriots	11	5	0	.688	371	272
Miami Dolphins	11	5	0	.688	344	290
New York Jets	10	6	0	.625	308	295
Indianapolis Colts	6	10	0	.375	413	486
Buffalo Bills	3	13	0	.188	265	420

Central Division	W	L	T	Pct	PF	PA
Pittsburgh Steelers	13	3	0	.813	352	212
Baltimore Ravens	10	6	0	.625	303	265
Cleveland Browns	7	9	0	.438	285	319
Tennessee Titans	7	9	0	.438	336	388
Jacksonville Jaguars	6	10	0	.375	294	286
Cincinnati Bengals	6	10	0	.375	226	309

Western Division	W	L	T	Pct	PF	PA
Oakland Raiders	10	6	0	.625	399	327
Seattle Seahawks	9	7	0	.563	301	324
Denver Broncos	8	8	0	.500	340	339
Kansas City Chiefs	6	10	0	.375	320	344
San Diego Chargers	5	11	0	.313	332	321

ROSTER

No	Name	Pos	Ht	Wt	DOB	College	G
31	Akins, Chris	S	5-11	195	11/29/76	Arkansas-Pine Bluff	11
9	Bidwell, Josh	P	6-3	220	03/13/76	Oregon	16
28	Bowen, Matt	S	6-1	208	11/12/76	Iowa	5
85	Bradford, Corey	WR	6-1	197	12/08/75	Jackson State	16
93	Brown, Gilbert	DT	6-2	339	02/22/71	Kansas	11
36	Butler, LeRoy	S	6-0	203	07/19/68	Florida State	9
76	Clifton, Chad	T	6-5	327	06/26/76	Tennessee	14
87	Collins, Bobby	TE	6-4	248	08/26/76	North Alabama	4
60	Davis, Rob	LS	6-3	285	12/10/68	Shippensburg	16
81	Davis, Tyrone	TE	6-4	260	06/30/72	Virginia	4
59	Diggs, Na'il	LB	6-4	238	07/08/78	Ohio State	16
72	Dotson, Earl	T	6-3	317	12/17/70	Texas A&I	12
71	Dotson, Santana	DT	6-5	287	12/19/69	Baylor	16
80	Driver, Donald	WR	6-0	185	02/02/75	Alcorn State	13
24	Edwards, Antuan	CB	6-1	210	05/26/77	Clemson	3
4	Favre, Brett	QB	6-2	225	10/10/69	Southern Mississippi	16
89	Ferguson, Robert	WR	6-1	209	12/17/79	Texas A&M	1
58	Flanagan, Mike	C	6-5	297	11/10/73	UCLA	16
75	Flanigan, Jim	DT	6-2	290	08/27/71	Notre Dame	16
88	Franks, Bubba	TE	6-6	260	01/06/78	Miami (FL)	16
86	Freeman, Antonio	WR	6-0?	198	05/27/72	Virginia Tech	16
94	Gbaja-Biamila, Kabeer	DE	6-4	253	09/24/77	San Diego State	16
57	Gizzi, Chris	LB	6-0	235	03/08/75	Air Force	12
29	Goodman, Herbert	RB	5-11	205	08/31/77	Graceland	7
30	Green, Ahman	RB	6-0	217	02/16/77	Nebraska	16
55	Harris, Bernardo	LB	6-2	250	10/15/71	North Carolina	16
33	Henderson, William	FB	6-1	253	02/19/71	North Carolina	16
90	Holliday, Vonnie	DE	6-5	290	12/11/75	North Carolina	16
56	Holmberg, Rob	LB	6-3	240	05/06/71	Penn State	4
97	Hunt, Cletidus	DE/DT	6-4	290	01/02/76	Kentucky State	12
23	Jenkins, Billy	S	5-10	205	07/08/74	Howard	6
21	Jue, Bhawoh	CB/S	6-0	200	05/24/79	Penn State	15
82	Lee, Charles	WR	6-2	205	11/19/77	Central Florida	7
25	Levens, Dorsey	RB	6-1	230	05/21/70	Georgia Tech	15
8	Longwell, Ryan	K	6-0	200	08/16/74	California	16
98	Lyon, Billy	DE/DT	6-5	295	12/10/73	Marshall	12
51	Marshall, Torrance	LB	6-2	255	06/12/77	Oklahoma	14
83	Martin, David	TE	6-4	250	03/13/79	Tennessee	14
27	McBride, Tod	DB	6-1	205	01/26/76	UCLA	16
34	McKenzie, Mike	CB	6-0	190	04/26/76	Memphis	16
32	Mealey, Rondell	RB	6-0	224	02/24/77	Louisiana State	11
53	O'Neal, Andre	LB	6-1	235	12/12/75	Marshall	2
18	Pederson, Doug	QB	6-3	220	01/31/68	Northeast Louisiana	16
99	Reynolds, Jamal	DE	6-3	266	02/20/79	Florida State	6
62	Rivera, Marco	G	6-4	310	04/26/72	Penn State	16
20	Rossum, Allen	CB/KR	5-8	178	10/22/75	Notre Dame	6
84	Schroeder, Bill	WR	6-2	205	01/09/71	Wisconsin-La Crosse	14
42	Sharper, Darren	DB	6-1	207	11/03/75	William & Mary	16
79	Stokes, Barry	G/T	6-4	310	12/20/73	Eastern Michigan	16
65	Tauscher, Mark	T	6-3	320	06/17/77	Wisconsin	16
22	Thibodeaux, Keith	CB	5-11	189	05/16/74	Northwestern (LA) State	7
91	Thierry, John	DE	6-4	262	09/04/71	Alcorn State	12
68	Wahle, Mike	G	6-6	310	03/29/77	Navy	16
95	Walker, Rod	DT	6-3	320	02/04/76	Troy State	11
54	Wayne, Nate	LB	6-0	237	01/12/75	Mississippi	12
50	Williams, K.D.	LB	6-0	245	04/22/73	Henderson State	12
37	Williams, Tyrone	CB	5-11	193	05/31/73	Nebraska	16
52	Winters, Frank	C	6-3	305	01/23/64	West Illinois	4

DRAFT

Rnd	Name	Pos	Ht	Wt	College
1a	Jamal Reynolds (10)	DE	6-3	266	Florida State

(Choice from Seahawks in Matt Hasselbeck trade)

1b (Choice (17) to Seahawks in Matt Hasselbeck trade)

Rnd	Name	Pos	Ht	Wt	College
2a	Robert Ferguson (41)	WR	6-1	209	Texas A&M

(Traded 2nd-round (47), two 3rd-round (80 & 82), 6th-round (179) and 7th-round (222) picks to 49ers for 49ers' 2nd-round (41), 3rd-round (71) and 4th-round (105) picks)

2b (Choice (47) to 49ers in deal mentioned above)

Rnd	Name	Pos	Ht	Wt	College
3a	Bhawoh Jue (71)	DB	6-0	200	Penn State

(Choice from 49ers in deal mentioned above)

Rnd	Name	Pos	Ht	Wt	College
3b	Torrance Marshall (72)	LB	6-2	250	Oklahoma

(Choice from Seahawks in Matt Hasselbeck trade)

3c (Choice (80) to 49ers in deal mentioned above)

3d (Choice (82) from Saints in Aaron Brooks/Lamont Hall/K.D. Williams trade; to 49ers in deal mentioned above)

Rnd	Name	Pos	Ht	Wt	College
4a	Bill Ferrario (105)	G	6-2	315	Wisconsin

(Choice from 49ers in deal mentioned above)

4b (Choice (113) to Broncos for Nate Wayne)

5 (Choice (147) to Eagles for Allen Rossum)

6a (Choice (179) to 49ers in deal mentioned above)

Rnd	Name	Pos	Ht	Wt	College
6b	David Martin (198)	TE	6-4	250	Tennessee

(Free agent compensatory pick)

7a (Choice (219) to Broncos for David Bowens)

7b (Choice (222) from Rams in Mike Morton trade; to 49ers in deal mentioned above)

2001 GREEN BAY PACKERS

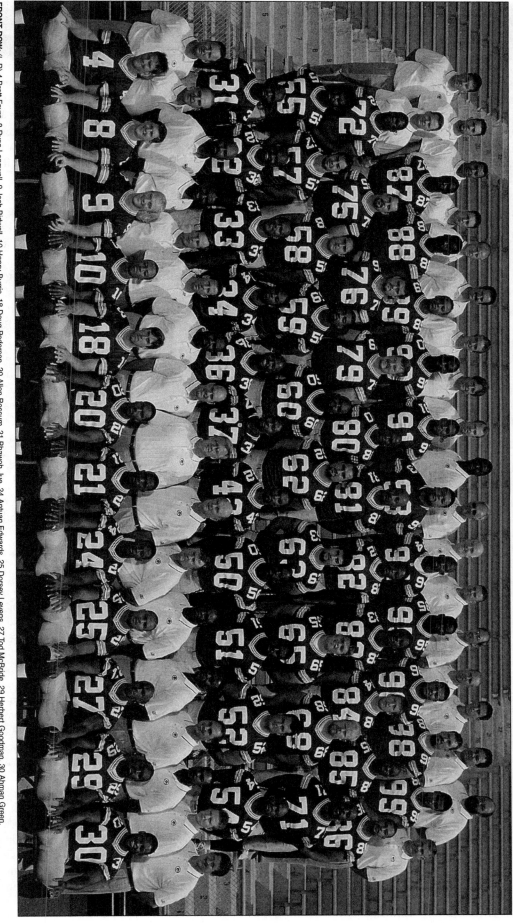

FRONT ROW: (L–R) 4 Brett Favre, 8 Ryan Longwell, 9 Josh Bidwell, 10 Henry Burris, 18 Doug Pederson, 20 Allen Rossum, 21 Bhawoh Jue, 24 Antuan Edwards, 25 Dorsey Levens, 27 Tod McBride, 29 Herbert Goodman, 30 Ahman Green.

SECOND ROW: (L–R) Strength and Conditioning Coach Barry Rubin, Special Teams Coach Frank Novak, Defensive Assistant/Quality Control Brad Miller, Assistant Defensive Backs Coach Lionel Washington, Defensive Backs Coach Bob Slowik, Linebackers Coach Bo Pelini, Defensive Line Coach Jethro Franklin, Defensive Coordinator Ed Donatell, Head Coach Mike Sherman, Offensive Coordinator Tom Rossley, Offensive Line Coach Larry Beightol, Running Backs Coach Sylvester Croom, Wide Receivers Coach Ray Sherman, Tight Ends Coach Jeff Jagodzinski, Quality Control Assistant/Special Teams–Offense Stan Drayton, Quality Control Assistant/Special Teams–Offense/Defense Darrell Bevell, Assistant Offensive Line Coach Pat Ruel.

THIRD ROW: (L–R) 31 Chris Akins, 32 Rondell Mealey, 33 William Henderson, 34 Mike McKenzie, 36 LeRoy Butler, 37 Tyrone Williams, 42 Darren Sharper, 50 K.D. Williams, 51 Torrance Marshall, 52 Frank Winters, 54 Nate Wayne.

FOURTH ROW: (L–R) 55 Bernardo Harris, 57 Chris Gizzi, 58 Mike Flanagan, 59 Na'il Diggs, 60 Rob Davis, 62 Marco Rivera, 63 Bill Ferrario, 65 Mark Tauscher, 68 Mike Wahle, 71 Santana Dotson.

FIFTH ROW: (L–R) 72 Earl Dotson, 75 Jim Flanigan, 76 Chad Clifton, 79 Barry Stokes, 80 Donald Driver, 81 Tyrone Davis, 82 Charles Lee, 83 David Martin, 84 Bill Schroeder, 85 Corey Bradford, 86 Antonio Freeman.

SIXTH ROW: (L–R) Director of Football Administration Bruce Warwick, 87 Bobby Collins, 88 Bubba Franks, 89 Robert Ferguson, 90 Vonnie Holliday, 91 John Thierry, 93 Gilbert Brown, 94 Kabeer Gbaja-Biamila, 95 Rod Walker, 96 Steve Warren, 98 Billy Lyon, 99 Jamal Reynolds, Director Research and Development Mike Eayrs.

BACK ROW: (L–R) Administrative Assistant/Football Matt Klein, Assistant Strength and Conditioning Coach Mark Lovat, Weight Room Assistant Vince Workman, Training Room Intern Jay Phillips, Assistant Trainer Bryan Engel, Assistant Trainer Kurt Fielding, Head Trainer Pepper Burruss, Associate Team Physician Dr. John Gray, Team Physician Dr. Patrick J. McKenzie, Director of Player Programs Edgar Bennett, Corporate Security Officer Jerry Parins, Equipment Manager Gordon (Red) Batty, Assistant Equipment Manager Tom Bakken, Assistant Equipment Manager Bryan Nehring, Equipment Assistant John Odea, Video Intern Andy Muckerheide, Video Assistant Director Chris Kirby, Video Director Bob Eckberg.

Adversity and the ability to overcome it was a theme Mike Sherman addressed repeatedly in the weeks leading up to the start of the season. He couldn't have chosen a more appropriate topic, as the Packers were rocked by an inordinate number of injuries in 2002.

To its credit, Green Bay buckled down and won 12 of its first 15 games. Playing in the new NFC North Division, the club salted away the division title by early December.

Not content to merely make the playoffs, the team sought to secure a bye and home-field advantage throughout the postseason. After Tampa Bay and Philadelphia each lost in the season's final weeks, Green Bay jumped into the driver's seat. Beat the Jets in the finale and the road to the Super Bowl would go through Lambeau Field.

But instead of seizing the moment, the Packers merely seized up, falling 42-17 in New York. The loss became even costlier when the Falcons stunned the football world by becoming the first visiting team to win a playoff game at Lambeau Field, a game that wouldn't have taken place had Green Bay beaten the Jets.

"To say it's disappointing is as big an understatement as I could ever make," said Sherman, after Atlanta ran over his team 27-7.

Brett Favre did not talk to reporters after the game. Some speculated he might retire.

"I'm upset we didn't go any further," he said at a press conference two days later. "But I'm still standing, still feel like I'm playing my best, will be back next year."

During the season, Favre was repeatedly asked whether he was coming back in 2003.

The Packers signed three big names during the offseason: defensive end Joe Johnson, wide receiver Terry Glenn and linebacker Hardy Nickerson. None of the three produced as they had in their prime, although Glenn was second on the team in receiving yards (817).

The injury list grew as the season wore on. The offensive and defensive lines were hit particularly hard. Mark Tauscher (MCL, Game 2), Joe Johnson (torn triceps, Game 5) and Chad Clifton (pelvis, Game 11) were lost for the season. Some players, such as Vonnie Holliday (torn pectoral muscle, knee injury) and Marco Rivera (both knees), suffered more than one injury.

Even Favre was not immune. He sustained a sprained lateral collateral ligament after being sacked by the Redskins' LaVar Arrington and Jeremiah Trotter. The injury occurred before the Packers' bye week, which gave Favre extra time to recover. The quarterback didn't miss a game and his streak of consecutive starts reached 173 by season's end.

Green Bay struggled early, especially defensively and on special teams. In the season opener, Atlanta piled up 374 yards before bowing out 37-34 in overtime. The Saints amassed 357 yards in a 35-20 win. The Lions' Az-Zahir Hakim scored on a 72-yard punt return and rookie quarterback Joey Harrington staged a rally that had Detroit thinking upset before finally falling 37-31 in Week 3.

For Green Bay, the Lions contest was the first of seven wins in a row. By the time the run was over, the Packers were 8-1 (the best record in the NFL) with a five-game lead over Detroit in the NFC North.

During the run, Sherman was assessed a 15-yard penalty for unsportsmanlike conduct for a sideline tantrum after a touchdown pass from Bubba Franks to Donald Driver was called back. (Replays reversed the call on the field.) Favre threw for a career-high 287 yards in the first half against the Bears in Champaign, Ill., then bettered that mark with 295 yards in the rematch with the Lions. And Driver emerged as the team's go-to receiver with 35 catches for 578 yards.

Even on such a roll, Green Bay couldn't win in the Metrodome or in Tampa. Favre was flagged for unnecessary roughness after hitting safety Jack Brewer out of bounds in the 31-21 loss to the Vikings, and Sherman confronted defensive lineman Warren Sapp after the 21-7 loss to the Buccaneers. Sapp ended Clifton's season with a vicious block on an interception return by Brad Kelly in the third quarter.

"I just went up to Warren and I told him that I didn't appreciate that lick that he put on Clifton," Sherman said. "That was the extent of it."

Green Bay bounced back as if it might win out. But the Jets chalked up six touchdowns on six trips inside the Packers' red zone to end that possibility on Dec. 29.

SECOND-HALF RALLIES

The Packers of 2002 rallied to win four games in which they trailed at halftime. None of the other 81 Packers teams before them won more than three such games.

Mike Sherman's group went 4-3 in games in which it fell behind at the break. Not since the 1972 club went 2-1 had the team produced a winning mark in this area.

On Sept. 8, the Falcons jumped in front 21-13. Ryan Longwell capped a second-half comeback with a 34-yard field goal in overtime to give Green Bay a 37-34 win.

The Packers then rallied during each of the first three weekends in December. They bounced back to beat the Bears 30-20 after trailing 14-6 at halftime. They rebounded to edge the Vikings 26-22 despite a 13-6 halftime deficit and they escaped with a 20-14 win in San Francisco after being down 6-3 at intermission.

Green Bay's three losses when trailing at halftime occurred in New Orleans (35-20), in Minneapolis (31-21), and against the Jets (42-17) in the finale. The team's only other loss of the season came in Tampa, where the Packers failed to protect a 7-3 lead in the final two quarters.

TEAM STATISTICS

	GB	OPP
First Downs	318	294
Rushing	94	122
Passing	197	143
Penalty	27	29
Rushes	451	413
Yards Gained	1,933	1,998
Average Gain	4.29	4.84
Average Yards per Game	120.8	124.9
Passes Attempted	580	531
Completed	361	287
% Completed	62.24	54.05
Total Yards Gained	3,823	3,228
Times Sacked	27	43
Yards Lost	196	241
Net Yards Gained	3,627	2,987
Yards Gained per Completion	10.59	11.25
Net Yards per Pass Play	5.98	5.20
Average Net Yards per Game	226.7	186.7
Combined Net Yards Gained	5,560	4,985
Total Plays	1,058	987
Average Yards per Play	5.26	5.05
Average Net Yards per Game	347.5	311.6
Third Down Efficiency	87/225	65/192
Percentage	38.67	33.85
Fourth Down Efficiency	7/13	6/16
Percentage	53.85	37.50
Intercepted By	24	16
Yards Returned	516	327
Returned for TD	4	0
Punts	79	76
Yards Punted	3,296	3,135
Average Yards per Punt	41.72	41.25
Punt Returns	46	41
Yards Returned	191	357
Average Yards per Return	4.15	8.71
Returned for TD	0	1
Kickoff Returns	63	83
Yards Returned	1,284	1,800
Average Yards per Return	20.38	21.69
Returned for TD	0	0
Penalties	108	98
Yards Penalized	913	945
Fumbles	28	39
Lost	12	21
Own Recovered for Touchdown	0	0
Opponent's Recovered by	21	12
Opponent's Recovered for Touchdown	0	1
Total Points Scored	398	328
Total Touchdowns	45	40
Touchdowns Rushing	12	14
Touchdowns Passing	29	24
Touchdowns on Returns & Recoveries	4	2
Extra Points (Kicking)	44	36
Two-Point Conversions	0/1	2/3
Safeties	0	0
Field Goals Attempted	34	22
Field Goals Made	28	16
% Successful	82.35	72.73
Average Time of Possession	31:50	28:10

Regular Season 12-4-0

Date	GB		OPP	Att.
9/8	37	Atlanta Falcons (OT)	34	(63,127)
9/15	20	at New Orleans Saints	35	(67,958)
9/22	37	at Detroit Lions	31	(61,505)
9/29	17	Carolina Panthers	14	(63,329)
10/07	34	at Chicago Bears (Champaign)	21	(63,226)
10/13	28	at New England Patriots	10	(68,436)
10/20	30	Washington Redskins	9	(63,363)
11/04	24	Miami Dolphins	10	(63,284)
11/10	40	Detroit Lions	14	(63,313)
11/17	21	at Minnesota Vikings	31	(64,153)
11/24	7	at Tampa Bay Buccaneers	21	(65,672)
12/01	30	Chicago Bears	20	(64,196)
12/08	26	Minnesota Vikings	22	(64,070)
12/15	20	at San Francisco 49ers	14	(67,947)
12/22	10	Buffalo Bills	0	(64,106)
12/29	17	at New York Jets	42	(78,733)

Postseason 0-1-0

Date	GB		OPP	Att.
1/4	7	Atlanta Falcons	27	(65,358)

Score By Periods

	1	2	3	4	OT	Total
Packers	50	141	107	97	3	398
Opponents	69	91	62	106	0	328

INDIVIDUAL STATISTICS

Rushing	Att	Yds	Avg	LG	TD
Green	286	1,240	4.3	43	7
Fisher	70	283	4.0	28	2
Davenport	39	184	4.7	43	1
Favre	25	73	2.9	17	0
Driver	8	70	8.8	17	0
Mealey	11	36	3.3	18	1
Henderson	7	27	3.9	10	1
J. Walker	1	11	11.0	11	0
Metcalf	2	7	3.5	5	0
Graham	1	3	3.0	3	0
Pederson	1	-1	-1.0	-1	0
Packers	451	1,933	4.3	43	12
Opponents	413	1,998	4.8	62	14

Receiving	No	Yds	Avg	LG	TD
Driver	70	1,064	15.2	t85	9
Green	57	393	6.9	t23	2
Glenn	56	817	14.6	49	2
Franks	54	442	8.2	t20	7
Henderson	26	168	6.5	17	3
J. Walker	23	319	13.9	30	1
Ferguson	22	293	13.3	t40	3
Fisher	18	70	3.9	11	0
T. Davis	9	107	11.9	24	1
D. Martin	8	33	4.1	7	1
Mealey	7	45	6.4	11	0
Davenport	5	33	6.6	13	0
Bailey	3	26	8.7	10	0
Graham	2	6	3.0	4	0
Wahle	1	7	7.0	7	0
Packers	361	3,823	10.6	t85	29
Opponents	287	3,228	11.2	t64	24

Passing	Att	Com	Yds	Pct	TD	In	Tk/Yds	Rate
Favre	551	341	3,658	61.9	27	16	26/188	85.6
Pederson	28	19	134	67.9	1	0	1/8	90.5
Franks	1	1	31	100.0	1	0	0/0	158.3
Packers	580	361	3,823	62.2	29	16	27/196	86.6
Opponents	531	287	3,228	54.0	24	24	43/241	68.7

Punting	No	Yds	Avg	Net	TB	In20	LG	HB
Bidwell	79	3,296	41.7	35.7	6	26	57	0
Packers	79	3,296	41.7	35.7	6	26	57	0
Opponents	76	3,135	41.3	38.2	2	27	84	0

Kickoff Returns	No	Yds	Avg	LG	TD
J. Walker	35	769	22.0	55	0
Davenport	6	130	21.7	27	0
Ferguson	6	113	18.8	25	0
Moses	4	69	17.3	27	0
Gordon	4	53	13.3	19	0
T. Carter	2	42	21.0	25	0
Fisher	2	42	21.0	21	0
Metcalf	2	41	20.5	21	0
K. McKenzie	2	25	12.5	18	0
Packers	63	1,284	20.4	55	0
Opponents	83	1,800	21.7	51	0

Punt Returns	No	Yds	Avg	FC	LG	TD
Gordon	35	180	5.1	9	27	0
Moses	5	12	2.4	0	8	0
Metcalf	3	-1	-0.3	0	0	0
T. Carter	1	0	0.0	0	0	0
Edwards	1	0	0.0	0	0	0
Sharper	1	0	0.0	2	0	0
Packers	46	191	4.2	11	27	0
Opponents	41	357	8.7	22	t72	1

Interceptions	No	Yds	Avg	LG	TD
Sharper	7	233	33.3	t89	1
M. Anderson	4	114	28.5	t78	2
Wayne	3	32	10.7	25	0
Diggs	2	62	31.0	33	0
M. McKenzie	2	0	0.0	0	0
Gbaja-Biamila	1	72	72.0	t72	1
Holliday	1	3	3.0	3	0
Bowen	1	0	0.0	0	0
McBride	1	0	0.0	0	0
Westbrook	1	0	0.0	0	0
T. Williams	1	0	0.0	0	0
Packers	24	516	21.5	t89	4
Opponents	16	327	20.4	65	0

Scoring	TDr	TDp	TDrt	PAT	2pt	FG	S	TP
Longwell	0	0	0	44/44	0	28/34	0	128
Driver	0	9	0	0/0	0	0/0	0	54
Green	7	2	0	0/0	0	0/0	0	54
Franks	0	7	0	0/0	0	0/0	0	42
Henderson	1	3	0	0/0	0	0/0	0	24
Ferguson	0	3	0	0/0	0	0/0	0	18
M. Anderson	0	0	2	0/0	0	0/0	0	12
Fisher	2	0	0	0/0	0	0/0	0	12
Glenn	0	2	0	0/0	0	0/0	0	12
Davenport	1	0	0	0/0	0	0/0	0	6
T. Davis	0	1	0	0/0	0	0/0	0	6
Gbaja-Biamila	0	0	1	0/0	0	0/0	0	6
D. Martin	0	1	0	0/0	0	0/0	0	6
Mealey	1	0	0	0/0	0	0/0	0	6
Sharper	0	0	1	0/0	0	0/0	0	6
J. Walker	0	1	0	0/0	0	0/0	0	6
Packers	12	29	4	44/44	0	28/34	0	398
Opponents	14	24	2	36/37	2	16/22	0	328

2-point conversions: Packers (0-1); Opponents (2-3)

Fumbles	Fum	Ow	Op	Yds	Tot
M. Anderson	0	0	2	0	2
Davenport	1	0	1	0	2
Diggs	0	0	2	0	2
Driver	1	2	0	0	2
Favre	10	5	0	-14	5
Ferguson	0	0	1	0	1
Fisher	2	0	0	0	1
Flanagan	1	0	0	0	1
Franz	0	0	1	0	1
Gbaja-Biamila	0	0	1	0	1
Glenn	1	0	0	0	1
Gordon	5	1	0	0	1
Green	4	0	1	0	1
Hunt	0	0	2	0	2
J. Johnson	0	0	1	0	1
Jue	0	1	0	0	1
Lenon	0	0	1	0	1
T. Marshall	0	0	1	0	1
D. Martin	0	1	0	0	1
McBride	0	0	3	9	3
K. McKenzie	0	1	0	0	1
M. McKenzie	0	0	1	0	1
Metcalf	1	0	0	0	1
Moses	1	0	0	0	0
Reynolds	0	0	2	1	2
J. Walker	1	0	0	0	1
R. Walker	0	0	2	0	2
Wayne	0	0	2	0	2
T. Williams	0	0	1	0	1
Packers	28	15	21	-4	36

Quarterback Sacks	No.
Gbaja-Biamila	12.0
Holliday	6.0
Hunt	5.5
Diggs	3.0
Wayne	2.5
J. Johnson	2.0
Lyon	2.0
Nickerson	1.5
Edwards	1.0
M. McKenzie	1.0
Reynolds	1.0
Warren	1.0
T. Williams	1.0
Kampman	0.5
team	3.0
Packers	43.0
Opponents	27.0

NFL STANDINGS

National Conference

NFC East	W	L	T	Pct	PF	PA
Philadelphia Eagles	12	4	0	.750	415	241
New York Giants	10	6	0	.625	320	279
Washington Redskins	7	9	0	.438	307	365
Dallas Cowboys	5	11	0	.313	217	329

NFC North	W	L	T	Pct	PF	PA
Green Bay Packers	12	4	0	.750	398	328
Minnesota Vikings	6	10	0	.375	390	442
Chicago Bears	4	12	0	.250	281	379
Detroit Lions	3	13	0	.188	306	451

NFC South	W	L	T	Pct	PF	PA
Tampa Bay Buccaneers	12	4	0	.750	346	196
Atlanta Falcons	9	6	1	.594	402	314
New Orleans	9	7	0	.563	432	388
Carolina Panthers	7	9	0	.438	258	302

NFC West	W	L	T	Pct	PF	PA
San Francisco 49ers	10	6	0	.625	367	351
St. Louis Rams	7	9	0	.438	316	369
Seattle Seahawks	7	9	0	.438	355	369
Arizona Cardinals	5	10	0	.313	262	417

American Conference

AFC East	W	L	T	Pct	PF	PA
New York Jets	9	7	0	.563	359	336
New England Patriots	9	7	0	.563	381	346
Miami Dolphins	9	7	0	.563	378	301
Buffalo Bills	8	8	0	.500	379	397

AFC North	W	L	T	Pct	PF	PA
Pittsburgh Steelers	10	5	1	.656	390	345
Cleveland Browns	9	7	0	.563	344	320
Baltimore Ravens	7	9	0	.438	316	354
Cincinnati Bengals	2	14	0	.125	279	456

AFC South	W	L	T	Pct	PF	PA
Tennessee Titans	11	5	0	.688	367	324
Indianapolis Colts	10	6	0	.625	349	313
Jacksonville Jaguars	6	10	0	.375	328	315
Houston Texans	4	12	0	.250	213	356

AFC West	W	L	T	Pct	PF	PA
Oakland Raiders	11	5	0	.688	450	304
Denver Broncos	9	7	0	.563	392	344
San Diego Chargers	8	8	0	.500	333	367
Kansas City Chiefs	8	8	0	.500	467	399

ROSTER

No	Name	Pos	Ht	Wt	DOB	College	G
20	Anderson, Marques	S	5-11	212	05/26/79	UCLA	14
85	Bailey, Karsten	WR	6-0	205	04/26/77	Auburn	7
71	Barry, Kevin	T	6-4	325	07/20/79	Arizona	14
9	Bidwell, Josh	P	6-3	220	03/13/76	Oregon	16
69	Blackshear, Jeff	G	6-6	323	03/29/69	Northeast Louisiana	1
28	Bowen, Matt	S	6-1	210	11/12/76	Iowa	16
77	Brooks, Barrett	T	6-4	320	05/05/72	Kansas State	2
93	Brown, Gilbert	DT	6-2	339	02/22/71	Kansas	12
39	Carter, Tony	RB	6-0	235	08/23/72	Minnesota	12
76	Clifton, Chad	T	6-5	327	06/26/76	Tennessee	10
44	Davenport, Najeh	FB	6-1	247	02/08/79	Miami	8
60	Davis, Rob	LS	6-3	285	12/10/68	Shippensburg	16
81	Davis, Tyrone	TE	6-4	260	06/30/72	Virginia	9
59	Diggs, Na'il	LB	6-4	238	07/08/78	Ohio State	16
72	Dotson, Earl	T	6-3	317	12/17/70	Texas A&I	14
80	Driver, Donald	WR	6-0	185	02/02/75	Alcorn State	16
24	Edwards, Antuan	CB	6-1	210	05/26/77	Clemson	12
4	Favre, Brett	QB	6-2	225	10/10/69	Southern Mississippi	16
89	Ferguson, Robert	WR	6-1	209	12/17/79	Texas A&M	16
63	Ferrario, Bill	G	6-2	315	09/22/78	Wisconsin	16
40	Fisher, Tony	RB	6-1	222	10/12/79	Notre Dame	15
58	Flanagan, Mike	C	6-5	297	11/10/73	UCLA	16
88	Franks, Bubba	TE	6-6	260	01/06/78	Miami (FL)	16
49	Franz, Todd	CB	6-0	194	04/12/76	Tulsa	2
94	Gbaja-Biamila, Kabeer	DE	6-4	253	09/24/77	San Diego State	15
83	Glenn, Terry	WR	5-11	195	07/23/74	Ohio State	15
23	Gordon, Darrien	CB/KR	5-11	190	11/14/70	Stanford	13
35	Graham, Jay	RB	6-0	225	07/14/76	Tennessee	3
30	Green, Ahman	RB	6-0	217	02/16/77	Nebraska	14
33	Henderson, William	FB	6-1	253	02/19/71	North Carolina	15
90	Holliday, Vonnie	DE	6-5	290	12/11/75	North Carolina	10
97	Hunt, Cletidus	DE/DT	6-4	299	01/02/76	Kentucky State	14
64	Jackson, Alcender	G/T	6-3	311	05/18/77	Louisiana State	2
86	Jackson, Chris	WR	6-2	204	02/26/75	Washington State	1
91	Johnson, Joe	DE	6-4	275	07/11/72	Louisville	5
21	Jue, Bhawoh	CB/S	6-0	200	05/24/79	Penn State	12
74	Kampman, Aaron	DE	6-4	287	11/30/79	Iowa	4
53	Lenon, Paris	LB	6-2	232	11/26/77	Richmond	16
8	Longwell, Ryan	K	6-0	200	08/16/74	California	16
98	Lyon, Billy	DE/DT	6-5	295	12/10/73	Marshall	16
41/51	Marshall, Torrance	LB	6-2	255	06/12/77	Oklahoma	16
87	Martin, David	TE	6-4	250	03/13/79	Tennessee	8
27	McBride, Tod	DB	6-1	205	01/26/76	UCLA	15
73	McKenzie, Keith	DE	6-3	270	10/17/73	Ball State	4
34	McKenzie, Mike	CB	6-0	190	04/26/76	Memphis	13
32	Mealey, Rondell	RB	6-0	224	02/24/77	Louisiana State	3
22	Metcalf, Eric	WR	5-10	195	01/23/68	Texas	1
86	Moses, J.J.	WR/KR	5-6	178	09/12/79	Iowa State	2
56	Nickerson, Hardy	LB	6-2	237	09/01/65	California	16
18	Pederson, Doug	QB	6-3	220	01/31/68	Northeast Louisiana	16
99	Reynolds, Jamal	DE	6-3	266	02/20/79	Florida State	7
62	Rivera, Marco	G	6-4	310	04/26/72	Penn State	16
42	Sharper, Darren	DB	6-2	207	11/03/75	William & Mary	13
43	Smith, Maurice (Mo)	RB	6-0	235	02/14/77	North Carolina A&T	1
26	Swiney, Erwin	DB	6-0	192	10/08/78	Nebraska	3
65	Tauscher, Mark	T	6-3	320	06/17/77	Wisconsin	2
75	Tomich, Jared	DE	6-3	283	04/24/74	Nebraska	2
68	Wahle, Mike	G	6-6	310	03/29/77	Navy	16
84	Walker, Javon	WR	6-3	210	10/14/78	Florida State	15
95	Walker, Rod	DT	6-3	320	02/04/76	Troy State	13
96	Warren, Steve	DT	6-1	298	01/22/78	Nebraska	12
54	Wayne, Nate	LB	6-0	237	01/12/75	Mississippi	16
32	Westbrook, Bryant	CB	6-1	198	12/19/74	Texas	6
55	Wilkins, Marcus	LB	6-2	231	01/02/80	Texas	5
37	Williams, Tyrone	CB	5-11	193	05/31/73	Nebraska	15
52	Winters, Frank	C	6-3	305	01/23/64	West Illinois	16
77	Wisne, Jerry	T	6-6	315	07/28/76	Notre Dame	2

DRAFT

Rnd	Name	Pos	Ht	Wt	College
1a	Javon Walker (20)	WR	6-3	215	Florida State
	(Traded 1st-round (28) and 2nd-round (60) picks to Seahawks for Seahawks' 1st-round (20) and 5th-round (156) picks)				
1b	(Choice (28) to Seahawks in deal mentioned above)				
2	(Choice (60) to Seahawks in deal mentioned above)				
3	Marques Anderson (92)	S	5-11	213	UCLA
4a	(Choice (126) to Patriots for Terry Glenn)				
4b	Najeh Davenport (135)	RB	6-1	248	Miami
	(Free agency compensatory pick)				
5a	Aaron Kampman (156)	DE	6-4	285	Iowa
	(Choice from Seahawks in deal mentioned above)				
5b	Craig Nall (164)	QB	6-3	237	Northwestern State
6	Mike Houghton (200)	G	6-5	318	San Diego State
7	(Choice (240) to Titans for Rod Walker)				

2002 GREEN BAY PACKERS

FRONT ROW: (L-R) 4 Brett Favre, 8 Ryan Longwell, 9 Josh Bidwell, 12 Craig Nall, 18 Doug Pederson, 20 Marques Anderson, 21 Bhawoh Jue, 23 Darren Gordon, 24 Antuan Edwards, 27 Tod McBride, 28 Matt Bowen, 30 Ahman Green, 32 Rondell Mealey, 33 William Henderson, 34 Mike McKenzie.

SECOND ROW: (L-R) Strength and Conditioning Coach Barry Rubin, Special Teams Coach Frank Novak, Defensive Assistant/Quality Control Brad Miller, Assistant Defensive Backs Coach Lionel Washington, Assistant Head Coach/Defensive Backs Coach Bob Slowik, Linebackers Coach Bo Pelini, Defensive Line Coach Jethro Franklin, Defensive Coordinator Ed Donatell, Head Coach Mike Sherman, Offensive Coordinator Tom Rossley, Offensive Line Coach Larry Beightol, Running Backs Coach Sylvester Croom, Wide Receivers Coach Ray Sherman, Tight Ends Coach Jeff Jagodzinski, Quality Control Assistant/Special Teams-Offense Stan Drayton, Offensive Assistant Darrell Bevell, Assistant Offensive Line Coach Pat Ruel.

THIRD ROW: (L-R) 37 Tyrone Williams, 40 Tony Fisher, 42 Darren Sharper, 44 Najeh Davenport, 51 Torrance Marshall, 52 Frank Winters, 53 Paris Lenon, 54 Nate Wayne, 55 Marcus Wilkins, 56 Hardy Nickerson, 58 Mike Flanagan.

FOURTH ROW: (L-R) 59 Na'il Diggs, 60 Rob Davis, 62 Marco Rivera, 63 Bill Ferrario, 65 Mark Tauscher, 68 Mike Wahle, 71 Kevin Barry, 72 Earl Dotson, 74 Aaron Kampman, 76 Chad Clifton.

FIFTH ROW: (L-R) 80 Donald Driver, 81 Tyrone Davis, 83 Terry Glenn, 84 Javon Walker, 85 Karsten Bailey, 87 David Martin, 88 Bubba Franks, 89 Robert Ferguson, 90 Vonnie Holliday, 91 Joe Johnson.

SIXTH ROW: (L-R) Administrative Assistant/Football Matt Klein, Vice President of Football Operations Mark Hatley, Personnel Analyst to General Manager John Schneider, Assistant to the General Manager/Director of Football Administration Bruce Warwick, 93 Gilbert Brown, 94 Kabeer Gbaja-Biamila, 95 Rod Walker, 96 Steve Warren, 97 Cletidus Hunt, 98 Billy Lyon, 99 Jamal Reynolds, Director of Research and Development Mike Eayrs, Director of Pro Personnel Reggie McKenzie, Assistant Director of Pro Personnel Sean Howard, Pro Personnel Assistant Marc Lillibridge.

BACK ROW: (L-R) Strength and Conditioning Assistant Mark Lovat, Weight Room Assistant Vince Workman, Training Room Intern Jacob Greer, Assistant Trainer Bryan Engel, Assistant Trainer Kurt Fielding, Head Trainer Pepper Burruss, Associate Team Physician Dr. John Gray, Team Physician Dr. Patrick J. McKenzie, Director of Player Development Edgar Bennett, Director of Corporate Security Jerry Parins, Equipment Manager Gordon (Red) Batty, Assistant Equipment Manager Tom Bakken, Assistant Equipment Manager Bryan Nehring, Equipment Assistant Tim Odea, Equipment Assistant John Odea, Video Assistant Andy Muckerheide, Assistant Video Director Chris Kirby, Video Director Bob Eckberg.

For much of the year, Destiny could have been just another Packers fan, rooting for an up and down team that was in danger of going nowhere. Not until Green Bay staged a December to remember—capturing a playoff berth in dramatic fashion—did Destiny become a way to describe a team some thought was preordained for greatness.

Coach Mike Sherman's team didn't win more than two games in a row until it closed with four straight victories. A 10-point loss to the Rams in October sent the Packers (3-4) into their bye week well behind the Vikings (6-0).

Green Bay came out of its break by outplaying Minnesota 30-27. The Vikings dropped seven of their last 10 games, including a season-ending, 18-17 loss to the Cardinals in which Arizona quarterback Josh McCown overcame fourth-and-25 by firing a 28-yard touchdown pass to Nathan Poole as time expired. That completion gave Green Bay (10-6) its second straight division crown and knocked the Vikings (9-7) out of the playoffs.

"Something's going on here," said quarterback Brett Favre, who led the Packers to a 31-3 rout of the Broncos at the same time Minnesota was stunned in the desert. "My emotions are numb. I've cried as many tears as I can cry. I'm so proud of this team and everything we've overcome."

A week earlier, Favre's father, Irv, had died of a heart attack in Mississippi. His death came one day before Green Bay's Monday night encounter with the Raiders. Saying that his father would have wanted him to play, Favre passed for 399 yards and four touchdowns in a 41-7 win. His passer rating of 154.9 that night was a franchise record.

In Game 7, Favre suffered a hairline fracture of the thumb on his throwing hand after hitting a teammate's shoulder pads during his follow-through on a pass. The injury didn't stop Favre who, playing with a splint on his thumb, ran his string of regular-season starts to 189.

Green Bay's running game flourished. Led by Ahman Green's club-record 1,883 yards, the Packers rushed for a team-record 2,558 yards.

Injuries were fewer than a year previous. Chad Clifton, Mike Wahle, Mike Flanagan, Marco Rivera and Mark Tauscher started all 16 games, the first time five offensive linemen started every game of a season since 1978.

Gilbert Brown and Joe Johnson did not enjoy such good health. Brown completely tore his right biceps during training camp, but started 14 games at nose tackle. Johnson tore the quadriceps tendon above his right knee in October and was lost for the year. In his place, the Packers acquired Grady Jackson from the Saints, who proved to be a valuable midseason pickup.

On Sept. 7, the Packers christened the renovated Lambeau Field. A stadium record 70,505 fans watched the Vikings register a 30-25 win to spoil the day.

Wide receiver Donald Driver was taken off the field on a stretcher, after landing on his head while trying to make a catch. He returned to action two weeks later.

Green Bay took out its frustrations on the Lions 31-6. Favre gave a pregame speech that inspired.

"We never hear Brett," wide receiver Robert Ferguson said. "He's a silent leader. He leads with action. When he speaks, everyone listens."

Green Bay dropped three of its next five games, including a 20-13 slipup in Arizona and a 40-34 overtime loss to the Chiefs in which it blew a 17-point lead. Safety Darren Sharper spoke out after the team fell 34-24 to the Rams in St. Louis.

"Every time I lace up those pads, I'm going out there to win, but (I) also understand that I've got to make something happen out there. If you get paid to do that, and they're not calling your name a lot on that loudspeaker, then I don't think you're earning your check."

The Packers got it together in December. They crushed the Bears, Chargers, Raiders and Broncos.

"Maybe we limped in last year," said Flanagan after beating Denver. "We were patched up across the board. Now we've got our guys healthy...and we're rolling."

Was someone watching out for the Packers, as Denver's wide receiver Ashley Lelie claimed?

Green Bay opened the playoffs by beating Seattle 33-27 in overtime at Lambeau Field. But the Eagles revealed the Packers to be anything but a team of destiny, as they rallied to bring down Green Bay 20-17 in overtime.

Defensive coordinator Ed Donatell and tight ends coach Jeff Jagodzinski were fired shortly after the loss.

WHAT A RUSH!

Green Bay didn't merely run the football against its opponents in 2003. In many cases, it overran them.

The Packers rushed for a team-record 2,558 yards. Their average gain of slightly more than five yards per carry (5.05) also was a team record. The Packers became only the fourth team since 1978 to average better than five yards a carry while amassing at least 2,500 yards rushing in the same season.

Ahman Green was the featured back. He set single-season records for yards rushing (1,883), carries (355) and most 100-yard games (10).

Green Bay rolled in November. In order, the club reeled off 261, 241, 190 and 243 yards. The 935 rushing yards were the most ever by the Packers over a four-game stretch.

Highest Average Gain Rushing, Season

Avg.	Year	Att.-Yards	TD	Records
5.05	2003	507-2,558	18	10-6
4.96	1961	474-2,350	27	11-3
4.74	1962	518-2,460	36	13-1

TEAM STATISTICS

	GB	OPP
First Downs	315	288
Rushing	127	91
Passing	166	172
Penalty	22	25
Rushes	507	413
Yards Gained	2,558	1,701
Average Gain	5.05	4.12
Average Yards per Game	159.9	106.3
Passes Attempted	473	589
Completed	310	326
% Completed	65.54	55.35
Total Yards Gained	3,377	3,600
Times Sacked	19	34
Yards Lost	137	200
Net Yards Gained	3,240	3,400
Yards Gained per Completion	10.89	11.04
Net Yards per Pass Play	6.59	5.46
Average Net Yards per Game	202.5	212.5
Combined Net Yards Gained	5,798	5,101
Total Plays	999	1,036
Average Yards per Play	5.80	4.92
Average Net Yards per Game	362.4	318.8
Third Down Efficiency	85/207	85/228
Percentage	41.06	37.28
Fourth Down Efficiency	4/7	4/17
Percentage	57.14	23.53
Intercepted By	21	21
Yards Returned	315	429
Returned for TD	2	2
Punts	71	83
Yards Punted	2,933	3,399
Average Yards per Punt	41.31	40.95
Punt Returns	35	32
Yards Returned	277	316
Average Yards per Return	7.91	9.88
Returned for TD	0	0
Kickoff Returns	64	82
Yards Returned	1,511	1,707
Average Yards per Return	23.61	20.82
Returned for TD	0	1
Penalties	88	97
Yards Penalized	699	767
Fumbles	19	21
Lost	11	11
Own Recovered for Touchdown	0	0
Opponent's Recovered by	11	11
Opponent's Recovered for Touchdown	1	0
Total Points Scored	442	307
Total Touchdowns	53	31
Touchdowns Rushing	18	10
Touchdowns Passing	32	18
Touchdowns on Returns & Recoveries	3	3
Extra Points (Kicking)	51	29
Two-Point Conversions	2-2	1-1
Safeties	0	0
Field Goals Attempted	26	33
Field Goals Made	23	30
% Successful	88.46	90.91
Average Time of Possession	30:52	29:08

Regular Season   10-6-0

Date	GB		OPP	Att.
9/7	25	Minnesota Vikings	30	(70,505)
9/14	31	Detroit Lions	6	(70,244)
9/21	13	at Arizona Cardinals	20	(58,784)
9/29	38	at Chicago Bears	23	(60,257)
10/5	35	Seattle Seahawks	13	(70,365)
10/12	34	Kansas City Chiefs (OT)	40	(70,407)
10/19	24	at St. Louis Rams	34	(66,201)
11/2	30	at Minnesota Vikings	27	(64,482)
11/10	14	Philadelphia Eagles	17	(70,291)
11/16	20	at Tampa Bay Buccaneers	13	(65,614)
11/23	20	San Francisco 49ers	10	(70,250)
11/27	14	at Detroit Lions	22	(62,123)
12/7	34	Chicago Bears	21	(70,458)
12/14	38	at San Diego Chargers	21	(64,978)
12/22	41	at Oakland Raiders	7	(62,298)
12/28	31	Denver Broncos	3	(70,299)

Postseason   1-1-0

Date	GB		OPP	Att.
1/4	33	Seattle Seahawks (OT)	27	(71,457)
1/11	17	at Philadelphia Eagles (OT)	20	(67,707)

Score By Periods

	1	2	3	4	OT	Total
Packers	103	138	69	132	0	442
Opponents	86	64	49	102	6	307

INDIVIDUAL STATISTICS

Rushing	Att	Yds	Avg	LG	TD
Green	355	1,883	5.3	t98	15
Davenport	77	420	5.5	t76	2
Fisher	40	200	5.0	19	1
Driver	5	51	10.2	45	0
Favre	18	15	0.8	7	0
Luchey	1	3	3.0	3	0
J. Walker	2	1	0.5	1	0
Nall	2	-2	-1.0	-1	0
Pederson	6	-5	-0.8	0	0
Ferguson	1	-8	-8.0	-8	0
Packers	507	2,558	5.0	198	18
Opponents	413	1,701	4.1	t67	10

Receiving	No	Yds	Avg	LG	TD
Driver	52	621	11.9	41	2
Green	50	367	7.3	27	5
J. Walker	41	716	17.5	t66	9
Ferguson	38	520	13.7	47	4
Franks	30	241	8.0	24	4
Henderson	24	214	8.9	22	3
Fisher	21	206	9.8	32	2
Walls	20	222	11.1	36	1
Freeman	14	141	10.1	15	0
D. Martin	13	79	6.1	14	2
Davenport	6	38	6.3	12	0
Luchey	1	12	12.0	12	0
Packers	310	3,377	10.9	t66	32
Opponents	326	3,600	11.0	t68	18

Passing	Att	Com	Yds	Pct	TD	In	Tk/Yds	Rate
Favre	471	308	3,361	65.4	32	21	19/137	90.4
Pederson	2	2	16	100.0	0	0	0/0	--
Packers	473	310	3,377	65.5	32	21	19/137	90.5
Opponents	589	326	3,600	55.3	18	21	34/200	69.0

Punting	No	Yds	Avg	Net	TB	In20	LG	HB
Bidwell	69	2,875	41.7	35.1	7	16	60	0
Longwell	2	58	29.0	19.0	1	1	30	0
Packers	71	2,933	41.3	34.6	8	17	60	0
Opponents	83	3,399	41.0	35.0	11	23	62	1

Kickoff Returns	No	Yds	Avg	LG	TD
Chatman	36	804	22.3	46	0
Davenport	16	505	31.6	60	0
Ferguson	7	148	21.1	31	0
Henderson	3	33	11.0	15	0
Luchey	2	21	10.5	12	0
Packers conversions	64	1,511	23.6	60	0
Opponents	82	1,707	20.8	t88	1

Punt Returns	No	Yds	Avg	FC	LG	TD
Chatman	33	277	8.4	18	33	0
A. Harris	1	0	0.0	0	0	0
Wilkins	1	0	0.0	0	0	0
Packers	35	277	7.9	18	33	0
Opponents	32	316	9.9	15	32	0

Interceptions	No	Yds	Avg	LG	TD
Sharper	5	78	15.6	50	0
M. McKenzie	4	98	24.5	t90	1
A. Harris	3	89	29.7	t56	1
Barnett	3	21	7.0	14	0
Diggs	2	13	6.5	13	0
Hawthorne	2	8	4.0	8	0
Edwards	1	5	5.0	5	0
M. Anderson	1	3	3.0	3	0
Packers	21	315	15.0	t90	2
Opponents	21	429	20.4	t79	2

Scoring	TDr	TDp	TDrt	PAT	2pt	FG	S	TP
Longwell	0	0	0	51/51	0	23/26	0	120
Green	15	5	0	0/0	0	0/0	0	120
J. Walker	0	9	0	0/0	0	0/0	0	54
Franks	0	4	0	0/0	2	0/0	0	28
Ferguson	0	4	0	0/0	0	0/0	0	24
Fisher	1	2	0	0/0	0	0/0	0	18
Henderson	0	3	0	0/0	0	0/0	0	18
Davenport	2	0	0	0/0	0	0/0	0	12
Driver	0	2	0	0/0	0	0/0	0	12
D. Martin	0	2	0	0/0	0	0/0	0	12
A. Harris	0	0	1	0/0	0	0/0	0	6
M. McKenzie	0	0	1	0/0	0	0/0	0	6
Walls	0	1	0	0/0	0	0/0	0	6
Wilkins	0	0	1	0/0	0	0/0	0	6
Packers	18	32	3	51/51	2	23/26	0	442
Opponents	10	18	3	29/29	1	30/33	0	307

2-point conversions: Packers (2-3); Opponents (1-1)

Fumbles	Fum	Ow	Op	Yds	Tot
M. Anderson	0	0	2	1	2
Barnett	0	0	1	0	1
Gi. Brown	0	0	1	0	1
Clifton	0	1	0	0	1
Davenport	4	0	0	-8	0
Driver	0	1	0	0	1
Favre	5	0	0	0	0
Ferguson	0	1	0	0	1
Flanagan	0	1	0	0	1
Gbaja-Biamila	0	0	2	0	2
Green	7	2	0	0	2
A. Harris	1	0	0	0	0
Hunt	0	0	1	0	1
Kampman	0	0	1	0	1
Marshall	0	0	1	0	1
Navies	0	0	1	0	1
Tauscher	0	1	0	0	1
J. Walker	1	0	0	0	0
M. Wilkins	1	0	0	0	0
Packers	19	7	11	-7	18

Quarterback Sacks	No.
Gbaja-Biamila	10.0
Hunt	4.0
G. Jackson	2.5
Nwokorie	2.5
Barnett	2.0
Kampman	2.0
Sharper	2.0
Jue	1.5
L. Smith	1.5
Diggs	1.0
Edwards	1.0
Hawthorne	1.0
Marshall	1.0
Navies	1.0
team	1.0
Packers	34.0
Opponents	19.0

NFL STANDINGS

National Conference

NFC East	W	L	T	Pct	PF	PA
Philadelphia Eagles	12	4	0	.750	374	287
Dallas Cowboys	10	6	0	.625	289	260
Washington Redskins	5	11	0	.313	287	372
New York Giants	4	12	0	.250	243	387

NFC North	W	L	T	Pct	PF	PA
Green Bay Packers	**10**	**6**	**0**	**.625**	**442**	**307**
Minnesota Vikings	9	7	0	.563	416	353
Chicago Bears	7	9	0	.438	283	346
Detroit Lions	5	11	0	.313	270	379

NFC South	W	L	T	Pct	PF	PA
Carolina Panthers	11	5	0	.688	325	304
New Orleans Saints	8	8	0	.500	340	326
Tampa Bay Buccaneers	7	9	0	.438	301	264
Atlanta Falcons	5	11	0	.313	299	422

NFC West	W	L	T	Pct	PF	PA
St. Louis Rams	12	4	0	.750	447	328
Seattle Seahawks	10	6	0	.625	404	327
San Francisco 49ers	7	9	0	.438	384	337
Arizona Cardinals	4	12	0	.250	225	452

American Conference

AFC East	W	L	T	Pct	PF	PA
New England Patriots	14	2	0	.875	348	238
Miami Dolphins	10	6	0	.625	311	261
Buffalo Bills	6	10	0	.375	243	279
New York Jets	6	10	0	.375	283	299

AFC North	W	L	T	Pct	PF	PA
Baltimore Ravens	10	6	0	.625	391	281
Cincinnati Bengals	8	8	0	.500	346	384
Pittsburgh Steelers	6	10	0	.375	300	327
Cleveland Browns	5	11	0	.313	254	322

AFC South	W	L	T	Pct	PF	PA
Indianapolis Colts	12	4	0	.750	447	336
Tennessee Titans	12	4	0	.750	435	324
Jacksonville Jaguars	5	11	0	.313	276	331
Houston Texans	5	11	0	.313	255	380

AFC West	W	L	T	Pct	PF	PA
Kansas City Chiefs	13	3	0	.813	484	332
Denver Broncos	10	6	0	.625	381	301
Oakland Raiders	4	12	0	.250	270	379
San Diego Chargers	4	12	0	.250	313	441

ROSTER

No	Name	Pos	Ht	Wt	DOB	College	G
20	Anderson, Marques	S	5-11	212	05/26/79	UCLA	1
85	Bailey, Karsten	WR	6-0	205	04/26/77	Auburn	1
56	Barnett, Nick	LB	6-2	240	05/27/81	Oregon State	15
71	Barry, Kevin	T	6-4	325	07/20/79	Arizona	16
9	Bidwell, Josh	P	6-3	220	03/13/76	Oregon	16
93	Brown, Gilbert	DT	6-2	340	02/22/71	Kansas	14
83	Chatman, Antonio	WR/KR	5-9	177	02/12/79	Cincinnati	16
76	Clifton, Chad	T	6-5	327	06/26/76	Tennessee	16
45	Combs, Derek	CB	6-0	185	02/28/79	Ohio State	8
44	Davenport, Najeh	FB	6-1	245	02/08/79	Miami	15
60	Davis, Rob	LS	6-3	285	12/10/68	Shippensburg	16
59	Diggs, Na'il	LB	6-4	238	07/08/78	Ohio State	16
80	Driver, Donald	WR	6-0	185	02/02/75	Alcorn State	15
24	Edwards, Antuan	CB	6-1	212	05/26/77	Clemson	10
4	Favre, Brett	QB	6-2	225	10/10/69	Southern Mississippi	16
89	Ferguson, Robert	WR	6-1	209	12/17/79	Texas A&M	15
40	Fisher, Tony	RB	6-1	222	10/12/79	Notre Dame	15
58	Flanagan, Mike	C	6-5	297	11/10/73	UCLA	16
88	Franks, Bubba	TE	6-6	260	01/06/78	Miami (FL)	16
86	Freeman, Antonio	WR	6-1	198	05/27/72	Virginia Tech	15
29	Fuller, Curtis	S	5-11	191	07/25/78	Texas Christian	9
94	Gbaja-Biamila, Kabeer	DE	6-4	253	09/24/77	San Diego State	16
30	Green, Ahman	RB	6-0	217	02/16/77	Nebraska	16
31	Harris, Al	CB	6-1	185	12/07/74	Texas A&M-Kingsville	16
27	Hawthorne, Michael	S/CB	6-3	200	01/26/77	Purdue	14
33	Henderson, William	FB	6-1	253	02/19/71	North Carolina	16
97	Hunt, Cletidus	DE/DT	6-4	299	01/02/76	Kentucky State	16
81	Jackson, Chris	WR	6-2	204	02/26/75	Washington State	1
75	Jackson, Grady	DT	6-2	350	01/21/73	Knoxville	8
91	Johnson, Joe	DE	6-4	275	07/11/72	Louisville	6
21	Jue, Bhawoh	CB/S	6-0	200	05/24/79	Penn State	16
74	Kampman, Aaron	DE	6-4	287	11/30/79	Iowa	12
53	Lenon, Paris	LB	6-2	240	11/26/77	Richmond	16
8	Longwell, Ryan	K	6-0	200	08/16/74	California	16
22	Luchey, Nick	FB	6-2	270	03/30/77	Miami (FL)	10
51	Marshall, Torrance	LB	6-2	255	06/12/77	Oklahoma	12
87	Martin, David	TE	6-4	260	03/13/79	Tennessee	16
34	McKenzie, Mike	CB	6-0	194	04/26/76	Memphis	14
16	Nall, Craig	QB	6-3	230	04/21/79	Northwestern (LA) State	1
50	Navies, Hannibal	LB	6-3	247	07/19/77	Colorado	16
90	Nwokorie, Chukie	DE	6-3	288	07/10/75	Purdue	14
18	Pederson, Doug	QB	6-3	220	01/31/68	Northeast Louisiana	16
98	Peterson, Kenny	DT	6-3	300	11/21/78	Ohio State	9
99	Reynolds, Jamal	DE	6-3	260	02/20/79	Florida State	5
62	Rivera, Marco	G	6-4	310	04/26/72	Penn State	16
67	Ruegamer, Grey	C/G	6-4	310	06/11/76	Arizona State	15
78	Sands, Terdell	DT	6-7	340	10/31/79	Tennessee-Chattanooga	1
42	Sharper, Darren	DB	6-2	207	11/03/75	William & Mary	15
57	Slaughter, T.J.	LB	6-0	233	02/20/77	Southern Mississippi	1
96	Smith, Larry	DT/DE	6-5	310	12/04/74	Florida State	10
79	Spriggs, Marcus	T/G	6-3	310	05/30/74	Houston	2
26	Swiney, Erwin	DB	6-0	192	10/08/78	Nebraska	6
65	Tauscher, Mark	T	6-3	320	06/17/77	Wisconsin	16
68	Wahle, Mike	G	6-6	310	03/29/77	Navy	16
84	Walker, Javon	WR	6-3	210	10/14/78	Florida State	16
95	Walker, Rod	DT	6-3	320	02/04/76	Troy State	7
85	Walls, Wesley	TE	6-5	240	03/26/66	Mississippi	14
25	Whitley, James	DB	5-11	190	05/13/79	Michigan	3
55	Wilkins, Marcus	LB	6-2	235	01/02/80	Texas	8

DRAFT

Rnd	Name	Pos	Ht	Wt	College
1	Nick Barnett (29)	LB	6-2	235	Oregon State
2	(Packers traded 2nd-round pick (62) to Eagles for Al Harris and Eagles' 4th-round pick (127))				
3	Kenny Peterson (79) (Choice from Bills for Packers 2nd-round pick (94) and 4th-round pick (127))	DT	6-3	300	Ohio State
3	(Choice (94) to Bills in deal mentioned above)				
4	(Choice (127) from Eagles in deal mentioned above; to Bills in deal mentioned above)				
4	(Choice (128) to Patriots for Terry Glenn)				
5a	James Lee (147) (Choice from Seahawks for Packers 5th-round pick (165) and 6th-round pick (203))	DT	6-4	330	Oregon State
5	(Choice (165) to Seahawks in deal mentioned above)				
5b	Hunter Hillenmeyer (166) (Choice from Eagles for Packers' 6th-round pick (185) and 7th-round pick (244))	LB	6-4	240	Vanderbilt

Rnd	Name	Pos	Ht	Wt	College
6	(Choice (185) from Redskins for Matt Bowen; traded to Eagles in deal mentioned above)				
6	(Choice (203) to Seahawks in deal mentioned above)				
6	Brennan Curtin (212) (Free agent compensatory pick)	T	6-9	315	Notre Dame
7	(Choice (244) to Redskins in deal mentioned above)				
7a	Chris Johnson (245) (Choice from Eagles for Packers 6th-round pick in 2004)	CB	5-11	195	Louisville
7b	DeAndrew Rubin (253) (Free agent compensatory pick)	WR	5-11	190	South Florida
7c	Carl Ford (256) (Free agent compensatory pick)	WR	6-0	180	Toledo
7d	Steve Josue (257) (Free agent compensatory pick)	LB	6-2	225	Carson-Newman

2003 GREEN BAY PACKERS

FRONT ROW: (L–R) 4 Brett Favre, 8 Ryan Longwell, 9 Josh Bidwell, 16 Craig Nall, 18 Doug Pederson, 20 Marques Anderson, 21 Bhawoh Jue, 22 Nick Luchey, 24 Antuan Edwards, 26 Erwin Swiney, 30 Ahman Green, 31 Al Harris, 33 William Henderson.

SECOND ROW: (L–R) Special Teams Consultant Frank Novak, Special Teams Coordinator John Bonamego, Assistant Defensive Line Coach Brad Miller, Assistant Head Coach/Defensive Backs Coach Bob Slowik, Linebackers Coach Mark Duffner, Defensive Line Coach Jethro Franklin, Defensive Coordinator Ed Donatell, Head Coach Mike Sherman, Offensive Coordinator Tom Rossley, Offensive Line Coach Larry Beightol, Running Backs Coach Sylvester Croom, Wide Receivers Coach Ray Sherman, Tight Ends Coach Jeff Jagodzinski, Quarterbacks Coach Darrell Bevell, Offense Quality Control/Assistant Special Teams Coach Stan Drayton, Assistant Offensive Line Coach Joe Philbin, Strength & Conditioning Coach Barry Rubin.

THIRD ROW: (L–R) 34 Mike McKenzie, 37 Chris Johnson, 40 Tony Fisher, 42 Darren Sharper, 44 Najeh Davenport, 45 Derek Combs, 50 Hannibal Navies, 53 Paris Lenon, 55 Marcus Wilkins, 56 Nick Barnett, 57 Hunter Hillenmeyer, 58 Mike Flanagan.

FOURTH ROW: (L–R) 59 Na'il Diggs, 60 Rob Davis, 62 Marco Rivera, 65 Mark Tauscher, 67 Grey Ruegamer, 68 Mike Wahle, 69 Brennan Curtin, 71 Kevin Barry, 74 Aaron Kampman, 76 Chad Clifton, 79 Marcus Spriggs.

FIFTH ROW: (L–R) 80 Donald Driver, 82 Wesley Walls, 83 Antonio Chatman, 84 Javon Walker, 85 Karsten Bailey, 87 David Martin, 88 Bubba Franks, 89 Robert Ferguson, 90 Chukie Nwokorie, 91 Joe Johnson, 93 Gilbert Brown.

SIXTH ROW: (L–R) Administrative Assistant/Football Matt Klein, Director of Research and Development Mike Eayrs, Director of Player Development Edgar Bennett, Assistant to the General Manager/Director of Football Administration Bruce Warwick, 94 Kabeer Gbaja-Biamila, 95 Rod Walker, 97 Cletidus Hunt, 98 Kenny Peterson, 99 Jamal Reynolds, Vice President of Football Operations Mark Hatley, Personnel Analyst to General Manager John Schneider, Director of Pro Personnel Reggie McKenzie, Assistant Director of Pro Personnel Sean Howard, Pro Personnel Assistant Marc Lillibridge.

BACK ROW: (L–R) Strength and Conditioning Assistant Mark Lovat, Weight Room Assistant Vince Workman, Intern Trainer Mike Keehan, Intern Trainer Jason Lisko, Assistant Trainer Bryan Engel, Assistant Trainer Kurt Fielding, Head Trainer Pepper Burruss, Associate Team Physician Dr. John Gray, Team Physician Dr. Patrick McKenzie, Director of Corporate Security Jerry Parins, Equipment Manager Gordon (Red) Batty, Assistant Equipment Manager Tom Bakken, Assistant Equipment Manager Bryan Nehring, Equipment Assistant Tim Odea, Equipment Department Assistant John Odea, Equipment Assistant Cale Kirby, Video Assistant Andy Muckerheide, Assistant Video Director Chris Kirby, Video Director Bob Eckberg.

The Packers enjoyed a record-setting season in 2003. Ahman Green, Ryan Longwell, Brett Favre and others all got into the act.

The setting of new standards reached its peak on Sunday, Dec. 15. Three longstanding marks fell as Green Bay buried the Chargers 38-21 in San Diego. Green broke Jim Taylor's single-season rushing record of 1,474 yards with a 9-yard run in the first quarter. Favre extended his string of consecutive games with a touchdown pass to 23 in the second quarter to eclipse Cecil Isbell's team record by one. Longwell's final extra point in the fourth quarter pushed him past Don Hutson (823 points) and into first place on the club's all-time scoring list.

Of course numbers can't sum up all of what transpired. Gilbert Brown completely tore his right biceps during training camp, but shrugged off surgery to start 14 games at nose tackle. Donald Driver bounced back from a scary tumble in the season opener, but not before the team welcomed Antonio Freeman back into the fold. The offensive line— Chad Clifton, Mike Wahle, Mike Flanagan, Marco Rivera and Mark Tauscher started all 16 games together.

Favre, the dean of all Packers at 12 years of service, suffered a hairline fracture of the thumb on his throwing hand in October and lost his father, Irv, to a heart attack two days before the Raiders game in December. He didn't miss a start, and his breathtaking, 4-touchdown, 399-yard passing performance in Oakland gave birth to the notion that the Packers might be a team of destiny.

Some of the Many Records Set in 2003

Source: Green Bay Packers 2003 Season Review

INDIVIDUAL NFL & PACKERS RECORDS, 2003

Most consecutive seasons completing 300 or more passes: 12, Brett Favre (extended from 2002)
Most consecutive starts, quarterback: 189, Brett Favre (extended from 2002)
Most consecutive seasons, 3,000 or more yards passing: 12, Brett Favre (extended from 2002)
Most consecutive playoff games with a TD pass: 15, Brett Favre (old record: 13, Dan Marino)

INDIVIDUAL PACKERS RECORDS, 2003

Regular Season

Most consecutive games scoring: 112, Ryan Longwell (extended from 2002)
Most points, career: 844, Ryan Longwell (old record: 823, Don Hutson)
Most field goals, career: 182, Ryan Longwell (old record: 173, Chris Jacke)
Most touchdowns season: 20, Ahman Green (old record: 19, Jim Taylor, 1962)
Most rushing attempts, season: 355, Ahman Green (old record: 329, Dorsey Levens, 1997)
Most rushing yards, season: 1,883, Ahman Green (old record: 1,474, Jim Taylor, 1962)
Most rushing yards, game: 218, Ahman Green (old record: 190, Dorsey Levens, 1997)

Most 100-yard rushing games, season: 10, Ahman Green (old record: 7 Jim Taylor, 1962 and Green, 2001)
Longest run from scrimmage: 98 yards, Ahman Green (old record: 97, Andy Uram, 1939)
Highest completion percentage, season: 65.39, Brett Favre (old record: 64.12, Brett Favre, 1992)
Most consecutive games, touchdown pass: 25, Brett Favre (old record: 22, Cecil Isbell)
Most yards from scrimmage, season: 2,250, Ahman Green (old record: 1,981, Ahman Green, 2001)
Most consecutive punts, none blocked: 308, Josh Bidwell (old record: 274, David Beverly)

Postseason

Most games played: 19, Brett Favre (extended from 2002)
Most rushing yards, game: 156, Ahman Green (old record: 116, Dorsey Levens, 1998)
Most passes completed, career: 379, Brett Favre (extended from 2002)
Most passes attempted, career: 630, Brett Favre (extended from 2002)
Most yards passing, career: 4,686, Brett Favre (extended from 2002)
Most touchdown passes, career: 33, Brett Favre (extended from 2002)
Most games, 300 or more yards passing, career: 3, Brett Favre (extended from 2002)
Most passes had intercepted, career: 22, Brett Favre (extended from 2002)

TEAM RECORDS, 2003

Regular Season

Most yards rushing, season: 2,558 (old record: 2,460, 1962)
Highest rushing average, season: 5.05 (old record: 4.96, 1961)
Highest completion percentage, season: 65.54 (old record: 64.52, 1992)
Most consecutive games scoring: 201 (extended from 2002)

Postseason

Most sacks of opposing passers, game: 8 vs. Eagles (old record: 6 vs. Chiefs, 1967)

Brett Favre, celebrating a teammate's touchdown with typical enthusiasm, continued to add to his Packers records in 2003. He eclipsed Cecil Isbell's record 22 consecutive regular-season games with a touchdown pass. He moved past Forrest Gregg's 187 consecutive games played record and now has 191 consecutive games played. And his near-perfect 154.9 passing rating against the Oakland Raiders was another team record.

Donald Driver celebrates a touchdown catch during the 2002 season by taking a Lambeau Leap into the appreciative crowd.

Quarterback Brett Favre, the Pack's all-time leader in passing yardage, rolls out and looks for a receiver.

Concentrating on the catch, receiver Boyd Dowler (86) makes a big play against the Chicago Bears during the Packers' 49-0 shutout on Sept. 30, 1962.

Trying to elude the Tampa Bay defense, Terdell Middleton (34) turns the corner for a 5-yard gain in the Packers' 9-7 win on Oct. 29, 1978. Quarterback David Whitehurst is No. 17 at right.

A Measure of Greatness

Photo from Tom Pigeon Collection

Halfback Paul Hornung (5) runs a sweep behind a block from tackle Forrest Gregg (75) for some of his game-high 89 yards rushing in the 1961 NFL Championship Game. The Packers shut out the New York Giants 37-0 on Dec. 31, 1961.

Photo from Tom Pigeon Collection

Only a referee remains upright as Tom Moore (25) bursts for yardage as the Packers downed the Colts 31-20 on Sept. 29, 1963.

Photo from Tom Pigeon Collection

Milt Plum (16) of the Lions tries to scramble as future Hall of Famer Willie Davis (87) closes in during a 9-7 Green Bay win on Oct. 7, 1962.

Photo from Tom Pigeon Collection

The famed Packers sweep gains momentum as back Tom Moore (25) follows the blocks of Fuzzy Thurston (63), Jerry Kramer (64), and Forrest Gregg (75) on Nov. 10, 1963, as the Packers crushed the Vikings 28-7.

Another NFL championship loomed for the Packers as Don Chandler (34) adds a field goal in the Pack's 23-12 win over Cleveland on Jan. 2, 1966. Bart Starr (15) is the holder.

The day's −13 temperature shows in the red deer-hunting attire worn by many fans during the famous "Ice Bowl" game against Dallas for the NFL championship on Dec. 31, 1967. Bart Starr (15), who scored the winning touchdown with seconds remaining, hands off to Travis Williams (23) for a short gain.

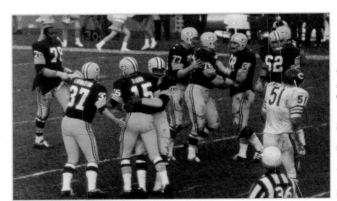

Quarterback Bart Starr is congratulated by teammates after his game-winning run with 3 seconds left beat the Bears 20-19 on Nov. 15, 1970. Walking off the field at right is the Bears' Dick Butkus (51).

A Measure of Greatness

Photo from Tom Pigeon Collection

This time it's Donny Anderson (44) running the Packers sweep, but it's still Jerry Kramer (64) making the lead block as the Packers beat the Eagles 30-13 on Sept. 15, 1968.

Photo from Tom Pigeon Collection

John Brockington (42), who rushed for more than 1,000 yards in each of his first three seasons, takes a handoff from Scott Hunter (16) as the Bears' Dick Butkus (51) fights off a block. The Packers beat the Bears 20-17 on Oct. 8, 1972.

Photo from Tom Pigeon Collection

The line of scrimmage is tense as Packers quarterback Lynn Dickey calls out signals against the Lions on Oct. 3, 1976. The Packers won 24-14.

Allen Rossum (20) celebrates, with the help of Chris Gizzi (57), his 55-yard punt return for a touchdown that beat Tampa Bay 21-20 during the 2001 season.

Ahman Green (30) is brought down after a size-able gain after a block from Marco Rivera (62). Green rushed for 1,387 yards in 2001 and added 1,240 yards in 2002.

Ryan Longwell adds another field goal to his collection, out of the hold of backup quarterback Doug Pederson.

A Measure of Greatness

Photo by Chip Manthey

Donald Driver (80) leaps high to snag a touchdown catch over two Chicago Bears in 2002. Driver emerged as the go-to receiver with 70 receptions and 9 touchdowns.

Photo by Chip Manthey

Quarterback Brett Favre prepares to hand off during the 2003 season, in which Favre set a number of all-time Packers records, including most consecutive number of games played and most consecutive number of games throwing a touchdown pass.

Photo by Chip Manthey

Tight end Bubba Franks picks up yardage after a reception. A first-round draft choice, Franks has emerged as a favorite touchdown pass target for Brett Favre.

Javon Walker, the 2002 first-round draft choice, fields a kickoff. Walker led the Packers with 35 kickoff returns and also caught 23 passes in his rookie year.

Head coach Mike Sherman, who is now also the Packers general manager, watches his team practice, with Lambeau Field towering in the background.

Vikings quarterback Daunte Culpepper (11) tries to lob a pass over the outstretched arms of rusher Kabeer Gbaja-Biamila (94). "KGB" was the Packers' top quarterback sacker in 2001 with 13.5 and 2002 with 12.

A Measure of Greatness

Ahman Green, running for a big gain as Packers coaches cheer him on, broke the single-season rushing records with 1,883 yards in 2003. The record had been held by Jim Taylor for about 40 years.

Working on a blocking scheme, offensive line coach Larry Beightol goes to the clipboard during a game. Looking on is tackle Mark Tauscher (65).

Center Mike Flanagan celebrates a first down. Flanagan and his teammates on the line started all 16 games in 2003, the first time five offensive lineman started every game of a season since 1978.

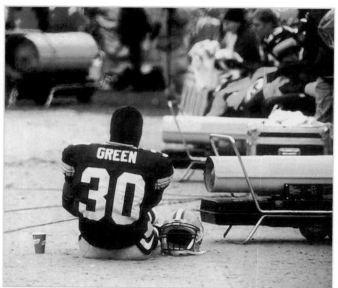

Taking a break, and warming up next to a portable heater, running back Ahman Green gets ready for another offensive series.

RUSHING

(leaders determined by total yards)

Year	Name	Att	Yds	Avg	LG	TD
1932	Clarke Hinkle	95	331	3.5	—	3
1933	Bob Monnett	108	413	3.8	—	3
	Clarke Hinkle	139	413	3.0	—	3
1934	Clarke Hinkle	144	359	2.5	—	1
1935	Bob Monnett	68	336	4.9	—	1
1936	Clarke Hinkle	100	476	4.8	—	5
1937	Clarke Hinkle	129	552	4.3	—	5
1938	Cecil Isbell	85	445	5.2	—	2
1939	Cecil Isbell	132	407	3.1	—	2
1940	Clarke Hinkle	109	383	3.5	—	2
1941	Clarke Hinkle	129	393	3.0	20	5
1942	Ted Fritsch	74	323	4.4	55	0
1943	Tony Canadeo	94	489	5.2	t35	3
1944	Ted Fritsch	94	322	3.4	18	4
1945	Ted Fritsch	88	282	3.2	31	7
1946	Tony Canadeo	122	476	3.9	27	0
1947	Tony Canadeo	103	464	4.5	35	2
1948	Tony Canadeo	123	589	4.8	49	4
1949	Tony Canadeo	208	1,052	5.1	54	4
1950	Billy Grimes	84	480	5.7	t73	5
1951	Tobin Rote	76	523	6.9	t55	3
1952	Tobin Rote	58	313	5.4	30	2
1953	Floyd (Breezy) Reid	95	492	5.2	43	3
1954	Floyd (Breezy) Reid	99	507	5.1	t69	5
1955	Howie Ferguson	192	859	4.5	57	4
1956	Tobin Rote	84	398	4.7	39	11
1957	Don McIlhenny	100	384	3.8	t40	1
1958	Paul Hornung	69	310	4.5	55	2
1959	Paul Hornung	152	681	4.5	63	7
1960	Jim Taylor	230	1,101	4.8	32	11
1961	Jim Taylor	243	1,307	5.4	53	15
1962	Jim Taylor	272	1,474	5.4	51	19
1963	Jim Taylor	248	1,018	4.1	t40	9
1964	Jim Taylor	235	1,169	5.0	t84	12
1965	Jim Taylor	207	734	3.5	35	4
1966	Jim Taylor	204	705	3.5	19	4
1967	Jim Grabowski	120	466	3.9	24	2
1968	Donny Anderson	170	761	4.5	42	5
1969	Travis Williams	129	536	4.2	t39	4
1970	Donny Anderson	222	853	3.8	54	5
1971	John Brockington	216	1,105	5.1	t52	4
1972	John Brockington	274	1,027	3.7	t30	8
1973	John Brockington	265	1,144	4.3	53	3
1974	John Brockington	266	883	3.3	33	5
1975	John Brockington	144	434	3.0	19	7
1976	Willard Harrell	130	435	3.3	56	3
1977	Barty Smith	166	554	3.3	11	2
1978	Terdell Middleton	284	1,116	3.9	t76	11
1979	Terdell Middleton	131	495	3.8	28	2
1980	Eddie Lee Ivery	202	831	4.1	t38	3
1981	Gerry Ellis	196	860	4.4	29	4
1982	Eddie Lee Ivery	127	453	3.6	32	9
1983	Gerry Ellis	141	696	4.9	71	4
1984	Gerry Ellis	123	581	4.7	50	4
1985	Eddie Lee Ivery	132	636	4.8	34	2
1986	Kenneth Davis	114	519	4.6	50	0
1987	Kenneth Davis	109	413	3.8	t39	3
1988	Brent Fullwood	101	483	4.8	t33	7
1989	Brent Fullwood	204	821	4.0	38	5
1990	Michael Haddix	98	311	3.2	13	0
1991	Darrell Thompson	141	471	3.3	t40	1
1992	Vince Workman	159	631	4.0	44	2
1993	Darrell Thompson	169	654	3.9	t60	3
1994	Edgar Bennett	178	623	3.5	t39	5
1995	Edgar Bennett	316	1,067	3.4	23	3
1996	Edgar Bennett	222	899	4.0	23	2
1997	Dorsey Levens	329	1,435	4.4	t52	7
1998	Darick Holmes	93	386	4.2	13	1
1999	Dorsey Levens	279	1,034	3.7	36	9
2000	Ahman Green	263	1,175	4.5	t39	10
2001	Ahman Green	304	1,387	4.6	t83	9
2002	Ahman Green	286	1,240	4.3	43	7
2003	Ahman Green	355	1,883	5.3	t98	15

Tony Canadeo, a Pro Football Hall of Famer, led the Packers in rushing in 1943 and 1946-49, capped by a 1,052-yard season in 1949. Stiller-Lefebvre Collection

RECEIVING

(leaders determined by number of receptions)

Year	Name	No	Yds	Avg	LG	TD
1932	Johnny Blood	14	168	12.0	—	3
1933	Roger Grove	18	215	11.9	—	0
1934	Clarke Hinkle	12	113	9.4	t69	1
1935	Johnny Blood	25	404	16.2	t70	3
1936	Don Hutson	34	526	15.5	t58	8
1937	Don Hutson	41	552	13.5	t78	7
1938	Don Hutson	32	548	17.1	54	9
1939	Don Hutson	34	846	24.9	t92	6
1940	Don Hutson	45	664	14.8	t36	7
1941	Don Hutson	58	738	12.7	t45	10
1942	Don Hutson	74	1,211	16.4	t73	17
1943	Don Hutson	47	776	16.5	t79	11
1944	Don Hutson	58	866	14.9	t55	9
1945	Don Hutson	47	834	17.7	t75	9
1946	Clyde Goodnight	16	308	19.3	t51	1
	Nolan Luhn	16	224	14.0	36	2
1947	Nolan Luhn	42	696	16.5	44	7
1948	Clyde Goodnight	28	448	16.0	57	3
1949	Ted Cook	25	442	17.7	50	1
1950	Al Baldwin	28	555	19.8	t85	3
1951	Bob Mann	50	696	13.9	52	8
1952	Bill Howton	53	1,231	23.2	t90	13
1953	Bill Howton	25	463	18.5	t80	4

Johnny (Blood) McNally led the Packers in pass receptions in 1932 and 1935. McNally was a charter member of the Pro Football Hall of Fame, elected in 1963. Stiller-Lefebvre Collection

1972	MacArthur Lane	26	285	11.0	49	0
1973	MacArthur Lane	27	255	9.4	30	1
1974	John Brockington	43	314	7.3	29	0
1975	Ken Payne	58	766	13.2	54	0
1976	Ken Payne	33	467	14.2	t57	4
1977	Barty Smith	37	340	9.2	42	1
1978	James Lofton	46	818	17.8	t58	6
1979	Paul Coffman	56	711	12.7	t78	4
1980	James Lofton	71	1,226	17.3	47	4
1981	James Lofton	71	1,294	18.2	t75	8
1982	James Lofton	35	696	19.9	t80	4
1983	James Lofton	58	1,300	22.4	t74	8
1984	James Lofton	62	1,361	22.0	t79	7
1985	James Lofton	69	1,153	16.7	t56	4
1986	James Lofton	64	840	13.1	36	4
1987	Walter Stanley	38	672	17.7	t70	3
1988	Sterling Sharpe	55	791	14.4	51	1
1989	Sterling Sharpe	90	1,423	15.8	t79	12
1990	Sterling Sharpe	67	1,105	16.5	t76	6
1991	Sterling Sharpe	69	961	13.9	t58	4
1992	Sterling Sharpe	108	1,461	13.5	t76	13
1993	Sterling Sharpe	112	1,274	11.4	54	11
1994	Sterling Sharpe	94	1,119	11.9	49	18
1995	Robert Brooks	102	1,497	14.7	t99	13
1996	Antonio Freeman	56	933	16.7	t51	9
1997	Antonio Freeman	81	1,243	15.3	t58	12
1998	Antonio Freeman	84	1,424	17.0	t84	14
1999	Antonio Freeman	74	1,074	14.5	51	6
	Bill Schroeder	74	1,051	14.2	51	5
2000	Ahman Green	73	559	7.7	31	3
2001	Ahman Green	62	594	9.6	42	2
2002	Donald Driver	70	1,064	15.2	t85	9
2003	Donald Driver	52	621	11.9	41	2

PASSING

(leaders determined by total yards)

Year	Name	Att	Com	Yds	Pct	TD	In	Rate
1932	Arnie Herber	101	37	637	45.5	9	9	51.5
1933	Arnie Herber	124	50	656	40.3	4	12	28.9
1934	Arnie Herber	115	42	799	36.5	8	12	45.1
1935	Arnie Herber	106	40	729	37.7	8	14	47.8
1936	Arnie Herber	173	77	1,239	44.5	11	13	58.9
1937	Arnie Herber	104	47	684	45.2	7	10	50.0
1938	Cecil Isbell	91	37	659	40.7	7	10	52.2
1939	Arnie Herber	139	57	1,107	41.0	8	9	61.6
1940	Cecil Isbell	150	68	1,037	45.3	9	12	55.3
1941	Cecil Isbell	206	117	1,479	56.8	15	11	81.4
1942	Cecil Isbell	268	146	2,021	54.5	24	14	87.0
1943	Tony Canadeo	129	56	875	43.4	9	12	51.0
1944	Irv Comp	177	80	1,159	45.2	12	21	50.0
1945	Irv Comp	106	44	865	41.5	7	11	53.1
1946	Irv Comp	94	27	333	28.7	1	8	9.9
1947	Jack Jacobs	242	108	1,615	44.6	16	17	59.8
1948	Jack Jacobs	184	82	848	44.6	5	21	27.9
1949	Earl (Jug) Girard	175	881	881	35.4	4	12	31.6
1950	Tobin Rote	224	83	1,231	37.1	7	24	26.7
1951	Tobin Rote	256	106	1,540	41.4	15	20	48.6
1952	Vito (Babe) Parilli	177	77	1,416	43.5	13	17	56.6
1953	Tobin Rote	185	72	1,005	38.9	5	15	32.4
1954	Tobin Rote	382	180	2,311	47.1	14	18	59.1
1955	Tobin Rote	342	157	1,977	45.9	17	19	57.8
1956	Tobin Rote	308	146	2,203	47.4	18	15	70.6
1957	Bart Starr	215	117	1,489	54.4	8	10	69.3
1958	Vito (Babe) Parilli	157	68	1,068	43.3	10	13	53.3
1959	Bart Starr	134	70	972	52.2	6	7	69.0
1960	Bart Starr	172	98	1,358	57.0	4	8	70.8
1961	Bart Starr	295	172	2,418	58.3	16	16	80.3
1962	Bart Starr	285	178	2,438	62.5	12	9	90.7
1963	Bart Starr	244	132	1,855	54.1	15	10	82.3
1964	Bart Starr	272	163	2,144	59.9	15	4	97.1
1965	Bart Starr	251	140	2,055	55.8	16	9	89.0
1966	Bart Starr	251	156	2,257	62.2	14	3	105.0
1967	Bart Starr	210	115	1,823	54.8	9	17	64.4
1968	Bart Starr	171	109	1,617	63.7	15	8	104.3
1969	Don Horn	168	89	1,505	53.0	11	11	78.1
1970	Bart Starr	255	140	1,645	54.9	8	13	63.9

1954	Bill Howton	52	768	14.8	59	2
1955	Bill Howton	44	697	15.8	60	5
1956	Bill Howton	55	1,188	21.6	t66	12
1957	Bill Howton	38	727	19.1	t77	5
1958	Max McGee	37	655	17.7	t80	7
1959	Boyd Dowler	32	549	17.2	35	4
1960	Max McGee	38	787	20.7	t57	4
1961	Max McGee	51	883	17.3	53	7
1962	Max McGee	49	820	16.7	64	3
	Boyd Dowler	49	724	14.8	41	2
1963	Boyd Dowler	53	901	17.0	t53	6
1964	Boyd Dowler	45	623	13.8	t50	5
1965	Boyd Dowler	44	610	13.9	t47	4
1966	Jim Taylor	41	331	8.1	21	2
1967	Boyd Dowler	54	836	15.5	t57	4
1968	Boyd Dowler	45	668	14.8	t72	6
1969	Carroll Dale	45	879	19.5	48	6
1970	Carroll Dale	49	814	16.6	t89	2
1971	Carroll Dale	31	598	19.3	t77	4

One of many great Packers quarterbacks, Arnie Herber led the team in passing from 1932-37 and again in 1939, throwing for 1,239 yards in 1936. Stiller-Lefebvre Collection

1971	Scott Hunter	163	75	1,210	46.0	7	17	46.1
1972	Scott Hunter	199	86	1,252	43.2	6	9	55.5
1973	Jerry Tagge	106	56	720	52.8	2	7	53.2
1974	John Hadl	184	89	1,072	48.4	3	8	54.0
1975	John Hadl	353	191	2,095	54.1	6	21	52.8
1976	Lynn Dickey	243	115	1,465	47.3	7	14	52.2
1977	Lynn Dickey	220	113	1,346	51.4	5	14	51.4
1978	David Whitehurst	328	168	2,093	51.2	10	17	59.9
1979	David Whitehurst	322	179	2,247	55.6	10	18	64.5
1980	Lynn Dickey	478	278	3,529	58.2	15	25	70.0
1981	Lynn Dickey	354	204	2,593	57.6	17	15	79.0
1982	Lynn Dickey	218	124	1,790	56.9	12	14	75.3
1983	Lynn Dickey	484	289	4,458	59.7	32	29	87.3
1984	Lynn Dickey	401	237	3,195	59.1	25	19	85.6
1985	Lynn Dickey	314	172	2,206	54.8	15	17	70.4
1986	Randy Wright	492	263	3,247	53.5	17	23	66.2
1987	Randy Wright	247	132	1,507	53.4	6	11	61.6
1988	Don Majkowski	336	178	2,119	53.0	9	11	67.8
1989	Don Majkowski	599	353	4,318	58.9	27	20	82.3
1990	Don Majkowski	264	150	1,925	56.8	10	12	73.5
1991	Mike Tomczak	238	128	1,490	53.8	11	9	72.6
1992	Brett Favre	471	302	3,227	64.1	18	13	85.3
1993	Brett Favre	522	318	3,303	60.9	19	24	72.2
1994	Brett Favre	582	363	3,882	62.4	33	14	90.7
1995	Brett Favre	570	359	4,413	63.0	38	13	99.5
1996	Brett Favre	543	325	3,899	59.9	39	13	95.8
1997	Brett Favre	513	304	3,867	59.3	35	16	92.6
1998	Brett Favre	551	347	4,212	63.0	31	23	87.8
1999	Brett Favre	595	341	4,091	57.3	22	23	74.7
2000	Brett Favre	580	338	3,812	58.3	20	16	78.0
2001	Brett Favre	510	314	3,921	61.6	32	15	94.1
2002	Brett Favre	551	341	3,658	61.9	27	16	85.6
2003	Brett Favre	471	308	3,361	65.4	32	21	90.4

PUNTING

(leaders determined by number of punts)

Year	Name	No	Yds	Avg	LG	HB
1939	Clarke Hinkle	43	1,751	40.7	65	0
1940	Clarke Hinkle	22	819	37.2	59	0
1941	Clarke Hinkle	22	980	44.5	63	0
1942	Lou Brock	32	1,226	38.3	52	2
1943	Lou Brock	32	1,164	36.4	72	1
1944	Lou Brock	14	494	35.3	50	0
1945	Roy McKay	44	1,814	41.2	73	0
1946	Roy McKay	64	2,735	42.7	64	1
1947	Jack Jacobs	57	2,481	43.5	74	1
1948	Jack Jacobs	69	2,782	40.3	78	1
1949	Earl (Jug) Girard	69	2,694	39.0	72	3
1950	Earl (Jug) Girard	71	2,715	38.2	63	2
1951	Earl (Jug) Girard	52	2,101	40.4	66	0
1952	Vito (Babe) Parilli	65	2,645	40.7	63	0
1953	Clive Rush	60	2,262	37.7	60	0
1954	Max McGee	72	2,999	41.7	63	0
1955	Dick Deschaine	56	2,420	43.2	73	0
1956	Dick Deschaine	62	2,649	42.7	57	0
1957	Dick Deschaine	63	2,645	42.0	71	2
1958	Max McGee	62	2,625	42.3	61	0
1959	Max McGee	64	2,716	42.4	61	1
1960	Max McGee	31	1,291	41.6	58	1
1961	Boyd Dowler	38	1,674	44.1	75	0
1962	Boyd Dowler	36	1,550	43.1	75	0
1963	Jerry Norton	51	2,279	44.7	61	0
1964	Jerry Norton	56	2,365	42.2	61	0
1965	Don Chandler	74	3,176	42.9	90	0
1966	Don Chandler	60	2,452	40.9	58	0
1967	Donny Anderson	65	2,378	36.6	63	1
1968	Donny Anderson	59	2,359	40.0	65	0
1969	Donny Anderson	58	2,329	40.2	58	0
1970	Donny Anderson	81	3,302	40.4	62	0
1971	Donny Anderson	50	2,022	40.4	58	0
1972	Ron Widby	65	2,714	41.8	64	2
1973	Ron Widby	56	2,414	43.1	60	0
1974	Randy Walker	69	2,648	38.4	58	0
1975	David Beverly	66	2,482	37.6	55	0
1976	David Beverly	83	3,074	37.0	60	1
1977	David Beverly	85	3,391	39.9	59	1
1978	David Beverly	106	3,759	35.5	57	0
1979	David Beverly	69	2,785	40.4	65	0
1980	David Beverly	86	3,294	38.3	55	0
1981	Ray Stachowicz	82	3,330	40.6	72	2
1982	Ray Stachowicz	42	1,687	40.2	53	0
1983	Bucky Scribner	69	2,869	41.6	70	1
1984	Bucky Scribner	85	3,596	42.3	61	0
1985	Joe Prokop	56	2,210	39.8	66	0
1986	Don Bracken	55	2,203	40.1	63	2
1987	Don Bracken	72	2,947	40.9	65	1
1988	Don Bracken	85	3,287	38.7	62	1
1989	Don Bracken	66	2,662	40.6	63	0
1990	Don Bracken	64	2,431	38.0	59	1
1991	Paul McJulien	86	3,473	40.4	62	0
1992	Paul McJulien	36	1,386	38.5	67	2
1993	Bryan Wagner	74	3,174	42.9	60	0
1994	Craig Hentrich	81	3,351	41.4	70	0
1995	Craig Hentrich	65	2,740	42.2	61	2
1996	Craig Hentrich	68	2,886	42.4	65	0
1997	Craig Hentrich	75	3,378	45.0	65	0
1998	Sean Landeta	65	2,788	42.9	72	0
1999	Louie Aguiar	75	2,954	39.4	64	0
2000	Josh Bidwell	78	3,003	38.5	53	0
2001	Josh Bidwell	82	3,485	42.5	68	0
2002	Josh Bidwell	79	3,296	41.7	57	0
2003	Josh Bidwell	69	2,875	41.7	60	0

KICKOFF RETURNS

(leaders determined by number of returns)

Year	Name	No	Yds	Avg	LG	TD
1941	Tony Canadeo	4	110	27.5	55	0
	Hal Van Every	4	99	24.8	31	0
	Lou Brock	4	94	23.5	36	0
1942	Lou Brock	9	179	19.9	26	0
1943	Tony Canadeo	10	242	24.2	43	0

Steve Odom (84) cuts back behind blockers during a kickoff return against the Bears in 1978. Odom was the team leader in kickoff returns from 1974-79, scoring two touchdowns. Tom Pigeon Collection

Year	Name	No	Yds	Avg	LG	TD
1944	Ted Fritsch	11	288	26.2	44	0
1945	Ted Fritsch	8	279	34.9	79	0
1946	Tony Canadeo	6	163	27.2	38	0
	Bob Nussbaumer	6	148	24.7	44	0
1947	Tony Canadeo	15	312	20.8	35	0
1948	O.E. Smith	12	287	23.9	36	0
1949	Jack Kirby	14	315	22.5	34	0
1950	Billy Grimes	26	600	23.1	36	0
1951	Billy Grimes	23	582	25.3	47	0
1952	Billy Grimes	18	422	23.4	34	0
1953	Al Carmichael	26	641	24.7	43	0
1954	Al Carmichael	20	531	26.6	49	0
	Veryl Switzer	20	500	25.0	88	0
1955	Veryl Switzer	17	445	26.2	57	0
1956	Al Carmichael	33	927	28.1	t106	1
1957	Al Carmichael	31	690	22.3	33	0
1958	Al Carmichael	29	700	24.1	60	0
1959	Bill Butler	21	472	22.5	35	0
1960	Tom Moore	12	397	33.1	84	0
	Lew Carpenter	12	249	20.8	29	0
1961	Herb Adderley	18	478	26.6	61	0
1962	Herb Adderley	15	418	27.9	t103	1
1963	Herb Adderley	20	597	29.9	t98	1
1964	Herb Adderley	19	508	26.7	43	0
1965	Elijah Pitts	20	396	19.8	29	0
1966	Donny Anderson	23	533	23.2	61	0
1967	Travis Williams	18	739	41.1	t104	4
1968	Travis Williams	28	599	21.4	60	0
1969	Dave Hampton	22	582	26.5	t87	1
1970	Ken Ellis	22	451	20.5	48	0
1971	Dave Hampton	46	1,314	28.6	t90	1
1972	Ike Thomas	21	572	27.2	89	0
1973	Ike Thomas	23	527	22.9	34	0
1974	Steve Odom	31	713	23.0	52	0
1975	Steve Odom	42	1,034	24.6	t93	1
1976	Steve Odom	29	610	21.0	88	0
1977	Steve Odom	23	468	20.3	37	0
1978	Steve Odom	25	677	27.1	t95	1
1979	Steve Odom	29	622	21.4	31	0
1980	Mark Lee	30	589	19.6	35	0
1981	Mark Lee	14	270	19.3	31	0
1982	Del Rodgers	20	436	21.8	76	0
1983	Harlan Huckleby	41	757	18.5	57	0
1984	Del Rodgers	39	843	21.6	t97	1
1985	Gary Ellerson	29	521	18.0	32	0
1986	Walter Stanley	28	559	20.0	55	0
1987	Brent Fullwood	24	510	21.3	46	0
1988	Brent Fullwood	21	421	20.0	31	0
1989	Vince Workman	33	547	16.6	46	0
1990	Charles Wilson	35	798	22.8	36	0
1991	Charles Wilson	23	522	22.7	t82	1
1992	Corey Harris	23	485	21.1	50	0
1993	Robert Brooks	23	611	26.6	t95	1
1994	Corey Harris	29	618	21.3	59	0
1995	Antonio Freeman	24	556	23.2	45	0
1996	Desmond Howard	22	460	20.9	40	0
1997	Bill Schroeder	24	562	23.4	40	0
1998	Roell Preston	57	1,497	26.3	t101	2
1999	Basil Mitchell	21	464	22.1	t88	1
2000	Allen Rossum	50	1,288	25.8	t92	1
2001	Allen Rossum	23	431	18.7	27	0
2002	Javon Walker	35	769	22.0	55	0
2003	Antonio Chatman	36	804	22.3	46	0

PUNT RETURNS

(leaders determined by number of returns)

Year	Name	No	Yds	Avg	LG	TD
1941	Lou Brock	15	153	10.2	45	0
1942	Lou Brock	8	86	10.8	22	0
1943	Joe Laws	10	84	8.4	19	0
1944	Joe Laws	15	118	7.9	23	0
1945	Joe Laws	12	78	6.5	21	0

Willie Wood, a member of the Pro Football Hall of Fame, led the Packers in punt returns for 10 seasons, from 1960-68 and 1970. He ran two back for touchdowns in 1961. Stiller-Lefebvre Collection

Year	Name	No	Yds	Avg	LG	TD
1946	Bob Nussbaumer	12	98	8.2	21	0
1947	Herman Rohrig	18	213	11.8	28	0
1948	Fred Provo	18	208	11.6	40	0
1949	Ralph Earhart	14	161	11.5	t57	1
1950	Billy Grimes	29	555	19.1	t85	2
1951	Billy Grimes	16	100	6.3	26	0
1952	Billy Grimes	18	179	9.9	72	0
1953	Al Carmichael	20	199	10.0	52	0
1954	Veryl Switzer	24	306	12.8	t93	1
1955	Veryl Switzer	24	158	6.6	38	0
1956	Al Carmichael	21	165	7.9	22	0
1957	Al Carmichael	25	190	7.6	48	0
1958	Al Carmichael	15	67	4.5	51	0
1959	Bill Butler	18	163	9.1	t61	1
1960	Willie Wood	16	106	6.6	33	0
1961	Willie Wood	14	225	16.1	t72	2
1962	Willie Wood	23	273	11.9	65	0
1963	Willie Wood	19	169	8.9	41	0
1964	Willie Wood	19	252	13.3	64	0
1965	Willie Wood	13	38	2.9	14	0
1966	Willie Wood	22	82	3.7	13	0
1967	Willie Wood	12	3	0.3	8	0
1968	Willie Wood	26	126	4.8	16	0
1969	Elijah Pitts	16	60	3.8	10	0
1970	Willie Wood	11	58	5.3	12	0
1971	Ken Ellis	22	107	4.9	30	0
1972	Ken Ellis	14	215	15.4	t80	1
1973	Jon Staggers	19	90	4.7	26	0
1974	Jon Staggers	22	222	10.1	t68	1
1975	Willard Harrell	21	136	6.5	25	0
1976	Johnnie Gray	37	307	8.3	27	0
1977	Willard Harrell	28	253	9.0	t75	1
1978	Steve Odom	33	298	9.0	48	0
1979	Steve Odom	15	80	5.3	19	0
1980	Ron Cassidy	17	139	8.2	20	0
1981	Mark Lee	20	187	9.4	t94	1
1982	Phil Epps	20	150	7.5	35	0
1983	Phil Epps	36	324	9.0	t90	1
1984	Phil Epps	29	199	6.9	39	0
1985	Phil Epps	15	146	9.7	46	0
1986	Walter Stanley	33	316	9.6	t83	1
1987	Walter Stanley	28	173	6.2	48	0
1988	Walter Stanley	12	52	4.3	15	0
1989	Jeff Query	30	247	8.2	15	0
1990	Jeff Query	32	308	9.6	25	0
1991	Vai Sikahema	26	239	9.2	62	0
1992	Terrell Buckley	21	211	10.0	t58	1
1993	Mike Prior	17	194	11.4	24	0
1994	Robert Brooks	40	352	8.8	t85	1
1995	Antonio Freeman	37	292	7.9	26	0
1996	Desmond Howard	58	875	15.1	t92	3
1997	Bill Schroeder	33	342	10.4	46	0
1998	Roell Preston	44	398	9.0	t71	1
1999	Desmond Howard	12	93	7.8	20	0
2000	Allen Rossum	29	248	8.6	43	0
2001	Antonio Freeman	17	114	6.7	29	0
2002	Darrien Gordon	35	180	5.1	27	0
2003	Antonio Chatman	33	277	8.4	33	0

INTERCEPTIONS

(leaders determined by number of interceptions)

Year	Name	No	Yds	Avg	LG	TD
1940	Don Hutson	6	24	4.0	—	0
1941	Hal Van Every	3	104	34.7	t91	1
1942	Don Hutson	7	71	10.1	27	0
1943	Irv Comp	10	149	14.9	35	1
1944	Ted Fritsch	6	115	19.2	t50	1
	Irv Comp	6	54	9.0	43	0
1945	Charley Brock	4	122	30.5	38	2
	Don Hutson	4	15	3.8	15	0
1946	Herman Rohrig	5	134	26.8	51	0
1947	Bob Forte	8	140	17.5	t68	1
1948	Ted Cook	6	81	13.5	27	0
1949	Ted Cook	5	52	10.4	30	0
1950	Rebel Steiner	7	190	27.1	t94	1
1951	Earl (Jug) Girard	5	25	5.0	15	0
1952	Ace Loomis	4	115	28.8	t45	1
	Bob Forte	4	50	12.5	25	0
	Bobby Dillon	4	35	8.8	17	0
1953	Bobby Dillon	9	112	12.4	t49	1
1954	Bobby Dillon	7	111	15.9	t59	1
1955	Bobby Dillon	9	153	17.0	61	0

Defensive back Herb Adderly's skills kept the Packers in many games during the Glory Years. He led the team or shared the team lead in interceptions in 1963, 1964, 1965, and 1969. Stiller-Lefebvre Collection

Year	Name	No	Yds	Avg	LG	TD
1956	Bobby Dillon	7	244	34.9	45	1
1957	John Symank	9	198	22.0	36	0
	Bobby Dillon	9	180	20.0	t55	1
1958	Bobby Dillon	6	134	22.3	46	1
1959	Bill Forester	2	48	24.0	34	0
	John Symank	2	46	23.0	25	0
	Bob Freeman	2	22	11.0	22	0
	Emlen Tunnell	2	20	10.0	18	0
1960	Jess Whittenton	6	101	16.8	52	0
1961	John Symank	5	99	19.8	41	0
	Jess Whittenton	5	98	19.6	t41	1
	Hank Gremminger	5	54	10.8	41	0
	Willie Wood	5	52	10.4	21	0
1962	Willie Wood	9	132	14.7	37	0
1963	Herb Adderley	5	86	17.2	35	0
	Willie Wood	5	67	13.4	22	0
1964	Herb Adderley	4	56	14.0	35	0
1965	Herb Adderley	6	175	29.2	t44	3
	Willie Wood	6	65	10.8	28	0
1966	Bob Jeter	5	142	28.4	t75	2
	Dave Robinson	5	60	12.0	23	0
1967	Bob Jeter	8	78	9.8	25	0
1968	Tom Brown	4	66	16.5	25	0
1969	Herb Adderley	5	169	33.8	t80	1
1970	Willie Wood	7	110	15.7	24	0
1971	Ken Ellis	6	10	1.7	5	0
1972	Ken Ellis	4	106	26.5	40	1
	Willie Buchanon	4	62	15.5	26	0
	Jim Hill	4	37	9.3	21	0
1973	Ken Ellis	3	53	17.7	t47	1
	Jim Hill	3	53	17.7	20	0
	Jim Carter	3	44	14.7	t42	1
1974	Ted Hendricks	5	74	14.8	44	0

Year	Name	No	Yds	Avg	Long	TD
1975	Perry Smith	6	97	16.2	61	0
1976	Johnnie Gray	4	101	25.3	67	1
1977	Steve Luke	4	9	2.3	7	0
	Mike C. McCoy	4	2	0.5	2	0
1978	Willie Buchanon	9	93	10.3	t77	1
1979	Johnnie Gray	5	66	13.2	35	0
1980	Johnnie Gray	5	54	10.8	21	0
1981	Maurice Harvey	6	217	36.2	53	0
	Mark Lee	6	50	8.3	25	0
1982	John Anderson	3	22	7.3	9	0
1983	Tim Lewis	5	111	22.2	46	0
	John Anderson	5	54	10.8	t27	1
1984	Tom Flynn	9	106	11.8	31	0
1985	Tim Lewis	4	4	1.0	4	0
1986	Mark Lee	9	33	3.7	11	0
1987	Jim Bob Morris	3	135	45.0	73	0
	Dave Brown	3	16	5.3	11	0
1988	Mark Murphy	5	19	3.8	9	0
1989	Dave Brown	6	12	2.0	12	0
1990	LeRoy Butler	3	42	14.0	28	0
	Jerry Holmes	3	39	13.0	24	0
	Mark Murphy	3	6	2.0	4	0
1991	Chuck Cecil	3	76	25.3	32	0
	Mark Murphy	3	27	9.0	16	0
	LeRoy Butler	3	6	2.0	6	0
1992	Chuck Cecil	4	52	13.0	29	0
1993	LeRoy Butler	6	131	21.8	39	0
1994	Terrell Buckley	5	38	7.6	26	0
1995	LeRoy Butler	5	105	21.0	76	0
1996	Eugene Robinson	6	107	17.8	39	0
1997	LeRoy Butler	5	4	0.8	2	0
1998	Tyrone Williams	5	40	8.0	15	0
1999	Mike McKenzie	6	4	0.7	4	0
2000	Darren Sharper	9	109	12.1	47	0
2001	Darren Sharper	6	78	13.0	23	0
2002	Darren Sharper	7	233	33.3	t89	1
2003	Darren Sharper	5	78	15.6	50	0

SCORING

(leaders determined by total points)

Year	Name	TDr	TDp	TDrt	PAT	2pt	FG	S	TP
1921	Curly Lambeau	2	0	0	7	0	3	0	28
1922	Curly Lambeau	3	0	0	3	0	1	0	24
1923	Cub Buck	0	0	0	5	0	6	0	23
1924	Tillie Voss	0	5	0	0	0	0	0	30
1925	Myrt Basing	4	2	0	0	0	0	0	36
	Marty Norton	1	4	1	0	0	0	0	36
1926	Verne Lewellen	3	3	1	0	0	0	0	42
1927	Verne Lewellen	5	0	0	0	0	0	0	30
1928	Verne Lewellen	6	3	0	0	0	0	0	54
1929	Verne Lewellen	6	1	1	0	0	0	0	48
1930	Verne Lewellen	8	1	0	0	0	0	0	54
1931	Johnny Blood	2	10	1	0	0	0	0	78
1932	Johnny Blood	0	3	1	0	0	0	0	24
	Hank Bruder	0	3	1	0	0	0	0	24
1933	Buckets Goldenberg	4	1	2	0	0	0	0	42
1934	Bob Monnett	2	0	0	6	0	4	0	30
1935	Don Hutson	0	6	1	1	0	0	0	43
1936	Don Hutson	0	8	1	0	0	0	0	54
1937	Clarke Hinkle	5	2	0	8	0	2	0	56
1938	Clarke Hinkle	3	4	0	7/8	0	3/9	0	58
1939	Don Hutson	0	6	0	2/2	0	0/0	0	38
1940	Don Hutson	0	7	0	15/16	0	0/0	0	57
1941	Don Hutson	2	10	0	20/24	0	1/1	0	95
1942	Don Hutson	0	17	0	33/34	0	1/4	0	138
1943	Don Hutson	0	11	1	36/36	0	3/5	0	117
1944	Don Hutson	0	9	0	31/33	0	0/3	0	85
1945	Don Hutson	1	9	0	31/35	0	2/4	0	97
1946	Ted Fritsch	9	1	0	13/15	0	9/17	0	100
1947	Ted Fritsch	6	0	0	2/2	0	6/13	0	56
1948	Ted Fritsch	0	0	1	5/6	0	6/16	0	29
1949	Ted Fritsch	1	0	0	11/13	0	5/20	0	32
1950	Billy Grimes	5	1	2	0/0	0	0/0	0	48
1951	Fred Cone	1	0	0	29/35	0	5/7	0	50
1952	Bill Howton	0	13	0	0/0	0	0/0	0	78
1953	Fred Cone	5	1	0	23/25	0	5/16	0	74
1954	Fred Cone	0	0	0	27/29	0	9/16	0	54
	Max McGee	0	9	0	0/0	0	0/0	0	54
1955	Fred Cone	0	0	0	30/30	0	16/24	0	78
1956	Fred Cone	2	2	0	33/35	0	5/8	0	72
	Bill Howton	0	12	0	0/0	0	0/0	0	72
1957	Fred Cone	2	0	0	26/26	0	12/17	0	74
1958	Paul Hornung	2	0	0	22/23	0	11/21	0	67
1959	Paul Hornung	7	0	0	31/32	0	7/17	0	94
1960	Paul Hornung	13	2	0	41/41	0	15/28	0	176

Year	Name	TDr	TDp	TDrt	PAT	2pt	FG	S	TP
1961	Paul Hornung	8	2	0	41/41	0	15/22	0	146
1962	Jim Taylor	19	0	0	0/0	0	0/0	0	114
1963	Jerry Kramer	0	0	0	43/46	0	16/34	0	91
1964	Paul Hornung	5	0	0	41/43	0	12/38	0	107
1965	Don Chandler	0	0	0	37/38	0	17/26	0	88
1966	Don Chandler	0	0	0	41/43	0	12/28	0	77
1967	Don Chandler	0	0	0	39/39	0	19/29	0	96
1968	Carroll Dale	0	8	0	0/0	0	0/0	0	48
1969	Travis Williams	4	3	2	0/0	0	0/0	0	54
1970	Dale Livingston	0	0	0	19/21	0	15/28	0	64
1971	Lou Michaels	0	0	0	19/20	0	8/14	0	43
1972	Chester Marcol	0	0	0	29/29	0	33/48	0	128
1973	Chester Marcol	0	0	0	19/20	0	21/35	0	82
1974	Chester Marcol	0	0	0	19/19	0	25/39	0	94
1975	Joe Danelo	0	0	0	20/23	0	11/16	0	53
1976	Chester Marcol	0	0	0	24/27	0	10/19	0	54
1977	Chester Marcol	0	0	0	11/14	0	13/21	0	50
1978	Terdell Middleton	11	1	0	0/0	0	0/0	0	72
1979	Tom Birney	0	0	0	7/10	0	7/9	0	28
	Chester Marcol	0	0	0	16/18	0	4/10	0	28
1980	Gerry Ellis	5	3	0	0/0	0	0/0	0	48
1981	Jan Stenerud	0	0	0	35/36	0	22/24	0	101
1982	Jan Stenerud	0	0	0	25/27	0	13/18	0	64
1983	Jan Stenerud	0	0	0	52/52	0	21/26	0	115
1984	Al Del Greco	0	0	0	34/34	0	9/12	0	61
1985	Al Del Greco	0	0	0	38/40	0	19/26	0	95
1986	Al Del Greco	0	0	0	29/29	0	17/27	0	80
1987	Max Zendejas	0	0	0	13/15	0	16/19	0	61
1988	Brent Fullwood	7	1	0	0/0	0	0/0	0	48
1989	Chris Jacke	0	0	0	42/42	0	22/28	0	108
1990	Chris Jacke	0	0	0	28/29	0	23/30	0	97
1991	Chris Jacke	0	0	0	31/31	0	18/24	0	85
1992	Chris Jacke	0	0	0	30/30	0	22/29	0	96
1993	Chris Jacke	0	0	0	35/35	0	31/37	0	128
1994	Sterling Sharpe	0	18	0	0/0	0	0/0	0	108
1995	Chris Jacke	0	0	0	43/43	0	17/23	0	94
1996	Chris Jacke	0	0	0	51/53	0	21/27	0	114
1997	Ryan Longwell	0	0	0	48/48	0	24/30	0	120
1998	Ryan Longwell	0	0	0	41/43	0	29/33	0	128
1999	Ryan Longwell	0	0	0	38/38	0	25/30	0	113
2000	Ryan Longwell	0	0	0	32/32	0	33/38	0	131
2001	Ryan Longwell	0	0	0	44/45	0	20/31	0	104
2002	Ryan Longwell	0	0	0	44/44	0	28/34	0	128
2003	Ryan Longwell	0	0	0	51/51	0	23/26	0	120
	Ahman Green	15	5	0	0/0	0	0/0	0	120

Known as the "Golden Boy," Paul Hornung led the Packers in scoring from 1958-61 and in 1964. He scored a record 176 points in 1960, with 15 touchdowns, 41 extra points, and 15 field goals. Stiller-Lefebvre Collection

QUARTERBACK SACKS

(leaders determined by number of sacks)

Year	Name	No
1982	Ezra Johnson	5.5
1983	Ezra Johnson	14.5
1984	Mike Douglass	9.0
1985	Ezra Johnson	9.5
1986	Tim Harris	8.0
1987	Tim Harris	7.0
1988	Tim Harris	13.5
1989	Tim Harris	19.5
1990	Tim Harris	7.0
1991	Tony Bennett	13.0
1992	Tony Bennett	13.5
1993	Reggie White	13.0
1994	Sean Jones	10.5
1995	Reggie White	12.0
1996	Reggie White	8.5
1997	Reggie White	11.0
1998	Reggie White	16.0
1999	Keith McKenzie	8.0
2000	John Thierry	6.5
2001	Kabeer Gbaja-Biamila	13.5
2002	Kabeer Gbaja-Biamila	12.0
2003	Kabeer Gbaja-Biamila	10.0

COMBINED NET YARDS

(leaders determined by total yards)

Year	Name	Rush	Rec	P-rt	K-rt	Int	Fum	Tot
1933	Bob Monnett	413	44	—	—	—	—	457
1934	Clarke Hinkle	359	113	—	—	—	—	472
1935	Johnny Blood	115	404	—	—	—	—	519
1936	Don Hutson	-3	526	—	—	—	—	523
1937	Clarke Hinkle	552	116	—	—	—	—	668
1938	Cecil Isbell	445	104	—	—	—	—	549
1939	Don Hutson	26	846	—	—	—	—	872
1940	Don Hutson	0	664	—	—	24	—	688
1941	Don Hutson	22	738	0	8	32	—	800
1942	Don Hutson	4	1,211	0	0	71	—	1,285
1943	Don Hutson	41	776	0	0	197	—	1,014
1944	Don Hutson	87	866	0	0	50	—	1,003
1945	Don Hutson	60	834	0	37	15	0	946
1946	Tony Canadeo	476	25	76	163	23	0	763
1947	Tony Canadeo	464	0	111	312	0	2	889
1948	Tony Canadeo	598	81	55	166	26	0	926
1949	Tony Canadeo	1,052	-2	0	20	0	0	1,070
1950	Billy Grimes	480	261	555	600	0	0	1,896
1951	Billy Grimes	123	170	100	582	0	0	975
1952	Bill Howton	0	1,231	0	0	0	0	1,231
1953	Al Carmichael	199	131	199	641	0	0	1,170
1954	Veryl Switzer	59	166	306	500	0	0	1,031
1955	Howie Ferguson	859	153	0	20	0	0	1,032
1956	Al Carmichael	199	180	165	927	0	0	1,471
1957	Al Carmichael	118	184	190	690	0	0	1,182
1958	Al Carmichael	21	26	67	700	0	0	814
1959	Paul Hornung	681	113	0	0	0	0	794
1960	Jim Taylor	1,101	121	0	0	0	1	1,223
1961	Jim Taylor	1,307	175	0	0	0	0	1,482
1962	Jim Taylor	1,474	106	0	0	0	0	1,580
1963	Jim Taylor	1,018	68	0	0	0	0	1,086
1964	Jim Taylor	1,169	354	0	0	0	0	1,523
1965	Jim Taylor	734	207	0	0	0	0	941
1966	Jim Taylor	705	331	0	0	0	0	1,036
1967	Donny Anderson	402	331	98	226	0	0	1,057
1968	Donny Anderson	761	333	0	0	0	0	1,094
1969	Travis Williams	536	275	189	517	0	0	1,517
1970	Donny Anderson	853	414	0	0	0	0	1,267
1971	Dave Hampton	307	37	0	1,314	0	0	1,658
1972	John Brockington	1,027	243	0	0	0	0	1,270
1973	John Brockington	1,144	128	0	0	0	0	1,272
1974	Steve Odom	66	249	191	713	0	0	1,219
1975	Steve Odom	55	299	0	1,034	0	0	1,388
1976	Steve Odom	78	456	0	610	0	0	1,144
1977	Steve Odom	6	549	0	468	0	0	1,023
1978	Terdell Middleton	1,116	332	0	22	0	0	1,470
1979	James Lofton	-1	968	0	0	0	0	967
1980	Eddie Lee Ivery	831	481	0	0	0	0	1,312
1981	Gerry Ellis	860	499	0	0	0	0	1,359
1982	James Lofton	101	696	0	0	0	0	797
1983	James Lofton	36	1,300	0	0	0	0	1,336
1984	James Lofton	82	1,361	0	0	0	0	1,443
1985	James Lofton	14	1,153	0	0	0	0	1,167
1986	Walter Stanley	19	723	316	559	0	0	1,617
1987	Walter Stanley	38	672	173	47	0	0	930
1988	Brent Fullwood	483	128	0	421	0	0	1,032
1989	Sterling Sharpe	25	1,423	0	0	0	5	1,453
1990	Sterling Sharpe	14	1,105	0	0	0	0	1,119
1991	Sterling Sharpe	4	961	0	0	0	0	965
1992	Sterling Sharpe	8	1,461	0	0	0	0	1,469
1993	Sterling Sharpe	8	1,274	0	0	0	0	1,282
1994	Robert Brooks	0	648	352	260	0	0	1,260
1995	Edgar Bennett	1,067	648	0	0	0	0	1,715
1996	Desmond Howard	0	95	875	460	0	0	1,430
1997	Dorsey Levens	1,435	370	0	0	0	-7	1,798
1998	Roell Preston	0	23	398	1,497	0	0	1,918
1999	Dorsey Levens	1,034	573	0	0	0	0	1,607
2000	Ahman Green	1,175	559	0	0	0	0	1,734
2001	Ahman Green	1,387	594	0	0	0	0	1,981
2002	Ahman Green	1,240	393	0	0	0	0	1,633
2003	Ahman Green	1,883	367	0	0	0	0	2,250

Using his multipurpose skills of rushing, receiving, and returning kickoffs and punts, Tony Canadeo led the Packers in combined net yardage for four consecutive seasons, 1946-49. Stiller-Lefebvre Collection

TOP SINGLE-GAME PERFORMANCES

RUSHING

100 OR MORE YARDS (153)

Date	Name	Att-Yds	Avg	LG	TD
12-3-33	C. Hinkle	15-116	7.7	—	0
11-28-35	B. Monnett	12-107	8.9	—	1
11-1-36	C. Hinkle	13-109	8.4	—	1
10-8-39	A. Uram	2-108	54.0	t97	1
11-10-40	C. Isbell	11-118	10.7	—	0
10-26-41	A. Uram	7-103	14.7	61	0
11-22-42	T. Fritsch	9-111	12.3	55	0
10-31-43	T. Canadeo	18-122	6.8	t35	1
10-22-44	T. Canadeo	12-107	8.9	34	0
10-26-47	E. Cody	9-111	12.3	51	2
10-3-48	T. Canadeo	17-118	6.9	49	1
10-17-48	T. Canadeo	16-105	6.6	36	0
10-7-49	T. Canadeo	16-100	6.3	27	1
10-23-49	T. Canadeo	26-122	4.7	45	0
10-30-49	T. Canadeo	21-117	5.6	30	1
11-20-49	T. Canadeo	21-116	5.5	25	0
11-27-49	T. Canadeo	20-122	6.1	54	1
10-1-50	L. Coutre	8-101	12.6	53	0
10-8-50	B. Grimes	10-167	16.7	t61	1
11-18-51	T. Rote	14-150	10.7	32	0
11-22-51	T. Rote	15-131	8.7	23	1
10-12-52	T. Rote	14-106	7.6	30	0
10-31-53	B. Reid	9-120	13.3	t38	1
11-13-54	H. Ferguson	15-112	7.5	25	0
10-2-55	H. Ferguson	15-153	10.2	57	0
11-6-55	H. Ferguson	17-120	7.1	24	2
11-3-57	P. Hornung	16-112	7.0	72	0
10-19-58	H. Ferguson	11-100	9.1	29	0
12-7-58	J. Taylor	22-137	6.2	25	0
10-11-59	P. Hornung	28-138	4.9	14	1
12-13-59	L. Carpenter	16-113	7.1	26	0
10-2-60	J. Taylor	26-151	5.8	27	1
10-30-60	J. Taylor	25-105	4.2	18	1
11-13-60	J. Taylor	15-121	8.1	t28	3
11-20-60	T. Moore	11-105	9.5	t59	1
12-4-60	J. Taylor	24-140	5.8	29	1
12-11-60	J. Taylor	27-161	6.0	25	0
10-1-61	J. Taylor	19-130	6.8	53	1
10-8-61	P. Hornung	11-111	10.1	t54	3
10-15-61	J. Taylor	21-158	7.5	t45	4
10-22-61	T. Moore	16-159	9.9	69	0
12-3-61	J. Taylor	27-186	6.9	43	2
12-10-61	J. Taylor	22-122	5.5	23	1
9-23-62	J. Taylor	23-122	5.3	12	0
9-30-62	J. Taylor	17-126	7.4	26	3
10-14-62	J. Taylor	17-164	9.6	31	0
10-21-62	J. Taylor	17-160	9.4	27	2
11-4-62	J. Taylor	25-124	5.0	51	4
11-11-62	J. Taylor	25-141	5.6	26	4
12-16-62	J. Taylor	23-156	6.8	t28	1
9-22-63	T. Moore	17-122	7.2	t77	2
10-27-63	J. Taylor	26-107	4.1	t16	2
11-3-63	J. Taylor	30-141	4.7	21	1
11-24-63	J. Taylor	15-119	7.9	t34	1
12-7-63	J. Taylor	17-113	6.6	t40	1
10-11-64	J. Taylor	23-133	5.8	t27	2
11-1-64	J. Taylor	17-108	6.4	16	1
11-8-64	J. Taylor	19-145	7.6	t84	2
12-13-64	J. Taylor	17-165	9.7	65	1
11-21-65	J. Taylor	25-111	4.4	13	0
9-24-67	J. Grabowski	32-111	3.5	9	1
10-22-67	J. Grabowski	21-123	5.9	14	1
11-12-67	B. Wilson	16-100	6.3	19	0
10-6-68	D. Anderson	15-101	6.7	18	1
10-26-69	D. Anderson	18-114	6.3	t16	1
10-12-70	T. Williams	21-109	5.2	37	0
11-1-70	D. Anderson	15-105	7.0	54	0
10-3-71	J. Brockington	19-120	6.3	29	0
11-1-71	J. Brockington	16-111	6.9	41	0
11-7-71	J. Brockington	30-142	4.7	22	1
11-14-71	J. Brockington	23-149	6.5	31	0
11-5-72	J. Brockington	24-133	5.5	t30	2
11-19-72	M. Lane	16-126	7.9	t36	1
12-10-72	J. Brockington	25-114	4.6	19	0
9-23-73	J. Brockington	22-118	5.4	26	0
10-14-73	J. Brockington	15-106	7.1	33	0
11-11-73	J. Brockington	28-137	4.9	16	1
12-8-73	J. Brockington	27-124	4.6	29	0
12-16-73	J. Brockington	22-142	6.5	53	0
12-16-73	M. Lane	19-101	6.3	18	0
11-17-74	J. Brockington	32-137	4.3	23	0
11-30-75	J. Brockington	26-111	4.3	19	3
10-3-76	W. Harrell	17-111	6.5	56	0
9-10-78	T. Middleton	19-114	6.0	34	0
10-1-78	T. Middleton	11-148	13.5	t76	1
10-15-78	T. Middleton	23-121	5.3	25	4
11-26-78	T. Middleton	39-110	2.8	11	1
9-9-79	S. Atkins	12-110	9.2	60	1
10-14-79	N. Simpson	19-121	6.4	22	0
11-11-79	T. Middleton	27-135	5.0	28	0
11-23-80	G. Ellis	15-101	6.7	19	1
11-23-80	E. L. Ivery	24-145	6.0	t38	1
11-1-81	G. Ellis	23-127	5.5	19	0
9-12-82	E. L. Ivery	17-109	6.4	32	2
12-4-83	G. Ellis	18-141	7.8	71	1
10-28-84	E. L. Ivery	9-116	12.9	49	0
11-11-84	G. Ellis	10-107	10.7	50	1
9-29-85	J. Clark	9-112	12.4	80	0
11-10-85	E. L. Ivery	15-111	7.4	34	0
12-1-85	G. Ellis	9-101	11.2	t35	1
12-1-85	E. L. Ivery	13-109	8.4	24	0
10-18-87	K. Willhite	16-100	6.3	61	0
10-25-87	K. Davis	23-129	5.6	t39	2
10-9-88	B. Fullwood	14-118	8.4	t33	3
9-17-89	B. Fullwood	18-125	6.9	38	2
10-8-89	B. Fullwood	28-119	4.3	13	0
12-17-89	K. Woodside	10-116	11.6	t68	1
11-1-92	V. Workman	23-101	4.4	14	0
11-22-92	E. Bennett	29-107	3.7	9	0
10-24-93	D. Thompson	21-105	5.0	22	0
12-26-93	D. Thompson	21-101	4.8	t60	1

John Brockington (42) cuts around the corner for big yardage, led by blocker Gale Gillingham, in a 1974 game. Brockington had 13 100-yard rushing games in his career. Photo from Tom Pigeon Collection

Date	Name	Att-Yds	Avg	LG	TD
10-31-94	E. Bennett	26-105	4.0	21	2
12-11-94	E. Bennett	22-106	4.8	28	1
12-24-94	E. Bennett	21-100	4.8	t39	1
10-29-95	E. Bennett	22-121	5.5	13	0
12-22-96	E. Bennett	18-109	6.1	21	1
9-14-97	D. Levens	21-121	5.8	23	0
9-28-97	D. Levens	16-107	6.7	39	0
10-27-97	D. Levens	26-100	3.8	15	1
11-16-97	D. Levens	14-103	7.4	t52	2
11-23-97	D. Levens	33-190	5.8	30	1
12-1-97	D. Levens	31-108	3.5	17	2
11-15-98	D. Holmes	27-111	4.1	13	1
11-29-98	D. Holmes	26-163	6.3	13	0
12-13-98	D. Levens	15-105	7.0	50	0
9-19-99	D. Levens	29-153	5.3	32	1
11-1-99	D. Levens	24-104	4.3	15	0
12-5-99	D. Parker	19-113	5.9	22	2
1-2-00	D. Levens	24-146	6.1	36	4
11-19-00	A. Green	24-153	6.4	36	0
12-10-00	A. Green	27-118	4.4	t39	1
12-17-00	A. Green	25-161	6.4	34	0
9-9-01	A. Green	17-157	9.2	t83	2
9-24-01	A. Green	25-116	4.6	18	0
11-4-01	A. Green	24-169	7.0	t63	1
11-22-01	A. Green	22-102	4.6	t26	1
12-9-01	A. Green	29-125	4.3	29	1
12-23-01	A. Green	21-150	7.1	43	0
1-6-02	A. Green	23-101	4.4	t25	2
9-8-02	A. Green	27-155	5.7	38	0
10-7-02	A. Green	27-107	4.0	43	0
10-13-02	A. Green	31-136	4.4	38	1
12-22-02	A. Green	26-116	4.5	28	0
9-14-03	A. Green	23-160	7.0	t65	1
9-29-03	A. Green	19-176	9.3	t60	2
10-5-03	A. Green	27-118	4.4	16	2
10-12-03	A. Green	26-139	5.3	26	1
11-2-03	A. Green	21-137	6.5	27	0
11-10-03	A. Green	29-192	6.6	t45	1
11-16-03	A. Green	21-109	5.2	10	1
11-23-03	A. Green	27-154	5.7	24	0
12-22-03	A. Green	24-127	5.3	19	1
12-28-03	A. Green	20-218	10.9	t98	2

RECEIVING

100 OR MORE YARDS (262)

Date	Name	Att-Yds	Avg	LG	TD
10-6-35	D. Hutson	4-109	27.3	t43	2
10-27-35	D. Hutson	5-103	20.6	t69	2
11-10-35	J. Blood	3-100	33.3	t70	2
11-7-37	D. Hutson	5-140	28.0	t78	1
10-30-38	D. Hutson	6-148	24.7	t53	3
10-8-39	D. Hutson	3-126	42.0	t92	2
10-22-39	D. Hutson	2-111	55.5	t60	2
11-12-39	D. Hutson	5-112	22.4	—	0
11-19-39	D. Hutson	3-149	49.7	t69	1
10-13-40	C. Mulleneaux	4-111	27.8	t47	2
10-12-41	D. Hutson	8-126	15.8	t32	1
11-30-41	D. Hutson	9-135	15.0	t40	3

Date	Name	Att-Yds	Avg	LG	TD
9-27-42	D. Hutson	8-147	18.4	t40	2
10-11-42	D. Hutson	5-149	29.8	t69	2
10-18-42	D. Hutson	13-209	16.1	33	2
11-1-42	D. Hutson	5-207	41.4	t73	3
11-1-42	A. Uram	4-174	43.5	t64	3
11-15-42	D. Hutson	10-117	11.7	20	1
11-22-42	D. Hutson	14-134	9.6	19	2
10-31-43	D. Hutson	8-103	12.9	t19	2
10-31-43	H. Jacunski	5-124	24.8	48	1
11-14-43	H. Jacunski	3-120	40.0	t86	1
11-21-43	D. Hutson	8-237	29.6	t79	2
10-8-44	D. Hutson	11-207	18.8	t55	2
11-12-44	D. Hutson	5-107	21.4	t35	2
10-7-45	D. Hutson	6-144	24.0	t59	4
10-14-45	D. Hutson	7-110	15.7	25	0
10-21-45	D. Hutson	6-169	28.2	t75	2
10-28-45	D. Hutson	7-141	20.1	t59	2
10-19-47	N. Luhn	9-140	15.6	32	1
11-30-47	C. Goodnight	5-107	21.4	38	1
12-14-47	N. Luhn	8-135	16.9	44	1
10-24-48	C. Goodnight	5-117	23.4	57	1
10-19-50	A. Baldwin	3-106	35.3	t85	1
10-28-51	E. (Jug) Girard	4-130	32.5	t75	1
12-16-51	B. Mann	11-123	11.2	52	0
10-5-52	B. Howton	3-128	42.7	t90	1
10-12-52	B. Howton	5-156	31.2	t69	1
10-26-52	B. Howton	7-151	21.6	t78	1
11-27-52	B. Howton	7-123	17.6	t54	3
12-7-52	B. Howton	6-200	33.3	76	0
12-14-52	B. Howton	8-162	20.3	t90	2
10-4-53	B. Bailey	4-100	25.0	50	0
10-11-53	C. Rush	7-101	14.4	24	0
11-8-53	B. Mann	6-101	16.8	45	0
10-3-54	B. Howton	4-100	25.0	44	0
10-17-54	B. Howton	5-105	21.0	42	1
10-24-54	B. Howton	11-147	13.4	59	0
10-30-54	M. McGee	3-104	34.7	t49	3
11-21-54	B. Howton	7-101	14.4	29	0
12-12-54	M. McGee	9-105	11.7	t22	1
10-16-55	B. Howton	8-158	19.8	t57	1
10-21-56	B. Howton	7-257	36.7	t63	2
11-11-56	B. Howton	4-151	37.8	t53	1
11-18-56	B. Howton	3-121	40.3	45	1
11-22-56	H. Ferguson	7-106	15.1	25	0
9-29-57	B. Howton	8-165	20.6	41	1
11-3-57	B. Howton	4-111	27.8	t77	1
10-19-58	B. Howton	5-130	26.0	50	0
10-26-58	M. McGee	6-100	16.7	t34	2
10-4-59	M. McGee	3-124	41.3	47	2
10-25-59	M. McGee	3-110	36.7	t81	1
11-15-59	B. Dowler	8-147	18.4	34	0
11-26-59	B. Dowler	4-107	26.8	35	0
10-23-60	M. McGee	5-110	22.0	30	1
12-4-60	M. McGee	6-121	20.2	46	1
12-18-60	M. McGee	4-125	31.3	t57	2
9-17-61	M. McGee	7-127	18.1	29	0
10-15-61	M. McGee	5-120	24.0	t48	1
10-22-61	B. Dowler	2-100	50.0	t78	1
10-29-61	B. Dowler	5-121	24.2	48	1
10-29-61	M. McGee	6-102	17.0	29	1
10-14-62	B. Dowler	7-124	17.7	41	1
10-14-62	M. McGee	10-159	15.9	t55	2
11-11-62	B. Dowler	7-101	14.4	25	1
11-11-62	M. McGee	7-174	24.9	64	0

Date	Name	Att-Yds	Avg	LG	TD
11-10-63	B. Dowler	8-134	16.8	49	1
11-28-63	B. Dowler	9-178	19.8	49	0
12-7-63	M. McGee	7-105	15.0	t25	3
12-14-63	B. Dowler	8-188	23.5	t53	2
10-4-64	B. Dowler	6-128	21.3	t50	2
10-18-64	M. McGee	4-123	30.8	t42	1
11-15-64	M. McGee	6-139	23.2	t44	2
9-19-65	B. Dowler	6-104	17.3	31	0
10-17-65	C. Dale	3-108	36.0	t77	1
10-17-65	B. Long	4-106	26.5	t62	1
11-28-65	E. Pitts	4-111	27.8	t80	1
12-12-65	P. Hornung	2-115	57.5	t65	2
12-19-65	B. Dowler	6-117	19.5	t43	1
10-23-66	C. Dale	4-110	27.5	t51	1
12-4-66	C. Dale	3-142	47.3	t83	1
12-18-66	C. Dale	3-121	40.3	74	1
9-17-67	C. Dale	4-109	27.3	51	0
10-1-67	B. Dowler	8-105	13.1	18	0
10-12-67	D. Anderson	5-103	20.6	37	0
11-26-67	B. Dowler	6-105	17.5	42	1
12-3-67	B. Dowler	3-100	33.3	t57	1
9-15-68	B. Dowler	5-110	22.0	t55	1
9-29-68	C. Dale	6-205	34.2	t63	2
11-17-68	C. Dale	8-161	20.1	t47	1
12-15-68	B. Dowler	6-182	30.3	t72	2
10-12-69	C. Dale	7-167	23.9	t40	2
10-19-69	B. Dowler	6-100	16.7	33	1
11-2-69	C. Dale	7-134	19.1	t43	1
12-21-69	C. Dale	9-195	21.7	44	2
12-21-69	B. Dowler	6-102	17.0	t43	2
9-27-70	C. Dale	4-186	46.5	t89	2
12-13-70	C. Dale	8-128	16.0	33	0
10-17-71	C. Dale	8-151	18.9	t56	1
9-29-75	K. Payne	12-167	13.9	29	0
11-23-75	K. Payne	4-103	25.8	54	0
10-24-76	K. Payne	6-120	20.0	t57	1
11-28-76	O. Smith	4-121	30.3	47	0
11-13-77	S. Odom	4-115	28.8	t65	1
9-10-78	J. Lofton	3-107	35.7	t47	3
10-21-79	P. Coffman	7-106	15.1	21	0
10-28-79	P. Coffman	5-116	23.2	t78	1
11-4-79	J. Lofton	6-114	19.0	45	0
11-18-79	J. Lofton	4-112	28.0	44	1
12-9-79	J. Lofton	6-112	18.7	40	0
10-5-80	J. Lofton	8-114	14.3	23	1
10-12-80	P. Coffman	9-109	12.1	18	1
10-12-80	E. L. Ivery	11-128	11.6	31	0
10-12-80	Au. Thompson	7-102	14.6	36	0
10-19-80	J. Lofton	8-136	17.0	31	1
11-2-80	G. Ellis	7-106	15.1	t69	2
11-9-80	J. Lofton	8-146	18.3	37	0
11-16-80	J. Lofton	8-175	21.9	47	1
12-7-80	J. Lofton	6-111	18.5	24	1
9-13-81	J. Lofton	8-179	22.4	53	0
9-27-81	J. Jefferson	7-121	17.3	24	0
9-27-81	J. Lofton	8-101	12.6	27	1
11-22-81	J. Lofton	6-102	17.0	21	0
11-29-81	J. Lofton	7-159	22.7	t47	1
12-6-81	J. Jefferson	8-113	14.1	22	0
9-12-82	J. Jefferson	6-116	19.3	50	0
9-20-82	J. Lofton	4-101	25.3	36	0
12-19-82	J. Jefferson	5-101	20.2	43	0
12-26-82	J. Lofton	3-146	48.7	t80	2
1-2-83	J. Lofton	7-128	18.3	30	1

Date	Name	Att-Yds	Avg	LG	TD
9-4-83	J. Lofton	8-154	19.3	t74	1
9-11-83	J. Lofton	5-169	33.8	t73	3
10-2-83	J. Lofton	4-112	28.0	t57	1
10-17-83	P. Coffman	6-124	20.7	t36	2
10-17-83	G. Ellis	4-105	26.3	56	0
11-6-83	J. Jefferson	7-102	14.6	28	1
11-27-83	J. Lofton	7-161	23.0	41	1
12-4-83	J. Lofton	6-120	20.0	67	0
12-18-83	P. Coffman	4-122	30.5	74	1
9-2-84	J. Lofton	7-134	19.1	43	0
10-7-84	P. Coffman	8-104	13.0	42	1
10-7-84	J. Lofton	5-158	31.6	46	1
10-15-84	J. Lofton	11-206	18.7	t54	1
10-21-84	J. Lofton	5-162	32.4	t79	2
11-11-84	J. Lofton	4-119	29.8	t63	1
11-18-84	J. Lofton	6-129	21.5	51	0
10-6-85	J. Lofton	10-151	15.1	27	0
10-21-85	J. Lofton	7-103	14.7	t27	1
11-10-85	P. Epps	6-118	19.7	63	0
12-1-85	J. Lofton	6-106	17.7	27	0
9-14-86	J. Lofton	8-100	12.5	21	1
10-5-86	J. Lofton	7-109	15.6	24	1
11-23-86	E. West	5-103	20.6	t46	1
11-27-86	W. Stanley	4-124	31.0	62	2
10-18-87	Lee Morris	6-132	22.0	t46	1
10-25-87	W. Stanley	6-150	25.0	t70	1
11-8-87	P. Epps	6-139	23.2	40	1
12-27-87	W. Stanley	4-109	27.3	t39	2
9-25-88	S. Sharpe	7-137	19.6	51	0
10-2-88	W. Stanley	6-107	17.8	56	0
10-16-88	W. Stanley	5-101	20.2	43	0
11-20-88	S. Sharpe	8-124	15.5	27	0
12-11-88	P. Kemp	6-108	18.0	29	0
9-17-89	S. Sharpe	8-107	13.4	39	1
9-24-89	S. Sharpe	8-164	20.5	57	1
10-8-89	S. Sharpe	6-132	22.0	t79	1
10-29-89	S. Sharpe	7-105	15.0	28	1
11-26-89	S. Sharpe	10-157	15.7	t34	2
12-3-89	S. Sharpe	8-169	21.1	t55	2
10-7-90	S. Sharpe	5-129	25.8	t76	1
10-14-90	S. Sharpe	7-139	19.9	35	0
11-18-90	S. Sharpe	10-157	15.7	t54	1
12-22-90	E. West	7-103	14.7	22	0
11-10-91	S. Sharpe	8-133	16.6	t58	1
9-20-92	S. Sharpe	7-109	15.6	42	1
10-4-92	S. Sharpe	9-107	11.9	24	1
10-25-92	S. Sharpe	9-144	16.0	45	1
11-8-92	S. Sharpe	11-160	14.5	43	0
11-15-92	S. Sharpe	7-116	16.6	34	1
12-6-92	S. Sharpe	6-107	17.8	t65	2
12-20-92	S. Sharpe	8-110	13.8	18	2
9-5-93	S. Sharpe	7-120	17.1	t50	1
10-10-93	J. Harris	5-128	25.6	t66	1
10-24-93	S. Sharpe	10-147	14.7	t32	4
12-5-93	S. Sharpe	10-114	11.4	t18	1
12-19-93	S. Sharpe	6-106	17.7	42	1
12-26-93	S. Sharpe	7-119	17.0	26	1
9-18-94	S. Sharpe	6-108	18.0	48	0
10-2-94	S. Sharpe	9-132	14.7	30	1
11-24-94	S. Sharpe	9-122	13.6	t36	4
12-4-94	S. Sharpe	10-115	11.5	29	1
12-4-94	A. Morgan	6-103	17.2	t47	2
12-11-94	R. Brooks	6-105	17.5	35	1
12-18-94	E. Bennett	8-101	12.6	40	0
12-24-94	S. Sharpe	9-132	14.7	49	3
9-11-95	R. Brooks	8-161	20.1	t99	2
10-8-95	R. Brooks	10-124	12.4	29	0
10-22-95	M. Chmura	5-101	20.2	23	1
10-29-95	R. Brooks	6-127	21.2	t77	1
11-5-95	R. Brooks	9-120	13.3	21	0
11-12-95	R. Brooks	6-138	23.0	t44	2

Date	Name	Att-Yds	Avg	LG	TD
11-26-95	R. Brooks	6-114	19.0	t54	2
12-3-95	M. Chmura	7-109	15.6	29	1
12-10-95	R. Brooks	9-122	13.6	35	0
12-16-95	R. Brooks	5-118	23.6	t40	2
12-24-95	R. Brooks	11-137	12.5	26	1
9-9-96	R. Brooks	5-130	26.0	38	2
9-15-96	R. Brooks	8-108	13.5	32	0
9-29-96	A. Freeman	7-108	15.4	28	2
10-6-96	A. Freeman	7-146	20.9	t50	2
10-14-96	D. Beebe	11-220	20.0	t59	1
11-3-96	D. Beebe	4-106	26.5	t65	1
12-1-96	A. Freeman	10-156	15.6	41	0
12-8-96	A. Freeman	9-175	19.4	t51	3
9-21-97	A. Freeman	7-122	17.4	t28	2
9-28-97	R. Brooks	9-164	18.2	45	0
11-9-97	A. Freeman	7-160	22.9	45	1
11-16-97	D. Mayes	3-119	39.7	74	0
12-14-97	A. Freeman	10-166	16.6	t58	2
9-6-98	A. Freeman	4-110	27.5	t84	2
10-15-98	A. Freeman	6-126	21.0	t67	2
10-25-98	A. Freeman	9-103	11.4	44	1
11-1-98	A. Freeman	7-193	27.6	t80	2
11-29-98	B. Schroeder	5-128	25.6	46	0
12-13-98	A. Freeman	8-103	12.9	22	1
12-20-98	A. Freeman	7-186	26.6	t68	3
12-12-99	A. Freeman	7-111	15.9	51	1
10-10-99	B. Schroeder	7-158	22.6	51	0
10-10-99	A. Freeman	7-152	21.7	43	2
11-1-99	C. Bradford	3-106	35.3	t74	1
11-14-99	A. Freeman	6-110	18.3	t28	1
10-1-00	B. Schroeder	8-108	13.5	32	2
10-15-00	A. Freeman	6-116	19.3	t67	1
11-6-00	A. Freeman	5-118	23.6	t43	1
11-19-00	B. Schroeder	8-155	19.4	32	0
12-3-00	B. Schroeder	6-119	19.8	38	0
9-9-01	B. Schroeder	4-104	26.0	35	1
10-7-01	B. Schroeder	4-119	29.8	t67	1
10-14-01	A. Freeman	9-138	15.3	47	1
11-11-01	B. Schroeder	4-100	25.0	t41	1
11-18-01	C. Bradford	3-117	39.0	56	0
12-3-01	B. Schroeder	6-106	17.7	t43	1
12-3-01	A. Freeman	3-104	34.7	63	0
1-6-02	C. Bradford	3-111	37.0	t54	1
1-6-02	B. Schroeder	5-102	20.4	45	1
10-7-02	T. Glenn	8-154	19.3	49	0
10-7-02	D. Driver	4-120	30.0	t85	1
11-10-02	D. Driver	11-130	11.8	38	0
11-17-02	D. Driver	4-121	30.3	t84	1
12-8-02	R. Ferguson	6-105	17.5	t40	2
12-14-03	D. Driver	8-112	14.0	23	1
12-22-03	J. Walker	4-124	31.0	46	2

PASSING

300 OR MORE YARDS (72)

Date	Name	Att-Yds	Avg	LG	TD
11-1-42	C. Isbell	21-10	333	5	1
12-16-51	T. Rote	40-20	335	2	2
11-22-56	T. Rote	40-21	301	2	3
10-12-58	B. Starr	46-26	320	1	4
10-29-61	B. Starr	24-18	311	2	0
12-14-63	B. Starr	27-17	306	2	0
10-17-65	B. Starr	23-15	301	3	1
9-17-67	B. Starr	23-14	321	0	4
12-21-69	D. Horn	31-22	410	5	1

Date	Name	Att-Yds	Avg	LG	TD
10-24-76	L. Dickey	34-22	303	1	2
10-12-80	L. Dickey	51-35	418	1	2
11-16-80	L. Dickey	36-20	331	2	2
12-14-80	L. Dickey	37-18	309	0	3
9-13-81	L. Dickey	44-30	342	2	3
9-4-83	L. Dickey	31-27	333	5	1
10-17-83	L. Dickey	31-22	387	3	1
10-23-83	L. Dickey	41-23	383	2	3
11-27-83	L. Dickey	37-25	366	3	3
12-4-83	L. Dickey	34-16	345	1	1
10-7-84	L. Dickey	39-25	384	3	2
10-15-84	L. Dickey	37-27	371	1	1
10-21-84	L. Dickey	38-24	364	3	3
11-11-84	L. Dickey	40-22	303	4	1
11-17-85	L. Dickey	35-22	302	2	2
10-26-86	R. Wright	54-30	328	1	3
10-25-87	D. Majkowski	29-19	323	1	1
10-2-88	R. Wright	51-28	321	1	2
11-20-88	D. Majkowski	43-30	327	1	1
9-17-89	D. Majkowski	32-25	354	3	1
9-24-89	D. Majkowski	43-25	335	2	3
10-8-89	D. Majkowski	32-21	313	4	0
10-29-89	D. Majkowski	45-29	367	2	1
11-12-89	D. Majkowski	59-34	357	1	2
12-3-89	D. Majkowski	53-25	331	2	2
10-14-90	D. Majkowski	42-25	355	1	5
11-10-91	M. Tomczak	38-23	317	2	2
12-5-93	B. Favre	54-36	402	2	3
9-11-94	B. Favre	51-31	362	2	1
9-25-94	B. Favre	39-30	306	3	0
12-4-94	B. Favre	43-29	366	3	2
12-18-94	B. Favre	44-29	321	2	1
9-11-95	B. Favre	37-21	312	3	1
10-15-95	B. Favre	34-23	342	2	0
10-29-95	B. Favre	43-26	304	1	3
11-12-95	B. Favre	33-25	336	5	0
12-3-95	B. Favre	43-31	339	3	1
12-16-95	B. Favre	30-21	308	4	0
12-24-95	B. Favre	32-23	301	2	0
10-14-96	B. Favre	61-28	395	1	2
11-10-96	B. Favre	49-27	314	2	1
11-9-97	B. Favre	37-18	306	1	2
11-16-97	B. Favre	25-18	363	3	2
9-27-98	B. Favre	45-27	388	2	1
10-15-98	B. Favre	43-22	300	2	3
11-22-98	B. Favre	39-31	303	2	1
11-29-98	B. Favre	33-20	321	2	2
9-12-99	B. Favre	47-28	333	4	3
9-26-99	B. Favre	39-24	304	1	0
10-10-99	B. Favre	40-22	390	2	0
11-21-99	B. Favre	40-26	309	1	0
12-12-99	B. Favre	38-26	302	2	1
1-2-00	B. Favre	34-21	311	2	1
10-1-00	B. Favre	48-31	333	3	1
11-19-00	B. Favre	36-23	301	2	1
9-30-01	B. Favre	39-25	308	3	2
10-14-01	B. Favre	34-27	337	3	0
12-3-01	B. Favre	42-24	362	3	0
1-6-02	B. Favre	30-15	315	2	0
9-22-02	B. Favre	47-31	357	3	1
10-7-02	B. Favre	33-22	359	3	0
11-10-02	B. Favre	39-26	351	2	0
12-22-03	B. Favre	30-22	399	4	0

TOP OPPONENTS' SINGLE-GAME

RUSHING

100 OR MORE YARDS (182)

Date	Name	Att-Yds	LG	TD
11-19-33	Jim Musick	21-132	NA	2
9-16-34	Swede Hanson	13-116	t81	1
10-28-34	Beattie Feathers	15-155	NA	1
11-11-34	Harry Newman	38-114	NA	2
12-6-36	George Grosvenor	35-100	24	0
11-20-38	Tuffy Leemans	13-159	t76	1
10-22-44	Tom Colella	10-147	t75	2
11-19-44	Ward Cuff	103		0
11-4-45	Bob Margarita	16-116	38	2
11-11-45	Fred Gehrke	9-132	t72	2
10-20-46	Bill Dudley	17-133	31	1
10-10-48	Elmer Angsman	18-146	t72	1
10-30-49	Wally Triplett	9-109	t80	1
11-20-49	Jerry Nuzum	20-168	t64	1
9-24-50	Rob Goode	8-102	t80	1
11-5-50	Jimmie Spavital	15-176	t96	2
12-10-50	Joe Perry	9-135	t78	1
10-21-51	Dan Towler	11-144	t79	1
11-18-51	John Dottley	17-117	18	0
12-9-51	Joe Arenas	12-108	14	2
12-16-51	Dan Towler	13-102	26	0
12-14-52	Joe Perry	20-109	44	1
10-24-53	Fran Rogel	19-168	58	0
11-22-53	Joe Perry	16-153	47	1
10-10-54	Joe Perry	23-100	15	1
11-13-54	Carl Taseff	15-122	32	0
12-5-54	Joe Perry	20-137	25	1
10-29-55	Alan Ameche	22-117	14	0
11-6-55	Bobby Watkins	14-115	t29	2
11-6-55	Rick Casares	16-115	16	1
11-24-55	Lew Carpenter	20-120	t49	1
10-7-56	Rick Casares	24-139	25	1
10-21-56	Tank Younger	11-106	33	1
10-28-56	Lenny Moore	13-185	t79	2
11-11-56	John Hoffman	18-108	39	1
11-18-56	Hugh McElhenny	18-140	t86	1
11-22-56	Gene Gedman	22-103	21	0
12-8-56	Hugh McElhenny	19-132	50	1
12-16-56	Tom Wilson	23-223	46	0
10-6-57	J. H. Johnson	18-109	14	0
11-17-57	Jon Arnett	17-149	t68	1
11-28-57	J. H. Johnson	8-105	t62	1
12-8-57	Ron Waller	5-105	76	0
12-15-57	Joe Perry	27-130	18	2
10-19-58	Johnny Olszewski	21-165	t45	1
11-9-58	Rick Casares	15-113	t64	1
11-23-58	Hugh McElhenny	22-159	34	1
12-7-58	J.D. Smith	7-113	t80	1

Date	Name	Att-Yds	LG	TD
10-18-59	Ollie Matson	20-121	t49	1
11-26-59	Nick Pietrosante	17-134	25	0
12-13-59	J.D. Smith	18-106	24	1
9-24-61	J.D. Smith	16-102	33	0
11-5-61	Joe Perry	21-105	t15	2
10-21-62	J.D. Smith	26-119	22	0
12-16-62	Jon Arnett	16-103	40	0
12-14-63	J.D. Smith	19-126	t52	2
10-24-65	Don Perkins	22-133	43	0
12-5-65	Tommy Mason	21-101	26	1
11-26-67	Gale Sayers	18-117	t43	1
12-3-67	Dave Osborn	21-155	t43	1
10-20-68	Mel Farr	29-145	26	0
11-3-68	Gale Sayers	24-205	63	0
12-7-69	Leroy Kelly	22-151	31	0
11-28-71	Bob Gresham	26-113	15	0
9-24-72	Marv Hubbard	24-125	19	0
10-28-73	Altie Taylor	23-160	29	1
11-4-73	Bobby Douglass	19-100	42	4
12-8-73	Chuck Foreman	19-100	t50	1
10-13-74	L. McCutcheon	21-109	18	0
10-21-74	Carl Garrett	23-101	18	0
10-5-75	Mercury Morris	31-125	13	0
10-5-75	Don Nottingham	21-102	14	3
10-12-75	Mike Strachan	24-105	11	1
10-19-75	Preston Pearson	15-101	32	0
10-26-75	Rocky Bleier	35-163	11	0
9-12-76	Delvin Williams	25-121	t59	2
11-14-76	Walter Payton	18-109	42	1
11-28-76	Walter Payton	27-110	23	0
10-30-77	Walter Payton	23-205	58	2
11-27-77	Chuck Foreman	26-101	12	0
12-11-77	Walter Payton	32-163	26	2
9-17-78	Mark Van Eeghen	26-151	17	0
10-15-78	David Sims	22-104	12	1
11-12-78	Tony Dorsett	23-149	t33	2
11-12-78	Robert Newhouse	18-101	t14	2
11-19-78	Rob Lytle	16-110	25	1
12-17-78	Cullen Bryant	30-121	17	2
9-2-79	Walter Payton	36-125	14	0
10-21-79	Ricky Bell	28-167	26	0
11-4-79	Clark Gaines	16-125	52	0
11-25-79	Leroy Harris	9-137	80	0
12-9-79	Walter Payton	25-115	23	0
9-14-80	Billy Sims	20-134	25	1
12-7-80	Walter Payton	22-130	17	3
12-14-80	Earl Campbell	36-181	t24	2
9-20-81	Wendell Tyler	25-108	16	2
9-27-81	Ted Brown	21-109	17	0
11-15-81	Walter Payton	22-105	16	1
11-22-81	James Owens	16-112	t35	1

Date	Name	Att-Yds	LG	TD
12-12-82	Billy Sims	29-109	12	1
9-4-83	Earl Campbell	27-123	11	3
9-11-83	Franco Harris	22-118	12	1
9-26-83	Rob Carpenter	28-116	t14	1
10-23-83	Ted Brown	29-179	43	1
10-30-83	Pete Johnson	26-112	11	2
11-13-83	Darrin Nelson	16-119	22	0
11-20-83	Billy Sims	36-189	20	0
11-27-83	William Andrews	20-129	t20	2
12-18-83	Walter Payton	30-148	13	0
9-16-84	Walter Payton	27-110	12	0
9-30-84	James Wilder	43-172	t33	1
11-18-84	Eric Dickerson	25-132	10	0
12-9-84	Walter Payton	35-175	15	1
9-29-85	Ottis Anderson	20-104	17	1
10-21-85	Walter Payton	25-112	20	2
10-27-85	Randy McMillan	24-126	35	1
11-3-85	Walter Payton	28-192	t27	1
11-10-85	Darrin Nelson	21-146	37	1
11-24-85	Eric Dickerson	31-150	15	1
12-15-85	James Jones	23-104	17	0
10-12-86	Gary James	20-140	t41	1
12-20-86	Joe Morris	22-115	19	1
9-13-87	Marcus Allen	33-136	17	1
11-15-87	Curt Warner	25-123	t57	1
9-25-88	Neal Anderson	20-105	t45	2
10-23-88	Kelvin Bryant	27-140	25	0
10-30-88	Thurman Thomas	23-116	16	0
11-27-88	Neal Anderson	17-139	t80	2
9-24-89	Greg Bell	28-221	46	2
10-15-89	Herschel Walker	18-148	47	0
10-29-89	Barry Sanders	30-184	31	0
12-10-89	Christian Okoye	38-131	12	1
12-17-89	Neal Anderson	12-119	73	0
9-23-90	Christian Okoye	23-122	32	1
10-7-90	Neal Anderson	21-141	52	1
11-18-90	Johnny Johnson	15-103	41	0
12-9-90	Derrick Fenner	20-112	36	1
12-22-90	Barry Sanders	19-133	37	1
10-6-91	Emmitt Smith	32-122	26	0
11-10-91	Thurman Thomas	24-106	21	1
9-6-92	Terry Allen	12-140	51	0
9-20-92	Harold Green	21-101	15	0
9-27-92	Barry Foster	12-117	69	0
12-6-92	Barry Sanders	16-114	26	0
12-27-92	Terry Allen	20-100	37	1
11-14-93	Derek Brown	21-106	60	0
12-19-93	Scottie Graham	30-139	13	0
1-2-94	Eric Lynch	30-115	15	2
11-24-94	Emmitt Smith	32-133	30	2
12-4-94	Barry Sanders	20-188	63	1
10-8-95	Emmitt Smith	31-106	t16	2
10-15-95	Barry Sanders	18-124	30	0
10-29-95	Barry Sanders	22-167	37	0
12-10-95	Errict Rhett	22-118	21	0
9-29-96	Chris Warren	18-103	t37	1

Date	Name	Att-Yds	LG	TD
11-3-96	Barry Sanders	20-152	35	1
9-1-97	Raymont Harris	13-122	t68	2
9-21-97	Robert Smith	28-132	50	1
9-28-97	Barry Sanders	28-139	46	0
10-5-97	Warrick Dunn	16-125	44	1
10-12-97	Raymont Harris	27-101	8	1
11-2-97	Barry Sanders	23-105	18	0
11-16-97	Marshall Faulk	17-116	45	0
12-14-97	Fred Lane	19-119	t35	1
10-15-98	Barry Sanders	25-155	t73	1
11-9-98	Jerome Bettis	34-100	12	0
10-17-99	Olandis Gary	37-124	14	1
11-1-99	Ricky Watters	31-125	45	0
9-3-00	Curtis Martin	30-110	23	1
11-6-00	Robert Smith	24-122	22	0
11-27-00	Brad Hoover	24-117	35	1
11-22-01	James Stewart	14-102	38	0
12-16-01	Skip Hicks	17-142	51	1
12-23-01	Jamel White	21-131	51	0
12-30-01	Michael Bennett	25-104	23	0
9-15-02	Deuce McAllister	21-123	62	2
11-10-02	James Stewart	15-122	56	0
11-17-02	Michael Bennett	20-130	62	0
12-8-02	Michael Bennett	19-120	35	0
9-29-03	Anthony Thomas	13-110	t67	1
10-5-03	Shaun Alexander	20-102	18	1
11-16-03	Thomas Jones	9-134	61	0

Times 100 or more

Walter Payton 13, Barry Sanders 10, Joe Perry 7, JD Smith 7, Neal Anderson 4, Michael Bennett 3, Rick Casares 3, Hugh McElhenny 3, Billy Sims 3, Emmitt Smith 3, Terry Allen 2, Jon Arnett 2, Ted Brown 2, Earl Campbell 2, Eric Dickerson 2, Chuck Foreman 2, Raymont Harris 2, John Henry Johnson 2, Darrin Nelson 2, Christian Okoye 2, Gale Sayers 2, Robert Smith 2, James Stewart 2, Thurman Thomas 2, Dan Towler 2

RECEIVING

100 OR MORE YARDS (208)

Date	Name	No-Yds	LG	TD
10-10-37	Gus Tinsley	6-148	39	1
11-14-37	Joe Carter	6-139	t86	1
10-8-39	Bill Smith	6-128	t61	2
9-15-40	Don Looney	8-115	t39	2
9-22-40	Bob Swisher	2-106	55	0
10-20-40	Chuck Hanneman	3-101	74	0
12-5-43	Tony Bova	3-106	t48	2
10-7-45	John Greene	4-123	t61	1
11-10-46	Mal Kutner	4-127	54	0
11-9-47	Ken Kavanaugh	4-103	39	1
11-16-47	Mal Kutner	5-100	28	2
12-7-47	Ralph Heywood	5-128	39	1
12-14-47	Pete Pihos	4-108	t66	1
10-31-48	Joe Margucci	3-100	t55	1
11-13-49	Gene Roberts	7-212	57	3
11-27-49	Bob Ravensberg	5-114	t48	2
12-11-49	Bob Mann	8-182	t64	2
9-24-50	Howie Livingston	4-141	t74	2
10-1-50	Jim Keane	8-129	70	0
11-12-50	Tom Fears	7-128	t53	1
12-3-50	Tom Fears	18-189	36	2
10-21-50	Elroy Hirsch	3-111	t81	1
10-28-51	Dan Garza	4-121	t52	2
12-2-51	Dan Edwards	6-124	t53	2
12-16-51	Elroy Hirsch	6-146	t72	3
10-18-52	George Taliaferro	5-129	t78	1
11-27-52	Cloyce Box	9-155	45	3
12-14-52	J.R. Boone	5-108	42	0
10-11-53	Elroy Hirsch	8-168	70	0
11-15-53	Doak Walker	3-105	t83	1
11-26-53	Cloyce Box	2-110	t97	1
12-13-53	Elroy Hirsch	9-196	50	0
10-17-54	Bob Boyd	3-149	t71	1
11-7-54	John Hoffman	9-110	31	1
12-12-54	Elroy Hirsch	5-119	38	0
12-12-54	Bob Boyd	4-106	44	0
11-20-55	Carroll Hardy	4-122	t58	2
11-11-56	Harlon Hill	4-121	t70	2
12-8-56	Clyde Conner	7-125	49	1
12-16-56	Bob Boyd	4-146	t56	2
11-17-57	Elroy Hirsch	6-106	45	0
10-5-58	Jim Doran	4-133	t65	1
10-12-58	Lenny Moore	6-108	45	0
10-26-58	Pete Retzlaff	6-121	49	0
11-16-58	Jim Phillips	8-208	t93	1
11-23-58	Billy Wilson	8-128	34	1
10-25-59	Raymond Berry	10-117	23	2
11-26-59	Jim Gibbons	7-103	24	0
11-6-60	Raymond Berry	10-137	t45	3
11-6-60	Lenny Moore	8-137	30	0
12-4-60	Angie Coia	3-104	59	0
12-17-60	Clendon Thomas	7-137	58	0
10-15-61	Ray Renfro	7-100	21	1
11-12-61	Mike Ditka	9-190	t47	3
12-10-61	R.C. Owens	7-127	32	1
12-10-61	Bernie Casey	5-118	t51	1
12-17-61	Jim Phillips	13-101	14	0
10-14-62	Hugh McElhenny	5-118	41	0
11-18-62	Jimmy Orr	5-100	t34	1
12-9-62	Bernie Casey	7-134	43	0
10-13-63	Ray Poage	3-106	52	0
10-20-63	Bobby Joe Conrad	8-112	t27	1
11-22-64	Paul Warfield	7-126	t48	2
10-3-65	Gale Sayers	5-104	t65	1
10-17-65	Terry Barr	5-112	t55	1
11-21-65	Paul Flatley	6-133	46	1
12-12-65	Raymond Berry	10-125	40	1
12-19-65	Dave Parks	9-149	38	1
10-30-66	Pat Studstill	7-164	53	0
12-4-66	Dave Parks	6-138	t65	1
10-30-67	Dave Williams	6-147	t49	2
12-15-68	Dick Gordon	6-147	t51	2
9-28-69	Clifton McNeil	3-109	t80	1
11-2-69	Roy Jefferson	7-164	t53	2
11-15-70	Dick Gordon	5-158	t69	1
11-26-70	Bob Hayes	4-105	55	0
12-6-70	Dave Smith	3-111	t87	1
12-13-70	George Farmer	9-142	t42	1
9-19-71	Rich Houston	6-151	t81	3
10-10-71	Larry Walton	5-103	t60	2
10-17-71	Bob Grim	7-101	t24	1
12-5-71	Mel Gray	3-102	t57	1
10-29-72	John Gilliam	5-106	35	0
11-5-72	Gene Washington	6-164	t62	2
11-18-73	Reggie Rucker	5-108	t63	1
10-27-74	Charlie Sanders	7-146	29	1
11-17-74	Jim Lash	6-136	31	0
10-24-76	Cliff Branch	4-135	t88	1
10-31-76	Ray Jarvis	6-163	t74	2
12-12-76	Alfred Jenkins	6-101	22	0
9-10-78	Tony Galbreath	14-122	18	0
10-8-78	James Scott	9-113	t17	2
10-15-78	Steve Largent	6-127	t48	1
11-19-78	Haven Moses	5-101	31	1
9-9-79	Henry Childs	7-112	t33	1
9-23-79	Ahmad Rashad	9-136	t50	2
10-28-79	Duriel Harris	10-180	t37	1
11-18-79	Frank Lewis	6-116	46	0
11-9-80	Freddie Solomon	5-104	44	1
11-16-80	Earnest Gray	6-119	t50	3
11-16-80	Mike Friede	6-108	29	0
12-7-80	Rickey Watts	4-126	t53	1
9-13-81	Alfred Jenkins	6-116	t30	1
9-4-83	Tim Smith	8-197	t47	1
10-17-83	Art Monk	5-105	34	0
11-13-83	Darrin Nelson	7-137	68	0
12-4-83	Willie Gault	4-129	t87	1
9-23-84	Doug Cosbie	7-103	36	0
10-7-84	Kellen Winslow	15-157	29	0
10-21-84	Steve Largent	7-129	t31	1
11-22-84	Mark Nichols	4-108	48	0
12-2-84	Kevin House	6-105	35	0
9-15-85	Lionel Manuel	5-105	43	1
10-6-85	Jeff Chadwick	7-112	41	0
10-27-85	Matt Bouza	6-109	40	0
10-27-85	Wayne Capers	5-104	t39	2
12-15-85	Carl Bland	7-109	24	0
9-14-86	Eric Martin	3-164	84	1
9-28-86	Steve Jordan	6-112	35	2
9-28-86	Hassan Jones	6-106	t36	2
11-16-86	Gerald Carter	7-143	46	1
11-27-86	Jeff Chadwick	6-121	28	1
10-4-87	James Brim	6-144	t63	1
10-18-87	Otis Grant	7-135	41	0
11-8-87	Neal Anderson	5-102	t59	1
10-1-89	Shawn Collins	5-126	47	0
11-19-89	Jerry Rice	9-106	20	1
11-26-89	Anthony Carter	6-103	25	0
12-3-89	Mark Carrier	7-104	17	0
9-9-90	Willie Anderson	5-128	t40	1
9-9-90	Henry Ellard	6-106	30	0

A Measure of Greatness

Top Opponents' Performances

Date	Name	No-Yds	LG	TD
10-28-90	Anthony Carter	9-141	t49	1
11-4-90	Jerry Rice	6-187	t64	1
11-18-90	Ernie Jones	7-117	t25	2
11-18-90	Roy Green	4-102	54	1
12-16-90	Fred Barnett	5-108	47	0
9-1-91	Keith Byars	8-111	t32	1
9-8-91	Robert Clark	10-143	36	0
10-6-91	Jay Novacek	11-121	26	1
11-3-91	Al Toon	8-109	21	0
11-10-91	James Lofton	6-114	29	0
12-1-91	Andre Rison	8-124	21	2
12-21-91	Cris Carter	7-112	50	0
9-13-92	Mark Carrier	7-115	40	1
9-13-92	Lawrence Dawsey	5-107	41	0
9-27-92	Dwight Stone	5-101	49	0
11-22-92	Wendell Davis	8-106	30	0
12-6-92	Herman Moore	8-114	45	1
12-13-92	Curtis Duncan	6-100	36	0
10-3-93	Michael Irvin	7-155	t61	1
10-10-93	Vance Johnson	10-148	49	1
12-12-93	Anthony Miller	8-103	23	0
12-19-93	Cris Carter	6-106	58	2
10-2-94	Vincent Brisby	6-117	t37	2
11-6-94	Herman Moore	8-151	49	2
11-20-94	Andre Reed	15-191	28	2
10-8-95	Michael Irvin	8-150	t48	1
10-29-95	Herman Moore	6-147	t69	3
11-12-95	Curtis Conway	6-126	t46	2
11-12-95	Jeff Graham	7-108	36	0
11-19-95	Keenan McCardell	4-102	36	0
11-26-95	Jackie Harris	10-122	23	0
12-10-95	Horace Copeland	8-122	23	0
12-16-95	Quinn Early	8-117	41	0
9-22-96	Jake Reed	7-129	t26	1
10-6-96	Curtis Conway	9-101	28	0
9-7-97	Irving Fryar	8-125	57	0
9-14-97	Charles Jordan	4-100	44	1
9-21-97	Jake Reed	9-119	t27	2
9-28-97	Herman Moore	6-105	45	0
10-27-97	Terry Glenn	7-163	50	0
11-9-97	Amp Lee	5-104	62	0
12-20-97	Quinn Early	7-120	29	0
9-6-98	Herman Moore	9-100	t25	1
10-5-98	Randy Moss	5-190	t52	2
10-5-98	Cris Carter	8-119	33	0
11-22-98	Randy Moss	8-153	t49	1
9-19-99	Johnnie Morton	4-118	t45	1
9-26-99	Jake Reed	6-108	50	0
10-17-99	Ed McCaffrey	5-116	t78	2
10-17-99	Byron Chamberlain	3-123	88	0
11-21-99	Germane Crowell	8-112	25	1
12-12-99	Patrick Jeffers	8-147	t38	2
12-20-99	Randy Moss	5-131	t57	2
1-2-00	Frank Sanders	13-118	18	1
1-2-00	Rob Moore	6-120	51	0
9-3-00	Dedric Ward	5-104	61	0
9-10-00	Eric Moulds	7-103	42	0
10-1-00	Marcus Robinson	2-126	t68	2
11-6-00	Randy Moss	6-130	42	0
11-27-00	Muhsin Muhammad	11-131	34	2
12-17-00	Randy Moss	4-136	t78	1
9-9-01	Johnnie Morton	5-111	42	0
12-3-01	Jimmy Smith	8-116	23	0
12-16-01	Derrick Mason	8-107	t35	1
9-15-02	Joe Horn	6-120	40	0
9-29-02	Steve Smith	5-116	61	0
10-7-02	Marty Booker	12-141	31	1
11-10-02	Az-Zahir Hakim	7-143	t64	1
11-17-02	Randy Moss	6-115	41	1
9-7-03	Randy Moss	9-150	27	1
10-12-03	Johnnie Morton	6-109	38	1
10-12-03	Tony Gonzalez	4-121	67	1
10-19-03	Isaac Bruce	9-129	26	0
12-7-03	Marty Booker	5-115	t61	1
12-14-03	LaDainian Tomlinson	11-144	t68	2
12-14-03	Antonio Gates	5-117	48	0
12-22-03	Jerry Rice	10-159	29	0

Times 100 or more

Randy Moss 7, Elroy Hirsch 6, Herman Moore 5, Raymond Berry 3, Bob Boyd 3, Cris Carter 3, Johnnie Morton 3, Jake Reed 3, Jerry Rice 3, Marty Booker 2, Cloyce Box 2, Mark Carrier 2, Anthony Carter 2, Bernie Casey 2, Jeff Chadwick 2, Curtis Conway 2, Quinn Early 2, Tom Fears 2, Dick Gordon 2, Michael Irvin 2, Alfred Jenkins 2, Mal Kutner 2, Steve Largent 2, Lenny Moore 2, Dave Parks 2, Jim Phillips 2

PASSING
300 OR MORE YARDS (60)

Date	Name	Att-Com	Yds	TD	In
11-13-49	Chuck Conerly	29-16	357	4	3
10-28-51	Bob Celeri	27-14	319	3	2
11-16-58	Bill Wade	42-19	372	1	2
11-15-59	Johnny Unitas	33-19	324	3	0
11-6-60	Johnny Unitas	29-20	324	4	1
12-10-61	John Brodie	29-19	328	2	0
10-30-67	Jim Hart	29-16	317	2	2
12-1-68	John Brodie	39-24	319	3	1
9-27-70	Bob Berry	44-28	302	2	3
12-13-70	Jack Concannon	34-21	338	4	1
10-10-71	Greg Landry	29-18	302	4	1
11-5-72	Steve Spurrier	37-19	315	2	1
11-18-73	Jim Plunkett	32-18	348	2	1
9-10-78	Archie Manning	53-33	303	1	1
10-15-78	Jim Zorn	31-17	308	1	2
10-19-80	Brian Sipe	39-24	391	2	0
11-16-80	Phil Simms	33-17	322	3	0
12-7-80	Vince Evans	22-18	316	3	0
11-29-81	Tommy Kramer	55-38	384	2	5
9-4-83	Archie Manning	34-22	348	1	2
10-17-83	Joe Theismann	39-27	398	2	0
11-13-83	Steve Dils	37-21	303	0	1
11-27-83	Mike Moroski	35-22	303	2	1
10-7-84	Dan Fouts	50-31	376	3	0
10-21-84	Dave Krieg	35-22	310	2	2
11-22-84	Gary Danielson	33-24	305	3	1
12-8-85	Dan Marino	44-30	345	5	1
10-25-87	Chuck Long	47-33	362	3	0
12-6-87	Joe Montana	35-26	308	2	1
10-2-88	Vinny Testaverde	37-20	300	1	4
10-22-89	Dan Marino	37-24	333	2	2
11-19-89	Joe Montana	42-30	325	2	1
11-26-89	Wade Wilson	38-23	309	0	2
9-9-90	Jim Everett	40-24	340	2	2
11-4-90	Joe Montana	40-25	411	3	0
9-13-92	Vinny Testaverde	25-22	363	2	0
12-13-92	Cody Carlson	36-25	330	0	2
10-3-93	Troy Aikman	23-18	317	1	0
10-10-93	John Elway	59-33	367	1	1
10-2-94	Drew Bledsoe	53-29	334	2	1
11-20-94	Jim Kelly	44-32	365	2	1
11-24-94	Jason Garrett	26-15	311	2	1
10-8-95	Troy Aikman	31-24	316	2	0
11-12-95	Erik Kramer	38-23	318	2	1
11-26-95	Trent Dilfer	48-27	312	0	0
12-16-95	Jim Everett	45-29	364	2	1
12-24-95	Neil O'Donnell	55-33	318	1	0
11-16-97	Paul Justin	30-24	340	1	0
10-5-98	Randall Cunningham	32-20	442	4	0
10-17-99	Brian Griese	31-19	363	2	1
12-12-99	Steve Beuerlein	42-29	373	3	0
1-2-00	Jake Plummer	57-35	396	2	3
10-15-00	Jeff Garcia	42-27	336	4	0
12-17-00	Daunte Culpepper	38-23	335	3	1
11-18-01	Chris Chandler	50-29	352	2	2
12-3-01	Mark Brunell	45-26	311	1	2
1-6-02	Kerry Collins	59-36	386	1	2
10-7-02	Jim Miller	49-27	353	3	3
10-12-03	Trent Green	45-27	400	3	0
12-14-03	Drew Brees	48-28	363	2	1

Times 300 or more

Joe Montana 3, Troy Aikman 2, John Brodie 2, Jim Everett 2, Archie Manning 2, Dan Marino 2, Vinny Testaverde 2, Johnny Unitas 2

ALL-TIME RUSHERS

(Statistic kept since 1933; rankings based on total yards)

Name	Att.	Yds.	Avg.	LG	TD	100
Jim Taylor, 1958-66	1,811	8,207	4.53	t84	81	26
Ahman Green, 2000-03	1,208	5,685	4.71	t98	41	24
John Brockington, 1971-77	1,293	5,024	3.89	53	29	13
Tony Canadeo, 1941-44, 46-52	1,025	4,197	4.09	54	26	9
Dorsey Levens, 1994-01	1,006	3,937	3.91	t52	28	10
Clarke Hinkle, 1932-41	1,171	3,860	3.30	57	34	2
Gerry Ellis, 1980-86	836	3,826	4.58	71	25	5
Paul Hornung, 1957-62, 64-66	893	3,711	4.16	72	50	3
Edgar Bennett, 1992-96	936	3,353	3.58	t39	19	6
Donny Anderson, 1966-71	787	3,165	4.02	54	24	3
Eddie Lee Ivery, 1979-86	667	2,933	4.40	49	23	5
Tobin Rote, 1950-56	419	2,205	5.26	t55	29	3
Ted Fritsch, 1942-50	619	2,200	3.55	55	31	1
Howie Ferguson, 1953-58	544	2,120	3.90	57	6	4
Tom Moore, 1960-65	503	2,069	4.11	t77	20	3
Terdell Middleton, 1977-81	559	2,044	3.66	t76	15	5
Floyd Reid, 1950-56	459	1,964	4.28	t69	13	1
Barty Smith, 1974-80	544	1,942	3.57	33	18	0
Joe Laws, 1934-45	470	1,932	4.11		9	0
MacArthur Lane, 1972-74	484	1,711	3.54	41	7	2
Brent Fullwood, 1987-90	433	1,702	3.93	38	18	3
Elijah Pitts, 1961-69, 71	479	1,684	3.52	t34	28	0
Brett Favre, 1992-03	469	1,647	3.51	40	12	0
Darrell Thompson, 1990-94	464	1,642	3.54	t60	7	2
Jessie Clark, 1983-87	379	1,588	4.19	80	9	1
Jim Grabowski, 1966-70	424	1,582	3.73	t36	8	2
Cecil Isbell, 1938-42	422	1,522	3.61		10	1
Bob Monnett, 1933-38	510	1,488	2.92		7	1
Walt Schlinkman, 1946-50	365	1,455	3.99	44	8	0
Bart Starr, 1956-71	247	1,308	5.30	39	15	0
Eric Torkelson, 1974-79, 81	351	1,307	3.72	29	8	0
Fred Cone, 1951-57	347	1,156	3.33	t41	12	0
Andy Uram, 1938-43	239	1,073	4.49	t97	4	2
Travis Williams, 1967-70	271	1,063	3.92	t39	6	1
Kenneth Davis, 1986-88	262	1,053	4.02	50	4	1
Don Majkowski, 1987-92	199	1,037	5.21	33	9	0
Ed Jankowski, 1937-41	275	1,002	3.64		8	0
Keith Woodside, 1988-91	259	976	3.77	t68	6	1
Willard Harrell, 1975-77	311	934	3.00	56	5	1
Vince Workman, 1989-92	242	927	3.83	44	10	1
Don McIlhenny, 1957-59	221	854	3.86	46	3	0
Lou Brock, 1940-45	254	804	3.17		10	0
Dave Hampton, 1969-71	195	787	4.04	53	7	0
Harlan Huckleby, 1980-85	242	779	3.22	23	10	0
Al Carmichael, 1953-58	166	712	4.29	t41	2	0
Billy Grimes, 1950-52	145	662	4.57	t73	6	1
George Sauer, 1935-37	190	656	3.45		6	0
Paul Ott Carruth, 1986-88	194	614	3.16	42	5	0
Najeh Davenport, 2002-03	116	604	5.21	t76	3	0
Reggie Cobb, 1994	153	579	3.78	30	1	0
Hank Bruder, 1931-39	190	569	2.99		5	0
Paul Miller, 1936-38	143	537	3.76		1	0
Bruce Smith, 1945-48	96	522	5.44	37	1	0
Irv Comp, 1943-49	255	502	1.97	34	7	0
Nate Simpson, 1977-79	153	497	3.25	40	1	1
Gary Ellerson, 1985-86	122	492	4.03	t37	5	0
Tony Fisher, 2002-03	110	483	4.39	28	3	0
Steve Atkins, 1979-81	120	467	3.89	60	2	1
Ben Wilson, 1967	103	453	4.40	40	2	1
Michael Haddix, 1989-90	142	446	3.14	13	0	0
Travis Jervey, 1995-98	109	431	3.95	16	1	0
William Henderson, 1995-03	122	431	3.53	17	5	0
Don Perkins, 1943-45	94	399	4.24	49	1	0
Darick Holmes, 1998	93	386	4.15	13	1	2
Joe Johnson, 1954-58	93	376	4.04	21	0	0
Vito (Babe) Parilli, 1952-53, 57-58	106	375	3.54	20	7	0
Charles Goldenberg, 1933-45	107	365	3.41		6	0
Lew Carpenter, 1959-63	64	359	5.61	t55	1	1
Earl Gros, 1962-63	77	358	4.65	26	4	0
Johnny Blood, 1929-33, 35-36	96	351	3.66		0	0
Bob Forte, 1946-50, 52-53	107	331	3.09	25	0	0
Perry Williams, 1969-73	103	329	3.19	14	1	0
Larry Coutre, 1950, 53	63	322	5.11	53	1	1
Ed Cody, 1947-48	82	321	3.91	51	2	1
Chester Johnston, 1931, 34-37	101	309	3.06		1	0
Roy McKay, 1944-47	100	288	2.88	41	3	0
Roger Grove, 1931-35	70	287	4.10		0	0
Don Hutson, 1935-45	62	284	4.58	27	3	0
Earl (Jug) Girard, 1948-51	76	283	3.72	35	1	0
Hal Van Every, 1940-41	63	281	4.46		2	0
DeMond Parker, 1999-00	54	269	4.98	26	2	1
Del Rodgers, 1982, 84	71	269	3.79	15	1	0
Chuck Sample, 1942, 45	59	257	4.36	31	4	0
Kevin Willhite, 1987	53	251	4.74	61	0	1
James Lofton, 1978-86	31	245	7.90	t83	1	0
Mike Meade, 1982-83	69	243	3.52	19	1	0
David Whitehurst, 1977-83	77	242	3.14	19	7	0
Bobby Jack Floyd, 1952	61	236	3.87	17	1	0
Raymont Harris, 1998	79	228	2.89	14	1	0
Jim Gillette, 1947	50	207	4.14	26	0	0
Steve Odom, 1974-79	16	205	12.81	28	1	0
Tony Falkenstein, 1943	58	198	3.41	59	1	0
Larry Mason, 1988	48	194	4.04	17	0	0
Ralph Earhart, 1948-49	50	194	3.88	t72	0	0
Les Goodman, 1973-74	38	189	4.97	47	1	0
Paul Duhart, 1944	51	183	3.59	16	2	0
John Stephens, 1993	48	173	3.60	22	1	0
Randy Wright, 1984-88	55	173	3.15	27	3	0
Ray Crouse, 1984	53	169	3.19	14	0	0
Donald Driver, 1999-03	17	163	9.59	45	1	0
Harry Sydney, 1992	51	163	3.20	19	2	0
Cliff Aberson, 1946	48	161	3.35	13	0	0
Veryl Switzer, 1954-55	31	160	5.16	38	0	0
Joe Francis, 1958-59	26	158	6.08	20	1	0
Jim Culbreath, 1977-79	47	153	3.26	18	0	0
Aaron Hayden, 1997	32	148	4.63	21	1	0
Frank Balazs, 1939-41	38	147	3.87		0	0
Herman Fontenot, 1989-90	34	145	4.26	19	0	0
Terry Wells, 1975	33	139	4.21	25	0	0
Jack Jacobs, 1947-49	42	137	3.26	23	2	0
Ricky Patton, 1979	37	134	3.62	14	0	0
Lamar McHan, 1959-60	24	131	5.46	t35	1	0
Basil Mitchell, 1999-00	31	125	4.03	15	0	0
Phillip Epps, 1982-88	10	121	12.10	34	1	0
Max McGee, 1954, 57-67	12	121	10.08	36	0	0
Bill Reichardt, 1952	39	121	3.10	14	1	0
Larry Buhler, 1939-41	41	121	2.95		0	0
Jerry Tagge, 1972-74	41	117	2.85	t41	3	0
George Paskvan, 1941	38	116	3.05	12	0	0
Anthony Dilweg, 1989-90	21	114	5.43	22	0	0
Jack Cloud, 1950-51	47	113	2.40	19	4	0
Jim Jensen, 1981-82	36	107	2.97	15	0	0
Chuck Mercein, 1967-69	31	105	3.39	15	2	0
Bob Summerhays, 1949-51	29	101	3.48	14	0	0
Allen Rice, 1991	30	100	3.33	21	0	0
Oscar E. Smith, 1948-49	36	100	2.78	11	0	0
Lynn Dickey, 1976-77, 79-85	129	98	0.76	13	9	0
LeShon Johnson, 1994-95	28	97	3.46	43	0	0
Mike Tomczak, 1991	17	93	5.47	48	1	0
Fred Provo, 1948	29	90	3.10	28	0	0
Scott Hunter, 1971-73	51	90	1.76	16	10	0
Walt Landers, 1978-79	24	81	3.38	14	0	0
Wuert Engelmann, 1930-33	23	79	3.43		0	0
Robert Brooks, 1992-98	17	75	4.41	21	0	0
Rondell Mealey, 2001-02	22	73	3.32	18	1	0
Sterling Sharpe, 1988-94	23	72	3.13	26	0	0
Alan Risher, 1987	11	64	5.82	15	1	0
Bob Hudson, 1972	15	62	4.13	17	0	0
Don Chandler, 1965-67	2	60	30.00	33	0	0
Walter Stanley, 1985-88	6	58	9.67	24	0	0
Blair Kiel, 1990-91	9	55	6.11	26	1	0
Bob Cifers, 1949	23	52	2.26	19	0	0
Arnie Herber, 1930-40	173	52	0.30		1	0
Bill Butler, 1959	7	49	7.00	16	0	0
Carlos Brown, 1975-76	12	49	4.08	21	0	0
Russ Mosely, 1945-46	16	49	3.06	9	0	0
Ben Starret, 1942-45	16	48	3.00	13	2	0
Cliff Taylor, 1976	14	47	3.36	17	1	0
Ray Pelfrey, 1951-52	3	44	14.67	24	0	0
Johnny Papit, 1953	6	44	7.33	21	0	0
John Hadl, 1974-75	28	44	1.57	9	0	0
John Losch, 1956	19	43	2.26	8	0	0
Bob Nussbaumer, 1946, 51	29	43	1.48	16	0	0
Perry Kemp, 1988-91	6	42	7.00	14	0	0
Don Milan, 1975	4	41	10.25	15	0	0
Don Barton, 1953	7	40	5.71	14	0	0
Jeff Query, 1989-91	3	39	13.00	18	0	0
Dave Kopay, 1972	10	39	3.90	20	0	0
John Jefferson, 1981-84	4	38	9.50	15	0	0
James Hargrove, 1987	11	38	3.45	t7	0	0
Herm Schneidman, 1935-39	13	37	2.85		0	0
Zeke Bratkowski, 1963-68, 71	25	35	1.40	13	1	0

Name	Att.	Yds.	Avg.	LG	TD	100
Dick Weisgerber, 1938-40, 42	11	34	3.09		0	0
Freddie Parker, 1987	8	33	4.13	17	0	0
John Roach, 1961-63	6	31	5.17	22	1	0
Jim Shanley, 1958	23	30	1.30	5	0	0
Herb Banet, 1937	9	29	3.22		0	0
Byron Bailey, 1953	13	29	2.23	13	0	0
Boyd Dowler, 1959-69	2	28	14.00	20	0	0
Ken Roskie, 1948	5	28	5.60	9	1	0
Bobby Douglass, 1978	4	27	6.25	17	0	0
Lee Weigel, 1987	10	26	2.60	7	0	0
Randy Johnson, 1976	5	25	5.00	11	1	0
Jon Staggers, 1972-74	5	25	5.00	t20	1	0
Clyde Goodnight, 1945-49	9	25	2.78	12	0	0
Stan Heath, 1949	10	25	2.50	18	1	0
Jerry Norton, 1963-64	3	24	8.00	24	0	0
J.R. Boone, 1953	7	24	3.43	24	0	0
Dom Moselle, 1951-52	12	23	1.92	7	1	0
Frank Purnell, 1957	5	22	4.40	7	0	0
Larry Hickman, 1960	7	22	3.14	4	0	0
Earl Witte, 1934	8	22	2.75		0	0
Clarence Self, 1952, 54-55	0	21	—	21	0	0
Bill Howton, 1952-58	4	20	5.00	11	0	0
John Sterling, 1987	5	20	4.00	9	0	0
Charles Casper, 1934	4	19	4.75		0	0
Beattie Feathers, 1940	4	19	4.75		0	0
Lavale Thomas, 1987	5	19	3.80	5	0	0
Buford McGee, 1992	8	19	2.38	4	0	0
Randy Walker, 1974	1	18	18.00	18	0	0
Carroll Dale, 1965-72	3	18	6.00	9	0	0
Gib Dawson, 1953	5	18	3.60	18	0	0
Paul Christman, 1950	7	18	2.57	4	1	0
Larry Morris, 1987	8	18	2.25	10	0	0
David Beverly, 1975-80	9	18	2.00	11	0	0
Bill Schroeder, 1994, 97-01	3	17	5.67	12	0	0
Antonio Freeman, 1995-01, 03	8	17	2.13	14	0	0
Allen Rossum, 2000-01	1	16	16.00	16	0	0
Steve Wagner, 1976-79	1	16	16.00	16	0	0
Gary Lewis, 1981-84	4	16	4.00	11	1	0
Dave Osborn, 1976	6	16	2.67	6	0	0
Bill Boedecker, 1950	8	16	2.00	8	0	0
Larry Craig, 1939-49	10	16	1.60	4	0	0
Claudis James, 1967-69	1	15	15.00	15	0	0
Larry Krause, 1970-74	6	15	2.50	12	0	0
Ken Keuper, 1945-47	6	14	2.33	8	0	0
Aundra Thompson, 1977-81	12	14	1.17	16	0	0
Jim Ringo, 1953-63	0	13	—	13	0	0
Leland Glass, 1972-73	2	13	6.50	13	0	0
Norm (Buster) Mott, 1933	5	13	2.60		0	0
Junior Coffey, 1965	3	12	4.00	10	0	0
Javon Walker, 2002-03	3	12	4.00	11	0	0
Ed Frutig, 1941, 45	1	11	11.00	11	0	0
Paul Staroba, 1973	1	11	11.00	11	0	0
Dexter McNabb, 1992-93	2	11	5.50	8	0	0
Chuck Fusina, 1986	7	11	1.57	6	0	0
Corey Harris, 1992-94	2	10	5.00	7	0	0
Ken Snelling, 1945	3	10	3.33	8	0	0
Hurdis McCrary, 1929-33	6	10	1.67		0	0
Matt Hasselbeck, 1999-00	10	10	1.00	13	0	0
Bob Mann, 1950-54	2	9	4.50	9	0	0
Ron Kramer, 1957, 59-64	6	9	1.50	12	0	0
Clarence Thompson, 1939	6	9	1.50		0	0
Bob Kahler, 1942-44	9	9	1.00	13	0	0
Jim Zorn, 1985	10	9	0.90	8	0	0
Paul Held, 1955	1	8	8.00	8	0	0
Ward Cuff, 1947	1	7	7.00	7	0	0
Eric Metcalf, 2002	2	7	3.50	5	0	0
Jack Concannon, 1974	3	7	2.33	6	1	0
Mark Brunell, 1993-94	6	7	1.17	t5	1	0
Don Highsmith, 1973	7	7	1.00	4	0	0
John Howell, 1938	7	7	1.00		0	0
T.J. Rubley, 1995	2	6	3.00	6	0	0
John Kirby, 1949	3	6	2.00	8	0	0
Bob Adkins, 1940-41, 45	1	5	5.00	5	0	0
Tommy Crutcher, 1964-67, 71-72	1	5	5.00	5	0	0
Charles Jordan, 1994-95, 99	1	5	5.00	5	0	0
Barry Smith, 1974-75	1	5	5.00	5	0	0
Gerald Tinker, 1975	1	5	5.00	5	0	0
Wayland Becker, 1936-38	2	5	2.50	3	0	0
Frank Patrick, 1970-72	2	5	2.50	3	0	0
Allen Jacobs, 1965	3	5	1.60	2	0	0
Vickey Ray Anderson, 1980	4	5	1.25	4	0	0
Frank Mestnick, 1963	1	4	4.00	4	0	0
Bill Robinson, 1952	3	4	1.33	4	0	0
Albin (Rip) Collins, 1951	5	4	0.80	6	0	0
Jim Salsbury, 1957-58	0	3	—	3	0	0
Paul Coffman, 1978-85	1	3	3.00	3	0	0
Jay Graham, 2002	1	3	3.00	3	0	0
Rich McGeorge, 1970-78	1	3	3.00	3	0	0
Nick Luchey, 2003	1	3	3.00	3	0	0
Don Zimmerman, 1976	1	3	3.00	3	0	0
Kelly Cook, 1987	2	3	1.50	2	0	0
Michael Blair, 1998	2	3	1.50	2	0	0
Aubrey Matthews, 1988	3	3	1.00	4	0	0
Charles Wilson, 1990-91	3	3	1.00	5	0	0
Marcus Wilson, 1992-95	6	3	0.50	5	0	0
Al Cannava, 1950	1	2	2.00	2	0	0
Harry Mattos, 1936	1	2	2.00	2	0	0
Claude Perry, 1927-35	1	2	2.00	2	0	0
Patrick Scott, 1987-88	1	2	2.00	2	0	0
Alex Urban, 1941, 44-45	1	2	2.00	2	0	0
Rich Campbell, 1981-84	2	2	1.00	5	0	0
Patrick Collins, 1988	2	2	1.00	2	0	0
Jim Lankas, 1943	2	2	1.00	2	0	0
Lee Morris, 1987	2	2	1.00	4	0	0
Lindell Pearson, 1952	2	2	1.00	2	0	0
Ed West, 1984-94	2	2	1.00	t2	1	0
Perry Moss, 1948	5	2	0.40	2	0	0
Jackie Harris, 1990-93	1	1	1.00	1	0	0
Dale Livingston, 1970	1	1	1.00	1	0	0
Jim Del Gaizo, 1973	4	1	0.25	3	0	0
Ty Detmer, 1993-95	4	1	0.25	5	0	0
Herman Rohrig, 1941, 46-47	42	1	0.02	18	0	0
Wally Dreyer, 1950	1	0	0.00	0	0	0
Vince Ferragamo, 1986	1	0	0.00	0	0	0
Tony Hunter, 1987	1	0	0.00	0	0	0
Charlie Leigh, 1974	1	0	0.00	0	0	0
Paul McJulien, 1991-92	1	0	0.00	0	0	0
Frankie Neal, 1987	1	0	0.00	0	0	0
Lester Peterson, 1932, 34	1	0	0.00	0	0	0
Guy Prather, 1981-85	1	0	0.00	0	0	0
Bill Renner, 1986-87	1	0	0.00	0	0	0
Al Romine, 1955, 58	0	0	—	0	0	0
Karl Swanke, 1980-86	1	0	0.00	0	0	0
Dave Davis, 1971-72	2	0	0.00	0	0	0
Dennis Sproul, 1978	2	0	0.00	0	0	0
Ray Stachowicz, 1981-82	2	0	0.00	0	0	0
Jim Lawrence, 1939	4	0	0.00	0	0	0
Jim McMahon, 1995-96	4	-1	-0.25	2	0	0
Ken Payne, 1974-77	1	-2	-2.00	-2	0	0
Gene Wilson, 1947-48	1	-2	-2.00	-2	0	0
Craig Nall, 2003	2	-2	-1.00	-1	0	0
Danny Wuerffel, 2000	2	-2	-1.00	-1	0	0
Bob Garrett, 1954	1	-3	-3.00	-3	0	0
Mark Ingram, 1995	1	-3	-3.00	-3	0	0
Dennis Claridge, 1965	2	-3	-1.50	1	0	0
Paul Winslow, 1960	2	-3	-1.50	1	0	0
Steve Bono, 1997	3	-3	-1.00	1	0	0
Herbert Goodman, 2000-01	4	-3	-0.75	3	0	0
Dick Gordon, 1973	1	-4	-4.00	-4	0	0
Bobby Thomason, 1951	5	-5	-1.00	10	0	0
Clive Rush, 1953	1	-6	-6.00	-6	0	0
Robert Ferguson, 2001-03	1	-8	-8.00	-8	0	0
Cal Clemmens, 1936	3	-8	-2.67	2	0	0
Tom O'Malley, 1950	1	-9	-9.00	-9	0	0
Don Horn, 1967-70	12	-12	-1.00	4	1	0
Doug Pederson, 1996-98, 01-03	19	-15	-0.79	3	0	0
Packers, 1933-2003*	31,646	122,066	3.86	t98	936	153
Opponents, 1933-2003	32,110	125,418	3.91	t96	922	—

*The 1933-2003 totals for the Packers include 95 rushes for 331 yards and three touchdowns by Clarke Hinkle in 1932. The totals also include 27 rushes for 130 yards and no touchdowns by Johnny Blood in 1932. For a more accurate comparison between the Packers and Opponents for the 71-year period, subtract 122 rushes, 461 yards, and three touchdowns. This will allow for an exact 1933-2003 comparison.

RUSHING TOUCHDOWNS

Below is a list of rushing touchdowns scored by Packers who played before 1933. Since Hinkle's three touchdowns are accounted for above, they do not appear below.

Name	No.	Name	No.
Verne Lewellen, 1924-32	37	Faye (Mule) Wilson, 1931	2
Bo Molenda, 1929-32	9	Norm Barry, 1921	1
Curly Lambeau, 1921-29	8	Lynn (Tubby) Howard, 1921-22	1
Myrt Basing, 1923-27	7	Claude Taugher, 1922	1
Carl (Cully) Lidberg, 1926, 29-30	7	Eddie Usher, 1922, 24	1
Hurdis McCrary, 1929-32	7	Stan Mills, 1922-23	1
Johnny (Blood) McNally, 1929-31	5	Charlie Mathys, 1922-26	1
Eddie Kotal, 1925-29	4	Marty Norton, 1925	1
Dutch Hendrian, 1924	3	Everett (Pid) Purdy, 1925	1
Jack Harris, 1925-26	3	Harry O'Boyle, 1928, 32	1
Rex Enright, 1926-27	3	Paul Fitzgibbons, 1930-32	1
Hank Bruder, 1931-32	3	Russ Saunders, 1931	1
Bill (Gus) DuMoe, 1921	2	Packers, 1921-32	115
Wuert Engelmann, 1930-32	2	Opponents, 1921-32	46
Arnie Herber, 1930-32	2		

(Statistic kept since 1933; rankings based on number of receptions)

Name	Att.	Yds.	Avg.	LG	TD	100
Sterling Sharpe, 1988-94	595	8,134	13.67	t79	65	29
James Lofton, 1978-86	530	9,656	18.22	t80	49	32
Don Hutson, 1935-45	488	7,991	16.38	t92	99	24
Boyd Dowler, 1959-69	448	6,918	15.44	t91	40	19
Antonio Freeman, 1995-01, 03	431	6,651	15.43	t84	57	20
Max McGee, 1954, 57-67	345	6,346	18.39	t82	50	16
Paul Coffman, 1978-85	322	4,223	13.11	t78	39	6
Robert Brooks, 1992-98	306	4,225	13.81	t99	32	13
Bill Howton, 1952-58	303	5,581	18.42	t90	43	17
Carroll Dale, 1965-72	275	5,422	19.72	t89	35	13
Dorsey Levens, 1994-01	271	2,079	7.67	56	16	0
Gerry Ellis, 1980-86	267	2,514	9.42	t69	10	2
William Henderson, 1995-03	244	1,844	7.56	27	11	0
Edgar Bennett, 1992-96	242	1,920	7.93	40	10	1
Ahman Green, 2000-03	242	1,913	7.90	42	12	0
Bill Schroeder, 1994, 97-01	225	3,435	15.27	t67	20	10
Ed West, 1984-94	202	2,321	11.49	50	25	2
Phillip Epps, 1982-88	192	2,884	15.02	63	14	2
Mark Chmura, 1993-99	188	2,253	11.98	33	17	2
Jim Taylor, 1958-66	187	1,505	8.05	41	10	0
Perry Kemp, 1988-91	182	2,341	12.86	39	6	1
Rich McGeorge, 1970-78	175	2,370	13.54	51	13	0
Ron Kramer, 1957, 59-64	170	2,594	15.23	55	15	0
Eddie Lee Ivery, 1979-86	162	1,612	9.95	62	7	1
Donald Driver, 1999-03	159	2,205	13.87	t85	14	4
Bubba Franks, 2000-03	154	1,368	8.89	31	21	0
John Jefferson, 1981-84	149	2,253	15.12	50	11	5
Keith Woodside, 1988-91	144	1,248	8.67	t49	2	0
John Brockington, 1971-77	138	1,075	7.79	t48	3	0
Gray Knafelc, 1954-62	134	1,930	14.40	53	21	0
Jackie Harris, 1990-93	133	1,620	12.18	t66	9	1
Paul Hornung, 1957-62, 64-66	130	1,480	11.38	t83	12	1
Howie Ferguson, 1953-58	127	1,079	8.50	49	1	1
Donny Anderson, 1966-71	125	1,725	13.80	51	6	1
Barty Smith, 1974-80	120	979	8.16	42	3	0
Bob Mann, 1950-54	109	1,629	14.94	52	17	2
Marv Fleming, 1963-69	109	1,300	11.93	t53	12	0
Ken Payne, 1974-77	103	1,395	13.54	57	5	3
Walter Stanley, 1985-88	101	1,831	18.13	t70	5	5
Nolan Luhn, 1945-49	100	1,525	15.25	44	13	2
Jessie Clark, 1983-87	99	925	9.34	t75	6	0
Elijah Pitts, 1961-69, 71	97	1,182	12.19	84	6	1
Vince Workman, 1989-92	97	691	7.12	25	5	0
Aundra Thompson, 1977-81	95	1,573	16.56	57	7	1
Clyde Goodnight, 1945-49	89	1,632	18.34	t75	13	2
MacArthur Lane, 1972-74	87	855	9.83	t68	4	0
Steve Odom, 1974-79	84	1,613	19.20	t95	11	1
Milt Gantenbein, 1931-40	79	1,228	15.54	t77	7	0
Joe Laws, 1934-45	79	1,041	13.18		10	0
Terdell Middleton, 1977-81	78	659	8.45	50	3	0
Al Carmichael, 1953-58	75	994	13.25	63	3	0
Fred Cone, 1951-57	75	852	11.36	t69	4	0
Floyd (Breezy) Reid, 1950-56	72	868	12.06	t81	5	0
Corey Bradford, 1998-01	71	1,190	16.76	t74	7	3
Tyrone Davis, 1997-02	71	780	10.99	t60	13	0
Herman Fontenot, 1989-90	71	665	9.37	59	4	0
Tom Moore, 1960-65	71	645	9.08	t45	7	0
Willard Harrell, 1975-77	70	656	9.37	t69	4	0
Tony Canadeo, 1941-44, 46-52	69	579	8.39	46	5	0
Jon Staggers, 1972-74	65	985	15.15	63	4	0
Jim Grabowski, 1966-70	65	575	8.85	t67	3	0
Javon Walker, 2002-03	64	1,035	16.17	t66	10	1
Jeff Query, 1989-91	64	902	14.09	t47	4	0
Joe Johnson, 1954-58	64	652	10.19	61	4	0
Robert Ferguson, 2001-03	60	813	13.55	47	7	1
Anthony Morgan, 1993-96	60	749	12.48	t47	8	1
Carleton Elliott, 1951-54	60	581	9.68	33	6	0
Lou Brock, 1940-45	59	761	12.90	t52	6	0
Eric Torkelson, 1974-79, 81	59	469	7.95	31	0	0
Andy Uram, 1938-43	58	1,083	18.67	t64	10	1
Paul Ott Carruth, 1986-88	58	423	7.29	31	3	0
Johnny Blood, 1929-33, 35-36	56	934	16.68	t70	11	1
Terry Glenn, 2002	56	817	14.59	49	2	1
Ted Cook, 1948-50	54	780	14.44	50	4	0
Derrick Mayes, 1996-98	54	730	13.52	74	5	1
Keith Jackson, 1995-96	53	647	12.21	t51	11	0
Harlan Huckleby, 1980-85	53	411	7.75	39	3	0
Harry Jacunski, 1939-44	52	985	18.94	t86	6	2
Clarke Hinkle, 1932-41	50	537	10.74	t69	3	0
Travis Williams, 1967-70	49	530	10.82	t60	5	0
Harry Sydney, 1992	49	384	7.84	20	1	0
Don McIlhenny, 1957-59	46	459	9.98	t55	4	0
Kenneth Davis, 1986-88	46	333	7.24	35	1	0
Clarence Weathers, 1990-91	45	540	12.00	29	1	0
Carl Mulleneaux, 1938-41, 45-46	44	850	19.32	56	11	1
Brent Fullwood, 1987-90	44	370	8.41	67	1	0
Ollie Smith, 1976-77	42	721	17.17	47	1	1
Don Beebe, 1996-97	41	727	17.73	t80	4	2
Barry Smith, 1973-75	41	604	14.73	t27	4	0
Darrell Thompson, 1990-94	41	330	8.05	43	1	0
Ray Pelfrey, 1951-52	39	472	12.10	49	5	0
Mark Ingram, 1995	39	469	12.03	29	3	0
Tony Fisher, 2002-03	39	276	7.08	32	2	0
Jeff Thomason, 1995-99	38	421	11.08	27	3	0
Frankie Neal, 1987	36	420	11.67	38	3	0
Reggie Cobb, 1994	35	299	8.54	t37	1	0
David Martin, 2001-03	34	256	7.53	31	4	0
Aubrey Matthews, 1988-89	33	367	11.12	25	2	0
Billy Grimes, 1950-52	32	431	13.47	t96	2	0
Mark Clayton, 1993	32	331	10.34	32	3	0
Veryl Switzer, 1954-55	31	269	8.68	28	3	0
Al Baldwin, 1950	28	555	19.82	t85	3	1
Patrick Scott, 1987-88	28	354	12.64	41	1	0
Michael Haddix, 1989-90	28	205	7.32	28	1	0
John Spilis, 1969-71	27	446	16.52	39	1	0
Bob Monnett, 1933-38	27	303	11.22		0	0
Charles Wilson, 1990-91	26	389	14.96	t75	1	0
Leland Glass, 1972-73	26	380	14.62	31	1	0
Terry Mickens, 1994-97	26	244	9.38	24	3	0
Bob Long, 1964-67	25	487	19.48	t62	4	1
John Hilton, 1970	25	350	14.00	t65	1	0
Dave Hampton, 1969-71	25	276	11.04	50	3	0
Ted Fritsch, 1942-50	25	227	9.08	35	1	0
Roger Grove, 1931-35	24	340	14.17		3	0
Bob Forte, 1946-50, 52-53	24	242	10.08	28	3	0
Hank Bruder, 1931-39	23	344	14.96		2	0
Steve Pritko, 1949-50	23	219	9.52	24	4	0
LaVern (Lavvie) Dilweg, 1927-34	22	360	16.36		2	0
Ralph Earhart, 1948-49	22	303	13.77	t64	2	0
Ron Lewis, 1992-94	22	281	12.77	38	0	0
Al Rose, 1932-36	21	297	14.14		3	0
Gary Lewis, 1981-84	21	285	13.57	49	1	0
Ray Riddick, 1940-42, 46	20	285	14.25		1	0
Wesley Walls, 2003	20	222	11.10	36	1	0
Darick Holmes, 1998	19	179	9.42	24	0	0
Mike Meade, 1982-83	19	105	5.53	t31	2	0
Paul Miller, 1936-38	18	215	11.94	34	3	0
Larry Coutre, 1950, 53	18	202	11.22	t77	2	0
Jim Keane, 1952	18	191	10.61	t29	1	0
Steve Atkins, 1979-81	18	138	7.67	19	1	0
Bill Kelley, 1949	17	222	13.06	32	1	0
Lew Carpenter, 1959-63	17	213	12.53	23	0	0
Dan Ross, 1986	17	143	8.41	16	1	0
Sanjay Beach, 1992	17	122	7.18	20	1	0
Nate Simpson, 1977-79	17	69	4.06	14	0	0
Earl (Jug) Girard, 1948-51	16	324	20.25	t75	2	1
Lee Morris, 1987	16	259	16.19	t46	1	1
Jack Clancy, 1970	16	244	15.25	t33	2	0
Joel Mason, 1942-45	16	202	12.63	21	2	0
Steve Meilinger, 1958, 60	15	182	12.13	23	1	0
Cecil Isbell, 1938-42	15	174	11.60	49	0	0
Wayland Becker, 1936-38	14	245	17.50	49	1	0
Dom Moselle, 1951-52	14	233	16.64	85	2	0
Ron Cassidy, 1979-81, 83-84	14	233	16.64	43	0	0
Clive Rush, 1953	14	190	13.57	24	0	1
Larry Craig, 1939-49	14	155	11.07	28	0	0
Gary Ellerson, 1985-86	14	145	10.36	32	0	0
Ben Wilson, 1967	14	88	6.29	21	0	0
Preston Dennard, 1985	13	182	14.00	34	2	0
LeShon Johnson, 1994-95	13	168	12.92	33	0	0
Charles Lee, 2000-01	13	166	12.77	38	1	0
Andre Rison, 1996	13	135	10.38	t22	1	0
Desmond Howard, 1996, 99	13	95	7.31	12	0	0
Herman Rohrig, 1941, 46-47	13	94	7.23	21	0	0
De'Mond Parker, 1999-00	13	65	5.00	10	0	0
Jim Gillette, 1947	12	224	18.67	50	1	0
Keith Paskett, 1987	12	188	15.67	t47	1	0
Oscar E. Smith, 1948-49	12	121	10.08	49	0	0
Perry Williams, 1969-73	12	118	9.83	24	0	0
Clint Didier, 1988-89	12	108	9.00	t24	2	0
Carl Bland, 1989-90	11	164	14.91	t46	1	0
Arnie Herber, 1930-40	11	155	14.09	25	2	0
Bobby Jack Floyd, 1952	11	129	11.73	44	0	0
Charles Goldenberg, 1933-45	11	111	10.09	21	1	0
Najeh Davenport, 2002-03	11	71	6.45	13	0	0
Bernie Scherer, 1936-38	10	193	19.30	t78	3	0
Dave Davis, 1971-72	10	178	17.80	t68	1	0
Walter Tullis, 1978-79	10	173	17.30	t52	1	0

Name	Att.	Yds.	Avg.	LG	TD	100
Bob Nussbaumer, 1946, 51	10	143	14.30	35	0	0
Bill Anderson, 1965-66	10	119	11.90	t27	1	0
Dick Evans, 1940, 43	10	111	11.10	30	0	0
Randy Vataha, 1977	10	109	10.90	20	0	0
Raymont Harris, 1998	10	68	6.80	12	0	0
Paul Duhart, 1944	9	176	19.56	32	2	0
Charles Wilson, 1994-95, 99	9	171	19.00	43	2	0
George Sauer, 1935-37	9	142	15.78		0	0
Ray Crouse, 1984	9	93	10.33	25	1	0
Jim Culbreath, 1977-79	9	84	9.33	19	0	0
Rondell Mealey, 2001-02	9	76	8.44	19	0	0
Travis Jervey, 1995-98	9	33	3.67	11	0	0
Claudis James, 1967-69	8	148	18.50	24	2	0
Lester Peterson, 1932, 34	8	139	17.38		0	0
Byron Bailey, 1953	8	119	14.88	50	0	1
Larry Mason, 1988	8	84	10.50	39	1	0
Del Rodgers, 1982, 84	8	79	9.88	22	0	0
Chester Johnston, 1931, 34-37	8	70	8.75		1	0
Jim Jensen, 1981-82	8	67	8.38	16	1	0
Herm Schneidman, 1935-39	7	119	17.00	t46	2	0
John Losch, 1956	7	85	12.14	43	0	0
Don Summers, 1987	7	83	11.86	17	1	0
Reggie Johnson, 1994, 97	7	79	11.29	24	0	0
Erik Affholter, 1991	7	68	9.71	20	0	0
Les Goodman, 1973-74	7	38	5.43	12	0	0
Fred Nixon, 1980-81	6	105	17.50	32	0	0
Ray Wehba, 1944	6	67	11.17	17	0	0
Buford McGee, 1990	6	60	10.00	15	0	0
J.R. Boone, 1953	6	55	9.17	18	1	0
Basil Mitchell, 1999-00	6	48	8.00	20	0	0
Ricky Patton, 1979	6	41	6.83	9	0	0
Kevin Willhite, 1987	6	37	6.17	12	0	0
Jack Cloud, 1950-51	6	35	5.83	13	1	0
Chuck Sample, 1942, 45	6	35	5.83	t10	0	0
Terry Wells, 1975	6	11	1.83	4	0	0
Bert Askson, 1975-77	5	78	15.60	34	1	0
Leon Manley, 1950-51	5	66	13.20	18	0	0
Walt Landers, 1978-79	5	60	12.00	t55	1	0
Gene Wilson, 1947-48	5	57	11.40	15	0	0
Dan Orlich, 1949-51	5	48	9.60	12	0	0
Hal Van Every, 1940-41	5	44	8.80	23	0	0
John Stephens, 1993	5	31	6.20	10	0	0
Jeff Wilner, 1994-95	5	31	6.20	9	0	0
Bill Reichardt, 1952	5	18	3.60	12	0	0
Alex Urban, 1941, 44-45	4	91	22.75	55	1	0
Mike Moffitt, 1986	4	87	21.75	34	0	0
Gerald Tinker, 1975	4	84	21.00	t35	1	0
Bob Adkins, 1940-41, 45	4	73	18.25	t55	1	0
Len Garrett, 1971-72	4	66	16.50	21	0	0
Wuert Engelmann, 1930-33	4	54	13.50		1	0
Bruce Smith, 1945-48	4	50	12.50	t36	1	0
Bill Larson, 1980	4	37	9.25	21	1	0
Henry Childs, 1984	4	32	8.00	17	0	0
Chuck Mercein, 1967-69	4	12	3.00	9	0	0
Fred Provo, 1948	4	(9)	-2.25	4	0	0
Irv Comp, 1943-49	3	66	22.00	50	2	0
Ed Jankowski, 1937-41	3	65	21.67	46	1	0
Allen Brown, 1966-67	3	43	14.33	17	0	0
Tony Falkenstein, 1943	3	39	13.00	18	0	0
Bob Tenner, 1935	3	38	12.67	29	0	0
Lamont Hall, 1999	3	33	11.00	13	0	0
Al Norgard, 1934	3	29	9.67	22	0	0
Abner Wimberly, 1950-52	3	28	9.33	10	0	0
Karsten Bailey, 2002	3	26	8.67	10	0	0
Freddie Parker, 1987	3	22	7.33	13	0	0
Ryan Wetnight, 2000	3	20	6.67	9	0	0
Dave Kopay, 1972	3	19	6.33	8	0	0
Jim Shanley, 1958	3	13	4.33	7	0	0
Don Perkins, 1943-45	3	12	4.00	10	0	0
Walt Schlinkman, 1946-50	3	(1)	-0.33	5	0	0
Don Wells, 1946-49	2	74	37.00	65	0	0
Kitrick Taylor, 1992	2	63	31.50	t35	1	0
Lavale Thomas, 1987	2	52	26.00	t30	1	0
Don Barton, 1953	2	51	25.50	t42	1	0
Ed Frutig, 1941, 45	2	40	20.00	34	0	0
Ken Keuper, 1945-47	2	37	18.50	26	0	0
Scott Bolton, 1988	2	33	16.50	18	0	0
Derrick Harden, 1987	2	29	14.50	15	0	0
Bob Jeter, 1963-70	2	25	12.50	23	0	0
John Thompson, 1979-82	2	24	12.00	t23	2	0
Roell Preston, 1997-98	2	23	11.50	13	0	0
Ben Smith, 1933	2	23	11.50	13	0	0
Larry Krause, 1970-71, 73-74	2	22	11.00	11	0	0
Bob Kahler, 1942-44	2	21	10.50	12	0	0
Cliff Taylor, 1976	2	21	10.50	18	0	0
Joe Carter, 1942	2	19	9.50	t10	1	0
Frank Balazs, 1939-41	2	18	9.00	11	0	0
Mike Donohoe, 1973-74	2	18	9.00	10	0	0
Marcus Wilson, 1992-95	2	18	9.00	11	0	0
Patrick Collins, 1988	2	17	8.50	9	0	0
Frank Purnell, 1957	2	16	8.00	15	0	0
Michael Blair, 1998	2	13	6.50	10	0	0
John Spagnola, 1989	2	13	6.50	14	0	0
Russell Copeland, 1998	2	11	5.50	12	0	0
Corey Harris, 1992-94	2	11	5.50	6	0	0
Aaron Hayden, 1997	2	11	5.50	7	0	0
Allen Rice, 1991	2	10	5.00	7	0	0
Mark Lewis, 1985-87	2	7	3.50	t4	2	0
Jay Graham, 2002	2	6	3.00	4	0	0
Blake Moore, 1984-85	2	6	3.00	t3	2	0
Vickey Ray Anderson, 1980	2	2	1.00	2	0	0
Tobin Rote, 1950-56	1	39	—	t28	1	0
Dick Weisgerber, 1938-40, 42	1	37	37.00	37	0	0
Bob Summerhays, 1949-51	1	34	34.00	34	0	0
Ray Nitschke, 1958-72	1	34	34.00	34	0	0
Al Cannava, 1950	1	28	28.00	28	0	0
Keith Ranspot, 1942	1	25	25.00	t25	1	0
Paul Staroba, 1973	1	23	23.00	23	0	0
Jim Gueno, 1976-80	1	23	23.00	23	0	0
Jim Lawrence, 1939	1	21	21.00	21	0	0
Earl Gros, 1962-63	1	19	19.00	19	0	0
Pete Lammons, 1972	1	19	19.00	19	0	0
Cal Clemmens, 1936	1	18	18.00	18	0	0
Charlie Hall, 1971-76	1	18	18.00	18	0	0
Cornelius Redick, 1987	1	18	18.00	18	0	0
Connie Mack Berry, 1940	1	17	17.00	17	0	0
Lee Weigel, 1987	1	17	17.00	17	0	0
Lindell Pearson, 1952	1	16	16.00	16	0	0
Harper Davis, 1951	1	15	15.00	15	0	0
Keith Crawford, 1995, 99	1	14	14.00	14	0	0
Bill Roberts, 1956	1	14	14.00	14	0	0
Don Zimmerman, 1976	1	13	13.00	13	0	0
Nick Luchey, 2003	1	12	12.00	12	0	0
Dick Moje, 1951	1	11	11.00	11	0	0
George Svendsen, 1935-37, 40-41	1	11	11.00	11	0	0
A.D. Williams, 1959	1	11	11.00	11	0	0
Bill Boedecker, 1950	1	10	10.00	10	0	0
Russ Mosley, 1945-46	1	10	10.00	10	0	0
Ace Loomis, 1951-52	1	9	9.00	9	0	0
Syd Kitson, 1980-81, 83-84	1	9	9.00	9	0	0
Mel Jackson, 1976-80	1	8	8.00	8	0	0
Ace Prescott, 1946	1	8	8.00	8	0	0
Lenny Taylor, 1984	1	8	8.00	8	0	0
Nolan Franz, 1986	1	7	7.00	7	0	0
Mike Wahle, 1998-2002	1	7	7.00	7	0	0
Herb Banet, 1937	1	6	6.00	6	0	0
James Hargrove, 1987	1	6	6.00	6	0	0
Val Jansante, 1951	1	6	6.00	6	0	0
Ben Starret, 1942-45	1	6	6.00	6	0	0
Bob Cifers, 1949	1	5	5.00	5	0	0
Albin (Rip) Collins, 1951	1	5	5.00	5	0	0
Bobby Collins, 2001	1	3	3.00	3	0	0
Ed Cody, 1947-48	1	2	2.00	2	0	0
Joey Hackett, 1987-88	1	2	2.00	t2	1	0
Karl Swanke, 1980-86	1	2	2.00	t2	1	0
Clarence Thompson, 1939	1	1	1.00	1	0	0
Herbert Goodman, 2000-01	1	0	0.00	0	0	0
Bill Butler, 1959	1	-2	-2.00	-2	0	0
Brett Favre, 1992-02	1	-7	-7.00	-7	0	0
Unaccounted for	1	30	—	—	0	-
Packers, 1933-2003*	**14,293**	**185,276**	**12.96**		**1,283**	**262**
Opponents, 1933-2003	14,022	173,857	12.40		1,046	—

*The 1933-2003 totals for the Packers include 14 receptions for 168 yards and three touchdowns by Johnny (Blood) McNally in 1932. For a more accurate comparison between the Packers and Opponents for the 71-year period, subtract Blood's 1932 statistics. This will allow for an exact 1933-2003 comparison.

RECEIVING TOUCHDOWNS

Below is a list of receiving touchdowns scored by Packers prior to 1933. Since Blood's three touchdowns are accounted for above, they do not appear below.

Name	TD	Name	TD
Johnny (Blood) McNally, 1929-31	17	Rex Enright, 1926-27	2
Verne Lewellen, 1924-32	12	Larry Marks, 1928	2
LaVern (Lavvie) Dilweg, 1927-32	10	Tom Nash, 1929-32	2
Walter (Tillie) Voss, 1924	5	Paul Fitzgibbons, 1930-32	2
Eddie Kotal, 1925-29	5	Art Schmaehl, 1921	1
Charley Mathys, 1922-26	4	Tommy Cronin, 1922	1
Marty Norton, 1925	4	Lyle (Cowboy) Wheeler, 1921-23	1
Dick O'Donnell, 1924-30	4	Lester Hearden, 1924	1
Hurdis McCrary, 1929-32	4	Jim Crowley, 1925	1
Wuert Engelmann, 1930-32	4	Joseph (Red) Dunn, 1927-31	1
Roger Grove, 1931-32	4	Roy Baker, 1928-29	1
Hank Bruder, 1931-32	4	Arnie Herber, 1930-31	1
Curly Lambeau, 1921-29	3	Robert (Cal) Hubbard, 1929-32	1
Stan Mills, 1922-23	2	Milt Gantenbein, 1931	1
Myrt Basing, 1923-27	2	**Packers, 1921-32**	**104**
Dick Flaherty, 1926-27	2	Opponents, 1921-32	50

ALL-TIME PASSERS

(Statistic kept since 1933; rankings based on total yards)

Name	Att.	Com.	Yds.	Pct.	TD	Int.	Rate
Brett Favre, 1992-2003	6,459	3,960	45,646	61.31	346	207	87.1
Bart Starr, 1956-71	3,149	1,808	24,718	57.42	152	138	80.5
Lynn Dickey, 1976-77, 79-85	2,831	1,592	21,369	56.23	133	151	73.8
Tobin Rote, 1950-56	1,854	826	11,535	44.55	89	119	54.4
Don Majkowski, 1987-92	1,607	889	10,870	55.32	56	56	73.4
Randy Wright, 1984-88	1,119	602	7,106	53.80	31	57	61.4
Arnie Herber, 1930-40	1,006	410	6,749	40.76	64	90	47.9
David Whitehurst, 1977-83	980	504	6,205	51.43	28	51	59.2
Cecil Isbell, 1938-42	818	411	5,945	50.24	61	52	72.6
Babe Parilli, 1952-53, 57-58	602	258	3,983	42.86	31	61	42.9
Irv Comp, 1943-49	519	213	3,354	41.04	28	52	41.6
John Hadl, 1974-75	537	280	3,167	52.14	9	29	53.2
Zeke Bratkowski, 1963-68, 71	416	220	3,147	52.88	21	29	65.5
Scott Hunter, 1971-73	446	196	2,904	43.95	15	30	49.0
Jack Jacobs, 1947-49	442	193	2,518	43.67	21	41	39.4
Don Horn, 1967-70	284	139	2,291	48.94	16	22	63.0
Bob Monnett, 1933-38	336	158	2,227	47.02	29	26	65.4
Tony Canadeo, 41-44, 46-52	268	105	1,642	39.18	16	20	49.1
Jerry Tagge, 1972-74	281	136	1,583	48.40	3	17	44.2
Mike Tomczak, 1991	238	128	1,490	53.78	11	9	72.6
Lamar McHan, 1959-60	199	81	1,322	40.70	11	14	52.8
Bobby Thomason, 1951	221	125	1,306	56.56	11	9	73.5
Anthony Dilweg, 1989-90	193	102	1,274	52.85	8	7	72.3
Earl (Jug) Girard, 1948-51	189	66	998	34.92	5	13	33.3
Blair Kiel, 1990-91	135	80	865	59.26	5	4	78.2
Jim Zorn, 1985	123	56	794	45.53	4	6	57.4
John Roach, 1961-63	100	41	653	41.00	4	8	43.5
Roy McKay, 1944-47	103	38	592	36.89	6	11	36.6
Alan Risher, 1987	74	44	564	59.46	3	3	80.0
Paul Christman, 1950	126	51	545	40.48	7	7	49.2
Lou Brock, 1940-45	67	19	519	28.36	7	5	63.1
Carlos Brown, 1975-76	78	29	396	37.18	3	6	35.0
Hal Van Every, 1940-41	71	23	394	32.39	4	8	31.4
Rich Campbell, 1981-84	68	31	386	45.59	3	9	38.8
Paul Hornung, 1957-62, 64-66	55	24	383	43.64	5	4	67.5
Jack Concannon, 1974	54	28	381	51.85	1	3	57.8
Stan Heath, 1949	106	26	355	24.53	1	14	4.6
Jim Del Gaizo, 1973	62	27	318	43.55	2	6	30.9
Clarke Hinkle, 1932-41	53	25	293	47.17	0	5	25.1
Vince Ferragamo, 1986	40	23	283	57.50	1	3	56.6
Joe Francis, 1958-59	49	20	266	40.82	2	3	46.8
Doug Pederson, 1996-98, 01-03	54	35	278	64.81	3	0	96.1
Tom Moore, 1960-65	16	10	261	62.50	4	1	119.8
Randy Johnson, 1976	35	21	249	60.00	0	1	69.8
George Sauer, 1935-37	25	11	203	44.00	1	6	46.3
Cliff Aberson, 1946	41	14	184	34.15	0	5	9.7
Johnny Blood, 1929-33, 35-36	41	14	184	34.15	1	3	26.9
Don Milan, 1975	32	15	181	46.88	1	1	62.1
Chuck Fusina, 1986	32	19	178	59.38	0	1	61.7
Joe Laws, 1934-45	36	10	163	27.78	3	6	34.1
Matt Hasselbeck, 1999-00	29	13	145	44.83	2	0	83.3
Bob Garrett, 1954	30	15	143	50.00	0	1	49.7
Willard Harrell, 1975-77	10	5	134	50.00	4	1	95.8
David Beverly, 1975-80	6	4	129	66.67	0	0	109.7
Elijah Pitts, 1961-69, 71	9	4	113	44.44	1	0	128.2
Ty Detmer, 1992-95	21	11	107	52.38	1	1	63.0
Frank Patrick, 1970-72	23	8	107	34.78	0	2	14.2
Ron Widby, 1972	2	2	102	100.00	1	0	158.3
Herman Rohrig, 1941, 46-47	9	3	100	33.33	1	1	73.6
Mark Brunell, 1993-94	27	12	95	44.44	0	0	53.8
Bobby Douglass, 1978	12	5	90	41.67	1	1	61.1
Dennis Sproul, 1978	13	5	87	38.46	0	0	62.0
Roger Grove, 1931-35	13	6	78	46.15	0	0	65.5
Gerry Ellis, 1980-86	12	4	71	33.33	1	1	47.6
Bob Forte, 1946-50, 52-53	14	8	64	57.14	1	1	62.8
Jerry Norton, 1963-64	5	3	64	60.00	1	0	143.8
John Losch, 1956	1	1	63	100.00	0	0	158.3
Andy Uram, 1938-43	7	2	60	28.57	1	1	62.8
Hank Bruder, 1931-39	20	6	53	30.00	0	2	0.0
Eddie Lee Ivery, 1979-86	4	2	50	50.00	0	0	95.8
Bill Troup, 1980	12	4	48	33.33	0	3	6.9
Ray Peterson, 1937	6	3	47	50.00	0	0	76.4
Jim McMahon, 1995-96	5	4	45	80.00	0	0	104.2

Name	Att.	Com.	Yds.	Pct.	TD	Int.	Rate
James Lofton, 1978-86	5	1	43	20.00	0	0	62.9
Paul Duhart, 1944	13	4	42	30.77	0	0	41.2
MacArthur Lane, 1972-74	5	3	42	60.00	1	0	126.7
Donny Anderson, 1966-71	10	4	40	40.00	2	0	91.7
T.J. Rubley, 1995	6	4	39	66.67	0	1	45.1
Don Hutson, 1935-45	11	1	38	9.09	1	2	32.2
Harry Mattos, 1936	12	4	32	33.33	0	2	2.8
Bubba Franks, 2000-03	1	1	31	100.00	1	0	158.3
Tom O'Malley, 1950	11	3	31	26.67	0	6	0.0
Steve Bono, 1997	15	5	29	50.00	0	0	56.3
Willie Gillus, 1987	5	2	28	40.00	0	0	58.8
Paul Held, 1955	4	2	27	50.00	0	0	71.9
Perry Moss, 1948	17	4	20	23.53	0	0	39.6
Fred Provo, 1948	1	1	20	100.00	1	0	158.3
Steve Pisarkiewicz, 1980	5	2	19	40.00	0	0	51.3
Jim Lawrence, 1939	4	1	15	25.00	0	1	3.1
Dennis Claridge, 1965	1	1	13	100.00	0	0	118.8
Bill Stevens, 1968-69	5	1	12	20.00	0	0	39.6
Bob Nussbaumer, 1946, 51	1	1	10	100.00	0	0	108.3
Paul Ott Carruth, 1986-88	3	1	3	33.33	1	0	81.9
Herb Banet, 1937	7	1	2	14.29	0	2	0.0
Sterling Sharpe, 1988-94	1	1	1	100.00	0	0	79.2
Charles Brackens, 1955	2	0	0	0.00	0	0	39.6
Howie Ferguson, 1953-58	2	0	0	0.00	0	0	39.6
Max McGee, 1954, 57-67	2	0	0	0.00	0	1	0.0
Ernie Smith, 1935-37, 39	2	0	0	0.00	0	1	0.0
Frank Balazs, 1939-41	1	0	0	0.00	0	1	0.0
Dick Bilda, 1944	1	0	0	0.00	0	0	39.6
John Brockington, 1971-77	1	0	0	0.00	0	0	39.6
Cal Clemmens, 1936	1	0	0	0.00	0	0	39.6
Brian Dowling, 1977	1	0	0	0.00	0	0	39.6
Ted Fritsch, 1942-50	1	0	0	0.00	0	0	39.6
Ahman Green, 2000-03	1	0	0	0.00	0	0	39.6
Craig Hentrich, 1994-97	1	0	0	0.00	0	0	39.6
Ron Kramer, 1957, 59-64	1	0	0	0.00	0	1	0.0
Paul McJulien, 1991-92	1	0	0	0.00	0	0	39.6
Paul Miller, 1936-38	1	0	0	0.00	0	1	0.0
Russ Mosley, 1945-46	1	0	0	0.00	0	0	39.6
Frankie Neal, 1987	1	0	0	0.00	0	0	39.6
Floyd (Breezy) Reid, 1950-56	1	0	0	0.00	0	0	39.6
Bucky Scribner, 1983-84	1	0	0	0.00	0	0	39.6
Bruce Smith, 1945-48	1	0	0	0.00	0	0	39.6
Jon Staggers, 1972-74	1	0	0	0.00	0	0	39.6
J.R. Boone, 1953	1	1	-2	100.00	0	0	79.2
Packers, 1933-2003*	**27,128**	**14,316**	**185,747**	**52.77**	**1289**	**1463**	**68.0**
Opponents, 1933-2003	26,893	14,022	173,857	52.14	1052	1584	61.0

*The 1933-2003 totals for the Packers include 101 attempts, 37 completions, 639 yards, nine touchdowns and nine interceptions by Arnie Herber in 1932. For a more accurate comparison between the Packers and Opponents for the 71-year period, subtract Herber's 1932 statistics. This will allow for an exact 1933-2003 comparison.

TOUCHDOWN PASSES

Below is a list of touchdown passes thrown by Packers prior to 1933. Since Herber's 1932 statistics are accounted for above, they do not appear below.

Name	TD	Name	TD
Joseph (Red) Dunn, 1927-31	31	Jack McAuliffe, 1926	1
Curly Lambeau, 1921-29	24	Everett (Pid) Purdy, 1926-27	1
Charlie Mathys, 1922-26	11	Hurdis McCrary, 1929-33	1
Verne Lewellen, 1924-32	8	Johnny (Blood) McNally, 1929-32	1
Bo Molenda, 1929-32	5	Faye (Mule) Wilson, 1931	1
Paul Fitzgibbons, 1930-32	4	Russ Saunders, 1931	1
Arnie Herber, 1930-31	3	Hank Bruder, 1931-32	1
Eddie Kotal, 1925-29	2	**Packers, 1921-32**	**98**
Roger Grove, 1931-32	2	Opponents, 1921-32	50
Howard (Cub) Buck, 1921-25	1		

A Measure of Greatness

All-Time Lists

ALL-TIME PUNTERS

(Statistic kept since 1939; rankings based on number of punts)

Name	No	Yds	GAvg	NAvg	TB	In20	LG	HB
David Beverly, 1975-80	495	18,785	37.95	33.06	37	96	65	2
Don Bracken, 1985-90	368	14,602	39.68	32.52	37	74	65	5
Donny Anderson, 1966-71	315	12,479	39.62	36.52	18	85	65	1
Josh Bidwell, 2000-03	308	12,659	41.10	35.50	28	85	68	0
Craig Hentrich, 1994-97	289	12,355	42.75	35.64	47	104	70	2
Max McGee, 1954, 57-67	256	10,647	41.59	35.30	31	52	63	2
Earl (Jug) Girard, 1948-51	200	7,830	39.15	—	—	—	72	5
Dick Deschaine, 1955-57	181	7,714	42.62	37.69	12	53	73	2
Bucky Scribner, 1983-84	154	6,465	41.98	34.41	19	29	70	1
Jack Jacobs, 1947-49	143	6,020	42.10	—	—	—	78	2
Don Chandler, 1965-67	135	5,659	41.92	35.84	18	24	90	0
Roy McKay, 1944-47	124	5,196	41.90	—	—	—	73	1
Ray Stachowicz, 1981-82	124	5,017	40.46	31.75	11	23	72	2
Paul McJulien, 1991-92	122	4,859	39.83	33.12	11	30	67	2
Ron Widby, 1972-73	121	5,128	42.38	36.23	11	15	64	2
Jerry Norton, 1963-64	107	4,644	43.40	35.95	9	25	61	0
Bryan Wagner, 1992-93	104	4,396	42.27	35.89	12	29	60	0
Boyd Dowler, 1959-69	93	3,987	42.87	34.25	15	11	75	2
Clarke Hinkle, 1932-41	87	3,550	40.80	—	—	—	65	0
Babe Parilli, 1952-53, 57-58	84	3,331	39.65	—	—	—	63	0
Lou Brock, 1940-45	84	3,137	37.35	—	—	—	72	3
Louie Aguiar, 1999	75	2,954	39.39	33.92	4	20	64	0
Randy Walker, 1974	69	2,648	38.38	31.48	6	14	58	0
Sean Landeta, 1998	65	2,788	42.89	37.09	7	30	72	0
Clive Rush, 1953	60	2,262	37.70	—	—	—	60	0
Joe Prokop, 1985	56	2,210	39.46	32.59	6	9	66	0
Tony Canadeo, 1941-44, 46-52	45	1,667	37.04	—	—	—	62	0
Arnie Herber, 1930-40	37	1,461	39.49	—	—	—	74	2
Bill Renner, 1986-87	35	1,334	38.11	30.89	2	6	50	3
Hal Van Every, 1940-41	30	1,125	37.50	—	—	—	65	0
Steve Broussard, 1975	29	922	31.79	26.24	2	8	51	3
Ted Fritsch, 1942-50	19	733	38.58	—	—	—	54	0
Irv Comp, 1943-49	12	453	37.75	—	—	—	46	0
Paul Staroba, 1973	12	373	31.08	27.67	2	1	49	0
Cecil Isbell, 1938-42	10	327	32.70	—	—	—	46	0
Ken Duncan, 1971	6	216	36.00	31.50	1	1	47	0
Dale Livingston, 1970	6	199	33.17	27.83	0	0	52	0
Ray Pelfrey, 1951-52	5	220	44.00	—	—	—	46	0
Herman Rohrig, 1941, 46-47	5	214	42.80	—	—	—	52	0
Chris Hanson, 1999	4	157	39.25	38.50	0	0	44	0
Ryan Longwell, 1997-03	4	107	26.75	16.75	2	2	30	0
Ben Starret, 1942-45	3	108	36.00	—	—	—	43	0
Bob Forte, 1946-50, 52-53	3	107	35.67	—	—	—	39	0
Tobin Rote, 1950-56	2	112	56.00	—	—	—	57	0
Albin (Rip) Collins, 1951	2	81	40.50	—	—	—	49	0
Don Perkins, 1943-45	2	44	22.00	—	—	—	31	0
Bob Cifers, 1949	1	49	49.00	—	—	—	49	0
Fred Cone, 1951-57	1	47	47.00	—	—	—	47	0
Frank Balazs, 1939-41	1	35	35.00	—	—	—	35	0
Chester Marcol, 1972-80	1	33	33.00	13.00	1	0	33	0
Ken Keuper, 1945-47	1	12	12.00	—	—	—	12	0
Team (blocked since 1976)	17							
Packers, 1939-2003	**4,512**	**181,458**	**40.22**				**90**	**42**
Opponents, 1939-2003	4,549	184,382	40.53				88	28

ALL-TIME KICKOFF RETURNERS

(Statistic kept since 1941; rankings based on number of returns)

Name	No.	Yds.	Avg.	LG	TD	100
Steve Odom, 1974-79	179	4,124	23.04	t95	2	10
Al Carmichael, 1953-58	153	3,907	25.54	t106	2	13
Herb Adderley, 1961-69	120	3,080	25.67	t103	2	5
Travis Williams, 1967-70	77	2,058	26.73	t104	5	8
Tony Canadeo, 1941-44, 46-52	75	1,736	23.15	48	0	2
Dave Hampton, 1969-71	74	2,084	28.16	t101	3	6
Allen Rossum, 2000-01	73	1,719	23.55	t92	1	6
Tom Moore, 1960-65	71	1,882	26.51	84	0	1
Harlan Huckleby, 1980-85	70	1,300	18.57	57	0	1
Corey Harris, 1992-94	68	1,585	23.31	65	0	4
Billy Grimes, 1950-52	67	1,604	23.94	47	0	2
Roell Preston, 1997-98	64	1,708	26.69	t101	2	5
Del Rodgers, 1982, 84	59	1,279	21.68	t97	1	4
Charles Wilson, 1990-91	58	1,320	22.76	t82	1	1
Brent Fullwood, 1987-90	56	1,174	20.96	46	0	0
Vince Workman, 1989-92	56	913	16.30	46	0	0
Mike C. McCoy, 1976-83	54	1,187	21.98	65	0	1
Robert Brooks, 1992-98	51	1,237	24.25	t96	2	3
Mark Lee, 1980-90	45	859	19.09	35	0	1
Ike Thomas, 1972-73	44	1,099	24.98	89	0	3
Walter Stanley, 1985-88	42	857	20.40	55	0	0
Desmond Howard, 1996, 99	41	824	20.10	40	0	3
Aundra Thompson, 1977-81	40	835	20.88	t100	1	3
Ted Fritsch, 1942-50	37	951	25.70	79	0	0
Veryl Switzer, 1954-55	37	945	25.54	88	0	1
Antonio Chatman, 2003	36	804	22.33	46	0	4
Ken Ellis, 1970-75	36	802	22.28	84	0	1
Gary Ellerson, 1985-86	36	675	18.75	57	0	2
Larry Krause, 1970-71, 73-74	35	864	24.69	t100	1	1
Javon Walker, 2002-03	35	769	21.97	55	0	2
Donny Anderson, 1966-71	34	759	22.32	61	0	1
Charles Jordan, 1994-95, 99	32	654	20.44	33	0	1
Antonio Freeman, 1995-01, 03	27	600	22.22	45	0	1
Elijah Pitts, 1961-69, 71	27	513	19.00	29	0	0
Dom Moselle, 1951-52	25	630	25.20	44	0	1
Bill Schroeder, 1994, 97-01	25	572	22.88	40	0	0
Phillip Epps, 1982-88	25	532	21.28	48	0	2
Don McIlhenny, 1957-59	24	558	23.25	53	0	1
Darrell Thompson, 1990-94	23	468	20.35	t76	1	0
Najeh Davenport, 2002-03	22	635	28.86	60	0	2
John Symank, 1957-62	22	562	25.55	39	0	1
Basil Mitchell, 1999-00	22	490	22.27	t88	1	1
Don Beebe, 1996-97	21	537	25.57	t90	1	0
Dorsey Levens, 1994-01	21	477	22.71	53	0	2
Bill Butler, 1959	21	472	22.48	35	0	1
Lou Brock, 1940-45	21	438	20.86	40	0	0
Keith Woodside, 1988-91	21	381	18.14	29	0	0
Johnnie Gray, 1975-83	21	317	15.10	26	0	0
Carl Bland, 1989-90	20	360	18.00	37	0	0
Tim Lewis, 1983-86	20	358	17.90	30	0	1
Joe Laws, 1934-45	19	362	19.05	29	0	0
Earl Gros, 1962-63	18	437	24.28	51	0	0
Fred Nixon, 1980-81	18	382	21.22	54	0	0
Lew Carpenter, 1959-63	18	348	19.33	29	0	1
William Henderson, 1995-03	18	236	13.11	23	0	0
Bill Forester, 1953-63	17	236	13.88	27	0	0
John Losch, 1956	15	390	26.00	51	0	0
Vai Sikahema, 1991	15	325	21.67	35	0	0
Robert Ferguson, 2001-03	15	293	19.53	31	0	0
De'Mond Parker, 1999-00	15	268	17.87	40	0	1
Howie Ferguson, 1953-58	15	257	17.13	34	0	0
Oscar E. Smith, 1948-49	14	323	23.07	36	0	0
John Kirby, 1949	14	315	22.50	34	0	0
Bob Forte, 1946-50, 52-53	14	290	20.71	36	0	0
Eric Torkelson, 1974-79, 81	14	268	19.14	29	0	0
Patrick Scott, 1987-88	14	239	17.07	27	0	0
Steve Wagner, 1976-79	14	181	12.93	27	0	0
Gerry Ellis, 1980-86	13	247	19.00	40	0	0
Ralph Earhart, 1948-49	13	238	18.31	30	0	0
Ed Cody, 1947-48	12	300	25.00	39	0	0
Irv Comp, 1943-49	12	255	21.25	31	0	0
Elbert Watts, 1986	12	239	19.92	40	0	0
Ken Davis, 1986-88	12	231	19.25	35	0	0
Ken Stills, 1985-88	12	227	18.92	38	0	0
Terdell Middleton, 1977-81	11	263	23.91	t85	1	0
Jon Staggers, 1972-74	11	260	23.64	39	0	0
Bob Hudson, 1972	11	247	22.45	55	0	0
Ace Loomis, 1951-53	11	226	20.55	34	0	0
Marcus Wilson, 1992-95	11	211	19.18	37	0	0
Paul Hornung, 1957-62, 64-66	10	248	24.80	39	0	0
Andy Uram, 1938-43	10	235	23.50	t98	1	0
Fred Provo, 1948	10	205	20.50	28	0	0
Kelly Cook, 1987	10	147	14.70	38	0	0
John Jurkovic, 1991-95	10	135	13.50	17	0	0
Charlie Leigh, 1974	9	201	22.33	30	0	0
Travis Jervey, 1995-98	9	182	20.22	28	0	0
Herman Rohrig, 1941, 46-47	9	181	20.11	27	0	0
Fred Cone, 1951-57	9	148	16.44	25	0	0

Name	No.	Yds.	Avg.	LG	TD	100
Jim Culbreath, 1977-79	9	140	15.56	30	0	0
Tommy Crutcher, 1964-67, 71-72	8	155	19.38	37	0	0
Jim Taylor, 1958-66	7	185	26.43	47	0	0
Tom Brown, 1964-68	7	167	23.86	34	0	0
Walt Schlinkman, 1946-50	7	155	22.14	34	0	0
Dave Robinson, 1963-72	7	80	11.43	20	0	0
Nolan Luhn, 1945-49	7	76	10.86	18	0	0
Bob Nussbaumer, 1946, 51	6	148	24.67	44	0	0
Norman Jefferson, 1987-88	6	146	24.33	46	0	0
Aaron Hayden, 1997	6	141	23.50	35	0	0
Joe Johnson, 1954-58	6	137	22.83	28	0	0
Bruce Smith, 1945-48	6	128	21.33	26	0	0
Willard Harrell, 1975-77	6	126	21.00	39	0	0
Jeff Query, 1989-91	6	125	20.83	28	0	0
Roy McKay, 1944-47	6	108	18.00	26	0	0
Lee Morris, 1987	6	104	17.33	28	0	0
Floyd (Breezy) Reid, 1950-56	6	103	17.17	23	0	0
Cecil Isbell, 1938-42	6	96	16.00	32	0	0
Perry Williams, 1969-73	6	94	15.67	24	0	0
Steve Luke, 1975-80	6	91	15.17	21	0	0
Larry Craig, 1939-49	6	70	11.67	17	0	0
Ray Nitschke, 1958-72	6	53	8.83	17	0	0
Herbert Goodman, 2000-01	5	150	30.00	54	0	1
Herman Fontenot, 1989-90	5	118	23.60	50	0	0
Edgar Bennett, 1992	5	104	20.80	33	0	0
Walt Michaels, 1951	5	86	17.20	26	0	0
Howard Sampson, 1978-79	5	84	16.80	23	0	0
Bobby Jack Floyd, 1952, 54	5	75	15.00	26	0	0
Barty Smith, 1974-80	5	53	10.60	18	0	0
Paul Ott Carruth, 1986-88	5	48	9.60	20	0	0
John Martinkovic, 1951-56	5	46	9.20	31	0	0
Don Hutson, 1935-45	5	45	9.00	12	0	0
Gib Dawson, 1953	4	102	25.50	33	0	0
Hal Van Every, 1940-41	4	99	24.75	31	0	0
Earl (Jug) Girard, 1948-51	4	90	22.50	25	0	0
Allan Clark, 1982	4	75	18.75	30	0	0
Derrick Harden, 1987	4	72	18.00	20	0	0
Max McGee, 1954, 57-67	4	69	17.25	32	0	0
J.J. Moses, 2002	4	69	17.25	27	0	0
Chris Darkins, 1997	4	68	17.00	20	0	0
Rondell Mealey, 2001-02	4	63	15.75	24	0	0
Phil Vandersea, 1966, 68-70	4	58	14.50	21	0	0
Darrien Gordon, 2002	4	53	13.25	19	0	0
Les Goodman, 1973-74	4	49	12.25	20	0	0
Frankie Neal, 1987	4	44	11.00	18	0	0
Bob Hyland, 1967-69, 76	4	31	7.75	11	0	0
Charlie Sample, 1942, 45	3	91	30.33	35	0	0
Clarence Self, 1952, 54-55	3	85	28.33	33	0	0
Paul Coffman, 1978-85	3	77	25.67	52	0	0
Estus Hood, 1978-84	3	74	24.67	33	0	0
Cliff Aberson, 1946	3	69	23.00	26	0	0
Jim Gillette, 1947	3	66	22.00	29	0	0
Cliff Taylor, 1976	3	59	19.67	23	0	0
Larry Hickman, 1960	3	54	18.00	27	0	0
Larry Coutre, 1950, 53	3	52	17.33	27	0	0
Anthony Morgan, 1993-96	3	46	15.33	20	0	0
Ray DiPierro, 1950-51	3	42	14.00	26	0	0
Keith McKenzie, 1996-99, 02	3	42	14.00	18	0	0
Clarke Hinkle, 1932-41	3	38	12.67	16	0	0
Allen Rice, 1991	3	36	12.00	15	0	0
Chet Winters, 1983	3	28	9.33	12	0	0
Clyde Goodnight, 1945-49	3	27	9.00	12	0	0
Aaron Brown, 1973-74	3	26	8.67	12	0	0
Don Davey, 1991-94	3	22	7.33	8	0	0
Mike P. McCoy, 1970-76	3	22	7.33	10	0	0
Willie Wood, 1960-71	3	20	6.67	20	0	0
Dave Osborn, 1976	3	19	6.33	10	0	0
Paul (Buddy) Burris, 1949-51	3	18	6.00	11	0	0
Deral Teteak, 1952-56	2	62	31.00	47	0	0
Joe Francis, 1958-59	2	52	26.00	28	0	0
Bill Robinson, 1952	2	49	24.50	26	0	0
Tony Falkenstein, 1943	2	47	23.50	24	0	0
Tony Carter, 2002	2	42	21.00	25	0	0
Tony Fisher, 2002-03	2	42	21.00	21	0	0
Eric Metcalf, 2002	2	41	20.50	21	0	0
Chuck Webb, 1991	2	40	20.00	23	0	0
Johnny Papit, 1953	2	38	19.00	21	0	0
Jeff Thomason, 1995-99	2	36	18.00	20	0	0
Byron Bailey, 1953	2	34	17.00	21	0	0
Don Perkins, 1943-45	2	34	17.00	18	0	0
Corey Bradford, 1998-01	2	33	16.50	24	0	0
MacArthur Lane, 1972-74	2	31	15.50	29	0	0
Mike Meade, 1982-83	2	31	15.50	17	0	0
Daryll Jones, 1984-85	2	30	15.00	19	0	0
Forrest Gregg, 1956, 58-70	2	21	10.50	16	0	0
Nick Luchey, 2003	2	21	10.50	12	0	0
Rich McGeorge, 1970-78	2	17	8.50	17	0	0
Ben Starret, 1942-45	2	16	8.00	13	0	0
Jim Temp, 1957-60	2	16	8.00	16	0	0
Dan Currie, 1958-64	2	14	7.00	7	0	0
Steve Okoniewski, 1974-75	2	11	5.50	11	0	0
Jim Gueno, 1976-80	2	9	4.50	9	0	0
Darren Sharper, 1997-03	2	7	3.50	4	0	0
Abner Wimberly, 1950-52	2	4	2.00	3	0	0
Jerry Kramer, 1958-68	2	0	0.00	0	0	0
Terry Mickens, 1994-97	2	0	0.00	0	0	0
Ed West, 1984-92	2	0	0.00	0	0	0
Albin (Rip) Collins, 1951	1	40	40.00	40	0	0
Harry Jacunski, 1939-44	1	33	33.00	33	0	0
Ray Pelfrey, 1951-52	1	26	26.00	26	0	0
Terry Wells, 1975	1	26	26.00	26	0	0
Bob Kroll, 1972-73	1	23	23.00	23	0	0
Gary Berry, 2000	1	22	22.00	22	0	0
Dave Davis, 1971-72	1	22	22.00	22	0	0
Pete Van Valkenburg, 1974	1	22	22.00	22	0	0
Bob Summerhays, 1949-51	1	21	21.00	21	0	0
Bill Boedecker, 1950	1	20	20.00	20	0	0
Bob Dees, 1952	1	20	20.00	20	0	0
Tom Flynn, 1984-86	1	20	20.00	20	0	0
Alex Urban, 1941, 44-45	1	20	20.00	20	0	0
Bill Reichardt, 1952	1	19	19.00	19	0	0
Paul Duhart, 1944	1	18	18.00	18	0	0
Don Highsmith, 1973	1	18	18.00	18	0	0
Eddie Lee Ivery, 1979-86	1	17	17.00	17	0	0
Ron Pitts, 1988-90	1	17	17.00	17	0	0
Sterling Sharpe, 1988-92	1	17	17.00	17	0	0
Ed Berry, 1986	1	16	16.00	16	0	0
Jim Jensen, 1981-82	1	15	15.00	15	0	0
Joel Mason, 1942-45	1	15	15.00	15	0	0
Dexter McNabb, 1992	1	15	15.00	15	0	0
Tim Moresco, 1977	1	15	15.00	15	0	0
John Anderson, 1978-89	1	14	14.00	14	0	0
Don Barton, 1953	1	14	14.00	14	0	0
Carleton Elliott, 1951-54	1	14	14.00	14	0	0
Ezra Johnson, 1977-87	1	14	14.00	14	0	0
Ray Riddick, 1940-42, 46	1	14	14.00	14	0	0
George Schmidt, 1952	1	14	14.00	14	0	0
Allen Brown, 1966-67	1	13	13.00	13	0	0
Gale Gillingham, 1966-74, 76	1	13	13.00	13	0	0
Derrel Gofourth, 1977-82	1	13	13.00	13	0	0
Raleigh McKenzie, 1999-00	1	13	13.00	13	0	0
Mike Morton, 2000	1	13	13.00	13	0	0
David Bowens, 2000	1	12	12.00	12	0	0
Ollie Smith, 1976-77	1	12	12.00	12	0	0
Joe Sims, 1992	1	11	11.00	11	0	0
Mike Arthur, 1995-96	1	10	10.00	10	0	0
Bill Bain, 1975	1	10	10.00	10	0	0
Larry Buhler, 1939-41	1	10	10.00	10	0	0
Al Cannava, 1950	1	10	10.00	10	0	0
Carlton Massey, 1957-58	1	10	10.00	10	0	0
Ernie Pannell, 1941-42, 45	1	10	10.00	10	0	0
Mike Wellman, 1979-80	1	10	10.00	10	0	0
Junior Coffey, 1965	1	9	9.00	9	0	0
Jim Flanigan, 2001	1	9	9.00	9	0	0
Joey Hackett, 1987	1	9	9.00	9	0	0
Doug Hart, 1964-71	1	8	8.00	8	0	0
Paul Berezney, 1942-44	1	7	7.00	7	0	0
Ted Cook, 1948-50	1	7	7.00	7	0	0
Guy Prather, 1981-85	1	7	7.00	7	0	0
Blaise Winter, 1988-90	1	7	7.00	7	0	0
Hank Gremminger, 1956-65	1	6	6.00	6	0	0
Ken Keuper, 1945-47	1	6	6.00	6	0	0
Dick Wildung, 1946-51, 53	1	6	6.00	6	0	0
Jim Carter, 1970-75, 77-78	1	5	5.00	5	0	0
Dick Himes, 1968-77	1	4	4.00	4	0	0
Cliff Lewis, 1981-84	1	4	4.00	4	0	0
John Jefferson, 1981-84	1	3	3.00	3	0	0
Dave Dreschler, 1983-84	1	1	1.00	1	0	0
Nate Hill, 1988	1	1	1.00	1	0	0
Brian Noble, 1985-92	1	1	1.00	1	0	0
Clayton Weishuhn, 1987	1	1	1.00	1	0	0
Chris Akins, 2000-01	1	0	0.00	0	0	0
Nate Borden, 1955-59	1	0	0.00	0	0	0
Byron Braggs, 1981-83	1	0	0.00	0	0	0
Bill Brown, 1953-56	1	0	0.00	0	0	0
Lee Roy Caffey, 1964-69	1	0	0.00	0	0	0
Bill Cherry, 1986-87	1	0	0.00	0	0	0
Mark Chmura, 1993-99	1	0	0.00	0	0	0
Walter Dean, 1991	1	0	0.00	0	0	0
Clint Didier, 1988-89	1	0	0.00	0	0	0
Marv Fleming, 1963-69	1	0	0.00	0	0	0
Len Garrett, 1971-72	1	0	0.00	0	0	0
Dan Grimm, 1963-65	1	0	0.00	0	0	0
Syd Kitson, 1980-81, 83-84	1	0	0.00	0	0	0
Walt Landers, 1978-79	1	0	0.00	0	0	0
James Lofton, 1978-86	1	0	0.00	0	0	0
Tony Mandarich, 1989-91	1	0	0.00	0	0	0
Steve Meilinger, 1958, 60	1	0	0.00	0	0	0
Frank Mestnick, 1963	1	0	0.00	0	0	0
Nate Simpson, 1977-79	1	0	0.00	0	0	0
John Sterling, 1987	1	0	0.00	0	0	0
Evan Vogds, 1948-49	1	0	0.00	0	0	0
Ryan Wetnight, 2000	1	0	0.00	0	0	0
Francis Winkler, 1968-69	1	0	0.00	0	0	0
Keith Wortman, 1972-75	1	0	0.00	0	0	0
Kevin Willhite, 1987	0	37	—	37	0	0
Packers, 1941-2003	**3,317**	**71,329**	**21.50**	**t106**	**28**	**111**
Opponents, 1941-2003	3,430	71,189	20.75	t101	13	—

A Measure of Greatness

(Statistic kept since 1941; rankings based on number of returns)

Name	No.	Yds.	Avg.	LG	TD	FC
Willie Wood, 1960-71	187	1,391	7.44	t72	2	102
Phillip Epps, 1982-88	100	819	8.19	t90	1	31
Al Carmichael, 1953-58	100	753	7.53	52	0	—
Walter Stanley, 1985-88	87	720	8.28	t83	1	17
Johnnie Gray, 1975-84	85	656	7.72	24	0	28
Jeff Query, 1989-91	76	712	9.37	28	0	17
Elijah Pitts, 1961-69, 71	75	394	5.25	t65	1	41
Desmond Howard, 1996, 99	70	968	13.83	t92	3	23
Robert Brooks, 1992-98	67	589	8.79	t85	1	18
Steve Odom, 1974-79	64	569	8.89	t95	1	14
Billy Grimes, 1950-52	63	834	13.24	t85	2	—
Ken Ellis, 1970-75	63	426	6.76	t80	1	11
Antonio Freeman, 1995-01, 03	54	406	7.52	29	0	10
Willard Harrell, 1975-77	52	382	7.35	t75	1	16
Jon Staggers, 1972-74	50	460	9.20	t85	2	38
Veryl Switzer, 1954-55	48	464	9.67	t93	1	—
Tony Canadeo, 1941-44, 46-52	46	513	11.15	26	0	—
Joe Laws, 1934-45	46	339	7.37	23	0	—
Roell Preston, 1997-98	45	398	8.84	t71	1	17
Allen Rossum, 2000-01	40	357	8.93	t55	1	32
Lou Brock, 1940-45	39	438	11.23	45	0	—
Bill Schroeder, 1994, 97-01	35	347	9.91	46	0	8
Darrien Gordon, 2002	35	180	5.14	27	0	9
Antonio Chatman, 2003	33	277	8.39	33	0	18
Terrell Buckley, 1992-94	32	287	8.97	t58	1	10
Herman Rohrig, 1941, 46-47	30	357	11.90	28	0	—
Lew Carpenter, 1959-63	28	339	12.11	51	0	5
Mike Prior, 1993-98	28	266	9.50	24	0	17
Charles Jordan, 1994-95, 99	27	242	8.96	18	0	5
Tom Brown, 1964-68	27	151	5.59	t52	1	8
Vai Sikahema, 1991	26	239	9.19	62	0	4
Mark Lee, 1980-90	26	215	8.27	t94	1	1
Fred Nixon, 1980-81	26	203	7.81	17	0	6
Ralph Earhart, 1948-49	25	298	11.92	t57	1	—
Tom Flynn, 1984-86	22	169	7.68	20	0	8
Andy Uram, 1938-43	19	219	11.53	t90	0	—
Ron Cassidy, 1979-81, 83-84	19	139	7.32	20	0	9
Fred Provo, 1948	18	208	11.56	40	0	—
Bill Butler, 1959	18	163	9.06	t61	1	—
Dom Moselle, 1951-52	16	157	9.81	24	0	—
Donny Anderson, 1966-71	15	222	14.80	t77	1	4
Derrick Mayes, 1996-98	15	150	10.00	26	0	3
Jim Shanley, 1958	14	105	7.50	26	0	—
Bob Nussbaumer, 1946, 51	13	101	7.77	21	0	—
Travis Williams, 1967-70	12	209	17.42	t83	1	5
Earl (Jug) Girard, 1948-51	12	79	6.58	11	0	—
Jim Gillette, 1947	11	168	15.27	26	0	—
Irv Comp, 1943-49	11	123	11.18	20	0	—
Antuan Edwards, 1999-03	11	90	8.18	45	0	4
Joe Johnson, 1954-58	10	82	8.20	13	0	—
Oscar E. Smith, 1948-49	10	80	8.00	27	0	—
Bruce Smith, 1945-48	9	101	11.22	22	0	—
Ron Pitts, 1988-90	9	93	10.33	t63	1	9
Roy McKay, 1944-47	9	85	9.44	17	0	—
Darren Sharper, 1997-03	9	50	5.56	23	0	8
Sterling Sharpe, 1988-92	9	48	5.33	14	0	7
Ace Loomis, 1951-53	8	83	10.38	31	0	—
John Losch, 1956	8	74	9.25	58	0	—
Charles Lee, 2000-01	8	58	7.25	16	0	2
John Kirby, 1949	8	48	6.00	13	0	—
Gib Dawson, 1953	7	72	10.29	t60	1	—
Patrick Scott, 1987-88	6	71	11.83	36	0	2
Dave Davis, 1971-72	6	36	6.00	19	0	0
Bill Boedecker, 1950	5	49	9.80	12	0	—
Mickey Sutton, 1989	5	42	8.40	17	0	1

Name	No.	Yds.	Avg.	LG	TD	FC
Dan Sandifer, 1952-53	5	40	8.00	23	0	—
J.R. Boone, 1953	5	24	4.80	9	0	—
Gary Hayes, 1984-86	5	24	4.80	10	0	0
Norman Jefferson, 1987-88	5	15	3.00	9	0	2
J.J. Moses, 2002	5	12	2.40	8	0	0
John Symank, 1957-62	5	0	0.00	0	0	—
Hal Van Every, 1940-41	4	58	14.50	20	0	—
Bobby Dillon, 1952-59	4	37	9.25	13	0	—
Cecil Isbell, 1938-42	4	33	8.25	14	0	—
Wally Dreyer, 1950-51	3	48	16.00	22	0	—
Paul Duhart, 1944	3	32	10.67	18	0	—
Billy Kinard, 1957-58	3	19	6.33	19	0	—
Jack Jacobs, 1947-49	3	16	5.33	9	0	—
Eric Metcalf, 2002	3	-1	-0.33	0	0	0
Clarke Hinkle, 1932-41	2	61	30.50	36	0	—
Ed Cody, 1947-48	2	30	15.00	20	0	—
Bob Forte, 1946-50, 52-53	2	28	14.00	15	0	—
Harper Davis, 1951	2	21	10.50	17	0	—
Kelly Cook, 1987	2	18	9.00	14	0	0
Don Barton, 1953	2	13	6.50	7	0	—
Al Cannava, 1950	2	9	4.50	9	0	—
Al Romine, 1955, 58	2	7	3.50	7	0	—
Bill Whitaker, 1981-82	2	1	0.50	1	0	0
Basil Mitchell, 99-00	2	0	0.00	0	0	0
Leon Harden, 1970	2	-7	-3.50	0	0	0
Ted Fritsch, 1942-50	1	31	31.00	31	0	—
Joel Mason, 1942-45	1	20	20.00	20	0	—
Bob Kahler, 1942-44	1	14	14.00	14	0	—
Russ Mosley, 1945-46	1	13	13.00	13	0	—
Bill Forester, 1953-63	1	7	7.00	7	0	—
Larry Coutre, 1950, 53	1	5	5.00	5	0	—
Robert Ferguson, 2001-03	1	4	4.00	4	0	2
Mark Murphy, 1980-85, 87-91	1	4	4.00	4	0	2
Emlen Tunnell, 1959-61	1	3	3.00	3	0	—
Tim Hauck, 1991-92	1	2	2.00	2	0	0
Leland Glass, 1972-73	1	1	1.00	1	0	0
Lee Morris, 1987	1	1	1.00	1	0	0
Herb Adderley, 1961-69	1	0	0.00	0	0	0
Ben Aldridge, 1953	1	0	0.00	0	0	—
Tony Carter, 2002	1	0	0.00	0	0	0
Chuck Cecil, 1988-92	1	0	0.00	0	0	0
Vinnie Clark, 1991-92	1	0	0.00	0	0	0
Doug Evans, 1993-97	1	0	0.00	0	0	0
Charlie Hall, 1971-76	1	0	0.00	0	0	0
Al Harris, 2003	1	0	0.00	0	0	0
Larry Hefner, 1972-75	1	0	0.00	0	0	0
Estus Hood, 1978-84	1	0	0.00	0	0	0
Bob Hudson, 1972	1	0	0.00	0	0	2
Mark Ingram, 1995	1	0	0.00	0	0	0
Ron Kostelnik, 1961-68	1	0	0.00	0	0	0
Cliff Lewis, 1981-84	1	0	0.00	0	0	0
Don McIlhenny, 1957-59	1	0	0.00	0	0	—
Mike McKenzie, 1999-03	1	0	0.00	0	0	0
Jim Psaltis, 1954	1	0	0.00	0	0	—
Al Randolph, 1971	1	0	0.00	0	0	0
Floyd (Breezy) Reid, 1950-56	1	0	0.00	0	0	—
Howard Sampson, 1978-79	1	0	0.00	0	0	0
Eric Torkelson, 1974-79, 81	1	0	0.00	0	0	0
Walter Tullis, 1978-79	1	0	0.00	0	0	0
Marcus Wilkins, 2002-03	1	0	0.00	0	0	0
Clarence Williams, 1970-77	1	0	0.00	0	0	0
Vince Workman, 1989-92	1	0	0.00	0	0	0
George Teague, 1993-95	1	-1	-1.00	-1	0	0
Packers, 1941-2003	**2,304**	**20,005**	**8.68**	**t95**	**29**	**576**
Opponents, 1941-2003	2,287	19,274	8.43	t95	23	539

ALL-TIME INTERCEPTORS

(Statistic kept since 1940; rankings based on number of interceptions)

Name	No.	Yds.	Avg.	LG	TD
Bobby Dillon, 1952-59	52	976	18.77	61	5
Willie Wood, 1960-71	48	699	14.56	t42	2
Herb Adderley, 1961-69	39	795	20.38	t80	7
LeRoy Butler, 1990-01	38	533	14.03	t90	1
Irv Comp, 1943-49	34	483	14.21	t54	2
Darren Sharper, 1997-03	32	580	18.13	t89	3
Mark Lee, 1980-90	31	249	8.03	40	0
Don Hutson, 1935-45	30	389	12.97	t84	1
Hank Gremminger, 1956-65	28	421	15.04	45	0
Ray Nitschke, 1958-72	25	385	15.40	t43	2
John Anderson, 1978-89	25	167	6.68	t27	1
Bob Jeter, 1963-70	23	333	14.48	t75	2
Bob Forte, 1946-50, 52-53	23	291	12.65	t68	1
Johnnie Gray, 1975-84	22	332	15.09	67	1
Dave Robinson, 1963-72	21	322	15.33	87	0
Bill Forester, 1953-63	21	279	13.29	37	0
Willie Buchanon, 1972-78	21	234	11.14	t77	2
Jess Whittenton, 1958-64	20	329	16.45	52	1
Ken Ellis, 1970-75	20	294	14.70	60	3
Charley Brock, 1939-47	20	230	11.50	41	2
Mark Murphy, 1980-85, 87-91	20	194	9.70	t50	1
Tyrone Williams, 1996-02	19	274	14.42	t69	2
John Symank, 1957-62	18	366	20.33	41	0
Joe Laws, 1934-45	18	266	14.78	38	0
Tim Lewis, 1983-86	16	266	16.63	t99	1
Doug Hart, 1964-71	15	436	29.07	t85	3
Val Joe Walker, 1953-56	15	234	15.60	t54	1
Mike McKenzie, 1999-03	15	166	11.07	t90	2
Tom Brown, 1964-68	13	210	16.15	51	0
Chuck Cecil, 1988-92	13	200	15.38	33	0
Lou Brock, 1940-45	13	193	14.85	74	0
Mike C. McCoy, 1976-83	13	116	8.92	38	0
Ace Loomis, 1951-53	12	257	21.42	66	1
Doug Evans, 1993-97	12	159	13.25	63	1
Dave Brown, 1987-89	12	55	4.58	15	0
Herman Rohrig, 1941, 46-47	11	231	21.00	51	0
Dan Currie, 1958-64	11	193	17.55	33	1
Ted Cook, 1948-50	11	133	12.09	30	0
Tom Flynn, 1984-86	11	113	10.27	31	0
Estus Hood, 1978-84	11	93	8.45	t41	1
Mike Douglass, 1978-85	10	274	27.40	t80	1
Ted Fritsch, 1942-50	10	263	26.30	t69	2
Rebel Steiner, 1950-51	10	194	19.40	t94	1
Al Matthews, 1970-75	10	169	16.90	t58	1
Steve Luke, 1975-80	10	149	14.90	t63	1
Terrell Buckley, 1992-94	10	102	10.20	t33	1
Lee Roy Caffey, 1964-69	9	177	19.67	t52	2
Andy Uram, 1938-43	9	138	15.33	28	0
Jim Hill, 1972-74	9	137	15.22	24	0
Johnny Holland, 1987-93	9	130	14.44	32	0
Tony Canadeo, 1941-44, 46-52	9	129	14.33	35	0
Cecil Isbell, 1938-42	9	61	6.78	19	0
Maurice Harvey, 1981-83	8	249	31.13	53	0
Earl (Jug) Girard, 1948-51	8	106	13.25	41	0
Fred Carr, 1968-77	8	98	12.25	28	1
Mike Prior, 1993-98	8	89	11.13	49	0
Charles Goldenberg, 1933-45	8	73	9.13	30	0
Eugene Robinson, 1996-97	7	133	19.00	39	0
Ken Stills, 1985-89	7	107	15.29	t58	1
Perry Smith, 1973-76	7	97	13.86	61	0
Antuan Edwards, 1999-03	7	35	5.00	t26	1
George Teague, 1993-95	6	155	25.83	74	0
Hal Van Every, 1940-41	6	134	22.33	t91	1
Jack Jacobs, 1947-49	6	90	15.00	29	0
Nate Wayne, 2000-02	6	87	14.50	35	0
Deral Teateak, 1952-56	6	84	14.00	32	0
Marvin Johnson, 1952-53	6	61	10.17	36	0
Jim Carter, 1970-75, 77-78	6	60	10.00	t42	1
Bob Flowers, 1942-49	6	33	5.50	19	0
Marques Anderson, 2002-03	5	117	23.40	t78	2

Name	No.	Yds.	Avg.	LG	TD
Ben Aldridge, 1953	5	85	17.00	34	0
Ted Hendricks, 1974	5	74	14.80	44	0
Scott Stephen, 1987-91	5	65	13.00	26	0
Ken Keuper, 1945-47	5	63	12.60	26	0
Wally Dreyer, 1950-51	5	62	12.40	34	1
Emlen Tunnell, 1959-61	5	42	8.40	22	0
Jay Rhodemyre, 1948-49, 51-52	5	36	7.20	9	0
Al Baldwin, 1950	5	35	7.00	22	0
George Cumby, 1980-85	5	33	6.60	17	0
Doyle Nix, 1955	5	33	6.60	12	0
Mossy Cade, 1985-86	5	26	5.20	18	0
Bob Adkins, 1940-41, 45	4	114	28.50	54	1
Vinnie Clark, 1991-92	4	112	28.00	43	0
George Koonce, 1992-99	4	96	24.00	t75	1
Ron Pitts, 1988-90	4	93	23.25	37	0
Brian Williams, 1995-00	4	90	22.50	60	0
Na'il Diggs, 2000-03	4	75	18.75	33	0
Bryce Paup, 1990-94	4	55	13.75	30	1
Roy McKay, 1944-47	4	53	13.25	20	0
Craig Newsome, 1995-98	4	51	12.75	26	0
Dick Weisgerber, 1938-40, 42	4	51	12.75	24	0
Rich Wingo, 1979, 81-84	4	51	12.75	38	0
Pete Tinsley, 1938-45	4	41	10.25	t24	0
Jerry Holmes, 1990-91	4	39	9.75	24	0
Tom Toner, 1973-77	4	39	9.75	28	0
Harper Davis, 1951	4	37	9.25	25	0
Roger Zatkoff, 1953-56	4	25	6.25	15	0
Paul Duhart, 1944	4	23	5.75	14	0
George (Tiger) Greene, 1986-90	4	11	2.75	11	0
Dave Hanner, 1952-64	4	3	0.75	2	0
Dom Moselle, 1951-52	4	2	0.50	2	0
Jim Bob Morris, 1987	3	135	45.00	73	0
Bob Summerhays, 1949-51	3	112	37.33	t88	1
Al Harris, 2003	3	89	29.67	t56	1
Randy Scott, 1981-86	3	62	20.67	30	0
Cliff Aberson, 1946	3	53	17.67	33	0
Billy Bookout, 1955-56	3	43	14.33	27	0
Tod McBride, 1999-02	3	43	14.33	43	0
Roland Mitchell, 1991-94	3	40	13.33	35	0
Bob Nussbaumer, 1946, 51	3	31	10.33	16	0
Clarence Self, 1952, 54-55	3	23	7.67	23	0
Nick Barnett, 2003	3	21	7.00	14	0
Wayne Simmons, 1993-97	3	21	7.00	19	0
Brian Noble, 1985-92	3	20	6.67	10	0
Clarke Hinkle, 1932-41	3	13	4.33	8	0
Bernardo Harris, 1995-01	3	12	4.00	8	0
Mike Jolly, 1980, 82-83	3	2	0.67	2	0
Don Perkins, 1943-45	2	123	61.50	t83	2
Jim Capuzzi, 1955-56	2	65	32.50	65	0
Larry Buhler, 1939-41	2	58	29.00	32	0
George Svendsen, 1935-37, 40-41	2	48	24.00	42	0
Robert Brown, 1982-92	2	42	21.00	37	1
Russ Mosley, 1945-46	2	40	20.00	20	0
Alex Wizbicki, 1950	2	38	19.00	34	0
Bhawoh Jue, 2001-03	2	35	17.50	35	0
Ben Starret, 1942-45	2	31	15.50	27	0
Dan Sandifer, 1952-53	2	25	12.50	17	0
Mike Hunt, 1978-80	2	23	11.50	13	0
Bob Freeman, 1959	2	22	11.00	22	0
Charlie Hall, 1971-76	2	22	11.00	19	0
Willie Davis, 1960-69	2	21	10.50	21	0
Fred Vinson, 1999	2	21	10.50	21	0
Larry Craig, 1939-49	2	20	10.00	20	0
James Willis, 1993-94	2	20	10.00	17	0
Tommy Crutcher, 1964-67, 71-72	2	19	9.50	15	0
Lenny McGill, 1994-95	2	16	8.00	16	0
Wylie Turner, 1979-80	2	13	6.50	13	0
Gene Wilson, 1947-48	2	13	6.50	13	0
Bill Quinlan, 1959-62	2	9	4.50	5	0

Name	No.	Yds.	Avg.	LG	TD
Michael Hawthorne, 2003	2	8	4.00	8	0
Tom MacLeod, 1973	2	8	4.00	8	0
Sherwood Fries, 1943	2	6	3.00	4	0
Vonnie Holliday, 1998-02	2	6	3.00	3	0
George Paskvan, 1941	2	6	3.00	4	0
Abner Wimberly, 1950-52	2	5	2.50	5	0
Ken Gorgal, 1956	2	2	1.00	2	0
Clayton Tonnemaker, 1950, 53-54	2	2	1.00	1	0
Albin (Rip) Collins, 1951	2	0	0.00	0	0
Arnie Herber, 1930-40	2	0	0.00	0	0
Gabe Wilkins, 1994-97	1	77	77.00	t77	1
Kabeer Gbaja-Biamila, 2000-03	1	72	72.00	t72	1
Burnell Dent, 1986-92	1	53	53.00	53	0
Reggie White, 1993-98	1	46	46.00	46	0
Al Randolph, 1971	1	34	34.00	34	0
Ed Jankowski, 1937-41	1	33	33.00	33	0
Keith McKenzie, 1996-99, 02	1	33	33.00	t33	1
Dick Bilda, 1944	1	25	25.00	25	0
Bob Ingalls, 1942	1	23	23.00	t23	1
Esera Tuaolo, 1991-92	1	23	23.00	23	0
Clarence Williams, 1970-77	1	23	23.00	23	0
Jim Laughlin, 1983	1	22	22.00	22	0
Bobby Leopold, 1986	1	21	21.00	21	0
Gene White, 1954	1	20	20.00	20	0
Charles Mitchell, 1946	1	18	18.00	18	0
Roderick Mullen, 1994-97	1	17	17.00	17	0
Bill Lee, 1937-42, 46	1	14	14.00	14	0
Von Mansfield, 1987	1	14	14.00	14	0
Paul Rudzinski, 1978-80	1	14	14.00	14	0
Jim Temp, 1957-60	1	13	13.00	13	0
Bernie Crimmins, 1945	1	12	12.00	t12	1
Ken Roskie, 1948	1	12	12.00	12	0
Frank Balazs, 1939-41	1	11	11.00	11	0
Sam Palumbo, 1957	1	11	11.00	11	0
Howard Ruetz, 1951-53	1	11	11.00	11	0
Howard (Smiley) Johnson, 1940-41	1	10	10.00	10	0
Damon Tassos, 1947-49	1	10	10.00	10	0
Shawn Patterson, 1988-91	1	9	9.00	t9	1
Pat Terrell, 1998	1	9	9.00	9	0
Keith Thibodeaux, 2001	1	9	9.00	9	0
Harry Jacunski, 1939-44	1	7	7.00	7	0

Name	No.	Yds.	Avg.	LG	TD
Fred Strickland, 1994-95	1	7	7.00	7	0
Ray Wehba, 1944	1	7	7.00	7	0
Alphonso Carreker, 1984-88	1	6	6.00	6	0
Elbert Watts, 1986	1	6	6.00	6	0
Carl Barzilauskas, 1978-79	1	5	5.00	5	0
Corey Dowden, 1996	1	5	5.00	5	0
Tom Greenfield, 1939-41	1	5	5.00	5	0
Roger Harding, 1949	1	5	5.00	5	0
Mike P. McCoy, 1970-76	1	5	5.00	5	0
Dick Afflis, 1951-54	1	3	3.00	3	0
Larry Hefner, 1972-75	1	3	3.00	3	0
KeShon Johnson, 1994, 97	1	3	3.00	3	0
Lamont Hollinquest, 1996-98	1	2	2.00	2	0
Kenneth Johnson, 1987	1	2	2.00	2	0
Buford (Baby) Ray, 1938-48	1	2	2.00	2	0
Jermaine Smith, 1997, 99	1	2	2.00	2	0
Tom Bettis, 1955-61	1	0	0.00	0	0
Matt Bowen, 2001-02	1	0	0.00	0	0
Matt Brock, 1989-94	1	0	0.00	0	0
Paul (Buddy) Burris, 1949-51	1	0	0.00	0	0
Anthony Harrison, 1987	1	0	0.00	0	0
Jerry Helluin, 1954-57	1	0	0.00	0	0
Van Jakes, 1989	1	0	0.00	0	0
Charles Johnson, 1979-80, 83	1	0	0.00	0	0
Henry Jordan, 1959-69	1	0	0.00	0	0
Joe Kelly, 1995	1	0	0.00	0	0
Billy Lyon, 1998-02	1	0	0.00	0	0
Mike McLeod, 1984-85	1	0	0.00	0	0
James Melka, 1987	1	0	0.00	0	0
Jim Nelson, 1998-99	1	0	0.00	0	0
Dan Orlich, 1949-51	1	0	0.00	0	0
Ernie Pannell, 1941-42, 45	1	0	0.00	0	0
John Petitbon, 1957	1	0	0.00	0	0
Al Romine, 1955, 58	1	0	0.00	0	0
Carl Schuette, 1950-51	1	0	0.00	0	0
Rod Smith, 1998	1	0	0.00	0	0
Joe Spencer, 1950-51	1	0	0.00	0	0
Bryant Westbrook, 2002	1	0	0.00	0	0
Packers, 1940-2003	1,403	20,083	14.31	t99	81
Opponents, 1940-2003	1,310	18,725	14.29	t99	101

ALL-TIME SCORERS

(Statistic kept since 1921; rankings based on total points)

Name	TDr	TDp	TDrt	PAT	2pt	FG	S	TP
Ryan Longwell, 1997-03	0	0	0	298/301	0	182/222	0	844
Don Hutson, 1935-45	3	99	3	172/184	0	7	0	823
Chris Jacke, 1989-96	0	0	0	301/306	0	173/224	0	820
Paul Hornung, 1957-62, 64-66	50	12	0	190/194	0	66/140	0	760
Jim Taylor, 1958-66	81	10	0	0/0	0	0/0	0	546
Chester Marcol, 1972-80	0	0	1	155/164	0	120/195	0	521
Fred Cone, 1951-57	12	4	0	200/214	0	53/89	0	455
Sterling Sharpe, 1988-94	0	65	1	0/0	0	0/0	0	396
Ted Fritsch, 1942-50	31	1	3	62/70	0	36/98	0	380
Clarke Hinkle, 1932-41	34	9	0	30	0	28	0	372
Antonio Freeman, 1995-01, 03	0	57	0	0/0	2	0/0	0	346
Ahman Green, 2000-03	41	12	0	0/0	0	0/0	0	318
Verne Lewellen, 1924-32	37	12	2	1	0	0	0	307
Max McGee, 1954, 57-67	0	50	1	0/0	0	0/0	0	306
James Lofton, 1978-86	1	49	0	0/0	0	0/0	0	300
Jan Stenerud, 1980-83	0	0	0	115/118	0	59/73	0	292
Dorsey Levens, 1994-01	28	16	0	0/0	1	0/0	0	266
Al Del Greco, 1984-87	0	0	0	112/114	0	50/75	0	262
Don Chandler, 1965-67	0	0	0	117/120	0	48/83	0	261
Bill Howton, 1952-58	0	43	0	0/0	0	0/0	0	258
Boyd Dowler, 1959-69	0	40	0	0/0	0	0/0	0	240
Paul Coffman, 1978-85	0	39	0	0/0	0	0/0	0	234
Johnny Blood, 1929-33, 35-36	5	28	4	2	0	0	0	224
Robert Brooks, 1992-98	0	32	3	0/0	0	0/0	0	210
Carroll Dale, 1965-72	0	35	0	0/0	0	0/0	0	210
Gerry Ellis, 1980-86	25	10	0	0/0	0	0/0	0	210
Elijah Pitts, 1961-69, 71	28	6	1	0/0	0	0/0	0	210
John Brockington, 1971-77	29	3	0	0/0	0	0/0	0	192
Donny Anderson, 1966-71	24	6	1	0/0	0	0/0	0	186
Tony Canadeo, 1941-44, 46-52	26	5	0	0/0	0	0/0	0	186
Eddie Lee Ivery, 1979-86	23	7	0	0/0	0	0/0	0	180

Name	TDr	TDp	TDrt	PAT	2pt	FG	S	TP
Tobin Rote, 1950-56	29	1	0	0/0	0	0/0	0	180
Edgar Bennett, 1992-96	19	10	0	0/0	2	0/0	0	178
Jerry Kramer, 1958-68	0	0	0	90/94	0	29/54	0	177
Tom Moore, 1960-65	20	7	0	0/0	0	0/0	0	162
Ed West, 1984-94	1	25	0	0/0	1	0/0	0	158
Bubba Franks, 2000-03	0	21	0	0/0	2	0/0	0	130
Gary Knafelc, 1954-62	0	21	0	0/0	0	0/0	0	126
Joe Laws, 1934-45	9	10	2	0/0	0	0/0	0	126
Barty Smith, 1974-80	18	3	0	0/0	0	0/0	0	126
Bill Schroeder, 1997-01	0	20	0	0/0	0	0/0	0	120
Brent Fullwood, 1987-90	18	1	0	0/0	0	0/0	0	114
Terdell Middleton, 1977-81	15	3	1	0/0	0	0/0	0	114
Floyd (Breezy) Reid, 1950-56	13	5	0	0/0	0	0/0	0	108
Max Zendejas, 1987-88	0	0	0	30/34	0	25/35	0	105
Mark Chmura, 1993-99	0	17	0	0/0	1	0/0	0	104
Curly Lambeau, 1921-29	8	3	0	20	0	6	0	104
Bob Mann, 1950-54	0	17	0	0/0	0	0/0	0	102
Travis Williams, 1967-70	6	5	6	0/0	0	0/0	0	102
Hank Bruder, 1931-39	8	6	2	4	0	0	0	100
Lou Brock, 1940-45	10	6	0	2/2	0	0/1	0	98
Andy Uram, 1938-43	4	10	2	2/3	0	0/0	0	98
Phillip Epps, 1982-88	1	14	1	0/0	0	0/0	0	96
William Henderson, 1995-03	5	11	0	0/0	0	0/0	0	96
Donald Driver, 1999-03	1	14	0	0/0	1	0/0	0	92
Bob Monnett, 1933-38	7	0	1	28	0	5	0	91
Jessie Clark, 1983-87	9	6	0	0/0	0	0/0	0	90
Ron Kramer, 1957, 59-64	0	15	0	0/0	0	0/0	0	90
Steve Odom, 1974-79	1	11	3	0/0	0	0/0	0	90
Bart Starr, 1956-71	15	0	0	0/0	0	0/0	0	90
Vince Workman, 1989-92	10	5	0	0/0	0	0/0	0	90
Tyrone Davis, 1997-02	0	13	1	0/0	1	0/0	0	86

Name	TDr	TDp	TDrt	PAT	2pt	FG	S	TP
Lavvie Dilweg, 1927-34	0	12	2	2	0	0	0	86
Paul Engebretsen, 1934-41	0	0	0	43	0	14	0	85
Clyde Goodnight, 1945-49	0	13	0	0/0	0	0/0	0	78
Dave Hampton, 1969-71	7	3	3	0/0	0	0/0	0	78
Harlan Huckleby, 1980-85	10	3	0	0/0	0	0/0	0	78
Nolan Luhn, 1945-49	0	13	0	0/0	0	0/0	0	78
Rich McGeorge, 1970-78	0	13	0	0/0	0	0/0	0	78
Brett Favre, 1992-02	12	0	0	0/0	0	0/0	0	72
Marv Fleming, 1963-69	0	12	0	0/0	0	0/0	0	72
Hurdis McCrary, 1929-33	7	4	1	0/0	0	0/0	0	72
Carl Mulleneaux, 1938-41, 45-46	0	11	1	0/0	0	0/0	0	72
Mike Mercer, 1968-69	0	0	0	35/37	0	12/29	0	71
Ed Jankowski, 1937-41	8	1	0	4	0	0	1	67
Irv Comp, 1943-49	7	2	2	0/0	0	0/0	0	66
Jim Grabowski, 1966-70	8	3	0	0/0	0	0/0	0	66
Keith Jackson, 1995-96	0	11	0	0/0	0	0/0	0	66
John Jefferson, 1981-84	0	11	0	0/0	0	0/0	0	66
MacArthur Lane, 1972-74	7	4	0	0/0	0	0/0	0	66
Roger Grove, 1931-35	1	7	0	16	0	0	0	64
Dale Livingston, 1970	0	0	0	19/21	0	15/28	0	64
Bo Molenda, 1928-32	9	0	0	10	0	0	0	64
Cecil Isbell, 1938-42	10	0	0	3/3	0	0/0	0	63
Ernie Smith, 1935-37, 39	0	0	0	43	0	6	0	61
Tom Birney, 1979-80	0	0	0	21/28	0	13/21	0	60
Joseph (Red) Dunn, 1927-31	0	1	0	48	0	2	0	60
Wuert Engelmann, 1930-33	2	5	3	0	0	0	0	60
Charles Goldenberg, 1933-45	6	1	3	0	0	0	0	60
Billy Grimes, 1950-52	6	2	0	0/0	0	0/0	0	60
Scott Hunter, 1971-73	10	0	0	0/0	0	0/0	0	60
Eddie Kotal, 1925-29	4	5	1	0	0	0	0	60
Javon Walker, 2002-03	0	10	0	0/0	0	0/0	0	60
Herb Adderley, 1961-69	0	0	9	0/0	0	0/0	0	54
Myrt Basing, 1923-27	7	2	0	0	0	0	0	54
Howard (Cub) Buck, 1921-25	0	0	0	24	0	10	0	54
Lynn Dickey, 1976-77, 79-85	9	0	0	0/0	0	0/0	0	54
Willard Harrell, 1975-77	5	3	1	0/0	0	0/0	0	54
Jackie Harris, 1990-93	0	9	0	0/0	0	0/0	0	54
Don Majkowski, 1987-92	9	0	0	0/0	0	0/0	0	54
Darrell Thompson, 1990-94	7	1	1	0/0	0	0/0	0	54
Eric Torkelson, 1974-79, 81	8	0	1	0/0	0	0/0	0	54
Joe Danelo, 1975	0	0	0	20/23	0	11/16	0	53
Ward Cuff, 1947	0	0	0	30/30	0	7/16	0	51
Paul Ott Carruth, 1986-88	5	3	0	0/0	0	0/0	0	48
Milt Gantenbein, 1931-40	0	8	0	0/0	0	0/0	0	48
Anthony Morgan, 1993-96	0	8	0	0/0	0	0/0	0	48
Walt Schlinkman, 1946-50	8	0	0	0/0	0	0/0	0	48
Aundra Thompson, 1977-81	0	7	1	0/0	0	0/0	0	48
Keith Woodside, 1988-91	6	2	0	0/0	0	0/0	0	48
Corey Bradford, 1998-01	0	7	0	0/0	1	0/0	0	44
Arnie Herber, 1930-40	3	3	1	2	0	0	0	44
Lou Michaels, 1971	0	0	0	19/20	0	8/14	0	43
Al Carmichael, 1953-58	2	3	2	0/0	0	0/0	0	42
Carleton Elliott, 1951-54	0	6	1	0/0	0	0/0	0	42
Howie Ferguson, 1953-58	6	1	0	0/0	0	0/0	0	42
Robert Ferguson, 2001-03	0	7	0	0/0	0	0/0	0	42
Cully Lidberg, 1926, 29-30	7	0	0	0/0	0	0/0	0	42
Don McIlhenny, 1957-59	3	4	0	0/0	0	0/0	0	42
Babe Parilli, 1952-53, 57-58	7	0	0	0/0	0	0/0	0	42
George Sauer, 1935-37	6	0	1	0	0	0	0	42
Jon Staggers, 1972-74	1	4	2	0/0	0	0/0	0	42
David Whitehurst, 1977-83	7	0	0	0/0	0	0/0	0	42
Don Beebe, 1996-97	0	4	2	0/0	0	0/0	0	36
Harry Jacunski, 1939-44	0	6	0	0/0	0	0/0	0	36
Perry Kemp, 1988-91	0	6	0	0/0	0	0/0	0	36
Marty Norton, 1925	1	4	1	0	0	0	0	36
Walter Stanley, 1985-88	0	5	1	0/0	0	0/0	0	36
Charlie Mathys, 1922-26	1	4	0	0	0	1	0	33
Doug Hart, 1964-71	0	0	5	0/0	0	0/0	1	32
Jack Cloud, 1950-51	4	0	1	0/0	0	0/0	0	30
Kenneth Davis, 1986-88	4	1	0	0/0	0	0/0	0	30
Bobby Dillon, 1952-59	0	0	5	0/0	0	0/0	0	30
Gary Ellerson, 1985-86	5	0	0	0/0	0	0/0	0	30
Ken Ellis, 1970-75	0	0	5	0/0	0	0/0	0	30
Rex Enright, 1926-27	3	2	0	0	0	0	0	30
Tony Fisher, 2002-03	3	2	0	0/0	0	0/0	0	30
Herman Fontenot, 1989-90	1	4	0	0/0	0	0/0	0	30
Derrick Mayes, 1996-98	0	5	0	0/0	0	0/0	0	30
Harry O'Boyle, 1928, 32	1	0	0	15	0	3	0	30
Ken Payne, 1974-77	0	5	0	0/0	0	0/0	0	30
Ray Pelfrey, 1951-52	0	5	0	0/0	0	0/0	0	30
Everett (Pid) Purdy, 1926-27	1	0	0	15	0	3	0	30
Jeff Query, 1989-90	0	4	1	0/0	0	0/0	0	30
Al Rose, 1932-36	0	3	2	0	0	0	0	30
Chuck Sample, 1942, 45	4	0	0	0/0	0	0/0	0	30
Veryl Switzer, 1954-55	0	3	2	0/0	0	0/0	0	30
Walter (Tillie) Voss, 1924	0	5	0	0	0	0	0	30
Bill Reichardt, 1952	1	0	0	5/5	0	5/20	0	26
Tim Webster, 1971	0	0	0	8/8	0	6/11	0	26
Chuck Mercein, 1967-69	2	0	0	7/7	0	2/5	0	25
Ade Schwammel, 1934-36, 43-44	0	0	0	7	0	6	0	25
Willie Wood, 1960-71	0	0	4	1/1	0	0/1	0	25
Charley Brock, 1939-47	0	0	4	0/0	0	0/0	0	24
Reggie Cobb, 1994	3	1	0	0/0	0	0/0	0	24
Ted Cook, 1948-50	0	4	0	0/0	0	0/0	0	24
Paul Duhart, 1944	2	2	0	0/0	0	0/0	0	24
Ralph Earhart, 1948-49	1	2	1	0/0	0	0/0	0	24
Bob Forte, 1946-50, 52-53	0	3	1	0/0	0	0/0	0	24
Earl Gros, 1962-63	4	0	0	0/0	0	0/0	0	24
John Hilton, 1970	0	4	0	0/0	0	0/0	0	24
Joe Johnson, 1954-58	0	4	0	0/0	0	0/0	0	24
Bob Long, 1964-67	0	4	0	0/0	0	0/0	0	24
David Martin, 2001-03	0	4	0	0/0	0	0/0	0	24
Keith McKenzie, 1996-99, 02	0	0	4	0/0	0	0/0	0	24
Paul Miller, 1936-38	1	3	0	0/0	0	0/0	0	24
Dick O'Donnell, 1924-30	0	4	0	0/0	0	0/0	0	24
Steve Pritko, 1949-50	0	4	0	0/0	0	0/0	0	24
Del Rodgers, 1982, 84	1	0	3	0/0	0	0/0	0	24
Bernie Scherer, 1936-38	0	3	1	0	0	0	0	24
Darren Sharper, 1997-03	0	0	4	0/0	0	0/0	0	24
Barry Smith, 1973-75	0	4	0	0/0	0	0/0	0	24
Ed Cody, 1947-48	2	0	0	11/13	0	0/0	0	23
Eddie Garcia, 1983-84	0	0	0	14/15	0	3/9	0	23
Tom Nash, 1928-32	0	2	1	0	0	0	2	22
Dutch Hendrian, 1924	3	0	0	0	0	1	0	21
Roy McKay, 1944-47	3	0	0	3/3	0	0/0	0	21
Paul Fitzgibbons, 1930-32	1	2	0	1	0	0	0	19
Steve Atkins, 1979-81	2	1	0	0/0	0	0/0	0	18
Al Baldwin, 1950	0	3	0	0/0	0	0/0	0	18
Willie Buchanon, 1972-78	0	0	3	0/0	0	0/0	0	18
LeRoy Butler, 1990-01	0	0	3	0/0	0	0/0	0	18
Mark Clayton, 1993	0	3	0	0/0	0	0/0	0	18
Larry Coutre, 1950, 53	1	2	0	0/0	0	0/0	0	18
Najeh Davenport, 2002-03	3	0	0	0/0	0	0/0	0	18
Mike Douglass, 1978-85	0	0	3	0/0	0	0/0	0	18
Earl (Jug) Girard, 1948-51	1	2	0	0/0	0	0/0	0	18
Michael Haddix, 1989-90	0	3	0	0/0	0	0/0	0	18
Jack Harris, 1925-26	3	0	0	0	0	0	0	18
Desmond Howard, 1996, 99	0	0	3	0/0	0	0/0	0	18
Mark Ingram, 1995	0	3	0	0/0	0	0/0	0	18
Mike Meade, 1982-83	1	2	0	0/0	0	0/0	0	18
Terry Mickens, 1994-97	0	3	0	0/0	0	0/0	0	18
Stan Mills, 1922-23	1	2	0	0	0	0	0	18
Dom Moselle, 1951-52	1	2	0	0/0	0	0/0	0	18
Frankie Neal, 1987	0	3	0	0/0	0	0/0	0	18
Don Perkins, 1943-45	1	0	2	0	0	0	0	18
Roell Preston, 1997-98	0	0	3	0/0	0	0/0	0	18
Harry Sydney, 1992	2	1	0	0/0	0	0/0	0	18
Jerry Tagge, 1972-74	3	0	0	0/0	0	0/0	0	18
Jeff Thomason, 1995-99	0	3	0	0/0	0	0/0	0	18
Hal Van Every, 1940-41	2	0	1	0/0	0	0/0	0	18
Randy Wright, 1984-88	3	0	0	0/0	0	0/0	0	18
Bob Adkins, 1940-41, 45	0	1	1	4/4	0	0/1	0	16
Willie Davis, 1960-69	0	0	2	0/0	0	0/0	2	16
Booth Lusteg, 1969	0	0	0	12/12	0	1/5	0	15
Craig Hentrich, 1994-97	0	0	0	5/5	0	3/5	0	14
Bruce Smith, 1945-48	1	1	0	0/0	0	0/0	1	14
Marques Anderson, 2002-03	0	0	2	0/0	0	0/0	0	12
Carl Bland, 1989-90	0	1	1	0/0	0	0/0	0	12
Tom Brown, 1964-68	0	0	2	0/0	0	0/0	0	12
Terrell Buckley, 1992-94	0	0	2	0/0	0	0/0	0	12
Lee Roy Caffey, 1965-69	0	0	2	0/0	0	0/0	0	12
Jack Clancy, 1970	0	2	0	0/0	0	0/0	0	12
Bill (Gus) DuMoe, 1921	2	0	0	0	0	0	0	12
Preston Dennard, 1985	0	2	0	0/0	0	0/0	0	12
Clint Didier, 1988-89	0	2	0	0/0	0	0/0	0	12
Dick Flaherty, 1926	0	2	0	0	0	0	0	12
Terry Glenn, 2002	0	2	0	0/0	0	0/0	0	12
Cal Hubbard, 1929-33, 35	0	1	1	0	0	0	0	12
Jack Jacobs, 1947-49	2	0	0	0/0	0	0/0	0	12
Claudis James, 1967-69	0	2	0	0/0	0	0/0	0	12
Bob Jeter, 1963-70	0	0	2	0/0	0	0/0	0	12
Chester Johnston, 1931, 34-37	1	1	0	0	0	0	0	12
Charles Jordan, 1994-95, 99	0	2	0	0/0	0	0/0	0	12
Walt Landers, 1978-79	0	1	1	0/0	0	0/0	0	12
Gary Lewis, 1981-84	1	1	0	0/0	0	0/0	0	12
Mark Lewis, 1985-87	0	2	0	0/0	0	0/0	0	12
Tim Lewis, 1983-86	0	0	2	0/0	0	0/0	0	12
Larry Marks, 1928	0	2	0	0	0	0	0	12
John Martinkovic, 1951-56	0	0	2	0/0	0	0/0	0	12
Joel Mason, 1942-45	0	2	0	0/0	0	0/0	0	12
Aubrey Matthews, 1988-89	0	2	0	0/0	0	0/0	0	12
Mike McKenzie, 1999-03	0	0	2	0/0	0	0/0	0	12
Rondell Mealey, 2001-02	1	0	1	0/0	0	0/0	0	12
Mike Michalske, 1929-35, 37	0	0	2	0	0	0	0	12
Blake Moore, 1984-85	0	0	0	0/0	0	0/0	0	12
Ray Nitschke, 1958-72	0	0	2	0/0	0	0/0	0	12

A Measure of Greatness

Name	TDr	TDp	TDrt	PAT	2pt	FG	S	TP
De'Mond Parker, 1999-00	2	0	0	0/0	0	0/0	0	12
Allen Rossum, 2000-01	0	0	2	0/0	0	0/0	0	12
Art Schmaehl, 1921	0	1	1	0	0	0	0	12
Herm Schneidman, 1935-39	0	2	0	0	0	0	0	12
Ben Starret, 1942-45	2	0	0	0/0	0	0/0	0	12
John Thompson, 1979-82	0	2	0	0/0	0	0/0	0	12
Cowboy Wheeler, 1921-23	0	1	1	0	0	0	0	12
Gabe Wilkins, 1994-97	0	0	2	0/0	0	0/0	0	12
Tyrone Williams, 1996-02	0	0	2	0/0	0	0/0	0	12
Ben Wilson, 1967	2	0	0	0/0	0	0/0	0	12
Charles Wilson, 1990-91	0	1	1	0/0	0	0/0	0	12
Faye (Mule) Wilson, 1931	2	0	0	0	0	0	0	12
Ben Agajanian, 1961	0	0	0	8/8	0	1/2	0	11
John Anderson, 1978-89	0	0	1	1/2	0	1/1	0	10
Dale Dawson, 1988	0	0	0	1/2	0	3/5	0	10
Tim Harris, 1986-90	0	0	1	0/0	0	0/0	2	10
Whitey Woodin, 1922-31	0	0	1	4	0	0	0	10
George Abramson, 1925	0	0	0	2	0	2	0	8
Robert Brown, 1982-92	0	0	1	0/0	0	0/0	1	8
Bryce Paup, 1990-94	0	0	1	0/0	0	0/0	1	8
Frank Balazs, 1939-41	1	0	0	1/1	0	0/0	0	7
Nate Abrams, 1921	0	0	1	0	0	0	0	6
Lionel Aldridge, 1963-71	0	0	1	0/0	0	0/0	0	6
Bill Anderson, 1965-66	0	1	0	0/0	0	0/0	0	6
Bert Askson, 1975-77	0	1	0	0/0	0	0/0	0	6
Frank Baker, 1931	0	1	0	0	0	0	0	6
Norm Barry, 1921	1	0	0	0	0	0	0	6
Don Barton, 1953	0	1	0	0/0	0	0/0	0	6
Sanjay Beach, 1992	0	1	0	0/0	0	0/0	0	6
Wayland Becker, 1936-38	0	1	0	0	0	0	0	6
Tony Bennett, 1990-93	0	0	1	0/0	0	0/0	0	6
J.R. Boone, 1953	0	1	0	0/0	0	0/0	0	6
Zeke Bratkowski, 1963-68, 71	1	0	0	0/0	0	0/0	0	6
Mark Brunell, 1994	1	0	0	0/0	0	0/0	0	6
Bill Butler, 1959	0	0	1	0/0	0	0/0	0	6
Mike Butler, 1977-82, 85	0	0	1	0/0	0	0/0	0	6
Ivan Cahoon, 1926-29	0	0	1	0	0	0	0	6
Lew Carpenter, 1959-63	1	0	0	0/0	0	0/0	0	6
Fred Carr, 1968-77	0	0	1	0/0	0	0/0	0	6
Jim Carter, 1970-75, 77-78	0	0	1	0/0	0	0/0	0	6
Joe Carter, 1942	0	1	0	0/0	0	0/0	0	6
Paul Christman, 1950	1	0	0	0/0	0	0/0	0	6
Jack Concannon, 1974	1	0	0	0/0	0	0/0	0	6
Larry Craig, 1939-49	0	0	1	0/0	0	0/0	0	6
Bernie Crimmins, 1945	0	0	1	0/0	0	0/0	0	6
Tommy Cronin, 1922	0	1	0	0	0	0	0	6
Ray Crouse, 1984	0	1	0	0/0	0	0/0	0	6
Jim Crowley, 1925	0	1	0	0	0	0	0	6
Dan Currie, 1958-64	0	0	1	0/0	0	0/0	0	6
Gib Dawson, 1953	0	1	0	0/0	0	0/0	0	6
Dave Davis, 1971	0	1	0	0/0	0	0/0	0	6
Dean Dorsey, 1988	0	0	0	3/4	0	1/3	0	6
Wally Dreyer, 1950	0	0	1	0/0	0	0/0	0	6
Antuan Edwards, 1999-03	0	0	1	0/0	0	0/0	0	6
Doug Evans, 1993-97	0	0	1	0/0	0	0/0	0	6
Tony Falkenstein, 1943	1	0	0	0/0	0	0/0	0	6
Bobby Jack Floyd, 1952	1	0	0	0/0	0	0/0	0	6
Joe Francis, 1958-59	1	0	0	0/0	0	0/0	0	6
Moose Gardner, 1922-26	0	0	1	0	0	0	0	6
Kabeer Gbaja-Biamila, 2000-03	0	0	1	0/0	0	0/0	0	6
Jim Gillette, 1947	0	1	0	0/0	0	0/0	0	6
Leland Glass, 1972-73	0	1	0	0/0	0	0/0	0	6
Les Goodman, 1973-74	1	0	0	0/0	0	0/0	0	6
Johnnie Gray, 1975-84	0	0	1	0/0	0	0/0	0	6
Tiger Greene, 1986-90	0	0	1	0/0	0	0/0	0	6
Tom Greenfield, 1939-41	0	0	1	0/0	0	0/0	0	6
Hank Gremminger, 1956-65	0	0	1	0/0	0	0/0	0	6
Joey Hackett, 1987-88	0	1	0	0/0	0	0/0	0	6
James Hargrove, 1987	1	0	0	0/0	0	0/0	0	6
Al Harris, 2003	0	0	1	0/0	0	0/0	0	6
Raymont Harris, 1998	1	0	0	0/0	0	0/0	0	6
Maurice Harvey, 1981-83	0	0	1	0/0	0	0/0	0	6
Aaron Hayden, 1997	1	0	0	0/0	0	0/0	0	6
Les Hearden, 1924	0	1	0	0	0	0	0	6
Stan Heath, 1949	1	0	0	0/0	0	0/0	0	6
Darick Holmes, 1998	1	0	0	0/0	0	0/0	0	6
Estus Hood, 1978-84	0	0	1	0/0	0	0/0	0	6
Don Horn, 1967-70	1	0	0	0/0	0	0/0	0	6
Lynn (Tubby) Howard, 1921-22	1	0	0	0	0	0	0	6
Bob Ingalls, 1942	0	0	1	0/0	0	0/0	0	6
Jim Jensen, 1981-82	1	0	0	0/0	0	0/0	0	6
Travis Jervey, 1995-98	1	0	0	0/0	0	0/0	0	6
Glen Johnson, 1949	0	0	1	0/0	0	0/0	0	6
Randy Johnson, 1976	1	0	0	0/0	0	0/0	0	6
Bruce Jones, 1927-28	0	0	1	0	0	0	0	6
Sean Jones, 1994-96	0	0	1	0/0	0	0/0	0	6
Henry Jordan, 1959-69	0	0	1	0/0	0	0/0	0	6
Jim Keane, 1952	0	1	0	0/0	0	0/0	0	6
Bill Kelley, 1949	0	1	0	0/0	0	0/0	0	6
Blair Kiel, 1990-91	1	0	0	0/0	0	0/0	0	6
George Koonce, 1992-99	0	0	1	0/0	0	0/0	0	6
Larry Krause, 1970-71, 73-74	0	0	1	0/0	0	0/0	0	6
Bill Larsen, 1980	0	1	0	0/0	0	0/0	0	6
Charles Lee, 2000-01	0	1	0	0/0	0	0/0	0	6
Mark Lee, 1980-90	0	0	1	0/0	0	0/0	0	6
Ace Loomis, 1951-53	0	0	1	0/0	0	0/0	0	6
Steve Luke, 1975-80	0	0	1	0/0	0	0/0	0	6
Larry Mason, 1988	0	1	0	0/0	0	0/0	0	6
Al Matthews, 1970-75	0	0	1	0/0	0	0/0	0	6
Mike P. McCoy, 1970-76	0	0	1	0/0	0	0/0	0	6
Lamar McHan, 1959-60	1	0	0	0/0	0	0/0	0	6
Steve Meilinger, 1958, 60	0	1	0	0/0	0	0/0	0	6
Basil Mitchell, 1999-00	0	0	1	0/0	0	0/0	0	6
Lee Morris, 1987	0	1	0	0/0	0	0/0	0	6
Mark Murphy, 1980-85, 87-91	0	0	1	0/0	0	0/0	0	6
Ed Neal, 1945-51	0	0	1	0/0	0	0/0	0	6
Brian Noble, 1985-93	0	0	1	0/0	0	0/0	0	6
Dan Orlich, 1949-51	0	1	0	0/0	0	0/0	0	6
Ernie Pannell, 1941-42, 45	0	0	1	0/0	0	0/0	0	6
Johnny Papit, 1953	1	0	0	0/0	0	0/0	0	6
Keith Paskett, 1987	0	1	0	0/0	0	0/0	0	6
Shawn Patterson, 1988-91, 93	0	0	1	0/0	0	0/0	0	6
Ron Pitts, 1988-90	0	0	1	0/0	0	0/0	0	6
Keith Ranspot, 1942	0	1	0	0/0	0	0/0	0	6
Ray Riddick, 1940-42, 46	0	1	0	0/0	0	0/0	0	6
Alan Risher, 1987	1	0	0	0/0	0	0/0	0	6
Andre Rison, 1996	0	1	0	0/0	0	0/0	0	6
John Roach, 1961-63	1	0	0	0/0	0	0/0	0	6
Ken Roskie, 1948	1	0	0	0/0	0	0/0	0	6
Dan Ross, 1986	0	1	0	0/0	0	0/0	0	6
Russ Saunders, 1931	1	0	0	0	0	0	0	6
Francis (Zud) Schammel, 1937	0	0	1	0	0	0	0	6
Patrick Scott, 1987-88	0	1	0	0/0	0	0/0	0	6
John Simmons, 1986	0	0	1	0/0	0	0/0	0	6
Nate Simpson, 1977-79	1	0	0	0/0	0	0/0	0	6
Ollie Smith, 1976-77	0	1	0	0/0	0	0/0	0	6
John Spilis, 1969-71	0	1	0	0/0	0	0/0	0	6
Rebel Steiner, 1950-51	0	0	1	0/0	0	0/0	0	6
John Stephens, 1993	1	0	0	0/0	0	0/0	0	6
Ken Stills, 1985-88	0	0	1	0/0	0	0/0	0	6
Bob Summerhays, 1949-51	0	0	1	0/0	0	0/0	0	6
Don Summers, 1987	0	1	0	0/0	0	0/0	0	6
Earl Svendsen, 1937, 39	0	0	1	0/0	0	0/0	0	6
Karl Swanke, 1980-86	0	1	0	0/0	0	0/0	0	6
Len Szafaryn, 1950, 53-56	0	0	1	0/0	0	0/0	0	6
Claude Taugher, 1922	1	0	0	0	0	0	0	6
Cliff Taylor, 1976	1	0	0	0/0	0	0/0	0	6
Kitrick Taylor, 1992	0	1	0	0/0	0	0/0	0	6
Lavale Thomas, 1987-88	0	1	0	0/0	0	0/0	0	6
Gerald Tinker, 1975	0	1	0	0/0	0	0/0	0	6
Mike Tomczak, 1991	1	0	0	0/0	0	0/0	0	6
Walter Tullis, 1978-79	0	1	0	0/0	0	0/0	0	6
Alex Urban, 1941, 44-45	0	1	0	0/0	0	0/0	0	6
Eddie Usher, 1922, 24	1	0	0	0	0	0	0	6
Val Joe Walker, 1953-56	0	0	1	0/0	0	0/0	0	6
Wesley Walls, 2003	0	1	0	0/0	0	0/0	0	6
Clarence Weathers, 1990-91	0	1	0	0/0	0	0/0	0	6
Jess Whittenton, 1958-64	0	0	1	0/0	0	0/0	0	6
Marcus Wilkins, 2002-03	0	0	1	0/0	0	0/0	0	6
Clarence Williams, 1970-77	0	0	1	0/0	0	0/0	0	6
Perry Williams, 1969-73	1	0	0	0/0	0	0/0	0	6
Paul Winslow, 1960	0	0	1	0/0	0	0/0	0	6
Dave Conway, 1971	0	0	0	5/5	0	0/1	0	5
Joe Etheridge, 1949	0	0	0	1/1	0	1/2	0	4
Errol Mann, 1968	0	0	0	4/4	0	0/3	0	4
Dave Pureifory, 1972-77	0	0	0	2/4	0	0/0	1	4
Herman Rohrig, 1941, 46-47	0	0	0	1/1	0	1/1	0	4
Chet Adams, 1943	0	0	0	0/0	0	1/6	0	3
Greg Boyd, 1983	0	0	0	0/0	0	0/0	1	2
Bob Brown, 1966-73	0	0	0	0/0	0	0/0	1	2
Curtis Burrow, 1988	0	0	0	2/4	0	0/1	0	2
Bill Forester, 1953-64	0	0	0	0/0	0	0/0	1	2
Dave Hanner, 1952-64	0	0	0	0/0	0	0/0	1	2
Ted Hendricks, 1974	0	0	0	0/0	0	0/0	1	2
Russell Maryland, 2000	0	0	0	0/0	0	0/0	1	2
Walter Niemann, 1922-24	0	0	0	0	0	0	1	2
Urban Odson, 1946-49	0	0	0	0/0	0	0/0	1	2
John Thierry, 2000-01	0	0	0	0/0	0	0/0	1	2
Tom Toner, 1973-77	0	0	0	0/0	0	0/0	1	2
Dick Weisgerber, 1938-40, 42	0	0	0	2/2	0	0/0	0	2
Dick Wildung, 1946-51, 53	0	0	0	0/0	0	0/0	1	2
Cal Clemmens, 1936	0	0	0	1	0	0	0	1
Glen Sorenson, 1943-45	0	0	0	1/1	0	0/5	0	1
Clayton Tonnemaker, 1950, 53-54	0	0	0	1/1	0	0/0	0	1
Rich Wingo, 1979, 81-83	0	0	0	1	0	0/0	0	1
Walt Michaels, 1951	0	0	0	0/0	0	0/1	0	0
team	0	0	0	0	0	1	20	41
Packers, 1921-2003	**1,051**	**1,387**	**240**	**2,420**	**12**	**1,031**	**42**	**21,689**
Opponents, 1921-2003	972	1,096	231	2,076	22	1,047	47	19,151

ALL-TIME FUMBLES AND RECOVERIES

(Statistic kept since 1945; players are listed alphabetically)

Name	Fum	Own Rec	Opp Rec	Yds	Tot Rec
Cliff Aberson, 1941, 46-47	2	0	1	0	1
Herb Adderley, 1961-69	9	5	8	60	13
Bob Adkins, 1940-41, 45	1	1	0	0	1
Chris Akins, 2000-01	1	0	0	0	0
Ben Aldridge, 1953	0	0	2	0	2
Lionel Aldridge, 1963-71	1	0	16	44	16
Kurt Allerman, 1980-81	0	0	1	0	1
Donny Anderson, 1966-71	31	5	0	-5	5
John Anderson, 1978-89	0	0	15	22	15
Marques Anderson, 2002-03	0	0	4	1	4
Vickey Ray Anderson, 1980	1	0	0	0	0
Joe Andruzzi, 1998-99	0	1	0	0	1
Charlie Ane, 1981	0	1	1	0	2
Billy Ard, 1989-91	0	2	0	0	2
Mike Arthur, 1995-96	1	0	0	0	0
Bert Askson, 1975-77	0	0	1	0	1
Steve Atkins, 1979-81	3	1	0	0	1
Buddy Aydelette, 1980	1	0	0	-28	0
Byron Bailey, 1953	1	0	0	0	0
Al Baldwin, 1950	3	1	0	-3	1
Bob Barber, 1976-79	0	0	4	0	4
Nick Barnett, 2003	0	0	1	0	1
Carl Barzilauskas, 1978-79	0	0	1	0	1
Lloyd Baxter, 1948	0	0	1	0	1
Sanjay Beach, 1992	1	1	0	0	1
Don Beebe, 1996-97	1	1	0	0	1
Ed Bell, 1947-49	0	1	0	0	1
Edgar Bennett, 1992-96	7	4	0	0	4
Tony Bennett, 1990-93	0	0	4	18	4
Ed Berry, 1986	0	0	1	0	1
Tom Bettis, 1955-61	0	0	5	4	5
David Beverly, 1975-80	3	2	0	-16	2
Josh Bidwell, 2000-03	1	1	0	0	1
Lewis Billups, 1992	0	0	1	0	1
Carl Bland, 1989-90	0	2	2	4	4
Steve Bono, 1997	1	0	0	0	0
Billy Bookout, 1955-56	0	1	2	0	3
J.R. Boone, 1953	1	1	0	0	1
Nate Borden, 1955-59	0	0	7	0	7
David Bowens, 2000	0	0	1	0	1
Ken Bowman, 1964-73	2	3	0	-28	3
Corey Bradford, 1998-01	3	0	0	0	0
Dave Bradley, 1969-71	0	0	1	0	1
Byron Braggs, 1981-83	0	0	2	0	2
Zeke Bratkowski, 1963-68, 71	10	5	0	0	5
Charley Brock, 1939-47	0	2	11	83	13
Lou Brock, 1940-45	1	0	0	0	0
Matt Brock, 1989-94	0	0	3	34	3
John Brockington, 1971-77	23	6	0	0	6
Robert Brooks, 1992-98	5	2	0	0	2
Bill Brown, 1953-56	0	2	1	0	3
Bob Brown, 1966-73	0	0	1	0	1
Carlos Brown, 1975-76	3	3	0	-2	3
Gilbert Brown, 1993-99, 2001-03	0	0	1	0	1
Ken Brown, 1980	1	0	0	-37	0
Robert Brown, 1982-92	0	0	13	0	13
Tom Brown, 1964-68	0	0	6	27	6
Mark Brunell, 1994	1	0	0	-2	0
Willie Buchanon, 1972-78	1	0	8	9	8
Terrell Buckley, 1992-94	8	3	2	0	5
Hank Bullough, 1955, 58	0	0	1	0	1
Paul (Buddy) Burris, 1949-51	0	1	1	0	2
Blair Bush, 1989-91	0	2	0	0	2
Bill Butler, 1959	1	1	0	0	1
LeRoy Butler, 1990-01	0	2	8	76	10
Mike Butler, 1977-82, 85	0	0	3	70	3
Mossy Cade, 1985-86	0	0	1	0	1
Lee Roy Caffey, 1964-69	0	1	3	0	4
Rich Campbell, 1981-84	0	0	0	0	0
James Campen, 1989-93	2	2	0	-21	2
Tony Canadeo, 1941-44, 46-52	23	5	0	2	5
Al Cannava, 1950	0	0	0	0	0
Mark Cannon, 1985-88	3	2	0	-39	2
Jim Capuzzi, 1955-56	0	0	1	0	1
Al Carmichael, 1953-58	16	3	0	0	3
Lew Carpenter, 1959-63	8	0	1	0	1
Fred Carr, 1968-77	0	0	15	64	15
Alphonso Carreker, 1984-88	0	0	3	0	3
Leo Carroll, 1968	0	0	1	0	1
Paul Ott Carruth, 1986-88	5	0	0	0	0
Jim Carter, 1970-75, 77-78	0	0	7	19	7
Ron Cassidy, 1979-81, 83-84	2	0	0	0	0
Chuck Cecil, 1988-92	1	0	1	0	1
Bill Cherry, 1986-87	1	0	0	-23	0
Mark Chmura, 1993-99	3	1	0	0	1
Putt Choate, 1987	0	0	1	4	1
Paul Christman, 1950	2	0	0	0	0
Gus Cifelli, 1953	0	1	0	0	1
Bob Cifers, 1949	0	0	1	5	1
Dennis Claridge, 1965	1	0	0	0	0
Allan Clark, 1982	1	1	0	0	1

Name	Fum	Own Rec	Opp Rec	Yds	Tot Rec
Jessie Clark, 1983-87	9	3	0	0	3
Chad Clifton, 2000-03	1	1	0	0	1
Jack Cloud, 1950-51	3	1	0	0	1
Reggie Cobb, 1994	1	0	0	0	0
Ed Cody, 1947-48	4	1	0	0	1
Junior Coffey, 1965	0	0	1	0	1
Paul Coffman, 1978-85	8	1	1	0	2
Keo Coleman, 1993	0	0	1	0	1
Irv Comp, 1943-49	16	9	4	-1	13
Fred Cone, 1951-57	14	6	2	5	8
Ted Cook, 1948-50	2	0	1	2	1
Kerry Cooks, 1998	0	0	1	0	1
Larry Coutre, 1950, 53	1	0	0	0	0
Larry Craig, 1939-49	0	2	9	21	11
Ted Cremer, 1948	0	0	1	0	1
Milburn (Tiny) Croft, 1942-47	0	0	3	16	3
Jim Culbreath, 1977-79	2	3	0	0	3
George Cumby, 1980-85	0	0	5	70	5
Dan Currie, 1958-64	0	0	6	0	6
Bill Curry, 1965-66	0	1	0	0	1
Carroll Dale, 1965-72	4	1	0	0	1
Ernie Danjean, 1957	0	0	1	0	1
Najeh Davenport, 2002-03	5	0	0	-8	0
Dave Davis, 1971-72	1	0	1	18	1
Harper Davis, 1951	0	0	1	0	1
Kenneth Davis, 1986-88	4	0	0	0	0
Rob Davis, 1997-03	0	0	1	0	1
Tyrone Davis, 1997-02	3	0	1	0	1
Willie Davis, 1960-69	0	1	21	19	22
Gib Dawson, 1953	1	0	0	0	0
Walter Dean, 1991	1	0	0	0	0
Jim Del Gaizo, 1973	3	2	0	0	2
Jeff Dellenbach, 1996-98	0	2	0	0	2
Preston Dennard, 1985	1	0	0	0	0
Burnell Dent, 1986-92	0	0	2	0	2
Ty Detmer, 1993, 95	1	1	0	0	1
Lynn Dickey, 1976-77, 79-85	56	26	0	-82	26
Clint Didier, 1988-89	1	0	1	4	1
Na'il Diggs, 2000-03	0	0	3	52	3
Bobby Dillon, 1952-59	0	0	3	0	3
Anthony Dilweg, 1989-90	10	4	0	-9	4
John Dittrich, 1959	0	0	1	0	1
Mike Donohoe, 1973-74	0	0	1	2	1
John Dorsey, 1984-88	0	0	4	0	4
Earl Dotson, 1993-02	0	3	0	0	3
Santana Dotson, 1996-01	0	0	2	8	2
Mike Douglass, 1978-85	1	1	15	63	16
Boyd Dowler, 1959-69	8	0	0	0	0
Donald Driver, 1999-03	1	4	0	0	4
Ralph Earhart, 1948-49	5	2	0	0	2
Antuan Edwards, 1999-03	1	0	1	-2	1
Gary Ellerson, 1985-86	6	2	1	0	3
Carleton Elliott, 1951-54	0	0	2	17	2
Gerry Ellis, 1980-86	33	9	0	0	9
Ken Ellis, 1970-75	7	2	4	11	6
Phillip Epps, 1982-88	6	1	0	0	1
Joe Etheridge, 1949	0	1	0	0	1
Doug Evans, 1993-97	2	0	4	5	4
Hal Faverty, 1952	0	0	3	0	3
Brett Favre, 1992-03	116	29	0	-100	29
Howie Ferguson, 1953-58	29	7	0	0	7
Robert Ferguson, 2001-03	0	1	0	0	1
Vince Ferragamo, 1985	3	0	0	-8	0
Lou Ferry, 1949	0	0	2	0	2
Tony Fisher, 2002-03	2	0	0	0	0
Mike Flanagan, 1998-03	3	1	0	-18	1
Jim Flanigan, 1967-70	0	0	1	0	1
Marv Fleming, 1963-69	0	0	1	0	1
Bob Flowers, 1942-49	0	0	2	1	2
Bobby Jack Floyd, 1952	5	1	0	0	1
Tom Flynn, 1984-86	1	0	4	3	4
Herman Fontenot, 1989-90	1	1	2	0	3
Len Ford, 1958	0	0	1	5	1
Bill Forester, 1953-63	3	2	13	45	15
Aldo Forte, 1947	0	0	2	1	2
Bob Forte, 1946-50, 52-53	4	2	9	3	11
Joe Francis, 1958-59	3	0	0	0	0
Bubba Franks, 2000-03	1	0	0	0	0
Todd Franz, 2002	0	0	1	0	1
Antonio Freeman, 1995-01, 03	14	7	0	14	7
Ted Fritsch, 1942-50	10	4	5	-1	9
Brent Fullwood, 1987-90	15	3	0	0	3
Chuck Fusina, 1986	4	4	0	-1	4
Bob Garrett, 1954	2	1	0	0	1
Len Garrett, 1971-72	0	0	1	0	1
Lester Gatewood, 1946-47	0	1	1	0	2
Kabeer Gbaja-Biamila, 2000-03	0	0	4	0	4
Jim Gillette, 1947	2	0	0	0	0
Gale Gillingham, 1966-74, 76	0	2	0	0	2

Name	Fum	Own Rec	Opp Rec	Yds	Tot Rec
Earl (Jug) Girard, 1948-51	8	3	1	5	4
Leland Glass, 1972-73	0	1	0	0	1
Terry Glenn, 2002	1	0	0	0	0
Derrel Gofourth, 1977-82	0	2	0	0	2
Herbert Goodman, 2000-01	2	0	0	0	0
Les Goodman, 1973-74	3	0	0	0	0
Clyde Goodnight, 1945-49	3	2	0	8	2
Darrien Gordon, 2002	5	1	0	0	1
Jim Grabowski, 1966-70	13	1	0	0	1
Johnnie Gray, 1975-84	6	2	20	30	22
Ahman Green, 2000-03	22	6	0	0	6
George (Tiger) Greene, 1986-90	1	0	3	0	3
Forrest Gregg, 1956, 58-70	0	8	0	0	8
Hank Gremminger, 1956-65	1	0	7	0	7
Billy Grimes, 1950-52	18	5	0	0	5
Dan Grimm, 1963-65	0	0	1	0	1
Earl Gros, 1962-63	7	1	1	0	2
Jim Gueno, 1976-80	0	3	1	0	4
Michael Haddix, 1989-90	5	0	0	0	0
John Hadl, 1974-75	11	3	0	-12	3
Charlie Hall, 1971-76	1	1	0	0	1
Ron Hallstrom, 1982-92	0	4	1	1	5
Dave Hampton, 1969-71	17	4	0	0	4
Dave Hanner, 1952-64	0	1	8	0	9
Derrick Harden, 1987	1	0	0	0	0
Leon Harden, 1970	0	0	0	0	0
Roger Harding, 1949	0	1	0	0	1
Willard Harrell, 1975-77	23	2	1	0	3
Al Harris, 2003	1	0	0	0	0
Bernardo Harris, 1995-01	0	1	3	0	4
Corey Harris, 1992-94	1	0	0	0	1
Jackie Harris, 1990-92	2	0	1	0	1
Leotis Harris, 1978-83	0	3	0	0	3
Raymont Harris, 1998	3	0	0	0	0
Tim Harris, 1986-90	0	0	6	28	6
Anthony Harrison, 1987	0	0	1	0	1
Doug Hart, 1964-71	0	0	5	20	5
Maurice Harvey, 1981-83	1	1	5	25	6
Matt Hasselbeck, 1999-00	1	1	0	-16	1
Tim Hauck, 1991-94	0	0	2	0	2
Gary Hayes, 1984-86	1	1	2	0	3
Bill Hayhoe, 1969-74	0	1	0	0	1
Stan Heath, 1949	2	0	0	0	0
Larry Hefner, 1972-75	0	1	1	4	2
Jerry Helluin, 1954-57	0	0	6	0	6
William Henderson, 1995-03	5	5	0	0	5
Ted Hendricks, 1974	0	0	1	0	1
Craig Hentrich, 1994-97	0	1	0	0	1
Don Highsmith, 1973	1	0	0	0	0
Jim Hill, 1972-74	0	0	5	15	5
John Hilton, 1970	1	0	2	0	2
Dick Himes, 1968-77	0	3	0	1	3
Jim Hobbins, 1987	0	1	0	0	1
Johnny Holland, 1987-93	4	1	14	3	15
Vonnie Holliday, 1998-02	0	0	6	11	6
Darick Holmes, 1998	1	1	0	0	1
Jerry Holmes, 1990-91	0	0	4	56	4
Estus Hood, 1978-84	0	0	2	0	2
Don Horn, 1967-70	11	4	0	0	4
Paul Hornung, 1957-62, 64-66	22	2	1	0	3
Desmond Howard, 1996, 99	2	1	0	0	1
Bill Howton, 1952-58	5	2	0	0	2
Harlan Huckleby, 1980-85	8	2	0	0	2
Bob Hudson, 1972	1	0	0	0	0
Donnie Humphrey, 1984-86	0	0	1	0	1
Cletidus Hunt, 1999-03	0	0	5	0	5
Mike Hunt, 1978-80	0	0	1	0	1
Art Hunter, 1954	0	1	0	0	1
Scott Hunter, 1971-73	13	5	0	-11	5
Don Hutson, 1935-45	1	0	0	0	0
Bob Hyland, 1967-69, 76	1	0	0	0	0
Ken Iman, 1960-63	0	0	1	0	1
Mark Ingram, 1995	1	0	0	0	0
Eddie Lee Ivery, 1979-86	9	2	2	0	4
Jack Jacobs, 1947-49	6	2	1	-3	3
Claudis James, 1967-69	2	0	0	0	0
John Jefferson, 1981-84	1	0	0	0	0
Norman Jefferson, 1987-88	5	1	1	0	2
Jim Jennings, 1955	0	0	1	0	1
Jim Jensen, 1981-82	2	0	0	0	0
Travis Jervey, 1995-98	4	0	2	0	2
Bob Jeter, 1963-70	0	0	2	7	2
Charles Johnson, 1979-80, 83	0	0	2	0	2
Ezra Johnson, 1977-87	0	0	7	0	7
Joe Johnson, 1954-58	6	0	0	0	0
Joe Johnson, 2002-03	0	0	1	0	1
KeShon Johnson, 1994	0	0	1	0	1
Marvin Johnson, 1952-53	0	0	1	0	1
Randy Johnson, 1976	2	1	0	-4	1
Mike Jolly, 1980, 82-83	0	1	0	0	1
Daryll Jones, 1984-85	0	1	2	0	3
Sean Jones, 1994-96	0	0	5	0	5
Terry Jones, 1978-84	0	0	5	0	5
Charles Jordan, 1994-95, 99	3	2	0	0	2
Henry Jordan, 1959-69	0	2	18	67	20
Bhawoh Jue, 2001-03	0	1	0	0	1
Aaron Kampman, 2002-03	0	0	1	0	1
Bill Kelley, 1949	1	0	0	0	0
Perry Kemp, 1988-91	10	0	0	0	0
Ken Keuper, 1945-47	0	0	3	0	3
Blair Kiel, 1990-91	4	2	0	0	2
J.D. Kimmel, 1958	0	0	1	0	1
Billy Kinard, 1957-58	2	0	2	14	2
John Kirby, 1949	3	0	0	0	0
Gary Knafelc, 1954-62	0	1	0	0	1
Gene Knutson, 1954, 56	0	0	1	0	1
Matt Koart, 1986	0	0	1	0	1
Greg Koch, 1978-85	0	1	0	0	1
Mark Koncar, 1976-77, 79-81	0	2	0	0	2
George Koonce, 1992-99	0	0	6	4	6
Dave Kopay, 1972	1	0	1	0	1
Ron Kostelnik, 1961-68	0	0	7	0	7
Jerry Kramer, 1958-68	0	3	0	13	3
Ron Kramer, 1957, 59-64	3	1	0	0	1
Kenneth Kranz, 1949	0	0	1	7	1
Larry Krause, 1970-71, 73-74	3	0	3	0	3
Bob Kroll, 1972-73	0	0	1	0	1
Pete Lammons, 1972	0	1	0	0	1
MacArthur Lane, 1972-74	13	2	0	0	2
Kit Lathrop, 1979-80	0	2	0	0	2
Larry Lauer, 1956-57	0	0	1	0	1
Joe Laws, 1934-45	2	1	1	2	1
Mark Lee, 1980-90	2	0	6	15	6
Paris Lenon, 2002-03	0	1	0	0	1
Dorsey Levens, 1994-01	12	2	0	-7	2
Gary Lewis, 1981-84	0	1	0	0	1
Tim Lewis, 1983-86	3	1	1	6	2
Paul Lipscomb, 1945-49	0	2	9	1	11
Dick Logan, 1952-53	0	1	0	0	1
James Lofton, 1978-86	14	3	0	8	3
Ace Loomis, 1951-53	2	0	5	0	5
John Losch, 1956	3	3	0	0	3
Bill Lueck, 1968-74	0	1	0	0	1
Nolan Luhn, 1945-49	2	1	1	4	2
Steve Luke, 1975-80	1	0	6	0	6
Tom MacLeod, 1973	0	0	2	0	2
Don Majkowski, 1987-92	48	19	0	-26	19
Tony Mandarich, 1989-91	0	1	0	0	1
Von Mansfield, 1987	1	0	0	0	0
Rich Marshall, 1965	0	0	1	0	1
Torrance Marshall, 2001-03	0	1	2	0	3
Charles Martin, 1984-86	0	0	2	0	2
David Martin, 2001-03	0	1	0	0	1
John Martinkovic, 1951-56	0	0	10	32	10
Dave Mason, 1974	0	0	1	19	1
Joel Mason, 1942-45	0	0	1	0	1
Carlton Massey, 1957-58	0	0	1	0	1
Norm Masters, 1957-64	0	4	0	0	4
Al Matthews, 1970-75	0	0	7	-7	7
Derrick Mayes, 1996-98	1	0	0	0	0
Tod McBride, 1999-02	0	0	5	9	5
Larry McCarren, 1973-84	1	1	0	0	1
Mike C. McCoy, 1976-83	0	1	4	0	5
Mike P. McCoy, 1970-76	1	0	12	36	12
John McDowell, 1964	0	0	1	0	1
Scott McGarrahan, 1998-00	0	1	0	0	1
Clink McGeary, 1950	0	1	0	0	1
Max McGee, 1954, 57-67	6	4	0	43	4
Rich McGeorge, 1970-78	2	5	2	0	7
Lenny McGill, 1994-95	0	1	0	0	1
Michael McGruder, 1989	0	1	0	0	1
Lamar McHan, 1959-60	3	0	0	0	0
Don McIlhenny, 1957-59	13	4	0	0	4
Paul McJulien, 1991-92	1	0	2	-2	2
Roy McKay, 1944-47	6	4	0	10	4
Keith McKenzie, 1996-99, 02	0	1	7	151	8
Mike McKenzie, 1999-03	1	0	1	0	1
Raleigh McKenzie, 1999-00	0	1	0	0	1
Mike McLeod, 1984-85	0	1	0	0	1
Jim McMahon, 1995-96	1	1	0	0	1
Steve McMichael, 1994	0	0	1	0	1
Mike Meade, 1982-83	2	1	0	0	1
Rondell Mealey, 2001-02	0	0	1	27	1
Chuck Mercein, 1967-69	1	0	1	0	1
Casey Merrill, 1979-83	0	0	4	0	4
Frank Mestnik, 1963	0	1	0	0	1
Eric Metcalf, 2002	1	1	0	0	1
Terry Mickens, 1994-97	0	1	0	0	1
Terdell Middleton, 1977-81	18	4	0	0	4
Don Milan, 1975	1	0	0	0	0
Keith Millard, 1992	0	0	1	0	1
Basil Mitchell, 1999-00	3	2	1	0	3
Roland Mitchell, 1991-92	0	0	1	0	1
Blake Moore, 1984-85	1	0	0	0	0
Rich Moore, 1969-70	0	0	1	0	1
Tom Moore, 1960-65	12	2	2	0	4
Rich Moran, 1985-92	1	3	0	3	3
Anthony Morgan, 1993-96	1	0	0	0	0
Lee Morris, 1987	0	1	1	0	2
Jim Morrisey, 1993	0	0	1	0	1
Dom Moselle, 1951-52	4	1	1	0	2
J.J. Moses, 2002	1	0	0	0	0
Perry Moss, 1948	3	1	0	-1	1
Roderick Mullen, 1995-97	0	0	1	1	1
Mark Murphy, 1980-85, 87-91	1	0	13	2	13
Hannibal Navies, 2003	0	0	1	0	1
Ed Neal, 1945-51	1	3	2	0	5
Frankie Neal, 1987	1	0	0	0	0

Name	Fum	Own Rec	Opp Rec	Yds	Tot Rec
Bob Nelson, 1988-90	0	0	1	0	1
Jim Nelson, 1999	0	0	1	0	1
Tom Neville, 1986-88, 92	0	1	0	0	1
Craig Newsome, 1995-98	0	0	1	0	1
Ray Nitschke, 1958-72	2	3	20	34	23
Doyle Nix, 1955	0	0	1	0	1
Fred Nixon, 1980-81	3	0	0	0	0
Brian Noble, 1985-93	0	0	11	1	11
Rick Norton, 1970	1	1	0	0	1
Bob Nussbaumer, 1946, 51	1	1	0	0	1
Rick Nuzum, 1978	0	0	1	15	1
Steve Odom, 1974-79	15	6	0	0	6
Urban Odson, 1946-49	0	0	3	0	3
Ralph Olsen, 1949	0	1	0	0	1
Larry Olsonoski, 1948-49	0	2	0	0	2
Andre O'Neal, 2001	0	0	1	0	1
Ed O'Neil, 1980	0	0	2	26	2
Dan Orlich, 1949-51	0	0	4	68	4
Vito (Babe) Parilli, 1952-53, 57-58	19	4	0	0	4
De'Mond Parker, 1999-00	1	1	1	0	2
Shawn Patterson, 1988-91, 93	0	0	1	0	1
Ricky Patton, 1979	1	0	0	0	0
Bryce Paup, 1990-94	0	1	3	0	4
Ken Payne, 1974-77	2	2	0	0	2
Francis Peay, 1968-72	0	1	0	0	1
Doug Pederson, 1996-98, 01-03	1	0	0	-2	0
Ray Pelfrey, 1951-52	1	0	0	0	0
Don Perkins, 1943-45	0	0	1	15	1
John Petitbon, 1957	0	0	1	0	1
Elijah Pitts, 1961-69, 71	14	3	1	0	4
Ron Pitts, 1988-90	1	2	3	0	5
Guy Prather, 1981-85	1	0	2	0	2
Roell Preston, 1997-98	7	1	0	0	1
Mike Prior, 1993-98	8	5	0	0	5
Steve Pritko, 1949-50	1	0	0	0	0
John Pointer, 1987	0	0	1	0	1
Fred Provo, 1948	1	0	1	0	1
Jim Psaltis, 1954	0	0	1	0	1
Dave Pureifory, 1972-77	0	0	4	11	4
Frank Purnell, 1957	1	1	0	0	1
Jeff Query, 1989-91	5	3	2	0	5
Bill Quinlan, 1959-62	1	0	2	0	2
Al Randolph, 1971	1	0	2	0	2
Buford (Baby) Ray, 1938-48	0	0	6	5	6
Bill Reichardt, 1952	1	0	0	0	0
Floyd (Breezy) Reid, 1950-56	15	7	0	2	7
Jamal Reynolds, 2001-03	0	0	2	1	2
Jay Rhodemyre, 1948-49, 51-52	0	1	1	0	2
Allen Rice, 1991	2	0	0	0	0
Jim Ringo, 1953-63	0	5	2	1	7
Alan Risher, 1987	4	1	0	0	1
Andre Rison, 1996	1	0	0	0	0
Marco Rivera, 1997-03	0	2	0	0	2
John Roach, 1961-63	4	1	0	0	1
Dave Robinson, 1963-72	1	1	8	23	9
Eugene Robinson, 1996-97	1	0	2	0	2
Alden Roche, 1971-76	0	0	8	17	8
Del Rodgers, 1982, 84	3	2	0	0	2
Herman Rohrig, 1941, 46-47	4	2	2	-2	4
Dave Roller, 1975-78	0	1	4	-4	5
Allen Rossum, 2000-01	4	3	0	0	3
Tobin Rote, 1950-56	44	10	0	-21	10
John Rowser, 1967-69	0	0	1	0	1
Larry Rubens, 1982-83	1	0	1	-15	1
T.J. Rubley, 1995	1	0	0	0	0
Ken Ruettgers, 1985-96	0	11	0	0	11
Howard Ruetz, 1951-53	0	0	3	13	3
Clive Rush, 1953	1	0	0	0	0
Steve Ruzich, 1952-54	1	2	1	0	3
Jim Salsbury, 1957-58	0	1	1	0	2
Howard Sampson, 1978-79	1	0	0	0	0
Hurles Scales, 1975	0	0	1	0	1
Walt Schlinkman, 1946-50	20	5	0	10	5
Bill Schroeder, 1997-01	10	1	0	0	1
Carl Schuette, 1950-51	0	0	3	8	3
Harry Schuh, 1974	0	2	0	0	2
Patrick Scott, 1987-88	2	2	0	0	2
Randy Scott, 1981-86	0	0	6	31	6
Clarence Self, 1952, 54-55	0	0	4	10	4
Washington Sereni, 1952	0	0	3	0	3
Jim Shanley, 1958	1	1	0	0	1
Sterling Sharpe, 1988-94	9	5	0	5	5
Darren Sharper, 1997-03	2	0	3	60	3
Vai Sikahema, 1991	3	0	0	0	0
Wayne Simmons, 1993-97	0	1	1	0	2
Nate Simpson, 1977-79	7	2	0	0	2
Joe Sims, 1992-95	0	1	0	0	1
Bob Skoglund, 1947	0	0	2	0	2
Bob Skoronski, 1956, 59-68	0	1	0	0	1
Barty Smith, 1974-80	13	3	0	0	3
Bruce Smith, 1945-48	4	1	0	-2	1
Jermaine Smith, 1997, 99	1	0	0	0	0
Ollie Smith, 1976-77	3	0	0	0	0
Oscar E. Smith, 1948-49	2	0	0	0	0
Perry Smith, 1973-76	0	0	1	0	1
Ken Snelling, 1945	1	0	0	0	0
Glen Sorenson, 1943-45	0	0	1	0	1
Joe Spencer, 1950-51	0	1	1	0	2
Ollie Spencer, 1957-58	0	1	0	0	1
John Spilis, 1969-71	1	0	0	0	0
Dennis Sproul, 1978	2	1	0	-5	1
Ray Stachowicz, 1981-82	1	0	0	-10	0
Jon Staggers, 1972-74	3	1	0	0	1
Don Stansauk, 1950-51	0	0	2	0	2
Walter Stanley, 1985-88	11	4	0	0	4
Bart Starr, 1956-71	64	18	0	-8	18
Ben Starret, 1942-45	1	1	0	0	1
Scott Stephen, 1987-91	1	0	4	91	4
John Stephens, 1993	0	1	0	0	1
John Sterling, 1987	1	0	0	0	0
Ken Stills, 1985-88	1	2	2	4	4
Tim Stokes, 1978-82	0	2	0	0	2
Fred Strickland, 1994-95	0	0	1	0	1
Bob Summerhays, 1949-51	1	0	3	0	3
Mickey Sutton, 1989	1	0	0	0	0
Karl Swanke, 1980-86	3	3	0	-4	3
Veryl Switzer, 1954-55	9	4	1	0	5
Harry Sydney, 1992	2	2	0	0	2
John Symank, 1957-62	7	1	11	50	12
Len Szafaryn, 1950, 53-56	0	3	1	0	4
Jerry Tagge, 1972-74	6	1	0	-6	1
Damon Tassos, 1947-49	0	0	2	0	2
Mark Tauscher, 2000-03	0	2	0	0	2
Aaron Taylor, 1995-97	0	3	0	0	3
Jim Taylor, 1958-66	33	7	0	1	7
George Teague, 1993-95	0	0	3	4	3
Jim Temp, 1957-60	0	1	1	4	2
Pat Terrell, 1998	0	0	1	6	1
Deral Teteak, 1952-56	0	0	5	0	5
John Thierry, 2000-01	0	0	2	0	2
Ike Thomas, 1972-73	2	3	0	0	3
Lavale Thomas, 1987-88	0	1	1	3	2
Bobby Thomason, 1951	2	0	0	0	0
Jeff Thomason, 1995-99	1	0	1	0	1
Arland Thompson, 1981	0	1	0	0	1
Aundra Thompson, 1977-81	6	4	0	5	4
Darrell Thompson, 1990-94	6	0	0	0	0
John Thompson, 1979-82	0	1	0	0	1
Gerald Tinker, 1975	0	0	1	0	1
Nelson Toburen, 1961-62	0	1	0	0	1
Mike Tomczak, 1991	5	2	0	-1	2
Tom Toner, 1973-77	0	0	2	0	2
Eric Torkelson, 1974-79, 81	10	6	2	29	8
Emlen Tunnell, 1959-61	0	0	1	0	1
Keith Uecker, 1984-85, 87-88, 90-91	0	2	1	0	3
Bruce Van Dyke, 1974-76	0	1	0	0	1
Alan Veingrad, 1986-87, 89-90	0	1	0	0	1
Ross Verba, 1997-00	0	1	0	2	1
Evan Vogds, 1948-49	0	0	1	0	1
Steve Wagner, 1976-79	0	0	3	0	3
Mike Wahle, 1998-03	0	1	0	0	1
Javon Walker, 2002-03	2	0	0	0	0
Malcolm Walker, 1970	0	1	0	4	1
Rod Walker, 2001-03	0	0	2	0	2
Val Joe Walker, 1953-56	1	0	7	3	7
Chuck Washington, 1987	0	1	0	0	1
Nate Wayne, 2000-02	0	0	5	9	5
Clarence Weathers, 1990-91	1	0	0	0	0
Jim Weatherwax, 1966-67, 69	0	0	1	0	1
Gary Weaver, 1975-79	0	0	3	0	3
Mike Weddington, 1986-90	0	0	4	0	4
Don Wells, 1946-49	0	0	5	47	5
Terry Wells, 1975	1	0	0	0	0
Ed West, 1984-94	6	2	0	0	2
Bill Whitaker, 1981-82	0	0	1	0	1
Gene White, 1954	0	0	1	0	1
Reggie White, 1993-98	2	1	7	12	8
David Whitehurst, 1977-83	20	5	0	-30	5
Jess Whittenton, 1958-64	0	0	10	47	10
Dick Wildung, 1946-51, 53	0	4	7	7	11
Gabe Wilkins, 1994-97	0	0	3	1	3
Marcus Wilkins, 2002-03	1	0	1	0	1
Kevin Willhite, 1987	2	0	0	0	0
Brian Williams, 1995-00	0	1	5	0	6
Clarence Williams, 1970-77	1	0	8	21	8
K.D. Williams, 2000-01	0	0	2	0	2
Mark Williams, 1994	0	1	0	0	1
Perry Williams, 1969-73	4	0	0	0	0
Travis Williams, 1967-70	9	2	1	0	3
Tyrone Williams, 1996-02	1	0	5	12	5
Matt Willig, 1998	0	1	0	0	1
James Willis, 1993-94	1	2	0	0	2
Ben Wilson, 1967	4	2	0	0	2
Charles Wilson, 1990-91	4	1	0	0	1
Gene Wilson, 1947-48	0	0	1	0	1
Marcus Wilson, 1992-95	2	0	1	0	1
Abner Wimberly, 1950-52	1	1	4	0	5
Rich Wingo, 1979, 81-84	0	0	1	0	1
Francis Winkler, 1968-69	0	0	1	0	1
Blaise Winter, 1988-90	0	0	1	0	1
Frank Winters, 1992-02	2	3	0	-2	3
Cal Withrow, 1971-73	0	1	0	0	1
Alex Wizbicki, 1950	0	0	2	12	2
Willie Wood, 1960-71	6	2	14	39	16
Keith Woodside, 1988-91	12	3	0	0	3
Vince Workman, 1989-92	8	7	0	9	7
Randy Wright, 1984-88	23	10	0	-19	10
Steve Wright, 1964-67	0	4	0	0	4
Roger Zatkoff, 1953-56	1	0	6	0	6
Jim Zorn, 1985	3	2	0	-1	2
Packers, 1945-2003	**1695**	**713**	**949**	**1742**	**1662**

ALL-TIME SACK LEADERS

(Statistic kept since 1982; rankings based on number of sacks)

Name	No.
Reggie White, 1993-98	68.5
Tim Harris, 1986-90	55.0
Ezra Johnson, 1977-87	41.5
Kabeer Gbaja-Biamila, 2000-03	37.0
Tony Bennett, 1990-93	36.0
Bryce Paup, 1990-94	32.5
Vonnie Holliday, 1998-02	32.0
Santana Dotson, 1996-01	26.0
Robert Brown, 1982-92	25.5
Sean Jones, 1994-96	24.5
Lee Roy Butler, 1990-01	20.5
John Anderson, 1978-89	19.5
Mike Douglass, 1978-85	19.0
Alphonso Carreker, 1984-88	18.5
Keith McKenzie, 1996-99, 02	18.5
Cletidus Hunt, 1999-03	15.0
Brian Noble, 1985-93	14.0
Matt Brock, 1989-94	12.5
Gabe Wilkins, 1994-97	12.5
Mark Murphy, 1980-85, 87-91	11.0
Shawn Patterson, 1988-91, 93	11.0
John Thierry, 2000-01	10.0
Nate Wayne, 2000-02	10.0
Billy Lyon, 1998-02	8.0
Charles Martin, 1984-87	8.0
Bernardo Harris, 1995-01	7.5
John Jurkovic, 1991-95	7.5
George Koonce, 1992-99	7.5
Wayne Simmons, 1993-96	7.5
Gilbert Brown, 1993-99, 01-03	7.0
Terry Jones, 1978-84	7.0
Randy Scott, 1981-86	7.0
Blaise Winter, 1988-90	7.0
Vaughn Booker, 1998-99	6.5
Na'il Diggs, 2000-03	6.0
Doug Evans, 1993-97	6.0
Darren Sharper, 1997-03	6.0
Brian Williams, 1995-00	6.0
Lester Archambeau, 1990-92	5.5
Byron Braggs, 1981-83	5.5
George Cumby, 1980-85	4.5
Burnell Dent, 1986-92	4.5
Jim Flanigan, 2001	4.5
Scott Stephen, 1987-91	4.5
Esera Tuaolo, 1991-92	4.5
Mike Butler, 1977-82, 85	4.0
George (Tiger) Greene, 1986-90	4.0
Casey Merrill, 1979-83	4.0
David Bowens, 2000	3.5
Johnny Holland, 1987-93	3.5
Charles Johnson, 1979-80, 83	3.5
David Greenwood, 1986-87	3.0
Donnie Humphrey, 1984-86	3.0
Seth Joyner, 1997	3.0
Matt LaBounty, 1995	3.0
Jamal Reynolds, 2001-03	3.0
Jerry Boyarsky, 1986-89	2.5
Grady Jackson, 2003	2.5
Aaron Kampman, 2002-03	2.5
Steve McMichael, 1994	2.5

Name	No.
Chukie Nwokorie, 2003	2.5
Eugene Robinson, 1996-97	2.5
Nick Barnett, 2003	2.0
Greg Boyd, 1983	2.0
Jeff Drost, 1987	2.0
Antuan Edwards, 1999-03	2.0
Joe Johnson, 2002-03	2.0
Bob Kuberski, 1995-98	2.0
Cliff Lewis, 1981-84	2.0
Tod McBride, 1999-02	2.0
Bob Nelson, 1988-90	2.0
Guy Prather, 1981-85	2.0
Jude Waddy, 1998-99	2.0
Don Davey, 1991-94	1.5
Darius Holland, 1995-97	1.5
Bhawoh Jue, 2001-03	1.5
Bobby Leopold, 1986-87	1.5
Hardy Nickerson, 2002	1.5
Mike Prior, 1993-98	1.5
Jermaine Smith, 1997, 99	1.5
Larry Smith, 2003	1.5
Ross Browner, 1987	1.0
Mossy Cade, 1985-86	1.0
Mark Hall, 1989-90	1.0
Maurice Harvey, 1981-83	1.0
Michael Hawthorne, 2003	1.0
Jerry Holmes, 1990-91	1.0
Kenneth Johnson, 1987	1.0
Kenneth Jordan, 1987	1.0
Torrance Marshall, 2001-03	1.0
Mike McKenzie, 1999-02	1.0
Roland Mitchell, 1991-94	1.0
Jim Bob Morris, 1987	1.0
Hannibal Navies, 2003	1.0
Bill Neill, 1984	1.0
Ken Stills, 1985-89	1.0
Pat Terrell, 1998	1.0
Ben Thomas, 1986-87	1.0
Rich Turner, 1981-83	1.0
Fred Vinson, 1999	1.0
Steve Warren, 2000, 02	1.0
Elbert Watts, 1986-87	1.0
Mike Weddington, 1986-90	1.0
Tyrone Williams, 1996-02	1.0
Rich Wingo, 1979, 81-84	1.0
David Caldwell, 1987	0.5
Shannon Clavelle, 1995-97	0.5
Scott McGarrahan, 1998-00	0.5
Ron Spears, 1983	0.5
Carl Sullivan, 1987	0.5
K.D. Williams, 2000-01	0.5
team, 2002	3.0
team, 1997	2.0
team, 1991	1.0
team, 1999	1.0
team, 2000	1.0
team, 2001	1.0
team, 2003	1.0
Packers, 1982-2003	**832.0**
Opponents, 1982-2003	836.0

ALL-TIME COMBINED NET YARDS

(Rankings based on total yards; 2,000 or more yards)

Name	Rush	Rec	P-Ret	K-Ret	Int	Fum-Rec	Total
James Lofton, 1978-86	31-245	530-9,656	0-0	1-0	0-0	3-8	565-9,909
Jim Taylor, 1958-66	1,811-8,207	187-1,505	0-0	7-185	0-0	7-1	2,012-9,898
Don Hutson, 1935-45	62-284	488-7,991	0-0	5-45	30-389	0-0	585-8,709
Sterling Sharpe, 1988-94	23-72	595-8,134	9-48	1-17	0-0	5-5	633-8,276
Antonio Freeman, 1995-01, 2003	8-17	431-6,651	54-406	27-600	0-0	7-14	527-7,688
Ahman Green, 2000-03	1,208-5,685	242-1,913	0-0	0-0	0-0	6-0	1,456-7,598
Tony Canadeo, 1941-44, 46-52	1,025-4,197	69-579	46-513	75-1,736	9-129	5-2	1,229-7,156
Boyd Dowler, 1959-69	2-28	448-6,918	0-0	0-0	0-0	0-0	450-6,946
Gerry Ellis, 1980-86	836-3,826	267-2,514	0-0	13-247	0-0	9-0	1,125-6,587
Max McGee, 1954, 57-67	12-121	345-6,346	0-0	4-69	0-0	4-43	365-6,579
Steve Odom, 1974-79	16-205	84-1,613	64-569	179-4,124	0-0	6-0	349-6,511
Dorsey Levens, 1994-01	1,006-3,937	271-2,079	0-0	21-477	0-0	2-(-7)	1,300-6,486
Al Carmichael, 1953-58	166-712	75-994	100-753	153-3,907	0-0	3-0	497-6,366
Robert Brooks, 1992-98	17-75	306-4,225	51-1,237	67-589	0-0	2-0	443-6,126
John Brockington, 1971-77	1,293-5,024	138-1,075	0-0	0-0	0-0	6-0	1,437-6,099
Donny Anderson, 1966-71	787-3,165	125-1,725	15-222	34-759	0-0	5-(-5)	966-5,866
Bill Howton, 1952-58	4-20	303-5,581	0-0	0-0	0-0	2-0	309-5,601
Carroll Dale, 1965-72	3-18	275-5,581	0-0	0-0	0-0	1-0	279-5,440
Paul Hornung, 1957-62, 64-66	893-3,711	130-1,480	0-0	10-248	0-0	3-0	1,036-5,439
Edgar Bennett, 1992-96	936-3,353	242-1,920	0-0	5-104	0-0	4-0	1,187-5,377
Tom Moore, 1960-65	503-2,069	71-645	0-0	71-1,882	0-0	4-2	649-4,598
Eddie Lee Ivery, 1979-86	667-2,933	162-1,612	0-0	1-17	0-0	4-0	834-4,562
Clarke Hinkle, 1932-41	1,171-3,860	50-537	2-61	3-38	3-13	—	1,229-4,509
Bill Schroeder, 1997-01	3-17	225-3,435	35-347	25-572	0-0	1-0	289-4,371
Phillip Epps, 1982-88	10-121	192-2,884	100-819	25-532	0-0	1-0	328-4,356
Paul Coffman, 1978-85	1-3	322-4,223	0-0	3-77	0-0	2-0	328-4,303
Joe Laws, 1934-45	470-1,932	79-1,041	46-339	19-362	18-266	1-2	633-3,942
Herb Adderley, 1961-69	0-0	0-0	1-0	120-3,080	39-795	13-60	173-3,935
Travis Williams, 1967-70	271-1,063	49-530	12-209	77-2,058	0-0	3-0	412-3,860
Elijah Pitts, 1961-69, 71	479-1,684	97-1,182	75-394	27-513	0-0	4-0	682-3,773
Ted Fritsch, 1942-50	619-2,200	25-227	1-31	37-951	10-263	9-(-1)	701-3,671
Billy Grimes, 1950-52	145-662	32-431	63-834	67-1,604	0-0	5-0	312-3,531
Walter Stanley, 1985-88	6-58	101-1,831	87-720	42-857	0-0	4-0	240-3,466
Howie Ferguson, 1953-58	544-2,120	127-1,079	0-0	15-257	0-0	7-0	693-3,456
Brent Fullwood, 1987-90	433-1,702	44-370	0-0	56-1,174	0-0	3-0	536-3,246
Dave Hampton, 1969-71	195-787	25-276	0-0	74-2,084	0-0	4-0	298-3,147
Barty Smith, 1974-80	544-1,942	120-979	0-0	5-53	0-0	3-0	672-2,974
Terdell Middleton, 1977-81	559-2,044	78-659	0-0	11-263	0-0	4-0	652-2,966
Floyd (Breezy) Reid, 1950-56	459-1,964	72-868	1-0	6-103	0-0	7-2	545-2,937
Andy Uram, 1938-43	239-1,073	58-1,083	19-219	10-235	9-122	—	335-2,732
Lou Brock, 1940-45	254-804	59-761	39-438	21-438	13-193	—	386-2,634
Keith Woodside, 1988-91	259-976	144-1,248	0-0	21-381	0-0	3-0	427-2,605
Ron Kramer, 1957, 59-64	6-9	170-2,594	0-0	0-0	0-0	1-0	177-2,603
MacArthur Lane, 1972-74	484-1,711	87-855	0-0	2-31	0-0	2-0	575-2,597
Vince Workman, 1989-92	242-927	97-691	1-0	56-913	0-0	7-9	403-2,540
Jessie Clark, 1983-87	379-1,588	99-925	0-0	0-0	0-0	3-0	481-2,513
Harlan Huckleby, 1980-85	242-779	53-411	0-0	70-1,300	0-0	2-0	367-2,490
William Henderson, 1995-2003	122-431	244-1,844	0-0	15-203	0-0	5-0	386-2,478
Darrell Thompson, 1990-94	464-1,642	41-330	0-0	23-468	0-0	2-0	530-2,440
Aundra Thompson, 1977-81	12-14	95-1,573	0-0	40-835	0-0	4-5	151-2,427
Rich McGeorge, 1970-78	1-3	175-2,370	0-0	2-17	0-0	7-0	185-2,390
Perry Kemp, 1988-91	6-42	182-2,341	0-0	0-0	0-0	1-0	189-2,383
Donald Driver, 1999-2003	17-163	159-2,205	0-0	0-0	0-0	4-0	180-2,368
Ed West, 1984-94	2-2	202-2,321	0-0	2-0	0-0	2-0	208-2,323
John Jefferson, 1981-84	4-38	149-2,253	0-0	1-3	0-0	0-0	154-2,294
Mark Chmura, 1993-99	0-0	188-2,253	0-0	1-0	0-0	1-0	190-2,253
Tobin Rote, 1950-56	419-2,205	1-39	0-0	0-0	0-0	10-(-21)	430-2,223
Fred Cone, 1951-57	347-1,156	75-852	0-0	9-148	0-0	8-5	439-2,161
Jim Grabowski, 1966-70	424-1,582	65-575	0-0	0-0	0-0	1-0	490-2,157
Willie Wood, 1960-71	0-0	0-0	187-1,391	3-20	48-699	16-39	254-2,149
Roell Preston, 1997-98	0-0	2-23	45-398	64-1,708	0-0	1-0	112-2,129
Willard Harrell, 1975-77	311-934	70-656	52-382	6-126	0-0	3-0	442-2,098
Allen Rossum, 2000-01	1-16	0-0	40-357	73-1,719	0-0	3-0	117-2,092
Eric Torkelson, 1974-79, 81	351-1,307	59-469	1-0	14-268	0-0	8-29	433-2,073

ALL-TIME ROSTER

The following have all played in at least one regular-season game with the Green Bay Packers. A player who was active during the course of a season but did not play will not appear in this list, but will be mentioned in a separate list at the end of this roster. If a player was on injured reserve for an entire season, he will not be given credit for that year in this roster.

A

Name	Pos	Years	College	Games
Aberson, Cliff	B	1946	No College	10
Abrams, Nate	E	1921	No College	1
Abramson, George	G/T	1925	Minnesota	—
Acks, Ron	LB	1974-76	Illinois	40
Adams, Chet	T	1943	Ohio State	10
Adderley, Herb	CB	1961-69	Michigan State	125
Adkins, Robert	E	1940-41, 45	Marshall	—
Affholter, Erik	WR	1991	USC	4
Afflis, Dick	G	1951-54	Nevada	48
Agajanian, Ben	K	1961	New Mexico	3
Aguiar, Louie	P	1999	Utah State	15
Akins, Chris	S	2000-01	Arkansas-Pine Bluff	13
Aldridge, Ben	DB	1953	Oklahoma State	8
Aldridge, Lionel	DE	1963-71	Utah	123
Allerman, Kurt	LB	1980-81	Penn State	29
Amsler, Marty	DE	1970	Evansville	9
Amundsen, Norm	G	1957	Wisconsin	12
Anderson, Aric	LB	1987	Iona	3
Anderson, Bill	TE	1965-66	Tennessee	24
Anderson, Curtis	DE	1987	Central State (OR)	3
Anderson, Donny	RB	1966-71	Texas Tech	84
Anderson, John	LB	1978-89	Michigan	146
Anderson, Marques	S	2002-03	UCLA	30
Anderson, Vickey Ray	RB	1980	Oklahoma	7
Andruzzi, Joe	G	1998-99	Southern Conn. State	23
Ane, Charlie	C	1981	Michigan State	16
Apsit, Marger	B	1932	USC	2
Archambeau, Lester	DE	1990-92	Stanford	36
Ard, Billy	G	1989-91	Wake Forest	35
Ariey, Mike	T	1989	San Diego State	1
Arnold, Jahine	WR	1999	Fresno State	1
Arthur, Mike	C	1995-96	Texas A&M	16
Artmore, Rodney	S	1999	Baylor	5
Ashmore, Roger	T	1928-29	Gonzaga	21
Askson, Bert	TE	1975-77	Texas Southern	42
Atkins, Steve	RB	1979-81	Maryland	19
Auer, Todd	LB	1987	Western Illinois	3
Austin, Hise	CB	1973	Prairie View	9
Avery, Steve	FB	1991	Northern Michigan	1
Aydelette, Buddy	T	1980	Alabama	9

B

Name	Pos	Years	College	Games
Bailey, Byron	HB	1953	Washington State	9
Bailey, Karsten	WR	2002-03	Auburn	8
Bain, Bill	G	1975	USC	14
Baker, Frank	E	1931	Northwestern	2
Baker, Roy (Bullet)	B	1928-29	USC	14
Balazs, Frank	B	1939-41	Iowa	13
Baldwin, Al	E	1950	Arkansas	12
Banet, Herb	B	1937	Manchester	—
Barber, Bob	DE	1976-79	Grambling	60
Barker, Roy	DE	1999	North Carolina	1
Barnes, Emery	DE	1956	Oregon	2
Barnes, Gary	E	1962	Clemson	13
Barnett, Nick	LB	2003	Oregon State	15
Barnett, Solon	T	1945-46	Baylor	5
Barragar, Nate	C	1931-32, 34-35	USC	—
Barrett, Jan	E	1963	Fresno State	3
Barrie, Sebastian	DE	1992	Liberty	3
Barry, Al	G	1954, 57	USC	24
Barry, Kevin	T	2002-03	Arizona	30
Barry, Norm	B	1921	Notre Dame	5
Barton, Don	HB	1953	Texas	5
Bartrum, Mike	TE	1995	Marshall	4
Barzilauskas, Carl	DT	1978-79	Indiana	21
Basing, Myrt	B	1923-27	Lawrence	41

Name	Pos	Years	College	Games
Basinger, Mike	DE	1974	California-Riverside	1
Baxter, Lloyd	C	1948	SMU	11
Beach, Sanjay	WR	1992	Colorado State	16
Beasey, Jack	B	1924	South Dakota	1
Beck, Ken	DT	1959-60	Texas A&M	24
Becker, Wayland	E	1936-38	Marquette	32
Beebe, Don	WR	1996-97	Chadron State	26
Beekley, Bruce	LB	1980	Oregon	15
Bell, Albert	WR	1988	Alabama	5
Bell, Edward	G	1947-49	Indiana	35
Bell, Tyrone	CB	1999	North Alabama	1
Bennett, Earl	G	1946	Hardin-Simmons	3
Bennett, Edgar	RB	1992-96	Florida State	80
Bennett, Tony	LB	1990-93	Mississippi	56
Berezney, Paul	T	1942-44	Fordham	31
Berry, Connie Mack	E	1940	North Carolina State	1
Berry, Ed	DB	1986	Utah State	16
Berry, Gary	S	2000	Ohio State	4
Bettencourt, Larry	C	1933	St. Mary's (CA)	2
Bettis, Tom	LB	1955-61	Purdue	84
Beverly, David	P	1975-80	Auburn	86
Bidwell, Josh	P	2000-03	Oregon	64
Bieberstein, Adolph	G	1926	Wisconsin	1
Bilda, Dick	B	1944	Marquette	—
Billups, Lewis	CB	1992	North Alabama	5
Biolo, John	G	1939	Lake Forest	1
Birney, Tom	K	1979-80	Michigan	13
Blackmon, Roosevelt	CB	1998	Morris Brown	3
Blackshear, Jeff	G	2002	Northeast Louisiana	1
Blaine, Ed	G	1962	Missouri	14
Blair, Michael	RB	1998	Ball State	11
Bland, Carl	WR	1989-90	Virginia Union	30
Bloodgood, Elbert	B	1930	Nebraska	—
Boedecker, Bill	B	1950	Kalamazoo	9
Bolden, Juran	CB	1998	Mississippi Delta CC	3
Bolton, Scott	WR	1988	Auburn	4
Bone, Warren	DE	1987	Texas Southern	1
Bono, Steve	QB	1997	UCLA	2
Booker, Vaughn	DE/DT	1998-99	Cincinnati	30
Bookout, Billy	DB	1955-56	Austin	19
Boone, J.R.	HB	1953	Tulsa	8
Borak, Fred (Fritz)	E	1938	Creighton	1
Borden, Nate	DE	1955-59	Indiana	57
Borgognone, Dirk	K	1995	Pacific	2
Bowdoin, James	G	1928-31	Alabama	45
Bowen, Matt	S	2001-02	Iowa	21
Bowens, David	DE	2000	Western Illinois	14
Bowman, Ken	C	1964-73	Wisconsin	127
Boyarsky, Jerry	NT	1986-89	Pittsburgh	29
Boyd, Elmo	WR	1978	Eastern Kentucky	2
Boyd, Greg	DE	1983	San Diego State	12
Bracken, Don	P	1985-90	Michigan	80
Brackins, Charles	QB	1955	Prairie View A&M	7
Bradford, Corey	WR	1998-01	Jackson State	42
Bradley, Dave	G	1969-71	Penn State	15
Brady, Jeff	LB	1992	Kentucky	8
Braggs, Byron	NT	1981-83	Alabama	41
Branstetter, Kent	T	1973	Houston	9
Bratkowski, Zeke	QB	1963-68, 71	Georgia	43
Bray, Ray	G	1952	Western Michigan	12
Breen, Gene	LB	1964	Virginia Tech	6
Brennan, John	G	1939	Michigan	3
Brock, Charley	C	1939-47	Nebraska	92
Brock, Lou	B	1940-45	Purdue	58
Brock, Matt	DE	1989-94	Oregon	76
Brockington, John	RB	1971-77	Ohio State	85
Brooks, Barrett	T	2002	Kansas State	2
Brooks, Bucky	CB	1996-97	North Carolina	5
Brooks, Robert	WR	1992-98	South Carolina	96
Bross, Marty	B	1927	Gonzaga	2
Broussard, Steve	P	1975	SMU	4
Brown, Aaron	DE	1973-74	Minnesota	10
Brown, Allen	TE	1966-67	Mississippi	19
Brown, Bill (Buddy)	G	1953-56	Arkansas	47
Brown, Bob	DE	1966-73	Arkansas-Pine Bluff	104

Brown, Carlos ....QB ...1975-76 ....Pacific 27
Brown, Dave ....CB ...1987-89 ....Michigan 44
Brown, Gary ....T ...1994-96 ....Georgia Tech 25
Brown, Gilbert....................NT ...1993-99, 01-03.........Kansas 125
Brown, Jonathan ....DE ...1998 ....Tennessee 4
Brown, Ken ....C ...1980 ....New Mexico 6
Brown, Robert ....DE ...1982-92 ....Virginia Tech 164
Brown, Tim ....HB ...1959 ....Ball State 1
Brown, Tom ....DB ...1964-68 ....Maryland 70
Browner, Ross ....DE ...1987 ....Notre Dame 11
Bruder, Hank ....B ...1931-39 ....Northwestern...............101
Brunell, Mark ....QB ...1994 ....Washington 2
Bucchianeri, Amadeo ....1941, 44-45 ....Indiana 14
Buchanon, Willie ....CB ...1972-78 ....San Diego State 80
Buck, Howard (Cub).........T ...1921-25 ....Wisconsin 49
Buckley, Terrell ....CB ...1992-94 ....Florida State 46
Buhler, Larry ....B ...1939-41 ....Minnesota 22
Buland, Walter ....T ...1924 ....No college 1
Bullough, Hank ....G ...1955, 58 ....Michigan State 20
Bultman, Arthur (Red) ......C ...1932-34 ....Marquette........................—
Burgess, Ronnie..............DB ...1985 ....Wake Forest 11
Burnette, Reggie ....LB ...1991 ....Houston 3
Burris, Paul (Buddy) ....G ...1949-51 ....Oklahoma 29
Burrow, Curtis ....K ...1988 ....Central Arkansas 1
Burrow, Jim ....S ...1976 ....Montana 3
Bush, Blair ....C ...1989-91 ....Washington 48
Butler, Bill ....HB ...1959 ....Chattanooga 11
Butler, Frank ....C ...1934-36, 38 ....Michigan State ....—
Butler, LeRoy ....CB ...1990-01 ....Florida State 181
Butler, Mike ....DE ...1977-82, 85 ....Kansas 97

C

Name	Pos	Years	College	Games
Cabral, Brian	LB	1980	Colorado	7
Cade, Mossy	CB	1985-86	Texas	30
Caffey, Lee Roy	LB	1964-69	Texas A&M	83
Cahoon, Ivan	T	1926-29	Gonzaga	31
Caldwell, David	NT	1987	TCU	3
Campbell, Rich	QB	1981-84	California	7
Campen, James	C	1989-93	Tulane	61
Canadeo, Tony	HB	1941-44, 46-52	Gonzaga	116
Cannava, Al	B	1950	Boston College	1
Cannon, Mark	C	1984-89	Texas-Arlington	82
Capp, Dick	TE	1967	Boston College	2
Capuzzi, Jim	QB	1956	Cincinnati	10
Carey, Joseph	G	1921	No college	6
Carlson, Wes	G	1926	St. John's	—
Carmichael, Al	HB	1953-58	USC	70
Carpenter, Lew	FB	1959-63	Arkansas	66
Carr, Fred	LB	1968-77	Texas-El Paso	140
Carreker, Alphonso	DE	1984-88	Florida State	72
Carroll, Leo	DE	1968	San Diego State	6
Carruth, Paul Ott	RB	1986-88	Alabama	43
Carter, Carl	CB	1992	Texas Tech	7
Carter, Jim	LB	1970-75, 77-78	Minnesota	106
Carter, Joe	E	1942	SMU	11
Carter, Mike	WR	1970	Sacramento State	2
Carter, Tony	RB	2002	Minnesota	12
Casper, Charles	B	1934	TCU	1
Cassidy, Ron	WR	1979-81, 83-84	Utah State	65
Cecil, Chuck	S	1988-92	Arizona	66
Chandler, Don	K	1965-67	Florida	42
Chatman, Antonio	KR	2003	Cincinnati	16
Cheek, Louis	T	1991	Texas A&M	12
Cherry, Bill	C	1986-87	Middle Tennessee State	28
Chesley, Francis	LB	1978	Wyoming	1
Childs, Henry	TE	1984	Kansas State	3
Choate, Putt	LB	1987	SMU	2
Christman, Paul	QB	1950	Missouri	11
Chmura, Mark	TE	1993-99	Boston College	89
Cifelli, Gus	T	1953	Notre Dame	12
Cifers, Bob	B	1949	Tennessee	9
Clancy, Jack	WR	1970	Michigan	14
Clanton, Chuck	DB	1985	Auburn	3
Claridge, Dennis	QB	1965	Nebraska	1
Clark, Allen	RB	1982	Northern Arizona	4
Clark, Greg	LB	1991	Arizona State	2
Clark, Jessie	RB	1983-87	Arkansas	60
Clark, Vinnie	CB	1991-92	Ohio State	32
Clavelle, Shannon	DE	1995-97	Colorado	15
Clayton, Mark	WR	1993	Louisville	16
Clemens, Bob	FB	1955	Georgia	2
Clemens, Cal	B	1936	USC	9
Clemons, Raymond	G	1947	St. Mary's (CA)	9
Clifton, Chad	T	2000-03	Tennessee	53

Name	Pos	Years	College	Games
Cloud, Jack	B	1950-51	William & Mary	13
Cobb, Reggie	RB	1994	Tennessee	16
Cody, Ed	B	1947-48	Purdue	20
Coffey, Junior	HB	1965	Washington	13
Coffman, Paul	TE	1978-85	Kansas State	119
Coleman, Keo	LB	1993	Mississippi	12
Collier, Steve	T	1987	Bethune-Cookman	10
Collins, Albin (Rip)	HB	1951	Louisiana State	7
Collins, Bobby	TE	2001	North Alabama	4
Collins, Brett	LB	1992-93	Washington	15
Collins, Mark	CB	1997	Cal State-Fullerton	1
Collins, Patrick	RB	1988	Oklahoma	6
Collins, Shawn	WR	1993	Northern Arizona	4
Combs, Derek	CB	2003	Ohio State	8
Comp, Irv	QB	1943-49	St. Benedict's	69
Compton, Chuck	DB	1987	Boise State	2
Comstock, Rudy	G	1931-33	Georgetown	40
Concannon, Jack	QB	1974	Boston College	14
Cone, Fred	FB	1951-57	Clemson	82
Conway, Dave	K	1971	Texas	1
Cook, Jim	G	1921	Wisconsin	2
Cook, Kelly	RB	1987	Oklahoma State	11
Cook, Ted	E	1948-50	Alabama	35
Cooke, Bill	T	1975	Massachusetts	5
Cooks, Kerry	S	1998	Iowa	9
Cooney, Mark	LB	1974	Colorado	13
Copeland, Russell	WR	1998	Memphis State	3
Corker, John	LB	1988	Oklahoma State	2
Coughlin, Frank	T	1921	Notre Dame	5
Coutre, Larry	HB	1950, 53	Notre Dame	19
Cox, Ron	LB	1996	Fresno State	16
Craig, Larry	E	1939-49	South Carolina	121
Crawford, Keith	CB	1995, 99	Howard Payne	16
Cremer, Ted	E	1948	Auburn	3
Crenshaw, Leon	DT	1968	Tuskegee	10
Crimmins, Bernard	G	1945	Notre Dame	6
Croft, Milburn (Tiny)	T	1942-47	Ripon	—
Cronin, Tommy	B	1922	Marquette	—
Croston, Dave	T	1988	Iowa	16
Crouse, Ray	RB	1984	Nevada-Las Vegas	16
Crowley, Jim	B	1925	Notre Dame	2
Crutcher, Tommy	LB	1964-67, 71-72	TCU	80
Cuff, Ward	B	1947	Marquette	10
Culbreath, Jim	RB	1977-79	Oklahoma	29
Culver, Al	T	1932	Notre Dame	1
Cumby, George	LB	1980-85	Oklahoma	81
Curcio, Mike	LB	1983	Temple	14
Currie, Dan	LB	1958-64	Michigan State	90
Curry, Bill	C	1965-66	Georgia Tech	28
Curry, Scott	T	1999	Montana	5
Cverko, Andy	G	1960	Northwestern	12
Cyre, Hector	G/E/T	1926	Gonzaga	10

D

Name	Pos	Years	College	Games
Dahms, Tom	T	1955	San Diego State	12
Dale, Carroll	WR	1965-72	Virginia Tech	111
Danelo, Joe	K	1975	Washington State	12
Daniell, Averell	T	1937	Pittsburgh	6
Danjean, Ernest	G	1957	Auburn	12
Darkins, Chris	RB	1997	Minnesota	14
Darling, Bernard (Boob)	C	1927-31	Beloit	—
Davenport, Najeh	FB	2002-03	Miami	23
Davenport, Wayne	B	1931	Hardin-Simmons	2
Davey, Don	DE	1991-94	Wisconsin	50
Davidson, Ben	DE	1961	Washington	14
Davis, Anthony	LB	1999	Utah	14
Davis, Dave	WR	1971-72	Tennessee State	24
Davis, Harper	B	1951	Mississippi State	12
Davis, Kenneth	RB	1986-88	TCU	35
Davis, Pahl	G	1922	Marquette	—
Davis, Ralph	G	1947-48	Wisconsin	22
Davis, Rob	LS	1997-03	Shippensburg	103
Davis, Tyrone	TE	1997-02	Virginia	69
Davis, Willie	DE	1960-69	Grambling	138
Dawson, Dale	K	1988	Eastern Kentucky	4
Dawson, Gib	HB	1953	Texas	7
Dean, Walter	FB	1991	Grambling	8
Deeks, Donald	G	1948	Washington	8
Dees, Robert	T	1952	Southwest Missouri State	9
Degrate, Tony	DE	1985	Texas	1
Del Gaizo, Jim	QB	1973	Tampa Bay	8
Del Greco, Al	K	1984-87	Auburn	46
DeLisle, Jim	DT	1971	Wisconsin	9
Dellenbach, Jeff	C	1996-98	Wisconsin	33
DeLuca, Tony	NT	1984	Rhode Island	1

Name	Pos	Years	College	Games
Dennard, Preston	WR	1985	New Mexico	16
Dent, Burnell	LB	1986-92	Tulane	95
Deschaine, Dick	P	1955-57	No college	36
Detmer, Ty	QB	1993, 95	BYU	7
Dickey, Lynn	QB	1976-77, 79-85	Kansas State	105
Didier, Clint	TE	1988-89	Portland State	31
Diggs, Na'il	LB	2000-03	Ohio State	61
Dillon, Bobby	DB	1952-59	Texas	94
Dilweg, Anthony	QB	1989-90	Duke	10
Dilweg, LaVern (Lavvie)	E	1927-34	Marquette	98
Dimler, Rich	DT	1980	USC	3
Dingle, Antonio	DT	1999	Virginia	6
DiPierro, Ray	G	1950-51	Ohio State	18
Disend, Leo	T	1940	Albright	—
Dittrich, John	G	1959	Wisconsin	12
Don Carlos, Waldo	C	1931	Drake	—
D'Onofrio, Mark	LB	1992	Penn State	2
Donohoe, Mike	TE	1973-74	San Francisco	27
Dorsett, Matthew	CB	1995	Southern	10
Dorsey, Dean	K	1988	Toronto	3
Dorsey, John	LB	1984-88	Connecticut	76
Dotson, Earl	T	1993-02	Texas A&I	120
Dotson, Santana	DT	1996-01	Baylor	88
Douglass, Bobby	QB	1978	Kansas	12
Douglass, Mike	LB	1978-85	San Diego State	120
Dowden, Corey	CB	1996	Tulane	9
Dowden, Steve	T	1952	Baylor	12
Dowler, Boyd	WR	1959-69	Colorado	150
Dowling, Brian	QB	1977	Yale	2
Dreschler, Dave	G	1983-84	North Carolina	32
Dreyer, Wally	B	1950	Wisconsin	12
Driver, Donald	WR	1999-03	Alcorn State	66
Drost, Jeff	DT	1987	Iowa	2
Drulis, Charles	G	1950	Temple	11
Duckett, Forey	CB	1994	Nevado-Reno	3
Duford, Wilfred	B	1924	Marquette	3
Duhart, Paul	B	1944	Florida	8
Dukes, Jamie	C	1994	Florida State	6
DuMoe, Bill (Gus)	E	1921	Notre Dame	6
Dunaway, Dave	WR	1968	Duke	2
Duncan, Ken	P	1971	Tulsa	2
Dunn, Joseph (Red)	B	1927-31	Marquette	58
Dunnigan, Merton (Pat)	E	1922	Minnesota	2

E

Name	Pos	Years	College	Games
Earhart, Ralph	HB	1948-49	Texas Tech	24
Earp, Francis (Jug)	C/T	1922-32	Monmouth	120
Eason, Roger	G	1949	Oklahoma	12
Ecker, Ed	T	1950-51	John Carroll	19
Edwards, Antuan	DB	1999-03	Clemson	53
Edwards, Earl	DT	1979	Wichita State	9
Ellerson, Gary	RB	1985-86	Wisconsin	31
Elliott, Carlton	E	1951-54	Virginia	48
Elliott, Tony	DB	1987	Central Michigan	1
Ellis, Gerry	FB	1980-86	Missouri	102
Ellis, Ken	CB	1970-75	Southern University	84
Enderle, Dick	G	1976	Minnesota	3
Engebretsen, Paul (Tiny)	G	1934-41	Northwestern	—
Englemann, Wuert	B	1930-33	South Dakota State	44
Enright, Rex	B	1926-27	Notre Dame	19
Epps, Phillip	WR	1982-88	TCU	85
Estep, Mike	G	1987	Bowling Green	1
Ethridge, Joe	T	1949	SMU	12
Evans, Dick	E	1940, 43	Iowa	—
Evans, Doug	CB	1993-97	Louisiana Tech	79
Evans, Jack	B	1929	California	—
Evans, Lon	T/G	1933-37	TCU	59

F

Name	Pos	Years	College	Games
Falkenstein, Tony	FB	1943	St. Mary's (CA)	10
Fanucci, Mike	DE	1974	Arizona State	13
Faverty, Hal	E	1952	Wisconsin	11
Favre, Brett	QB	1992-03	Southern Mississippi	191
Faye, Allen	E	1922	Marquette	1
Feasel, Greg	T	1986	Abilene Christian	15
Feathers, Beattie	B	1940	Tennessee	1
Ferguson, Howie	FB	1953-58	No college	65
Ferguson, Robert	WR	2001-03	Texas A&M	32
Ferragamo, Vince	QB	1986	Nebraska	3
Ferrario, Bill	G	2002	Wisconsin	16

Name	Pos	Years	College	Games
Ferry, Louis	T	1949	Villanova	12
Finnin, Tom	DT	1957	Detroit Mercy	3
Fisher, Tony	RB	2002-03	Notre Dame	30
Fitzgerald, Kevin	TE	1987	Wisconsin-Eau Claire	1
Fitzgibbons, Paul	B	1930-32	Creighton	—
Flaherty, Dick	E	1926	Marquette	12
Flanagan, Mike	C	1998-03	UCLA	81
Flanigan, Jim	LB	1967-70	Pittsburgh	40
Flanigan, Jim	DT	2001	Notre Dame	16
Fleming, Marv	TE	1963-69	Utah	95
Flowers, Bob	C	1942-49	Texas Tech	—
Floyd, Bobby Jack	FB	1952	TCU	12
Flynn, Tom	S	1984-86	Pittsburgh	37
Folkins, Lee	DE	1961	Washington	14
Fontenot, Herman	RB	1989-90	LSU	30
Ford, Len	DE	1958	Michigan	11
Forester, Bill	LB	1953-63	SMU	138
Forte, Aldo	G	1947	Montana	10
Forte, Bob	HB	1946-50, 52-53	Arkansas	80
Francis, Joe	QB	1958-59	Oregon State	24
Frankowski, Ray	G	1945	Washington	2
Franks, Bubba	TE	2000-03	Miami (FL)	64
Franta, Herb	T	1930	St. Thomas (MN)	2
Franz, Nolan	WR	1986	Tulane	1
Franz, Todd	CB	2002	Tulsa	2
Frase, Paul	DE	1997	Syracuse	9
Freeman, Antonio	WR	1995-01, 2003	Virginia Tech	116
Freeman, Bob	DB	1959	Auburn	12
Fries, Sherwood	G	1943	Colorado State	5
Fritsch, Ted	FB	1942-50	Stevens Point	99
Frutig, Ed	E	1941, 45	Michigan	9
Fuller, Curtis	S	2003	TCU	9
Fuller, Joe	CB	1991	Northern Iowa	16
Fullwood, Brent	FB	1987-90	Auburn	45
Fusina, Chuck	QB	1986	Penn State	7

G

Name	Pos	Years	College	Games
Gabbard, Steve	G/T	1991	Florida State	4
Galbraith, Scott	TE	1998	USC	1
Galbreath, Harry	G	1993-95	Tennessee	48
Gantenbein, Milt	E	1931-40	Wisconsin	104
Garcia, Eddie	K	1983-84	SMU	19
Gardella, Gus	B	1922	No college	7
Gardner, Milton (Moose)	G	1922-26	Wisconsin	55
Garrett, Bob	QB	1954	Stanford	9
Garrett, Len	TE	1971-73	New Mexico Highlands	30
Gassert, Ron	DT	1962	Virginia	11
Gatewood, Lester	C	1946-47	Baylor	23
Gavin, Patrick (Buck)	B	1923	Marquette	9
Gaydos, Kent	WR	1975	Florida State	6
Gbaja-Biamila, Kabeer	DE	2000-03	San Diego State	54
Getty, Charlie	T	1983	Penn State	16
Gibson, Paul	S	1972	Texas-El Paso	1
Gillette, Jim	B	1947	Virginia	10
Gillingham, Gale	G	1966-74, 76	Minnesota	128
Gillus, Willie	QB	1987	Norfolk State	1
Girard, Earl (Jug)	QB	1948-51	Wisconsin	46
Gizzi, Chris	LB	2000-01	Air Force	23
Glass, Leland	WR	1972-73	Oregon	26
Glenn, Terry	WR	2002	Ohio State	15
Glick, Eddie	B	1922	Marquette	—
Gofourth, Derrel	C	1977-82	Oklahoma State	86
Goldenberg, Charles	G	1933-45	Wisconsin	122
Goodman, Herbert	RB	2000-01	Graceland	12
Goodman, Les	RB	1973-74	Yankton	19
Goodnight, Clyde	E	1945-49	Tulsa	38
Gordon, Darrien	CB/KR	2002	Stanford	13
Gordon, Dick	WR	1973	Michigan State	2
Gordon, Lou	T	1936-37	Illinois	22
Gorgal, Ken	DB	1956	Purdue	5
Grabowski, Jim	RB	1966-70	Illinois	65
Graham, Jay	RB	2002	Tennessee	3
Grant, David	NT	1993	West Virginia	7
Gray, Cecil	T	1992	North Carolina	2
Gray, Jack (Dolly)	E	1923	No college	1
Gray, Johnnie	S	1975-83	Cal State Fullerton	124
Green, Ahman	RB	2000-03	Nebraska	62
Greene, George (Tiger)	DB	1986-90	Western Carolina	72
Greeney, Norm	G	1933	Notre Dame	7
Greenfield, Tom	C	1939-41	Arizona	22
Greenwood, David	S	1986	Wisconsin	9
Gregg, Forrest	T	1956, 58-70	SMU	187
Gremminger, Hank	DB	1956-65	Baylor	123
Griffen, Harold	C	1928	Iowa	5

Name	Pos	Years	College	Games
Grimes, Billy	HB	1950-52	Oklahoma A&M	36
Grimm, Dan	G	1963-65	Colorado	42
Gros, Earl	FB	1962-63	Louisiana	27
Grove, Roger	B	1931-35	Michigan State	—
Gruber, Bob	T	1987	Pittsburgh	1
Gueno, Jim	LB	1976-80	Tulane	7

H

Name	Pos	Years	College	Games
Hackbart, Dale	DB	1960	Wisconsin	12
Hackett, Joey	TE	1987-88	Elon	20
Haddix, Michael	RB	1989-90	Mississippi State	32
Hadl, John	QB	1974-75	Kansas	21
Haley, Darryl	T	1988	Utah	13
Hall, Charlie	CB	1971-76	Pittsburgh	83
Hall, Lamont	TE	1999	Clemson	14
Hall, Mark	DE	1989-90	Southwestern Louisiana	10
Hallstrom, Ron	G	1982-92	Iowa	162
Hamilton, Ruffin	LB	1994	Tulane	5
Hampton, Dave	RB	1969-71	Wyoming	33
Hanner, Dave	DT	1952-64	Arkansas	160
Hanny, Frank	T	1930	Indiana	2
Hansen, Don	LB	1976-77	Illinois	20
Hansen, Hal	B	1923	Minnesota	1
Hanson, Chris	P	1999	Marshall	1
Harden, Derrick	WR	1987	Eastern New Mexico	3
Harden, Leon	DB	1970	Texas-El Paso	8
Harding, Roger	C	1949	California	6
Hardy, Kevin	DT	1970	Notre Dame	14
Hargrove, James	RB	1987	Wake Forest	2
Harrell, Willard	RB	1975-77	Pacific	40
Harris, Al	CB	2003	Texas A&M-Kingsville	16
Harris, Bernardo	LB	1995-01	North Carolina	107
Harris, Corey	WR	1992-94	Vanderbilt	37
Harris, Welton John (Jack)	B	1925-26	Wisconsin	21
Harris, Jackie	TE	1990-93	Northeast Louisiana	60
Harris, Leotis	G	1978-83	Arkansas	75
Harris, Raymont	RB	1998	Ohio State	8
Harris, Tim	LB	1986-90	Memphis State	76
Harris, William	TE	1990	Bishop	4
Harrison, Anthony	DB	1987	Georgia Tech	3
Hart, Doug	DB	1964-71	Texas-Arlington	112
Hartnett, Perry	G	1987	SMU	1
Hartwig, Keith	WR	1977	Arizona	4
Harvey, Maurice	S	1981-83	Ball State	29
Hasselbeck, Matt	QB	1999-00	Boston College	32
Hathcock, Dave	DB	1966	Memphis State	14
Hauck, Tim	S	1991-94	Montana	58
Havig, Dennis	G	1977	Colorado	7
Hawthorne, Michael	DB	2003	Purdue	14
Haycraft, Ken	E	1930	Minnesota	1
Hayden, Aaron	RB	1997	Tennessee	14
Hayes, Chris	S	1996	Washington State	2
Hayes, Dave	E	1921-22	Notre Dame	13
Hayes, Gary	CB	1984-86	Fresno State	42
Hayes, Norbert	E	1923	Marquette	6
Hayhoe, Bill	T	1969-73	USC	62
Hays, George	DE	1953	St. Bonaventure	9
Hearden, Lester	B	1924	St. Ambrose	2
Hearden, Thomas	B	1927-28	Notre Dame	5
Heath, Stan	QB	1949	Nevada	12
Hefner, Larry	LB	1972-75	Clemson	34
Heimburger, Craig	G/T	1999	Missouri	2
Held, Paul	QB	1955	San Diego	5
Helluin, Jerry	DT	1954-57	Tulane	48
Henderson, William	FB	1995-03	North Carolina	142
Hendrian, Oscar (Dutch)	B	1924	Princeton	11
Hendricks, Ted	LB	1974	Miami	14
Henry, Urban	DE	1963	Georgia Tech	14
Hentrich, Craig	P	1994-97	Notre Dame	64
Herber, Arnie	HB	1930-40	Regis	—
Hickman, Larry	FB	1960	Baylor	12
Highsmith, Don	RB	1973	Michigan State	7
Hill, Don	B	1929	Stanford	3
Hill, Jim	S	1972-74	Texas A&I	41
Hill, Nate	DE	1988	Auburn	3
Hilton, John	TE	1970	Richmond	14
Himes, Dick	T	1968-77	Ohio State	140
Hinkle, Clarke	FB	1932-41	Bucknell	114
Hinte, Harold	E	1942	Pittsburgh	1
Hobbins, Jim	T	1987	Minnesota	3
Hoffman, Gary	T	1984	Santa Clara	1
Holland, Darius	DT	1995-97	Colorado	42
Holland, Johnny	LB	1987-93	Texas A&M	103
Holler, Ed	LB	1963	South Carolina	2
Holliday, Vonnie	DE	1998-02	North Carolina	66

Name	Pos	Years	College	Games
Hollinquest, Lamont	LB	1996-98	USC	46
Holmberg, Rob	LB	2001	Penn State	4
Holmes, Darick	RB	1998	Portland State	11
Holmes, Jerry	CB	1990-91	West Virginia	29
Hood, Estus	CB	1978-84	Illinois State	104
Hope, Charles	G	1994	Central State	6
Horn, Don	QB	1967-70	San Diego State	22
Hornung, Paul	RB	1957-62, 64-66	Notre Dame	104
Houston, Bobby	LB	1990	North Carolina State	1
Howard, Desmond	WR	1996, 99	Michigan	24
Howard, Lynn (Tubby)	B	1921-22	Indiana	12
Howell, John	B	1938	Nebraska	8
Howton, Bill	E	1952-58	Rice	80
Hubbard, Robert (Cal)	E/T	1929-33, 35	Geneva	—
Huckleby, Harlan	RB	1980-85	Michigan	84
Hudson, Bob	RB	1972	Southeast Oklahoma	12
Huffman, Tim	T	1981-85	Notre Dame	46
Hull, Tom	LB	1975	Penn State	13
Humphrey, Donnie	DE	1984-86	Auburn	48
Hunt, Cletidus	DE	1999-03	Kentucky State	69
Hunt, Ervin	DB	1970	Fresno State	6
Hunt, Kevin	T	1972	Doane	3
Hunt, Mike	LB	1978-80	Minnesota	22
Hunter, Art	T	1954	Notre Dame	12
Hunter, Scott	QB	1971-73	Alabama	35
Hunter, Tony	RB	1987	Minnesota	1
Hutchins, Paul	T	1993-94	Western Michigan	17
Hutson, Don	E	1935-45	Alabama	117
Hyland, Bob	C	1967-69, 76	Boston College	56

I

Name	Pos	Years	College	Games
Ilkin, Tunch	T	1993	Indiana State	1
Iman, Ken	C	1960-63	SE Missouri State	54
Ingalls, Bob	C	1942	Michigan	11
Ingram, Darryl	TE	1992-93	California	18
Ingram, Mark	WR	1995	Michigan State	16
Isbell, Cecil	B	1938-42	Purdue	54
Ivery, Eddie Lee	RB	1979-86	Georgia Tech	72

J

Name	Pos	Years	College	Games
Jacke, Chris	K	1989-96	Texas-El Paso	126
Jackson, Alcender	G/T	2002	Louisiana State	2
Jackson, Chris	WR	2002-03	Washington State	2
Jackson, Grady	DT	2003	Knoxville	8
Jackson, Johnnie	S	1992	Houston	1
Jackson, Keith	TE	1995-96	Oklahoma	25
Jackson, Mel	G	1976-80	USC	65
Jacobs, Allen	HB	1965	Utah	14
Jacobs, Jack	QB	1947-49	Oklahoma	36
Jacunski, Harry	E	1939-44	Fordham	—
Jakes, Van	CB	1989	Kent State	16
James, Claudis	WR	1967-68	Jackson State	15
Janet, Ernie	G	1975	Washington	1
Jankowski, Ed	B	1937-41	Wisconsin	51
Jansante, Val	E	1951	Duquesne	3
Jay, Craig	TE	1987	Mount Senario	3
Jefferson, John	WR	1981-84	Arizona State	50
Jefferson, Norman	DB	1987-88	LSU	14
Jenison, Ray	T	1931	South Dakota State	2
Jenke, Noel	LB	1973-74	Minnesota	10
Jenkins, Billy	S	2001	Howard	6
Jennings, Jim	E	1955	Missouri	6
Jensen, Greg	OL	1987	No college	1
Jensen, Jim	RB	1981-82	Iowa	23
Jervey, Travis	RB	1995-98	The Citadel	56
Jeter, Bob	DB	1963-70	Iowa	107
Johnson, Bill	E	1941	Minnesota	6
Johnson, Charles	DT	1979-80, 83	Maryland	46
Johnson, Danny	LB	1978	Tennessee State	3
Johnson, Ezra	DE	1977-87	Morris Brown	148
Johnson, Glen	T	1949	Temple Tech	8
Johnson, Howard	G	1940-41	Georgia	17
Johnson, Joe	HB	1954-58	Boston College	53
Johnson, Joe	DE	2002-03	Louisville	11
Johnson, Kenneth	CB	1987	Mississippi State	12
Johnson, KeShon	CB	1994	Arizona	7
Johnson, LeShon	RB	1994-95	Northern Illinois	14
Johnson, Marvin	DB	1952-53	San Jose State	12
Johnson, Randy	QB	1976	Texas A&I	3
Johnson, Reggie	TE	1994, 97	Florida State	13

Name	Pos	Years	College	Games
Johnson, Sammy	RB	1979	North Carolina	3
Johnson, Tom	DT	1952	Michigan	8
Johnston, Chester	B	1931, 34-38	Marquette	—
Jolly, Mike	S	1980, 82-83	Michigan	35
Jones, Boyd	T	1984	Texas Southern	2
Jones, Bruce	G	1927-28	Alabama	22
Jones, Calvin	RB	1996	Nebraska	1
Jones, Daryll	S	1984-85	Georgia	24
Jones, Robert	G	1934	Indiana	12
Jones, Ron	TE	1969	Texas-El Paso	6
Jones, Scott	T	1991	Washington	2
Jones, Sean	DE	1994-96	Northeastern	47
Jones, Terry	DT	1978-84	Alabama	85
Jones, Tom	G	1938	Bucknell	—
Jordan, Charles	WR	1994-95, 1999	Long Beach City College	20
Jordan, Henry	DT	1959-69	Virginia	139
Jordan, Kenneth	LB	1987	Tuskegee	3
Jorgensen, Carl	T/G	1934	St. Mary's (CA)	10
Joyner, Seth	LB	1997	Texas-El Paso	11
Jue, Bhawoh	CB/S	2001-03	Penn State	35
Jurkovic, John	NT	1991-95	Eastern Illinois	68

K

Name	Pos	Years	College	Games
Kahler, Bob	B	1942-44	Nebraska	9
Kahler, Royal	T	1942	Nebraska	—
Kampman, Aaron	DE	2002-03	Iowa	24
Katalinas, Leo	T	1938	Catholic University	8
Kauahi, Kani	C	1988	Hawaii	16
Keane, Jim	E	1952	Iowa	11
Keefe, Emmett	G	1921	Notre Dame	1
Kekeris, James	T	1948	Missouri	5
Kell, Paul	T	1939-40	Notre Dame	21
Kelley, Bill	E	1949	Texas Tech	12
Kelly, Joe	LB	1995	Washington	13
Kemp, Perry	WR	1988-91	California State (PA)	62
Kercher, Bob	E	1944	Georgetown	—
Kern, William	T	1929-30	Pittsburgh	—
Keuper, Ken	B	1945-47	Georgia	31
Kiel, Blair	QB	1990-91	Notre Dame	7
Kiesling, Walt	G	1935-36	St. Thomas (MN)	19
Kilbourne, Warren	T	1939	Minnesota	4
Kimball, Bobby	WR	1979-80	Oklahoma	8
Kimmel, J.D.	DT	1958	Houston	12
Kinard, Billy	DB	1957-58	Mississippi	24
Kinder, Randy	CB	1997	Notre Dame	6
King, David	DB	1987	Auburn	3
King, Don	DT	1956	Kentucky	6
King, Don	DB	1987	SMU	1
Kirby, Jack	B	1949	USC	6
Kitson, Syd	G	1980-81, 83-84	Wake Forest	47
Kitts, Jim	FB	1998	Ferrum	2
Klaus, Feryl (Fee)	C	1921	No college	4
Kleibhan, Adolph	B	1921	No college	1
Knafelc, Gary	E	1954-62	Colorado	89
Knapp, Lindsey	G	1996	Notre Dame	9
Knutson, Gene	E	1954, 56	Michigan	18
Knutson, Steve	T	1976-77	USC	24
Koart, Matt	DE	1986	USC	6
Koch, Greg	T	1977-85	Arkansas	133
Koncar, Mark	T	1976-77, 79-81	Colorado	54
Konopasek, Ed	T	1987	Ball State	3
Koonce, George	LB	1992-99	East Carolina	112
Kopay, Dave	RB	1972	Washington	14
Kostelnik, Ron	DT	1961-68	Cincinnati	110
Kotal, Eddie	B	1925-29	Lawrence	46
Kovatch, John	E	1947	Notre Dame	3
Kowalkowski, Bob	G	1977	Virginia	9
Kramer, Jerry	G	1958-68	Idaho	129
Kramer, Ron	E	1957, 59-64	Michigan	89
Kranz, Kenneth	B	1949	Wisconsin-Milwaukee	7
Krause, Larry	RB	1970-71, 73-74	St. Norbert	51
Kroll, Bob	S	1972	Northern Michigan	5
Kuberski, Bob	NT	1995-98	Navy	37
Kuechenberg, Rudy	LB	1970	Indiana	6
Kurth, Joe	T	1933-34	Notre Dame	20
Kuusisto, William	G	1941-46	Minnesota	—

L

Name	Pos	Years	College	Games
LaBounty, Matt	DE	1995	Oregon	14
Ladrow, Wally	B	1921	No college	1
Lally, Bob	LB	1976	Cornell	2
Lambeau, Earl (Curly)	B	1921-29	Notre Dame	77
Lammons, Pete	TE	1972	Texas	12
Landers, Walt	RB	1978-79	Clark	13
Landeta, Sean	P	1998	Towson State	16
Lane, MacArthur	RB	1972-74	Utah State	41
Lankas, Jim	FB	1943	St. Mary's (CA)	3
Larson, Bill	TE	1980	Colorado State	9
Larson, Fred (OJ)	C	1925	Notre Dame	13
Larson, Kurt	LB	1991	Michigan State	13
Laslavic, Jim	LB	1982	Penn State	6
Lathrop, Kit	DT	1979-80	Arizona State	17
Lauer, Harold (Dutch)	E	1922	Detroit	2
Lauer, Lary	C	1956-57	Alabama	18
Laughlin, Jim	LB	1983	Ohio State	15
Lawrence, Jim	B	1939	TCU	5
Laws, Joe	B	1934-45	Iowa	123
Leaper, Wes	E	1923	Wisconsin	2
Lee, Bill	T	1937-42, 46	Alabama	53
Lee, Charles	WR	2000-01	Central Florida	22
Lee, Mark	CB	1980-90	Washington	157
Leigh, Charlie	RB	1974	No college	11
Leiker, Tony	DT	1987	Stanford	1
LeJeune, Walter	T/C/G	1925-26	Heidelberg	19
Lenon, Paris	LB	2002-03	Richmond	32
Leopold, Bobby	LB	1986	Notre Dame	12
Lester, Darrell	C	1937-38	TCU	18
Letlow, Russ	G	1936-42, 46	San Francisco	74
Levens, Dorsey	RB	1994-01	Georgia Tech	102
Lewellen, Verne	B	1924-32	Nebraska	102
Lewis, Cliff	LB	1981-84	Southern Mississippi	57
Lewis, Gary	TE	1981-84	Texas-Arlington	44
Lewis, Mark	TE	1986-87	Texas A&M	17
Lewis, Mike	DT	1980	Arkansas A&M	10
Lewis, Ron	WR	1992-94	Florida State	21
Lewis, Tim	CB	1983-86	Pittsburgh	51
Lidberg, Carl (Cully)	B	1926, 29-30	Minnesota	—
Lipscomb, Paul	T	1945-49	Tennessee	57
Livingston, Dale	K	1970	Western Michigan	14
Lofton, James	WR	1978-86	Stanford	136
Logan, Dave	NT	1987	Pittsburgh	2
Logan, Dick	T	1952-53	Ohio State	19
Lollar, John	B	1928	Samford	3
London, Antonio	LB	1998	Alabama	1
Long, Bob	WR	1964-67	Wichita	35
Longwell, Ryan	K	1997-03	California	112
Loomis, Ace	HB	1951-53	Wisconsin-LaCrosse	33
Losch, John	HB	1956	Miami (FL)	12
Luchey, Nick	FB	2003	Miami (FL)	10
Lucky, Bill	DT	1955	Baylor	12
Lueck, Bill	G	1968-74	Arizona	90
Luhn, Nolan	E	1945-49	Tulsa	56
Luke, Steve	DB	1975-80	Ohio State	89
Lusteg, Booth	K	1969	Connecticut	4
Lyle, Dewey	G	1922-23	Minnesota	11
Lyman, Del	T	1941	UCLA	5
Lyon, Billy	DT	1998-02	Marshall	59

M

Name	Pos	Years	College	Games
Maas, Bill	NT	1993	Pittsburgh	14
Mack, Red	WR	1966	Notre Dame	8
MacLeod, Tom	LB	1973	Minnesota	11
Maddox, George (Buster)	T	1935	Kansas State	1
Majkowski, Don	QB	1987-92	Virginia	68
Malancon, Rydell	LB	1987	LSU	3
Malone, John (Grover)	B	1921	Notre Dame	6
Mandarich, Tony	T	1989-91	Michigan State	45
Mandeville, Chris	S	1987	California-Davis	4
Manley, Leon	G-T	1950-51	Oklahoma	24
Mann, Bob	E	1950-54	Michigan	39
Mann, Errol	K	1968	North Dakota	2
Manning, Brian	WR	1998	Stanford	3
Mansfield, Von	DB	1987	Wisconsin	3
Marcol, Chester	K	1972-80	Hillsdale	106
Marks, Larry	B	1928	Indiana	11
Marshall, Rich	DT	1965	Stephen A. Austin	14
Marshall, Torrance	LB	2001-03	Oklahoma	42
Martel, Herman	E	1921	No college	1
Martin, Charles	DE	1984-87	Livingston	48
Martin, David	TE	2001-03	Tennessee	38
Martinkovic, John	DE	1951-56	Xavier	72
Maryland, Russell	DT	2000	Miami (FL)	16
Mason, Dave	DB	1974	Nebraska	12
Mason, Joel	E	1942-45	Western Michigan	41

Name	Pos	Years	College	Games
Mason, Larry	RB	1988	Troy State	15
Massey, Carlton	DE	1957-58	Texas	14
Masters, Norm	T	1957-64	Michigan State	104
Mataele, Stan	DL	1987	Arizona	2
Mathys, Charlie	QB	1922-26	Indiana	47
Matson, Pat	G	1975	Oregon	14
Matthews, Al	DB	1970-75	Texas A&I	84
Matthews, Aubrey	WR	1988-89	Delta State	20
Mattos, Harry	B	1936	St. Mary's (CA)	2
Matuszak, Marv	LB	1958	Tulsa	3
Mayer, Frank	T/G	1927	Notre Dame	10
Mayes, Derrick	WR	1996-98	Notre Dame	29
Mays, Kivuusama	LB	1999	North Carolina	3
McAuliffe, Jack	B	1926	Beloit	8
McBride, Ron	RB	1973	Minnesota	11
McBride, Tod	DB	1999-02	UCLA	61
McCaffrey, Bob	C	1975	USC	11
McCarren, Larry	C	1973-84	Illinois	162
McCaslin, Eugene	LB	2000	Florida	1
McCloughan, Dave	CB	1992	Colorado	5
McConkey, Phil	WR	1986	Navy	4
McCoy, Mike C.	CB	1976-83	Colorado	110
McCoy, Mike P.	DT	1970-76	Notre Dame	94
McCrary, Hurdis	B	1929-33	Georgia	52
McDonald, Dustin	G	1935	Indiana	1
McDougal, Robert	B	1947	Miami (FL)	1
McDowell, John	G-T	1964	St. John's	12
McElmurry, Blaine	S	1997	Montana	1
McGarrahan, Scott	S	1998-00	New Mexico	44
McGarry, John	OL	1987	St. Joseph's	2
McGaw, Walter	G	1926	Beloit	1
McGeary, Clarence	T	1950	North Dakota	12
McGee, Buford	RB	1992	Missouri	4
McGee, Max	WR	1954, 57-67	Tulane	148
McGeorge, Rich	TE	1970-78	Elon	116
McGill, Lenny	CB	1994-95	Arizona State	21
McGrew, Sylvester	DE	1987	Tulane	3
McGruder, Michael	DB	1989	Kent State	2
McGuire, Gene	C	1996	Notre Dame	8
McHan, Lamar	QB	1959-60	Arkansas	24
McIlhenny, Don	RB	1957-59	SMU	36
McIntyre, Guy	G	1994	Georgia	10
McJulien, Paul	P	1991-92	Jackson State	25
McKay, Roy	HB	1944-47	Texas	35
McKenzie, Keith	DE	1996-99, 02	Ball State	62
McKenzie, Mike	CB	1999-03	Memphis	69
McKenzie, Raleigh	G	1999-00	Tennessee	19
McLaughlin, Joe	LB	1979	Massachusetts	3
McLaughlin, Lee	G	1941	Virginia	9
McLean, Ray (Toody)	B	1921	No college	3
McLeod, Mike	S	1984-85	Montana State	19
McMahon, Jim	QB	1995-96	BYU	6
McMath, Herb	DT	1977	Morningside	8
McMichael, Steve	DT	1994	Texas	16
McMillan, Ernie	T	1975	Illinois	13
McNabb, Dexter	FB	1992-93	Florida	32
McNally (Blood), Johnny	B	1929-33, 35-36	St. John's	75
McPherson, Forrest	T/C	1943-45	Nebraska	—
Meade, Mike	RB	1982-83	Penn State	18
Mealey, Rondell	RB	2001-02	Louisiana State	14
Meilinger, Steve	E	1958, 60	Kentucky	24
Melka, James	LB	1987	Wisconsin	1
Mendoza, Ruben	G	1986	Wayne State	6
Mercein, Chuck	RB	1967-69	Yale	22
Mercer, Mike	K	1968-69	Arizona State	16
Merrill, Casey	DE	1979-83	California-Davis	59
Merrill, Mark	LB	1982	Minnesota	2
Mestnik, Frank	FB	1963	Marquette	11
Metcalf, Eric	WR	2002	Texas	1
Meyer, Jim	T	1987	Illinois State	2
Michaels, Lou	K	1971	Kentucky	10
Michaels, Walt	G	1951	Washington-Lee	12
Michalske, August (Mike)	G	1929-35, 37	Penn State	—
Michels, John	T	1996-97	USC	24
Mickens, Terry	WR	1994-97	Florida A&M	47
Middleton, Terdell	RB	1977-81	Memphis State	69
Midler, Lou	G	1940	Minnesota	7
Mihajlovich, Lou	E	1954	Indiana	3
Milan, Don	QB	1975	Cal-Poly-SLO	14
Millard, Keith	DT	1992	Washington State	2
Miller, Charles (Ookie)	C	1938	Purdue	11
Miller, Don	DB	1954	SMU	1
Miller, John	T	1960	Boston College	5
Miller, John	LB	1987	Mississippi State	1
Miller, Paul	B	1936-38	South Dakota State	32
Miller, Tom	E	1946	Hampden-Sydney	2
Mills, Stan	B	1922-23	Penn State	17
Minick, Paul	G	1928-29	Iowa	—
Mitchell, Basil	RB	1999-00	Texas Christian	16
Mitchell, Charles	B	1946	Tulsa	2
Mitchell, Roland	CB	1991-94	Texas Tech	48
Moffitt, Mike	WR	1986	Freso State	4
Moje, Dick	E	1951	Loyola (LA)	2
Molenda, John (Bo)	B	1928-32	Michigan	45
Monaco, Ron	LB	1987	South Carolina	2
Monnett, Bob	B	1933-38	Michigan State	63
Monroe, Henry	DB	1979	Mississippi State	3
Moore, Allen	E	1939	Texas A&M	5
Moore, Blake	C	1984-85	Wooster	27
Moore, Brent	LB	1987	USC	4
Moore, Jason	S	2000	San Diego State	3
Moore, Rich	DT	1969-70	Villanova	20
Moore, Tom	HB	1960-65	Vanderbilt	78
Moran, Rich	G	1985-93	San Diego State	108
Moresco, Tim	S	1977	Syracuse	14
Morgan, Anthony	WR	1993-96	Tennessee	37
Morris, Jim Bob	LB	1987	Kansas State	11
Morris, Larry	RB	1987	Syracuse	2
Morris, Lee	WR	1987	Oklahoma	5
Morrissey, Jim	LB	1993	Michigan State	6
Morton, Mike	LB	2000	North Carolina	16
Moselle, Dom	B	1951-52	Wisconsin-Superior	20
Moses, J.J.	WR/KR	2002	Iowa State	2
Mosley, Russ	B	1945-46	Alabama	8
Moss, Perry	QB	1948	Illinois	6
Mott, Joe	LB	1993	Iowa	2
Mott, Norm (Buster)	B	1933	Georgia	3
Mullen, Roderick	CB	1995-97	Grambling State	38
Mulleneaux, Carl (Moose)	E	1938-41, 45-46	Utah State	47
Mulleneaux, Lee	C	1938	Northern Arizona	5
Murphy, Mark	DB	1980-85, 87-91	West Liberty State	146
Murray, Richard (Jab)	T	1921-24	Marquette	21

N

Name	Pos	Years	College	Games
Nadolney, Romanus	T/G	1922	Notre Dame	8
Nall, Craig	QB	2003	Northwestern (LA) State	1
Nash, Tom	E	1928-32	Georgia	53
Navies, Hannibal	LB	2003	Colorado	16
Neal, Ed	T	1945-51	Tulane	68
Neal, Frankie	WR	1987	Fort Hays State	12
Neill, Bill	NT	1984	Pittsburgh	16
Nelson, Bob	NT	1988-90	Miami	46
Nelson, Jim	LB	1999	Penn State	16
Neville, Tom	G	1986-88, 92	Fresno State	38
Newsome, Craig	CB	1995-98	Arizona State	46
Nichols, Hamilton	G	1951	Rice	9
Nickerson, Hardy	LB	2002	California	16
Niemann, Walter	C	1922-24	Michigan	22
Nitschke, Ray	LB	1958-72	Illinois	190
Nix, Doyle	DB	1955	SMU	12
Nixon, Fred	WR	1980-81	Oklahoma	23
Noble, Brian	LB	1985-93	Arizona State	117
Noonan, Danny	NT	1992	Nebraska	6
Norgard, Al	E	1934	Stanford	10
Norton, Jerry	P	1963-64	SMU	28
Norton, Marty	B	1925	Hamline	—
Norton, Rick	QB	1970	Kentucky	1
Nussbaumer, Bob	B	1946, 51	Michigan	14
Nuzum, Rick	C	1978	Kentucky	16
Nwokorie, Chukie	DE	2003	Purdue	14
Nystrom, Lee	T	1974	Macalester	13

O

Name	Pos	Years	College	Games
Oats, Carleton	DT	1973	Florida A&M	8
O'Boyle, Harry	B	1928, 32	Notre Dame	22
O'Connor, Bob	G	1935	Stanford	7
Odom, Steve	WR	1974-79	Utah	75
O'Donahue, Pat	DE	1955	Wisconsin	12
O'Donnell, Dick	E	1924-30	Minnesota	74
Odson, Urban	T	1946-49	Minnesota	39
Oglesby, Alfred	NT	1992	Houston	7
Ohlgren, Earl	E	1942	Minnesota	—
Okoniewski, Steve	DT	1974-75	Montana	28
Oliver, Muhammad	CB	1993	Oregon	2
Olsen, Ralph	E	1949	Utah	4
Olsonoski, Larry	G	1948-49	Minnesota	16
O'Malley, Tom	QB	1950	Cincinnati	1
O'Neal, Andre	LB	2001	Marshall	2
O'Neil, Ed	LB	1980	Penn State	12
Orlich, Dan	E	1949-51	Nevada	36
Osborn, Dave	RB	1976	North Dakota	6

Name	Pos	Years	College	Games
O'Steen, Dwayne	CB	1983-84	San Jose State	11
Owens, Ralph (Rip)	G	1922	Lawrence	3

P

Name	Pos	Years	College	Games
Palumbo, Sam	C	1957	Notre Dame	9
Pannell, Ernie	T	1941-42, 45	Texas A&M	23
Pape, Oran	B	1930	Iowa	2
Papit, Johnny	HB	1953	Virginia	4
Parilli, Vito (Babe)	QB	1952-53, 57-58	Kentucky	48
Parker, De'Monday	RB	1999-00	Oklahoma	19
Parker, Freddie	RB	1987	Mississippi Valley	1
Parlavecchio, Chet	LB	1983	Penn State	3
Paskett, Keith	WR	1987	Western Kentucky	12
Paskvan, George	B	1941	Wisconsin	—
Patrick, Frank	QB	1970-72	Nebraska	4
Patterson, Shawn	DE	1988-91, 93	Arizona State	49
Patton, Ricky	RB	1979	Jackson State	6
Paulekas, Tony	G/C	1936	Washington & Jefferson	11
Paup, Bryce	LB	1990-94	Northern Iowa	64
Payne, Ken	WR	1974-77	Langston	44
Pearson, Lindell	HB	1952	Oklahoma	2
Peay, Francis	T	1968-72	Missouri	62
Pederson, Doug	QB	1996-98, 01-03	Northeast Louisiana	62
Pelfrey, Ray	E	1951-52	East Kentucky State	13
Perkins, Don	FB	1944-45	Platteville	17
Perko, Tom	LB	1976	Pittsburgh	14
Perry, Claude	T	1927-35	Alabama	93
Pesonen, Dick	DB	1960	Minnesota-Duluth	12
Peterson, Kenny	DT	2003	Ohio State	9
Peterson, Lester	E	1932, 34	Texas	20
Peterson, Ray	B	1937	San Francisco	2
Petitbon, John	DB	1957	Notre Dame	12
Petway, David	S	1981	Northern Illinois	5
Pickens, Bruce	CB	1993	Nebraska	2
Pisarkewicz, Steve	QB	1980	Missouri	1
Pitts, Elijah	HB	1961-69, 71	Philander Smith	126
Pitts, Ron	DB	1988-90	UCLA	44
Ploeger, Kurt	DE	1986	Gustavus Adolphus	1
Pointer, John	LB	1987	Vanderbilt	3
Pope, Bucky	WR	1968	Catawba	3
Powers, Sammy	G	1921	Northern Michigan	4
Prather, Guy	LB	1981-85	Grambling	73
Pregulman, Merv	G	1946	Michigan	11
Prescott Harold (Ace)	E	1946	Hardin-Simmons	2
Preston, Roell	WR	1997-98	Mississippi	17
Prior, Mike	S	1993-98	Illinois State	96
Pritko, Steve	E	1949-50	Villanova	20
Prokop, Joe	P	1985	Cal Poly-Pomona	9
Provo, Fred	B	1948	Washington	9
Psaltis, Jim	DB	1954	USC	11
Purdy, Everett (Pid)	B	1926-27	Beloit	17
Pureifory, Dave	DE	1972-77	Eastern Michigan	78
Purnell, Frank	FB	1957	Alcorn A&M	9

Q

Name	Pos	Years	College	Games
Quatse, Jess	T	1933	Pittsburgh	—
Query, Jeff	WR	1989-91	Millikin	48
Quinlan, Bill	DE	1959-62	Michigan State	52

R

Name	Pos	Years	College	Games
Radick, Ken	E/T	1930-31	Marquette	5
Rafferty, Vince	C/G	1987	Colorado	3
Randolph, Al	S	1971	Iowa	14
Randolph, Terry	CB	1977	American International	14
Ranspot, Keith	E	1942	SMU	5
Rash, Lou	DB	1987	Mississippi Valley	3
Ray, Buford (Baby)	T	1938-48	Vanderbilt	116
Redick, Cornelius	WR	1987	Cal State Fullerton	1
Regnier, Pete (Doc)	B	1922	Minnesota	5
Reichardt, Bill	FB	1952	Iowa	12
Reid, Floyd (Breezy)	HB	1950-56	Georgia	78
Renner, Bill	P	1986-87	Virginia Tech	6
Reynolds, Jamal	DE	2001-03	Florida State	18
Rhodemyre, Jay	C	1948-49, 51-52	Kentucky	45
Rice, Allen	RB	1991	Baylor	6

Name	Pos	Years	College	Games
Richard, Gary	CB	1988	Pittsburgh	10
Riddick, Ray	E	1940-42, 46	Fordham	26
Ringo, Jim	C	1953-63	Syracuse	131
Risher, Alan	QB	1987	LSU	3
Rison, Andre	WR	1996	Michigan State	5
Rivera, Marco	G	1997-03	Penn State	109
Roach, John	QB	1961-63	SMU	22
Robbins, Austin	DT	2000	North Carolina	2
Robbins, Tootie	T	1992-93	East Carolina	27
Roberts, Bill	HB	1956	Dartmouth	4
Robinson, Bill	HB	1952	Lincoln	2
Robinson, Dave	LB	1963-72	Penn State	117
Robinson, Eugene	S	1996-97	Colgate	32
Robinson, Michael	CB	1996	Hampton	6
Robison, Tommy	G	1987	Texas A&M	3
Roche, Alden	DE	1971-76	Southern University	83
Rodgers, Del	RB	1982, 84	Utah	23
Rohrig, Herman	B	1941, 46-47	Nebraska	25
Roller, Dave	DT	1975-78	Kentucky	48
Romine, Al	HB	1955, 58	North Alabama	16
Rosatti, Roman	T	1924, 26-27	Michigan	27
Rose, Al	E	1932-36	Texas	49
Rose, Bob	C	1926	Ripon	—
Roskie, Ken	B	1948	South Carolina	6
Ross, Dan	TE	1986	Northeastern	15
Rossum, Allen	CB/KR	2000-01	Notre Dame	22
Rote, Tobin	QB	1950-56	Rice	84
Rowser, John	DB	1967-69	Michigan	42
Rubens, Larry	C	1982-83	Montana State	25
Rudzinski, Paul	LB	1978-80	Michigan State	33
Ruegamer, Grey	C/G	2003	Arizona State	15
Ruettgers, Ken	T	1985-96	USC	157
Ruetz, Howard	T	1951-53	Loras	20
Rule, Gordon	S	1968-69	Dartmouth	15
Rush, Clive	E	1953	Miami (OH)	11
Ruzich, Steve	G	1952-54	Ohio State	36

S

Name	Pos	Years	College	Games
Salem, Harvey	T	1992	California	4
Salsbury, Jim	G	1957-58	UCLA	24
Sample, Chuck	FB	1942, 45	Toledo	10
Sampson, Howard	DB	1978-79	Arkansas	31
Sams, Ron	G	1983	Pittsburgh	5
Sandifer, Dan	DB	1952-53	LSU	13
Sands, Terdell	DT	2003	Tennessee-Chattanooga	1
Sandusky, John	DT	1956	Villanova	12
Sarafiny, Al	C	1933	St. Edward's	—
Satterfield, Brian	FB	1996	North Alabama	1
Sauer, George	B	1935-37	Nebraska	22
Saunders, Russell	B	1931	USC	9
Scales, Hurles	DT	1975	North Texas State	8
Schammel, Francis (Zud)	T/G	1937	Iowa	11
Scherer, Bernie	E	1936-38	Nebraska	31
Schlinkman, Walt	FB	1946-49	Texas Tech	47
Schmael, Art	B	1921	No college	6
Schmidt, George	C	1952	Lewis	7
Schmitt, John	C	1974	Hofstra	14
Schneidman, Herm	B	1935-39	Iowa	40
Schoemann, Roy	C	1938	Marquette	3
Schroeder, Bill	WR	1997-01	Wisconsin-La Crosse	74
Schroll, Charles	G	1951	LSU	12
Schuette, Carl	C	1950-51	Marquette	24
Schuh, Jeff	LB	1986	Minnesota	12
Schuh, Harry	T	1974	Memphis State	14
Schultz, Charles	T	1939-41	Minnesota	23
Schwammel, Ade	T	1934-36, 43-44	Oregon State	47
Scott, Patrick	WR	1987-88	Grambling	24
Scott, Randy	LB	1981-86	Alabama	78
Scribner, Bucky	P	1983-84	Kansas	32
Secord, Joe	C	1922	No college	2
Seeman, George	E	1940	Nebraska	1
Seibold, Champ	G/T	1934-38, 40	Wisconsin	41
Self, Clarence	DB	1952, 54-55	Wisconsin	26
Serini, Washington	G	1952	Kentucky	11
Shanley, Jim	HB	1958	Oregon	12
Sharpe, Sterling	WR	1988-94	South Carolina	112
Sharper, Darren	S	1997-03	William & Mary	106
Shelly, Dexter	B	1932	Texas	2
Shield, Joe	QB	1986	Trinity	3
Shirey, Fred	T	1940	Nebraska	10
Shumate, Mark	NT	1985	Wisconsin	6
Sikahema, Vai	RB	1991	BYU	11
Simmons, Davie	LB	1979	North Carolina	16
Simmons, John	CB	1986	SMU	6

Name	Pos	Years	College	Games
Simmons, Wayne	LB	1993-97	Clemson	64
Simpkins, Ron	LB	1988	Michigan	7
Simpson, Nate	RB	1977-79	Tennessee State	43
Simpson, Travis	OL	1987	Oklahoma	3
Sims, Joe	OL	1992-95	Nebraska	47
Skaugstad, Daryle	NT	1983	California	9
Skeate, Gil	B	1927	Gonzaga	2
Skibinski, Joe	G	1955-56	Purdue	24
Skinner, Gerald	T	1978	Arkansas	15
Skoglund, Robert	E	1947	Notre Dame	9
Skoronski, Bob	T	1956, 59-68	Indiana	146
Sleight, Elmer (Red)	T	1930-31	Purdue	26
Smith, Barry	WR	1973-75	Florida State	42
Smith, Barty	FB	1974-80	Richmond	67
Smith, Ben	E	1933	Alabama	9
Smith, Blane	G	1977	Purdue	1
Smith, Bruce	B	1945-48	Minnesota	23
Smith, Donnell	DE	1971	Southern University	4
Smith, Earl	E	1922	Ripon	—
Smith, Ed	B	1937	New York	—
Smith, Ernie	T	1935-37, 39	USC	41
Smith, Jermaine	DT	1997, 99	Georgia	19
Smith, Jerry	G	1956	Wisconsin	3
Smith, Kevin	TE	1996	UCLA	1
Smith, Larry	DT/DE	2003	Florida State	10
Smith, Maurice (Mo)	RB	2002	North Carolina A&T	1
Smith, Ollie	WR	1976-77	Tennessee State	25
Smith, Oscar E.	B	1948-49	Texas-El Paso	14
Smith, Perry	CB	1973-76	Colorado State	47
Smith, Rex	E	1922	UW-La Crosse	2
Smith, Richard (Red)	G	1927, 29	Notre Dame	10
Smith, Rod	CB	1998	Notre Dame	8
Smith, Warren	C	1921	Western Michigan	2
Smith, Wes	WR	1987	East Texas	1
Snelling, Kenneth	B	1945	UCLA	2
Snider, Malcolm	G	1972-74	Stanford	42
Snider, Matt	FB	1999-00	Richmond	24
Sorenson, Glen	G	1943-45	Utah State	27
Spagnola, John	TE	1989	Yale	6
Sparlis, Al	G	1946	UCLA	3
Spears, Ron	DE	1983	San Diego State	13
Spencer, Joe	T	1950-51	Oklahoma State	24
Spencer, Ollie	T	1957-58	Kansas	24
Spilis, John	WR	1969-71	Northern Illinois	40
Spinks, Jack	G	1955-56	Alcorn State	7
Spriggs, Marcus	T/G	2003	Houston	2
Sproul, Dennis	QB	1978	Arizona	6
Stachowicz, Ray	P	1981-82	Michigan State	25
Staggers, Jon	WR	1972-74	Missouri	39
Stahlman, Dick	T	1931-32	De Paul	27
Stanley, Walter	WR	1985-88	Mesa	49
Stansauk, Don	T	1950-51	Denver	15
Starch, Ken	RB	1976	Wisconsin	6
Staroba, Paul	WR	1973	Michigan	2
Starr, Bart	QB	1956-71	Alabama	196
Starret, Ben	B	1942-45	St. Mary's (CA)	—
Steen, Frank	E	1939	Rice	3
Steiner, Rebel	E	1950-51	Alabama	24
Stenerud, Jan	K	1980-83	Montana	45
Stephen, Scott	LB	1987-91	Arizona State	64
Stephens, John	RB	1993	Northwestern (LA) State	5
Stephenson, Dave	G	1951-55	West Virginia	49
Sterling, John	RB	1987	Central State (OK)	2
Stevens, Bill	QB	1968-69	Texas-El Paso	2
Stewart, Steve	LB	1979	Minnesota	3
Stills, Ken	S	1985-89	Wisconsin	65
Stokes, Barry	G/T	2000-01	Eastern Michigan	24
Stokes, Tim	T	1978-82	Oregon	63
Stonebreaker, John	E	1942	USC	9
Strickland, Fred	LB	1994-95	Purdue	30
Sturgeon, Lyle	T	1937	North Dakota State	8
Sullivan, Carl	DE	1987	San Jose State	3
Sullivan, John	S	1986	California	6
Summerhays, Bob	B	1949-51	Utah	35
Summers, Don	TE	1987	Boise State	3
Sutton, Mickey	CB	1989	Montana	3
Svendsen, Earl	C	1937, 39	Minnesota	21
Svendsen, George	C	1935-37, 40-41	Minnesota	47
Swanke, Karl	T	1980-86	Boston College	84
Swiney, Erwin	DB	2002-03	Nebraska	9
Switzer, Veryl	HB	1954-55	Kansas State	24
Sydney, Harry	FB	1992	Kansas	16
Symank, John	DB	1957-62	Florida	76
Szafaryn, Len	G-T	1950, 53-56	North Carolina	55

T

Name	Pos	Years	College	Games
Tagge, Jerry	QB	1972-74	Nebraska	17
Tassos, Damon	G	1947-49	Texas A&M	26
Taugher, Claude	B	1922	Marquette	2
Tauscher, Mark	T	2000-03	Wisconsin	50

Name	Pos	Years	College	Games
Taylor, Aaron	G	1995-97	Notre Dame	46
Taylor, Cliff	RB	1976	Memphis State	7
Taylor, Jim	FB	1958-66	LSU	118
Taylor, Kitrick	WR	1992	Washington State	10
Taylor, Lenny	WR	1984	Tennessee	2
Taylor, Willie	WR	1978	Pittsburgh	1
Teague, George	S	1993-95	Alabama	47
Temp, Jim	DE	1957-60	Wisconsin	43
Tenner, Bob	E	1935	Minnesota	11
Terrell, Pat	S	1998	Notre Dame	40
Teteak, Deral	G	1952-56	Wisconsin	49
Thibodeaux, Keith	LB	2001	Northwestern (LA) State	7
Thierry, John	DE	2000-01	Alcorn State	28
Thomas, Ben	DE	1986	Auburn	9
Thomas, Ike	CB	1972-73	Bishop	25
Thomas, Lavale	RB	1987-88	Fresno State	2
Thomason, Bobby	QB	1951	Virginia Military	11
Thomason, Jeff	TE	1995-99	Oregon	75
Thompson, Arland	G	1981	Baylor	10
Thompson, Aundra	WR	1977-81	East Texas	63
Thompson, Clarence	B	1939	Minnesota	2
Thompson, Darrell	FB	1990-94	Minnesota	60
Thompson, John	TE	1979-81	Utah State	25
Thurston, Fred (Fuzzy)	G	1959-67	Valparaiso	112
Timberlake, George	G	1955	USC	6
Timmerman, Adam	G	1995-98	South Dakota State	61
Tinker, Gerald	WR	1975	Kent State	6
Tinsley, Pete	G	1938-45	Georgia	76
Toburen, Nelson	LB	1961-62	Wichita	24
Tollefson, Charles	G	1944-46	Iowa	18
Tomczak, Mike	QB	1991	Ohio State	12
Tomich, Jared	DE	2002	Nebraska	2
Toner, Tom	LB	1973, 75-77	Idaho	53
Tonnemaker, Clayton	C	1950, 53-54	Minnesota	36
Torkelson, Eric	RB	1974-79, 81	Connecticut	92
Traylor, Keith	DE	1993	Central Oklahoma	5
Troup, Bill	QB	1980	South Carolina	2
Tuaolo, Esera	NT	1991-92	Oregon State	20
Tullis, Walter	WR	1978-79	Delaware State	32
Tunnell, Emlen	DB	1959-61	Iowa	37
Turner, Maurice	RB	1985	Utah State	13
Turner, Rich	NT	1981-83	Oklahoma	31
Turner, Wylie	CB	1979-80	Angelo State	28
Turpin, Miles	LB	1986	California	1
Tuttle, George	E	1927	Minnesota	1
Twedell, Francis	G	1939	Minnesota	—

U

Name	Pos	Years	College	Games
Uecker, Keith	G	1984-85, 87-88, 90-91	Auburn	64
Uram, Andy	HB	1938-43	Minnesota	—
Urban, Alex	E	1941, 44-45	South Carolina	11
Usher, Eddie	B	1922, 24	Michigan	6

V

Name	Pos	Years	College	Games
Vairo, Dominic	E	1935	Notre Dame	1
Vandersea, Phil	LB	1966, 68-69	Massachusetts	34
Van Dyke, Bruce	G	1975-76	Missouri	28
Van Every, Hal	HB	1940-41	Minnesota	21
Vanoy, Vernon	DT	1972	Kansas	13
Van Sickle, Clyde	C	1932-33	Arkansas	10
Vant Hull, Fred	T/G	1942	Minnesota	10
Van Valkenburg, Pete	RB	1974	Brigham Young	6
Vataha, Randy	WR	1977	Stanford	6
Veingrad, Alan	T	1986-87, 89-90	East Texas State	59
Verba, Ross	T/G	1997-00	Iowa	59
Vereen, Carl	T	1957	Georgia Tech	12
Vergara, George	E	1925	Notre Dame	12
Viane, David	OL	1992	Minnesota-Duluth	1
Villanucci, Vince	NT	1987	Bowling Green	2
Vinson, Fred	CB	1999	Vanderbilt	16
Vogds, Evan	G	1948-49	Wisconsin	24
Voss, Lloyd	T	1964-65	Nebraska	28
Voss, Walter (Tillie)	E	1924	Detroit Mercy	11

W

Name	Pos	Years	College	Games
Waddy, Jude	LB	1998-99	William & Mary	27
Wade, Charlie	WR	1975	Tennessee State	2
Wafer, Carl	T	1974	Tennessee State	2
Wagner, Bryan	P	1992-93	Cal State-Northridge	23
Wagner, Almore (Buff)	B	1921	Carroll (WI)	4
Wagner, Steve	S	1976-79	Wisconsin	57
Wahle, Mike	G	1998-03	Navy	81
Walker, Cleo	LB	1970	Louisville	12
Walker, Javon	WR	2002-03	Florida State	31
Walker, Malcolm	C	1970	Rice	11
Walker, Randy	P	1974	Northwestern Louisiana	14
Walker, Rod	DT	2001-03	Troy State	31
Walker, Sammy	CB	1993	Texas Tech	8
Walker, Val Joe	DB	1953-56	SMU	46
Wallace, Calvin	DE	1987	West Virginia Tech	1
Walls, Wesley	TE	2003	Mississippi	14
Walsh, Ward	RB	1972	Montana	2
Warren, Steve	DT	2000, 02	Nebraska	25
Washington, Chuck	DB	1987	Arkansas	3
Watts, Elbert	CB	1986	USC	9
Wayne, Nate	LB	2000-02	Mississippi	44
Weathers, Clarence	WR	1990-91	Delaware State	28
Weatherwax, Jim	DT	1966-67, 69	Cal State-Los Angeles	34
Weaver, Gary	LB	1975-79	Fresno State	63
Webb, Chuck	FB	1991	Tennessee	2
Webber, Howard	E	1928	Kansas State	3
Webster, Tim	K	1971	Arkansas	4
Weddington, Mike	LB	1986-90	Oklahoma	52
Wehba, Ray	E	1944	USC	10
Weigel, Lee	RB	1987	Wisconsin-Eau Claire	2
Weisgerber, Dick	B	1938-40, 42	Willamette	27
Weishuhn, Clayton	LB	1987	Angelo State	9
Wellman, Mike	C	1979-80	Kansas	20
Wells, Don	E	1946-49	Georgia	37
Wells, Terry	RB	1975	Southern Mississippi	14
West, Ed	TE	1984-94	Auburn	167
West, Pat	B	1948	USC	3
Westbrook, Bryant	CB	2002	Texas	6
Wetnight, Ryan	TE	2000	Stanford	10
Wheeler, Lyle (Cowboy)	E	1921-23	Ripon	21
Whitaker, Bill	S	1981-82	Missouri	25
White, Adrian	S	1992	Florida	15
White, Gene	DE	1954	Georgia	8
White, Reggie	DE	1993-98	Tennessee	95
Whitehurst, David	QB	1977-83	Furman	53
Whitley, James	DB	2003	Michigan	3
Whittenton, Jesse	DB	1958-64	Texas Western	88
Wicks, Bob	WR	1974	Utah State	1
Widby, Ron	P	1972-73	Tennessee	26
Widdell, Doug	G	1993	Boston College	16
Willhite, Kevin	RB	1987	Oregon	3
Wildung, Dick	G	1946-51, 53	Minnesota	74
Wilkens, Elmer	E	1925	Indiana	6
Wilkerson, Bruce	T	1996-97	Tennessee	30
Wilkins, Gabe	DE	1994-97	Gardner-Webb	60
Wilkins, Marcus	LB	2002-03	Texas	13
Williams, A.D.	DE	1959	Pacific	12
Williams, Brian	LB	1995-00	USC	72
Williams, Clarence	DE	1970-77	Prairie View A&M	112
Williams, Delvin	RB	1981	San Francisco	1
Williams, Gerald	DL	1997	Auburn	4
Williams, Howard	DB	1962-63	Howard Junior College	10
Williams, K.D.	LB	2000-01	Henderson State	28
Williams, Kevin	RB	1993	UCLA	3
Williams, Mark	LB	1994	Ohio State	16
Williams, Perry	RB	1969-73	Purdue	69
Williams, Travis	RB	1967-70	Arizona State	48
Williams, Tyrone	CB	1996-02	Nebraska	111
Willig, Matt	T	1998	USC	16
Willis, James	LB	1993-94	Auburn	25
Wilner, Jeff	TE	1994-95	Wesleyan	13
Wilson, Ben	RB	1967	USC	14
Wilson, Charles	WR	1990-91	Memphis State	30
Wilson, Faye (Mule)	B	1931	Texas A&M	12
Wilson, Gene	E	1947-48	SMU	21
Wilson, Marcus	RB	1992-95	Virginia	48
Wilson, Ray	S	1994	New Mexico	3
Wilson, Richard (Milt)	G	1921	Wisconsin-Oshkosh	6
Wimberly, Abner	E	1950-52	LSU	35
Wingle, Blake	G	1985	UCLA	2
Wingo, Rich	LB	1979, 81-84	Alabama	69
Winkler, Francis	DE	1967-68	Memphis State	21
Winkler, Randy	G	1971	Tarleton State	7
Winslow, Paul	HB	1960	North Carolina College	12
Winter, Blaise	DE	1988-90	Syracuse	45
Winters, Chet	RB	1983	Oklahoma	4
Winters, Frank	OL	1992-02	Western Illinois	156
Winther, Richard (Wimpy)	C	1971	Mississippi	11
Wisne, Jerry	T	2002	Notre Dame	2
Withrow, Cal	C	1971-73	Kentucky	42
Witte, Earl	B	1934	Gustavus-Adolphus	5
Wizbicki, Alex	B	1950	Holy Cross	11
Wood, Bobby	T	1940	Alabama	2
Wood, Willie	S	1960-71	USC	166
Woodin, Howard (Whitey)	G	1922-31	Marquette	—
Woods, Jerry	S	1990	Northern Michigan	16
Woodside, Keith	RB	1988-91	Texas A&M	64
Workman, Vince	RB	1989-92	Ohio State	56
Wortman, Keith	G	1972-75	Nebraska	46
Wright, Randy	QB	1984-88	Wisconsin	48
Wright, Steve	DE	1964-67	Alabama	56
Wuerffel, Danny	QB	2000	Florida	1
Wunsch, Harry	G	1934	Notre Dame	2

Y

Name	Pos	Years	College	Games
Young, Bill	G	1929	Ohio State	2
Young, Glenn	DB	1956	Purdue	4
Young, Paul	C	1933	Oklahoma	2

Z

Name	Pos	Years	College	Games
Zarnas, Gus	G	1939-40	Ohio State	—
Zatkoff, Roger	T	1953-56	Michigan	48
Zeller, Joe	G	1932	Indiana	14
Zendejas, Max	K	1987-88	Arizona	18
Zeno, Lance	C	1933	UCLA	5
Zimmerman, Don	WR	1976	Northeast Louisiana	2
Zoll, Carl	G	1922	No college	1
Zoll, Dick	G	1939	Indiana	1
Zoll, Martin	G	1921	No college	1
Zorn, Jim	QB	1985	Cal Poly-Pomona	13
Zuidmulder, Dave	B	1929-31	St. Ambrose	7
Zupek, Al	B	1946	Lawrence	3
Zuver, Merle	G/C	1930	Nebraska	10

ACTIVE, BUT DID NOT PLAY

The following were active for at least one game, but did not actually play during a particular year.

Name	Pos	Years	College	Games
Ambrose, J.R.	WR	1988	Mississippi	1
Brunell, Mark	QB	1993	Washington	1
Carlson, Dean	QB	1974	Iowa State	6
Cheyunski, Jim	LB	1977	Syracuse	1
Collier, Steve	T	1988	Bethune-Cookman	1
Detmer, Ty	QB	1992 (2), 1994 (5)	BYU	7
Dimler, Rich	DT	1980	USC	3
Ferragamo, Vince	QB	1985	Nebraska	2
Fields, Angelo	T	1982	Michigan State	1
Graff, Neil	QB	1978	Wisconsin	1
Gray, Johnnie	S	1984	Cal State-Fullerton	1
Harrison, Reggie	RB	1978	Cincinnati	2
Henderson, Carlos	CB	1987	Marquette	1
Hudson, Craig	TE	1990	Wisconsin	1
Hunt, Sam	LB	1980	Stephen A. Austin	1
Kiel, Blair	QB	1989	Notre Dame	9
Koncar, Mark	T	1978	Colorado	14
Labbe, Rico	S	1990	Boston College	1
Mann, Errol	K	1976	North Dakota	1
McCarthy, John	QB	1987	Williams College	1
Miller, Mark	QB	1980	Bowling Green	1
Mirer, Rick	QB	1998	Notre Dame	4
Norseth, Mike	QB	1990	Kansas	2
Nystrom, Lee	T	1973	Macalester	1
Oates, Brad	T	1981	BYU	1
Pass, Randy	G	1978	Georgia Tech	2
Shield, Joe	QB	1985	Trinity College	3
Singletary, Reggie	T	1991	North Carolina	6
Smith, Jimmy	RB	1984	Elon	1
White Russell	RB	1995	California	1
Young, Steve	T	1979	Colorado	1

THE RECORD BOOK

ALL-TIME INDIVIDUAL RECORDS

SERVICE

Most Seasons
- 16   Bart Starr, 1956-71
- 15   Ray Nitschke, 1958-72
- 14   Forrest Gregg, 1956, '58-70
- 13   Charles (Buckets) Goldenberg, 1933-45
-       Dave Hanner, 1952-64

Most Games Played, Career
- 196   Bart Starr, 1956-71
- 191   Brett Favre, 1992-2003
- 190   Ray Nitschke, 1958-72
- 187   Forrest Gregg, 1956, '58-70

Most Consecutive Games Played, Career
- 191   Brett Favre, 1992-2003
- 187   Forrest Gregg, 1956, '58-70
- 166   Willie Wood, 1960-71
- 162   Larry McCarren, 1973-84

Most Seasons, Coach
- 29   Curly Lambeau, 1921-49
- 9   Vince Lombardi, 1959-67
-       Bart Starr, 1975-83
- 7   Mike Holmgren, 1992-98

SCORING

Most Seasons Leading Team
- 9   Don Hutson, 1935-36, '39-45
- 7   Chris Jacke, 1989-93, '95-96
-       Ryan Longwell, 1997-2003
- 6   Fred Cone, 1951, '53-57
-       Chester Marcol, 1972-74, '76-77, '79
- 5   Verne Lewellen, 1926-30
-       Paul Hornung, 1958-61, '64

Most Consecutive Seasons Leading Team
- 7   Don Hutson, 1939-45
-       Ryan Longwell, 1997-2003
- 5   Verne Lewellen, 1926-30
-       Fred Cone, 1953-57
-       Chris Jacke, 1989-93
- 4   Ted Fritsch, 1946-49
-       Paul Hornung, 1958-61

Most Points, Career
- 844   Ryan Longwell, 1997-2003
- 823   Don Hutson, 1935-45
- 820   Chris Jacke, 1989-96
- 760   Paul Hornung, 1957-62, '64-66

Points

Most Points, Season
- 176   Paul Hornung, 1960
- 146   Paul Hornung, 1961
- 138   Don Hutson, 1942
- 131   Ryan Longwell, 2000

Most Points, No Touchdowns, Season
- 131   Ryan Longwell, 2000
- 128   Chester Marcol, 1972
-       Chris Jacke, 1993
-       Ryan Longwell, 1998
-       Ryan Longwell, 2002
- 120   Ryan Longwell, 2003
- 115   Jan Stenerud, 1983

Most Seasons, 100 or More Points
- 7   Ryan Longwell, 1997-2003
- 3   Paul Hornung, 1960-61, '64
-       Chris Jacke, 1989, '93, '96
- 2   Don Hutson, 1942-43
-       Jan Stenerud, 1981, '83
- 1   Ted Fritsch, 1946
-       Jim Taylor, 1962
-       Chester Marcol, 1972
-       Sterling Sharpe, 1994

Most Points, Rookie, Season
- 128   Chester Marcol, 1972
- 120   Ryan Longwell, 1997
- 108   Chris Jacke, 1989
- 78   Bill Howton, 1952

Most Points, Game
- 33   Paul Hornung, vs. Colts, Oct. 8, 1961
- 31   Don Hutson, vs. Lions, Oct. 7, 1945
- 30   Paul Hornung, vs. Colts, Dec. 12, 1965
- 28   Paul Hornung, vs. Vikings, Sept. 16, 1962

Most Consecutive Games Scoring
- 112   Ryan Longwell, 1997-2003 (current)
- 45   Jan Stenerud, 1980-83
- 42   Don Chandler, 1965-67
- 41   Al Del Greco, 1984-86

Touchdowns

Most Seasons Leading Team
- 11   Don Hutson, 1935-45
- 5   Verne Lewellen, 1926-30
-       Jim Taylor, 1959, '61-64
-       Sterling Sharpe, 1989-90, '92-94

Most Consecutive Seasons Leading Team
- 11   Don Hutson, 1935-45
- 5   Verne Lewellen, 1926-30
- 4   Jim Taylor, 1961-64
-       Ahman Green, 2000-03
- 3   Sterling Sharpe, 1992-94

Most Touchdowns, Career
- 105   Don Hutson, 1935-45
- 91   Jim Taylor, 1958-66
- 66   Sterling Sharpe, 1988-94
- 62   Paul Hornung, 1957-62, '64-66

Most Touchdowns, Season
- 20 Ahman Green, 2003
- 19 Jim Taylor, 1962
- 18 Sterling Sharpe, 1994
- 17 Don Hutson, 1942

Most Touchdowns, Rookie, Season
- 13 Bill Howton, 1952
- 9 Max McGee, 1954
- 8 Gerry Ellis, 1980
- 7 Don Hutson, 1935
  Dave Hampton, 1969

Most Touchdowns, Game
- 5 Paul Hornung, vs. Colts, Dec. 12, 1965
- 4 Accomplished many times

Most Consecutive Games Scoring Touchdowns
- 7 Don Hutson, 1941-42
  Don Hutson, 1943-44
  Paul Hornung, 1960
  Ahman Green, 2003
- 6 Clarke Hinkle, 1937
  Bill Howton, 1956
  Terdell Middleton, 1978
  Brent Fullwood, 1988
  Sterling Sharpe, 1994
  Ahman Green, 2000-01

Points After Touchdown

Most Seasons Leading Team
- 8 Chris Jacke, 1989-96
- 7 Fred Cone, 1951-57
  Chester Marcol, 1972-74, '76-79
  Ryan Longwell, 1997-2003
- 6 Don Hutson, 1940-45
- 5 Paul Hornung, 1958-61, '64

Most Consecutive Seasons Leading Team
- 8 Chris Jacke, 1989-96
- 7 Fred Cone, 1951-57
  Ryan Longwell, 1997-2003
- 6 Don Hutson, 1940-45
- 4 Howard (Cub) Buck, 1922-25
  Paul Hornung, 1958-61
  Chester Marcol, 1976-79

Most (Kicking) Points After Touchdown Attempted, Career
- 306 Chris Jacke, 1989-96
- 301 Ryan Longwell, 1997-2003
- 214 Fred Cone, 1951-57
- 194 Paul Hornung, 1957-62, '64-66

Most (Kicking) Points After Touchdown Attempted, Season
- 53 Chris Jacke, 1996
- 52 Jan Stenerud, 1983
- 51 Ryan Longwell, 2003
- 48 Ryan Longwell, 1997

Most (Kicking) Points After Touchdown Attempted, Game
- 8 Don Hutson, vs. Lions, Oct. 7, 1945
  Don Chandler, vs. Falcons, Oct. 23, 1966
- 7 Don Hutson, vs. Cardinals, Nov. 1, 1942
  Paul Hornung, vs. Browns, Oct. 15, 1961
  Paul Hornung, vs. Bears, Sept. 30, 1962
  Jerry Kramer, vs. Eagles, Nov. 11, 1962
  Don Chandler, vs. Browns, Nov. 12, 1967
  Jan Stenerud, vs. Buccaneers, Oct. 2, 1983
  Ryan Longwell, vs. Cardinals, Jan. 2, 2000

Most (One-Point) Points After Touchdown, Career
- 301 Chris Jacke, 1989-96
- 298 Ryan Longwell, 1997-2003
- 200 Fred Cone, 1951-57
- 190 Paul Hornung, 1957-62, '64-66

Most (One-Point) Points After Touchdown, Season
- 52 Jan Stenerud, 1983
- 51 Chris Jacke, 1996
  Ryan Longwell, 2003
- 48 Ryan Longwell, 1997
- 44 Ryan Longwell, 2001
  Ryan Longwell, 2002

Most (One-Point) Points After Touchdown, Game
- 8 Don Chandler, vs. Falcons, Oct. 23, 1966
- 7 Don Hutson, vs. Lions, Oct. 7, 1945
  Paul Hornung, vs. Browns, Oct. 15, 1961
  Paul Hornung, vs. Bears, Sept. 30, 1962
  Jerry Kramer, vs. Eagles, Nov. 11, 1962
  Don Chandler, vs. Browns, Nov. 12, 1967
  Jan Stenerud, vs. Buccaneers, Oct. 2, 1983
  Ryan Longwell, vs. Cardinals, Jan. 2, 2000

Most Consecutive (Kicking) Points After Touchdown
- 134 Chris Jacke, 1990-94
- 105 Ryan Longwell, 1999-2003 (current)
- 104 Ryan Longwell, 1999-01
- 99 Paul Hornung, 1960-62, '64

Highest (Kicking) PAT Percentage, Career (min. 100 atts.)
- 99.00 Ryan Longwell, 1997-2003 (298-301)
- 98.37 Chris Jacke, 1989-96 (301-306)
- 98.25 Al Del Greco, 1984-87 (112-114)
- 97.94 Paul Hornung, 1957-62, 64-66 (190-194)

Most (Kicking) Points After Touchdown, No Misses, Season
- 52 Jan Stenerud, 1983
- 51 Ryan Longwell, 2003
- 48 Ryan Longwell, 1997
- 44 Ryan Longwell, 2002

Most 2-Point Conversions, Career
- 2 Edgar Bennett, 1992-96
  Antonio Freeman, 1995-01, 2003
  Bubba Franks, 2000-03

Most 2-Point Conversions, Season
- 2 Edgar Bennett, 1996
  Bubba Franks, 2003

Field Goals

Most Seasons Leading Team
- 8 Chris Jacke, 1989-96
- 7 Ryan Longwell, 1997-2003
- 6 Ted Fritsch, 1942, '45-46, '48-50
  Fred Cone, 1951, '53-57
  Chester Marcol, 1972-74, '76-78
- 5 Clarke Hinkle, 1933, '37-38, '40-41
  Paul Hornung, 1958-61, '64

Most Consecutive Seasons Leading Team
- 8 Chris Jacke, 1989-96
- 7 Ryan Longwell, 1997-2003
- 5 Fred Cone, 1953-57
- 4 Howard (Cub) Buck, 1922-25
  Paul Hornung, 1958-61

Most Field Goals Attempted, Career
- 224 Chris Jacke, 1989-96
- 222 Ryan Longwell, 1997-2003

195 Chester Marcol, 1972-80
140 Paul Hornung, 1957-62, '64-66

Most Field Goals Attempted, Season
48 Chester Marcol, 1972
39 Chester Marcol, 1974
38 Paul Hornung, 1964
     Ryan Longwell, 2000
37 Chris Jacke, 1993

Most Field Goals Attempted, Game
6 Paul Hornung, vs. Steelers, Oct. 30, 1960
    Chester Marcol, vs. Browns, Sept. 17, 1972
    Chester Marcol, vs. Cowboys, Oct. 1, 1972
    Chester Marcol, vs. Lions, Dec. 3, 1972
    Chester Marcol, vs. Lions, Sept. 29, 1974
    Chester Marcol, vs. Vikings, Nov. 17, 1974

Most Field Goals, Career
182 Ryan Longwell, 1997-2003
173 Chris Jacke, 1989-96
120 Chester Marcol, 1972-80
66 Paul Hornung, 1957-62, '64-66

Most Field Goals, Season
33 Chester Marcol, 1972
     Ryan Longwell, 2000
31 Chris Jacke, 1993
29 Ryan Longwell, 1998
28 Ryan Longwell, 2002

Most Field Goals, Rookie, Season
33 Chester Marcol, 1972
24 Ryan Longwell, 1997
22 Chris Jacke, 1989
11 Joe Danelo, 1975

Most Field Goals, Game
5 Chris Jacke, vs. Raiders, Nov. 11, 1990
    Chris Jacke, vs. 49ers, Oct. 14, 1996
    Ryan Longwell, vs. Cardinals, Sept. 24, 2000

Most Field Goals, One Quarter
3 Paul Hornung, vs. Steelers, Oct. 30, 1960 (1)
    Chester Marcol, vs. Lions, Dec. 17, 1972 (1)
    Chris Jacke, vs. Vikings, Nov. 5, 1995 (2)

Most Consecutive Games Scoring Field Goals
14 Ryan Longwell, 1997-98
12 Jan Stenerud, 1980-81
     Chris Jacke, 1991-92
11 Ryan Longwell, 2000
10 Fred Cone, 1955
     Chris Jacke, 1989-90
     Chris Jacke, 1993
     Ryan Longwell, 2001-02

Most Consecutive Field Goals
17 Chris Jacke, 1993
15 Chris Jacke, 1989-90
14 Ryan Longwell, 2002
     Ryan Longwell, 2002-03
13 Ryan Longwell, 1997-98
     Ryan Longwell, 2000

Longest Field Goal
54 Chris Jacke, vs. Lions, Jan. 2, 1994
     Ryan Longwell, vs. Titans, Dec. 16, 2001
53 Jan Stenerud, vs. Buccaneers, Nov. 22, 1981
     Chris Jacke, vs. Rams, Sept. 9, 1990
     Chris Jacke, vs. Jets, Nov. 3, 1991
     Chris Jacke, vs. Lions, Nov. 1, 1992
     Chris Jacke, vs. 49ers, Oct. 14, 1996
52 Ted Fritsch, vs. Bulldogs, Oct. 19, 1950
     Paul Hornung, vs. Bears, Sept. 13, 1964
     Chester Marcol, vs. Colts, Sept. 22, 1974

Chris Jacke, vs. Falcons, Oct. 1, 1989
Chris Jacke, vs. Lions, Nov. 21, 1993
Ryan Longwell, vs. Buccaneers, Nov. 12, 2000

Highest Field Goal Percentage, Career (min. 50 FGs)
81.98 Ryan Longwell, 1997-2003 (182-222)
80.82 Jan Stenerud, 1980-83 (59-73)
77.23 Chris Jacke, 1989-96 (173-224)
66.67 Al Del Greco, 1984-87 (50-75)

Highest Field Goal Percentage, Season (min. 1 att./game)
91.67 Jan Stenerud, 1981 (22-24)
88.46 Ryan Longwell, 2003 (23-26)
87.88 Ryan Longwell, 1998 (29-33)
86.84 Ryan Longwell, 2000 (33-38)

Most Field Goals, No Misses, Game
5 Chris Jacke, vs. Raiders, Nov. 11, 1990
    Chris Jacke, vs. 49ers, Oct. 14, 1996
    Ryan Longwell, vs. Cardinals, Sept. 24, 2000

Most Field Goals, 50 or More Yards, Career
17 Chris Jacke, 1989-96
7 Ryan Longwell, 1997-2003
3 Chester Marcol, 1972-80
2 Ted Fritsch, 1942-50
    Paul Hornung, 1957-62, '64-66
    Jan Stenerud, 1980-83
    Al Del Greco, 1984-87

Most Field Goals, 50 or More Yards, Season
6 Chris Jacke, 1993
3 Chris Jacke, 1995
    Ryan Longwell, 2000
2 Chester Marcol, 1972
    Jan Stenerud, 1981
    Al Del Greco, 1986
    Chris Jacke, 1990, '92

RUSHING

Most Seasons Leading Team
7 Clarke Hinkle, 1932-34, '36-37, '40-41
    Jim Taylor, 1960-66
5 Tony Canadeo, 1943, '46-49
    John Brockington, 1971-75
3 Ted Fritsch, 1942, '44-45
    Tobin Rote, 1951-52, '56
    Gerry Ellis, 1981, '83-84
    Eddie Lee Ivery, 1980, '82, '85
    Edgar Bennett, 1994-96

Most Consecutive Seasons Leading Team
7 Jim Taylor, 1960-66
5 John Brockington, 1971-75
4 Tony Canadeo, 1946-49
    Ahman Green, 2000-03
3 Clarke Hinkle, 1932-34
    Edgar Bennett, 1994-96

Attempts

Most Seasons Leading Team
8 Clarke Hinkle, 1932-34, '37-41
7 Jim Taylor, 1960-66
5 John Brockington, 1971-75

4 Tony Canadeo, 1943, '48-50
　Ahman Green, 2000-03
Most Consecutive Seasons Leading Team
7 Jim Taylor, 1960-66
5 Clarke Hinkle, 1937-41
　John Brockington, 1971-75
4 Ahman Green, 2000-03
3 Clarke Hinkle, 1932-34
　Ted Fritsch, 1944-46
　Tony Canadeo, 1948-50
　Edgar Bennett, 1994-96
　Dorsey Levens, 1997-99
Most Attempts, Career
1,811 Jim Taylor, 1958-66
1,293 John Brockington, 1971-77
1,208 Ahman Green, 2000-03
1,171 Clarke Hinkle, 1932-41
Most Attempts, Season
355 Ahman Green, 2003
329 Dorsey Levens, 1997
316 Edgar Bennett, 1995
304 Ahman Green, 2001
Most Attempts, Rookie, Season
216 John Brockington, 1971
126 Gerry Ellis, 1980
121 Willard Harrell, 1975
114 Kenneth Davis, 1986
Most Attempts, Game
39 Terdell Middleton, vs. Vikings, Nov. 26, 1978
33 Dorsey Levens, vs. Cowboys, Nov. 23, 1997
32 Jim Grabowski, vs. Bears, Sept. 24, 1967
　John Brockington, vs. Vikings, Nov. 17, 1974
31 Dorsey Levens, vs. Vikings, Dec. 1, 1997
　Ahman Green, vs. Patriots, Oct. 13, 2002

Yards Gained

Most Yards Gained, Career
8,207 Jim Taylor, 1958-66
5,685 Ahman Green, 2000-03
5,024 John Brockington, 1971-77
4,197 Tony Canadeo, 1941-44, '46-52
Most Seasons, 1,000 or More Yards Rushing
5 Jim Taylor, 1960-64
4 Ahman Green, 2000-03
3 John Brockington, 1971-73
2 Dorsey Levens, 1997, 1999
Most Yards Gained, Season
1,883 Ahman Green, 2003
1,474 Jim Taylor, 1962
1,435 Dorsey Levens, 1997
1,387 Ahman Green, 2001
Most Yards Gained, Rookie, Season
1,105 John Brockington, 1971
545 Gerry Ellis, 1980
519 Kenneth Davis, 1986
445 Cecil Isbell, 1938
Most Yards Gained, Game
218 Ahman Green, vs. Broncos, Dec. 28, 2003
192 Ahman Green, vs. Eagles, Nov. 10, 2003
190 Dorsey Levens, vs. Cowboys, Nov. 23, 1997
186 Jim Taylor, vs. Giants, Dec. 3, 1961

Most Games, 100 or More Yards Rushing, Career
26 Jim Taylor, 1958-66
24 Ahman Green, 2000-03
13 John Brockington, 1971-77
10 Dorsey Levens, 1994-01
Most Games, 100 or More Yards Rushing, Season
10 Ahman Green, 2003
7 Jim Taylor, 1962
　Ahman Green, 2001
6 Dorsey Levens, 1997
5 Tony Canadeo, 1949
　Jim Taylor, 1960
Most Consecutive Games, 100 or More Yards Rushing
4 Ahman Green, 2003
3 John Brockington, 1971
　Dorsey Levens, 1997
　Ahman Green, 2003
Longest Run From Scrimmage
98 Ahman Green, vs. Broncos, Dec. 28, 2003
97 Andy Uram, vs. Cardinals, Oct. 8, 1939
84 Jim Taylor, vs. Lions, Nov. 8, 1964
83 James Lofton, vs. Giants, Sept. 20, 1982
　Ahman Green, vs. Lions, Sept. 9, 2001

Average Gain

Highest Average Gain, Career (min. 400 atts.)
5.26 Tobin Rote, 1950-56 (419-2,205)
4.71 Ahman Green, 2000-03 (1,208-5,685)
4.58 Gerry Ellis, 1980-86 (836-3,826)
4.53 Jim Taylor, 1958-66 (1,811-8,207)
Highest Average Gain, Season (min. 100 atts.)
5.49 Gerry Ellis, 1985 (104-571)
5.42 Jim Taylor, 1962 (272-1,474)
5.38 Jim Taylor, 1961 (243-1,307)
5.30 Ahman Green, 2003 (355-1,883)
Highest Average Gain, Game (min. 10 att.)
16.70 Billy Grimes, vs. Yanks, Oct. 8, 1950 (10-167)
13.45 Terdell Middleton, vs. Lions, Oct. 1, 1978 (11-148)
11.60 Keith Woodside, vs. Bears, Dec. 17, 1989 (10-116)
10.90 Ahman Green, vs. Broncos, Dec. 28, 2003 (20-218)

Touchdowns

Most Seasons Leading Team
6 Clarke Hinkle, 1932, '36-39, '41
5 Verne Lewellen, 1927-31
　Ted Fritsch, 1943-47
　Tobin Rote, 1951-52, '54-56
　Paul Hornung, 1957-60, '65
4 Jim Taylor, 1961-64
　Donny Anderson, 1967-68, '70-71
　John Brockington, 1972-75
　Brent Fullwood, 1987-90
　Dorsey Levens, 1995-97, '99
　Ahman Green, 2000-03
3 Tony Canadeo, 1948-49, '52
　Gerry Ellis, 1980, '83, '85
　Edgar Bennett, 1993-95
Most Consecutive Seasons Leading Team
5 Verne Lewellen, 1927-31
　Ted Fritsch, 1943-47
4 Clarke Hinkle, 1936-39
　Paul Hornung, 1957-60
　Jim Taylor, 1961-64
　John Brockington, 1972-75
　Brent Fullwood, 1987-90

Ahman Green, 2000-03
3   Tobin Rote, 1954-56
     Edgar Bennett, 1993-95

Most Touchdowns, Career
81   Jim Taylor, 1958-66
50   Paul Hornung, 1957-62, '64-66
41   Ahman Green, 2000-03
37   Verne Lewellen, 1924-32

Most Touchdowns, Season
19   Jim Taylor, 1962
15   Jim Taylor, 1961
      Ahman Green, 2003
13   Paul Hornung, 1960
12   Jim Taylor, 1964

Most Touchdowns, Rookie, Season
5   Charles (Buckets) Goldenberg, 1933
     Gerry Ellis, 1980
     Brent Fullwood, 1987

Most Touchdowns, Game
4   Jim Taylor, vs. Browns, Oct. 15, 1961
     Jim Taylor, vs. Bears, Nov. 4, 1962
     Jim Taylor, vs. Eagles, Nov. 11, 1962
     Terdell Middleton, vs. Seahawks, Oct. 15, 1978
     Dorsey Levens, vs. Cardinals, Jan. 2, 2000

Most Consecutive Games Rushing for Touchdowns
7   Paul Hornung, 1960
6   Terdell Middleton, 1978
5   Tobin Rote, 1956
     Jim Taylor, 1961
     Jim Taylor, 1964
     Brent Fullwood, 1988

PASSING

Highest Passer Rating, Career
87.1   Brett Favre, 1992-2003
80.5   Bart Starr, 1956-71
73.8   Lynn Dickey, 1976-77, '79-85
73.5   Don Majkowski, 1987-92

Highest Passer Rating, Season (min. 8 atts./game)
105.1   Bart Starr, 1966
104.3   Bart Starr, 1968
99.5   Brett Favre, 1995
97.1   Bart Starr, 1964

Highest Passer Rating, Game (min. 20 attempts)
154.9   Brett Favre, vs. Raiders, Dec. 22, 2003
152.1   Lynn Dickey, vs. Steelers, Sept. 11, 1983
150.0   Bart Starr, vs. Rams, Dec. 2, 1962
149.5   Lynn Dickey, vs. Saints, Dec. 13, 1981

Attempts

Most Seasons Leading Team
13   Bart Starr, 1957-68, '70
12   Brett Favre, 1992-2003
8   Lynn Dickey, 1976-77, '80-85
7   Arnie Herber, 1932-37, '39

Most Consecutive Seasons Leading Team
12   Bart Starr, 1957-68
      Brett Favre, 1992-2003
6   Arnie Herber, 1932-37
      Lynn Dickey, 1980-85
4   Tobin Rote, 1953-56

Most Passes Attempted, Career
6,459   Brett Favre, 1992-2003
3,149   Bart Starr, 1956-71
2,831   Lynn Dickey, 1976-77, '79-85
1,854   Tobin Rote, 1950-56

Most Passes Attempted, Season
599   Don Majkowski, 1989
595   Brett Favre, 1999
582   Brett Favre, 1994
580   Brett Favre, 2000

Most Passes Attempted, Rookie, Season
224   Tobin Rote, 1950
177   Vito (Babe) Parilli, 1952
163   Scott Hunter, 1971
127   Don Majkowski, 1987

Most Passes Attempted, Game
61   Brett Favre, vs. 49ers, Oct. 14, 1996
59   Don Majkowski, vs. Lions, Nov. 12, 1989
54   Randy Wright, vs. 49ers, Oct. 26, 1986
      Brett Favre, vs. Bears, Dec. 5, 1993
53   Don Majkowski, vs. Buccaneers, Dec. 3, 1989

Completions

Most Seasons Leading Team
14   Bart Starr, 1957-70
12   Brett Favre, 1992-2003
8   Lynn Dickey, 1976-77, '80-85
7   Arnie Herber, 1932-37, '39

Most Consecutive Seasons Leading Team
14   Bart Starr, 1957-70
12   Brett Favre, 1992-2003
6   Arnie Herber, 1932-37
      Lynn Dickey, 1980-85
3   Cecil Isbell, 1940-42
      Irv Comp, 1944-46
      Tobin Rote, 1954-56
      Don Majkowski, 1988-90

Most Passes Completed, Career
3,960   Brett Favre, 1992-2003
1,808   Bart Starr, 1956-71
1,592   Lynn Dickey, 1976-77, '79-85
889   Don Majkowski, 1987-92

Most Passes Completed, Season
363   Brett Favre, 1994
359   Brett Favre, 1995
353   Don Majkowski, 1989
347   Brett Favre, 1998

Most Passes Completed, Rookie, Season
83   Tobin Rote, 1950
77   Vito (Babe) Parilli, 1952
75   Scott Hunter, 1971
55   Don Majkowski, 1987

Most Passes Completed, Game
36   Brett Favre, vs. Bears, Dec. 5, 1993
35   Lynn Dickey, vs. Buccaneers, Oct. 14, 1980
34   Don Majkowski, vs. Lions, Nov. 12, 1989
33   Brett Favre, vs. Falcons, Oct. 4, 1992

Most Consecutive Passes Completed
18   Lynn Dickey, vs. Oilers, Oct. 4, 1983
      Don Majkowski, vs. Saints, Sept. 17, 1989
15   Lynn Dickey, vs. 49ers, Nov. 9, 1980
14   Don Majkowski, vs. Vikings, Nov. 26, 1989
      Brett Favre, vs. Bills, Sept. 10, 2000
      Brett Favre, vs. Lions (4), Sept. 14, 2003 and
      vs. Cardinals (10), Sept. 21, 2003

Completion Percentage

Highest Completion Percentage, Career (min. 500 atts.)
61.31 Brett Favre, 1992-2003 (3,960-6,459)
57.42 Bart Starr, 1956-71 (1,808-3,149)
56.23 Lynn Dickey, 1976-77, 79-85 (1,592-2,831)
55.32 Don Majkowski, 1987-92 (889-1,607)

Highest Completion Percentage, Season (min. 8 atts./game)
65.39 Brett Favre, 2003 (308-471)
64.12 Brett Favre, 1992 (302-471)
63.74 Bart Starr, 1968 (109-171)
62.98 Brett Favre, 1995 (359-570)
       Brett Favre, 1998 (347-551)

Highest Completion Percentage, Game (min. 20 att.)
90.48 Lynn Dickey, vs. Saints, Dec. 13, 1981 (19-21)
87.10 Lynn Dickey, vs. Oilers, Sept. 4, 1983 (27-31)
82.14 Brett Favre, vs. Browns, Nov. 11, 1995 (23-28)
81.48 Randy Wright, vs. Buccaneers, Sept. 11, 1988 (22-27)

Yards Gained

Most Seasons Leading Team
12 Bart Starr, 1957, '59-68, '70
   Brett Favre, 1992-2003
 8 Lynn Dickey, 1976-77, '80-85
 7 Arnie Herber, 1932-37, '39

Most Consecutive Seasons Leading Team
12 Brett Favre, 1992-2003
10 Bart Starr, 1959-68
 6 Arnie Herber, 1932-37
   Lynn Dickey, 1980-85
 4 Tobin Rote, 1953-56

Most Yards Gained, Career
45,646 Brett Favre, 1992-2003
24,718 Bart Starr, 1956-71
21,369 Lynn Dickey, 1976-77, '79-85
11,535 Tobin Rote, 1950-56

Most Seasons, 3,000 or More Yards Passing
12 Brett Favre, 1992-2003
 3 Lynn Dickey, 1980, '83-84
 1 Randy Wright, 1986
   Don Majkowski, 1989

Most Yards Gained, Season
4,458 Lynn Dickey, 1983
4,413 Brett Favre, 1995
4,318 Don Majkowski, 1989
4,212 Brett Favre, 1998

Most Yards Gained, Rookie, Season
1,416 Vito (Babe) Parilli, 1952
1,231 Tobin Rote, 1950
1,210 Scott Hunter, 1971
  875 Don Majkowski, 1987

Most Yards Gained, Game
418 Lynn Dickey, vs. Buccaneers, Oct. 12, 1980
410 Don Horn, vs. Cardinals, Dec. 21, 1969
402 Brett Favre, vs. Bears, Dec. 5, 1993
399 Brett Favre, vs. Raiders, Dec. 22, 2003

Most Games, 300 or More Yards Passing, Career
36 Brett Favre, 1992-2003
15 Lynn Dickey, 1976-77, '79-85
 9 Don Majkowski, 1987-92
 5 Bart Starr, 1956-71

Most Games, 300 or More Yards Passing, Season
7 Brett Favre, 1995
6 Don Majkowski, 1989
  Brett Favre, 1999
5 Lynn Dickey, 1983
4 Lynn Dickey, 1984
  Brett Favre, 1994
  Brett Favre, 1998
  Brett Favre, 2001

Most Consecutive Games, 300 or More Yards Passing
3 Lynn Dickey, 1984

Longest Pass Completion
99 Brett Favre to Robert Brooks, vs. Bears, Sept. 11, 1995
96 Tobin Rote to Billy Grimes, vs. 49ers, Dec. 10, 1950
95 Lynn Dickey to Steve Odom, vs. Vikings, Oct. 2, 1977

Average Gain

92 Arnie Herber to Don Hutson, vs. Cardinals, Oct. 8, 1939

Highest Average Gain, Career (min. 500 atts.)
7.85 Bart Starr, 1956-71 (24,718-3,149)
7.55 Lynn Dickey, 1976-77, '79-85 (21,369-2,831)
7.27 Cecil Isbell, 1938-42 (5,945-818)
7.07 Brett Favre, 1992-2003 (45,646-6,459)

Highest Average Gain, Season (min. 8 att./game)
9.46 Bart Starr, 1968 (1,617-171)
9.21 Lynn Dickey, 1983 (4,458-484)
8.99 Bart Starr, 1966 (2,257-251)
8.96 Don Horn, 1969 (1,505-168)

Highest Average Gain, Game (min. 20 att.)
15.86 Cecil Isbell, vs. Cardinals, Nov. 1, 1942 (333-21)
14.85 Vito (Babe) Parilli, vs. Redskins, Oct. 19, 1958 (297-20)
14.52 Brett Favre, vs. Colts, Nov. 16, 1997 (363-25)

Touchdowns

14.50 Lynn Dickey, vs. Steelers, Sept. 11, 1983 (290-20)

Most Seasons Leading Team
12 Brett Favre, 1992-2003
11 Bart Starr, 1957, '60-68, '70
 8 Lynn Dickey, 1976-77, '80-85
 7 Tobin Rote, 1950-56

Most Consecutive Seasons Leading Team
12 Brett Favre, 1992-2003
 9 Bart Starr, 1960-68
 7 Tobin Rote, 1950-56
 6 Lynn Dickey, 1980-85

Most Touchdown Passes, Career
346 Brett Favre, 1992-2003
152 Bart Starr, 1956-71
133 Lynn Dickey, 1976-77, '79-85
 89 Tobin Rote, 1950-56

Most Touchdown Passes, Season
39 Brett Favre, 1996
38 Brett Favre, 1995
35 Brett Favre, 1997
33 Brett Favre, 1994

Most Touchdown Passes Rookie, Season
13 Vito (Babe) Parilli, 1952
 7 Cecil Isbell, 1938
   Irv Comp, 1943
   Tobin Rote, 1950
   Scott Hunter, 1971

Most Touchdown Passes, Game
5   Cecil Isbell, vs. Rams, Nov. 1, 1942
     Don Horn, vs. Cardinals, Dec. 21, 1969
     Lynn Dickey, vs. Saints, Dec. 13, 1981
     Lynn Dickey, vs. Oilers, Sept. 4, 1983
     Brett Favre, vs. Bears, Nov. 12, 1995
     Brett Favre, vs. Vikings, Sept. 21, 1997
     Brett Favre, vs. Panthers, Sept. 27, 1998

Most Games, 4 or More TD Passes, Career
16   Brett Favre, 1992-2003
5   Lynn Dickey, 1976-77, '79-85
2   Bart Starr, 1956-71

Most Games, 4 or More TD Passes, Season
5   Brett Favre, 1996
3   Brett Favre, 1995
2   Lynn Dickey, 1983
     Lynn Dickey, 1984
     Brett Favre, 1997
     Brett Favre, 2003

Most Consecutive Games, Touchdown Passes
25   Brett Favre, 2002-03 (current)
22   Cecil Isbell, 1941-42
18   Brett Favre, 1997-98
17   Brett Favre, 1994-95

Highest Touchdown Percentage, Career (min. 500 att.)
7.46   Cecil Isbell, 1938-42 (818-61)
6.36   Arnie Herber, 1932-40 (1,006-64)
5.39   Irv Comp, 1943-49 (519-28)
5.36   Brett Favre, 1992-2003 (6,459-346)

Highest Touchdown Percentage, Season (min. 8 att./game)
8.96   Cecil Isbell, 1942 (268-24)
8.77   Bart Starr, 1968 (171-15)
8.28   Tobin Rote, 1952 (157-13)
7.69   Cecil Isbell, 1938 (91-7)

Top Quarterback-to-Receiver Scoring Combinations
57   Brett Favre to Antonio Freeman
41   Brett Favre to Sterling Sharpe
35   Lynn Dickey to Paul Coffman
33   Cecil Isbell to Don Hutson
32   Lynn Dickey to James Lofton
     Brett Favre to Robert Brooks

Interceptions

Most Consecutive Passes Attempted, None Intercepted
294   Bart Starr, 1964-65
163   Brett Favre, 1995-96
152   Bart Starr, 1963-64
148   Brett Favre, 2001-02

Most Passes Had Intercepted, Career
207   Brett Favre, 1992-2003
151   Lynn Dickey, 1976-77, '79-85
138   Bart Starr, 1956-71
119   Tobin Rote, 1950-56

Most Passes Had Intercepted, Season
29   Lynn Dickey, 1983
25   Lynn Dickey, 1980
24   Tobin Rote, 1950
     Brett Favre, 1993
23   Randy Wright, 1986
     Brett Favre, 1998
     Brett Favre, 1999

Most Passes Had Intercepted, Game
6   Tom O'Malley, vs. Lions, Sept. 17, 1950

Most Attempts, No Interceptions, Game
46   Don Majkowski, vs. Lions, Sept. 30, 1990
43   Brett Favre, vs. Vikings, Oct. 22, 1995
42   Tobin Rote, vs. Bears, Nov. 7, 1954
     Don Majkowski, vs. Dolphins, Oct. 22, 1989
     Brett Favre, vs. Jaguars, Dec. 3, 2001
41   Randy Wright, vs. Bears, Nov. 8, 1987
     Don Majkowski, vs. Colts, Nov. 13, 1988
     Brett Favre, vs. Buccaneers, Nov. 29, 1992
     Brett Favre, vs. Buccaneers, Dec. 7, 1998

Lowest Interception Percentage, Career (min. 500 att.)
3.20   Brett Favre, 1992-2003 (207-6,459)
3.48   Don Majkowski, 1987-92 (56-1,607)
4.38   Bart Starr, 1956-71 (138-3,149)
5.09   Randy Wright, 1984-88 (57-1,119)

Lowest Interception Percentage, Season (min. 8 att./game)
1.20   Bart Starr, 1966 (3-251)
1.47   Bart Starr, 1964 (4-272)
2.28   Brett Favre, 1995 (13-570)
2.39   Brett Favre, 1996 (13-543)

Times Sacked

Most Times Sacked, Career
366   Brett Favre, 1992-2003
268   Lynn Dickey, 1976-77, '79-85
235   Bart Starr, 1963-71
159   Don Majkowski, 1987-92

Most Times Sacked, Season
47   Don Majkowski, 1989
42   Bart Starr, 1964
40   Lynn Dickey, 1981
     Lynn Dickey, 1983
     Brett Favre, 1996
38   Brett Favre, 1998

Most Times Sacked, Game
11   Bart Starr, vs. Lions, Dec. 7, 1965
10   David Whitehurst, vs. Chargers, Sept. 24, 1978
9   Lynn Dickey, vs. Jets, Dec. 20, 1981
8   Bart Starr, vs. Vikings, Oct. 5, 1969
     David Whitehurst, vs. Falcons, Oct. 7, 1979
     Don Majkowski, vs. Vikings, Oct. 15, 1989
     Don Majkowski, vs. Raiders, Nov. 11, 1990
     Brett Favre, vs. Buccaneers, Dec. 7, 1998

PASS RECEIVING

Most Seasons Leading Team
10   Don Hutson, 1936-45
8   James Lofton, 1978, '80-86
7   Boyd Dowler, 1959, '62-65, '67-68
     Sterling Sharpe, 1988-94
6   Bill Howton, 1952-57

Most Consecutive Seasons Leading Team
10   Don Hutson, 1936-45
7   James Lofton, 1980-86
     Sterling Sharpe, 1988-94
6   Bill Howton, 1952-57

Most Pass Receptions, Career
595   Sterling Sharpe, 1988-94
530   James Lofton, 1978-86
488   Don Hutson, 1935-45
448   Boyd Dowler, 1959-69

Most Seasons, 50 or More Pass Receptions

- 7 James Lofton, 1979-81, 83-86
  Sterling Sharpe, 1988-94
- 6 Antonio Freeman, 1996-2001

Most Pass Receptions, Season

- 112 Sterling Sharpe, 1993
- 108 Sterling Sharpe, 1992
- 102 Robert Brooks, 1995
- 94 Sterling Sharpe, 1994

Most Pass Receptions, Rookie, Season

- 55 Sterling Sharpe, 1988
- 53 Bill Howton, 1952
- 48 Gerry Ellis, 1980
- 46 James Lofton, 1978

Most Pass Receptions, Game

- 14 Don Hutson, vs. Giants, Nov. 22, 1942
- 13 Don Hutson, vs. Rams, Oct. 18, 1942
- 12 Ken Payne, vs. Broncos, Sept. 29, 1975
  Vince Workman, vs. Vikings, Sept. 6, 1992

Most Consecutive Games, Pass Receptions

- 103 Sterling Sharpe, 1988-94
- 60 Edgar Bennett, 1993-96
- 58 James Lofton, 1979-83
- 50 Don Hutson, 1941-45
  Paul Coffman, 1979-82

Yards Gained

Most Seasons Leading Team

- 11 Don Hutson, 1935-45
- 9 James Lofton, 1978-86
- 7 Sterling Sharpe, 1988-94
- 6 Bill Howton, 1952-57
  Carroll Dale, 1966, '68-72

Most Consecutive Seasons Leading Team

- 11 Don Hutson, 1935-45
- 9 James Lofton, 1978-86
- 7 Sterling Sharpe, 1988-94
- 6 Bill Howton, 1952-57

Most Yards Gained, Career

- 9,656 James Lofton, 1978-86
- 8,134 Sterling Sharpe, 1988-94
- 7,991 Don Hutson, 1935-45
- 6,918 Boyd Dowler, 1959-69

Most Yards Gained, Season

- 1,497 Robert Brooks, 1995
- 1,461 Sterling Sharpe, 1992
- 1,424 Antonio Freeman, 1998
- 1,423 Sterling Sharpe, 1989

Most Yards Gained, Rookie, Season

- 1,231 Bill Howton, 1952
- 818 James Lofton, 1978
- 791 Sterling Sharpe, 1988
- 614 Max McGee, 1954

Most Yards Gained, Game

- 257 Bill Howton, vs. Rams, Oct. 21, 1956
- 237 Don Hutson, vs. Dodgers, Nov. 21, 1943
- 220 Don Beebe, vs. 49ers, Oct. 14, 1996
- 209 Don Hutson, vs. Rams, Nov. 11, 1942

Most Seasons, 1,000 or More Yards, Receiving

- 5 James Lofton, 1980-81, '83-85
  Sterling Sharpe, 1989-90, '92-94
- 3 Antonio Freeman, 1997-99
- 2 Bill Howton, 1952, '56

Robert Brooks, 1995, '97
- 1 Don Hutson, 1942
  Bill Schroeder, 1999
  Donald Driver, 2002

Most Games, 200 or More Yards Receiving, Career

- 4 Don Hutson, 1935-45
- 2 Bill Howton, 1952-58
- 1 Carroll Dale, 1965-72
  James Lofton, 1978-86
  Don Beebe, 1996

Most Games, 200 or More Yards Receiving, Season

- 2 Don Hutson, 1942

Most Games, 100 or More Yards Receiving, Career

- 32 James Lofton, 1978-86
- 29 Sterling Sharpe, 1988-94
- 24 Don Hutson, 1935-45
- 20 Antonio Freeman, 1995-2001

Most Games, 100 or More Yards Receiving, Season

- 9 Robert Brooks, 1995
- 7 Sterling Sharpe, 1992
- 6 Don Hutson, 1942
  Bill Howton, 1952
  James Lofton, 1984
  Sterling Sharpe, 1989
  Antonio Freeman, 1998
- 5 James Lofton, 1980
  James Lofton, 1983
  Sterling Sharpe, 1993
  Sterling Sharpe, 1994
  Bill Schroeder, 2001

Most Consecutive Games, 100 or More Yards Receiving

- 4 Don Hutson, 1945
  James Lofton, 1982-83
- 3 Bill Howton, 1952
  James Lofton, 1984
  Robert Brooks, 1995 (twice)
  Antonio Freeman, 1998

Longest Pass Reception

- 99 Robert Brooks from Brett Favre, vs. Bears, Sept. 11, 1995
- 96 Billy Grimes from Tobin Rote, vs. 49ers, Dec. 10, 1950
- 95 Steve Odom from Lynn Dickey, vs. Vikings, Oct. 2, 1977
- 92 Don Hutson from Arnie Herber, vs. Cardinals, Oct. 8, 1939

Average Gain

Highest Average Gain, Career (min. 150 receptions)

- 19.72 Carroll Dale, 1965-72 (275-5,422)
- 18.42 Bill Howton, 1952-58 (303-5,581)
- 18.39 Max McGee, 1954, '57-67 (345-6,346)
- 18.22 James Lofton, 1978-86 (530-9,656)

Highest Average Gain, Season (min. 24 receptions)

- 24.88 Don Hutson, 1939 (34-846)
- 23.68 Carroll Dale, 1966 (37-876)
- 23.22 Bill Howton, 1952 (53-1,231)
- 23.17 Max McGee, 1959 (30-695)

Highest Average Gain, Game (min. 3 receptions)

- 49.67 Don Hutson, vs. Dodgers, Nov. 19, 1939 (3-149)
- 48.67 James Lofton, vs. Falcons, Dec. 26, 1982 (3-146)
- 47.33 Carroll Dale, vs. 49ers, Dec. 4, 1966 (3-142)
- 46.50 Carroll Dale, vs. Falcons, Sept. 27, 1970 (4-186)

Touchdowns

Most Seasons Leading Team

11	Don Hutson, 1935-45
7	Max McGee, 1954, '58-61, '63-64
6	James Lofton, 1978-82, '86
	Sterling Sharpe, 1989-94
5	Carroll Dale, 1966-69, '71

Most Consecutive Seasons Leading Team

11	Don Hutson, 1935-45
6	Sterling Sharpe, 1989-94
5	James Lofton, 1978-82
4	Johnny (Blood) McNally, 1930-33
	Max McGee, 1958-61
	Carroll Dale, 1966-69
	Antonio Freeman, 1997-2000

Most Touchdowns, Career

99	Don Hutson, 1935-45
65	Sterling Sharpe, 1988-94
57	Antonio Freeman, 1995-2002
50	Max McGee, 1954, '57-67

Most Touchdowns, Season

18	Sterling Sharpe, 1994
17	Don Hutson, 1942
14	Antonio Freeman, 1998
13	Bill Howton, 1952
	Sterling Sharpe, 1992
	Robert Brooks, 1995

Most Touchdowns, Rookie, Season

13	Bill Howton, 1952
9	Max McGee, 1954
6	Don Hutson, 1935
	James Lofton, 1978

Most Touchdowns, Game

4	Don Hutson, vs. Lions, Oct. 7, 1945
	Sterling Sharpe, vs. Buccaneers, Oct. 24, 1993
	Sterling Sharpe, vs. Cowboys, Nov. 24, 1994

Most Consecutive Games, Touchdowns

7	Don Hutson, 1941-42
	Don Hutson, 1943-44
6	Bill Howton, 1956
	Sterling Sharpe, 1994
5	Don Hutson, 1942
	Bill Howton, 1952

INTERCEPTIONS

Most Seasons Leading Team

7	Bobby Dillon, 1952-58
5	Willie Wood, 1961-63, '65, '70
	LeRoy Butler, 1990-91, '93, '95, '97
4	Herb Adderley, 1963-65, '69
	Darren Sharper, 2000-03

Most Consecutive Seasons Leading Team

7	Bobby Dillon, 1952-58
4	Darren Sharper, 2000-03
3	Willie Wood, 1961-63
	Herb Adderley, 1963-65
	Ken Ellis, 1971-73

Most Interceptions, Career

52	Bobby Dillon, 1952-59
48	Willie Wood, 1960-71
39	Herb Adderley, 1961-69
38	LeRoy Butler, 1990-01

Most Interceptions, Season

10	Irv Comp, 1943

Most Interceptions, Rookie, Season

10	Irv Comp, 1943
9	John Symank, 1957
	Tom Flynn, 1984
7	Rebel Steiner, 1950
6	Mike McKenzie, 1999

Most Interceptions, Game

4	Bobby Dillon. vs. Lions, Nov. 26, 1953
	Willie Buchanon, vs. Chargers, Sept. 24, 1978

Most Consecutive Games Interceptions

4	Accomplished many times. Last: Willie Wood, 1970

YARDS GAINED

Most Seasons Leading Team

5	Bobby Dillon, 1953-56, '58
	LeRoy Butler, 1990, '93-96
3	Herb Adderley, 1962, '65, '69
	Mike Douglass, 1979, '82, '85

Most Yards Gained, Career

976	Bobby Dillon, 1952-59
795	Herb Adderley, 1961-69
699	Willie Wood, 1960-71
580	Darren Sharper, 1997-2003

Most Yards Gained, Season

244	Bobby Dillon, 1956
233	Darren Sharper, 2002
217	Maurice Harvey, 1981
198	John Symank, 1957

Most Yards Gained, Rookie, Season

198	John Symank, 1957
190	Rebel Steiner, 1950
149	Irv Comp, 1943
114	Marques Anderson, 2002

Most Yards Gained, Game

99	Maurice Harvey, vs. Saints, Dec. 13, 1981 (2)
	Tim Lewis, vs. Rams, Nov. 18, 1984 (1)
98	Mike McKenzie, vs. Bears, Dec. 7, 2003 (2)
94	Rebel Steiner, vs. Bears, Oct. 1, 1950 (1)
91	Hal Van Every, vs. Steelers, Nov. 23, 1941 (1)

Longest Return

99	Tim Lewis, vs. Rams, Nov. 18, 1984
94	Rebel Steiner, vs. Bears, Oct. 1, 1950
91	Hal Van Every, vs. Steelers, Nov. 23, 1941
90	LeRoy Butler, vs. Chargers, Sept. 15, 1996
	Mike McKenzie, vs. Bears, Dec. 7, 2003

Touchdowns

Most Touchdowns, Career

7	Herb Adderley, 1961-69
5	Bobby Dillon, 1952-59
4	Johnny (Blood) McNally, 1929-33, '35-36
3	Charley Brock, 1939-47
	Doug Hart, 1964-71

Ken Ellis, 1970-75
Darren Sharper, 1997-2003

Most Touchdowns, Season

3 Herb Adderley, 1965
2 Don Perkins, 1944
  Charley Brock, 1945
  Bob Jeter, 1966
  Darren Sharper, 1997
  Marques Anderson, 2002

PUNTING

Most Seasons Leading Team

6 David Beverly, 1975-80
5 Donny Anderson, 1967-71
  Don Bracken, 1986-90
4 Max McGee, 1954, '58-60
  Craig Hentrich, 1994-97
3 Clarke Hinkle, 1939-41
  Lou Brock, 1942-44
  Earl (Jug) Girard, 1949-51
  Dick Deschaine, 1955-57

Most Consecutive Seasons Leading Team

6 David Beverly, 1975-80
5 Donny Anderson, 1967-71
  Don Bracken, 1986-90
4 Craig Hentrich, 1994-97
  Josh Bidwell, 2000-03

Most Punts, Career

495 David Beverly, 1975-80
368 Don Bracken, 1985-90
315 Donny Anderson, 1966-71
308 Josh Bidwell, 2000-03

Most Punts, Season

106 David Beverly, 1978
86 David Beverly, 1980
  Paul McJulien, 1991
85 David Beverly, 1977
  Bucky Scribner, 1984
  Don Bracken, 1988
83 David Beverly, 1976

Most Punts, Game

11 Clarke Hinkle, vs. Bears, Dec. 10, 1933
  Earl (Jug) Girard, vs. Bears, Oct. 15, 1950
  Earl (Jug) Girard, vs. Rams, Dec. 3, 1950

Longest Punt

90 Don Chandler, vs. 49ers, Oct. 10, 1965
78 Jack Jacobs, vs. Cardinals, Oct. 10, 1948
75 Boyd Dowler, vs. Vikings, Oct. 22, 1961
  Boyd Dowler, vs. 49ers, Oct. 21, 1962
74 Arnie Herber, vs. Lions, Oct. 22, 1939
  Jack Jacobs, vs. Rams, Oct. 5, 1947

Average Yardage

Highest Gross Average, Career (min. 150 punts)

42.73 Craig Hentrich, 1994-97 (289-12,349)
42.62 Dick Deschaine, 1955-57 (181-7,714)
41.98 Bucky Scribner, 1983-84 (153-6,202)
41.59 Max McGee, 1954, '57-67 (256-10,647)

Highest Gross Average, Season (min. 2.5 punts/game)

45.04 Craig Hentrich, 1997 (75-3,378)

44.69 Jerry Norton, 1963 (51-2,279)
44.05 Boyd Dowler, 1961 (38-1,674)
43.54 Jack Jacobs, 1947 (57-2,481)

Highest Gross Average, Game (min. 4 punts)

61.60 Roy McKay, vs. Cardinals, Oct. 28, 1945 (5-308)
54.83 Craig Hentrich, vs. Jets, Nov. 13, 1994 (6-329)
54.25 Earl (Jug) Girard, vs. Eagles, Oct. 14, 1951 (4-217)
53.25 Boyd Dowler, vs. Colts, Oct. 9, 1960 (4-213)
  Josh Bidwell, vs. Saints, Sept. 15, 2002 (4-213)

Highest Net Average, Career (min. 150 punts)

37.69 Dick Deschaine, 1955-57 (181-6,822)
36.52 Donny Anderson, 1966-71 (315-11,504)
35.64 Craig Hentrich, 1994-97 (291-10,372)
35.50 Josh Bidwell, 2000-03 (308-10,933)

Highest Net Average, Season (min. 2.5 punts/game)

39.20 Jerry Norton, 1963 (51-1,999)
38.47 Donny Anderson, 1969 (58-2,231)
38.03 Dick Deschaine, 1957 (63-2,396)
37.85 Donny Anderson, 1968 (59-2,233)

Had Blocked

Most Consecutive Punts, None Blocked

308 Josh Bidwell, 2000-03
274 David Beverly, 1977-80
254 Donny Anderson, 1967-71
200 Craig Hentrich, 1995-97

Most Punts, Had Blocked, Career

5 Earl (Jug) Girard, 1948-51
  Don Bracken, 1985-90
3 Lou Brock, 1940-45
  Steve Broussard, 1975
  Bill Renner, 1986-87

Most Punts, Inside Opponents' 20, Career

104 Craig Hentrich, 1994-97
96 David Beverly, 1975-80
85 Donny Anderson, 1966-71
  Josh Bidwell, 2000-03
74 Don Bracken, 1985-90

Most Punts, Inside Opponents' 20, Season

30 Sean Landetta, 1998
28 Craig Hentrich, 1996
26 Craig Hentrich, 1995
  Craig Hentrich, 1997
  Josh Bidwell, 2002
24 Craig Hentrich, 1994

Most Punts, Inside Opponents' 20, Game

6 Donny Anderson, vs. Browns, Dec. 7, 1969
5 Donny Anderson, vs. Vikings, Oct. 15, 1967
  David Beverly, vs. Bears, Oct. 8, 1978

Most Touchbacks, Career

47 Craig Hentrich, 1994-97
37 David Beverly, 1975-80
  Don Bracken, 1985-90
31 Max McGee, 1954, '57-67
28 Josh Bidwell, 2000-03

Most Touchbacks, Season

21 Craig Hentrich, 1997
13 Don Chandler, 1965
12 Max McGee, 1960
  Bucky Scribner, 1984
  Don Bracken, 1988
11 Don Bracken, 1989

Most Touchbacks, Game

  4 Don Bracken, vs. Bears, Sept. 25, 1988
     Don Bracken, vs. Buccaneers, Dec. 3, 1989
     Craig Hentrich, vs. Eagles, Sept. 7, 1997
  3 Max McGee, vs. Rams, Dec. 12, 1954
     Boyd Dowler, vs. Rams, Dec. 17, 1961
     Donny Anderson, vs. Vikings, Oct. 17, 1971
     David Beverly, vs. Buccaneers, Dec. 3, 1978
     Bucky Scribner, vs. Chargers, Oct. 7, 1984

PUNT RETURNS

Most Seasons Leading Team, Number of Returns

 10 Willie Wood, 1960-68, '70
  4 Al Carmichael, 1953, '56-58
     Phillip Epps, 1982-85
  3 Joe Laws, 1943-45
     Billy Grimes, 1950-52
     Walter Stanley, 1986-88

Most Punt Returns, Career

 187 Willie Wood, 1960-71
 100 Al Carmichael, 1953-58
     Phillip Epps, 1982-88
  87 Walter Stanley, 1985-88
  85 Johnnie Gray, 1975-83

Most Punt Returns, Season

  58 Desmond Howard, 1996
  44 Roell Preston, 1998
  40 Robert Brooks, 1994
  37 Johnnie Gray, 1976
     Antonio Freeman, 1995

Most Punt Returns, Rookie, Season

  37 Antonio Freeman, 1995
  30 Jeff Query, 1989
  24 Veryl Switzer, 1954
  21 Willard Harrell, 1975
     Terrell Buckley, 1992

Most Punt Returns, Game

  8 Phillip Epps, vs. Vikings, Nov. 21, 1982
  7 Johnnie Gray, vs. Vikings, Nov. 21, 1976
     Robert Brooks, vs. Patriots, Oct. 2, 1994
     Desmond Howard, vs. Chargers, Sept. 15, 1996

Fair Catches

Darrien Gordon, vs. Panthers, Sept. 29, 2002

Most Fair Catches, Career

 102 Willie Wood, 1960-71
  41 Elijah Pitts, 1961-69, 71
  38 Jon Staggers, 1972-74
  32 Allen Rossum, 2000-01

Most Fair Catches, Season

  24 Allen Rossum, 2000
  20 Jon Staggers, 1972
  18 Willie Wood, 1970
     Antonio Chatman, 2003
  17 Roell Preston, 1998

Most Fair Catches, Game

  5 Willie Wood, vs. Bears, Nov. 15, 1970
  4 Willie Wood, vs. Saints, Nov. 17, 1968
     Jon Staggers, vs. Redskins, Nov. 26, 1972
     Phillip Epps, vs. Cowboys, Sept. 23, 1984
     Terrell Buckley, vs. Buccaneers, Oct. 24, 1993
     Terrell Buckley, vs. Buccaneers, Dec. 24, 1994

Roell Preston, vs. Panthers, Sept. 27, 1998
Roell Preston, vs. Buccaneers, Dec. 7, 1998

Yards Gained

Antonio Chatman, vs. Lions, Sept. 14, 2003

Most Seasons Leading Team

  9 Willie Wood, 1960-66, '68, '70
  3 By five players

Most Yards Gained, Career

1,391 Willie Wood, 1960-71
  968 Desmond Howard, 1996, '99
  834 Billy Grimes, 1950-52
  819 Phillip Epps, 1982-88

Most Yards Gained, Season

  875 Desmond Howard, 1996
  555 Billy Grimes, 1950
  398 Roell Preston, 1998
  352 Robert Brooks, 1994

Most Yards Gained, Rookie, Season

  306 Veryl Switzer, 1954
  292 Antonio Freeman, 1995
  247 Jeff Query, 1989
  211 Terrell Buckley, 1992

Most Yards Gained, Game

  167 Desmond Howard, vs. Lions, Dec. 15, 1996
  129 Phillip Epps, vs. Buccaneers, Oct. 2, 1983
  122 Robert Brooks, vs. Rams, Oct. 9, 1994
  118 Desmond Howard, vs. Chargers, Sept. 15, 1996

Longest Punt Return

  95 Steve Odom, vs. Bears, Nov. 10, 1974
  94 Mark Lee, vs. Giants, Nov. 8, 1981
  93 Veryl Switzer, vs. Bears, Nov. 7, 1954

Average Gain

  92 Desmond Howard, vs. Lions, Dec. 15, 1996

Highest Average, Career (min. 50 returns)

13.83 Desmond Howard, 1996, '99 (70-968)
13.24 Billy Grimes, 1950-52 (63-834)
 9.37 Jeff Query, 1989-91 (76-712)
 9.20 Jon Staggers, 1972-74 (50-460)

Highest Average, Season (min. 1 return/game)

19.14 Billy Grimes, 1950 (29-555)
16.07 Willie Wood, 1961 (14-225)
15.36 Ken Ellis, 1972 (14-215)
15.09 Desmond Howard, 1996 (58-875)

Highest Average, Rookie, Season (min. 1 return/game)

12.75 Veryl Switzer, 1954 (24-306)
12.73 Steve Odom, 1974 (15-191)
11.56 Fred Provo, 1948 (18-208)
10.04 Terrell Buckley, 1992 (21-211)

Highest Average, Game (min. 3 returns)

37.00 Mark Lee, vs. Giants, Nov. 8, 1981 (3-111)
36.67 Willie Wood, vs. Bears, Dec. 5, 1964 (3-110)
33.40 Desmond Howard, vs. Lions, Dec. 15, 1996 (5-167)

Touchdowns

30.50 Robert Brooks, vs. Rams, Oct. 9, 1994 (4-122)

Most Touchdowns, Career

  3 Desmond Howard, 1996
  2 Billy Grimes, 1950-52
     Willie Wood, 1960-71
     Jon Staggers, 1972-74

Most Touchdowns, Season

3 Desmond Howard, 1996
2 Billy Grimes, 1950

KICKOFF RETURNS

Willie Wood, 1961
Most Seasons Leading Team, Number of Returns
6 Steve Odom, 1974-79
5 Al Carmichael, 1953-54, '56-58
4 Herb Adderley, 1961-64
Tony Canadeo, 1941, '43, '46-47
3 Billy Grimes, 1950-52
Most Kickoff Returns, Career
179 Steve Odom, 1974-79
153 Al Carmichael, 1953-58
120 Herb Adderley, 1961-69
77 Travis Williams, 1967-70
Most Kickoff Returns, Season
57 Roell Preston, 1998
50 Allen Rossum, 2000
46 Dave Hampton, 1971
42 Steve Odom, 1975
Most Kickoff Returns, Rookie, Season
35 Charles Wilson, 1990
Javon Walker, 2002
33 Vince Workman, 1989
31 Steve Odom, 1974
30 Mark Lee, 1980
Most Kickoff Returns, Game
8 Harlan Huckleby, vs. Redskins, Oct. 17, 1983
Gary Ellerson, vs. Cardinals, Sept. 29, 1985
Roell Preston, vs. Vikings, Oct. 5, 1998
7 Steve Odom, vs. Lions, Sept. 29, 1974

Yards Gained

Roell Preston, vs. Colts, Nov. 16, 1997
Most Seasons Leading Team
6 Steve Odom, 1974-79
5 Al Carmichael, 1953-54, '56-58
4 Tony Canadeo, 1941, '43, '46-47
Herb Adderley, 1961-64
3 Billy Grimes, 1950-52
Most Consecutive Seasons Leading Team
6 Steve Odom, 1974-79
4 Herb Adderley, 1961-64
3 Billy Grimes, 1950-52
Al Carmichael, 1956-58
Most Yards Gained, Career
4,124 Steve Odom, 1974-79
3,907 Al Carmichael, 1953-58
3,080 Herb Adderley, 1961-69
2,084 Dave Hampton, 1969-71
Most Yards Gained, Season
1,497 Roell Preston, 1998
1,314 Dave Hampton, 1971
1,288 Roell Preston, 2000
1,034 Steve Odom, 1975
Most Yards Gained, Rookie, Season
798 Charles Wilson, 1990
769 Javon Walker, 2002
739 Travis Williams, 1967
713 Steve Odom, 1974
Most Yards Gained, Game

256 Roell Preston, vs. Vikings, Oct. 5, 1998
211 Roell Preston, vs. Colts, Nov. 16, 1997
208 Harlan Huckleby, vs. Redskins, Oct. 17, 1983
194 Dave Hampton, vs. Giants, Sept. 19, 1971
Longest Kickoff Return (all touchdowns)
106 Al Carmichael, vs. Bears, Oct. 7, 1956
104 Travis Williams, vs. Rams, Dec. 9, 1967
103 Herb Adderley, vs. Colts, Nov. 18, 1962
101 Dave Hampton, vs. Vikings, Oct. 4, 1970

Average Gain

Roell Preston, vs. Vikings, Oct. 5, 1998
Highest Average, Career (min. 50 returns)
28.16 Dave Hampton, 1969-71 (74,2,084)
26.73 Travis Williams, 1967-70 (77-2,058)
26.69 Roell Preston, 1997-98 (64-1,708)
26.51 Tom Moore, 1960-65 (71-1,882)
Highest Average, Season (min. 1 return per game)
41.06 Travis Williams, 1967 (18-739)
33.08 Tom Moore, 1960 (12-397)
31.56 Najeh Davenport, 2003 (12-397)
29.86 Al Carmichael, 1955 (14-418)
Highest Average, Rookie, Season (min. 1 return per game)
41.06 Travis Williams, 1967 (18-739)
33.08 Tom Moore, 1960 (12-397)
28.50 Larry Krause, 1970 (18-513)
26.56 Herb Adderley, 1961 (18-478)
Highest Average, Game (min. 3 returns)
50.33 Travis Williams, vs. Cardinals, Oct. 30, 1967 (3-151)
44.67 Steve Odom, vs. Lions, Oct. 3, 1976 (3-134)
43.33 Del Rodgers, vs. Bears, Dec. 9, 1984 (3-130)

Touchdowns

43.25 Allen Rossum, vs. Colts, Nov. 19, 2000 (4-173)
Most Touchdowns, Career
5 Travis Williams, 1967-70
3 Dave Hampton, 1969-71
2 Al Carmichael, 1953-58
Herb Adderley, 1961-69
Steve Odom, 1974-79
Robert Brooks, 1992-96
Roell Preston, 1998
Most Touchdowns, Season
4 Travis Williams, 1967
2 Roell Preston, 1998
Most Touchdowns, Game

COMBINED KICK RETURNS

2 Travis Williams, vs. Browns, Nov. 12, 1967
Most Combined Kick Returns, Career
253 Al Carmichael, 1953-58 (p-100, k-153)
243 Steve Odom, 1974-79 (p-64, k-179)
190 Willie Wood, 1960-71 (p-187, k-3)
130 Billy Grimes, 1950-52 (p-63, k-67)
Most Combined Kick Returns, Season
101 Roell Preston, 1998 (p-44, k-57)
80 Desmond Howard, 1996 (p-58, k-22)
79 Allen Rossum, 2000 (p-29, k-50)
69 Antonio Chatman, 2003 (p-33, k-36)
Most Combined Kick Returns, Game
10 Charles Jordan, vs. Rams, Sept. 3, 1995 (p-6, k-4)

Roell Preston, vs. Panthers, Sept. 27, 1998 (p-4, k-6)
9 Al Carmichael, vs. 49ers, Dec. 9, 1956 (p-4, k-5)
Phillip Epps, vs. Buccaneers, Sept. 30, 1984 (p-3, k-6)
Charles Jordan, vs. Cowboys, Oct. 8, 1995 (p-4, k-5)
Antonio Freeman, vs. Vikings, Nov. 5, 1995 (p-6, k-3)
Desmond Howard, vs. Cowboys, Nov. 18, 1996 (p-3, k-6)

Yards Gained

Roell Preston, vs. 49ers, Nov. 1, 1998 (p-4, k-5)
Darrien Gordon, vs. Panthers, Sept. 29, 2002 (p-7, k-2)

Most Yards Gained, Career
4,693 Steve Odom, 1974-79
4,660 Al Carmichael, 1953-58
3,080 Herb Adderley, 1961-69
2,438 Billy Grimes, 1950-52

Most Yards Gained, Season
1,895 Roell Preston, 1998 (p-398, k-1,497)
1,536 Allen Rossum, 2000 (p-248, k-1,288)
1,335 Desmond Howard, 1996 (p-875, k-460)
1,314 Dave Hampton, 1971 (p-0, k-1,314)

Most Yards Gained, Game
256 Roell Preston, vs. Vikings, Oct. 5, 1998 (p-0, k-256)
247 Travis Williams, vs. Steelers, Nov. 2, 1969 (p-83, k-164)
211 Al Carmichael, vs. Bears, Oct. 7, 1956 (p-22, k-189)

Touchdowns

Roell Preston, vs. Colts, Nov. 16, 1997 (p-0, k-211)
208 Harlan Huckleby, vs. Redskins, Oct. 17, 1983 (p-0, k-208)

Most Touchdowns, Career
6 Travis Williams, 1967-70 (p-1, k-5)
3 Dave Hampton, 1969-71 (p-0, k-3)
Steve Odom, 1974-79 (p-1, k-2)
Robert Brooks, 1992-96 (p-1, k-2)
Desmond Howard, 1996 (p-3)
Roell Preston, 1997-98 (p-1, k-2)

Most Touchdowns, Season
4 Travis Williams, 1967 (p-0, k-4)
3 Desmond Howard, 1996 (p-3, k-0)
Roell Preston, 1998 (p-1, k-2)
2 Billy Grimes, 1950 (p-2, k-0)
Willie Wood, 1961 (p-2, k-0)
Travis Williams, 1969 (p-1, k-1)
Robert Brooks, 1994 (p-1, k-1)

Most Touchdowns, Game

FUMBLES

2 Travis Williams, vs. Browns, Nov. 12, 1967 (p-0, k-2)
Travis Williams, vs. Steelers, Nov. 2, 1969 (p-1, k-1)

Most Fumbles, Career
116 Brett Favre, 1992-2003
64 Bart Starr, 1956-71
56 Lynn Dickey, 1976-77, '79-85
48 Don Majkowski, 1987-92

Most Fumbles, Season
16 Brett Favre, 2001
15 Don Majkowski, 1989

14 Brett Favre, 1993
13 Lynn Dickey, 1980

Most Fumbles, Game
6 Brett Favre, vs. Buccaneers, Dec. 7, 1998
4 Don Majkowski, vs. Vikings, Sept. 6, 1992
Brett Favre, vs. Bengals, Sept. 20, 1992

Most Fumbles Recovered, Career, Own and Opponents
29 Brett Favre, 1992-2002 (29-own)
26 Lynn Dickey, 1976-77, '79-85 (26-own)
23 Ray Nitschke, 1958-72 (3-own, 20-opp)
22 Willie Davis, 1960-69 (1-own, 21-opp)
Johnnie Gray, 1975-83 (2-own, 20-opp)

Most Fumbles Recovered, Season, Own and Opponents
6 Charley Brock, 1946 (1-own, 5-opp)
Larry Craig, 1946 (2-own, 4-opp)
Lynn Dickey, 1983 (6-own)
Don Majkowski, 1989 (6-own)
Brett Favre, 2001 (6-own)

Most Fumbles Recovered, Game, Own and Opponents
3 Billy Grimes, vs. Yanks, Oct. 19, 1950 (3-own, 0-opp)
Gary Ellerson, vs. Lions, Oct. 6, 1985 (2-own, 1-opp)

Fumbles Recovered

Chuck Fusina, vs. Redskins, Nov. 9, 1986 (3-own, 0-opp)
Don Majkowski, vs. Vikings, Sept. 6, 1992 (3-own, 0-opp)

Most Own Fumbles Recovered, Career
29 Brett Favre, 1992-2002
26 Lynn Dickey, 1976-77, '79-85
19 Don Majkowski, 1987-92
18 Bart Starr, 1956-71

Most Own Fumbles Recovered, Season
6 Lynn Dickey, 1983
Don Majkowski, 1989
Brett Favre, 2001
5 Lynn Dickey, 1980
Gerry Ellis, 1980
Lynn Dickey, 1985
Brett Favre, 1996
Brett Favre, 2002

Most Own Fumbles Recovered, Game
3 Billy Grimes, vs. Yanks, Oct. 19, 1950
Chuck Fusina, vs. Redskins, Nov. 9, 1986
Don Majkowski, vs. Vikings, Sept. 6, 1992

Most Opponents Fumbles Recovered, Career
21 Willie Davis, 1960-69
20 Ray Nitschke, 1958-72
Johnnie Gray, 1975-83
18 Henry Jordan, 1959-69
16 Lionel Aldridge, 1963-71

Most Opponents Fumbles Recovered, Season
5 Charley Brock, 1945
Charley Brock, 1946
Paul Lipscomb, 1946
Lionel Aldridge, 1964
Randy Scott, 1985
Brian Noble, 1987

Most Opponents Fumbles Recovered, Game
2 Accomplished many times

Longest Fumble Return
88 Keith McKenzie, vs. Steelers, Nov. 9, 1998

Touchdowns

76 Scott Stephen, vs. Bears, Dec. 17, 1989
70 Mike Butler, vs. Vikings, Nov. 11, 1979

68 George Cumby, vs. Buccaneers, Oct. 11, 1981

Most Touchdowns, Career
3 Keith McKenzie, 1996-99
2 Mike Douglass, 1978-85
   Del Rodgers, 1982, '84
   LeRoy Butler, 1990-98

Most Touchdowns, Season
2 Del Rodgers, 1982
   Mike Douglass, 1983
   Keith McKenzie, 1999

Most Touchdowns, Career, Own Recovered
2 Del Rodgers, 1982, '84
1 Max McGee, 1954, '57-67
   Willie Davis, 1960-69
   Sterling Sharpe, 1988-94
   Carl Bland, 1989-90
   Don Beebe, 1996-97

Most Touchdowns, Season, Own Recovered
2 Del Rodgers, 1982
1 Max McGee, 1962
   Willie Davis, 1964
   Carl Bland, 1989
   Sterling Sharpe, 1989
   Don Beebe, 1996

Most Touchdowns, Career, Opponents Recovered
3 Keith McKenzie, 1996-99
2 Mike Douglass, 1978-85
   LeRoy Butler, 1990-98

COMBINED NET YARDS GAINED

Most Touchdowns, Season, Opponents Recovered
2 Mike Douglass, 1983
   Keith McKenzie, 1999

Most Seasons Leading Team
8 Don Hutson, 1936, '39-45
7 Jim Taylor, 1960-66
5 Sterling Sharpe, 1989-93
4 Tony Canadeo, 1946-49
   Al Carmichael, 1953, '56-58
   Steve Odom, 1974-77
   James Lofton, 1979, '82-84
   Ahman Green, 2000-03

Most Consecutive Seasons Leading Team
7 Don Hutson, 1939-45
   Jim Taylor, 1960-66
5 Sterling Sharpe, 1989-93
4 Tony Canadeo, 1946-49
   Steve Odom, 1974-77

ATTEMPTS

Ahman Green, 2000-03
3 Al Carmichael, 1956-58
   James Lofton, 1982-84

Most Attempts, Career
2,012 Jim Taylor, 1958-66
1,456 Ahman Green, 2000-03
1,437 John Brockington, 1971-77
1,300 Dorsey Levens, 1994-01

Most Attempts, Season
407 Ahman Green, 2003
383 Dorsey Levens, 1997
378 Edgar Bennett, 1995
368 Ahman Green, 2001

Most Attempts, Game
41 Terdell Middleton, vs. Vikings, Nov. 26, 1978

Yards Gained

38 Vince Workman, vs. Vikings, Sept. 6, 1992
37 Dorsey Levens, vs. Cowboys, Nov. 23, 1997
36 Ahman Green, vs. Buccaneers, Dec. 24, 2000

Most Yards Gained, Career
9,909 James Lofton, 1978-86
9,898 Jim Taylor, 1958-66
8,709 Don Hutson, 1935-45
8,276 Sterling Sharpe, 1988-94

Most Yards Gained, Season
2,250 Ahman Green, 2003
1,981 Ahman Green, 2001
1,918 Roell Preston, 1998
1,896 Billy Grimes, 1950

Most Yards Gained, Rookie, Season
1,231 Bill Howton, 1952
1,219 Steve Odom, 1974
1,203 John Brockington, 1971
1,170 Al Carmichael, 1953

Most Yards Gained, Game
314 Travis Williams, vs. Steelers, Nov. 2, 1969
287 Walter Stanley, vs. Lions, Nov. 27, 1986
257 Bill Howton, vs. Rams, Oct. 21, 1956
256 Roell Preston, vs. Vikings, Oct. 5, 1998

Most Seasons, 1,000 or More Yards, Career
6 Jim Taylor, 1960-64, '66
5 Steve Odom, 1974-78
   James Lofton, 1980-81, '83-85
   Sterling Sharpe, 1989-90, '92-94
4 Donny Anderson, 1967-68, '70-71
   John Brockington, 1971-74
   Gerry Ellis, 1980-81, '83, '85
   Edgar Bennett, 1993-96
   Ahman Green, 2000-03

Most Consecutive Seasons, 1,000 or More Yards, Career
5 Jim Taylor, 1960-64
   Steve Odom, 1974-78
4 John Brockington, 1971-74
   Edgar Bennett, 1993-96
   Ahman Green, 2000-03
3 Don Hutson, 1942-44

SACKS

Sterling Sharpe, 1992-94
Antonio Freeman, 1997-99

Most Sacks, Career
68.5 Reggie White, 1993-98
55.0 Tim Harris, 1986-90
41.5 Ezra Johnson, 1982-87
37.0 Kabeer Gbaja-Biamila, 2000-03

Most Sacks, Season
19.5 Tim Harris, 1989
16.0 Reggie White, 1998
14.5 Ezra Johnson, 1983
13.5 Tim Harris, 1988
   Tony Bennett, 1992
   Kabeer Gbaja-Biamila, 2001

Most Sacks, Game
5.0 Vonnie Holliday, vs. Bills, Dec. 22, 2002
4.5 Bryce Paup, vs. Buccaneers, Sept. 15, 1991

ALL-TIME TEAM RECORDS

CHAMPIONSHIPS

Most Seasons League Champions
12 1929-31, 1936, 1939, 1944, 1961-62, 1965-67, 1996

Most Consecutive Seasons League Champions
3 1929-31, 1965-67
2 1961-62

Most Times Finishing First, Regular Season
19 1929-31, 1936, 1938-39, 1944, 1960-62, 1965-67, 1972, 1995-97, 2002-03

Most Consecutive Times Finishing First, Regular Season
3 1929-31, 1960-62, 1965-67, 1995-97
2 1938-39, 2002-03

GAMES WON

Most Consecutive Games Won (incl. postseason)
12 1961-62
11 1929
10 1929-30
9 1931, 1936, 1943-44, 1996-97

Most Consecutive Games Won (regular season only)
11 1929, 1961-62
10 1929-30
9 1931, 1936, 1943-44, 1997-98
8 1941, 1963

Most Consecutive Games Without Defeat (incl. postseason)
23 1928-30 (won 21, tied 2)
12 1961-62 (won 12)
11 1936 (won 10, tied 1), 1966-67 (won 10, tied 1)
10 1930-31 (won 9, tied 1), 1964-65 (won 9, tied 1)

Most Consecutive Games Without Defeat (regular season only)
23 1928-30 (won 21, tied 2)
11 1961-62 (won 11)
10 1930-31 (won 9, tied 1), 1936 (won 9, tied 1) 1964-65 (won 9, tied 1)
9 1922-23 (won 5, tied 4), 1932 (won 8, tied 1) 1943-44 (won 9), 1997-98 (won 9)

Most Games Won, Season (incl. postseason games)
16 1996
15 1997
14 1962, 1966
13 1995, 2001

Curly Lambeau coached the Packers to many records, including most consecutive games won (11) and most consecutive games without a defeat (23). His team won six NFL championships. Stiller-Lefebvre Collection

Vince Lombardi's Glory Years teams won five NFL championships and the first two Super Bowls. Stiller-Lefebvre Collection

Most Consecutive Games Won, Season
(incl. postseason games)
    10   1929, 1962
     9   1931, 1936
     8   1930, 1941, 1963, 1996
     7   1932, 1937, 1966, 1997, 2002
Most Consecutive Games Won, Season (regular season only)
    10   1929, 1962
     9   1931, 1936
     8   1930, 1941, 1963
     7   1932, 1937, 2002
Most Consecutive Games Won, Start of Season
    10   1929, 1962
     9   1931
     8   1930
     6   1944, 1965
Most Consecutive Games Won, End of Season
(regular season only)
     8   1941
     5   1923, 1966, 1996, 1997
     4   1939, 1959, 2000, 2003
Most Consecutive Games Without Defeat, Season
(incl. postseason)
    13   1929 (won 12, tied 1)
    11   1936 (won 10, tied 1)
    10   1962 (won 10)
     9   1931 (won 9), 1932 (won 8, tied 1)
Most Consecutive Games Without Defeat, Season
(regular season only)
    13   1929 (won 12, tied 1)
    10   1936 (won 9, tied 1), 1962 (won 10)
     9   1931 (won 9), 1932 (won 8, tied 1)
     8   1930 (won 8), 1941 (won 8), 1963 (won 8)
Most Consecutive Games Without Defeat, Start of Season
    13   1929 (won 12, tied 1)
    10   1962 (won 10)
     9   1931 (won 9), 1932 (won 8, tied 1)
     8   1930 (won 8)
Most Consecutive Games Without Defeat, End of Season (regular season only)
    13   1929 (won 12, tied 1)
    10   1936 (won 9, tied 1)
     8   1941 (won 8)
     7   1922 (won 4, tied 3)
Most Consecutive Home Games Won
(includes Milwaukee)(regular season games only)
    25   1995-98
    20   1929-32
    14   1923-26
    13   1961-62
Most Consecutive Home Games Won
(includes Milwaukee)(includes postseason games)
    29   1995-98
    20   1929-32
    14   1923-26
          1961-62
    11   2001-02
Most Consecutive Home Games Without Defeat
(includes Milwaukee)(regular season games only)
    30   1928-33 (won 27, tied 3)
    25   1995-98 (won 25)
    16   1923-26 (won 14, tied 2)
    13   1961-62 (won 13)
Most Consecutive Home Games Without Defeat
(includes Milwaukee)(includes postseason games)
    30   1928-33 (won 27, tied 3)
    29   1995-98 (won 29)
    16   1923-26 (won 14, tied 2)
    14   1961-62 (won 14)

Most Consecutive Games Won at Milwaukee
(regular season only)
    16   1935-42
     9   1961-64
     8   1964-67
     6   1981-83, 1991-93
Most Consecutive Games Won at Milwaukee
(includes postseason)
    17   1935-42
     9   1961-64
     8   1964-67
     6   1981-83, 1991-93
Most Consecutive Games Won at Green Bay
(regular season only)
    25   1995-98
    11   1960-62
          2001-02
     9   1993-94
          2000-01
Most Consecutive Games Won at Green Bay
(includes postseason)
    29   1995-98
    12   1960-62
    11   2001-02
    10   1993-94
Most Consecutive Road Games Won
(regular season only)
     8   1941-42, 1966-67
     6   1928-29, 1935-36
     5   1960-61, 1961-62, 1962-63, 1989-90, 1997-98
Most Consecutive Road Games Won
(includes postseason)
     9   1966-67
     6   1928-29, 1935-36, 1962-63, 1997-98
     5   1941, 1960-61, 1961-62, 1989-90
Most Consecutive Road Games Without Defeat
(regular season only)
    12   1929-30 (won 10, tied 2)
    10   1935-37 (won 9, tied 1), 1940-42 (won 9, tied 1)
     8   1966-67 (won 8)
     6   1922-23 (won 4, tied 2)
Most Consecutive Road Games Without Defeat
(includes postseason)
    12   1929-30 (won 10, tied 2)
    10   1935-37 (won 9, tied 1)
     9   1966-67 (won 9)
     7   1940-41 (won 6, tied 1)
Most Shutout Games, Won or Tied, Season
     8   1926 (won 7, tied 1), 1929 (won 7, tied 1)
     7   1923 (won 6, tied 1), 1932 (won 6, tied 1)
     5   1922 (won 3, tied 2), 1925 (won 5), 1927 (won 5),
          1928 (won 4, tied 1), 1931 (won 5)
     4   1924 (won 4), 1930 (won 4), 1934 (won 4)
Most Consecutive Shutout Games Won or Tied
     5   1926 (won 5), 1929-30 (won 4, tied 1)
     4   1922-23 (won 3, tied 1)
     3   1922 (won 1, tied 2), 1924 (won 3), 1927 (won 3),
          1928-29 (won 3), 1932 (won 3)

GAMES LOST

Most Consecutive Games Lost
     9   1948-49
     8   1951-52, 1953-54
     7   1949-50, 1958, 1974-75, 1984, 1987-88, 1988, 1990-91
     6   1950, 1952-53, 1986

Most Consecutive Games Without Victory

9   1948-49 (lost 9), 1953-54 (lost 8, tied 1)
8   1951-52 (lost 8)
7   1921-22 (lost 4, tied 3), 1949-50 (lost 7),
     1957-58 (lost 6, tied 1), 1958 (lost 7), 1974-75 (lost 7),
     1984 (lost 7), 1987-88 (lost 7), 1988 (lost 7)
     1990-91 (lost 7)
6   1950 (lost 6), 1952-53 (lost 6), 1986 (lost 6)

Most Games Lost, Season

12   1986, 1988, 1991
11   1979
10   1949, 1958, 1975, 1977, 1980, 1990
9   1948, 1950-51, 1953, 1957, 1976, 1987

Most Consecutive Games Lost, Season

7   1948, 1951, 1958, 1984, 1988
6   1949, 1950, 1986
5   1953, 1959, 1977, 1988, 1990

Most Consecutive Games Lost, Start of Season

6   1986
5   1988
4   1975
3   1922, 1953-54, 1976

Most Consecutive Games Lost, End of Season

7   1948, 1951, 1958
6   1949
5   1953, 1990
4   1954, 1980

Most Consecutive Games Without Victory, Season

7   1948 (lost 7), 1951 (lost 7), 1958 (lost 7),
     1984 (lost 7), 1988 (lost 7)
6   1949 (lost 6), 1950 (lost 6), 1953 (lost 5, tied 1),
     1986 (lost 6)
5   1922 (lost 3, tied 2), 1959 (lost 5), 1977 (lost 5),
     1988 (lost 5), 1990 (lost 5)

Most Consecutive Games Without Victory, Start of Season

6   1986 (lost 6)
5   1922 (lost 3, tied 2), 1988 (lost 5)
4   1958 (lost 3, tied 1), 1975 (lost 4)
3   1928 (lost 2, tied 1), 1933 (lost 2, tied 1), 1953 (lost 3),
     1954 (lost 3), 1976 (lost 3)

Most Consecutive Games Without Victory, End of Season

7   1948 (lost 7), 1951 (lost 7), 1958 (lost 7)
6   1949 (lost 6), 1953 (lost 5, tied 1)
5   1990 (lost 5)
4   1954 (lost 4), 1980 (lost 4)

Most Consecutive Home Games Lost
(includes Milwaukee)

7   1976-77, 1985-86
6   1957-58, 1980-81
5   1948-49, 1953-54
4   1951-52, 1968, 1975

Most Consecutive Home Games, Without Victory
(includes Milwaukee)

8   1957-58 (lost 7, tied 1)
7   1976-77 (lost 7), 1985-86 (lost 7)
6   1980-81 (lost 6)
5   1948-49 (lost 5), 1953-54 (lost 5)

Most Consecutive Road Games Lost

12   1957-59
11   1949-50
10   1975-76
9   1978-79

Most Consecutive Road Games, Without Victory
     see record above

Most Shutout Games Lost or Tied, Season

4   1928 (lost 3, tied 1), 1932 (lost 3, tied 1)
3   1924 (lost 3), 1925 (lost 3), 1934 (lost 3), 1988 (lost 3)
2   1922 (tied 2), 1923 (lost 1, tied 1), 1944 (lost 2),
     1949 (lost 2), 1970 (lost 2)

Most Consecutive Shutout Games Lost or Tied

2   1922 (lost 2), 1923 (lost 1, tied 1), 1925 (lost 2),
     1928 (lost 2), 1932 (lost 2), 1988 (lost 2)

Most Consecutive Games Lost at Milwaukee
(since 1933)

8   1956-59
5   1947-49
4   1953-54
3   1976-77, 1980-81, 1990-91

Most Consecutive Games Lost at Green Bay (since 1933)

8   1985-87
7   1987-88
5   1990-91
4   1949-50, 1951-52, 1953-54, 1973-74, 1976-77, 1991-92

TIE GAMES

Most Tie Games, Season

3   1922, 1926, 1928
2   1971, 1973

Most Consecutive Tie Games

2   1922, 1926

LENGTH OF GAME

Longest Game Played (since 1938)
(includes overtime games)

4:09   vs. Lions, Oct. 11, 1987 (OT)
4:02   vs. Buccaneers, Sept. 30, 1984 (OT)
3:53   vs. Dolphins, Oct. 29, 2000 (OT)
3:48   vs. Broncos, Sept. 20, 1987 (OT)

Longest Game Played (since 1938)
(no overtime games)

3:43   vs. Lions, Nov. 27, 1986
3:41   vs. Lions, Nov. 12, 1989
3:39   vs. 49ers, Oct. 26, 1986
3:36   vs. Bills, Oct. 6, 1974

Shortest Game Played (since 1938)

1:45   vs. Lions, Nov. 17, 1946
1:50   vs. Lions, Oct. 25, 1942
1:52   vs. Lions, Dec. 2, 1945
2:00   vs. Rams, Oct. 30, 1938

Greatest Time of Possession (since 1977)
(includes overtime games)

50:12   vs. Buccaneers, Oct. 12, 1980 (OT)
41:25   vs. Giants, Oct. 4, 1981
41:10   vs. 49ers, Oct. 26, 1986
40:42   vs. Lions, Dec. 3, 1972 (unofficial, but accurate)

Greatest Time of Possession (since 1977)
(no overtime games)

41:25   vs. Giants, Oct. 4, 1981
41:10   vs. 49ers, Oct. 26, 1986
40:42   vs. Lions, Dec. 3, 1972 (unofficial, but accurate)
39:58   vs. Cowboys, Oct. 8, 1989

Shortest Time of Possession

14:46   vs. Broncos, Oct. 17, 1999
15:13   vs. Lions, Nov. 22, 1984
17:29   vs. Cowboys, Nov. 12, 1978
18:24   vs. Chargers, Oct. 7, 1984

SCORING

Most Points, Season

456   1996
442   2003
429   1983
422   1997

Fewest Points, Season

70	1921, 1922
85	1923
102	1924
113	1927

Fewest Points, Season (since 1932)

114	1949
134	1977
148	1946
152	1932

Most Points, Game

57	vs. Lions, Oct. 7, 1945
56	vs. Falcons, Oct. 23, 1966
55	vs. Cardinals, Nov. 1, 1942
	vs. Browns, Nov. 12, 1967
	vs. Buccaneers, Oct. 2, 1983
54	vs. Steelers, Nov. 23, 1941

Most Points, Both Teams, Game

95	GB (48) vs. Redskins (47), Oct. 17, 1983
88	GB (41) vs. Falcons (47), Nov. 27, 1983
87	GB (35) vs. Lions (52), Nov. 22, 1951
84	GB (44) vs. Lions (40), Nov. 27, 1986

Fewest Points, Both Teams, Game

0	Accomplished many times

Most Points, Shutout Victory, Game

49	vs. Bears, Sept. 30, 1962
	vs. Eagles, Nov. 11, 1962
47	vs. Pirates, Oct. 15, 1933
41	vs. Reds, Oct. 14, 1934
37	vs. Redskins, Sept. 24, 2001

Fewest Points, Shutout Victory, Game

2	vs. Bears, Oct. 16, 1932

Most Points Overcome to Win Game

23	vs. Rams, Sept. 12, 1982 (down 0-23, won 35-23)
21	vs. Saints, Sept. 17, 1989 (down 0-21, won 35-34)
18	vs. Lions, Oct. 17, 1965 (down 3-21, won 31-21)
17	vs. Redskins, Nov. 30, 1941 (down 0-17, won 22-17)
	vs. Lions, Oct. 16, 1972 (down 0-17, won 24-23)

Most Points, First Half

49	vs. Buccaneers, Oct. 2, 1983
45	vs. Browns, Nov. 12, 1967
41	vs. Lions, Oct. 7, 1945
35	vs. Eagles, Nov. 11, 1962
	vs. Lions, Dec. 6, 1992

Most Points, Second Half

38	vs. Giants, Oct. 22, 1967
35	vs. Bears, Sept. 30, 1962
	vs. Rams, Sept. 12, 1982
	vs. Cowboys, Nov. 23, 1997
	vs. Cardinals, Jan. 2, 2000
34	vs. Cardinals, Nov. 1, 1942
	vs. Steelers, Sept. 19, 1965
33	vs. Jeffersons, Oct. 25, 1925

Most Points, Both Teams, First Half

56	GB (49) vs. Buccaneers (7), Oct. 2, 1983
55	GB (21) vs. Cardinals (34), Nov. 27, 1949
	GB (28) vs. Colts (27), Nov. 16, 1997
52	GB (21) vs. Lions (31), Nov. 22, 1951
	GB (45) vs. Browns (7), Nov. 12, 1967
51	GB (28) vs. Steelers (23), Oct. 7, 1951
	GB (7) vs. Rams (44), Sept. 21, 1980

Most Points, Both Teams, Second Half

56	GB (35) vs. Cardinals (21), Jan. 2, 2000
55	GB (28) vs. Yanks (27), Oct. 9, 1950
52	GB (28) vs. Bears (24), Nov. 6, 1955
	GB (28) vs. Cardinals (24), Sept. 29, 1985
51	GB (24) vs. Redskins (27), Oct. 17, 1983

Most Points, One Quarter

41	vs. Lions, Oct. 7, 1945 (2)
35	vs. Browns, Nov. 12, 1967 (1)
	vs. Buccaneers, Oct. 2, 1983 (2)

Most Points, Both Teams, One Quarter

48	GB (41) vs. Lions (7), Oct. 7, 1945 (2)
44	GB (7) vs. Rams (37), Sept. 21, 1980 (2)
42	GB (28) vs. Bears (14), Nov. 6, 1955 (4)
	GB (35) vs. Browns (7), Nov. 12, 1967 (1)
	GB (35) vs. Buccaneers (7), Oct. 2, 1983 (2)
41	GB (21) vs. Yanks (20), Oct. 8, 1950 (3)

Most Points, First Quarter

35	vs. Browns, Nov. 12, 1967
28	vs. Seahawks, Oct. 15, 1978
21	vs. Steam Roller, Oct. 25, 1931
	vs. Eagles, Sept. 15, 1940
	vs. Steelers, Oct. 7, 1951
	vs. Lions, Oct. 25, 1987
	vs. Lions, Sept. 9, 2001
20	vs. Yellow Jackets, Oct. 12, 1930
	vs. Giants, Nov. 8, 1981

Most Points, Second Quarter

41	vs. Lions, Oct. 7, 1945
35	vs. Buccaneers, Oct. 2, 1983
28	vs. Rams, Nov. 19, 1961
	vs. Eagles, Nov. 11, 1962
	vs. Rams, Dec. 20, 1992
27	vs. Lions, Nov. 10, 2002

Most Points, Third Quarter

23	vs. Lions, Oct. 6, 1985
21	Accomplished many times

Most Points, Fourth Quarter

28	vs. Bears, Nov. 6, 1955
	vs. Vikings, Nov. 21, 1965
	vs. Giants, Oct. 22, 1967
26	vs. Jeffersons, Oct. 25, 1925
24	vs. Colts, Oct. 27, 1957
23	vs. Yanks, Oct. 28, 1951

Most Points, Both Teams, First Quarter

42	GB (35) vs. Browns (7), Nov. 12, 1967
33	GB (7) vs. Rams (26), Dec. 13, 1953
28	GB (14) vs. Card-Pitt (14), Dec. 5, 1943
	GB (7) vs. Colts (21), Oct. 8, 1955
	GB (28) vs. Seahawks (0), Oct. 15, 1978
	GB (0) vs. Vikings (28), Sept. 28, 1986
27	GB (7) vs. Rams (20), Nov. 11, 1945
	GB (0) vs. Cardinals (27), Nov. 27, 1949
	GB (0) vs. 49ers (27), Dec. 7, 1958

Most Points, Both Teams, Second Quarter

48	GB (41) vs. Lions (7), Oct. 7, 1945
44	GB (7) vs. Rams (37), Sept. 21, 1980
42	GB (35) vs. Buccaneers (7), Oct. 2, 1983
35	GB (14) vs. Lions (21), Nov. 27, 1952
	GB (7) vs. Giants (28), Sept. 19, 1971
	GB (7) vs. Bears (28), Dec. 7, 1980
	GB (7) vs. Rams (28), Sept. 28, 1989

Most Points, Both Teams, Third Quarter

41	GB (21) vs. Yanks (20), Oct. 8, 1950
28	GB (21) vs. Bears (7), Oct. 1, 1950
	GB (7) vs. Lions (21), Nov. 22, 1951
	GB (7) vs. Colts (21), Oct. 25, 1959
	GB (7) vs. Broncos (21), Oct. 17, 1999
26	GB (7) vs. Cowboys (19), Nov. 24, 1994

Most Points, Both Teams, Fourth Quarter

42	GB (28) vs. Bears (14), Nov. 6, 1955
39	GB (26) vs. Jeffersons (13), Oct. 25, 1925
36	GB (21) vs. Chargers (15), Dec. 14, 2003
35	GB (14) vs. Yanks (21), Dec. 2, 1951
	GB (21) vs. Colts (14), Oct. 9, 1960
	GB (28) vs. Giants (7), Oct. 22, 1967
	GB (21) vs. Cardinals (14), Jan. 2, 2000

Most Consecutive Games, Scoring
201	1991-2003 (current)
156	1958-69
122	1978-86
69	1938-44

TOUCHDOWNS

Most Touchdowns, Season
56	1996
53	1962, 2003
52	1983
51	1984

Fewest Touchdowns, Season
9	1921, 1922
10	1923
14	1924, 1949, 1977
17	1927, 1928, 1946

Fewest Touchdowns, Season (since 1932)
14	1949, 1977
17	1946
19	1934, 1974
20	1948, 1973

Most Touchdowns, Game
8	vs. Steelers, Nov. 23, 1941
	vs. Cardinals, Nov. 1, 1942
	vs. Lions, Oct. 7, 1945
	vs. Falcons, Oct. 23, 1966

Most Touchdowns, Both Teams, Game
12	GB (5) vs. Lions (7), Nov. 22, 1951
11	Accomplished six times

Most Consecutive Games Scoring Touchdowns
75	1992-97
61	2000-03
48	1997-2000
45	1965-68

POINTS AFTER TOUCHDOWN

Most (One-Point) Points After Touchdown, Season
52	1962, 1983
51	1996, 2003
49	1961
48	1984, 1995, 1997

Fewest (One-Point) Points After Touchdown, Season
5	1923
6	1922
7	1921
8	1927

Fewest (One-Point) Points After Touchdown, Season (since 1932)
11	1977
12	1949
14	1932
15	1946

Most (One-Point) Points After Touchdown, Game
8	vs. Falcons, Oct. 22, 1966
7	Accomplished seven times

Most (One-Point) Points After Touchdown, Both Teams, Game
12	GB (5) vs. Lions (7), Nov. 22, 1951
11	GB (4) vs. Bears (7), Nov. 6, 1955
	GB (5) vs. Giants (6), Sept. 19, 1971
	GB (6) vs. Redskins (5), Oct. 17, 1983

Most Two-Point Conversions, Season
2	1996, 2000, 2003

Most Two-Point Conversions, Game
1	Many times

Most Two-Point Conversions, Both Teams, Game
2	GB (0) vs. Lions (2), Nov. 6, 1994
	GB (1) vs. Bears (1), Sept. 9, 1997
	GB (0) vs. Colts (2), Nov. 16, 1997

FIELD GOALS

Most Field Goals Attempted, Season
48	1972
39	1964, 1974
38	2000
37	1993

Fewest Field Goals Attempted Season
5	1944
8	1951, 1956
10	1942
13	1945

Most Field Goals Attempted, Game
6	vs. Lions, Sept. 14, 1941
	vs. Lions, Oct. 26, 1947
	vs. Steelers, Oct. 30, 1960
	vs. Browns, Sept. 17, 1972
	vs. Cowboys, Oct. 1, 1972
	vs. Lions, Dec. 3, 1972
	vs. Lions, Sept. 29, 1974
	vs. Vikings, Nov. 17, 1974

Most Field Goals Attempted, Both Teams, Game
11	GB (6) vs. Lions (5), Sept. 29, 1974
10	GB (5) vs. Cardinals (5), Dec. 5, 1971
9	GB (5) vs. Colts (4), Oct. 18, 1964
	GB (3) vs. Bears (6), Nov. 8, 1987
	GB (4) vs. Jets (5), Nov. 3, 1991

Most Field Goals, Season
33	1972, 2000
31	1993
29	1998
28	2002

Fewest Field Goals, Season
0	1930, 1931, 1932, 1944
1	1927
2	1926, 1929, 1933
3	1921, 1922, 1925, 1928, 1950

Fewest Field Goals, Season (since 1932)
0	1932, 1944
2	1933
3	1950
4	1937, 1943

Most Field Goals, Game
5	vs. Raiders, Nov. 11, 1990
	vs. 49ers, Oct. 14, 1996
	vs. Cardinals, Sept. 24, 2000

Most Field Goals, Both Teams, Game
8	GB (4) vs. Lions (4), Sept. 29, 1974

Most Consecutive Games Scoring Field Goals
14	1987, 1997-98
12	1980-81, 1991-92

SAFETIES

Most Safeties, Season
3	1932, 1975
2	1929, 1939, 1947, 1959, 1988

Most Safeties, Game
1	Accomplished 31 times

Most Safeties, Both Teams, Game
2	GB (0) vs. Rams (2), Oct. 21, 1973

FIRST DOWNS

Most First Downs, Season
- 342   1989 (114 rush, 207 pass, 21 penalty)
- 340   1983 (98 rush, 214 pass, 27 penalty)
- 339   1995 (84 rush, 235 pass, 20 penalty)
- 338   1996 (118 rush, 197 pass, 23 penalty)

Fewest First Downs, Season
- 125   1935
- 131   1945 (73 rush, 44 pass, 14 penalty)
- 134   1938, 1943 (60 rush, 66 pass, 8 penalty)
- 140   1937

Most First Downs, Game
- 37   vs. Eagles, Nov. 11, 1962 (21,15,1)
- 32   vs. Buccaneers, Oct. 12, 1980 (11,21,0)
  - vs. Falcons, Nov. 27, 1983 (11,18,3)
- 31   vs. Buccaneers, Dec. 1, 1985 (12,17,2)
  - vs. Lions, Nov. 12, 1989 (10,19,2)
- 30   vs. Lions, Oct. 28, 1984 (10,16,4)
  - vs. Lions, Oct. 6, 1985 (16,13,1)

Fewest First Downs, Game
- 3   vs. Cardinals, Sept. 18, 1932
  - vs. Redskins, Nov. 4, 1934
  - vs. Cardinals, Nov. 18, 1934
- 4   vs. Lions, Nov. 17, 1935

Most First Downs, Both Teams, Game
- 57   GB (32) vs. Falcons (25), Nov. 27, 1983
- 56   GB (23) vs. Redskins (33), Oct. 17, 1983
  - GB (26) vs. Cardinals (30), Jan. 2, 2000
- 52   GB (19) vs. Rams (33), Dec. 16, 1956
  - GB (19) vs. Bears (33), Dec. 7, 1980
- 51   GB (27) vs. Vikings (24), Oct. 23, 1983
  - GB (29) vs. Falcons (22), Sept. 8, 2002

Fewest First Downs, Both Teams, Game
- 5   GB (5) vs. Giants (0), Oct. 1, 1933
  - GB (3) vs. Cardinals (2), Nov. 18, 1934
- 8   GB (3) vs. Cardinals (5), Sept. 18, 1932
- 10   GB (5) vs. Spartans (5), Dec. 4, 1932
  - GB (6) vs. Cardinals (4), Nov. 5, 1933

Most First Downs Rushing, Season
- 145   1962
- 142   1961
- 135   1960
- 133   1964

Fewest First Downs Rushing, Season
- 59   1982
- 60   1943
- 65   1942
- 70   1944

Most First Downs Rushing, Game
- 21   vs. Eagles, Nov. 11, 1962
- 19   vs. 49ers, Oct. 11, 1959
  - vs. Giants, Oct. 22, 1967
- 18   vs. Colts, Oct. 18, 1953
  - vs. Lions, Oct. 2, 1960
  - vs. Vikings, Dec. 22, 1996

Fewest First Downs Rushing, Game
- 0   vs. Seahawks, Dec. 9, 1990
- 1   Accomplished many times

Most First Downs Rushing, Both Teams, Game
- 30   GB (13) vs. Saints (17), Sept. 9, 1979
- 29   GB (11) vs. Rams (18), Dec. 16, 1956
  - GB (19) vs. Giants (10), Oct. 22, 1967
- 28   GB (15) vs. Lions (13), Oct. 26, 1947
  - GB (9) vs. Bears (19), Nov. 6, 1955
  - GB (16) vs. Falcons (12), Oct. 26, 1969
- 27   GB (9) vs. Bears (18), Nov. 18, 1951
  - GB (8) vs. Bears (19), Oct. 30, 1977
  - GB (6) vs. Raiders (21), Sept. 13, 1978

Fewest First Downs Rushing, Both Teams, Game
- 4   GB (1) vs. Eagles (3), Oct. 13, 1946
  - GB (2) vs. Giants (2), Nov. 8, 1981
  - GB (3) vs. Buccaneers (1), Sept. 13, 1998
  - GB (3) vs. Lions (1), Sept. 9, 2001
  - GB (3) vs. Panthers (1), Sept. 30, 2001
  - GB (2) vs. Bears (2), Oct. 7, 2002
- 5   GB (3) vs. Eagles (2), Nov. 12, 1939
  - GB (4) vs. Lions (1), Oct. 24, 1943
  - GB (4) vs. Buccaneers (1), Oct. 14, 1990
  - GB (2) vs. Vikings (3), Sept. 27, 1996
  - GB (3) vs. Buccaneers (2), Dec. 7, 1997
  - GB (3) vs. Panthers (2), Sept. 27, 1998
  - GB (3) vs. Jaguars (2), Dec. 3, 2001

Most First Downs, Passing, Season
- 235   1995
- 214   1983
- 210   1998
- 207   1989

Fewest First Downs, Passing, Season
- 34   1946
- 58   1948
- 63   1944
- 66   1939, 1940, 1943

Most First Downs, Passing, Game
- 21   vs. Cardinals, Dec. 21, 1969
  - vs. Buccaneers, Oct. 12, 1980
  - vs. Panthers, Sept. 27, 1998
- 20   vs. Broncos, Oct. 15, 1984
  - vs. Bears, Dec. 5, 1993
  - vs. Dolphins, Sept. 11, 1994
- 19   vs. Lions, Nov. 12, 1989
  - vs. Falcons, Dec. 18, 1994
  - vs. Vikings, Nov. 22, 1998
  - vs. Raiders, Sept. 12, 1999
  - vs. Panthers, Sept. 30, 2001

Fewest First Downs Passing, Game
- 0   vs. Spartans, Oct. 8, 1933
  - vs. Bears, Sept. 25, 1949
- 1   Accomplished many times

Most First Downs Passing, Both Teams, Game
- 38   GB (17) vs. Redskins (21), Oct. 17, 1983
- 35   GB (13) vs. Cardinals (22), Jan. 2, 2000
- 33   GB (14) vs. Vikings (19), Nov. 29, 1981
  - GB (18) vs. Saints (15), Sept. 17, 1989
  - GB (19) vs. Falcons (14), Dec. 18, 1994
  - GB (15) vs. Saints (18), Dec. 16, 1995
  - GB (16) vs. Steelers (17), Dec. 24, 1995
  - GB (16) vs. Bears (17), Oct. 7, 2002

Fewest First Downs Passing, Both Teams, Game
- 1   GB (1) vs. Rams (0), Sept. 21, 1941
- 3   GB (2) vs. Cardinals (1), Dec. 6, 1936
  - GB (1) vs. 49ers (2), Dec. 11, 1960
- 4   GB (4) vs. Bears (0), Nov. 7, 1937
  - GB (3) vs. Eagles (1), Nov. 29, 1942
  - GB (1) vs. Bears (3), Sept. 29, 1946
  - GB (3) vs. Bears (1), Nov. 3, 1946

Most First Downs Penalty, Season
- 32   1985
- 31   1997, 1999
- 30   1981, 2000
- 28   1951

Fewest First Downs Penalty, Season
- 6   1940
- 8   1939, 1943
- 11   1964
- 12   1955

Most First Downs Penalty, Game
- 6 vs. Rams, Sept. 20, 1981
    vs. Cowboys, Nov. 23, 1997
    vs. Lions, Nov. 21, 1999
    vs. Eagles, Sept. 17, 2000

Most First Downs Penalty, Both Teams, Game
- 10 GB (4) vs. Redskins (6), Oct. 20, 2002
- 9 GB (6) vs. Lions (3), Nov. 21, 1999
    GB (5) vs. Lions (4), Nov. 22, 2001
- 8 GB (5) vs. Bears (3), Nov. 17, 1963
    GB (5) vs. Lions (3), Oct. 12, 1969
    GB (6) vs. Rams (2), Sept. 20, 1981
    GB (5) vs. Cowboys (3), Nov. 14, 1999
    GB (5) vs. Vikings (3), Nov. 17, 2002

NET YARDS RUSHING AND PASSING

Most Yards Gained, Season
- 6,172 1983
- 5,798 2003
- 5,780 1989
- 5,750 1995

Fewest Yards Gained, Season
- 2,340 1934
- 2,618 1946
- 2,702 1933
- 2,869 1945

Most Yards Gained, Game
- 628 vs. Eagles, Nov. 11, 1962
- 569 vs. Buccaneers, Oct. 12, 1980
- 548 vs. Raiders, Dec. 22, 2003
- 541 vs. Rams, Oct. 18, 1942

Fewest Yards Gained, Game
- 36 vs. Bengals, Sept. 26, 1976
- 61 vs. Redskins, Nov. 4, 1934
- 63 vs. Cowboys, Oct. 24, 1965
    vs. Rams, Oct. 21, 1973
    vs. Lions, Oct. 28, 1973
- 68 vs. Lions, Nov. 7, 1965

Most Yards Gained, Both Teams, Game
- 1,025 GB (473) vs. Redskins (552), Oct. 17, 1983
- 977 GB (479) vs. Oilers (498), Sept. 4, 1983
- 966 GB (355) vs. Rams (611), Dec. 16, 1956
    GB (457) vs. Colts (509), Nov. 15, 1959
- 949 GB (471) vs. Lions (478), Nov. 22, 1951

Fewest Yards Gained, Both Teams, Game
- 136 GB (86) vs. Cardinals (50), Nov. 18, 1934
- 175 GB (109) vs. Giants (66), Oct. 1, 1933
- 184 GB (75) vs. Cardinals (109), Sept. 18, 1932
- 195 GB (118) vs. Bears (77), Sept. 18, 1938

Most Consecutive Games, 400 or More Yards
- 4 1984, 1989
- 3 1961, 1980

Most Consecutive Games, 300 or More Yards
- 12 2000-01
- 10 1984
- 9 1996-97
- 8 1963, 1980, 1995-96

RUSHING

Most Rushing Attempts, Season
- 560 1946
- 550 1978
- 544 1972
- 527 1973

Fewest Rushing Attempts, Season
- 283 1982
- 313 1951
- 321 1954
- 337 1956

Most Rushing Attempts, Game
- 64 vs. Redskins, Dec. 1, 1946
- 63 vs. Steelers, Oct. 20, 1946
- 62 vs. Cardinals, Sept. 12, 1937
    vs. Rams, Sept. 21, 1941
    vs. Cardinals, Nov. 10, 1946
- 61 vs. Lions, Nov. 17, 1946

Fewest Rushing Attempts, Game
- 7 vs. Dolphins, Sept. 11, 1994
- 10 vs. Seahawks, Dec. 9, 1990
- 11 vs. Bears, Nov. 27, 1988
    vs. Broncos, Oct. 17, 1999
- 12 vs. Chargers, Oct. 7, 1984
    vs. Bills, Nov. 20, 1994
    vs. Buccaneers, Dec. 26, 1999

Most Rushing Attempts, Both Teams, Game
- 108 GB (38) vs. Cardinals (70), Dec. 5, 1948
- 102 GB (51) vs. Steelers (51), Nov. 20, 1949
- 101 GB (32) vs. Cardinals (69), Dec. 5, 1936
- 100 GB (62) vs. Cardinals (38), Sept. 12, 1937

Fewest Rushing Attempts, Both Teams, Game
- 37 GB (24) vs. Panthers (13), Dec. 12, 1999
- 39 GB (18) vs. Vikings (21), Nov. 22, 1998
- 40 GB (15) vs. Dolphins (25), Sept. 22, 1991
- 41 GB (13) vs. Buccaneers (28), Oct. 14, 1990
    GB (7) vs. Dolphins (34), Sept. 11, 1994
    GB (18) vs. Rams (23), Sept. 3, 1995
    GB (22) vs. Buccaneers (19), Oct. 7, 2001

Most Yards Gained Rushing, Season
- 2,558 2003
- 2,460 1962
- 2,350 1961
- 2,276 1964

Fewest Yards Gained Rushing, Season
- 1,081 1982
- 1,183 1934
- 1,196 1951
- 1,274 1942

Most Yards Gained Rushing, Game
- 366 vs. Lions, Oct. 26, 1947
- 312 vs. Yanks, Oct. 8, 1950
- 303 vs. Colts, Oct. 18, 1953
- 301 vs. Redskins, Dec. 1, 1946

Fewest Yards Gained Rushing, Game
- 12 vs. Buccaneers, Dec. 26, 1999
- 13 vs. Seahawks, Dec. 9, 1990
- 17 vs. Redskins, Sept. 17, 1933
- 18 vs. Cardinals, Oct. 21, 1934

Most Yards Gained Rushing, Both Teams, Game
- 557 GB (151) vs. Bears (406), Nov. 6, 1955
- 508 GB (366) vs. Lions (142), Oct. 26, 1947
- 506 GB (294) vs. Rams (212), Oct. 22, 1944
- 502 GB (312) vs. Yanks (190), Oct. 8, 1950

Fewest Yards Gained Rushing, Both Teams, Game
- 81 GB (44) vs. Dolphins (37), Sept. 22, 1991
- 85 GB (18) vs. Cardinals (67), Oct. 21, 1934
    GB (35) vs. Eagles (50), Oct. 13, 1946
- 87 GB (37) vs. Buccaneers (50), Sept. 13, 1998
- 92 GB (79) vs. Panthers (13), Dec. 12, 1999

Most Games, 200 or More Yards Rushing, Season
- 5 1960, 1962, 1963, 1971
- 4 1946, 1961

Most Consecutive Games, 200 or More Yards Rushing
3   1961

Most Consecutive Games, Fewer Than 200 Yards Rushing
72   1989-94
62   1997-01
54   1980-84
39   1985-88

Most Games, 100 or More Yards Rushing, Season
14   1964, 1972
13   1961
12   1949, 1962, 1971, 1984

Most Consecutive Games, 100 or More Yards Rushing
19   1971-73
18   1963-65
13   1948-49, 1959-60, 1961-62
12   1946-47

Most Consecutive Games, Fewer Than 100 Yards Rushing
16   1990-91
7   1986

Highest Average Gain, Season
5.05   2003 (507-2,558)
4.96   1961 (474-2,350)
4.74   1962 (518-2,460)
4.70   1985 (470-2,208)

Lowest Average Gain, Season
2.59   1934 (456-1,183)
3.11   1933 (487-1,513)
3.12   1977 (469-1,464)
3.15   1939 (500-1,574), 1946 (560-1,765)

Most Touchdowns Rushing, Season
36   1962
29   1960
27   1961
23   1964

Fewest Touchdowns Rushing, Season
5   1922-24, 1977, 1990
6   1921
7   1925, 1932, 1935, 1949, 1958, 1992, 1998
8   1934, 1951, 1970, 1986

Most Touchdowns Rushing, Game
6   vs. Browns, Oct. 15, 1961
    vs. Eagles, Nov. 11, 1962
5   vs. Pirates, Oct. 15, 1933
    vs. Bears, Sept. 30, 1962
    vs. Bears, Nov. 4, 1962
    vs. Giants, Oct. 22, 1967
    vs. Patriots, Oct. 9, 1988

Most Touchdowns Rushing, Both Teams, Game
8   GB (3) vs. Bears (5), Nov. 6, 1955
7   GB (4) vs. Bears (3), Sept. 30, 1945
    GB (4) vs. Seahawks (3), Oct. 15, 1978

PASSING

Most Passes Attempted, Season
609   1994
605   1999
600   1989, 2000
593   1995

Fewest Passes Attempted, Season
178   1946
197   1934
209   1933
210   1938

Most Passes Attempted, Game
61   vs. 49ers, Oct. 14, 1996
60   vs. Lions, Nov. 12, 1989
59   vs. Saints, Sept. 14, 1986
57   vs. 49ers, Oct. 26, 1986

Fewest Passes Attempted, Game
0   vs. Spartans, Oct. 8, 1933
4   vs. Dodgers, Oct. 23, 1932
5   vs. Bears, Oct. 16, 1932
    vs. Lions, Nov. 1, 1971
6   vs. Giants, Oct. 2, 1932

Most Passes Attempted, Both Teams, Game
100   GB (47) vs. Patriots (53), Oct. 2, 1994
      GB (61) vs. 49ers (39), Oct. 14, 1996
98   GB (45) vs. Panthers (53), Sept. 27, 1998
95   GB (43) vs. Vikings (52), Oct. 22, 1995
92   GB (53) vs. Buccaneers (39), Dec. 3, 1989

Fewest Passes Attempted, Both Teams, Game
11   GB (0) vs. Spartans (11), Oct. 8, 1933
13   GB (9) vs. Bears (4), Sept. 25, 1932
     GB (8) vs. Cardinals (5), Nov. 18, 1934
14   GB (8) vs. Bears (6), Sept. 18, 1938
15   GB (10) vs. Cardinals (5), Dec. 6, 1936

Most Passes Completed, Season
375   1994
372   1995
361   1998, 2002
354   1989

Fewest Passes Completed, Season
54   1946
74   1934
81   1945
89   1933

Most Passes Completed, Game
36   vs. Bears, Dec. 5, 1993
35   vs. Buccaneers, Oct. 12, 1980
     vs. Lions, Nov. 12, 1989
33   vs. Falcons, Oct. 4, 1992
32   vs. 49ers, Oct. 26, 1986

Fewest Passes Completed, Game
0   vs. Spartans, Oct. 8, 1933
    vs. Bears, Sept. 25, 1949

Most Passes Completed, Both Teams, Game
57   GB (24) vs. Steelers (33), Dec. 24, 1995
56   GB (18) vs. Vikings (38), Nov. 29, 1981
     GB (25) vs. Chargers (31), Oct. 7, 1984
     GB (21) vs. Cardinals (35), Jan. 2, 2000
55   GB (26) vs. Panthers (29), Dec. 12, 1999
54   GB (25) vs. Patriots (29), Oct. 2, 1994
     GB (22) vs. Bills (32), Nov. 20, 1994

Fewest Passes Completed, Both Teams, Game
2   GB (1) vs. Bears (1), Sept. 25, 1932
    GB (2) vs. Cardinals (0), Nov. 18, 1934
4   GB (3) vs. Cardinals (1), Nov. 29, 1934
    GB (3) vs. Bears (1), Sept. 18, 1938
5   GB (0) vs. Spartans (5), Oct. 8, 1933
    GB (3) vs. Cardinals (2), Dec. 6, 1936
    GB (4) vs. Cardinals (1), Sept. 12, 1937

Most Yards Gained Passing, Season
4,365   1983
4,322   1995
4,110   1998
4,048   1989

Fewest Yards Gained Passing, Season
841   1946
1,165   1934
1,186   1933
1,283   1973

Most Yards Gained Passing, Game
423   vs. Cardinals, Nov. 1, 1942
422   vs. Cardinals, Dec. 21, 1969
415   vs. Buccaneers, Oct. 12, 1980
403   vs. Redskins, Oct. 17, 1983

Fewest Yards Gained Passing, Game
-35   vs. Bengals, Sept. 26, 1976
-12   vs. Bears, Nov. 4, 1973
-10   vs. Cowboys, Oct. 24, 1965
-2   vs. Lions, Nov. 7, 1965

Most Yards Gained Passing, Both Teams, Game
771   GB (403) vs. Redskins (368), Oct. 17, 1983
720   GB (368) vs. Chargers (352), Oct. 7, 1984
692   GB (344) vs. Oilers (348), Sept. 4, 1983
686   GB (308) vs. Giants (378), Jan. 6, 2002

Fewest Yards Gained Passing, Both Teams, Game
-11   GB (-10) vs. Cowboys (-1), Oct. 24, 1965
10   GB (16) vs. Cardinals (-6), Nov. 29, 1934
20   GB (13) vs. Bears (7), Sept. 25, 1932
     GB (20) vs. Cardinals (0), Nov. 18, 1934
29   GB (-35) vs. Bengals (64), Sept. 26, 1976

Most Games, 300 or More Yards Passing, Season
6   1983, 1989
4   1984, 1994, 1995, 2001
3   1942, 1999, 2002
2   1952, 1981, 1988, 1998

Most Consecutive Games, 300 or More Yards Passing
3   1984

Most Consecutive Games, Fewer Than 300 Yards Passing
149   1970-80
95   1943-51
86   1933-40
62   1956-61

Most Games, 200 or More Yards Passing, Season
15   1998
14   1983, 1995
13   1989
12   1994, 1996, 2000

Most Consecutive Games, 200 or More Yards Passing
15   1995-96, 1998
10   1983
9   1996-97
8   1988-89, 1994-95

Most Consecutive Games, Fewer Than 200 Yards Passing
50   1946-50
21   1933-35
19   1972-73
16   1937-39

Most Consecutive Games, Fewer Than 100 Yards Passing
9   1946
8   1933, 1949, 1973
7   1972

Most Times Sacked, Season
62   1990
52   1981
51   1988
50   1985

Fewest Times Sacked, Season
17   1972, 1974
18   1971
19   2003
20   1963

Most Times Sacked, Game
11   vs. Lions, Nov. 7, 1965
10   vs. Chargers, Sept. 24, 1978
9   vs. Bears, Dec. 13, 1970
    vs. Jets, Dec. 20, 1981
    vs. Lions, Dec. 12, 1982

Most Times Sacked, Both Teams, Game
18   GB (10) vs. Chargers (8), Sept. 24, 1978
14   GB (5) vs. Cowboys (9), Oct. 24, 1965
13   GB (11) vs. Lions (2), Nov. 7, 1965
     GB (8) vs. Raiders (5), Nov. 11, 1990
12   GB (4) vs. Rams (8), Sept. 25, 1966
     GB (5) vs. Lions (7), Dec. 15, 1979
     GB (6) vs. Buccaneers (6), Oct. 27, 1991

Most Yards Lost Attempting to Pass, Season
395   1965 (43 sacks)
394   1967 (41 sacks)
390   1990 (62 sacks)
389   1985 (50 sacks)

Fewest Yards Lost Attempting to Pass, Season
104   1947
118   1960
124   1972 (17 sacks)
126   1974 (17 sacks)

Highest Completion Percentage, Season
65.54   2003 (473-310)
64.52   1992 (527-340)
62.78   1998 (361-575)
62.73   1995 (593-372)

Lowest Completion Percentage, Season
30.34   1946 (178-54)
30.43   1949 (299-91)
37.16   1945 (218-81)
37.56   1934 (197-74)

Highest Completion Percentage, Game
90.48   vs. Saints, Dec. 13, 1981 (21-19)
88.24   vs. Oilers, Sept. 4, 1983 (34-30)
82.14   vs. Browns, Nov. 11, 1995 (28-23)
81.48   vs. Buccaneers, Sept. 11, 1988 (27-22)

Lowest Completion Percentage, Game (min. 20 att.)
19.05   vs. Bears, Nov. 3, 1946 (21-4)
19.23   vs. Colts, Nov. 2, 1958 (26-5)
20.00   vs. Rams, Oct. 2, 1949 (20-4)
20.83   vs. Rams, Dec. 13, 1953 (24-5)

Highest Completion Percentage, Both Teams, Game (min. 40 att.)
78.57   GB (25-20) vs. 49ers (17-13), Dec. 13, 1959
        GB (21-19) vs. Saints (21-14), Dec. 13, 1981
78.13   GB (27-21) vs. Browns (37-29), Oct. 19, 1986
76.47   GB (34-30) vs. Oilers (34-22), Sept. 4, 1983
76.36   GB (25-18) vs. Colts (30-24), Nov. 16, 1997

Lowest Completion Percentage, Both Teams, Game (min. 40 att.)
24.49   GB (25-8) vs. Pirates (24-4), Oct. 6, 1935
26.15   GB (34-10) vs. Eagles (31-7), Nov. 2, 1952
27.91   GB (17-7) vs. Bears (26-5), Sept. 22, 1935
28.26   GB (20-5) vs. Cardinals (26-8), Oct. 12, 1947

Most Touchdowns Passing, Season
39   1995, 1996
35   1997
33   1983, 1994, 1998
32   2001, 2003

Fewest Touchdowns Passing, Season
1   1921
3   1922
4   1927, 1946
5   1923, 1949, 1974

Most Touchdowns Passing, Game
6   vs. Cardinals, Nov. 1, 1942
    vs. Lions, Oct. 7, 1945
5   vs. Cardinals, Dec. 21, 1969
    vs. Saints, Dec. 13, 1981
    vs. Oilers, Sept. 4, 1983
    vs. Bears, Nov. 12, 1995
    vs. Vikings, Sept. 21, 1997
    vs. Panthers, Sept. 27, 1998

Most Touchdowns Passing, Both Teams, Game

    8   GB (4) vs. Lions (4), Nov. 22, 1951
        GB (3) vs. Lions (5), Nov. 27, 1952
        GB (5) vs. Vikings (3), Sept. 21, 1997

Most Passes Had Intercepted, Season

    37 1950
    34 1953
    32 1983
    30 1984

Fewest Passes Had Intercepted, Season

    5   1966
    6   1964
    9   1972
    13 1941, 1960, 1962, 1996

Most Passes Had Intercepted, Game

    8   vs. Giants, Nov. 21, 1948
    7   vs. Bears, Sept. 22, 1940
        vs. Lions, Oct. 20, 1940
        vs. Rams, Nov. 11, 1945
        vs. Lions, Sept. 17, 1950
        vs. Saints, Sept. 14, 1986
    6   vs. Cardinals, Oct. 13, 1935
        vs. Eagles, Dec. 14, 1947

Most Passes Had Intercepted, Both Teams, Game

    11 GB (4) vs. Rams (7), Oct. 30, 1938
        GB (7) vs. Lions (4), Oct. 20, 1940
    10 GB (1) vs. Lions (9), Oct. 24, 1943
        GB (3) vs. Rams (7), Nov. 12, 1944
        GB (7) vs. Rams (3), Nov. 11, 1945

Highest Passer Rating, Season

    102.1   1966
    97.6   1995
    95.7   1996
    94.1   2001

Lowest Passer Rating, Season

    11.4   1949
    15.0   1946
    26.1   1948
    27.5   1953

PUNTING

Most Punts, Season

    106 1978
    95   1975
    93   1987
    87   1949, 1970, 1980

Fewest Punts, Season

    42   1982
    46   1945
    48   1944
    49   1960

Most Punts, Game

    14   vs. Bears, Oct. 22, 1933
         vs. Cardinals, Nov. 5, 1933
         vs. Lions, Nov. 17, 1935
    13   vs. Redskins, Nov. 4, 1934
    12   vs. Bears, Nov. 10, 1933
    11   vs. Spartans, Nov. 12, 1933
         vs. Bears, Sept. 23, 1934
         vs. Bears, Oct. 15, 1950
         vs. Rams, Dec. 3, 1950
         vs. Steelers, Oct. 24, 1953

Fewest Punts, Game

    0   vs. Colts, Nov. 6, 1960
         vs. Bears, Sept. 24, 1967
         vs. Bills, Dec. 5, 1982
         vs. Bears, Dec. 17, 1989

Most Punts, Both Teams, Game

    31   GB (14) vs. Bears (17), Oct. 22, 1933
    26   GB (14) vs. Cardinals (12), Nov. 5, 1933
         GB (11) vs. Spartans (15), Nov. 12, 1933
         GB (12) vs. Bears (14), Dec. 10, 1933
         GB (14) vs. Lions (12), Nov. 17, 1935
    24   GB (13) vs. Redskins (11), Nov. 4, 1934
    23   GB (9) vs. Eagles (13), Dec. 3, 1933

Fewest Punts, Both Teams, Game

    1   GB (0) vs. Bills (1), Dec. 5, 1982
         GB (0) vs. Bears (1), Dec. 17, 1989
    2   GB (1) vs. Redskins (1), Oct. 17, 1983
         GB (1) vs. Colts (1), Nov. 16, 1997

Highest Gross Average, Season

    45.04   1997 (75-3,378)
    44.67   1963 (51-2,279)
    43.55   1947 (65-2,831)
    43.21   1956 (62-2,649)

Lowest Gross Average, Season

    35.46   1978 (106-3,759)
    35.83   1975 (95-3,404)
    35.96   1943 (52-1,870)
    36.50   1967 (66-2,409)

Highest Net Average, Season

    39.20   1963 (51-1,999)
    38.32   1969 (59-2,261)
    38.03   1957 (63-2,396)
    37.85   1968 (59-2,233)

Lowest Net Average, Season

    31.00   1989 (66-2,046)
    31.07   1978 (106-3,293)
    31.42   1981 (84-2,639)
    31.48   1974 (69-2,172)

PUNT RETURNS

Most Punt Returns, Season

    61   1995
    58   1996
    56   1997
    49   1994

Fewest Punt Returns, Season

    20   1961
    22   1965
    25   1970, 1972
    26   1960, 1963, 1982

Most Punt Returns, Game

    8   vs. Yanks, Nov. 18, 1945
         vs. Texans, Nov. 23, 1952
         vs. Vikings, Nov. 4, 1982

Most Punt Returns, Both Teams, Game

    14   GB (7) vs. Patriots (7), Oct. 2, 1994
    13   GB (5) vs. Eagles (8), Nov. 29, 1942
         GB (6) vs. Bears (7), Nov. 14, 1948
         GB (6) vs. Bears (7), Dec. 4, 1983

Most Fair Catches, Season

    26   2000
    23   1972
    21   1998
    20   1970, 2001

Fewest Fair Catches, Season

    5   1971
    6   1982, 1987, 1992
    7   1975, 1986, 1991, 1995
    8   1974, 1976

Most Fair Catches, Game
- 6 vs. Bears, Dec. 16, 1973
- 5 vs. Saints, Nov. 17, 1968
- vs. Bears, Nov. 15, 1970

Most Yards, Punt Returns, Season
- 875 1996
- 729 1950
- 563 1939, 1947
- 527 1948

Fewest Yards, Punt Returns, Season
- 65 1965
- 98 1970
- 137 1973
- 141 1979

Most Yards, Punt Returns, Game
- 167 vs. Lions, Dec. 15, 1996
- 147 vs. Bears, Nov. 8, 1959
- 144 vs. Texans, Nov. 23, 1952
- 141 vs. Rams, Oct. 9, 1994

Most Yards, Punt Returns, Both Teams, Game
- 182 GB (167) vs. Lions (15), Dec. 15, 1996
- 181 GB (92) vs. Giants (89), Nov. 13, 1949
- 177 GB (122) vs. Redskins (55), Sept. 24, 1950
- 175 GB (0) vs. Lions (175), Nov. 22, 1951

Highest Average, Punt Returns, Season
- 17.75 1961 (20-355)
- 16.57 1950 (44-729)
- 15.09 1996 (58-875)
- 14.56 1972 (25-364)

Lowest Average, Punt Returns, Season
- 2.95 1965 (22-65)
- 3.92 1970 (25-98)
- 4.03 1967 (39-157)
- 4.15 2002 (46-191)

Most Touchdowns, Punt Returns, Season
- 3 1996
- 2 1950, 1961, 1972, 1974

Most Touchdowns, Punt Returns, Game
- 1 Accomplished many times

Most Touchdowns, Punt Returns, Both Teams, Game
- 2 GB (0) vs. Lions (2), Nov. 22, 1951
- GB (1) vs. Bengals (1), Sept. 20, 1992

KICKOFF RETURNS

Most Kickoff Returns, Season
- 79 1983
- 76 1986
- 73 1980
- 69 1989

Fewest Kickoff Returns, Season
- 28 1941, 1943
- 30 1944, 1962
- 33 1945
- 34 1946, 1982

Most Kickoff Returns, Game
- 10 vs. Giants, Dec. 20, 1986
- 9 vs. Lions, Nov. 22, 1951
- vs. Lions, Nov. 27, 1952
- vs. Lions, Sept. 20, 1970
- vs. Rams, Sept. 21, 1980
- vs. Bears, Dec. 7, 1980

Most Kickoff Returns, Both Teams, Game
- 17 GB (8) vs. Redskins (9), Oct. 17, 1983
- GB (8) vs. Lions (9), Nov. 27, 1986
- 15 GB (8) vs. Oilers (7), Sept. 4, 1983
- GB (10) vs. Giants (5), Dec. 20, 1986

Most Yards, Kickoff Returns, Season
- 1,570 2000
- 1,547 1998
- 1,546 1971
- 1,511 2003

Fewest Yards, Kickoff Returns, Season
- 381 1940
- 567 1941
- 610 1944
- 661 1943

Most Yards, Kickoff Returns, Game
- 258 vs. Cowboys, Oct. 3, 1993
- 256 vs. Vikings, Oct. 5, 1998
- 245 vs. Giants, Sept. 19, 1971
- 244 vs. Bears, Oct. 7, 1956

Most Yards, Kickoff Returns, Both Teams, Game
- 427 GB (245) vs. Giants (182), Sept. 19, 1971
- 410 GB (106) vs. Bears (304), Nov. 9, 1952
- 407 GB (163) vs. Lions (244), Sept. 6, 1998
- 401 GB (208) vs. Redskins (193), Oct. 17, 1983

Highest Average, Kickoff Returns, Season
- 26.98 1967 (46-1,241)
- 26.66 1971 (58-1,546)
- 26.27 1961 (41-1,077)
- 25.78 1998 (60-1,547)
- 25.78 1964 (45-1,160)

Lowest Average, Kickoff Returns, Season
- 16.95 1983 (79-1,339)
- 17.49 1987 (59-1,032)
- 17.96 1989 (69-1,239)
- 18.38 1981 (58-1,066)

Most Touchdowns, Kickoff Returns, Season
- 4 1967
- 2 1969, 1970, 1971, 1998

Most Touchdowns, Kickoff Returns, Game
- 2 vs. Browns, Nov. 12, 1967

Most Touchdowns, Kickoff Returns, Both Teams, Game
- 2 GB (0) vs. Bears (2), Sept. 22, 1940
- GB (0) vs. Bears (2), Nov. 9, 1952
- GB (2) vs. Browns (0), Nov. 12, 1967
- GB (0) vs. Rams (2), Nov. 24, 1985
- GB (1) vs. Lions (1), Sept. 6, 1998

FUMBLES

Most Fumbles, Season
- 44 1988
- 42 1992
- 41 1991
- 40 1952

Fewest Fumbles, Season
- 11 1944
- 13 1942
- 15 1943
- 16 1939

Most Fumbles, Game
- 8 vs. Eagles, Dec. 1, 1974
- vs. Buccaneers, Dec. 7, 1998

Most Fumbles, Both Teams, Game
- 13 GB (7) vs. Lions (6), Oct. 6, 1985
- 12 GB (6) vs. Lions (6), Nov. 24, 1955
- GB (4) vs. Lions (8), Dec. 6, 1992
- 11 GB (2) vs. Eagles (9), Oct. 13, 1946
- GB (6) vs. Cardinals (5), Nov. 10, 1946
- GB (5) vs. 49ers (6), Nov. 15, 1964
- GB (6) vs. Seahawks (5), Nov. 1, 1999

Most Fumbles Lost, Season
   31   1952
   26   1988
   25   1955
   24   1978
Fewest Fumbles Lost, Season
    6   1943, 1995
    7   1939, 1944, 1945, 1984
    8   1942, 1994
    9   1940, 1977
Most Fumbles Lost, Game
    6   vs. Lions, Nov. 27, 1952
    5   vs. Bears, Nov. 6, 1955
        vs. Lions, Nov. 24, 1955
        vs. Rams, Sept. 22, 1966
        vs. Eagles, Dec. 1, 1974
Most Fumbles Recovered, Season, Own and Opponents
   45   1985 (20 own, 25 opp)
   41   1946 (13 own, 28 opp)
        1975 (14 own, 27 opp)
   40   1987 (16 own, 24 opp)
   38   1981 (14 own, 24 opp)
Fewest Fumbles Recovered, Season, Own and Opponents
   16   1940 (9 own, 7 opp)
        1944 (4 own, 12 opp)
   17   1969 (10 own, 7 opp)
Most Fumbles Recovered, Game, Own and Opponents
    9   vs. Lions, Oct. 6, 1985 (5 own, 4 opp)
    8   vs. Cardinals, Nov. 10, 1946 (3 own, 5 opp)
    7   vs. Steelers, Nov. 23, 1941 (1 own, 6 opp.)
        vs. Colts, Sept. 29, 1963 (2 own, 5 opp)
        vs. 49ers, Nov. 15, 1964 (3 own, 4 opp)
        vs. Jets, Dec. 20, 1981 (4 own, 3 opp)
Most Own Fumbles Recovered, Season
   22   1980, 1991
   20   1985
   19   1989, 1992, 1996
Fewest Own Fumbles Recovered, Season
    4   1944, 1966
    5   1942
    6   1960, 1965
    7   1938, 1971, 1978, 1997, 2003
Most Own Fumbles Recovered, Game
    6   vs. Buccaneers, Dec. 7, 1998
    5   vs. Lions, Oct. 6, 1985
        vs. Jets, Nov. 3, 1991
Most Opponents Fumbles Recovered, Season
   28   1946
   27   1975
   25   1964, 1985
   24   1981, 1987
Fewest Opponents Fumbles Recovered, Season
    3   1995
    7   1940, 1969, 2000
    8   1956
    9   1939, 1943
Most Opponents Fumbles Recovered, Game
    6   vs. Steelers, Nov. 23, 1941
        vs. Chargers, Sept. 24, 1978
Most Touchdowns Fumble Recoveries, Season, Own and Opponents
    3   1964, 1982, 1997
    2   1939, 1983, 1989, 1998, 1999
Most Touchdowns, Own Fumbles Recovered, Season
    2   1982, 1989
Most Touchdowns, Opponents Fumbles Recovered, Season
    3   1997
    2   1939, 1964, 1983, 1998, 1999

Most Touchdowns Fumble Recoveries, Game, Own and Opponents
    2   vs. Cowboys, Nov. 26, 1964 (2 opp)
Most Touchdowns, Own Fumbles Recovered, Game
    1   Accomplished many times
Most Touchdowns Opponents Fumbles Recovered, Game
    2   vs. Cowboys, Nov. 26, 1964

TURNOVERS

Most Turnovers, Season
   57   1950
   56   1952
   50   1983, 1988
   48   1948, 1953
Fewest Turnovers, Season
   19   1972
   21   1995
   22   1994
   23   1964
Most Turnovers, Game
    9   vs. Bears, Sept. 22, 1940
        vs. Rams, Nov. 12, 1950
        vs. Lions, Oct. 26, 1952
    8   vs. Rams, Nov. 11, 1945
        vs. Giants, Nov. 21, 1948
        vs. Lions, Nov. 27, 1952
        vs. Bears, Sept. 24, 1967
Most Turnovers, Both Teams, Game
   14   GB (4) vs. Lions (10), Oct. 24, 1943
        GB (4) vs. Cardinals (10), Nov. 10, 1946
        GB (9) vs. Rams (5), Nov. 12, 1950

PENALTIES

Most Penalties, Season
  135   1987
  128   1986
  110   1984
  108   2002
Fewest Penalties, Season
   38   1942
   41   1955
   42   1956, 1982
   43   1957
Most Penalties, Game
   17   vs. Yanks, Oct. 21, 1945
   16   vs. Bears, Nov. 8, 1987
   15   vs. Rams, Oct. 5, 1947
   14   vs. 49ers, Oct. 26, 1986
        vs. Lions, Nov. 27, 1986
        vs. Giants, Dec. 20, 1986
        vs. Buccaneers, Nov. 1, 1987
Fewest Penalties, Game
    0   vs. Giants, Oct. 1, 1933
        vs. Bears, Nov. 29, 1934
        vs. Lions, Nov. 17, 1935
        vs. Bears, Sept. 18, 1938
        vs. Rams, Nov. 26, 1939
        vs. Bears, Nov. 15, 1942
        vs. 49ers, Dec. 14, 1963
        vs. Colts, Sept. 20, 1964
        vs. Vikings, Nov. 27, 1977
        vs. Buccaneers, Nov. 25, 1990

Most Penalties, Both Teams, Game
- 33   GB (11) vs. Tigers (22), Sept. 17, 1944
- 28   GB (11) vs. Seahawks (17), Oct. 21, 1984
- 27   GB (17) vs. Yanks (10), Oct. 21, 1945
- 26   GB (13) vs. Raiders (13), Oct. 24, 1976

Fewest Penalties, Both Teams, Game
- 1   GB (0) vs. Lions (1), Nov. 17, 1935
-     GB (1) vs. Cardinals (0), Nov. 28, 1935
-     GB (0) vs. 49ers (1), Dec. 14, 1963
-     GB (1) vs. Colts (0), Sept. 10, 1966
-     GB (1) vs. Panthers (0), Dec. 14, 1997

Most Yards Penalized, Season
- 1,103   1987
- 1,019   1947
- 949   1986
- 941   1948

Fewest Yards Penalized, Season
- 250   1938
- 259   1939
- 291   1937
- 295   1935, 1940

Most Yards Penalized, Game
- 184   vs. Yanks, Oct. 21, 1945
- 151   vs. Raiders, Oct. 24, 1976
- 146   vs. Lions, Oct. 3, 1948
-     vs. Rams, Dec. 3, 1950
- 143   vs. Eagles, Nov. 15, 1992

Fewest Yards Penalized, Game
-     see Fewest Penalties, Game

Most Yards Penalized, Both Teams, Game
- 309   GB (184) vs. Yanks (125), Oct. 21, 1945
- 270   GB (151) vs. Raiders (119), Oct. 24, 1976
- 269   GB (146) vs. Rams (123), Dec. 3, 1950
- 252   GB (84) vs. Tigers (168), Sept. 17, 1944

Fewest Yards Penalized, Both Teams, Game
- 5   GB (0) vs. Lions (5), Nov. 17, 1935
-     GB (0) vs. 49ers (5), Dec. 14, 1963
-     GB (5) vs. Colts (0), Sept. 10, 1966
- 10   GB (10) vs. Giants (0), Nov. 11, 1934
-     GB (5) vs. Eagles (5), Dec. 8, 1935
-     GB (10) vs. Redskins (0), Nov. 8, 1936
-     GB (5) vs. Rams (5), Dec. 16, 1962
-     GB (10) vs. Panthers (0), Dec. 14, 1997
- 13   GB (5) vs. Vikings (8), Nov. 10, 1963

TEAM DEFENSIVE RECORDS

SCORING

Fewest Points Allowed, Season
- 22   1929
- 34   1923
- 38   1924
- 43   1927

Fewest Points Allowed, Season (since 1932)
- 63   1932
- 96   1935
- 107   1933
- 112   1934

Most Points Allowed, Season
- 439   1983
- 418   1986
- 406   1950
- 382   1958

Most Points Allowed, Game
- 61   vs. Bears, Dec. 7, 1980
- 56   vs. Colts, Nov. 2, 1958
- 55   vs. Giants, Dec. 20, 1986
- 52   vs. Lions, Nov. 22, 1951
-     vs. Lions, Oct. 26, 1952
-     vs. Bears, Nov. 6, 1955

Most Points Shut Out by Opponent
- 56   vs. Colts, Nov. 2, 1958
- 40   vs. Lions, Sept. 28, 1970
- 35   vs. 49ers, Dec. 5, 1954
- 34   vs. Lions, Oct. 28, 1973

Fewest Points Shut Out by Opponent
- 2   vs. Yellow Jackets, Nov. 29, 1928
-     vs. Bears, Sept. 18, 1938

Most Points Opponent Overcame to Beat Packers
- 22   Rams, Oct. 12, 1952 (trailed 28-6, won 30-28)
- 21   Rams, Nov. 17, 1957 (trailed 24-3, won 31-27)
-     Falcons, Nov. 27, 1983 (trailed 21-0, won 47-41)
- 17   Colts, Oct. 12, 1958 (trailed 17-0, won 24-17)
-     Rams, Oct. 25, 1964 (trailed 17-0, won 27-17)
-     Falcons, Sept. 13, 1981 (trailed 17-0, won 31-17)
-     Lions, Nov. 20, 1983 (trailed 20-3, won 23-20)
-     Dolphins, Oct. 29, 2000 (trailed 17-0, won 28-20)
-     Chiefs, Oct. 12, 2003 (trailed 31-14, won 40-34)
- 16   Saints, Oct. 12, 1975 (trailed 16-0, won 20-19)

Most Points, Opponents, First Half
- 44   Rams, Sept. 21, 1980
- 38   Rams, Sept. 24, 1989
- 35   Rams, Dec. 16, 1956
-     Vikings, Sept. 28, 1986
- 34   Cardinals, Nov. 27, 1949
-     49ers, Dec. 7, 1958

Most Points, Opponents, Second Half
- 38   Colts, Oct. 13, 1957
- 36   Cowboys, Nov. 24, 1994
- 35   Rams, Dec. 3, 1950
- 33   Bears, Dec. 7, 1980

Most Points, Opponents, One Quarter
- 37   Rams, Sept. 21, 1980 (2)
- 31   Falcons, Sept. 13, 1981 (4)
- 28   Giants, Sept. 19, 1971 (2)
-     Bears, Dec. 7, 1980 (2)
-     Vikings, Sept. 28, 1986 (1)
-     Rams, Sept. 24, 1989 (2)
- 27   Cardinals, Nov. 27, 1949 (1)
-     Colts, Nov. 5, 1950 (4)
-     49ers, Dec. 7, 1958 (1)
-     Bengals, Oct. 5, 1986 (2)

Most Points, Opponents, First Quarter
- 28   Vikings, Sept. 28, 1986
- 27   Cardinals, Nov. 27, 1949
-     49ers, Dec. 7, 1958
- 26   Rams, Dec. 13, 1953
- 21   49ers, Dec. 5, 1954
-     Colts, Oct. 8, 1955
-     Giants, Dec. 20, 1986

Most Points, Opponents, Second Quarter
- 37   Rams, Sept. 21, 1980
- 28   Giants, Sept. 19, 1971
-     Bears, Dec. 7, 1980
-     Rams, Sept. 24, 1989
- 27   Bengals, Oct. 5, 1986
- 24   Rams, Dec. 14, 1958
-     Buccaneers, Nov. 22, 1981

Most Points, Opponents, Third Quarter
- 21   Rams, Dec. 3, 1950
        Lions, Nov. 22, 1951
        Rams, Dec. 7, 1952
        Colts, Oct. 25, 1959
        Rams, Sept. 18, 1983
        Broncos, Oct. 17, 1999
        Dolphins, Oct. 29, 2000
- 20   Yanks, Oct. 8, 1950
- 19   Cowboys, Nov. 24, 1994

Most Points, Opponents, Fourth Quarter
- 31   Falcons, Sept. 13, 1981
- 27   Colts, Nov. 5, 1950
- 24   Rams, Oct. 12, 1952
        Rams, Oct. 18, 1959
        Redskins, Dec. 2, 1979

Most Consecutive Games, Opponents, Scoring
- 125   1949-59
         1977-85
- 114   1993-2001
- 89   1985-91
- 68   1969-73

TOUCHDOWNS

Most Touchdowns, Opponents, Season
- 56   1950
- 55   1983
- 52   1986
- 50   1951, 1958

Fewest Touchdowns, Opponents, Season
- 3   1929
- 4   1923, 1924
- 6   1922, 1927
- 7   1926

Fewest Touchdowns, Opponents, Season (since 1932)
- 8   1932
- 13   1935
- 14   1933, 1934, 1936
- 15   1938

Most Touchdowns, Opponents, Game
- 9   Bears, Dec. 7, 1980
- 8   Colts, Nov. 2, 1958

Most Consecutive Games, Opponents, Scoring Touchdowns
- 51   1980-84
- 46   1955-59
- 40   1949-52, 1988-91
- 36   1974-77

POINTS AFTER TOUCHDOWN

Most (One-Point) Points After Touchdown, Opponents, Season
- 50   1950, 1983
- 49   1951
- 48   1986
- 46   1958

Fewest (One-Point) Points After Touchdown, Opponents, Season
- 0   1929
- 2   1924
- 3   1922
- 4   1921, 1923, 1926, 1927, 1932

Fewest (One-Point) Points After Touchdown, Opponents, Season (since 1932)
- 4   1932
- 9   1935
- 10   1934
- 12   1933, 1936

Most (One-Point) Points After Touchdown, Opponents, Game
- 8   Colts, Nov. 2, 1958

Most Two-Point Conversions, Season
- 6   1997
- 5   2001
- 3   1994, 1998
- 2   2002

Most Two-Point Conversions, Game
- 2   Lions, Nov. 6, 1994
       Colts, Nov. 16, 1997

FIELD GOALS

Most Field Goals Attempted, Opponents, Season
- 42   1970
- 40   1993
- 37   1971
- 36   1987

Fewest Field Goals Attempted, Opponents, Season
- 2   1944, 1945
- 3   1940, 1943
- 7   1942, 1946
- 10   1938, 1939

Most Field Goals Attempted, Opponents, Game
- 7   Bears, Nov. 17, 1963
       Cowboys, Nov. 18, 1996
- 6   49ers, Nov. 23, 1958
       Saints, Nov. 28, 1971
       Cardinals, Sept. 19, 1976
       Bears, Nov. 8, 1987
       Vikings, Sept. 26, 1993

Most Field Goals, Opponents, Season
- 31   1993
- 30   2003
- 28   1970
- 27   1987

Fewest Field Goals, Opponents, Season
- 0   1928, 1929, 1930, 1943, 1945
- 1   1921, 1927, 1931, 1944
- 2   1923, 1937, 1940
- 3   1932, 1933, 1935

Most Field Goals, Opponents, Game
- 7   Cowboys, Nov. 18, 1996
- 5   Saints, Nov. 28, 1971
       Cardinals, Sept. 19, 1976
       Lions, Sept. 14, 1980
       Vikings, Sept. 26, 1993
       Cowboys, Oct. 3, 1993
       Lions, Nov. 27, 2003

Most Consecutive Games, Opponents, Scoring Field Goals
- 14   1971-72, 1999-2000
- 13   1990-91, 1996-97
- 12   1965-66, 1970, 2003
- 11   1984, 1992, 1998

SAFETIES

Most Safeties, Opponents, Season
- 4   1985
- 3   1973
- 2   1929, 1936, 1938, 1949, 1965, 1986, 1987

Most Safeties, Opponents, Game
- 2   Rams, Oct. 21, 1973

FIRST DOWNS

Most First Downs, Opponents, Season
- 366 1983 (171 rush, 187 pass, 8 penalty)
- 327 1979 (162 rush, 146 pass, 19 penalty)
- 326 1981 (140 rush, 168 pass, 18 penalty)
- 323 1984 (136 rush, 166 pass, 21 penalty)

Fewest First Downs, Opponents, Season
- 96 1935
- 110 1937
- 113 1939 (40 rush, 64 pass, 9 penalty)
- 114 1944 (56 rush, 49 pass, 9 penalty)

Most First Downs, Opponents, Game
- 33 Rams, Dec. 16, 1956 (18,13,2)
  - Bears, Dec. 7, 1980 (17,16,0)
  - Redskins, Oct. 17, 1983 (12,21,0)
  - Lions, Nov. 22, 1984 (18,15,0)
- 32 Cowboys, Nov. 12, 1978 (17,12,3)
- 31 Rams, Dec. 3, 1950 (11,16,4)
- 30 Rams, Dec. 12, 1954 (12,18,0)
  - Colts, Nov. 2, 1958 (14,9,7)
  - Bengals, Oct. 30, 1983 (13,16,1)
  - Giants, Dec. 20, 1986 (15,12,3)
  - Cardinals, Jan. 2, 2000 (7,22,1)

Fewest First Downs, Opponents, Game
- 0 Giants, Oct. 1, 1933
- 2 Bears, Dec. 10, 1933
  - Cardinals, Nov. 18, 1934
- 3 Eagles, Nov. 11, 1962
- 4 Giants, Oct. 2, 1932
  - Stapletons, Oct. 30, 1932
  - Cardinals, Nov. 5, 1933
  - Giants, Nov. 26, 1933
  - Bears, Sept. 18, 1938

Most First Downs Rushing, Opponents, Season
- 171 1983
- 162 1979
- 140 1977, 1981
- 137 1978

Fewest First Downs Rushing, Opponents, Season
- 40 1939
- 56 1944
- 58 1982
- 61 1940

Most First Downs Rushing, Opponents, Game
- 21 Raiders, Sept. 17, 1978
- 19 Cardinals, Dec. 5, 1948
  - 49ers, Dec. 9, 1951
  - Steelers, Oct. 24, 1953
  - Bears, Nov. 6, 1955
  - Bears, Oct. 30, 1977
- 18 Bears, Nov. 18, 1951
  - Rams, Dec. 16, 1956
  - Steelers, Sept. 11, 1983
  - Lions, Nov. 22, 1984

Fewest First Downs Rushing, Opponents, Game
- 0 Giants, Oct. 1, 1933
  - Eagles, Nov. 11, 1962
  - Lions, Dec. 3, 1972
  - Bears, Dec. 11, 1994

Most First Downs Passing, Opponents, Season
- 188 1995
- 187 1983
- 186 2000
- 182 1994

Fewest First Downs Passing, Opponents, Season
- 49 1941, 1944
- 53 1940
- 56 1943
- 57 1945

Most First Downs Passing, Opponents, Game
- 22 Cardinals, Jan. 2, 2000
- 21 Redskins, Oct. 17, 1983
- 20 Chargers, Oct. 7, 1984

Fewest First Downs Passing, Opponents, Game
- 0 Bears, Sept. 25, 1932
  - Giants, Oct. 2, 1932
  - Giants, Oct. 1, 1933
  - Cardinals, Nov. 18, 1934
  - Bears, Sept. 28, 1941
  - Giants, Nov. 19, 1944

Most First Downs Penalty, Opponents, Season
- 29 2002
- 27 1986, 1997
- 26 1947, 1987
- 25 2003

Fewest First Downs Penalty, Opponents, Season
- 4 1943
- 6 1940
- 7 1955, 1967
- 8 1954, 1983

Most First Downs Penalty, Opponents, Game
- 7 Colts, Nov. 2, 1958
- 6 Bears, Oct. 25, 1992
  - Redskins, Oct. 20, 2002
- 5 Lions, Oct. 30, 1949
  - Vikings, Oct. 22, 1978
  - Raiders, Sept. 13, 1987
  - Bills, Dec. 20, 1997

NET YARDS RUSHING AND PASSING

Most Yards Gained, Opponents, Season
- 6,403 1983
- 5,782 1980
- 5,647 1979
- 5,442 1990

Fewest Yards Gained, Opponents, Season
- 1,929 1933
- 2,091 1935
- 2,299 1937
- 2,334 1934

Most Yards Gained, Opponents, Game
- 611 Rams, Dec. 16, 1956
- 599 Rams, Dec. 8, 1957
- 594 Bears, Dec. 7, 1980
- 570 Rams, Dec. 12, 1954

Fewest Yards Gained, Opponents, Game
- 33 Yanks, Nov. 18, 1945
- 50 Cardinals, Nov. 18, 1934
- 54 Eagles, Nov. 11, 1962
- 58 Falcons, Oct. 1, 1967

Most Consecutive Games, Opponents, 400 or More Yards
- 5 1983
- 3 1950

Most Consecutive Games, Opponents, 300 or More Yards
- 11 1949-50
- 10 1951-52
- 9 1983
- 7 1958, 1979

RUSHING

Most Rushing Attempts, Opponents, Season
639 1979
620 1978
597 1983
582 1977

Fewest Rushing Attempts, Opponents, Season
275 1982
333 1939
350 1943, 1960
356 1941

Most Rushing Attempts, Opponents, Game
70 Cardinals, Dec. 5, 1948
69 Cardinals, Dec. 6, 1936
62 Redskins, Oct. 24, 1948
59 Giants, Nov. 11, 1934
    Steelers, Oct. 26, 1976
    Steelers, Sept. 11, 1983

Fewest Rushing Attempts, Opponents, Game
11 Lions, Dec. 3, 1972
    Vikings, Nov. 29, 1981
12 Cardinals, Oct. 20, 1963
    Lions, Oct. 25, 1987
    Lions, Nov. 1, 1992
13 Eagles, Nov. 11, 1962
    Bears, Nov. 22, 1992
    Bengals, Dec. 3, 1995
    Chargers, Sept. 15, 1996
    Panthers, Dec. 12, 1999
    Cardinals, Sept. 24, 2000
14 Buccaneers, Oct. 2, 1983
    Lions, Oct. 28, 1984
    Bears, Dec. 11, 1994

Most Yards Gained Rushing, Opponents, Season
2,885 1979
2,641 1983
2,619 1956
2,439 1978

Fewest Yards Gained Rushing, Opponents, Season
932 1982
1,040 1940
1,112 1943
1,130 1944

Most Yards Gained Rushing, Opponents, Game
406 Bears, Nov. 6, 1955
375 Bears, Oct. 30, 1977
323 Rams, Oct. 21, 1951
314 Rams, Dec. 16, 1956

Fewest Yards Gained Rushing, Opponents, Game
-7 Eagles, Sept. 15, 1940
12 Yanks, Nov. 18, 1945
    Cardinals, Nov. 10, 1946
13 Panthers, Dec. 12, 1999
16 Cardinals, Sept. 23, 1962

Highest Average Gain, Opponents, Season
5.12 1956 (512-2,619)
4.84 2002 (413-1,998)
4.78 1958 (427-2,040)
4.67 1957 (462-2,159)

Lowest Average Gain, Opponents, Season
2.69 1940 (387-1,040)
2.72 1935 (448-1,219)
2.77 1933 (443-1,226)
2.96 1937 (400-1,184)

Most Touchdowns Rushing, Opponents, Season
28 1983
24 1950, 1953, 1958
21 1948, 1951, 1956, 1981
20 1949

Fewest Touchdowns Rushing, Opponents, Season
1 1923, 1929
2 1924, 1926, 1927
4 1932, 1933, 1962
5 1921, 1922, 1936

Most Touchdowns Rushing, Opponents, Game
5 Bears, Nov. 6, 1955
   Bears, Dec. 7, 1980

PASSING

Most Passes Attempted, Opponents, Season
616 1995
605 1994
589 2003
583 2001

Fewest Passes Attempted, Opponents, Season
173 1934
179 1933
191 1935
197 1937

Most Passes Attempted, Opponents, Game
59 Broncos, Oct. 10, 1993
    Giants, Jan. 6, 2002
57 Cardinals, Jan. 2, 2000
55 Vikings, Nov. 29, 1981
    Steelers, Dec. 24, 1995
    Lions, Sept. 14, 2003
54 Chargers, Oct. 24, 1999

Fewest Passes Attempted, Opponents, Game
2 Cardinals, Nov. 29, 1934
3 Cardinals, Oct. 13, 1935
   Cardinals, Sept. 12, 1937
4 Bears, Sept. 25, 1932
   Cardinals, Nov. 18, 1934
   Browns, Nov. 4, 1956
5 Cardinals, Dec. 6, 1936
   Giants, Nov. 17, 1940

Most Passes Completed, Opponents, Season
351 1995
341 2001
337 1994
326 2003

Fewest Passes Completed, Opponents, Season
48 1933
56 1934
61 1935
70 1937

Most Passes Completed, Opponents, Game
38 Vikings, Nov. 29, 1981
36 Giants, Jan. 6, 2002
35 Saints, Sept. 10, 1978
    Cardinals, Jan. 2, 2000
33 Lions, Oct. 25, 1987
    Broncos, Oct. 10, 1993
    Steelers, Dec. 24, 1995

Fewest Passes Completed, Opponents, Game
0 Cardinals, Nov. 18, 1934

Most Yards Gained Passing, Opponents, Season
3,762 1983
3,640 1995
3,553 1989
3,505 1999

Fewest Yards Gained Passing, Opponents, Season

    676 1934
    711 1933
    837 1935
  1,115 1937

Most Yards Gained Passing, Opponents, Game

    442 Vikings, Oct. 5, 1998
    434 Rams, Dec. 12, 1954
    411 49ers, Nov. 4, 1990
    400 Chiefs, Oct. 12, 2003

Fewest Yards Gained Passing, Opponents, Game

     -6 Cardinals, Nov. 29, 1934
     -1 Cowboys, Oct. 24, 1965
      0 Cardinals, Nov. 18, 1934
      6 Cardinals, Sept. 12, 1937

Most Times Sacked, Opponents, Season

     52 2001
     50 1998
     48 1978, 1985
     47 1966

Fewest Times Sacked, Opponents, Season

     19 1971
     20 1982
     25 1973
     27 1990

Most Times Sacked, Opponents, Game

      9 Cowboys, Oct. 24, 1965
         49ers, Nov. 1, 1998

Most Yards Lost Attempting to Pass, Opponents, Season

    443 1952
    386 1978 (48 sacks)
    383 1985 (48 sacks)
    357 1966 (47 sacks), 1976 (43 sacks)

Fewest Yards Lost Attempting to Pass, Opponents, Season

     75 1956
     78 1958
     80 1955
    112 1948

Highest Completion Percentage, Opponents, Season

  63.45 1989 (302-476)
  59.60 1986 (267-448)
  59.49 1987 (279-469)
  58.49 2001 (341-583)

Lowest Completion Percentage, Opponents, Season

  26.82 1933 (48-179)
  31.94 1935 (61-191)
  32.37 1934 (56-173)
  35.53 1937 (70-197)

**Highest Completion Percentage, Opponents, Game
(min. 20 atts.)**

  84.62 Buccaneers, Sept. 13, 1992 (22-26)
  83.33 Bears, Dec. 7, 1980 (20-24)
  81.48 Buccaneers, Sept. 10, 1989 (22-27)
  80.77 Giants, Dec. 19, 1987 (21-26)

**Lowest Completion Percentage, Opponents, Game
(min. 20 atts.)**

  16.67 Pirates, Oct. 6, 1935 (4-24)
  19.23 Bears, Sept. 22, 1935 (5-26)
  22.58 Eagles, Nov. 2, 1952 (7-31)
  22.73 Lions, Oct. 7, 1934 (5-22)
         Lions, Sept. 14, 1941 (5-22)

Most Touchdowns Passing, Opponents, Season

     31 1986
     28 2000
     25 1951, 1995
     24 1950, 1958, 2002

Fewest Touchdowns Passing, Opponents, Season

      1 1922
      2 1921, 1924, 1929
      3 1923, 1932, 1934
      4 1926, 1927

Most Touchdowns Passing, Opponents, Game

      6 Vikings, Sept. 28, 1986

Most Passes Had Intercepted, Opponents, Season

     42 1943
     40 1940
     33 1942
     31 1936, 1955, 1962

Fewest Passes Had Intercepted, Opponents, Season

     11 1976
     12 1960, 1982
     13 1958, 1977, 1980, 1995, 1998
     14 1959, 1975

Most Passes Had Intercepted, Opponents, Game

      9 Lions, Oct. 24, 1943
      7 Rams, Oct. 30, 1938
         Rams, Nov. 8, 1942
         Rams, Nov. 12, 1944
         Rams, Oct. 17, 1948

Highest Passer Rating, Opponents, Season

   86.1 1958
   85.4 1986
   83.8 1980
   81.2 1985

Lowest Passer Rating, Opponents, Season

   11.5 1934
   17.1 1933
   19.6 1935
   24.0 1936

PUNTING

Most Punts, Opponents, Season

     94 2000
     90 1978, 1996, 1997, 1998
     89 1984
     88 1994, 1995

Fewest Punts, Opponents, Season

     42 1958
     46 1982
     49 1961
     50 1956, 1957

Most Punts, Opponents, Game

     17 Bears, Oct. 22, 1933
     15 Spartans, Nov. 12, 1933
     14 Eagles, Dec. 3, 1933
         Bears, Dec. 10, 1933
     13 Texans, Nov. 23, 1952

Fewest Punts, Opponents, Game

      0 Bears, Nov. 6, 1955
         Rams, Dec. 16, 1956
         Vikings, Sept. 27, 1981
         Buccaneers, Nov. 22, 1981

Highest Gross Average, Opponents, Season

  44.30 1959 (56-2,481)
  43.56 1998 (90-3,920)
  43.54 1947 (65-2,830)
  43.49 1964 (72-3,131)
  43.36 1963 (59-2,558)

Lowest Gross Average, Opponents, Season

  36.53 1977 (76-2,776)
  36.60 1974 (84-3,074)
  36.67 1943 (55-2,017)
  37.20 1944 (56-2,083)

Highest Net Average, Opponents, Season
  38.97 1965 (60-2,338)
  38.43 1967 (75-2,882)
  38.21 2002 (76-2,904)
  38.12 1963 (59-2,249)
Lowest Net Average, Opponents, Season
  29.71 1961 (49-1,456)
  29.98 1974 (84-2,518)
  31.25 1977 (76-2,375)
  31.33 1986 (70-2,193)

PUNT RETURNS

Most Punt Returns, Opponents, Season
  54 1987
  53 1977
  51 1978
  50 1949, 1980, 1981
Fewest Punt Returns, Opponents, Season
  13 1967
  18 1944, 1969
  19 1968
  20 1962
Most Punt Returns, Opponents, Game
  9 Giants, Nov. 1, 1959
  8 Eagles, Nov. 29, 1942
     Bears, Oct. 15, 1950
Most Fair Catches, Opponents, Season
  27 1967, 2000
  25 1969
  24 1991, 1999
  22 1978, 2002
Fewest Fair Catches, Opponents, Season
  2 1974
  3 1982
  4 1961, 1977, 1981
  5 1984, 1986
Most Yards Punt Returns, Opponents, Season
  932 1949
  564 1951
  511 1981
  483 1947
Fewest Yards Punt Returns, Opponents, Season
  22 1967
  62 1969
  66 1968
  144 1960
Most Yards Punt Returns, Opponents, Game
  175 Lions, Nov. 22, 1951
  148 Cardinals, Nov. 27, 1949
       Colts, Oct. 14, 1956
  113 Lions, Dec. 11, 1949
  109 Redskins, Dec. 4, 1949
Highest Average Punt Returns, Opponents, Season
  18.64 1949 (50-932)
  14.84 1951 (38-564)
  13.94 1941 (31-432)
  13.87 1989 (30-416)
Lowest Average Punt Returns, Opponents, Season
  1.69 1967 (13-22)
  3.44 1969 (18-62)
  3.47 1968 (19-66)
  3.73 1957 (40-149)
Most Touchdowns Punt Returns, Opponents, Season
  3 1949
Most Touchdowns Punt Returns, Opponents, Game
  2 Lions, Nov. 22, 1951

KICKOFF RETURNS

Most Kickoff Returns, Opponents, Season
  83 2002
  82 2003
  78 1983, 1997
  76 1962, 1996, 2000, 2001
Fewest Kickoff Returns, Opponents, Season
  22 1948
  28 1946
  29 1949
  31 1943
Most Kickoff Returns, Opponents, Game
  9 Redskins, Oct. 17, 1983
     Lions, Nov. 27, 1986
     Bears, Dec. 11, 1994
     Lions, Nov. 10, 2002
Most Yards Kickoff Returns, Opponents, Season
  1,807 1998
  1,800 2002
  1,707 2003
  1,649 1996
Fewest Yards Kickoff Returns, Opponents, Season
  583 1949
  606 1943
  611 1948
  683 1946
Most Yards Kickoff Returns, Opponents, Game
  304 Bears, Nov. 9, 1952
  282 Cardinals, Nov. 1, 1942
  260 Lions, Nov. 24, 1940
  244 Lions, Sept. 6, 1998
Highest Average Kickoff Returns, Opponents, Season
  27.77 1948 (22-611)
  25.73 1952 (51-1,312)
  24.67 1970 (36-888)
  24.42 1998 (74-1,807)
Lowest Average Kickoff Returns, Opponents, Season
  15.81 1992 (57-901)
  16.04 1984 (73-1,171)
  16.90 1981 (70-1,183)
  17.35 1980 (52-902)
Most Touchdowns Kickoff Returns, Opponents, Season
  2 1940, 1952, 1985, 1998
Most Touchdowns Kickoff Returns, Opponents, Game
  2 Bears, Sept. 22, 1940
     Bears, Nov. 9, 1952
     Rams, Nov. 24, 1985

FUMBLES

Most Fumbles, Opponents, Season
  45 1946
  44 1975, 1985
  42 1981, 1987
  41 1941, 1947
Fewest Fumbles, Opponents, Season
  12 1995
  15 1940
  16 2000
  17 1956

Most Fumbles, Opponents, Game

  9 Eagles, Oct. 13, 1946

     Chargers, Sept. 24, 1978

  8 Steelers, Nov. 23, 1941

     Lions, Dec. 6, 1992

  7 Redskins, Dec. 1, 1946

     Lions, Sept. 17, 1950

     Bears, Nov. 4, 1962

     Vikings, Nov. 13, 1983

     Bears, Oct. 21, 1985

Most Fumbles Recovered, Own and Packers, by Opponents, Season

  43 1978 (19 own, 24 Packers)

  40 1952 (9 own, 31 Packers)

  39 1950 (19 own, 20 Packers)

Fewest Fumbles Recovered, Own and Packers, by Opponents, Season

  15 1942 (7 own, 8 Packers)

     1995 (9 own, 6 Packers)

  19 1943 (13 own, 6 Packers)

     1967 (9 own, 10 Packers)

Most Fumbles Recovered, Own and Packers, by Opponents, Game

  8 Lions, Sept. 17, 1950 (7 own, 1 Packers)

     49ers, Dec. 10, 1950 (4 own, 4 Packers)

  7 Cardinals, Sept. 17, 1939 (5 own, 2 Packers)

     Lions, Nov. 27, 1952 (1 own, 6 Packers)

     Giants, Sept. 19, 1971 (3 own, 4 Packers)

     Bears, Nov. 15, 1981 (6 own, 1 Packers)

Most Own Fumbles Recovered, by Opponents, Season

  19 1947, 1950, 1978, 1983

Fewest Own Fumbles Recovered, by Opponents, Season

  6 1974

  7 1942, 1948

  8 1940, 1949, 1954, 1960, 1998, 2000

Most Own Fumbles Recovered, by Opponents, Game

  7 Lions, Sept. 17, 1950

  6 Eagles, Oct. 13, 1946

     Bears, Nov. 15, 1981

  5 Cardinals, Sept. 17, 1939

     Lions, Oct. 14, 1979

     Vikings, Nov. 13, 1983

Most TDs, Fumbles Recovered, Own and Packers, by Opponents, Season

  3 1950, 1955, 1971, 1981

Most TDs, Fumbles Recovered, Own and Packers, by Opponents, Game

  2 Lions, Sept. 17, 1950 (1 own, 1 Packers)

     Giants, Sept. 19, 1971 (2 Packers)

     Broncos, Oct. 15, 1984 (2 Packers)

TURNOVERS

Most Turnovers, Opponents, Season

  54 1981

  52 1946

  51 1943, 1947

  50 1962, 1965

Fewest Turnovers, Opponents, Season

  16 1995

  23 1982, 1998

  24 1939, 1977

  26 1969, 1976

Most Turnovers, Opponents, Game

  11 Chargers, Sept. 24, 1978

  10 Steelers, Nov. 23, 1941

     Lions, Oct. 24, 1943

     Cardinals, Nov. 10, 1948

  9 Bears, Nov. 9, 1947

     Rams, Oct. 17, 1948

PENALTIES

Most Penalties, Opponents, Season

  145 1984

  116 1978

  114 1997

  112 1988

Fewest Penalties, Opponents, Season

  50 1972

  51 1943, 1959

  52 1956, 1961

  54 1962, 1973

Most Penalties, Opponents, Game

  22 Tigers, Sept. 17, 1944

  17 Seahawks, Oct. 21, 1984

  16 Cardinals, Sept. 13, 1936

     Falcons, Dec. 26, 1982

  15 Bears, Nov. 5, 1944

     Bears, Sept. 30, 1951

     Bears, Sept. 28, 1952

     Vikings, Oct. 16, 1988

     Rams, Nov. 9, 1997

Fewest Penalties, Opponents, Game

  0 Giants, Nov. 11, 1934

     Cardinals, Nov. 28, 1935

     Redskins, Nov. 8, 1936

     Lions, Oct. 31, 1937

     Steelers, Sept. 19, 1965

     Colts, Sept. 10, 1966

     Lions, Dec. 20, 1970

     Panthers, Dec. 14, 1997

Most Yards Penalized, Opponents, Season

  1,129 1984

  993 1999

  992 2000

  965 1983

Fewest Yards Penalized, Opponents, Season

  190 1935

  286 1937

  315 1939

  334 1938

Most Yards Penalized, Opponents, Game

  168 Tigers, Sept. 17, 1944

  153 Falcons, Dec. 26, 1982

  135 Rams, Dec. 8, 1946

     Cowboys, Nov. 14, 1999

  134 Falcons, Nov. 27, 1983

THE POSTSEASON

THE PLAYOFF GAMES

Ice Bowl
The Lambeau Field scoreboard at the end of the legendary "Ice Bowl" game has the Packers prevailing over the Cowboys 21-17, thanks to Bart Starr's quarterback sneak with seconds remaining. The playoff game on Dec. 31, 1967, gave the Packers the NFL title and sent them to Super Bowl II. Photo from the Tom Pigeon Collection

1936 NFL Championship Game

Sunday, December 13, 1936

At Polo Grounds, New York
Attendance = 29,545

GREEN BAY PACKERS	7	0	7	7	—	21
BOSTON REDSKINS	0	6	0	0	—	6

GB - Hutson 43 pass from Herber (Ernie Smith kick)
BR - Rentner 1 run (Riley Smith kick wide)
GB - Gantenbein 8 pass from Herber (Ernie Smith kick)
GB - Monnett 2 run (Engebretsen kick)

In 1933, the NFL spilt into two divisions and decreed the winners of each would meet at season's end in a championship game. The Packers, who won three consecutive titles (1929-31) in the days when finishing first in the standings determined the league champion, made their playoff debut against the Boston Redskins on Dec. 13, 1936.

The Redskins weren't expected to give Green Bay much of a challenge. The Packers had defeated the Easterners twice during the regular season, once by a 31-2 margin.

Boston owner George Marshall, disgusted by the support his team had received at home, moved the contest to the neutral Polo Grounds. A crowd of 29,545 turned out—nearly six times the number that had attended Boston's final regular-season home game against the Steelers.

Boston was in trouble almost from the start. On the team's fifth offensive play—a play in which the Redskins lost their top rusher, Cliff Battles, to injury—Riley Smith mishandled a lateral and the Packers' Lou Gordon recovered. Three plays later, Arnie Herber passed 43 yards to Don Hutson for a touchdown.

Pug Rentner, Battle's replacement, carried five times for 18 yards and completed two passes, including a 32-yarder to Ed Justice, to ignite a 78-yard drive. Rentner capped the advance with a 2-yard scoring run. Riley Smith's conversion attempt sailed wide and Green Bay led 7-6.

Green Bay took charge in the second half. Herber moved the Packers 74 yards in six plays, with the payoff coming on an 8-yard pass to Milt Gantenbein. Early in the fourth quarter, Lon Evans blocked a Riley Smith punt and Clarke Hinkle recovered on the Boston 2-yard line. Bobby Monnett scored two plays later.

Green Bay blocked Riley Smith's next punt also, but gave up the ball on downs.

STATISTICS

	Packers	Redskins
First Downs	7	8
Total Net Yards	220	116
Yards Rushing	41-67	35-39
Yards Passing	153	77
Att/Com/HI	23-9-2	22-7-1
Punts	7	10
Penalties	3-15	4-25
Fumbles/Lost	2-1	5-2

1938 NFL Championship Game

Sunday, December 11, 1938

At Polo Grounds, New York
Attendance = 48,120

GREEN BAY PACKERS	0	14	3	0	—	17
NEW YORK GIANTS	9	7	7	0	—	23

NY - FG (13) Cuff
NY - Leemans 6 run (Gildea kick wide)
GB - Mulleneaux 50 pass from Herber (Engebretsen kick)
NY - Barnard 20 pass from Danowski (Cuff kick)
GB - Hinkle 6 run (Engebretsen kick)
GB - FG (15) Engebretsen
NY - Soar 23 pass from Danowski (Cuff kick)

"It just isn't fair for us to lose a game on account of incompetent officiating. That's my sincere opinion."

If nothing else, the 1938 championship game will be remembered for Curly Lambeau's outbursts. He erupted at least twice during the game and carried on for days afterward.

"I don't howl about offside decisions and 15-yard penalties for holding and those things, but two decisions by (head-linesman Larry) Conover, the official, were completely wrong and we are going to have a showdown on it," Lambeau said.

The first play in question helped the Giants go up 16-7. Tuffy Leemans fired a 20-yard pass to Len Barnum. A jarring hit by Clarke Hinkle knocked the ball free, but Conover ruled

the pass complete despite Lambeau's argument that Barnum never had possession. Three plays later, Eddie Danowski tossed a 20-yard pass to Hap Barnard and New York led by nine.

The second controversy arose in the fourth quarter with the Packers trailing 23-17. An 18-yard pass from Arnie Herber to Milt Gantenbein put the Packers on the Giants' 39-yard line. But Conover ruled Gantenbein ineligible because of an illegal shift, and New York was awarded the ball on the Green Bay 43.

The calls hurt, but Green Bay hampered its own cause with three turnovers and two blocked punts. The Giants turned the blocked kicks into a 9-0 lead. Two of the turnovers occurred in the second half in New York territory.

The Packers were without a healthy Don Hutson, who had injured his knee against the Lions on Nov. 13. Hutson's only offensive contribution was to turn a lateral from Carl Mulleneaux into a 10-yard gain on the second-to-last play of the game.

"They (the Packers) were lucky to have given us as much trouble as they did," Ward Cuff said later in the week.

STATISTICS

	Packers	Giants
First Downs	14	10
Total Net Yards	378	212
Yards Rushing	46-164	43-115
Yards Passing	214	97
Att/Com/Int	19-8-1	15-8-1
Punts	6	8
Penalties	2-10	3-20
Fumbles/Lost	4-2	2-0

1939 NFL Championship Game

Sunday, December 10, 1939

At State Fair Park, Milwaukee
Attendance = 32,279

NEW YORK GIANTS	0	0	0	0	—	0
GREEN BAY PACKERS	7	0	10	10	—	27

GB - Gantenbein 7 pass from Herber (Engebretsen kick)
GB - FG (29) Engebretsen
GB - Laws 31 pass from Isbell (Engebretsen kick)
GB - FG (42) Ernie Smith
GB - Jankowski 1 run (Ernie Smith kick)

In the years since the league had split into two divisions, no team had successfully defended its title. Green Bay ensured that trend continued by pounding the 1938 champion Giants 27-0.

The game was close for two quarters. The Packers had a punt blocked and threw two interceptions. The Giants botched three field goal tries and had two passes intercepted, the last by Charley Brock deep in Packers territory just before the half.

But the second half was a different story. Aside from the final drive of the game, Green Bay held New York to just 20 yards rushing and zero yards passing. Milt Gantenbein, Andy Uram, Earl Svendsen, and Brock all halted Giant advances with interceptions. Ernie Smith, Pete Tinsley, and Carl Mulleneaux were among those who registered tackles for losses. Larry Craig set the tone on the first play from scrimmage in the third quarter when he smacked Tuffy Leemans for a 2-yard loss.

"We broke their hearts in the third period this afternoon when we scored 10 points against the wind," said Don Hutson, who caught two passes for 21 yards, including a 15-yarder that set up the team's first score.

The Giants played without head coach Steve Owen, who was attending his mother's funeral. Assistant Bo Molenda, who played with the Packers from 1928-32, handled Owen's duties.

"The Packers were the better team out there today," he said, then later added, "We have no excuses. We were just outplayed all the way through."

The Packers executive board decided the game would be played in Milwaukee. Corporation directors approved the board's decision and issued a statement that said in part, "the decision to play the game in Milwaukee was reached reluctantly." The statement went on to say, "the amount of money which would accrue to the players by selecting Milwaukee (over Green Bay) was greater by several thousand dollars."

STATISTICS

	Packers	Giants
First Downs	10	9
Total Net Yards	232	164
Yards Rushing	52-136	34-70
Yards Passing	96	94
Att/Com/Int	10-7-3	25-8-6
Punts	7	6
Penalties	4-50	5-21
Fumbles/Lost	2-0	1-0

1941 Western Division Playoff Game

Sunday, December 14, 1941

At Wrigley Field, Chicago
Attendance = 43,425

GREEN BAY PACKERS	7	0	7	0	—	14
CHICAGO BEARS	6	24	0	3	—	33

GB - Hinkle 1 run (Hutson kick)
CB - Gallarneau 81 punt return (Snyder kick blocked)
CB - FG (24) Snyder
CB - Standlee 3 run (Stydahar kick)
CB - Standlee 2 run (Stydahar kick)
CB - Swisher 9 run (Stydahar kick)
GB - Van Every 10 pass from Isbell (Hutson kick)
CB - FG (26) Snyder

When two long-time rivals are about to clash, words can get thrown about like so many footballs.

"The Packers tricked us once this season with their seven-man line, but they are not going to do it this time," Sid Luckman supposedly said in the days leading up to the matchup.

"The Halas strategy," Lambeau noted, "includes frightening the opposition with propaganda. A good many of the teams the Bears played this year were licked on Saturday afternoon."

The Bears and Packers shared the NFL's best record at 10-1. Neither was likely to be intimidated by verbal jabs. Because they had tied, a divisional playoff game became necessary.

The Packers drew first blood. Hugh Gallarneau fumbled the opening kickoff and Ray Riddick recovered. Clarke Hinkle reached pay dirt five plays later, and Green Bay led 7-0.

Shortly thereafter, Norm Standlee fumbled and Larry Craig recovered on the Chicago 35. But the Packers failed to capitalize as Don Hutson dropped a pass from Cecil Isbell in the end zone and Hinkle's field goal try was blocked by John Siegal.

From there it was downhill for the Packers. Gallarneau returned a punt 81 yards for a touchdown and the Bears added 24 points in the second quarter.

Green Bay reached Chicago's one-yard line late in the first half, but Isbell was thrown for a loss by Luckman as time ran out. Green Bay's only second-half score came on a pass from Isbell to Hal Van Every.

"Green Bay is a one-man team," growled Bears fullback Bill Osmanski. "You always know that if you stop Don Hutson, you should win the game."

STATISTICS

	Packers	Bears
First Downs	12	14
Total Net Yards	255	325
Yards Rushing	36-33	48-277
Yards Passing	222	48
Att/Com/Int	27-11-2	12-5-0
Punts	4	6
Penalties	3-46	12-128
Fumbles/Lost	3-2	5-3

1944 NFL Championship Game

Sunday, December 17, 1944

At Polo Grounds, New York
Attendance = 46,016

GREEN BAY PACKERS	0	14	0	0	—	14
NEW YORK GIANTS	0	0	0	7	—	7

GB - Fritsch 2 run (Hutson kick)
GB - Fritsch 28 pass from Comp (Hutson kick)
NY - Cuff 1 run (Strong kick)

Joe Laws was 33 years old and in his 11th NFL campaign, but you'd have had a hard time convincing the Giants of that.

Laws intercepted a playoff-record three passes, led the Packers in rushing with 72 yards, and returned four kicks as Green Bay edged New York 14-7 in the Polo Grounds. His 21-yard run to open the second quarter started the Packers on a 49-yard march that put them up 7-0. He had interceptions in each of the final two quarters to snuff out late Giant advances.

"I thought Laws was the best player on the field," said Chicago Cardinals coach Phil Handler, who was in attendance. "Why he actually looked faster than when he broke into pro football."

The game was far from a one-man show, however. Ted Fritsch reeled off a 27-yard run and scored two touchdowns. Paul Duhart intercepted former Packer Arnie Herber late in the fourth quarter. And the entire defense held New York to just 18 total yards on 20 plays in the first half.

"For the first time this year, the ball club operated at full efficiency," Packers coach Curly Lambeau said.

The Giants crossed midfield only three times. In the third quarter, Herber passed to Howie Livingston to reach the Packer 47, but Laws intercepted Herber on the next play. Later in the period, Herber's 41-yard pass to Frank Liebel set up Ward Cuff's 1-yard run. New York's last trip into enemy territory occurred in the fourth quarter and ended with Duhart's interception.

Said Lambeau: "On defense, all the boys were superb. Special credit should be given to Larry Craig, whose trap blocking on runs by Joe Laws up the middle paved the way for Joe."

Craig, Hutson, and Charley Brock all played 60 minutes.

The Giants, on the other hand, played much of the game without the services of Bill Paschal, the NFL's leading rusher, who had sprained his ankle at season's end. Paschal gained four yards on two carries.

STATISTICS

	Packers	Giants
First Downs	11	10
Total Net Yards	237	199
Yards Rushing	49-163	30-85
Yards Passing	74	114
Att/Com/Int	11-3-3	22-8-4
Punts	10	10
Penalties	4-48	11-90
Fumbles/Lost	2-0	2-0

1960 NFL Championship Game

Monday, December 26, 1960

At Franklin Field, Philadelphia
Attendance = 67,325

GREEN BAY PACKERS	3	3	0	7	—	13
PHILADELPHIA EAGLES	0	10	0	7	—	17

GB - FG (20) Hornung
GB - FG (23) Hornung
PE - McDonald 35 pass from Van Brocklin (Walston kick)
PE - FG (15) Walston
GB - McGee 7 pass from Starr (Hornung kick)
PE - Dean 5 run (Walston kick)

In 1958, the Packers (1-10-1) and Eagles (2-9-1) were among the worst teams in the NFL. Two years later, they ranked among the elite, thanks to Vince Lombardi and Buck Shaw.

On the day after Christmas 1960, the two met at Franklin Field. Twelve-year veteran Norm Van Brocklin presided over the league's second-best passing attack. Jim Taylor and Paul Hornung spearheaded the NFL's second-ranked running game.

Statistically, the visitors dominated. They outgained the Eagles 401-296 and outrushed them 223-99. They ran 77 offensive plays and crossed the Eagles' 26-yard line seven times.

But in the end, the Eagles prevailed 17-13 thanks to a lightning-quick, second-quarter drive, a 58-yard kickoff return by Ted Dean, and a costly Packers' turnover.

Philadelphia needed only seconds to move ahead 7-6. Van Brocklin passed 22 and 35 yards to Tommy McDonald to complete a two-play drive that gave the Eagles their first lead with 6:52 remaining in the first half.

In the second half, Dean's long kickoff return sparked a 7-play, 39-yard, scoring march that he capped with a 5-yard run. Max McGee then fumbled away one of Green Bay's last chances after he crossed midfield with a pass from Starr.

Even so, the Packers battled to the end. Green Bay started its last drive from its own 35 with 75 seconds left. Starr passed to Taylor for five, then to Moore for four. Taylor gained nine and Starr followed with a 17-yard toss to Gary Knafelc to the Eagles' 30. Two plays later, Starr and Knafelc clicked for eight yards. Starr then tossed a short pass to Taylor who charged to the 9-yard line before Chuck Bednarik jumped on him to end the game.

Green Bay would never again come up short in a last-minute, playoff drive under Lombardi.

STATISTICS

	Packers	Eagles
First Downs	22	13
Total Net Yards	401	296
Yards Rushing	42-223	28-99
Yards Passing	178	204
Att/Com/Int	35-21-0	20-9-1
Punts	5	6
Penalties	4-27	0-0
Fumbles/Lost	1-1	3-2

1961 NFL Championship Game

Sunday, December 31, 1961

At City Stadium, Green Bay
Attendance = 39,029

NEW YORK GIANTS	0	0	0	0	—	0
GREEN BAY PACKERS	0	24	10	3	—	37

GB - Hornung 6 run (Hornung kick)
GB - Dowler 13 pass from Starr (Hornung kick)
GB - R. Kramer 14 pass from Starr (Hornung kick)
GB - FG (17) Hornung
GB - FG (22) Hornung
GB - R. Kramer 13 pass from Starr (Hornung kick)
GB - FG (19) Hornung

On New Year's Eve 1961, the Packers of the '60s arrived in full force. The team that would dominate the NFL for much of the decade crushed the New York Giants 37-0 to earn Vince Lombardi his first championship.

"You're the greatest team in the National Football League today," Vince Lombardi told his team afterwards. To the press, he said simply: "They played a hell of a ball game. Defensively, I thought we were outstanding."

Herb Adderley, Hank Gremminger, Ray Nitschke, and Jess Whittenton each had an interception. Bart Starr fired three touchdown passes, two to Ron Kramer. Jim Taylor and Paul Hornung combined for 158 yards rushing. Hornung scored a then-playoff record 19 points and was voted the most valuable player.

The Packers, installed as 3 1/2-point favorites, turned the second quarter into a nightmare for the Giants. Hornung opened the period by capping an 11-play, 80-yard drive with a 6-yard run. Three plays later, Nitschke intercepted Y.A. Tittle, which led to a Starr-to-Dowler touchdown pass and a 14-0 lead. Gremminger's theft then set up the first of Ron Kramer's scores. Hornung closed the half with a 17-yard field goal that pushed Green Bay's lead to 24-0.

In the second half, the Packers allowed the Giants past midfield only once. Tittle moved New York to Green Bay's 31-yard line with pass completions to Rote and Del Shofner. But on fourth down, Dave Hanner dropped Tittle for a 9-yard loss.

"We just got behind early and had to open up in an attempt to catch them," Shofner said. "That's where the mistakes came in."

"We couldn't do anything right and they couldn't do anything wrong," was New York end Joe Walton's assessment.

STATISTICS

	Packers	Giants
First Downs	19	6
Total Net Yards	345	130
Yards Rushing	44-181	14-31
Yards Passing	164	99
Att/Com/Int	19-10-0	29-10-4
Punts	5	5
Penalties	4-16	4-38
Fumbles/Lost	1-0	5-1

1962 NFL Championship Game

Sunday, December 30, 1962

At Yankee Stadium, New York
Attendance = 64,892

GREEN BAY PACKERS	3	7	3	3	—	16
NEW YORK GIANTS	0	0	7	0	—	7

GB - FG (26) J. Kramer
GB - Taylor 7 run (J. Kramer kick)
NY - Collier blocked punt recovery (Chandler kick)
GB - FG (29) J. Kramer
GB - FG (30) J. Kramer

Jim Taylor's running was as brutal as the conditions in which the game was played.

Amid 20 degree temperatures and winds that gusted between 20 and 40 miles per hour, Taylor repeatedly slammed his body into the likes of defensive linemen Rosie Grier, Dick Modzelewski, and linebacker Sam Huff. The indestructible fullback pounded out 85 yards rushing in 31 carries to spur the Packers past the Giants 16-7.

Taylor's 7-yard burst in the second quarter was Green Bay's only touchdown. But it and three field goals from Jerry Kramer provided more than enough points for the Packers to secure a second consecutive world championship.

"I got it in the elbow, the stomach, and the hip," a battered Taylor said afterward. "I'm bruised all over."

Taylor was instrumental in each of the Packers' two first-half scoring drives. In the first, he carried five times for 26 yards and caught two passes for another 20 yards as the team moved into position for a 26-yard field goal. In the second, he followed a Paul Hornung-to-Boyd Dowler pass with his touchdown blast.

In the third quarter, Erich Barnes blocked Max McGee's fourth punt and rookie Jim Collier recovered in the end zone.

McGee's next punt was fumbled by Sam Horner and Ray Nitschke pounced on the ball. Five plays later, Kramer kicked a 29-yard field goal and the Packers led 13-7.

Late in the third quarter, Wood drew a 29-yard pass interference call while guarding end Joe Walton. In addition, Wood was ejected for bumping into back judge Tom Kelleher. Fortunately for Green Bay, New York was called for holding on two straight plays, and Chandler had to punt on fourth-and-52.

The Packers put the game out of reach with a final scoring drive that featured 11 running plays, six by Taylor.

STATISTICS

	Packers	Giants
First Downs	18	18
Total Net Yards	244	291
Yards Rushing	46-148	26-94
Yards Passing	96	197
Att/Com/Int	22-10-0	41-18-1
Punts	6	7
Penalties	5-44	4-62
Fumbles/Lost	2-0	3-2

1965 Western Conference Playoff Game

Sunday, December 26, 1965

At Lambeau Field, Green Bay
Attendance = 50,484

BALTIMORE COLTS	7	3	0	0	0	— 10
GREEN BAY PACKERS	0	0	7	3	3	— 13

BC - Shinnick 25 fumble return (Michaels kick)
BC - FG (15) Michaels
GB - Hornung 1 run (Chandler kick)
GB - FG (22) Chandler
GB - FG (25) Chandler

"If we can't win a must game against a team as handicapped as the Colts, then we don't deserve to win the championship," Packers defensive end Willie Davis said in the week before his team hosted the Baltimore Colts.

Davis should have known better. Nothing is easy in the NFL.

Absent quarterback Johnny Unitas and backup Gary Cuozzo, the Colts hung tough and took the Packers to overtime before bowing out 13-10. Lou Michaels missed a 47-yard field goal try in the extra period that would have won it for the Colts.

Baltimore lost Unitas (knee) midway through the season and Cuozzo (shoulder) in its 42-27 loss to Green Bay. The Colts signed veteran Ed Brown, but the league would not let him play in the playoffs because he did not play a minimum of two regular-season games with the team. Thus

Tom Matte, a running back who had last quarterbacked at Ohio State, got the call.

He would not be the only backup on center stage. On the first offensive play, Bart Starr completed a 10-yard pass to Bill Anderson, then was knocked from the game as Don Shinnick returned the receiver's fumble for a touchdown.

Enter Zeke Bratkowski. Bratkowski had the unenviable task of leading the Packers from behind. Twice in the first half, the team blew scoring opportunities. Don Chandler missed a 47-yard field goal attempt and Jim Taylor fumbled on fourth down from the Colts' 1-yard line late in the second period.

Paul Hornung finally cashed in on a 1-yard run early in the third quarter. Chandler tied the game on a 22-yard field goal with 1:58 left, a kick that Colts fans claimed went wide.

Chandler won the game on a 25-yarder after 13 minutes and 39 seconds of overtime had been played.

"Well, gentlemen, you can't say we don't give the world a thrill," Vince Lombardi said in the aftermath.

STATISTICS

	Packers	Colts
First Downs	23	9
Total Net Yards	362	175
Yards Rushing	39-112	47-143
Yards Passing	250	32
Att/Com/Int	41-23-2	12-5-0
Punts	5	8
Penalties	4-40	3-59
Fumbles/Lost	3-2	1-1

1965 NFL Championship Game

Sunday, January 2, 1966

At Lambeau Field, Green Bay
Attendance = 50,777

CLEVELAND BROWNS	9	3	0	0	— 12
GREEN BAY PACKERS	7	6	7	3	— 23

GB - Dale 47 pass from Starr (Chandler kick)
CB - Collins 17 pass from Ryan (Groza pass failed)
CB - FG (24) Groza
GB - FG (15) Chandler
GB - FG (23) Chandler
CB - FG (28) Groza
GB - Hornung 13 run (Chandler kick)
GB - FG (29) Chandler

The defending champion Browns had enough offensive firepower to cause many a defender to lose sleep: perennial 1,000-yard rusher Jim Brown, dangerous receivers Gary Collins and Paul Warfield, and veteran quarterback Frank Ryan.

But Green Bay proved it was up to the challenge, holding Cleveland to just 161 yards in forging a 23-12 win on a sloppy track at Lambeau Field.

"That's the best defensive club we've faced in the last couple of years," said Ryan, who was sacked three times.

After Green Bay went ahead 7-0 on a 47-yard pass from Bart Starr to Carroll Dale, Cleveland showed how potent it

could be. Ryan tossed a 30-yard pass to Brown, hit Warfield with a 19-yarder, then fired a 17-yard strike to Collins in the end zone.

The Packers clamped down in the second half. Green Bay held the Brown to 26 yards after intermission. Ryan completed just three passes for 24 yards. In the fourth quarter, the Browns ran four plays and gained minus-5 yards. Herb Adderley intercepted Ryan's last pass with less than two minutes left.

Green Bay's offense got going as well. It put together drives of 11, 14, and 8 plays. The first two resulted in 10 points, while the third chewed up much of the fourth quarter. Jim Taylor, the game's most valuable player, gained 62 of his 96 yards rushing in the final two periods.

Injuries were a concern for Green Bay coming into the game. Starr's ribs remained painful from the Colts' game and Vince Lombardi did not tab the veteran as his starter until Saturday. In addition, Taylor, Hornung, Boyd Dowler, and Ron Kostelnik all were nursing a variety of ailments.

STATISTICS

	Packers	Browns
First Downs	21	8
Total Net Yards	332	161
Yards Rushing	47-204	18-64
Yards Passing	128	97
Att/Com/Int	19-10-1	18-8-2
Punts	3	4
Penalties	2-20	3-35
Fumbles/Lost	0-0	0-0

1966 NFL Championship Game

Sunday, January 1, 1967

At Cotton Bowl, Dallas
Attendance = 74,152

GREEN BAY PACKERS	14	7	7	6	—	34
DALLAS COWBOYS	14	3	3	7	—	27

GB - Pitts 17 pass from Starr (Chandler kick)
GB - Grabowski 18 fumble return (Chandler kick)
DC - Reeves 3 run (Villanueva kick)
DC - Perkins 23 run (Villanueva kick)
GB - Dale 51 pass from Starr (Chandler kick)
DC - FG (11) Villanueva
DC - FG (32) Villanueva
GB - Dowler 16 pass from Starr (Chandler kick)
GB - McGee 28 pass from Starr (Chandler kick blocked)
DC - Clarke 68 pass from Meredith (Villanueva kick)

Mere seconds were all linebacker Dave Robinson and defensive back Tom Brown needed to turn in one of the most memorable moments in Packers history. With one play, the duo squelched the Cowboys' last gasp as Green Bay secured its 10th NFL championship.

New Year's Day 1967 saw the Packers and Cowboys battle for league supremacy in the Cotton Bowl. The affair, won by the Packers 34-27, turned into an offensive showcase from the start. But after 58 minutes, nearly 800 yards of offense, and 42 combined first downs, the game came down to four plays.

With 1:52 left, a pass interference call on Brown put Dallas at the Packers' 2-yard line. On first down, Dan Reeves gained a yard. On second down, the Cowboys were penalized five yards and Don Meredith then passed incomplete. On third down, Pettis Norman took a throw from Meredith and the Cowboys were again at the Packers' two-yard line with 45 seconds remaining.

On fourth down, Meredith rolled right but couldn't shake the hard-charging Robinson. The 240-pounder draped himself over the quarterback, who lobbed a weak pass toward the end zone. The ball fluttered into the outstretched hands of Brown.

"I had his left arm completely paralyzed and I had his right arm at the elbow," Robinson said. "So he just flipped it with his wrist. I thought it was a good move on his part."

Added Brown: "(Bob) Hayes was on my left and (Frank) Clarke was on my right. I think Meredith saw a white jersey and just threw it."

STATISTICS

	Packers	Cowboys
First Downs	19	23
Total Net Yards	367	418
Yards Rushing	24-102	40-187
Yards Passing	265	231
Att/Com/Int	28-19-0	31-15-1
Punts	4	4
Penalties	2-23	6-29
Fumbles/Lost	1-1	3-1

Super Bowl I

Sunday, January 15, 1967

At Memorial Coliseum, Los Angeles
Attendance = 74,152

GREEN BAY PACKERS	7	7	14	7	—	35
KANSAS CITY CHIEFS	0	10	0	0	—	10

GB - McGee 37 pass from Starr (Chandler kick)
KC - McClinton 7 pass from Dawson (Mercer kick)
GB - Taylor 14 run (Chandler kick)
KC - FG (31) Mercer
GB - Pitts 5 run (Chandler kick)
GB - McGee 13 pass from Starr (Chandler kick)
GB - Pitts 1 run (Chandler kick)

The Packers were expected to win Super Bowl I. The first championship game between the NFL and AFL didn't simply pit the 13 1/2 point favorite Packers against the Chiefs. It was a contest between two rival leagues.

Former running back Frank Gifford served as color commentator for CBS. He got a pregame interview with Lombardi.

"He (Lombardi) told me, 'Every owner in the (NFL) is calling me. They're telling me you've got to not only win, but win big. You know this (Kansas City) is a really good football team. This isn't just a bunch of humpty-dumpties.' I've got my arm around him and underneath I can feel him shaking like a leaf."

Lombardi had reason to worry. The Chiefs were talented. They outweighed the Packers by an average of 15 pounds per man. And they were a younger, perhaps faster team.

Green Bay led by just four points at halftime.

"He (Lombardi) told us to relax," linebacker Ray Nitschke recalled years later. "Well, he was the guy who'd gotten us so nervous in the first place, who'd made us so uptight."

Len Dawson, who had finished the first half with eight straight completions, was intercepted by Willie Wood on his first throw of the third quarter. Wood's play turned the tide. Green Bay finished off Kansas City 35-10 with second-half touchdowns from Max McGee and Elijah Pitts. McGee hadn't expected to play.

"I was sitting on the bench, enjoying the shady side of the field for a while—we normally sit on the sun side when we play in the Coliseum—and I heard somebody yell, 'McGee.'"

McGee replaced Boyd Dowler who injured his shoulder on the third play of the game. McGee, who caught only four passes all season, led all receivers with seven catches for 138 yards.

STATISTICS

	Packers	Chiefs
First Downs	21	17
Total Net Yards	358	239
Yards Rushing	33-130	19-72
Yards Passing	228	167
Att/Com/Int	28-16-1	32-17-1
Punts	4	7
Penalties	4-40	4-26
Fumbles/Lost	1-0	1-0

1967 Western Conference Playoff Game

Saturday, December 23, 1967

At County Stadium, Milwaukee
Attendance = 49,861

LOS ANGELES RAMS	7	0	0	0	—	7
GREEN BAY PACKERS	0	14	7	7	—	28

LA - Casey 29 pass from Gabriel (Gossett kick)
GB - Williams 46 run (Chandler kick)
GB - Dale 17 pass from Starr (Chandler kick)
GB - Mercein 6 run (Chandler kick)
GB - Williams 2 run (Chandler kick)

In 1967, the Packers sought to become the first team to win three straight championships since the playoff format was instituted in 1933. Few would have been surprised if that quest ended at the hands of the Los Angeles Rams.

Los Angeles (11-1-2) and its "Fearsome Foursome" was the cream of the NFL. The club finished with eight straight wins and scored more points and allowed fewer than any other team.

Green Bay, on the other hand, was hurting. It lost 27-24 to the Rams on Dec. 9, then fell to the lowly Steelers. Injuries had decimated its backfield. Elijah Pitts (torn Achilles heel) and Jim Grabowski (knee) were out, and Donny Anderson (hip pointer) and Ben Wilson (rib/foot) were not at full strength.

The Packers rose to the occasion, but not before a shaky start. The team committed three turnovers in the first 16 minutes. Roman Gabriel turned one of the miscues into a touchdown with a 29-yard pass to Bernie Casey.

Tom Brown's 39-yard punt return got Green Bay going. Travis Williams scored from 46 yards out on the next play. The Packers then increased their lead to 14-7 just before halftime when Carroll Dale hauled in a 17-yard pass from Bart Starr.

In the second half, Starr engineered two long scoring drives. The first, a 13-play, 80-yard effort was topped off by Mercein's 6-yard run. The second covered 73 yards and ended when Williams crashed in from two yards out.

"You know some of our most loyal rooters were picking the Rams," Vince Lombardi said.

Linemen Forrest Gregg, Jerry Kramer, Bob Skoronski, Gale Gillingham, and Ken Bowman were a major reason for the Packers' offensive success. They allowed only one sack of Starr (who completed 17 of 23 passes for 222 yards) and opened holes for a ground game that netted 163 yards.

STATISTICS

	Packers	Rams
First Downs	20	12
Total Net Yards	374	217
Yards Rushing	45-163	28-75
Yards Passing	211	142
Att/Com/Int	23-17-1	31-11-1
Punts	5	6
Penalties	7-44	3-25
Fumbles/Lost	3-3	0-0

1967 NFL Championship Game

Sunday, December 31, 1967

At Lambeau Field, Green Bay
Attendance = 50,861

DALLAS COWBOYS	0	10	0	7	—	17
GREEN BAY PACKERS	7	7	0	7	—	21

GB - Dowler 8 pass from Starr (Chandler kick)
GB - Dowler 43 pass from Starr (Chandler kick)
DC - Andrie 7 fumble return (Villanueva kick)
DC - FG (21) Villanueva
DC - Rentzel 50 pass from Reeves (Villanueva kick)
GB - Starr 1 run (Chandler kick)

"Just remember, the whole world loves a gambler, except when he loses."

Vince Lombardi was addressing the inherent risk involved with the blitz, but he might as well have been speaking about the climatic play that gave Green Bay an unprecedented third straight championship. Lombardi's statement came in answer to a reporter's query concerning how often the defending champions might blitz the Cowboys in the upcoming title game.

The "Ice Bowl" was a classic. Temperatures dipped to 13 degrees below zero. Dallas, not succumbing to the elements as might be expected, battled back to take the lead early in the fourth quarter. And, of course, the Packers staged a last-minute, all-or-nothing drive in the final five minutes.

Just four minutes and 50 seconds remained when Bart Starr and the offense took the field for the last time. Trailing 17-14, the Packers needed to traverse 68 icy yards to the end zone.

Five passes by Starr (all completions) and a couple of runs put Green Bay on the Dallas 11-yard line. An 8-yard run by Donny Anderson and a 2-yarder by Chuck Mercein gave the Packers a first-down on the Cowboys' 1.

Two Anderson runs gained nothing. After using his last timeout, Starr called his own number and slid into the end zone behind blocks by Jerry Kramer and Ken Bowman to deliver a 21-17 win with just 13 seconds left.

Lance Rentzel had passed 50 yards to Dan Reeves to open the fourth quarter and force Green Bay into a comeback mode.

Fully aware that had Starr failed to score, his team probably would not have had time to set up for a field goal, Lombardi admitted: "We took the gamble."

And Packers fans to this day love him for it.

STATISTICS

	Packers	Cowboys
First Downs	18	11
Total Net Yards	195	192
Yards Rushing	32-80	33-92
Yards Passing	115	100
Att/Com/Int	24-14-0	26-11-1
Punts	8	8
Penalties	2-10	7-58
Fumbles/Lost	3-2	3-1

Super Bowl II

Sunday, January 14, 1968

At Orange Bowl, Miami
Attendance = 75,546

GREEN BAY PACKERS	3	13	10	7	—	33
OAKLAND RAIDERS	0	7	0	7	—	14

GB - FG (39) Chandler
GB - FG (20) Chandler
GB - Dowler 62 pass from Starr (Chandler kick)
OR - Miller 23 pass from Lamonica (Blanda kick)
GB - FG (43) Chandler
GB - Anderson 2 run (Chandler kick)
GB - FG (31) Chandler
GB - Adderley 60 interception return (Chandler kick)
OR - Miller 23 pass from Lamonica (Blanda kick)

Was he or wasn't he?

In nine years, Vince Lombardi and his Packers had earned six conference titles and five NFL championships. As he prepared to add a second Super Bowl victory to that list, the question of his possible retirement was on the minds of many.

"I expect we'll have some retirements," he said in his final pregame press conference. "Maybe we'll need a new coach."

Lombardi, of course, did retire. And his team made sure his exit was a memorable one.

Offensively, Bart Starr, Ben Wilson, and Don Chandler had big days. Starr completed 13 of 24 passes for 202 yards.

Wilson, a Rams' castoff, had a game-high 62 yards rushing. Chandler scored 15 points on four field goals and three extra points.

Defensively, Willie Davis, Herb Adderley, Dave Robinson, and Ray Nitschke stood out. Davis sacked Daryle Lamonica three times. Adderley returned an interception 60 yards for a score. Nitschke led the Packers with nine tackles (five solo).

As had been the case in the first Super Bowl, Green Bay broke open a close game in the second half. Donny Anderson's 2-yard run finished off an 82-yard drive, and Chandler's fourth field goal put Green Bay ahead 26-7. Adderley's interception return for a touchdown early in the fourth quarter put the game out of reach.

"It was a day of learning for me," Oakland quarterback Daryle Lamonica said. "Bart Starr is one of my favorites. I hope to be of his caliber some day."

Starr was voted the game's most valuable player for the second year in a row. Lombardi announced he was stepping down as head coach on Feb. 1, 1968.

STATISTICS

	Packers	Raiders
First Downs	19	16
Total Net Yards	322	293
Yards Rushing	41-160	20-107
Yards Passing	162	186
Att/Com/Int	24-13-0	34-15-1
Punts	6	6
Penalties	1-12	4-31
Fumbles/Lost	0-0	3-2

1972 NFC Divisional Playoff Game

Sunday, December 24, 1972

At RFK Stadium, Washington D.C.
Attendance = 53,140

GREEN BAY PACKERS	0	3	0	0	—	3
WASHINGTON REDSKINS	0	10	0	6	—	16

GB - FG (17) Marcol
WR - Jefferson 32 pass from Kilmer (Knight kick)
WR - FG (42) Knight
WR - FG (35) Knight
WR - FG (46) Knight

Did Dan Devine's stubbornness in sticking with the run cost the Packers in a 16-3 playoff loss to the Redskins?

It's easy to see why Devine wanted to run. He had John Brockington and MacArthur Lane, the second-most productive running tandem in the NFL.

Knowing this, the Redskins played much of the game in a five-man front. The strategy paid off as Green Bay was held to its poorest rushing output of the season (78 yards), with Brockington managing just 9 yards on 13 carries.

Years later, Packers players remained amazed at Devine's refusal to call more pass plays and force the Redskins into a different defense.

"We never adjusted and passed the ball to the weak side," center Ken Bowman said more than 20 years later. "The gun went off at the end of the game, and they were still in the 5-1."

The lack of a consistent running attack was only one reason the Packers faltered. Green Bay failed to come away with any points following the Redskins' only turnover—Chester Marcol hit the upright on a 47-yard field goal attempt. The team allowed Washington's Larry Brown to rush for 101 yards on 25 carries. And Marcol's counterpart, Curt Knight, who was good on just 14-of-30 field goals during the regular season, was a perfect 3-for-3, with two coming from beyond 40 yards.

Roy Jefferson scored the only touchdown of the day after the Packers went up 3-0. His 32-yard reception from Billy Kilmer gave the Redskins a lead they never relinquished.

The Packers moved past midfield just twice in the second half. Hunter completed three passes to reach the Redskins' 46-yard line, but Brockington was dumped for a five-yard loss and Ron Widby followed up a Hunter incompletion with a punt.

Chris Hanburger ended the second advance by intercepting Hunter with one minute and 35 seconds remaining.

STATISTICS

	Packers	Redskins
First Downs	10	13
Total Net Yards	211	232
Yards Rushing	29-78	36-138
Yards Passing	133	94
Att/Com/Int	24-12-1	14-7-0
Punts	8	6
Penalties	6-54	4-39
Fumbles/Lost	0-0	1-1

1982 NFC First-Round Playoff Game

Saturday, January 8, 1983

At Lambeau Field, Green Bay
Attendance = 54,282

ST. LOUIS CARDINALS	3	6	0	7	—	16
GREEN BAY PACKERS	7	21	10	3	—	41

StL - FG (18) O'Donoghue
GB - Jefferson 60 pass from Dickey (Stenerud kick)
GB - Lofton 20 pass from Dickey (Stenerud kick)
GB - Ivery 2 run (Stenerud kick)
GB - Ivery 4 pass from Dickey (Stenerud kick)
StL - Tilley 5 pass from Lomax (O'Donoghue kick blocked)
GB - FG (46) Stenerud
GB - Jefferson 7 pass from Dickey (Stenerud kick)
GB - FG (34) Stenerud
StL - Schumann 18 pass from Lomax (O'Donoghue)

John Jefferson's reemergence in the Packers' high-powered passing attack could not have come at a better time. The former Chargers standout caught six passes for 148 yards and two touchdown as Green Bay blasted St. Louis 41-16 in the first round of the 1982 Super Bowl Tournament.

On the third play of Green Bay's second possession, Jefferson hauled in a pass from Lynn Dickey and outraced cornerback Carl Allen to the end zone to complete a 60-yard play. In the third quarter, Jefferson pulled down a 7-yard strike from Dickey as Green Bay went up 38-9.

"I wasn't saying that we had to throw the ball to J.J. all the time," said Jefferson, who had caught only one pass in the team's 30-20 loss to the Lions a week earlier. "But I just thought we would have beaten Detroit if we had spread it around more."

Dickey completed 17 of 23 passes for 260 yards and four touchdowns and was not sacked.

Before catching fire offensively, Green Bay had to shut down the Cardinals. St. Louis moved to the Packers' 3-yard line on its opening drive. On third down, linebacker George Cumby stuffed Stump Mitchell short of the goal. The Cardinals settled for an 18-yard field goal.

"I think it (the goal-line stand) ultimately proved to be a special moment in the game," coach Bart Starr said. "Had they scored, you're looking at some different prospects."

St. Louis lost Ottis Anderson—its top rusher—to an ankle injury in the second quarter and Pat Tilley—its top receiver—to a knee injury in the third quarter.

STATISTICS

	Packers	Cardinals
First Downs	22	28
Total Net Yards	394	453
Yards Rushing	31-108	23-106
Yards Passing	286	347
Att/Com/Int	26-19-0	51-32-2
Punts	1	0
Penalties	5-35	6-78
Fumbles/Lost	1-1	3-2

1982 NFC Divisional Playoff Game

Sunday, January 16, 1983

At Texas Stadium, Irving, Texas
Attendance = 63,972

GREEN BAY PACKERS	0	7	6	13	—	26
DALLAS COWBOYS	6	14	3	14	—	37

DC - FG (50) Septien
DC - FG (34) Septien
GB - Lofton 6 pass from Dickey (Stenerud kick)
DC - Newsome 2 run (Septien kick)
DC - Thurman 39 interception return (Septien kick)
GB - FG (30) Stenerud
GB - FG (33) Stenerud
DC - FG (24) Septien
GB - Lofton 71 run (Stenerud kick blocked)
DC - Cosbie 7 pass from White (Septien kick)
GB - Lee 22 interception return (Stenerud kick)
DC - Newhouse 1 run (Septien kick)

The Dallas Cowboys were big time: 16 playoff appearances and two Super Bowl wins since 1966. Though Dallas (6-3) may have slipped a notch in 1982, it remained a Super Bowl contender.

"We're not fearful of anything," Green Bay coach Bart Starr said early in the week leading to the matchup. "You have to recognize they have awesome firepower and a solid defense. They are a championship, Super Bowl-type team."

The game was a tale of two halves for the Packers. In the first, Green Bay ran 20 plays, gained 109 yards, and scored seven points. In the second, the underdogs produced 37 plays, 363 yards, and 19 points.

Turnovers hurt. Dennis Thurman intercepted Lynn Dickey three times, returning one for a score and a 20-7 Cowboys lead.

"All those things started to total up," Starr said. "Dallas is too good to make those kinds of mistakes against."

The Packers forged their only lead (7-6) in the second quarter. The team used nine plays, including a 16-yard pass from Dickey to Phillip Epps on third down, to move 79 yards. Dickey finished off the effort with a touchdown pass to James Lofton.

In the second half, Lofton reeled off a 71-yard reverse, Mark Lee returned an interception for a touchdown and Dickey threw for 269 yards.

Said Starr: "I don't know how we could have given any more of an effort. We gave everything we had."

STATISTICS

	Packers	Cowboys
First Downs	21	24
Total Net Yards	466	375
Yards Rushing	17-158	39-109
Yards Passing	308	266
Att/Com/Int	36-19-3	37-24-1
Punts	4	4
Penalties	3-35	5-30
Fumbles/Lost	4-2	1-1

1993 NFC Wild Card Game

Sunday, January 8, 1994

At Pontiac Silverdome, Pontiac, Michigan
Attendance = 68,479

GREEN BAY PACKERS	0	7	14	7	—	28
DETROIT LIONS	3	7	7	7	—	24

DL - FG (47) Hanson
GB - Sharpe 12 pass from Favre (Jacke kick)
DL - Perriman 1 pass from Kramer (Hanson kick)
DL - Jenkins 15 interception return (Hanson kick)
GB - Sharpe 28 pass from Favre (Jacke kick)
GB - Teague 101 interception return (Jacke kick)
DL - Moore 5 run (Hanson kick)
GB - Sharpe 40 pass from Favre (Jacke kick)

Brett Favre had thrown nearly 1,000 passes in his first two years in Green Bay. None was more important than the 40-yard bomb he dropped on the Lions in the 1993 Wild Card game.

Favre's across-the-field heave to Sterling Sharpe with 55 seconds remaining lifted the Packers to a 28-24 win.

"I don't want to say a hope and a prayer, but that's what it really was," Favre said. "I knew where Sterling was going to be and he knew not to give up on me, because who knows where I'll throw it. Sometimes I never know."

Green Bay started its comeback from its own 29-yard line with 2:26 remaining. Three passes and a 4-yard Edgar Bennett run set the stage for Favre's final fling.

For most of the game, the Lions controlled the ball. Barry Sanders, who'd missed the previous five games with a knee injury, rushed 27 times for 169 yards including a 44-yard, second-quarter burst that set up Detroit's first touchdown.

Erik Kramer was also hot, completing 22 of 31 passes for 248 yards and a touchdown. But rookie George Teague returned one of his few errant throws a playoff-record 101 yards to turn a potential 10-point deficit into a 21-17 Green Bay lead.

"All I thought was, 'I've got to get past somebody, get downfield and get into the end zone,'" Teague said.

The Lions roared back. Kramer engineered a 15-play, 89-yard march that culminated in Derrick Moore's 5-yard run. With 8:27 remaining, the Packers trailed 24-21.

Green Bay went nowhere on its next possession. The Lions again attacked, but back-to-back tackles by Matt Brock and Wayne Simmons on Sanders for no gain and an incomplete Kramer pass gave the Packers the last chance they needed.

STATISTICS

	Packers	Lions
First Downs	16	25
Total Net Yards	293	410
Yards Rushing	25-89	29-175
Yards Passing	204	235
Att/Com/HI	26-15-1	31-22-2
Punts	4	3
Penalties	6-49	5-35
Fumbles/Lost	2-0	2-0

1993 NFC Divisional Playoff Game

Sunday, January 16, 1994

At Texas Stadium, Irvin, Texas
Attendance = 64,790

GREEN BAY PACKERS	3	0	7	7	—	17
DALLAS COWBOYS	0	17	7	3	—	27

GB - FG (30) Jacke
DC - Harper 25 pass from Aikman (Murray kick)
DC - FG (41) Murray
DC - Novacek 6 pass from Aikman (Murray kick)
DC - Irvin 19 pass from Aikman (Murray kick)
GB - Brooks 13 pass from Favre (Jacke kick)
DC - FG (38) Murray
GB - Sharpe 29 pass from Favre (Jacke kick)

Corey Harris' fumble may have cost the Packers more than seven points. It may have taken the steam out of a team that was not giving an inch to the NFL defending champion Cowboys.

With 23 seconds left in the first half, Eddie Murray, who had just made a 41-yard field goal to give Dallas a 10-3 lead, kicked off. Harris fielded the ball at the 11. At the 25, defensive back Kenneth Gant knocked the ball loose and Joe Fishback recovered. Two plays later, Troy Aikman hooked up with Jay Novacek for a touchdown and a 17-3 lead.

"This is probably my worst day ever playing football," lamented Harris, who saw his team fall 27-17, "but God-willing, there'll be next year."

Said coach Mike Holmgren: "Not only the points (hurt), but we sagged just a little bit, and it took us a while to regroup after that."

For a quarter-and-a-half, Green Bay didn't back down. Tony Bennett forced an Emmitt Smith fumble on the game's opening drive, and LeRoy Butler recovered. Johnny Holland snuffed out the Cowboys' next two chances with third-down tackles on Daryl Johnston and Smith, respectively. And Butler halted a fourth drive by snagging an Aikman pass intended for Kevin Williams.

But after Harris' fumble, the Packers lost some of their fire. Dallas launched a 6-play, 69-yard drive midway in the third quarter that culminated in Aikman's third touchdown pass and a 24-3 lead. The Packers' first two second-half possessions ended in a Jim Jeffcoat sack of Brett Favre and a fourth-down pass to Ed West that came up two yards short of a first down.

Favre, who completed 28 of 45 passes for 331 yards, threw two touchdown passes, the last coming with 22 seconds left.

STATISTICS

	Packers	Cowboys
First Downs	19	23
Total Net Yards	358	381
Yards Rushing	13-31	27-97
Yards Passing	327	284
Att/Com/HI	45-28-2	37-28-2
Punts	3	3
Penalties	4-30	5-39
Fumbles/Lost	3-2	2-1

1994 NFC Wild Card Game

Saturday, December 31, 1994

At Lambeau Field, Green Bay
Attendance = 58,125

DETROIT LIONS	0	0	3	9	—	12
GREEN BAY PACKERS	7	3	3	3	—	16

GB - Levens 3 run (Jacke kick)
GB - FG (51) Jacke
DL - FG (38) Hanson
GB - FG (32) Jacke
DL - Perriman 3 pass from Krieg (Hanson kick)
GB - FG (28) Jacke
DL - safety (Hentrich ran out of end zone)

There had never been a defensive performance like it in NFL postseason history. It's unlikely there ever will be again.

What the Packers accomplished on New Year's Eve 1994 at the expense of the Lions and a healthy Barry Sanders was simply unheard of. Sanders, who led the league with 1,883 yards rushing, was harassed, harried, and hit—often. Bryce Paup, George Koonce, Doug Evans, Don Davey, John Jurkovic, Sean Jones, and LeRoy Butler all figured in on at least two tackles of Sanders. When the final gun sounded in Green Bay's 16-12 victory, its defenders had held the Offensive Player of the Year to minus-1 yards on 13 carries and the entire Detroit team to a playoff record low minus-4 yards rushing in 15 attempts.

"I think I saw something I've never seen in my five or six years in the NFL," Butler said. "I saw some good (hits) on Barry Sanders. No one ever gets good shots on him."

While the Packers attacked with abandon on defense, they were a bit more conservative on offense. With Sterling Sharpe (neck) out, Holmgren played it close to the vest. His plan worked as the Packers controlled the clock (37:28 to 22:32), and outgained the Lions 336 yards to 171.

Dorsey Levens' 3-yard run and Chris Jacke's 51-yard field goal gave the Packers a 10-0 cushion at halftime.

Detroit rallied. A 36-yard pass from Dave Krieg to Herman Moore set up a Jason Hanson field goal. Mel Gray's 68-yard kickoff return led to a Lions touchdown.

At the two-minute warning, Krieg had the Lions at the Packers' 11. On third down, Paup sacked Krieg. On fourth down, Herman Moore hauled in Krieg's last pass, but the 6-foot-3 receiver came down out of the end zone.

STATISTICS

	Packers	Lions
First Downs	18	9
Total Net Yards	336	171
Yards Rushing	35-81	15- (-4)
Yards Passing	255	175
Att/Com/HI	38-23-0	35-17-0
Punts	5	8
Penalties	3-35	4-30
Fumbles/Lost	0-0	1-0

1994 NFC Divisional Playoff Game

Sunday, January 8, 1995

At Texas Stadium, Irving, Texas
Attendance = 64,745

GREEN BAY PACKERS	3	6	0	0	—	9
DALLAS COWBOYS	14	14	0	7	—	35

DC - Smith 5 run (Boniol kick)
GB - FG (50) Jacke
DC - Harper 94 pass from Aikman (Boniol kick)
DC - Thomas 1 run (Boniol kick)
GB - Bennett 1 run (Favre pass failed)
DC - Galbraith 1 pass from Aikman (Boniol kick)
DC - Thomas 2 run (Boniol kick)

Coach Mike Holmgren's Packers rarely got blown out. On Jan. 8, 1995, Green Bay suffered one of its worst-ever playoff losses, falling to the Cowboys by 26 points, 35-9.

The Cowboys simply had too many weapons. Even with Emmitt Smith (7 carries-44 yards) spending most of the game on the sidelines with a sore hamstring, Dallas was virtually unstoppable. Troy Aikman passed for 337 yards and two touchdowns. Alvin Harper (2 catches-108 yards), Jay Novacek (11-104), and Michael Irvin (6-111) all had at least one reception of more than 20 yards. Blair Thomas, a New England Patriots' reject, picked up 70 yards rushing and scored twice.

"Our whole deal was to prevent the big play," Holmgren said. "Now that sounds foolish, but that was our plan coming in."

Dallas scored on four of its first six possessions. It racked up 328 yards by halftime.

The Packers didn't find the going so easy. Their only touchdown occurred late in the first half. Robert Brooks reached the Dallas 4-yard line on a 59-yard catch. Four plays later, Edgar Bennett rumbled into the end zone. On the two-point conversion attempt, Brett Favre failed to connect with Mark Chmura and Green Bay trailed 21-9.

In the second half, the Packers entered Dallas territory five times. Corey Harris got them there first with a 51-yard kickoff return, but Favre was intercepted by Kevin Smith two plays later. A second trip resulted in a missed 37-yard field goal. Two more drives ended on fourth-down incompletions. The team's fifth and final venture came late in the game when reserve quarterback Mark Brunell passed to Reggie Johnson for a touchdown that was called back because of an illegal formation. The game ended three plays later with the Packers on the Cowboys' 2-yard line.

STATISTICS

	Packers	Cowboys
First Downs	18	27
Total Net Yards	327	450
Yards Rushing	23-99	32-120
Yards Passing	228	330
Att/Com/HI	46-21-1	32-23-1
Punts	8	7
Penalties	8-43	7-46
Fumbles/Lost	0-0	1-1

1995 NFC Wild Card Game

Sunday, December 31, 1995

At Lambeau Field, Green Bay
Attendance = 60,453

ATLANTA FALCONS	7	3	0	10	—	20
GREEN BAY PACKERS	14	13	0	10	—	37

AF - Metcalf 65 pass from George (Andersen kick)
GB - E. Bennett 8 run (Jacke kick)
GB - Brooks 14 pass from Favre (Jacke kick)
AF - FG (31) Andersen
GB - Freeman 76 punt return (high snap, no kick)
GB - Chmura 2 pass from Favre (Jacke kick)
AF - Birden 27 pass from George (Andersen kick)
GB - Levens 18 pass from Favre (Jacke kick)
AF - FG (22) Andersen
GB - FG (25) Jacke

Teams in the NFL will not publicly admit that they're looking past an opponent. But after Green Bay defeated the Falcons 37-20 at Lambeau Field, it was clear the Packers considered Atlanta merely a team that stood in the way of getting to San Francisco.

"In terms of winning this game, so what," defensive end Sean Jones said. "This is a game we expected to win. Let's go to San Francisco and see what they try to do to us."

The Falcons' run-and-shoot offense produced 360 yards, but only 21 on the ground. The Packers' defense held the 260-pound Craig Heyward to 21 yards on nine carries, causing Atlanta to become a one-dimensional outfit.

Jeff George passed for 366 yards, including a 65-yard bomb to Eric Metcalf that put Atlanta ahead 7-0. But George was also intercepted by George Teague and Doug Evans, and sacked three times, twice by Jones.

For Green Bay, Edgar Bennett rushed for 108 yards on 24 carries. Brett Favre threw three touchdown passes without an interception. Antonio Freeman set up Bennett's 8-yard touchdown run with a 42-yard kickoff return, then became the first Packer to return a punt for a touchdown in the playoffs.

"Once Freeman had that punt return, we felt like we had enough breathing room to win it," safety LeRoy Butler said.

Left guard Aaron Taylor tore the patellar tendon in his left knee and was carted off the field. Taylor went down late in the first half, as he was pass blocking Jumpy Geathers.

"Certainly it's a blow," coach Mike Holmgren said about losing Taylor. "That offensive line has been together the whole season."

STATISTICS

	Packers	Falcons
First Downs	23	18
Total Net Yards	307	360
Yards Rushing	29-117	10-21
Yards Passing	190	339
Att/Com/HI	35-24-0	54-30-2
Punts	4	5
Penalties	5-36	5-67
Fumbles/Lost	0-0	1-0

1995 NFC Divisional Playoff Game

Saturday, January 6, 1996

At 3Com Park, San Francisco
Attendance = 69,311

GREEN BAY PACKERS	14	7	3	3	—	27
SAN FRANCISCO 49ERS	0	3	7	7	—	17

GB - Newsome 31 fumble recovery (Jacke kick)
GB - K. Jackson 3 pass from Favre (Jacke kick)
GB - Chmura 13 pass from Favre (Jacke kick)
SF - FG (21) Wilkins
SF - Young 1 run (Wilkins kick)
GB - FG (27) Jacke
GB - FG (26) Jacke
SF - Loville 2 run (Wilkins kick)

Green Bay blindsided the 49ers in much the same manner as linebacker Wayne Simmons did with his hit on running back Adam Walker, a fumble-inducing blast that triggered the onslaught which buried San Francisco 27-17.

The Packers made sure that head coach Mike Holmgren's return to San Francisco, where he served as an assistant for six years, was successful. They jumped to a 21-0 lead and forced 49ers quarterback Steve Young to throw an NFL playoff-record 65 passes in trying to catch up.

Simmons, who led all defenders with 12 solo tackles, jarred the ball free from Walker on the 49ers' first play from scrimmage. Craig Newsome scooped up the ball and bolted for the end zone.

Green Bay needed little more than three minutes to increase its lead to 14-0. Brett Favre hit tight end Keith Jackson with a 3-yard scoring pass to finish a drive that included completions of 35 yards to Jackson and 20 yards to Robert Brooks.

Favre again found Jackson for 35 yards on the Packers' next drive. The play set up a 13-yard touchdown toss to Mark Chmura.

In the first half, Favre was 15-of-17 for 222 yards. His passer rating was 158.0

"(Favre) played like an MVP," Chmura said. "We've said all along if we're going to win it all, he's going to show us the way."

Young passed for 328 yards, but his receivers rarely found room after the catch. Jerry Rice, his favorite target, caught 11 passes (117 yards), but only once gained more than 11 yards.

49ers running back Derek Loville was held to five yards on eight carries. Young gained 77 of the 49ers' 87 yards rushing.

Rookie Adam Timmerman started at left guard in place of the injured Aaron Taylor.

STATISTICS

	Packers	49ers
First Downs	18	26
Total Net Yards	368	395
Yards Rushing	28-74	18-87
Yards Passing	294	308
Att/Com/HI	28-21-0	65-32-2
Punts	5	5
Penalties	5-35	8-72
Fumbles/Lost	0-0	2-2

1995 NFC Championship Game

Sunday, January 14, 1996

At Texas Stadium, Irving, Texas
Attendance = 65,135

GREEN BAY PACKERS	10	7	10	0	—	27
DALLAS COWBOYS	14	10	0	14	—	38

GB - FG (46) Jacke
DC - Irvin 6 pass from Aikman (Boniol kick)
DC - Irvin 4 pass from Aikman (Boniol kick)
GB - Brooks 73 pass from Favre (Jacke kick)
GB - K. Jackson 24 pass from Favre (Jacke kick)
DC - FG (34) Boniol
DC - Smith 1 run (Boniol kick)
GB - FG (37) Jacke
GB - Brooks 1 pass from Favre (Jacke kick)
DC - Smith 5 run (Boniol kick)
DC - Smith 16 run (Boniol kick)

For the third year in a row, the Packers' postseason run came to a screeching halt in the unfriendly confines of Texas Stadium. This time, the Cowboys took control in the final 20 minutes, scoring 14 points in winning 38-27 and denying Green Bay its first trip to the Super Bowl in 28 years.

"One week you're euphoric," Packers general manager Ron Wolf said. "The next week you feel like a piece of slime on the bottom of the ocean. That's exactly what I feel like."

Dallas had to rally because Brett Favre and Co. pro-duced 10 third-quarter points to stake Green Bay to a 27-24 lead. Favre hooked up with Robert Brooks on a short touch-down pass with 5:19 left in the period. The score was set up by Keith Jackson's 54-yard reception.

The Cowboys responded with a 14-play, 90-yard drive that ended with Emmitt Smith's 5-yard run. Shortly there-after, Larry Brown intercepted Favre and Smith scored an insurance touchdown. Smith gained 61 of his game-high 150 yards rushing after Green Bay took its second-half lead.

Packers nose tackle John Jurkovic tore the medial col-lateral ligament in his knee on a chop block by Dallas tack-le Erik Williams in the second quarter. Green Bay assistant coach Gil Haskell fractured his skull when he was knocked down after Brooks was pushed out of bounds by Darren Woodson.

"We made a lot of progress," said Reggie White who added: "Before I retire, you'll see. This team will win a championship."

STATISTICS

	Packers	Cowboys
First Downs	17	26
Total Net Yards	328	419
Yards Rushing	12-48	43-169
Yards Passing	280	250
Att/Com/HI	39-21-2	33-21-0
Punts	3	5
Penalties	11-84	6-65
Fumbles/Lost	0-0	0-0

1996 NFC Divisional Playoff Game

Sunday, January 4, 1997

At Lambeau Field, Green Bay
Attendance = 60,787

SAN FRANCISCO 49ERS	0	7	7	0	—	14
GREEN BAY PACKERS	14	7	7	7	—	35

GB - Howard 71 punt return (Jacke kick)
GB - Rison 4 pass from Favre (Jacke kick)
GB - E. Bennett 2 run (Jacke kick)
SF - Kirby 8 pass from Grbac (Wilkins kick)
SF - Grbac 4 run (Wilkins kick)
GB - Freeman fumble recovery in end zone (Jacke kick)
GB - E. Bennett 11 run (Jacke kick)

Desmond Howard turned the mud and slop of rain-soaked Lambeau Field into his own personal playground with two huge punt returns that had the 49ers in catch-up mode for the second year in a row. Howard returned Tommy Thompson's first punt 71 yards for a touchdown. He brought back the punter's third kick 46 yards to set up a 4-yard touchdown pass from Brett Favre to Andre Rison.

Just like that, Green Bay led 14-0.

"This is crazy," said Don Beebe, the team's third wide receiver. "It's gotten to the point where it's almost ridicu-lous. Why kick it to him? If I'm the special teams coach playing the Green Bay Packers, I'd just (punt) it out of bounds."

Howard's presence was needed on a day in which both teams combined for just 406 yards of offense. Favre's 18-yard pass to Antonio Freeman was the longest play from scrimmage.

The only negative to Howard's day came at the start of the third quarter. The return specialist was in the locker room changing jerseys when the 49ers kicked off. Without Howard, the disorganized return unit allowed San Francisco's Steve Israel to recover the kick at the Packers' 4-yard line. Elvis Grbac scored on the next play to cut Green Bay's lead to 21-14.

Loose balls were a factor on two other scores. The Packers' Chris Hayes was hit by a punt while blocking and the 49ers' Curtis Buckley recovered to set up San Francisco's first touchdown. Edgar Bennett fumbled near the goal line in the third quarter and Freeman fell on the ball for a touchdown and a 28-14 lead.

Steve Young, who injured his ribs against the Eagles a week earlier, started at quarterback but left after five pass attempts. Grbac, his replacement, was intercepted three times.

STATISTICS

	Packers	49ers
First Downs	15	12
Total Net Yards	210	196
Yards Rushing	39-139	18-68
Yards Passing	71	128
Att/Com/HI	15-11-0	41-21-3
Punts	6	6
Penalties	1-5	6-42
Fumbles/Lost	5-1	3-2

1996 NFC Championship Game

Sunday, January 12, 1997

At Lambeau Field, Green Bay
Attendance = 60,216

CAROLINA PANTHERS	7	3	3	0	—	13
GREEN BAY PACKERS	0	17	10	3	—	30

CP - Griffith 3 pass from Collins (Kasay kick)
GB - Levens 29 pass from Favre (Jacke kick)
CP - FG (22) Kasay
GB - Freeman 6 pass from Favre (Jacke kick)
GB - FG (31) Jacke
GB - FG (32) Jacke
CP - FG (23) Kasay
GB - E. Bennett 4 run (Jacke kick)
GB - FG (28) Jacke

Dorsey Levens started only one game for the Packers in 1996, but he showed he was a back to be reckoned with in the NFC Championship Game.

Levens produced a franchise-record 205 yards from scrimmage as Green Bay routed the Panthers 30-13 to earn its first trip to the Super Bowl since January 1968. The running back gained 88 yards rushing and added 117 yards on five catches.

"A great athlete," said Edgar Bennett, the starter at running back. "A great athlete. Probably one of the best backs, as far as versatility, in the NFL. He can do everything.

Block. Run. Catch."

Bennett was no slouch either. He gained 99 yards rushing as the Packers dominated on the ground with 201 yards.

Two turnovers kept the Packers behind early. Linebacker Sam Mills intercepted a Brett Favre pass and returned it to the Green Bay 2-yard line. Kerry Collins threw a 3-yard touchdown pass to Howard Griffith two plays later.

Lamar Lathon recovered a Favre fumble in the second quarter. The Panthers cashed in on John Kasay's 22-yard field goal to go up 10-7.

Green Bay then used nearly eight minutes to traverse 71 yards. The payoff was a 6-yard pass from Favre to Freeman.

In the third quarter, Levens, who jumped over cornerback Eric Davis to get the Packers' first touchdown, ripped off 66 yards on a screen pass. Bennett took it from there, scoring on a 4-yard run that put Green Bay out front 27-13.

"Green Bay, I hope you're proud of us, because we're proud of you," Reggie White said in a postgame speech to the crowd.

STATISTICS

	Packers	Panthers
First Downs	22	12
Total Net Yards	479	251
Yards Rushing	45-201	14-45
Yards Passing	278	206
Att/Com/HI	29-19-1	37-19-2
Punts	2	5
Penalties	5-45	4-25
Fumbles/Lost	2-1	2-1

Super Bowl XXXI

Sunday, January 26, 1997

At Louisiana Superdome
Attendance = 72,301

NEW ENGLAND PATRIOTS	7	0	7	7	—	21
GREEN BAY PACKERS	10	17	8	0	—	35

GB - Rison 54 pass from Favre (Jacke kick)
GB - FG (37) Jacke
NE - Byars 1 pass from Bledsoe (Vinatieri kick)
NE - Coates 4 pass from Bledsoe (Vinatieri kick)
GB - Freeman 81 pass from Favre (Jacke kick)
GB - FG (31) Jacke
GB - Favre 2 run (Jacke kick)
NE - Martin 18 run (Vinatieri kick)
GB - Howard 99 kickoff return (Chmura pass from Favre)

"I think it's time that the Lombardi Trophy goes home to Lambeau Field, where it belongs."

Packers president Bob Harlan captured the thoughts of many as he spoke in the wake of the Packers' 35-21 dismissal of the Patriots in Super Bowl XXXI. After 29 often frustrating years, the Packers were once again world champions.

"I look at the faces of my players and my coaches and ownership in the locker room and I'm humbled by that," coach Mike Holmgren said. "There is a great sense of accomplishment. I'm so happy for these guys. They've

worked so very, very hard for this."

Key contributions were made by a variety of players. Brett Favre passed for 246 yards, and fired scoring passes of 54 yards to Andre Rison and 81 yards to Antonio Freeman. Super Bowl MVP Desmond Howard's 99-yard kickoff return restored momentum to a team nursing a 7-point lead. And Reggie White's three sacks of quarterback Drew Bledsoe in the last 18 minutes helped blunt whatever resistance remained within the Patriots.

"A lot of guys questioned our heart and our ability," defensive lineman Sean Jones said. "So it's good to finally win this game and shut a lot of people up."

Green Bay trailed only once, after Bledsoe found Ben Coates in the end zone for a 14-10 Patriots lead late in the first quarter.

Favre and Freeman erased that deficit with an 81-yard collaboration, the longest pass play in Super Bowl history.

Howard became the first special teams player to be named MVP. He returned four kickoffs for 154 yards and gained 90 yards on six punt returns.

STATISTICS

	Packers	Patriots
First Downs	16	16
Total Net Yards	323	257
Yards Rushing	36-115	13-43
Yards Passing	208	214
Att/Com/HI	27-14-0	48-25-4
Punts	7	8
Penalties	3-41	2-22
Fumbles/Lost	0-0	0-0

1997 NFC Divisional Playoff Game

Sunday, January 4, 1998

At Lambeau Field, Green Bay
Attendance = 60,327

TAMPA BAY BUCCANEERS	0	0	7	0	—	7
GREEN BAY PACKERS	7	6	0	8	—	21

GB - Chmura 3 pass from Favre (Longwell kick)
GB - FG (21) Longwell
GB - FG (32) Longwell
TB - Alstott 6 run (Husted kick)
GB - Levens 2 run (Favre run)

The Packers began defense of their Super Bowl title with an uninspiring 21-7 victory over the Tampa Bay Buccaneers at Lambeau Field.

The team dropped a half dozen passes, committed three turnovers, and was called for seven penalties.

"It really felt like we hadn't played in two weeks," said Antonio Freeman, who had a 90-yard kickoff for a touchdown called back because of a penalty. "It was a different type of football, but guys were able to overcome that feeling and push through it."

Freeman was guilty of having the biggest drop. The wideout had a clear path to the end zone, had he hung on to a Brett Favre pass in the third quarter. Instead, Tampa Bay's Warren Sapp sacked Favre on the next play and Green Bay had to punt.

But Green Bay made its share of big plays as well. Defensive lineman Bob Kuberski blocked Michael Husted's only field goal attempt. Keith McKenzie held tight end John Davis to no gain on a fake field goal attempt. And Dorsey Levens came up with 88 of his game-high 112 yards rushing after halftime, including a 2-yard run that gave Green Bay a 21-7 lead.

"Aside from two plays that I can think of where we had breakdowns, we played a very fine football game," Packers coach Mike Holmgren said.

With Gilbert Brown in the lineup for the first time in nearly a month, Green Bay held Warrick Dunn and Mike Alstott to 85 yards rushing on 25 carries. Brown had been out since Dec. 7 with a badly sprained ankle.

Donnie Abraham intercepted Favre twice. His first pick led to the Buccaneers' only touchdown.

Favre's counterpart, Trent Dilfer, completed only 11 of 36 passes and was also intercepted twice.

With Desmond Howard lost to free agency, Freeman and Robert Brooks returned kickoffs and punts, respectively.

STATISTICS

	Packers	Buccaneers
First Downs	16	15
Total Net Yards	289	263
Yards Rushing	32-118	27-90
Yards Passing	171	173
Att/Com/HI	28-15-2	37-12-2
Punts	5	4
Penalties	7-90	3-38
Fumbles/Lost	3-1	2-0

1997 NFC Championship Game

Sunday, January 11, 1998

At 3Com Park, San Francisco
Attendance = 68,987

GREEN BAY PACKERS	3	10	0	10	—	23
SAN FRANCISCO 49ERS	0	3	0	7	—	10

GB - FG (19) Longwell
GB - Freeman 27 pass from Favre (Longwell kick)
SF - FG (28) Anderson
GB - FG (43) Longwell
GB - FG (25) Longwell
GB - Levens 5 run (Longwell kick)
SF - Levy 95 kickoff return (Anderson kick)

It had been 31 years since the Packers last rolled into another team's home and laid claim to an NFL or NFC championship. But Green Bay did just that by out-defensing the 49ers in a 23-10 win at 3Com Park.

Eugene Robinson's 58-yard interception return got the Packers going and Keith McKenzie's sack of Steve Young on fourth down at the San Francisco 11-yard line with four minutes remaining essentially ended the game. In between, Green Bay stifled the 49ers' running attack and again forced Young to the air.

"We knew coming into it that in order for them to have a chance to win the game, they would have to run the ball," defensive lineman Santana Dotson said. "We made a concerted

effort on our front seven to stop them from doing that."

Garrison Hearst, back after missing four games with a broken collarbone, gained 12 yards on eight carries. Terry Kirby, who replaced Hearst in the second half, got 21 yards on six tries.

Dorsey Levens had better success. He picked up 114 yards on 27 carries and scored on a 5-yard run in the fourth quarter.

Robinson stepped in front of a pass intended for Brent Jones. His return put the ball on the 49ers' 28-yard line. After a run by Levens, Favre found Antonio Freeman in the end zone.

"That (the interception) was probably the biggest play of the game," linebacker Bernardo Harris said. "He made a great play."

The 49ers went for it from their own 20 with just over four minutes left. McKenzie swooped in to drop Young for a 9-yard loss. Levens then carried twice in getting his touchdown.

Chuck Levy returned Ryan Longwell's kickoff for a score. Jeff Thomason then recovered Tommy Thompson's onside try.

Favre, whom 49ers coach Steve Mariucci said was prone to throwing interceptions, had none in passing for 222 yards.

STATISTICS

	Packers	49ers
First Downs	19	15
Total Net Yards	325	257
Yards Rushing	32-106	18-33
Yards Passing	219	224
Att/Com/HI	27-16-0	38-23-1
Punts	5	6
Penalties	9-62	6-64
Fumbles/Lost	1-0	4-1

Super Bowl XXXII

Sunday, January 25, 1998

At Qualcomm Stadium, San Diego
Attendance = 68,912

GREEN BAY PACKERS	7	7	3	7	—	24
DENVER BRONCOS	7	10	7	7	—	31

GB - Freeman 22 pass from Favre (Longwell kick)
DB - T. Davis 1 run (Elam kick)
DB - Elway 1 run (Elam kick)
DB - FG (51) Elam
GB - Chmura 6 pass from Favre (Longwell kick)
GB - FG (27) Longwell
DB - T. Davis 1 run (Elam kick)
GB - Freeman 13 pass from Favre (Longwell kick)
DB - T. Davis 1 run (Elam kick)

The Packers had no answer for Denver's Terrell Davis, who ran for 157 yards in the Broncos' 31-24 victory over Green Bay. In fact, the Green and Gold conceded a touchdown to the AFC's leading rusher in order to get one more shot with the ball.

Davis' rushing output was the fifth highest in the first 32 Super Bowls. Only John Riggins, Franco Harris, and Larry Csonka had carried more often, and none of those three had missed an entire quarter because of a migraine headache.

"A lot of times you play against a slasher or a guy who will kill you with speed," Packers linebacker Seth Joyner said.

"Other guys will kill you with power. He can do all of them."

Davis, who did not play the entire second quarter, rushed for 51 yards in the final period. His 17-yard run brought the ball to the Packers' 1-yard line. He scored on the next play.

"We had to let them score," coach Mike Holmgren said. "That way, we get the ball back with some time to work with. We had a game earlier (Colts) where a team ran the clock out and kicked a field goal."

Brett Favre had one minute and 39 seconds to negotiate 70 yards. Four straight passes to Dorsey Levens earned a second down at the Broncos' 31. Favre then failed to connect with Antonio Freeman, Robert Brooks, and Mark Chmura.

Defensively, the Broncos kept blitzing despite three touchdown passes from Favre.

"Most teams, if you burn them early they'll back off," said Sherman Lewis, the Packers' offensive coordinator. "But they decided they were going to blitz no matter what, and they did."

Green Bay was a 12-point favorite heading into the game.

STATISTICS

	Packers	Broncos
First Downs	21	21
Total Net Yards	95	179
Yards Rushing	20-95	39-179
Yards Passing	255	123
Att/Com/HI	42-25-1	22-12-1
Punts	4	4
Penalties	9-59	7-65
Fumbles/Lost	2-2	1-1

1998 NFC Wild Card Game

Sunday, January 3, 1999

At 3Com Park, San Francisco
Attendance = 66,506

GREEN BAY PACKERS	3	14	0	10	—	27
SAN FRANCISCO 49ERS	7	3	10	10	—	30

GB - FG (23) Longwell
SF - G. Clark 1 pass from Young (Richey kick)
GB - Freeman 2 pass from Favre (Longwell kick)
SF - FG (34) Richey
GB - Levens 2 run (Longwell kick)
SF - G. Clark 8 pass from Young (Richey kick)
SF - FG (48) Richey
GB - FG (37) Longwell
GB - Freeman 15 pass from Favre (Longwell kick)
SF - Owens 25 pass from Young (Richey kick)

With one last-second, bullet-like pass, quarterback Steve Young decisively ended San Francisco's three-year run of frustration against the Packers in the playoffs. The left-hander fired a 25-yard touchdown pass to Terrell Owens with three seconds left to beat Green Bay 30-27. Hits from safeties Darren Sharper and Pat Terrell failed to jar the ball loose from Owens.

"It feels like somebody stuck a knife in ya," said Packers defensive coordinator Fritz Shurmur, who rushed only three linemen on the game-winning play.

Owen's reception was not the only to garner attention.

Four plays earlier, rookie Scott McGarrahan caused Jerry Rice to fumble after Rice made his only catch of the game. The officials ruled the veteran was down before the ball slipped out.

The 49ers' last drive came after the Packers went ahead 27-23 on a 15-yard pass from Brett Favre to Antonio Freeman. Young needed just under two minutes to move the team 76 yards.

The game was the last as a Packer for Reggie White.

"Losing this game hurts," he said. "You put too much into it for it not to hurt. Knowing that I'm going on my way makes it hurt even more."

A first-quarter fumble by Dorsey Levens and a third-quarter interception of Favre led to two 49ers touchdowns by Greg Clark.

This time out, San Francisco had a running game. Garrison Hearst rushed for 128 yards on 22 carries.

Levens, who missed nine games with a broken leg and ankle injury, finished with a season-high 116 yards rushing. Three days later, the running back had a screw removed from his leg.

STATISTICS

	Packers	49ers
First Downs	24	20
Total Net Yards	403	347
Yards Rushing	28-121	31-178
Yards Passing	282	169
Att/Com/HI	35-20-2	32-18-2
Punts	2	3
Penalties	4-42	6-50
Fumbles/Lost	3-2	1-1

2001 NFC Wild Card Game

Sunday, January 13, 2002

At Lambeau Field, Green Bay
Attendance = 59,825

SAN FRANCISCO 49ERS	0	7	0	8	—	15
GREEN BAY PACKERS	6	0	9	10	—	25

GB - Freeman 5 pass from Favre (Longwell kick blocked)
SF - Hearst 2 run (Cortez kick)
GB - FG (26) Longwell
GB - Franks 19 pass from Favre (Favre pass failed)
SF - Streets 14 pass from Garcia (Garcia pass Streets)
GB - FG (45) Longwell
GB - Green 9 run (Longwell kick)

Cornerback Mike McKenzie's tip of a Jeff Garcia pass not only resulted in an interception by teammate Tyrone Williams, it also swung the balance of power back to the Packers, who went on to post a 25-15 win over the 49ers at Lambeau Field.

Garcia's pass was intended for Terrell Owens, who had cut inside the Packers' 10-yard line with about five minutes remaining. The ball never found its mark as McKenzie deflected it to Williams, who snatched it from the air.

"I didn't want to look (for the ball) until I was in striking distance to know that I could make a play on the ball," said McKenzie, whose team held a scant 18-15 lead at the time.

Instead of possibly finding themselves behind by four or five points, the Packers turned around and marched 93 yards to Ahman Green's game-clinching touchdown. Green struck pay dirt from nine yards out with 1:55 left.

Green, who was kept in check in the first half, amassed 53 of his game-high 86 yards rushing in the final two quarters.

Brett Favre also enjoyed a fine second half. The 11-year veteran completed 16 of 21 passes for 223 yards and a touchdown.

"It's do or die in the playoffs," said Favre, who threw one interception in the first quarter. "I don't ever want to look back and say we left something on the field."

Favre's interception led to a field goal attempt by Jose Cortez. Defensive lineman Cletidus Hunt blocked the kick.

Ryan Longwell's first extra point try was blocked by Dana Stubblefield. After the Packers' second touchdown, the team went for two. When that failed, the 49ers were able to tie the game 15-15 early in the fourth quarter.

"I was very frustrated we missed that extra point," Packers coach Mike Sherman said. "I thought we could make it up."

STATISTICS

	Packers	49ers
First Downs	21	19
Total Net Yards	368	290
Yards Rushing	28-106	21-71
Yards Passing	262	219
Att/Com/HI	29-22-1	32-22-1
Punts	3	5
Penalties	3-25	3-30
Fumbles/Lost	1-0	2-1

2001 NFC Divisional Playoff Game

Sunday, January 20, 2002

At Dome at America's Center, St. Louis
Attendance = 66,338

GREEN BAY PACKERS	7	3	0	7	—	17
ST. LOUIS RAMS	7	17	14	7	—	45

StL - A. Williams 29 interception return (Wilkins kick)
GB - Freeman 22 pass from Favre (Longwell kick)
StL - Holt 4 pass from Warner (Wilkins kick)
StL - Hodgins 4 pass from Warner (Wilkins kick)
GB - FG (28) Longwell
StL - FG (27) Wilkins
StL - Faulk 7 run (Wilkins kick)
StL - Pollen 34 interception return (Wilkins kick)
StL - A. Williams 32 interception return (Wilkins kick)
GB - Freeman 8 pass from Favre (Longwell kick)

In seven decades of postseason play, only three quarterbacks had ever been intercepted six times in one game. Brett Favre became the first of the new millennium as Green Bay committed eight turnovers in falling 45-17 to the Rams in St. Louis.

Favre joined Frank Filchock, Bobby Layne, and Norm Van Brocklin with his dubious achievement. Three of Favre's misfires were returned for touchdowns.

"It was a disappointing loss, but we'll be back next year," Favre said. "I will be back, and my plan is to make everyone forget about what happened today."

St. Louis converted all of the Packers' turnovers into 35 points. The Greatest Show on Turf—as the Rams offense was called—didn't have to sweat, finishing with a season-low 292 yards.

Green Bay also had a 95-yard kickoff return for a touchdown called back. Allen Rossum's scamper would have cut the lead to 21-14, but rookie Torrance Marshall was caught holding.

The Rams committed just one turnover. Safety Darren Sharper intercepted Kurt Warner in the first quarter. Favre found Antonio Freeman to tie the game 7-7 five plays later.

"We (the defense) played our ass off," Sharper said. "We held a team everyone said was unstoppable to two plays."

Four, not two, was the number of plays from scrimmage the Rams had that covered more than 20 yards. Three came on scoring drives, including a 50-yard bomb to Tory Holt that set up Marshall Faulk's 7-yard run, which put the Rams ahead 31-10.

Aeneas Williams set a playoff record with two interception returns for touchdowns.

STATISTICS

	Packers	Rams
First Downs	19	13
Total Net Yards	383	292
Yards Rushing	22-118	22-91
Yards Passing	265	201
Att/Com/HI	44-26-6	30-18-1
Punts	3	5
Penalties	3-20	4-30
Fumbles/Lost	3-2	0-0

2002 NFC Wild Card Game

Saturday, January 4, 2003

At Lambeau Field, Green Bay
Attendance = 65,358

ATLANTA FALCONS	14	10	3	0	—	27
GREEN BAY PACKERS	0	0	7	0	—	7

AF - Jefferson 10 pass from Vick (Feely kick)
AF - Ulmer 1 blocked punt return (Feely kick)
AF - Duckett 6 run (Feely kick)
AF - FG (22) Feely
GB - Driver 14 pass from Favre (Longwell kick)
AF - FG (23) Feely

Deep down, Packers fans had to know it would eventually happen. Just not in their lifetime, one assumes they believed.

Atlanta, an expansion team that Green Bay welcomed into the league 56-3 in 1966, did the unthinkable. It became the first team to beat the Packers in a playoff game at Lambeau Field.

The Falcons did more than win. They made the Packers look bad. From blocking a punt, to controlling the clock, to forcing five turnovers, Atlanta had its way, especially in the first half.

"To say it's disappointing is as big an understatement as I could make," Packers coach Mike Sherman said.

Atlanta scored three touchdowns in the first 18 minutes. Michael Vick guided the Falcons on a 10-play, 76-yard drive that he capped with a 10-yard pass to Shawn Jefferson. Mark Simoneau blocked Josh Bidwell's only punt and Artie Ulmer recovered in the end zone for a touchdown. T.J. Duckett then powered over from six yards out for a 21-0 advantage with just over 12 minutes remaining in the first half.

Green Bay regrouped to earn a first-and-goal at the Falcons' 1-yard line after that third score. Three plays knocked the team back a yard. Defensive tackle Ellis Johnson then wrapped up Ahman Green for a 4-yard loss on fourth down.

"It's first-and-goal at the 1," left guard Mike Wahle said. "How do you not score from there?"

Safety Darren Sharper (sprained knee) did not play. Receiver Donald Driver, who dislocated his right shoulder a week earlier, was helped off the field after scoring the Packers' only touchdown.

In the second quarter, Falcons safety Kevin McCadam blocked Tyrone Williams into Eric Metcalf, who was waiting to field a punt. The ball was ruled to have hit Williams and Atlanta recovered. Replays, however, appeared to show the ball hit McCadam first, but the Packers never challenged the call.

STATISTICS

	Packers	Falcons
First Downs	17	21
Total Net Yards	289	309
Yards Rushing	19-56	44-192
Yards Passing	233	117
Att/Com/HI	42-20-2	25-13-0
Punts	1	5
Penalties	3-15	3-20
Fumbles/Lost	3-3	1-0

2003 NFC Wild Card Game

Sunday, January 4, 2004

At Lambeau Field, Green Bay
Attendance = 71,457

SEATTLE SEAHAWKS	3	3	14	7	0	—	27
GREEN BAY PACKERS	0	13	0	14	6	—	7

SS - FG (30) J. Brown
GB - FG (31) Longwell
SS - FG (35) J. Brown
GB - Franks 23 pass from Favre (Longwell kick)
GB - FG (27) Longwell
SS - Alexander 1 run (J. Brown kick)
SS - Alexander 1 run (J. Brown kick)
GB - Green 1 run (Longwell kick)
GB - Green 1 run (Longwell kick)
GB - Alexander 1 run (J. Brown kick)
GB - A. Harris 52 interception return

Al Harris' 52-yard interception return for a touchdown did more than push Green Bay past Seattle, 33-27, in an NFC wildcard playoff game. His runback made NFL history.

The six-year veteran became the first player to win an overtime playoff game with a defensive touchdown.

"It's every cornerback's dream," said Harris, who came to the Packers in an off-season trade with the Eagles. "You hope they call the coverage. You hope the pressure gets there, and the quarterback calls that check."

The interception was the only glaring mistake made by Seattle quarterback Matt Hasselbeck, who passed for 305 yards.

Packers coach Mike Sherman elected to go for it on two fourth downs in the fourth quarter. Needing a yard, Ahman Green gained two yards, then scored on the next play from a yard out to tie the game at 20-20. Green converted another fourth-and-one from the Seattle 42 midway through the period. Eight plays later, he put Green Bay ahead 27-20 with 2:44 remaining.

"To win a playoff game, you have to be aggressive," Sherman said. "Playoff games don't come to you."

The Seahawks used seven plays to cover 67 yards and force overtime. A 5-yard pass interference call on rookie linebacker Nick Barnett gave them a first down on the Packers' 1-yard line. Hasselbeck guided the Seahawks to a first down on their second overtime possession. Harris then made his game-winning steal, jumping on Hasselbeck's throw intended for Alex Bannister on third-and-11 from the Seattle 45.

STATISTICS

	Packers	Seahawks
First Downs	22	22
Total Net Yards	397	340
Yards Rushing	32-78	21-49
Yards Passing	319	291
Att/Com/HI	38-26-0	45-25-1
Punts	5	6
Penalties	5-30	2-15
Fumbles/Lost	0-0	1-0

2003 NFL Divisional Playoff Game

Sunday, January 11, 2004

At Lincoln Financial Field, Philadelphia
Attendance = 67,707

GREEN BAY PACKERS	14	0	0	3	0	—	17
PHILADELPHIA EAGLES	0	7	0	10	3	—	20

GB - Ferguson 40 pass from Favre (Longwell kick)
GB - Ferguson 17 pass from Favre (Longwell kick)
PE - Staley 7 pass from McNabb (Akers kick)
PE - Pinkston 12 pass from McNabb (Akers kick)
GB - FG (21) Longwell
PE - FG (37) Akers
PE - FG (31) Akers

How does a team overcome 4th-and-26 and pull off an overtime victory in an NFC divisional playoff game? Well, if you're the Philadelphia Eagles playing the Green Bay Packers, you toss a 28-yard pass, kick a field goal, then convert your opponent's only turnover into a game-winning score.

For the third year in a row, Green Bay's postseason ended in a devastating loss. The club didn't commit eight turnovers, as was the case in 2001, or get embarrassed at Lambeau Field, as they had a year later. This time, the Packers squandered a 14-point lead before succumbing to the Eagles 20-17 in a game in which they rushed for 210 yards.

"You would have thought fourth-down-and-26 was pretty good odds," Packers defensive backs coach Bob Slowik said.

Quarterback Donovan McNabb defied the odds, dropping back to pass from his own 26-yard line and finding Freddie Mitchell. Marques Anderson, Darren Sharper and Bhawoh Jue were all close by, but could not prevent the big gain. David Akers' 37-yard field goal tied the score 17-17 with five seconds left.

Fourth down was again key. Ahman Green failed to gain from the Eagles' 1-yard line with 1:56 left in the first half, after tripping over guard Mike Wahle's foot. With 2:30 to go in the game, coach Mike Sherman called for a punt rather than try to get a yard at the Philadelphia 41.

The Packers ran only one play in overtime. Under heavy pressure, Brett Favre threw up a pass intended for Javon Walker that Brian Dawkins intercepted and returned 35 yards.

Akers' game-winning field goal came four minutes and 48 seconds into the extra period.

McNabb had 107 yards rushing and 248 yards passing.

STATISTICS

	Packers	Eagles
First Downs	16	19
Total Net Yards	381	363
Yards Rushing	37-210	25-164
Yards Passing	171	199
Att/Com/HI	28-15-1	39-21-0
Punts	7	7
Penalties	6-45	3-25
Fumbles/Lost	0-0	3-1

Well-dressed fans at the Wildcard Playoff Game bring Cheese Power to Lambeau Field to help the Packers defeat the Seattle Seahawks.

Lambeau Field may have a new look, but tailgating remains a tradition before Packers games. Fans party before the Packers vs. Seahawks playoff game.

Green Bay Mayor Jim Schmitt, left, and Arizona Cardinals wide receiver Nathon Poole sign autographs before the 2003 NFC Wildcard Playoff Game against Seattle. Schmitt invited Poole to attend the game after Poole's last-second touchdown catch for the Cardinals knocked the Minnesota Vikings out of the playoffs and made the Packers the NFC North Division champion.

Photos by Eric Goska

All-Time Rushers–Playoffs

(Rankings based on total yards)

Name	Att.	Yds.	Avg.	LG	TD	G
Dorsey Levens	144	647	4.51	35	4	14
Edgar Bennett	163	561	3.44	18	5	10
Jim Taylor	146	508	3.48	33	2	7
Ahman Green	96	436	4.54	49	3	5
Paul Hornung	67	323	4.82	34	3	5
Donny Anderson	48	165	3.44	18	1	5
Clarke Hinkle	59	161	2.73	16	2	4
Travis Williams	30	137	4.57	t46	2	3
Elijah Pitts	29	123	4.24	32	2	6
Joe Laws	21	112	5.33	21	0	5
Eddie Lee Ivery	20	91	4.55	18	1	2
Tom Moore	22	79	3.59	14	0	5
Ben Wilson	21	75	3.57	13	0	3
Darrell Thompson	19	69	3.63	12	0	3
Brett Favre	47	66	1.40	12	1	19
Najeh Davenport	16	63	3.94	12	0	2
Del Rodgers	10	60	6.00	22	0	2
Ted Fritsch	18	59	3.28	27	1	1
James Lofton	2	58	29.00	t71	1	2
Robert Brooks	5	56	11.20	20	0	11
MacArthur Lane	14	56	4.00	18	0	1
Gerry Ellis	9	48	5.33	17	0	2
Cecil Isbell	36	40	1.11	14	0	3
Andy Uram	12	37	3.08	13	0	3
Max McGee	1	35	35.00	35	0	7
Chuck Mercein	19	33	1.74	8	1	3
Tony Fisher	8	32	4.00	7	0	3
Ed Jankowski	13	32	2.46	12	1	3
Mark Brunell	4	26	6.50	11	0	1
Bart Starr	8	26	3.25	14	1	10
Reggie Cobb	12	26	2.17	6	0	2
Donald Driver	2	25	12.50	16	0	3
Bob Monnett	13	23	1.77	33	1	2
Irv Comp	9	21	2.33	29	0	1
William Henderson	11	21	1.91	7	0	15
Arnie Herber	8	19	2.38	16	0	3
Paul Duhart	7	15	2.14	8	0	1
Scott Hunter	2	13	6.50	9	0	1
Harry Jacunski	1	11	11.00	11	0	3
Jim Jensen	3	10	3.33	6	0	2
John Brockington	13	9	0.69	3	0	1
Johnny Blood	2	8	4.00	6	0	1
George Sauer	4	8	2.00	4	0	1
George Paskvan	2	7	3.50	8	0	1
Tony Canadeo	5	7	1.40	16	0	1
Hal Van Every	6	6	1.00	6	0	1
Antonio Freeman	1	5	5.00	5	0	14
Chester Johnston	2	4	2.00	4	0	2
Don Hutson	1	3	3.00	3	0	5
Jim Grabowski	2	2	1.00	4	0	3
Hank Bruder	1	0	0.00	0	0	3
John Roach	1	0	0.00	0	0	1
Lynn Dickey	2	0	0.00	0	0	2
Jim McMahon	4	0	0.00	0	0	6
Doug Pederson	1	-1	-1.00	-1	0	6
Harlan Huckleby	2	-1	-0.50	3	0	2
Don Perkins	2	-4	-2.00	1	0	1
Paul Miller	2	-6	-3.00	-3	0	2
Javon Walker	1	-8	-8.00	-8	0	3
Craig Hentrich	1	-22	-22.00	-22	0	11
Packers	**1,230**	**4,415**	**3.59**	**t71**	**32**	**—**
Opponents	1,032	3,794	3.68	44	33	—

All-Time Receivers–Playoffs

(Rankings based on number of receptions)

Name	Att.	Yds.	Avg.	LG	TD	G
Antonio Freeman	47	748	15.91	t81	10	14
Robert Brooks	45	651	14.47	t73	4	11
Dorsey Levens	41	387	9.44	66	2	14
Edgar Bennett	31	170	5.48	18	0	10
Boyd Dowler	30	440	14.67	t62	5	10
Carroll Dale	29	534	18.41	t51	3	8
Mark Chmura	25	259	10.36	33	4	14
William Henderson	21	171	8.14	33	0	15
Jim Taylor	19	137	7.21	20	0	7
Ahman Green	19	130	6.84	13	0	5
Keith Jackson	17	267	15.71	54	2	6
Anthony Morgan	14	151	10.79	20	0	5
Donald Driver	13	181	13.92	25	1	5
Max McGee	12	233	19.42	t37	4	7
Marv Fleming	12	137	11.42	24	0	7
Paul Hornung	12	111	9.25	20	0	5
Javon Walker	11	259	23.55	44	0	3
Sterling Sharpe	11	229	20.82	48	4	2
Don Hutson	10	167	16.70	t43	1	5
Corey Bradford	9	188	20.89	51	0	3
Paul Coffman	9	111	12.33	23	0	2
John Jefferson	8	188	23.50	t60	2	2
James Lofton	8	161	20.13	50	2	2
Gerry Ellis	8	99	12.38	31	0	2
Bubba Franks	8	99	12.38	t23	2	5
Donny Anderson	8	92	11.50	25	0	5
Robert Ferguson	8	90	11.25	t40	2	3
Bill Anderson	8	78	9.75	18	0	4
Andre Rison	7	143	20.43	t54	2	3
Ed West	7	81	11.57	23	0	4
Tony Fisher	7	36	5.14	13	0	3
Ron Kramer	6	105	17.50	37	2	3
Darrell Thompson	6	86	14.33	30	0	3
Gary Knafelc	6	76	12.67	20	0	2
Bill Schroeder	5	70	14.00	0	0	4
Mark Ingram	5	22	4.40	8	0	3
Derrick Mayes	4	67	16.75	23	0	4
Terry Mickens	4	61	15.25	25	0	11
MacArthur Lane	4	42	10.50	22	0	1
Milt Gantenbein	4	34	8.50	13	0	3
Chuck Mercein	4	32	8.00	19	0	3
Carl Mulleneaux	3	84	28.00	t40	1	3
Ed Frutig	3	75	25.00	40	0	1
Elijah Pitts	3	49	16.33	22	1	6
Tyrone Davis	3	34	11.33	17	0	7
Tom Moore	3	5	1.67	5	0	5
Wayland Becker	2	79	39.50	66	0	1
Johnny Blood	2	64	32.00	52	0	1
Don Beebe	2	31	15.50	29	0	3
Reggie Cobb	2	30	15.00	18	0	2
Eddie Lee Ivery	2	29	14.50	25	1	2
Hal Van Every	2	24	12.00	14	1	1
Leland Glass	2	23	11.50	14	0	1
John Brockington	2	17	8.50	12	0	1
Wesley Walls	2	12	6.00	7	0	2
Travis Williams	2	12	6.00	8	0	3
Darryl Ingram	2	9	4.50	7	0	1
Larry Craig	2	6	3.00	5	0	3
Ray Riddick	1	45	45.00	45	0	1
Harry Jacunski	1	31	31.00	31	0	3
Joe Laws	1	31	31.00	t31	1	5
Ted Fritsch	1	28	28.00	t28	1	1
Andy Uram	1	24	24.00	24	0	3
Jon Staggers	1	23	23.00	23	0	1
Cecil Isbell	1	22	22.00	22	0	3
Ed Jankowski	1	19	19.00	19	0	3
Bernie Scherer	1	19	19.00	19	0	1
Len Garrett	1	17	17.00	17	0	1
Phillip Epps	1	16	16.00	16	0	2
Karsten Bailey	1	11	11.00	11	0	1
Terry Glenn	1	11	11.00	11	0	1
Del Rodgers	1	10	10.00	10	0	2
Mark Clayton	1	9	9.00	9	0	1
Reggie Johnson	1	9	9.00	9	0	2
Bob Long	1	9	9.00	9	0	7
Larry Buhler	1	8	8.00	8	0	2
Ron Lewis	1	7	7.00	7	0	2
Jim Jensen	1	4	4.00	4	0	2
David Martin	1	2	2.00	2	0	3
Herman Rohrig	1	2	2.00	2	0	1
Packers	**623**	**8,263**	**13.26**	**t81**	**60**	**—**
Opponents	619	7,347	11.87	t94	38	—

All-Time Passers–Playoffs

(Rankings based on total yards)

Name	Att.	Com	Yds	Pct	TD	HI	Tk/Yds	Rate	G
Brett Favre	630	379	4,686	60.16	33	22	30-199	86.1	19
Bart Starr	213	130	1,753	61.03	15	3	24-207	104.8	10
Lynn Dickey	59	36	592	61.02	5	3	2-15	101.8	2
Arnie Herber	37	16	317	43.24	4	4	NA	70.3	3
Zeke Bratkowski	40	22	248	55.00	0	2	2-18	52.9	5
Cecil Isbell	26	13	235	50.00	2	1	NA	91.0	3
Scott Hunter	24	12	150	50.00	0	1	2-17	52.4	1
Hal Van Every	6	2	75	33.33	0	1	NA	42.4	1
Irv Comp	10	3	74	30.00	1	3	NA	51.7	1
Tony Canadeo	2	1	40	50.00	0	1	NA	56.3	1
Mark Brunell	11	3	25	27.27	0	0	0-0	39.6	1
Bobby Monnett	8	3	21	37.50	0	1	NA	6.3	2
Paul Hornung	6	1	21	16.67	0	0	0-0	41.7	5
Rich Campbell	2	1	15	50.00	0	0	0-0	75.0	1
Gerry Ellis	1	1	11	100.00	0	0	0-0	112.5	2
Lou Brock	1	0	0	0.00	0	0	NA	39.6	1
Gary Lewis	0	0	0	0.00	0	0	1-4	0.0	2
David Whitehurst	0	0	0	0.00	0	0	1-5	0.0	1
Packers	**1,076**	**623**	**8,263**	**57.90**	**60**	**42**	**62-465**	**84.7**	
Opponents	1,185	619	7,347	52.24	38	55	82-573	62.8	

All-Time Punters–Playoffs

(Rankings based on number of punts)

Name	No	Yds	GAvg	NAvg	LG	HB	TB	In20	G
Craig Hentrich	50	2,049	40.98	36.12	63	0	6	19	11
Donny Anderson	20	670	33.50	31.90	48	0	1	3	5
Josh Bidwell	18	759	42.17	35.72	57	1	3	6	5
Don Chandler	15	618	41.20	38.40	54	0	0	3	7
Clarke Hinkle	14	413	29.50	25.07	55	3	0	4	4
Max McGee	11	379	34.45	33.55	55	1	0	4	7
Ron Widby	8	293	36.63	34.25	47	0	0	2	1
Bryan Wagner	7	278	39.71	34.57	51	0	0	1	2
Arnie Herber	6	231	38.50	29.33	52	0	0	1	3
Lou Brock	6	221	36.83	28.67	43	0	1	2	1
Boyd Dowler	5	210	42.00	40.00	64	1	0	1	10
Ray Stachowicz	5	196	39.20	34.60	49	0	0	1	2
Ted Fritsch	4	164	41.00	35.50	51	0	1	3	1
Sean Landeta	2	101	50.50	37.50	54	0	0	0	1
Herman Rohrig	2	66	33.00	NA	35	0	NA	NA	1
Hal Van Every	2	49	24.50	NA	34	0	NA	NA	1
Cecil Isbell	1	0	0.00	0.00	0	1	0	0	3
Team (blocks)	1								
Packers	**177**	**6,697**	**37.84**		**64**	**7**	**12**	**50**	
Opponents	209	8,263	39.54		61	3	14	43	

All-Time Kickoff Returns–Playoffs

(Rankings based on number of returns)

Name	No.	Yds.	Avg.	LG	TD	G
Antonio Freeman	20	413	20.65	42	0	14
Corey Harris	11	253	23.00	51	0	4
Desmond Howard	9	277	30.78	t99	1	3
Del Rodgers	9	195	21.67	30	0	2
Herb Adderley	8	161	20.13	26	0	9
Roell Preston	7	194	27.71	40	0	1
Tom Moore	7	170	24.29	33	0	5
Najeh Davenport	7	139	19.86	29	0	5
Allen Rossum	5	83	16.60	25	0	2
Donny Anderson	4	70	17.50	25	0	5
Robert Ferguson	4	54	13.50	22	0	3
Ike Thomas	3	50	16.67	19	0	1
Dorsey Levens	3	37	12.33	22	0	14
Travis Jervey	3	35	11.67	19	0	9
John Symank	2	49	24.50	25	0	3
Clarke Hinkle	2	43	21.50	22	0	4
Joe Laws	2	38	19.00	29	0	5
Robert Brooks	2	36	18.00	19	0	11
Herbert Goodman	2	33	16.50	20	0	2
Herman Rohrig	2	33	16.50	19	0	1
Tony Fisher	2	30	15.00	20	0	3

Name	No.	Yds	Avg	LG	TD	G
Charles Jordan	2	27	13.50	15	0	2
Tommy Crutcher	2	10	5.00	7	0	7
Don Beebe	1	25	25.00	25	0	3
Ed Jankowski	1	25	25.00	25	0	3
George Sauer	1	25	25.00	25	0	1
Hal Van Every	1	25	25.00	25	0	1
Aaron Hayden	1	19	19.00	19	0	3
Eric Metcalf	1	18	18.00	18	0	1
Ray Nitschke	1	18	18.00	18	0	11
Travis Williams	1	18	18.00	18	0	3
Marcus Wilson	1	17	17.00	17	0	5
Tod McBride	1	16	16.00	16	0	2
Hank Bruder	1	15	15.00	15	0	3
Arnie Herber	1	15	15.00	15	0	3
Paul Coffman	1	12	12.00	12	0	2
Bob Hudson	1	12	12.00	12	0	1
Nick Luchey	1	12	12.00	12	0	2
Ernie Pannell	1	12	12.00	12	0	1
Dave Robinson	1	10	10.00	10	0	8
Jim Flanigan, Sr.	1	9	9.00	9	0	3
Lee Roy Caffey	1	7	7.00	7	0	7
John Jurkovic	1	2	2.00	2	0	7
Jim Weatherwax	1	0	0.00	0	0	5
Wesley Walls	0	5	--	--	0	2
Packers	**139**	**2,747**	**19.76**	**t99**	**1**	—
Opponents	168	3,508	20.88	t95	1	—

All-Time Punt Returns–Playoffs

(Rankings based on number of returns)

Name	No.	Yds.	Avg.	LG	FC	TD	G
Willie Wood	20	74	3.70	31	8	0	10
Robert Brooks	14	214	15.29	43	4	0	11
Antonio Freeman	10	143	14.30	t76	2	1	14
Desmond Howard	9	210	23.33	t71	2	1	3
Antonio Chatman	9	66	7.33	21	2	0	2
Elijah Pitts	6	43	7.17	36	0	0	6
Irv Comp	4	55	13.75	21	0	0	1
Joe Laws	4	44	11.00	15	0	0	5
Andy Uram	4	31	7.75	23	NA	0	3
Bobby Monnett	3	33	11.00	12	0	0	2
Donny Anderson	3	25	8.33	15	1	0	5
Jon Staggers	3	20	6.67	12	2	0	1
Allen Rossum	2	41	20.50	35	2	0	2
Tom Brown	2	37	18.50	39	0	0	7
Tony Canadeo	2	27	13.50	21	NA	0	1
Lew Carpenter	2	7	3.50	6	0	0	1
Ken Ellis	1	13	13.00	13	0	0	1
Phillip Epps	1	8	8.00	8	0	0	2
Hal Van Every	1	6	6.00	6	NA	0	1
Paul Duhart	1	5	5.00	5	0	0	1
Johnny Blood	1	4	4.00	4	0	0	1
Chris Hayes	1	0	0.00	0	0	0	3
Arnie Herber	1	0	0.00	0	0	0	3
Paul Miller	1	0	0.00	0	0	0	1
Roell Preston	1	0	0.00	0	0	0	1
Johnny Gray	0	0	0.00	0	1	0	2
Mike Prior	0	0	0.00	0	4	0	14
Tyrone Williams	1	0	0.00	0	35	0	10
Packers	**107**	**1,106**	**10.34**	**t76**	**28**	**2**	—
Opponents	73	592	8.11	t81	35	1	—

All-Time Interceptors–Playoffs

(Rankings based on number of interceptions)

Name	No.	Yds.	Avg.	LG	TD	G
Herb Adderley	4	89	22.25	t60	1	9
Eugene Robinson	4	75	18.75	58	0	6
Craig Newsome	4	40	10.00	35	0	7
Joe Laws	3	28	9.33	19	0	5
Mike Prior	3	25	8.33	13	0	14
Tyrone Williams	3	14	4.67	14	0	10
George Teague	2	131	65.50	t101	1	7
Willie Wood	2	65	32.50	50	0	10
Tom Brown	2	20	10.00	20	0	7
Charley Brock	2	15	7.50	10	0	3
Terrell Buckley	2	0	0.00	0	0	4
Doug Evans	2	0	0.00	0	0	13
Darren Sharper	2	0	0.00	0	0	8
Al Harris	1	52	52.00	t52	1	2

Name	Att.	Yds.	Avg.	LG	TD	G
Bryce Paup	1	34	34.00	34	0	4
Dan Currie	1	30	30.00	30	0	3
Mark Lee	1	22	22.00	t22	1	2
Mark Murphy	1	22	22.00	22	0	2
Brian Williams	1	16	16.00	16	0	10
Earl Svendsen	1	15	15.00	15	0	2
LeRoy Butler	1	14	14.00	14	0	14
Hank Gremminger	1	13	13.00	13	0	5
Andy Uram	1	10	10.00	10	0	3
Ray Nitschke	1	9	9.00	9	0	11
Milt Gantenbein	1	5	5.00	5	0	3
Hank Bruder	1	0	0.00	0	0	3
Paul Duhart	1	0	0.00	0	0	1
Paul Engebretsen	1	0	0.00	0	0	3
Estus Hood	1	0	0.00	0	0	2
George Koonce	1	0	0.00	0	0	10
Jim Lawrence	1	0	0.00	0	0	1
John Symank	1	0	0.00	0	0	3
Jess Whittenton	1	0	0.00	0	0	3
Packers	**55**	**744**	**13.53**	**t101**	**4**	
Opponents	42	438	10.43	t39	5	

Name	TDr	TDp	TDrt	PAT	2pt	FG	TP	G
George Teague	0	0	1	0/0	0	0/0	6	7
Hal Van Every	0	1	0	0/0	0	0/0	6	1
Chester Marcol	0	0	0	0/0	0	1/2	3	1
Packers	**32**	**60**	**10**	**93/96**	**2**	**54/74**	**871**	—
Opponents*	33	38	11	76/80	1	40/64	692	—

*includes one safety

All-Time Scorers–Playoffs

(Rankings based on total points)

Name	TDr	TDp	TDrt	PAT	2pt	FG	TP	G
Chris Jacke	0	0	0	28/28	0	15/22	73	10
Antonio Freeman	0	10	2	0/0	0	0/0	72	14
Ryan Longwell	0	0	0	18/19	0	14/19	60	9
Don Chandler	0	0	0	22/23	0	9/12	49	7
Paul Hornung	3	0	0	5/5	0	5/6	38	5
Dorsey Levens	4	2	0	0/0	0	0/0	36	14
Edgar Bennett	5	0	0	0/0	0	0/0	30	10
Boyd Dowler	0	5	0	0/0	0	0/0	30	10
Mark Chmura	0	4	0	0/0	1	0/0	26	14
Robert Brooks	0	4	0	0/0	0	0/0	24	11
Max McGee	0	4	0	0/0	0	0/0	24	7
Sterling Sharpe	0	4	0	0/0	0	0/0	24	2
Jan Stenerud	0	0	0	7/8	0	4/4	19	2
Carroll Dale	0	3	0	0/0	0	0/0	18	8
Ahman Green	3	0	0	0/0	0	0/0	18	5
James Lofton	1	2	0	0/0	0	0/0	18	2
Elijah Pitts	2	1	0	0/0	0	0/0	18	6
Robert Ferguson	0	2	0	0/0	0	0/0	12	3
Bubba Franks	0	2	0	0/0	0	0/0	12	5
Ted Fritsch	1	1	0	0/0	0	0/0	12	1
Milt Gantenbein	0	2	0	0/0	0	0/0	12	3
Clarke Hinkle	2	0	0	0/0	0	0/1	12	4
Desmond Howard	0	0	2	0/0	0	0/0	12	3
Eddie Lee Ivery	1	1	0	0/0	0	0/0	12	2
Keith Jackson	0	2	0	0/0	0	0/0	12	6
John Jefferson	0	2	0	0/0	0	0/0	12	2
Ron Kramer	0	2	0	0/0	0	0/0	12	3
Andre Rison	0	2	0	0/0	0	0/0	12	3
Jim Taylor	2	0	0	0/0	0	0/0	12	7
Travis Williams	2	0	0	0/0	0	0/0	12	3
Paul Engebretsen	0	0	0	5/5	0	2/2	11	3
Don Hutson	0	1	0	4/4	0	0/0	10	5
Jerry Kramer	0	0	0	1/1	0	3/5	10	9
Brett Favre	1	0	0	0/0	1	0/0	8	19
Herb Adderley	0	0	1	0/0	0	0/0	6	9
Donny Anderson	1	0	0	0/0	0	0/0	6	5
Donald Driver	0	1	0	0/0	0	0/0	6	5
Jim Grabowski	0	0	1	0/0	0	0/0	6	3
Al Harris	0	0	1	0/0	0	0/0	6	2
Ed Jankowski	1	0	0	0/0	0	0/0	6	3
Joe Laws	0	1	0	0/0	0	0/0	6	5
Mark Lee	0	0	1	0/0	0	0/0	6	2
Chuck Mercein	1	0	0	0/0	0	0/0	6	3
Bobby Monnett	1	0	0	0/0	0	0/0	6	2
Carl Mulleneaux	0	1	0	0/0	0	0/0	6	3
Craig Newsome	0	0	1	0/0	0	0/0	6	7
Ernie Smith	0	0	0	3/3	0	1/1	6	2
Bart Starr	1	0	0	0/0	0	0/0	6	10

All-Time Fumbles and Recoveries–Playoffs

(Players are listed alphabetically)

Name	Fum	Own Rec	Opp Rec	Yds	Tot Rec	G
Herb Adderley	0	0	1	0	1	9
Bill Anderson	1	0	0	0	0	4
Donny Anderson	1	0	0	0	0	5
Nick Barnett	0	0	1	0	1	2
Wayland Becker	1	0	0	0	0	1
Edgar Bennett	2	2	0	-3	2	10
Corey Bradford	0	0	1	0	1	3
Tom Brown	0	0	1	0	1	7
Hank Bruder	1	1	0	0	1	3
LeRoy Butler	0	0	2	0	2	14
Dick Capp	0	0	1	0	1	1
Larry Craig	0	0	1	0	1	3
George Cumby	0	0	1	2	1	3
Carroll Dale	1	0	0	0	0	8
Lynn Dickey	1	1	0	-2	1	2
Donald Driver	0	0	1	0	1	5
Gerry Ellis	1	0	0	0	0	2
Brett Favre	9	2	0	0	2	19
Mike Flanagan	1	0	0	-2	0	5
Marv Fleming	0	0	0	0	0	7
Bill Forester	0	0	1	0	1	3
Paul Frase	0	0	1	0	1	2
Antonio Freeman	2	1	0	0	1	14
Milt Gantenbein	0	0	1	0	1	3
Lou Gordon	0	0	1	0	1	1
Jim Grabowski	1	0	0	18	1	3
Ahman Green	1	0	0	0	0	5
Forrest Gregg	0	0	1	0	1	10
Corey Harris	2	0	0	0	0	4
Chris Hayes	1	0	1	0	1	3
Arnie Herber	2	1	0	0	1	3
Clarke Hinkle	2	0	0	-4	1	4
Darius Holland	0	0	1	0	1	8
Paul Hornung	2	1	0	0	1	5
Cecil Isbell	1	0	0	0	0	3
Eddie Lee Ivery	1	0	0	0	0	2
Ed Jankowski	1	0	0	0	0	3
Ezra Johnson	0	0	1	3	1	2
Sean Jones	0	0	1	0	1	8
Jerry Kramer	0	0	1	0	1	9
Joe Laws	2	0	0	0	1	5
Dorsey Levens	4	0	0	0	1	14
Max McGee	1	0	0	0	0	7
Chuck Mercein	1	0	1	0	1	3
Casey Merrill	0	0	1	0	1	2
Carl Mulleneaux	0	0	1	0	1	3
Craig Newsome	1	0	1	31	1	7
Ray Nitschke	0	0	2	0	2	11
Don Perkins	1	0	0	0	1	1
Elijah Pitts	1	0	0	0	0	6
Roell Preston	2	0	0	0	0	1
Bill Quinlan	0	0	1	0	1	3
Ray Riddick	0	0	1	0	1	1
Dave Robinson	0	0	1	16	1	8
Alden Roche	0	0	1	0	1	1
Del Rodgers	2	0	0	0	0	2
Allen Rossum	1	0	0	0	0	2
Ade Schwammel	0	0	1	0	1	2
Joe Sims	0	0	1	0	1	4

Name	Fum	Own Rec	Opp Rec	Yds	Tot Rec	G
Bob Skoronski	0	1	0	0	1	10
Bart Starr	1	0	0	0	0	10
George Svendsen	1	0	1	0	1	2
Aaron Taylor	0	1	0	0	1	7
Jim Taylor	3	1	0	0	1	7
Pat Terrell	0	0	1	0	1	1
Fuzzy Thurston	0	1	0	0	1	10
Andy Uram	1	0	0	0	0	3
Brian Williams	0	0	1	0	1	10
Mark Williams	0	0	1	0	1	2
Tyrone Williams	1	0	1	0	1	10
Frank Winters	1	0	0	-15	0	14
Willie Wood	1	0	0	0	0	10
Packers	**61**	**23**	**32**	**44**	**55**	**—**

All-Time Sack Leaders–Playoffs

(Statistic kept since 1982; rankings based on number of sacks)

Name	No.
Reggie White	8.0
Sean Jones	4.0
Keith McKenzie	4.0
Tony Bennett	3.0
LeRoy Butler	3.0
Aaron Kampman	3.0
Bryce Paup	3.0
Mike Butler	2.0
Na'il Diggs	2.0
Bernardo Harris	2.0
Darren Sharper	2.0
Wayne Simmons	2.0
Mike Douglass	1.5
Ezra Johnson	1.5
Marques Anderson	1.0
Gilbert Brown	1.0
Santana Dotson	1.0
Doug Evans	1.0
Kabeer Gbaja-Biamila	1.0
Vonnie Holliday	1.0
Cletidus Hunt	1.0
Bhawoh Jue	1.0
John Jurkovic	1.0
Matt LaBounty	1.0
Mike McKenzie	1.0
Chukie Nwokorie	1.0
Fred Strickland	1.0
John Anderson	0.5
Matt Brock	0.5
Johnny Holland	0.5
Randy Scott	0.5
Packers	**56.0**
Opponents	34.0

All-Time Combined Net Yards–Playoffs

(Rankings based on total yards; 200 or more yards)

Name	Rush	Rec	P-Ret	K-Ret	Int	Fum-Rec	Total	G
Antonio Freeman	1-5	47-748	10-143	20-413	0-0	1-0	79-1,309	14
Dorsey Levens	144-647	41-387	0-0	3-37	0-0	1-0	189-1,071	14
Robert Brooks	5-56	42-651	14-214	2-36	0-0	0-0	66-957	11
Edgar Bennett	163-561	31-170	0-0	0-0	0-0	2-(-3)	196-728	10
Jim Taylor	146-508	19-137	0-0	0-0	0-0	1-0	166-645	7
Ahman Green	96-436	19-130	0-0	0-0	0-0	0-0	115-566	5
Carroll Dale	0-0	29-534	0-0	0-0	0-0	0-0	29-534	8
Desmond Howard	0-0	0-0	9-210	9-277	0-0	0-0	18-487	3
Boyd Dowler	0-0	30-440	0-0	0-0	0-0	0-0	30-440	10
Paul Hornung	67-323	12-111	0-0	0-0	0-0	1-0	80-434	5

Name	Rush	Rec	P-Ret	K-Ret	Int	Fum-Rec	Total	G
Donny Anderson	48-165	8-92	3-25	4-70	0-0	0-0	63-352	5
Max McGee	1-35	12-233	0-0	0-0	0-0	0-0	13-268	7
Keith Jackson	0-0	17-267	0-0	0-0	0-0	0-0	17-267	6
Del Rodgers	10-60	1-10	0-0	9-195	0-0	0-0	20-265	2
Mark Chmura	0-0	25-259	0-0	0-0	0-0	0-0	25-259	14
Tom Moore	22-79	3-5	0-0	7-170	0-0	0-0	32-254	5
Corey Harris	0-0	0-0	0-0	11-253	0-0	0-0	11-253	4
Joe Laws	21-112	1-31	4-44	2-38	3-28	1-0	32-253	5
Javon Walker	1-(-8)	11-259	0-0	0-0	0-0	0-0	12-251	3
Herb Adderley	0-0	0-0	0-0	8-161	4-89	1-0	13-250	9
Sterling Sharpe	0-0	11-229	0-0	0-0	0-0	0-0	11-229	2
James Lofton	2-58	8-161	0-0	0-0	0-0	0-0	10-219	2
Elijah Pitts	29-123	3-49	6-43	0-0	0-0	0-0	38-215	6
Donald Driver	2-25	13-181	0-0	0-0	0-0	1-0	16-206	5
Najeh Davenport	16-63	0-0	0-0	7-139	0-0	0-0	23-202	2
Clarke Hinkle	59-161	0-0	0-0	0-0	2-43	1-(-4)	62-200	4

TOP SINGLE-GAME PERFORMANCES PLAYOFFS

RUSHING

100 OR MORE YARDS (7)

Date	Name	Att-Yds	Avg	LG	TD
12-26-60	Jim Taylor	24-105	4.4	16	0
1-2-66	Paul Hornung	18-105	5.8	34	1
12-31-95	Edgar Bennett	24-108	4.5	15	1
1-4-98	Dorsey Levens	25-112	4.5	21	1
1-11-98	Dorsey Levens	27-114	4.2	12	1
1-3-99	Dorsey Levens	27-116	4.3	22	1
1-11-04	Ahman Green	25-156	6.2	33	0

RECEIVING

100 OR MORE YARDS (17)

Date	Name	No-Yds	Avg	LG	TD
1-1-67	Carroll Dale	5-128	25.6	t51	1
1-15-67	Max McGee	7-138	19.7	t37	2
12-23-67	Carroll Dale	6-109	18.2	48	1
1-8-83	John Jefferson	6-148	24.7	t60	2
1-16-83	James Lofton	5-109	21.8	50	1
1-8-94	Sterling Sharpe	5-101	20.2	t40	3
1-16-94	Sterling Sharpe	6-128	21.3	48	1
1-8-95	Robert Brooks	8-138	17.3	59	0
1-6-96	Robert Brooks	4-103	25.8	53	0
1-6-96	Keith Jackson	4-101	25.3	35	1
1-14-96	Robert Brooks	6-105	17.5	t73	2
1-12-97	Dorsey Levens	5-117	23.4	66	1
1-26-97	Antonio Freeman	3-105	35.0	t81	1
1-11-98	Antonio Freeman	4-107	26.8	40	1
1-25-98	Antonio Freeman	9-126	14.0	27	2
1-4-03	Javon Walker	5-104	20.8	37	0
1-4-04	Javon Walker	5-111	22.2	44	0

PASSING

300 OR MORE YARDS (5)

Date	Name	Att-Com	Yds	TD	In
1-1-67	Bart Starr	28-19	304	4	0
1-16-83	Lynn Dickey	36-19	332	1	3
1-16-94	Brett Favre	45-28	331	2	2
1-14-96	Brett Favre	39-21	307	3	2
1-4-04	Brett Favre	38-26	319	1	0

ALL-TIME INDIVIDUAL RECORDS POSTSEASON

SERVICE

Most Games Played, Career
19   Brett Favre
15   Earl Dotson
      William Henderson
Most Games Coached, Career
14   Mike Holmgren, 1993-98
10   Vince Lombardi, 1960-62, 65-67
Most Games Won, Career
9   Vince Lombardi, 1961-62, 65-67
9   Mike Holmgren, 1993-97
3   Curly Lambeau, 1936, 1939, 1944

SCORING

Most Points, Career
73   Chris Jacke (0 TD, 28 PAT, 15 FG)
72   Antonio Freeman (12 TD)
Most Points, Game
19   Paul Hornung vs. Giants 12-31-61
18   Sterling Sharpe vs. Lions 1-8-94
Most Consecutive Games Scoring
10   Chris Jacke
9   Ryan Longwell

Touchdowns

Most Touchdowns, Career
12   Antonio Freeman (14 games)
6   Dorsey Levens (14 games)
Most Touchdowns, Game
3   Sterling Sharpe vs. Lions 1-8-94
2   By many players

Sterling Sharpe hauls in a touchdown catch for the Packers. Sharpe's 595 receptions leads the Packers' all-time list. Photo by Chip Manthey

Most Consecutive Games Scoring Touchdowns
5   Antonio Freeman, 1997-98, 2001
3   Antonio Freeman, 1996

Points After Touchdown

Most Points After Touchdown, Career
28   Chris Jacke (10 games)
22   Don Chandler (7 games)
Most (1-Point) Points After Touchdown, Game
5   Don Chandler vs. Chiefs 1-15-67
     Jan Stenerud vs. Cardinals 1-8-83
     Chris Jacke vs. 49ers 1-4-97
Most (1-point) Points After Touchdown, No Misses, Career
28   Chris Jacke (10 games)
5   Paul Engebretsen (3 games)
     Paul Hornung (5 games)

Field Goals

Most Field Goals Attempted, Career
22   Chris Jacke (10 games)
19   Ryan Longwell (9 games)
Most Field Goals Attempted, Game
5   Jerry Kramer vs. Giants 12-30-62
4   Don Chandler vs. Raiders 1-14-68
     Chris Jacke vs. Lions 12-31-94
     Chris Jacke vs. Panthers 1-12-97
     Ryan Longwell vs. 49ers 1-11-98
Most Field Goals, Career
15   Chris Jacke (10 games)
14   Ryan Longwell (9 games)
Most Field Goals, Game
4   Don Chandler vs. Raiders 1-14-68
Most Field Goals, One Quarter
2   Don Chandler vs. Browns 1-2-66 (2)
     Don Chandler vs. Raiders 1-14-68 (2)
     Jan Stenerud vs. Cowboys 1-16-83 (3)
     Ryan Longwell vs. Buccaneers 1-4-98 (2)
     Ryan Longwell vs. Seahawks 1-4-04 (2)
Most Consecutive Games Scoring Field Goals
6   Chris Jacke
6   Ryan Longwell
Most Consecutive Field Goals
5   Don Chandler, 1965
     Chris Jacke, 1996
Longest Field Goal
51   Chris Jacke vs. Lions 12-31-94
50   Chris Jacke vs. Cowboys 1-8-95
Highest Field Goal Percentage, Career (min. 5 FGs)
83.33   Paul Hornung (5-6) (5 games)
75.00   Don Chandler (9-12) (7 games)

Jim Taylor ran for 8,207 yards in his career, more than 2,500 yards ahead of any other Packers running back. He posted 26 100-yard games and scored 81 touchdowns. Stiller-Lefebvre Collection

FIRST DOWNS

Most First Downs, Career
52　Dorsey Levens (14 games)
43　Jim Taylor (7 games)
Most First Downs, Game
11　Dorsey Levens vs. 49ers 1-3-99
10　Jim Taylor vs. Eagles 12-26-60
Most First Downs Rushing, Career
38　Dorsey Levens (14 games)
35　Jim Taylor (7 games)
Most First Downs Rushing, Game
9　Dorsey Levens vs. 49ers 1-3-99
8　Jim Taylor vs. Eagles 12-26-60
Most First Downs Receiving, Career
36　Antonio Freeman (14 games)
32　Robert Brooks (11 games)
Most First Downs Receiving, Game
7　Antonio Freeman vs. Broncos 1-25-98
6　Robert Brooks vs. Falcons 12-31-95

RUSHING

Attempts

Most Attempts, Career
163　Edgar Bennett (10 games)
146　Jim Taylor (7 games)
Most Attempts, Game
31　Jim Taylor vs. Giants 12-30-62
27　Jim Taylor vs. Browns 1-2-66
　　Dorsey Levens vs. 49ers 1-11-98
　　Dorsey Levens vs. 49ers 1-3-99

Yards Gained

Most Yards Gained, Career
647　Dorsey Levens (14 games)
561　Edgar Bennett (10 games)
Most Yards Gained, Game
156　Ahman Green vs. Eagles 1-11-04
116　Dorsey Levens vs. 49ers 1-3-99
Most Games, 100 or More Yards Rushing, Career
3　Dorsey Levens (12 games)
1　Jim Taylor (7 games)
1　Paul Hornung (5 games)
1　Edgar Bennett (10 games)
1　Ahman Green (5 games)
Most Consecutive Games, 100 or More Yards Rushing
2　Dorsey Levens, 1997
Longest Run From Scrimmage
71　James Lofton vs. Cowboys 1-16-83
49　Ahman Green vs. Rams 1-20-02

Average Gain

Highest Average Gain, Career (min. 20 atts.)
5.33　Joe Laws (21-112) (4 games)
4.82　Paul Hornung (67-323) (5 games)
Highest Average Gain, Game (min. 10 atts.)
8.80　Dorsey Levens vs. Panthers 1-12-97 (10-88)
6.24　Ahman Green vs. Eagles 1-11-04 (25-156)

Touchdowns

Most Touchdowns, Career
5　Edgar Bennett (10 games)
4　Dorsey Levens (14 games)
Most Touchdowns, Game
2　Elijah Pitts vs. Chiefs 1-15-67
　　Travis Williams vs. Rams 12-23-67
　　Edgar Bennett vs. 49ers 1-4-97
　　Ahman Green vs. Seahawks 1-4-04
Most Consecutive Games Rushing for Touchdowns
2　Paul Hornung, 1965
　　Edgar Bennett (twice), 1994-95, 1996
　　Dorsey Levens, 1997

PASSING

Highest Passer Rating, Career (min. 40 atts.)
104.8　Bart Starr (10 games)
101.8　Lynn Dickey (2 games)
Highest Passer Rating, Game (min. 20 atts.)
150.4　Lynn Dickey vs. Cardinals 1-8-83
143.5　Bart Starr vs. Cowboys 1-1-67

Attempts

Most Passes Attempted, Career
630　Brett Favre (19 games)
213　Bart Starr (10 games)
Most Passes Attempted, Game
45　Brett Favre vs. Cowboys 1-16-94
44　Brett Favre vs. Rams 1-20-02

Completions

Most Passes Completed, Career
379 Brett Favre (19 games)
130 Bart Starr (10 games)
Most Passes Completed, Game
28 Brett Favre vs. Cowboys 1-16-94
26 Brett Favre vs. Rams 1-20-02
Brett Favre vs. Seahawks 1-4-04
Most Consecutive Passes Completed
11 Brett Favre vs. 49ers 1-6-96
Brett Favre vs. Seahawks 1-4-04
9 Brett Favre vs. Cowboys (3) 1-16-94 and Lions (6)
12-31-94
Brett Favre vs. Panthers 1-12-97

Completion Percentage

Highest Completion Percentage, Career (min. 40 atts.)
61.03 Bart Starr (130-213) (10 games)
61.02 Lynn Dickey (36-59) (2 games)
Highest Completion Percentage, Game (min. 20 atts.)
75.86 Brett Favre vs. 49ers 1-13-02 (22-29)
75.00 Brett Favre vs. 49ers 1-6-96 (21-28)

Yards Gained

Most Yards Gained, Career
4.686 Brett Favre (19 games)
1,753 Bart Starr (10 games)
Most Yards Gained, Game
332 Lynn Dickey vs. Cowboys 1-16-83
331 Brett Favre vs. Cowboys 1-16-94
Most Games, 300 or More Yards Passing, Career
3 Brett Favre (19 games)
1 Bart Starr (10 games)
1 Lynn Dickey (1 game)
Longest Pass Completion
81 Brett Favre to Antonio Freeman vs. Patriots 1-26-97
73 Brett Favre to Robert Brooks vs. Cowboys 1-14-96

Average Gain

Highest Average Gain, Career (min. 40 atts.)
10.03 Lynn Dickey (59-592) (2 games)
8.23 Bart Starr (213-1,753) (10 games)
Highest Average Gain, Game (min. 20 atts.)
11.30 Lynn Dickey vs. Cardinals 1-8-83 (23-260)
10.87 Bart Starr vs. Chiefs 1-15-67 (23-250)

Touchdowns

Most Touchdown Passes, Career
33 Brett Favre (19 games)
15 Bart Starr (10 games)
Most Touchdown Passes, Game
4 Bart Starr vs. Cowboys 1-1-67
Lynn Dickey vs. Cardinals 1-8-83
3 Bart Starr vs. Giants 12-31-61
Brett Favre vs. Lions 1-8-94
Brett Favre vs. Falcons 12-31-95

Brett Favre vs. Cowboys 1-14-96
Brett Favre vs. Broncos 1-25-98
Most Consecutive Games, Touchdown Passes
15 Brett Favre, 1995-98, 2001-03
6 Bart Starr, 1965-67

Had Intercepted

Most Passes Had Intercepted, Career
22 Brett Favre (19 games)
4 Arnie Herber (3 games)
Most Passes Had Intercepted, Game
6 Brett Favre vs. Rams 1-20-02
3 Arnie Herber vs. Giants 12-10-39
Irv Comp vs. Giants 12-17-44
Lynn Dickey vs. Cowboys 1-16-83
Most Attempts, No Interceptions, Game
38 Brett Favre vs. Lions 12-31-94
Brett Favre vs. Seahawks 1-4-04
35 Brett Favre vs. Falcons 12-31-95
Lowest Interception Percentage, Career (min. 40 atts.)
1.41 Bart Starr (213-3) (10 games)
3.49 Brett Favre (21-564) (19 games)

Hall of Famer Bart Starr, who led the Packers to five NFL championships, led the team in passing until his statistics were surpassed by Brett Favre. Stiller-Lefebvre Collection

Most Consecutive Passes Attempted, None Intercepted
86 Brett Favre, 1994-95
85 Bart Starr, 1960-65

Times Sacked

Most Times Sacked, Career
30 Brett Favre (19 games)
24 Bart Starr (10 games)
Most Times Sacked, Game
8 Bart Starr vs. Cowboys 12-31-67
5 Bart Starr vs. Cowboys 1-1-67
Brett Favre vs. Patriots 1-26-97

PASSES RECEIVED

Most Pass Receptions, Career
47 Antonio Freeman (4 games)
45 Robert Brooks (11 games)
Most Pass Receptions, Game
9 Edgar Bennett vs. Cowboys 1/16/94
Antonio Freeman vs. Broncos 1/25/98
8 Bill Anderson vs. Colts 12/26/65
Robert Brooks vs. Cowboys 1/8/95
Ahman Green vs. Rams 1/20/02
Most Consecutive Games, Pass Receptions
13 Dorsey Levens, 1994-98, 2001
12 Antonio Freeman, 1995-98, 2001

Yards Gained

Most Yards Gained, Career
748 Antonio Freeman (12 games)
651 Robert Brooks (11 games)
Most Yards Gained, Game
148 John Jefferson vs. Cardinals 1-8-83
138 Max McGee vs. Chiefs 1-15-67
Robert Brooks vs. Cowboys 1-8-95
Most Games, 100 or More Yards Receiving, Career
3 Robert Brooks (11 games)
Antonio Freeman (12 games)
2 Carroll Dale (8 games)
Sterling Sharpe (2 games)
Javon Walker (3 games)
Most Consecutive Games, 100 or More Yards Receiving
2 Sterling Sharpe, 1993
Robert Brooks, 1996
Antonio Freeman, 1997
Javon Walker, 2002-03
Longest Pass Reception
81 Antonio Freeman from Brett Favre vs. Patriots 1-26-97
73 Robert Brooks from Brett Favre vs. Cowboys 1-14-96

Average Gain

Highest Average Gain, Career (min. 10 receptions)
23.55 Javon Walker (11-259) (3 games)
20.82 Sterling Sharpe (11-229) (2 games)
Highest Average Gain, Game (min. 3 receptions)
35.00 Antonio Freeman vs. Patriots 1-26-97 (3-105)
26.75 Antonio Freeman vs. 49ers 1-11-98 (4-107)

Touchdowns

Most Touchdowns, Career
10 Antonio Freeman (12 games)
5 Boyd Dowler (10 games)
Most Touchdowns, Game
3 Sterling Sharpe vs. Lions 1-8-94
Most Consecutive Games, Touchdown Passes Caught
5 Antonio Freeman, 1997-98, 2001

INTERCEPTIONS

Most Interceptions, Career
4 Herb Adderley (9 games)
Craig Newsome (7 games)
Eugene Robinson (6 games)
3 Joe Laws (5 games)
Mike Prior (14 games)
Tyrone Williams (10 games)
Most Interceptions, Game
3 Joe Laws vs. Giants 12-17-44
2 Charley Brock vs. Giants 12-10-39
Eugene Robinson vs. 49ers 1-4-97
Most Consecutive Games Interceptions
3 Craig Newsome, 1996
2 Herb Adderley, 1967
Terrell Buckley, 1993
Mike Prior, 1996-97
Eugene Robinson, 1997

Yards Gained

Most Yards Gained, Career
131 George Teague (7 games)
89 Herb Adderley (9 games)
Most Yards Gained, Game
101 George Teague vs. Lions 1-8-94
60 Herb Adderley vs. Raiders 1-14-68
Longest Return
See record above

Touchdowns

Most Touchdowns, Career
1 Herb Adderley (9 games)
George Teague (7 games)
Mark Lee (2 games)
Al Harris (2 games)

Punting

Most Punts, Career
50 Craig Hentrich (11 games)
20 Donny Anderson (4 games)
Most Punts, Game
8 Donny Anderson vs. Cowboys 12-31-67
Ron Widby vs. Redskins 12-24-72
7 Clarke Hinkle vs. Redskins 12-13-36
Craig Hentrich vs. Patriots 1-26-97
Josh Bidwell vs. Eagles 1-11-04
Longest Punt
64 Boyd Dowler vs. Giants 12-31-61
63 Craig Hentrich vs. 49ers 1-4-97

Average Yardage

Highest Gross Average, Career (min. 10 punts)
42.17 Josh Bidwell (5 games) (18-759)
41.20 Don Chandler (7 games) (15-618)
Highest Gross Average, Game (min. 4 punts)
45.20 Max McGee vs. Eagles 12-26-60 (5-226)
44.00 Craig Hentrich vs. Cowboys 1-8-95 (4-176)

Had Blocked

Most Consecutive Punts, None Blocked
50   Craig Hentrich (11 games)
20   Donny Anderson (4 games)
Most Punts, Had Blocked, Career
3   Clarke Hinkle (4 games)
1   Cecil Isbell (3 games)
    Max McGee (7 games)
    Boyd Dowler (10 games)
    Josh Bidwell (3 games)

Inside Opponents' 20-Yard Line

Most Punts, Inside Opponents' 20, Career
19   Craig Hentrich (11 games)
6   Josh Bidwell (5 games)
Most Punts, Inside Opponents' 20, Game
5   Craig Hentrich vs. 49ers 1-11-98
3   Clarke Hinkle vs. Redskins 12-13-36
    Ted Fritsch vs. Giants 12-17-44
    Ron Widby vs. Redskins 12-24-72
    Craig Hentrich vs. 49ers 1-4-97
    Craig Hentrich vs. Buccaneers 1-4-98

PUNT RETURNS

Most Punt Returns, Career
19   Willie Wood (10 games)
14   Robert Brooks (11 games)
Most Punt Returns, Game
6   Desmond Howard vs. Patriots 1-26-97
    Antonio Chatman vs. Eagles 1-11-04
5   Willie Wood vs. Raiders 1-14-68

Willie Wood is the all-time Packers leader in punt returns, with 187 for 1,391 yards and two touchdowns. Stiller-Lefebvre Collection

Fair Catches

Most Fair Catches, Career
8   Willie Wood (10 games)
4   Robert Brooks (11 games)
    Mike Prior (14 games)
Most Fair Catches, Game
3   Willie Wood, vs. Rams 12-23-67

Yards Gained

Most Yards Gained, Career
214   Robert Brooks (11 games)
210   Desmond Howard (3 games)
Most Yards Gained, Game
117   Desmond Howard vs. 49ers 1-4-97
90   Desmond Howard vs. Patriots 1-26-97
Longest Punt Return
76   Antonio Freeman vs. Falcons 12-31-95
71   Desmond Howard vs. 49ers 1-4-97

Average Gain

Highest Average, Career (min. 10 returns)
15.29   Robert Brooks (14-214) (11 games)
14.30   Antonio Freeman (10-143) (12 games)
Highest Average, Game (min. 3 returns)
24.00   Antonio Freeman vs. Falcons 12-31-95 (3-72)
15.67   Robert Brooks vs. Buccaneers 1-4-98 (3-47)

Touchdowns

Most Touchdowns, Career
1   Antonio Freeman (14 games)
    Desmond Howard (3 games)

Kickoff Returns

Most Kickoff Returns, Career
20   Antonio Freeman (14 games)
11   Corey Harris (4 games)
Most Kickoff Returns, Game
7   Del Rodgers vs. Cowboys 1-16-83
    Antonio Freeman vs. Cowboys 1-16-96
    Roell Preston vs. 49ers 1-3-99
6   Antonio Freeman vs. Broncos 1-25-98

Yards Gained

Most Yards Gained, Career
413   Antonio Freeman (14 games)
277   Desmond Howard (3 games)
Most Yards Gained, Game
194   Roell Preston vs. 49ers 1-3-99
154   Desmond Howard vs. Patriots 1-26-97
Longest Return
99   Desmond Howard vs. Patriots 1-26-97 (TD)
51   Corey Harris vs. Cowboys 1-8-95

Average Gain

Highest Average, Career (min. 10 returns)
23.00   Corey Harris (11-253) (4 games)
20.65   Antonio Freeman (20-413) (14 games)
Highest Average, Game (min. 3 returns)
38.50   Desmond Howard vs. Patriots 1-26-97 (4-154)
29.67   Corey Harris vs. Lions 1-8-94 (3-89)

Touchdowns

Most Touchdowns, Career
1   Desmond Howard (4 games)

COMBINED KICK RETURNS

Most Combined Kick Returns, Career
30   Antonio Freeman (p-10, k-20) (14 games)
19   Willie Wood (p-19) (10 games)
Most Combined Kick Returns, Game
11   Antonio Freeman vs. Cowboys 1-14-96 (p-4, k-7)
10   Desmond Howard vs. Patriots 1-26-97 (p-6, k-4)

Yards Gained

Most Yards Gained, Career
556   Antonio Freeman (p-143, k-413) (14 games)
487   Desmond Howard (p-210, k-277) (3 games)
Most Yards Gained, Game
244   Desmond Howard vs. Patriots 1-26-97 (p-90, k-154)
202   Antonio Freeman vs. Cowboys 1-14-96 (p-54, k-148)

Touchdowns

Most Touchdowns, Career
2   Desmond Howard (p-1, k-1) (3 games)
1   Antonio Freeman (p-1) (14 games)

FUMBLES

Most Fumbles, Career
9   Brett Favre (19 games)
4   Dorsey Levens (14 games)
Most Fumbles, Game
2   Jim Taylor vs. Giants 12-30-62
    Del Rodgers vs. Cowboys 1-16-83
    Corey Harris vs. Cowboys 1-16-94
    Brett Favre vs. 49ers 1-4-97
    Roell Preston vs. 49ers 1-3-99

Fumbles Recovered

Most Own Fumbles Recovered, Career
2   Brett Favre (19 games)
    Edgar Bennett (10 games)
Most Opponent Fumbles Recovered, Career
2   Ray Nitschke (11 games)
    LeRoy Butler (14 games)
Longest Fumble Return
31   Craig Newsome vs. 49ers 1-6-96 (TD)
18   Jim Grabowski vs. Cowboys 1-1-67 (TD)

Touchdowns

Most Touchdowns, Career
1   Jim Grabowski (3 games)
    Craig Newsome (6 games)
    Antonio Freeman (14 games)

COMBINED NET YARDS GAINED

Attempts

Most Attempts, Career
196   Edgar Bennett (10 games)
189   Dorsey Levens (14 games)
Most Attempts, Game
34   Jim Taylor vs. Giants 12-30-62
33   Dorsey Levens vs. 49ers 1-3-99

Yards Gained

Most Yards Gained, Career
1,309   Antonio Freeman (12 games)
1,071   Dorsey Levens (14 games)
Most Yards Gained, Game
244   Desmond Howard vs. Patriots 1-26-97
230   Antonio Freeman vs. Broncos 1-25-98

SACKS

Most Sacks, Career
8.0   Reggie White (14 games)
4.0   Sean Jones (8 games)
      Keith McKenzie (7 games)
Most Sacks, Game
3.0   Reggie White vs. Patriots 1-26-97
2.0   Mike Butler vs. Cardinals 1-8-83
      Reggie White vs. Lions 1-8-94
      Bryce Paup vs. Lions 12-31-94
      Sean Jones vs. Falcons 12-31-95
      Keith McKenzie vs. 49ers 1-11-98
      Aaron Kampman vs. Eagles 1-11-04

Don Hutson's scoring record for the Packers, with 823 total points, was surpassed by Ryan Longwell in 2003. He caught 99 touchdown passes.
Stiller-Lefebvre Collection

SCORING

Most Points, Game
- 41 vs. Cardinals 1-8-83
- 37 vs. Giants 12-31-61
- vs. Falcons 12-31-95

Fewest Points, Game
- 3 vs. Redskins 12-24-72
- 7 vs. Falcons 1-4-03

Most Points, Both Teams, Game
- 65 GB (27) vs. Cowboys (38) 1-14-96
- 63 GB (26) vs. Cowboys (37) 1-16-83

Fewest Points, Both Teams, Game
- 19 GB (3) vs. Redskins (16) 12-24-72
- 21 GB (14) vs. Giants (7) 12-17-44

Largest Margin of Victory
- 37 vs. Giants 12-31-61
- 27 vs. Giants 12-10-39

Most Points Overcome to Win Game
- 10 vs. Colts 12-26-65 (trailed 10-0, won 13-10)
- vs. Lions 1-8-94 (trailed 17-7, won 28-24)
- 7 vs. Rams 12-23-67 (trailed 7-0, won 28-7)
- vs. Falcons 12-31-95 (trailed 7-0, won 37-20)
- vs. Panthers 1-12-97 (trailed 7-0, won 30-13)
- vs. Seahawks 1-4-04 (trailed 20-13, won 33-27)

Most Points First Half
- 28 vs. Cardinals 1-8-83
- 27 vs. Falcons 12-31-95
- vs. Patriots 1-26-97

Most Points, Second Half
- 21 vs. Chiefs 1-15-67
- vs. Lions 1-8-94
- 20 vs. Giants 12-10-39

Most Points, Each Quarter
- 1st: 14 vs. Cowboys 1-1-67
- 14 vs. Falcons 12-31-95
- 14 vs. 49ers 1-6-96
- 14 vs. 49ers 1-4-97
- 14 vs. Eagles 1-11-04
- 2nd: 24 vs. Giants 12-31-61
- 3rd: 14 vs. Chiefs 1-15-67
- 14 vs. Lions 1-8-94
- 4th: 14 vs. Seahawks 1-4-04

Most Touchdowns, Game
- 5 vs. Cowboys 1-1-67
- vs. Chiefs 1-15-67
- vs. Cardinals 1-8-83
- vs. Falcons 12-31-95
- vs. 49ers 1-4-97

Most Touchdowns, Both Teams, Game
- 8 GB (5) vs. Cowboys (3) 1-1-67
- GB (3) vs. Cowboys (5) 1-14-96
- GB (2) vs. Rams (6) 1-20-02

Fewest Touchdowns, Both Teams, Game
- 1 GB (0) vs. Redskins (1) 12-24-72
- 2 GB (1) vs. Giants (1) 12-30-62

- GB (1) vs. Colts (1) 12-26-65
- GB (1) vs. Lions (1) 12-31-94

Most (One-Point) Points After Touchdown, Game
- 5 vs. Chiefs 1-15-67
- vs. Cardinals 1-8-83
- vs. 49ers 1-4-97

Most (One-Point) Points After Touchdown, Both Teams, Game
- 8 GB (3) vs. Cowboys (5) 1-14-96
- GB (2) vs. Rams (6) 1-20-02
- 7 GB (4) vs. Cowboys (3) 1-1-67
- GB (4) vs. Lions (3) 1-8-94
- GB (5) vs. 49ers (2) 1-4-97
- GB (3) vs. Broncos (4) 1-25-98

Fewest Points After Touchdown, Both Team, Game
- 1 GB (0) vs. Redskins (1) 12-24-72

Most Field Goals, Game
- 4 vs. Raiders 1-14-68

Most Field Goals, Both Teams, Game
- 5 GB (3) vs. Browns (2) 1-2-66
- GB (2) vs. Cowboys (3) 1-16-83
- GB (3) vs. Panthers (2) 1-12-97
- GB (2) vs. 49ers (3) 1-3-99
- 4 GB (4) vs. Raiders (0) 1-14-68
- GB (1) vs. Redskins (3) 12-24-72
- GB (3) vs. Lions (1) 12-31-94
- GB (3) vs. 49ers (1) 1-11-98
- GB (2) vs. Seahawks (2) 1-4-04

Most Field Goals, Attempted, Game
- 5 vs. Giants 12-30-62
- 4 vs. Raiders 1-14-68
- vs. Lions 12-31-94
- vs. Panthers 1-12-97
- vs. 49ers 1-11-98

Most Field Goals Attempted, Both Teams, Game
- 6 GB (5) vs. Giants (1) 12-30-62
- GB (3) vs. Browns (3) 1-2-66
- GB (2) vs. Cardinals (4) 1-8-83
- GB (4) vs. Lions (2) 12-31-94
- GB (3) vs. 49ers (3) 1-3-99
- GB (2) vs. Falcons (4) 1-4-03

First Downs

Most First Downs, Game
- 24 vs. 49ers 1-3-99
- 23 vs. Colts 12-26-65
- vs. Falcons 12-31-95

Fewest First Downs, Game
- 7 vs. Redskins 12-13-36
- 10 vs. Giants 12-10-39
- vs. Redskins 12-24-72

Most First Downs, Both Teams, Game
- 50 GB (22) vs. Cardinals (28) 1-8-83
- 45 GB (21) vs. Cowboys (24) 1-16-83
- GB (18) vs. Cowboys (27) 1-8-95

Fewest First Downs, Both Teams, Game
15 GB (7) vs. Redskins (8) 12-13-36
19 GB (10) vs. Giants (9) 12-10-39

Most First Downs, Rushing, Game
14 vs. Eagles 12-26-60
11 vs. Giants 12-30-62
vs. Rams 12-23-67
vs. Raiders 1-14-68

Fewest First Downs, Rushing, Game
2 vs. Redskins 12-13-36
vs. Redskins 12-24-72
vs. Cowboys 1-16-94
3 vs. Cowboys 1-1-67
vs. 49ers 1-6-96
vs. Cowboys 1-14-96

Most First Downs, Rushing, Both Teams, Game
20 GB (10) vs. 49ers (10) 1-3-99
19 GB (14) vs. Eagles (5) 12-26-60

Fewest First Downs, Rushing, Both Teams, Game
6 GB (2) vs. Redskins (4) 12-13-36
7 GB (6) vs. Lions (1) 12-31-94
GB (6) vs. Falcons (1) 12-31-95

Most First Downs, Passing, Game
17 vs. Cowboys 1-16-94
16 vs. Cowboys 1-8-83

Fewest First Downs, Passing, Game
2 vs. Giants 12-10-39
vs. Giants 12-17-44
4 vs. Redskins 12-13-36
vs. Giants 12-11-38

Most First Downs, Passing, Both Teams, Game
33 GB (17) vs. Cowboys (16) 1-16-94
32 GB (13) vs. Cardinals (19) 1-8-83

Fewest First Downs, Passing, Both Teams, Game
5 GB (2) vs. Giants (3) 12-10-39
6 GB (4) vs. Giants (2) 12-11-38
GB (2) vs. Giants (4) 12-17-44

Most First Downs, Penalty, Game
3 vs. Colts 12-26-65
vs. Cowboys 12-31-67
vs. Falcons 12-31-95
vs. Cowboys 1-14-96
vs. Broncos 1-25-98

Most First Downs, Penalty, Both Teams, Game
5 GB (3) vs. Cowboys (2) 1-14-96
GB (3) vs. Broncos (2) 1-25-98

Net Yards Rushing and Recieving

Most Yards Gained, Game
479 vs. Panthers 1-12-97
466 vs. Cowboys 1-16-83

Fewest Yards Gained, Game
195 vs. Cowboys 12-31-67
210 vs. 49ers 1-4-97

Most Yards Gained, Both Teams, Game
847 GB (394) vs. Cardinals (453) 1-8-83
841 GB (466) vs. Cowboys (375) 1-16-83

Fewest Yards Gained, Both Teams, Game

336 GB (220) vs. Redskins (116) 12-13-36
387 GB (195) vs. Cowboys (192) 12-31-67

Longest Drive (Most Net Yards)
95 vs. Broncos 1-25-98 (17 plays, TD)
93 vs. 49ers 1-13-02 (8 plays, TD)

Longest Drive (Most Plays)
17 vs. Raiders 1-14-68 (84 yards, FG)
vs. Broncos 1-25-98 (95 yards, TD)
15 vs. Panthers 1-12-97 (71 yards, TD)

Longest Drive (Time of Possession)
8:40 vs. Raiders 1-14-68 (17-84, TD)
7:55 vs. Browns 1-2-66 (14-59, FG)

Rushing

Most Attempts, Game
52 vs. Giants 12-10-39
49 vs. Giants 12-17-44

Fewest Attempts, Game
12 vs. Cowboys 1-14-96
13 vs. Cowboys 1-16-94

Most Attempts, Both Teams, Game
89 GB (46) vs. Giants (43) 12-11-38
86 GB (52) vs. Giants (34) 12-10-39
GB (39) vs. Colts (47) 12-26-65

Fewest Attempts, Both Teams, Game
39 GB (29) vs. Falcons (10) 12-31-95
40 GB (13) vs. Cowboys (27) 1-16-94

Most Yards Gained, Game
223 vs. Eagles 12-26-60
210 vs. Eagles 1-11-04

Fewest Yards Gained, Game
31 vs. Cowboys 1-16-94
33 vs. Bears 12-14-41

Most Yards Gained, Both Teams, Game
374 GB (210) vs. Eagles (164) 1-11-04
332 GB (223) vs. Eagles (99) 12-26-60

Fewest Yards Gained, Both Teams, Game
77 GB (81) vs. Lions (-4) 12-31-94
106 GB (67) vs. Redskins (39) 12-13-36

Highest Average Gain, Game
9.29 vs. Cowboys 1-16-83 (17-158)
5.68 vs. Eagles 1-11-04 (37-210)

Lowest Average Gain, Game
0.92 vs. Bears 12-14-41 (36-33)
1.63 vs. Redskins 12-13-36 (41-67)

Most Touchdowns, Game
3 vs. Chiefs 1-15-67
vs. Rams 12-23-67

Most Touchdowns, Both Teams, Game
5 GB (2) vs. Seahawks (3) 1-4-04
4 GB (1) vs. Bears (3) 12-14-41
GB (1) vs. Cowboys (3) 1-8-95
GB (0) vs. Broncos (4) 1-25-98

Passing

Most Attempts, Game
46 vs. Cowboys 1-8-95
45 vs. Cowboys 1-16-94

A Measure of Greatness **The Postseason Record Book**

Fewest Attempts, Game

  10 vs. Giants 12-10-39

  11 vs. Giants 12-17-44

Most Attempts, Both Teams, Game

  93 GB (28) vs. 49ers (65) 1-6-96

  89 GB (35) vs. Falcons (54) 12-31-95

Fewest Attempts, Both Teams, Game

  33 GB (11) vs. Giants (22) 12-17-44

  34 GB (19) vs. Giants (15) 12-11-38

Most Completions, Game

  28 vs. Cowboys 1-16-94

  26 vs. Rams 1-20-02

      vs. Seahawks 1-4-04

Fewest Completions, Game

   3 vs. Giants 12-17-44

   7 vs. Giants 12-10-39

Most Completions, Both Teams, Game

  56 GB (28) vs. Cowboys (28) 1-16-94

  54 GB (24) vs. Falcons (30) 12-31-95

Fewest Completions, Both Teams, Game

  11 GB (3) vs. Giants (8) 12-17-44

  15 GB (7) vs. Giants (8) 12-10-39

Highest Completion Percentage, Game (min. 20 atts.)

  75.86 vs. 49ers 1-13-02 (22-29)

  75.00 vs. 49ers 1-6-96 (21-28)

Highest Completion Percentage, Both Teams, Game (min. 40 atts.)

  72.13 GB (22-29) vs. 49ers (22-32) 1-13-02

  68.29 GB (28-45) vs. Cowboys (28-37) 1-16-94

Lowest Completion Percentage, Game (min. 20 atts.)

  39.13 vs. Redskins 12-13-36 (9-23)

  40.74 vs. Bears 12-14-41 (11-27)

Lowest Completion Percentage, Both Teams, Game (min. 40 atts.)

  35.56 GB (9-23) vs. Redskins (7-22) 12-13-36

  41.54 GB (15-28) vs. Buccaneers (12-37) 1-4-98

Most Yards Gained, Game

  327 vs. Cowboys 1-16-94

  319 vs. Seahawks 1-4-04

Fewest Yards Gained, Game

  74 vs. Giants 12-17-44

  96 vs. Giants 12-10-39

      vs. Giants 12-30-62

Most Yards Gained, Both Teams, Game

  633 GB (286) vs. Cardinals (347) 1-8-83

  611 GB (327) vs. Cowboys (284) 1-16-94

Fewest Yards Gained, Both Teams, Game

  188 GB (74) vs. Giants (114) 12-17-44

  190 GB (96) vs. Giants (94) 12-10-39

Most Times Sacked, Game

   8 vs. Cowboys 12-31-67

   5 vs. Cowboys 1-1-67

      vs. Patriots 1-26-97

Fewest Times Sacked, Game

   0 vs. Eagles 12-26-60

      vs. Giants 12-31-61

      vs. Cardinals 1-8-83

      vs. Lions 1-8-94

Most Times Sacked, Both Teams, Game

  10 GB (5) vs. Patriots (5) 1-26-97

      GB (2) vs. Eagles (8) 1-11-04

   9 GB (3) vs. Chiefs (6) 1-15-67

      GB (8) vs. Cowboys (1) 12-31-67

Fewest Times Sacked, Both Teams, Game

   1 GB (0) vs. Eagles (1) 12-26-60

      GB (1) vs. Giants (0) 12-30-62

      GB (1) vs. Broncos (0) 1-25-98

   2 GB (1) vs. Colts (1) 12-26-65

      GB (1) vs. Cowboys (1) 1-8-95

      GB (1) vs. 49ers (1) 1-4-97

      GB (2) vs. Falcons (0) 1-4-03

      GB (0) vs. Seahawks (2) 1-4-04

Most Touchdowns, Game

   4 vs. Cowboys 1-1-67

      vs. Cardinals 1-8-83

Most Touchdowns, Both Teams, Game

   6 GB (4) vs. Cardinals (2) 1-8-83

Most Passes Had Intercepted, Game

   6 vs. Rams 1-20-02

   3 vs. Giants 12-10-39

      vs. Giants 12-17-44

      vs. Cowboys 1-16-83

Most Passes Had Intercepted, Both Teams, Game

   9 GB (3) vs. Giants (6) 12-10-39

   7 GB (3) vs. Giants (4) 12-17-44

      GB (6) vs. Rams (1) 1-20-02

Interceptions

Most Passes Intercepted, Game

   6 vs. Giants 12-10-39

   4 vs. Giants 12-17-44

      vs. Giants 12-31-61

      vs. Patriots 1-26-97

Most Yards Gained, Game

  123 vs. Giants 12-10/39

  101 vs. Lions 1-8-94

Most Yards Gained, Both Teams, Game

  128 GB (123) vs. Giants (5) 12-10-39

  116 GB (101) vs. Lions (15) 1-8-94

Most Touchdowns, Game

   1 vs. Raiders 1-14-68

      vs. Cowboys 1-16-83

      vs. Lions 1-8-94

      vs. Seahawks 1-4-04

Most Touchdowns, Both Teams, Game

   3 GB (0) vs. Rams (3) 1-20-02

   2 GB (1) vs. Cowboys (1) 1-16-83

      GB (1) vs. Lions (1) 1-8-94

Punts

Most Punts, Game

  10 vs. Giants 12-17-44

   8 vs. Redskins 12-13-36

vs. Cowboys 12-31-67
vs. Redskins 12-24-72

Fewest Punts, Game
1   vs. Cardinals 1-8-83
    vs. Falcons 1-4-03
2   vs. Carolina 1-12-97
    vs. 49ers 1-3-99

Most Punts, Both Teams, Game
20   GB (10) vs. Giants (10) 12-17-44
18   GB (8) vs. Redskins (10) 12-13-36

Fewest Punts, Both Teams, Game
1   GB (1) vs. Cardinals (0) 1-8-83
5   GB (2) vs. 49ers (3) 1-3-99

Highest Average Distance, Game (min. 4 punts)
45.20   vs. Eagles 12-26-60 (5-226)
44.00   vs. Cowboys 1-8-95 (4-176)

Lowest Average Distance, Game (min. 4 punts)
25.50   vs. Giants 12-30-62 (6-153)
26.00   vs. Giants 12-10-39 (7-182)

Punt Returns

Most Punt Returns, Game
8   vs. Giants 12-17-44
6   vs. Colts 12-26-65
    vs. Patriots 1-26-97
    vs. Eagles 1-11-04

Most Punt Returns, Both Teams, Game
12   GB (8) vs. Giants (4) 12-17-44
11   GB (6) vs. Colts (5) 12-26-65

Fewest Punt Returns, Game
0   vs. Cowboys 1-1-67
    vs. Cardinals 1-8-83
    vs. Broncos 1-25-98

Fewest Punt Returns, Both Teams, Game
0   GB (0) vs. Cardinals (0) 1-8-83
    GB (0) vs. Broncos (0) 1-25-98
1   GB (1) vs. 49ers (0) 1-13-02
    GB (1) vs. Falcons (0) 1-4-03

Most Yards Gained, Game
117   vs. 49ers 1-4-97
90   vs. Patriots 1-26-97

Fewest Yards Gained, Game
-10   vs. Browns 1-2-66
0   vs. Cowboys 1-1-67
    vs. Cardinals 1-8-83
    vs. Broncos 1-25-98
    vs. 49ers 1-3-99
    vs. Falcons 1-4-03

Most Yards Gained, Both Teams, Game
141   GB (54) vs. Bears (87) 12-14-41
140   GB (117) vs. 49ers (23) 1-4-97

Fewest Yards Gained, Both Teams, Game
-9   GB (0) vs. Cowboys (-9) 1-1-67
0   GB (0) vs. Cardinals (0) 1-8-83
    GB (0) vs. Broncos (0) 1-25-98
    GB (0) vs. Falcons (0) 1-4-03

Kickoff Returns

Most Kickoff Returns, Game
7   vs. Cowboys 1-16-83
    vs. Cowboys 1-14-96
    vs. 49ers 1-3-99
    vs. Rams 1-20-02

Most Kickoff Returns, Both Teams, Game
13   GB (7) vs. Cowboys (6) 1-16-83
    GB (7) vs. 49ers (6) 1-3-99
    GB (7) vs. Seahawks 1-4-04
12   GB (6) vs. Cowboys (6) 1-1-67

Fewest Kickoff Returns, Game
0   vs. Giants 12-10-39
1   vs. Giants 12-17-44
    vs. Giants 12-31-61

Fewest Kickoff Returns, Both Teams, Game
4   GB (0) vs. Giants (4) 12-10-39

Most Yards Gained, Game
194   vs. 49ers 1-3-99
154   vs. Patriots 1-26-97

Fewest Yards Gained, Game
0   vs. Giants 12-10-39
9   vs. Giants 12-17-44

Most Yards Gained, Both Teams, Game
322   GB (194) vs. 49ers (128) 1-3-99
321   GB (148) vs. Cowboys (173) 1-16-83

Fewest Yards Gained, Both Teams, Game
53   GB (10) vs. Cowboys (43) 12-31-67
54   GB (0) vs. Giants (54) 12-10-39

Penalties

Most Penalties, Game
11   vs. Cowboys 1-14-96
9   vs. 49ers 1-11-98
    vs. Broncos 1-25-98

Fewest Penalties, Game
1   vs. Raiders 1-14-68
    vs. 49ers 1-4-97

Most Penalties, Both Teams, Game
17   GB (11) vs. Cowboys (6) 1-14-96
16   GB (9) vs. Broncos (7) 1-25-98

Fewest Penalties, Both Teams, Game
4   GB (4) vs. Eagles (0) 12-26-60

Most Yards Penalized, Game
90   vs. Buccaneers 1-4-98
84   vs. Cowboys 1-14-96

Fewest Yards Penalized, Game
5   vs. 49ers 1-4-97
10   vs. Giants 12-11-38
    vs. Cowboys 12-31-67

Most Yards Penalized, Both Teams, Game
174   GB (46) vs. Bears (128) 12/14/41
149   GB (84) vs. Cowboys (65) 1/14/96

Fewest Yards Penalized, Both Teams, Game
27   GB (27) vs. Eagles (0) 12/26/60
30   GB (10) vs. Giants (20) 12/11/38

Fumbles

Most Fumbles, Game
5   vs. 49ers 1-4-97
4   vs. Giants 1-16-83
    vs. Cowboys 1-16-83

Fewest Fumbles, Game

   0 Accomplished 11 times (last vs. Eagles 1-11-04)

Most Fumbles, Both Teams, Game

   8 GB (2) vs. Redskins (6) 12-13-36
      GB (3) vs. Bears (5) 12-14-41
      GB (5) vs. 49ers (3) 1-4-97

Fewest Fumbles, Both Teams, Game

   0 GB (0) vs. Browns (0) 1-2-66
      GB (0) vs. Cowboys (0) 1-14-96
      GB (0) vs. Patriots (0) 1-26-97

Most Own Fumbles Recovered, Game

   4 vs. 49ers 1-4-97

Most Opponents Fumbles Recovered, Game

   3 vs. Redskins 12-13-36
      vs. Bears 12-14-41

Most Fumbles Recovered, Own and Opponents

   6 vs. 49ers 1-4-97 (4 own, 2 opponent)
   4 vs. Bears 12-14-41 (1 own, 3 opponent)
      vs. Giants 12-30-62 (2 own, 2 opponent)

Turnovers

Most Turnovers, Game

   8 vs. Rams 1-20-02
   5 vs. Cowboys 1-16-83
      vs. Falcons 1-4-03

Fewest Turnovers, Game

   0 Accomplished 9 times (last vs. Seahawks 1-4-04)

Most Turnovers, Both Teams, Game

   9 GB (3) vs. Giants (6) 12-10-39
      GB (8) vs. Rams (1) 1-20-02

Fewest Turnovers, Both Teams, Game

   0 GB (0) vs. Lions (0) 12-31-94

TEAM DEFENSIVE RECORDS

Points

Most Points, Allowed, Game

  45 vs. Rams 1-20-02
  38 vs. Cowboys 1-16-83

Fewest Points Allowed, Game

   0 vs. Giants 12-10-39
      vs. Giants 12-30-62
   6 vs. Redskins 12-13-36

Largest Margin of Defeat, Game

  28 vs. Rams 1-20-02
  26 vs. Cowboys 1-8-95

Most Points Opponents Overcame to Beat Packers

  14 Eagles 1-11-04 (trailed 14-0, won 20-17)
   7 Bears 12-14-41 (trailed 7-0, won 33-14)
      Broncos 1-25-98 (trailed 7-0, won 31-24)
      49ers 1-3-99 (trailed 17-10, won 30-27)

Most Points, Opponents, First Half

  30 Bears 12-14-41
  28 Cowboys 1-8-95

Most Points, Opponents, Second Half

  21 Rams 1-20-02
      Seahawks 1-4-04
  20 49ers 1-3-99

Most Points, Opponents, Each Quarter

  1st: 14 Cowboys 1-1-67
        14 Cowboys 1-8-95
        14 Cowboys 1-14-96
        14 Patriots 1-26-97
        14 Falcons 1-4-03
  2nd: 24 Bears 12-14-41
  3rd: 14 Rams 1-20-02
        14 Seahawks 1-4-04
  4th: 14 Cowboys 1-16-83
        14 Cowboys 1-14-96

Most Touchdowns, Opponents, Game

   6 Rams 1-20-02
   5 Cowboys 1-8-95
      Cowboys 1-14-96

Most Points After Touchdown, Opponents, Game

   6 Rams 1-20-02
   5 Cowboys 1-8-95
      Cowboys 1-14-96

Most Field Goals, Opponents, Game

   3 Redskins 12-24-72
      Cowboys 1-16-83
      49ers 1-3-99

Most Field Goals Attempted, Opponents, Game

   4 Cardinals 1-8-83
      Falcons 1-4-03

First Downs

Most First Downs, Opponents, Game

  28 Cardinals 1-8-83
  27 Cowboys 1-8-95
      Cowboys 1-14-96

Fewest First Downs, Opponents, Game

   6 Giants 12-31-61
   8 Redskins 12-13-36
      Browns 1-2-66

Most First Downs, Rushing, Opponents, Game

  14 Broncos 1-25-98
  13 Falcons 1-4-03

Fewest First Downs, Rushing, Opponents, Game

   1 Giants 12-31-61
      Lions 12-31-94
      Falcons 12-31-95
      Panthers 1-12-97
      49ers 1-11-98
   2 Browns 1-2-66
      Rams 12-23-67

Most First Downs, Passing, Opponents, Game

  19 Cardinals 1-8-83
  17 Falcons 12-31-95

Fewest First Downs, Passing, Opponents, Game

   2 Giants 12-11-38
      Colts 12-26-65
   3 Redskins 12-13-36

Giants 12-10-39
Bears 12-14-41
Most First Downs, Penalty, Opponents, Game
3   Redskins 12-24-72
Cowboys 1-8-95
49ers 1-11-98

Net Yards Rushing and Receiving

Most Yards Gained, Opponents, Game
453   Cardinals 1-8-83
450   Cowboys 1-8-95
Fewest Yards Gained, Opponents, Game
116   Redskins 12-13-36
130   Giants 12-31-61

Rushing

Most Rushing Attempts, Opponents, Game
48   Bears 12-14-41
47   Colts 12-26-65
Fewest Rushing Attempts, Opponents, Game
10   Falcons 12-31-95
13   Patriots 1-26-97
Most Yards Gained, Rushing, Opponents, Game
277   Bears 12-14-41
192   Falcons 1-4-03
Fewest Yards Gained, Rushing, Opponents, Game
-4   Lions 12-31-94
21   Falcons 12-31-95
Highest Average Gain, Opponents, Game
6.56   Eagles 1-11-04 (25-164)
6.03   Lions 1-8-94 (29-175)
Lowest Average Gain, Opponents, Game
-0.27   Lions 12-31-94 (15-[-4])
1.11   Redskins 12-13-36 (35-39)
Most Touchdowns, Rushing, Opponents, Game
4   Broncos 1-25-98
3   Bears 12-14-41
Cowboys 1-8-95
Cowboys 1-14-96
Seahawks 1-4-04

Passing

Most Passing Attempts, Opponents, Game
65   49ers 1-6-96
54   Falcons 12-31-95
Fewest Passing Attempts, Opponents, Game
12   Bears 12-14-41
Colts 12-26-65
14   Redskins 12-24-72
Most Completions, Opponents, Game
32   Cardinals 1-8-83
49ers 1-6-96
30   Falcons 12-31-95
Fewest Completions, Opponents, Game
5   Bears 12-14-41
Colts 12-26-65

7   Redskins 12-13-36
Redskins 12-24-72
Highest Completion Percentage, Opponents, Game (min. 20 atts.)
75.68   Cowboys 1-16-94 (28-37)
71.88   Cowboys 1-8-95 (23-32)
Lowest Completion Percentage, Opponents, Game (min. 20 atts.)
31.82   Redskins 12-13-36 (7-22)
32.00   Giants 12-10-39 (8-25)
Most Yards Gained, Passing, Opponents, Game
347   Cardinals 1-8-83
339   Falcons 12-31-95
Fewest Yards Gained, Passing, Opponents, Game
32   Colts 12-26-65
48   Bears 12-14-41
Most Times Packers Sacked Opponents, Game
8   Eagles 1-11-04
6   Chiefs 1-15-67
Fewest Times Packers Sacked Opponents, Game
0   Giants 12-30-62
Broncos 1-25-98
Falcons 1-4-03
Most Touchdowns, Passing, Opponents, Game
3   Cowboys 1-16-94
49ers 1-3-99
Most Passes Had Intercepted, Opponents, Game
6   Giants 12-10-39
4   Giants 12-17-44
Giants 12-31-61
Patriots 1-26-97

Interceptions

Most Passes Intercepted By, Opponents, Game
6   Rams 1-20-02
3   Giants 12-10-39
Giants 12-17-44
Cowboys 1-16-83
Most Yards Gained on Interceptions, Opponents, Game
161   Rams 1-20-02
58   Cowboys 1-16-83
Most Touchdowns on Interceptions, Opponents, Game
3   Rams 1-20-02
1   Cowboys 1-16-83
Lions 1-8-94

Punting

Most Punts, Opponents, Game
10   Redskins 12-13-36
Giants 12-17-44
Fewest Punts, Opponents, Game
0   Cardinals 1-8-83
3   Lions 1-8-94

Cowboys 1-16-94

49ers 1-3-99

Highest Average Distance, Opponents, Game
(min. 4 punts)

46.50   Redskins 12-24-72 (6-279)

46.00   Browns 1-2-66 (4-184)

Lowest Average Distance, Opponents, Game
(min. 4 punts)

32.25   Cowboys 1-1-67 (4-129)

33.80   Falcons 1-4-03 (5-169)

Punts Returns

Most Punt Returns, Opponents, Game

5   Redskins 12-13-36

    Colts 12-26-65

4   Patriots 1-26-97

    Eagles 1-11-04

Fewest Punt Returns, Opponents, Game

0   Cowboys 12-31-67

    Cardinals 1-8-83

    Cowboys 1-8-95

    Broncos 1-25-98

    49ers 1-13-02

    Falcons 1-4-03

Most Yards Gained, Punt Returns, Opponents, Game

87   Bears 12-14-41

58   Redskins 12-13-36

Fewest Yards Gained, Punt Returns, Opponents, Game

-9   Browns 1-2-66

0   Accomplished 8 times

Kickoff Returns

Most Kickoff Returns, Opponents, Game

7   Raiders 1-14-68

    Cardinals 1-8-83

    Panthers 1-12-97

    Seahawks 1-4-04

Fewest Kickoff Returns, Opponents, Game

2   Colts 12-26-65

    Redskins 12-24-72

    Cowboys 1-16-94

    Falcons 1-4-03

Most Yards Gained, Kickoff Returns, Opponents, Game

186   Lions 12-31-94

178   Cardinals 1-8-83

Fewest Yards Gained, Kickoff Returns, Opponents, Game

29   Falcons 1-4-03

34   Cowboys 1-16-94

PENALTIES

Most Penalties, Opponents, Game

12   Bears 12-14-41

11   Giants 12-17-44

Fewest Penalties, Opponents, Game

0   Eagles 12-26-60

2   Patriots 1-26-97

    Seahawks 1-4-04

Most Yards Penalized, Opponents, Game

128   Bears 12-14-41

90   Giants 12-17-44

Fewest Yards Penalized, Opponents, Game

0   Eagles 12-26-60

15   Seahawks 1-4-04

FUMBLES

Most Fumbles, Opponents, Game

6   Redskins 12-13-36

5   Bears 12-14-41

    Giants 12-31-61

Fewest Fumbles, Opponents, Game

0   Browns 1-2-66

    Rams 12-23-67

    Cowboys 1-14-96

    Patriots 1-26-97

    Rams 1-20-02

Most Own Fumbles, Recovered, Opponents, Game

4   Giants 12-31-61

3   Redskins 12-13-36

Most Packers Fumbles Recovered, Game

3   Rams 12-23-67

    Falcons 1-4-03

Most Fumbles Recovered, Own and Packers, Opponents, Game

4   Redskins 12-13-36 (3 own, 1 Packers)

    Bears 12-14-41 (2 own, 2 Packers)

    Giants 12-31-61 (4 own)

    Cowboys 12-31-67 (2 own, 2 Packers)

    Falcons 1-4-03 (1 own, 3 Packers)

Turnovers

Most Turnovers, Opponents, Game

6   Giants 12-10-39

5   Giants 12-11-38

    Giants 12-31-61

    49ers 1-4-97

Fewest Turnovers, Opponents, Game

0   Lions 12-31-94

    Cowboys 1-14-96

    Falcons 1-4-03

    Accomplished 7 times

    (last vs. Eagles 1-11-04)

All-Time Playoffs

Player	Number of Games
Anderson, Marques	3
Andruzzi, Joe	1
Arthur, Mike	3
Bailey, Karsten	1
Barnett, Nick	2
Barry, Kevin	3
Beebe, Don	3
Bennett, Edgar	10
Bennett, Tony	2
Bidwell, Josh	5
Blackshear, Jeff	1
Blair, Michael	1
Booker, Vaughn	1
Bowen, Matt	3
Bradford, Corey	3
Brock, Matt	4
Brooks, Robert	11
Brown, Gary	5
Brown, Gilbert	14
Brunell, Mark	1
Buckley, Terrell	4
Butler, LeRoy	14
Chatman, Antonio	2
Chmura, Mark	14
Clavelle, Shannon	1
Clayton, Mark	2
Clifton, Chad	4
Cobb, Reggie	2
Collins, Mark	1
Cox, Ron	3
Crawford, Keith	3
Darkins, Chris	3
Davenport, Najeh	2
Davey, Don	4
Davis, Rob	9
Davis, Tyrone	7
Delenbach, Jeff	4
Detmer, Ty	1
Diggs, Na'il	5
Dorsett, Matthew	1
Dotson, Earl	15
Dotson, Santana	9
Driver, Donald	5
Edwards, Antuan	1
Evans, Doug	13
Favre, Brett	19
Ferguson, Robert	3
Ferrario, Bill	1
Fisher, Tony	3
Flanagan, Mike	5
Flanigan, Jim	2
Franks, Bubba	5
Frase, Paul	2
Freeman, Antonio	14
Fuller, Curtis	2
Galbreath, Harry	7
Gbaja-Biamila, Kabeer	5
Glenn, Terry	1

Player	Number of Games
Goodman, Herbert	2
Green, Ahman	5
Hamilton, Ruffin	2
Harris, Al	2
Harris, Bernardo	12
Harris, Corey	4
Hauck, Tim	4
Hawthorne, Michael	2
Hayden, Aaron	3
Hayes, Chris	3
Henderson, William	15
Hentrich, Craig	11
Holland, Darius	8
Holland, Johnny	2
Holliday, Vonnie	4
Hollinquest, Lamont	7
Holmberg, Rob	2
Hope, Charles	2
Howard, Desmond	3
Hunt, Cletidius	5
Hutchins, Paul	2
Ilkin, Tunch	2
Ingram, Darryl	1
Ingram, Mark	3
Jacke, Chris	10
Jackson, Grady	2
Jackson, Keith	6
Jenkins, Billy	2
Jervey, Travis	9
Johnson, KeShon	1
Johnson, Reggie	2
Jones, Calvin	2
Jones, Sean	8
Jordan, Charles	2
Joyner, Seth	3
Jue, Bhawoh	4
Jurkovic, John	7
Kampman, Aaron	3
Kitts, Jim	1
Knapp, Lindsey	3
Koonce, George	10
Kuberski, Bob	5
LaBounty, Matt	3
Landeta, Sean	1
Lenon, Paris	3
Levens, Dorsey	14
Lewis, Ron	2
Longwell, Ryan	9
Nick Luchey	2
Lyon, Billy	3
Maas, Bill	2
Marshall, Torrance	5
Martin, David	3
Mayes, Derrick	4
McBride, Tod	2
McGarrahan, Scott	1
McGill, Lenny	3
McIntyre, Guy	2
McKenzie, Keith	7
McKenzie, Mike	5
McMahon, Jim	2

Player	Number of Games	Player	Number of Games
McMichael, Steve	2	Strickland, Fred	5
McNabb, Dexter	2	Swiney, Erwin	1
Merriweather, Mike	2	Tauscher, Mark	4
Metcalf, Eric	1	Taylor, Aaron	7
Michels, John	3	Teague, George	7
Mickens, Terry	11	Terrell, Pat	1
Mitchell, Roland	2	Thomason, Jeff	9
Morgan, Anthony	5	Thompson, Darrell	3
Morrissey, Jim	2	Timmerman, Adam	10
Mott, Joe	2	Verba, Ross	4
Mullen, Roderick	8	Wagner, Bryan	2
Navies, Hannibal	2	Wahle, Mike	5
Nelson, Jim	1	Walker, Javon	3
Newsome, Craig	7	Walker, Rod	1
Nickerson, Hardy	1	Walker, Sammy	2
Nwokorie, Chukie	1	Walls, Wesley	2
Paup, Bryce	4	Warren, Steve	1
Pederson, Doug	6	Wayne, Nate	3
Peterson, Kenny	1	West, Ed	4
Preston, Roell	1	Westbrook, Bryant	1
Prior, Mike	14	White, Reggie	14
Reynolds, Jamal	4	Whitley, James	2
Rison, Andre	3	Widell, Doug	2
Rivera, Marco	9	Wilkerson, Bruce	6
Robinson, Eugene	6	Wilkins, Gabe	10
Rossum, Allen	2	Williams, Brian	10
Ruegamer, Gray	2	Williams, K.D.	2
Ruettgers, Ken	7	Williams, Mark	2
Schroeder, Bill	4	Williams, Tyrone	10
Sharpe, Sterling	2	Willig, Matt	1
Sharper, Darren	8	Wilner, Jeff	1
Simmons, Wayne	10	Wilson, Marcus	5
Sims, Joe	4	Wilson, Ray	1
Smith, Larry	2	Winters, Frank	14
Stokes, Barry	2	Zeno, Lance	2

THE OFF-SEASON

Head coach Vince Lombardi rides the blocking sled as he puts the Packers linemen through a workout during training camp. Lambeau Field forms the backdrop for the practice session. Stiller-Lefebvre Collection

THE HEAD COACHES

EARL LOUIS (CURLY) LAMBEAU 1919-1949

Born: April 9, 1898   **Died:** June 1, 1965

On Aug. 14, 1919, Earl Louis (Curly) Lambeau was elected captain of the Green Bay city football team. The club was sponsored by the Indian Packing Corp., which contributed $500 toward jerseys, equipment, and other items. Lambeau's employers also provided company land on which to practice.

In its first two seasons, Green Bay played teams primarily from Wisconsin. Dubbed the "Packers" by publicist George Whitney Calhoun, the team went 19-2-1 in 1919 and 1920.

In 1921, the Acme Packing Co. bought out the Indian Packing Corp. Acme's John and Emmett Clair were granted a franchise in the new American Professional Football Organization, forerunner to the NFL. Pro football had arrived in the oldest city in Wisconsin, and Lambeau became its guide.

Lambeau was born in Green Bay in 1898. He attended Green Bay East High School and made the varsity football team as a freshman.

In the fall of 1918, Lambeau enrolled at Notre Dame. There, he joined a backfield that included the great George Gipp.

While at school, Lambeau developed tonsillitis. He returned to Green Bay and took a job with the Indian Packing Corp.

As head coach of the Packers, Lambeau made liberal use of the forward pass. He held daily practices and later used film as a means to evaluate his team as well as opponents. He had a keen eye for talent and, over the years, he acquired players who won six NFL championships (1929-31, 1936, 1939, and 1944).

Green Bay's fortunes declined after World War II. By the late '40s, Lambeau had fallen out of favor with some members of the team's executive committee. He resigned in 1950 and went on to coach the Cardinals and Redskins.

From 1955 through 1957, Lambeau coached the College All-Stars in their annual clash with the NFL champions. In 1963, he was enshrined in the Pro Football Hall of Fame. City Stadium was renamed Lambeau Field in 1965.

NFL COACHING RECORD

	Reg. Season	Playoffs	Overall	Pct.
Packers, 1921-49	209-104-21	3-2	212-106-21	.656
Cardinals, 1950-51	7-15-0	0-0	7-15-0	.318
Redskins, 1952-53	10-13-1	0-0	10-13-1	.438
TOTALS	**226-132-22**	**3-2**	**229-134-22**	**.623**

AS PACKERS COACH

Largest Margin of Victory = 47   **Largest Margin of Defeat** = 46

GB 47, Steelers 0 (10-15-33)   Giants 49, GB 3 (11-21-48)

GENE RONZANI 1950-1953

Born: March 28, 1909   **Died:** Sept. 12, 1975

Gene Ronzani became the second head coach in Packers history on Feb. 6, 1950. Prior to that, he spent 16 years with the Chicago Bears as a player, coach, and public relations figure.

Ronzani was born in Iron Mountain, Mich., in 1909. He attended Iron Mountain High School and won eight letters in football, basketball, and track. In 1929, he enrolled at Marquette University, where he earned nine letters in the same three sports. He was captain of the football team in 1932, the same year he earned his law degree.

In the fall of 1933, Ronzani joined the Bears. He played in the same backfield as veterans Bronko Nagurski and Beattie Feathers, the latter the first to gain 1,000 yards rushing in a single season. On Dec. 10, the rookie's 23-yard pass to Keith Molesworth beat the Packers 7-6.

In 1939, Ronzani became head coach of the Newark Bears, a Chicago Bears farm club. In 1944, the Chicago Bears re-signed him, and he played two more years, filling in for quarterback Sid Luckman who was in the Coast Guard.

In his eight-year playing career (1933-38, 1944-45), Ronzani rushed for 1,144 yards and passed for 1,201 yards.

Ronzani was named head coach of the Bears' Akron, Ohio, farm team in 1946. A year later, he joined George Halas as Chicago's backfield assistant and quarterbacks coach.

In Green Bay, Ronzani's four-year tour was filled with more downs than ups. His club won only three games in 1950. A year later, the Packers again finished 3-9, but boasted a passing game second only to that of the Rams.

In 1952, the club went 6-6 and remained in the National Conference race until late November. But the following year, the losses again mounted and Ronzani came under fire. Some of his decisions were openly second-guessed. He was released on Nov. 27, 1953. Hugh Devore and Ray McLean served as co-coaches for the final two games.

Ronzani served as the Steelers' backfield coach in 1954. He died of a heart attack at his cottage in Lac du Flambeau in 1975.

NFL COACHING RECORD

	Reg. Season	Playoffs	Overall	Pct.
Packers, 1950-53	14-31-1	0-0	14-31-1	.315
TOTALS	**14-31-1**	**0-0**	**14-31-1**	**.315**

AS PACKERS COACH

Largest Margin of Victory = 28   **Largest Margin of Defeat** = 38

GB 42, Texans 14 (11-23-52)   Lions 45, GB 7 (9-17-50)

LISLE (LIZ) BLACKBOURN 1954-1957

Born: June 3, 1899   **Died:** June 13, 1983

For the first time, the fortunes of the Packers rested with a man who had never coached or played football at the professional level. Lisle (Liz) Blackbourn, named head coach on Jan. 7, 1954, had spent 22 years as coach and athletic director at Washington High School in Milwaukee before logging another seven at the collegiate level as scout, assistant coach, and head coach.

Blackbourn was born in Beetown Township in Grant County, Wis., and attended Lawrence University. He graduated in 1925 and moved to Milwaukee where he began his association with Washington High School. He compiled a 140-30-6 record, and his teams won 10 city championships and tied for an eleventh.

In 1946, Blackbourn became a scout for the University of Wisconsin at Madison. In 1948, he was named backfield coach by then head coach Harry Stuhldreher. Stuhldreher departed the following year and, though a candidate for the vacancy, Blackbourn lost out to Ivy Williamson.

In 1949, Blackbourn became line coach at Marquette University under Frank Murray. Murray retired after the 1949 campaign, and this time Blackbourn was named head coach. His teams went 18-17-4 between 1950-53.

The Packers won just four games in Blackbourn's first year in Green Bay. His team, however, lost just once by more than eight points. Blackbourn finished second to Cleveland's Paul Brown by a single vote in the United Press "Coach of the Year" poll of sportswriters.

In 1955, the Packers (6-6) remained in the race for the Western Conference championship until Thanksgiving. A year later, the club dropped to 4-8. In 1957, the team inaugurated play at New City Stadium, but managed just three wins.

Blackbourn was released on Jan. 6, 1958.

In later years, Blackbourn gained recognition for his role in the 1958 draft that brought Jim Taylor, Ray Nitschke, Dan Currie, and Jerry Kramer to Green Bay.

NFL COACHING RECORD

	Reg. Season	Playoffs	Overall	Pct.
Packers, 1954-57	17-31-0	0-0	17-31-0	.354
TOTALS	**17-31-0**	**0-0**	**17-31-0**	**.354**

AS PACKERS COACH
Largest Margin of Victory = 25 **Largest Margin of Defeat** = 35
GB 42, Rams 17 (10-21-56)   GB 0, 49ers 35 (12-5-54)

RAY (SCOOTER) MCLEAN 1958

Born: Dec. 6, 1915   **Died:** March 4, 1964

Ray (Scooter) McLean enjoyed a seven-year relationship with the Packers before becoming the team's fourth head coach on Jan. 7, 1958. McLean signed a one-year deal, just long enough for the team to post its worst record ever at 1-10-1.

McLean was the Packers offensive backfield coach from 1951 through 1957. He helped develop talents such as Fred Cone, Al Carmichael, Floyd (Breezy) Reid, and Howie Ferguson. He tutored quarterbacks such as Tobin Rote and Bart Starr.

McLean's easy-going, affable manner was both a help and a hindrance. As an assistant, he related well to his players. As head coach, he saw a number of players take advantage of his relaxed rules.

Prior to coming to Green Bay, McLean had served three years as head coach at Lewis College in Lockport, Ill. And like Ronzani before him, McLean had also played for the Chicago Bears. The Bruins made the St. Anselm graduate their 19th selection in the 1940 draft.

In an eight-year career with the club, McLean turned out to be a better receiver than running back. He caught 103 passes for 2,222 yards for an impressive 21.6-yard average per catch. He gained just 422 yards rushing.

McLean's Packers won but one game and had to hang on to do it. Green Bay led Philadelphia 38-14 after three quarters, but the Eagles soared back with three touchdowns to close to 38-35 with 54 seconds left. Only Ray Nitschke's recovery of the Eagles' subsequent onside kick allowed the Packers to prevail.

Green Bay was outscored 382-193 in 1958. The team had the distinction of being clobbered 56-0 by Baltimore. That setback was the first of seven, which closed out the campaign.

After losing the season finale 34-20 in Los Angeles, McLean resigned and joined the Lions as an assistant. He coached Detroit's offensive backfield until Sept. 22, 1963. At that point, weakened with cancer, he entered a Michigan hospital. McLean died in early March of the following year.

NFL COACHING RECORD

	Reg. Season	Playoffs	Overall	Pct.
Packers, 1958	1-10-1	0-0	1-10-1	.125
TOTALS	**1-10-1**	**0-0**	**1-10-1**	**.125**

AS PACKERS COACH
Largest Margin of Victory = 3 **Largest Margin of Defeat** = 56
GB 38, Eagles 35 (10-26-58)   Colts 56, GB 0 (11-2-56)

VINCENT THOMAS LOMBARDI 1959-1967

Born: June 11, 1913   **Died:** Sept. 3, 1970

Five NFL championships. Six Western Conference crowns. Two Super Bowl victories and a glittering winning percentage of .758.

Those were some of the major achievements of the Vince Lombardi era in Green Bay.

When he arrived in January 1959, he professed to be "no miracle man." Even so, his prior record indicated he wasn't one to tolerate failure.

Lombardi was born in Brooklyn, N.Y. He was an all-city performer at St. Francis Prep School and earned a scholarship to Fordham University. Though only 5-11 and 188 pounds, he played guard on the team's famed line—the Seven Blocks of Granite— under coach Jimmy Crowley.

Lombardi graduated in 1937. Beginning in 1939, he taught a variety of subjects, including Latin and chemistry, at St. Cecilia High School in Englewood, N.J. He coached football, baseball, and basketball. His football team once won 36 straight games, and it earned six state championships in eight years.

In 1947, Lombardi was freshman football coach at Fordham. The next year he became a varsity assistant under Ed Danowski.

Earl Blaik made him offensive line coach at the U. S. Military Academy in 1949 and he spent five years in that capacity.

Jim Lee Howell hired Lombardi to direct the New York Giants' offense in 1954. Though his unit never finished better than fourth, the Giants won the NFL title in 1956.

In his first year with the Packers, Lombardi took a 1-10-1 team and turned it into a 7-5 winner. In 1960, his team won the West, then lost a heartbreaker to the Eagles (17-13) in the championship game. The Packers won titles in 1961 and 1962 and grabbed three in a row from 1965-67.

In 1968, Lombardi stepped down as coach but remained general manager. A year later, the lure of coaching and the prospect of another challenge prompted him to leave Green Bay for Washington, where he transformed a losing Redskins program into a winner with a 7-5-2 record in 1969.

NFL COACHING RECORD

	Reg. Season	Playoffs	Overall	Pct.
Packers, 1959-67	89-29-4	9-1	98-30-4	.758
Redskins, 1969	7-5-2	0-0	7-5-2	.571
TOTALS	**96-34-6**	**9-1**	**105-35-6**	**.740**

AS PACKERS COACH
Largest Margin of Victory = 53 **Largest Margin of Defeat** = 39
GB 56, Falcons 3 (10-23-66)   Rams 45, GB 6 (10-18-59)

JOHN PHILLIP (PHIL) BENGTSON 1968-1970

Born: July 17, 1913   **Died:** Dec. 18, 1994

During the nine years Vince Lombardi's teams were winning championships, Phil Bengtson was busy perfecting the club's defense. Bengtson's unit finished third or better seven times and twice wound up first. When Lombardi named Bengtson his successor on Feb. 1, 1968, the announcement came as no surprise.

Bengtson had the unenviable task of following a legend. His final record of 20-21-1 was a far cry from that of his predecessor. He announced his resignation two days after his team went 6-8 in 1970. Bengtson cited a disappointing season and a need for change as reasons for leaving.

Bengtson began his association with pro football in 1951 when 49ers head coach Buck Shaw persuaded him to leave his position at Stanford. Bengtson remained with San Francisco until Lombardi appointed him defensive line coach in 1959. A year later, he had control of the entire defense.

In 1958, the Packers surrendered more yards (4,615) than any team except the Cardinals. A year later, the team gave up 3,552 yards and improved to third. It finished first in fewest yards allowed in 1964 and 1967.

Bengtson's units were strong against the pass. From 1962-69, the team was either first or second in that category.

Born in Rousseau, Minn., Bengtson enrolled at the University of Minnesota in 1931 and was named an All-American at tackle three years later. He was selected to play in that year's East-West Shrine game and the College All-Star game.

Bengtson was an assistant coach at the University of Missouri (1935-39) and Stanford (1940-41, 1946-50). He also coached an Iowa preflight service football team during World War II. He became a gunnery officer, eventually reaching the rank of lieutenant commander.

After leaving Green Bay, Bengtson served a year on the Chargers' coaching staff. He became a scout the next year and, in an unusual move, was lent to the Patriots late in 1972 to take over as head coach for the departed John Mazur.

NFL COACHING RECORD

	Reg. Season	Playoffs	Overall	Pct.
Packers, 1968-70	20-21-1	0-0	20-21-1	.488
Patriots, 1972	1-4-0	0-0	1-4-0	.200
TOTALS	**21-25-1**	**0-0**	**21-25-1**	**.457**

AS PACKERS COACH
Largest Margin of Victory = 31 **Largest Margin of Defeat** = 40
GB 38, Falcons 7 (10-6-68)   Lions 40, GB 0 (9-20-70)

DANIEL JOHN DEVINE 1971-1974

Born: Dec. 23, 1924   **Died:** May 9, 2002

Dan Devine brought an impressive 120-40-8 mark with him when he was named the Packers' seventh head coach on Jan. 14, 1971. Despite the gaudy numbers, forged at Arizona State and the University of Missouri, some still questioned whether a college coach could make a successful leap to the professional ranks.

By his second year in Green Bay, it appeared Devine could. In 1972, the team won the NFC Central Division with a 10-4 mark. One of the losses came at the hands of the Redskins, and they also dumped the Packers in the first round of the playoffs, 16-3.

The loss, in which Washington shut down Green Bay's running game, confirmed the Packers lacked a standout quarterback. Over the next two years, Devine sought to rectify that situation, but his inability to do so, in part, contributed to two losing seasons in 1973 and 1974.

The day after a season-ending loss to the Falcons in 1974, Devine resigned and became head coach at Notre Dame.

Devine was born in 1924 in Augusta, Wis. He attended the University of Minnesota at Duluth where he competed in baseball, basketball, and football. He graduated in 1948 after having served for more than two years in the Army Air Corps.

He began coaching at East Jordan High School in Michigan the same year. In 1950, he became an assistant at Michigan State, first as freshman coach and then as backfield coach.

Devine became head coach at Arizona State in 1955. In three years, his teams went 27-3-1. His 1957 squad (10-0) was the first unbeaten and nationally ranked team (12th) in Sun Devil history.

At Missouri (1958-70), Devine compiled an impressive 93-37-7 regular-season mark. Nine of his teams were nationally ranked and his Tigers won four bowl games.

After leaving the Packers, Devine guided the Irish to a 53-16-1 record over five seasons, including the 1977 national championship.

NFL COACHING RECORD

	Reg. Season	Playoffs	Overall	Pct.
Packers, 1971-74	25-27-4	0-1	25-28-4	.474
TOTALS	**25-27-4**	**0-1**	**25-28-4**	**.474**

AS PACKERS COACH

Largest Margin of Victory = 34   Largest Margin of Defeat = 34

GB 34, Chargers 0 (11-24-74)   Lions 34, GB 0 (10-28-73)

BRYAN BARTLETT (BART) STARR 1975-1983

Born: Jan. 9, 1934

The Packers reached back into their glorious past in making Bart Starr their eighth head coach on Dec. 24, 1974. Starr won five NFL championships as a player in the 1960s, but had just one year of coaching experience—as the Packers' quarterbacks coach in 1972—on his resume.

In his first three years, Starr's teams notched just 13 wins and lost 29 times. Early on, he was handicapped by a lack of top draft choices (traded away by his predecessor to obtain quarterback John Hadl and others).

In 1978, the team jumped to a 6-1 start before finishing 8-7-1. Performances from rookies such as James Lofton, Paul Coffman, and John Anderson helped fuel the quick getaway.

Losing seasons in 1979 and 1980 had fans getting impatient. Starr was stripped of his general manager duties after the 1980 season.

The 1981 team—after rallying to win six of its last eight games—just missed making the playoffs. The strong finish carried over into 1982 and the Packers reached the playoffs for the first time in a decade. A 41-16 win over the Cardinals in Lambeau Field marked the first time since Super Bowl II that Green Bay had won a postseason game.

The Cowboys ended Green Bay's season 37-26 in Dallas.

In 1983, the Packers went 8-8. Starr was fired a day after a 23-21 loss to the Bears cost his team a trip to the playoffs.

Starr was born in Montgomery, Ala., in 1934. He won All-America honors in high school then moved on to the University of Alabama where he became a four-year letter-winner. He led his team to a win over Syracuse in the 1953 Orange Bowl and finished second in the nation in punting. He also played in the 1955 Blue-Grey game.

In 1956, the Packers selected him with the 199th pick overall in the draft.

Starr led the league in passing three times: 1962, 1964 and 1966. He played in four Pro Bowls: 1961-63 and 1967.

NFL COACHING RECORD

	Reg. Season	Playoffs	Overall	Pct.
Packers, 1975-83	52-76-3	1-1	53-77-3	.410
TOTALS	**52-76-3**	**1-1**	**53-77-3**	**.410**

AS PACKERS COACH

Largest Margin of Victory = 41   Largest Margin of Defeat = 54

GB 55, Buccaneers 14 (10-2-83)   Bears 61, GB 7 (12-7-80)

ALVIS FORREST GREGG 1984-1987

Born: Oct. 18, 1933

Forrest Gregg was named head coach of the Packers just five days after Bart Starr was fired. Like Starr, Gregg had played under Vince Lombardi. But unlike Starr, the former offensive tackle had many years of NFL coaching experience to his credit, including two tours of duty as head coach.

Gregg came to Green Bay as a second-round draft choice in 1956. He played in a team-record 187 consecutive games and appeared in nine Pro Bowls. He was elected to the Pro Football Hall of Fame in his first year of eligibility (1977).

Following his playing career — which included a year with the Cowboys in 1971 — Gregg joined the Chargers' staff as an assistant. In 1974, he became the Browns offensive line coach.

In 1975, Browns owner Art Modell named Gregg head coach. Gregg's first team won just three games. In 1976, his team went 9-5 and the former lineman earned "Coach of the Year" honors.

Injuries beset the team in 1977, and Gregg resigned with one game left on the schedule.

Gregg returned to coaching in 1979 and led the Toronto Argonauts of the CFL to a 5-11 record. He rejoined the NFL a year later. During a four-year run, he guided the Cincinnati Bengals to two playoff appearances, including a trip to Super Bowl XVI.

Gregg left Cincinnati after a disappointing 7-9 finish in 1983.

In his four years in Green Bay, Gregg's teams never won more than eight games in a single year. Slow starts in 1984 (1-7) and 1985 (3-5) hampered his first two squads. A rebuilding effort in 1986 had the Packers stumbling to a 4-12 finish. After Green Bay posted a 5-9-1 record in 1987, Gregg departed for his alma mater, Southern Methodist University.

As a collegian, Gregg twice made the All-Southwest Conference team. He captained the Southern Methodist football team as a senior in 1955.

NFL COACHING RECORD

	Reg. Season	Playoffs	Overall	Pct.
Browns, 1975-77	18-23-0	0-0	18-23-0	.439
Bengals, 1980-83	32-25-0	2-2	34-27-0	.557
Packers, 1984-87	25-37-1	0-0	25-37-1	.405
TOTALS	**75-85-1**	**2-2**	**77-87-1**	**.470**

AS PACKERS COACH
Largest Margin of Victory = 33 Largest Margin of Defeat = 35
GB 43, Lions 10 (10-6-85)   Vikings 42, GB 7 (9-28-86)

GELINDO (LINDY) INFANTE 1988-1991

Born: May 27, 1940

The Packers broke from the past when they made Lindy Infante their 10th head coach on Feb. 3, 1988. Unlike Forrest Gregg and Bart Starr before him, the Miami native had no ties to the team. He had, however, served as quarterbacks coach and then offensive coordinator with Forrest Gregg at Cincinnati in the early '80s.

Infante implemented what some called a "Pass to Daylight" offense. Unfamiliarity with that system, injuries, holdouts, and a deficient kicking game all contributed to a 4-12 record in 1988.

A year later, Don Majkowski, Sterling Sharpe, Tim Harris, and others carried the team out of the Central Division cellar. Green Bay (10-6) tied the Vikings for first place, but Minnesota made the playoffs because of a better division record.

In 1990, the Packers slumped to 6-10. Majkowski missed the last six games with a shoulder injury, the offensive line labored, and the running game was ineffective.

The situation worsened in 1991, and Infante was fired shortly after a 4-12 finish.

Infante graduated from the University of Florida in 1963 and began coaching at Miami Senior High School in 1965. In 1966, he coached freshmen at Florida before becoming the team's defensive backfield coach.

From there, Infante made stops at Memphis State (1972-73), the World Football League (Charlotte, 1975), Tulane (1976, 1979), and the Giants (1977-78). He joined the Bengals in 1980.

In 1984, Infante was named head coach of the Jacksonville Bulls of the USFL. His two-year record there was 15-21.

Infante served as offensive coordinator and quarterbacks coach at Cleveland in 1986 and 1987.

After leaving the Packers, Infante won a dozen games as head coach of the Colts (1996-97).

Infante was selected by both the Browns (12th round) and Bills (11th round) in 1963. He signed with the Bills, but was released. He then played one game for the Tiger-Cats of the Canadian Football League, gaining all of 12 yards rushing.

NFL COACHING RECORD

	Reg. Season	Playoffs	Overall	Pct.
Packers, 1988-91	24-40-0	0-0	24-40-0	.375
Colts, 1996-97	12-20-0	0-1	12-21-0	.364
TOTALS	**36-60-0**	**0-1**	**36-61-0**	**.371**

AS PACKERS COACH
Largest Margin of Victory = 42 Largest Margin of Defeat = 31
GB 45, Patriots 3 (10-9-88)   Eagles 31, GB 0 (12-16-90)

MICHAEL (MIKE) HOLMGREN 1992-1998

Born: June 15, 1948

On Jan. 11, 1992, Packers general manager Ron Wolf announced the hiring of Mike Holmgren as the team's 11th head coach. Holmgren had been an assistant coach with the 49ers for six years starting in 1986.

San Francisco was the NFL's winningest team in the 1980s: seven division titles, eight playoff berths, and four Super Bowl victories. Holmgren, as quarterbacks coach (1986-88) and offensive coordinator/quarterbacks coach (1989-91), was a key assistant on the 49ers back-to-back Super Bowl champion teams of 1988-89.

Packers fans couldn't have been more pleased. Holmgren recharged the team, helped turn Brett Favre into one of the all-time greats, acquired defensive leader Reggie White, and led the team to its first Super Bowl victory in nearly three decades.

Holmgren won more games as a Packers head coach (84) than all but Curly Lambeau (212) and Vince Lombardi (98). His winning percentage (.667) trailed only that of Lombardi (.758).

Holmgren got his coaching start at San Francisco's Lincoln High School in 1971. From there, Holmgren moved on to Sacred Heart High (1972-74) and Oakgrove High (1975-80).

In 1981, Holmgren became offensive coordinator and quarterbacks coach at San Francisco State University. A year later, he joined the staff of Brigham Young University where he tutored quarterbacks such as Robbie Bosco and Steve Young. In 1984, BYU won its first national championship.

Holmgren jumped to the professional ranks in 1986 with the 49ers. As quarterbacks coach, he was instrumental in the continuing development of Joe Montana and backup Young.

Holmgren left the Packers in 1998 for the Seahawks.

The St. Louis Cardinals drafted Holmgren, a backup quarterback at the University of Southern California, in the eighth round of the 1970 draft. He spent time in the training camps of both the Cardinals and Jets in 1970 prior to embarking on his coaching career.

NFL COACHING RECORD

	Reg. Season	Playoffs	Overall	Pct.
Packers, 1992-98	75-37-0	9-5	84-42-0	.667
Seahawks, 1999-02	31-33-0	0-1	31-34-0	.477
TOTALS	**106-70-0**	**9-6**	**115-76-0**	**.602**

AS PACKERS COACH

Largest Margin of Victory = 37 **Largest Margin of Defeat** = 28

GB 40, Bears 3 (12-11-94)   Buccaneers 31, GB 3 (9-13-92)

RAYMOND (RAY) EARL RHODES 1999

Born: Oct. 20, 1950

Ray Rhodes was Packers general manager Ron Wolf's only choice to succeed Mike Holmgren as the team's 12th head coach. Rhodes, who had served as Green Bay's defensive coordinator for two years (1992-93), had been the coach at Philadelphia, where he twice led the Eagles to the playoffs.

"The things that impressed me was the fact that he is a genuine leader, he is extremely knowledgeable, he is a darn good football coach, and that's what this is all about, him being a darn good football coach," Wolf said.

A running back at Texas Christian University and a wide receiver at the University of Tulsa, Rhodes was drafted by the Giants in 1974 (10th round). He played seven years in the NFL, the first six in New York where he was first a wide receiver, then a defensive back. He played one year (1980) with the 49ers.

Rhodes spent the next 11 years with San Francisco as an assistant coach. He was the assistant secondary coach (1981-82) and defensive backs coach (1983-91).

As defensive coordinator in Green Bay, Rhodes' units ranked 23rd and 2nd in yards allowed.

After a year as defensive coordinator with the 49ers (1994), Rhodes was named head coach of the Eagles in 1995. Philadelphia posted 10-6 records in each of his first two seasons and Rhodes was named Coach of the Year in 1995.

He was fired after going 3-13 in 1998.

In Green Bay, Rhodes team finished 8-8 and failed to qualify for the playoffs. Special teams woes, penalties, and a suspect defense contributed to the disappointing season. An intense competitor himself, Rhodes was content to run the team in a looser, more relaxed atmosphere than his predecessor, and the focus wasn't always there.

He was fired in early January 2000.

Now defensive coordinator at Seattle, Rhodes also served in that capacity with both Washington (2001) and Denver (2002).

NFL COACHING RECORD

	Reg. Season	Playoffs	Overall	Pct.
Eagles, 1995-98	29-34-1	1-2	30-36-1	.455
Packers, 1999	8-8-0	0-0	8-8-0	.500
TOTALS	**37-42-1**	**1-2**	**38-44-1**	**.464**

AS PACKERS COACH

Largest Margin of Victory = 28 **Largest Margin of Defeat** = 21

GB 31, Chargers 3 (10-24-99)   Broncos 31, GB 10 (10-17-99)

MICHAEL FRANCIS SHERMAN
2000-PRESENT

Born: Dec. 19, 1954

"He just blew my socks off."

Mike Sherman was named the Packers 13th head coach on Jan. 18, 2000, and general manager Ron Wolf was obviously quite pleased with his new hire. It mattered little to Wolf that Sherman had just three previous years of coaching experience at the professional level.

"I just met the guy I want to hire as coach," Wolf told team president Bob Harlan on Jan. 15. "It was one of the best interviews I've ever had. If I had any guts, I'd hire him right now."

Wolf, who had considered a number of candidates before talking with Sherman, was also interested in former Cleveland and Kansas City coach Marty Schottenheimer. But when talks broke down, Wolf offered the job to Sherman.

Sherman was hired by Mike Holmgren in 1997 to coach the Packers tight ends and assist with the offensive line. He served in that capacity for two years before leaving with Holmgren for Seattle in 1999, where he became offensive coordinator.

Quiet, organized, and well prepared, Sherman didn't attract much attention in his two years as an assistant in Green Bay.

"I don't think we ever said five words to one another the whole time we were here in a day," Wolf said.

In his first season, Sherman had Green Bay again winning in Lambeau Field and playing its best football in December. In 2001, the team won 12 games and returned to the playoffs for the first time in three years. A year later, the Packers secured their first divisional title (NFC North) in five years with a 12-4 mark.

In 2001, Sherman was named executive vice president and general manager, succeeding Wolf who stepped down that June.

Sherman played collegiately at Central Connecticut State University (defensive end and offensive guard/tackle). He was a graduate assistant at the University of Pittsburgh (1981-82).

For the next 15 years, he served as offensive line coach at Tulane (1983-84), Holy Cross (1985-87), Texas A&M (1989-93 and 1995-96), and UCLA (1994). He also had a one-year stint as offensive coordinator at Holy Cross in 1988.

NFL COACHING RECORD

	Reg. Season	Playoffs	Overall	Pct.
Packers, 2000-03	43-21-0	2-3	45-24-0	.652
TOTALS	**43-21-0**	**2-3**	**45-24-0**	**.652**

AS PACKERS COACH

Largest Margin of Victory = 37 **Largest Margin of Defeat** = 28
GB 37, Redskins 0 (9-24-01)   Rams 45, Packers 17 (1-20-02)

Name	Assignment(s)	Years
Austin, Bill	Offensive line	1959-64
Baggett, Charlie	Wide receivers	1999
Beightol, Larry	Offensive line	1999-2003
Bengtson, Phil	Defensive line/defense	1959-67
Bevell, Darrell	Offensive assistant/quality control	2000-01
	Offensive assistant	2002
	Quarterbacks	2003
Blache, Greg	Defensive line	1988-93
Bonamego, John	Special teams coordinator	2003
Bratkowski, Zeke	Offensive backfield	1969-70
	Quarterbacks	1975-78
	Quarterbacks/offensive backfield	1979-81
Brock, Charley	Defense	1949
Brooks, Larry	Defensive line	1994-98
Brown, Kippy	Running backs	2000
Brunner, John	Offensive backfield	1983
Bullough, Hank	Defensive coordinator	*1984, 1988-91
Burns, Jerry	Defensive backfield	1966-67
Carpenter, Lew	Receivers/passing game	1975-79
	Receivers	1980-85
Champion, Jim	Defensive line	1980
Clark, Joe	General offensive assistant	1988-89
	Assistant offensive line	1990-91
Cochran, John (Red)	Offensive backfield	1959-66, 71-74
Colbert, Jim	Defensive backs	1975
Coughlin, Tom	Receivers/passing game	1986-87
Cromwell, Nolan	Special teams	1992-97
	Wide receivers	1998
Croom, Sylvester	Running backs	2001-03
Curry, Bill	Offensive line	1977-79
Davis, Billy	Defensive assistant/quality control	2000
Davis, Charlie	Offensive line	1988-91
Devore, Hugh	Ends	1953
Doll, Don	Defensive secondary	1971-73
Donatell, Ed	Defensive coordinator	2000-03
Dotsch, Rollie	Offensive line	1971-74
Drayton, Stan	Quality control/special teams-offense	2001-03
Drulis, Charles	Line	1951-53
Duffner, Mark	Linebackers	2003
Eatman, Irv	Assistant offensive line	1999
Evans, Dick	Defensive secondary	1970
Fears, Tom	Offensive ends	1962-65
Fichtner, Ross	Defensive backs	1980-83
Fajole, Ken	Defensive assistant/quality control	1998
Franklin, Jethro	Defensive line	2000-03
Geis, Wayne (Buddy)	Receivers	1988-91
Gregg, Forrest	Offensive line	1969-70
Gruden, Jon	Offensive assistant/quality control	1992
	Wide receivers	1993-94
Gustafson, Burt	Linebackers	1971-74
	Special teams	1977-78
Hanner, Dave	Defensive line	1965-71
	Defensive coordinator	1972-74
	Defensive coordinator/asst. head coach	1975-79
	Quality control	1982
Haskell, Gil	Running backs	1992-94
	Wide receivers	1995-97
Hearden, Tom	Ends	1954-55, 57
Hecker, Norb	Defensive backfield	1959-65
Hilton, John	Offensive backfield/special teams	1986
Holland, Johnny	Defensive assistant/quality control	1995-97
	Special teams	1998
	Linebackers	1999
Hutson, Don	Backfield/ends	1945-48
Jagodzinski, Jeff	Tight ends	1999-2003
Jauron, Dick	Defensive backs	1986-94
Johnston, Kent	Strength/conditioning	1992-98
Kettela, Pete	Special assistant	1981
	Offensive backs	1982
Kiesling, Walt	Line	1945-48
Kiffin, Monte	Linebackers	1983
Kinard, Billy	Defensive secondary	1974
Klapstein, Earl	Defensive line	1956
Knight, Virgil	Strength/conditioning	1984-85
	Strength/conditioning/offensive line	1986-87
	Strength/conditioning/tight ends	1988-90
	Tight Ends	1991
Knox, Chuck Jr.	Defensive assistant/quality control	1999
Kotal, Eddie	Backfield	1942-43
Kuhlmann, Hank	Special teams	1972-74
LeBeau, Dick	Defensive backfield	1976-79
Lewis, Sherman	Offensive coordinator	1992-99
Lind, Jim	Defensive assistant/quality control	1992-94
	Linebackers	1995-98
Lindsey, Dale	Linebackers	1986-87
Lord, Bob	Special teams	1975-76
	Offensive backfield	1977-78
Lovat, Tom	Assistant offensive line	1980
	Offensive line	1992-98
Mariucci, Steve	Quarterbacks	1992-95
Marshall, John	Special teams/linebackers	1980

Name	Assignment(s)	Years
	Linebackers	1981-82
McCarthy, Mike	Quarterbacks	1999
McCormick, Tom	Offensive backfield	1967-68
McGeorge, Rich	Assistant offensive line	2000
McLaughlin, Leon	Offensive line	1975-76
McLean, Ray (Scooter)	Backfield	1951-57
McMillan, Ernie	Offensive line	1978-83
Meyer, John	Linebackers	1975-79
	Defensive coordinator	1980-83
Meyers, Bill	Assistant offensive line	1982-83
Miles, Trent	Offensive assistant/quality control	2000
Miller, Brad	Defensive assistant/quality control	2001-02
	Assistant defensive line	2003
Modzelewski, Dick	Defensive coordinator/defensive line	1984-87
Molenda, Bo	Backfield	1947-48
Mornhinweg, Marty	Offensive assistant/quality control	1995
	Quarterbacks	1996
Morton, Jack	Defensive line	1957-58
Moseley, Dick	Outside linebackers	1988-91
Moss, Perry	Quarterbacks	1974
Nolting, Ray	Backfield	1950
Novak, Frank	Special teams	2000-02
	Special teams consultant	2003
Ortmayer, Steve	Special teams	1999
Paterra, Herb	Linebackers/special teams	1984-85
Peete, Willie	Offensive backfield/special teams	1987
	Offensive backfield	1988-91
Pelini, Bo	Linebackers	2000-02
Philbin, Joe	Assistant offensive line	2003
Plasman, Dick	Ends	1950-52
Polonchek, John	Receivers/passing game	1972-74
Priefer, Chuck	Special teams/linebackers	1984
	Special teams	1985
Rehbein, Dick	Special assistant	1979-80
	Special teams	1981-83
Reid, Andy	Tight ends/assistant offensive line	1992-96
	Quarterbacks	1997-98
Reid, Floyd (Breezy)	Backfield	1958
Reynolds, Gary	Offensive assistant/quality control	1998
Rhodes, Ray	Defensive coordinator	1992-93
Richards, Ray	Defense	1958
Riederer, Russ	Strength/Conditioning	1991
Riley, Ken	Secondary	1984-85
Roach, Paul	Offensive coordinator	1975-76
Robinson, Wayne	Defensive secondary	1968-69
Roland, Johnny	Special assignments	1974
Rossley, Tom	Offensive coordinator	2000-03
Rubin, Barry	Strength/conditioning assistant	1995-98
	Strength/conditioning	1999-03
Ruel, Pat	Assistant offensive line	2001-02
Rymkus, Lou	Line	1954-57
Schnelker, Bob	Receivers	1966-68
	Receivers/passing game	1969-71
	Offensive coordinator	1982-85
Sefcik, George	Offensive backfield	1984-85
	Quarterbacks	1986-87
Sherman, Mike	Tight ends/assistant offensive line	1997-98
Sherman, Ray	Wide receivers	2000-03
Shurmur, Fritz	Defensive coordinator	1994-98
Skorich, Nick	Offensive line	1958
Slowik, Bob	Defensive backs	2000-01
	Assistant head coach/defensive backs	2002-03
Smith, Richard (Red)	Assistant coach	1935-43
Snyder, Bob	Backfield	1949
Starr, Bart	Quarterbacks	1972
Stidham, Tom	Line	1949
Stuber, Emmett (Abe)	Defensive backfield	1956
Sydney, Harry	General assistant	1994
	Running backs	1995-99
Taylor, John (Tarz)	Line	1950-52
Thomas, Emmitt	Defensive coordinator	1999
Tippett, Howard	Special teams	1988-91
Trafton, George	Line	1944
Trgovac, Mike	Defensive line	1999
Urich, Richard (Doc)	Defensive line	1981-83
Valesente, Bob	Linebackers	1992-94
	Defensive backs	1995-98
Vitt, Joe	Defensive backs	1999
vonAppen, Fred	Special teams	1979
	Defensive line	**1980
Voris, Dick	Ends	1961-62
Wampfler, Jerry	Offensive line	1984-87
Washington, Lionel	Assistant defensive backs	1999-2003
Wietecha, Ray	Offensive line	1965-68
	Running game	1969-70
Zampese, Ken	Offensive assistant/quality control	1999

* Hank Bullough resigned May 23, 1984, then returned in 1988.
**resigned Sept. 3, 1980.

First team recognition in **bold**.

AP — Associated Press (1940-present)
CP — *College and Pro Football News Weekly* (1987-present)
FD — *Football Digest* (1980-present)
FN — *Football News*, All-NFC (1985-present)
INS— International News Service (1937-40, 1942-45, 1949)
NEA—Newspaper Enterprise Association (1954-92)
NFL— Official League Selection by the NFL (1931-42)
NY — *New York Daily News* (1937-61, 1963-69)
PF — *Pro Football Illustrated* (1943-48)
PFW— *Pro Football Weekly* (1968-84, 1986-91, choices combined with Pro Football Writers of America 1992-present)
PFWA —Pro Football Writers of America (1938-40, 1966-present)
PG — *Green Bay Press-Gazette* (1923-31, 1933-35)
SI — *Sports Illustrated* (1981-present)
SN — *The Sporting News* (1948, 1954-81, 1983-present)
UP — United Press (1931-41, 1943-57)
UPI— United Press International (1958-96)
USA—*USA Today* (1990-present)

1923
  B - Curly Lambeau (PG)
1924
  B - Curly Lambeau (PG)
  E - Tillie Voss (**PG**)
1925
  G - George Abramson (PG)
  B - Verne Lewellen (PG)
  T - Dick Stahlman (PG)
1926
  B - Verne Lewellen (**PG**)
1927
  E - Lavvie Dilweg (**PG**)
  B - Verne Lewellen (**PG**)
1928
  E - Lavvie Dilweg (**PG**)
  B - Eddie Kotal (PG)
  B - Verne Lewellen (**PG**)
1929
  B - Johnny Blood (PG)
  E - Lavvie Dilweg (**PG**)
  C - Jug Earp (PG)
  T - Bill Kern (PG)
  B - Verne Lewellen (**PG**)
  G - Mike Michalske (**PG**)
1930
  E - Lavvie Dilweg (**PG**)
  B - Red Dunn (PG)
  T - Bill Kern (PG)
  G - Mike Michalske (**PG**)
  E - Tom Nash (PG)

1931
  C - Nate Barragar (UP)
  B - Johnny Blood (**NFL**, UP)
  E - Lavvie Dilweg (**NFL**, **UP**)
  B - Red Dunn (NFL, UP)
  T - Cal Hubbard (**NFL**, **UP**)
  G - Mike Michalske (**NFL**, **UP**)
  B - Bo Molenda (NFL)
  T - Dick Stahlman (NFL)
1932
  C - Nate Barragar (**NFL**, UP)
  E - Lavvie Dilweg (NFL, UP)
  B - Arnie Herber (**NFL**, **UP**)
  B - Clarke Hinkle (NFL, UP)
  T - Cal Hubbard (**NFL**, **UP**)
  E - Tom Nash (**UP**)
  G - Joe Zeller (UP)
1933
  E - Lavvie Dilweg (UP)
  B - Clarke Hinkle (PG, UP)
  T - Cal Hubbard (**PG**, **NFL**, **UP**)
1934
  C - Nate Barragar (NFL)
  B - Clarke Hinkle (NFL, PG)
  G - Mike Michalske (NFL, **PG**)
1935
  C - Nate Barragar (PG)
  G - Lon Evans (NFL)
  B - Arnie Herber (NFL, PG)
  B - Clarke Hinkle (**UP**)
  E - Don Hutson (NFL, UP)
  G - Mike Michalske (**NFL**, **PG**, UP)
  B - George Sauer (**PG**)
  T - Ade Schwammel (**UP**)
1936
  G - Lon Evans (**NFL**, **UP**)
  E - Milt Gantenbein (NFL, **UP**)
  B - Arnie Herber (NFL)
  FB - Clarke Hinkle (**NFL**, **UP**)
  E - Don Hutson (**NFL**, **UP**)
  T - Ernie Smith (**NFL**, **UP**)
1937
  G - Lon Evans (**NFL**, NY)
  E - Milt Gantenbein (NFL)
  FB - Clarke Hinkle (**INS**, **NFL**, **NY**, **UP**)
  E - Don Hutson (**INS**, NFL, **NY**, UP)
  T - Ernie Smith (INS, NFL, NY)
1938
  E - Milt Gantenbein (NFL, UP)
  FB - Clarke Hinkle
       (**INS**, **NFL**, **NY**, **PFWA**, **UP**)
  E - Don Hutson (**INS**, **NFL**, **NY**, **PFWA**, **UP**)
  B - Cecil Isbell (INS, NFL, NY, PFWA, UP)
  G - Russ Letlow (**INS**, **NFL**, NY, **PFWA**, UP)
1939
  B - Clarke Hinkle (UP)
  E - Don Hutson (**INS**, **NFL**, **NY**, **PFWA**, **UP**)
  B - Cecil Isbell (INS)
  G - Russ Letlow (NY)
  T - Baby Ray (UP)

1940
  B - Clarke Hinkle (INS, NFL)
  E - Don Hutson (**AP**, INS, **NFL**, **NY**, **UPN**)
  B - Cecil Isbell (NFL, UP)
  G - Russ Letlow (NY)
  E - Carl Mulleneaux (UP)
1941
  FB - Clarke Hinkle (**AP**, **NFL**, **NY**)
  E - Don Hutson (**AP**, **NFL**, **NY**, **UP**)
  B - Cecil Isbell (AP, NFL, NY, UP)
  T - Baby Ray (NY, **UP**)
  E - Ray Riddick (NFL)
  C - George Svendsen (NFL, UP)
  G - Pete Tinsley (AP, NY)
1942
  E - Don Hutson (**AP**, **INS**, **NFL**, **NY**)
  G - Buckets Goldenberg (AP, INS, **NFL**, **NY**)
  B - Cecil Isbell (AP, INS, **NFL**, **NY**)
1943
  T - Chet Adams (AP, NY)
  C - Charley Brock (AP, PF)
  B - Tony Canadeo (**AP**, **INS**, **NY**, PF, UP)
  E - Don Hutson (**AP**, **INS**, **NY**, **PF**, **UP**)
  T - Baby Ray (INS, NY, **PF**, UP)
1944
  C - Charley Brock (UP)
  E - Don Hutson (**AP**, **INS**, **NY**, **PF**, **UP**)
  T - Baby Ray (INS, NY, **PF**, UP)

Packers fullback Clarke Hinkle was named to various All-Pro teams nine times from 1932 through 1941. He was inducted into the Pro Football Hall of Fame in 1964. Stiller-Lefebvre Collection

1945
C - Charley Brock (**AP, INS, NY, PF, UP**)
B - Ted Fritsch (INS, NY, **UP**)
E - Don Hutson (**AP**, INS, **NY, PF, UP**)

1946
C - Charley Brock (**PF**, UP)
FB - Ted Fritsch (**AP, NY, PF, UP**)
E - Nolan Luhn (PF)

1947
E - Larry Craig (**PF**)
B - Tony Canadeo (UP)
B - Walt Schlinkman (PF, UP)
G - Dick Wildung (PF, UP)

1948
HB - Tony Canadeo (PF, UP)
T - Dick Wildung (NY)

1949
HB - Tony Canadeo (AP, **INS**, NY, **UP**)
T - Dick Wildung (**NY**, UP)

1950
HB - Billy Grimes (AP, **NY**)
DT - Ed Neal (NY)
C - Clayton Tonnemaker (AP, **NY, UP**)

1951
C - Jay Rhodemyre (NY)

1952
E - Bill Howton (AP, NY, UP)

1953
DB - Bobby Dillon (**NY**)

1954
DB - Bobby Dillon (**AP**, NY)
DE - John Martinkovic (NY)
LB - Clayton Tonnemaker (AP, **NY**, UP)
DB - Val Joe Walker (AP)
LB - Roger Zatkoff (AP, **UP**)

1955
DB - Bobby Dillon (**AP, NEA, NY, SN, UP**)
RB - Howie Ferguson (AP, **NEA**, NY, **SN**, UP)
E - Bill Howton (NEA, NY)
QB - Tobin Rote (AP, **NEA**, NY)
LB - Roger Zatkoff (**AP**, NEA, NY, **SN**)

1956
DB - Bobby Dillon (AP, **NEA, NY, UP**)
E - Bill Howton (**AP, NEA, NY, UP**)
QB - Tobin Rote (AP, NEA, NY, UP)
LB - Roger Zatkoff (NEA, NY)

1957
DB - Bobby Dillon (**AP, NEA, NY, UP**)
E - Bill Howton (**AP, NEA, NY, UP**)
C - Jim Ringo (**AP, NEA**, UP)

1958
DB - Bobby Dillon (**AP, NEA, NY, UPI**)
C - Jim Ringo (AP, NEA, **NY**, UPI)

1959
DB - Bobby Dillon (NY)
LB - Bill Forester (NY)
T - Forrest Gregg (AP, NEA, UPI)
RB - Paul Hornung (AP, UPI)
C - Jim Ringo (**AP, NEA, NY, UPI**)

1960
LB - Bill Forester (**AP**, NEA, NY, **UPI**)
T - Forrest Gregg (**AP**, NEA, NY, UPI)
RB - Paul Hornung (**AP, NEA, NY, UPI**)
DT - Henry Jordan (**AP**, NEA, **NY, UPI**)
G - Jerry Kramer (**AP**, NY, UPI)
C - Jim Ringo (**AP, NEA, NY, UPI**)
RB - Jim Taylor (AP, NEA, NY, UPI)
CB - Jesse Whittenton (AP, UPI)

1961
LB - Dan Currie (**NEA, UPI**)
LB - Bill Forester (**AP**, NEA, **NY, UPI**)
T - Forrest Gregg (NY, **UPI**)
RB - Paul Hornung (**AP**, NEA, **NY, UPI**)
DT - Henry Jordan (**AP, NEA, NY, UPI**)
G - Jerry Kramer (NY)
C - Jim Ringo (**AP, NEA, NY, UPI**)
QB - Bart Starr (NEA, NY)
RB - Jim Taylor (**NEA**, NY, UPI)
G - Fuzzy Thurston (**AP, NEA, NY, UPI**)
CB - Jess Whittenton (**AP**, NEA, **UPI**)

1962
CB - Herb Adderley (**AP**, NEA, **UPI**)
LB - Dan Currie (**AP, NEA, UPI**)
DE - Willie Davis (**AP, UPI**)
LB - Bill Forester (**AP, NEA, UPI**)
T - Forrest Gregg (**AP, NEA, UPI**)
DT - Henry Jordan (**AP, NEA, UPI**)
G - Jerry Kramer (**AP, NEA, UPI**)
TE - Ron Kramer (**AP, NEA, UPI**)
LB - Ray Nitschke (AP, NEA)
C - Jim Ringo (**AP, NEA, UPI**)
QB - Bart Starr (AP, NEA, UPI)
RB - Jim Taylor (**AP, NEA, UPI**)
G - Fuzzy Thurston (AP, NEA, **UPI**)
S - Willie Wood (AP, NEA, UPI)

1963
CB - Herb Adderley (**AP**, NY, UPI)
LB - Dan Currie (AP, **NEA, NY**)
DE - Willie Davis (NEA, NY, UPI)
LB - Bill Forester (NEA, UPI)
T - Forrest Gregg (**AP, NEA, NY, UPI**)
DT - Henry Jordan (**AP, NEA, NY, UPI**)
G - Jerry Kramer (**AP, NEA, NY, UPI**)
TE - Ron Kramer (AP, NEA, NY, UPI)
FB - Tom Moore (AP)
LB - Ray Nitschke (NY)
C - Jim Ringo (**AP, NEA, NY, UPI**)
RB - Jim Taylor (AP, NEA, NY, UPI)
G - Fuzzy Thurston (UPI)
S - Willie Wood (**NEA**, UPI)

1964
CB - Herb Adderley (AP, NEA, NY, UPI)
DE - Willie Davis (**AP, NEA, NY, UPI**)
T - Forrest Gregg (**AP, NEA, NY, UPI**)
DT - Henry Jordan (**AP**, NY, **UPI**)
LB - Ray Nitschke (**AP**, NY, **UPI**)
QB - Bart Starr (AP)
RB - Jim Taylor (NEA, NY, UPI)
G - Fuzzy Thurston (NY)
S - Willie Wood (**AP, NEA**, NY, **UPI**)

One of the defensive line anchors during the Glory Years, Willie Davis was a member of a number of All-Pro teams from 1962-67. He's another Packer who's in the Hall of Fame. Stiller-Lefebvre Collection

1965
CB - Herb Adderley (**AP, NEA, NY, UPI**)
DE - Willie Davis (**AP, NEA, NY, UPI**)
T - Forrest Gregg (**AP**, NY, **UPI**)
LB - Ray Nitschke (AP, NY, **UPI**)
S - Willie Wood (**AP, NEA, NY, UPI**)

1966
CB - Herb Adderley (**AP, NEA, NY, PFWA, UPI**)
LB - Lee Roy Caffey (**AP**, NY, **UPI**)
DE - Willie Davis (**AP, NEA, NY, PFWA, UPI**)
T - Forrest Gregg (**AP, NEA, NY, PFWA, UPI**)
DT - Henry Jordan (AP, NY, UPI)
LB - Ray Nitschke (**AP, NEA, NY, PFWA, UPI**)
QB - Bart Starr (**AP, NEA, NY, PFWA, UPI**)
FB - Jim Taylor (UPI)
G - Fuzzy Thurston (NY)
S - Willie Wood (**AP, NEA, NY, PFWA, UPI**)

1967
CB - Herb Adderley (AP, NEA, NY)
DE - Willie Davis (**AP, NEA, NY, UPI**)
T - Forrest Gregg (**AP, NEA, NY, UPI**)
DB - Bob Jeter (**AP, NEA, NY, UPI**)
DT - Henry Jordan (NY)
G - Jerry Kramer (**AP, NEA, NY, UPI**)
LB - Ray Nitschke (AP, NY)
LB - Dave Robinson (**AP, NEA, NY, UPI**)
S - Willie Wood (**AP, NEA, NY, UPI**)

1968
E - Carroll Dale (NEA)
G - Gale Gillingham (NEA, UPI)
CB - Bob Jeter (NEA)
G - Jerry Kramer (AP)

LB - Dave Robinson (**NEA**, **NY**, PFWA, **UPI**)
S - Willie Wood (**AP**, NEA, **NY**, **PFWA**, **UPI**)
1969
CB - Herb Adderley (**AP**, NY, **PFW**, PFWA)
G - Gale Gillingham (**AP**, **NEA**, UPI)
LB - Ray Nitschke (NEA, PFWA)
LB - Dave Robinson (**AP**, **NEA**, **NY**, **PFW**, PFWA, **UPI**)
S - Willie Wood (NEA)
1970
G - Gale Gillingham (**AP**, **NEA**)
S - Willie Wood (NEA)
1971
RB - John Brockington (**AP**, **NEA**, **PFW**, **PFWA**)
G - Gale Gillingham (NEA, PFW)
1972
CB - Ken Ellis (**AP**, PFWA)
K - Chester Marcol (**AP**, **NEA**, **PFW**, **PFWA**)
1973
RB - John Brockington (AP, **NEA**, PFWA)
CB - Ken Ellis (PFWA)
G - Gale Gillingham (PFWA)
1974
G - Gale Gillingham (**NEA**)
LB - Ted Hendricks (**AP**, **NEA**, **PFW**, **PFWA**)
K - Chester Marcol (**AP**, **PFW**, **PFWA**)
1975
LB - Fred Carr (NEA)
1978
CB - Willie Buchanon (**AP**, NEA, **PFW**, **PFWA**)
1980
WR - James Lofton (AP, **NEA**, **PFW**, **PFWA**, **SN**)
1981
WR - James Lofton (**AP**, **NEA**, **PFW**, **PFWA**, **SN**)
1982
WR - James Lofton (**AP**, **NEA**)
LB - George Cumby (NEA)
LB - Mike Douglass (**PFW**)
1983
WR - James Lofton (**AP**, PFWA)
C - Larry McCarren (NEA)
LB - Mike Douglass (**SI**)
1984
TE - Paul Coffman (NEA)
WR - James Lofton (**NEA**)
1985
WR - James Lofton (NEA)
1988
LB - Tim Harris (AP, **NEA**, **SI**)
1989
LB - Tim Harris (**AP**, **NEA**, **PFW**, **PFWA**, **SI**, **SN**)
QB - Don Majkowski (AP)
G - Rich Moran (**NEA**)
LB - Sterling Sharpe (**AP**, **NEA**, **PFW**, **PFWA**, **SI**, **SN**)
1990
C - James Campen (**USA**)
WR - Sterling Sharpe (NEA)
1992
S - Chuck Cecil (**CP**)
TE - Jackie Harris (NEA)
WR - Sterling Sharpe (**AP**, **CP**, **FD**, **NEA**, **PFW**, **SN**)
1993
S - LeRoy Butler (**AP**, **FD**, **PFW**, **SI**, **SN**)

K - Chris Jacke (**AP**, **CP**)
WR - Sterling Sharpe (**AP**, **CP**, **FD**, **PFW**, **SN**)
DE - Reggie White (AP, **CP**, **FD**, **SN**)
1994
LB - Bryce Paup (**USA**)
DE - Reggie White (AP, **SI**)
1995
WR - Robert Brooks (**USA**)
TE - Mark Chmura (**CP**, **FD**)
QB - Brett Favre (**AP**, **FD**, **PFW**, **SI**, **SN**, **USA**)
DE - Reggie White (**AP**, **CP**, **FD**, **PFW**, **SN**, **USA**)
1996
S - LeRoy Butler (**AP**, **FD**, **PFW**, **SI**, **SN**, **USA**)
QB - Brett Favre (**AP**, **CP**, **FD**, **PFW**, **SI**, **SN**, **USA**)
PR - Desmond Howard (**CP**, **FD**, **PFW**, **SN**, **USA**)
S - Eugene Robinson (**SI**)
DE - Reggie White (**AP**, **CP**)
1997
S - LeRoy Butler (**AP**, **CP**, **PFW**, **SI**, **SN**, **USA**)
CB - Doug Evans (**FD**)
QB - Brett Favre (**AP**, **CP**, **FD**, **PFW**, **SN**, **USA**)
P - Craig Hentrich (**CP**)
ST - Travis Jervey (**PFW**)
DE - Reggie White (**AP**)
LB - Brian Williams (**USA**)
1998
S - LeRoy Butler (**AP**, **PFW**, **SN**, **USA**)
WR - Antonio Freeman (**AP**, **CP**, **FD**, **PFW**, **SI**, **SN**)
ST - Travis Jervey (**FD**)
KR - Roell Preston (**FD**, **PFW**)
DE - Reggie White (**AP**, **CP**, **FD**, **PFW**, **SN**)
1999
C - Frank Winters (**USA**)
2000
S - Darren Sharper (**AP**, **CP**, **PFW**, **SI**, **SN**, **USA**)
2002
QB - Brett Favre (AP)
S - Darren Sharper (AP, FD, **SN**)
2003
RB-Ahman Green (FD)
K- Ryan Longwell (FD)
G- Marco Rivera (FD, AP)

First Team All-NFC

1970
G - Gale Gillingham (AP, PFW, SN, UPI)
S - Willie Wood (SN)
1971
RB - John Brockington (AP, PFW, SN, PFW)
G - Gale Gillingham (PFW, SN, UPI)
1972
RB - John Brockington (AP, UPI, SN)
CB - Ken Ellis (AP, UPI)
K - Chester Marcol (AP, PFW, SN)
1973
RB - John Brockington (AP, PFW, SN, UPI)
CB - Ken Ellis (AP, PFW, SN, UPI)
G - Gale Gillingham (PFW)

1974
G - Gale Gillingham (AP, SN, UPI)
LB - Ted Hendricks (AP, PFW, SN, UPI)
K - Chester Marcol (PFW, SN, UPI)
1975
LB - Fred Carr (SN)
1978
CB - Willie Buchanon (AP, PFW, SN, UPI)
RB - Terdell Middleton (SN)
1980
WR - James Lofton (PFW, UPI)
1981
WR - James Lofton (PFW, UPI)
C - Larry McCarren (PFW)
1982
WR - James Lofton (UPI)
C - Larry McCarren (UPI)
1983
TE - Paul Coffman (PFW, UPI)
1984
TE - Paul Coffman (PFW, UPI)
P - Bucky Scribner (UPI)
1988
LB - Tim Harris (PFW)
1989
LB - Tim Harris (PFW, UPI)
WR - Sterling Sharpe (PFW, UPI)
1992
S - Chuck Cecil (PFW)
WR - Sterling Sharpe (PFW, UPI)
1993
S - LeRoy Butler (PFW, UPI)
WR - Sterling Sharpe (PFW, UPI)
DE - Reggie White (PFW, UPI)
1994
LB - Bryce Paup (PFW, UPI)
1995
TE - Mark Chmura (PFW)
QB - Brett Favre (PFW, UPI)
DE - Reggie White (PFW, UPI)
1996
S - LeRoy Butler (PFW)
QB - Brett Favre (PFW)
PR - Desmond Howard (PFW)
DE - Reggie White (PFW)
1997
S - LeRoy Butler (FN)
QB - Brett Favre (FN)
RB - Dorsey Levens (FN)
DE - Reggie White (FN)
1998
S - LeRoy Butler (FN)
WR - Antonio Freeman (FN)
DE - Reggie White (FN)
2000
K - Ryan Longwell (FN)
S - Darren Sharper (FN)
2001
RB - Ahman Green (FN)

2002
QB - Brett Favre (PFW)
S - Darren Sharper (PFW)

2003
QB - Brett Favre (PFW)
RB - Ahman Green (PFW)
G - Marco Rivera (PFW)

The Pro Bowl debuted on Jan. 14, 1951. The top players from the American and National Conferences participated in that game. When the conferences were renamed in 1954, the best of the Western and Eastern Conferences clashed on an annual basis. Beginning in 1971, with the merger of the NFL and AFL, the elite of the AFC and NFC battled.

Below is a list of the Pro Bowls and the Packers who participated in them (starters listed in bold face):

Packers Pro Bowl Selections

1951
HB - **Billy Grimes**
C - Ed Neal
*C - Clayton Tonnemaker
1952
HB - Billy Grimes
T - Dick Wildung
1953
E - Bill Howton
LB - Deral Teteak
E - Abner Wimberly
1954
DT - Dave Hanner
DE - John Martinkovic
LB - Clayton Tonnemaker
1955
DT - Dave Hanner
DE - John Martinkovic
LB - Roger Zatkoff
1956
DB - Bobby Dillon
FB - **Howie Ferguson**
E - Bill Howton
DE - John Martinkovic
LB - Roger Zatkoff
1957
DB - Bobby Dillon
E - **Bill Howton**
QB - Tobin Rote
LB - Roger Zatkoff
1958
DB - Bobby Dillon
E - **Bill Howton**
C - **Jim Ringo**
1959
DB - **Bobby Dillon**
C - Jim Ringo
1960
LB - Bill Forester
T - Forrest Gregg
HB - Paul Hornung
C - **Jim Ringo**
DB - Emlen Tunnell
1961
LB - Dan Currie
LB - Bill Forester
T - Forrest Gregg
HB - **Paul Hornung**
DT - Henry Jordan
C - **Jim Ringo**
QB - Bart Starr
FB - **Jim Taylor**
1962
LB - **Bill Forester**
T - Forrest Gregg
DT - **Henry Jordan**
WR - Max McGee
C - **Jim Ringo**
QB - **Bart Starr**
FB - **Jim Taylor**
DB - **Jesse Whittenton**

1963
LB - **Bill Forester**
T - **Forrest Gregg**
G - **Jerry Kramer**
TE - Ron Kramer
$FB - Tom Moore
C - **Jim Ringo**
QB - Bart Starr
*FB - Jim Taylor
S - **Willie Wood**
1964
CB - **Herb Adderley**
DE - Willie Davis
T - **Forrest Gregg**
DT - Henry Jordan
G - **Jerry Kramer**
C - **Jim Ringo**
FB - **Jim Taylor**
DB - **Jesse Whittenton**
1965
CB - Herb Adderley
DE - **Willie Davis**
T - **Forrest Gregg**
LB - **Ray Nitschke**
FB - **Jim Taylor**
S - **Willie Wood**
1966
CB - **Herb Adderley**
LB - **Lee Roy Caffey**
DE - **Willie Davis**
WR - Boyd Dowler
S - **Willie Wood**
1967
CB - **Herb Adderley**
DE - **Willie Davis**
T - **Forrest Gregg**
DT - Henry Jordan
LB - **Dave Robinson**
T - Bob Skoronski
QB - Bart Starr
S - **Willie Wood**
1968
CB - **Herb Adderley**
K - Don Chandler
DE - **Willie Davis**
WR - **Boyd Dowler**
T - **Forrest Gregg**
DB - Bob Jeter
G - **Jerry Kramer**
LB - **Dave Robinson**
S - **Willie Wood**
1969
RB - Donny Anderson
WR - Carroll Dale
T - **Forrest Gregg**
S - **Willie Wood**

1970
WR - **Carroll Dale**
G - **Gale Gillingham**
CB - Bob Jeter
LB - Dave Robinson
S - Willie Wood
1971
LB - Fred Carr
WR - Carroll Dale
G - Gale Gillingham
S - Willie Wood
1972
FB - John Brockington
G - Gale Gillingham
1973
FB - John Brockington
DT - Bob Brown
LB - Fred Carr
K - Chester Marcol
1974
RB - John Brockington
*CB - Willie Buchanon
LB - Jim Carter
CB - Ken Ellis
*G - Gale Gillingham
1975
CB - Willie Buchanon
CB - Ken Ellis
G - Gale Gillingham
LB - Ted Hendricks
K - Chester Marcol
1976
LB - Fred Carr
KR - Steve Odom
1979
CB - Willie Buchanon
DE - Ezra Johnson
WR - James Lofton
RB - Terdell Middleton
1981
WR - James Lofton
1982
WR - James Lofton
1983
TE - Paul Coffman
WR - John Jefferson
WR - James Lofton
C - Larry McCarren
1984
TE - Paul Coffman
WR - James Lofton
C - Larry McCarren
1985
TE - Paul Coffman
WR - James Lofton
1986
WR - James Lofton

1990
RB - Brent Fullwood
LB - **Tim Harris**
*QB - Don Majkowski
WR - **Sterling Sharpe**
1991
WR - Sterling Sharpe
1993
S - **Chuck Cecil**
QB - Brett Favre
WR - **Sterling Sharpe**
1994
S - LeRoy Butler
QB - Brett Favre
*WR - Sterling Sharpe
DE - **Reggie White**
1995
LB - **Bryce Paup**
*WR - Sterling Sharpe
*DE - Reggie White
1996
TE - **Mark Chmura**
QB - **Brett Favre**
DE - **Reggie White**
1997
S - **LeRoy Butler**
QB - **Brett Favre**
TE - Keith Jackson
DE - **Reggie White**
C - Frank Winters
1998
S - **LeRoy Butler**
TE - Mark Chmura
*QB - **Brett Favre**
ST - Travis Jervey
RB - **Dorsey Levens**
*DE - **Reggie White**
1999
S - **LeRoy Butler**
TE - **Mark Chmura**
WR - **Antonio Freeman**
KR - **Roell Preston**
DE - **Reggie White**
2001
S - **Darren Sharper**
2002
*QB - **Brett Favre**
RB - **Ahman Green**
TE - **Bubba Franks**
2003
*QB - **Brett Favre**
C - Mike Flanigan
TE - Bubba Franks
DE - Kabeer Gbaja-Biamila

$ - Moore replaced Taylor.
* - Selected, but did not play.
Starters in bold.

The Packers' preseason results since 1939 are listed below. Prior to that year, the team played non-professional teams such as Ironwood or Madison on an irregular basis as regular-season warmups. Starting with a unique doublehead-er against the Pirates in 1939, the team began to schedule at least one league opponent for its preseason schedule. The list below includes only exhibitions against league opponents or college all-star teams.

1939 (2-0-1)

8/25	7	Pittsburgh Pirates	7
8/25	17	Pittsburgh Pirates	0
9/4	31	at Southwest College All-Stars	20
	55		**27**

1940 (2-0-0)

8/29	45	at Chicago College All-Stars	28
9/2	28	Washington Redskins (M)	20
	73		**48**

1941 (1-0-1)

8/25	17	New York Giants	17
9/7	28	Philadelphia Eagles (M)	21
	45		**38**

1942 (2-1-0)

8/30	21	at Brooklyn Dodgers	16
9/7	7	Redskins at Baltimore	28
9/13	36	Western Army All-Stars (M)	21
	64		**65**

1943 (2-0-0)

9/5	23	Redskins at Baltimore	21
9/11	28	at Phil-Pitt Steagles	10
	51		**31**

1944 (1-1-0)

9/4	7	Redskins at Baltimore	20
9/10	28	Boston Yanks at Buffalo, NY	0
	35		**20**

1945 (2-2-0)

8/30	19	at Chicago College All-Stars	7
9/13	21	at Philadelphia Eagles	28
9/19	38	Steelers at Hershey, PA	12
9/23	7	at Washington Redskins	21
	85		**68**

1946 (0-3-0)

9/6	6	Philadelphia Eagles (M)	7
9/10	31	Redskins at Denver	35
9/20	21	at New York Giants	35
	58		**77**

1947 (3-1-0)

8/23	17	New York Giants	14
8/29	17	at Pittsburgh Steelers	24
9/14	14	New York Yanks (M)	10
9/21	31	Redskins at Baltimore	21
	79		**69**

1948 (3-0-0)

8/29	7	NY Giants at Minneapolis	0
9/5	9	Pittsburgh Steelers	7
9/11	43	Redskins at Birmingham, AL	0
	59		**7**

1949 (2-3-0)

8/20	0	Philadelphia Eagles	35
8/24	14	NY Giants at Syracuse, NY	7
8/28	3	at Pittsburgh Steelers	9
9/11	7	Bulldogs at Rock Island, IL	3
9/18	24	Washington Redskins (M)	35
	48		**89**

1950 (3-1-0)

8/12	7	Browns at Toledo, OH	38
8/16	17	Chicago Cardinals	14
8/29	10	New York Giants at Boston	0
9/10	16	Baltimore Colts (M)	14
	50		**66**

1951 (2-3-0)

8/25	17	Chicago Cardinals	14
9/9	10	Philadelphia Eagles (M)	14
9/12	0	49ers at Minneapolis, MN	20
9/16	6	Steelers at Buffalo, NY	35
9/23	14	Redskins at Alexandria, VA	7
	47		**90**

1952 (2-4-0)

8/16	0	New York Giants (M)	7
8/23	14	Cleveland Browns	21
8/29	6	Steelers at Latrobe, PA	7
9/7	7	at Chicago Cardinals	38
9/14	13	Redskins at Kansas City	7
9/17	23	Steelers at Minneapolis, MN	10
	63		**90**

1953 (1-4-0)

8/22	31	Giants at Minneapolis, MN	7
8/29	7	Cardinals at Spokane, WA	13
9/5	6	Washington Redskins	13
9/12	23	Pittsburgh Steelers (M)	26
9/19	13	at Cleveland Browns	21
	80		**80**

1954 (2-4-0)

8/14	10	Cardinals at Minneapolis, MN	27
8/21	13	Cleveland Browns	14
8/28	36	at Pittsburgh Steelers	14
9/4	13	Eagles at Hershey, PA	24
9/11	31	Redskins at Raleigh, NC	3
9/18	27	New York Giants (M)	38
	130		**120**

1955 (2-4-0)

8/13	31	Giants at Spokane, WA	24
8/20	7	Browns at Akron, OH	13
8/27	14	Pittsburgh Steelers	16
9/3	10	Eagles at Charleston, WV	24
9/10	31	Redskins at Winston Salem, NC	33
9/17	37	Chicago Cardinals (M)	28
	130		**138**

1956 (4-1-0)

8/18	27	Philadelphia Eagles (M)	6
8/25	17	New York Giants	13
9/1	21	at Cleveland Browns	20
9/8	10	Redskins at Winston Salem, NC	17
9/15	29	Chicago Cardinals at St. Louis	21
	104		**77**

1957 (5-0-1)

8/16	24	Chicago Cardinals at Miami	16
8/24	17	Cardinals at Austin, TX	14
8/28	16	Philadelphia Eagles (M)	13
9/7	13	New York Giants at Boston	10
9/14	20	Redskins at Winston Salem, NC	17
9/21	10	Steelers at Minneapolis, MN	10
	100		**80**

1958 (2-3-0)

8/20	0	Pittsburgh Steelers (M)	3
9/1	20	Philadelphia Eagles	17
9/6	41	New York Giants at Boston	20
9/13	14	Redskins at Winston Salem, NC	23
9/21	24	Cardinals at Minneapolis, MN	31
	99		**94**

1959 (4-2-0)

8/15	16	Chicago Bears (M)	19
8/23	24	at San Francisco 49ers	17
8/29	45	Eagles at Portland, OR	28
9/5	0	Giants at Bangor, ME	14
9/12	20	Redskins at Winston Salem, NC	13
9/20	13	Steelers at Minneapolis, MN	10
	118		**101**

1960 (6-0-0)

8/13	20	Steelers at New Orleans	13
8/22	16	New York Giants at Jersey City	7
8/27	35	Chicago Bears (M)	7
9/5	35	Chicago Cardinals	14
9/11	28	Cowboys at Minneapolis, MN	23
9/17	41	Redskins at Winston Salem, NC	7
	175		**71**

1961 (5-0-0)

8/11	30	at Dallas Cowboys	7
8/18	31	at St. Louis Cardinals	10
8/26	24	Chicago Bears (M)	14
9/4	20	New York Giants	17
9/9	31	Redskins at Columbus, GA	24
	136	**5-0-0**	**72**

1962 (6-0-0)

8/3	42	at Chicago College All-Stars	20
8/10	31	at Dallas Cowboys	7
8/18	41	Cardinals at Jacksonville, FL	14
8/25	35	Chicago Bears (M)	21
9/3	20	New York Giants	17
9/8	20	Redskins at Columbus, GA	14
	189		**93**

1963 (5-1-0)

8/2	17	at Chicago All-Stars	20
8/10	27	Pittsburgh Steelers at Miami	7
8/17	31	at Dallas Cowboys	10
8/24	26	Chicago Bears (M)	7
9/2	24	New York Giants	17
9/7	28	Redskins at Cedar Rapids, IA	17
	153		**78**

1964 (3-2-0)

8/8	7	Cardinals at New Orleans	20
8/15	34	New York Giants	10
8/22	21	Chicago Bears (M)	7
8/29	35	at Dallas Cowboys	3
9/5	17	at Cleveland Browns	20
	114		**60**

1965 (4-1-0)

8/14	44	New York Giants	7
8/21	31	Chicago Bears (M)	14
8/28	12	at Dallas Cowboys	21
9/4	30	at Cleveland Browns	14
9/11	31	St. Louis Cardinals	13
	148		**69**

1966 (3-2-0)

8/5	38	at Chicago College All-Stars	0
8/12	10	Chicago Bears (M)	13
8/20	3	at Dallas Cowboys	21
8/27	17	Pittsburgh Steelers	6
9/3	37	New York Giants (M)	10
	105		**50**

1967 (6-0-0)

8/4	27	at Chicago College All-Stars	0
8/12	31	Pittsburgh Steelers	20
8/18	18	Chicago Bears (M)	0
8/28	20	at Dallas Cowboys	3
9/2	30	at Cleveland Browns	21
9/9	31	New York Giants	14
	157		**58**

1968 (4-2-0)

8/2	34	at Chicago College All-Stars	17
8/10	14	New York Giants	15
8/19	7	Chicago Bears (M)	10
8/24	31	at Dallas Cowboys	27
8/31	21	Pittsburgh Steelers (M)	17
9/7	31	at Cleveland Browns	9
	138		**95**

1969 (4-2-0)

8/9	22	New York Giants	21
8/16	9	Chicago Bears (M)	19
8/23	13	at Dallas Cowboys	31
8/30	27	at Cleveland Browns	17
9/6	31	Pittsburgh Steelers	19
9/13	38	Atlanta Falcons at Canton, OH	24
	140		**131**

1970 (3-0-3)

8/8	31	New York Giants	31
8/15	6	Chicago Bears (M)	6
8/22	35	at Dallas Cowboys	34
8/30	37	at Oakland Raiders	7
9/5	10	Cincinnati Bengals (M)	10
9/12	34	Buffalo Bills	0
	153		88

1971 (2-4-0)

8/7	0	Chicago Bears (M)	2
8/14	13	Pittsburgh Steelers	16
8/21	10	Miami Dolphins (M)	7
8/28	13	Oakland Raiders	17
9/4	24	at Cincinnati Bengals	27
9/10	20	at Buffalo Bills	14
	80		83

1972 (4-2-0)

8/5	24	Cincinnati Bengals	14
8/12	14	at Miami Dolphins	13
8/19	3	at Houston Oilers	20
8/27	10	Chicago Bears (M)	7
9/2	10	St. Louis Cardinals	31
9/9	20	Kansas City Chiefs (M)	0
	81		85

1973 (3-2-1)

8/4	13	Chicago Bears (M)	13
8/11	10	Buffalo Bills	3
8/18	33	Houston Oilers (M)	14
8/26	21	at Kansas City Chiefs	16
9/1	22	Pittsburgh Steelers	30
9/8	10	at Cincinnati Bengals	13
	109		89

1974 (4-2-0)

8/2	16	at Buffalo Bills	13
8/10	13	St. Louis Cardinals (M)	0
8/17	20	Chicago Bears	10
8/24	21	Denver Broncos	31
8/30	10	at Miami Dolphins	21
9/6	26	Cincinnati Bengals (M)	24
	106		99

1975 (2-4-0)

8/9	23	Buffalo Bills	6
8/16	13	Chicago Bears (M)	9
8/23	10	at Cincinnati Bengals	27
8/30	17	New England Patriots (OT)	20
9/6	3	at Kansas City Chiefs	31
9/13	3	San Francisco 49ers	24
	69		117

1976 (2-4-0)

7/31	17	Cincinnati Bengals	23
8/7	10	Tampa Bay Buccaneers (M)	6
8/15	16	at New England Patriots	14
8/20	0	at Buffalo Bills	37
8/28	16	New York Giants	20
9/3	7	Atlanta Falcons (M)	26
	66		126

1977 (2-4-0)

8/6	23	Cincinnati Bengals	20
8/13	3	New England Patriots (M)	38
8/20	7	at Tampa Bay Buccaneers	10
8/27	9	Washington Redskins (M)	13
9/3	14	Cleveland Browns	19
9/9	24	Philadelphia Eagles	16
	80		116

1978 (1-3-0)

8/5	14	Kansas City Chiefs	17
8/11	12	at Washington Redskins	20
8/19	23	St. Louis Cardinals	17
8/26	14	Cincinnati Bengals (M)	17
	63		71

1979 (3-1-0)

8/4	14	Kansas City Chiefs	10
8/11	5	at Cincinnati Bengals	20
8/18	7	Buffalo Bills	6
8/25	45	Atlanta Falcons (M)	35
	71		71

1980 (0-4-1)

8/2	*0	San Diego Chargers at Canton	0
8/9	14	at Dallas Cowboys	17
8/16	3	Baltimore Colts (M)	17
8/23	0	at Buffalo Bills	14
8/30	0	Denver Broncos	38
	17		86

* called with 5:29 remaining because of electrical storm.

1981 (3-1-0)

8/8	21	at Dallas Cowboys	17
8/15	34	Oakland Raiders (M)	14
8/22	7	at Denver Broncos	17
8/29	35	Cleveland Browns	18
	97		66

1982 (2-2-0)

8/14	21	New York Jets	19
8/20	41	Cincinnati Bengals (M)	27
8/28	3	at Oakland Raiders	24
9/4	27	at New England Patriots	41
	92		111

1983 (1-3-0)

8/6	20	Cleveland Browns	21
8/12	21	at Seattle Seahawks	38
8/20	14	Philadelphia Eagles	27
8/27	39	at St. Louis Cardinals	27
	94		113

1984 (2-2-0)

8/4	17	at Dallas Cowboys	31
8/11	17	Chicago Bears (M)	10
8/18	24	at Los Angeles Rams	27
8/25	34	Indianapolis Colts	17
	92		85

1985 (1-3-0)

8/10	3	at Dallas Cowboys	27
8/17	2	at New York Giants	10
8/24	28	Atlanta Falcons (M)	24
8/31	20	New York Jets	30
	53	1-3-0	91

1986 (1-3-0)

8/9	38	New York Jets at Madison	14
8/16	14	New York Giants (M)	22
8/23	12	at Cincinnati Bengals	34
8/30	9	New England Patriots	16
	73		86

1987 (0-4-0)

8/15	14	Denver Broncos at Tempe, AZ	20
8/22	0	Redskins at Madison	33
8/29	20	Cincinnati Bengals	28
9/5	24	Cleveland Browns (M) (OT)	30
	58		111

1988 (1-2-1)

8/6	3	New York Giants	34
8/13	21	at Indianapolis Colts	25
8/19	21	Kansas City Chiefs (M) (OT)	21
8/27	27	New York Jets at Madison	24
	72		104

1989 (3-1-0)

8/12	28	New York Jets (M)	27
8/19	23	Indianapolis Colts	24
8/26	27	Buffalo Bills at Madison	24
9/1	16	at New England Patriots	0
	94		75

1990 (1-3-0)

8/11	10	Cleveland Browns	25
8/18	27	New Orleans Saints at Madison	13
8/25	14	Atlanta Falcons (M)	17
8/31	14	at Kansas City Chiefs	27
	65		82

1991 (2-2-0)

8/3	28	New England Patriots	7
8/10	20	at New Orleans Saints	31
8/17	35	Buffalo Bills at Madison	24
8/24	16	Cincinnati Bengals (M) (OT)	19
	99		81

1992 (1-3-0)

8/8	21	Kansas City Chiefs	13
8/16	7	New York Jets at Madison	24
8/22	13	at Los Angeles Rams (OT)	16
8/29	10	New England Patriots (M)	24
	51		77

1993 (1-4-0)

7/31	3	L.A. Raiders at Canton, OH	19
8/7	21	Kansas City Chiefs (M)	29
8/14	17	New Orleans Saints at Madison	26
8/20	17	at New England Patriots	21
8/27	41	Indianapolis Colts	10
	99		105

1994 (3-1-0)

8/6	14	L.A. Rams at Madison	6
8/13	24	Miami Dolphins (M)	31
8/19	13	at New Orleans Saints	10
8/26	24	New England Patriots	20
	75		67

1995 (3-1-0)

8/5	27	New Orleans Saints at Madison	17
8/13	36	at Pittsburgh Steelers	13
8/19	17	Indianapolis Colts	20
8/25	35	Washington Redskins	23
	115		73

1996 (3-1-0)

8/2	24	New England Patriots	7
8/11	24	Pittsburgh Steelers	17
8/17	17	at Baltimore Ravens	15
8/24	6	at Indianapolis Colts	30
	71		69

1997 (5-0-0)

7/26	20	Miami Dolphins	0
7/31	7	New England Patriots	3
8/8	37	at Oakland Raiders	24
8/16	35	Buffalo Bills at Toronto	3
8/22	22	N.Y. Giants at Madison	17
	121		47

1998 (2-3-0)

8/2	27	K.C. Chiefs at Tokyo (OT)	24
8/8	31	New Orleans Saints	7
8/16	21	Oakland Raiders	27
8/24	31	at Denver Broncos	34
8/28	7	at Miami Dolphins	21
	117		113

1999 (4-0-0)

8/14	27	New York Jets	16
8/23	27	Denver Broncos at Madison	12
8/28	38	at New Orleans Saints	17
9/2	25	Miami Dolphins	17
	117		62

2000 (2-2-0)

8/4	37	New York Jets	24
8/13	20	at Denver Broncos	26
8/21	14	at Miami Dolphins	17
8/26	34	Cleveland Browns	33
	105		100

2001 (2-2-0)

8/11	3	at Cleveland Browns	10
8/20	22	Denver Broncos	7
8/25	17	Miami Dolphins	12
8/31	13	at Oakland Raiders	24
	55		53

2002 (3-1-0)

8/10	13	at Philadelphia Eagles	20
8/17	29	at Arizona Cardinals	21
8/26	27	Cleveland Browns	20
8/30	21	Tennessee Titans	20
	90		81

2003 (2-3-0)

8/4	*0	Kansas City Chiefs at Canton	9
8/9	27	at Atlanta Falcons	21
8/15	38	at Cleveland Browns	31
8/23	7	Carolina Panthers	20
8/28	**3	Tennessee Titans	27
	75		108

* called with 20:49 remaining because of rain/lightning.

**delayed for 2 hours, 33 minutes by rain/lightning.

ALL-TIME RECORDS

The following lists include regular-season results only.

OVERALL RECORD

1921-2003

Year	W	L	T	Pct	PF	PA
1921	3	2	1	.600	70	55
1922	4	3	3	.571	70	54
1923	7	2	1	.778	85	34
1924	7	4	0	.636	108	38
1925	8	5	0	.615	151	110
1926	7	3	3	.700	151	61
1927	7	2	1	.778	113	43
1928	6	4	3	.600	120	92
1929	12	0	1	1.000	198	22
1930	10	3	1	.769	234	111
1931	12	2	0	.857	291	87
1932	10	3	1	.769	152	63
1933	5	7	1	.417	170	107
1934	7	6	0	.538	156	112
1935	8	4	0	.667	181	96
1936	10	1	1	.909	248	118
1937	7	4	0	.636	220	122
1938	8	3	0	.727	223	118
1939	9	2	0	.818	233	153
1940	6	4	1	.600	238	155
1941	10	1	0	.909	258	120
1942	8	2	1	.800	300	215
1943	7	2	1	.778	264	172
1944	8	2	0	.800	238	141
1945	6	4	0	.600	258	173
1946	6	5	0	.545	148	158
1947	6	5	1	.545	274	210
1948	3	9	0	.250	154	290
1949	2	10	0	.167	114	329
1950	3	9	0	.250	244	406
1951	3	9	0	.250	254	375
1952	6	6	0	.500	295	312
1953	2	9	1	.182	200	338
1954	4	8	0	.333	234	251
1955	6	6	0	.500	258	276
1956	4	8	0	.333	264	342
1957	3	9	0	.250	218	311
1958	1	10	1	.091	193	382
1959	7	5	0	.583	248	246
1960	8	4	0	.667	332	209
1961	11	3	0	.786	391	223
1962	13	1	0	.929	415	148
1963	11	2	1	.846	369	206
1964	8	5	1	.615	342	245
1965	10	3	1	.769	316	224
1966	12	2	0	.857	335	163
1967	9	4	1	.692	332	209
1968	6	7	1	.462	281	227
1969	8	6	0	.571	269	221
1970	6	8	0	.429	196	293
1971	4	8	2	.333	274	298
1972	10	4	0	.714	304	226
1973	5	7	2	.429	202	259
1974	6	8	0	.429	210	206
1975	4	10	0	.286	226	285
1976	5	9	0	.357	218	299
1977	4	10	0	.286	134	219
1978	8	7	1	.531	249	269
1979	5	11	0	.313	246	316
1980	5	10	1	.344	231	371
1981	8	8	0	.500	324	361
1982	5	3	1	.611	226	169
1983	8	8	0	.500	429	439
1984	8	8	0	.500	390	309
1985	8	8	0	.500	337	355
1986	4	12	0	.250	254	418
1987	5	9	1	.367	255	300
1988	4	12	0	.250	240	315
1989	10	6	0	.625	362	356
1990	6	10	0	.375	271	347
1991	4	12	0	.250	273	313
1992	9	7	0	.563	276	296
1993	9	7	0	.563	340	282
1994	9	7	0	.563	382	287
1995	11	5	0	.688	404	314
1996	13	3	0	.813	456	210
1997	13	3	0	.813	422	282
1998	11	5	0	.688	408	319
1999	8	8	0	.500	357	341
2000	9	7	0	.563	353	323
2001	12	4	0	.750	390	266
2002	12	4	0	.750	398	328
2003	10	6	0	.625	442	307
Totals	**602**	**474**	**36**	**.558**	**21,689**	**19,151**

GREEN BAY RECORD

1921-2003

Year	W	L	T	Pct	PF	PA
1921	3	1	0	.750	67	32
1922	3	1	1	.750	36	16
1923	4	2	1	.667	56	27
1924	5	0	0	1.000	71	3
1925	6	0	0	1.000	119	23
1926	4	1	2	.800	90	19
1927	6	1	0	.857	84	14
1928	3	2	2	.600	84	51
1929	5	0	0	1.000	79	4
1930	6	0	0	1.000	128	32
1931	8	0	0	1.000	207	40
1932	5	0	1	1.000	82	17
1933	3	1	1	.750	113	30
1934	3	2	0	.600	85	33
1935	4	1	0	.800	87	21
1936	3	1	0	.750	64	57
1937	2	2	0	.500	70	41
1938	2	2	0	.500	53	36
1939	3	1	0	.750	85	60
1940	2	2	0	.500	82	98
1941	2	1	0	.667	57	34
1942	2	1	0	.667	128	96
1943	1	0	1	1.000	56	35
1944	3	0	0	1.000	106	56
1945	2	1	0	.667	78	62
1946	1	2	0	.333	30	61
1947	2	1	0	.667	73	51
1948	2	1	0	.667	56	66
1949	0	3	0	.000	17	95
1950	2	2	0	.500	94	131
1951	1	3	0	.250	102	110
1952	1	2	0	.333	73	90
1953	1	2	0	.333	57	45
1954	0	3	0	.000	40	52
1955	3	0	0	1.000	75	34
1956	0	3	0	.000	53	74
1957	1	2	0	.333	52	72
1958	1	2	1	.333	78	102
1959	4	0	0	1.000	79	36
1960	3	1	0	.750	118	54
1961	4	0	0	1.000	134	34
1962	4	0	0	1.000	109	27
1963	3	1	0	.750	104	47
1964	2	2	0	.500	96	64
1965	3	1	0	.750	81	55
1966	3	1	0	.750	77	53
1967	2	1	1	.667	60	51
1968	1	3	0	.250	60	65
1969	3	1	0	.750	100	54
1970	2	2	0	.500	68	114
1971	2	2	0	.500	104	93
1972	2	2	0	.500	80	71
1973	1	2	1	.375	62	96
1974	1	3	0	.250	64	76
1975	2	2	0	.500	74	79
1976	2	2	0	.500	76	69
1977	1	3	0	.250	26	64
1978	2	1	1	.625	46	59
1979	1	4	0	.200	83	98
1980	3	1	0	.750	45	40
1981	3	2	0	.600	113	110
1982	0	1	0	.000	10	30
1983	3	2	0	.600	172	134
1984	3	2	0	.600	127	89
1985	3	2	0	.600	111	80
1986	0	5	0	.000	42	125
1987	1	4	0	.200	68	98
1988	1	4	0	.200	54	97
1989	3	2	0	.600	104	104
1990	1	4	0	.200	89	120
1991	1	4	0	.200	56	99
1992	3	2	0	.600	99	92
1993	4	1	0	.800	105	60
1994	5	0	0	1.000	127	43
1995	7	1	0	.875	214	135
1996	8	0	0	1.000	252	101
1997	8	0	0	1.000	233	145
1998	7	1	0	.875	229	161
1999	5	3	0	.625	203	182
2000	6	2	0	.750	172	149
2001	7	1	0	.875	208	99
2002	8	0	0	1.000	214	123
2003	5	3	0	.625	224	140
Totals	**248**	**130**	**13**	**.651**	**7,939**	**5,835**

AWAY RECORD

1921-2003

Year	W	L	T	Pct	PF	PA
1921	0	1	1	.000	3	23
1922	1	2	2	.333	34	38
1923	3	0	0	1.000	29	7
1924	2	4	0	.333	37	35
1925	2	5	0	.286	32	87
1926	3	2	1	.600	61	42
1927	1	1	1	.500	29	29
1928	3	2	1	.600	36	41
1929	7	0	1	1.000	119	18
1930	4	3	1	.571	106	79
1931	4	2	0	.667	84	47
1932	5	3	0	.625	70	46
1933	2	5	0	.286	50	67
1934	3	3	0	.500	51	64
1935	3	2	0	.600	81	63
1936	5	0	1	1.000	118	51
1937	3	2	0	.600	79	61
1938	4	1	0	.800	107	68
1939	4	1	0	.800	97	59
1940	2	2	1	.500	101	48
1941	5	0	0	1.000	133	59
1942	4	1	1	.800	110	91
1943	5	1	0	.833	166	90
1944	3	2	0	.600	91	72
1945	2	3	0	.400	85	76
1946	4	2	0	.667	91	69
1947	2	3	1	.400	140	117
1948	1	5	0	.167	81	135
1949	1	5	0	.167	57	151
1950	0	6	0	.000	101	209
1951	1	5	0	.167	117	204
1952	3	3	0	.500	147	162
1953	1	4	1	.200	116	191
1954	2	4	0	.333	118	146
1955	1	5	0	.167	106	169
1956	2	4	0	.333	124	194
1957	2	4	0	.333	108	139
1958	0	6	0	.000	86	223
1959	3	3	0	.500	139	137
1960	4	2	0	.667	142	108
1961	5	2	0	.714	196	145
1962	6	1	0	.857	217	98
1963	5	1	1	.833	173	125
1964	4	2	1	.667	177	119
1965	4	2	1	.667	196	146
1966	6	1	0	.857	158	97
1967	5	2	0	.714	187	141
1968	4	2	1	.667	165	113
1969	3	4	0	.429	128	141
1970	2	5	0	.286	75	139
1971	1	5	1	.214	101	149
1972	6	1	0	.857	165	108
1973	2	5	0	.286	77	136
1974	2	5	0	.286	88	102
1975	1	6	0	.143	83	146
1976	1	6	0	.143	73	166
1977	2	5	0	.286	79	100
1978	3	5	0	.375	81	109
1979	1	7	0	.125	92	176
1980	1	6	1	.188	132	238
1981	4	4	0	.500	169	184
1982	2	2	1	.500	122	88
1983	3	5	0	.375	175	237
1984	3	5	0	.375	163	167
1985	3	5	0	.375	165	220
1986	3	5	0	.375	136	221
1987	3	4	0	.429	137	152
1988	2	6	0	.250	115	176
1989	4	4	0	.500	192	192
1990	3	5	0	.375	124	187
1991	2	6	0	.250	162	150
1992	3	5	0	.375	93	156
1993	3	5	0	.375	156	178
1994	2	6	0	.250	182	173
1995	4	4	0	.500	190	179
1996	5	3	0	.625	204	109
1997	5	3	0	.625	189	137
1998	4	4	0	.500	179	158
1999	3	5	0	.375	154	159
2000	3	5	0	.375	181	174
2001	5	3	0	.625	182	167
2002	4	4	0	.500	184	205
2003	5	3	0	.625	218	167
Totals	**249**	**283**	**20**	**.469**	**9,997**	**10,345**

MILWAUKEE RECORD

1933-1994

Year	W	L	T	Pct	PF	PA
1933	0	1	0	.000	7	10
1934	1	1	0	.500	20	15
1935	1	1	0	.500	13	12
1936	2	0	0	1.000	66	10
1937	2	0	0	1.000	71	20
1938	2	0	0	1.000	63	14
1939	2	0	0	1.000	51	34
1940	2	0	0	1.000	55	9
1941	3	0	0	1.000	68	27
1942	2	0	0	1.000	62	28
1943	1	1	0	.500	42	47
1944	2	0	0	1.000	41	13
1945	2	0	0	1.000	95	35
1946	1	1	0	.500	27	28
1947	2	1	0	.667	61	42
1948	0	3	0	.000	17	89
1949	1	2	0	.333	40	83
1950	1	1	0	.500	49	66
1951	1	1	0	.500	35	61
1952	2	1	0	.667	75	60
1953	0	3	0	.000	27	102
1954	2	1	0	.667	76	53
1955	2	1	0	.667	77	73
1956	2	1	0	.667	87	74
1957	0	3	0	.000	58	100
1958	0	2	0	.000	29	57
1959	0	2	0	.000	30	73
1960	1	1	0	.500	72	47
1961	2	1	0	.667	61	44
1962	3	0	0	1.000	89	23
1963	3	0	0	1.000	92	34
1964	2	1	0	.667	69	62
1965	3	0	0	1.000	39	23
1966	3	0	0	1.000	100	13
1967	2	1	0	.667	85	17
1968	1	2	0	.333	56	49
1969	2	1	0	.667	41	26
1970	2	1	0	.667	53	40
1971	1	1	1	.500	69	56
1972	2	1	0	.667	59	47
1973	2	0	1	.833	63	27
1974	3	0	0	1.000	58	28
1975	1	2	0	.333	69	60
1976	2	1	0	.667	69	64
1977	1	2	0	.333	29	55
1978	3	1	0	.750	122	101
1979	3	0	0	1.000	71	42
1980	1	3	0	.250	54	93
1981	1	2	0	.333	42	67
1982	3	0	0	1.000	94	51
1983	2	1	0	.667	82	68
1984	2	1	0	.667	100	53
1985	2	1	0	.667	61	55
1986	1	2	0	.333	76	72
1987	1	1	1	.500	50	50
1988	1	2	0	.333	71	42
1989	3	0	0	1.000	66	60
1990	2	1	0	.667	58	40
1991	1	2	0	.333	55	64
1992	3	0	0	1.000	84	48
1993	2	1	0	.667	79	44
1994	2	1	0	.667	73	71
Totals	**105**	**61**	**3**	**.630**	**3,753**	**2,971**

The Pro Football Hall of Fame in Canton, Ohio, opened on Sept. 7, 1963. Seventeen charter members were inducted, including four who had ties to the Packers. At present, 25 players and coaches (in bold) in Canton spent part or all of their careers in Green Bay.

1963
Sammy Baugh, QB, coach, 1937-52, '60-61, '64
Bert Bell, coach, NFL Commissioner, 1936-41, '46-59
Joe Carr, League President, 1921-39
Earl (Dutch) Clark, back, coach, 1931-42
Harold (Red) Grange, back, 1925, '27, '29-34
George Halas, player, coach, founder, 1919-67
Mel Hein, C, co-coach, 1931-45, '47
Wilbur (Pete) Henry, T, coach, 1920-23, '25-28
Robert (Cal) Hubbard, T, 1927-36
Don Hutson, E, 1935-45
Earl (Curly) Lambeau, HB, coach, founder, 1919-53
Tim Mara, founder, 1925-29
George Marshall, founder, 1933-69
Johnny (Blood) McNally, HB, coach, 1925-39
Bronko Nagurski, FB, 1930-37, '43
Ernie Nevers, FB, coach, 1926-27, '29-31, '39
Jim Thorpe, HB, coach, 1920-26, '28

1964
Jimmy Conzelman, player, coach, 1920-30, '40-42, '46-48
Ed Healy, T, 1920-27
Clarke Hinkle, FB, 1932-41
Roy (Link) Lyman, T, 1922-28, '30-31, '33-34
August (Mike) Michalske, G, 1927-35, '37
Art Rooney, founder, 1933-88
George (Brute) Trafton, C, 1920-32

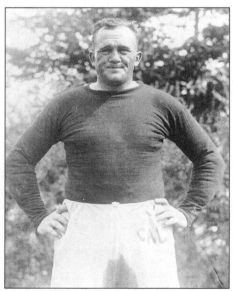

Tackle Cal Hubbard was among the charter members named to the Pro Football Hall of Fame in 1963. He made the NFL's All-Pro team three times while a Packer (1931-33). Stiller-Lefebvre Collection

1965
Guy Chamberlain, player, coach, 1920-27
John (Paddy) Driscoll, player, coach, 1920-29, '56-57
Danny Fortmann, G, 1936-43
Otto Graham, QB, coach, 1946-55, '66-68
Sid Luckman, QB, 1939-50
Steve Van Buren, HB, 1944-51
Bob Waterfield, QB, coach, 1945-52, '60-62

1966
Bill Dudley, HB, 1942, '45-51, '53
Joe Guyon, HB, 1920-25, '27
Arnie Herber, HB, 1930-40, '44-45
Walt Kiesling, T, coach, 1926-44, '54-56
George McAfee, HB, 1940-41, '45-50
Steve Owen, T, coach, 1924-53
Hugh (Shorty) Ray, statistician, 1938-56
Clyde (Bulldog) Turner, C, coach, 1940-52, '62

1967
Chuck Bednarik, C-LB, 1949-62
Charles Bidwell, owner, 1933-47
Paul Brown, coach, 1946-62, '68-75
Bobby Layne, QB, 1948-62
Dan Reeves, owner, 1941-71
Ken Strong, HB, 1929-35, 39, '44-47
Joe Stydahar, T, 1936-42, '45-46
Emlen Tunnell, DB, 1948-61

1968
Cliff Battles, HB, 1932-37
Art Donovan, T, 1950-61
Elroy Hirsch, E, 1946-57
Wayne Millner, E, 1936-41, '45
Marion Motley, FB, 1946-54
Charles Trippi, HB, 1947-55
Alex Wojciechowicz, C, 1938-50

1969
Glen (Turk) Edwards, T, coach, 1932-40, '46-48
Earl (Greasy) Neal, coach, 1941-50
Leo Nomellini, T, 1950-63
Joe Perry, HB, 1948-63
Ernie Stautner, T, 1950-63

1970
Jack Christiansen, HB, 1951-58
Tom Fears, E, coach, 1948-56, '67-70
Hugh McElhenny, HB, 1952-64
Pete Pihos, E, 1947-55

1971
Jim Brown, FB, 1957-65
Bill Hewitt, E, 1932-39, '43
Frank (Bruiser) Kinard, T, 1938-44, '46-47
Vince Lombardi, coach, 1959-67, '69
Andy Robustelli, DE, 1951-64
Y.A. Tittle, QB, 1948-64
Norm Van Brocklin, QB, coach, 1949-66, '68-74

1972
Lamar Hunt, founder, 1960-91
Gino Marchetti, E, 1952-64, '66
Ollie Matson, HB, 1952, '54-66
Clarence (Ace) Parker, HB, 1937-41, '45-46

1973
Raymond Berry, E, 1955-67
Jim Parker, G-T, 1957-67
Joe Schmidt, LB, coach, 1953-65, '67-72

1974
Tony Canadeo, HB, 1941-44, '46-52
Bill George, LB, 1952-66
Lou Groza, T-K, 1946-59, '61-67
Dick (Night Train) Lane, DB, 1952-65

Mike Michalske, a 60-minute-per-game lineman on the Packers championship teams in 1929-31, was elected to the Pro Football Hall of Fame in 1964. He was named to various All-Pro teams in five different seasons with the Packers. Stiller-Lefebvre Collection

1975
Roosevelt Brown, T, 1953-65
George Connor, T-LB, 1948-55
Dante Lavelli, E, 1946-56
Lenny Moore, HB, 1956-67

1976
Ray Flaherty, E, coach, 1927-29, 31-42, 46-49
Len Ford, DE, 1948-58
Jim Taylor, FB, 1958-67

1977
Frank Gifford, HB, 1952-60, '62-63
Forrest Gregg, T, coach, 1956, '58-70, '75-77, '80-87
Gale Sayers, HB, 1965-71
Bart Starr, QB, coach, 1956-71, '75-83
Bill Willis, G, 1946-53

1978
Lance Alworth, E, 1962-72
Weeb Ewbank, coach, 1954-73
Alphonse (Tuffy) Leemans, back, 1936-43
Ray Nitschke, LB, 1958-72
Larry Wilson, DB, 1960-73

1979
Dick Butkus, LB, 1965-73
Yale Lary, DB, 1952-53, '56-64
Ron Mix, T, 1960-70
Johnny Unitas, QB, 1956-73

1980
Herb Adderley, DB, 1961-72
David (Deacon) Jones, DE, 1961-74
Bob Lilly, DT, 1961-74
Jim Otto, C, 1960-74

1981
Morris (Red) Badgro, HB, 1927, '30-36
George Blanda, QB-K, 1949-58, '60-75
Willie Davis, DE, 1958-69
Jim Ringo, C, 1953-67

1982
Doug Atkins, DE, 1953-69
Sam Huff, LB, 1956-67, '69
George Musso, G-T, 1933-44
Merlin Olsen, DT, 1952-76

1983
Bobby Bell, LB, 1963-74
Sid Gillman, coach, 1955-69, '71, '73-74
Sonny Jurgensen, QB, 1957-74
Bobby Mitchell, HB-FL, 1958-68
Paul Warfield, WR, 1964-74, '76-77

1984
Willie Brown, DB, 1963-78
Mike McCormack, T, coach, 1951, '53-62, '73-75, '80-82
Charley Taylor, WR, 1964-77
Arnie Weinmeister, T, 1948-53

1985
Frank Gatski, C, 1946-57
Joe Namath, QB, 1965-77
Pete Rozelle, NFL Commissioner, 1960-89
O.J. Simpson, HB, 1969-79
Roger Staubach, QB, 1969-79

1986
Paul Hornung, HB, 1957-62, '64-66
Ken Houston, DB, 1967-80
Willie Lanier, LB, 1967-77
Fran Tarkenton, QB, 1961-78
Doak Walker, HB, 1950-55

1987
Larry Csonka, FB, 1968-79
Len Dawson, QB, 1957-75
Joe Greene, DT, 1969-81
John Henry Johnson, FB, 1954-66
Jim Langer, C, 1970-81
Don Maynard, WR, 1958-73
Gene Upshaw, G, 1967-81

After spending much of his Hall of Fame career with the Giants, safety Emlen Tunnell spent 1959-61 with the Packers. He made the Pro Bowl squad nine times. Stiller-Lefebvre Collection

1988
Fred Biletnikoff, WR, 1965-78
Mike Ditka, TE, 1961-72
Jack Ham, LB, 1971-82
Alan Page, DE, 1967-81

1989
Mel Blount, CB, 1970-83
Terry Bradshaw, QB, 1970-83
Art Shell, T, 1968-82
Willie Wood, S, 1960-71

1990
Buck Buchanon, DT, 1963-75
Bob Griese, QB, 1967-80
Franco Harris, FB, 1972-83
Ted Hendricks, LB, 1969-83
Jack Lambert, LB, 1974-84
Tom Landry, DB, coach, 1949-55, '60-88
Bob St. Clair, T, 1953-63

1991
Earl Campbell, RB, 1978-85
John Hannah, G, 1973-85
Stan Jones, G, 1954-66
Tex Schramm, general manager, 1960-89
Jan Stenerud, K, 1967-85

1992
Lem Barney, CB, 1967-77
Al Davis, team/league administrator, 1963-present
John Mackey, TE, 1963-72
John Riggins, RB, 1971-79, '81-85

1993
Dan Fouts, QB, 1973-87
Larry Little, G, 1967-80
Chuck Noll, coach, 1969-91
Walter Payton, RB, 1975-87
Bill Walsh, coach, 1979-88

1994
Tony Dorsett, RB, 1977-88
Bud Grant, coach, 1967-83, '85
Jimmy Johnson, CB, 1961-76
Leroy Kelly, RB, 1964-73
Jackie Smith, TE, 1963-78
Randy White, DT, 1975-88

1995
Jim Finks, QB/executive, 1949-55/1964-93
Henry Jordan, DT, 1957-69
Steve Largent, WR, 1976-84
Lee Roy Selmon, DE, 1976-84
Kellen Winslow, TE, 1979-87

1996
Lou Creekmur, T/G, 1950-59
Dan Dierdorf, T, 1971-83
Joe Gibbs, coach, 1981-92
Charlie Joiner, WR, 1969-86
Mel Renfro, DB, 1964-77

1997
Mike Haynes, CB, 1976-89
Wellington Mara, owner, 1937-present
Don Shula, DB/coach, 1951-57/1963-95
Mike Webster, C, 1974-90

1998
Paul Krause, S, 1964-79
Tommy McDonald, WR, 1957-68
Anthony Munoz, T, 1980-92
Mike Singletary, LB, 1981-92
Dwight Stephenson, C, 1980-87

Walt Kiesling played and coached in the NFL for 34 years, including a stint with the Packers as a player in the late 1930s and assistant coach from 1945-48. He was elected to the Hall of Fame in 1966. Stiller-Lefebvre Collection

1999
Eric Dickerson, RB, 1983-93
Tom Mack, G, 1966-78
Ozzie Newsome, TE, 1978-90
Billy Shaw, G, 1961-69
Lawrence Taylor, LB, 1981-93

2000
Howie Long, DE, 1981-93
Ronnie Lott, DB, 1981-94
Joe Montana, QB, 1979-94
Dan Rooney, owner, 1955-present
Dave Wilcox, LB, 1964-74

2001
Nick Buoniconti, LB, 1962-74, 76
Marv Levy, coach, 1978-82, '86-97
Mike Munchak, G, 1982-93
Jackie Slater, T, 1976-95
Lynn Swann, WR, 1974-82
Ron Yary, T, 1968-82
Jack Youngblood, DE, 1971-84

2002
George Allen, coach, 1966-77
Dave Casper, TE, 1974-84
Dan Hampton, DE/DT, 1979-90
Jim Kelly, QB, 1986-96
John Stallworth, WR, 1974-87

2003
Marcus Allen, RB, 1982-97
Elvin Bethea, DE, 1968-83
Joe DeLamielleure, G, 1973-85
James Lofton, WR, 1978-93
Hank Stram, coach, 1960-74, '76-77

2004
Bob Brown, T, 1964-73
Carl Eller, DE, 1964-79
John Elway, QB, 1983-98
Barry Sanders, RB, 1989-98

PACKER HALL OF FAME

The permanent Green Bay Packer Hall of Fame was dedicated on April 3, 1976. Earlier, a temporary hall had been set up each summer at the Brown County Veterans Memorial Arena. That display was first opened to the public on July 1, 1967.

On Sept. 19, 1970, the Packer Hall of Fame Association held its first induction banquet and honored eight former players.

The Hall of Fame closed its building adjacent to the Arena after the 2002 season and moved into the new atrium on the east side of Lambeau Field in 2003.

September, 1970
Bernard (Boob) Darling, C, 1927-31
LaVern (Lavvie) Dilweg, E, 1927-34
Francis (Jug) Earpe, T, 1922-32
Robert (Cal) Hubbard, T, 1929-33, '35
Earl (Curly) Lambeau, HB, coach, 1919-49
Verne Lewellen, B, 1924-32
August (Mike) Michalske, G, 1929-35, '37

January, 1972
Hank Bruder, B, 1931-39
Milt Gantenbein, E, 1931-40
Charles (Buckets) Goldenberg, B-G, 1933-45
Arnie Herber, HB, 1930-40
Clarke Hinkle, FB, 1932-41
Don Hutson, E, 1935-45
Cecil Isbell, HB, 1938-42
Joe Laws, HB, 1934-45
Russ Letlow, G, 1936-42, '46
George Svendsen, C, 1935-37, '40-41

January, 1973
Charley Brock, C, 1939-47
Tony Canadeo, HB, 1941-44, '46-52
Larry Craig, E, 1939-49
Bob Forte, HB, 1946-50, '52-53
Ted Fritsch, FB, 1942-50
Bob Monnett, HB, 1933-38
Buford (Baby) Ray, T, 1938-48
Andy Uram, B, 1938-43
Dick Wildung, G, 1946-51, '53
Howard (Whitey) Woodin, G, 1922-31

January, 1974
Al Carmichael, HB, 1953-58
Fred Cone, FB, 1951-57
Bobby Dillon, DB, 1952-59
Howie Ferguson, FB, 1953-58
Bill Forester, LB, 1953-63
Dave Hanner, DT, 1952-64
Bill Howton, E, 1952-58
John Martinkovic, DE, 1951-56
Jim Ringo, C, 1953-63
Tobin Rote, QB, 1950-56

January, 1975
Don Chandler, K, 1965-67
Willie Davis, DE, 1960-69
Paul Hornung, HB, 1957-62, '64-66
Henry Jordan, DT, 1959-69
Jerry Kramer, G, 1958-68
Ron Kramer, TE, 1957, '59-64
Vince Lombardi, coach, general manager, 1959-68
Max McGee, E, 1954, '57-67
Jim Taylor, FB, 1958-66
Fred (Fuzzy) Thurston, G, 1959-67

January, 1976
Joseph (Red) Dunn, B, 1927-31
Hank Gremminger, DB, 1956-65
Carl (Bud) Jorgensen, trainer, 1924-70
Gary Knafelc, E, 1954-62
Bob Skoronski, T, 1956, '59-68
Jesse Whittenton, DB, 1958-64

January, 1977
Howard (Cub) Buck, T, 1921-25
Forrest Gregg, T, coach, 1956, '58-70, '84-87
Charlie Mathys, B, 1922-26
Bart Starr, QB, coach, 1956-71, '75-83
A.B. Turnbull, president, 1923-27
Willie Wood, S, 1960-71

February, 1978
George Whitney Calhoun, publicity dir., 1919-46
Boyd Dowler, WR, 1959-69
Paul (Tiny) Engebretsen, G, 1934-41
Lon Evans, G, 1933-37
Ray Nitschke, LB, 1958-72

February, 1979
Nate Barrager, C, 1931-32, '34-35
Carroll Dale, WR, 1965-72
Dominic Olejniczak, president, 1958-81
Elijah Pitts, HB, 1961-69, '71
Pete Tinsley, G, 1938-45

February, 1981
Herb Adderley, CB, 1961-69
Ken Bowman, C, 1964-73
Chester (Swede) Johnston, B, 1931, '34-37
Lee H. Joannes, president, 1930-47

February, 1982
Lou Brock, B, 1940-45
Gale Gillingham, G, 1966-74, '76
Dave Robinson, LB, 1963-72
Jack Vainisi, scout, 1950-60

February, 1983
Donny Anderson, RB, 1966-71
Fred Carr, LB, 1968-77
Fred Leicht, contributor
Carl (Moose) Mulleneaux, E, 1938-41, '45-46

February, 1984
John Brockington, FB, 1971-77
Dan Currie, LB, 1958-64
Ed Jankowski, B, 1937-41
Fred N. Trowbridge Sr., contributor

February, 1985
Phil Bengtson, coach, general manager, 1959-70
Bob Jeter, DB, 1963-70
Earl Svendsen, C, 1937, '39

February, 1986
Wilner Burke, band director, 1938-81
Lee Roy Caffey, LB, 1964-69
Irv Comp, B, 1943-49

March, 1987
Dr. Euguene Brusky, team physician, 1962-90
Chester Marcol, K, 1972-80
Deral Teteak, LB, 1952-56

February, 1988
Lionel Aldridge, DE, 1963-71
Jerry Atkinson, contributor
Bob Mann, E, 1950-54

February, 1989
Zeke Bratkowski, QB, 1963-68, '71
Ron Kostelnik, DT, 1961-68

February, 1991
Jerry Clifford, member board of directors, 1929-52
Harry Jacunski, E, 1939-44
Jan Stenerud, K, 1980-83

February, 1992
Lynn Dickey, QB, 1976-77, '79-85
Larry McCarren, C, 1973-84
Al J. Schneider, contributor

March, 1993
Willie Buchanon, DB, 1972-78
Art Daley, contributor
Johnnie Gray, S, 1975-83

March, 1994
Paul Coffman, TE, 1978-85
Gerry Ellis, FB, 1980-86
Dr. W. Webber Kelly, contributor

March, 1995
William Brault, HOF founder

March, 1996
John Anderson, LB, 1978-89
Lee Remmel, contributor

March, 1997
John (Red) Cochran, coach/scout, 1959-66, '71-present
Ezra Johnson, DE, 1977-87
Travis Williams, RB/KR, 1967-70

March, 1998
Ken Ellis, CB, 1970-75
Mark Murphy, S, 1980-85, '87-91
Hon. Robert J. Parins, president, 1982-89

March, 1999
James Lofton, WR, 1978-86
Tom Miller, contributor

July, 2000
Ron Wolf, executive VP-GM, 1991-2001

July, 2001
Johnny Holland, LB, 1987-93
Ray Scott, contributor

Ken Bowman, who played center with the Packers from 1964-73, was in the 1981 class in the Packer Hall of Fame. Stiller-Lefebvre Collection

July, 2002
Sterling Sharpe, WR, 1988-94
Vernon Biever, contributor

July, 2003
Mike Douglass, LB, 1978-85
Jim Irwin, contributor

July, 2004
Bob Harlan, contributor, president 1989-

Jerry Kramer, an offensive guard in the Glory Years from 1958-68, was named to the Packer Hall of Fame in 1975. Stiller-Lefebvre Collection

Center Jim Ringo, who played with the Packers from 1953-63, was elected to the Packer Hall of Fame in 1974. He was named to the Pro Football Hall of Fame in 1981. Stiller-Lefebvre Collection

Lockers, featuring period jerseys and memorabilia, for each of the Packers who are members of the Pro Football Hall of Fame are displayed at the new Packer Hall of Fame.

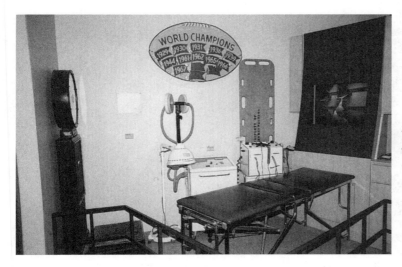

An exhibit at the Packer Hall of Fame includes equipment from the training room used in the 1960s.

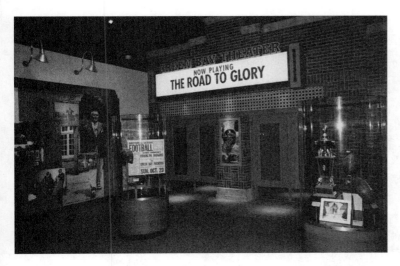

The theater at the Packer Hall of Fame shows the movie, "The Road to Glory," that chronicles the Packers' history.

Packers running back John Brockington runs to daylight in a photo displayed at the Hall of Fame.

Memorabilia in the Hall of Fame includes this preview of the 1967 Ice Bowl playoff game.

A giant color photo in the Packer Hall of Fame shows wide receiver James Lofton running after a reception.

LAMBEAU FIELD

Lambeau Field, then new City Stadium, opened on Sept. 29, 1957, when the Green Bay Packers defeated the Chicago Bears 21-17 before a crowd of 32,132. The structure was renamed Lambeau Field after the death of Curly Lambeau in 1965.

The stadium begins its 48th year of operation in 2004. The facility has undergone numerous facelifts to reach its present look. Built for a bargain $960,000, the stadium seated 32,150 originally.

In 1961, part of the south end was filled in and capacity increased to 38,669.

In 1963, 3,658 seats were added, increasing seating capacity to 42,327.

In 1965, 8,525 seats were added, increasing seating capacity to 50,852.

In 1970, 5,411 seats were added, increasing seating capacity to 56,263 and fully enclosing the stadium bowl.

In 1985, 72 skyboxes were added, increasing seating capacity to 56,926.

In 1990, 36 additional skyboxes were added as well as 1,920 club seats in the south end zone. Seating capacity increased to 59,543.

In 1995, 90 additional skyboxes were added, increasing seating capacity to 60,890.

In 2003, a two-year renovation of the stadium was completed and seating capacity increased to approximately 71,500.

From 1925-56, the Packers played in old City Stadium. The team played at Hagemeister Park in 1921-22 and at Bellevue Park in 1923-24.

The team also played at least one home game annually in Milwaukee from 1933 through 1994: at Borchert Field (1933), State Fair Park (1934-51), Marquette Stadium (1952), and County Stadium (1953-94).

Packers All-Time Record in Lambeau Field

Regular Season:	147-85-4	(.631)
Postseason:	12-1-0	(.923)
OVERALL	**159-86-4**	**(.647)**

The new City Stadium, later to be renamed Lambeau Field, looked quite different from the present day on its opening day, Sept. 29, 1957. Capacity of the stadium, built for $960,000, was then 32,150 and was more than doubled over the years. Stiller-Lefebvre Collection

At New City Stadium
Sunday, Sept. 29, 1957
Attendance = 32,132

Babe Parilli and Gary Knafelc provided the game-winning touchdown. The Packers' defense made sure the score held up.

Green Bay defeated the Chicago Bears 21-17 in the first game played at Lambeau Field (then called new City Stadium). The game was a thrilling climax to a weekend filled with celebration.

The Bears of 1957 were a formidable team. Ed Brown and Rick Casares, league leaders in passing and rushing the previous year, returned. Willie Galimore manned the left halfback spot and Harlon Hill was always dangerous at left end for the 1956 championship runners-up.

Green Bay twice had to come from behind before Parilli put his team ahead for good with a 6-yard pass to Knafelc with 8:21 left. As time wound down, the Packers' defense forced a Bears punt, Bobby Dillon intercepted a Brown pass intended for Hill and center Larry Lauer recovered Perry Jeter's fumble as the latter tried to field Dick Deschaine's punt.

This was a battle from the start. Green Bay lost its starting fullback, Howie Ferguson, on the second play of the game to a leg injury. In the third quarter, Packers tackle Ollie Spencer and Bears defensive back Stan Wallace were ejected for fighting.

From the middle of the first quarter to the halfway mark of the second, the teams combined for 28 points. Brown marched Chicago 77 yards to its first score. Parilli, who replaced starter Bart Starr, then directed a 79-yard advance that ended in a 37-yard pass to Bill Howton. The Bears responded by moving 72 yards in 10 plays to go up 14-7 on an 11-yard, Brown-to-Hill pass. Fred Cone then knotted the score at 14-all with a 1-yard run.

The Packers owned the fourth quarter. They stuffed Bobby Watkins on fourth-and-inches near midfield. Parilli then passed 41 yards to Howton, and Cone gained another two yards to set up game-winning touchdown.

Chicago Bears	7	7	3	0	—	17
Green Bay Packers	0	14	0	7	—	21

First Quarter
CB - Brown 5 run (Blanda kick)
Second Quarter
GB - Howton 37 pass from Parilli (Cone kick)
CB - Hill 11 pass from Brown (Blanda kick)
GB - Cone 1 run (Cone kick)
Third Quarter
CB - FG (13) Blanda
Fourth Quarter
GB - Knafelc 6 pass from Parilli (Cone kick)

	GB	Bears
First Downs	16	19
3rd Down Efficiency	7-15	6-12
4th Down Efficiency	1-2	0-1
Plays-Net Yards	65-297	65-362
Rushes-Yards	39-97	35-141
Passing	200	221
Sacked-Yards Lost	4-35	2-10

	GB	Bears
Comp-Att-Int	22-12-2	28-14-5
Punts	5-51.2	3-40.0
Punt Returns	4-34	1-0
Kickoff Returns	4-114	2-39
Interceptions Ret.	5-26	2-6
Penalties-Yards	2-26	7-55
Fumbles-Lost	2-2	2-1

INDIVIDUAL STATISTICS

RUSHING — GB: Cone 20-52, Carmichael 11-50, McIlhenny 3-7, Ferguson 2-0, Howton 1-(-2), Hornung 2-(-10); **Bears:** Casares 18-72, Galimore 8-28, Watkins 4-24, Bratkowski 1-10, Jeter 2-7, Brown 2-0.
PASSING — GB: Parilli 17-9-197-2-1, Starr 5-3-38-0-1; **Bears:** Brown 24-12-197-1-4, Bratkowski 4-2-34-0-1.
RECEIVING — GB: Howton 8-165, Knafelc 4-70; **Bears:** McColl 4-84, Hill 4-82, Dooley 4-59, Galimore 1-7, Watkins 1-(-1).
MISSED FIELD GOALS — GB: Hornung 50, 47; Cone 45.
Length of Game: 2 hours, 38 minutes

Vice President Richard Nixon, center, shakes hands with Packers team president Dominick Olejneczak after arriving for the dedication ceremonies for the new City Stadium on Sept. 29, 1957. At left is Congressman John Byrnes.

Stiller-Lefebvre Collection

Stiller-Lefebvre Collection

City Stadium seated 32,150 fans when it was built in 1957 at a cost of $960,000. Additions to what was later renamed Lambeau Field, including remodeling completed in 2003, has boosted its capacity to 71,500.

James Arness, star of the hit TV show "Gunsmoke," was among the celebrities riding in the parade during dedication events of the new City Stadium in 1957. The stadium's name was changed to Lambeau Field in 1965.

Stiller-Lefebvre Collection

LAMBEAU FIELD'S 'REBIRTH'

"Rebirth of a Legend" was how the Packers referred to the rededication of Lambeau Field. On Sept. 7, 2003, the Packers hosted the Minnesota Vikings in a game that capped a week's work of activities celebrating the completion of the stadium's renovation.

On Jan. 22, 2000, the Packers unveiled a $295 million plan to completely make over the stadium. Funding would come from a variety of sources, but the residents of Brown County—the county in which the stadium resides—would be asked to shoulder the bulk of the cost ($160 million) through a 0.5 percent sales tax.

Packers president Bob Harlan spent much of the year touring the state to build support for the project. On Sept. 12, 2000, Brown County voters said yes to the sales tax. Work started four months later, with an official groundbreaking ceremony taking place in May 2001.

The renovation was the most ambitious ever undertaken at the field the Packers had called home since 1957. A five-story atrium was built. Seating capacity was increased from 60,890 to more than 71,000. A brick exterior with wrought-iron gates was added.

The atrium, with its 80-foot-tall glass wall, is one of the highlights of the renovation. the 366,000-square-foot addition is home to restaurants, meeting and event facilities, the Packer Hall of Fame, team administration offices and the Packers Pro Shop.

Bronze statues of Curly Lambeau and Vince Lombardi stand in the plaza in front of the atrium.

A number of events were held in the week leading up to the rededication. The stadium was opened up to Brown County residents a week before the Packers-Vikings game and more than 30,000 turned out. Packers president Bob Harlan was honored two days later when the plaza was named after him. A Lambeau Field Inaugural Ball was held and the new Hall of Fame was dedicated.

The night before the game, 33,899 fans and dozens of former Packers players came out for The Rebirth of a Legend event at Lambeau Field. Video clips of memorable moments were played and Bart Starr's quarterback sneak from the Ice Bowl was recreated. The festivities were broadcast live on all the team's preseason network stations.

Most disappointing, of course, was the team's 30-25 loss to the Vikings in the first regular-season game at the renovated stadium.

"We went out there and laid a big egg," right guard Marco Rivera said.

In the end, the hole was just too deep.

The Packers committed four turnovers in a first half that saw them outscored 20-3 by the Vikings. By the time the team finally awakened, Minnesota had added another touchdown and a Packers' victory would have required a comeback like no other in club history.

Randy Moss and the Minnesota Vikings sprinted past Green Bay 30-25 in a game in which Lambeau Field was rededicated following more than two years of extensive renovation. The star receiver caught nine passes for 150 yards and the touchdown that gave his team a 27-3 lead midway through the third quarter.

"Moss is a great player. He had a great game," Packers coach Mike Sherman said. "We tried to corral him. He got the best of us today."

Green Bay was its worst enemy in the first half. Brett Favre threw three interceptions and Ahman Green lost a fumble. Minnesota scored a pair of field goals as a result of the turnovers.

Unlike the Packers, the Vikings had little trouble moving the ball. They had three scoring drives of 10 plays each and amassed 201 yards of offensive before halftime.

Behind 27-3, Green Bay finally got going. Favre used 14 plays to move the team 78 yards with Green cashing in from eight yards out.

After Aaron Elling kicked his third field goal of the day, Favre piloted a 74-yard drive that Green capped with a 1-yard run with 6:27 remaining.

Erwin Swiney recovered Longwell's onside kick. But Favre then threw his fourth interception.

Green Bay got one last chance after Kabeer Gbaja-Biamila forced Daunte Culpepper to fumble and Cletidus Hunt recovered. Favre passed to Javon Walker for a touchdown with 1:55 left, but Longwell's onside kick attempt went out of bounds and Minnesota took over.

Minnesota Vikings	10	10	7	3	—	30
Green Bay Packers	0	3	8	14	—	25

First Quarter
MV - Avery 11 pass with Culpepper (Elling kick)
MV - FG (22) Elling
Second Quarter
GB - FG (27) Longwell
MV - Bates 2 pass from Culpepper (Elling kick)
MV - FG (46) Elling
Third Quarter
MV - Moss 13 pass from Culpepper (Elling kick)
GB - Green 8 run (Franks pass from Favre)
Fourth Quarter
MV - FG (34) Elling
GB - Green 1 run (Longwell kick)
GB - Walker 24 pass from Favre (Longwell kick)

	GB	Vikings
First Downs	22	21
3rd Down Efficiency	5-10	8-14
4th Down Efficiency	0-0	0-0
Plays-Net Yards	61-304	68-337
Rushes-Yards	19-62	36-154
Passing	242	183

	GB	Vikings
Sacked-Yards Lost	1-6	2-12
Comp-Att-Int	41-25-4	30-15-0
Punts	2-39.5	2-37.0
Punt Returns	2-13	1-0
Kickoff Returns	7-143	2-47
Interceptions Ret.	0-0	4-98
Penalties-Yards	6-60	7-65
Fumbles-Lost	1-1	2-2

INDIVIDUAL STATISTICS

RUSHING — GB: Green 15-53, Davenport 3-8, Driver 1-1; **Vikings:** M. Williams 22-80, Culpepper 9-50, Campbell 1-15, Chapman 4-9.

PASSING — GB: Favre 41-25-248-1-4; **Vikings:** Culpepper 30-15-195-3-0.

RECEIVING — GB: Green 7-62, Ferguson 6-53, Walker 5-84, Franks 3-18, Driver 2-27, Martin 2-4; **Vikings:** Moss 9-150, Bates 2-15, Avery 1-11, Campbell 1-8, Chapman 1-8, Goodwin 1-3.

MISSED FIELD GOALS — None

Length of Game: 3 hours, 21 minutes

Bob Harlan, Packers president, addresses a record crowd of 70,505 at the dedication of the remodeled Lambeau Field on Sept. 7, 2003.

Among celebrities on hand to help dedicate the new Lambeau Field was Paul Tagliabue, commissioner of the National Football League. About 10,000 seats were added, as well as an Atrium housing restaurants and the Packer Hall of Fame.

An aerial photo shows the remodeled Lambeau Field, featuring a five-story Atrium on its east side. Stadium capacity has more than doubled since it opened in 1957.

Photo by Eric Goska

Fans mill around the statue honoring coach Vince Lombardi, which stands outside the north entrance of Lambeau Field.

Photo by Eric Goska

Outside the remodeled Lambeau Field, a huge statue of former player and coach Curly Lambeau points the way to another winning season.

Photo by Eric Goska

Glass doors inside the new Atrium at Lambeau Field lead to the seating area.

Lambeau Field's Atrium includes several restaurants, including Curly's Pub, a food court that's open on game days, the new Packer Hall of Fame and the Packers Pro Shop.

A plaque at Lambeau Field notes as a "moment in time," the dedication of the original stadium in 1957.

A blown-up caricature honoring the Packers stands across the street from Lambeau Field on a game day.

Early arrivals head toward the west side of the new Lambeau Field after remodeling enlarged and enhanced the stadium in 2003.

TRAINING CAMP

cooter McLean did little right in his one year as Packers head coach, but it should be noted that the team began its training camp association with St. Norbert College in De Pere, Wis., during his brief time in charge. Since 1958, Packers players have eaten, slept and attended meetings at the Catholic liberal arts college on the shores of the Fox River as they prepared for the upcoming season.

The Packers held their first training camp outside Green Bay in 1935. On Aug. 24 of that year, Curly Lambeau and his team piled into a bus and headed for Pinewood Lodge on Lake Thompson. The lodge was located four miles to the east of Rhinelander, Wis.

The team practiced at Pinewood Lodge for a week, then played three exhibition games in a five-day span against teams from Merrill, Chippewa Falls and Stevens Point. After their game in Stevens Point, the Packers returned to practicing at Joannes Park for one additional tune-up against the La Crosse Old Style Lagers, which was played in Green Bay on Sept. 8.

In late May of 1946, the Packers purchased Rockwood Lodge, which was located 15 miles northeast of Green Bay. The lodge and the five cottages on the 53-acre site served as training camp for the team from 1946 through 1949. In 1946, the team held its morning practices on a field near City Stadium and the afternoon sessions were conducted at Rockwood Lodge. The lodge burned to the ground in January of 1950.

From 1951 through 1953, the Packers trained at Grand Rapids, Minn. For four years after that, they set up camp at the University of Wisconsin-Stevens Point.

In 1987, Forrest Gregg had his team spend two weeks at Olympia Village in southern Wisconsin. Gregg believed that the vacation resort, located about two miles from downtown Oconomowoc, would have fewer distractions as the Packers attempted to rebound from a dismal preseason showing against the Washington Redskins.

Training Camp Sites Outside Green Bay

1935 - Pinewood Lodge near Rhinelander, Wis.

1946-49 - Rockwood Lodge

1951-53 - Grand Rapids, Minn.

1954-57 - Stevens Point, Wis.

1958-present - St. Norbert College, De Pere, Wis.

A sign shows fans the way to the Packers practice field in 1961. It proclaims, "Visitors Welcome" and "Admission FREE."

Photos from the Tom Pigeon Collection

Linebacker Ray Nitschke takes his turn getting photographed during Photo Day at the 1962 Packers training camp.

Quarterback Bart Starr readies a pass for photographers at the 1961 Packers training camp.

A Measure of Greatness

Training Camp

Legendary coach Vince Lombardi, center, poses for a picture with his coaching staff in 1962. From left are Phil Bengtson, Tom Fears, Bill Austin, Lombardi, Red Cochran, Norb Hecker and Dick Voris.

Modest by today's standards, the Packers' ticket office was located in a storefront in downtown Green Bay in 1961.

Today's Packers practice outside, and inside in inclement weather, the massive Don Hutson Center across from Lambeau Field.

Photos by Eric Goska

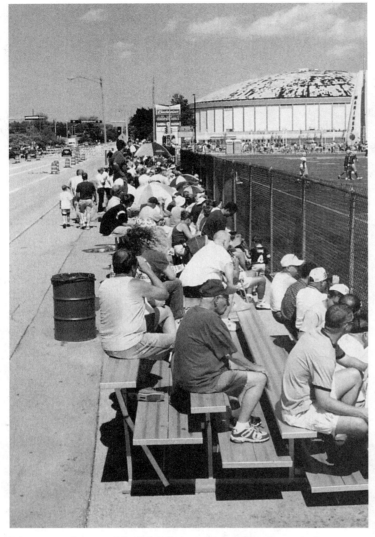

A large contingent of "railbirds" sit on bleachers to watch the Packers practice during the 2003 training camp.

New to the training camp site in 2003 is a sign advertising the restaurants that opened in Lambeau Field's Atrium after remodeling of the stadium was completed.

A newspaper's tent is part of the scenery at the Packers training camp outside Clarke Hinkle Field, one of two outdoor practice fields near the Don Hutson Center.

A Measure of Greatness   **Training Camp**